# Weiss Ratings' Guide to Banks

# Weiss Ratings' Guide to Banks

A Quarterly Compilation of Financial Institutions Ratings and Analyses

**Summer 2020**

GREY HOUSE PUBLISHING

Weiss Ratings
4400 Northcorp Parkway
Palm Beach Gardens, FL 33410
561-627-3300



WeissRatings
Independent. Unbiased. Accurate. Trusted.

Published by Grey House Publishing, Inc., located at 4919 Route 22, Amenia, NY 12501; telephone 518-789-8700. Grey House Publishing neither guarantees the accuracy of the data contained herein nor assumes any responsibility for errors, omissions or discrepancies. Grey House Publishing accepts no payment for listing; inclusion in the publication of any organization, agency, institution, publication, service or individual does not imply endorsement of the publisher.

Grey House Publishing
4919 Route 22
PO Box 56
Amenia, NY 12501-0056

Edition No. 118, Summer 2020

ISBN: 978-1-64265-549-0
ISSN: 2158-5962

# Contents

# Terms and Conditions

This document is prepared strictly for the confidential use of our customer(s). It has been provided to you at your specific request. It is not directed to, or intended for distribution to or use by, any person or entity who is a citizen or resident of or located in any locality, state, country or other jurisdiction where such distribution, publication, availability or use would be contrary to law or regulation or which would subject Weiss Ratings or its affiliates to any registration or licensing requirement within such jurisdiction.

No part of the analysts' compensation was, is, or will be, directly or indirectly, related to the specific recommendations or views expressed in this research report.

This document is not intended for the direct or indirect solicitation of business. Weiss Ratings, LLC and its affiliates disclaims any and all liability to any person or entity for any loss or damage caused, in whole or in part, by any error (negligent or otherwise) or other circumstances involved in, resulting from or relating to the procurement, compilation, analysis, interpretation, editing, transcribing, publishing and/or dissemination or transmittal of any information contained herein.

Weiss Ratings has not taken any steps to ensure that the securities or investment vehicle referred to in this report are suitable for any particular investor. The investment or services contained or referred to in this report may not be suitable for you and it is recommended that you consult an independent investment advisor if you are in doubt about such investments or investment services. Nothing in this report constitutes investment, legal, accounting or tax advice or a representation that any investment or strategy is suitable or appropriate to your individual circumstances or otherwise constitutes a personal recommendation to you.

The ratings and other opinions contained in this document must be construed solely as statements of opinion from Weiss Ratings, LLC., and not statements of fact. Each rating or opinion must be weighed solely as a factor in your choice of an institution and should not be construed as a recommendation to buy, sell or otherwise act with respect to the particular product or company involved.

Past performance should not be taken as an indication or guarantee of future performance, and no representation or warranty, expressed or implied, is made regarding future performance. Information, opinions and estimates contained in this report reflect a judgment at its original date of publication and are subject to change without notice. Weiss Ratings offers a notification service for rating changes on companies you specify. For more information visit WeissRatings.com or call 1-877-934-7778. The price, value and income from any of the securities or financial instruments mentioned in this report can fall as well as rise.



**Date of Data Analyzed: December 31, 2019**

Data Source: Call Report data provided by SNL Financial.

# Welcome to Weiss Ratings'
# *Guide to Banks*

Most people automatically assume their bank will survive, year after year. However, prudent consumers and professionals realize that in this world of shifting risks, the solvency of financial institutions can't be taken for granted. After all, your bank's failure could have a heavy impact on you in terms of lost time, lost money (in cases of deposits exceeding the federal insurance limit), tied-up deposits, lost credit lines, and the possibility of being shifted to another institution under not-so-friendly terms.

If you are looking for accurate, unbiased ratings and data to help you choose a commercial bank, savings bank, or savings and loan for yourself, your family, your company or your clients, Weiss Ratings' Guide to Banks gives you precisely what you need.

## Weiss Ratings' Mission Statement

Weiss Ratings' mission is to empower consumers, professionals, and institutions with high quality advisory information for selecting or monitoring a financial services company or financial investment.

In doing so, Weiss Ratings will adhere to the highest ethical standards by maintaining our independent, unbiased outlook and approach to advising our customers.

## Why rely on Weiss Ratings?

Weiss Ratings provides fair, objective ratings to help professionals and consumers alike make educated financial decisions.

At Weiss Ratings, integrity is number one. Weiss Ratings never takes a penny from rated companies for issuing its ratings. And, we publish Weiss Safety Ratings without regard for institutions' preferences. Our analysts review and update Weiss ratings each and every quarter, so you can be sure that the information you receive is accurate and current – providing you with advance warning of financial vulnerability early enough to do something about it.

Other rating agencies focus primarily on a company's current financial solvency and consider only mild economic adversity. Weiss Ratings also considers these issues, but in addition, our analysis covers a company's ability to deal with severe economic adversity in terms of a sharp decline in the value of its investments and a drop in the collectability of its loans.

Our use of more rigorous standards stems from the viewpoint that a financial institution's obligations to its customers should not depend on favorable business conditions. A bank must be able to honor its loan and deposit commitments in bad times as well as good.

Weiss's rating scale, from A to F, is easy to understand. Only a few outstanding companies receive an A (Excellent) rating, although there are many to choose from within the B (Good) category. A large group falls into the broad average range which receives C (Fair) ratings. Companies that demonstrate marked vulnerabilities receive either D (Weak) or E (Very Weak) ratings. So, there's no numbering system, star counting, or color-coding to keep track of.

# How to Use This Guide

The purpose of the *Guide to Banks* is to provide consumers, businesses, financial institutions, and municipalities with a reliable source of banking industry ratings and analysis on a timely basis. We realize that the financial safety of a bank is an important factor to consider when establishing a relationship. The ratings and analysis in this Guide can make that evaluation easier when you are considering:

- A checking, merchant banking, or other transaction account
- An investment in a certificate of deposit or savings account
- A line of credit or commercial loan
- Counterparty risk

The rating for a particular company indicates our opinion regarding that company's ability to meet its obligations – not only under current economic conditions, but also during a declining economy or in an environment of increased liquidity demands.

To use this Guide most effectively, we recommend you follow the steps outlined below:

**Step 1** To ensure you evaluate the correct company, verify the company's exact name as it was given to you. It is also helpful to ascertain the city and state of the company's main office or headquarters since no two banks with the same name can be headquartered in the same city. Many companies have similar names but are not related to one another, so you will want to make sure the company you look up is really the one you are interested in evaluating.

**Step 2** Turn to Section I, the Index of Banks, and locate the company you are evaluating. This section contains all federally-insured commercial banks and savings banks. It is sorted alphabetically by the name of the company and shows the main office city and state following the name for additional verification.
If you have trouble finding a particular institution or determining which is the right one, consider these possible reasons:

- You may have an incorrect or incomplete institution name. There are often several institutions with the same or very similar names. So, make sure you have the exact name and proper spelling, as well as the city in which it is headquartered.
- You may be looking for a *bank holding company.* If so, try to find the exact name of the main bank in the group and look it up under that name.

**Step 3** Once you have located your specific company, the first column after the state shows its current Weiss Safety Rating. Turn to *About Weiss Safety Ratings* for information about what this rating means. If the rating has changed since the last edition of this Guide, a downgrade will be indicated with a down triangle ▼ to the left of the company name; an upgrade will be indicated with an up triangle ▲.

**Step 4** Following the current Weiss Safety Rating are two prior ratings for the company based on year-end data from the two previous years. Use this to discern the longer-term direction of the company's overall financial condition.

**Step 5** The remainder of Section I; provides insight into the areas our analysts reviewed as the basis for assigning the company's rating. These areas include size, capital adequacy, asset quality, profitability, liquidity, and stability. An index within each of these categories represents a composite evaluation of that particular facet of the company's financial condition. Refer to the Critical Ranges In Our Indexes table for an interpretation of which index values are considered strong, good, fair, or weak. In most cases, lower-rated companies will have a low index value in one or more of the indexes shown. Bear in mind, however, that Weiss Safety Rating is the result of a complex qualitative and quantitative analysis which cannot be reproduced using only the data provided here.

**Step 6** If the company you are evaluating is not highly rated and you want to find a bank with a higher rating, turn to the page in Section II that has your state's name at the top. This section contains Weiss Recommended Banks by State (rating of A+, A, A- or B+) that have a branch office in your state. If the main office telephone number provided is not a local telephone call or to determine if a branch of the bank is near you, consult your local telephone Yellow Pages Directory under "Banks," "Savings Banks," or "Savings and Loan Associations." Here you will find a complete list of the institution's branch locations along with their telephone numbers.

**Step 7** Once you've identified a Weiss Recommended Company in your local area, you can then refer back to Section I to analyze it.

**Step 8** In order to use Weiss Safety Ratings most effectively, we strongly recommend you consult the *Important Warnings and Cautions* listed. These are more than just "standard disclaimers." They are very important factors you should be aware of before using this Guide. If you have any questions regarding the precise meaning of specific terms used in the Guide, refer to the Glossary.

**Step 9** Make sure you stay up to date with the latest information available since the publication of this Guide. For information on how to set up a rating change notification service, acquire follow-up reports, check ratings online or receive a more in-depth analysis of an individual company, call 1-877-934-7778 or visit www.weissratings.com.

# About Weiss Safety Ratings

The Weiss Ratings are calculated based on a complex analysis of hundreds of factors that are synthesized into five indexes: capitalization, asset quality, profitability, liquidity and stability. Each index is then used to arrive at a letter grade rating. A weak score on any one index can result in a low rating, as financial problems can be caused by any one of a number of factors, such as inadequate capital, non-performing loans and poor asset quality, operating losses, poor liquidity, or the failure of an affiliated company.

Our **Capitalization Index** gauges the institution's capital adequacy in terms of its cushion to absorb future operating losses under adverse business and economic scenarios that may impact the company's net interest margin, securities' values, and the collectability of its loans.

Our **Asset Quality Index** measures the quality of the company's past underwriting and investment practices based on the estimated liquidation value of the company's loan and securities portfolios.

Our **Profitability Index** measures the soundness of the company's operations and the contribution of profits to the company's financial strength. The index is a composite of five sub-factors: 1) gain or loss on operations; 2) rates of return on assets and equity; 3) management of net interest margin; 4) generation of noninterest-based revenues; and 5) overhead expense management.

Our **Liquidity Index** evaluates a company's ability to raise the necessary cash to satisfy creditors and honor depositor withdrawals.

Finally, our **Stability Index** integrates a number of sub-factors that affect consistency (or lack thereof) in maintaining financial strength over time. These include 1) risk diversification in terms of company size and loan diversification; 2) deterioration of operations as reported in critical asset, liability, income and expense items, such as an increase in loan delinquency rates or a sharp increase in loan originations; 3) years in operation; 4) former problem areas where, despite recent improvement, the company has yet to establish a record of stable performance over a suitable period of time; and 5) relationships with holding companies and affiliates.

In order to help guarantee our objectivity, we reserve the right to publish ratings expressing our opinion of a company's financial stability based exclusively on publicly available data and our own proprietary standards for safety.

Each of these indexes is measured according to the following range of values.

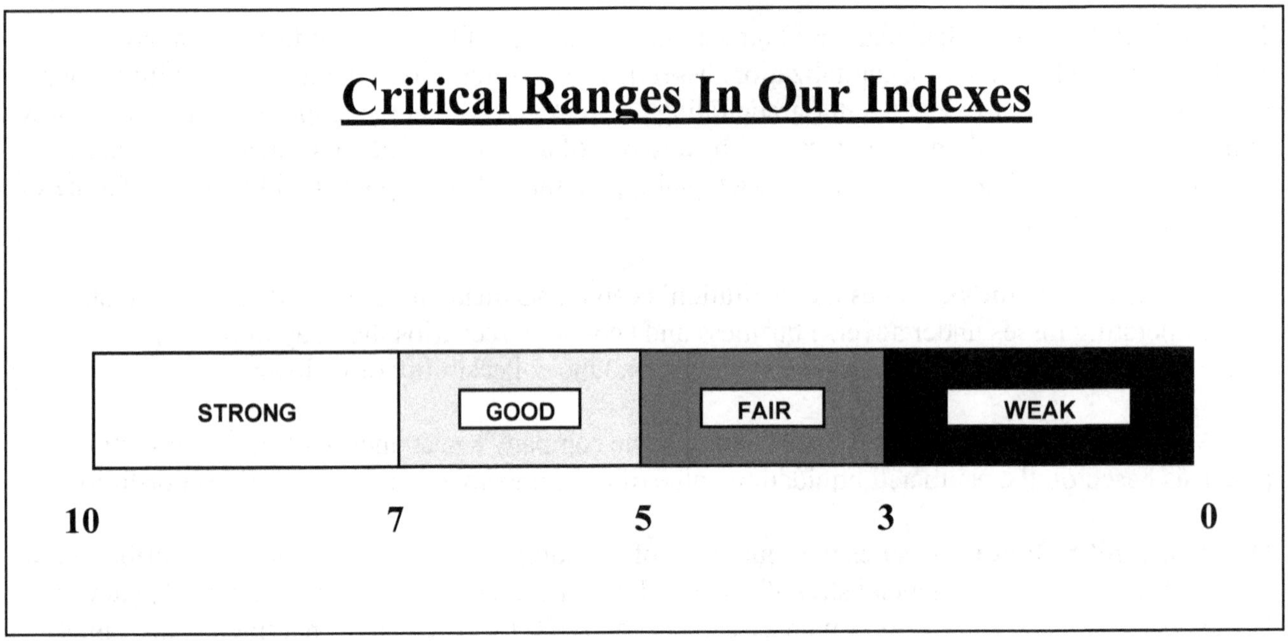


Finally, the indexes are combined to form a composite company rating which is then verified by one of our analysts. The resulting distribution of ratings assigned to all banks looks like this:

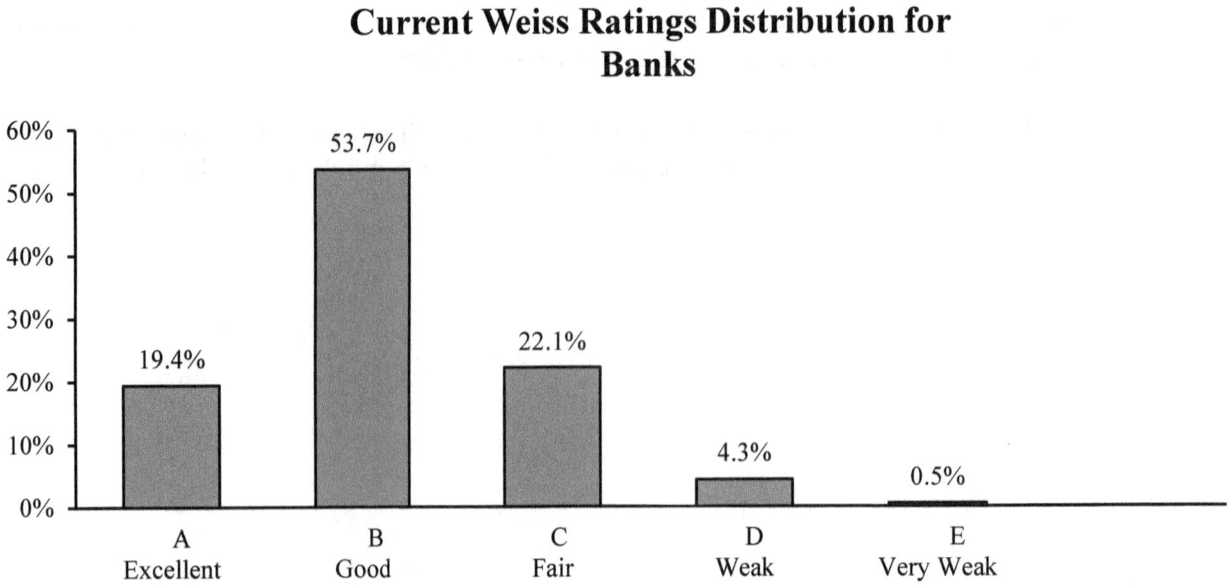

# What Our Ratings Mean

**A** **Excellent.** The institution offers excellent financial security. It has maintained a conservative stance in its business operations and underwriting practices as evidenced by its strong equity base, high asset quality, steady earnings, and high liquidity. While the financial position of any company is subject to change, we believe that this institution has the resources necessary to deal with severe economic conditions.

**B** **Good.** The institution offers good financial security and has the resources to deal with a variety of adverse economic conditions. It comfortably exceeds the minimum levels for all of our rating criteria, and is likely to remain healthy for the near future. Nevertheless, in the event of a severe recession or major financial crisis, we feel that this assessment should be reviewed to make sure that the company is still maintaining adequate financial strength.

**C** **Fair.** The institution offers fair financial security, is currently stable, and will likely remain relatively healthy as long as the economic environment remains relatively stable. In the event of a severe recession or major financial crisis, however, we feel this company may encounter difficulties in maintaining its financial stability.

**D** **Weak.** The institution currently demonstrates what, in our opinion, we consider to be significant weaknesses which could negatively impact depositors or creditors. In the event of a severe recession or major financial crisis, these weaknesses could be magnified.

**E** **Very Weak.** The institution currently demonstrates what we consider to be significant weaknesses and has also failed some of the basic tests that we use to identify fiscal stability. Therefore, even in a favorable economic environment, it is our opinion that depositors or creditors could incur significant risks.

**F** **Failed.** The institution has been placed under the custodianship of regulatory authorities. This implies that it will be either liquidated or taken over by another financial institution.

**+** The **plus sign** is an indication that the institution is in the upper third of the letter grade.

**-** The **minus sign** is an indication that the institution is in the lower third of the letter grade.

**U** **Unrated.** The institution is unrated due to the absence of sufficient data for our ratings.

# Peer Comparison of Bank Safety Ratings

| Weiss Ratings | Veribanc | Bauer Financial | IDC Financial | Bankrate.com | Lace Financial |
|---|---|---|---|---|---|
| A+, A, A- | Green, Three Stars w/ Blue Ribbon recognition | 5 stars, 4 stars | 201-300 | 1, Five stars | A+, A |
| B+, B, B- | Green, Three Stars w/out Blue Ribbon recognition | 3 ½ stars | 166-200 | 2, Four stars | B+ |
| C+, C, C- | Green Two Stars, Yellow Two Stars | 3 stars | 126-165 | 3, Three stars | B, C+ |
| D+, D, D- | Green one star, Yellow one star, Green no stars | 2 stars | 76-125 | 4, Two stars | C, D |
| E+, E, E- | Yellow no stars, Red no stars | 1 star | 1-75 | 5, One star | E |

# Important Warnings and Cautions

1. **A rating alone cannot tell the whole story.** Please read the explanatory information contained here, in the section introductions and in the appendix. It is provided in order to give you an understanding of our rating philosophy as well as to paint a more complete picture of how we arrive at our opinion of a company's strengths and weaknesses. In addition, please remember that our safety rating is not an end-all measure of an institution's safety. Rather, it should be used as a "flag" of possible troubles, suggesting a need for further research.

2. **Safety ratings shown in this directory were current as of the publication date.** In the meantime, the rating may have been updated based on more recent data. Weiss Ratings offers a notification service for ratings changes on companies that you specifiy. For more information call 1-877-934-7778 or visit www.weissratings.com.

3. **When deciding to do business with a financial institution, your decision should be based on a wide variety of factors in addition to Weiss Safety Rating**. These include the institution's pricing of its deposit instruments and loans, the fees you will be charged, the degree to which it can help you meet your long-term planning needs, how these costs/benefits may change over the years, and what other choices are available to you given your current location and financial circumstances.

4. **Weiss Safety Ratings represent our opinion of a company's insolvency risk.** As such, a high rating means we feel that the company has less chance of running into financial difficulties. A high rating is not a guarantee of solvency nor is a low rating a prediction of insolvency. Weiss Safety Ratings are not deemed to be a recommendation concerning the purchase or sale of the securities of any bank that is publicly owned.

5. **All firms that have the same Weiss Safety Rating should be considered to be essentially equal in safety.** This is true regardless of any differences in the underlying numbers which might appear to indicate greater strengths. Weiss Safety Rating already takes into account a number of lesser factors which, due to space limitations, cannot be included in this publication.

6. **A good rating requires consistency.** If a company is excellent on four indicators and fair on one, the company may receive a fair rating. This requirement is necessary due to the fact that fiscal problems can arise from any *one* of several causes including poor underwriting, inadequate capital resources, or operating losses.

7. **Our rating standards are more conservative than those used by other agencies.** We believe that no one can predict with certainty the economic environment of the near or long-term future. Rather, we assume that various scenarios – from the extremes of double-digit inflation to a severe recession – are within the range of reasonable possibilities over the next one or two decades. To achieve a top rating according to our standards, a company must be adequately prepared for the worst-case reasonable scenario, without impairing its current operations.

8. **We are an independent rating agency and do not depend on the cooperation of the companies we rate**. Our data are derived, from quarterly financial statements filed with federal regulators. Although we seek to maintain an open line of communication with the companies being rated, we do not grant them the right to influence the ratings or stop their publication. This policy stems from the fact that this Guide is designed for the protection of our customers.

9. **Inaccuracies in the data issued by the federal regulators could negatively impact the quality of a company's Safety Rating.** While we attempt to find and correct as many data errors as possible, some data errors inevitably slip through. We have no method of intercepting fraudulent or falsified data and must take for granted that all information is reported honestly to the federal regulatory agencies.

10. **Institutions that operate exclusively or primarily as a trust company may have skewed financial information.** Due to the nature of their business, these companies often record high profit levels compared to other more "traditional" banks. Trust companies can usually be recognized by the initials "TC" or "& TC" in their names.

11. **This Guide does not cover nonbank affiliates of banking companies.** Although some nonbank companies may be affiliated with the banks cited in this Guide, the firms are separate corporations whose financial strength is only partially dependent on the strength of their affiliates.

12. **There are many companies with the same or similar sounding names, despite no affiliation whatsoever.** Therefore, it is important that you have the exact name, city, and state of the institution's headquarters before you begin to research the company in this Guide.

13. **Affiliated companies do not automatically receive the same rating.** We recognize that a troubled institution may expect financial support from its parent or affiliates. Weiss Safety Ratings reflect our opinion of the measure of support that may become available to a subsidiary bank, if the subsidiary were to experience serious financial difficulties. In the case of a strong parent and a weaker subsidiary, the affiliate relationship will generally result in a higher rating for the subsidiary than it would have on a stand-alone basis. Seldom, however, would the rating be brought up to the level of the parent.

    This treatment is appropriate because we do not assume the parent would have either the resources or the will to "bail out" a troubled subsidiary during a severe economic crisis. Even when there is a binding legal obligation for a parent corporation to honor the obligations of its subsidiary banks, the possibility exists that the subsidiary could be sold and lose its parental support. Therefore, it is quite common for one affiliate to have a higher rating than another. This is another reason why it is especially important that you have the precise name of the company you are evaluating.

14. **This publication does not include foreign banking companies, or their U.S. branches.** Therefore, our evaluation of foreign banking companies is limited to those U.S. chartered domestic banks owned by foreign banking companies. In most cases, the U.S. operations of a foreign banking company are relatively small in relation to the overall size of the company, so you may want to consult other sources as well. In any case, do not be confused by a domestic bank with a name which is the same as – or similar to – that of a foreign banking company. Even if there is an affiliation between the two, we have evaluated the U.S. institution based on its own merits.

# Section I

# Index of Banks

An analysis of all rated

**U.S. Commercial Banks and Savings Banks**

Institutions are listed in alphabetical order.

# Section I Contents

This section contains Weiss Safety Ratings, key rating factors, and summary financial data for all U.S. federally-insured commercial banks and savings banks. Companies are sorted in alphabetical order, first by company name, then by city and state.

*Left Pages*

1. **Institution Name** — The name under which the institution was chartered. If you cannot find the institution you are interested in, or if you have any doubts regarding the precise name, verify the information with the bank itself before proceeding. Also, determine the city and state in which the institution is headquartered for confirmation. (See columns 2 and 3.)

2. **City** — The city in which the institution's headquarters or main office is located. With the adoption of intrastate and interstate branching laws, many institutions operating in your area may actually be headquartered elsewhere. So, don't be surprised if the location cited is not in your particular city.

   Also use this column to confirm that you have located the correct institution. It is possible for two unrelated companies to have the same name if they are headquartered in different cities.

3. **State** — The state in which the institution's headquarters or main office is located. With the adoption of interstate branching laws, some institutions operating in your area may actually be headquartered in another state.

4. **Safety Rating** — Weiss rating assigned to the institution at the time of publication. Our ratings are designed to distinguish levels of insolvency risk and are measured on a scale from A to F based upon a wide range of factors. See *About Weiss Safety Ratings* for specific descriptions of each letter grade.

   Highly rated companies are, in our opinion, less likely to experience financial difficulties than lower rated firms. See *About Weiss Safety Ratings* for more information. Also, please be sure to consider the warnings regarding the ratings' limitations and the underlying assumptions.

5. **Prior Year Safety Rating** — Weiss rating assigned to the institution based on data from December 31 of the previous year. Compare this rating to the company's current rating to identify any recent changes.

6. **Safety Rating Two Years Prior** — Weiss rating assigned to the institution based on data from December 31 two years ago. Compare this rating to the ratings in the prior columns to identify longer term trends in the company's financial condition.

**7. Total Assets**

The total of all assets listed on the institution's balance sheet, in millions of dollars. This figure primarily consists of loans, investments (such as municipal and treasury bonds), and fixed assets (such as buildings and other real estate).

Overall size is an important factor which affects the company's ability to diversify risk and avoid vulnerability to a single borrower, industry, or geographic area. Larger institutions are usually, although not always, more diversified and thus less susceptible to a downturn in a particular area. Nevertheless, do not be misled by the general public perception that "bigger is better." Larger institutions are known for their inability to quickly adapt to changes in the marketplace and typically underperform their smaller brethren.

**8. One Year Asset Growth**

The percentage change in total assets over the previous 12 months. Moderate growth is generally a positive since it can reflect the maintenance or expansion of the company's market share, leading to the generation of additional revenues. Excessive growth, however, is generally a sign of trouble as it can indicate a loosening of underwriting practices in order to attract new business.

**9. Commercial Loans/ Total Assets**

The percentage of the institution's asset base invested in loans to businesses. Commercial loans are the traditional bread and butter of commercial banks, although many have increased their business lending in recent years.

**10. Consumer Loans/ Total Assets**

The percentage of the institution's asset base invested in loans to consumers, primarily credit cards. Consumer lending has grown rapidly in recent years due to the high interest rates and fees institutions are able to charge. On the down side, consumer loans usually experience higher delinquency and default rates than other loans, negatively impacting earnings down the road.

**11. Home Mortgage Loans/ Total Assets**

The percentage of the institution's asset base invested in residential mortgage loans to consumers, excluding home equity loans. Savings banks have traditionally dominated mortgage lending.

This type of loan typically experiences lower default rates. However, the length of the loan's term can be a subject for concern during periods of rising interest rates.

**12. Securities/ Total Assets**

The percentage of the institution's asset base invested in securities, including U.S. Treasury securities, mortgage-backed securities, and municipal bonds. This does not include securities the institution may be holding on behalf of individual customers.

Although securities are similar to loans in that they represent obligations to pay a debt at some point in the future, they are a more liquid investment than loans and usually present less risk of default. In addition, mortgage-backed securities can present less credit risk than holding mortgage loans themselves due to the diversification of the underlying mortgages.

**13. Capitalization Index**

An index that measures the adequacy of the institution's capital resources to deal with potentially adverse business and economic situations that could arise. It is based on an evaluation of the company's degree of leverage compared to total assets as well as risk-adjusted assets. See the Critical Ranges In Our Indexes for a description of the different critical levels presented in this index.

**14. Leverage Ratio**

A regulatory ratio defined by the federal banking regulators as core (tier 1) capital divided by tangible assets. This ratio answers the question: How much does the institution have in stockholders' equity for every dollar of assets? Thus, the Leverage Ratio represents the amount of actual "capital cushion" the institution has to fall back on in times of trouble. We feel that this is the single most important ratio in determining financial strength because it provides the best measure of an institution's ability to withstand losses.

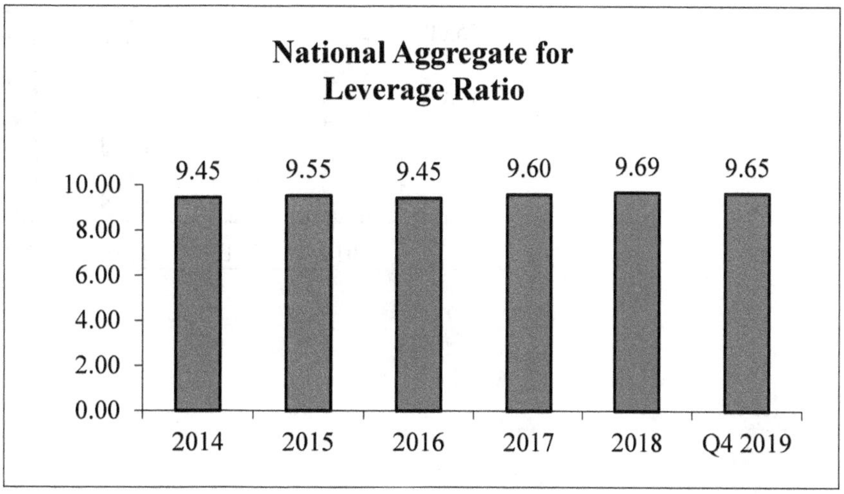

**15. Risk-Based Capital Ratio**

A regulatory ratio defined by the federal banking regulators as total (tier 1 + tier 2) capital divided by risk-weighted assets. This ratio addresses the issue that not all assets present the same level of credit risk to an institution. As such, all assets and certain off-balance sheet commitments are assigned to risk categories based on the level of credit risk they pose and then weighted accordingly to arrive at risk-weighted assets.

For instance, assets with virtually no risk, such as cash and U.S. Treasury securities, are risk-weighted at 0% and therefore, not included in the calculation. Assets with low risk, for example, high quality mortgage-backed securities and state and municipal bonds, are partially weighted at 20%.

Those assets possessing moderate risk, such as residential mortgages and state and local revenue bonds are partially weighted at 50%. And finally, assets considered to possess "normal" or "high" risk, including certain off-balance sheet commitments such as unfunded loans, are risk-weighted at 100%. The summation of these categories of risk-weighted assets results in the figure used in the denominator of this ratio.

Please be aware that not all banks and savings banks are required to report risk-weighted assets as defined by the federal regulators. Consequently, we have estimated this figure when necessary based on estimates used by the regulators themselves.

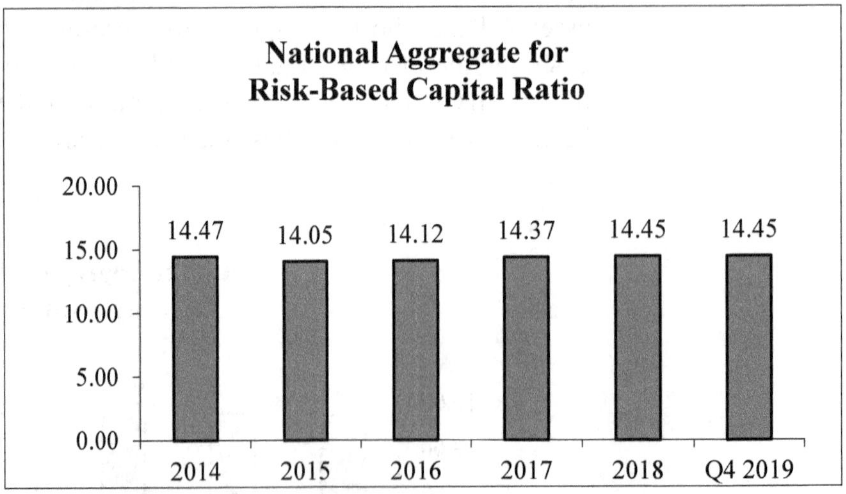

*Right Pages*

1. **Asset Quality Index** An index that measures the quality of the institution's past underwriting and investment practices, as well as its loss reserve coverage. See the Critical Ranges In Our Indexes for a description of the different critical levels presented in this index.

2. **Adjusted Nonperforming Loans/ Total Loans** The percentage of the institution's loan portfolio which is either past due on its payments by 90 days or more, or no longer accruing interest due to doubtful collectability plus a portion of all restructured loans, less government guaranteed GNMA loans and those loans protected by the FDIC. This ratio is affected primarily by the quality of the institution's underwriting practices and the prosperity of the local economies where it is doing business. While only a portion of these loans will actually end up in default, a high ratio here will have several negative consequences including increased loan loss provisions, increased loan collection expenses, and decreased interest revenues.

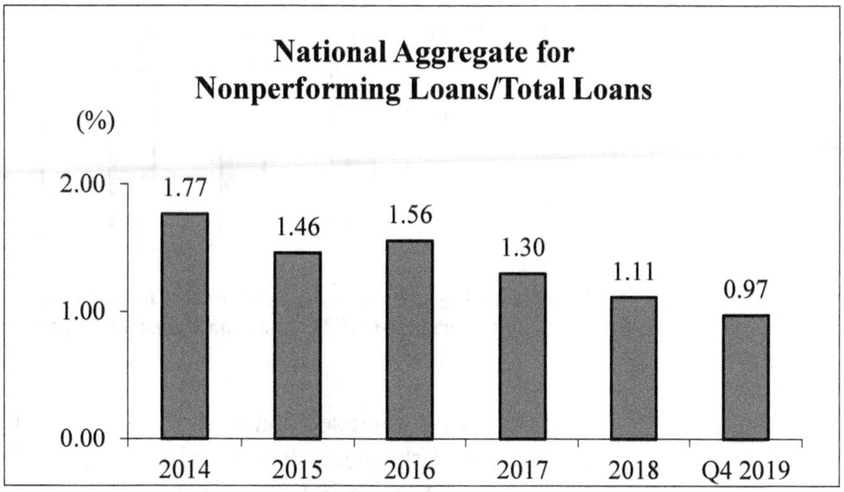


**[1]Nonperforming loans were adjusted in 2011 to include a portion of all restructured loans, less government guaranteed GNMA loans and those loans protected by the FDIC.**

**3. Adjusted Nonperforming Loans/ Capital**

The percentage of past due 90 days and nonaccruing loans plus a portion of all restructured loans, less government guaranteed GNMA loans and those loans protected by the FDIC to the company's core (tier 1) capital plus reserve for loan losses. This ratio answers the question: If all of the bank's significantly past due and nonaccruing loans were to go into default, how much would that eat into capital? A large percentage of nonperforming loans signal imprudent lending practices which are a direct threat to the equity of the institution.

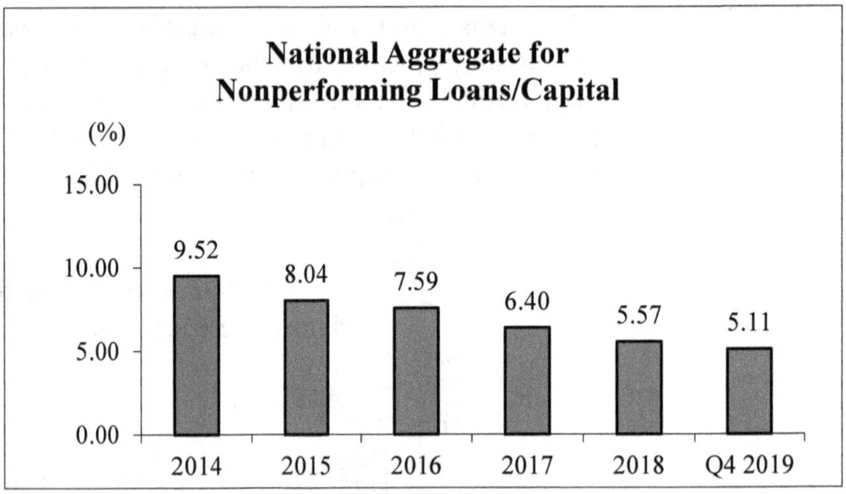


**[1] Nonperforming loans were adjusted in 2011 to include a portion of all restructured loans, less government guaranteed GNMA loans and those loans protected by the FDIC.**

**4. Net Charge-offs/ Average Loans**

The ratio of foreclosed loans written off the institution's books since the beginning of the year (less previous write-offs that were recovered) as a percentage of average loans for the year. This ratio answers the question: What percentage of the bank's past loans have actually become uncollectible? Past loan charge-off experience is often a very good indication of what can be expected in the future, and high loan charge-off levels are usually an indication of poor underwriting practices.

**5. Profitability Index**

An index that measures the soundness of the institution's operations and the contribution of profits to the company's financial strength. It is based on five sub-factors: 1) gain or loss on operations; 2) rates of return on assets and equity; 3) management of net interest margin; 4) generation of noninterest-based revenues; and 5) overhead expense management. See the Critical Ranges In Our Indexes for a description of the different critical levels presented in this index.

**6. Net Income**

The year-to-date net profit or loss recorded by the institution, in millions of dollars. This figure includes the company's operating profit (income from lending, investing, and fees less interest and overhead expenses) as well as nonoperating items such as capital gains on the sale of securities, income taxes, and extraordinary items.

**7. Return on Assets** The ratio of net income for the year (year-to-date quarterly figures are converted to a 12-month equivalent) as a percentage of average assets for the year. This ratio, known as ROA, is the most commonly used benchmark for bank profitability since it measures the company's return on investment in a format that is easily comparable with other companies.

Historically speaking, a ratio of 1.0% or greater has been considered good performance. However, this ratio will fluctuate with the prevailing economic times. Also, larger banks tend to have a lower ratio.

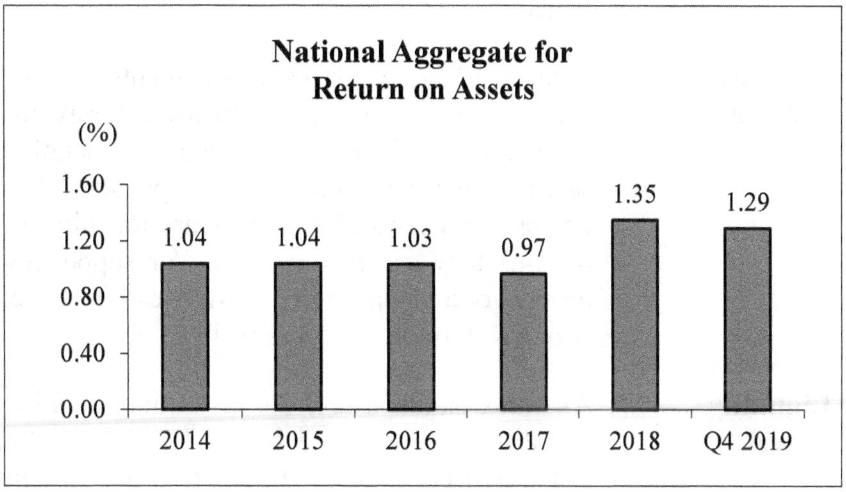


**8. Return on Equity** The ratio of net income for the year (year-to-date quarterly figures are converted to a 12-month equivalent) as a percentage of average equity for the year. This ratio, known as ROE, is commonly used by a company's shareholders as a measure of their return on investment. It is not always a good measure of profitability, however, because inadequate equity levels at some institutions can result in unjustly high ROE's.

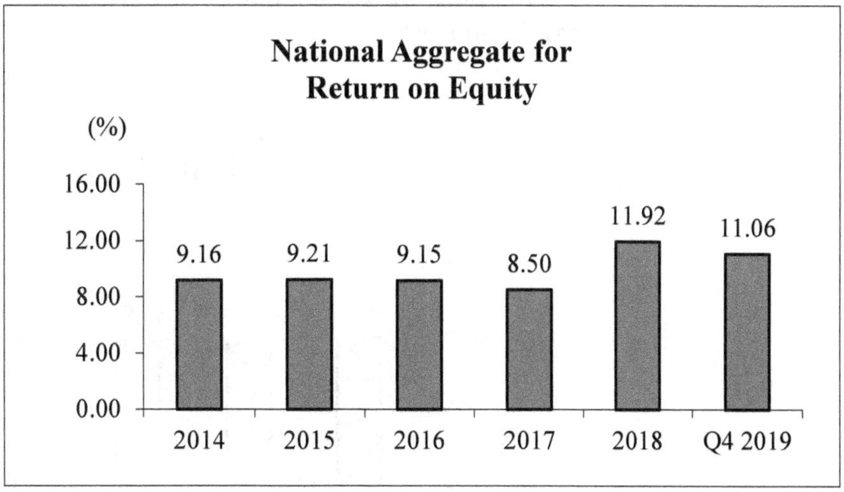

**9. Net Interest Spread**

The difference between the institution's interest income and interest expense for the year (year-to-date quarterly figures are converted to a 12-month equivalent) as a percentage of its average revenue-generating assets. Since the margin between interest earned and interest paid is generally where the company generates the majority of its income, this figure provides insight into the company's ability to effectively manage interest spreads.

A low Net Interest Spread can be the result of poor loan and deposit pricing, high levels of non-accruing loans, or poor asset/liability management.

**10. Overhead Efficiency Ratio**

Total overhead expenses as a percentage of total revenues net of interest expense. This is a common measure for evaluating an institution's ability to operate efficiently while keeping a handle on overhead expenses like salaries, rent, and other office expenses. A high ratio suggests that the company's overhead expenses are too high in relation to the amount of revenue they are generating and/or supporting. Conversely, a low ratio means good management of overhead expenses which usually results in a strong Return on Assets as well.

**11. Liquidity Index**

An index that measures the institution's ability to raise the necessary cash to satisfy creditors and honor depositor withdrawals. It is based on an evaluation of the company's short-term liquidity position, including its existing reliance on less stable deposit sources. See the Critical Ranges In Our Indexes for a description of the different critical levels presented in this index.

**12. Liquidity Ratio**

The ratio of short-term liquid assets to deposits and short-term borrowings. This ratio answers the question: How many cents can the institution easily raise in cash to cover each dollar on deposit plus pay off its short-term debts? Due to the nature of the business, it is rare (and not expected) for an established bank to achieve 100% on this ratio. Nevertheless, it serves as a good measure of an institution's liquidity in relation to the rest of the banking industry.

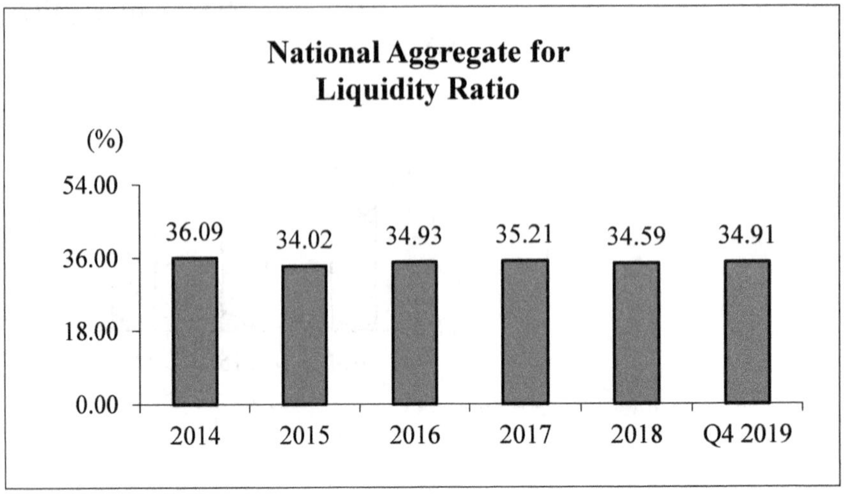

**13. Hot Money Ratio**

The percentage of the institution's deposit base that is being funded by jumbo CDs and brokered deposits. Jumbo CDs (high-yield certificates of deposit with principal amounts of at least $100,000) and brokered deposits (pooled funds sold by brokers seeking the highest interest rate available) are generally considered less stable (and more costly) and thus less desirable as a source of funds.

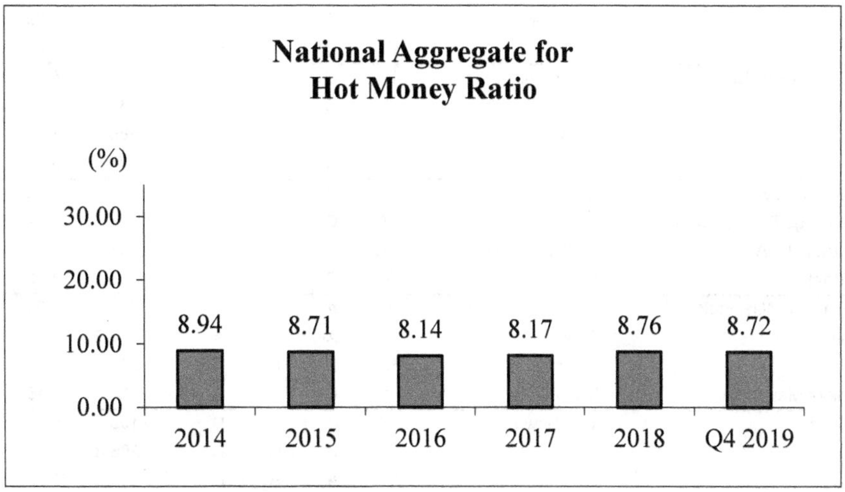


**14. Stability Index**

An index that integrates a number of factors such as 1) risk diversification in terms of company size and loan diversification; 2) deterioration of operations as reported in critical asset, liability, income and expense items, such as an increase in loan delinquency rates or a sharp increase in loan originations; 3) years in operation; 4) former problem areas where, despite recent improvement, the company has yet to establish a record of stable performance over a suitable period of time; and 5) relationships with holding companies and affiliates. See the Critical Ranges In Our Indexes for a description of the different critical levels presented in this index.

| Name | City | State | Rating | 2018 Rating | 2017 Rating | Total Assets ($Mil) | One Year Asset Growth | Asset Mix (As a % of Total Assets) Commercial Loans | Consumer Loans | Mortgage Loans | Securities | Capitalization Index | Leverage Ratio | Risk-Based Capital Ratio |
|---|---|---|---|---|---|---|---|---|---|---|---|---|---|---|
| ▲ 1880 Bank | Cambridge | MD | **A-** | B | B | 374.5 | -0.77 | 5.0 | 0.5 | 25.2 | 11.4 | **10.0** | 13.6 | 20.9 |
| 1st Advantage Bank | Saint Peters | MO | **C** | C | D+ | 112.4 | 0.28 | 12.6 | 0.1 | 10.4 | 2.0 | **8.2** | 10.4 | 13.5 |
| 1st Bank | Broadus | MT | **A-** | A- | B+ | 51.7 | 1.81 | 4.8 | 1.2 | 0.5 | 0.0 | **10.0** | 14.7 | 38.4 |
| 1st Bank in Hominy | Hominy | OK | **C-** | D+ | D | 40.1 | 0.38 | 14.4 | 7.6 | 9.6 | 24.0 | **7.0** | 9.0 | 22.6 |
| ▲ 1st Bank of Sea Isle City | Sea Isle City | NJ | **C+** | C | C | 243.3 | 0.94 | 0.0 | 0.2 | 50.1 | 7.1 | **10.0** | 11.0 | 20.4 |
| ▲ 1st Bank Yuma | Yuma | AZ | **B+** | B | B- | 368.4 | 14.52 | 13.6 | 0.3 | 2.8 | 4.9 | **7.9** | 10.2 | 13.3 |
| 1st Cameron State Bank | Cameron | MO | **C** | C- | C | 52.8 | -7.29 | 0.8 | 1.8 | 29.1 | 23.7 | **8.3** | 9.9 | 28.0 |
| 1st Capital Bank | Salinas | CA | **B+** | B- | C+ | 645.4 | 3.71 | 6.4 | 0.0 | 21.8 | 10.2 | **9.9** | 10.9 | 15.3 |
| 1st Colonial Community Bank | Cherry Hill | NJ | **C+** | C+ | C | 574.9 | 5.74 | 4.5 | 0.7 | 35.8 | 16.4 | **6.2** | 8.3 | 14.4 |
| 1st Community Bank | Sherrard | IL | **C** | C | C | 65.4 | 4.41 | 3.5 | 2.2 | 13.5 | 10.2 | **8.4** | 9.9 | 14.5 |
| 1st Constitution Bank | Cranbury | NJ | **B** | B | B | 1585.7 | 34.69 | 20.6 | 0.1 | 9.1 | 14.8 | **5.9** | 10.5 | 11.7 |
| 1st Equity Bank | Skokie | IL | **C-** | D | D | 96.8 | -3.50 | 13.8 | 0.1 | 16.9 | 0.2 | **10.0** | 15.3 | 21.1 |
| 1st Equity Bank Northwest | Buffalo Grove | IL | **B-** | C+ | C+ | 41.0 | -2.18 | 6.7 | 0.2 | 20.6 | 0.0 | **10.0** | 21.3 | 29.1 |
| 1st Federal Savings Bank of SC, Inc. | Walterboro | SC | **B-** | C+ | D+ | 97.0 | 8.37 | 0.1 | 1.6 | 64.6 | 7.3 | **7.5** | 9.3 | 17.7 |
| 1st Financial Bank USA | Dakota Dunes | SD | **C** | C | C | 661.8 | -2.52 | 0.1 | 68.5 | 0.1 | 7.7 | **10.0** | 25.7 | 29.6 |
| ▲ 1st National Bank | Lebanon | OH | **C** | C | C+ | 203.2 | 13.60 | 2.7 | 0.6 | 27.4 | 12.4 | **5.5** | 7.5 | 13.5 |
| 1st Security Bank of Washington | Mountlake Terrace | WA | **A** | A | A- | 1712.9 | 5.64 | 6.8 | 19.0 | 20.1 | 7.4 | **9.6** | 11.6 | 14.6 |
| 1st Source Bank | South Bend | IN | **A-** | A- | A- | 6622.2 | 5.28 | 47.7 | 2.1 | 6.0 | 15.7 | **8.3** | 11.0 | 13.6 |
| ▲ 1st State Bank | Saginaw | MI | **B-** | C+ | B- | 323.7 | 14.29 | 31.2 | 0.2 | 4.8 | 0.9 | **6.5** | 9.7 | 12.2 |
| ▼ 1st State Bank of Mason City | Mason City | IL | **C+** | B- | B | 24.9 | -7.46 | 1.2 | 6.9 | 15.1 | 40.8 | **10.0** | 13.8 | 33.0 |
| 1st Summit Bank | Johnstown | PA | **B** | B | B | 1103.5 | 4.35 | 8.9 | 2.7 | 24.7 | 44.5 | **8.4** | 9.9 | 19.1 |
| 1st Trust Bank, Inc. | Hazard | KY | **C-** | C | C- | 268.8 | 4.52 | 19.9 | 2.0 | 18.5 | 3.9 | **6.5** | 8.5 | 12.4 |
| 1st United Bank | Faribault | MN | **A-** | B | B | 144.4 | 1.44 | 10.4 | 1.9 | 7.1 | 39.0 | **10.0** | 11.8 | 18.4 |
| ▲ 21st Century Bank | Loretto | MN | **B+** | B+ | B+ | 530.7 | 8.54 | 19.5 | 0.1 | 8.7 | 12.1 | **10.0** | 12.0 | 16.8 |
| 22nd State Bank | Louisville | AL | **D-** | C- | C | 140.3 | -1.75 | 9.2 | 1.8 | 25.3 | 12.9 | **9.7** | 10.8 | 16.1 |
| 5Star Bank | Colorado Springs | CO | **A-** | A- | A- | 271.5 | 29.62 | 7.3 | 0.2 | 12.8 | 0.7 | **10.0** | 14.8 | 17.6 |
| AB&T | Albany | GA | **B** | B- | B- | 195.3 | 0.71 | 19.1 | 2.2 | 17.9 | 0.6 | **6.1** | 8.9 | 11.8 |
| Abacus Federal Savings Bank | New York | NY | **B-** | B- | B | 353.4 | 4.03 | 0.0 | 0.0 | 61.3 | 0.0 | **10.0** | 11.9 | 23.0 |
| Abbeville Building & Loan | Abbeville | LA | **B-** | B- | B- | 53.9 | -2.18 | 0.0 | 0.0 | 41.3 | 1.8 | **10.0** | 27.4 | 38.4 |
| Abbeville First Bank, SSB | Abbeville | SC | **C** | C | B | 78.5 | 1.31 | 3.4 | 0.9 | 44.0 | 26.7 | **7.3** | 9.2 | 17.8 |
| AbbyBank | Abbotsford | WI | **B-** | B- | B- | 549.9 | 8.23 | 3.6 | 0.6 | 14.9 | 14.2 | **5.3** | 8.4 | 11.2 |
| Abington Bank | Abington | MA | **B-** | C+ | C+ | 566.0 | 112.34 | 1.4 | 0.1 | 42.4 | 8.5 | **10.0** | 11.5 | 17.2 |
| Academy Bank, N.A. | Kansas City | MO | **A-** | A- | A- | 2095.4 | 43.31 | 17.3 | 0.9 | 11.5 | 9.7 | **10.0** | 13.2 | 16.3 |
| ACB Bank | Cherokee | OK | **D+** | C | C+ | 129.4 | -2.19 | 6.7 | 2.0 | 9.7 | 15.7 | **8.0** | 10.5 | 13.3 |
| Access Bank | Omaha | NE | **B** | B | B- | 658.9 | 23.61 | 16.2 | 0.3 | 10.9 | 7.3 | **6.9** | 10.3 | 12.4 |
| AccessBank Texas | Denton | TX | **B-** | B- | B- | 468.2 | 23.09 | 10.1 | 2.0 | 11.4 | 10.2 | **9.9** | 10.9 | 14.9 |
| ACNB Bank | Gettysburg | PA | **A-** | B+ | B | 1706.1 | 4.42 | 4.6 | 0.8 | 23.7 | 12.3 | **8.4** | 9.9 | 15.3 |
| Adams Bank & Trust | Ogallala | NE | **B+** | B | B+ | 839.2 | 7.53 | 10.0 | 1.9 | 13.5 | 2.1 | **8.2** | 11.2 | 13.5 |
| Adams Community Bank | Adams | MA | **C** | C | C | 630.1 | 8.69 | 1.5 | 1.4 | 68.4 | 6.8 | **6.5** | 8.6 | 14.9 |
| Adams County Bank | Kenesaw | NE | **B** | C+ | B- | 185.3 | 11.12 | 3.5 | 0.7 | 3.6 | 33.4 | **8.3** | 9.9 | 14.5 |
| Adams State Bank | Adams | NE | **B+** | B+ | B+ | 49.0 | -1.33 | 7.8 | 4.4 | 16.0 | 16.4 | **10.0** | 19.8 | 25.8 |
| Adirondack Bank | Utica | NY | **C** | C | C | 815.4 | -0.74 | 11.9 | 1.3 | 27.6 | 27.6 | **5.9** | 7.9 | 16.3 |
| Adirondack Trust Co. | Saratoga Springs | NY | **B** | B | B- | 1237.5 | 7.76 | 8.1 | 2.9 | 14.3 | 21.4 | **8.4** | 10.0 | 15.5 |
| ▲ Adrian Bank | Adrian | MO | **A-** | B- | B- | 140.5 | -1.44 | 6.7 | 5.3 | 10.3 | 22.9 | **10.0** | 11.6 | 17.2 |
| Adrian State Bank | Adrian | MN | **C+** | C | C+ | 54.9 | 9.15 | 5.8 | 1.0 | 2.8 | 3.1 | **6.2** | 9.2 | 11.9 |
| Advantage Community Bank | Dorchester | WI | **A-** | A- | B+ | 155.1 | 2.80 | 8.6 | 2.2 | 14.2 | 16.9 | **10.0** | 12.8 | 19.8 |
| ▲ Affiliated Bank, N.A. | Arlington | TX | **B** | B | B- | 973.1 | 29.46 | 12.2 | 0.5 | 23.9 | 0.0 | **7.6** | 11.4 | 13.0 |
| AIG Federal Savings Bank | Wilmington | DE | **U** | U | U | 36.4 | 3.67 | 0.0 | 0.0 | 0.0 | 89.9 | **10.0** | 95.2 | 575.6 |
| AimBank | Littlefield | TX | **A-** | B | B | 1775.8 | 26.75 | 12.6 | 1.1 | 11.8 | 27.8 | **7.8** | 9.5 | 14.0 |
| Alamerica Bank | Birmingham | AL | **D** | D+ | C- | 19.6 | -17.99 | 10.0 | 0.7 | 7.6 | 3.0 | **10.0** | 15.6 | 21.3 |
| Alamosa State Bank | Alamosa | CO | **A-** | A- | A- | 253.2 | 3.06 | 4.4 | 3.7 | 6.6 | 28.0 | **9.2** | 10.5 | 19.7 |
| ▲ Albany Bank and Trust Co., N.A. | Chicago | IL | **A-** | B+ | B+ | 617.7 | 2.81 | 6.1 | 0.1 | 3.4 | 7.7 | **10.0** | 16.0 | 23.3 |
| Alden State Bank | Sterling | KS | **C** | C- | C- | 20.1 | -2.98 | 6.7 | 7.9 | 18.5 | 20.2 | **10.0** | 11.8 | 22.9 |
| ▲ Alden State Bank | Alden | MI | **A-** | B+ | A- | 204.8 | 9.14 | 4.3 | 2.6 | 21.3 | 6.4 | **10.0** | 12.7 | 17.9 |
| Alden State Bank | Alden | NY | **B-** | B- | B | 344.7 | 3.86 | 9.1 | 1.3 | 53.1 | 12.0 | **10.0** | 12.8 | 19.5 |
| Alerus Financial, N.A. | Grand Forks | ND | **A-** | A- | B+ | 2354.9 | 8.20 | 18.1 | 3.7 | 22.9 | 13.2 | **7.8** | 10.2 | 13.2 |
| Algonquin State Bank | Algonquin | IL | **C** | D+ | D- | 134.2 | -8.93 | 2.6 | 14.7 | 13.2 | 20.1 | **10.0** | 11.5 | 15.6 |
| ▲ All America Bank | Oklahoma City | OK | **B-** | C+ | B | 467.5 | 6.61 | 5.5 | 2.4 | 16.6 | 9.4 | **6.1** | 8.9 | 11.8 |
| Allegiance Bank | Houston | TX | **C+** | B- | B- | 4985.7 | 7.13 | 13.1 | 0.9 | 12.7 | 7.5 | **8.1** | 10.9 | 13.4 |
| Alliance Bank | Francesville | IN | **A-** | B+ | A- | 311.2 | 2.29 | 8.0 | 0.4 | 5.3 | 31.8 | **10.0** | 12.6 | 18.7 |

| Asset Quality Index | Adjusted Non-Performing Loans as a % of Total Loans | Adjusted Non-Performing Loans as a % of Capital | Net Charge-Offs Avg Loans | Profitability Index | Net Income ($Mil) | Return on Assets (R.O.A.) | Return on Equity (R.O.E.) | Net Interest Spread | Overhead Efficiency Ratio | Liquidity Index | Liquidity Ratio | Hot Money Ratio | Stability Index |
|---|---|---|---|---|---|---|---|---|---|---|---|---|---|
| 6.8 | 1.09 | 2.9 | 0.00 | 5.8 | 4.1 | 1.09 | 7.63 | 3.73 | 62.1 | 3.3 | 23.3 | 13.2 | 8.3 |
| 7.4 | 0.03 | 0.2 | -0.02 | 3.2 | 0.7 | 0.60 | 5.86 | 3.54 | 83.3 | 0.9 | 15.7 | 31.5 | 5.3 |
| 9.0 | 0.00 | 0.0 | -0.25 | 8.9 | 1.1 | 2.27 | 15.36 | 4.11 | 47.6 | 5.9 | 71.3 | 10.9 | 8.0 |
| 4.4 | 2.42 | 11.9 | 0.19 | 3.8 | 0.4 | 0.87 | 9.72 | 3.81 | 75.6 | 3.0 | 42.7 | 20.7 | 3.7 |
| 7.2 | 1.03 | 5.9 | 0.00 | 3.3 | 1.3 | 0.52 | 4.82 | 3.95 | 81.4 | 4.4 | 22.8 | 7.3 | 5.7 |
| 6.0 | 0.46 | 1.9 | 0.05 | 7.5 | 5.2 | 1.46 | 14.15 | 4.98 | 62.5 | 4.3 | 22.2 | 7.5 | 6.8 |
| 7.4 | 0.88 | 3.4 | 0.00 | 2.9 | 0.3 | 0.46 | 4.74 | 3.09 | 81.7 | 5.9 | 53.7 | 7.2 | 4.3 |
| 6.6 | 0.10 | 0.2 | -0.01 | 5.8 | 7.1 | 1.15 | 11.09 | 4.03 | 62.8 | 4.9 | 16.1 | 2.8 | 7.3 |
| 5.1 | 1.71 | 12.1 | 0.51 | 3.6 | 3.4 | 0.60 | 7.36 | 3.49 | 65.5 | 1.3 | 11.7 | 21.9 | 5.4 |
| 5.1 | 0.65 | 5.7 | 0.00 | 3.3 | 0.4 | 0.68 | 6.70 | 3.56 | 83.5 | 1.6 | 21.5 | 25.0 | 5.1 |
| 4.8 | 0.87 | 3.8 | 0.05 | 5.8 | 14.2 | 1.11 | 9.11 | 4.00 | 63.0 | 2.0 | 11.1 | 18.7 | 8.8 |
| 0.6 | 7.28 | 31.3 | 0.00 | 5.2 | 1.2 | 1.18 | 7.96 | 3.18 | 63.3 | 0.9 | 22.6 | 38.4 | 8.4 |
| 6.9 | 1.06 | 4.1 | 0.00 | 4.1 | 0.3 | 0.68 | 3.12 | 2.94 | 79.6 | 0.7 | 18.6 | 62.8 | 7.3 |
| 8.7 | 0.23 | 1.9 | 0.01 | 4.0 | 0.5 | 0.52 | 5.66 | 4.05 | 84.6 | 2.5 | 14.6 | 16.5 | 5.2 |
| 2.1 | 3.84 | 11.6 | 4.88 | 7.9 | 9.4 | 1.42 | 5.74 | 17.97 | 70.8 | 0.4 | 16.0 | 22.2 | 8.1 |
| 5.2 | 0.51 | 4.2 | 0.02 | 3.5 | 1.5 | 0.77 | 9.06 | 3.17 | 84.8 | 1.3 | 16.6 | 28.7 | 4.0 |
| 6.9 | 0.21 | 1.4 | 0.15 | 8.5 | 23.4 | 1.41 | 12.05 | 4.55 | 65.0 | 1.1 | 12.3 | 19.5 | 10.0 |
| 7.2 | 0.39 | 1.5 | 0.10 | 7.6 | 96.4 | 1.48 | 12.42 | 3.75 | 57.5 | 1.8 | 15.0 | 13.1 | 10.0 |
| 4.3 | 1.78 | 11.8 | 0.34 | 5.1 | 2.9 | 1.01 | 10.46 | 4.29 | 64.0 | 5.4 | 30.7 | 3.4 | 5.6 |
| 6.6 | 2.59 | 5.7 | 0.50 | 1.4 | -0.1 | -0.25 | -1.72 | 3.01 | 73.9 | 5.2 | 75.5 | 13.4 | 5.7 |
| 8.3 | 0.43 | 2.9 | 0.13 | 4.6 | 10.9 | 1.00 | 10.22 | 2.88 | 63.5 | 3.3 | 31.7 | 19.1 | 8.3 |
| 2.7 | 2.14 | 19.9 | 0.22 | 2.7 | 0.9 | 0.34 | 3.82 | 2.86 | 81.5 | 0.7 | 18.8 | 41.2 | 4.6 |
| 7.1 | 0.17 | 0.5 | 0.00 | 6.1 | 2.2 | 1.54 | 11.34 | 3.84 | 65.0 | 6.4 | 46.2 | 2.5 | 8.0 |
| 7.3 | 0.35 | 1.1 | 0.04 | 6.1 | 6.5 | 1.26 | 10.91 | 3.43 | 54.2 | 0.8 | 13.1 | 3.4 | 7.5 |
| 2.3 | 4.37 | 20.8 | 0.44 | 0.2 | -1.3 | -0.93 | -9.24 | 3.43 | 109.0 | 0.7 | 15.7 | 44.4 | 5.1 |
| 7.2 | 0.18 | 0.5 | 0.02 | 6.4 | 2.7 | 1.12 | 6.84 | 4.70 | 62.3 | 1.7 | 14.9 | 21.9 | 7.8 |
| 6.8 | 0.62 | 4.4 | 0.04 | 4.8 | 1.8 | 0.96 | 9.73 | 3.87 | 69.7 | 4.2 | 15.2 | 7.1 | 7.3 |
| 9.1 | 0.35 | 1.3 | 0.00 | 3.3 | 2.0 | 0.59 | 4.43 | 3.29 | 78.4 | 0.7 | 15.3 | 35.0 | 7.7 |
| 4.3 | 0.76 | 7.5 | 0.06 | 2.9 | 0.1 | 0.18 | 0.60 | 4.74 | 95.7 | 2.3 | 5.0 | 16.4 | 8.0 |
| 5.8 | 2.82 | 9.0 | 0.10 | 0.0 | -0.8 | -0.97 | -8.27 | 3.21 | 136.6 | 2.5 | 35.2 | 22.2 | 5.8 |
| 5.2 | 0.71 | 5.3 | 0.09 | 3.5 | 2.9 | 0.57 | 6.41 | 3.36 | 70.3 | 1.2 | 16.7 | 21.9 | 6.1 |
| 5.7 | 1.87 | 5.7 | 0.00 | 3.3 | 2.3 | 0.53 | 3.55 | 3.23 | 74.1 | 1.5 | 15.4 | 23.6 | 6.9 |
| 7.0 | 0.65 | 3.6 | 0.51 | 5.6 | 16.1 | 0.96 | 6.76 | 3.39 | 72.7 | 0.9 | 18.3 | 32.6 | 8.5 |
| 1.7 | 5.05 | 42.2 | 0.94 | 5.0 | 1.6 | 1.18 | 11.91 | 3.94 | 50.7 | 0.7 | 17.6 | 49.8 | 6.3 |
| 6.7 | 0.39 | 2.7 | -0.10 | 5.4 | 6.7 | 1.17 | 9.38 | 4.19 | 67.2 | 4.1 | 23.6 | 8.8 | 7.6 |
| 3.6 | 2.44 | 10.9 | 0.15 | 3.7 | 2.4 | 0.58 | 6.10 | 3.68 | 78.5 | 2.0 | 29.1 | 24.3 | 6.2 |
| 6.9 | 0.60 | 3.7 | 0.06 | 6.7 | 23.6 | 1.41 | 14.08 | 3.87 | 58.1 | 3.1 | 10.6 | 13.3 | 8.9 |
| 7.8 | 0.23 | 0.9 | 0.02 | 6.9 | 10.7 | 1.33 | 12.02 | 4.67 | 66.4 | 2.2 | 10.2 | 17.6 | 8.5 |
| 5.6 | 0.77 | 5.9 | 0.09 | 3.1 | 4.2 | 0.69 | 7.45 | 3.13 | 79.4 | 2.6 | 10.6 | 11.0 | 5.8 |
| 5.8 | 0.00 | 2.5 | 0.00 | 6.1 | 2.6 | 1.52 | 15.80 | 3.00 | 47.8 | 1.0 | 10.9 | 25.0 | 5.8 |
| 8.3 | 0.00 | 0.1 | 0.03 | 5.5 | 0.6 | 1.26 | 6.48 | 3.72 | 65.2 | 2.5 | 18.2 | 15.4 | 8.3 |
| 3.8 | 2.08 | 14.8 | 0.11 | 2.8 | 4.7 | 0.55 | 7.00 | 3.36 | 88.0 | 1.5 | 7.9 | 17.3 | 4.9 |
| 8.0 | 0.21 | 1.0 | -0.01 | 5.1 | 12.8 | 1.07 | 9.91 | 3.42 | 71.0 | 4.5 | 23.7 | 9.1 | 9.0 |
| 6.1 | 0.89 | 4.9 | 0.05 | 8.3 | 3.1 | 2.15 | 18.50 | 4.36 | 53.1 | 3.9 | 20.9 | 10.3 | 7.8 |
| 7.1 | 0.01 | 0.1 | -0.01 | 7.2 | 0.9 | 1.79 | 18.95 | 4.35 | 56.8 | 2.0 | 16.1 | 19.3 | 5.7 |
| 8.6 | 0.00 | 0.0 | 0.00 | 6.0 | 1.8 | 1.24 | 9.52 | 3.62 | 57.1 | 5.3 | 39.3 | 6.7 | 7.4 |
| 6.3 | 0.31 | 2.0 | 0.01 | 5.1 | 7.5 | 0.86 | 6.17 | 4.36 | 75.1 | 0.7 | 13.0 | 41.9 | 8.0 |
| 10.0 | na | 0.0 | na | 9.8 | 3.1 | 8.58 | 8.87 | 2.45 | 31.6 | 4.0 | na | 100.0 | 6.7 |
| 8.1 | 0.11 | 0.5 | 0.06 | 6.8 | 22.0 | 1.42 | 13.35 | 4.14 | 56.3 | 1.7 | 17.7 | 22.9 | 9.0 |
| 2.6 | 1.16 | 21.3 | 1.35 | 0.0 | -1.1 | -5.35 | -27.99 | 3.56 | 416.9 | 0.9 | 28.3 | 48.6 | 3.9 |
| 8.5 | 0.30 | 1.2 | 0.05 | 8.4 | 5.0 | 1.99 | 19.45 | 3.87 | 48.1 | 3.7 | 28.4 | 12.7 | 8.3 |
| 7.4 | 0.39 | 1.6 | -0.01 | 5.9 | 6.7 | 1.10 | 6.85 | 3.29 | 53.9 | 1.7 | 30.0 | 27.6 | 8.4 |
| 8.5 | 0.00 | 0.0 | 0.05 | 2.3 | 0.0 | 0.17 | 1.39 | 3.54 | 94.0 | 1.9 | 32.0 | 23.4 | 5.5 |
| 6.3 | 1.99 | 5.7 | 0.03 | 6.4 | 2.6 | 1.31 | 10.24 | 4.46 | 59.3 | 3.9 | 27.8 | 11.5 | 7.1 |
| 3.0 | 3.97 | 25.7 | 0.45 | 6.8 | 4.8 | 1.39 | 11.07 | 4.28 | 52.6 | 3.5 | 8.2 | 11.0 | 7.8 |
| 6.9 | 0.47 | 2.8 | 0.32 | 7.9 | 34.1 | 1.54 | 12.87 | 3.80 | 73.0 | 4.6 | 15.4 | 5.4 | 9.7 |
| 7.7 | 0.38 | 1.0 | 0.00 | 2.3 | 0.6 | 0.42 | 3.84 | 3.56 | 90.3 | 4.9 | 20.6 | 3.3 | 4.4 |
| 4.1 | 1.01 | 10.3 | 0.47 | 6.4 | 6.7 | 1.49 | 14.86 | 4.46 | 58.1 | 3.3 | 14.2 | 12.3 | 6.5 |
| 3.5 | 1.24 | 4.4 | 0.07 | 5.5 | 55.6 | 1.15 | 7.60 | 4.28 | 61.2 | 1.1 | 16.3 | 26.4 | 9.6 |
| 7.2 | 1.07 | 3.1 | -0.03 | 7.2 | 5.4 | 1.77 | 13.46 | 4.05 | 60.3 | 5.1 | 38.3 | 8.8 | 8.9 |

| Name | City | State | Rating | 2018 Rating | 2017 Rating |
|---|---|---|---|---|---|
| Alliance Bank | Topeka | KS | **B+** | B | B |
| Alliance Bank | Saint Paul | MN | **B** | B | B- |
| Alliance Bank | Cape Girardeau | MO | **B+** | B+ | B+ |
| Alliance Bank | Sulphur Springs | TX | **B-** | B- | B- |
| Alliance Bank | Mondovi | WI | **B** | B- | B- |
| ▲ Alliance Bank & Trust Co. | Gastonia | NC | **C+** | D+ | D |
| Alliance Bank Central Texas | Waco | TX | **C+** | C+ | C+ |
| Alliance Community Bank | Petersburg | IL | **C+** | B- | B |
| Alliant Bank | Madison | MO | **B+** | B+ | B+ |
| Allied First Bank,sb | Oswego | IL | **C** | C- | C |
| AllNations Bank | Calumet | OK | **D** | D | D |
| Ally Bank | Sandy | UT | **B+** | A- | A- |
| ▲ Alma Bank | Astoria | NY | **D** | D- | D- |
| Almena State Bank | Almena | KS | **D-** | D+ | C+ |
| Alpine Bank | Glenwood Springs | CO | **A-** | A- | B+ |
| Alpine Capital Bank | New York | NY | **A** | A- | A- |
| Altabank | American Fork | UT | **A** | A | A |
| Altamaha Bank and Trust Co. | Vidalia | GA | **B** | B- | B+ |
| Alton Bank | Alton | MO | **B+** | B+ | B+ |
| Altoona First Savings Bank | Altoona | PA | **B** | B | B- |
| ▼ Alva State Bank & Trust Co. | Alva | OK | **C** | C+ | B+ |
| Amalgamated Bank | New York | NY | **B** | B- | C- |
| Amalgamated Bank of Chicago | Chicago | IL | **B** | C+ | B- |
| Amarillo National Bank | Amarillo | TX | **B+** | A- | A- |
| Ambler Savings Bank | Ambler | PA | **B** | B | B |
| Amboy Bank | Old Bridge | NJ | **B-** | B- | B |
| Amerant Bank, N.A. | Coral Gables | FL | **C+** | C+ | C+ |
| Amerant Trust, N.A. | Coral Gables | FL | **U** | U | U |
| ▲ Amerasia Bank | Flushing | NY | **A-** | A | A- |
| ▲ America's Community Bank | Blue Springs | MO | **C+** | C+ | B- |
| American B&T of the Cumberlands | Livingston | TN | **B** | B- | B |
| American Bank | Bozeman | MT | **A-** | A- | A- |
| American Bank | Wagoner | OK | **C+** | C | C- |
| American Bank | Allentown | PA | **B+** | B | B |
| American Bank & Trust | Huron | SD | **B** | B | B+ |
| American Bank & Trust Co. | Opelousas | LA | **A-** | A- | B+ |
| American Bank & Trust Co., Inc. | Bowling Green | KY | **B** | B | B+ |
| American Bank & Trust Co., Inc. | Covington | LA | **C** | C | C |
| American Bank and Trust Co. | Tulsa | OK | **A-** | B+ | B+ |
| ▼ American Bank and Trust Co., N.A. | Davenport | IA | **C+** | C+ | C- |
| American Bank Center | Dickinson | ND | **B-** | B- | B- |
| ▼ American Bank of Baxter Springs | Baxter Springs | KS | **B-** | B | B- |
| American Bank of Beaver Dam | Beaver Dam | WI | **B-** | C+ | C+ |
| American Bank of Commerce | Wolfforth | TX | **B** | B | B- |
| American Bank of Missouri | Wellsville | MO | **B** | B | B- |
| American Bank of Oklahoma | Collinsville | OK | **C** | C+ | C |
| ▲ American Bank of the North | Nashwauk | MN | **B-** | C- | D+ |
| American Bank, N.A. | Le Mars | IA | **C+** | C+ | C+ |
| American Bank, N.A. | Corpus Christi | TX | **B-** | B | B |
| American Bank, N.A. | Dallas | TX | **B** | C+ | C+ |
| American Bank, N.A. | Waco | TX | **B** | B | B |
| American Business Bank | Los Angeles | CA | **B** | B- | B- |
| ▲ American Commerce Bank, N.A. | Bremen | GA | **B-** | C+ | B- |
| American Community Bank | Glen Cove | NY | **B** | B | B+ |
| American Community Bank & Trust | Woodstock | IL | **B+** | B+ | B |
| American Community Bank of Indiana | Saint John | IN | **B-** | B- | B |
| American Continental Bank | City of Industry | CA | **A-** | B+ | A- |
| ▲ American Eagle Bank | South Elgin | IL | **C-** | C- | C+ |
| ▲ American Eagle Bank of Chicago | Chicago | IL | **C** | C- | C+ |
| American Equity Bank | Minnetonka | MN | **D+** | D | D+ |

| Name | Total Assets ($Mil) | One Year Asset Growth | Asset Mix (As a % of Total Assets) Commercial Loans | Consumer Loans | Mortgage Loans | Securities |
|---|---|---|---|---|---|---|
| Alliance Bank | 110.7 | 11.87 | 17.6 | 2.7 | 18.7 | 3.6 |
| Alliance Bank | 639.9 | 7.75 | 18.5 | 1.0 | 4.3 | 10.9 |
| Alliance Bank | 253.2 | 2.76 | 5.9 | 2.3 | 17.1 | 2.8 |
| Alliance Bank | 979.8 | 31.38 | 5.5 | 1.2 | 13.2 | 36.9 |
| Alliance Bank | 186.6 | 6.59 | 3.0 | 3.4 | 17.4 | 13.2 |
| ▲ Alliance Bank & Trust Co. | 157.4 | 9.80 | 9.6 | 0.5 | 7.1 | 14.9 |
| Alliance Bank Central Texas | 325.0 | 2.94 | 9.3 | 2.4 | 28.9 | 17.3 |
| Alliance Community Bank | 276.2 | -0.49 | 3.7 | 5.0 | 18.0 | 33.5 |
| Alliant Bank | 160.4 | 0.64 | 4.1 | 1.1 | 25.8 | 5.3 |
| Allied First Bank,sb | 109.7 | 28.70 | 3.9 | 0.7 | 44.2 | 7.2 |
| AllNations Bank | 43.4 | -8.70 | 11.0 | 2.0 | 3.1 | 23.3 |
| Ally Bank | 167492.0 | 5.15 | 24.0 | 36.0 | 10.1 | 16.7 |
| ▲ Alma Bank | 1203.6 | 5.38 | 13.4 | 0.1 | 3.2 | 4.0 |
| Almena State Bank | 78.5 | -42.08 | 17.4 | 3.5 | 4.8 | 16.8 |
| Alpine Bank | 3864.1 | 4.25 | 3.3 | 1.0 | 19.7 | 17.2 |
| Alpine Capital Bank | 258.3 | -3.00 | 1.2 | 2.5 | 2.1 | 36.9 |
| Altabank | 2406.3 | 10.19 | 9.9 | 0.7 | 3.7 | 16.9 |
| Altamaha Bank and Trust Co. | 173.4 | 4.05 | 11.2 | 3.8 | 15.1 | 20.7 |
| Alton Bank | 72.8 | 5.38 | 3.9 | 7.8 | 12.9 | 23.2 |
| Altoona First Savings Bank | 233.5 | 8.53 | 5.0 | 4.8 | 29.9 | 4.1 |
| ▼ Alva State Bank & Trust Co. | 410.9 | -0.99 | 7.0 | 2.1 | 2.7 | 16.6 |
| Amalgamated Bank | 5325.0 | 13.57 | 8.0 | 3.0 | 25.4 | 28.5 |
| Amalgamated Bank of Chicago | 930.7 | 1.63 | 3.7 | 4.4 | 3.5 | 17.1 |
| Amarillo National Bank | 5700.7 | 30.51 | 26.8 | 14.8 | 5.0 | 4.9 |
| Ambler Savings Bank | 410.6 | 2.06 | 0.7 | 0.0 | 46.9 | 24.6 |
| Amboy Bank | 2322.2 | 0.58 | 1.4 | 0.0 | 13.9 | 20.8 |
| Amerant Bank, N.A. | 7975.3 | -1.71 | 15.5 | 1.1 | 3.7 | 20.6 |
| Amerant Trust, N.A. | 9.2 | 7.49 | 0.0 | 0.0 | 0.0 | 60.1 |
| ▲ Amerasia Bank | 691.9 | 11.10 | 1.8 | 0.2 | 18.1 | 0.5 |
| ▲ America's Community Bank | 31.3 | 14.73 | 3.7 | 2.0 | 29.2 | 0.8 |
| American B&T of the Cumberlands | 254.0 | 11.84 | 11.4 | 4.8 | 31.0 | 6.1 |
| American Bank | 440.6 | 1.40 | 13.9 | 0.2 | 13.2 | 7.0 |
| American Bank | 29.0 | 1.11 | 1.1 | 5.6 | 2.5 | 49.6 |
| American Bank | 640.4 | 3.16 | 8.0 | 0.1 | 12.2 | 9.4 |
| American Bank & Trust | 985.3 | 8.58 | 13.4 | 1.4 | 2.8 | 16.6 |
| American Bank & Trust Co. | 210.0 | 9.59 | 8.3 | 3.4 | 26.6 | 14.3 |
| American Bank & Trust Co., Inc. | 436.4 | 12.04 | 7.4 | 1.1 | 23.0 | 8.2 |
| American Bank & Trust Co., Inc. | 189.3 | 14.92 | 5.2 | 1.5 | 23.3 | 1.0 |
| American Bank and Trust Co. | 253.4 | 5.30 | 12.0 | 0.2 | 2.5 | 33.0 |
| ▼ American Bank and Trust Co., N.A. | 359.3 | 3.02 | 8.6 | 0.9 | 20.9 | 10.3 |
| American Bank Center | 1671.9 | 17.24 | 6.5 | 15.3 | 4.0 | 27.0 |
| ▼ American Bank of Baxter Springs | 115.7 | 7.54 | 7.3 | 1.0 | 6.3 | 38.8 |
| American Bank of Beaver Dam | 156.2 | -3.64 | 2.8 | 1.3 | 19.5 | 14.7 |
| American Bank of Commerce | 981.4 | 1.22 | 8.4 | 0.6 | 12.3 | 31.8 |
| American Bank of Missouri | 388.1 | 24.45 | 10.9 | 0.1 | 27.2 | 6.6 |
| American Bank of Oklahoma | 325.4 | 13.47 | 21.3 | 8.8 | 14.9 | 2.0 |
| ▲ American Bank of the North | 529.1 | -2.10 | 10.8 | 1.6 | 15.3 | 17.3 |
| American Bank, N.A. | 346.0 | 8.16 | 7.5 | 1.3 | 4.9 | 1.9 |
| American Bank, N.A. | 1572.5 | 14.85 | 19.7 | 0.6 | 7.0 | 33.3 |
| American Bank, N.A. | 99.0 | 80.93 | 0.2 | 31.3 | 1.2 | 25.7 |
| American Bank, N.A. | 445.5 | 3.11 | 11.7 | 1.5 | 24.4 | 13.4 |
| American Business Bank | 2401.9 | 11.33 | 16.5 | 0.6 | 0.7 | 32.3 |
| ▲ American Commerce Bank, N.A. | 355.5 | 18.97 | 3.7 | 1.1 | 14.6 | 0.0 |
| American Community Bank | 217.6 | 4.63 | 1.1 | 0.1 | 15.8 | 8.1 |
| American Community Bank & Trust | 591.9 | 8.30 | 13.9 | 0.1 | 8.6 | 16.0 |
| American Community Bank of Indiana | 228.4 | 0.89 | 5.4 | 0.3 | 28.4 | 3.6 |
| American Continental Bank | 269.9 | 17.43 | 4.4 | 0.0 | 26.2 | 3.0 |
| ▲ American Eagle Bank | 275.1 | 3.97 | 1.4 | 48.5 | 8.5 | 5.6 |
| ▲ American Eagle Bank of Chicago | 93.4 | -10.72 | 3.5 | 30.7 | 12.8 | 8.2 |
| American Equity Bank | 54.2 | 18.16 | 27.1 | 0.6 | 29.6 | 4.6 |

| Name | Capitalization Index | Leverage Ratio | Risk-Based Capital Ratio |
|---|---|---|---|
| Alliance Bank | **10.0** | 11.7 | 16.1 |
| Alliance Bank | **8.5** | 11.5 | 13.8 |
| Alliance Bank | **10.0** | 13.0 | 15.8 |
| Alliance Bank | **7.8** | 9.6 | 16.4 |
| Alliance Bank | **7.9** | 9.6 | 14.7 |
| ▲ Alliance Bank & Trust Co. | **6.4** | 8.4 | 12.2 |
| Alliance Bank Central Texas | **6.1** | 8.2 | 13.4 |
| Alliance Community Bank | **8.9** | 10.3 | 17.1 |
| Alliant Bank | **9.3** | 10.5 | 15.7 |
| Allied First Bank,sb | **10.0** | 11.9 | 24.6 |
| AllNations Bank | **10.0** | 11.0 | 21.0 |
| Ally Bank | **7.9** | 10.0 | 13.2 |
| ▲ Alma Bank | **8.2** | 10.4 | 13.5 |
| Almena State Bank | **0.5** | 4.6 | 7.1 |
| Alpine Bank | **8.3** | 9.9 | 13.6 |
| Alpine Capital Bank | **10.0** | 20.1 | 43.9 |
| Altabank | **10.0** | 12.5 | 18.1 |
| Altamaha Bank and Trust Co. | **10.0** | 12.0 | 17.7 |
| Alton Bank | **10.0** | 14.9 | 15.7 |
| Altoona First Savings Bank | **10.0** | 14.2 | 19.6 |
| ▼ Alva State Bank & Trust Co. | **10.0** | 13.0 | 16.2 |
| Amalgamated Bank | **6.9** | 8.9 | 14.0 |
| Amalgamated Bank of Chicago | **9.6** | 10.8 | 17.4 |
| Amarillo National Bank | **5.6** | 9.6 | 11.5 |
| Ambler Savings Bank | **10.0** | 12.7 | 26.8 |
| Amboy Bank | **10.0** | 15.5 | 19.1 |
| Amerant Bank, N.A. | **8.0** | 10.0 | 13.3 |
| Amerant Trust, N.A. | **10.0** | 95.3 | 177.1 |
| ▲ Amerasia Bank | **10.0** | 12.0 | 15.9 |
| ▲ America's Community Bank | **10.0** | 11.5 | 15.6 |
| American B&T of the Cumberlands | **7.5** | 9.3 | 13.9 |
| American Bank | **8.8** | 10.2 | 14.7 |
| American Bank | **10.0** | 22.1 | 78.4 |
| American Bank | **7.9** | 10.8 | 13.2 |
| American Bank & Trust | **6.2** | 9.2 | 11.9 |
| American Bank & Trust Co. | **10.0** | 12.1 | 18.7 |
| American Bank & Trust Co., Inc. | **5.5** | 8.5 | 11.4 |
| American Bank & Trust Co., Inc. | **5.7** | 8.7 | 11.5 |
| American Bank and Trust Co. | **10.0** | 11.7 | 19.2 |
| ▼ American Bank and Trust Co., N.A. | **10.0** | 11.1 | 15.8 |
| American Bank Center | **7.5** | 9.3 | 13.1 |
| ▼ American Bank of Baxter Springs | **10.0** | 12.0 | 29.5 |
| American Bank of Beaver Dam | **9.8** | 10.9 | 16.7 |
| American Bank of Commerce | **7.9** | 9.6 | 14.2 |
| American Bank of Missouri | **8.3** | 10.4 | 13.6 |
| American Bank of Oklahoma | **4.0** | 8.4 | 10.5 |
| ▲ American Bank of the North | **9.9** | 10.9 | 16.0 |
| American Bank, N.A. | **8.0** | 11.1 | 13.4 |
| American Bank, N.A. | **7.6** | 9.4 | 15.0 |
| American Bank, N.A. | **10.0** | 12.3 | 21.8 |
| American Bank, N.A. | **9.0** | 10.3 | 15.6 |
| American Business Bank | **6.7** | 8.7 | 13.8 |
| ▲ American Commerce Bank, N.A. | **10.0** | 12.1 | 15.7 |
| American Community Bank | **10.0** | 12.7 | 18.1 |
| American Community Bank & Trust | **10.0** | 13.0 | 18.3 |
| American Community Bank of Indiana | **7.4** | 9.3 | 13.0 |
| American Continental Bank | **10.0** | 13.0 | 17.7 |
| ▲ American Eagle Bank | **4.8** | 8.2 | 10.9 |
| ▲ American Eagle Bank of Chicago | **9.1** | 10.4 | 15.0 |
| American Equity Bank | **10.0** | 11.6 | 17.7 |

| Asset Quality Index | Adjusted Non-Performing Loans as a % of Total Loans | Adjusted Non-Performing Loans as a % of Capital | Net Charge-Offs Avg Loans | Profitability Index | Net Income ($Mil) | Return on Assets (R.O.A.) | Return on Equity (R.O.E.) | Net Interest Spread | Overhead Efficiency Ratio | Liquidity Index | Liquidity Ratio | Hot Money Ratio | Stability Index |
|---|---|---|---|---|---|---|---|---|---|---|---|---|---|
| **7.0** | 0.74 | 3.0 | 0.06 | **5.4** | 1.1 | 1.08 | 9.21 | 4.37 | 64.1 | **1.8** | 23.9 | 22.7 | **5.9** |
| **4.3** | 1.43 | 8.3 | -0.81 | **7.1** | 10.5 | 1.72 | 15.09 | 4.07 | 66.9 | **2.5** | 14.3 | 14.2 | **8.9** |
| **6.9** | 0.62 | 3.5 | 0.02 | **4.6** | 2.3 | 0.89 | 6.86 | 3.73 | 67.1 | **2.9** | 9.0 | 14.0 | **8.0** |
| **7.8** | 0.49 | 1.3 | 0.09 | **4.4** | 9.8 | 1.02 | 9.75 | 3.36 | 73.6 | **4.4** | 28.5 | 9.1 | **7.0** |
| **4.3** | 2.26 | 13.4 | 0.01 | **5.5** | 2.3 | 1.26 | 12.91 | 3.64 | 65.6 | **3.5** | 26.6 | 13.1 | **6.9** |
| **3.0** | 1.15 | 8.2 | 0.26 | **3.9** | 1.0 | 0.72 | 8.18 | 4.38 | 76.9 | **4.5** | 33.1 | 10.3 | **4.5** |
| **8.5** | 0.13 | 1.0 | 0.00 | **3.4** | 2.1 | 0.67 | 8.28 | 3.34 | 75.1 | **1.1** | 23.4 | 33.5 | **4.8** |
| **3.1** | 2.58 | 10.5 | 0.07 | **4.7** | 3.2 | 1.16 | 8.84 | 3.51 | 69.3 | **4.7** | 36.6 | 10.1 | **6.9** |
| **6.6** | 0.49 | 3.4 | 0.00 | **5.3** | 2.0 | 1.28 | 12.38 | 4.24 | 75.0 | **1.5** | 15.6 | 23.6 | **7.1** |
| **4.6** | 3.87 | 9.6 | -0.01 | **6.3** | 3.2 | 3.42 | 29.13 | 3.44 | 93.2 | **2.2** | 31.3 | 15.4 | **4.7** |
| **0.3** | 18.11 | 55.8 | 2.80 | **0.0** | -1.7 | -3.55 | -28.73 | 3.59 | 170.4 | **5.2** | 23.3 | 1.7 | **3.8** |
| **4.6** | 1.01 | 5.8 | 0.71 | **6.8** | 2160.0 | 1.32 | 12.91 | 3.31 | 45.4 | **1.0** | 18.9 | 20.8 | **9.1** |
| **0.9** | 5.69 | 24.5 | 0.29 | **3.0** | 5.3 | 0.45 | 4.42 | 3.15 | 78.4 | **0.7** | 12.4 | 38.9 | **7.9** |
| **0.3** | 22.86 | 119.8 | 6.02 | **1.3** | -6.2 | -5.81 | -103.35 | 3.82 | 91.6 | **0.4** | 18.4 | 65.9 | **4.7** |
| **7.8** | 0.87 | 3.1 | 0.10 | **8.3** | 60.8 | 1.63 | 16.28 | 4.74 | 63.5 | **5.1** | 19.5 | 2.3 | **9.4** |
| **7.2** | 4.82 | 6.0 | 0.00 | **8.0** | 4.6 | 1.81 | 9.20 | 3.55 | 41.9 | **4.7** | 92.1 | 16.3 | **9.0** |
| **5.8** | 1.88 | 5.5 | 0.05 | **9.9** | 45.0 | 1.96 | 14.60 | 4.99 | 47.9 | **4.8** | 18.7 | 4.6 | **10.0** |
| **4.6** | 2.60 | 10.7 | 0.46 | **4.9** | 1.8 | 1.08 | 9.12 | 4.69 | 75.9 | **2.5** | 19.6 | 16.9 | **7.7** |
| **6.0** | 0.90 | 6.1 | 0.32 | **7.2** | 1.0 | 1.55 | 10.50 | 4.42 | 62.0 | **2.2** | 29.2 | 21.2 | **7.7** |
| **6.2** | 1.70 | 8.2 | 0.05 | **4.5** | 2.0 | 0.89 | 6.23 | 4.09 | 68.1 | **1.7** | 21.8 | 23.5 | **7.7** |
| **0.9** | 5.11 | 25.4 | 1.81 | **5.1** | 3.9 | 0.94 | 7.18 | 4.06 | 40.8 | **1.5** | 22.6 | 27.5 | **7.7** |
| **5.4** | 1.82 | 9.1 | 0.22 | **4.6** | 47.2 | 0.95 | 10.04 | 3.54 | 65.3 | **4.6** | 19.2 | 6.0 | **7.2** |
| **6.8** | 0.21 | 1.5 | 0.26 | **5.4** | 8.6 | 1.06 | 10.24 | 4.36 | 74.0 | **5.3** | 32.0 | 3.0 | **5.3** |
| **4.7** | 0.99 | 6.5 | 0.25 | **8.3** | 97.1 | 1.80 | 16.48 | 3.93 | 54.9 | **2.6** | 14.7 | 16.1 | **9.7** |
| **8.7** | 0.91 | 3.7 | -0.17 | **3.9** | 3.2 | 0.77 | 6.04 | 2.91 | 66.4 | **2.4** | 19.3 | 17.3 | **7.4** |
| **3.8** | 5.56 | 11.9 | 0.05 | **7.9** | 46.0 | 1.99 | 12.36 | 3.31 | 54.8 | **3.0** | 20.6 | 15.3 | **10.0** |
| **6.6** | 0.57 | 3.6 | 0.11 | **3.9** | 62.7 | 0.79 | 7.33 | 2.94 | 73.1 | **1.3** | 22.7 | 24.2 | **7.9** |
| **10.0** | na | 0.0 | na | **9.5** | 0.2 | 1.78 | 1.88 | 2.34 | 90.5 | **4.0** | na | 0.0 | **5.7** |
| **7.5** | 0.31 | 1.1 | -0.01 | **10.0** | 13.5 | 2.06 | 17.15 | 4.63 | 39.4 | **0.6** | 11.7 | 47.3 | **9.3** |
| **5.1** | 0.51 | 1.8 | 0.11 | **3.5** | 0.2 | 0.53 | 4.56 | 3.93 | 81.2 | **0.7** | 11.8 | 39.2 | **5.9** |
| **7.4** | 0.07 | 1.4 | -0.14 | **5.9** | 3.4 | 1.37 | 15.28 | 3.77 | 67.4 | **0.8** | 18.1 | 39.7 | **6.4** |
| **7.4** | 0.25 | 1.5 | 0.09 | **7.1** | 7.0 | 1.61 | 15.63 | 4.53 | 59.4 | **5.3** | 28.2 | 2.5 | **8.1** |
| **9.8** | 0.00 | 0.0 | 0.06 | **2.9** | 0.2 | 0.59 | 2.63 | 3.32 | 82.6 | **6.9** | 97.1 | 8.4 | **6.5** |
| **7.3** | 0.23 | 1.1 | 0.00 | **6.2** | 8.5 | 1.33 | 12.68 | 3.12 | 46.4 | **1.9** | 6.8 | 18.8 | **7.7** |
| **7.7** | 0.03 | 1.3 | 0.08 | **7.0** | 15.7 | 1.69 | 17.00 | 3.93 | 55.7 | **2.9** | 13.2 | 13.7 | **7.5** |
| **8.8** | 0.08 | 0.7 | 0.04 | **5.7** | 2.7 | 1.45 | 11.80 | 4.18 | 66.7 | **4.4** | 22.7 | 7.0 | **7.3** |
| **6.7** | 0.40 | 2.8 | 0.10 | **5.6** | 4.7 | 1.12 | 13.31 | 3.58 | 59.3 | **1.2** | 15.8 | 27.1 | **6.5** |
| **4.0** | 0.87 | 8.0 | 0.01 | **3.1** | 0.8 | 0.43 | 5.00 | 4.49 | 87.2 | **1.3** | 15.8 | 22.4 | **4.0** |
| **9.0** | 0.17 | 0.9 | -0.01 | **5.7** | 2.8 | 1.14 | 10.19 | 3.56 | 58.7 | **2.6** | 37.1 | 23.0 | **6.5** |
| **7.5** | 0.87 | 4.7 | -0.02 | **1.5** | -1.2 | -0.32 | -2.76 | 3.70 | 109.8 | **3.6** | 9.4 | 9.6 | **6.6** |
| **4.0** | 1.95 | 8.4 | 0.28 | **6.8** | 21.6 | 1.43 | 15.32 | 3.62 | 60.4 | **2.3** | 10.8 | 16.2 | **7.9** |
| **8.2** | 2.47 | 4.9 | 0.00 | **3.1** | 0.7 | 0.65 | 5.58 | 2.91 | 87.4 | **3.0** | 31.9 | 17.5 | **6.5** |
| **6.2** | 0.83 | 4.6 | 0.14 | **4.5** | 1.4 | 0.87 | 8.30 | 4.07 | 76.1 | **4.5** | 24.2 | 6.4 | **5.7** |
| **7.5** | 0.95 | 3.4 | 0.11 | **5.0** | 9.7 | 1.00 | 10.43 | 3.76 | 68.4 | **3.3** | 24.2 | 13.6 | **6.6** |
| **8.3** | 0.15 | 0.5 | 0.07 | **4.4** | 3.0 | 0.82 | 7.84 | 3.47 | 68.7 | **1.1** | 6.6 | 27.9 | **6.5** |
| **3.6** | 1.35 | 11.2 | 0.25 | **4.4** | 2.3 | 0.73 | 8.47 | 4.60 | 78.7 | **0.7** | 11.5 | 39.6 | **4.6** |
| **3.2** | 2.30 | 11.4 | -0.23 | **7.2** | 7.9 | 1.51 | 13.93 | 4.12 | 66.1 | **4.9** | 19.0 | 3.5 | **6.5** |
| **3.7** | 0.88 | 6.4 | 0.01 | **6.2** | 4.7 | 1.45 | 12.91 | 3.16 | 55.7 | **1.8** | 12.9 | 16.0 | **7.8** |
| **6.6** | 1.24 | 6.8 | 0.01 | **4.5** | 15.2 | 1.05 | 11.70 | 3.83 | 73.8 | **5.8** | 35.5 | 6.5 | **8.3** |
| **6.8** | 0.06 | 0.1 | 2.10 | **4.3** | 0.7 | 0.96 | 5.88 | 6.08 | 60.3 | **3.3** | 61.5 | 26.3 | **5.3** |
| **7.0** | 0.38 | 2.5 | 0.02 | **4.5** | 4.3 | 0.98 | 9.24 | 3.83 | 74.4 | **2.3** | 20.2 | 17.9 | **6.9** |
| **8.6** | 0.14 | 0.9 | 0.00 | **5.1** | 22.1 | 0.97 | 11.73 | 3.64 | 60.3 | **6.3** | 31.5 | 1.7 | **7.0** |
| **4.8** | 1.25 | 6.0 | 0.02 | **7.2** | 4.6 | 1.42 | 12.56 | 4.08 | 52.6 | **0.8** | 17.9 | 36.1 | **7.3** |
| **7.7** | 0.00 | 0.0 | -0.01 | **3.5** | 1.2 | 0.54 | 4.33 | 3.59 | 83.0 | **1.9** | 20.2 | 20.0 | **7.9** |
| **8.7** | 0.16 | 0.6 | -0.01 | **3.8** | 3.8 | 0.67 | 5.01 | 3.22 | 71.6 | **3.0** | 35.8 | 18.6 | **8.1** |
| **4.2** | 1.64 | 15.1 | 0.03 | **4.2** | 1.6 | 0.72 | 7.87 | 3.51 | 73.9 | **2.3** | 13.7 | 17.5 | **5.9** |
| **8.8** | 0.04 | 0.1 | -0.04 | **7.1** | 3.1 | 1.24 | 9.06 | 3.59 | 56.5 | **1.0** | 27.8 | 59.8 | **8.3** |
| **5.3** | 0.21 | 1.4 | 0.34 | **5.0** | 2.4 | 0.88 | 11.12 | 3.20 | 56.9 | **0.7** | 20.9 | 47.7 | **4.3** |
| **4.7** | 0.14 | 0.5 | 0.26 | **2.3** | 0.2 | 0.23 | 2.34 | 2.69 | 84.4 | **0.7** | 21.1 | 49.9 | **4.7** |
| **4.6** | 0.72 | 4.7 | 0.94 | **0.0** | -0.6 | -1.20 | -8.99 | 4.16 | 111.7 | **1.1** | 8.2 | 23.0 | **5.0** |

| | | | | | | | One | Asset Mix (As a % of Total Assets) | | | | | | Risk- |
|---|---|---|---|---|---|---|---|---|---|---|---|---|---|---|
| Name | City | State | Rating | 2018 Rating | 2017 Rating | Total Assets ($Mil) | Year Asset Growth | Commercial Loans | Consumer Loans | Mortgage Loans | Securities | Capitalization Index | Leverage Ratio | Based Capital Ratio |
| American Exchange Bank | Elmwood | NE | **B** | B- | B- | 45.6 | 3.52 | 18.8 | 2.0 | 9.0 | 15.5 | **10.0** | 11.6 | 18.0 |
| American Exchange Bank | Henryetta | OK | **B-** | B- | B- | 70.1 | 3.81 | 5.7 | 9.2 | 38.6 | 7.8 | **10.0** | 11.6 | 17.9 |
| American Exchange Bank | Lindsay | OK | **B+** | B+ | B | 72.4 | 8.23 | 5.7 | 4.1 | 6.0 | 59.5 | **9.2** | 10.4 | 19.9 |
| American Express National Bank | Sandy | UT | **B-** | B+ | B+ | 121931.2 | 4.52 | 23.5 | 58.2 | 0.0 | 4.2 | **10.0** | 11.1 | 15.4 |
| American Federal Bank | Fargo | ND | **B** | B+ | B+ | 628.6 | 6.04 | 3.9 | 0.9 | 14.1 | 7.9 | **6.3** | 8.3 | 12.6 |
| American First National Bank | Houston | TX | **A-** | B+ | B+ | 1904.3 | 19.96 | 6.3 | 0.4 | 3.5 | 5.8 | **7.2** | 10.8 | 12.6 |
| American Heritage Bank | Clovis | NM | **B+** | B | B | 91.0 | 4.01 | 11.3 | 0.5 | 9.5 | 28.3 | **10.0** | 11.9 | 17.6 |
| American Heritage Bank | Sapulpa | OK | **B-** | B- | B- | 1149.4 | 3.15 | 5.4 | 2.7 | 14.4 | 51.8 | **6.8** | 8.8 | 20.1 |
| American Heritage National Bank | Long Prairie | MN | **A-** | A- | A- | 378.6 | 4.91 | 7.3 | 0.3 | 9.7 | 9.0 | **10.0** | 11.0 | 17.3 |
| American Interstate Bank | Elkhorn | NE | **A** | A | A | 101.6 | -13.49 | 11.5 | 0.9 | 26.2 | 0.0 | **10.0** | 19.6 | 22.5 |
| American Investors Bank and Mortgage | Eden Prairie | MN | **B-** | B- | B- | 74.8 | 8.14 | 0.4 | 0.2 | 24.1 | 20.5 | **10.0** | 12.2 | 17.1 |
| ▲ American Metro Bank | Chicago | IL | **C+** | C | C | 80.5 | 0.39 | 1.1 | 0.0 | 24.4 | 0.0 | **10.0** | 11.1 | 17.3 |
| American Momentum Bank | College Station | TX | **B+** | A- | A- | 1742.0 | 59.97 | 13.4 | 0.2 | 11.8 | 10.1 | **10.0** | 13.1 | 15.8 |
| American Nation Bank | Ardmore | OK | **B** | B | B | 445.9 | 8.43 | 3.1 | 4.4 | 19.6 | 33.9 | **8.8** | 10.2 | 15.7 |
| ▲ American National Bank | Oakland Park | FL | **A-** | A- | A- | 305.0 | -2.54 | 6.9 | 0.0 | 2.5 | 4.3 | **10.0** | 14.8 | 20.0 |
| American National Bank | Omaha | NE | **B** | B | B | 4043.2 | 8.81 | 14.9 | 18.2 | 5.6 | 16.8 | **6.4** | 9.5 | 12.1 |
| American National Bank & Trust | Wichita Falls | TX | **B** | B+ | A- | 885.1 | 20.86 | 4.4 | 2.8 | 9.6 | 9.6 | **8.9** | 11.5 | 14.1 |
| American National Bank and Trust Co. | Danville | VA | **B+** | A- | A- | 2464.9 | 33.02 | 11.0 | 0.4 | 13.2 | 15.0 | **7.7** | 10.3 | 13.1 |
| American National Bank of Minnesota | Brainerd | MN | **B-** | B | B- | 306.1 | 4.90 | 3.1 | 2.4 | 33.8 | 2.4 | **9.5** | 10.7 | 15.4 |
| American National Bank of Mount Pleasant | Mount Pleasant | TX | **A-** | B+ | B+ | 103.9 | 3.72 | 8.1 | 8.5 | 15.1 | 38.2 | **10.0** | 13.5 | 25.4 |
| American National Bank of Texas | Terrell | TX | **B+** | B | B | 3467.0 | 9.85 | 6.0 | 0.8 | 12.6 | 33.1 | **6.4** | 8.5 | 13.4 |
| American National Bank-Fox Cities | Appleton | WI | **A-** | B+ | A- | 301.9 | 3.91 | 20.2 | 0.2 | 5.5 | 18.5 | **10.0** | 14.0 | 16.8 |
| American Plus Bank, N.A. | Arcadia | CA | **A-** | B+ | A- | 563.5 | 9.56 | 14.4 | 1.8 | 14.4 | 3.8 | **10.0** | 14.5 | 16.2 |
| American Pride Bank | Macon | GA | **A-** | B+ | A- | 193.9 | 2.27 | 4.9 | 0.2 | 4.9 | 6.0 | **10.0** | 14.7 | 17.8 |
| American River Bank | Rancho Cordova | CA | **B** | B | B | 721.0 | 4.73 | 3.1 | 3.6 | 4.1 | 36.4 | **7.4** | 9.3 | 16.1 |
| American Riviera Bank | Santa Barbara | CA | **B** | B | B+ | 719.0 | 16.61 | 11.4 | 0.1 | 13.7 | 6.0 | **6.9** | 10.0 | 12.4 |
| American Savings Bank | Tripoli | IA | **B+** | B+ | A- | 51.3 | 4.17 | 7.2 | 1.7 | 8.6 | 37.4 | **10.0** | 20.0 | 29.3 |
| American Savings Bank, F.S.B. | Honolulu | HI | **B+** | B+ | B+ | 7233.0 | 2.92 | 8.5 | 3.5 | 33.7 | 19.0 | **7.1** | 9.1 | 14.3 |
| ▲ American State Bank | Osceola | IA | **B+** | B+ | B+ | 221.4 | 4.41 | 13.6 | 4.3 | 11.6 | 16.5 | **7.6** | 9.4 | 13.9 |
| American State Bank | Sioux Center | IA | **C** | C | C+ | 948.4 | 1.66 | 16.7 | 2.0 | 3.3 | 1.1 | **8.5** | 11.7 | 13.8 |
| American State Bank | Arp | TX | **C+** | C+ | C+ | 445.0 | 54.98 | 15.0 | 3.2 | 21.2 | 3.2 | **5.0** | 8.3 | 11.0 |
| American State Bank & Trust Co | Williston | ND | **B+** | B+ | A- | 619.9 | 0.96 | 6.0 | 3.9 | 5.6 | 47.7 | **10.0** | 12.0 | 21.6 |
| ▲ American State Bank & Trust Co. | Wichita | KS | **B** | B | B | 664.9 | -1.79 | 8.3 | 2.1 | 4.6 | 22.1 | **9.7** | 11.4 | 14.7 |
| American State Bank of Grygla | Grygla | MN | **B-** | C+ | B- | 57.3 | 8.50 | 8.0 | 5.6 | 11.8 | 12.7 | **9.6** | 10.7 | 18.9 |
| American Trust and Savings Bank | Lowden | IA | **B-** | B- | C+ | 33.5 | -2.10 | 3.0 | 1.8 | 0.6 | 31.2 | **10.0** | 19.1 | 52.0 |
| ▲ Americana Community Bank | Sleepy Eye | MN | **C+** | C | D+ | 124.6 | 8.07 | 11.5 | 0.5 | 8.4 | 13.4 | **6.0** | 8.0 | 12.6 |
| AmeriFirst Bank | Montgomery | AL | **C+** | C | C | 184.2 | 5.14 | 15.9 | 1.9 | 16.3 | 10.8 | **8.9** | 10.6 | 14.1 |
| Ameriprise Bank, FSB | Minneapolis | MN | **U** | U | U | 4108.3 | 15989. | 0.0 | 2.3 | 0.0 | 91.4 | **6.7** | 8.8 | 16.7 |
| Ameris Bank | Atlanta | GA | **B+** | B+ | B | 18157.0 | 59.87 | 7.3 | 8.5 | 23.0 | 7.7 | **6.6** | 9.7 | 12.2 |
| AmeriServ Financial Bank | Johnstown | PA | **C+** | C+ | C+ | 1156.4 | 0.94 | 14.3 | 1.6 | 13.6 | 15.3 | **6.6** | 9.5 | 12.2 |
| AmeriState Bank | Atoka | OK | **C+** | C+ | B | 282.5 | 4.46 | 7.5 | 7.6 | 17.2 | 2.3 | **7.3** | 9.2 | 13.5 |
| AMG National Trust Bank | Greenwood Village | CO | **A-** | A- | A- | 548.6 | 11.39 | 1.0 | 4.2 | 2.0 | 31.0 | **7.9** | 9.6 | 14.9 |
| Amistad Bank | Del Rio | TX | **A-** | B+ | B+ | 31.1 | 9.99 | 2.3 | 0.9 | 6.0 | 0.0 | **10.0** | 15.0 | 19.2 |
| ▼ Amory Federal S&L Assn. | Amory | MS | **D+** | C- | C+ | 80.6 | -0.16 | 0.0 | 0.7 | 67.5 | 4.8 | **10.0** | 13.1 | 29.2 |
| Anahuac National Bank | Anahuac | TX | **B+** | B+ | A- | 189.7 | 56.68 | 3.7 | 4.4 | 10.9 | 32.1 | **7.2** | 9.1 | 18.6 |
| ANB Bank | Denver | CO | **B+** | B+ | B+ | 2646.2 | 3.08 | 6.3 | 0.3 | 15.6 | 31.6 | **6.0** | 8.0 | 13.1 |
| Anchor Bank | Juno Beach | FL | **C** | C | C | 136.7 | 5.60 | 9.9 | 1.8 | 13.2 | 5.0 | **7.4** | 9.6 | 12.8 |
| Anchor D Bank | Texhoma | OK | **B+** | B+ | A- | 226.0 | 20.16 | 8.0 | 4.4 | 5.0 | 26.8 | **8.6** | 10.1 | 15.5 |
| Anchor State Bank | Anchor | IL | **C+** | C+ | C+ | 19.6 | 26.24 | 6.4 | 1.6 | 1.3 | 15.0 | **10.0** | 28.1 | 40.5 |
| Anderson Brothers Bank | Mullins | SC | **C+** | C+ | C | 876.5 | 15.02 | 6.2 | 28.9 | 15.6 | 3.3 | **7.1** | 9.6 | 12.5 |
| Anderson State Bank | Oneida | IL | **B** | B- | C+ | 86.4 | 1.92 | 2.3 | 2.2 | 4.7 | 29.7 | **10.0** | 15.4 | 35.3 |
| Andes State Bank | Lake Andes | SD | **D+** | D+ | C- | 22.9 | -13.78 | 5.7 | 5.2 | 5.9 | 7.6 | **10.0** | 12.6 | 23.5 |
| Andover Bank | Andover | OH | **B-** | B | B | 427.2 | 7.76 | 0.3 | 1.0 | 30.9 | 39.8 | **7.1** | 9.1 | 20.2 |
| Andover State Bank | Andover | KS | **C+** | C+ | C+ | 117.6 | 25.16 | 10.7 | 1.1 | 15.9 | 3.4 | **5.4** | 8.0 | 11.3 |
| Andrew Johnson Bank | Greeneville | TN | **A-** | B+ | B+ | 387.6 | 4.63 | 5.1 | 0.9 | 30.0 | 9.0 | **9.9** | 10.9 | 16.1 |
| Androscoggin Savings Bank | Lewiston | ME | **C+** | C+ | C+ | 1084.2 | 3.19 | 12.4 | 0.2 | 27.2 | 8.8 | **8.2** | 10.6 | 13.5 |
| Angelina Savings Bank, SSB | Lufkin | TX | **C+** | C+ | C+ | 65.8 | -2.90 | 13.1 | 19.6 | 19.9 | 0.0 | **7.3** | 9.2 | 18.3 |
| Anna State Bank | Anna | IL | **B+** | B+ | B+ | 87.0 | 12.92 | 1.1 | 2.4 | 19.7 | 45.6 | **10.0** | 15.1 | 35.4 |
| Anna-Jonesboro National Bank | Anna | IL | **B+** | B | B- | 219.1 | -1.81 | 3.3 | 4.7 | 27.2 | 36.1 | **10.0** | 14.2 | 29.2 |
| Anstaff Bank | Green Forest | AR | **B** | B | B | 715.9 | 12.19 | 7.6 | 3.6 | 17.4 | 13.6 | **6.5** | 9.0 | 12.1 |

| Asset Quality Index | Adjusted Non-Performing Loans as a % of Total Loans | Adjusted Non-Performing Loans as a % of Capital | Net Charge-Offs Avg Loans | Profitability Index | Net Income ($Mil) | Return on Assets (R.O.A.) | Return on Equity (R.O.E.) | Net Interest Spread | Overhead Efficiency Ratio | Liquidity Index | Liquidity Ratio | Hot Money Ratio | Stability Index |
|---|---|---|---|---|---|---|---|---|---|---|---|---|---|
| **8.4** | 0.00 | 0.1 | -0.39 | **5.6** | 0.7 | 1.40 | 12.30 | 4.11 | 66.6 | **3.3** | 25.2 | 13.6 | **6.8** |
| **4.0** | 1.66 | 16.5 | 0.41 | **4.1** | 0.5 | 0.74 | 6.39 | 4.93 | 74.5 | **3.2** | 18.1 | 9.8 | **6.5** |
| **9.2** | 0.04 | 0.1 | 0.02 | **4.3** | 0.7 | 0.94 | 8.76 | 3.88 | 74.3 | **6.1** | 67.2 | 8.6 | **6.4** |
| **3.0** | 1.25 | 7.9 | 2.64 | **10.0** | 5896.6 | 4.87 | 48.84 | 7.34 | 59.1 | **1.0** | 20.1 | 1.8 | **10.0** |
| **6.1** | 0.36 | 3.0 | 0.15 | **5.2** | 7.3 | 1.18 | 13.82 | 4.22 | 67.9 | **1.9** | 6.6 | 12.3 | **7.4** |
| **6.5** | 0.43 | 3.2 | 0.03 | **7.1** | 24.3 | 1.35 | 12.15 | 3.99 | 51.1 | **0.7** | 13.5 | 54.5 | **9.9** |
| **6.1** | 1.91 | 7.2 | 0.10 | **7.5** | 1.6 | 1.78 | 14.70 | 4.64 | 60.4 | **2.8** | 38.5 | 21.5 | **7.5** |
| **8.9** | 0.45 | 1.8 | 0.08 | **4.4** | 11.8 | 1.04 | 11.29 | 3.22 | 70.0 | **3.5** | 24.1 | 14.7 | **7.7** |
| **8.1** | 0.28 | 1.0 | 0.00 | **7.0** | 4.6 | 1.27 | 10.37 | 3.77 | 56.6 | **5.0** | 29.7 | 5.4 | **7.9** |
| **7.5** | 0.00 | 0.0 | -0.01 | **10.0** | 3.4 | 3.23 | 17.36 | 4.97 | 34.1 | **4.0** | 9.0 | 8.2 | **9.7** |
| **9.8** | 0.02 | 0.1 | -0.08 | **3.1** | 0.3 | 0.46 | 3.84 | 3.26 | 81.7 | **1.4** | 20.9 | 28.1 | **6.7** |
| **4.9** | 1.98 | 6.6 | -0.04 | **3.0** | 0.4 | 0.45 | 4.27 | 3.87 | 87.3 | **0.8** | 21.5 | 52.8 | **5.6** |
| **5.0** | 0.91 | 4.9 | 0.21 | **8.3** | 26.4 | 1.57 | 10.98 | 4.72 | 54.9 | **3.1** | 20.0 | 14.7 | **9.9** |
| **6.3** | 0.24 | 6.4 | 0.18 | **4.8** | 5.1 | 1.18 | 11.39 | 3.35 | 64.3 | **1.5** | 33.6 | 44.5 | **6.8** |
| **7.5** | 0.00 | 0.0 | 0.00 | **7.0** | 4.1 | 1.29 | 9.25 | 4.18 | 54.8 | **4.5** | 28.3 | 8.3 | **8.7** |
| **6.0** | 0.69 | 3.3 | 0.07 | **6.5** | 60.0 | 1.57 | 15.58 | 3.65 | 56.7 | **3.0** | 18.9 | 8.5 | **9.3** |
| **4.4** | 0.50 | 3.1 | 0.01 | **5.8** | 10.1 | 1.27 | 11.55 | 3.65 | 66.6 | **1.6** | 12.6 | 10.8 | **7.9** |
| **7.7** | 0.16 | 0.8 | 0.01 | **5.5** | 23.7 | 1.04 | 7.89 | 3.77 | 68.5 | **2.6** | 12.5 | 16.3 | **10.0** |
| **5.7** | 0.83 | 4.8 | -0.01 | **3.8** | 2.1 | 0.71 | 6.54 | 4.20 | 83.0 | **0.7** | 13.8 | 30.6 | **7.1** |
| **8.3** | 0.00 | 0.0 | 0.12 | **6.1** | 1.5 | 1.42 | 10.68 | 4.04 | 66.6 | **2.0** | 32.5 | 26.8 | **8.4** |
| **7.4** | 0.44 | 1.7 | 0.10 | **5.7** | 37.9 | 1.19 | 12.57 | 3.78 | 65.7 | **4.0** | 5.1 | 7.2 | **8.5** |
| **6.4** | 1.02 | 2.5 | -0.23 | **9.0** | 6.7 | 2.28 | 16.41 | 3.51 | 48.9 | **0.8** | 21.8 | 21.0 | **9.6** |
| **7.2** | 0.00 | 0.0 | 0.00 | **9.7** | 9.6 | 1.75 | 12.51 | 3.56 | 34.1 | **0.5** | 11.6 | 56.9 | **9.8** |
| **4.6** | 2.33 | 8.8 | 0.00 | **6.2** | 2.7 | 1.41 | 9.70 | 4.20 | 65.6 | **0.8** | 18.4 | 39.6 | **9.0** |
| **5.3** | 1.49 | 3.4 | -0.02 | **4.5** | 6.1 | 0.86 | 7.52 | 3.61 | 64.7 | **4.0** | 23.6 | 10.0 | **8.0** |
| **7.2** | 0.05 | 0.1 | 0.00 | **5.5** | 6.4 | 0.96 | 8.91 | 4.30 | 67.2 | **3.6** | 16.5 | 11.1 | **7.3** |
| **8.1** | 0.00 | 3.9 | 0.00 | **6.3** | 0.7 | 1.43 | 6.88 | 3.42 | 54.2 | **4.6** | 58.1 | 14.9 | **9.3** |
| **6.2** | 1.09 | 5.7 | 0.45 | **6.2** | 89.0 | 1.25 | 13.45 | 3.83 | 57.9 | **4.3** | 14.2 | 7.2 | **8.2** |
| **6.4** | 0.68 | 4.7 | 0.27 | **8.2** | 4.0 | 1.79 | 18.78 | 4.08 | 56.3 | **1.3** | 15.1 | 27.7 | **7.6** |
| **3.1** | 0.90 | 6.8 | 0.20 | **6.8** | 15.3 | 1.62 | 13.68 | 3.37 | 49.4 | **1.4** | 6.0 | 19.2 | **8.4** |
| **4.1** | 1.03 | 7.7 | 0.25 | **3.6** | 2.9 | 0.68 | 6.79 | 4.84 | 80.4 | **1.0** | 11.1 | 31.3 | **5.1** |
| **4.5** | 3.06 | 14.1 | 0.16 | **9.6** | 14.3 | 2.38 | 19.79 | 3.53 | 44.1 | **5.8** | 40.4 | 4.8 | **9.7** |
| **4.6** | 2.01 | 6.5 | 0.00 | **4.6** | 5.9 | 0.90 | 6.63 | 3.93 | 68.8 | **3.5** | 17.6 | 11.6 | **8.4** |
| **3.5** | 1.66 | 9.0 | 0.05 | **5.2** | 0.7 | 1.20 | 10.91 | 4.08 | 71.4 | **5.2** | 34.3 | 5.8 | **5.5** |
| **9.3** | 0.17 | 0.2 | -0.60 | **2.5** | 0.1 | 0.38 | 1.98 | 3.08 | 89.1 | **6.3** | 81.3 | 9.7 | **6.5** |
| **3.9** | 2.73 | 15.0 | -0.04 | **4.2** | 0.8 | 0.62 | 7.69 | 3.93 | 79.4 | **2.7** | 21.3 | 12.6 | **4.5** |
| **5.2** | 1.38 | 4.6 | 0.13 | **3.8** | 1.3 | 0.69 | 6.31 | 4.12 | 76.3 | **1.7** | 15.9 | 22.4 | **5.8** |
| **10.0** | 0.14 | 0.3 | 2.24 | **6.6** | 18.6 | 1.09 | 12.96 | 2.36 | 52.8 | **8.7** | 104.9 | 0.0 | **7.0** |
| **5.2** | 0.68 | 2.9 | 0.09 | **6.9** | 186.2 | 1.28 | 9.31 | 4.02 | 63.0 | **2.7** | 8.7 | 11.8 | **9.9** |
| **8.2** | 0.26 | 1.7 | 0.02 | **3.4** | 7.1 | 0.61 | 6.64 | 3.44 | 77.3 | **2.6** | 7.1 | 15.3 | **7.3** |
| **3.8** | 2.26 | 12.4 | 0.24 | **5.4** | 3.1 | 1.10 | 12.43 | 4.34 | 72.7 | **0.9** | 20.8 | 32.2 | **6.5** |
| **9.0** | 0.00 | 0.0 | 0.00 | **9.5** | 9.4 | 1.91 | 19.93 | 2.17 | 67.8 | **7.5** | 62.2 | 0.2 | **7.1** |
| **7.5** | 0.04 | 0.2 | 0.00 | **7.3** | 0.4 | 1.47 | 9.63 | 5.17 | 73.3 | **4.6** | 23.6 | 6.0 | **7.6** |
| **7.6** | 0.00 | 7.9 | 0.03 | **0.7** | -0.2 | -0.24 | -1.81 | 1.92 | 116.3 | **1.5** | 34.7 | 55.6 | **5.4** |
| **8.1** | 0.00 | 0.1 | -0.01 | **5.1** | 1.9 | 1.20 | 11.74 | 4.19 | 73.1 | **2.5** | 32.6 | 20.3 | **6.0** |
| **8.5** | 0.42 | 3.0 | -0.04 | **6.1** | 39.0 | 1.51 | 18.32 | 3.90 | 64.6 | **5.3** | 22.0 | 3.0 | **7.7** |
| **4.2** | 0.07 | 2.0 | -0.13 | **2.7** | 0.2 | 0.15 | 1.59 | 3.30 | 101.5 | **1.0** | 14.2 | 30.3 | **6.5** |
| **5.7** | 0.52 | 5.8 | 0.12 | **5.3** | 2.9 | 1.36 | 12.82 | 3.58 | 68.1 | **0.6** | 14.9 | 41.2 | **7.2** |
| **8.7** | 0.00 | 0.7 | 0.00 | **3.8** | 0.1 | 0.62 | 4.34 | 3.79 | 76.0 | **4.4** | 61.6 | 15.0 | **6.3** |
| **3.2** | 1.02 | 7.5 | 1.24 | **8.3** | 12.6 | 1.52 | 15.89 | 7.43 | 61.1 | **1.4** | 13.8 | 23.8 | **6.6** |
| **9.2** | 0.37 | 0.6 | 0.03 | **4.2** | 1.0 | 1.11 | 7.12 | 2.91 | 56.8 | **5.8** | 67.8 | 10.6 | **7.7** |
| **3.1** | 3.86 | 14.5 | 0.03 | **3.1** | 0.1 | 0.46 | 3.87 | 3.41 | 79.0 | **2.2** | 49.2 | 31.9 | **4.3** |
| **7.2** | 0.71 | 2.9 | 0.02 | **4.0** | 3.8 | 0.91 | 9.07 | 3.08 | 74.9 | **4.6** | 34.6 | 10.3 | **6.2** |
| **6.9** | 0.62 | 4.3 | 0.00 | **4.3** | 0.9 | 0.81 | 10.58 | 3.94 | 73.0 | **3.1** | 18.4 | 14.1 | **4.1** |
| **7.1** | 0.77 | 4.1 | 0.02 | **6.4** | 4.6 | 1.21 | 11.28 | 4.48 | 65.0 | **3.4** | 20.0 | 12.5 | **7.1** |
| **5.8** | 1.35 | 7.8 | 0.00 | **3.5** | 7.1 | 0.68 | 6.34 | 3.37 | 76.3 | **1.3** | 12.4 | 9.0 | **8.5** |
| **4.5** | 2.07 | 8.2 | 0.15 | **4.9** | 0.7 | 1.02 | 11.05 | 4.48 | 72.9 | **5.3** | 40.5 | 8.0 | **4.8** |
| **9.1** | 1.22 | 2.8 | 0.00 | **4.6** | 0.8 | 1.02 | 6.50 | 3.22 | 61.4 | **3.3** | 51.0 | 20.5 | **7.6** |
| **6.2** | 1.26 | 4.5 | 0.37 | **4.6** | 2.1 | 0.94 | 6.60 | 3.91 | 63.1 | **2.7** | 29.5 | 18.2 | **6.7** |
| **5.8** | 0.68 | 4.0 | 0.04 | **5.5** | 9.0 | 1.33 | 13.48 | 3.90 | 63.8 | **1.4** | 12.6 | 24.6 | **7.1** |

| Name | City | State | Rating | 2018 Rating | 2017 Rating | Total Assets ($Mil) | One Year Asset Growth | Asset Mix (As a % of Total Assets) Commercial Loans | Consumer Loans | Mortgage Loans | Securities | Capitalization Index | Leverage Ratio | Risk-Based Capital Ratio |
|---|---|---|---|---|---|---|---|---|---|---|---|---|---|---|
| Anthem Bank & Trust | Plaquemine | LA | **C** | C- | C- | 153.9 | 7.22 | 20.0 | 1.0 | 22.3 | 20.1 | **9.1** | 10.4 | 16.9 |
| Antwerp Exchange Bank Co. | Antwerp | OH | **B-** | B | B- | 119.5 | 11.94 | 7.4 | 3.5 | 25.7 | 13.5 | **8.8** | 10.2 | 14.2 |
| ANZ Guam, Inc. | Hagatna | GU | **B-** | C+ | C | 335.2 | 5.57 | 8.2 | 0.2 | 6.9 | 0.0 | **10.0** | 15.2 | 41.4 |
| Apex Bank | Camden | TN | **B-** | C- | C+ | 581.1 | 3.77 | 3.4 | 1.7 | 53.0 | 0.3 | **10.0** | 14.0 | 23.0 |
| Apollo Bank | Miami | FL | **B-** | C | B- | 745.3 | 6.29 | 7.9 | 2.3 | 15.4 | 17.9 | **7.3** | 9.5 | 12.8 |
| ▲ Apollo Trust Co. | Apollo | PA | **B+** | B | B- | 159.2 | -2.38 | 4.3 | 1.9 | 44.2 | 19.7 | **10.0** | 11.2 | 20.1 |
| Apple Bank for Savings | New York | NY | **B-** | C+ | C+ | 15808.1 | 10.49 | 32.7 | 0.1 | 0.7 | 24.3 | **5.3** | 7.3 | 14.2 |
| Apple Creek Banking Co. | Apple Creek | OH | **B-** | C+ | C+ | 144.6 | 8.38 | 7.3 | 0.4 | 25.3 | 15.3 | **5.9** | 7.9 | 12.1 |
| ▲ Apple River State Bank | Apple River | IL | **A-** | B | B | 362.8 | 9.71 | 7.8 | 3.0 | 11.5 | 28.3 | **9.2** | 10.5 | 16.9 |
| Applied Bank | Wilmington | DE | **A** | A | A- | 165.7 | -6.53 | 0.2 | 0.0 | 3.7 | 0.4 | **10.0** | 21.9 | 62.4 |
| Aquesta Bank | Cornelius | NC | **B** | B- | B- | 523.6 | 13.83 | 10.0 | 0.0 | 7.0 | 10.8 | **9.5** | 10.7 | 14.6 |
| Arbor Bank | Nebraska City | NE | **C** | C- | C | 365.0 | 10.06 | 17.3 | 1.4 | 10.4 | 7.6 | **5.2** | 8.4 | 11.2 |
| Arcola First Bank | Arcola | IL | **B-** | B- | B- | 112.9 | 4.95 | 0.8 | 0.4 | 2.7 | 73.7 | **10.0** | 11.4 | 28.7 |
| Argentine Federal Savings | Kansas City | KS | **C** | C | C | 55.3 | 2.21 | 0.0 | 0.4 | 53.6 | 24.8 | **10.0** | 13.6 | 30.1 |
| Arizona Bank & Trust | Phoenix | AZ | **B+** | B+ | B | 784.2 | 19.01 | 22.0 | 1.1 | 8.9 | 20.2 | **5.3** | 9.9 | 11.2 |
| Arkansas County Bank | De Witt | AR | **B** | B- | C+ | 169.4 | 5.19 | 5.0 | 2.3 | 18.4 | 31.0 | **8.7** | 10.1 | 18.3 |
| ▲ Arlington State Bank | Arlington | MN | **B+** | C+ | B- | 51.0 | -5.89 | 4.3 | 1.6 | 3.5 | 29.7 | **10.0** | 11.7 | 25.2 |
| Armed Forces Bank, N.A. | Fort Leavenworth | KS | **A-** | B+ | A- | 1074.3 | -0.30 | 13.0 | 0.5 | 10.0 | 18.9 | **10.0** | 16.5 | 22.8 |
| Armor Bank | Forrest City | AR | **C** | C | D+ | 161.2 | 78.10 | 9.2 | 1.1 | 8.4 | 13.0 | **9.2** | 10.5 | 18.3 |
| Armstrong Bank | Muskogee | OK | **B-** | B- | B- | 989.9 | 0.65 | 5.9 | 5.7 | 21.1 | 14.8 | **7.7** | 9.5 | 13.9 |
| Armstrong County Building and Loan Assn. | Ford City | PA | **C** | C | C | 86.8 | 1.47 | 0.0 | 0.6 | 54.7 | 28.2 | **10.0** | 14.9 | 36.2 |
| Aroostook County Federal S&L Assn. | Caribou | ME | **C+** | B- | B- | 141.5 | 11.63 | 12.8 | 11.3 | 50.4 | 11.2 | **9.3** | 10.6 | 17.5 |
| Arrowhead Bank | Llano | TX | **A-** | B | B- | 198.5 | 7.91 | 5.0 | 4.1 | 21.1 | 12.6 | **9.1** | 10.4 | 17.7 |
| Arthur State Bank | Union | SC | **B+** | B | B- | 516.4 | 2.30 | 5.7 | 1.5 | 30.0 | 16.1 | **7.5** | 9.4 | 14.2 |
| Artisans' Bank | Wilmington | DE | **C** | C | C | 540.9 | 1.13 | 6.5 | 0.1 | 17.5 | 19.5 | **6.7** | 9.2 | 12.3 |
| ▼ Arundel Federal Savings Bank | Glen Burnie | MD | **C** | C+ | C+ | 424.2 | -2.48 | 0.0 | 0.1 | 66.5 | 13.1 | **10.0** | 15.4 | 32.5 |
| Arvest Bank | Fayetteville | AR | **B-** | B- | B- | 19446.4 | 5.40 | 11.4 | 8.6 | 17.9 | 19.7 | **6.4** | 8.4 | 12.1 |
| Ashton State Bank | Ashton | IA | **B** | B+ | B+ | 50.6 | 2.91 | 7.2 | 2.8 | 9.0 | 26.4 | **10.0** | 13.0 | 16.8 |
| Ashton State Bank | Ashton | NE | **D-** | D- | D- | 19.0 | -13.80 | 2.9 | 1.7 | 0.2 | 4.7 | **7.7** | 10.7 | 13.1 |
| ▲ Asian Bank | Philadelphia | PA | **B-** | C+ | C+ | 238.5 | 12.94 | 1.2 | 0.0 | 14.9 | 2.9 | **6.7** | 8.7 | 13.1 |
| Asian Pacific National Bank | San Gabriel | CA | **C** | C+ | B- | 56.5 | -1.64 | 0.7 | 0.0 | 6.7 | 33.6 | **10.0** | 17.6 | 31.4 |
| Aspire Bank | Fargo | ND | **D+** | C | C | 40.6 | 37.41 | 21.2 | 1.0 | 2.2 | 0.3 | **5.2** | 8.0 | 11.1 |
| Associated Bank, N.A. | Green Bay | WI | **B** | B- | B- | 32343.1 | -3.75 | 16.7 | 1.1 | 25.7 | 17.1 | **6.3** | 8.6 | 12.0 |
| Associated Trust Co., N.A. | Milwaukee | WI | **U** | U | U | 66.3 | -9.67 | 0.0 | 0.0 | 0.0 | 1.5 | **10.0** | 85.2 | 151.2 |
| Astra Bank | Scandia | KS | **B-** | C+ | C | 295.2 | -5.76 | 8.5 | 1.1 | 11.7 | 24.9 | **7.7** | 9.7 | 13.1 |
| Atascosa Bank | Pleasanton | TX | **B** | B- | C | 91.4 | -0.43 | 3.2 | 2.3 | 2.7 | 44.6 | **8.6** | 10.1 | 34.8 |
| Athol Savings Bank | Athol | MA | **B-** | C+ | C+ | 448.3 | 1.44 | 1.8 | 2.7 | 44.4 | 22.6 | **10.0** | 13.8 | 22.6 |
| Atkins Savings Bank & Trust | Atkins | IA | **B+** | B+ | A- | 100.5 | 7.29 | 7.1 | 4.0 | 12.4 | 27.6 | **10.0** | 12.6 | 18.0 |
| ▲ Atlanta National Bank | Atlanta | IL | **B-** | C+ | C+ | 60.3 | 4.49 | 2.3 | 3.0 | 11.1 | 55.3 | **10.0** | 12.8 | 33.1 |
| Atlantic Capital Bank, N.A. | Atlanta | GA | **B+** | B | C+ | 2909.5 | -1.55 | 24.2 | 1.1 | 1.1 | 13.7 | **9.6** | 12.7 | 14.6 |
| ▼ Atlantic Community Bankers Bank | Camp Hill | PA | **B-** | B | B | 794.1 | 5.56 | 1.7 | 0.1 | 2.5 | 16.1 | **10.0** | 12.6 | 22.7 |
| Atlantic Union Bank | Richmond | VA | **B+** | B+ | B+ | 17516.1 | 27.56 | 12.1 | 4.1 | 9.5 | 14.5 | **7.0** | 10.5 | 12.5 |
| ▲ Auburn Banking Co. | Auburn | KY | **B** | C+ | B- | 84.5 | 7.47 | 5.5 | 4.2 | 22.8 | 16.1 | **7.8** | 9.6 | 13.8 |
| Auburn Savings Bank, FSB | Auburn | ME | **C** | C | C | 84.2 | 7.95 | 5.3 | 0.8 | 58.0 | 6.9 | **6.9** | 9.0 | 15.3 |
| Auburn State Bank | Auburn | NE | **A-** | A- | A- | 177.2 | 5.55 | 2.7 | 1.3 | 9.4 | 37.3 | **10.0** | 18.2 | 29.9 |
| AuburnBank | Auburn | AL | **A-** | B+ | B+ | 828.5 | 1.17 | 4.5 | 1.1 | 10.9 | 28.5 | **10.0** | 11.2 | 18.1 |
| ▲ Audubon State Bank | Audubon | IA | **B+** | B | B | 119.1 | 4.60 | 4.9 | 2.8 | 11.9 | 6.3 | **8.0** | 9.6 | 14.0 |
| Austin Bank, Texas N.A. | Jacksonville | TX | **A** | A- | B+ | 1860.0 | 3.79 | 7.9 | 6.0 | 23.1 | 15.1 | **10.0** | 14.2 | 20.2 |
| Austin Capital Bank SSB | Austin | TX | **B+** | B+ | A- | 139.1 | 31.55 | 3.1 | 12.6 | 39.0 | 1.4 | **9.1** | 10.4 | 24.4 |
| Austin County State Bank | Bellville | TX | **B+** | B+ | B+ | 184.4 | 9.38 | 19.3 | 1.3 | 24.0 | 14.4 | **7.6** | 9.4 | 14.1 |
| Auto Club Trust, FSB | Dearborn | MI | **D-** | D | D | 567.3 | 12.15 | 0.0 | 22.0 | 24.3 | 40.5 | **8.5** | 10.0 | 16.0 |
| Availa Bank | Carroll | IA | **B+** | B+ | B+ | 1083.7 | 21.08 | 8.2 | 0.6 | 9.9 | 16.3 | **6.8** | 9.1 | 12.4 |
| AVB Bank | Broken Arrow | OK | **B** | B | B | 404.6 | 4.74 | 15.4 | 0.5 | 24.0 | 10.0 | **8.7** | 10.3 | 13.9 |
| Avidbank | San Jose | CA | **B+** | B | B- | 1129.1 | 23.42 | 31.7 | 0.2 | 0.6 | 4.6 | **6.9** | 11.1 | 12.4 |
| Avidia Bank | Hudson | MA | **B** | B | B- | 1668.7 | 4.25 | 26.0 | 0.8 | 21.7 | 13.3 | **8.3** | 9.9 | 13.6 |
| Axiom Bank, N.A. | Maitland | FL | **C+** | B- | B- | 672.0 | 6.41 | 9.3 | 15.9 | 22.6 | 7.7 | **10.0** | 12.9 | 18.2 |
| Axos Bank | San Diego | CA | **A-** | A- | A- | 11550.8 | 17.91 | 8.6 | 3.5 | 41.0 | 2.2 | **6.7** | 9.2 | 12.3 |
| b1Bank | Baton Rouge | LA | **B** | B- | C+ | 2274.5 | 8.43 | 16.0 | 1.0 | 10.2 | 12.2 | **7.4** | 11.3 | 12.8 |
| ▲ BAC Community Bank | Stockton | CA | **B** | B | B- | 625.0 | -1.76 | 4.9 | 1.5 | 6.6 | 21.3 | **9.3** | 10.5 | 15.0 |
| BAC Florida Bank | Coral Gables | FL | **B+** | B | B- | 2260.0 | 1.06 | 2.6 | 0.4 | 52.6 | 6.3 | **8.7** | 10.1 | 16.6 |

| Asset Quality Index | Adjusted Non-Performing Loans as a % of Total Loans | Adjusted Non-Performing Loans as a % of Capital | Net Charge-Offs Avg Loans | Profitability Index | Net Income ($Mil) | Return on Assets (R.O.A.) | Return on Equity (R.O.E.) | Net Interest Spread | Overhead Efficiency Ratio | Liquidity Index | Liquidity Ratio | Hot Money Ratio | Stability Index |
|---|---|---|---|---|---|---|---|---|---|---|---|---|---|
| **5.0** | 1.77 | 10.0 | 0.00 | **3.0** | 0.8 | 0.55 | 5.28 | 3.96 | 87.3 | **1.0** | 15.5 | 32.8 | **5.9** |
| **4.0** | 1.34 | 12.9 | 0.01 | **4.0** | 0.7 | 0.66 | 6.22 | 3.85 | 79.6 | **3.6** | 16.8 | 11.3 | **6.0** |
| **5.9** | 7.03 | 9.9 | -0.05 | **3.2** | 1.5 | 0.48 | 3.15 | 3.34 | 83.5 | **7.2** | 90.2 | 7.3 | **7.5** |
| **3.9** | 1.03 | 16.7 | 0.07 | **10.0** | 23.1 | 3.98 | 28.62 | 7.67 | 40.6 | **0.6** | 15.3 | 40.1 | **9.8** |
| **5.3** | 0.88 | 5.6 | 0.00 | **4.2** | 5.7 | 0.79 | 8.09 | 3.45 | 69.4 | **3.1** | 28.1 | 13.9 | **6.8** |
| **8.9** | 0.12 | 2.6 | 0.01 | **5.2** | 1.7 | 1.08 | 10.28 | 4.10 | 70.2 | **4.1** | 14.5 | 5.1 | **6.7** |
| **7.8** | 0.02 | 0.1 | 0.00 | **4.0** | 111.7 | 0.76 | 8.74 | 2.39 | 57.2 | **1.6** | 17.9 | 25.5 | **6.4** |
| **7.3** | 0.56 | 4.8 | 0.00 | **4.5** | 1.2 | 0.87 | 10.72 | 4.54 | 70.5 | **4.8** | 15.6 | 3.6 | **4.4** |
| **8.0** | 0.40 | 1.5 | -0.15 | **6.0** | 5.0 | 1.45 | 13.83 | 3.31 | 62.0 | **2.7** | 25.7 | 16.8 | **7.2** |
| **9.5** | 0.00 | 0.0 | 0.01 | **8.4** | 3.6 | 2.04 | 8.61 | 3.99 | 67.7 | **8.1** | 86.2 | 0.2 | **9.0** |
| **6.0** | 0.31 | 2.2 | -0.01 | **4.5** | 4.4 | 0.91 | 9.08 | 3.61 | 69.9 | **4.0** | 10.9 | 7.7 | **5.7** |
| **3.8** | 1.72 | 13.1 | 0.16 | **4.7** | 3.8 | 1.09 | 13.10 | 4.00 | 75.4 | **1.4** | 9.4 | 18.4 | **5.2** |
| **10.0** | 0.00 | 0.0 | 0.00 | **2.8** | 0.5 | 0.48 | 4.11 | 2.30 | 82.2 | **5.9** | 60.8 | 10.6 | **6.7** |
| **8.9** | 0.21 | 1.0 | 0.35 | **2.3** | 0.1 | 0.22 | 1.61 | 3.01 | 88.6 | **1.6** | 35.1 | 38.5 | **7.2** |
| **5.7** | 1.27 | 5.7 | 0.06 | **7.7** | 10.1 | 1.46 | 13.81 | 4.41 | 58.3 | **5.3** | 28.3 | 2.8 | **7.5** |
| **4.2** | 2.07 | 10.3 | 0.14 | **6.4** | 2.7 | 1.59 | 14.16 | 4.23 | 60.7 | **2.5** | 21.4 | 17.0 | **7.1** |
| **8.9** | 0.54 | 1.8 | -0.28 | **5.9** | 0.8 | 1.46 | 13.28 | 3.57 | 63.4 | **5.7** | 57.8 | 9.6 | **5.7** |
| **5.5** | 1.28 | 4.7 | 0.45 | **8.8** | 16.7 | 1.56 | 8.39 | 3.69 | 69.7 | **4.8** | 23.7 | 7.0 | **9.0** |
| **6.5** | 1.46 | 6.0 | 0.21 | **1.6** | 0.1 | 0.05 | 0.34 | 3.61 | 88.9 | **3.3** | 37.7 | 17.5 | **5.5** |
| **3.7** | 1.70 | 10.4 | 0.29 | **7.5** | 14.0 | 1.38 | 11.93 | 4.55 | 64.7 | **1.7** | 20.9 | 23.1 | **8.0** |
| **9.3** | 0.36 | 2.5 | 0.01 | **2.2** | 0.2 | 0.22 | 1.50 | 1.50 | 82.7 | **2.1** | 42.6 | 39.7 | **6.9** |
| **4.9** | 0.90 | 6.4 | 0.16 | **3.3** | 0.7 | 0.52 | 4.73 | 3.15 | 77.0 | **1.9** | 24.3 | 20.9 | **5.5** |
| **8.6** | 0.03 | 0.2 | 0.03 | **6.5** | 3.1 | 1.65 | 15.98 | 4.45 | 61.4 | **5.7** | 32.5 | 1.9 | **6.0** |
| **5.6** | 1.50 | 6.5 | 0.03 | **5.2** | 5.0 | 0.98 | 10.29 | 4.28 | 72.8 | **4.9** | 21.6 | 3.6 | **6.2** |
| **4.7** | 1.31 | 9.0 | 0.00 | **3.2** | 2.8 | 0.52 | 5.55 | 3.38 | 81.7 | **2.7** | 24.2 | 16.5 | **6.2** |
| **5.8** | 2.44 | 12.3 | 0.01 | **2.0** | 0.7 | 0.17 | 1.10 | 2.27 | 89.9 | **1.6** | 25.3 | 26.2 | **7.3** |
| **4.2** | 1.32 | 5.8 | 0.31 | **4.6** | 166.8 | 0.87 | 7.57 | 3.78 | 76.9 | **5.0** | 20.6 | 3.9 | **8.9** |
| **4.9** | 2.03 | 9.9 | 0.03 | **5.7** | 0.6 | 1.28 | 9.76 | 3.15 | 55.4 | **2.4** | 32.5 | 21.7 | **7.8** |
| **0.0** | 8.53 | 124.4 | 1.26 | **0.8** | -0.1 | -0.55 | -5.17 | 3.77 | 97.5 | **2.1** | 24.1 | 18.6 | **3.0** |
| **4.3** | 0.82 | 5.5 | -0.01 | **5.3** | 2.5 | 1.11 | 13.04 | 3.43 | 56.1 | **0.9** | 24.2 | 40.6 | **5.6** |
| **9.5** | 0.00 | 0.0 | 0.00 | **1.9** | 0.1 | 0.10 | 0.60 | 2.76 | 96.1 | **1.0** | 28.2 | 56.9 | **7.8** |
| **7.1** | 0.00 | 0.0 | 0.27 | **2.6** | 0.1 | 0.32 | 3.03 | 3.73 | 88.2 | **2.2** | 27.2 | 19.7 | **4.4** |
| **5.7** | 0.62 | 3.4 | 0.24 | **4.9** | 341.8 | 1.03 | 9.31 | 2.86 | 64.8 | **3.6** | 12.6 | 5.7 | **9.9** |
| **7.3** | na | 0.0 | na | **9.5** | 14.9 | 23.16 | 26.92 | 2.49 | 76.0 | **4.0** | 275.3 | 0.0 | **6.3** |
| **4.3** | 1.04 | 10.3 | 0.01 | **4.2** | 2.9 | 0.97 | 9.53 | 4.06 | 72.6 | **4.3** | 13.3 | 6.8 | **5.8** |
| **9.9** | 0.00 | 0.0 | 0.21 | **5.0** | 1.1 | 1.16 | 11.88 | 3.04 | 51.1 | **6.7** | 94.1 | 9.3 | **5.2** |
| **8.9** | 0.66 | 3.1 | 0.04 | **3.4** | 3.1 | 0.69 | 5.24 | 2.82 | 83.8 | **2.6** | 34.5 | 17.2 | **7.2** |
| **5.2** | 1.69 | 9.3 | 0.03 | **6.2** | 1.2 | 1.24 | 9.41 | 3.27 | 39.9 | **2.7** | 38.4 | 22.9 | **8.5** |
| **9.3** | 0.51 | 1.2 | -0.04 | **3.4** | 0.4 | 0.69 | 5.03 | 3.04 | 73.6 | **5.8** | 61.9 | 9.6 | **6.6** |
| **7.2** | 0.99 | 3.4 | 0.11 | **5.5** | 53.2 | 1.15 | 8.17 | 3.54 | 57.7 | **6.1** | 32.8 | 0.4 | **8.9** |
| **9.0** | 0.06 | 0.2 | -0.12 | **2.7** | 2.2 | 0.31 | 2.33 | 2.28 | 92.1 | **2.3** | 41.2 | 29.6 | **8.0** |
| **5.7** | 0.32 | 2.1 | 0.17 | **6.1** | 212.5 | 1.27 | 7.92 | 3.78 | 60.1 | **3.1** | 13.4 | 12.2 | **9.8** |
| **5.3** | 1.07 | 4.8 | 0.03 | **7.7** | 1.5 | 1.82 | 19.98 | 4.37 | 61.1 | **1.7** | 20.7 | 22.9 | **6.7** |
| **3.2** | 4.22 | 23.2 | -0.01 | **3.0** | 0.2 | 0.31 | 3.39 | 3.56 | 88.8 | **0.7** | 9.1 | 34.3 | **4.4** |
| **8.9** | 0.53 | 1.3 | 0.03 | **5.7** | 2.4 | 1.37 | 7.59 | 3.55 | 56.3 | **2.3** | 23.3 | 18.3 | **8.3** |
| **8.8** | 0.04 | 0.2 | 0.03 | **5.4** | 9.6 | 1.16 | 10.47 | 3.44 | 62.5 | **3.0** | 24.6 | 14.8 | **7.8** |
| **5.6** | 0.50 | 1.6 | 0.07 | **7.4** | 2.1 | 1.73 | 14.63 | 3.99 | 53.5 | **1.3** | 16.9 | 22.7 | **8.9** |
| **6.5** | 0.98 | 4.1 | 0.17 | **9.0** | 31.0 | 1.69 | 11.86 | 4.62 | 59.5 | **3.6** | 14.6 | 11.1 | **10.0** |
| **8.7** | 0.08 | 0.5 | 0.00 | **4.7** | 1.0 | 0.84 | 7.40 | 3.58 | 93.8 | **1.3** | 29.5 | 37.5 | **5.7** |
| **8.6** | 0.02 | 0.1 | 0.09 | **5.3** | 2.1 | 1.17 | 11.74 | 4.33 | 69.8 | **0.7** | 15.1 | 39.8 | **7.5** |
| **6.6** | 0.55 | 2.7 | 0.07 | **0.0** | -7.2 | -1.31 | -12.41 | 1.38 | 149.4 | **0.7** | 24.8 | 41.8 | **6.0** |
| **6.8** | 0.35 | 3.4 | -0.02 | **5.1** | 11.1 | 1.12 | 9.78 | 3.48 | 64.1 | **2.3** | 18.5 | 16.7 | **9.5** |
| **5.5** | 0.70 | 4.9 | 0.23 | **4.1** | 2.7 | 0.71 | 6.77 | 4.23 | 72.3 | **1.8** | 13.0 | 19.7 | **7.1** |
| **6.8** | 0.43 | 2.8 | -0.01 | **7.5** | 13.8 | 1.33 | 12.22 | 4.70 | 57.8 | **2.0** | 20.4 | 20.0 | **9.0** |
| **5.9** | 1.15 | 5.0 | 0.24 | **4.3** | 13.5 | 0.82 | 7.96 | 3.85 | 78.7 | **1.1** | 19.1 | 8.4 | **8.4** |
| **4.3** | 1.70 | 6.6 | 0.24 | **2.3** | 1.2 | 0.18 | 1.15 | 4.15 | 92.7 | **0.8** | 20.5 | 42.8 | **7.8** |
| **6.4** | 0.51 | 4.6 | 0.25 | **9.7** | 188.7 | 1.79 | 18.71 | 4.26 | 41.1 | **1.6** | 10.9 | 14.3 | **9.0** |
| **6.0** | 0.53 | 2.8 | 0.10 | **5.8** | 26.8 | 1.25 | 9.38 | 4.21 | 60.6 | **1.4** | 13.4 | 27.1 | **9.0** |
| **4.9** | 0.67 | 4.0 | 0.03 | **5.5** | 8.7 | 1.36 | 13.12 | 4.07 | 65.9 | **5.0** | 25.7 | 3.7 | **7.7** |
| **6.4** | 1.52 | 6.8 | -0.01 | **6.9** | 31.4 | 1.40 | 14.30 | 3.14 | 50.9 | **1.0** | 21.8 | 45.1 | **8.7** |

| Name | City | State | Rating | 2018 Rating | 2017 Rating | Total Assets ($Mil) | One Year Asset Growth | Asset Mix (As a % of Total Assets) Comm-ercial Loans | Cons-umer Loans | Mort-gage Loans | Secur-ities | Capital-ization Index | Lever-age Ratio | Risk-Based Capital Ratio |
|---|---|---|---|---|---|---|---|---|---|---|---|---|---|---|
| Badger Bank | Fort Atkinson | WI | **A-** | B+ | B+ | 136.7 | 0.56 | 4.6 | 1.3 | 33.9 | 13.0 | **10.0** | 13.2 | 21.9 |
| Baker-Boyer National Bank | Walla Walla | WA | **B+** | B | B | 607.3 | 1.15 | 8.4 | 0.8 | 11.6 | 20.4 | **7.6** | 9.4 | 18.9 |
| Balboa Thrift and Loan Assn. | Chula Vista | CA | **B-** | B- | B+ | 323.7 | 6.53 | 0.0 | 76.5 | 0.7 | 0.0 | **9.4** | 12.6 | 14.5 |
| Baldwin State Bank | Baldwin City | KS | **C+** | B- | B- | 82.1 | 4.05 | 6.8 | 2.8 | 25.2 | 28.3 | **9.6** | 10.7 | 25.6 |
| Ballston Spa National Bank | Ballston Spa | NY | **B-** | C+ | C+ | 584.9 | 9.95 | 6.7 | 4.8 | 34.3 | 12.9 | **7.7** | 9.4 | 13.2 |
| Baltic State Bank | Baltic | OH | **C+** | B+ | B+ | 76.6 | 17.50 | 6.6 | 3.2 | 38.5 | 3.5 | **5.3** | 8.3 | 11.2 |
| Banc of California, N.A. | Santa Ana | CA | **C** | B- | B+ | 7802.1 | -26.60 | 6.0 | 0.1 | 20.4 | 11.7 | **10.0** | 12.0 | 17.5 |
| BancCentral, N.A. | Alva | OK | **C** | C | C | 526.8 | -4.44 | 12.7 | 1.7 | 3.3 | 32.0 | **6.1** | 8.4 | 11.8 |
| BancFirst | Oklahoma City | OK | **A-** | A- | B+ | 7724.8 | 2.24 | 16.0 | 4.7 | 12.1 | 5.9 | **8.8** | 10.2 | 14.1 |
| Banco Do Brasil Americas | Miami | FL | **C+** | C+ | B- | 665.9 | -2.98 | 1.5 | 0.9 | 46.9 | 4.1 | **8.2** | 9.8 | 19.4 |
| Banco Popular de Puerto Rico | San Juan | PR | **C-** | D+ | D+ | 41627.0 | 9.78 | 5.8 | 13.2 | 14.9 | 39.6 | **8.0** | 9.7 | 20.0 |
| ▲ Banco Santander Puerto Rico | San Juan | PR | **B-** | C | C | 6005.7 | 15.99 | 2.5 | 4.3 | 14.6 | 36.5 | **10.0** | 17.1 | 43.0 |
| Bancorp Bank | Wilmington | DE | **B** | B- | D+ | 5662.1 | 27.58 | 4.9 | 16.6 | 1.2 | 24.8 | **7.7** | 9.5 | 19.1 |
| BancorpSouth Bank | Tupelo | MS | **B+** | B+ | B+ | 21061.2 | 16.95 | 8.8 | 1.2 | 17.9 | 21.3 | **8.0** | 9.7 | 14.2 |
| Bandera Bank | Bandera | TX | **B+** | B | B | 69.5 | -3.36 | 3.3 | 4.1 | 32.6 | 9.4 | **9.9** | 10.9 | 26.7 |
| ▼ Banesco USA | Coral Gables | FL | **B-** | B- | C | 1718.2 | 34.58 | 11.2 | 0.0 | 19.9 | 15.3 | **6.3** | 8.3 | 12.9 |
| Bangor Savings Bank | Bangor | ME | **B-** | B- | B- | 4733.5 | 7.33 | 5.6 | 0.5 | 23.6 | 22.9 | **7.1** | 9.1 | 13.7 |
| BANK | Wapello | IA | **C+** | C+ | C- | 97.4 | 7.95 | 7.6 | 6.4 | 18.2 | 0.0 | **10.0** | 12.5 | 15.8 |
| Bank & Trust Co. | Litchfield | IL | **B** | B- | B- | 346.6 | 8.06 | 8.7 | 5.9 | 15.0 | 22.4 | **9.3** | 10.6 | 15.3 |
| ▲ Bank 1st | West Union | IA | **A** | A- | A- | 127.7 | 5.77 | 3.8 | 2.4 | 16.3 | 20.3 | **10.0** | 15.1 | 21.5 |
| Bank 21 | Carrollton | MO | **C+** | B- | B | 142.0 | -6.92 | 6.5 | 1.0 | 36.6 | 3.8 | **6.1** | 8.1 | 12.7 |
| BANK 34 | Alamogordo | NM | **C+** | C+ | C+ | 393.2 | 2.78 | 4.2 | 0.0 | 10.6 | 11.3 | **9.0** | 10.3 | 14.6 |
| Bank and Trust, SSB | Del Rio | TX | **B+** | B+ | B+ | 416.8 | 0.99 | 5.4 | 3.2 | 39.2 | 19.9 | **7.4** | 9.3 | 16.8 |
| Bank First, N.A. | Manitowoc | WI | **B** | B | B+ | 2206.4 | 23.22 | 12.3 | 1.3 | 18.0 | 10.3 | **4.4** | 9.7 | 10.7 |
| Bank Forward | Hannaford | ND | **B** | B | B- | 717.0 | 17.24 | 8.5 | 2.8 | 9.3 | 5.7 | **7.3** | 10.0 | 12.8 |
| Bank Independent | Sheffield | AL | **B** | B | B | 1735.2 | 8.61 | 18.6 | 1.4 | 13.1 | 2.5 | **7.4** | 9.2 | 12.9 |
| Bank Iowa | West Des Moines | IA | **B** | B | B | 1392.0 | 9.30 | 6.7 | 1.0 | 8.4 | 19.3 | **7.3** | 9.4 | 12.7 |
| Bank Leumi USA | New York | NY | **B** | B | B- | 6884.1 | -2.76 | 25.9 | 0.0 | 0.4 | 19.5 | **9.9** | 12.5 | 14.9 |
| Bank Michigan | Brooklyn | MI | **C-** | D | D- | 102.3 | -0.17 | 9.2 | 0.1 | 15.2 | 9.3 | **7.6** | 9.4 | 13.2 |
| Bank Midwest | Spirit Lake | IA | **B-** | B- | B | 948.8 | 2.34 | 22.7 | 0.7 | 5.7 | 11.2 | **5.4** | 9.0 | 11.3 |
| Bank Northwest | Hamilton | MO | **A-** | A- | B+ | 171.8 | 3.48 | 7.8 | 2.2 | 11.8 | 10.7 | **8.2** | 10.1 | 13.5 |
| Bank of Abbeville & Trust Co. | Abbeville | LA | **B-** | B- | C+ | 173.2 | -1.18 | 6.8 | 2.0 | 14.5 | 36.8 | **10.0** | 17.2 | 32.5 |
| Bank of Advance | Advance | MO | **A-** | B+ | A- | 326.0 | -2.91 | 7.4 | 6.4 | 31.2 | 14.2 | **10.0** | 12.3 | 18.1 |
| Bank of Akron | Akron | NY | **B-** | C | C | 388.5 | 11.15 | 9.0 | 0.4 | 25.6 | 9.7 | **7.7** | 9.9 | 13.1 |
| Bank of Alapaha | Alapaha | GA | **B+** | B+ | A- | 181.4 | 10.47 | 23.7 | 7.8 | 18.1 | 13.2 | **9.6** | 10.7 | 16.8 |
| Bank of Alma | Alma | WI | **A** | A- | A | 302.6 | 28.61 | 3.6 | 0.6 | 5.1 | 22.9 | **10.0** | 40.8 | 60.8 |
| Bank of America California, N.A. | San Francisco | CA | **A-** | A- | B+ | 13858.0 | -18.44 | 0.0 | 0.0 | 70.2 | 0.0 | **10.0** | 14.7 | 36.0 |
| Bank of America, N.A. | Charlotte | NC | **B+** | B | B- | 1852983.0 | 3.95 | 16.0 | 9.2 | 12.4 | 24.2 | **6.7** | 8.7 | 13.4 |
| Bank of Anguilla | Anguilla | MS | **C-** | C- | C+ | 139.6 | -7.46 | 6.6 | 5.6 | 8.2 | 19.7 | **9.4** | 10.6 | 15.2 |
| Bank of Ann Arbor | Ann Arbor | MI | **A-** | A- | B+ | 1756.5 | 4.13 | 16.1 | 0.7 | 6.4 | 3.9 | **8.1** | 11.1 | 13.4 |
| Bank of Austin | Austin | TX | **D+** | D | | 168.7 | 34.55 | 29.4 | 0.0 | 4.7 | 9.4 | **10.0** | 19.7 | 24.2 |
| ▲ Bank of Baker | Baker | MT | **B-** | C | C- | 147.5 | 13.40 | 12.2 | 0.8 | 2.4 | 14.5 | **10.0** | 11.7 | 18.0 |
| Bank of Bartlett | Bartlett | TN | **C+** | C | C | 357.8 | 1.70 | 6.2 | 3.0 | 23.7 | 19.4 | **6.4** | 8.4 | 14.1 |
| ▲ Bank of Bearden | Bearden | AR | **B+** | B | B | 47.8 | -10.02 | 11.3 | 6.5 | 10.7 | 21.6 | **10.0** | 12.8 | 20.6 |
| Bank of Beaver City | Beaver | OK | **B** | B | B | 129.3 | -6.29 | 12.0 | 2.7 | 14.7 | 30.1 | **10.0** | 11.7 | 18.1 |
| Bank of Belle Glade | Belle Glade | FL | **B-** | C+ | C | 113.4 | 4.54 | 3.8 | 0.4 | 11.2 | 30.0 | **7.7** | 9.5 | 27.1 |
| Bank of Belleville | Belleville | IL | **C+** | C+ | C+ | 230.5 | 10.24 | 15.1 | 1.5 | 12.5 | 14.8 | **5.7** | 8.2 | 11.5 |
| Bank of Bennington | Bennington | NE | **B-** | C | C+ | 146.8 | 7.88 | 18.3 | 2.3 | 13.1 | 10.7 | **9.0** | 12.4 | 14.1 |
| Bank of Bennington | Bennington | VT | **B** | B | B- | 420.6 | 1.53 | 2.3 | 0.2 | 58.2 | 12.3 | **10.0** | 11.2 | 20.9 |
| Bank of Benoit | Benoit | MS | **C-** | C- | C- | 18.4 | 12.09 | 2.9 | 8.0 | 0.5 | 31.5 | **9.3** | 10.5 | 28.5 |
| Bank of Billings | Billings | MO | **B-** | C+ | C+ | 60.2 | 6.58 | 13.2 | 3.8 | 30.6 | 0.0 | **8.8** | 10.2 | 14.6 |
| Bank of Bird-in-Hand | Bird in Hand | PA | **B** | B | C+ | 466.3 | 30.17 | 6.8 | 0.1 | 22.6 | 0.0 | **9.6** | 12.0 | 14.7 |
| Bank of Blue Valley | Overland Park | KS | **B+** | B | B | 1314.5 | 130.21 | 16.2 | 1.6 | 3.2 | 27.4 | **9.4** | 11.1 | 14.5 |
| Bank of Bluffs | Bluffs | IL | **B-** | B- | C+ | 55.2 | -3.42 | 3.3 | 5.6 | 16.7 | 23.0 | **10.0** | 14.2 | 24.3 |
| Bank of Bolivar | Bolivar | MO | **B-** | C+ | C+ | 309.3 | 6.12 | 5.9 | 3.3 | 27.3 | 8.5 | **6.5** | 8.7 | 12.2 |
| ▲ Bank of Botetourt | Buchanan | VA | **B** | C+ | C+ | 492.8 | 13.09 | 5.4 | 4.4 | 29.3 | 3.6 | **8.7** | 10.4 | 13.9 |
| ▲ Bank of Bourbonnais | Bourbonnais | IL | **A-** | B+ | A- | 70.1 | 17.91 | 3.6 | 4.0 | 11.8 | 0.9 | **10.0** | 12.1 | 19.1 |
| Bank of Bozeman | Bozeman | MT | **C+** | C+ | C+ | 80.3 | 4.82 | 14.9 | 0.8 | 20.2 | 1.7 | **6.9** | 9.8 | 12.4 |
| Bank of Brenham, N.A. | Brenham | TX | **B** | B+ | B+ | 486.3 | 19.89 | 2.3 | 0.8 | 6.9 | 78.1 | **8.9** | 10.2 | 27.7 |
| Bank of Brewton | Brewton | AL | **C+** | B | C+ | 47.7 | -1.14 | 6.4 | 10.7 | 5.6 | 48.3 | **10.0** | 23.3 | 38.4 |

| Asset Quality Index | Adjusted Non-Performing Loans as a % of Total Loans | Adjusted Non-Performing Loans as a % of Capital | Net Charge-Offs Avg Loans | Profitability Index | Net Income ($Mil) | Return on Assets (R.O.A.) | Return on Equity (R.O.E.) | Net Interest Spread | Overhead Efficiency Ratio | Liquidity Index | Liquidity Ratio | Hot Money Ratio | Stability Index |
|---|---|---|---|---|---|---|---|---|---|---|---|---|---|
| **6.4** | 1.04 | 5.0 | 0.00 | **8.2** | 2.9 | 2.16 | 16.36 | 4.15 | 54.1 | **4.1** | 21.7 | 8.6 | **7.5** |
| **7.3** | 0.83 | 3.0 | -0.04 | **5.8** | 7.2 | 1.21 | 12.70 | 3.98 | 75.4 | **6.6** | 47.9 | 2.2 | **6.9** |
| **4.1** | 0.45 | 2.4 | 1.54 | **4.1** | 1.8 | 0.56 | 4.43 | 6.10 | 58.7 | **0.3** | 7.2 | 76.2 | **6.3** |
| **5.9** | 1.46 | 6.8 | 1.07 | **3.0** | 0.4 | 0.55 | 5.19 | 2.84 | 73.7 | **5.3** | 40.3 | 7.8 | **6.2** |
| **5.8** | 0.40 | 3.3 | 0.04 | **3.8** | 3.9 | 0.71 | 7.89 | 3.61 | 75.4 | **4.1** | 2.2 | 6.5 | **6.3** |
| **8.7** | 0.03 | 0.1 | 0.00 | **3.8** | 0.4 | 0.55 | 6.39 | 4.56 | 86.5 | **1.3** | 12.3 | 26.7 | **4.3** |
| **7.5** | 0.97 | 4.4 | 0.58 | **2.7** | 32.8 | 0.36 | 3.15 | 2.99 | 69.8 | **2.3** | 18.2 | 18.0 | **8.4** |
| **3.9** | 1.33 | 8.2 | 0.13 | **2.7** | 2.8 | 0.51 | 5.63 | 3.37 | 85.0 | **0.9** | 21.3 | 31.4 | **6.0** |
| **6.8** | 0.67 | 3.4 | 0.11 | **8.7** | 129.2 | 1.69 | 15.41 | 3.87 | 56.2 | **5.1** | 23.6 | 4.8 | **9.4** |
| **8.7** | 0.00 | 0.1 | 0.17 | **3.7** | 4.6 | 0.69 | 6.46 | 3.48 | 78.0 | **1.9** | 27.2 | 23.5 | **7.2** |
| **1.7** | 8.19 | 27.8 | 1.07 | **7.0** | 601.0 | 1.50 | 14.94 | 4.32 | 58.5 | **4.2** | 20.6 | 9.0 | **8.2** |
| **4.5** | 5.90 | 7.4 | 1.17 | **5.7** | 66.7 | 1.13 | 6.64 | 3.92 | 60.6 | **5.1** | 32.2 | 9.4 | **7.2** |
| **5.5** | 1.05 | 3.9 | 0.11 | **7.3** | 59.0 | 1.25 | 13.17 | 3.81 | 69.3 | **2.4** | 40.3 | 0.0 | **5.7** |
| **5.6** | 0.66 | 3.2 | 0.02 | **6.2** | 234.3 | 1.23 | 9.88 | 3.83 | 67.7 | **3.7** | 13.8 | 10.3 | **9.8** |
| **6.9** | 0.66 | 3.0 | -0.02 | **6.9** | 1.2 | 1.74 | 16.31 | 4.20 | 62.0 | **5.3** | 47.3 | 9.6 | **6.8** |
| **7.9** | 0.56 | 4.2 | -0.09 | **3.8** | 14.2 | 0.91 | 11.02 | 3.24 | 84.5 | **1.1** | 20.6 | 34.4 | **6.9** |
| **8.2** | 0.42 | 2.2 | 0.00 | **3.9** | 34.0 | 0.75 | 7.51 | 3.02 | 77.9 | **3.4** | 13.4 | 5.3 | **8.1** |
| **3.8** | 2.92 | 15.5 | 0.21 | **2.9** | 0.4 | 0.47 | 3.70 | 4.05 | 85.8 | **1.5** | 15.2 | 22.5 | **7.3** |
| **6.0** | 0.71 | 3.1 | 0.13 | **5.1** | 3.4 | 1.01 | 9.55 | 3.55 | 63.5 | **1.6** | 17.3 | 23.7 | **6.7** |
| **8.5** | 0.12 | 0.7 | 0.03 | **7.5** | 2.1 | 1.72 | 11.72 | 4.04 | 56.0 | **4.6** | 34.1 | 10.3 | **9.2** |
| **3.7** | 2.72 | 22.4 | 0.04 | **4.5** | 1.5 | 1.02 | 13.13 | 3.41 | 71.8 | **2.8** | 12.0 | 14.7 | **6.2** |
| **5.7** | 1.21 | 2.6 | 0.00 | **3.6** | 0.8 | 0.53 | 5.14 | 3.89 | 82.0 | **1.9** | 19.8 | 13.3 | **6.5** |
| **8.5** | 0.23 | 1.3 | 0.10 | **5.8** | 5.9 | 1.41 | 14.47 | 4.07 | 71.4 | **3.1** | 7.9 | 13.0 | **6.4** |
| **6.0** | 0.30 | 2.1 | 0.39 | **7.4** | 27.9 | 1.43 | 13.08 | 3.99 | 50.8 | **3.6** | 8.9 | 9.5 | **9.4** |
| **5.4** | 0.38 | 3.4 | 0.03 | **7.1** | 10.7 | 1.66 | 15.90 | 4.46 | 70.1 | **1.4** | 12.6 | 15.0 | **8.5** |
| **5.0** | 1.33 | 9.2 | 0.54 | **6.8** | 22.0 | 1.32 | 13.47 | 5.48 | 67.6 | **2.0** | 20.7 | 18.9 | **8.4** |
| **7.4** | 0.65 | 3.6 | 0.03 | **4.3** | 12.7 | 0.95 | 10.32 | 3.37 | 71.8 | **1.7** | 11.4 | 21.5 | **8.7** |
| **4.8** | 1.57 | 9.4 | 0.41 | **5.1** | 75.1 | 1.08 | 8.94 | 3.52 | 60.7 | **1.4** | 22.3 | 23.8 | **8.8** |
| **3.6** | 1.35 | 8.7 | 0.05 | **1.3** | 0.5 | 0.46 | 4.82 | 3.76 | 103.3 | **0.8** | 18.5 | 36.1 | **4.0** |
| **5.1** | 0.37 | 2.7 | 0.04 | **5.7** | 10.3 | 1.11 | 11.49 | 3.98 | 68.4 | **1.6** | 11.9 | 16.0 | **7.4** |
| **7.9** | 0.21 | 1.2 | 0.02 | **9.6** | 3.9 | 2.34 | 24.67 | 4.48 | 47.2 | **4.2** | 22.9 | 8.6 | **7.5** |
| **6.7** | 3.75 | 7.6 | 0.01 | **3.1** | 1.1 | 0.60 | 3.52 | 3.35 | 79.3 | **3.8** | 40.4 | 16.3 | **7.9** |
| **6.4** | 0.84 | 5.0 | 0.08 | **9.9** | 7.5 | 2.27 | 16.91 | 4.76 | 53.1 | **1.5** | 6.0 | 21.3 | **9.2** |
| **4.9** | 1.18 | 7.2 | 0.38 | **5.2** | 4.9 | 1.32 | 13.19 | 3.90 | 69.2 | **1.5** | 5.6 | 15.9 | **6.2** |
| **4.5** | 1.17 | 6.9 | 0.31 | **5.2** | 1.6 | 0.94 | 8.55 | 3.65 | 62.9 | **1.1** | 18.3 | 32.0 | **6.4** |
| **8.7** | 2.39 | 2.1 | 0.00 | **10.0** | 7.6 | 3.06 | 6.81 | 4.39 | 14.4 | **7.3** | 78.2 | 4.7 | **9.5** |
| **6.4** | 3.18 | 10.3 | 0.04 | **9.5** | 286.0 | 2.03 | 14.52 | 2.99 | 15.9 | **6.2** | 34.5 | 0.0 | **8.7** |
| **5.5** | 0.90 | 3.4 | 0.38 | **7.8** | 26756.0 | 1.49 | 12.68 | 3.09 | 49.3 | **6.2** | 40.1 | 2.8 | **10.0** |
| **1.7** | 3.44 | 24.3 | 0.88 | **3.7** | 0.9 | 0.63 | 6.39 | 4.50 | 76.4 | **1.0** | 8.0 | 29.9 | **5.0** |
| **8.1** | 0.11 | 0.7 | 0.08 | **9.7** | 32.9 | 1.94 | 17.15 | 4.39 | 50.4 | **4.5** | 18.5 | 6.3 | **10.0** |
| **8.3** | 0.00 | 0.0 | 0.00 | **1.2** | 0.4 | 0.23 | 1.11 | 3.61 | 85.4 | **4.6** | 27.5 | 6.9 | **2.7** |
| **3.6** | 4.58 | 22.5 | 0.26 | **9.4** | 2.8 | 2.01 | 16.73 | 4.52 | 49.1 | **4.9** | 27.3 | 4.8 | **7.9** |
| **2.8** | 2.99 | 20.6 | 0.07 | **4.2** | 2.7 | 0.77 | 8.76 | 4.05 | 79.9 | **4.5** | 18.9 | 5.8 | **4.4** |
| **8.2** | 0.30 | 1.3 | 0.15 | **6.3** | 0.8 | 1.54 | 12.52 | 3.91 | 55.9 | **2.6** | 29.6 | 18.6 | **7.1** |
| **8.3** | 0.65 | 2.9 | 0.55 | **4.2** | 1.1 | 0.84 | 7.54 | 3.81 | 76.8 | **1.9** | 25.2 | 21.4 | **7.1** |
| **6.9** | 3.04 | 5.1 | 0.00 | **4.0** | 0.9 | 0.83 | 8.94 | 2.97 | 65.7 | **6.0** | 62.8 | 10.5 | **4.6** |
| **8.5** | 0.00 | 0.1 | 0.00 | **2.9** | 0.9 | 0.44 | 5.51 | 2.77 | 81.0 | **1.0** | 15.0 | 27.8 | **4.5** |
| **7.5** | 0.03 | 0.2 | 0.35 | **4.3** | 1.2 | 0.88 | 6.86 | 4.52 | 69.2 | **4.7** | 13.7 | 4.1 | **5.4** |
| **8.0** | 0.73 | 3.0 | 0.11 | **3.9** | 3.2 | 0.76 | 6.86 | 3.10 | 70.9 | **2.4** | 14.8 | 16.0 | **6.8** |
| **4.3** | 0.47 | 7.0 | 0.66 | **3.5** | 0.1 | 0.71 | 6.61 | 4.11 | 76.3 | **3.2** | 78.0 | 31.8 | **3.8** |
| **2.9** | 1.37 | 7.1 | 0.00 | **4.6** | 0.5 | 0.88 | 6.15 | 5.52 | 75.5 | **3.4** | 14.7 | 12.1 | **6.7** |
| **8.7** | 0.04 | 0.1 | 0.00 | **4.5** | 3.6 | 0.87 | 6.67 | 2.86 | 57.2 | **2.3** | 16.8 | 17.5 | **6.0** |
| **6.4** | 0.31 | 1.0 | 0.03 | **5.1** | 11.8 | 1.12 | 7.87 | 3.92 | 68.7 | **5.1** | 25.4 | 6.1 | **7.6** |
| **6.2** | 1.33 | 5.8 | 0.44 | **3.3** | 0.4 | 0.64 | 4.34 | 3.93 | 77.5 | **3.1** | 32.4 | 12.1 | **6.9** |
| **6.8** | 0.15 | 1.2 | 0.04 | **4.2** | 2.7 | 0.89 | 10.43 | 3.83 | 73.2 | **1.5** | 7.2 | 20.3 | **5.5** |
| **5.3** | 0.28 | 4.6 | 0.06 | **5.0** | 5.0 | 1.07 | 10.31 | 3.84 | 65.6 | **1.1** | 10.1 | 28.5 | **5.9** |
| **7.2** | 0.00 | 0.0 | 0.05 | **3.3** | 0.3 | 0.47 | 3.53 | 3.15 | 79.4 | **1.4** | 26.7 | 30.8 | **6.7** |
| **4.1** | 1.77 | 11.7 | -0.01 | **4.6** | 1.8 | 2.26 | 19.88 | 4.61 | 85.7 | **1.1** | 11.4 | 29.9 | **6.6** |
| **9.0** | 0.40 | 0.4 | 0.09 | **4.1** | 4.0 | 0.90 | 6.84 | 2.31 | 53.3 | **2.4** | 50.3 | 47.9 | **7.4** |
| **5.2** | 1.47 | 2.3 | 0.00 | **2.4** | 0.1 | 0.25 | 1.10 | 3.96 | 94.5 | **6.0** | 57.0 | 7.0 | **6.9** |

| Name | City | State | Rating | 2018 Rating | 2017 Rating | Total Assets ($Mil) | One Year Asset Growth | Asset Mix (As a % of Total Assets) Comm-ercial Loans | Cons-umer Loans | Mort-gage Loans | Secur-ities | Capital-ization Index | Lever-age Ratio | Risk-Based Capital Ratio |
|---|---|---|---|---|---|---|---|---|---|---|---|---|---|---|
| Bank of Bridger, N.A. | Bridger | MT | B | B | B | 610.0 | 19.67 | 4.7 | 2.6 | 8.0 | 42.9 | 7.3 | 9.2 | 17.8 |
| Bank of Brodhead | Brodhead | WI | B+ | B+ | A- | 155.3 | 1.02 | 9.3 | 1.2 | 9.4 | 27.9 | 10.0 | 12.4 | 19.5 |
| Bank of Brookfield-Purdin, N.A. | Brookfield | MO | B- | B- | B- | 86.4 | -5.90 | 1.1 | 1.4 | 6.1 | 52.7 | 10.0 | 12.6 | 34.7 |
| Bank of Brookhaven | Brookhaven | MS | B+ | B+ | B | 163.6 | 7.63 | 7.8 | 2.7 | 15.9 | 30.2 | 10.0 | 11.3 | 18.4 |
| Bank of Buffalo | Buffalo | KY | B | B | B | 72.9 | -0.51 | 1.5 | 6.0 | 27.7 | 38.8 | 10.0 | 11.6 | 18.8 |
| Bank of Burlington | Burlington | CO | B+ | B | B | 66.5 | 14.52 | 12.3 | 0.9 | 0.0 | 11.5 | 10.0 | 13.9 | 20.8 |
| Bank of Cadiz and Trust Co. | Cadiz | KY | B- | B- | C+ | 114.3 | 10.86 | 3.7 | 2.9 | 24.0 | 30.0 | 7.1 | 9.1 | 17.3 |
| Bank of Calhoun County | Hardin | IL | C+ | C | C | 66.3 | -1.33 | 1.0 | 2.5 | 31.2 | 11.8 | 7.6 | 9.4 | 19.3 |
| Bank of Camilla | Camilla | GA | B+ | B+ | B+ | 109.6 | 2.72 | 10.9 | 1.1 | 13.8 | 30.9 | 10.0 | 16.1 | 23.7 |
| Bank of Canton | Canton | MA | B | B | B+ | 677.9 | 8.03 | 1.1 | 0.2 | 28.6 | 9.2 | 10.0 | 12.1 | 15.7 |
| Bank of Carbondale | Carbondale | IL | B+ | B+ | B+ | 245.8 | 4.10 | 9.0 | 1.8 | 17.7 | 20.6 | 10.0 | 13.0 | 22.9 |
| Bank of Cashton | Cashton | WI | A- | A- | A- | 93.0 | 4.92 | 22.0 | 2.3 | 13.7 | 15.6 | 10.0 | 11.1 | 15.0 |
| Bank of Castile | Castile | NY | B | B | B | 1510.8 | -0.68 | 12.0 | 0.6 | 16.6 | 18.0 | 6.6 | 9.2 | 12.2 |
| Bank of Cattaraugus | Cattaraugus | NY | D+ | D+ | D+ | 21.8 | 2.57 | 8.0 | 7.7 | 20.7 | 36.8 | 6.6 | 8.6 | 20.2 |
| Bank of Cave City | Cave City | AR | B- | C+ | B- | 127.0 | 11.15 | 6.6 | 4.3 | 18.1 | 15.5 | 7.4 | 9.3 | 16.5 |
| Bank of Central Florida | Lakeland | FL | B+ | B | B | 571.4 | 10.59 | 14.3 | 2.2 | 13.2 | 16.0 | 7.2 | 9.1 | 12.9 |
| Bank of Charles Town | Charles Town | WV | B- | B- | B- | 515.7 | 6.48 | 4.0 | 1.5 | 34.0 | 9.8 | 9.2 | 10.5 | 14.8 |
| Bank of Charlotte County | Phenix | VA | A- | A- | A- | 140.8 | 3.98 | 6.2 | 3.5 | 37.3 | 14.6 | 10.0 | 15.3 | 22.4 |
| Bank of Cherokee County | Hulbert | OK | C+ | C+ | C+ | 118.7 | 6.07 | 3.8 | 9.2 | 24.7 | 1.6 | 6.4 | 8.4 | 12.8 |
| Bank of Chestnut | Chestnut | IL | D | D | D- | 18.3 | 0.05 | 3.3 | 10.3 | 33.0 | 11.8 | 8.7 | 10.1 | 14.9 |
| Bank of Clarendon | Manning | SC | A | A- | A- | 278.9 | 2.66 | 5.8 | 2.9 | 11.8 | 29.4 | 10.0 | 13.8 | 21.8 |
| Bank of Clarke County | Berryville | VA | B+ | B | B+ | 871.3 | 9.96 | 5.3 | 1.1 | 21.4 | 18.9 | 9.3 | 10.6 | 14.4 |
| Bank of Clarks | Clarks | NE | C+ | C+ | C+ | 39.4 | 5.80 | 5.5 | 12.8 | 4.6 | 2.8 | 7.8 | 10.7 | 13.1 |
| Bank of Clarkson | Clarkson | KY | B+ | B+ | A- | 121.5 | 1.74 | 1.7 | 5.9 | 27.4 | 20.7 | 10.0 | 13.9 | 17.9 |
| ▲ Bank of Cleveland | Cleveland | TN | A- | C+ | B | 286.9 | 4.75 | 4.1 | 0.8 | 18.1 | 1.4 | 10.0 | 15.3 | 20.7 |
| Bank of Clovis | Clovis | NM | A- | B+ | B | 211.7 | 8.00 | 11.2 | 3.3 | 13.6 | 32.3 | 10.0 | 12.9 | 27.2 |
| Bank of Colorado | Fort Collins | CO | A- | A- | A- | 4520.4 | 12.26 | 3.6 | 0.9 | 11.4 | 30.3 | 7.2 | 9.1 | 15.3 |
| ▲ Bank of Columbia | Columbia | KY | B | C+ | B- | 148.8 | 7.02 | 11.3 | 5.6 | 19.2 | 13.4 | 8.2 | 10.2 | 13.5 |
| Bank of Commerce | Ammon | ID | A | A | A | 1283.6 | 2.68 | 12.8 | 0.8 | 2.0 | 9.1 | 10.0 | 15.4 | 18.7 |
| Bank of Commerce | Chanute | KS | B- | B- | B- | 184.3 | 6.57 | 10.4 | 2.8 | 14.1 | 28.4 | 7.8 | 9.5 | 18.3 |
| Bank of Commerce | White Castle | LA | B- | B- | B | 66.0 | -2.65 | 12.7 | 2.8 | 9.8 | 29.0 | 10.0 | 12.2 | 20.5 |
| ▲ Bank of Commerce | Greenwood | MS | A- | B | B+ | 569.9 | 19.41 | 7.0 | 2.7 | 18.0 | 32.3 | 9.0 | 10.4 | 18.3 |
| Bank of Commerce | Chelsea | OK | B+ | B | B- | 146.4 | 4.35 | 11.8 | 8.0 | 16.7 | 11.7 | 10.0 | 12.7 | 17.7 |
| Bank of Commerce | Chouteau | OK | C+ | C | C | 37.7 | -3.08 | 6.3 | 3.5 | 16.4 | 34.2 | 7.0 | 9.0 | 20.9 |
| Bank of Commerce | Duncan | OK | C- | D+ | C- | 316.0 | -0.92 | 17.4 | 1.7 | 4.7 | 4.9 | 8.4 | 12.0 | 13.7 |
| ▲ Bank of Commerce | Stilwell | OK | B+ | B+ | B+ | 131.9 | 176.06 | 14.2 | 3.9 | 7.4 | 21.4 | 10.0 | 12.5 | 16.8 |
| Bank of Commerce | Rawlins | WY | A- | A- | A- | 141.8 | 7.09 | 6.2 | 1.9 | 18.1 | 32.3 | 10.0 | 11.5 | 22.1 |
| Bank of Commerce & Trust Co. | Crowley | LA | B- | B- | B- | 341.6 | 5.36 | 3.7 | 1.9 | 5.0 | 70.5 | 10.0 | 12.8 | 43.0 |
| Bank of Commerce and Trust Co. | Wellington | KS | B- | B- | B- | 82.0 | 7.08 | 5.4 | 5.3 | 18.0 | 33.4 | 6.7 | 8.7 | 15.5 |
| ▲ Bank of Cordell | Cordell | OK | B+ | B- | B- | 37.4 | -9.66 | 12.4 | 1.1 | 41.1 | 0.0 | 10.0 | 11.5 | 17.0 |
| ▲ Bank of Coushatta | Coushatta | LA | B | B | B | 241.2 | 7.31 | 2.3 | 1.6 | 15.0 | 52.7 | 8.7 | 10.1 | 14.9 |
| Bank of Crocker | Waynesville | MO | C+ | B- | C- | 121.9 | -1.75 | 3.0 | 1.7 | 14.4 | 33.2 | 10.0 | 11.8 | 26.3 |
| Bank of Crockett | Bells | TN | B+ | B+ | A- | 189.3 | 11.89 | 6.3 | 2.5 | 5.0 | 50.5 | 8.0 | 9.6 | 17.9 |
| Bank of Cushing | Cushing | OK | B+ | A- | A- | 117.8 | -0.05 | 8.7 | 3.0 | 1.1 | 51.1 | 10.0 | 14.1 | 25.7 |
| Bank of Dade | Trenton | GA | A- | B+ | A- | 114.9 | 5.53 | 1.6 | 4.6 | 25.0 | 43.7 | 10.0 | 11.4 | 25.1 |
| ▲ Bank of Dawson | Dawson | GA | A- | B+ | A- | 130.8 | 10.65 | 4.0 | 3.7 | 17.4 | 14.8 | 10.0 | 18.2 | 29.2 |
| Bank of Deerfield | Deerfield | WI | A- | B+ | A | 161.1 | 13.22 | 5.9 | 1.1 | 27.8 | 6.3 | 9.5 | 12.0 | 14.6 |
| Bank of Delight | Delight | AR | A- | B+ | A- | 140.8 | 13.18 | 7.7 | 2.3 | 15.9 | 7.6 | 10.0 | 13.6 | 17.8 |
| ▲ Bank of Delmarva | Salisbury | MD | C | C- | C | 796.1 | 7.72 | 8.0 | 0.2 | 15.6 | 6.9 | 7.2 | 9.1 | 12.8 |
| Bank of Denton | Denton | KS | C | C | C+ | 18.5 | 1.74 | 3.8 | 11.0 | 31.2 | 18.2 | 10.0 | 18.6 | 29.0 |
| Bank of Denver | Denver | CO | C+ | B- | C- | 237.3 | 6.55 | 0.8 | 6.6 | 11.0 | 21.7 | 8.2 | 9.8 | 15.7 |
| ▲ Bank of DeSoto, N.A. | Desoto | TX | A- | B | B- | 180.4 | 4.34 | 8.1 | 14.6 | 20.0 | 1.3 | 10.0 | 11.2 | 18.3 |
| Bank of Dickson | Dickson | TN | B | B | B | 233.9 | 4.96 | 3.4 | 2.6 | 39.5 | 34.3 | 10.0 | 12.3 | 25.5 |
| ▲ Bank of Dixon County | Ponca | NE | B+ | B- | B | 94.3 | 0.08 | 10.0 | 5.9 | 15.5 | 11.8 | 10.0 | 12.5 | 19.2 |
| Bank of Doniphan | Doniphan | NE | B | B- | B- | 117.8 | 6.42 | 10.1 | 3.0 | 9.7 | 21.5 | 6.3 | 9.6 | 12.0 |
| ▲ Bank of Dudley | Dublin | GA | A- | B | B | 222.8 | -0.11 | 8.8 | 4.3 | 14.7 | 11.8 | 10.0 | 13.2 | 19.7 |
| Bank of Eastern Oregon | Heppner | OR | D+ | C | C- | 491.4 | 18.53 | 11.3 | 0.8 | 4.7 | 4.3 | 3.6 | 9.5 | 10.3 |
| ▲ Bank of Eastman | Eastman | GA | C | D+ | D+ | 161.5 | -4.98 | 8.7 | 5.8 | 24.6 | 7.5 | 10.0 | 11.3 | 17.4 |
| Bank of Easton | North Easton | MA | B- | B- | B- | 161.1 | 11.55 | 0.0 | 0.4 | 41.9 | 21.0 | 10.0 | 11.6 | 26.2 |
| Bank of Edison | Edison | GA | C | C | C | 50.7 | 5.61 | 4.3 | 5.9 | 9.7 | 46.6 | 7.2 | 9.1 | 20.4 |

| Asset Quality Index | Adjusted Non-Performing Loans as a % of Total Loans | Adjusted Non-Performing Loans as a % of Capital | Net Charge-Offs Avg Loans | Profitability Index | Net Income ($Mil) | Return on Assets (R.O.A.) | Return on Equity (R.O.E.) | Net Interest Spread | Overhead Efficiency Ratio | Liquidity Index | Liquidity Ratio | Hot Money Ratio | Stability Index |
|---|---|---|---|---|---|---|---|---|---|---|---|---|---|
| **6.5** | 1.42 | 2.5 | 0.15 | **5.1** | 5.2 | 0.96 | 9.55 | 3.50 | 61.1 | **4.2** | 33.6 | 12.0 | **6.8** |
| **8.5** | 1.26 | 2.7 | 0.00 | **5.0** | 1.6 | 1.03 | 6.91 | 3.40 | 64.4 | **2.5** | 39.5 | 26.4 | **7.7** |
| **9.6** | 0.00 | 0.0 | -0.01 | **3.8** | 0.8 | 0.88 | 7.12 | 2.85 | 68.9 | **6.0** | 61.0 | 7.7 | **6.8** |
| **8.7** | 0.00 | 1.5 | 0.08 | **4.6** | 1.5 | 0.94 | 7.75 | 3.51 | 71.0 | **2.5** | 34.6 | 21.4 | **6.9** |
| **6.4** | 0.89 | 5.3 | 0.23 | **6.2** | 1.1 | 1.45 | 12.68 | 3.11 | 53.1 | **1.7** | 35.7 | 29.8 | **7.9** |
| **8.7** | 0.00 | 0.0 | 0.00 | **5.4** | 0.8 | 1.29 | 9.08 | 3.73 | 61.4 | **3.0** | 40.0 | 20.1 | **7.5** |
| **5.7** | 0.92 | 5.7 | 0.17 | **4.1** | 1.0 | 0.86 | 9.28 | 3.63 | 76.7 | **2.7** | 37.4 | 21.6 | **4.7** |
| **6.8** | 0.88 | 2.4 | 0.09 | **3.2** | 0.4 | 0.55 | 5.46 | 3.22 | 75.2 | **4.2** | 33.0 | 11.8 | **4.9** |
| **6.4** | 2.76 | 6.6 | -0.02 | **4.8** | 1.1 | 1.04 | 6.50 | 4.10 | 72.6 | **2.2** | 31.1 | 23.5 | **7.8** |
| **7.8** | 0.12 | 0.8 | -0.04 | **4.7** | 5.5 | 0.85 | 7.70 | 3.99 | 73.1 | **4.6** | 12.3 | 4.4 | **7.2** |
| **3.7** | 5.15 | 20.3 | 0.17 | **4.8** | 2.1 | 0.93 | 7.01 | 3.58 | 55.2 | **5.1** | 27.1 | 3.9 | **7.1** |
| **8.2** | 0.13 | 0.6 | 0.14 | **7.1** | 1.5 | 1.67 | 14.94 | 3.70 | 55.6 | **3.0** | 23.7 | 13.2 | **8.2** |
| **8.5** | 0.19 | 1.6 | 0.02 | **7.4** | 21.9 | 1.46 | 17.14 | 3.69 | 53.3 | **3.9** | 5.2 | 8.1 | **7.5** |
| **7.4** | 0.36 | 2.0 | 0.02 | **3.4** | 0.1 | 0.49 | 6.02 | 4.52 | 88.0 | **5.1** | 15.8 | 1.2 | **4.1** |
| **4.2** | 1.41 | 10.0 | 0.15 | **5.1** | 1.3 | 1.13 | 12.36 | 4.37 | 72.1 | **1.3** | 14.5 | 23.8 | **5.6** |
| **8.5** | 0.04 | 0.3 | 0.07 | **5.7** | 6.4 | 1.23 | 14.10 | 3.40 | 58.1 | **4.8** | 30.3 | 6.8 | **5.9** |
| **6.5** | 0.59 | 3.8 | 0.01 | **4.0** | 3.3 | 0.67 | 6.59 | 3.40 | 78.1 | **1.9** | 12.9 | 18.8 | **6.0** |
| **7.9** | 1.08 | 3.3 | 0.05 | **6.3** | 1.7 | 1.19 | 7.76 | 4.62 | 70.0 | **3.2** | 17.2 | 13.1 | **8.7** |
| **4.6** | 0.65 | 8.3 | -0.02 | **3.2** | 0.6 | 0.50 | 5.89 | 4.35 | 87.6 | **2.0** | 22.3 | 19.8 | **4.6** |
| **1.7** | 2.52 | 19.2 | 0.65 | **2.4** | 0.1 | 0.28 | 2.80 | 3.92 | 80.5 | **4.4** | 16.3 | 4.1 | **3.9** |
| **8.7** | 0.46 | 1.2 | 0.01 | **6.1** | 3.4 | 1.23 | 8.60 | 3.77 | 63.7 | **4.2** | 28.5 | 10.1 | **8.2** |
| **6.3** | 0.75 | 3.6 | 0.18 | **5.9** | 10.0 | 1.22 | 11.30 | 4.00 | 67.4 | **3.3** | 25.1 | 13.3 | **7.9** |
| **3.8** | 0.53 | 2.9 | -0.11 | **5.6** | 0.4 | 1.00 | 8.81 | 4.91 | 71.5 | **3.9** | 15.8 | 9.7 | **6.3** |
| **6.6** | 2.53 | 6.5 | 0.01 | **8.1** | 2.1 | 1.72 | 12.66 | 4.37 | 58.9 | **2.6** | 19.7 | 16.4 | **8.4** |
| **5.9** | 0.68 | 1.7 | -0.11 | **8.9** | 4.5 | 1.61 | 10.67 | 4.43 | 58.0 | **3.8** | 15.8 | 10.3 | **9.3** |
| **8.7** | 0.61 | 1.8 | 0.00 | **6.1** | 2.6 | 1.25 | 9.79 | 4.32 | 65.2 | **2.1** | 27.0 | 20.5 | **7.5** |
| **7.4** | 0.41 | 2.2 | 0.01 | **7.0** | 60.6 | 1.43 | 14.54 | 3.38 | 55.0 | **4.9** | 30.4 | 10.9 | **8.8** |
| **4.7** | 1.04 | 7.1 | 0.02 | **9.2** | 3.0 | 2.12 | 20.72 | 4.51 | 56.5 | **1.6** | 11.0 | 22.2 | **8.2** |
| **8.2** | 0.29 | 1.3 | 0.08 | **10.0** | 24.6 | 2.03 | 12.67 | 5.08 | 40.8 | **4.5** | 33.7 | 13.6 | **10.0** |
| **8.8** | 0.02 | 0.1 | 0.00 | **3.9** | 1.6 | 0.88 | 9.42 | 3.19 | 72.3 | **4.0** | 21.3 | 9.8 | **5.6** |
| **6.2** | 1.27 | 10.8 | 0.50 | **3.2** | 0.4 | 0.55 | 4.53 | 3.95 | 80.4 | **3.0** | 22.3 | 14.9 | **6.2** |
| **6.8** | 0.05 | 2.1 | 0.14 | **6.8** | 7.1 | 1.39 | 12.66 | 3.33 | 52.8 | **2.9** | 28.4 | 16.9 | **7.4** |
| **7.7** | 0.41 | 2.0 | 0.05 | **4.9** | 1.6 | 1.11 | 8.47 | 5.26 | 77.2 | **2.7** | 16.0 | 15.5 | **6.6** |
| **8.6** | 0.02 | 0.6 | 0.16 | **4.2** | 0.4 | 0.91 | 10.32 | 4.14 | 77.8 | **4.5** | 28.8 | 8.7 | **5.0** |
| **1.6** | 2.21 | 24.1 | 0.69 | **5.9** | 4.2 | 1.37 | 11.36 | 4.47 | 61.3 | **1.4** | 13.0 | 25.4 | **7.3** |
| **6.0** | 0.91 | 4.8 | 1.36 | **10.0** | 3.0 | 4.46 | 43.03 | 10.90 | 56.3 | **1.7** | 19.1 | 22.3 | **8.4** |
| **9.0** | 0.06 | 0.3 | -0.02 | **6.2** | 1.8 | 1.29 | 10.35 | 3.99 | 60.2 | **1.6** | 19.6 | 24.9 | **7.8** |
| **6.3** | 5.02 | 11.1 | 0.07 | **3.4** | 1.8 | 0.58 | 4.84 | 2.62 | 74.5 | **5.3** | 43.6 | 9.3 | **5.9** |
| **6.4** | 0.42 | 2.3 | 0.06 | **3.9** | 0.7 | 0.83 | 9.10 | 3.80 | 78.7 | **2.8** | 27.0 | 16.6 | **5.7** |
| **8.6** | 0.00 | 0.0 | -0.07 | **9.3** | 0.9 | 2.33 | 21.60 | 5.32 | 57.9 | **0.6** | 7.2 | 37.1 | **7.0** |
| **5.0** | 3.48 | 12.3 | 0.43 | **5.4** | 3.2 | 1.38 | 13.79 | 3.36 | 59.0 | **3.3** | 43.6 | 19.5 | **6.4** |
| **6.4** | 2.65 | 10.4 | 0.17 | **2.8** | 0.6 | 0.47 | 4.02 | 3.33 | 85.4 | **3.1** | 42.4 | 21.0 | **6.5** |
| **9.0** | 0.10 | 0.3 | 0.01 | **6.7** | 2.4 | 1.41 | 12.62 | 3.50 | 49.5 | **2.6** | 38.7 | 24.8 | **6.7** |
| **7.1** | 0.01 | 0.0 | 0.46 | **4.9** | 1.2 | 1.12 | 5.06 | 3.95 | 60.5 | **5.2** | 60.5 | 13.9 | **6.7** |
| **6.3** | 2.03 | 7.6 | -0.46 | **7.3** | 1.9 | 1.71 | 15.83 | 4.15 | 61.4 | **4.9** | 33.0 | 7.4 | **8.3** |
| **5.5** | 3.04 | 8.8 | 0.33 | **7.6** | 2.2 | 1.78 | 9.51 | 4.66 | 59.8 | **2.0** | 33.0 | 27.9 | **8.1** |
| **7.6** | 0.59 | 1.9 | 0.00 | **9.4** | 3.1 | 2.05 | 16.35 | 3.99 | 51.1 | **0.7** | 16.1 | 48.1 | **9.1** |
| **7.1** | 1.54 | 4.8 | 0.05 | **7.3** | 2.4 | 1.76 | 12.87 | 3.66 | 53.0 | **1.1** | 18.8 | 31.6 | **9.2** |
| **2.4** | 1.71 | 8.9 | 0.19 | **5.2** | 7.8 | 1.01 | 10.38 | 4.13 | 63.5 | **1.5** | 18.9 | 20.1 | **6.1** |
| **6.4** | 1.04 | 3.9 | 0.04 | **3.3** | 0.1 | 0.66 | 3.52 | 3.36 | 77.5 | **4.7** | 22.2 | 4.6 | **6.6** |
| **8.0** | 0.12 | 1.3 | 0.17 | **5.7** | 2.5 | 1.08 | 10.81 | 4.62 | 65.9 | **3.9** | 13.2 | 9.4 | **6.0** |
| **7.0** | 0.61 | 3.4 | 0.33 | **9.1** | 3.6 | 2.06 | 17.70 | 6.92 | 63.1 | **2.5** | 37.1 | 24.4 | **8.0** |
| **5.3** | 3.22 | 11.4 | 0.00 | **4.2** | 2.1 | 0.90 | 6.83 | 3.45 | 69.3 | **3.4** | 31.6 | 15.1 | **7.3** |
| **5.7** | 1.55 | 5.3 | -0.09 | **6.5** | 1.3 | 1.40 | 11.56 | 4.05 | 57.7 | **2.2** | 15.3 | 18.0 | **7.0** |
| **7.9** | 0.00 | 0.3 | 0.06 | **4.5** | 1.0 | 0.91 | 8.30 | 4.40 | 74.0 | **3.6** | 15.8 | 11.1 | **6.9** |
| **5.8** | 1.49 | 6.1 | 0.37 | **6.6** | 2.9 | 1.29 | 10.22 | 4.75 | 65.5 | **3.8** | 16.0 | 10.3 | **7.7** |
| **1.2** | 2.61 | 20.9 | 0.10 | **5.6** | 4.7 | 1.00 | 10.30 | 5.43 | 73.3 | **4.5** | 7.3 | 4.5 | **5.6** |
| **3.1** | 2.13 | 14.8 | 0.33 | **4.1** | 1.3 | 0.78 | 7.15 | 5.21 | 82.9 | **2.6** | 24.3 | 16.7 | **5.4** |
| **9.7** | 0.45 | 2.1 | 0.01 | **3.8** | 1.1 | 0.71 | 6.07 | 2.50 | 64.9 | **3.1** | 46.2 | 23.7 | **6.3** |
| **6.0** | 0.91 | 3.1 | 0.17 | **3.8** | 0.4 | 0.88 | 9.64 | 3.80 | 79.8 | **2.8** | 37.7 | 20.9 | **4.7** |

| Name | City | State | Rating | 2018 Rating | 2017 Rating | Total Assets ($Mil) | One Year Asset Growth | Asset Mix (As a % of Total Assets) Comm-ercial Loans | Cons-umer Loans | Mort-gage Loans | Secur-ities | Capital-ization Index | Lever-age Ratio | Risk-Based Capital Ratio |
|---|---|---|---|---|---|---|---|---|---|---|---|---|---|---|
| ▲ Bank of Edmonson County | Brownsville | KY | **B** | B- | B+ | 217.4 | 2.40 | 2.5 | 3.6 | 28.1 | 19.1 | **10.0** | 12.1 | 19.6 |
| ▲ Bank of Elgin | Elgin | NE | **B+** | B+ | B+ | 61.3 | -0.01 | 3.1 | 1.1 | 0.6 | 4.0 | **10.0** | 15.4 | 20.3 |
| Bank of Elk River | Elk River | MN | **B+** | B | B | 456.8 | 7.47 | 15.8 | 2.4 | 9.7 | 28.3 | **7.5** | 9.4 | 14.9 |
| Bank of England | England | AR | **B+** | B | B+ | 464.5 | 48.84 | 5.1 | 0.8 | 54.0 | 9.6 | **7.9** | 12.5 | 13.3 |
| Bank of Erath | Erath | LA | **B** | B | B | 99.9 | -1.89 | 11.4 | 2.6 | 18.4 | 14.2 | **10.0** | 13.5 | 21.8 |
| Bank of Estes Park | Estes Park | CO | **A-** | B+ | B- | 133.9 | 5.52 | 1.7 | 0.1 | 14.0 | 24.3 | **8.8** | 10.2 | 20.9 |
| ▼ Bank of Eufaula | Eufaula | OK | **C+** | B- | C+ | 98.7 | -1.25 | 2.9 | 6.5 | 14.1 | 46.8 | **10.0** | 13.6 | 31.8 |
| Bank of Evergreen | Evergreen | AL | **B-** | C+ | B- | 62.8 | 0.90 | 9.8 | 3.9 | 21.4 | 25.9 | **10.0** | 13.5 | 25.5 |
| Bank of Farmington | Farmington | IL | **B-** | B- | B+ | 180.2 | 2.54 | 11.3 | 3.3 | 14.8 | 23.1 | **10.0** | 11.5 | 18.1 |
| Bank of Fayette County | Piperton | TN | **B-** | B- | B- | 656.5 | 6.34 | 6.1 | 7.2 | 32.3 | 6.4 | **7.1** | 9.0 | 12.7 |
| ▲ Bank of Feather River | Yuba City | CA | **A-** | B+ | B+ | 145.3 | 17.05 | 8.1 | 0.0 | 3.7 | 0.0 | **8.5** | 10.8 | 13.7 |
| ▲ Bank of Fincastle | Fincastle | VA | **D+** | D- | E | 221.3 | 6.85 | 9.9 | 0.7 | 19.9 | 10.3 | **10.0** | 11.7 | 16.2 |
| Bank of Forest | Forest | MS | **B+** | B+ | B | 204.6 | 4.56 | 5.2 | 4.6 | 9.7 | 29.7 | **10.0** | 13.2 | 19.8 |
| ▲ Bank of Frankewing | Frankewing | TN | **B+** | B+ | B+ | 309.8 | 11.97 | 9.9 | 4.2 | 19.1 | 3.4 | **10.0** | 11.4 | 15.4 |
| Bank of Franklin | Meadville | MS | **A-** | B+ | B- | 146.2 | 5.44 | 7.4 | 4.4 | 22.3 | 23.5 | **10.0** | 11.6 | 17.4 |
| Bank of Franklin County | Washington | MO | **C+** | C | C- | 261.0 | -0.73 | 12.1 | 2.3 | 18.5 | 11.3 | **6.2** | 9.1 | 11.9 |
| ▲ Bank of George | Las Vegas | NV | **A** | B+ | A | 343.7 | 44.14 | 4.3 | 0.0 | 1.7 | 1.0 | **10.0** | 12.2 | 20.1 |
| Bank of Gibson City | Gibson City | IL | **C+** | C | B- | 90.7 | 11.60 | 5.4 | 4.3 | 11.8 | 14.2 | **5.9** | 7.9 | 13.5 |
| Bank of Gleason | Gleason | TN | **B+** | B+ | A- | 113.7 | 2.06 | 3.3 | 7.2 | 12.5 | 52.6 | **10.0** | 23.5 | 47.3 |
| ▲ Bank of Glen Burnie | Glen Burnie | MD | **C** | C | C- | 384.9 | -6.80 | 3.8 | 27.2 | 20.7 | 18.6 | **7.4** | 9.3 | 13.2 |
| Bank of Glen Ullin | Glen Ullin | ND | **C** | D+ | D- | 61.9 | 18.24 | 5.7 | 1.4 | 2.5 | 9.1 | **9.0** | 10.3 | 14.4 |
| Bank of Grain Valley | Kansas City | MO | **A-** | A- | A- | 95.5 | 5.43 | 12.7 | 1.1 | 17.5 | 14.8 | **10.0** | 22.1 | 39.6 |
| Bank of Grand Lake | Grove | OK | **B-** | B- | B- | 170.2 | 1.43 | 6.2 | 2.8 | 27.7 | 12.7 | **6.0** | 8.0 | 11.8 |
| ▲ Bank of Grandin | Grandin | MO | **B-** | B- | B | 172.3 | 8.11 | 12.0 | 7.1 | 13.0 | 29.5 | **10.0** | 15.5 | 21.4 |
| Bank of Gravette | Gravette | AR | **C+** | C+ | B- | 134.2 | 4.20 | 4.0 | 2.5 | 16.4 | 18.6 | **6.9** | 8.9 | 14.4 |
| Bank of Greeley | Greeley | KS | **B** | B | B | 38.7 | 2.53 | 4.9 | 4.1 | 17.8 | 11.8 | **10.0** | 13.0 | 25.3 |
| ▲ Bank of Greeleyville | Greeleyville | SC | **B+** | C+ | B- | 93.0 | 0.17 | 12.6 | 8.6 | 13.7 | 19.1 | **10.0** | 12.5 | 19.9 |
| Bank of Greene County | Catskill | NY | **B+** | B+ | B+ | 1439.7 | 20.81 | 6.1 | 0.4 | 23.5 | 37.3 | **6.3** | 8.3 | 15.5 |
| Bank of Guam | Hagatna | GU | **C+** | C+ | C+ | 1944.7 | 2.98 | 12.3 | 11.9 | 7.7 | 22.0 | **6.7** | 8.7 | 13.8 |
| Bank of Gueydan | Gueydan | LA | **B** | B- | B- | 75.3 | -3.46 | 4.7 | 7.1 | 1.0 | 61.8 | **10.0** | 20.7 | 51.5 |
| Bank of Halls | Halls | TN | **B** | B | B+ | 90.7 | 1.55 | 10.3 | 2.6 | 6.5 | 33.9 | **8.0** | 9.6 | 15.1 |
| Bank of Hamilton | Hamilton | ND | **C+** | C- | C- | 21.0 | -4.73 | 3.0 | 5.9 | 0.0 | 3.0 | **10.0** | 13.2 | 65.5 |
| Bank of Hancock County | Sparta | GA | **B+** | B+ | B+ | 75.5 | 0.75 | 4.4 | 5.7 | 15.6 | 57.4 | **10.0** | 20.8 | 48.8 |
| Bank of Hartington | Hartington | NE | **B-** | C+ | B- | 96.2 | 3.12 | 11.3 | 1.6 | 6.6 | 12.0 | **7.1** | 9.6 | 12.5 |
| Bank of Hawaii | Honolulu | HI | **B** | B | B | 18066.0 | 5.55 | 4.8 | 6.2 | 25.4 | 31.4 | **5.0** | 7.0 | 12.9 |
| ▲ Bank of Hays | Hays | KS | **B** | B- | B- | 259.5 | 0.99 | 12.0 | 2.1 | 8.7 | 28.2 | **10.0** | 11.0 | 16.7 |
| Bank of Hazelton | Hazelton | ND | **B** | B- | C+ | 50.3 | -1.89 | 1.5 | 0.6 | 0.8 | 22.7 | **9.0** | 10.3 | 20.8 |
| Bank of Hazlehurst | Hazlehurst | GA | **D+** | D | D- | 119.9 | -12.36 | 11.3 | 2.5 | 7.7 | 22.6 | **10.0** | 11.8 | 23.5 |
| ▲ Bank of Hemet | Riverside | CA | **A-** | B+ | A | 692.5 | -4.36 | 1.5 | 0.1 | 0.2 | 9.6 | **9.4** | 11.0 | 14.5 |
| Bank of Herrin | Herrin | IL | **B-** | B- | B | 249.7 | 0.70 | 9.7 | 2.3 | 14.2 | 22.1 | **9.6** | 10.8 | 15.6 |
| Bank of Hillsboro, N.A. | Hillsboro | IL | **B** | B- | B | 369.7 | 9.00 | 6.9 | 0.8 | 8.4 | 17.4 | **9.9** | 11.2 | 14.9 |
| Bank of Hindman | Hindman | KY | **C+** | C | C | 212.7 | 8.15 | 6.7 | 1.5 | 14.9 | 39.2 | **7.8** | 9.5 | 16.6 |
| Bank of Holland | Holland | NY | **B-** | B- | B- | 143.3 | 5.89 | 2.8 | 2.0 | 43.3 | 20.1 | **6.3** | 8.3 | 13.6 |
| Bank of Holly Springs | Holly Springs | MS | **B** | B- | B | 243.8 | 11.97 | 11.1 | 7.7 | 22.1 | 13.4 | **10.0** | 13.7 | 21.7 |
| ▼ Bank of Holyrood | Holyrood | KS | **B** | B+ | B+ | 62.6 | 0.54 | 19.4 | 6.6 | 23.4 | 8.2 | **10.0** | 14.7 | 22.9 |
| Bank of Hope | Los Angeles | CA | **B** | B | B- | 15666.5 | 2.34 | 14.6 | 0.3 | 6.1 | 11.0 | **9.3** | 12.3 | 14.4 |
| Bank of Houston | Houston | MO | **D-** | D- | E+ | 31.3 | 2.99 | 5.2 | 0.6 | 6.4 | 36.1 | **8.6** | 10.0 | 18.2 |
| Bank of Houston, N.A. | Houston | TX | **D+** | C | B- | 149.4 | 115.86 | 12.5 | 1.9 | 8.8 | 2.8 | **10.0** | 29.3 | 29.8 |
| ▲ Bank of Hydro | Hydro | OK | **A** | B+ | A- | 127.5 | 1.00 | 4.4 | 1.9 | 31.3 | 0.0 | **10.0** | 11.4 | 15.4 |
| Bank of Iberia | Iberia | MO | **C** | D+ | D+ | 55.6 | -0.28 | 3.5 | 5.7 | 25.5 | 19.0 | **7.3** | 9.2 | 17.3 |
| Bank of Idaho | Idaho Falls | ID | **B-** | B- | B+ | 405.3 | 21.26 | 9.5 | 2.0 | 6.2 | 21.0 | **10.0** | 12.5 | 15.9 |
| Bank of Jackson | Jackson | TN | **B-** | B- | B- | 192.6 | 4.58 | 5.9 | 1.3 | 8.7 | 62.5 | **8.1** | 9.7 | 18.3 |
| ▲ Bank of Jackson Hole | Jackson | WY | **B** | C+ | B+ | 982.4 | 19.12 | 4.7 | 0.3 | 16.7 | 4.2 | **8.1** | 9.7 | 14.9 |
| Bank of Jamestown | Jamestown | KY | **B-** | B- | B- | 205.1 | 5.25 | 4.3 | 1.1 | 10.2 | 27.4 | **9.2** | 11.5 | 14.4 |
| Bank of Kampsville | Kampsville | IL | **B** | B | B | 109.8 | 2.76 | 3.2 | 7.0 | 18.5 | 36.7 | **10.0** | 17.4 | 30.0 |
| Bank of Kaukauna | Kaukauna | WI | **C** | D+ | D+ | 107.5 | 3.42 | 14.7 | 1.7 | 10.0 | 2.4 | **7.9** | 9.6 | 14.1 |
| Bank of Kilmichael | Kilmichael | MS | **B+** | B+ | B | 178.9 | 0.40 | 12.4 | 5.7 | 14.3 | 23.1 | **8.8** | 10.2 | 16.4 |
| Bank of Kirksville | Kirksville | MO | **B+** | B | B | 439.5 | -4.34 | 3.6 | 0.6 | 14.4 | 31.4 | **10.0** | 12.1 | 37.8 |
| ▲ Bank of Kremlin | Kremlin | OK | **B-** | C+ | C- | 314.4 | 1.15 | 8.9 | 2.0 | 7.0 | 10.0 | **7.5** | 9.9 | 12.9 |
| Bank of Labor | Kansas City | KS | **C** | C | C- | 664.4 | 9.00 | 19.7 | 0.1 | 3.0 | 43.8 | **6.6** | 8.6 | 15.3 |

| Asset Quality Index | Adjusted Non-Performing Loans as a % of Total Loans | Adjusted Non-Performing Loans as a % of Capital | Net Charge-Offs Avg Loans | Profitability Index | Net Income ($Mil) | Return on Assets (R.O.A.) | Return on Equity (R.O.E.) | Net Interest Spread | Overhead Efficiency Ratio | Liquidity Index | Liquidity Ratio | Hot Money Ratio | Stability Index |
|---|---|---|---|---|---|---|---|---|---|---|---|---|---|
| **5.0** | 1.70 | 7.2 | 0.32 | **6.4** | 3.1 | 1.46 | 12.13 | 3.93 | 60.7 | **1.1** | 19.4 | 31.7 | **8.5** |
| **6.9** | 0.00 | 0.0 | 0.00 | **9.2** | 1.3 | 2.30 | 15.11 | 4.05 | 49.0 | **4.7** | 21.5 | 5.2 | **9.5** |
| **6.6** | 0.65 | 4.1 | 0.04 | **7.1** | 6.8 | 1.54 | 16.14 | 4.02 | 65.9 | **4.5** | 33.7 | 10.2 | **6.5** |
| **6.0** | 0.82 | 3.6 | 0.15 | **9.4** | 11.0 | 2.72 | 20.12 | 3.27 | 91.3 | **0.7** | 12.4 | 35.3 | **9.2** |
| **5.3** | 2.21 | 11.1 | -0.01 | **3.4** | 0.6 | 0.54 | 4.02 | 4.60 | 83.2 | **2.0** | 21.0 | 19.4 | **6.9** |
| **9.3** | 0.00 | 0.0 | 0.00 | **6.1** | 2.0 | 1.51 | 14.60 | 3.85 | 63.9 | **6.9** | 55.4 | 2.4 | **7.1** |
| **8.5** | 0.10 | 3.2 | 0.13 | **1.7** | 0.1 | 0.09 | 0.67 | 3.57 | 97.8 | **3.5** | 41.4 | 17.8 | **5.4** |
| **4.1** | 5.05 | 17.5 | 0.33 | **4.2** | 0.4 | 0.73 | 5.39 | 4.25 | 68.0 | **2.4** | 37.6 | 25.8 | **6.0** |
| **5.7** | 2.57 | 7.5 | 0.13 | **3.5** | 1.1 | 0.60 | 5.13 | 3.44 | 72.9 | **1.9** | 23.4 | 21.2 | **6.7** |
| **4.6** | 0.67 | 7.8 | 0.09 | **5.9** | 7.1 | 1.10 | 12.29 | 3.98 | 59.8 | **0.5** | 4.3 | 38.5 | **6.0** |
| **8.4** | 0.00 | 0.0 | 0.00 | **7.5** | 1.7 | 1.30 | 11.84 | 4.90 | 62.4 | **1.6** | 21.3 | 25.5 | **7.4** |
| **5.1** | 2.01 | 7.7 | 0.08 | **2.9** | 2.1 | 0.99 | 8.11 | 3.83 | 92.0 | **3.2** | 16.0 | 13.2 | **4.8** |
| **5.7** | 0.95 | 7.9 | 0.07 | **5.2** | 2.7 | 1.33 | 9.87 | 4.12 | 68.6 | **2.5** | 35.5 | 22.3 | **8.1** |
| **6.2** | 1.10 | 5.6 | 0.07 | **6.8** | 3.9 | 1.33 | 11.76 | 4.20 | 60.7 | **0.8** | 20.0 | 35.5 | **7.5** |
| **6.8** | 0.56 | 3.0 | 0.18 | **6.3** | 1.9 | 1.28 | 11.27 | 4.57 | 66.5 | **2.9** | 21.9 | 15.4 | **6.8** |
| **4.4** | 2.32 | 10.0 | 0.20 | **3.9** | 2.0 | 0.76 | 8.44 | 3.59 | 69.9 | **3.1** | 14.0 | 13.5 | **5.2** |
| **7.1** | 0.00 | 0.0 | 0.33 | **10.0** | 5.8 | 2.03 | 15.97 | 5.21 | 54.5 | **4.0** | 34.4 | 13.1 | **9.3** |
| **4.5** | 0.90 | 2.7 | 0.18 | **5.6** | 0.9 | 1.10 | 9.07 | 3.54 | 54.8 | **3.4** | 25.5 | 13.2 | **5.3** |
| **8.8** | 0.49 | 1.6 | 0.20 | **4.7** | 1.3 | 1.14 | 4.84 | 3.47 | 67.3 | **4.5** | 75.5 | 19.5 | **8.1** |
| **2.6** | 1.45 | 11.0 | 0.12 | **2.8** | 1.8 | 0.46 | 5.09 | 3.41 | 84.6 | **3.8** | 24.1 | 10.8 | **4.0** |
| **2.1** | 2.88 | 16.0 | -0.04 | **9.2** | 1.2 | 2.01 | 17.11 | 4.39 | 50.5 | **0.6** | 14.3 | 45.8 | **8.1** |
| **8.9** | 0.00 | 0.0 | 0.00 | **7.3** | 1.6 | 1.78 | 8.07 | 4.17 | 56.4 | **5.3** | 37.9 | 6.8 | **9.1** |
| **4.7** | 0.94 | 10.7 | 0.09 | **5.0** | 1.9 | 1.05 | 13.50 | 3.58 | 70.7 | **0.8** | 13.2 | 23.3 | **5.4** |
| **3.6** | 9.14 | 21.1 | 0.53 | **5.3** | 2.1 | 1.24 | 7.82 | 3.68 | 60.6 | **1.4** | 20.3 | 27.5 | **8.5** |
| **3.6** | 0.82 | 5.4 | 0.08 | **3.2** | 0.5 | 0.39 | 2.89 | 3.87 | 81.2 | **1.5** | 25.2 | 27.2 | **7.1** |
| **8.7** | 0.00 | 0.0 | 0.01 | **5.1** | 0.5 | 1.27 | 9.75 | 3.28 | 62.4 | **4.5** | 44.3 | 13.0 | **7.5** |
| **5.8** | 1.44 | 4.8 | 0.03 | **6.5** | 1.3 | 1.42 | 11.54 | 4.65 | 70.6 | **3.5** | 33.0 | 15.3 | **6.9** |
| **8.6** | 0.48 | 2.9 | 0.11 | **6.4** | 17.4 | 1.34 | 16.04 | 3.43 | 54.6 | **4.9** | 3.1 | 1.0 | **7.6** |
| **3.6** | 2.87 | 16.0 | 0.45 | **4.7** | 16.1 | 0.83 | 10.34 | 4.94 | 76.0 | **2.8** | 14.6 | 15.2 | **6.4** |
| **6.5** | 4.84 | 5.7 | 0.43 | **3.6** | 0.6 | 0.78 | 3.81 | 3.03 | 66.1 | **4.1** | 82.0 | 23.1 | **6.2** |
| **3.8** | 3.83 | 13.4 | 0.00 | **5.9** | 1.0 | 1.18 | 10.91 | 3.60 | 60.4 | **2.0** | 29.2 | 24.0 | **6.8** |
| **9.5** | 0.00 | 0.0 | -0.15 | **1.4** | 0.0 | 0.12 | 0.86 | 2.70 | 101.2 | **7.6** | 97.2 | 2.5 | **5.2** |
| **9.1** | 0.55 | 1.3 | 0.06 | **3.9** | 0.7 | 0.93 | 4.36 | 4.24 | 80.9 | **5.1** | 48.2 | 10.6 | **7.9** |
| **7.1** | 0.00 | 0.2 | 0.00 | **5.1** | 1.1 | 1.18 | 12.18 | 4.44 | 71.6 | **3.5** | 12.9 | 11.1 | **6.2** |
| **7.8** | 0.67 | 4.0 | 0.12 | **6.3** | 227.1 | 1.30 | 18.66 | 3.05 | 55.1 | **4.2** | 21.7 | 9.8 | **6.2** |
| **5.6** | 2.34 | 4.7 | 0.91 | **5.1** | 2.7 | 1.04 | 9.82 | 3.37 | 55.2 | **1.9** | 23.7 | 21.2 | **6.9** |
| **8.8** | 0.00 | 0.0 | 0.00 | **5.5** | 0.7 | 1.45 | 13.57 | 3.43 | 58.5 | **4.3** | 53.4 | 15.5 | **6.1** |
| **0.7** | 9.69 | 32.1 | 2.98 | **2.8** | 0.8 | 0.62 | 4.59 | 4.05 | 62.6 | **5.4** | 34.0 | 4.7 | **6.0** |
| **7.3** | 0.00 | 0.0 | 0.01 | **9.8** | 19.4 | 2.68 | 24.65 | 4.36 | 40.4 | **4.7** | 7.0 | 2.7 | **9.6** |
| **4.4** | 1.95 | 10.3 | 0.30 | **5.0** | 2.8 | 1.13 | 10.71 | 4.16 | 65.3 | **4.6** | 11.8 | 4.6 | **6.7** |
| **4.7** | 3.34 | 10.4 | 0.01 | **5.1** | 3.7 | 1.03 | 9.18 | 3.42 | 62.5 | **2.3** | 12.2 | 17.3 | **6.8** |
| **3.4** | 3.03 | 12.8 | 0.02 | **3.8** | 1.8 | 0.85 | 6.98 | 2.94 | 63.8 | **1.8** | 32.8 | 30.1 | **6.9** |
| **5.8** | 0.93 | 7.0 | 0.01 | **4.4** | 1.4 | 0.98 | 12.53 | 3.74 | 70.2 | **3.4** | 15.0 | 12.0 | **5.0** |
| **4.3** | 2.86 | 13.1 | 0.34 | **6.9** | 3.6 | 1.54 | 10.72 | 4.65 | 66.7 | **1.2** | 11.6 | 28.2 | **9.2** |
| **4.4** | 2.07 | 12.8 | 1.24 | **5.8** | 0.8 | 1.34 | 9.07 | 3.80 | 48.8 | **0.9** | 24.6 | 31.2 | **7.7** |
| **4.9** | 0.96 | 3.3 | 0.04 | **6.5** | 185.7 | 1.22 | 8.22 | 3.39 | 52.5 | **0.9** | 16.1 | 28.9 | **10.0** |
| **5.6** | 0.00 | 9.4 | 0.00 | **0.0** | -0.2 | -1.31 | -14.68 | 3.71 | 138.6 | **6.0** | 52.4 | 6.2 | **3.1** |
| **7.4** | 0.00 | 0.0 | 0.00 | **0.9** | -0.2 | -0.24 | -0.85 | 5.28 | 95.5 | **2.7** | 26.2 | 17.0 | **6.0** |
| **7.3** | 0.03 | 5.5 | 0.10 | **10.0** | 3.3 | 2.64 | 23.25 | 4.99 | 48.5 | **1.2** | 12.9 | 27.7 | **8.9** |
| **4.8** | 1.81 | 9.1 | 0.15 | **2.9** | 0.2 | 0.40 | 4.38 | 4.28 | 89.1 | **3.5** | 40.4 | 17.4 | **3.7** |
| **5.1** | 1.99 | 9.0 | 0.21 | **3.9** | 2.8 | 0.78 | 6.98 | 4.87 | 86.5 | **5.1** | 19.1 | 1.7 | **7.3** |
| **8.8** | 0.90 | 1.9 | 0.00 | **4.1** | 1.7 | 0.90 | 8.35 | 2.90 | 68.6 | **2.9** | 50.1 | 28.6 | **5.9** |
| **6.3** | 1.18 | 4.2 | 0.00 | **6.9** | 11.6 | 1.32 | 12.83 | 3.88 | 55.5 | **4.4** | 30.2 | 9.5 | **6.9** |
| **7.5** | 0.74 | 2.8 | 0.13 | **4.5** | 2.1 | 1.04 | 9.27 | 3.41 | 62.8 | **1.5** | 8.2 | 22.4 | **6.4** |
| **7.4** | 2.19 | 5.8 | -0.08 | **4.1** | 0.9 | 0.83 | 4.70 | 3.15 | 67.7 | **4.5** | 48.7 | 14.7 | **8.1** |
| **2.8** | 4.41 | 17.0 | 0.00 | **4.8** | 0.9 | 1.15 | 11.64 | 3.35 | 81.5 | **3.2** | 34.1 | 5.2 | **5.6** |
| **4.9** | 1.47 | 8.7 | 0.27 | **6.5** | 2.6 | 1.46 | 14.61 | 4.43 | 60.8 | **1.8** | 23.6 | 22.2 | **7.3** |
| **6.7** | 3.73 | 8.4 | 0.01 | **4.7** | 5.1 | 1.14 | 9.80 | 2.29 | 53.7 | **4.4** | 39.9 | 12.9 | **7.5** |
| **4.4** | 0.96 | 4.4 | 0.00 | **4.2** | 0.6 | 1.13 | 9.98 | 3.93 | 62.2 | **0.7** | 15.2 | 36.7 | **8.0** |
| **5.6** | 2.49 | 6.9 | 0.20 | **2.9** | 2.0 | 0.35 | 3.99 | 3.83 | 91.2 | **5.9** | 49.1 | 7.1 | **4.7** |

| Name | City | State | Rating | 2018 Rating | 2017 Rating | Total Assets ($Mil) | One Year Asset Growth | Asset Mix (As a % of Total Assets) Comm-ercial Loans | Cons-umer Loans | Mort-gage Loans | Secur-ities | Capital-ization Index | Lever-age Ratio | Risk-Based Capital Ratio |
|---|---|---|---|---|---|---|---|---|---|---|---|---|---|---|
| Bank of LaFayette, Georgia | Lafayette | GA | **B** | B | B | 284.7 | 4.46 | 1.1 | 6.1 | 19.6 | 53.2 | **10.0** | 13.2 | 42.8 |
| Bank of Lake Mills | Lake Mills | WI | **A-** | B+ | B | 230.7 | 4.71 | 1.6 | 9.9 | 33.6 | 9.0 | **10.0** | 12.6 | 17.3 |
| ▲ Bank of Lake Village | Lake Village | AR | **A-** | B+ | B+ | 64.1 | -3.11 | 2.9 | 1.8 | 4.6 | 28.9 | **10.0** | 13.2 | 24.9 |
| Bank of Landisburg | Landisburg | PA | **B+** | B+ | A- | 304.1 | 4.77 | 1.9 | 1.8 | 44.7 | 16.4 | **10.0** | 18.1 | 29.5 |
| Bank of Laverne | Laverne | OK | **B** | B | B | 59.6 | 0.23 | 6.7 | 5.4 | 0.8 | 27.4 | **10.0** | 16.1 | 26.9 |
| Bank of Lewellen | Lewellen | NE | **C+** | B- | B | 23.3 | 1.27 | 2.9 | 1.3 | 0.0 | 22.3 | **10.0** | 27.0 | 55.9 |
| Bank of Lexington, Inc. | Lexington | KY | **B** | B | B | 248.2 | -0.58 | 1.5 | 0.2 | 39.6 | 3.8 | **10.0** | 12.3 | 19.3 |
| Bank of Lincoln County | Fayetteville | TN | **A-** | B | B+ | 153.2 | 11.19 | 7.6 | 1.6 | 13.3 | 8.3 | **5.1** | 12.5 | 11.1 |
| Bank of Lindsay | Lindsay | NE | **C+** | C+ | C+ | 76.0 | 1.11 | 5.4 | 1.6 | 0.1 | 2.6 | **7.8** | 11.5 | 13.2 |
| ▲ Bank of Little Rock | Little Rock | AR | **B-** | C- | C+ | 197.4 | -2.68 | 14.1 | 2.3 | 16.0 | 31.7 | **10.0** | 11.2 | 19.0 |
| Bank of Locust Grove | Locust Grove | OK | **B** | B | B | 40.1 | 24.07 | 27.9 | 37.2 | 2.9 | 9.4 | **10.0** | 12.6 | 16.4 |
| Bank of Louisiana | New Orleans | LA | **C-** | D- | D- | 78.4 | -0.18 | 0.6 | 4.9 | 34.9 | 1.9 | **6.5** | 9.2 | 12.1 |
| Bank of Louisiana | Louisiana | MO | **B-** | C+ | C+ | 51.7 | 0.43 | 10.2 | 1.7 | 17.2 | 25.0 | **9.6** | 10.7 | 15.4 |
| Bank of Lumber City | Lumber City | GA | **C** | C | C | 23.8 | -1.12 | 8.0 | 11.7 | 15.8 | 12.5 | **10.0** | 16.0 | 24.5 |
| Bank of Luxemburg | Luxemburg | WI | **C+** | B- | B- | 391.5 | 9.89 | 14.5 | 1.6 | 14.7 | 15.1 | **6.0** | 9.3 | 11.8 |
| ▲ Bank of Madison | Madison | GA | **A-** | B+ | B+ | 230.6 | 2.19 | 5.2 | 0.8 | 15.1 | 18.6 | **10.0** | 13.2 | 17.5 |
| Bank of Magnolia Co. | Magnolia | OH | **B** | B- | C+ | 80.2 | -2.60 | 4.4 | 4.7 | 27.4 | 21.5 | **10.0** | 11.8 | 24.8 |
| ▲ Bank of Maple Plain | Maple Plain | MN | **A-** | B+ | A- | 88.7 | -0.48 | 10.3 | 1.3 | 19.4 | 38.3 | **10.0** | 13.4 | 25.3 |
| Bank of Marin | Novato | CA | **A-** | A- | A- | 2707.3 | 7.40 | 5.6 | 1.0 | 6.2 | 21.1 | **9.6** | 11.3 | 14.6 |
| Bank of Marion | Marion | VA | **A-** | B | B | 392.3 | 4.00 | 2.2 | 3.8 | 32.4 | 29.3 | **10.0** | 11.9 | 21.4 |
| ▲ Bank of Mauston | Mauston | WI | **A** | A | A- | 295.3 | 1.47 | 5.0 | 2.0 | 9.6 | 31.4 | **10.0** | 13.3 | 19.1 |
| Bank of Maysville | Maysville | KY | **B+** | B+ | B | 129.4 | 2.83 | 0.4 | 1.0 | 30.2 | 30.7 | **10.0** | 18.0 | 31.1 |
| Bank of Mead | Mead | NE | **B** | B- | B- | 27.0 | 0.18 | 10.7 | 5.3 | 17.3 | 29.9 | **10.0** | 11.6 | 21.8 |
| Bank of Milan | Milan | TN | **B-** | B- | B | 77.0 | 15.81 | 8.2 | 1.3 | 20.2 | 26.4 | **6.9** | 8.9 | 15.6 |
| Bank of Millbrook | Millbrook | NY | **B** |  | B- | 227.4 | 3.95 | 1.9 | 1.6 | 22.1 | 40.8 | **9.8** | 10.8 | 25.5 |
| Bank of Milton | Milton | WI | **B** | B | B | 132.9 | 13.00 | 6.4 | 2.0 | 21.8 | 14.8 | **6.2** | 9.1 | 11.9 |
| Bank of Mingo | Williamson | WV | **C-** | C- | D- | 88.0 | 7.74 | 13.5 | 10.1 | 33.4 | 12.1 | **8.3** | 9.9 | 15.0 |
| Bank of Missouri | Perryville | MO | **B+** | B+ | B | 1813.6 | 2.28 | 8.5 | 3.1 | 17.4 | 18.8 | **9.4** | 11.7 | 14.5 |
| Bank of Monroe | Union | WV | **A-** | A- | B+ | 145.6 | 4.02 | 6.3 | 3.2 | 26.3 | 23.9 | **10.0** | 14.4 | 24.3 |
| Bank of Montana | Missoula | MT | **A-** | B+ | A- | 96.5 | 11.54 | 30.0 | 3.2 | 8.7 | 0.0 | **10.0** | 11.9 | 16.4 |
| Bank of Montgomery | Montgomery | IL | **D** | C- | C- | 40.9 | -5.35 | 11.9 | 1.9 | 13.2 | 24.3 | **6.7** | 8.8 | 23.5 |
| ▲ Bank of Monticello | Monticello | GA | **B+** | B | C+ | 110.1 | 1.35 | 6.2 | 6.7 | 27.5 | 13.6 | **10.0** | 11.3 | 18.8 |
| Bank of Monticello | Monticello | MO | **A-** | B+ | B+ | 119.5 | 5.23 | 6.6 | 4.0 | 11.4 | 18.5 | **10.0** | 11.4 | 15.9 |
| Bank of Morton | Morton | MS | **B+** | B+ | A- | 67.5 | -0.38 | 5.1 | 9.4 | 42.6 | 12.0 | **10.0** | 15.1 | 22.7 |
| ▼ Bank of Moundville | Moundville | AL | **C-** | C | C- | 92.7 | 1.80 | 6.6 | 2.7 | 4.6 | 64.9 | **8.0** | 9.7 | 23.6 |
| Bank of New Cambria | New Cambria | MO | **B** | B- | B- | 30.4 | -2.72 | 2.4 | 0.7 | 6.6 | 24.8 | **10.0** | 13.7 | 24.6 |
| Bank of New Castle | New Castle | DE | **D+** | C- | C- | 18.0 | 1.70 | 0.0 | 0.0 | 0.0 | 0.8 | **10.0** | 97.3 | 484.6 |
| ▲ Bank of New England | Salem | NH | **B** | C+ | B | 956.0 | 4.41 | 5.4 | 0.0 | 0.3 | 1.3 | **10.0** | 15.0 | 16.4 |
| Bank of New Glarus | New Glarus | WI | **B-** | B- | B | 317.4 | 10.70 | 17.1 | 1.8 | 14.0 | 10.3 | **8.4** | 11.4 | 13.6 |
| Bank of New Hampshire | Laconia | NH | **B-** | B- | C+ | 1755.6 | 7.10 | 5.7 | 2.9 | 32.4 | 8.6 | **6.6** | 9.1 | 12.2 |
| Bank of New Madrid | New Madrid | MO | **A-** | A- | A- | 100.5 | 3.26 | 2.2 | 2.8 | 19.4 | 34.4 | **10.0** | 12.3 | 15.7 |
| Bank of New York Mellon | New York | NY | **B** | B | B- | 311387.0 | 8.72 | 0.5 | 0.0 | 0.3 | 39.0 | **4.9** | 7.0 | 15.2 |
| Bank of New York Mellon Trust Co., N.A. | Los Angeles | CA | **U** | U | U | 1393.7 | 4.79 | 0.0 | 0.0 | 0.0 | 12.3 | **10.0** | 67.6 | 335.0 |
| ▲ Bank of Newington | Newington | GA | **C+** | C | C- | 145.9 | 12.55 | 5.1 | 2.1 | 23.9 | 0.7 | **6.6** | 8.6 | 13.0 |
| Bank of Newman Grove | Newman Grove | NE | **C** | C- | C | 32.7 | -6.74 | 0.4 | 2.8 | 0.0 | 16.3 | **8.9** | 11.7 | 14.0 |
| Bank of O'Fallon | O'Fallon | IL | **A-** | A- | B+ | 312.8 | -1.44 | 4.7 | 5.5 | 42.2 | 5.5 | **10.0** | 14.6 | 23.8 |
| Bank of Oak Ridge | Oak Ridge | LA | **B-** | C+ | C+ | 55.0 | 5.28 | 23.7 | 0.9 | 9.2 | 12.1 | **10.0** | 11.1 | 15.7 |
| Bank of Oak Ridge | Oak Ridge | NC | **B-** | B- | B- | 471.9 | 4.93 | 11.3 | 0.9 | 19.4 | 8.9 | **7.9** | 10.3 | 13.2 |
| Bank of Ocean City | Ocean City | MD | **A-** | A- | B+ | 362.3 | 7.70 | 3.8 | 0.5 | 18.5 | 13.1 | **9.4** | 10.6 | 15.2 |
| Bank of Odessa | Odessa | MO | **B+** | B+ | B+ | 273.5 | 9.49 | 8.8 | 3.8 | 41.2 | 15.5 | **10.0** | 18.9 | 31.4 |
| ▲ Bank of Okolona | Okolona | MS | **C-** | C | B- | 206.6 | 5.23 | 18.2 | 5.4 | 14.9 | 13.9 | **9.0** | 10.4 | 15.6 |
| Bank of Old Monroe | Old Monroe | MO | **A** | A | A | 391.9 | 7.26 | 6.7 | 0.5 | 10.5 | 24.6 | **10.0** | 15.2 | 20.7 |
| ▲ Bank of Ontario | Ontario | WI | **B** | C+ | B- | 49.2 | -1.31 | 7.1 | 3.8 | 29.0 | 10.0 | **10.0** | 12.4 | 21.5 |
| Bank of Orchard | Orchard | NE | **B-** | B- | B- | 25.0 | 2.97 | 6.0 | 4.7 | 0.2 | 17.8 | **10.0** | 14.6 | 34.7 |
| Bank of Orrick | Orrick | MO | **C-** | C- | C- | 32.8 | 1.77 | 1.3 | 2.2 | 18.7 | 40.7 | **8.1** | 9.8 | 21.5 |
| Bank of Palmer | Palmer | KS | **C+** | C+ | C+ | 44.8 | 2.04 | 2.2 | 3.9 | 7.7 | 39.8 | **9.6** | 10.7 | 18.8 |
| Bank of Pensacola | Pensacola | FL | **C** | C- | D+ | 88.9 | 5.90 | 3.7 | 1.5 | 22.0 | 28.7 | **10.0** | 13.6 | 28.9 |
| ▲ Bank of Perry County | Lobelville | TN | **C+** | C+ | B | 176.8 | 6.82 | 7.8 | 15.9 | 41.0 | 3.9 | **7.2** | 9.2 | 13.6 |
| ▲ Bank of Pontiac | Pontiac | IL | **A-** | B+ | A- | 565.7 | 3.38 | 11.3 | 4.4 | 23.4 | 13.0 | **10.0** | 13.0 | 19.2 |
| ▲ Bank of Prague | Prague | NE | **A-** | B | B | 29.5 | 5.96 | 13.1 | 10.6 | 1.5 | 16.5 | **10.0** | 14.4 | 19.2 |

Arrows denote recent upgrades ▲ or downgrades ▼

| Asset Quality Index | Adjusted Non-Performing Loans as a % of Total Loans | Adjusted Non-Performing Loans as a % of Capital | Net Charge-Offs Avg Loans | Profitability Index | Net Income ($Mil) | Return on Assets (R.O.A.) | Return on Equity (R.O.E.) | Net Interest Spread | Overhead Efficiency Ratio | Liquidity Index | Liquidity Ratio | Hot Money Ratio | Stability Index |
|---|---|---|---|---|---|---|---|---|---|---|---|---|---|
| 6.4 | 2.34 | 6.4 | 0.28 | 3.8 | 1.9 | 0.72 | 5.87 | 2.98 | 71.1 | 3.9 | 29.7 | 12.0 | 6.4 |
| 5.8 | 1.44 | 6.3 | 0.02 | 7.9 | 4.2 | 1.90 | 15.28 | 4.08 | 59.4 | 2.3 | 7.6 | 12.9 | 8.2 |
| 8.5 | 1.28 | 1.6 | 0.31 | 5.6 | 0.8 | 1.26 | 9.98 | 4.19 | 62.5 | 4.2 | 34.2 | 11.9 | 7.3 |
| 5.4 | 4.82 | 12.7 | 0.03 | 6.2 | 3.7 | 1.25 | 6.85 | 3.55 | 57.9 | 1.9 | 13.2 | 19.4 | 8.4 |
| 5.9 | 2.00 | 5.7 | -0.14 | 4.9 | 0.7 | 1.11 | 6.62 | 4.35 | 74.6 | 3.8 | 45.7 | 16.9 | 7.1 |
| 8.8 | 0.00 | 0.0 | 0.00 | 3.8 | 0.2 | 0.67 | 2.53 | 3.77 | 77.4 | 4.2 | 57.6 | 15.5 | 5.7 |
| 9.1 | 0.00 | 0.3 | 0.00 | 3.9 | 2.2 | 0.83 | 7.37 | 3.47 | 71.3 | 0.5 | 15.7 | 50.3 | 7.0 |
| 6.2 | 1.43 | 4.6 | -0.03 | 9.1 | 2.3 | 1.56 | 11.84 | 4.98 | 59.5 | 1.1 | 15.6 | 31.2 | 7.6 |
| 6.9 | 0.14 | 0.9 | 0.00 | 3.0 | 0.3 | 0.45 | 3.87 | 3.28 | 88.0 | 0.6 | 8.9 | 37.6 | 6.5 |
| 3.7 | 3.79 | 18.0 | 1.33 | 3.4 | 1.2 | 0.61 | 5.58 | 3.75 | 90.9 | 5.1 | 35.5 | 6.3 | 4.6 |
| 4.8 | 0.89 | 5.0 | 0.24 | 9.3 | 0.6 | 1.61 | 12.61 | 5.87 | 59.9 | 1.6 | 12.9 | 23.1 | 6.7 |
| 2.2 | 1.51 | 22.0 | 0.42 | 6.0 | 1.5 | 1.92 | 18.46 | 4.88 | 139.2 | 4.8 | 27.7 | 6.1 | 4.9 |
| 4.2 | 1.41 | 3.8 | 1.82 | 2.3 | 0.0 | -0.07 | -0.70 | 4.10 | 80.2 | 1.8 | 12.5 | 19.7 | 6.9 |
| 6.4 | 2.82 | 6.4 | 0.14 | 3.3 | 0.1 | 0.59 | 3.83 | 5.42 | 90.4 | 2.4 | 37.6 | 19.7 | 5.0 |
| 2.8 | 2.67 | 18.6 | 0.25 | 4.8 | 3.5 | 0.93 | 9.94 | 3.86 | 71.4 | 3.2 | 19.6 | 13.5 | 5.6 |
| 6.1 | 1.43 | 7.1 | -0.03 | 5.8 | 2.8 | 1.25 | 9.23 | 4.26 | 63.8 | 3.8 | 8.5 | 9.0 | 7.7 |
| 9.0 | 0.46 | 1.7 | 0.10 | 3.9 | 0.6 | 0.71 | 6.07 | 3.70 | 74.9 | 5.5 | 38.8 | 5.9 | 6.6 |
| 7.9 | 0.21 | 1.4 | 0.14 | 5.3 | 1.2 | 1.39 | 10.28 | 3.43 | 58.6 | 5.1 | 42.1 | 9.6 | 7.8 |
| 6.9 | 0.62 | 1.7 | 0.00 | 7.2 | 35.4 | 1.39 | 11.27 | 4.03 | 53.9 | 5.7 | 26.3 | 2.9 | 10.0 |
| 7.2 | 0.00 | 3.7 | 0.31 | 5.8 | 4.9 | 1.29 | 10.57 | 4.44 | 67.2 | 4.4 | 24.5 | 7.2 | 6.8 |
| 7.8 | 0.80 | 3.2 | 0.07 | 9.8 | 8.4 | 2.84 | 21.85 | 3.87 | 39.9 | 2.4 | 21.8 | 17.8 | 9.2 |
| 8.6 | 0.57 | 1.0 | 0.00 | 4.9 | 1.2 | 0.95 | 4.89 | 3.58 | 67.4 | 3.8 | 28.9 | 12.5 | 8.2 |
| 8.5 | 0.00 | 0.0 | -0.12 | 5.0 | 0.3 | 0.98 | 8.48 | 3.56 | 64.1 | 5.0 | 28.9 | 4.9 | 6.5 |
| 7.7 | 0.81 | 4.4 | 0.06 | 4.5 | 0.7 | 0.96 | 9.89 | 3.71 | 74.2 | 2.8 | 42.9 | 24.5 | 5.2 |
| 9.1 | 0.14 | 1.5 | 0.10 | 4.5 | 2.3 | 1.00 | 9.02 | 3.33 | 68.4 | 6.3 | 44.8 | 2.7 | 6.2 |
| 7.5 | 0.00 | 0.0 | 0.00 | 6.4 | 1.6 | 1.29 | 13.94 | 4.07 | 58.7 | 2.4 | 23.6 | 17.8 | 6.6 |
| 4.4 | 1.12 | 7.0 | 0.68 | 2.1 | 0.1 | 0.15 | 1.51 | 4.24 | 93.8 | 1.2 | 13.6 | 28.7 | 2.8 |
| 5.7 | 1.54 | 5.0 | 0.28 | 6.6 | 28.1 | 1.59 | 12.41 | 3.90 | 64.5 | 4.1 | 11.4 | 7.9 | 9.4 |
| 8.4 | 1.00 | 2.7 | 0.02 | 6.2 | 1.9 | 1.32 | 9.43 | 4.09 | 64.8 | 3.2 | 29.4 | 15.5 | 8.5 |
| 8.1 | 0.00 | 0.0 | 0.00 | 10.0 | 2.1 | 2.38 | 19.18 | 4.75 | 58.4 | 1.6 | 17.7 | 21.6 | 8.3 |
| 7.3 | 1.32 | 2.2 | 2.13 | 0.9 | -0.2 | -0.45 | -4.81 | 2.87 | 83.9 | 4.6 | 58.5 | 15.1 | 4.4 |
| 5.4 | 1.33 | 7.3 | 0.09 | 7.2 | 1.8 | 1.69 | 15.74 | 4.52 | 60.7 | 3.7 | 20.8 | 10.9 | 6.7 |
| 6.2 | 1.31 | 5.7 | 0.18 | 7.2 | 2.0 | 1.81 | 15.18 | 4.19 | 55.5 | 3.0 | 23.8 | 12.6 | 7.2 |
| 4.9 | 2.10 | 12.5 | 0.10 | 9.5 | 1.3 | 1.89 | 12.56 | 5.48 | 64.5 | 1.1 | 9.9 | 28.6 | 9.3 |
| 9.4 | 0.17 | 0.5 | 0.00 | 2.0 | 0.3 | 0.31 | 3.34 | 2.57 | 92.2 | 2.6 | 41.9 | 27.5 | 4.6 |
| 9.1 | 0.00 | 0.0 | -0.01 | 3.8 | 0.2 | 0.65 | 4.84 | 3.86 | 78.4 | 6.4 | 55.3 | 4.0 | 7.0 |
| 7.5 | 0.00 | 0.0 | 0.00 | 7.7 | 0.3 | 1.63 | 1.68 | 2.42 | 5.7 | 2.3 | 74.6 | 100.0 | 3.0 |
| 5.1 | 1.05 | 3.4 | 0.01 | 9.7 | 16.9 | 1.76 | 11.99 | 4.07 | 37.4 | 0.5 | 8.6 | 21.5 | 10.0 |
| 4.2 | 2.45 | 11.7 | 0.78 | 8.0 | 4.4 | 1.48 | 12.07 | 4.51 | 54.5 | 3.3 | 18.2 | 12.9 | 7.3 |
| 6.7 | 0.48 | 3.2 | 0.01 | 4.2 | 14.3 | 0.84 | 8.22 | 3.58 | 70.9 | 3.0 | 4.6 | 6.7 | 8.2 |
| 9.0 | 0.00 | 0.2 | 0.00 | 6.7 | 1.6 | 1.65 | 13.49 | 4.31 | 58.7 | 1.9 | 13.5 | 19.4 | 8.1 |
| 9.0 | 0.41 | 0.3 | 0.05 | 4.6 | 2583.0 | 0.95 | 10.04 | 1.22 | 70.6 | 3.6 | 57.7 | 25.4 | 7.6 |
| 6.5 | na | 0.0 | na | 10.0 | 187.0 | 13.70 | 16.70 | 2.19 | 48.5 | 9.5 | 161.5 | 0.0 | 7.0 |
| 4.2 | 1.40 | 9.7 | 0.38 | 6.0 | 1.5 | 1.08 | 12.36 | 5.05 | 67.3 | 1.0 | 16.9 | 32.0 | 5.7 |
| 4.7 | 0.12 | 5.3 | 0.00 | 4.0 | 0.3 | 0.89 | 8.02 | 3.92 | 78.4 | 3.2 | 19.1 | 13.3 | 5.4 |
| 8.7 | 0.08 | 0.5 | -0.01 | 5.2 | 4.0 | 1.30 | 9.08 | 2.90 | 54.4 | 1.3 | 19.2 | 29.0 | 8.5 |
| 8.5 | 0.03 | 0.2 | 0.01 | 3.1 | 0.3 | 0.48 | 4.11 | 3.68 | 83.5 | 1.3 | 18.7 | 29.3 | 6.2 |
| 4.0 | 1.06 | 7.4 | 0.17 | 5.1 | 4.8 | 1.04 | 9.99 | 3.93 | 70.1 | 0.7 | 13.9 | 32.6 | 6.6 |
| 7.8 | 0.05 | 0.4 | -0.08 | 8.0 | 5.5 | 1.54 | 14.53 | 3.95 | 47.9 | 3.8 | 24.8 | 10.8 | 7.1 |
| 6.3 | 1.28 | 6.1 | 0.16 | 6.2 | 3.2 | 1.20 | 6.31 | 3.41 | 50.1 | 1.6 | 7.4 | 20.5 | 7.9 |
| 2.1 | 3.95 | 25.6 | 0.90 | 7.1 | 3.6 | 1.80 | 17.87 | 4.24 | 64.6 | 1.1 | 27.4 | 37.8 | 8.0 |
| 8.7 | 0.83 | 1.9 | -0.15 | 9.3 | 8.8 | 2.29 | 15.00 | 4.27 | 51.0 | 3.4 | 25.8 | 8.7 | 9.9 |
| 4.0 | 2.72 | 14.8 | -0.02 | 8.5 | 1.2 | 2.40 | 20.46 | 4.81 | 56.0 | 1.1 | 7.5 | 27.6 | 7.7 |
| 8.7 | 0.00 | 0.3 | 0.53 | 3.2 | 0.2 | 0.59 | 4.08 | 3.02 | 74.5 | 5.3 | 80.4 | 14.9 | 7.3 |
| 5.2 | 2.63 | 10.0 | 0.29 | 2.3 | 0.1 | 0.18 | 1.67 | 4.02 | 92.3 | 5.9 | 41.4 | 4.4 | 5.0 |
| 3.7 | 0.03 | 19.8 | -0.04 | 3.8 | 0.4 | 0.88 | 8.21 | 3.48 | 73.9 | 5.6 | 46.4 | 7.6 | 5.5 |
| 9.1 | 0.00 | 0.0 | 0.02 | 2.4 | 0.2 | 0.28 | 2.05 | 2.68 | 82.5 | 4.4 | 50.4 | 14.7 | 5.5 |
| 5.0 | 0.59 | 4.8 | 0.19 | 7.8 | 2.7 | 1.58 | 16.94 | 4.51 | 59.9 | 1.1 | 7.7 | 21.5 | 7.3 |
| 6.1 | 1.17 | 5.0 | 0.20 | 6.5 | 6.8 | 1.24 | 9.38 | 3.84 | 54.8 | 1.7 | 13.8 | 14.8 | 8.0 |
| 7.5 | 0.00 | 0.0 | 0.04 | 10.0 | 0.7 | 2.44 | 16.77 | 4.78 | 59.7 | 4.0 | 28.6 | 11.4 | 9.0 |

| Name | City | State | Rating | 2018 Rating | 2017 Rating | Total Assets ($Mil) | One Year Asset Growth | Asset Mix (As a % of Total Assets): Commercial Loans | Consumer Loans | Mortgage Loans | Securities | Capitalization Index | Leverage Ratio | Risk-Based Capital Ratio |
|---|---|---|---|---|---|---|---|---|---|---|---|---|---|---|
| Bank of Prairie Du Sac | Prairie Du Sac | WI | **A+** | A+ | A+ | 463.7 | 2.40 | 10.2 | 0.5 | 5.7 | 28.1 | **10.0** | 15.7 | 21.9 |
| Bank of Prairie Village | Prairie Village | KS | **A-** | B+ | B+ | 104.9 | -1.07 | 10.4 | 1.3 | 21.2 | 25.1 | **10.0** | 12.0 | 22.4 |
| Bank of Princeton | Princeton | NJ | **B+** | A- | B | 1454.9 | 16.25 | 1.6 | 0.1 | 10.0 | 7.7 | **10.0** | 12.9 | 15.1 |
| Bank of Protection | Protection | KS | **B** | B | B | 68.6 | -1.87 | 5.2 | 3.4 | 6.3 | 14.0 | **10.0** | 15.3 | 19.4 |
| Bank of Putnam County | Cookeville | TN | **B** | B- | B- | 1060.0 | 28.78 | 4.7 | 3.0 | 23.3 | 24.9 | **6.1** | 8.1 | 14.6 |
| Bank of Rantoul | Rantoul | IL | **B-** | B- | B+ | 232.8 | 1.24 | 12.0 | 0.6 | 1.7 | 46.0 | **9.6** | 10.7 | 19.3 |
| Bank of Richmondville | Cobleskill | NY | **B-** | B- | B- | 141.9 | 0.63 | 3.0 | 7.5 | 36.2 | 27.1 | **10.0** | 11.5 | 23.6 |
| Bank of Ripley | Ripley | TN | **B** | B | B- | 224.9 | 2.29 | 1.4 | 7.9 | 7.7 | 51.7 | **10.0** | 15.6 | 29.1 |
| Bank of Romney | Romney | WV | **B** | B- | B- | 294.0 | 2.61 | 2.2 | 6.7 | 46.7 | 15.6 | **10.0** | 12.2 | 20.7 |
| Bank of Salem | Salem | AR | **B+** | B | B- | 144.9 | 7.42 | 12.7 | 5.6 | 24.7 | 1.5 | **10.0** | 11.4 | 15.8 |
| Bank of Salem | Salem | MO | **B-** | C+ | C+ | 105.9 | -0.24 | 2.1 | 3.7 | 31.4 | 30.7 | **8.1** | 9.7 | 18.0 |
| Bank of San Antonio | San Antonio | TX | **B** | B | B | 836.2 | 9.82 | 25.2 | 0.4 | 7.7 | 8.4 | **5.6** | 9.4 | 11.4 |
| Bank of San Francisco | San Francisco | CA | **A-** | B+ | B | 397.4 | 20.74 | 18.5 | 0.0 | 32.3 | 0.0 | **9.8** | 10.8 | 16.5 |
| Bank of San Jacinto County | Coldspring | TX | **B** | B | B | 40.4 | 2.50 | 3.9 | 2.5 | 34.4 | 18.0 | **10.0** | 14.6 | 43.1 |
| Bank of Santa Clarita | Santa Clarita | CA | **B+** | B | C+ | 304.4 | -0.98 | 5.5 | 1.2 | 2.9 | 3.0 | **10.0** | 12.2 | 15.6 |
| Bank of South Carolina | Charleston | SC | **A** | A- | B+ | 445.1 | 3.74 | 11.8 | 1.2 | 13.7 | 22.6 | **10.0** | 11.1 | 16.5 |
| Bank of South Texas | Pharr | TX | **B-** | C+ | B- | 138.0 | 3.94 | 4.5 | 1.2 | 22.4 | 5.8 | **9.5** | 10.7 | 15.5 |
| ▲ Bank of Southern California, N.A. | San Diego | CA | **B** | C+ | B | 830.2 | 8.10 | 13.1 | 0.3 | 8.8 | 2.0 | **10.0** | 12.8 | 16.2 |
| ▲ Bank of Southside Virginia | Carson | VA | **A** | B+ | A | 573.8 | 3.27 | 2.3 | 18.0 | 5.2 | 25.0 | **10.0** | 18.2 | 31.1 |
| Bank of Springfield | Springfield | IL | **C-** | C- | C | 1040.3 | 3.44 | 19.2 | 0.8 | 10.1 | 5.9 | **6.3** | 9.2 | 12.0 |
| Bank of St. Elizabeth | Saint Elizabeth | MO | **A-** | B+ | A | 149.0 | 6.39 | 1.9 | 7.4 | 52.9 | 0.0 | **9.3** | 10.5 | 16.8 |
| Bank of St. Francisville | Saint Francisville | LA | **B** | B- | B | 153.2 | 15.24 | 5.7 | 2.4 | 16.0 | 9.7 | **9.7** | 10.8 | 15.4 |
| Bank of Star Valley | Afton | WY | **B+** | B | B+ | 237.1 | 11.29 | 7.3 | 7.1 | 9.9 | 36.0 | **8.4** | 9.9 | 16.7 |
| Bank of Steinauer | Steinauer | NE | **C** | D+ | C- | 12.5 | -1.96 | 5.7 | 8.6 | 38.0 | 3.2 | **8.5** | 10.0 | 15.0 |
| Bank of Stockton | Stockton | CA | **A** | A- | A- | 3357.5 | 6.19 | 6.4 | 10.5 | 5.9 | 14.0 | **10.0** | 17.4 | 15.7 |
| Bank of Stronghurst | Stronghurst | IL | **C+** | C+ | C+ | 74.1 | 3.14 | 2.6 | 1.7 | 6.3 | 56.9 | **10.0** | 17.3 | 36.8 |
| ▼ Bank of Sun Prairie | Sun Prairie | WI | **B** | B+ | A- | 440.5 | 6.78 | 7.0 | 1.0 | 7.8 | 8.7 | **9.7** | 12.5 | 14.7 |
| Bank of Sunset and Trust Co. | Sunset | LA | **B+** | B | B | 149.9 | 10.17 | 14.5 | 0.6 | 26.4 | 11.4 | **8.2** | 9.8 | 14.1 |
| Bank of Tampa | Tampa | FL | **B+** | B+ | B | 1870.1 | 13.76 | 15.2 | 3.5 | 4.1 | 28.9 | **7.2** | 9.4 | 12.7 |
| Bank of Tennessee | Kingsport | TN | **B** | B | B | 1414.9 | 2.85 | 10.5 | 0.5 | 21.8 | 13.1 | **6.0** | 9.1 | 11.7 |
| Bank of Tescott | Tescott | KS | **A-** | B | B+ | 399.9 | -1.67 | 2.4 | 1.7 | 22.2 | 22.9 | **10.0** | 14.1 | 20.3 |
| Bank of Texas | Midland | TX | **A-** | A- | B+ | 395.2 | 5.16 | 31.9 | 0.1 | 2.0 | 1.2 | **8.4** | 12.7 | 13.7 |
| Bank of the Bluegrass & Trust Co. | Lexington | KY | **A-** | B+ | A- | 266.0 | 2.90 | 3.4 | 0.7 | 22.4 | 19.6 | **10.0** | 12.0 | 17.8 |
| Bank of the Federated States of Micronesi | Pohnpei | FM | **A-** | B+ | A- | 171.5 | 4.39 | 7.7 | 9.8 | 1.1 | 31.4 | **10.0** | 14.2 | 41.2 |
| Bank of the Flint Hills | Wamego | KS | **B-** | C+ | B | 304.0 | -2.26 | 15.0 | 1.9 | 17.3 | 11.6 | **6.6** | 10.0 | 12.2 |
| Bank of the James | Lynchburg | VA | **B-** | B- | B- | 725.7 | 7.47 | 11.8 | 2.4 | 17.1 | 8.8 | **5.7** | 9.1 | 11.5 |
| Bank of the Lowcountry | Walterboro | SC | **B** | B- | B- | 227.0 | 5.04 | 5.2 | 0.9 | 14.0 | 28.7 | **9.8** | 10.8 | 22.3 |
| Bank of the Mountains, Inc. | West Liberty | KY | **C-** | C- | B- | 71.7 | 2.36 | 4.4 | 18.9 | 28.8 | 6.9 | **9.8** | 10.8 | 15.7 |
| ▼ Bank of the Orient | San Francisco | CA | **B-** | B+ | B- | 894.1 | 1.97 | 7.5 | 0.0 | 17.6 | 4.3 | **8.3** | 9.9 | 14.1 |
| Bank of the Pacific | Aberdeen | WA | **A-** | B+ | B | 928.7 | 2.38 | 10.7 | 6.3 | 7.9 | 11.1 | **9.4** | 11.1 | 14.5 |
| Bank of the Panhandle | Guymon | OK | **A-** | A- | A | 169.8 | 2.92 | 11.0 | 1.1 | 8.7 | 26.2 | **10.0** | 12.5 | 17.5 |
| ▲ Bank of the Prairie | Olathe | KS | **B** | B- | B | 118.2 | -16.40 | 18.4 | 0.7 | 19.8 | 0.0 | **9.6** | 11.1 | 14.6 |
| Bank of the Rockies | White Sulphur Spring | MT | **C-** | C | C | 157.5 | 5.57 | 9.9 | 1.6 | 9.2 | 14.9 | **9.0** | 10.3 | 14.3 |
| Bank of the Sierra | Porterville | CA | **A-** | A- | A- | 2593.4 | 2.82 | 4.4 | 0.3 | 7.7 | 23.2 | **10.0** | 11.7 | 15.3 |
| Bank of the South | Pensacola | FL | **C** | C- | D+ | 74.8 | -10.60 | 0.0 | 0.1 | 5.0 | 50.8 | **10.0** | 18.8 | 58.7 |
| Bank of the Southwest | Roswell | NM | **B** | B | B | 157.2 | 6.15 | 24.2 | 6.8 | 15.9 | 0.1 | **7.2** | 9.1 | 13.4 |
| Bank of the Valley | Bellwood | NE | **C** | C- | C+ | 310.6 | 13.23 | 6.2 | 1.9 | 4.0 | 12.5 | **5.3** | 8.0 | 11.2 |
| Bank of the West | San Francisco | CA | **B** | B | B | 92968.6 | 6.53 | 14.7 | 16.4 | 10.0 | 22.1 | **7.9** | 10.0 | 13.3 |
| Bank of the West | Thomas | OK | **A** | A- | B+ | 163.4 | 7.03 | 8.6 | 0.4 | 4.8 | 0.0 | **9.0** | 12.8 | 14.1 |
| Bank of the West | Grapevine | TX | **B** | B | B | 505.6 | 2.87 | 7.3 | 0.5 | 8.3 | 7.7 | **7.6** | 9.4 | 13.8 |
| Bank of Tioga | Tioga | ND | **C+** | B- | B | 330.9 | -6.55 | 2.5 | 0.7 | 3.1 | 73.4 | **7.8** | 9.6 | 19.4 |
| Bank of Travelers Rest | Travelers Rest | SC | **B+** | B | B | 804.9 | 10.16 | 6.4 | 4.4 | 13.7 | 22.7 | **8.4** | 9.9 | 15.6 |
| Bank of Turtle Lake | Turtle Lake | ND | **B-** | C- | C+ | 52.7 | 6.47 | 10.0 | 1.8 | 0.5 | 8.0 | **10.0** | 11.6 | 15.1 |
| Bank of Utah | Ogden | UT | **A** | B+ | A | 1423.2 | 0.04 | 5.8 | 0.4 | 2.1 | 9.1 | **10.0** | 12.6 | 16.9 |
| ▲ Bank of Utica | Utica | NY | **A-** | B+ | A- | 1144.4 | 6.68 | 3.9 | 0.4 | 0.2 | 81.9 | **10.0** | 21.1 | 20.1 |
| Bank of Vernon | Vernon | AL | **A-** | B+ | B+ | 162.0 | 8.58 | 17.1 | 2.0 | 15.5 | 14.6 | **10.0** | 15.8 | 23.2 |
| Bank of Versailles | Versailles | MO | **B** | B | B | 263.7 | -1.43 | 1.0 | 0.8 | 62.6 | 0.0 | **10.0** | 13.4 | 24.0 |
| Bank of Vici | Vici | OK | **C+** | C- | C+ | 34.0 | -7.88 | 23.5 | 13.9 | 2.3 | 20.2 | **10.0** | 13.5 | 20.5 |
| Bank of Walker County | Jasper | AL | **C** | C+ | B- | 70.5 | 0.56 | 13.8 | 3.7 | 23.6 | 12.6 | **8.8** | 11.1 | 14.0 |
| Bank of Washington | Washington | MO | **D** | D | D | 712.2 | 3.62 | 26.4 | 0.7 | 8.6 | 6.1 | **9.8** | 13.4 | 14.9 |

| Asset Quality Index | Adjusted Non-Performing Loans as a % of Total Loans | Adjusted Non-Performing Loans as a % of Capital | Net Charge-Offs Avg Loans | Profitability Index | Net Income ($Mil) | Return on Assets (R.O.A.) | Return on Equity (R.O.E.) | Net Interest Spread | Overhead Efficiency Ratio | Liquidity Index | Liquidity Ratio | Hot Money Ratio | Stability Index |
|---|---|---|---|---|---|---|---|---|---|---|---|---|---|
| **8.7** | 0.19 | 0.4 | 0.00 | **9.7** | 7.9 | 1.79 | 11.19 | 3.71 | 42.4 | **5.7** | 42.9 | 6.5 | **9.7** |
| **9.0** | 0.00 | 0.0 | 0.00 | **6.6** | 1.6 | 1.52 | 13.02 | 3.74 | 56.0 | **2.4** | 25.6 | 18.4 | **7.9** |
| **6.3** | 0.99 | 3.4 | 0.37 | **4.1** | 10.1 | 0.75 | 5.35 | 3.35 | 61.9 | **1.0** | 14.7 | 25.5 | **9.9** |
| **7.2** | 0.00 | 0.0 | 0.15 | **5.4** | 0.8 | 1.17 | 8.05 | 4.24 | 60.9 | **1.4** | 11.1 | 25.4 | **7.4** |
| **8.7** | 0.08 | 0.9 | 0.11 | **5.9** | 12.7 | 1.40 | 18.68 | 3.85 | 66.3 | **3.4** | 31.2 | 18.1 | **6.4** |
| **4.8** | 2.74 | 7.5 | 0.76 | **7.4** | 4.0 | 1.74 | 15.08 | 3.77 | 49.0 | **2.3** | 19.2 | 16.8 | **8.5** |
| **6.3** | 1.22 | 8.0 | 0.23 | **3.6** | 0.9 | 0.63 | 5.57 | 3.78 | 77.4 | **3.9** | 14.6 | 9.2 | **6.3** |
| **5.7** | 5.40 | 11.6 | 0.23 | **3.7** | 1.6 | 0.74 | 4.72 | 3.93 | 76.2 | **3.7** | 48.0 | 18.6 | **7.5** |
| **4.6** | 2.74 | 14.1 | 0.03 | **5.1** | 3.2 | 1.07 | 10.22 | 3.78 | 66.2 | **1.6** | 15.2 | 15.4 | **6.5** |
| **5.3** | 1.14 | 7.8 | 0.24 | **8.5** | 2.1 | 1.49 | 12.88 | 4.56 | 60.3 | **1.1** | 15.4 | 27.4 | **7.6** |
| **5.8** | 1.25 | 6.9 | 0.06 | **3.9** | 0.9 | 0.88 | 9.36 | 3.11 | 71.9 | **3.0** | 21.7 | 14.8 | **5.2** |
| **7.0** | 0.00 | 0.0 | 0.02 | **6.5** | 10.4 | 1.29 | 12.85 | 3.83 | 63.0 | **4.7** | 17.1 | 4.1 | **7.0** |
| **8.7** | 0.00 | 0.0 | 0.00 | **6.0** | 4.1 | 1.16 | 10.48 | 4.24 | 59.8 | **2.0** | 20.7 | 19.3 | **6.2** |
| **9.7** | 0.00 | 0.0 | 0.00 | **4.2** | 0.3 | 0.85 | 5.93 | 4.68 | 83.5 | **4.8** | 60.0 | 14.3 | **6.8** |
| **6.7** | 0.70 | 3.2 | 0.00 | **5.3** | 3.2 | 1.04 | 9.18 | 3.22 | 55.3 | **1.4** | 14.5 | 19.3 | **7.0** |
| **8.3** | 0.80 | 3.6 | 0.14 | **9.1** | 7.5 | 1.73 | 15.56 | 4.54 | 52.8 | **5.2** | 28.4 | 3.7 | **8.1** |
| **4.0** | 1.61 | 8.4 | 0.13 | **6.5** | 1.8 | 1.32 | 10.60 | 6.06 | 72.6 | **0.8** | 23.5 | 40.4 | **7.6** |
| **6.1** | 0.28 | 0.8 | 0.00 | **5.0** | 6.8 | 0.87 | 6.34 | 4.23 | 67.8 | **1.5** | 14.6 | 18.8 | **8.1** |
| **7.8** | 0.42 | 0.6 | 0.06 | **7.3** | 9.3 | 1.63 | 8.96 | 4.01 | 59.6 | **6.8** | 62.4 | 5.3 | **9.3** |
| **1.5** | 4.17 | 28.6 | 0.10 | **4.2** | 7.6 | 0.74 | 7.92 | 3.87 | 71.9 | **4.3** | 12.3 | 6.9 | **7.1** |
| **7.8** | 0.15 | 1.0 | 0.02 | **9.1** | 3.0 | 1.98 | 16.51 | 4.51 | 60.7 | **1.8** | 8.8 | 19.6 | **9.1** |
| **4.8** | 1.35 | 8.6 | 0.07 | **6.2** | 2.1 | 1.53 | 14.46 | 4.47 | 69.4 | **2.6** | 20.5 | 16.8 | **6.4** |
| **6.1** | 1.08 | 3.3 | 0.02 | **8.3** | 4.7 | 2.05 | 20.14 | 4.06 | 47.7 | **2.8** | 34.0 | 18.8 | **8.1** |
| **8.2** | 0.00 | 0.0 | 0.00 | **3.1** | 0.0 | 0.35 | 3.49 | 4.53 | 90.4 | **4.3** | 14.2 | 6.0 | **3.8** |
| **7.7** | 0.63 | 1.2 | 0.11 | **9.2** | 125.9 | 3.92 | 22.99 | 4.00 | 48.4 | **6.0** | 43.3 | 7.4 | **10.0** |
| **9.3** | 0.21 | 0.3 | 0.03 | **3.0** | 0.4 | 0.53 | 3.12 | 2.75 | 81.0 | **5.0** | 58.5 | 13.2 | **7.1** |
| **4.4** | 1.54 | 9.2 | 0.17 | **4.5** | 3.8 | 0.90 | 7.31 | 3.45 | 67.5 | **2.7** | 15.5 | 12.5 | **8.0** |
| **8.7** | 0.09 | 0.7 | 0.04 | **5.4** | 1.7 | 1.14 | 11.80 | 4.07 | 64.8 | **1.0** | 11.6 | 28.8 | **5.8** |
| **7.5** | 0.63 | 3.9 | 0.18 | **6.0** | 21.8 | 1.24 | 13.16 | 4.02 | 62.1 | **6.5** | 32.5 | 1.1 | **8.0** |
| **7.7** | 0.49 | 3.6 | 0.02 | **5.9** | 20.5 | 1.45 | 16.39 | 3.85 | 65.2 | **3.7** | 11.4 | 7.1 | **8.6** |
| **6.0** | 1.35 | 6.4 | 0.17 | **6.2** | 5.6 | 1.43 | 10.42 | 3.74 | 52.9 | **1.2** | 22.2 | 31.3 | **9.4** |
| **8.2** | 0.00 | 0.0 | 0.00 | **9.8** | 9.8 | 2.63 | 20.55 | 3.91 | 31.9 | **0.8** | 21.1 | 53.1 | **9.3** |
| **7.4** | 0.01 | 0.0 | -0.05 | **7.0** | 3.6 | 1.38 | 11.44 | 3.74 | 66.5 | **3.5** | 24.6 | 10.4 | **8.3** |
| **6.7** | 3.22 | 3.9 | 0.67 | **6.5** | 2.7 | 1.53 | 10.71 | 4.26 | 60.7 | **6.6** | 81.2 | 9.8 | **8.2** |
| **6.5** | 0.06 | 1.4 | 0.25 | **4.3** | 2.8 | 0.93 | 9.13 | 3.82 | 71.9 | **1.7** | 13.7 | 20.4 | **6.6** |
| **6.8** | 0.29 | 2.1 | 0.05 | **4.4** | 6.0 | 0.86 | 9.46 | 3.84 | 75.9 | **2.2** | 12.2 | 16.4 | **6.0** |
| **5.7** | 2.17 | 6.0 | -0.04 | **4.7** | 2.3 | 1.01 | 9.59 | 3.67 | 67.7 | **2.7** | 33.4 | 19.3 | **6.3** |
| **2.6** | 1.92 | 13.9 | 0.35 | **4.2** | 0.5 | 0.71 | 6.65 | 5.82 | 78.7 | **1.5** | 13.3 | 23.5 | **5.4** |
| **5.7** | 0.54 | 4.3 | 1.75 | **2.6** | -1.1 | -0.13 | -1.18 | 3.89 | 66.0 | **1.1** | 15.7 | 30.2 | **7.7** |
| **7.5** | 0.19 | 0.9 | 0.01 | **7.7** | 14.4 | 1.57 | 12.80 | 4.76 | 66.4 | **4.4** | 13.5 | 4.7 | **8.3** |
| **7.8** | 0.79 | 3.8 | 0.12 | **7.1** | 2.8 | 1.71 | 13.21 | 4.14 | 59.3 | **1.4** | 22.0 | 24.9 | **9.0** |
| **5.0** | 0.45 | 2.8 | 1.50 | **3.1** | 0.8 | 0.56 | 5.41 | 3.82 | 80.1 | **1.5** | 14.6 | 25.1 | **7.0** |
| **2.0** | 3.80 | 22.2 | 0.07 | **4.8** | 1.5 | 1.02 | 8.90 | 5.61 | 80.4 | **4.6** | 24.5 | 6.3 | **7.6** |
| **7.4** | 0.80 | 2.8 | 0.14 | **7.8** | 38.1 | 1.48 | 11.73 | 4.26 | 56.3 | **2.0** | 19.8 | 17.6 | **10.0** |
| **9.5** | 0.00 | 0.0 | 0.00 | **1.5** | 0.1 | 0.16 | 0.87 | 2.52 | 92.1 | **7.1** | 79.3 | 4.3 | **5.7** |
| **6.9** | 0.25 | 2.0 | 0.22 | **6.0** | 2.1 | 1.38 | 14.69 | 6.67 | 76.1 | **4.8** | 13.4 | 2.9 | **5.4** |
| **2.3** | 0.91 | 13.1 | 0.01 | **3.9** | 2.3 | 0.78 | 9.23 | 3.37 | 67.6 | **0.6** | 9.7 | 32.7 | **4.9** |
| **5.4** | 0.80 | 3.1 | 0.24 | **3.9** | 617.2 | 0.69 | 4.91 | 2.84 | 65.4 | **3.5** | 26.4 | 10.9 | **9.8** |
| **7.1** | 0.00 | 0.0 | 0.01 | **10.0** | 3.5 | 2.35 | 18.28 | 4.97 | 52.3 | **1.3** | 12.7 | 26.7 | **9.2** |
| **4.8** | 0.47 | 2.8 | 0.12 | **5.3** | 6.5 | 1.30 | 13.83 | 4.41 | 70.1 | **3.9** | 24.2 | 10.4 | **6.3** |
| **6.5** | 3.75 | 4.5 | 0.16 | **4.1** | 5.9 | 1.71 | 17.58 | 2.75 | 76.9 | **2.9** | 61.4 | 31.0 | **5.5** |
| **7.1** | 0.47 | 2.1 | 0.18 | **6.1** | 11.2 | 1.45 | 14.63 | 3.60 | 62.7 | **3.6** | 32.7 | 14.8 | **7.2** |
| **6.9** | 0.27 | 1.7 | -0.01 | **6.0** | 0.5 | 1.05 | 8.59 | 4.51 | 65.8 | **1.5** | 15.1 | 24.8 | **6.6** |
| **7.2** | 0.12 | 0.5 | -0.01 | **10.0** | 30.8 | 2.22 | 17.00 | 4.72 | 52.8 | **4.5** | 18.2 | 5.6 | **10.0** |
| **9.9** | 3.53 | 1.0 | 0.66 | **6.1** | 21.3 | 1.89 | 9.11 | 1.72 | 46.8 | **4.7** | 87.5 | 24.1 | **8.7** |
| **7.6** | 0.67 | 1.4 | 0.05 | **7.0** | 2.2 | 1.38 | 8.53 | 3.94 | 61.0 | **1.9** | 24.1 | 21.6 | **7.8** |
| **5.7** | 2.76 | 10.5 | 0.05 | **4.9** | 2.6 | 1.02 | 7.79 | 3.30 | 59.3 | **3.4** | 14.1 | 12.1 | **8.3** |
| **0.6** | 1.93 | 34.8 | 0.32 | **4.7** | 0.4 | 1.05 | 8.13 | 4.79 | 76.9 | **2.5** | 35.8 | 22.7 | **6.5** |
| **3.2** | 2.53 | 16.2 | 0.01 | **3.8** | 0.6 | 0.83 | 7.77 | 4.39 | 78.8 | **0.6** | 6.4 | 39.1 | **6.2** |
| **1.0** | 5.31 | 28.8 | 0.09 | **6.9** | 12.3 | 1.73 | 13.49 | 4.04 | 59.4 | **2.3** | 13.0 | 15.6 | **8.1** |

| Name | City | State | Rating | 2018 Rating | 2017 Rating | Total Assets ($Mil) | One Year Asset Growth | Asset Mix (As a % of Total Assets) Comm-ercial Loans | Cons-umer Loans | Mort-gage Loans | Secur-ities | Capital-ization Index | Lever-age Ratio | Risk-Based Capital Ratio |
|---|---|---|---|---|---|---|---|---|---|---|---|---|---|---|
| Bank of Waynesboro | Waynesboro | TN | **A-** | B+ | A- | 174.8 | 5.35 | 6.8 | 5.9 | 19.8 | 14.5 | **10.0** | 13.1 | 20.2 |
| Bank of Western Oklahoma | Elk City | OK | **B-** | B- | B- | 304.8 | 5.78 | 7.6 | 0.8 | 14.2 | 9.3 | **4.8** | 7.7 | 10.9 |
| Bank of Weston | Weston | MO | **B** | B- | C+ | 149.6 | 5.41 | 7.0 | 0.8 | 18.5 | 11.7 | **6.6** | 8.6 | 12.4 |
| Bank of Whittier, N.A. | Whittier | CA | **C+** | B- | B- | 73.9 | 25.55 | 0.0 | 0.6 | 16.2 | 0.0 | **10.0** | 17.2 | 25.6 |
| Bank of Wiggins | Wiggins | MS | **B+** | B+ | B+ | 166.4 | -8.87 | 8.3 | 5.5 | 17.2 | 34.1 | **10.0** | 17.7 | 31.1 |
| Bank of Winnfield & Trust Co. | Winnfield | LA | **B-** | B | B | 137.5 | -1.12 | 10.4 | 3.8 | 17.2 | 32.4 | **10.0** | 13.9 | 28.7 |
| Bank of Winona | Winona | MS | **B** | B | B- | 122.9 | 5.17 | 1.9 | 3.2 | 20.7 | 41.1 | **9.3** | 10.6 | 16.2 |
| ▲ Bank of Wisconsin Dells | Wisconsin Dells | WI | **A-** | B | B- | 594.0 | 7.01 | 6.1 | 0.3 | 7.3 | 12.5 | **8.7** | 12.1 | 13.9 |
| ▲ Bank of Wolcott | Wolcott | IN | **A-** | B | B+ | 183.5 | 11.23 | 4.9 | 1.1 | 11.0 | 24.6 | **10.0** | 11.5 | 17.3 |
| ▲ Bank of Wrightsville | Wrightsville | GA | **B-** | C | C | 56.8 | 2.89 | 9.1 | 2.7 | 14.6 | 26.2 | **9.0** | 10.4 | 16.3 |
| Bank of Wyandotte | Wyandotte | OK | **C-** | C- | C- | 12.7 | 2.10 | 11.2 | 12.2 | 14.1 | 20.7 | **7.5** | 9.3 | 15.7 |
| Bank of Yates City | Yates City | IL | **C-** | C- | D+ | 69.6 | 2.47 | 8.8 | 8.1 | 22.8 | 21.9 | **7.4** | 9.3 | 14.9 |
| Bank of Yazoo City | Yazoo City | MS | **B** | B | B- | 239.1 | -4.12 | 5.6 | 1.9 | 17.3 | 34.7 | **10.0** | 12.2 | 19.8 |
| Bank of York | York | SC | **B+** | B- | B- | 224.7 | -2.95 | 4.0 | 3.0 | 10.2 | 20.5 | **10.0** | 11.4 | 26.9 |
| Bank of Zachary | Zachary | LA | **B-** | B- | B- | 240.4 | -1.16 | 2.4 | 1.9 | 36.5 | 21.4 | **8.7** | 10.2 | 18.0 |
| Bank of Zumbrota | Zumbrota | MN | **B+** | B | B | 166.7 | 3.55 | 14.2 | 2.6 | 13.7 | 16.2 | **8.0** | 12.6 | 13.4 |
| Bank OZK | Little Rock | AR | **A-** | B+ | B+ | 23559.4 | 5.23 | 2.8 | 12.5 | 3.5 | 9.7 | **10.0** | 15.4 | 15.6 |
| ▲ Bank Plus | Estherville | IA | **B-** | C | C- | 126.1 | -10.75 | 2.1 | 1.9 | 7.1 | 11.5 | **6.9** | 9.4 | 12.4 |
| Bank Rhode Island | Providence | RI | **B** | B | B | 2537.1 | 8.39 | 17.2 | 0.0 | 10.3 | 10.8 | **7.2** | 10.0 | 12.7 |
| Bank Star | Pacific | MO | **B** | B- | C+ | 135.0 | -2.09 | 4.9 | 2.3 | 31.4 | 4.9 | **8.3** | 9.9 | 15.1 |
| Bank, N.A. | McAlester | OK | **A-** | B+ | B+ | 391.1 | 5.50 | 4.2 | 2.8 | 16.3 | 34.4 | **10.0** | 11.1 | 19.2 |
| Bank3 | Memphis | TN | **D+** | D- | D | 225.2 | 19.31 | 28.5 | 0.7 | 7.0 | 12.4 | **10.0** | 12.7 | 15.3 |
| Bank7 | Oklahoma City | OK | **A** | A | A- | 865.4 | 12.46 | 30.1 | 0.2 | 4.6 | 0.0 | **10.0** | 11.7 | 15.4 |
| bankcda | Coeur d'Alene | ID | **A-** | B- | C | 140.5 | 11.18 | 14.1 | 0.9 | 6.1 | 33.6 | **10.0** | 12.4 | 17.4 |
| BankChampaign, N.A. | Champaign | IL | **B+** | B | B | 237.2 | 3.90 | 13.4 | 0.7 | 17.5 | 12.3 | **8.7** | 10.1 | 14.8 |
| BankCherokee | Saint Paul | MN | **B-** | B- | C+ | 281.5 | 5.42 | 16.7 | 0.8 | 11.1 | 17.1 | **6.6** | 8.7 | 13.5 |
| Bankers Trust Co. | Des Moines | IA | **B** | B- | C+ | 4981.7 | 10.39 | 19.9 | 0.4 | 8.8 | 12.9 | **5.8** | 9.5 | 11.6 |
| Bankers' Bank | Madison | WI | **B** | B | B | 827.0 | 14.73 | 2.1 | 0.7 | 8.4 | 10.9 | **8.8** | 10.2 | 15.7 |
| Bankers' Bank of Kansas | Wichita | KS | **B+** | B+ | B+ | 173.6 | 1.59 | 13.0 | 12.3 | 3.6 | 2.4 | **10.0** | 15.6 | 20.5 |
| Bankers' Bank of Kentucky, Inc. | Frankfort | KY | **C+** | C+ | C+ | 176.8 | 40.02 | 1.8 | 0.0 | 1.2 | 0.6 | **8.7** | 10.1 | 34.0 |
| Bankers' Bank of the West | Denver | CO | **A-** | B+ | B+ | 403.0 | 10.46 | 7.1 | 0.1 | 0.4 | 7.1 | **10.0** | 13.1 | 17.9 |
| BankFinancial, N.A. | Olympia Fields | IL | **B+** | A- | B | 1486.0 | -6.11 | 28.1 | 0.2 | 2.9 | 0.8 | **9.8** | 10.9 | 16.4 |
| BankFirst | Norfolk | NE | **B+** | B+ | A- | 765.4 | 8.32 | 9.3 | 0.6 | 7.3 | 15.0 | **6.0** | 10.0 | 11.7 |
| BankFirst Financial Services | Macon | MS | **B** | B | B- | 1278.2 | 31.06 | 8.2 | 1.0 | 14.2 | 17.0 | **8.5** | 10.0 | 14.0 |
| BankFlorida | Jupiter | FL | **D-** | D | C | 90.2 | 3.04 | 6.2 | 0.5 | 33.5 | 11.6 | **6.4** | 8.5 | 12.0 |
| ▲ BankGloucester | Gloucester | MA | **C+** | C | C | 277.9 | 1.53 | 3.5 | 0.2 | 45.3 | 7.6 | **6.6** | 8.6 | 13.1 |
| BankIowa of Cedar Rapids | Cedar Rapids | IA | **B** | B | B+ | 678.7 | 2.10 | 9.1 | 2.0 | 17.5 | 15.3 | **8.3** | 11.0 | 13.5 |
| BankNewport | Middletown | RI | **B+** | B | B | 1748.2 | 4.97 | 8.4 | 4.2 | 27.6 | 13.3 | **7.9** | 10.7 | 13.2 |
| BankNorth | Arthur | ND | **C** | C+ | B+ | 415.8 | 0.14 | 8.0 | 1.4 | 3.6 | 1.9 | **6.0** | 10.8 | 11.8 |
| BankORION | Orion | IL | **B** | B- | B- | 470.3 | 3.94 | 7.5 | 2.7 | 18.5 | 33.8 | **10.0** | 11.2 | 19.3 |
| ▼ BankPacific, Ltd | Hagatna | GU | **C+** | B- | B- | 154.6 | 6.65 | 7.5 | 25.5 | 37.0 | 0.7 | **10.0** | 11.6 | 17.4 |
| BankPlus | Belzoni | MS | **B+** | B+ | B | 2971.3 | 7.61 | 11.0 | 1.9 | 16.0 | 12.8 | **8.0** | 9.6 | 13.4 |
| BankSouth | Dothan | AL | **A-** | A- | A- | 182.3 | 5.47 | 8.7 | 1.6 | 33.9 | 21.2 | **10.0** | 20.1 | 33.2 |
| BankSouth | Greensboro | GA | **A-** | A- | A- | 717.8 | 13.09 | 3.2 | 0.7 | 39.2 | 3.7 | **9.1** | 10.4 | 14.3 |
| BankStar Financial | Elkton | SD | **B-** | B- | B | 199.1 | 10.07 | 7.5 | 2.3 | 17.1 | 15.1 | **6.1** | 8.1 | 12.9 |
| ▲ BankTennessee | Collierville | TN | **B** | C+ | B- | 324.5 | 7.04 | 11.3 | 2.7 | 22.1 | 5.0 | **7.8** | 9.6 | 13.1 |
| BankUnited, N.A. | Miami Lakes | FL | **B+** | B+ | B+ | 32782.2 | 2.20 | 12.9 | 0.0 | 17.3 | 23.5 | **7.5** | 9.3 | 13.4 |
| BankVista | Sartell | MN | **C** | C- | C+ | 347.1 | 14.92 | 17.4 | 1.8 | 12.2 | 4.4 | **4.9** | 8.6 | 10.9 |
| Bankwell Bank | New Canaan | CT | **B** | B | B | 1879.2 | 0.42 | 12.2 | 0.0 | 8.1 | 5.4 | **8.0** | 11.0 | 13.4 |
| BANKWEST | Rockford | MN | **B+** | B+ | B | 155.4 | 5.47 | 10.8 | 1.6 | 11.8 | 18.5 | **8.2** | 9.8 | 16.8 |
| Bankwest of Kansas | Goodland | KS | **B+** | B | B | 117.0 | -1.90 | 3.0 | 1.5 | 2.5 | 9.8 | **10.0** | 12.9 | 15.4 |
| BankWest, Inc. | Pierre | SD | **C** | C | C | 1205.0 | 14.73 | 5.5 | 8.4 | 4.2 | 15.1 | **7.8** | 9.9 | 13.2 |
| Banner Bank | Walla Walla | WA | **B+** | B+ | B+ | 12304.7 | 6.22 | 11.0 | 1.2 | 8.3 | 14.1 | **7.1** | 10.5 | 12.6 |
| Banner Banks | Birnamwood | WI | **B-** | B- | B- | 105.9 | 9.59 | 2.0 | 0.3 | 5.0 | 35.1 | **10.0** | 12.2 | 26.6 |
| Banner Capital Bank | Harrisburg | NE | **C+** | B- | B- | 189.1 | 16.04 | 12.6 | 2.0 | 3.5 | 5.9 | **5.9** | 9.9 | 11.7 |
| Banterra Bank | Eldorado | IL | **B-** | B- | B- | 1950.8 | 8.61 | 24.2 | 22.1 | 5.9 | 17.4 | **5.3** | 8.5 | 11.2 |
| Bar Harbor Bank & Trust | Bar Harbor | ME | **B** | B | B | 3665.5 | 1.69 | 6.8 | 0.3 | 33.5 | 18.1 | **6.4** | 8.4 | 12.4 |
| Bar Harbor S&L Assn. | Bar Harbor | ME | **B-** | B | B | 103.5 | -0.69 | 0.0 | 0.5 | 62.8 | 5.4 | **10.0** | 11.4 | 25.2 |
| Baraboo State Bank | Baraboo | WI | **B** | B | B | 386.5 | -2.12 | 7.7 | 1.2 | 8.3 | 13.6 | **9.9** | 11.2 | 14.9 |
| Barclays Bank Delaware | Wilmington | DE | **C** | C | C | 33871.0 | 2.34 | 0.6 | 79.6 | 0.0 | 0.4 | **10.0** | 14.6 | 19.5 |

| Asset Quality Index | Adjusted Non-Performing Loans as a % of Total Loans | Adjusted Non-Performing Loans as a % of Capital | Net Charge-Offs Avg Loans | Profitability Index | Net Income ($Mil) | Return on Assets (R.O.A.) | Return on Equity (R.O.E.) | Net Interest Spread | Overhead Efficiency Ratio | Liquidity Index | Liquidity Ratio | Hot Money Ratio | Stability Index |
|---|---|---|---|---|---|---|---|---|---|---|---|---|---|
| **7.3** | 0.94 | 3.1 | 0.35 | **8.5** | 2.7 | 1.58 | 11.98 | 4.82 | 58.6 | **2.2** | 28.6 | 20.5 | **8.3** |
| **5.5** | 0.03 | 3.4 | 0.04 | **8.2** | 5.8 | 1.91 | 22.83 | 4.79 | 57.9 | **0.7** | 10.0 | 36.0 | **7.1** |
| **6.8** | 0.53 | 2.1 | 0.00 | **6.5** | 2.5 | 1.66 | 19.83 | 4.44 | 64.8 | **2.9** | 14.1 | 14.3 | **5.5** |
| **8.4** | 0.00 | 0.0 | -0.13 | **3.2** | 0.4 | 0.52 | 3.19 | 2.18 | 80.7 | **2.9** | 71.0 | 51.5 | **6.9** |
| **7.7** | 0.46 | 3.1 | 0.05 | **4.0** | 1.2 | 0.69 | 3.99 | 3.79 | 79.4 | **3.2** | 47.3 | 23.1 | **7.5** |
| **5.6** | 1.97 | 6.8 | 1.31 | **3.1** | 0.9 | 0.62 | 5.06 | 3.39 | 78.7 | **3.7** | 42.7 | 16.9 | **7.4** |
| **5.8** | 1.44 | 4.4 | 0.24 | **3.8** | 0.9 | 0.73 | 6.35 | 3.90 | 77.6 | **4.3** | 42.8 | 14.1 | **6.5** |
| **6.5** | 0.01 | 0.0 | 0.00 | **9.2** | 10.2 | 1.76 | 14.77 | 3.84 | 46.8 | **2.1** | 13.5 | 11.2 | **8.7** |
| **5.4** | 2.41 | 8.3 | 0.08 | **7.2** | 2.8 | 1.66 | 14.40 | 3.90 | 55.9 | **3.5** | 40.7 | 14.6 | **7.9** |
| **5.8** | 0.79 | 4.2 | -0.08 | **5.1** | 0.7 | 1.28 | 13.81 | 4.14 | 68.1 | **3.1** | 24.2 | 14.2 | **5.2** |
| **7.5** | 0.00 | 0.0 | 0.17 | **4.6** | 0.1 | 0.64 | 7.14 | 5.40 | 79.4 | **4.3** | 31.6 | 6.6 | **3.7** |
| **2.1** | 3.41 | 21.7 | 0.40 | **2.7** | 0.3 | 0.40 | 4.37 | 3.60 | 80.6 | **3.3** | 25.9 | 13.8 | **4.4** |
| **8.8** | 0.00 | 0.8 | 0.64 | **4.3** | 2.3 | 0.91 | 8.24 | 3.44 | 71.1 | **2.9** | 26.9 | 16.1 | **6.8** |
| **6.4** | 3.14 | 7.8 | 0.11 | **4.3** | 2.1 | 0.94 | 7.76 | 3.42 | 65.8 | **5.9** | 55.1 | 9.2 | **6.8** |
| **6.7** | 1.02 | 6.0 | 0.14 | **3.7** | 1.6 | 0.64 | 6.62 | 3.98 | 79.0 | **2.8** | 20.4 | 15.5 | **6.1** |
| **5.4** | 0.93 | 4.0 | -0.09 | **6.4** | 2.4 | 1.49 | 11.45 | 3.82 | 63.4 | **1.9** | 11.2 | 16.5 | **8.1** |
| **5.8** | 0.33 | 1.3 | 0.11 | **9.8** | 425.9 | 1.87 | 10.70 | 4.35 | 40.5 | **1.0** | 16.0 | 21.9 | **10.0** |
| **4.8** | 0.06 | 4.1 | 0.01 | **4.5** | 1.4 | 1.05 | 9.70 | 3.88 | 66.2 | **1.6** | 6.3 | 16.3 | **6.6** |
| **4.8** | 0.47 | 4.4 | 0.06 | **5.0** | 24.9 | 1.02 | 7.85 | 3.40 | 61.0 | **2.1** | 8.3 | 13.7 | **8.3** |
| **7.6** | 0.00 | 1.3 | 0.04 | **4.7** | 1.2 | 0.91 | 7.88 | 4.34 | 67.3 | **4.1** | 14.2 | 8.0 | **6.3** |
| **7.3** | 1.24 | 6.1 | 0.23 | **7.4** | 6.3 | 1.67 | 15.40 | 3.88 | 59.2 | **5.1** | 47.3 | 11.4 | **8.1** |
| **8.3** | 0.00 | 0.0 | 0.00 | **1.3** | 1.0 | 0.48 | 4.08 | 3.02 | 89.2 | **0.9** | 21.8 | 22.3 | **4.8** |
| **8.0** | 0.64 | 2.3 | 0.00 | **8.4** | 8.1 | 1.01 | 8.40 | 5.60 | 65.9 | **1.4** | 19.2 | 23.4 | **8.9** |
| **7.7** | 1.18 | 2.9 | -0.05 | **5.4** | 1.4 | 1.09 | 9.44 | 4.38 | 67.8 | **6.2** | 40.6 | 2.6 | **6.5** |
| **7.7** | 0.18 | 1.3 | 0.04 | **5.5** | 3.0 | 1.34 | 13.32 | 3.90 | 70.0 | **0.8** | 14.5 | 23.0 | **6.9** |
| **8.1** | 0.19 | 1.1 | -0.13 | **4.6** | 2.4 | 0.87 | 10.08 | 4.04 | 73.0 | **5.6** | 33.1 | 3.0 | **5.1** |
| **6.0** | 1.22 | 4.7 | 0.15 | **6.5** | 63.0 | 1.32 | 13.65 | 3.32 | 55.8 | **2.1** | 11.7 | 18.2 | **8.6** |
| **6.3** | 1.04 | 5.5 | 0.03 | **4.9** | 7.8 | 1.01 | 9.73 | 2.29 | 70.6 | **2.2** | 39.4 | 12.0 | **6.4** |
| **6.9** | 1.06 | 3.0 | 0.34 | **5.9** | 1.9 | 1.09 | 7.24 | 3.69 | 79.3 | **0.9** | 25.1 | 10.9 | **7.7** |
| **9.7** | 0.00 | 0.0 | 0.00 | **3.1** | 0.8 | 0.56 | 5.41 | 1.35 | 69.5 | **8.1** | 82.3 | 0.0 | **5.2** |
| **8.5** | 0.14 | 0.7 | -0.01 | **5.6** | 4.2 | 1.12 | 8.39 | 3.52 | 77.5 | **1.9** | 39.5 | 31.9 | **7.4** |
| **7.2** | 0.07 | 0.5 | 0.37 | **4.9** | 12.8 | 0.85 | 7.76 | 3.63 | 63.5 | **2.4** | 18.8 | 16.2 | **9.5** |
| **6.2** | 0.56 | 3.3 | 0.00 | **9.1** | 13.2 | 1.77 | 15.74 | 3.89 | 43.3 | **2.4** | 14.8 | 16.9 | **9.0** |
| **5.0** | 1.30 | 7.1 | 0.05 | **5.6** | 14.0 | 1.15 | 10.94 | 3.65 | 65.3 | **3.0** | 15.0 | 14.6 | **8.5** |
| **4.8** | 1.12 | 9.0 | 0.08 | **0.0** | -1.2 | -1.35 | -13.92 | 3.25 | 166.7 | **1.0** | 17.2 | 29.9 | **4.3** |
| **3.9** | 2.20 | 15.9 | 0.00 | **3.8** | 1.6 | 0.58 | 6.94 | 3.69 | 77.6 | **1.4** | 13.2 | 24.8 | **4.8** |
| **6.5** | 0.96 | 4.7 | 0.01 | **4.7** | 7.6 | 1.14 | 10.07 | 3.19 | 66.5 | **1.4** | 8.1 | 20.8 | **8.1** |
| **5.5** | 1.50 | 7.7 | 0.22 | **5.4** | 18.5 | 1.08 | 9.92 | 3.67 | 66.1 | **2.7** | 16.9 | 14.6 | **9.2** |
| **2.8** | 1.92 | 9.2 | 0.14 | **8.0** | 7.4 | 1.81 | 14.80 | 5.07 | 60.0 | **2.8** | 6.2 | 14.1 | **9.0** |
| **6.0** | 1.95 | 5.9 | 0.00 | **4.6** | 4.5 | 0.96 | 7.95 | 3.28 | 62.0 | **2.8** | 19.0 | 15.2 | **7.0** |
| **1.5** | 3.77 | 22.6 | 0.12 | **3.5** | 0.7 | 0.51 | 4.32 | 5.42 | 86.8 | **5.0** | 16.5 | 2.1 | **6.3** |
| **6.3** | 0.69 | 5.1 | 0.18 | **6.4** | 40.1 | 1.37 | 14.50 | 3.97 | 69.5 | **4.1** | 16.5 | 8.7 | **7.4** |
| **8.9** | 0.08 | 0.1 | -0.08 | **5.6** | 2.2 | 1.23 | 6.07 | 3.50 | 61.3 | **2.6** | 28.9 | 18.2 | **8.8** |
| **6.6** | 0.55 | 3.7 | -0.06 | **7.7** | 15.4 | 2.30 | 24.20 | 4.23 | 82.3 | **2.0** | 12.2 | 19.0 | **8.7** |
| **5.4** | 0.37 | 2.8 | 0.15 | **5.4** | 2.3 | 1.21 | 12.57 | 3.72 | 63.6 | **0.8** | 7.4 | 25.5 | **6.4** |
| **5.7** | 0.38 | 2.5 | 0.19 | **6.0** | 4.1 | 1.32 | 12.24 | 4.33 | 68.3 | **1.6** | 15.6 | 23.1 | **7.0** |
| **6.3** | 1.13 | 7.6 | 0.05 | **5.1** | 335.7 | 1.03 | 10.91 | 2.53 | 52.6 | **1.3** | 18.8 | 14.2 | **8.6** |
| **3.7** | 0.75 | 6.0 | 0.05 | **4.9** | 2.9 | 0.89 | 10.53 | 3.77 | 68.8 | **0.9** | 15.7 | 29.0 | **5.0** |
| **4.4** | 1.16 | 8.4 | 0.15 | **5.6** | 21.7 | 1.16 | 11.05 | 3.12 | 53.7 | **0.8** | 10.7 | 33.6 | **8.7** |
| **6.3** | 1.26 | 4.0 | 0.00 | **6.7** | 2.5 | 1.67 | 16.53 | 4.39 | 64.9 | **5.8** | 36.9 | 3.4 | **6.9** |
| **7.5** | 0.00 | 0.0 | 0.00 | **5.0** | 1.3 | 1.11 | 8.94 | 5.00 | 72.3 | **1.3** | 22.7 | 11.9 | **7.7** |
| **3.4** | 2.02 | 13.7 | 0.05 | **5.7** | 13.0 | 1.18 | 11.24 | 4.02 | 72.7 | **2.7** | 19.6 | 6.7 | **9.8** |
| **6.1** | 0.43 | 2.2 | 0.07 | **6.5** | 149.4 | 1.28 | 9.60 | 4.39 | 63.8 | **4.4** | 16.3 | 5.0 | **9.9** |
| **6.1** | 3.06 | 9.0 | 0.00 | **3.7** | 0.8 | 0.80 | 6.59 | 2.88 | 72.5 | **6.5** | 66.0 | 7.4 | **7.2** |
| **2.7** | 1.57 | 11.8 | 0.04 | **4.2** | 1.4 | 0.82 | 7.44 | 4.04 | 76.4 | **0.7** | 10.0 | 36.8 | **6.5** |
| **5.5** | 0.53 | 3.8 | 0.06 | **6.0** | 26.4 | 1.43 | 15.55 | 3.49 | 60.3 | **1.5** | 16.1 | 18.9 | **9.2** |
| **6.0** | 0.62 | 3.1 | 0.03 | **3.9** | 26.6 | 0.73 | 6.43 | 2.84 | 71.8 | **1.1** | 12.0 | 12.2 | **8.9** |
| **6.9** | 1.59 | 9.2 | -0.05 | **3.3** | 0.5 | 0.52 | 4.68 | 2.34 | 79.0 | **1.1** | 27.7 | 40.8 | **6.9** |
| **4.1** | 1.86 | 8.0 | -0.14 | **5.3** | 3.6 | 0.95 | 8.38 | 3.85 | 65.2 | **4.1** | 25.0 | 9.6 | **7.7** |
| **2.5** | 1.06 | 7.9 | 3.99 | **6.1** | 369.0 | 1.07 | 7.02 | 8.40 | 52.7 | **1.5** | 22.1 | 10.7 | **9.6** |

| Name | City | State | Rating | 2018 Rating | 2017 Rating | Total Assets ($Mil) | One Year Asset Growth | Asset Mix (As a % of Total Assets) Comm-ercial Loans | Cons-umer Loans | Mort-gage Loans | Secur-ities | Capital-ization Index | Lever-age Ratio | Risk-Based Capital Ratio |
|---|---|---|---|---|---|---|---|---|---|---|---|---|---|---|
| Barrington Bank & Trust Co., N.A. | Barrington | IL | B | B | B- | 2445.4 | 14.51 | 28.0 | 18.9 | 25.4 | 4.1 | 6.6 | 13.6 | 12.2 |
| Barwick Banking Co. | Barwick | GA | D | D | D- | 14.0 | 6.01 | 1.1 | 1.4 | 0.6 | 41.4 | 10.0 | 11.5 | 111.0 |
| ▲ Basile State Bank | Basile | LA | B- | C+ | C | 56.2 | 4.55 | 4.7 | 9.7 | 41.8 | 1.6 | 10.0 | 11.5 | 18.7 |
| ▲ Bath Savings Institution | Bath | ME | A | A- | A- | 937.3 | 1.77 | 5.5 | 1.2 | 31.9 | 20.1 | 10.0 | 15.3 | 23.8 |
| Bath State Bank | Bath | IN | B- | B- | B+ | 166.0 | 2.98 | 3.8 | 1.8 | 19.4 | 8.7 | 8.4 | 9.9 | 13.7 |
| Battle Creek State Bank | Battle Creek | NE | B- | B- | B- | 34.0 | 7.95 | 54.4 | 1.5 | 2.5 | 4.8 | 10.0 | 13.0 | 17.1 |
| Baxter State Bank | Baxter Springs | KS | C+ | C+ | C+ | 24.4 | -7.78 | 2.8 | 8.7 | 35.2 | 18.6 | 10.0 | 21.2 | 37.1 |
| Bay Bank | Green Bay | WI | B+ | B | B | 108.3 | 13.68 | 11.1 | 4.5 | 14.0 | 14.6 | 10.0 | 13.5 | 23.1 |
| Bay Port State Bank | Bay Port | MI | C+ | C- | C- | 113.4 | 10.87 | 10.3 | 2.5 | 19.6 | 0.1 | 5.6 | 7.6 | 11.6 |
| Bay State Savings Bank | Worcester | MA | C | C | C+ | 437.7 | 4.69 | 2.4 | 1.0 | 52.9 | 2.9 | 7.1 | 9.1 | 12.7 |
| Baybank | Gladstone | MI | C | C | C+ | 106.3 | 7.17 | 19.4 | 11.7 | 21.4 | 15.6 | 7.4 | 9.3 | 13.1 |
| BayCoast Bank | Swansea | MA | C+ | C | C | 1782.1 | 5.92 | 9.2 | 2.7 | 23.0 | 5.5 | 5.2 | 8.9 | 11.2 |
| BayVanguard Bank | Sparrows Point | MD | B | C+ | C+ | 294.2 | 83.64 | 1.0 | 4.2 | 46.1 | 4.2 | 10.0 | 20.7 | 33.0 |
| BBVA USA | Birmingham | AL | C+ | C+ | C+ | 92658.0 | 2.89 | 18.0 | 7.8 | 15.0 | 15.0 | 7.0 | 9.0 | 13.9 |
| BCB Community Bank | Bayonne | NJ | B- | C+ | C+ | 2906.7 | 8.71 | 3.9 | 0.0 | 18.1 | 3.2 | 7.8 | 9.5 | 13.8 |
| BCBank, Inc. | Philippi | WV | C+ | C+ | C+ | 139.3 | 3.00 | 5.9 | 3.6 | 16.2 | 16.1 | 7.1 | 9.1 | 14.0 |
| ▲ Beach Community Bank | Fort Walton Beach | FL | D- | E | E- | 510.4 | 2.00 | 7.5 | 0.3 | 16.3 | 11.7 | 10.0 | 11.5 | 16.5 |
| ▲ Beacon Business Bank, N.A. | San Francisco | CA | B | C+ | B | 156.1 | 21.99 | 5.0 | 0.0 | 6.9 | 6.7 | 10.0 | 12.4 | 20.3 |
| Beacon Community Bank | Charleston | SC | D | D | | 135.8 | 90.87 | 5.6 | 0.3 | 31.9 | 5.4 | 10.0 | 23.9 | 27.6 |
| ▲ Beal Bank USA | Las Vegas | NV | C+ | C- | C | 5515.7 | 3.45 | 48.0 | 0.0 | 2.9 | 12.5 | 10.0 | 42.2 | 41.8 |
| Beal Bank, SSB | Plano | TX | C+ | C- | C | 1568.4 | -28.16 | 16.5 | 0.6 | 37.2 | 13.3 | 10.0 | 28.0 | 41.9 |
| Beardstown Savings s.b. | Beardstown | IL | C+ | C | C | 53.9 | 3.49 | 4.0 | 11.6 | 47.7 | 16.8 | 10.0 | 11.0 | 18.5 |
| Beartooth Bank | Billings | MT | B- | B- | B- | 52.3 | 13.42 | 13.3 | 0.7 | 13.8 | 0.0 | 10.0 | 15.3 | 19.0 |
| Beauregard Federal Savings Bank | DeRidder | LA | B+ | B+ | B+ | 66.2 | -4.28 | 7.1 | 7.8 | 43.5 | 17.4 | 10.0 | 17.0 | 33.4 |
| Bedford Federal Savings Bank | Bedford | IN | B | B | B | 130.6 | 7.16 | 3.4 | 3.6 | 47.1 | 0.0 | 10.0 | 11.6 | 20.7 |
| Bedford Loan & Deposit Bank | Bedford | KY | B | B- | B- | 95.9 | 1.89 | 0.5 | 9.1 | 31.6 | 31.9 | 10.0 | 13.9 | 24.8 |
| Belgrade State Bank | Belgrade | MO | B | B- | C+ | 277.9 | 4.18 | 8.6 | 4.3 | 30.7 | 8.2 | 7.7 | 9.5 | 15.4 |
| Bell Bank | Fargo | ND | B+ | B+ | B+ | 6492.2 | 20.34 | 14.9 | 2.6 | 15.9 | 1.0 | 5.2 | 9.6 | 11.2 |
| Bellevue State Bank | Bellevue | IA | A- | B+ | B+ | 121.9 | 3.33 | 12.0 | 5.6 | 19.1 | 8.2 | 10.0 | 14.8 | 16.2 |
| ▲ Belmont Bank & Trust Co. | Chicago | IL | C+ | B- | B- | 549.6 | 20.40 | 13.6 | 1.1 | 8.8 | 18.8 | 8.3 | 9.9 | 14.1 |
| Belmont Savings Bank | Bellaire | OH | B | B | B | 377.0 | -0.67 | 1.7 | 2.2 | 14.1 | 64.6 | 10.0 | 18.5 | 59.8 |
| Belmont Savings Bank, SSB | Belmont | NC | C+ | B- | B- | 91.4 | -0.05 | 0.0 | 0.0 | 67.7 | 4.5 | 10.0 | 20.4 | 39.7 |
| Belt Valley Bank | Belt | MT | B | B | B+ | 65.6 | 4.52 | 3.4 | 3.3 | 30.2 | 7.2 | 10.0 | 15.0 | 20.0 |
| Ben Franklin Bank of Illinois | Arlington Heights | IL | D- | D | D- | 96.9 | 2.78 | 1.6 | 0.0 | 31.8 | 3.6 | 7.8 | 9.5 | 15.7 |
| Benchmark Bank | Plano | TX | B+ | B+ | B+ | 800.9 | 37.43 | 8.2 | 2.4 | 15.1 | 0.2 | 6.9 | 8.9 | 13.4 |
| Benchmark Community Bank | Kenbridge | VA | A- | A- | A | 711.9 | 10.56 | 7.2 | 2.3 | 39.6 | 5.6 | 9.1 | 10.4 | 15.5 |
| Bendena State Bank | Bendena | KS | B- | B- | B- | 65.6 | 1.65 | 4.6 | 2.9 | 12.7 | 16.2 | 8.5 | 10.0 | 14.5 |
| Beneficial State Bank | Oakland | CA | C- | C- | C- | 1036.5 | 2.57 | 12.9 | 8.7 | 3.6 | 5.7 | 9.5 | 10.7 | 15.3 |
| Bennington State Bank | Salina | KS | B- | C+ | B+ | 729.0 | 4.15 | 9.4 | 1.3 | 15.2 | 27.0 | 10.0 | 11.8 | 17.8 |
| Benton County State Bank | Blairstown | IA | B | B | B+ | 45.9 | 2.17 | 3.4 | 0.1 | 5.4 | 16.6 | 10.0 | 14.2 | 18.3 |
| Benton State Bank | Benton | WI | C- | D+ | D+ | 64.3 | -3.01 | 5.4 | 4.6 | 33.7 | 3.6 | 7.3 | 9.5 | 12.8 |
| Berkshire Bank | Boston | MA | B- | B- | C+ | 13181.4 | 8.15 | 13.7 | 3.2 | 23.2 | 12.8 | 7.2 | 9.1 | 12.8 |
| Berkshire Bank | New York | NY | B | B | B- | 640.3 | -11.07 | 1.0 | 0.1 | 6.5 | 29.3 | 10.0 | 18.7 | 32.7 |
| ▲ Bessemer Trust Co. | New York | NY | A | B+ | A- | 975.9 | 16.48 | 9.0 | 22.7 | 0.0 | 27.4 | 7.5 | 9.3 | 21.0 |
| Bessemer Trust Co. of California, N.A. | San Francisco | CA | U | U | U | 11.6 | 12.03 | 0.0 | 0.0 | 0.0 | 61.2 | 10.0 | 100. | 660.4 |
| Bessemer Trust Co. of Delaware, N.A. | Wilmington | DE | U | U | U | 19.8 | 1.00 | 0.0 | 0.0 | 0.0 | 64.7 | 10.0 | 80.6 | 291.8 |
| Bessemer Trust Co., N.A. | New York | NY | A | A- | A- | 2105.9 | -29.63 | 9.5 | 13.2 | 0.0 | 39.4 | 9.1 | 10.4 | 30.5 |
| ▲ Best Hometown Bank | Collinsville | IL | D+ | D- | D | 112.3 | 2.70 | 3.2 | 0.4 | 41.0 | 9.3 | 9.3 | 10.5 | 17.2 |
| Better Banks | Peoria | IL | B- | C+ | C+ | 288.1 | -3.82 | 3.6 | 29.7 | 19.4 | 21.3 | 7.1 | 9.0 | 13.6 |
| Beverly Bank & Trust Co., N.A. | Chicago | IL | B | B | B | 1631.1 | 20.08 | 33.0 | 12.9 | 3.0 | 9.9 | 5.6 | 10.3 | 11.5 |
| Big Bend Banks, N.A. | Marfa | TX | A- | A- | A- | 139.9 | 8.03 | 1.5 | 3.1 | 2.6 | 60.3 | 10.0 | 14.6 | 48.1 |
| Big Horn Federal Savings Bank | Greybull | WY | C+ | C+ | C+ | 260.5 | 2.97 | 10.8 | 2.6 | 10.6 | 30.4 | 9.6 | 10.8 | 22.2 |
| ▲ Bippus State Bank | Huntington | IN | B | B- | B | 189.9 | 8.26 | 12.4 | 2.7 | 12.5 | 13.8 | 10.0 | 11.4 | 15.5 |
| Bison State Bank | Bison | KS | D | D | D- | 14.4 | 48.09 | 13.0 | 5.9 | 27.1 | 6.2 | 8.5 | 10.0 | 19.0 |
| ▲ Black Hills Community Bank, N.A. | Rapid City | SD | B | B- | B | 299.7 | 3.99 | 10.4 | 0.3 | 10.7 | 3.6 | 8.0 | 10.4 | 13.3 |
| Black Mountain Savings Bank, SSB | Black Mountain | NC | C+ | C+ | C+ | 40.8 | 0.72 | 0.0 | 0.6 | 64.4 | 0.0 | 10.0 | 12.6 | 33.0 |
| Black River Country Bank | Black River Falls | WI | B+ | B+ | B+ | 81.0 | 4.70 | 4.2 | 4.2 | 37.0 | 7.8 | 9.8 | 10.9 | 16.9 |
| Blackhawk Bank | Beloit | WI | B | B- | B- | 961.5 | 17.96 | 24.1 | 0.9 | 10.2 | 24.5 | 8.6 | 10.1 | 13.8 |
| Blackhawk Bank & Trust | Milan | IL | A- | B+ | B | 1403.6 | 3.19 | 10.8 | 0.8 | 7.6 | 45.6 | 10.0 | 11.2 | 19.0 |
| ▲ BlackRidgeBANK | Fargo | ND | C- | D+ | C- | 484.3 | 0.25 | 8.6 | 3.0 | 22.7 | 5.7 | 4.2 | 8.1 | 10.6 |

| Asset Quality Index | Adjusted Non-Performing Loans as a % of Total Loans | Adjusted Non-Performing Loans as a % of Capital | Net Charge-Offs Avg Loans | Profitability Index | Net Income ($Mil) | Return on Assets (R.O.A.) | Return on Equity (R.O.E.) | Net Interest Spread | Overhead Efficiency Ratio | Liquidity Index | Liquidity Ratio | Hot Money Ratio | Stability Index |
|---|---|---|---|---|---|---|---|---|---|---|---|---|---|
| **5.7** | 0.67 | 3.5 | 0.07 | **9.4** | 36.8 | 1.66 | 10.79 | 3.59 | 78.4 | **2.9** | 6.1 | 10.1 | **8.6** |
| **10.0** | 0.00 | 0.0 | 0.09 | **0.7** | 0.0 | -0.09 | -1.18 | 2.08 | 106.1 | **7.1** | 95.4 | 5.4 | **2.6** |
| **4.0** | 2.75 | 14.6 | 0.23 | **8.8** | 1.2 | 2.07 | 18.09 | 5.64 | 61.9 | **1.7** | 20.7 | 23.3 | **8.0** |
| **9.0** | 0.27 | 1.0 | 0.00 | **7.6** | 16.2 | 1.72 | 12.08 | 3.46 | 64.3 | **1.7** | 13.4 | 16.1 | **9.1** |
| **4.4** | 0.78 | 4.4 | 0.05 | **4.6** | 1.6 | 0.95 | 9.65 | 3.55 | 75.6 | **1.5** | 10.2 | 22.5 | **7.5** |
| **7.8** | 0.41 | 2.3 | 0.00 | **3.5** | 0.2 | 0.60 | 4.44 | 3.40 | 78.7 | **0.9** | 19.1 | 38.1 | **7.0** |
| **2.2** | 6.28 | 19.5 | 0.03 | **3.1** | 0.1 | 0.48 | 2.09 | 5.33 | 87.5 | **5.5** | 34.4 | 1.7 | **5.5** |
| **5.5** | 2.98 | 8.9 | 0.10 | **5.6** | 1.0 | 1.00 | 6.90 | 4.36 | 76.2 | **3.0** | 35.1 | 18.1 | **7.6** |
| **4.8** | 0.94 | 7.3 | 0.21 | **4.9** | 1.0 | 0.96 | 12.80 | 4.27 | 67.5 | **1.7** | 14.8 | 21.6 | **4.1** |
| **5.3** | 1.10 | 8.9 | 0.00 | **2.5** | 1.6 | 0.38 | 4.10 | 3.04 | 86.0 | **1.3** | 5.8 | 17.3 | **5.5** |
| **3.2** | 2.17 | 13.5 | 0.16 | **5.6** | 1.2 | 1.15 | 12.53 | 4.36 | 65.1 | **2.1** | 19.8 | 19.2 | **5.7** |
| **6.2** | 0.65 | 3.9 | 0.11 | **3.5** | 13.9 | 0.80 | 8.67 | 3.28 | 85.5 | **1.3** | 8.2 | 21.3 | **7.0** |
| **5.8** | 1.98 | 4.5 | 0.26 | **4.3** | 2.5 | 0.83 | 4.22 | 3.83 | 68.4 | **4.8** | 16.0 | 3.5 | **6.3** |
| **3.9** | 1.09 | 5.3 | 0.87 | **2.3** | 110.5 | 0.12 | 0.88 | 3.19 | 76.7 | **3.1** | 22.8 | 9.9 | **10.0** |
| **4.8** | 1.13 | 5.8 | 0.03 | **4.3** | 23.1 | 0.84 | 9.04 | 3.18 | 61.4 | **1.2** | 22.0 | 38.5 | **7.0** |
| **5.0** | 1.48 | 7.0 | 0.04 | **3.4** | 0.7 | 0.51 | 5.55 | 3.85 | 83.2 | **3.4** | 16.8 | 11.9 | **4.8** |
| **6.0** | 0.30 | 1.2 | 0.28 | **1.6** | 23.7 | 4.88 | 40.40 | 3.15 | 115.0 | **1.3** | 24.1 | 30.7 | **2.0** |
| **5.6** | 0.73 | 2.8 | -0.10 | **4.3** | 1.2 | 0.85 | 6.41 | 4.80 | 84.2 | **3.1** | 43.4 | 21.4 | **7.8** |
| **9.0** | 0.11 | 0.4 | 0.00 | **0.0** | -3.1 | -3.26 | -10.92 | 3.36 | 177.6 | **0.7** | 15.1 | 38.9 | **1.5** |
| **3.1** | 3.88 | 7.5 | 0.52 | **10.0** | 99.8 | 1.95 | 4.54 | 7.90 | 55.1 | **0.6** | 17.5 | 20.2 | **9.0** |
| **2.9** | 8.69 | 17.8 | 0.33 | **6.1** | 13.4 | 0.72 | 2.58 | 5.59 | 79.1 | **1.8** | 32.0 | 11.7 | **8.0** |
| **3.6** | 1.82 | 20.0 | 0.19 | **3.3** | 0.3 | 0.50 | 4.58 | 3.81 | 79.4 | **2.7** | 22.7 | 16.4 | **5.6** |
| **7.5** | 1.29 | 2.9 | 0.00 | **5.3** | 0.5 | 1.08 | 6.47 | 4.41 | 66.4 | **1.2** | 21.6 | 30.6 | **7.4** |
| **5.5** | 2.03 | 8.2 | 0.04 | **9.5** | 1.4 | 2.09 | 12.18 | 5.02 | 59.0 | **2.8** | 22.9 | 15.6 | **9.5** |
| **7.2** | 0.62 | 3.0 | 0.12 | **4.3** | 1.0 | 0.76 | 6.40 | 3.94 | 75.4 | **1.9** | 20.7 | 20.7 | **6.7** |
| **6.8** | 1.30 | 4.0 | 0.18 | **4.7** | 1.0 | 1.04 | 7.29 | 4.01 | 71.8 | **3.9** | 30.6 | 12.6 | **7.5** |
| **6.6** | 0.32 | 3.2 | 0.40 | **5.7** | 2.9 | 1.06 | 11.31 | 4.55 | 66.2 | **1.5** | 16.9 | 24.7 | **5.1** |
| **6.8** | 0.15 | 1.2 | 0.05 | **6.9** | 72.6 | 1.20 | 12.78 | 4.03 | 67.5 | **4.4** | 2.0 | 4.0 | **8.4** |
| **6.0** | 1.44 | 7.7 | -0.03 | **9.8** | 2.6 | 2.18 | 14.82 | 3.74 | 41.2 | **3.7** | 22.6 | 11.5 | **10.0** |
| **4.2** | 0.75 | 4.6 | 0.06 | **8.1** | 7.2 | 1.41 | 13.89 | 3.83 | 44.8 | **0.9** | 21.6 | 38.4 | **7.2** |
| **8.3** | 4.37 | 6.2 | -0.08 | **3.6** | 2.4 | 0.62 | 3.41 | 3.05 | 72.4 | **3.6** | 66.6 | 28.4 | **7.1** |
| **9.9** | 0.46 | 1.3 | 0.00 | **2.5** | 0.3 | 0.31 | 1.51 | 3.05 | 86.3 | **0.9** | 22.7 | 47.5 | **7.3** |
| **4.9** | 2.12 | 9.5 | 0.01 | **8.4** | 0.9 | 1.47 | 9.75 | 4.80 | 56.4 | **2.6** | 14.4 | 16.0 | **7.9** |
| **7.8** | 0.64 | 2.3 | -0.13 | **0.0** | -0.9 | -0.94 | -9.10 | 3.47 | 131.6 | **0.9** | 21.1 | 26.5 | **4.3** |
| **7.2** | 0.52 | 3.9 | -0.06 | **8.7** | 12.9 | 1.93 | 20.93 | 4.17 | 74.1 | **5.2** | 32.9 | 5.0 | **6.2** |
| **7.0** | 0.57 | 3.5 | 0.13 | **7.5** | 9.8 | 1.41 | 13.42 | 4.54 | 64.3 | **3.9** | 14.1 | 9.4 | **8.2** |
| **3.7** | 1.11 | 7.3 | 0.02 | **8.3** | 1.3 | 2.01 | 20.46 | 4.08 | 54.5 | **3.8** | 8.9 | 9.4 | **6.6** |
| **5.5** | 0.98 | 5.0 | 0.33 | **2.0** | 2.5 | 0.24 | 2.11 | 4.17 | 90.9 | **2.4** | 28.3 | 26.3 | **7.5** |
| **3.9** | 3.74 | 11.4 | 0.35 | **8.0** | 13.5 | 1.91 | 16.38 | 3.40 | 43.3 | **2.6** | 19.3 | 16.1 | **9.1** |
| **7.5** | 0.00 | 0.0 | 0.00 | **5.7** | 0.5 | 1.13 | 7.91 | 3.63 | 64.5 | **2.0** | 27.5 | 22.8 | **7.6** |
| **3.6** | 2.40 | 15.5 | 0.20 | **3.4** | 0.4 | 0.67 | 7.33 | 4.30 | 85.1 | **1.2** | 13.6 | 26.2 | **4.9** |
| **5.1** | 0.49 | 3.8 | 0.34 | **4.1** | 101.1 | 0.81 | 6.24 | 3.18 | 63.4 | **0.9** | 17.7 | 25.8 | **9.0** |
| **8.0** | 0.82 | 1.2 | 0.02 | **4.1** | 4.9 | 0.72 | 4.10 | 3.28 | 68.7 | **4.5** | 54.8 | 16.4 | **7.9** |
| **7.6** | 0.00 | 0.0 | 0.00 | **10.0** | 29.7 | 3.47 | 36.56 | 1.80 | 70.7 | **6.7** | 43.4 | 0.0 | **8.0** |
| **10.0** | na | 0.0 | na | **10.0** | 1.2 | 10.82 | 10.96 | 1.98 | 59.5 | **4.0** | na | 0.0 | **7.0** |
| **10.0** | na | 0.0 | na | **10.0** | 10.3 | 46.54 | 52.89 | 1.90 | 64.2 | **4.0** | na | 0.0 | **7.0** |
| **7.5** | 0.00 | 0.0 | 0.00 | **9.8** | 90.2 | 4.57 | 34.67 | 1.56 | 82.5 | **6.9** | 37.3 | 0.0 | **8.9** |
| **8.7** | 0.26 | 1.5 | 0.04 | **0.6** | 0.0 | -0.02 | -0.24 | 2.33 | 110.4 | **0.8** | 17.6 | 43.2 | **4.3** |
| **6.2** | 0.22 | 1.9 | 0.09 | **4.0** | 2.7 | 0.91 | 9.52 | 3.50 | 77.5 | **3.3** | 23.8 | 13.2 | **6.2** |
| **6.8** | 0.48 | 2.5 | 0.02 | **5.7** | 16.3 | 1.10 | 9.83 | 3.46 | 66.3 | **1.7** | 13.3 | 12.7 | **8.2** |
| **9.7** | 1.24 | 0.6 | 0.53 | **5.2** | 1.7 | 1.30 | 8.35 | 3.31 | 65.0 | **7.1** | 82.2 | 6.6 | **8.8** |
| **5.4** | 2.96 | 10.0 | 0.19 | **3.8** | 1.9 | 0.75 | 6.94 | 3.43 | 71.8 | **4.4** | 40.3 | 13.2 | **6.6** |
| **6.0** | 0.98 | 6.5 | 0.09 | **8.2** | 3.7 | 2.04 | 18.54 | 4.33 | 58.7 | **3.9** | 17.7 | 8.6 | **8.6** |
| **8.4** | 0.00 | 0.0 | 0.39 | **4.5** | 0.2 | 1.36 | 12.86 | 6.06 | 87.2 | **4.3** | 34.2 | 9.1 | **3.9** |
| **7.3** | 0.13 | 0.9 | 0.03 | **5.4** | 3.9 | 1.29 | 13.00 | 3.74 | 65.4 | **0.7** | 12.4 | 35.8 | **7.3** |
| **10.0** | 0.00 | 0.0 | 0.00 | **2.2** | 0.1 | 0.17 | 1.35 | 2.74 | 91.9 | **1.6** | 35.6 | 44.8 | **6.0** |
| **6.5** | 0.41 | 1.8 | 0.00 | **5.7** | 1.0 | 1.30 | 11.50 | 3.92 | 65.1 | **1.6** | 14.3 | 22.8 | **7.7** |
| **3.8** | 2.13 | 10.2 | 0.24 | **5.2** | 9.7 | 1.08 | 10.46 | 4.13 | 71.9 | **4.2** | 14.6 | 7.5 | **7.0** |
| **7.1** | 1.24 | 5.1 | -0.09 | **5.2** | 17.4 | 1.28 | 10.25 | 2.92 | 54.1 | **3.0** | 17.3 | 14.9 | **9.3** |
| **1.4** | 2.81 | 10.1 | 0.02 | **3.7** | 1.5 | 1.22 | 10.72 | 4.07 | 69.1 | **1.7** | 16.2 | 18.5 | **7.1** |

| Name | City | State | Rating | 2018 Rating | 2017 Rating | Total Assets ($Mil) | One Year Asset Growth | Asset Mix (As a % of Total Assets) Comm-ercial Loans | Cons-umer Loans | Mort-gage Loans | Secur-ities | Capital-ization Index | Lever-age Ratio | Risk-Based Capital Ratio |
|---|---|---|---|---|---|---|---|---|---|---|---|---|---|---|
| Blackrock Institutional Trust Co., N.A. | San Francisco | CA | **U** | U | U | 4277.2 | -0.38 | 0.0 | 0.0 | 0.0 | 7.8 | **10.0** | 72.8 | 137.7 |
| BLC Community Bank | Little Chute | WI | **A-** | A- | A- | 269.2 | 5.75 | 10.8 | 0.4 | 12.7 | 17.9 | **10.0** | 11.8 | 16.4 |
| Blissfield State Bank | Blissfield | MI | **B-** | C+ | C+ | 98.0 | 0.31 | 7.2 | 3.0 | 16.7 | 43.3 | **10.0** | 11.2 | 20.1 |
| ▲ Bloomsdale Bank | Bloomsdale | MO | **B+** | B+ | A- | 231.6 | 3.22 | 7.4 | 2.0 | 18.0 | 22.4 | **8.4** | 10.0 | 14.3 |
| ▼ Blue Foundry Bank | Rutherford | NJ | **C+** | C+ | C+ | 1838.8 | 8.60 | 0.0 | 0.0 | 42.3 | 11.6 | **10.0** | 12.3 | 21.5 |
| ▲ Blue Grass Federal S&L Assn. | Paris | KY | **B-** | C | D+ | 35.1 | 1.38 | 7.0 | 3.1 | 47.9 | 13.5 | **10.0** | 25.2 | 48.0 |
| Blue Grass Savings Bank | Blue Grass | IA | **B** | B | B+ | 201.8 | 3.81 | 10.1 | 0.5 | 18.5 | 33.7 | **10.0** | 15.1 | 26.7 |
| ▲ Blue Grass Valley Bank | Blue Grass | VA | **C+** | D+ | D+ | 45.3 | -0.42 | 6.3 | 6.0 | 31.0 | 9.0 | **10.0** | 11.1 | 21.5 |
| Blue Ridge Bank | Walhalla | SC | **C+** | C+ | B- | 132.6 | -1.13 | 1.4 | 2.0 | 32.8 | 27.9 | **8.5** | 10.0 | 19.7 |
| ▲ Blue Ridge Bank and Trust Co. | Independence | MO | **C** | C | B- | 574.6 | 3.85 | 12.7 | 12.4 | 5.9 | 15.7 | **8.8** | 10.3 | 14.0 |
| Blue Ridge Bank, N.A. | Martinsville | VA | **C+** | C+ | B- | 960.2 | 78.19 | 7.5 | 4.1 | 24.5 | 12.6 | **6.0** | 8.0 | 11.8 |
| Blue Sky Bank | Pawhuska | OK | **B** | B+ | A- | 234.9 | 5.79 | 28.1 | 0.7 | 6.9 | 3.8 | **7.4** | 11.6 | 12.8 |
| BlueHarbor Bank | Mooresville | NC | **A-** | B+ | B+ | 245.7 | 14.76 | 9.8 | 0.2 | 15.1 | 7.4 | **10.0** | 13.2 | 15.8 |
| ▲ Bluff View Bank | Galesville | WI | **A-** | A- | B+ | 107.3 | 6.08 | 5.7 | 2.6 | 17.1 | 11.7 | **10.0** | 18.7 | 20.5 |
| BMO Harris Bank, N.A. | Chicago | IL | **B** | B- | C+ | 137588.1 | 11.73 | 27.6 | 4.9 | 6.7 | 15.5 | **7.0** | 9.9 | 12.5 |
| BMO Harris Central N.A. | Roselle | IL | **U** | U | U | 8.0 | 0.72 | 0.0 | 0.0 | 0.0 | 0.0 | **10.0** | 87.2 | 443.8 |
| BMW Bank of North America | Salt Lake City | UT | **A-** | A- | A- | 10573.6 | 4.00 | 0.6 | 74.0 | 0.0 | 23.6 | **10.0** | 15.9 | 17.1 |
| BNA Bank | New Albany | MS | **A-** | A- | A- | 515.4 | 1.75 | 2.4 | 4.9 | 26.1 | 31.4 | **10.0** | 12.2 | 19.1 |
| BNB Bank | Bridgehampton | NY | **B+** | B+ | B+ | 4921.3 | 4.72 | 12.5 | 0.5 | 10.3 | 15.7 | **7.6** | 10.1 | 13.0 |
| ▲ BNC National Bank | Glendale | AZ | **B+** | B- | B | 965.3 | -0.50 | 9.2 | 4.8 | 17.0 | 27.5 | **8.2** | 9.8 | 15.9 |
| BNY Mellon Trust of Delaware | Wilmington | DE | **B** | B | B- | 141.3 | 15.75 | 0.0 | 0.0 | 14.4 | 0.0 | **10.0** | 52.5 | 111.5 |
| BNY Mellon, N.A. | Pittsburgh | PA | **B** | B | B- | 29303.0 | 1.48 | 0.3 | 7.6 | 28.1 | 4.4 | **5.8** | 7.8 | 12.5 |
| BOC Bank | Amarillo | TX | **A-** | B+ | B+ | 49.9 | -10.04 | 37.9 | 0.1 | 14.4 | 11.6 | **10.0** | 16.9 | 25.1 |
| Bodcaw Bank | Stamps | AR | **B-** | B | B+ | 117.0 | 23.27 | 17.9 | 4.8 | 27.0 | 24.4 | **7.6** | 9.5 | 13.0 |
| Boelus State Bank | Boelus | NE | **C+** | C+ | C+ | 17.5 | 19.02 | 1.4 | 4.6 | 0.5 | 0.5 | **10.0** | 14.9 | 29.5 |
| ▼ Bogota Savings Bank | Teaneck | NJ | **C+** | B | B | 766.7 | 15.16 | 0.3 | 0.1 | 50.8 | 9.2 | **9.7** | 10.8 | 17.8 |
| BOKF, N.A. | Tulsa | OK | **B** | B | B | 42074.1 | 23.37 | 20.9 | 1.0 | 4.6 | 27.5 | **6.0** | 8.0 | 11.8 |
| BOM Bank | Natchitoches | LA | **B** | B | B+ | 506.6 | 18.91 | 7.9 | 3.6 | 25.1 | 3.5 | **8.8** | 10.2 | 14.2 |
| Bonanza Valley State Bank | Brooten | MN | **C** | C | C | 68.0 | 7.25 | 9.1 | 2.8 | 33.8 | 6.3 | **6.4** | 8.9 | 12.0 |
| Bonduel State Bank | Bonduel | WI | **B+** | B+ | B+ | 64.8 | 7.05 | 6.9 | 4.1 | 11.0 | 35.7 | **10.0** | 22.0 | 42.4 |
| Boone Bank & Trust Co. | Boone | IA | **A-** | A- | A- | 134.7 | 7.20 | 4.0 | 1.7 | 3.3 | 46.0 | **7.7** | 9.5 | 14.1 |
| Boonville Federal Savings Bank | Boonville | IN | **D+** | D | D+ | 54.7 | 7.63 | 6.8 | 8.9 | 43.7 | 10.8 | **7.2** | 9.1 | 15.4 |
| Border State Bank | Greenbush | MN | **B-** | B- | C+ | 632.9 | 6.60 | 10.7 | 4.6 | 10.1 | 14.2 | **7.0** | 9.0 | 12.7 |
| Boston Private Bank & Trust Co. | Boston | MA | **B** | B | B | 8796.2 | 4.44 | 6.2 | 1.5 | 33.7 | 11.7 | **7.1** | 9.0 | 13.1 |
| Boston Trust Walden Co. | Boston | MA | **A-** | A- | A- | 48.3 | 1.34 | 0.1 | 0.0 | 0.0 | 4.1 | **10.0** | 71.0 | 123.3 |
| ▲ Boundary Waters Bank | Ely | MN | **C+** | C | C | 107.6 | -3.11 | 2.0 | 1.1 | 12.5 | 2.9 | **10.0** | 12.9 | 15.3 |
| ▲ Bradford National Bank of Greenville | Greenville | IL | **A-** | B | B | 367.8 | 24.33 | 3.7 | 1.2 | 11.5 | 55.0 | **10.0** | 12.3 | 20.0 |
| Brady National Bank | Brady | TX | **B-** | B- | B- | 134.9 | 10.93 | 11.6 | 1.8 | 8.0 | 34.2 | **7.7** | 9.5 | 16.5 |
| Brainerd S&L Assn., A Federal Assn. | Brainerd | MN | **D** | D | D | 67.3 | -0.48 | 0.3 | 1.4 | 54.6 | 7.5 | **5.3** | 7.3 | 12.6 |
| Brannen Bank | Inverness | FL | **B-** | C+ | C+ | 542.4 | 3.43 | 0.3 | 1.1 | 40.8 | 25.5 | **4.1** | 6.1 | 15.4 |
| Branson Bank | Branson | MO | **B** | B | B | 232.4 | 10.02 | 6.7 | 2.2 | 25.2 | 4.9 | **8.1** | 9.8 | 13.8 |
| Brantley Bank and Trust Co. | Brantley | AL | **B+** | B+ | B+ | 70.0 | -1.77 | 9.5 | 3.6 | 7.0 | 46.5 | **10.0** | 14.5 | 25.1 |
| ▲ Brattleboro S&L Assn. | Brattleboro | VT | **C+** | C | C | 216.6 | 5.26 | 4.0 | 0.7 | 44.4 | 0.1 | **6.0** | 8.0 | 12.5 |
| Brazos National Bank | Richwood | TX | **B+** | B+ | A- | 29.5 | 10.49 | 0.7 | 1.5 | 76.5 | 0.0 | **10.0** | 27.3 | 54.2 |
| Breda Savings Bank | Breda | IA | **A-** | A- | A | 62.6 | 0.69 | 5.0 | 1.0 | 15.4 | 31.9 | **10.0** | 11.7 | 18.4 |
| Bremer Bank, N.A. | Saint Paul | MN | **B+** | B+ | B+ | 13105.6 | 8.11 | 9.7 | 1.2 | 7.4 | 25.2 | **7.5** | 9.3 | 13.1 |
| ▲ Brenham National Bank | Brenham | TX | **A-** | B | B | 371.5 | 3.92 | 3.1 | 1.1 | 7.9 | 48.7 | **8.7** | 10.1 | 19.0 |
| Brentwood Bank | Bethel Park | PA | **B** | B | B- | 706.0 | 10.59 | 3.2 | 0.0 | 33.6 | 14.5 | **10.0** | 12.3 | 17.0 |
| Brickyard Bank | Lincolnwood | IL | **C-** | D+ | D+ | 133.9 | 18.61 | 10.1 | 0.6 | 10.9 | 3.1 | **10.0** | 11.6 | 19.8 |
| Bridge City State Bank | Bridge City | TX | **B** | B | B | 215.0 | 3.19 | 4.2 | 0.9 | 8.9 | 48.7 | **9.2** | 10.5 | 22.6 |
| Bridge Community Bank | Mount Vernon | IA | **B+** | B+ | B+ | 100.9 | 8.92 | 11.3 | 3.9 | 23.7 | 10.7 | **10.0** | 11.2 | 16.2 |
| Bridgewater Bank | Bloomington | MN | **A-** | A- | B+ | 2263.9 | 14.91 | 11.4 | 0.2 | 9.7 | 12.8 | **6.5** | 11.0 | 12.2 |
| Bridgewater Savings Bank | Raynham | MA | **C+** | C+ | C+ | 632.5 | 3.24 | 5.7 | 2.9 | 31.2 | 19.9 | **7.7** | 9.4 | 15.6 |
| ▼ Brighton Bank | Brighton | TN | **E-** | E | E- | 41.7 | 0.48 | 9.9 | 1.3 | 34.9 | 13.9 | **4.9** | 6.9 | 12.7 |
| Brighton Bank | Salt Lake City | UT | **A-** | B+ | A | 219.7 | 5.21 | 3.5 | 0.3 | 4.5 | 16.6 | **10.0** | 12.7 | 18.1 |
| Bristol County Savings Bank | Taunton | MA | **B-** | C+ | C+ | 2297.4 | 5.54 | 6.3 | 14.4 | 31.2 | 8.6 | **8.0** | 13.0 | 13.4 |
| Bristol Morgan Bank | Oakfield | WI | **C** | C+ | B | 112.3 | 11.02 | 9.5 | 2.0 | 16.7 | 12.6 | **9.4** | 10.8 | 14.5 |
| Broadway Federal Bank, F.S.B. | Los Angeles | CA | **C** | C+ | B- | 438.0 | 7.58 | 0.1 | 0.0 | 16.7 | 2.5 | **10.0** | 11.6 | 18.3 |
| Broadway National Bank | San Antonio | TX | **B+** | B | B | 3831.9 | 4.88 | 7.5 | 4.0 | 11.9 | 32.1 | **9.8** | 10.9 | 16.2 |
| Brookline Bank | Brookline | MA | **B** | B | B | 4966.1 | 6.93 | 25.3 | 0.8 | 10.8 | 5.2 | **6.8** | 10.4 | 12.4 |

| Asset Quality Index | Adjusted Non-Performing Loans as a % of Total Loans | Adjusted Non-Performing Loans as a % of Capital | Net Charge-Offs Avg Loans | Profitability Index | Net Income ($Mil) | Return on Assets (R.O.A.) | Return on Equity (R.O.E.) | Net Interest Spread | Overhead Efficiency Ratio | Liquidity Index | Liquidity Ratio | Hot Money Ratio | Stability Index |
|---|---|---|---|---|---|---|---|---|---|---|---|---|---|
| **6.5** | na | 0.0 | na | **10.0** | 522.3 | 12.23 | 14.88 | 2.75 | 53.6 | **4.0** | 57.8 | 0.0 | **7.0** |
| **7.5** | 0.00 | 0.0 | 0.01 | **6.3** | 4.1 | 1.51 | 12.78 | 3.02 | 50.7 | **0.9** | 21.7 | 18.7 | **9.8** |
| **4.7** | 3.95 | 15.3 | 0.01 | **3.6** | 0.8 | 0.81 | 7.29 | 3.50 | 79.6 | **5.5** | 55.7 | 10.0 | **6.7** |
| **6.7** | 0.43 | 2.7 | -0.01 | **9.5** | 5.5 | 2.43 | 25.13 | 4.01 | 45.1 | **1.6** | 19.5 | 21.1 | **8.1** |
| **8.9** | 0.40 | 2.3 | 0.00 | **2.6** | 5.5 | 0.32 | 2.47 | 2.65 | 81.6 | **1.2** | 20.0 | 31.3 | **8.8** |
| **8.2** | 0.50 | 4.5 | 0.00 | **6.4** | 0.7 | 1.94 | 7.56 | 3.76 | 80.0 | **2.0** | 37.8 | 32.5 | **5.4** |
| **5.8** | 1.97 | 6.9 | 0.00 | **4.1** | 1.6 | 0.80 | 5.07 | 2.66 | 60.6 | **2.7** | 43.9 | 24.9 | **7.8** |
| **3.4** | 3.22 | 13.0 | 0.43 | **3.5** | 0.3 | 0.57 | 5.07 | 3.76 | 76.6 | **4.2** | 39.1 | 13.7 | **5.8** |
| **5.6** | 2.26 | 8.2 | 0.18 | **3.6** | 0.8 | 0.62 | 6.11 | 3.73 | 82.8 | **4.6** | 46.7 | 13.4 | **6.1** |
| **3.7** | 1.76 | 10.6 | 0.44 | **5.7** | 6.0 | 1.09 | 10.86 | 3.83 | 65.8 | **4.0** | 19.6 | 9.0 | **6.9** |
| **3.7** | 0.94 | 5.8 | 0.14 | **4.7** | 6.8 | 0.94 | 10.74 | 3.23 | 76.4 | **1.2** | 13.2 | 24.5 | **6.6** |
| **3.6** | 0.97 | 5.3 | 0.09 | **7.0** | 3.5 | 1.58 | 13.91 | 5.05 | 68.5 | **1.0** | 17.2 | 30.7 | **7.4** |
| **8.0** | 0.05 | 0.3 | -0.02 | **6.3** | 3.1 | 1.32 | 10.11 | 4.00 | 57.5 | **1.5** | 10.7 | 15.3 | **7.8** |
| **7.1** | 1.18 | 4.6 | 0.10 | **7.9** | 1.9 | 1.81 | 9.49 | 4.32 | 65.3 | **3.8** | 14.2 | 9.3 | **10.0** |
| **4.6** | 1.46 | 6.5 | 0.10 | **4.4** | 1208.7 | 0.94 | 7.33 | 2.84 | 61.6 | **3.9** | 30.8 | 9.6 | **9.8** |
| **10.0** | na | 0.0 | na | **5.6** | 0.1 | 0.95 | 1.09 | 9.04 | -556.3 | **4.0** | na | 0.0 | **7.0** |
| **5.6** | 0.12 | 0.5 | 0.19 | **8.4** | 173.8 | 1.44 | 9.23 | 2.06 | 27.4 | **1.7** | 31.1 | 2.3 | **10.0** |
| **6.3** | 1.47 | 5.5 | -0.01 | **6.7** | 7.6 | 1.46 | 11.92 | 3.42 | 53.0 | **3.1** | 26.2 | 14.8 | **8.5** |
| **5.7** | 0.97 | 4.4 | 0.13 | **5.3** | 55.3 | 1.17 | 10.02 | 3.39 | 55.8 | **4.0** | 11.2 | 5.6 | **8.6** |
| **7.0** | 0.54 | 2.5 | 0.05 | **5.6** | 12.2 | 1.19 | 11.79 | 3.12 | 70.8 | **1.6** | 22.6 | 13.2 | **8.0** |
| **3.8** | 17.29 | 3.4 | -0.01 | **9.5** | 5.8 | 4.83 | 7.00 | 2.69 | 36.6 | **8.6** | 107.4 | 0.0 | **8.4** |
| **6.8** | 0.07 | 0.3 | 0.00 | **5.6** | 293.0 | 1.05 | 7.60 | 1.04 | 63.8 | **2.0** | 36.5 | 62.8 | **8.4** |
| **8.3** | 0.00 | 0.0 | 0.11 | **9.0** | 1.2 | 2.25 | 13.44 | 4.28 | 58.9 | **2.6** | 34.0 | 20.4 | **8.0** |
| **5.4** | 0.59 | 4.1 | 0.04 | **5.0** | 1.2 | 1.11 | 11.62 | 3.93 | 54.5 | **0.9** | 23.9 | 50.9 | **5.2** |
| **8.5** | 0.12 | 0.3 | 0.00 | **4.0** | 0.1 | 0.69 | 4.74 | 3.05 | 63.8 | **4.2** | 72.8 | 17.6 | **6.3** |
| **9.3** | 0.25 | 1.3 | -0.01 | **3.0** | 2.4 | 0.36 | 3.30 | 1.75 | 72.0 | **0.9** | 25.9 | 46.1 | **6.2** |
| **5.7** | 0.96 | 4.0 | 0.18 | **6.0** | 506.8 | 1.21 | 11.66 | 3.07 | 59.9 | **3.7** | 18.4 | 6.0 | **9.3** |
| **5.1** | 0.67 | 6.5 | 0.27 | **7.7** | 8.2 | 1.77 | 18.12 | 4.86 | 66.2 | **3.8** | 11.8 | 9.7 | **7.1** |
| **6.0** | 0.53 | 4.3 | 0.01 | **5.1** | 0.8 | 1.14 | 12.83 | 4.25 | 70.1 | **3.5** | 12.5 | 10.9 | **5.0** |
| **8.9** | 0.34 | 0.6 | 0.04 | **6.6** | 1.0 | 1.65 | 7.53 | 3.47 | 49.0 | **5.6** | 64.6 | 11.1 | **8.0** |
| **8.9** | 0.10 | 0.4 | 0.01 | **5.6** | 1.5 | 1.12 | 10.19 | 3.06 | 59.1 | **2.1** | 28.4 | 21.0 | **7.7** |
| **5.7** | 0.06 | 3.2 | 0.14 | **1.8** | 0.1 | 0.17 | 1.82 | 3.22 | 88.3 | **1.8** | 32.7 | 30.9 | **4.0** |
| **4.2** | 1.62 | 9.7 | 0.04 | **4.4** | 5.9 | 0.96 | 9.82 | 3.79 | 73.0 | **1.4** | 17.4 | 14.1 | **6.6** |
| **8.3** | 0.32 | 2.1 | 0.00 | **4.4** | 78.7 | 0.92 | 9.59 | 2.96 | 67.6 | **3.5** | 13.4 | 7.0 | **8.2** |
| **6.5** | 0.00 | 0.0 | 0.00 | **10.0** | 22.0 | 45.84 | 54.22 | 14.73 | 55.9 | **4.6** | 175.3 | 100.0 | **10.0** |
| **3.4** | 1.94 | 11.4 | -0.03 | **5.1** | 1.0 | 0.96 | 7.34 | 4.48 | 71.0 | **1.2** | 15.6 | 29.0 | **7.2** |
| **6.1** | 2.88 | 7.9 | 0.04 | **6.0** | 4.7 | 1.50 | 11.61 | 3.70 | 58.1 | **2.3** | 41.8 | 20.0 | **7.7** |
| **3.8** | 3.42 | 16.1 | 0.01 | **4.3** | 1.3 | 1.08 | 11.72 | 3.02 | 69.5 | **4.0** | 27.9 | 10.8 | **5.2** |
| **4.6** | 2.05 | 17.4 | -0.01 | **0.1** | -0.3 | -0.41 | -5.64 | 3.19 | 119.8 | **1.3** | 14.7 | 15.3 | **2.7** |
| **5.7** | 1.42 | 8.6 | -0.01 | **7.8** | 10.6 | 1.98 | 30.60 | 3.87 | 53.8 | **5.5** | 42.0 | 7.6 | **5.4** |
| **6.3** | 0.77 | 4.1 | 0.12 | **4.9** | 2.1 | 0.91 | 9.26 | 4.03 | 72.4 | **2.3** | 13.8 | 16.3 | **6.1** |
| **8.8** | 0.02 | 0.3 | 0.45 | **5.9** | 0.9 | 1.27 | 8.27 | 4.94 | 64.5 | **4.9** | 51.4 | 12.6 | **6.8** |
| **5.7** | 0.51 | 4.6 | 0.05 | **3.3** | 1.1 | 0.50 | 5.71 | 3.55 | 85.5 | **3.3** | 9.9 | 11.9 | **5.0** |
| **8.0** | 0.05 | 0.1 | 0.00 | **10.0** | 0.9 | 2.95 | 9.90 | 5.22 | 87.6 | **1.2** | 10.1 | 27.9 | **8.0** |
| **8.8** | 0.12 | 0.6 | 0.00 | **6.0** | 0.9 | 1.41 | 12.59 | 3.49 | 58.1 | **4.3** | 38.2 | 12.8 | **8.2** |
| **6.1** | 0.89 | 4.7 | 0.05 | **6.0** | 163.6 | 1.29 | 13.46 | 3.41 | 59.0 | **2.6** | 18.8 | 7.5 | **9.4** |
| **8.0** | 1.22 | 3.5 | 0.15 | **6.0** | 5.5 | 1.51 | 14.52 | 3.76 | 59.3 | **5.2** | 53.4 | 12.6 | **7.3** |
| **8.8** | 0.30 | 1.6 | 0.00 | **3.9** | 5.0 | 0.73 | 6.10 | 2.94 | 70.4 | **2.6** | 14.0 | 14.6 | **7.8** |
| **5.0** | 3.04 | 9.7 | -0.01 | **3.9** | 1.1 | 0.90 | 7.54 | 3.64 | 76.5 | **1.9** | 38.9 | 40.4 | **4.4** |
| **6.0** | 1.59 | 8.8 | 0.12 | **4.6** | 2.1 | 1.02 | 10.20 | 3.25 | 63.6 | **6.7** | 60.4 | 5.1 | **5.9** |
| **8.4** | 0.00 | 0.3 | 0.03 | **5.7** | 1.2 | 1.21 | 10.65 | 3.78 | 63.5 | **2.3** | 17.6 | 17.8 | **6.8** |
| **7.3** | 0.04 | 0.2 | 0.01 | **7.8** | 32.0 | 1.52 | 13.76 | 3.71 | 47.2 | **0.9** | 15.9 | 27.7 | **9.6** |
| **8.5** | 0.00 | 0.1 | 0.00 | **3.2** | 3.5 | 0.56 | 5.89 | 3.13 | 82.4 | **3.2** | 24.0 | 13.8 | **6.4** |
| **1.7** | 3.62 | 35.9 | -0.36 | **1.9** | 0.0 | 0.10 | 1.56 | 4.76 | 98.6 | **3.6** | 13.8 | 10.7 | **0.3** |
| **6.0** | 2.68 | 6.6 | 0.00 | **10.0** | 5.6 | 2.69 | 21.16 | 5.50 | 51.1 | **6.0** | 35.6 | 1.4 | **9.2** |
| **6.7** | 0.69 | 2.8 | 0.10 | **4.2** | 23.9 | 1.16 | 8.74 | 3.19 | 77.8 | **3.1** | 19.4 | 12.3 | **10.0** |
| **5.0** | 2.84 | 8.0 | 0.62 | **2.3** | 0.1 | 0.12 | 1.09 | 3.57 | 95.2 | **2.2** | 38.7 | 27.6 | **4.8** |
| **5.2** | 1.18 | 4.8 | -0.07 | **2.0** | 0.5 | 0.11 | 0.90 | 2.61 | 96.7 | **0.4** | 6.9 | 54.4 | **7.0** |
| **7.5** | 0.13 | 0.7 | -0.03 | **5.6** | 52.6 | 1.42 | 12.75 | 3.66 | 66.5 | **5.4** | 29.4 | 7.1 | **9.5** |
| **5.8** | 0.58 | 3.5 | 0.12 | **7.2** | 64.9 | 1.35 | 12.15 | 3.61 | 48.9 | **1.0** | 3.5 | 22.2 | **8.6** |

| Name | City | State | Rating | 2018 Rating | 2017 Rating | Total Assets ($Mil) | One Year Asset Growth | Asset Mix (As a % of Total Assets) Comm-ercial Loans | Cons-umer Loans | Mort-gage Loans | Secur-ities | Capital-ization Index | Lever-age Ratio | Risk-Based Capital Ratio |
|---|---|---|---|---|---|---|---|---|---|---|---|---|---|---|
| Brookville Building and Savings Assn. | Brookville | OH | **B** | B- | B- | 45.0 | -3.61 | 3.4 | 1.0 | 51.5 | 15.3 | **10.0** | 19.2 | 35.2 |
| Brown Brothers Harriman Trust Co. | Wilmington | DE | **U** | U | U | 11.8 | 17.16 | 0.0 | 0.0 | 0.0 | 63.2 | **10.0** | 53.4 | 132.0 |
| Brown Brothers Harriman Trust Co., N.A. | New York | NY | **U** | U | U | 15.2 | 1.97 | 0.0 | 0.0 | 0.0 | 62.4 | **10.0** | 51.5 | 102.1 |
| ▲ Bruning Bank | Bruning | NE | **B** | B- | B- | 369.2 | 2.96 | 9.0 | 0.8 | 1.4 | 20.6 | **8.9** | 12.3 | 14.1 |
| Brunswick Bank and Trust Co. | New Brunswick | NJ | **B-** | B- | C+ | 235.1 | 19.28 | 1.5 | 0.0 | 16.1 | 4.7 | **10.0** | 14.1 | 17.1 |
| Brunswick State Bank | Brunswick | NE | **C** | C+ | B | 136.9 | 2.35 | 15.2 | 5.0 | 0.1 | 3.5 | **5.7** | 9.7 | 11.5 |
| Bryant Bank | Tuscaloosa | AL | **A-** | A- | B | 1839.1 | 9.36 | 10.6 | 0.8 | 7.1 | 18.8 | **8.5** | 10.0 | 15.0 |
| Bryant State Bank | Bryant | SD | **B+** | B | B | 38.1 | 10.34 | 15.8 | 5.9 | 1.2 | 10.1 | **10.0** | 11.6 | 17.6 |
| Bryn Mawr Trust Co. | Bryn Mawr | PA | **B+** | B | B | 5248.3 | 13.17 | 8.2 | 1.1 | 14.3 | 19.4 | **6.5** | 9.4 | 12.1 |
| ▲ BTC Bank | Bethany | MO | **B+** | B | A- | 563.4 | 12.68 | 9.3 | 1.8 | 11.2 | 12.7 | **10.0** | 13.8 | 16.6 |
| BTH Bank, N.A. | Quitman | TX | **A-** | B+ | B | 1792.3 | -6.41 | 33.6 | 0.7 | 17.5 | 21.1 | **10.0** | 13.8 | 17.9 |
| ▲ Buckeye Community Bank | Lorain | OH | **A-** | B+ | B+ | 174.2 | 2.36 | 26.3 | 0.1 | 7.7 | 12.0 | **10.0** | 12.8 | 17.7 |
| Buckeye State Bank | Powell | OH | **D-** | D- | D- | 137.6 | 37.06 | 9.9 | 19.6 | 7.9 | 13.3 | **8.6** | 10.1 | 14.1 |
| Buckholts State Bank | Buckholts | TX | **A-** | A- | A- | 77.0 | -4.87 | 21.1 | 2.3 | 16.0 | 31.8 | **10.0** | 17.6 | 32.7 |
| Buckley State Bank | Buckley | IL | **B-** | C+ | C+ | 41.3 | -3.30 | 6.5 | 0.8 | 0.3 | 27.2 | **10.0** | 12.8 | 19.1 |
| Buena Vista National Bank | Chester | IL | **A-** | B+ | A- | 212.4 | 5.97 | 4.7 | 6.7 | 21.9 | 29.0 | **10.0** | 12.0 | 17.6 |
| Buffalo Federal Bank | Buffalo | WY | **B** | B | B | 123.2 | 1.97 | 9.8 | 4.5 | 15.9 | 18.4 | **9.9** | 11.0 | 16.2 |
| ▼ Burke & Herbert Bank & Trust Co. | Alexandria | VA | **B** | B+ | B+ | 2866.0 | -4.68 | 1.1 | 0.1 | 15.2 | 24.2 | **10.0** | 12.3 | 17.6 |
| Burling Bank | Chicago | IL | **A-** | B | B- | 134.0 | -5.02 | 8.6 | 0.4 | 32.8 | 19.6 | **10.0** | 11.5 | 19.5 |
| ▲ Burton State Bank | Burton | TX | **B+** | B- | B- | 72.5 | 9.43 | 2.1 | 5.1 | 11.5 | 9.8 | **10.0** | 12.2 | 30.8 |
| Busey Bank | Champaign | IL | **A-** | A- | A- | 9679.1 | 25.86 | 12.5 | 0.5 | 14.0 | 17.0 | **9.9** | 11.2 | 14.9 |
| Business Bank of Texas, N.A. | Austin | TX | **B-** | C | C+ | 93.9 | -18.10 | 13.7 | 0.0 | 2.3 | 25.7 | **10.0** | 14.6 | 23.6 |
| Butte State Bank | Butte | NE | **B-** | C+ | B- | 42.8 | 3.10 | 8.1 | 2.9 | 1.4 | 26.2 | **10.0** | 12.3 | 18.1 |
| Byline Bank | Chicago | IL | **B** | B- | C+ | 5516.5 | 11.67 | 22.6 | 0.1 | 5.9 | 21.6 | **8.6** | 10.9 | 13.9 |
| Byron Bank | Byron | IL | **B-** | C+ | B | 271.7 | 5.69 | 8.4 | 2.7 | 12.6 | 29.9 | **8.7** | 10.1 | 16.4 |
| C3bank, N.A. | Encinitas | CA | **B+** | B+ | A- | 356.4 | 5.77 | 0.4 | 0.0 | 5.5 | 1.5 | **10.0** | 13.1 | 16.7 |
| Cache Bank & Trust | Greeley | CO | **C** | C- | D+ | 112.1 | -7.39 | 7.0 | 1.9 | 7.0 | 19.7 | **10.0** | 13.0 | 25.2 |
| Cache Valley Bank | Logan | UT | **B** | B- | B | 1408.0 | 11.68 | 10.9 | 0.5 | 5.8 | 2.0 | **9.3** | 11.1 | 14.4 |
| Cadence Bank, N.A. | Atlanta | GA | **B+** | B+ | B- | 17778.0 | 39.82 | 31.1 | 0.5 | 13.4 | 13.3 | **8.3** | 11.3 | 13.6 |
| ▲ Caldwell Bank & Trust Co. | Columbia | LA | **B-** | D+ | D+ | 162.9 | 2.88 | 6.0 | 4.4 | 27.6 | 5.9 | **10.0** | 11.0 | 15.8 |
| Calhoun County Bank, Inc. | Grantsville | WV | **B-** | B- | B+ | 153.0 | 7.77 | 2.3 | 15.3 | 51.3 | 5.9 | **8.6** | 10.0 | 17.1 |
| ▲ California Bank of Commerce | Lafayette | CA | **B-** | C+ | B- | 1152.4 | 14.61 | 34.6 | 0.0 | 1.0 | 2.5 | **6.1** | 10.4 | 11.8 |
| California Business Bank | Irvine | CA | **D** | D | D | 82.6 | -6.27 | 13.4 | 11.5 | 1.3 | 0.0 | **10.0** | 14.9 | 22.1 |
| California First National Bank | Irvine | CA | **A** | A | A- | 138.6 | -49.05 | 4.0 | 0.0 | 0.0 | 0.1 | **10.0** | 49.5 | 65.5 |
| California International Bank, N.A. | Westminster | CA | **D** | D | D | 42.9 | -7.23 | 22.5 | 0.0 | 5.6 | 1.4 | **10.0** | 30.0 | 41.9 |
| ▼ California Pacific Bank | San Francisco | CA | **A-** | A | A | 77.4 | 5.53 | 4.4 | 0.0 | 4.5 | 0.0 | **10.0** | 41.4 | 51.2 |
| Callaway Bank | Fulton | MO | **B-** | B- | B- | 380.1 | 3.05 | 9.6 | 1.2 | 21.8 | 12.3 | **7.2** | 9.7 | 12.7 |
| ▼ CalPrivate Bank | La Jolla | CA | **C+** | B+ | A- | 1065.5 | 25.83 | 22.9 | 0.6 | 4.9 | 4.8 | **7.1** | 10.6 | 12.6 |
| Calvin B. Taylor Banking Co. | Berlin | MD | **A** | A- | A- | 546.0 | 3.07 | 3.3 | 0.3 | 21.6 | 12.4 | **10.0** | 15.9 | 25.2 |
| Calwest Bank | Irvine | CA | **B** | B- | B- | 234.2 | 19.98 | 15.3 | 0.4 | 9.8 | 5.7 | **6.3** | 9.1 | 12.0 |
| Cambridge Savings Bank | Cambridge | MA | **B-** | B- | B- | 4297.8 | 10.72 | 9.8 | 0.2 | 20.1 | 13.8 | **7.8** | 10.1 | 13.1 |
| Cambridge State Bank | Cambridge | MN | **B-** | C | B | 77.1 | -2.91 | 15.4 | 0.8 | 12.7 | 19.4 | **10.0** | 12.0 | 22.2 |
| Cambridge Trust Co. | Cambridge | MA | **B+** | B+ | B+ | 2855.6 | 35.89 | 4.4 | 1.2 | 32.8 | 14.2 | **6.9** | 8.9 | 13.5 |
| Camden National Bank | Camden | ME | **B+** | B+ | B | 4410.3 | 3.00 | 7.7 | 0.6 | 27.5 | 20.9 | **7.3** | 9.2 | 13.5 |
| ▲ Camp Grove State Bank | Camp Grove | IL | **D+** | D+ | D+ | 19.4 | 0.05 | 3.5 | 3.1 | 3.0 | 12.0 | **10.0** | 13.9 | 26.6 |
| Campbell & Fetter Bank | Kendallville | IN | **B-** | B- | B- | 316.5 | -1.63 | 3.8 | 5.9 | 42.8 | 26.0 | **9.5** | 10.7 | 24.5 |
| ▼ Campbell County Bank, Inc. | Herreid | SD | **B** | B+ | A | 135.2 | 32.01 | 5.7 | 1.0 | 0.1 | 19.7 | **10.0** | 13.7 | 17.9 |
| Campus State Bank | Campus | IL | **C** | C- | C- | 20.3 | -2.32 | 0.0 | 13.3 | 16.2 | 7.4 | **10.0** | 11.5 | 18.7 |
| Canandaigua National Bank and Trust Co. | Canandaigua | NY | **B+** | B | B | 2998.7 | 5.28 | 9.0 | 19.7 | 20.2 | 12.4 | **7.9** | 9.7 | 13.3 |
| Canandaigua National Trust Co. of Florida | Sarasota | FL | **U** | U | U | 4.0 | 7.84 | 0.0 | 0.0 | 0.0 | 12.9 | **10.0** | 92.1 | 366.7 |
| Canton Co-operative Bank | Canton | MA | **B-** | C+ | C+ | 124.8 | 5.65 | 0.0 | 0.0 | 38.9 | 18.1 | **10.0** | 15.7 | 28.2 |
| Canton State Bank | Canton | MO | **C-** | C- | D+ | 35.5 | 8.00 | 3.9 | 1.7 | 30.0 | 31.4 | **6.6** | 8.6 | 14.8 |
| Canyon Community Bank, N.A. | Tucson | AZ | **D** | D | D+ | 95.0 | 0.15 | 15.7 | 0.0 | 1.5 | 12.8 | **10.0** | 12.1 | 35.4 |
| Cape Ann Savings Bank | Gloucester | MA | **A-** | B+ | B | 683.0 | 8.22 | 2.1 | 0.2 | 41.9 | 15.5 | **10.0** | 24.4 | 40.7 |
| Cape Cod Five Cents Savings Bank | Orleans | MA | **B-** | B- | B- | 3658.4 | 6.78 | 3.0 | 0.7 | 54.4 | 10.0 | **8.1** | 9.7 | 15.5 |
| Capital Bank | Houston | TX | **B-** | B- | B- | 466.6 | 9.15 | 6.1 | 1.4 | 8.9 | 12.0 | **6.5** | 9.1 | 12.1 |
| Capital Bank and Trust Co. | Irvine | CA | **U** | U | U | 194.3 | 5.60 | 0.0 | 0.0 | 0.0 | 64.2 | **10.0** | 51.1 | 136.7 |
| Capital Bank of Texas | Carrizo Springs | TX | **B+** | B | B | 81.8 | 7.85 | 0.4 | 0.7 | 5.7 | 15.5 | **10.0** | 12.2 | 52.5 |
| Capital Bank, N.A. | Rockville | MD | **B** | B | B | 1396.9 | 30.01 | 10.8 | 3.3 | 24.4 | 4.4 | **6.3** | 8.7 | 12.0 |
| ▲ Capital City Bank | Tallahassee | FL | **B+** | B | C+ | 3080.9 | 4.72 | 6.1 | 9.1 | 11.0 | 20.7 | **9.4** | 10.6 | 16.9 |

| Asset Quality Index | Adjusted Non-Performing Loans as a % of Total Loans | Adjusted Non-Performing Loans as a % of Capital | Net Charge-Offs Avg Loans | Profitability Index | Net Income ($Mil) | Return on Assets (R.O.A.) | Return on Equity (R.O.E.) | Net Interest Spread | Overhead Efficiency Ratio | Liquidity Index | Liquidity Ratio | Hot Money Ratio | Stability Index |
|---|---|---|---|---|---|---|---|---|---|---|---|---|---|
| 9.5 | 0.20 | 0.9 | 0.00 | 3.9 | 0.4 | 0.77 | 4.11 | 3.40 | 74.5 | 3.0 | 32.0 | 13.9 | 7.3 |
| 10.0 | na | 0.0 | na | 10.0 | 2.3 | 23.03 | 34.19 | 2.11 | 78.5 | 4.0 | 152.9 | 0.0 | 6.5 |
| 10.0 | na | 0.0 | na | 9.5 | 2.3 | 16.70 | 26.96 | 2.15 | 86.3 | 4.0 | 139.2 | 0.0 | 6.7 |
| 8.4 | 0.00 | 0.0 | 0.00 | 4.7 | 3.3 | 0.95 | 7.79 | 3.50 | 69.6 | 2.4 | 10.9 | 14.7 | 7.4 |
| 5.6 | 1.10 | 4.6 | 0.02 | 3.6 | 1.3 | 0.60 | 4.18 | 3.98 | 80.6 | 1.2 | 13.7 | 28.1 | 7.1 |
| 3.2 | 1.53 | 12.3 | 0.29 | 9.2 | 2.8 | 2.16 | 22.63 | 4.16 | 41.8 | 0.7 | 14.2 | 38.5 | 8.1 |
| 8.5 | 0.49 | 2.7 | 0.04 | 6.3 | 24.6 | 1.45 | 14.23 | 3.60 | 60.2 | 3.7 | 29.1 | 15.8 | 9.0 |
| 8.0 | 0.35 | 1.5 | 1.86 | 5.2 | 0.4 | 1.23 | 10.70 | 5.71 | 57.9 | 5.0 | 36.3 | 8.3 | 6.5 |
| 6.5 | 0.42 | 2.0 | 0.15 | 6.0 | 54.7 | 1.17 | 8.80 | 3.73 | 65.3 | 3.3 | 20.0 | 6.5 | 9.3 |
| 5.0 | 0.99 | 5.4 | 0.02 | 6.5 | 7.0 | 1.32 | 9.45 | 4.09 | 58.3 | 0.9 | 6.2 | 27.5 | 9.1 |
| 5.8 | 2.03 | 10.2 | 0.34 | 7.1 | 29.1 | 1.61 | 11.88 | 3.44 | 35.8 | 0.8 | 14.5 | 39.7 | 9.2 |
| 7.7 | 0.50 | 2.3 | 0.02 | 6.1 | 2.1 | 1.22 | 9.51 | 4.19 | 65.3 | 1.4 | 11.1 | 16.9 | 7.5 |
| 5.1 | 0.66 | 3.4 | 0.55 | 0.0 | -1.4 | -1.32 | -10.39 | 3.23 | 132.8 | 0.9 | 21.5 | 35.2 | 4.5 |
| 6.5 | 0.53 | 8.4 | 0.62 | 8.3 | 1.4 | 1.78 | 10.18 | 4.14 | 51.3 | 4.2 | 35.7 | 12.7 | 9.8 |
| 7.4 | 0.00 | 0.0 | -0.01 | 3.8 | 0.4 | 1.00 | 8.13 | 3.38 | 63.8 | 5.5 | 41.5 | 7.2 | 5.4 |
| 6.5 | 1.15 | 3.8 | 0.12 | 6.4 | 2.6 | 1.28 | 9.27 | 4.30 | 63.8 | 4.3 | 28.9 | 9.5 | 7.7 |
| 8.4 | 0.09 | 0.5 | 0.01 | 4.8 | 1.2 | 0.96 | 9.09 | 4.09 | 75.6 | 3.0 | 21.1 | 14.9 | 6.8 |
| 6.3 | 0.88 | 3.8 | -0.03 | 3.1 | 17.0 | 0.58 | 4.78 | 3.34 | 81.0 | 3.8 | 13.7 | 10.4 | 9.9 |
| 9.0 | 0.00 | 0.0 | 0.00 | 6.4 | 2.2 | 1.59 | 15.10 | 4.27 | 62.1 | 2.3 | 23.4 | 18.6 | 6.4 |
| 9.3 | 0.02 | 0.1 | 0.00 | 6.6 | 1.2 | 1.80 | 14.95 | 2.77 | 45.3 | 4.0 | 71.5 | 21.0 | 6.9 |
| 6.3 | 0.49 | 2.2 | 0.12 | 8.0 | 121.6 | 1.48 | 10.46 | 4.01 | 59.4 | 3.8 | 17.8 | 10.8 | 10.0 |
| 5.8 | 2.88 | 8.4 | -0.20 | 2.9 | 0.4 | 0.34 | 2.60 | 3.12 | 86.7 | 1.6 | 36.5 | 40.9 | 6.0 |
| 5.1 | 0.71 | 5.9 | 0.01 | 7.4 | 1.0 | 2.30 | 18.13 | 4.10 | 57.0 | 1.3 | 30.4 | 17.7 | 6.8 |
| 4.4 | 0.99 | 7.0 | 0.37 | 6.0 | 60.4 | 1.14 | 8.32 | 4.55 | 63.2 | 2.2 | 15.5 | 15.9 | 9.1 |
| 4.0 | 2.52 | 11.6 | 0.17 | 5.2 | 3.3 | 1.26 | 11.83 | 3.23 | 66.6 | 1.5 | 16.5 | 24.8 | 6.9 |
| 7.5 | 0.00 | 0.0 | 1.12 | 5.0 | 2.1 | 0.62 | 4.65 | 4.01 | 61.4 | 2.7 | 23.5 | 5.7 | 8.3 |
| 8.4 | 1.52 | 3.4 | 0.00 | 2.4 | 0.3 | 0.24 | 2.14 | 3.23 | 89.8 | 4.3 | 49.8 | 15.9 | 5.8 |
| 4.4 | 2.05 | 8.2 | 0.21 | 10.0 | 26.2 | 1.95 | 17.26 | 5.04 | 46.6 | 3.5 | 22.2 | 13.8 | 10.0 |
| 5.0 | 0.98 | 5.4 | 0.62 | 7.1 | 224.9 | 1.27 | 9.16 | 4.10 | 49.7 | 3.5 | 18.1 | 10.7 | 9.6 |
| 3.5 | 2.17 | 21.5 | 0.70 | 4.0 | 1.2 | 0.78 | 6.90 | 4.84 | 76.3 | 0.7 | 15.2 | 50.2 | 5.2 |
| 4.5 | 0.50 | 4.8 | 0.04 | 4.0 | 1.0 | 0.63 | 6.46 | 4.22 | 78.2 | 1.8 | 12.5 | 19.7 | 6.4 |
| 6.1 | 0.36 | 2.2 | 0.23 | 4.3 | 7.4 | 0.70 | 5.94 | 4.10 | 72.4 | 3.5 | 13.2 | 11.6 | 8.9 |
| 6.5 | 0.00 | 0.0 | 0.00 | 0.0 | -0.9 | -1.04 | -6.79 | 3.64 | 125.4 | 3.5 | 21.8 | 12.1 | 5.9 |
| 9.2 | 0.00 | 0.0 | 0.24 | 10.0 | 5.1 | 2.95 | 7.00 | 5.02 | 44.8 | 3.5 | 67.2 | 30.8 | 9.3 |
| 7.5 | 0.00 | 0.0 | -0.04 | 0.0 | -1.0 | -2.31 | -7.64 | 4.89 | 137.0 | 1.6 | 33.3 | 34.4 | 5.4 |
| 5.4 | 3.85 | 6.1 | 0.00 | 10.0 | 1.8 | 2.32 | 5.50 | 6.07 | 50.5 | 3.3 | 45.9 | 16.4 | 9.2 |
| 5.3 | 1.02 | 6.2 | 0.05 | 3.9 | 2.6 | 0.69 | 7.06 | 3.83 | 78.7 | 2.7 | 4.7 | 12.6 | 5.5 |
| 7.2 | 0.00 | 0.0 | 1.22 | 2.8 | 0.6 | 0.06 | 0.57 | 4.76 | 72.8 | 1.3 | 12.8 | 13.5 | 7.8 |
| 7.9 | 0.70 | 3.0 | 0.01 | 8.1 | 8.3 | 1.57 | 9.78 | 4.03 | 50.2 | 5.5 | 32.3 | 3.6 | 9.4 |
| 7.4 | 0.10 | 0.4 | -0.05 | 4.9 | 6.8 | 3.06 | 30.66 | 4.02 | 83.3 | 4.7 | 16.4 | 2.5 | 6.7 |
| 5.5 | 0.71 | 4.9 | 0.01 | 4.5 | 38.9 | 0.97 | 9.62 | 3.25 | 63.8 | 2.4 | 12.2 | 13.4 | 8.1 |
| 8.9 | 0.47 | 1.1 | -0.01 | 3.7 | 0.6 | 0.82 | 7.06 | 3.69 | 76.6 | 6.2 | 49.0 | 4.0 | 5.3 |
| 8.6 | 0.20 | 1.9 | 0.08 | 5.1 | 25.4 | 0.98 | 11.78 | 3.27 | 67.8 | 4.7 | 17.9 | 5.2 | 7.6 |
| 7.8 | 0.36 | 1.7 | 0.08 | 6.5 | 59.5 | 1.35 | 12.02 | 3.24 | 55.0 | 3.4 | 7.7 | 9.2 | 9.6 |
| 4.7 | 3.94 | 10.0 | 1.80 | 1.0 | 0.0 | -0.06 | -0.46 | 3.11 | 76.8 | 1.3 | 39.6 | 32.7 | 3.8 |
| 9.0 | 0.00 | 0.1 | 0.01 | 3.9 | 2.4 | 0.76 | 7.94 | 3.04 | 69.9 | 4.4 | 25.3 | 7.4 | 5.5 |
| 2.2 | 3.20 | 15.9 | 0.03 | 9.6 | 2.4 | 1.97 | 11.91 | 4.64 | 54.4 | 1.5 | 15.6 | 12.6 | 9.5 |
| 6.0 | 0.50 | 6.0 | 0.00 | 3.1 | 0.1 | 0.42 | 3.64 | 3.79 | 88.1 | 2.2 | 35.4 | 20.8 | 5.2 |
| 6.2 | 0.44 | 3.6 | 0.29 | 7.1 | 41.0 | 1.40 | 14.45 | 3.65 | 60.2 | 2.7 | 5.2 | 14.9 | 8.5 |
| 10.0 | na | 0.0 | na | 0.0 | -0.1 | -1.59 | -1.62 | 0.64 | 103.4 | 4.0 | na | 0.0 | 7.0 |
| 6.4 | 4.29 | 12.5 | 0.00 | 3.2 | 0.7 | 0.56 | 3.62 | 3.41 | 78.1 | 4.1 | 43.9 | 15.6 | 7.6 |
| 6.3 | 0.93 | 6.3 | -0.08 | 2.8 | 0.2 | 0.48 | 4.77 | 3.69 | 88.1 | 4.8 | 28.7 | 6.2 | 4.8 |
| 9.1 | 0.00 | 0.0 | -0.01 | 0.3 | -0.3 | -0.35 | -2.90 | 2.86 | 114.4 | 6.3 | 45.3 | 1.7 | 6.4 |
| 8.2 | 1.36 | 3.4 | 0.00 | 7.5 | 12.6 | 1.95 | 8.15 | 2.73 | 69.8 | 2.4 | 42.2 | 30.8 | 9.2 |
| 7.7 | 0.57 | 4.2 | -0.01 | 3.9 | 26.9 | 0.76 | 7.92 | 3.14 | 74.0 | 2.3 | 12.3 | 17.1 | 7.4 |
| 5.5 | 0.66 | 5.4 | 0.15 | 6.0 | 5.2 | 1.16 | 12.74 | 4.30 | 64.8 | 1.3 | 18.6 | 28.4 | 6.0 |
| 10.0 | na | 0.0 | na | 9.5 | 44.7 | 23.14 | 36.45 | 2.50 | 78.1 | 9.2 | 143.2 | 0.0 | 6.7 |
| 9.4 | 0.00 | 0.0 | 0.00 | 4.8 | 0.9 | 1.07 | 8.17 | 2.91 | 61.1 | 6.7 | 67.4 | 4.8 | 7.3 |
| 7.0 | 0.34 | 3.6 | 0.07 | 7.3 | 16.1 | 1.36 | 15.84 | 5.66 | 73.1 | 1.4 | 13.6 | 19.7 | 7.4 |
| 5.7 | 1.13 | 3.4 | 0.13 | 5.5 | 33.2 | 1.12 | 9.48 | 3.94 | 71.1 | 5.8 | 24.2 | 1.1 | 8.9 |

| Name | City | State | Rating | 2018 Rating | 2017 Rating | Total Assets ($Mil) | One Year Asset Growth | Asset Mix (As a % of Total Assets) Commercial Loans | Consumer Loans | Mortgage Loans | Securities | Capitalization Index | Leverage Ratio | Risk-Based Capital Ratio |
|---|---|---|---|---|---|---|---|---|---|---|---|---|---|---|
| ▲ Capital Community Bank | Provo | UT | B- | C+ | B | 415.7 | -1.09 | 6.5 | 30.1 | 1.0 | 3.5 | 9.5 | 10.7 | 14.5 |
| Capital One Bank (USA), N.A. | Glen Allen | VA | B- | B- | C+ | 124626.7 | 3.50 | 7.1 | 77.6 | 0.0 | 12.0 | 10.0 | 14.8 | 18.1 |
| Capital One, N.A. | McLean | VA | B- | B- | C+ | 328999.0 | 7.99 | 8.6 | 25.2 | 0.1 | 19.3 | 7.4 | 9.2 | 14.5 |
| Capitol Bank | Madison | WI | A- | B+ | B- | 399.7 | 8.55 | 14.0 | 0.1 | 8.4 | 14.8 | 9.6 | 12.3 | 14.7 |
| Capitol Federal Savings Bank | Topeka | KS | B | B | B | 9255.7 | -0.70 | 0.6 | 0.1 | 71.2 | 13.3 | 10.0 | 12.5 | 24.3 |
| Capitol National Bank | Lansing | MI | B- | C | D+ | 119.6 | 8.65 | 9.9 | 0.2 | 3.6 | 0.8 | 10.0 | 12.6 | 18.6 |
| ▲ Capon Valley Bank | Wardensville | WV | B | B- | B | 158.4 | 3.09 | 7.8 | 9.8 | 39.9 | 4.4 | 10.0 | 11.1 | 16.1 |
| ▲ CapStar Bank | Nashville | TN | B+ | B- | C | 2036.6 | 3.73 | 19.4 | 1.4 | 7.9 | 10.6 | 7.2 | 10.7 | 12.7 |
| Captex Bank, N.A. | Trenton | TX | D | D | D+ | 184.4 | 5.25 | 4.2 | 9.7 | 12.6 | 16.1 | 10.0 | 12.1 | 17.6 |
| Carmine State Bank | Carmine | TX | B | B | B | 82.0 | 5.02 | 2.3 | 6.8 | 11.9 | 34.7 | 10.0 | 12.5 | 43.3 |
| ▲ Carolina Bank & Trust Co. | Florence | SC | A- | B+ | B+ | 490.5 | 3.22 | 7.8 | 1.5 | 18.8 | 7.4 | 10.0 | 13.2 | 21.0 |
| ▲ Carroll Bank and Trust | Huntingdon | TN | B | B- | B- | 306.7 | 7.54 | 6.7 | 5.9 | 29.0 | 8.2 | 8.7 | 10.2 | 15.1 |
| ▲ Carroll Community Bank | Eldersburg | MD | C- | C- | C- | 184.0 | -6.24 | 2.9 | 0.1 | 25.0 | 8.0 | 7.7 | 9.5 | 13.1 |
| Carroll County Trust Co. | Carrollton | MO | C | C | C+ | 159.6 | -0.93 | 3.5 | 1.9 | 5.7 | 42.7 | 6.6 | 10.8 | 12.2 |
| Carrollton Bank | Carrollton | IL | B- | B- | C+ | 1996.8 | 21.93 | 25.3 | 0.4 | 13.6 | 9.5 | 5.3 | 8.1 | 11.2 |
| Carrollton Federal Bank | Carrollton | KY | C+ | C+ | B- | 32.0 | 0.10 | 0.2 | 3.9 | 49.2 | 5.8 | 10.0 | 16.3 | 28.2 |
| Carson Bank | Mulvane | KS | C+ | C+ | C- | 122.5 | 2.21 | 9.4 | 1.7 | 17.0 | 16.6 | 6.1 | 8.1 | 12.2 |
| Carter Bank & Trust | Martinsville | VA | C | D+ | D | 4006.1 | -0.83 | 6.4 | 1.8 | 12.0 | 18.5 | 9.1 | 10.4 | 14.8 |
| Carthage Federal S&L Assn. | Carthage | NY | B | B | B | 245.4 | 6.72 | 0.0 | 2.4 | 56.0 | 10.6 | 10.0 | 11.6 | 27.8 |
| Carver Federal Savings Bank | New York | NY | D | D | D- | 572.0 | -3.42 | 1.7 | 0.6 | 21.4 | 14.2 | 10.0 | 11.3 | 17.1 |
| ▲ Carver State Bank | Savannah | GA | C | C- | D+ | 42.4 | 7.18 | 19.0 | 6.4 | 21.5 | 7.2 | 10.0 | 11.0 | 16.6 |
| ▲ Casey County Bank, Inc. | Liberty | KY | B+ | B- | B | 196.9 | 4.94 | 5.6 | 6.5 | 24.6 | 21.1 | 10.0 | 12.2 | 19.0 |
| Casey State Bank | Casey | IL | B- | B | B+ | 328.0 | 6.48 | 17.9 | 6.3 | 9.9 | 16.6 | 8.7 | 10.5 | 13.9 |
| Cashmere Valley Bank | Cashmere | WA | A | A- | A- | 1651.5 | 8.60 | 3.7 | 12.8 | 7.6 | 32.8 | 10.0 | 11.7 | 19.9 |
| ▲ Cass Commercial Bank | Saint Louis | MO | A | B+ | A | 915.3 | 3.28 | 30.2 | 0.0 | 0.0 | 0.0 | 10.0 | 16.6 | 19.3 |
| Castle Rock Bank | Castle Rock | MN | A- | B+ | B+ | 203.2 | -1.34 | 10.4 | 4.1 | 11.6 | 51.2 | 10.0 | 15.5 | 29.9 |
| Castroville State Bank | Castroville | TX | B | B- | B | 181.5 | 15.16 | 4.8 | 5.1 | 26.5 | 25.2 | 7.6 | 9.4 | 15.3 |
| Cathay Bank | Los Angeles | CA | A- | A- | B+ | 18066.5 | 7.77 | 14.7 | 0.0 | 27.2 | 8.0 | 8.6 | 11.2 | 13.8 |
| Catlin Bank | Catlin | IL | B- | C+ | C+ | 62.8 | 11.36 | 9.1 | 1.5 | 31.6 | 18.4 | 8.6 | 10.0 | 18.8 |
| Catskill Hudson Bank | Kingston | NY | C | C | C- | 503.1 | 8.42 | 6.4 | 0.3 | 5.6 | 26.0 | 5.2 | 7.2 | 12.0 |
| Cattaraugus County Bank | Little Valley | NY | B- | C+ | C+ | 251.7 | 2.04 | 10.9 | 1.0 | 17.5 | 10.7 | 7.1 | 9.0 | 12.5 |
| Cattle Bank & Trust | Seward | NE | A- | B+ | A- | 289.2 | 2.98 | 4.2 | 0.8 | 20.4 | 16.7 | 10.0 | 13.1 | 17.5 |
| ▼ Cayuga Lake National Bank | Union Springs | NY | B- | B | B | 155.7 | 6.06 | 5.8 | 2.8 | 32.9 | 39.1 | 7.5 | 9.3 | 20.5 |
| CB&S Bank, Inc. | Russellville | AL | B | B | B- | 1898.8 | 14.69 | 6.1 | 1.6 | 10.2 | 39.5 | 9.8 | 10.8 | 17.0 |
| CBank | Cincinnati | OH | B | B- | B | 217.1 | 10.74 | 16.9 | 1.4 | 8.7 | 4.4 | 8.8 | 11.5 | 14.0 |
| CBBC Bank | Maryville | TN | B | B | B | 357.1 | 2.86 | 3.1 | 0.5 | 6.9 | 31.7 | 10.0 | 15.5 | 23.3 |
| CBC Bank | Bowling Green | MO | C | C- | D+ | 36.8 | 0.76 | 4.4 | 1.6 | 8.8 | 40.5 | 6.9 | 8.9 | 30.8 |
| CBI Bank & Trust | Muscatine | IA | B+ | B- | B+ | 526.1 | 0.93 | 11.1 | 1.8 | 14.1 | 20.5 | 8.2 | 9.8 | 14.3 |
| CBW Bank | Weir | KS | A | A- | A- | 86.9 | 67.30 | 1.9 | 4.7 | 0.6 | 5.0 | 10.0 | 17.1 | 173.0 |
| ▲ CCB Community Bank | Andalusia | AL | A- | A- | B+ | 496.4 | -0.95 | 7.8 | 1.4 | 16.9 | 6.0 | 9.6 | 11.4 | 14.6 |
| Cecil Bank | Elkton | MD | E- | E- | E- | 179.3 | -8.33 | 13.8 | 0.1 | 13.6 | 15.7 | 4.3 | 6.3 | 14.3 |
| Cecilian Bank | Cecilia | KY | B+ | B- | B- | 935.9 | 6.88 | 4.9 | 4.4 | 18.8 | 23.4 | 8.8 | 10.2 | 15.2 |
| Cedar Hill National Bank | Charlotte | NC | U | U | U | 13.1 | 6.80 | 0.0 | 0.0 | 0.0 | 80.2 | 10.0 | 84.2 | 132.1 |
| Cedar Rapids Bank and Trust Co. | Cedar Rapids | IA | B+ | B+ | B+ | 1575.3 | 14.11 | 26.9 | 0.5 | 5.8 | 12.5 | 6.2 | 10.4 | 11.9 |
| ▲ Cedar Rapids State Bank | Cedar Rapids | NE | C- | C- | C- | 49.4 | 1.25 | 12.0 | 3.1 | 10.1 | 6.0 | 5.3 | 8.6 | 11.2 |
| Cedar Security Bank | Fordyce | NE | B- | C+ | D+ | 48.4 | 2.80 | 9.3 | 2.8 | 12.5 | 5.1 | 10.0 | 15.4 | 18.7 |
| ▲ Cedar Valley Bank & Trust | La Porte City | IA | C+ | C | C+ | 71.7 | -2.29 | 7.0 | 4.6 | 24.8 | 17.0 | 6.5 | 8.5 | 12.3 |
| CedarStone Bank | Lebanon | TN | B | B | B | 206.9 | 2.31 | 6.3 | 3.1 | 31.2 | 16.6 | 9.4 | 10.6 | 15.7 |
| ▲ Celtic Bank | Salt Lake City | UT | B+ | B- | B | 973.0 | 16.04 | 45.5 | 2.8 | 0.5 | 0.6 | 10.0 | 19.8 | 22.0 |
| CenBank | Buffalo Lake | MN | B | B- | B | 67.2 | -3.86 | 6.4 | 5.6 | 1.9 | 22.9 | 5.2 | 8.0 | 11.1 |
| Cendera Bank, N.A. | Bells | TX | B+ | B | B- | 108.8 | 12.21 | 6.8 | 1.2 | 39.6 | 2.7 | 10.0 | 12.3 | 18.4 |
| Cenlar FSB | Ewing | NJ | A- | A- | A | 1167.2 | 2.80 | 0.0 | 0.0 | 39.8 | 44.8 | 7.3 | 9.2 | 22.2 |
| ▲ Centennial Bank | Conway | AR | A- | B+ | B | 15015.8 | -1.80 | 10.2 | 3.4 | 10.5 | 13.9 | 10.0 | 12.5 | 15.3 |
| Centennial Bank | Trezevant | TN | B- | C+ | B- | 587.2 | 26.71 | 11.1 | 5.1 | 16.4 | 9.2 | 8.4 | 10.4 | 13.7 |
| Centennial Bank | Lubbock | TX | B | B+ | A- | 786.6 | -2.11 | 6.8 | 0.9 | 13.3 | 14.0 | 9.4 | 10.9 | 14.5 |
| Center National Bank | Litchfield | MN | A- | A- | A- | 194.7 | -1.22 | 9.0 | 6.0 | 7.3 | 33.5 | 10.0 | 11.8 | 16.4 |
| Center Point Bank and Trust Co. | Center Point | IA | B | B- | B- | 34.5 | 0.61 | 4.5 | 3.2 | 23.5 | 29.6 | 6.2 | 8.2 | 12.9 |
| Centera Bank | Sublette | KS | B- | B | B | 273.1 | 0.22 | 4.8 | 1.0 | 6.2 | 45.4 | 7.1 | 9.0 | 16.9 |
| CenterBank | Milford | OH | B | B- | B | 224.8 | 23.82 | 20.4 | 0.1 | 19.4 | 4.8 | 7.5 | 9.8 | 12.9 |
| CenterState Bank, N.A. | Winter Haven | FL | B+ | B+ | B | 17136.3 | 39.02 | 7.1 | 1.5 | 11.7 | 12.2 | 6.6 | 10.2 | 12.2 |

| Asset Quality Index | Adjusted Non-Performing Loans as a % of Total Loans | Adjusted Non-Performing Loans as a % of Capital | Net Charge-Offs Avg Loans | Profitability Index | Net Income ($Mil) | Return on Assets (R.O.A.) | Return on Equity (R.O.E.) | Net Interest Spread | Overhead Efficiency Ratio | Liquidity Index | Liquidity Ratio | Hot Money Ratio | Stability Index |
|---|---|---|---|---|---|---|---|---|---|---|---|---|---|
| **5.8** | 0.18 | 1.1 | 1.69 | **6.2** | 5.4 | 1.19 | 11.70 | 5.72 | 44.6 | **0.7** | 18.9 | 55.2 | **6.8** |
| **2.3** | 0.58 | 9.9 | 4.80 | **10.0** | 3312.1 | 2.79 | 19.21 | 11.37 | 47.8 | **0.5** | 16.3 | 76.4 | **8.1** |
| **4.7** | 0.93 | 3.9 | 1.00 | **4.3** | 2548.7 | 0.81 | 6.07 | 3.72 | 72.0 | **5.8** | 43.8 | 6.8 | **8.0** |
| **7.5** | 0.03 | 0.2 | -0.04 | **6.7** | 4.9 | 1.29 | 10.78 | 3.67 | 55.1 | **1.9** | 22.4 | 18.1 | **7.7** |
| **9.8** | 0.10 | 0.6 | 0.00 | **4.6** | 92.0 | 0.97 | 7.74 | 2.24 | 47.9 | **1.5** | 11.1 | 24.4 | **9.7** |
| **3.6** | 3.70 | 11.5 | -0.12 | **5.0** | 1.0 | 0.89 | 6.84 | 4.73 | 75.8 | **4.4** | 23.3 | 5.2 | **7.5** |
| **4.3** | 2.17 | 9.7 | 0.42 | **3.9** | 0.9 | 0.59 | 5.25 | 4.67 | 80.8 | **1.8** | 9.9 | 19.3 | **6.2** |
| **7.7** | 0.28 | 1.1 | 0.02 | **5.4** | 23.2 | 1.16 | 9.39 | 3.65 | 66.1 | **2.6** | 14.0 | 13.2 | **7.8** |
| **6.9** | 0.38 | 1.7 | -0.07 | **0.1** | -1.2 | -0.63 | -4.36 | 4.23 | 107.9 | **2.6** | 17.9 | 16.4 | **5.9** |
| **9.1** | 0.00 | 1.2 | 0.03 | **3.8** | 0.7 | 0.88 | 6.94 | 2.85 | 68.4 | **3.2** | 81.3 | 43.3 | **7.2** |
| **6.1** | 1.44 | 6.1 | 0.14 | **6.3** | 6.0 | 1.25 | 9.76 | 3.89 | 58.8 | **4.3** | 26.6 | 8.7 | **7.7** |
| **5.2** | 0.90 | 4.9 | 0.05 | **4.7** | 2.3 | 0.80 | 7.73 | 4.51 | 75.0 | **1.5** | 14.2 | 23.8 | **5.7** |
| **3.8** | 1.15 | 8.3 | 0.02 | **2.0** | 0.3 | 0.18 | 1.95 | 3.18 | 94.4 | **0.6** | 5.5 | 28.6 | **5.0** |
| **3.1** | 3.24 | 16.2 | -0.04 | **2.9** | 0.8 | 0.53 | 4.97 | 3.05 | 80.0 | **3.1** | 33.5 | 13.1 | **5.9** |
| **8.3** | 0.10 | 0.8 | 0.06 | **4.8** | 20.2 | 1.11 | 13.56 | 3.18 | 67.9 | **2.7** | 20.0 | 16.4 | **7.7** |
| **5.3** | 4.92 | 14.1 | 0.20 | **2.9** | 0.1 | 0.38 | 2.33 | 4.14 | 84.9 | **2.7** | 17.1 | 15.5 | **6.7** |
| **7.4** | 0.10 | 0.8 | 0.22 | **3.8** | 1.0 | 0.85 | 10.58 | 3.90 | 78.5 | **1.7** | 19.1 | 22.7 | **4.2** |
| **4.1** | 1.47 | 8.3 | 0.13 | **2.8** | 26.6 | 0.65 | 5.77 | 3.03 | 76.3 | **1.9** | 20.3 | 22.4 | **7.7** |
| **9.5** | 0.60 | 2.6 | 0.06 | **3.7** | 1.5 | 0.63 | 5.58 | 2.86 | 72.1 | **1.1** | 20.7 | 31.9 | **6.9** |
| **2.8** | 2.24 | 12.3 | 0.05 | **0.4** | -4.2 | -0.72 | -6.45 | 3.16 | 119.3 | **0.8** | 19.7 | 26.8 | **6.3** |
| **3.2** | 3.04 | 14.6 | 1.10 | **3.9** | 0.3 | 0.62 | 5.79 | 5.26 | 82.0 | **0.9** | 25.2 | 25.7 | **4.4** |
| **5.3** | 1.60 | 6.7 | 0.16 | **6.7** | 2.8 | 1.41 | 11.50 | 4.40 | 59.3 | **2.9** | 12.4 | 14.5 | **7.1** |
| **2.7** | 2.41 | 15.8 | 0.08 | **5.4** | 4.1 | 1.29 | 12.22 | 3.87 | 59.9 | **1.5** | 12.1 | 24.1 | **6.9** |
| **7.0** | 1.42 | 3.2 | 0.08 | **6.5** | 23.4 | 1.49 | 11.54 | 3.29 | 57.3 | **5.6** | 43.1 | 10.2 | **10.0** |
| **7.2** | 0.00 | 0.0 | -0.01 | **9.8** | 15.6 | 1.86 | 11.53 | 3.81 | 43.2 | **1.7** | 24.3 | 8.7 | **10.0** |
| **8.0** | 1.14 | 3.6 | 0.29 | **5.6** | 2.9 | 1.44 | 9.41 | 3.05 | 44.1 | **3.7** | 54.1 | 20.4 | **8.1** |
| **6.3** | 0.60 | 3.3 | 0.06 | **5.7** | 1.9 | 1.11 | 11.87 | 3.56 | 57.3 | **1.3** | 19.1 | 28.3 | **5.8** |
| **7.1** | 0.49 | 2.6 | -0.05 | **8.9** | 284.1 | 1.64 | 12.19 | 3.59 | 43.9 | **0.7** | 12.8 | 36.6 | **10.0** |
| **6.1** | 0.70 | 3.0 | 0.49 | **4.7** | 0.6 | 0.96 | 9.54 | 4.20 | 73.2 | **2.8** | 15.8 | 15.3 | **5.0** |
| **4.5** | 1.15 | 6.2 | 0.19 | **3.2** | 2.6 | 0.54 | 7.13 | 3.20 | 80.5 | **1.8** | 12.1 | 19.6 | **3.7** |
| **5.1** | 1.01 | 6.0 | 0.30 | **4.2** | 1.8 | 0.73 | 8.35 | 4.16 | 77.2 | **4.2** | 6.4 | 6.2 | **6.0** |
| **7.1** | 0.83 | 4.8 | -0.07 | **6.4** | 4.0 | 1.43 | 11.07 | 3.65 | 61.5 | **1.5** | 12.5 | 23.5 | **8.8** |
| **9.6** | 0.00 | 0.4 | 0.02 | **3.6** | 0.9 | 0.63 | 7.15 | 3.23 | 78.6 | **3.3** | 31.6 | 15.5 | **5.1** |
| **5.7** | 1.98 | 7.1 | 0.15 | **4.5** | 17.6 | 0.99 | 7.93 | 3.65 | 69.3 | **4.5** | 33.4 | 13.4 | **8.8** |
| **8.3** | 0.00 | 0.0 | 0.05 | **4.9** | 2.1 | 1.12 | 9.39 | 3.59 | 68.7 | **1.1** | 22.5 | 33.3 | **6.9** |
| **7.9** | 0.59 | 1.1 | 0.00 | **4.7** | 3.6 | 1.01 | 6.51 | 3.47 | 64.7 | **2.9** | 38.7 | 20.1 | **7.7** |
| **9.8** | 0.00 | 0.0 | 0.00 | **2.2** | 0.1 | 0.35 | 4.03 | 2.67 | 88.1 | **6.8** | 60.3 | 2.3 | **3.8** |
| **4.7** | 1.20 | 5.8 | 0.10 | **5.3** | 5.6 | 1.05 | 8.71 | 3.39 | 66.3 | **2.5** | 26.4 | 17.8 | **7.3** |
| **9.8** | 0.26 | 0.2 | -0.02 | **9.5** | 4.0 | 5.41 | 29.48 | 2.98 | 55.1 | **8.3** | 110.2 | 0.6 | **8.7** |
| **6.1** | 0.47 | 3.4 | 0.16 | **7.4** | 8.0 | 1.60 | 14.40 | 4.30 | 59.5 | **1.3** | 11.1 | 24.8 | **9.2** |
| **6.0** | 1.57 | 5.9 | -0.14 | **0.0** | -2.7 | -1.43 | -22.54 | 2.44 | 153.9 | **3.9** | 39.8 | 15.3 | **0.0** |
| **6.6** | 0.57 | 2.9 | -0.09 | **6.1** | 12.3 | 1.36 | 12.69 | 3.60 | 61.7 | **2.9** | 14.5 | 14.5 | **7.5** |
| **10.0** | na | 0.0 | na | **10.0** | 0.7 | 5.43 | 6.58 | 2.39 | 70.4 | **10.0** | 437.3 | 0.0 | **7.0** |
| **7.9** | 0.09 | 0.6 | 0.00 | **9.0** | 27.7 | 1.84 | 16.71 | 3.29 | 54.1 | **1.7** | 18.0 | 13.6 | **8.5** |
| **7.0** | 0.00 | 0.0 | 0.62 | **3.7** | 0.4 | 0.75 | 9.04 | 3.74 | 75.5 | **0.6** | 7.9 | 34.0 | **4.8** |
| **6.8** | 1.22 | 4.2 | 0.02 | **5.0** | 0.5 | 0.96 | 6.41 | 4.10 | 69.7 | **3.4** | 34.0 | 15.2 | **6.4** |
| **7.4** | 0.00 | 0.3 | -0.41 | **5.4** | 0.9 | 1.26 | 15.30 | 4.06 | 67.4 | **3.3** | 3.5 | 11.4 | **3.9** |
| **8.2** | 0.39 | 2.1 | 0.09 | **4.5** | 1.8 | 0.87 | 8.50 | 3.68 | 69.1 | **1.2** | 16.5 | 29.0 | **6.4** |
| **5.2** | 1.61 | 5.7 | 0.59 | **10.0** | 42.0 | 4.70 | 24.35 | 6.78 | 49.5 | **0.4** | 8.4 | 0.9 | **8.8** |
| **5.5** | 0.63 | 2.9 | -0.01 | **4.1** | 0.6 | 0.85 | 10.80 | 3.88 | 76.6 | **2.8** | 12.6 | 14.7 | **5.1** |
| **8.8** | 0.04 | 0.3 | 0.12 | **5.1** | 1.2 | 1.16 | 9.27 | 5.13 | 74.0 | **0.7** | 12.5 | 25.2 | **7.1** |
| **9.8** | 0.33 | 1.3 | 0.00 | **8.6** | 38.1 | 3.21 | 35.44 | 2.74 | 91.7 | **7.5** | 50.2 | 0.0 | **8.9** |
| **5.8** | 0.55 | 2.1 | 0.07 | **9.8** | 315.4 | 2.10 | 11.67 | 4.45 | 38.1 | **2.2** | 13.9 | 13.3 | **10.0** |
| **4.6** | 1.28 | 6.8 | 0.76 | **6.4** | 5.8 | 1.11 | 9.73 | 4.82 | 60.8 | **1.4** | 18.4 | 24.0 | **6.9** |
| **5.8** | 0.77 | 7.9 | 0.00 | **5.0** | 9.9 | 1.25 | 12.35 | 4.23 | 73.9 | **2.5** | 8.2 | 15.7 | **7.9** |
| **8.4** | 0.19 | 0.9 | 0.03 | **5.9** | 2.7 | 1.40 | 11.88 | 3.63 | 63.5 | **3.1** | 10.2 | 13.2 | **8.0** |
| **6.7** | 0.00 | 2.7 | 0.11 | **4.2** | 0.3 | 0.87 | 10.75 | 3.47 | 72.8 | **3.2** | 35.0 | 17.3 | **5.0** |
| **8.0** | 0.53 | 2.3 | 0.74 | **4.0** | 2.5 | 0.90 | 9.48 | 3.46 | 68.6 | **1.7** | 24.5 | 24.5 | **6.1** |
| **6.3** | 0.01 | 1.0 | -0.02 | **7.0** | 2.7 | 1.34 | 13.26 | 4.29 | 62.1 | **0.7** | 10.3 | 30.3 | **6.3** |
| **6.1** | 0.33 | 1.6 | 0.09 | **7.6** | 230.5 | 1.46 | 8.90 | 4.32 | 58.7 | **3.3** | 11.0 | 10.1 | **9.9** |

| Name | City | State | Rating | 2018 Rating | 2017 Rating | Total Assets ($Mil) | One Year Asset Growth | Asset Mix (As a % of Total Assets) Comm-ercial Loans | Cons-umer Loans | Mort-gage Loans | Secur-ities | Capital-ization Index | Lever-age Ratio | Risk-Based Capital Ratio |
|---|---|---|---|---|---|---|---|---|---|---|---|---|---|---|
| Centier Bank | Merrillville | IN | **B+** | B+ | A- | 4694.7 | 6.05 | 4.9 | 7.9 | 12.4 | 9.4 | **7.5** | 10.1 | 12.9 |
| Centinel Bank of Taos | Taos | NM | **A-** | B+ | A- | 279.5 | 10.39 | 2.9 | 1.0 | 16.4 | 47.3 | **6.7** | 8.7 | 23.4 |
| Central Bank | Little Rock | AR | **B** | B+ | B+ | 245.0 | 15.42 | 10.4 | 0.2 | 21.4 | 17.6 | **7.6** | 10.6 | 13.0 |
| Central Bank | Tampa | FL | **C+** | B- | B+ | 200.4 | 18.84 | 8.3 | 0.1 | 21.6 | 4.1 | **6.3** | 9.0 | 12.0 |
| ▲ Central Bank | Storm Lake | IA | **B** | C+ | C+ | 929.9 | 6.77 | 20.5 | 2.0 | 11.7 | 7.7 | **5.9** | 10.1 | 11.7 |
| Central Bank | Savannah | TN | **B** | C+ | C- | 98.6 | 4.75 | 3.6 | 4.6 | 42.8 | 12.9 | **10.0** | 12.1 | 23.6 |
| Central Bank | Houston | TX | **B+** | B+ | B+ | 776.4 | 1.95 | 11.3 | 0.4 | 29.7 | 14.4 | **8.5** | 10.0 | 14.1 |
| ▲ Central Bank | Provo | UT | **A** | B+ | A | 1195.6 | 10.00 | 5.0 | 1.2 | 4.7 | 26.1 | **10.0** | 16.3 | 23.9 |
| ▲ Central Bank & Trust Co. | Lexington | KY | **A-** | B | B- | 2762.2 | 6.25 | 9.3 | 3.9 | 15.4 | 10.0 | **10.0** | 11.6 | 15.2 |
| Central Bank and Trust | Lander | WY | **B** | B- | B | 159.1 | 5.36 | 9.2 | 1.6 | 17.0 | 32.8 | **8.3** | 9.8 | 17.7 |
| ▲ Central Bank Illinois | Geneseo | IL | **B+** | B | A- | 917.3 | 3.01 | 6.1 | 0.7 | 7.7 | 34.1 | **8.1** | 9.7 | 14.4 |
| Central Bank of Audrain County | Mexico | MO | **B** | B | B | 204.9 | 10.86 | 5.2 | 3.4 | 10.2 | 37.7 | **5.1** | 7.1 | 13.8 |
| Central Bank of Boone County | Columbia | MO | **B+** | B+ | B+ | 2221.2 | 7.49 | 5.0 | 5.1 | 10.6 | 25.3 | **6.5** | 8.5 | 13.2 |
| Central Bank of Branson | Branson | MO | **B+** | B | B- | 355.9 | 4.71 | 8.5 | 6.4 | 15.2 | 24.1 | **8.9** | 10.3 | 14.7 |
| Central Bank of Kansas City | Kansas City | MO | **A** | A | A- | 238.2 | 34.38 | 28.2 | 0.0 | 1.0 | 0.0 | **10.0** | 14.4 | 15.5 |
| Central Bank of Lake of the Ozarks | Osage Beach | MO | **B+** | B+ | B | 798.3 | 5.49 | 4.4 | 4.8 | 16.7 | 33.4 | **6.8** | 8.8 | 14.4 |
| Central Bank of Moberly | Moberly | MO | **B** | B | B- | 197.5 | 0.14 | 5.1 | 12.7 | 6.4 | 40.8 | **6.8** | 8.8 | 14.7 |
| Central Bank of Oklahoma | Tulsa | OK | **B** | B | B- | 703.9 | 0.79 | 10.7 | 0.3 | 13.6 | 4.0 | **8.1** | 12.0 | 13.4 |
| Central Bank of Sedalia | Sedalia | MO | **B+** | B+ | B | 429.0 | 6.40 | 7.9 | 16.2 | 8.1 | 22.2 | **6.4** | 8.5 | 12.7 |
| Central Bank of St. Louis | Clayton | MO | **B+** | B+ | B | 1978.8 | 1.24 | 13.0 | 1.0 | 10.8 | 10.1 | **7.1** | 10.6 | 12.6 |
| Central Bank of the Midwest | Lee's Summit | MO | **B+** | B+ | B | 2410.6 | 36.84 | 11.4 | 7.8 | 4.7 | 13.5 | **5.7** | 11.3 | 11.5 |
| Central Bank of the Ozarks | Springfield | MO | **B+** | B+ | B | 1373.9 | 6.19 | 9.9 | 12.5 | 11.9 | 18.4 | **7.2** | 9.5 | 12.6 |
| Central Bank of Warrensburg | Warrensburg | MO | **B** | B | B | 256.9 | 2.90 | 4.4 | 2.3 | 8.5 | 32.3 | **8.4** | 9.9 | 17.5 |
| Central Federal S&L Assn. | Cicero | IL | **C-** | C | C- | 188.8 | 6.47 | 0.0 | 0.0 | 58.7 | 10.4 | **8.6** | 10.1 | 20.8 |
| Central Federal S&L Assn. of Rolla | Rolla | MO | **C** | C | C- | 70.3 | 1.93 | 1.8 | 1.0 | 38.5 | 6.4 | **10.0** | 30.3 | 44.9 |
| Central National Bank | Junction City | KS | **B** | B | B- | 947.9 | -1.87 | 6.8 | 2.0 | 5.7 | 29.9 | **9.9** | 10.9 | 17.8 |
| Central National Bank | Waco | TX | **A-** | B+ | B+ | 938.7 | 6.19 | 15.8 | 0.9 | 31.7 | 7.0 | **7.5** | 9.3 | 13.4 |
| ▲ Central National Bank of Poteau | Poteau | OK | **B+** | B+ | A- | 259.8 | 4.99 | 12.6 | 3.1 | 14.7 | 29.0 | **9.3** | 10.5 | 17.6 |
| Central Pacific Bank | Honolulu | HI | **A-** | A- | A- | 6003.6 | 3.54 | 9.1 | 9.5 | 26.8 | 18.8 | **7.5** | 9.3 | 13.4 |
| ▼ Central Savings Bank | Sault Sainte Marie | MI | **B-** | B- | C+ | 261.7 | 4.50 | 8.4 | 5.9 | 20.2 | 25.3 | **10.0** | 12.5 | 20.0 |
| Central Savings, F.S.B. | Chicago | IL | **B** | B- | B+ | 107.8 | -5.44 | 0.0 | 0.0 | 30.4 | 3.4 | **10.0** | 25.5 | 33.2 |
| Central State Bank | Calera | AL | **A-** | A- | A- | 330.8 | 7.19 | 6.2 | 2.2 | 16.0 | 14.8 | **10.0** | 11.3 | 17.4 |
| Central State Bank | Elkader | IA | **B** | B | B | 331.2 | 19.79 | 11.2 | 2.1 | 15.9 | 13.9 | **6.2** | 8.5 | 11.9 |
| Central State Bank | State Center | IA | **C** | C+ | B- | 313.2 | 8.35 | 18.4 | 1.2 | 3.6 | 25.6 | **7.7** | 12.1 | 13.1 |
| ▼ Central State Bank | Clayton | IL | **C** | C+ | B- | 144.6 | 3.52 | 10.8 | 8.2 | 26.0 | 2.0 | **10.0** | 15.3 | 21.2 |
| Central Trust Bank | Jefferson City | MO | **B+** | B+ | B | 2678.3 | 3.76 | 6.2 | 7.5 | 8.7 | 45.1 | **5.4** | 7.4 | 13.9 |
| Central Valley Community Bank | Fresno | CA | **A** | A | A- | 1596.4 | 3.84 | 6.3 | 2.7 | 2.4 | 29.5 | **10.0** | 11.3 | 15.7 |
| ▲ CentreBank | Veedersburg | IN | **A-** | A- | B | 78.6 | 2.13 | 12.2 | 3.1 | 23.1 | 0.3 | **10.0** | 13.0 | 22.3 |
| ▲ Centreville Bank | West Warwick | RI | **C+** | D+ | C | 1341.8 | 10.22 | 0.5 | 0.1 | 31.2 | 22.1 | **10.0** | 24.5 | 26.6 |
| Centric Bank | Harrisburg | PA | **B+** | B+ | B- | 830.7 | 18.18 | 24.3 | 0.1 | 8.6 | 4.1 | **8.4** | 11.4 | 13.6 |
| CenTrust Bank, N.A. | Northbrook | IL | **C+** | C- | D+ | 130.5 | 5.60 | 28.0 | 0.3 | 7.5 | 10.9 | **7.8** | 9.8 | 13.2 |
| Century Bank | Shenandoah | IA | **B** | B | B+ | 109.3 | 21.03 | 2.8 | 0.9 | 2.7 | 44.0 | **7.1** | 9.0 | 15.4 |
| ▲ Century Bank | Lucedale | MS | **B-** | B- | B+ | 333.1 | 6.43 | 6.8 | 11.6 | 12.9 | 21.9 | **9.5** | 10.7 | 15.6 |
| Century Bank | Santa Fe | NM | **B+** | B | B | 908.3 | 6.91 | 18.2 | 2.3 | 4.1 | 26.5 | **7.7** | 10.2 | 13.1 |
| Century Bank and Trust | Milledgeville | GA | **B-** | B- | B+ | 254.4 | -3.53 | 3.9 | 1.2 | 13.2 | 24.5 | **10.0** | 11.6 | 17.8 |
| Century Bank and Trust | Coldwater | MI | **B** | B | B | 322.1 | 2.05 | 9.8 | 2.3 | 16.7 | 17.2 | **10.0** | 13.1 | 17.2 |
| Century Bank and Trust Co. | Medford | MA | **C+** | C+ | C+ | 5476.1 | 6.40 | 4.3 | 0.1 | 7.3 | 47.9 | **5.0** | 7.0 | 13.6 |
| Century Bank of Florida | Tampa | FL | **C+** | C | C- | 79.6 | 1.87 | 12.6 | 1.9 | 24.7 | 7.8 | **6.9** | 8.9 | 14.6 |
| Century Bank of Georgia | Cartersville | GA | **A-** | A- | A- | 201.4 | 4.46 | 6.1 | 1.4 | 11.6 | 20.3 | **8.5** | 10.0 | 18.6 |
| Century Bank of Kentucky, Inc. | Lawrenceburg | KY | **C+** | C | C+ | 138.4 | -1.08 | 2.9 | 1.4 | 37.9 | 11.7 | **8.9** | 10.3 | 17.7 |
| ▲ Century Bank of the Ozarks | Gainesville | MO | **A-** | B | B | 178.9 | -0.48 | 8.8 | 3.1 | 18.7 | 2.3 | **6.4** | 9.8 | 12.1 |
| Century Next Bank | Ruston | LA | **B** | B | B | 488.8 | 5.98 | 10.9 | 3.3 | 29.1 | 0.1 | **8.9** | 10.3 | 14.8 |
| Century S&L Assn. | Trinidad | CO | **C+** | C | C | 89.0 | -5.87 | 0.0 | 0.4 | 18.4 | 56.5 | **10.0** | 15.3 | 42.9 |
| Century Savings Bank | Vineland | NJ | **C+** | C+ | C+ | 443.6 | -0.06 | 0.9 | 0.0 | 22.2 | 39.1 | **10.0** | 15.3 | 28.4 |
| CerescoBank | Ceresco | NE | **B** | B | B+ | 51.3 | 3.76 | 10.9 | 4.6 | 14.5 | 17.5 | **10.0** | 15.8 | 20.6 |
| ▲ CFBank, N.A. | Worthington | OH | **B** | C+ | C+ | 879.2 | 32.36 | 18.2 | 0.0 | 27.4 | 0.9 | **7.6** | 10.6 | 13.0 |
| ▲ CFG Community Bank | Baltimore | MD | **C+** | C- | C+ | 1228.1 | 47.56 | 26.1 | 0.1 | 1.6 | 4.8 | **10.0** | 12.8 | 15.4 |
| cfsbank | Charleroi | PA | **C+** | C | C+ | 480.9 | -1.53 | 0.9 | 1.2 | 51.7 | 21.0 | **10.0** | 15.6 | 30.7 |
| Chain Bridge Bank, N.A. | McLean | VA | **C+** | C+ | C+ | 829.8 | 51.67 | 1.5 | 0.4 | 20.5 | 54.3 | **6.0** | 8.0 | 22.9 |
| Chambers Bank | Danville | AR | **B-** | C+ | B | 971.7 | 18.17 | 8.8 | 0.7 | 16.2 | 3.9 | **5.5** | 9.3 | 11.4 |

| Asset Quality Index | Adjusted Non-Performing Loans as a % of Total Loans | Adjusted Non-Performing Loans as a % of Capital | Net Charge-Offs Avg Loans | Profitability Index | Net Income ($Mil) | Return on Assets (R.O.A.) | Return on Equity (R.O.E.) | Net Interest Spread | Overhead Efficiency Ratio | Liquidity Index | Liquidity Ratio | Hot Money Ratio | Stability Index |
|---|---|---|---|---|---|---|---|---|---|---|---|---|---|
| **6.0** | 0.44 | 3.3 | 0.06 | **7.4** | 66.0 | 1.43 | 14.51 | 3.66 | 55.9 | **3.6** | 12.1 | 9.5 | **9.2** |
| **9.5** | 0.27 | 1.0 | 0.00 | **8.1** | 5.4 | 2.04 | 22.69 | 3.62 | 49.7 | **5.7** | 52.9 | 9.7 | **6.6** |
| **5.9** | 1.38 | 4.6 | 0.02 | **4.9** | 1.9 | 0.85 | 7.84 | 2.95 | 60.9 | **0.6** | 14.7 | 60.8 | **6.0** |
| **4.6** | 0.37 | 2.6 | 0.35 | **4.6** | 1.0 | 0.58 | 6.29 | 3.62 | 79.3 | **0.8** | 17.7 | 45.2 | **4.9** |
| **7.8** | 0.11 | 0.9 | 0.05 | **6.7** | 11.2 | 1.27 | 12.84 | 3.97 | 62.6 | **1.4** | 14.3 | 23.8 | **7.5** |
| **4.9** | 4.69 | 12.1 | 0.02 | **4.2** | 0.8 | 0.87 | 6.77 | 4.42 | 80.4 | **2.0** | 25.4 | 20.2 | **7.0** |
| **7.7** | 0.14 | 1.0 | 0.02 | **6.4** | 11.0 | 1.47 | 15.17 | 5.59 | 70.8 | **1.5** | 14.0 | 23.5 | **7.3** |
| **7.6** | 0.08 | 0.7 | -0.07 | **10.0** | 23.6 | 2.05 | 12.49 | 5.38 | 51.9 | **4.4** | 29.7 | 13.0 | **10.0** |
| **7.1** | 0.43 | 2.3 | 0.18 | **5.5** | 31.1 | 1.18 | 10.10 | 4.02 | 72.4 | **2.6** | 18.1 | 17.0 | **9.2** |
| **8.0** | 0.42 | 2.5 | 0.16 | **7.3** | 3.7 | 2.39 | 24.58 | 4.28 | 55.8 | **4.5** | 13.8 | 5.5 | **5.5** |
| **5.9** | 0.85 | 4.1 | 0.04 | **7.5** | 13.8 | 1.52 | 13.15 | 3.90 | 54.2 | **4.3** | 22.1 | 7.6 | **8.3** |
| **5.7** | 0.88 | 4.8 | 0.03 | **6.7** | 2.4 | 1.34 | 16.83 | 3.12 | 52.5 | **4.8** | 21.5 | 3.3 | **6.1** |
| **8.2** | 0.47 | 2.4 | 0.11 | **8.2** | 32.2 | 1.58 | 17.89 | 3.22 | 50.1 | **4.8** | 21.4 | 5.5 | **7.9** |
| **3.7** | 2.60 | 13.4 | 0.18 | **7.4** | 5.1 | 1.48 | 14.60 | 4.00 | 57.3 | **3.9** | 13.5 | 7.5 | **7.2** |
| **6.8** | 0.00 | 0.0 | -0.42 | **10.0** | 11.5 | 5.80 | 35.16 | 4.82 | 50.9 | **1.1** | 15.7 | 11.5 | **9.5** |
| **6.5** | 0.71 | 3.2 | 0.12 | **9.2** | 13.2 | 1.71 | 18.72 | 3.90 | 54.2 | **3.6** | 22.5 | 11.4 | **7.4** |
| **7.3** | 0.22 | 1.4 | 0.08 | **5.8** | 2.5 | 1.26 | 14.34 | 3.20 | 53.0 | **4.5** | 8.8 | 3.4 | **6.4** |
| **3.5** | 0.67 | 2.5 | 0.10 | **8.2** | 10.6 | 1.52 | 8.02 | 4.16 | 47.6 | **0.9** | 7.2 | 21.0 | **8.5** |
| **5.3** | 0.58 | 4.1 | 0.16 | **9.6** | 7.9 | 1.90 | 20.40 | 4.01 | 49.3 | **3.6** | 10.1 | 9.2 | **7.7** |
| **7.2** | 0.54 | 3.3 | 0.00 | **8.1** | 33.4 | 1.72 | 14.49 | 3.58 | 52.3 | **4.2** | 8.9 | 6.4 | **7.0** |
| **5.1** | 1.17 | 4.0 | 0.25 | **6.9** | 26.3 | 1.44 | 9.93 | 4.31 | 59.4 | **4.8** | 13.8 | 3.6 | **8.4** |
| **7.5** | 0.05 | 0.4 | 0.10 | **7.0** | 18.8 | 1.36 | 13.65 | 3.63 | 59.7 | **4.2** | 14.2 | 7.1 | **8.0** |
| **2.6** | 2.79 | 8.6 | 0.08 | **5.9** | 3.3 | 1.31 | 9.13 | 3.33 | 58.9 | **4.0** | 28.1 | 9.8 | **8.2** |
| **5.4** | 3.55 | 12.5 | -0.03 | **1.7** | 0.1 | 0.08 | 0.72 | 2.75 | 96.5 | **2.3** | 32.9 | 22.9 | **6.0** |
| **9.0** | 0.15 | 0.4 | 0.00 | **2.3** | 0.2 | 0.27 | 0.88 | 3.45 | 89.6 | **3.8** | 33.9 | 14.0 | **6.8** |
| **8.0** | 0.50 | 1.0 | 0.04 | **4.3** | 9.4 | 0.97 | 8.61 | 3.46 | 78.0 | **4.1** | 14.5 | 8.1 | **7.8** |
| **8.7** | 0.00 | 0.1 | 0.00 | **8.6** | 18.9 | 2.10 | 22.92 | 3.86 | 45.5 | **1.6** | 15.8 | 16.4 | **8.2** |
| **5.7** | 0.87 | 5.3 | 0.05 | **8.2** | 4.6 | 1.84 | 17.05 | 4.27 | 61.7 | **2.8** | 19.4 | 15.2 | **8.1** |
| **8.2** | 0.17 | 0.9 | 0.15 | **5.5** | 62.0 | 1.05 | 11.35 | 3.40 | 61.1 | **2.4** | 9.4 | 16.8 | **8.5** |
| **2.8** | 5.19 | 21.8 | 0.30 | **6.2** | 3.4 | 1.31 | 9.96 | 3.98 | 62.0 | **3.3** | 32.6 | 16.2 | **7.1** |
| **4.7** | 1.72 | 5.6 | 0.09 | **4.0** | 0.5 | 0.43 | 1.70 | 3.83 | 84.3 | **0.6** | 13.3 | 40.3 | **7.5** |
| **8.8** | 0.14 | 0.4 | 0.18 | **7.3** | 5.4 | 1.69 | 15.48 | 4.16 | 58.7 | **1.4** | 21.0 | 27.5 | **7.8** |
| **6.0** | 0.10 | 3.0 | 0.12 | **4.2** | 3.3 | 1.00 | 9.92 | 3.42 | 63.9 | **1.5** | 19.2 | 15.3 | **7.0** |
| **3.0** | 3.23 | 15.2 | 0.24 | **5.2** | 4.2 | 1.38 | 11.32 | 2.77 | 51.6 | **1.3** | 30.9 | 51.3 | **9.0** |
| **1.7** | 5.10 | 26.7 | 0.19 | **10.0** | 3.4 | 2.39 | 15.51 | 4.51 | 48.4 | **1.3** | 12.4 | 27.4 | **9.2** |
| **7.1** | 0.84 | 3.4 | 0.08 | **4.8** | 40.5 | 1.56 | 19.45 | 2.75 | 67.1 | **4.7** | 17.2 | 4.8 | **7.1** |
| **7.4** | 0.40 | 1.1 | 0.11 | **7.0** | 22.0 | 1.40 | 9.47 | 4.52 | 63.3 | **5.9** | 32.2 | 4.7 | **10.0** |
| **6.8** | 0.41 | 3.2 | -0.01 | **8.2** | 1.2 | 1.48 | 11.85 | 5.04 | 64.4 | **4.1** | 27.5 | 10.3 | **7.1** |
| **9.5** | 0.28 | 0.6 | 0.00 | **5.9** | 26.2 | 2.10 | 8.88 | 2.83 | 75.1 | **4.1** | 44.8 | 18.3 | **9.2** |
| **3.9** | 1.13 | 9.0 | 0.11 | **5.5** | 8.1 | 1.06 | 9.36 | 3.87 | 62.6 | **0.7** | 10.6 | 28.4 | **7.3** |
| **4.4** | 1.51 | 6.9 | 0.04 | **5.3** | 5.7 | 4.48 | 46.33 | 4.14 | 73.7 | **0.6** | 16.3 | 59.2 | **4.6** |
| **8.2** | 0.00 | 0.0 | 0.12 | **5.2** | 1.1 | 1.13 | 11.69 | 3.24 | 55.9 | **5.0** | 34.4 | 7.8 | **5.1** |
| **4.8** | 1.65 | 6.5 | 0.15 | **5.6** | 3.6 | 1.09 | 10.13 | 4.36 | 72.4 | **3.5** | 19.8 | 12.0 | **6.8** |
| **8.1** | 0.20 | 0.9 | 0.10 | **6.5** | 14.2 | 1.63 | 15.72 | 4.83 | 69.3 | **4.2** | 26.8 | 9.4 | **7.6** |
| **5.7** | 2.61 | 10.0 | 0.00 | **7.3** | 3.8 | 1.47 | 14.31 | 4.12 | 60.0 | **2.9** | 22.8 | 12.7 | **7.3** |
| **6.4** | 1.22 | 5.5 | 0.15 | **6.6** | 4.6 | 1.44 | 11.44 | 4.04 | 64.4 | **5.3** | 29.4 | 3.1 | **7.3** |
| **9.0** | 0.18 | 0.8 | 0.01 | **3.6** | 41.1 | 0.79 | 12.08 | 2.13 | 62.2 | **3.5** | 9.5 | 10.4 | **4.6** |
| **5.2** | 1.06 | 7.3 | -0.01 | **3.4** | 0.5 | 0.62 | 7.16 | 3.94 | 83.6 | **1.9** | 23.2 | 20.8 | **4.7** |
| **8.6** | 0.45 | 1.5 | -0.03 | **7.1** | 2.9 | 1.45 | 13.32 | 4.19 | 59.9 | **4.8** | 33.7 | 8.3 | **7.4** |
| **3.2** | 3.71 | 17.0 | 0.01 | **7.1** | 2.3 | 1.64 | 15.88 | 3.73 | 59.6 | **1.4** | 13.8 | 20.4 | **8.2** |
| **7.9** | 0.21 | 1.4 | 0.11 | **9.9** | 3.7 | 2.11 | 21.12 | 5.12 | 54.2 | **3.7** | 5.2 | 9.6 | **8.1** |
| **5.7** | 0.83 | 5.8 | 0.09 | **6.1** | 5.9 | 1.22 | 11.31 | 4.46 | 63.7 | **1.4** | 12.6 | 10.9 | **6.4** |
| **7.6** | 3.15 | 5.4 | 0.25 | **2.8** | 0.4 | 0.43 | 2.89 | 2.94 | 80.5 | **2.5** | 57.4 | 41.6 | **6.7** |
| **7.3** | 2.43 | 7.6 | 0.14 | **2.8** | 1.9 | 0.43 | 3.07 | 3.19 | 85.5 | **5.8** | 43.8 | 5.7 | **7.0** |
| **8.3** | 0.29 | 1.7 | 0.21 | **4.1** | 0.4 | 0.78 | 4.88 | 3.55 | 73.0 | **3.3** | 25.6 | 13.6 | **7.5** |
| **6.3** | 0.65 | 4.0 | -0.02 | **6.7** | 11.2 | 1.52 | 15.88 | 3.19 | 59.5 | **0.6** | 6.0 | 26.5 | **6.7** |
| **3.7** | 0.99 | 4.7 | 0.18 | **9.6** | 21.4 | 2.09 | 12.73 | 4.82 | 60.9 | **1.6** | 26.1 | 41.8 | **10.0** |
| **7.2** | 1.09 | 4.2 | 0.58 | **2.6** | 2.6 | 0.54 | 3.58 | 2.80 | 87.8 | **2.3** | 31.7 | 21.6 | **6.6** |
| **9.9** | 0.00 | 0.0 | 0.00 | **3.8** | 5.0 | 0.75 | 9.16 | 2.70 | 66.6 | **7.1** | 70.9 | 4.7 | **4.6** |
| **5.1** | 0.66 | 3.4 | 0.12 | **4.4** | 8.0 | 0.91 | 8.24 | 3.84 | 76.3 | **0.9** | 10.2 | 31.6 | **8.0** |

| Name | City | State | Rating | 2018 Rating | 2017 Rating | Total Assets ($Mil) | One Year Asset Growth | Asset Mix (As a % of Total Assets) Commercial Loans | Consumer Loans | Mortgage Loans | Securities | Capitalization Index | Leverage Ratio | Risk-Based Capital Ratio |
|---|---|---|---|---|---|---|---|---|---|---|---|---|---|---|
| Chambers State Bank | Chambers | NE | **B+** | B+ | B+ | 61.8 | 7.15 | 11.4 | 3.9 | 2.0 | 0.3 | **10.0** | 29.2 | 37.2 |
| Champion Bank | Parker | CO | **A-** | B- | C+ | 66.4 | 9.86 | 0.0 | 0.0 | 6.8 | 0.0 | **10.0** | 20.4 | 65.7 |
| Champlain National Bank | Willsboro | NY | **B-** | C+ | C+ | 362.3 | 1.41 | 6.3 | 9.4 | 19.5 | 22.0 | **7.0** | 9.0 | 14.8 |
| Chappell Hill Bank | Chappell Hill | TX | **C+** | C | C | 33.6 | 7.18 | 3.6 | 3.0 | 28.8 | 1.7 | **8.2** | 9.8 | 16.6 |
| Charis Bank | Justin | TX | **C+** | B | A- | 111.3 | 16.12 | 12.7 | 0.9 | 9.3 | 0.0 | **10.0** | 29.3 | 51.3 |
| Charles River Bank | Medway | MA | **C-** | C- | C- | 256.9 | 8.79 | 3.0 | 2.6 | 35.7 | 16.1 | **6.1** | 8.1 | 13.7 |
| Charles Schwab Bank | Henderson | NV | **B+** | B+ | B+ | 216654.0 | -7.43 | 0.5 | 1.6 | 5.6 | 82.3 | **5.1** | 7.1 | 20.8 |
| Charles Schwab Premier Bank | Henderson | NV | **U** | U | U | 14289.0 | -6.20 | 0.0 | 0.0 | 0.0 | 92.4 | **5.4** | 7.4 | 33.7 |
| Charlevoix State Bank | Charlevoix | MI | **B+** | B | B | 194.5 | 4.21 | 6.5 | 2.7 | 18.8 | 21.6 | **7.1** | 9.0 | 15.6 |
| Charlotte State Bank & Trust | Port Charlotte | FL | **A-** | A- | B+ | 381.7 | 9.58 | 0.3 | 0.3 | 21.5 | 29.3 | **8.7** | 10.1 | 20.4 |
| Charter Bank | Johnston | IA | **B+** | B+ | B+ | 166.4 | 5.04 | 5.8 | 2.5 | 19.6 | 29.0 | **10.0** | 11.5 | 19.5 |
| Charter Bank | Corpus Christi | TX | **B** | B | A- | 294.6 | 4.43 | 16.9 | 0.2 | 5.4 | 38.2 | **7.2** | 9.1 | 15.0 |
| Charter Bank | Eau Claire | WI | **A** | A | A | 938.0 | 2.65 | 12.1 | 0.6 | 14.4 | 17.0 | **10.0** | 12.7 | 16.9 |
| ▲ Charter West Bank | West Point | NE | **B** | B | B+ | 288.6 | 11.02 | 11.2 | 2.3 | 13.8 | 8.8 | **7.7** | 9.5 | 13.6 |
| Chasewood Bank | Houston | TX | **C-** | C | D | 90.4 | -20.33 | 5.4 | 0.2 | 8.9 | 24.8 | **9.8** | 10.9 | 16.4 |
| Cheaha Bank | Oxford | AL | **A** | A | A | 209.3 | 3.63 | 7.2 | 4.2 | 19.5 | 33.4 | **10.0** | 13.0 | 22.2 |
| Chelsea Groton Bank | Norwich | CT | **A-** | B | B- | 1142.8 | 2.32 | 5.4 | 0.4 | 48.8 | 11.4 | **10.0** | 16.4 | 22.2 |
| Chelsea Savings Bank | Belle Plaine | IA | **A-** | A- | A | 119.4 | 1.76 | 11.9 | 1.5 | 12.2 | 40.4 | **10.0** | 15.0 | 29.2 |
| Chelsea State Bank | Chelsea | MI | **A** | A- | A- | 297.1 | -0.92 | 11.9 | 0.4 | 5.9 | 21.5 | **10.0** | 12.3 | 20.5 |
| Chemung Canal Trust Co. | Elmira | NY | **B-** | B- | C+ | 1783.3 | 1.80 | 12.1 | 8.2 | 14.1 | 16.0 | **7.0** | 9.0 | 13.5 |
| Cherokee State Bank | Cherokee | IA | **B** | B+ | A | 221.5 | -4.73 | 4.1 | 0.7 | 6.1 | 28.1 | **10.0** | 12.0 | 17.5 |
| Chesapeake Bank | Kilmarnock | VA | **B+** | A- | B | 955.1 | 12.24 | 12.7 | 0.9 | 11.0 | 30.6 | **9.4** | 10.6 | 15.4 |
| Chesapeake Bank & Trust Co. | Chestertown | MD | **B+** | B | B | 106.9 | -0.95 | 3.0 | 1.3 | 40.6 | 21.0 | **7.8** | 9.6 | 16.0 |
| Chesapeake Bank of Maryland | Baltimore | MD | **B-** | B- | C+ | 220.3 | 2.29 | 3.2 | 0.2 | 32.6 | 16.8 | **10.0** | 19.1 | 28.7 |
| Chester National Bank | Chester | IL | **B-** | B- | C+ | 64.1 | -12.48 | 2.0 | 2.4 | 53.8 | 13.2 | **10.0** | 13.2 | 24.9 |
| Chesterfield State Bank | Chesterfield | IL | **C-** | D+ | D+ | 17.5 | -4.19 | 12.4 | 6.0 | 29.7 | 0.0 | **10.0** | 11.1 | 20.4 |
| Cheyenne State Bank | Cheyenne | WY | **B-** | C+ | B- | 39.2 | -5.12 | 3.9 | 0.8 | 25.4 | 3.1 | **10.0** | 16.9 | 23.2 |
| Chicago Trust Co., N.A. | Lake Forest | IL | **U** | U | U | 111.9 | 2.76 | 0.0 | 0.0 | 0.0 | 1.7 | **10.0** | 99.1 | 471.1 |
| Chickasaw Community Bank | Oklahoma City | OK | **B** | B+ | A- | 199.0 | 3.34 | 11.3 | 2.3 | 28.7 | 9.1 | **6.4** | 8.4 | 13.5 |
| Chillicothe State Bank | Chillicothe | MO | **B** | B | B | 121.0 | -3.84 | 3.6 | 5.4 | 26.2 | 29.1 | **6.7** | 8.7 | 17.5 |
| Chino Commercial Bank, N.A. | Chino | CA | **B+** | B | B | 229.4 | 13.63 | 2.4 | 0.1 | 8.5 | 16.0 | **9.4** | 10.6 | 16.8 |
| Chippewa Valley Bank | Hayward | WI | **B-** | B- | B- | 452.2 | 6.82 | 8.0 | 0.4 | 19.7 | 8.6 | **6.4** | 8.4 | 12.6 |
| Chisholm Trail State Bank | Park City | KS | **C-** | C | C | 97.9 | 26.19 | 5.4 | 2.0 | 19.4 | 17.6 | **8.7** | 10.4 | 13.9 |
| Choice Financial Group | Fargo | ND | **B+** | B+ | A- | 2379.1 | 11.04 | 21.6 | 0.6 | 5.8 | 3.7 | **5.5** | 9.8 | 11.4 |
| ▲ ChoiceOne Bank | Sparta | MI | **B+** | B | B | 674.0 | 1.08 | 11.9 | 3.5 | 12.4 | 22.9 | **7.9** | 10.0 | 13.2 |
| CIBC Bank USA | Chicago | IL | **B** | B+ | B+ | 33588.6 | 15.99 | 25.1 | 0.6 | 4.1 | 15.5 | **6.5** | 10.8 | 12.1 |
| CIBC National Trust Co. | Atlanta | GA | **U** | U | U | 244.2 | 4.01 | 0.0 | 0.0 | 0.0 | 0.0 | **10.0** | 76.4 | 244.1 |
| ▼ CIBM Bank | Champaign | IL | **C** | C+ | C+ | 696.0 | -2.84 | 5.9 | 0.1 | 26.8 | 17.0 | **9.0** | 10.3 | 14.7 |
| ▲ Ciera Bank | Graham | TX | **B-** | B | B+ | 632.0 | 11.42 | 12.5 | 0.7 | 9.7 | 9.7 | **7.9** | 11.1 | 13.2 |
| Cincinnati Federal | Cincinnati | OH | **C+** | B- | B- | 242.0 | 22.16 | 0.2 | 0.3 | 45.0 | 2.8 | **8.9** | 10.2 | 16.3 |
| Cincinnatus S&L Co. | Cincinnati | OH | **B-** | B- | B- | 97.4 | 5.24 | 0.6 | 2.0 | 42.4 | 0.0 | **10.0** | 22.4 | 35.8 |
| CIT Bank, N.A. | Pasadena | CA | **B+** | B+ | B+ | 45268.9 | 7.32 | 23.6 | 0.0 | 13.1 | 13.3 | **10.0** | 11.0 | 15.2 |
| Citibank, N.A. | Sioux Falls | SD | **B+** | B | B | 1453998.0 | 3.36 | 11.4 | 13.1 | 5.6 | 22.7 | **7.2** | 9.1 | 15.4 |
| Citicorp Trust Delaware, N.A. | Greenville | DE | **U** | U | U | 22.6 | -7.33 | 0.0 | 0.0 | 0.0 | 1.0 | **10.0** | 96.1 | 489.2 |
| Citizens & Northern Bank | Wellsboro | PA | **A-** | A- | A- | 1638.3 | 28.38 | 7.7 | 1.0 | 32.9 | 20.3 | **10.0** | 12.2 | 18.8 |
| Citizens 1st Bank | Tyler | TX | **A+** | A+ | A+ | 714.9 | -1.87 | 1.6 | 0.6 | 8.5 | 54.0 | **10.0** | 20.7 | 49.5 |
| Citizens Alliance Bank | Clara City | MN | **B-** | B- | B- | 847.1 | 7.22 | 11.8 | 1.4 | 7.7 | 17.8 | **4.9** | 8.3 | 11.0 |
| Citizens and Farmers Bank | Toano | VA | **A-** | A- | B+ | 1625.5 | 7.11 | 3.8 | 19.9 | 19.9 | 11.7 | **8.9** | 10.3 | 14.1 |
| ▲ Citizens B&T Co. of Grainger County | Rutledge | TN | **A-** | B+ | B+ | 208.1 | 0.11 | 3.2 | 1.8 | 11.2 | 60.5 | **10.0** | 17.2 | 35.6 |
| ▲ Citizens Bank | Enterprise | AL | **B** | C+ | B- | 149.4 | 0.66 | 10.6 | 1.1 | 19.5 | 10.9 | **9.0** | 10.3 | 15.0 |
| Citizens Bank | Greensboro | AL | **A-** | A- | A- | 95.0 | 1.71 | 5.5 | 5.2 | 6.8 | 44.7 | **10.0** | 13.9 | 26.6 |
| Citizens Bank | Batesville | AR | **B-** | B- | B- | 920.6 | 7.55 | 8.4 | 2.7 | 18.5 | 11.6 | **4.3** | 8.2 | 10.6 |
| Citizens Bank | Nashville | GA | **B** | B- | B | 252.4 | 0.32 | 6.6 | 4.3 | 30.3 | 11.0 | **10.0** | 14.3 | 25.0 |
| Citizens Bank | Sac City | IA | **C** | C | C | 50.7 | -0.87 | 13.0 | 2.7 | 11.6 | 30.1 | **6.8** | 8.8 | 16.0 |
| ▲ Citizens Bank | Mooresville | IN | **B** | C+ | B- | 486.6 | 1.25 | 2.3 | 41.4 | 5.2 | 20.8 | **9.6** | 10.7 | 14.7 |
| Citizens Bank | Hickman | KY | **B** | B+ | B+ | 144.2 | 7.48 | 5.7 | 2.8 | 14.3 | 20.0 | **10.0** | 12.4 | 19.7 |
| Citizens Bank | Morehead | KY | **B-** | B- | B- | 149.6 | 7.89 | 2.3 | 4.8 | 35.0 | 10.0 | **6.0** | 8.0 | 13.8 |
| Citizens Bank | Mount Vernon | KY | **C+** | C- | C+ | 144.3 | 1.88 | 4.0 | 5.2 | 41.2 | 7.5 | **9.2** | 10.5 | 15.4 |
| Citizens Bank | Butler | MO | **B-** | C+ | C+ | 151.0 | 24.59 | 9.1 | 2.3 | 27.3 | 1.3 | **6.7** | 8.7 | 12.3 |
| Citizens Bank | New Haven | MO | **C+** | B- | B | 225.1 | 4.09 | 6.3 | 1.7 | 19.7 | 8.0 | **7.2** | 11.9 | 12.7 |

| Asset Quality Index | Adjusted Non-Performing Loans as a % of Total Loans | Adjusted Non-Performing Loans as a % of Capital | Net Charge-Offs Avg Loans | Profitability Index | Net Income ($Mil) | Return on Assets (R.O.A.) | Return on Equity (R.O.E.) | Net Interest Spread | Overhead Efficiency Ratio | Liquidity Index | Liquidity Ratio | Hot Money Ratio | Stability Index |
|---|---|---|---|---|---|---|---|---|---|---|---|---|---|
| **6.9** | 0.12 | 0.4 | 0.31 | **7.7** | 0.9 | 1.45 | 4.91 | 4.22 | 52.2 | **1.1** | 28.9 | 30.4 | **8.4** |
| **9.5** | 0.89 | 1.2 | 0.00 | **9.5** | 1.4 | 2.07 | 9.94 | 2.80 | 68.0 | **3.8** | 81.8 | 27.0 | **9.0** |
| **6.0** | 1.16 | 4.7 | 0.03 | **4.6** | 3.4 | 0.95 | 11.91 | 3.93 | 70.5 | **0.8** | 14.8 | 25.4 | **4.9** |
| **5.1** | 2.79 | 17.7 | 0.00 | **5.7** | 0.5 | 1.43 | 15.40 | 4.58 | 63.7 | **2.0** | 26.5 | 22.1 | **5.0** |
| **5.8** | 1.13 | 1.2 | 0.00 | **0.6** | -1.0 | -0.99 | -3.77 | 4.93 | 117.5 | **6.7** | 63.2 | 5.8 | **8.0** |
| **7.0** | 0.39 | 4.9 | 0.01 | **2.3** | 0.7 | 0.30 | 3.68 | 3.08 | 88.4 | **2.1** | 27.6 | 20.6 | **4.3** |
| **9.9** | 0.13 | 0.2 | -0.01 | **8.2** | 3557.0 | 1.66 | 22.79 | 2.37 | 10.1 | **7.5** | 82.3 | 0.0 | **6.0** |
| **10.0** | na | 0.0 | na | **8.1** | 268.0 | 1.92 | 25.33 | 2.65 | 7.1 | **8.4** | 85.5 | 0.0 | **8.0** |
| **5.9** | 1.32 | 5.9 | 0.04 | **8.0** | 3.7 | 1.91 | 20.66 | 4.24 | 62.0 | **6.2** | 42.1 | 2.8 | **7.2** |
| **7.8** | 1.08 | 2.6 | -0.38 | **9.5** | 9.4 | 2.53 | 25.46 | 3.88 | 56.3 | **6.7** | 48.1 | 1.5 | **8.4** |
| **8.9** | 0.03 | 0.1 | 0.06 | **4.9** | 1.9 | 1.16 | 10.10 | 3.12 | 62.4 | **3.7** | 46.3 | 17.9 | **7.1** |
| **5.4** | 0.47 | 4.4 | 0.01 | **10.0** | 10.4 | 3.65 | 33.86 | 6.69 | 49.0 | **4.1** | 44.9 | 15.9 | **8.5** |
| **7.4** | 1.11 | 5.0 | -0.04 | **8.5** | 17.8 | 1.94 | 14.71 | 3.64 | 47.3 | **2.2** | 22.8 | 15.0 | **10.0** |
| **8.2** | 0.09 | 0.6 | 0.04 | **7.7** | 5.4 | 1.93 | 20.42 | 3.62 | 74.2 | **0.9** | 16.1 | 27.4 | **6.6** |
| **6.8** | 0.53 | 3.1 | 0.00 | **1.9** | 0.1 | 0.13 | 1.30 | 3.52 | 95.5 | **1.7** | 36.0 | 43.5 | **4.6** |
| **8.8** | 0.54 | 1.4 | 0.18 | **7.6** | 3.0 | 1.45 | 10.87 | 4.36 | 60.9 | **1.4** | 30.8 | 35.0 | **9.1** |
| **7.4** | 1.51 | 5.3 | 0.05 | **6.6** | 18.1 | 1.59 | 10.01 | 3.72 | 71.2 | **4.5** | 22.3 | 7.9 | **9.9** |
| **7.1** | 1.73 | 4.6 | 0.03 | **7.1** | 2.4 | 1.98 | 13.24 | 3.81 | 54.1 | **5.8** | 61.7 | 11.0 | **8.9** |
| **8.0** | 1.25 | 3.3 | -0.22 | **7.1** | 4.9 | 1.64 | 13.47 | 4.00 | 59.3 | **6.1** | 41.9 | 3.1 | **9.0** |
| **4.5** | 1.44 | 9.3 | 0.11 | **4.4** | 15.0 | 0.85 | 8.89 | 3.65 | 69.6 | **4.6** | 12.5 | 4.7 | **8.1** |
| **4.7** | 2.28 | 11.7 | 0.13 | **6.6** | 3.1 | 1.34 | 11.50 | 3.38 | 54.7 | **1.8** | 21.6 | 14.6 | **8.1** |
| **6.7** | 0.59 | 1.7 | 0.10 | **5.9** | 12.0 | 1.32 | 11.77 | 4.09 | 77.8 | **3.0** | 24.3 | 12.8 | **7.7** |
| **7.1** | 0.51 | 3.1 | 0.00 | **7.0** | 1.7 | 1.65 | 16.42 | 3.86 | 58.2 | **3.5** | 13.9 | 11.5 | **7.0** |
| **8.7** | 0.33 | 1.2 | -0.01 | **2.9** | 0.8 | 0.39 | 2.04 | 3.57 | 82.6 | **1.3** | 28.6 | 34.5 | **7.0** |
| **9.5** | 0.00 | 0.0 | 0.00 | **2.8** | 0.3 | 0.42 | 3.28 | 3.21 | 86.6 | **2.5** | 23.5 | 17.3 | **6.2** |
| **6.9** | 0.04 | 1.0 | -0.02 | **3.1** | 0.1 | 0.42 | 3.82 | 3.62 | 87.8 | **1.8** | 30.6 | 23.9 | **4.1** |
| **7.7** | 0.00 | 0.0 | 0.07 | **4.3** | 0.3 | 0.76 | 4.58 | 5.50 | 86.7 | **2.8** | 13.1 | 14.7 | **6.3** |
| **8.9** | na | 0.0 | na | **9.5** | 2.7 | 2.41 | 2.44 | 2.87 | 73.9 | **4.0** | na | 0.0 | **7.0** |
| **5.5** | 0.85 | 4.4 | 0.12 | **6.3** | 2.5 | 1.24 | 12.01 | 5.06 | 77.5 | **0.6** | 8.1 | 18.0 | **6.6** |
| **5.2** | 1.33 | 7.8 | 0.12 | **5.2** | 1.6 | 1.29 | 14.69 | 3.49 | 64.7 | **5.4** | 36.9 | 6.0 | **6.0** |
| **6.2** | 0.95 | 2.7 | -0.05 | **6.8** | 2.7 | 1.25 | 11.27 | 4.11 | 63.1 | **4.5** | 24.6 | 5.8 | **7.2** |
| **4.7** | 0.93 | 7.4 | -0.02 | **6.2** | 6.3 | 1.41 | 16.66 | 3.88 | 59.7 | **3.1** | 10.7 | 8.4 | **6.4** |
| **6.0** | 0.80 | 5.4 | 0.01 | **2.3** | 0.3 | 0.32 | 3.16 | 4.15 | 88.4 | **4.1** | 21.9 | 6.7 | **4.5** |
| **4.7** | 0.73 | 5.9 | 0.02 | **9.1** | 35.5 | 1.62 | 12.89 | 4.52 | 53.4 | **2.5** | 13.7 | 12.2 | **10.0** |
| **4.9** | 1.22 | 5.2 | 0.14 | **5.2** | 7.1 | 1.06 | 8.90 | 3.73 | 73.0 | **3.5** | 31.8 | 14.2 | **8.2** |
| **4.4** | 1.22 | 3.6 | 0.25 | **5.0** | 328.7 | 1.07 | 5.45 | 3.37 | 46.6 | **3.6** | 24.1 | 7.5 | **10.0** |
| **6.5** | na | 0.0 | na | **9.5** | 23.1 | 9.29 | 11.67 | 2.46 | 78.1 | **5.0** | 387.4 | 100.0 | **6.3** |
| **5.1** | 1.28 | 6.8 | 0.15 | **2.5** | 2.3 | 0.32 | 2.69 | 2.90 | 87.4 | **1.4** | 16.2 | 20.3 | **7.9** |
| **4.8** | 0.77 | 2.3 | -0.02 | **8.6** | 12.9 | 2.16 | 17.45 | 4.58 | 58.0 | **1.6** | 13.8 | 22.9 | **8.7** |
| **6.4** | 0.85 | 3.4 | 0.01 | **3.0** | 1.0 | 0.46 | 4.27 | 2.86 | 86.1 | **1.8** | 20.3 | 21.8 | **4.8** |
| **6.3** | 2.97 | 6.8 | -0.04 | **3.0** | 0.4 | 0.47 | 2.06 | 3.66 | 85.8 | **1.9** | 22.8 | 20.4 | **7.1** |
| **5.8** | 1.27 | 7.4 | 0.42 | **5.0** | 434.4 | 0.98 | 8.45 | 3.10 | 64.9 | **2.0** | 23.9 | 18.3 | **9.4** |
| **6.4** | 0.99 | 4.4 | 1.03 | **5.6** | 17405.0 | 1.20 | 11.68 | 3.16 | 50.9 | **3.7** | 42.9 | 8.3 | **8.6** |
| **10.0** | na | 0.0 | na | **10.0** | 1.9 | 7.76 | 8.36 | 2.76 | 75.4 | **4.0** | na | 0.0 | **7.0** |
| **5.9** | 0.85 | 4.2 | 0.03 | **6.8** | 20.3 | 1.33 | 9.87 | 3.88 | 65.5 | **2.3** | 9.2 | 16.1 | **10.0** |
| **9.5** | 0.40 | 1.0 | 0.00 | **6.9** | 11.3 | 1.64 | 7.77 | 2.91 | 41.0 | **3.0** | 47.8 | 26.2 | **10.0** |
| **4.6** | 1.00 | 8.9 | 0.02 | **6.0** | 10.7 | 1.33 | 14.95 | 3.79 | 57.8 | **1.1** | 18.3 | 18.4 | **7.6** |
| **6.8** | 0.55 | 2.2 | 0.83 | **6.8** | 20.9 | 1.34 | 11.79 | 5.60 | 68.3 | **2.3** | 15.1 | 17.9 | **8.8** |
| **6.2** | 5.38 | 7.9 | 0.00 | **5.2** | 2.4 | 1.19 | 6.73 | 3.60 | 64.5 | **5.4** | 58.2 | 12.5 | **8.1** |
| **4.8** | 2.15 | 7.5 | 0.62 | **5.0** | 1.6 | 1.05 | 10.71 | 4.02 | 70.3 | **2.4** | 17.8 | 13.7 | **6.1** |
| **7.5** | 0.37 | 4.9 | -0.04 | **5.7** | 1.1 | 1.19 | 8.24 | 3.34 | 53.5 | **3.1** | 49.8 | 23.3 | **7.7** |
| **4.9** | 0.54 | 5.0 | 0.04 | **4.5** | 7.5 | 0.85 | 8.64 | 3.86 | 70.7 | **1.5** | 12.0 | 18.7 | **6.3** |
| **5.0** | 2.51 | 12.2 | 0.10 | **4.3** | 2.3 | 0.92 | 6.56 | 3.76 | 74.3 | **1.3** | 22.8 | 29.4 | **7.5** |
| **5.0** | 0.11 | 10.0 | 0.07 | **4.4** | 0.5 | 0.96 | 10.75 | 3.55 | 66.0 | **1.9** | 23.8 | 21.1 | **4.3** |
| **6.2** | 0.19 | 1.3 | 0.01 | **5.5** | 5.3 | 1.10 | 10.26 | 3.50 | 67.0 | **3.8** | 8.9 | 9.3 | **6.8** |
| **6.5** | 0.56 | 5.6 | 0.33 | **4.3** | 1.5 | 1.04 | 8.39 | 3.72 | 68.5 | **1.5** | 16.3 | 24.0 | **6.0** |
| **4.5** | 1.21 | 8.5 | 0.08 | **4.4** | 1.3 | 0.94 | 9.81 | 4.54 | 79.8 | **3.9** | 15.8 | 9.4 | **5.2** |
| **3.8** | 1.09 | 7.6 | 0.34 | **4.3** | 1.4 | 0.96 | 8.79 | 4.32 | 75.3 | **1.2** | 10.2 | 27.1 | **6.5** |
| **4.8** | 0.77 | 6.3 | 0.23 | **8.6** | 2.7 | 2.01 | 23.79 | 5.89 | 62.4 | **3.2** | 12.4 | 12.7 | **5.6** |
| **3.2** | 1.57 | 9.8 | -0.02 | **4.7** | 2.1 | 0.90 | 7.79 | 3.91 | 64.7 | **1.6** | 5.3 | 12.2 | **7.8** |

| Name | City | State | Rating | 2018 Rating | 2017 Rating | Total Assets ($Mil) | One Year Asset Growth | Asset Mix (As a % of Total Assets) Commercial Loans | Consumer Loans | Mortgage Loans | Securities | Capitalization Index | Leverage Ratio | Risk-Based Capital Ratio |
|---|---|---|---|---|---|---|---|---|---|---|---|---|---|---|
| Citizens Bank | Byhalia | MS | **B+** | B | B | 76.2 | 4.18 | 3.7 | 7.3 | 19.7 | 25.9 | **10.0** | 12.3 | 26.1 |
| Citizens Bank | Columbia | MS | **B-** | B- | B- | 421.2 | 0.18 | 9.5 | 4.5 | 22.8 | 9.5 | **9.3** | 10.6 | 16.0 |
| Citizens Bank | Farmington | NM | **A-** | B+ | A- | 692.1 | 1.84 | 8.0 | 0.8 | 11.6 | 54.9 | **8.7** | 10.2 | 21.9 |
| Citizens Bank | Corvallis | OR | **A** | A- | B | 790.2 | 2.38 | 6.9 | 0.4 | 4.4 | 36.2 | **10.0** | 11.1 | 18.8 |
| Citizens Bank | Olanta | SC | **B** | B- | B | 577.2 | 7.98 | 7.8 | 4.0 | 21.7 | 12.4 | **8.1** | 9.7 | 15.1 |
| Citizens Bank | Carthage | TN | **A** | A | A+ | 622.2 | 5.90 | 4.6 | 3.1 | 11.4 | 50.2 | **10.0** | 18.2 | 28.5 |
| Citizens Bank | Elizabethton | TN | **A** | A- | A- | 859.9 | 2.25 | 9.1 | 2.3 | 6.8 | 23.0 | **10.0** | 12.7 | 16.9 |
| ▲ Citizens Bank | Hartsville | TN | **A-** | B | B | 256.0 | 18.06 | 4.9 | 2.8 | 19.8 | 11.1 | **9.6** | 11.3 | 14.7 |
| ▲ Citizens Bank | Amarillo | TX | **A-** | B | B+ | 181.2 | 13.36 | 3.1 | 0.2 | 2.7 | 7.1 | **8.3** | 10.1 | 13.6 |
| Citizens Bank | Kilgore | TX | **B** | B | B | 411.3 | -2.23 | 20.5 | 0.9 | 8.2 | 7.3 | **10.0** | 13.8 | 18.6 |
| ▲ Citizens Bank | Mukwonago | WI | **B+** | B | B | 793.0 | 5.57 | 7.7 | 0.2 | 7.3 | 18.3 | **10.0** | 13.2 | 18.3 |
| Citizens Bank & Trust | Guntersville | AL | **B** | B- | B- | 559.7 | 7.72 | 9.8 | 2.1 | 12.4 | 24.5 | **8.3** | 9.9 | 14.9 |
| Citizens Bank & Trust | Rock Port | MO | **B** | B | B | 100.3 | 10.66 | 10.3 | 2.6 | 6.4 | 44.0 | **10.0** | 11.3 | 22.7 |
| Citizens Bank & Trust Co. | Van Buren | AR | **A-** | A | A- | 404.1 | 1.81 | 6.3 | 4.9 | 15.7 | 31.4 | **10.0** | 12.9 | 20.7 |
| Citizens Bank & Trust Co. | Eastman | GA | **B-** | C | C- | 164.5 | 19.04 | 12.3 | 2.2 | 19.4 | 11.2 | **8.1** | 9.8 | 15.8 |
| Citizens Bank & Trust Co. | Campbellsville | KY | **B** | B | B | 228.5 | 10.80 | 16.9 | 3.2 | 19.1 | 35.1 | **10.0** | 15.6 | 26.0 |
| ▲ Citizens Bank & Trust Co. | Covington | LA | **B** | C | C+ | 123.8 | 5.68 | 6.1 | 0.6 | 20.0 | 7.2 | **9.3** | 10.6 | 15.9 |
| ▲ Citizens Bank & Trust Co. | Plaquemine | LA | **B** | B- | B | 341.5 | 6.30 | 4.7 | 0.8 | 16.6 | 7.3 | **10.0** | 12.1 | 16.0 |
| Citizens Bank & Trust Co. | Vivian | LA | **B-** | B- | B- | 138.6 | 1.77 | 4.7 | 2.6 | 22.5 | 31.0 | **10.0** | 12.6 | 21.8 |
| ▲ Citizens Bank & Trust Co. | Hutchinson | MN | **B-** | C+ | B | 215.3 | 4.18 | 13.0 | 1.4 | 20.8 | 26.7 | **6.9** | 8.9 | 13.7 |
| Citizens Bank & Trust Co. | Marks | MS | **D** | D+ | C | 147.0 | 15.94 | 6.7 | 2.7 | 12.3 | 11.7 | **6.3** | 8.3 | 12.6 |
| Citizens Bank & Trust Co. | Big Timber | MT | **C+** | C+ | B- | 117.2 | -0.75 | 4.2 | 2.1 | 7.4 | 11.9 | **8.8** | 10.2 | 17.9 |
| Citizens Bank & Trust Co. | Saint Paul | NE | **D+** | C | B- | 207.1 | 0.77 | 10.5 | 2.1 | 5.9 | 15.4 | **8.1** | 11.7 | 13.5 |
| ▼ Citizens Bank & Trust Co. | Atwood | TN | **C-** | C- | D+ | 25.1 | 1.08 | 0.9 | 12.4 | 21.3 | 43.8 | **9.0** | 10.4 | 27.1 |
| Citizens Bank & Trust Co. of Ardmore | Ardmore | OK | **B** | B | B | 224.0 | 1.66 | 5.9 | 2.6 | 31.8 | 20.5 | **7.7** | 9.5 | 15.4 |
| Citizens Bank & Trust Co. of Jackson | Jackson | KY | **C** | D+ | D | 144.8 | -1.01 | 8.4 | 6.7 | 31.1 | 7.0 | **6.4** | 8.4 | 12.5 |
| Citizens Bank & Trust, Inc. | Trenton | GA | **A-** | B+ | B+ | 105.2 | 7.70 | 4.0 | 8.1 | 35.0 | 26.4 | **9.6** | 10.8 | 20.9 |
| Citizens Bank and Trust | Lake Wales | FL | **B-** | C+ | C+ | 686.0 | 8.03 | 7.1 | 7.3 | 10.8 | 36.2 | **5.7** | 7.7 | 12.7 |
| Citizens Bank and Trust Co. | Kansas City | MO | **B** | B- | B- | 893.4 | 7.41 | 11.4 | 0.8 | 14.7 | 15.6 | **9.6** | 11.3 | 14.7 |
| Citizens Bank and Trust Co. | Blackstone | VA | **A-** | A- | A- | 411.6 | 4.89 | 4.1 | 2.8 | 24.6 | 27.9 | **10.0** | 13.7 | 24.6 |
| Citizens Bank Co. | Beverly | OH | **A-** | A- | A- | 226.9 | 4.75 | 7.9 | 2.0 | 32.9 | 18.8 | **10.0** | 12.9 | 20.4 |
| Citizens Bank Minnesota | New Ulm | MN | **B** | B | B | 432.2 | 3.53 | 6.7 | 0.9 | 20.9 | 19.1 | **6.3** | 9.9 | 11.9 |
| Citizens Bank of Ada | Ada | OK | **B** | B- | B- | 197.7 | -1.95 | 13.3 | 3.1 | 19.2 | 20.4 | **9.4** | 10.6 | 17.0 |
| Citizens Bank of Americus | Americus | GA | **B+** | B | B | 342.3 | 5.57 | 10.7 | 1.7 | 8.9 | 19.1 | **7.8** | 9.5 | 17.3 |
| Citizens Bank of Cape Vincent | Cape Vincent | NY | **C+** | C+ | C+ | 69.5 | -1.70 | 0.6 | 2.4 | 40.9 | 39.7 | **7.5** | 9.3 | 24.7 |
| Citizens Bank of Charleston | Charleston | MO | **A-** | B+ | A- | 142.7 | 5.38 | 8.2 | 5.0 | 7.8 | 6.8 | **10.0** | 17.4 | 26.4 |
| Citizens Bank of Chatsworth | Chatsworth | IL | **D** | E+ | E- | 33.5 | 5.32 | 10.1 | 1.7 | 2.8 | 17.4 | **10.0** | 11.9 | 17.2 |
| Citizens Bank of Clovis | Clovis | NM | **A-** | B+ | A- | 347.1 | -1.61 | 4.2 | 0.5 | 3.2 | 32.5 | **10.0** | 12.9 | 22.3 |
| Citizens Bank of Cochran | Cochran | GA | **B-** | B- | B- | 106.8 | 20.56 | 10.2 | 4.3 | 26.2 | 8.3 | **8.6** | 10.1 | 15.7 |
| Citizens Bank of Cumberland County | Burkesville | KY | **B** | B- | B | 76.0 | 0.01 | 4.1 | 12.1 | 24.9 | 9.3 | **10.0** | 13.4 | 19.8 |
| ▲ Citizens Bank of Edina | Edina | MO | **B+** | B+ | A- | 73.6 | 2.82 | 7.0 | 3.1 | 5.9 | 4.7 | **10.0** | 12.5 | 16.0 |
| Citizens Bank of Edinburg | Edinburg | IL | **C** | C- | C- | 25.0 | 0.91 | 1.5 | 2.3 | 11.9 | 18.5 | **7.5** | 9.3 | 17.6 |
| Citizens Bank of Edmond | Edmond | OK | **B-** | C+ | B | 301.9 | 9.60 | 5.8 | 0.6 | 21.0 | 6.7 | **8.7** | 10.1 | 14.1 |
| Citizens Bank of Eldon | Eldon | MO | **A-** | A- | A- | 156.0 | 6.78 | 7.3 | 9.3 | 24.3 | 6.5 | **10.0** | 13.3 | 18.9 |
| Citizens Bank of Fayette | Fayette | AL | **B+** | B+ | B | 190.4 | 2.96 | 5.4 | 3.6 | 3.3 | 69.0 | **10.0** | 20.4 | 45.6 |
| Citizens Bank of Florida | Oviedo | FL | **C+** | C | C+ | 357.0 | 16.43 | 5.0 | 0.5 | 9.0 | 19.6 | **6.4** | 8.4 | 13.0 |
| Citizens Bank of Georgia | Cumming | GA | **B** | B | B | 324.7 | 6.84 | 5.7 | 1.5 | 9.5 | 30.1 | **9.5** | 10.6 | 16.3 |
| Citizens Bank of Kansas | Kingman | KS | **B-** | B- | B- | 380.2 | 60.83 | 4.7 | 1.4 | 16.9 | 26.9 | **8.7** | 10.1 | 14.9 |
| Citizens Bank of Kentucky | Paintsville | KY | **B** | B | B | 656.1 | 11.30 | 8.0 | 2.9 | 17.0 | 21.7 | **10.0** | 11.2 | 17.8 |
| Citizens Bank of Lafayette | Lafayette | TN | **B+** | B+ | B | 941.4 | 2.31 | 5.1 | 5.1 | 14.3 | 25.7 | **10.0** | 11.7 | 18.0 |
| ▲ Citizens Bank of Las Cruces | Las Cruces | NM | **A-** | B+ | A- | 613.5 | 9.59 | 12.0 | 0.6 | 8.0 | 19.5 | **8.7** | 10.4 | 13.9 |
| Citizens Bank of Morgantown, Inc. | Morgantown | WV | **B-** | B- | B | 37.9 | 1.53 | 1.6 | 1.7 | 45.2 | 29.9 | **10.0** | 19.7 | 35.7 |
| ▼ Citizens Bank of Newburg | Rolla | MO | **C** | C | C | 143.6 | -4.17 | 9.8 | 2.0 | 25.2 | 10.4 | **8.2** | 9.8 | 13.6 |
| Citizens Bank of Philadelphia, Mississippi | Philadelphia | MS | **B-** | B- | B- | 1195.3 | 24.72 | 5.8 | 1.3 | 8.3 | 38.9 | **6.2** | 8.2 | 14.1 |
| Citizens Bank of Rogersville | Rogersville | MO | **B-** | B- | B- | 94.6 | 1.52 | 11.9 | 4.8 | 28.5 | 7.2 | **8.2** | 10.4 | 13.5 |
| ▲ Citizens Bank of Swainsboro | Swainsboro | GA | **B+** | B | B | 217.9 | 3.28 | 14.3 | 5.9 | 25.9 | 8.3 | **9.9** | 10.9 | 16.8 |
| Citizens Bank of The South | Sandersville | GA | **B+** | B | B | 258.7 | 5.46 | 10.2 | 3.8 | 30.3 | 10.4 | **10.0** | 11.3 | 17.6 |
| Citizens Bank of West Virginia, Inc. | Elkins | WV | **B-** | C+ | B | 285.0 | 7.91 | 5.1 | 18.6 | 37.0 | 5.5 | **9.9** | 10.9 | 16.8 |
| Citizens Bank of Weston, Inc. | Weston | WV | **B+** | B- | B | 205.3 | 3.12 | 20.8 | 3.6 | 19.8 | 16.4 | **10.0** | 11.5 | 18.9 |
| Citizens Bank of Winfield | Winfield | AL | **A** | A | A | 266.7 | 10.57 | 2.6 | 6.6 | 4.7 | 71.9 | **10.0** | 21.2 | 43.1 |

| Asset Quality Index | Adjusted Non-Performing Loans as a % of Total Loans | Adjusted Non-Performing Loans as a % of Capital | Net Charge-Offs Avg Loans | Profitability Index | Net Income ($Mil) | Return on Assets (R.O.A.) | Return on Equity (R.O.E.) | Net Interest Spread | Overhead Efficiency Ratio | Liquidity Index | Liquidity Ratio | Hot Money Ratio | Stability Index |
|---|---|---|---|---|---|---|---|---|---|---|---|---|---|
| **7.5** | 0.62 | 2.2 | 0.06 | **4.7** | 0.7 | 0.92 | 7.26 | 4.68 | 77.0 | **5.4** | 48.8 | 9.0 | **6.4** |
| **4.3** | 1.69 | 10.8 | 0.18 | **6.4** | 6.6 | 1.54 | 16.45 | 4.15 | 67.7 | **1.5** | 12.6 | 23.5 | **7.2** |
| **5.4** | 3.10 | 11.0 | 0.80 | **6.5** | 10.7 | 1.56 | 15.01 | 3.49 | 53.5 | **5.5** | 53.1 | 10.9 | **8.2** |
| **8.9** | 0.38 | 1.6 | -0.01 | **6.7** | 10.6 | 1.35 | 12.12 | 4.20 | 55.8 | **6.4** | 41.8 | 1.5 | **7.2** |
| **5.6** | 0.67 | 3.4 | 0.04 | **5.3** | 5.8 | 1.03 | 9.95 | 4.04 | 70.6 | **3.8** | 25.6 | 11.0 | **7.1** |
| **9.0** | 0.01 | 1.4 | 0.05 | **9.8** | 12.6 | 2.07 | 11.29 | 3.80 | 34.8 | **3.1** | 59.2 | 33.5 | **10.0** |
| **6.3** | 0.62 | 3.4 | 0.34 | **8.8** | 15.9 | 2.02 | 15.61 | 4.25 | 60.9 | **2.1** | 13.4 | 18.5 | **9.8** |
| **7.1** | 0.39 | 2.3 | 0.07 | **7.5** | 3.1 | 1.36 | 12.38 | 4.46 | 58.2 | **0.9** | 21.3 | 36.6 | **7.2** |
| **7.4** | 0.00 | 0.0 | 0.00 | **8.9** | 3.6 | 2.15 | 20.40 | 4.44 | 51.7 | **2.4** | 28.2 | 19.2 | **7.7** |
| **5.7** | 2.16 | 9.8 | 0.11 | **4.4** | 3.8 | 0.91 | 6.77 | 4.27 | 68.4 | **4.0** | 30.6 | 11.8 | **7.1** |
| **6.3** | 0.61 | 1.5 | -0.18 | **6.1** | 9.4 | 1.22 | 9.60 | 3.62 | 59.9 | **3.7** | 15.5 | 10.3 | **7.5** |
| **7.5** | 0.50 | 3.2 | 0.05 | **4.7** | 6.0 | 1.14 | 11.56 | 3.83 | 65.9 | **2.0** | 18.6 | 19.2 | **6.3** |
| **8.6** | 0.66 | 2.1 | 0.06 | **4.4** | 1.0 | 1.02 | 8.52 | 3.37 | 71.7 | **3.3** | 16.7 | 12.6 | **7.1** |
| **5.8** | 1.70 | 7.0 | 0.12 | **9.5** | 7.0 | 1.74 | 13.31 | 3.96 | 49.4 | **1.8** | 11.4 | 19.6 | **9.2** |
| **8.7** | 0.07 | 0.4 | -0.02 | **4.1** | 1.5 | 0.97 | 9.36 | 4.69 | 76.9 | **3.2** | 24.7 | 14.0 | **4.9** |
| **7.4** | 1.43 | 3.0 | -0.01 | **5.0** | 2.5 | 1.13 | 6.87 | 3.40 | 65.3 | **4.1** | 33.0 | 12.0 | **7.3** |
| **5.4** | 0.38 | 2.6 | 0.00 | **4.8** | 1.2 | 1.01 | 9.57 | 4.32 | 75.8 | **1.8** | 18.0 | 21.1 | **6.2** |
| **5.2** | 2.10 | 12.8 | 0.12 | **5.2** | 3.4 | 1.06 | 9.68 | 4.02 | 65.2 | **2.1** | 20.5 | 19.0 | **7.0** |
| **5.1** | 2.89 | 11.7 | 0.17 | **3.5** | 1.1 | 0.77 | 5.93 | 4.00 | 86.0 | **4.1** | 39.0 | 14.0 | **6.8** |
| **4.6** | 2.39 | 10.3 | 0.02 | **7.0** | 3.5 | 1.63 | 18.72 | 4.03 | 56.0 | **4.2** | 17.9 | 7.9 | **7.0** |
| **1.7** | 2.56 | 37.9 | 4.02 | **1.0** | -2.8 | -2.00 | -23.01 | 3.90 | 69.0 | **2.0** | 31.8 | 26.3 | **4.1** |
| **3.0** | 3.35 | 14.0 | -0.12 | **5.5** | 1.2 | 1.01 | 8.57 | 4.07 | 62.5 | **4.1** | 34.5 | 12.9 | **7.1** |
| **1.1** | 2.23 | 21.0 | 0.29 | **6.5** | 2.7 | 1.32 | 11.38 | 4.19 | 56.1 | **1.1** | 12.5 | 21.0 | **7.8** |
| **6.6** | 0.20 | 2.2 | 0.11 | **3.6** | 0.2 | 0.76 | 7.73 | 3.11 | 75.2 | **1.5** | 29.0 | 31.5 | **5.1** |
| **8.9** | 0.00 | 0.0 | 0.01 | **4.9** | 2.7 | 1.19 | 12.37 | 3.83 | 71.9 | **3.0** | 20.1 | 14.5 | **6.4** |
| **2.6** | 1.71 | 14.9 | 0.79 | **2.9** | 0.7 | 0.50 | 5.08 | 4.38 | 78.0 | **1.1** | 12.5 | 28.8 | **4.4** |
| **6.2** | 0.83 | 3.1 | 0.16 | **6.5** | 1.2 | 1.20 | 10.52 | 4.88 | 69.9 | **3.6** | 29.0 | 13.5 | **7.0** |
| **6.0** | 0.55 | 2.7 | 0.04 | **4.7** | 7.7 | 1.18 | 14.11 | 3.81 | 74.5 | **5.6** | 32.2 | 2.4 | **5.7** |
| **5.8** | 1.69 | 5.2 | 0.17 | **4.3** | 7.2 | 0.84 | 7.31 | 3.58 | 75.3 | **2.3** | 17.0 | 16.3 | **7.3** |
| **8.9** | 0.87 | 2.1 | -0.01 | **6.5** | 5.5 | 1.37 | 10.38 | 3.95 | 61.9 | **3.7** | 33.4 | 14.5 | **8.0** |
| **8.8** | 0.04 | 0.2 | 0.04 | **5.6** | 2.6 | 1.18 | 8.85 | 4.37 | 61.9 | **3.6** | 8.1 | 10.4 | **8.5** |
| **7.8** | 0.13 | 0.4 | 0.00 | **4.1** | 3.1 | 0.74 | 7.13 | 3.12 | 71.9 | **3.0** | 20.5 | 14.6 | **6.4** |
| **6.7** | 0.71 | 3.6 | 0.20 | **4.8** | 2.1 | 1.06 | 10.12 | 4.68 | 76.9 | **4.2** | 17.9 | 7.7 | **5.2** |
| **5.8** | 1.40 | 5.8 | 0.13 | **7.1** | 4.6 | 1.40 | 14.91 | 3.74 | 55.0 | **4.7** | 33.6 | 9.2 | **7.0** |
| **5.9** | 1.79 | 8.5 | 0.54 | **2.5** | 0.2 | 0.30 | 3.17 | 3.45 | 81.5 | **4.7** | 23.0 | 4.8 | **4.9** |
| **7.7** | 0.64 | 2.3 | 0.02 | **8.9** | 2.3 | 1.63 | 9.27 | 4.12 | 51.6 | **3.3** | 33.0 | 16.1 | **9.1** |
| **2.8** | 4.94 | 16.1 | 0.35 | **0.0** | -0.3 | -0.99 | -7.20 | 4.36 | 111.7 | **4.9** | 29.6 | 6.3 | **3.1** |
| **7.7** | 0.01 | 0.0 | -0.07 | **7.4** | 6.1 | 1.76 | 14.42 | 3.68 | 51.1 | **2.3** | 36.0 | 24.0 | **8.5** |
| **7.7** | 0.09 | 1.0 | 0.01 | **3.3** | 0.5 | 0.52 | 4.92 | 4.35 | 84.2 | **1.1** | 21.4 | 32.2 | **4.9** |
| **4.8** | 2.35 | 8.9 | 0.39 | **8.7** | 1.5 | 2.00 | 14.90 | 5.34 | 59.4 | **2.3** | 26.0 | 18.8 | **8.7** |
| **6.8** | 0.09 | 2.2 | 0.19 | **10.0** | 1.5 | 2.11 | 17.25 | 4.67 | 37.5 | **2.1** | 10.7 | 18.1 | **8.0** |
| **6.3** | 0.00 | 8.3 | 0.00 | **5.6** | 0.3 | 1.17 | 12.08 | 3.88 | 56.3 | **5.3** | 34.5 | 3.0 | **4.9** |
| **6.6** | 0.15 | 1.3 | 0.14 | **4.5** | 3.1 | 1.05 | 12.21 | 4.20 | 76.0 | **2.7** | 15.5 | 15.4 | **6.1** |
| **5.2** | 1.49 | 8.4 | 0.38 | **6.3** | 1.9 | 1.25 | 9.26 | 4.40 | 59.1 | **3.3** | 17.9 | 13.0 | **7.6** |
| **7.6** | 5.52 | 4.4 | 0.67 | **4.4** | 1.7 | 0.91 | 4.34 | 3.05 | 60.8 | **4.0** | 79.1 | 26.8 | **8.4** |
| **4.9** | 0.93 | 3.7 | 0.11 | **4.5** | 2.9 | 0.86 | 10.03 | 3.83 | 70.0 | **3.3** | 31.3 | 15.6 | **4.9** |
| **7.9** | 0.47 | 1.3 | 0.05 | **7.2** | 4.5 | 1.37 | 13.04 | 3.91 | 54.2 | **3.4** | 34.8 | 16.2 | **7.2** |
| **6.2** | 0.51 | 1.7 | 0.16 | **4.0** | 3.3 | 0.86 | 6.53 | 4.28 | 79.2 | **4.7** | 24.1 | 5.3 | **7.6** |
| **5.9** | 1.04 | 3.7 | 0.03 | **4.6** | 6.4 | 1.02 | 7.37 | 3.70 | 68.2 | **1.6** | 22.7 | 24.2 | **8.0** |
| **4.6** | 2.30 | 11.4 | 0.05 | **6.6** | 11.9 | 1.29 | 10.66 | 3.97 | 61.1 | **1.5** | 25.6 | 27.9 | **8.3** |
| **7.4** | 0.28 | 1.2 | 0.00 | **9.6** | 13.6 | 2.33 | 22.10 | 4.47 | 55.0 | **4.4** | 15.0 | 5.8 | **9.3** |
| **7.6** | 0.68 | 2.2 | 0.02 | **4.4** | 0.3 | 0.82 | 4.48 | 4.86 | 76.0 | **3.3** | 36.9 | 17.6 | **7.4** |
| **5.2** | 0.94 | 6.3 | 1.49 | **0.5** | -1.4 | -0.90 | -7.93 | 3.59 | 77.7 | **1.5** | 9.7 | 23.3 | **5.5** |
| **5.1** | 2.08 | 10.7 | 0.04 | **3.4** | 6.3 | 0.59 | 6.67 | 2.62 | 77.0 | **2.3** | 11.7 | 17.6 | **6.3** |
| **5.9** | 0.37 | 2.5 | 0.12 | **4.5** | 1.0 | 1.05 | 9.50 | 4.11 | 71.9 | **1.8** | 11.8 | 16.7 | **7.3** |
| **6.0** | 0.29 | 4.8 | 0.15 | **6.8** | 2.9 | 1.36 | 12.82 | 4.67 | 64.4 | **2.2** | 15.2 | 18.1 | **6.7** |
| **6.9** | 0.91 | 4.8 | 0.13 | **5.3** | 2.6 | 1.03 | 8.88 | 4.71 | 68.9 | **1.9** | 14.6 | 19.4 | **6.3** |
| **3.3** | 1.53 | 11.4 | 0.31 | **5.7** | 3.1 | 1.12 | 11.11 | 4.27 | 63.4 | **2.0** | 11.0 | 18.5 | **6.7** |
| **5.0** | 3.60 | 13.2 | 0.16 | **8.7** | 3.4 | 1.68 | 14.96 | 4.14 | 47.9 | **5.3** | 37.8 | 7.1 | **7.4** |
| **8.9** | 2.83 | 1.8 | 1.08 | **8.3** | 4.1 | 1.69 | 7.27 | 3.84 | 42.2 | **1.9** | 39.5 | 43.5 | **8.2** |

| Name | City | State | Rating | 2018 Rating | 2017 Rating | Total Assets ($Mil) | One Year Asset Growth | Asset Mix (As a % of Total Assets) Commercial Loans | Consumer Loans | Mortgage Loans | Securities | Capitalization Index | Leverage Ratio | Risk-Based Capital Ratio |
|---|---|---|---|---|---|---|---|---|---|---|---|---|---|---|
| Citizens Bank, N.A. | Providence | RI | **B-** | B- | B- | 165742.4 | 28.06 | 22.0 | 16.6 | 13.7 | 14.4 | **7.1** | 9.9 | 12.6 |
| ▲ Citizens Bank, N.A. | Abilene | TX | **A-** | B | A- | 107.2 | 2.77 | 10.4 | 6.4 | 17.5 | 18.3 | **7.7** | 9.5 | 13.6 |
| Citizens Building and Loan, SSB | Greer | SC | **B+** | A- | B+ | 141.7 | 9.05 | 0.0 | 0.2 | 54.5 | 13.8 | **10.0** | 20.8 | 41.0 |
| Citizens Business Bank | Ontario | CA | **A-** | A | A | 11279.4 | -2.08 | 7.4 | 0.1 | 3.8 | 21.4 | **10.0** | 12.2 | 15.8 |
| Citizens Commerce Bank | Versailles | KY | **C-** | C- | D | 265.7 | 7.51 | 4.4 | 0.9 | 26.5 | 15.9 | **8.3** | 9.8 | 14.6 |
| ▲ Citizens Community Bank | Hahira | GA | **A-** | B+ | A- | 138.1 | 4.09 | 5.5 | 4.0 | 21.3 | 24.3 | **10.0** | 12.9 | 20.9 |
| Citizens Community Bank | Mascoutah | IL | **B+** | B+ | B+ | 403.3 | 1.31 | 5.6 | 1.1 | 10.4 | 32.8 | **10.0** | 11.9 | 17.8 |
| Citizens Community Bank | Pilot Grove | MO | **B** | B- | B | 106.5 | 6.75 | 4.6 | 2.3 | 16.1 | 9.5 | **10.0** | 12.2 | 16.6 |
| ▲ Citizens Community Bank | Winchester | TN | **B+** | B- | B | 241.5 | 5.02 | 11.9 | 3.5 | 17.9 | 15.4 | **10.0** | 12.7 | 19.7 |
| Citizens Community Federal N.A. | Altoona | WI | **B-** | B- | C+ | 1531.1 | 18.87 | 7.2 | 3.8 | 15.3 | 12.0 | **7.7** | 10.4 | 13.1 |
| Citizens Deposit Bank & Trust | Vanceburg | KY | **B** | B- | B- | 552.9 | 24.29 | 2.9 | 2.6 | 17.4 | 35.8 | **6.5** | 8.5 | 14.1 |
| Citizens Deposit Bank of Arlington, Inc. | Arlington | KY | **A-** | B+ | A | 236.4 | 10.72 | 14.1 | 5.4 | 14.9 | 25.7 | **10.0** | 15.4 | 22.8 |
| Citizens Federal S&L Assn. | Covington | KY | **B** | B+ | B+ | 39.5 | 6.89 | 0.0 | 0.0 | 49.5 | 18.9 | **10.0** | 27.9 | 67.5 |
| Citizens Federal S&L Assn. | Bellefontaine | OH | **C** | C | C | 137.0 | 2.26 | 0.0 | 0.1 | 61.3 | 13.9 | **10.0** | 13.2 | 27.2 |
| Citizens Federal Savings Bank | Leavenworth | KS | **C** | C | C | 170.9 | -0.51 | 0.7 | 1.3 | 50.9 | 38.3 | **10.0** | 22.0 | 59.6 |
| ▲ Citizens First Bank | The Villages | FL | **A+** | A | A- | 2462.8 | 9.20 | 8.1 | 0.1 | 6.6 | 63.6 | **10.0** | 12.2 | 18.5 |
| Citizens First Bank | Clinton | IA | **B-** | C+ | B- | 214.3 | 4.70 | 25.9 | 2.8 | 12.9 | 2.8 | **6.8** | 10.0 | 12.3 |
| Citizens First Bank | Viroqua | WI | **B-** | C+ | C | 222.8 | 5.54 | 5.5 | 2.6 | 8.4 | 15.9 | **9.2** | 11.1 | 14.4 |
| Citizens First National Bank | Storm Lake | IA | **A** | A- | A | 209.2 | -3.70 | 10.3 | 4.2 | 4.1 | 31.1 | **10.0** | 11.6 | 17.8 |
| ▲ Citizens First State Bank of Walnut | Walnut | IL | **C+** | D+ | D | 46.8 | 0.84 | 5.1 | 4.5 | 24.2 | 26.7 | **7.3** | 9.2 | 18.6 |
| Citizens Guaranty Bank | Irvine | KY | **D+** | C- | C- | 197.6 | 16.43 | 11.6 | 8.7 | 37.2 | 9.6 | **3.6** | 6.8 | 10.3 |
| Citizens Independent Bank | Saint Louis Park | MN | **B-** | C+ | C+ | 287.3 | 4.73 | 11.6 | 7.2 | 12.8 | 25.8 | **10.0** | 12.0 | 18.4 |
| Citizens National Bank | Greenleaf | KS | **B-** | B- | B- | 174.1 | 3.30 | 2.8 | 2.5 | 10.1 | 56.7 | **9.6** | 10.7 | 24.3 |
| Citizens National Bank | Sevierville | TN | **A** | A | B+ | 1109.0 | 5.14 | 5.7 | 0.5 | 13.8 | 12.4 | **10.0** | 11.6 | 15.6 |
| Citizens National Bank | Cameron | TX | **B** | B | B- | 444.9 | 6.87 | 4.3 | 0.6 | 6.2 | 28.1 | **10.0** | 11.3 | 16.4 |
| Citizens National Bank | Crockett | TX | **B** | B- | C | 90.8 | 2.27 | 8.8 | 6.7 | 6.6 | 17.0 | **10.0** | 12.1 | 24.7 |
| Citizens National Bank at Brownwood | Brownwood | TX | **A-** | B+ | A- | 226.6 | 10.19 | 8.5 | 6.1 | 11.9 | 41.6 | **10.0** | 12.2 | 24.2 |
| Citizens National Bank of Albion | Albion | IL | **B** | B+ | A- | 320.2 | -1.16 | 7.9 | 3.8 | 14.8 | 23.8 | **10.0** | 16.6 | 25.1 |
| ▲ Citizens National Bank of Bluffton | Bluffton | OH | **B-** | C | B | 877.5 | 2.22 | 9.5 | 0.3 | 8.0 | 15.1 | **7.9** | 10.3 | 13.2 |
| Citizens National Bank of Cheboygan | Cheboygan | MI | **C+** | C | C+ | 311.2 | 6.76 | 3.5 | 2.1 | 19.8 | 29.7 | **6.3** | 8.3 | 16.3 |
| Citizens National Bank of Crosbyton | Crosbyton | TX | **B+** | B | B | 51.9 | 0.23 | 2.2 | 2.0 | 2.4 | 5.8 | **10.0** | 17.3 | 51.3 |
| Citizens National Bank of Greater St. Louis | Maplewood | MO | **C+** | C+ | B- | 510.0 | 1.03 | 17.0 | 0.7 | 14.4 | 15.9 | **8.5** | 10.7 | 13.7 |
| ▲ Citizens National Bank of Hammond | Hammond | NY | **C-** | D | D | 23.4 | 0.20 | 5.2 | 12.0 | 47.9 | 22.9 | **7.1** | 9.1 | 19.9 |
| Citizens National Bank of Hillsboro | Hillsboro | TX | **B+** | B | B | 174.4 | -0.15 | 5.1 | 3.2 | 7.6 | 60.9 | **10.0** | 14.3 | 34.9 |
| Citizens National Bank of Lebanon | Lebanon | KY | **B** | B | B | 127.8 | 1.65 | 2.6 | 4.1 | 12.4 | 48.0 | **10.0** | 11.5 | 28.4 |
| Citizens National Bank of McConnelsville | McConnelsville | OH | **B** | B | B- | 98.8 | 5.67 | 1.8 | 6.1 | 44.9 | 17.8 | **10.0** | 11.9 | 23.3 |
| Citizens National Bank of Meridian | Meridian | MS | **A-** | B+ | B+ | 1421.2 | 5.34 | 9.6 | 1.8 | 16.1 | 21.8 | **8.4** | 10.6 | 13.7 |
| ▲ Citizens National Bank of Park Rapids | Park Rapids | MN | **A-** | B- | B | 268.6 | 1.73 | 6.4 | 8.8 | 25.5 | 8.8 | **10.0** | 11.3 | 16.5 |
| Citizens National Bank of Quitman | Quitman | GA | **B+** | B | B | 103.7 | -0.18 | 2.2 | 14.1 | 14.3 | 11.8 | **10.0** | 13.5 | 20.2 |
| ▲ Citizens National Bank of Somerset | Somerset | KY | **B+** | B+ | B+ | 445.2 | 9.67 | 2.9 | 4.2 | 22.5 | 37.0 | **8.5** | 10.0 | 18.6 |
| Citizens National Bank of Texas | Waxahachie | TX | **B-** | C+ | B | 1168.8 | 4.57 | 7.2 | 0.8 | 11.2 | 0.8 | **8.3** | 10.7 | 13.5 |
| Citizens National Bank of Woodsfield | Woodsfield | OH | **C+** | C | C | 135.1 | 5.32 | 4.5 | 1.3 | 28.5 | 42.5 | **4.7** | 6.7 | 18.3 |
| Citizens National Bank, N.A. | Bossier City | LA | **B+** | B | B- | 1041.9 | 7.51 | 7.8 | 0.6 | 13.2 | 17.6 | **9.5** | 10.6 | 15.2 |
| Citizens Progressive Bank | Winnsboro | LA | **C** | D+ | D | 165.3 | 3.01 | 8.6 | 3.8 | 20.1 | 6.4 | **8.0** | 9.6 | 13.7 |
| ▲ Citizens Savings Bank | Anamosa | IA | **A-** | B+ | B+ | 122.4 | 1.95 | 5.5 | 1.0 | 8.8 | 34.2 | **9.0** | 10.3 | 16.5 |
| Citizens Savings Bank | Hawkeye | IA | **A-** | B+ | B+ | 29.2 | -4.47 | 0.9 | 1.5 | 9.2 | 50.5 | **10.0** | 14.9 | 25.6 |
| Citizens Savings Bank | Marshalltown | IA | **C+** | C+ | C+ | 63.3 | 3.49 | 7.5 | 1.6 | 18.5 | 0.3 | **6.4** | 8.4 | 12.0 |
| Citizens Savings Bank | Spillville | IA | **A-** | B+ | A | 106.8 | -6.22 | 2.5 | 0.4 | 4.2 | 31.9 | **10.0** | 17.3 | 21.0 |
| Citizens Savings Bank | Bogalusa | LA | **B-** | C+ | C+ | 234.4 | 1.29 | 2.0 | 4.9 | 41.9 | 9.7 | **10.0** | 14.4 | 22.4 |
| Citizens Savings Bank | Clarks Summit | PA | **B-** | B- | B- | 318.3 | -3.57 | 0.0 | 0.1 | 77.3 | 9.4 | **10.0** | 15.9 | 32.1 |
| Citizens Savings Bank and Trust Co. | Nashville | TN | **E+** | E+ | D- | 97.3 | -5.59 | 4.5 | 2.0 | 9.2 | 8.8 | **2.8** | 6.7 | 9.8 |
| Citizens State Bank | Vernon | AL | **B** | B- | B- | 72.1 | 2.46 | 7.9 | 5.2 | 10.6 | 51.7 | **10.0** | 15.1 | 38.9 |
| Citizens State Bank | Monticello | IA | **A-** | A- | B+ | 421.3 | 5.27 | 5.6 | 0.9 | 3.0 | 39.7 | **10.0** | 11.0 | 16.6 |
| Citizens State Bank | Sheldon | IA | **A-** | B+ | A- | 132.7 | 10.49 | 7.8 | 6.1 | 14.5 | 12.1 | **10.0** | 13.1 | 18.3 |
| Citizens State Bank | Wyoming | IA | **B** | B+ | A | 95.5 | -0.05 | 8.3 | 2.5 | 4.0 | 31.4 | **10.0** | 23.1 | 35.5 |
| ▲ Citizens State Bank | Lena | IL | **B** | B | B+ | 273.5 | 6.00 | 8.2 | 5.7 | 11.2 | 16.8 | **10.0** | 11.5 | 16.9 |
| ▲ Citizens State Bank | Gridley | KS | **B+** | B- | B- | 207.3 | 3.22 | 9.1 | 2.6 | 14.6 | 17.5 | **8.1** | 9.8 | 16.6 |
| Citizens State Bank | Hugoton | KS | **B-** | B- | B+ | 133.1 | 6.62 | 6.5 | 0.8 | 4.3 | 19.5 | **10.0** | 14.3 | 17.7 |
| Citizens State Bank | Marysville | KS | **A-** | B+ | A- | 354.2 | 1.86 | 8.3 | 1.1 | 8.2 | 13.3 | **7.6** | 10.0 | 13.0 |
| ▲ Citizens State Bank | Moundridge | KS | **B+** | B | B | 429.6 | 0.93 | 4.4 | 1.1 | 6.7 | 37.5 | **8.5** | 10.9 | 13.8 |

| Asset Quality Index | Adjusted Non-Performing Loans as a % of Total Loans | Adjusted Non-Performing Loans as a % of Capital | Net Charge-Offs Avg Loans | Profitability Index | Net Income ($Mil) | Return on Assets (R.O.A.) | Return on Equity (R.O.E.) | Net Interest Spread | Overhead Efficiency Ratio | Liquidity Index | Liquidity Ratio | Hot Money Ratio | Stability Index |
|---|---|---|---|---|---|---|---|---|---|---|---|---|---|
| 4.4 | 1.11 | 4.4 | 0.36 | 5.3 | 1811.8 | 1.11 | 8.67 | 3.16 | 58.1 | 3.3 | 16.7 | 7.9 | 9.7 |
| 7.1 | 0.00 | 0.0 | 0.00 | 8.3 | 2.2 | 2.06 | 15.39 | 4.46 | 54.6 | 1.5 | 11.0 | 23.7 | 9.8 |
| 9.8 | 0.07 | 0.2 | -0.01 | 3.9 | 0.9 | 0.68 | 3.25 | 3.18 | 70.6 | 0.8 | 23.7 | 56.7 | 8.0 |
| 5.8 | 0.11 | 0.3 | 0.00 | 10.0 | 213.2 | 1.89 | 10.99 | 4.38 | 38.7 | 4.6 | 10.4 | 3.5 | 10.0 |
| 8.1 | 0.18 | 1.0 | 0.00 | 3.9 | 1.8 | 0.69 | 6.68 | 3.37 | 77.7 | 1.3 | 12.6 | 27.4 | 6.0 |
| 5.7 | 2.26 | 10.0 | 0.09 | 5.7 | 1.8 | 1.30 | 10.45 | 4.36 | 71.4 | 3.4 | 34.7 | 16.5 | 8.6 |
| 5.9 | 3.09 | 10.3 | 0.24 | 5.3 | 4.2 | 1.07 | 9.25 | 2.97 | 50.0 | 1.5 | 12.2 | 23.2 | 6.9 |
| 6.9 | 1.22 | 3.9 | -0.04 | 4.6 | 0.9 | 0.87 | 7.09 | 3.75 | 70.3 | 2.4 | 17.5 | 17.4 | 7.3 |
| 5.6 | 1.41 | 7.8 | 0.13 | 9.9 | 4.0 | 1.73 | 13.51 | 4.92 | 43.8 | 3.1 | 22.4 | 14.1 | 8.4 |
| 4.1 | 1.81 | 9.7 | 0.08 | 4.3 | 12.2 | 0.87 | 7.12 | 3.55 | 67.4 | 2.5 | 16.5 | 13.1 | 8.2 |
| 6.4 | 0.56 | 3.3 | 0.11 | 6.5 | 6.0 | 1.25 | 12.95 | 3.60 | 61.5 | 1.6 | 15.7 | 23.0 | 6.3 |
| 7.6 | 0.19 | 3.0 | 0.14 | 7.2 | 3.7 | 1.63 | 10.21 | 3.82 | 55.3 | 0.6 | 19.0 | 47.5 | 9.4 |
| 10.0 | 0.00 | 0.0 | 0.00 | 3.8 | 0.4 | 0.99 | 3.48 | 2.98 | 71.9 | 3.4 | 56.9 | 22.2 | 8.0 |
| 8.3 | 1.15 | 4.3 | 0.00 | 2.4 | 0.4 | 0.30 | 2.49 | 2.79 | 88.7 | 1.3 | 25.0 | 31.0 | 6.4 |
| 10.0 | 0.22 | 0.5 | 0.01 | 1.9 | 0.4 | 0.20 | 0.95 | 2.70 | 91.5 | 3.4 | 41.9 | 18.5 | 7.0 |
| 9.6 | 0.58 | 0.8 | 0.00 | 8.6 | 46.1 | 1.98 | 16.45 | 3.05 | 42.3 | 6.8 | 63.5 | 7.2 | 9.9 |
| 5.6 | 0.42 | 4.1 | 0.35 | 5.1 | 2.5 | 1.22 | 12.29 | 3.71 | 66.8 | 0.9 | 10.8 | 31.5 | 6.2 |
| 4.4 | 1.31 | 7.0 | 0.06 | 5.6 | 2.8 | 1.30 | 11.07 | 4.04 | 66.3 | 1.2 | 23.2 | 20.9 | 7.9 |
| 8.3 | 0.00 | 0.6 | 0.01 | 9.6 | 4.6 | 2.23 | 19.37 | 4.00 | 47.7 | 4.9 | 40.8 | 10.9 | 8.7 |
| 8.0 | 0.24 | 1.4 | -0.70 | 4.2 | 0.5 | 0.97 | 10.88 | 3.78 | 82.7 | 6.0 | 44.0 | 4.0 | 3.8 |
| 2.9 | 1.16 | 13.9 | 0.11 | 3.0 | 1.0 | 0.51 | 7.46 | 4.10 | 83.8 | 0.9 | 6.7 | 30.9 | 3.9 |
| 6.3 | 1.07 | 4.0 | -0.02 | 3.9 | 1.8 | 0.64 | 5.35 | 3.66 | 82.7 | 5.5 | 32.2 | 3.2 | 6.7 |
| 9.2 | 0.01 | 0.0 | 0.05 | 3.9 | 1.2 | 0.71 | 6.64 | 3.19 | 77.0 | 5.0 | 45.6 | 11.5 | 6.3 |
| 7.6 | 0.05 | 1.1 | -0.01 | 8.0 | 20.6 | 1.91 | 16.71 | 3.93 | 55.0 | 3.3 | 17.1 | 13.3 | 10.0 |
| 8.8 | 0.00 | 0.0 | 0.01 | 4.5 | 4.2 | 1.01 | 8.97 | 3.42 | 62.7 | 3.2 | 32.4 | 16.3 | 7.2 |
| 8.7 | 0.00 | 0.0 | 0.04 | 4.6 | 1.0 | 1.14 | 9.82 | 4.18 | 70.3 | 5.5 | 49.4 | 9.0 | 6.7 |
| 8.1 | 0.29 | 1.1 | -0.01 | 8.0 | 6.4 | 2.97 | 23.44 | 4.09 | 44.6 | 5.0 | 43.7 | 11.1 | 6.4 |
| 4.5 | 2.90 | 11.6 | 0.30 | 5.2 | 3.3 | 1.02 | 6.02 | 3.28 | 57.6 | 2.0 | 27.2 | 20.6 | 8.3 |
| 5.2 | 0.89 | 3.7 | 0.00 | 8.5 | 17.6 | 2.07 | 20.62 | 3.94 | 53.4 | 2.3 | 7.6 | 9.0 | 9.1 |
| 5.7 | 1.67 | 6.3 | 0.03 | 3.3 | 1.9 | 0.63 | 7.51 | 3.75 | 82.7 | 5.9 | 47.0 | 6.4 | 4.0 |
| 9.3 | 0.00 | 0.0 | 0.13 | 6.3 | 0.8 | 1.62 | 9.57 | 2.89 | 46.8 | 3.4 | 80.1 | 32.5 | 8.2 |
| 4.8 | 0.51 | 4.8 | 1.32 | 3.7 | 3.5 | 0.68 | 6.49 | 3.53 | 60.5 | 1.9 | 11.5 | 19.0 | 7.6 |
| 4.9 | 0.87 | 6.4 | 0.25 | 3.9 | 0.2 | 0.76 | 8.43 | 4.30 | 74.0 | 5.0 | 12.0 | 1.5 | 3.6 |
| 9.4 | 0.25 | 0.3 | 0.07 | 5.1 | 2.2 | 1.33 | 9.25 | 2.78 | 62.4 | 6.9 | 68.8 | 5.2 | 8.1 |
| 9.3 | 0.45 | 1.9 | 0.01 | 4.3 | 1.3 | 1.01 | 9.27 | 3.21 | 72.0 | 5.2 | 39.8 | 8.6 | 6.9 |
| 5.8 | 0.41 | 10.5 | 0.13 | 4.4 | 0.8 | 0.90 | 7.48 | 3.94 | 71.9 | 3.6 | 10.7 | 10.4 | 6.9 |
| 6.7 | 0.73 | 4.1 | 0.15 | 7.9 | 26.5 | 1.86 | 16.69 | 3.53 | 58.7 | 2.1 | 18.9 | 19.1 | 10.0 |
| 6.7 | 0.52 | 3.6 | 0.05 | 6.8 | 4.4 | 1.66 | 15.01 | 4.15 | 57.9 | 1.9 | 7.6 | 18.9 | 7.8 |
| 5.8 | 1.38 | 3.7 | 0.04 | 5.8 | 1.2 | 1.18 | 8.82 | 4.03 | 62.3 | 1.5 | 24.3 | 26.6 | 7.5 |
| 6.6 | 0.85 | 4.6 | 0.22 | 6.0 | 6.1 | 1.41 | 14.29 | 3.74 | 66.7 | 2.8 | 25.8 | 16.4 | 6.9 |
| 6.7 | 0.52 | 2.8 | 0.04 | 9.7 | 27.3 | 2.42 | 22.36 | 5.05 | 54.6 | 4.9 | 13.8 | 3.1 | 10.0 |
| 9.8 | 0.00 | 0.8 | 0.00 | 3.8 | 1.1 | 0.82 | 12.29 | 2.94 | 65.6 | 7.0 | 54.4 | 1.2 | 3.5 |
| 5.7 | 1.63 | 8.9 | 0.07 | 5.7 | 12.3 | 1.23 | 11.10 | 3.98 | 63.2 | 3.2 | 19.7 | 13.9 | 9.1 |
| 2.7 | 0.62 | 9.8 | 0.34 | 4.8 | 1.8 | 1.10 | 8.94 | 4.42 | 73.2 | 0.7 | 16.7 | 48.9 | 6.3 |
| 8.2 | 0.29 | 1.4 | 0.01 | 6.9 | 1.9 | 1.57 | 14.08 | 3.81 | 56.0 | 5.1 | 31.9 | 6.1 | 8.0 |
| 9.5 | 0.00 | 0.0 | 0.05 | 4.0 | 0.3 | 0.93 | 6.33 | 2.83 | 64.4 | 5.8 | 72.7 | 11.1 | 6.9 |
| 8.5 | 0.00 | 0.0 | 0.05 | 4.8 | 0.7 | 1.10 | 12.76 | 3.85 | 69.1 | 3.6 | 21.7 | 11.9 | 4.8 |
| 6.5 | 0.08 | 5.4 | 0.00 | 6.6 | 1.5 | 1.35 | 8.09 | 3.59 | 52.7 | 2.6 | 41.0 | 14.0 | 8.9 |
| 3.7 | 7.54 | 20.5 | 0.19 | 4.2 | 1.5 | 0.66 | 4.61 | 4.52 | 75.7 | 1.5 | 19.3 | 25.7 | 7.6 |
| 9.1 | 0.74 | 3.0 | 0.01 | 2.9 | 1.3 | 0.41 | 2.65 | 3.02 | 83.6 | 2.6 | 7.3 | 15.3 | 7.7 |
| 0.4 | 3.96 | 31.8 | 0.41 | 1.6 | 0.2 | 0.17 | 2.67 | 4.50 | 94.9 | 0.6 | 15.0 | 55.1 | 0.3 |
| 9.1 | 0.00 | 0.6 | 0.13 | 4.6 | 0.8 | 1.13 | 7.41 | 2.32 | 53.7 | 2.2 | 46.7 | 37.0 | 6.5 |
| 5.8 | 3.00 | 5.2 | 0.21 | 7.2 | 7.2 | 1.75 | 13.78 | 3.29 | 53.1 | 2.6 | 35.0 | 20.2 | 9.2 |
| 7.8 | 0.00 | 0.2 | 0.05 | 6.7 | 2.0 | 1.57 | 11.08 | 3.64 | 56.4 | 4.9 | 29.5 | 6.2 | 8.7 |
| 6.6 | 0.60 | 1.4 | 0.78 | 4.9 | 1.0 | 1.01 | 4.26 | 3.84 | 61.5 | 4.1 | 46.0 | 15.3 | 8.2 |
| 5.2 | 1.16 | 6.7 | 1.22 | 4.3 | 1.9 | 0.72 | 5.72 | 3.84 | 56.8 | 2.2 | 15.8 | 18.1 | 8.6 |
| 7.1 | 0.39 | 2.4 | 0.00 | 6.3 | 2.6 | 1.26 | 13.70 | 4.22 | 61.6 | 4.2 | 24.2 | 8.5 | 5.7 |
| 2.9 | 3.81 | 17.4 | -0.08 | 6.2 | 1.5 | 1.26 | 9.07 | 4.04 | 68.8 | 1.2 | 15.2 | 29.2 | 8.0 |
| 7.5 | 0.26 | 2.0 | 0.02 | 9.7 | 7.8 | 2.25 | 21.88 | 3.80 | 37.1 | 1.0 | 9.0 | 30.3 | 8.7 |
| 6.0 | 0.89 | 4.3 | 0.16 | 7.5 | 7.3 | 1.68 | 14.69 | 3.65 | 64.1 | 3.9 | 25.4 | 10.8 | 7.4 |

| Name | City | State | Rating | 2018 Rating | 2017 Rating | Total Assets ($Mil) | One Year Asset Growth | Asset Mix (As a % of Total Assets) Comm-ercial Loans | Cons-umer Loans | Mort-gage Loans | Secur-ities | Capital-ization Index | Lever-age Ratio | Risk-Based Capital Ratio |
|---|---|---|---|---|---|---|---|---|---|---|---|---|---|---|
| Citizens State Bank | Carleton | NE | **D+** | D | D+ | 23.2 | 11.77 | 9.4 | 4.9 | 1.9 | 0.0 | **7.8** | 9.6 | 15.1 |
| Citizens State Bank | Wisner | NE | **C** | B- | B- | 382.6 | 15.70 | 7.9 | 1.2 | 8.1 | 6.4 | **8.5** | 11.1 | 13.7 |
| Citizens State Bank | Okemah | OK | **C+** | B- | B+ | 58.7 | -33.28 | 4.5 | 3.4 | 13.1 | 32.1 | **10.0** | 22.9 | 45.9 |
| ▲ Citizens State Bank | Anton | TX | **C-** | D | D | 34.9 | 3.97 | 8.4 | 1.4 | 0.0 | 3.1 | **7.9** | 9.6 | 17.4 |
| Citizens State Bank | Buffalo | TX | **B+** | B+ | A- | 1077.4 | 18.01 | 5.0 | 1.5 | 3.9 | 74.9 | **9.5** | 10.7 | 25.6 |
| Citizens State Bank | Corrigan | TX | **A-** | B+ | A- | 133.2 | 5.99 | 13.2 | 12.3 | 14.6 | 28.6 | **10.0** | 11.9 | 20.4 |
| Citizens State Bank | Ganado | TX | **D** | D- | D- | 56.3 | 0.94 | 0.4 | 1.9 | 5.8 | 70.6 | **6.0** | 8.0 | 25.8 |
| ▲ Citizens State Bank | Miles | TX | **A-** | A- | A- | 159.0 | 6.43 | 11.3 | 2.7 | 26.7 | 0.0 | **8.1** | 9.7 | 14.0 |
| Citizens State Bank | Roma | TX | **B-** | B- | B- | 87.9 | 4.49 | 4.6 | 13.7 | 18.8 | 33.7 | **7.2** | 9.2 | 17.7 |
| Citizens State Bank | Sealy | TX | **A-** | A- | A- | 299.3 | 4.47 | 3.5 | 2.7 | 25.6 | 46.5 | **9.5** | 10.7 | 23.4 |
| Citizens State Bank | Somerville | TX | **B+** | B | B+ | 653.9 | 11.69 | 9.7 | 3.3 | 21.1 | 19.9 | **10.0** | 11.0 | 17.2 |
| Citizens State Bank | Waco | TX | **C+** | C+ | C+ | 146.9 | 1.90 | 3.5 | 3.1 | 37.7 | 25.0 | **7.9** | 9.6 | 18.7 |
| Citizens State Bank | Cadott | WI | **B-** | B- | B- | 121.0 | 2.26 | 5.8 | 3.2 | 15.9 | 17.5 | **10.0** | 11.7 | 17.4 |
| Citizens State Bank | Hudson | WI | **B-** | B- | B- | 223.1 | 6.25 | 6.4 | 0.9 | 27.7 | 11.9 | **5.9** | 8.2 | 11.7 |
| ▲ Citizens State Bank and Trust Co. | Council Grove | KS | **D+** | D+ | D | 47.0 | -2.16 | 16.8 | 2.3 | 8.1 | 1.9 | **5.9** | 9.4 | 11.6 |
| Citizens State Bank and Trust Co. | Ellsworth | KS | **B** | B- | B | 209.5 | 9.41 | 1.9 | 2.3 | 15.3 | 37.4 | **6.8** | 8.9 | 16.4 |
| Citizens State Bank and Trust Co. | Hiawatha | KS | **A-** | A- | B | 86.6 | -6.95 | 3.6 | 2.7 | 13.7 | 31.2 | **10.0** | 17.3 | 28.6 |
| Citizens State Bank at Mohall | Mohall | ND | **B-** | C | C+ | 59.8 | 0.52 | 10.2 | 3.3 | 13.8 | 22.6 | **10.0** | 11.9 | 16.7 |
| ▲ Citizens State Bank Midwest | Cavalier | ND | **A-** | B+ | B+ | 130.7 | 3.81 | 14.8 | 1.6 | 4.2 | 10.7 | **10.0** | 13.4 | 16.2 |
| Citizens State Bank Norwood Young Ameri | Norwood Young Ame | MN | **C** | C | B- | 85.0 | 2.87 | 13.7 | 2.4 | 8.5 | 0.0 | **10.0** | 11.2 | 17.3 |
| Citizens State Bank of Arlington | Arlington | SD | **B** | B- | B | 112.7 | 6.44 | 3.1 | 1.1 | 3.6 | 25.8 | **10.0** | 13.2 | 20.2 |
| Citizens State Bank of Cheney, Kansas | Cheney | KS | **B** | C+ | B- | 61.0 | 3.25 | 9.4 | 10.0 | 11.6 | 27.4 | **9.5** | 10.7 | 16.3 |
| ▲ Citizens State Bank of Finley | Finley | ND | **A-** | B- | C | 130.2 | -4.40 | 4.7 | 1.4 | 0.8 | 28.0 | **10.0** | 13.5 | 19.3 |
| Citizens State Bank of Hayfield | Hayfield | MN | **D+** | D+ | D+ | 103.3 | 9.05 | 13.5 | 2.9 | 9.9 | 15.3 | **5.3** | 7.4 | 11.3 |
| Citizens State Bank of La Crosse | La Crosse | WI | **B** | B | B | 330.0 | 17.83 | 14.6 | 0.7 | 19.7 | 1.4 | **4.1** | 8.7 | 10.6 |
| Citizens State Bank of Lankin | Lankin | ND | **C+** | C+ | C- | 48.3 | 5.26 | 8.1 | 5.1 | 2.1 | 26.0 | **8.7** | 10.8 | 13.9 |
| Citizens State Bank of Loyal | Loyal | WI | **B+** | B+ | A- | 207.9 | 0.58 | 3.2 | 0.2 | 7.7 | 23.4 | **10.0** | 13.3 | 17.9 |
| Citizens State Bank of Luling | Luling | TX | **B** | B | B | 74.1 | 13.97 | 5.0 | 1.4 | 8.2 | 5.9 | **10.0** | 14.5 | 19.6 |
| Citizens State Bank of Milford | Milford | IL | **C-** | C- | D+ | 46.0 | 1.12 | 6.9 | 1.6 | 0.6 | 14.9 | **7.4** | 9.3 | 13.9 |
| Citizens State Bank of New Castle, Indiana | New Castle | IN | **B** | B | B | 577.9 | 6.81 | 5.4 | 11.5 | 19.5 | 15.9 | **8.1** | 9.7 | 16.9 |
| Citizens State Bank of Ontonagon | Ontonagon | MI | **C** | C+ | C | 52.6 | -4.51 | 2.0 | 7.0 | 15.2 | 30.5 | **10.0** | 12.9 | 43.6 |
| Citizens State Bank of Ouray | Ouray | CO | **C** | C- | D | 115.9 | 13.44 | 0.9 | 0.7 | 23.0 | 23.1 | **8.3** | 9.9 | 16.9 |
| Citizens State Bank of Roseau | Roseau | MN | **B+** | B | B+ | 224.6 | 5.99 | 7.2 | 6.0 | 6.3 | 38.6 | **10.0** | 13.0 | 17.9 |
| Citizens State Bank of Tyler, Inc. | Tyler | MN | **C-** | D+ | D | 23.0 | -1.68 | 5.1 | 4.2 | 3.2 | 26.3 | **8.3** | 9.9 | 41.9 |
| Citizens State Bank of Waverly | Waverly | MN | **B+** | B+ | B- | 82.1 | 7.69 | 4.8 | 1.5 | 19.7 | 15.7 | **6.5** | 8.5 | 13.2 |
| ▲ Citizens Tri-County Bank | Dunlap | TN | **C+** | C+ | B- | 927.6 | 8.58 | 2.1 | 10.2 | 21.0 | 22.0 | **7.4** | 9.2 | 18.4 |
| Citizens Trust Bank | Atlanta | GA | **B+** | B+ | B- | 418.1 | 1.95 | 9.3 | 1.8 | 15.1 | 19.8 | **10.0** | 11.0 | 16.6 |
| Citizens Union Bank of Shelbyville | Shelbyville | KY | **B** | B | B- | 855.2 | 8.08 | 8.8 | 0.6 | 15.6 | 7.1 | **8.2** | 11.2 | 13.5 |
| Citizens' Bank, Inc. | Robertsdale | AL | **B** | B | B- | 107.4 | 1.61 | 6.6 | 1.6 | 17.5 | 19.0 | **10.0** | 12.5 | 20.7 |
| Citizens-Farmers Bank of Cole Camp | Cole Camp | MO | **B+** | B+ | A | 133.2 | 1.13 | 4.1 | 7.6 | 28.6 | 24.7 | **10.0** | 15.7 | 27.3 |
| City Bank | Lubbock | TX | **B+** | B | B | 3235.1 | 19.34 | 10.9 | 9.1 | 12.8 | 21.9 | **9.6** | 11.5 | 14.7 |
| City Bank & Trust Co. | Natchitoches | LA | **B** | B | B- | 262.9 | 6.61 | 2.6 | 2.6 | 11.1 | 59.1 | **8.5** | 10.0 | 17.7 |
| City Bank & Trust Co. | Lincoln | NE | **B** | B | B- | 192.6 | 33.74 | 10.7 | 2.1 | 12.4 | 11.7 | **10.0** | 12.9 | 17.4 |
| City First Bank of D.C., N.A. | Washington | DC | **C+** | C+ | B- | 366.2 | -0.30 | 6.3 | 0.0 | 2.4 | 25.8 | **7.0** | 9.0 | 19.9 |
| ▲ City National B&T Co. of Lawton, Oklahom | Lawton | OK | **A** | A- | A- | 344.0 | 0.84 | 3.2 | 3.3 | 21.3 | 20.4 | **10.0** | 14.2 | 24.1 |
| City National Bank | Los Angeles | CA | **B+** | B | B | 61390.1 | 21.08 | 13.3 | 1.3 | 20.2 | 22.2 | **5.8** | 7.8 | 12.4 |
| City National Bank | Corsicana | TX | **B-** | B- | B | 52.1 | 7.62 | 10.6 | 6.2 | 37.2 | 3.9 | **9.2** | 10.5 | 18.7 |
| City National Bank of Colorado City | Colorado City | TX | **B-** | B | A- | 138.6 | 10.63 | 4.4 | 7.7 | 28.4 | 22.0 | **6.0** | 8.0 | 13.2 |
| City National Bank of Florida | Miami | FL | **B** | B | B | 15841.0 | 10.58 | 13.2 | 0.4 | 11.7 | 21.1 | **9.1** | 10.9 | 14.3 |
| City National Bank of Metropolis | Metropolis | IL | **B** | B | B | 387.3 | 1.78 | 3.7 | 3.6 | 20.5 | 47.4 | **10.0** | 13.7 | 30.3 |
| City National Bank of San Saba | San Saba | TX | **C+** | C+ | C+ | 68.4 | 12.11 | 1.9 | 3.7 | 0.4 | 59.8 | **10.0** | 14.1 | 36.0 |
| ▲ City National Bank of Sulphur Springs | Sulphur Springs | TX | **A-** | B | B+ | 769.4 | 6.44 | 6.3 | 5.8 | 28.9 | 17.1 | **9.0** | 10.4 | 15.4 |
| City National Bank of Taylor | Taylor | TX | **A-** | B+ | B | 197.1 | -6.09 | 2.3 | 0.7 | 37.4 | 28.4 | **10.0** | 11.2 | 25.2 |
| City National Bank of West Virginia | Charleston | WV | **B+** | B+ | B+ | 4956.2 | 2.49 | 5.8 | 1.1 | 33.2 | 16.5 | **7.8** | 9.5 | 14.3 |
| City State Bank | Norwalk | IA | **B** | B | B | 448.7 | 11.22 | 9.9 | 1.2 | 11.6 | 8.8 | **6.8** | 9.0 | 12.4 |
| City State Bank | Fort Scott | KS | **C+** | C+ | C+ | 39.6 | -3.57 | 3.4 | 4.0 | 26.0 | 14.7 | **8.2** | 9.8 | 16.9 |
| Citywide Banks | Denver | CO | **B+** | B+ | B | 2295.2 | -0.52 | 12.8 | 0.5 | 8.4 | 26.0 | **8.7** | 10.7 | 13.9 |
| Civis Bank | Rogersville | TN | **E-** | E- | E- | 88.8 | -4.27 | 4.4 | 1.5 | 25.6 | 10.9 | **0.0** | 2.8 | 6.0 |
| Civista Bank | Sandusky | OH | **A-** | A- | B+ | 2304.0 | 7.99 | 8.2 | 0.6 | 14.9 | 15.6 | **9.0** | 10.8 | 14.2 |
| Clackamas County Bank | Sandy | OR | **A** | A | A | 229.8 | 2.08 | 0.6 | 0.4 | 13.6 | 27.0 | **10.0** | 12.8 | 24.6 |

| Asset Quality Index | Adjusted Non-Performing Loans as a % of Total Loans | Adjusted Non-Performing Loans as a % of Capital | Net Charge-Offs Avg Loans | Profitability Index | Net Income ($Mil) | Return on Assets (R.O.A.) | Return on Equity (R.O.E.) | Net Interest Spread | Overhead Efficiency Ratio | Liquidity Index | Liquidity Ratio | Hot Money Ratio | Stability Index |
|---|---|---|---|---|---|---|---|---|---|---|---|---|---|
| **6.7** | 0.00 | 0.0 | -0.01 | **4.2** | 0.2 | 0.77 | 7.97 | 4.12 | 76.2 | **0.7** | 15.1 | 35.9 | **3.7** |
| **2.5** | 1.64 | 12.3 | -0.07 | **5.9** | 4.8 | 1.41 | 12.67 | 4.29 | 65.5 | **1.2** | 9.0 | 24.9 | **7.8** |
| **3.3** | 10.01 | 19.0 | 0.58 | **1.2** | -3.7 | -5.52 | -26.99 | 3.29 | 188.1 | **3.7** | 33.9 | 14.5 | **5.9** |
| **7.6** | 0.78 | 3.2 | 1.60 | **2.5** | 0.1 | 0.33 | 3.41 | 3.89 | 79.5 | **3.1** | 60.4 | 28.8 | **2.3** |
| **8.5** | 1.72 | 2.1 | 0.11 | **3.7** | 8.5 | 0.87 | 7.06 | 2.53 | 67.6 | **3.3** | 61.7 | 34.9 | **8.1** |
| **5.6** | 0.05 | 9.1 | 0.02 | **8.3** | 2.6 | 2.01 | 16.99 | 4.16 | 56.4 | **1.6** | 21.3 | 24.9 | **8.4** |
| **9.9** | 0.00 | 0.0 | 0.09 | **0.8** | 0.0 | 0.03 | 0.33 | 2.64 | 100.1 | **5.2** | 85.3 | 16.1 | **2.1** |
| **7.3** | 0.10 | 0.3 | 0.09 | **9.8** | 3.5 | 2.30 | 23.95 | 4.31 | 45.8 | **1.1** | 28.6 | 47.2 | **7.8** |
| **5.1** | 0.86 | 3.7 | 0.52 | **4.1** | 0.6 | 0.71 | 7.51 | 5.03 | 81.6 | **1.7** | 37.5 | 47.0 | **4.9** |
| **9.3** | 0.00 | 0.0 | 0.00 | **6.4** | 4.3 | 1.45 | 13.84 | 3.28 | 48.3 | **3.5** | 52.7 | 21.4 | **7.3** |
| **5.0** | 1.56 | 10.3 | 0.19 | **8.2** | 9.8 | 1.58 | 14.55 | 4.52 | 55.7 | **2.8** | 17.8 | 15.3 | **7.5** |
| **4.0** | 3.66 | 19.6 | 0.05 | **3.4** | 0.9 | 0.64 | 6.72 | 4.59 | 83.7 | **4.1** | 21.4 | 8.6 | **5.1** |
| **5.0** | 1.74 | 9.4 | 0.22 | **3.4** | 0.6 | 0.51 | 4.37 | 3.87 | 85.4 | **4.3** | 21.5 | 7.6 | **6.5** |
| **7.9** | 0.21 | 1.9 | 0.00 | **4.5** | 2.0 | 0.92 | 11.20 | 3.82 | 69.2 | **3.1** | 13.2 | 13.4 | **5.1** |
| **4.9** | 0.70 | 5.9 | 0.14 | **6.3** | 0.7 | 1.45 | 15.43 | 4.82 | 62.4 | **0.8** | 7.1 | 32.0 | **3.7** |
| **6.2** | 0.85 | 3.3 | 0.04 | **4.7** | 2.1 | 1.11 | 11.50 | 3.12 | 67.4 | **4.2** | 20.1 | 8.2 | **6.1** |
| **8.6** | 0.72 | 2.3 | 0.00 | **6.4** | 1.3 | 1.49 | 8.45 | 4.23 | 62.2 | **5.4** | 28.1 | 2.1 | **8.1** |
| **5.6** | 0.95 | 5.5 | 0.16 | **4.5** | 0.6 | 0.93 | 7.81 | 3.95 | 75.2 | **2.0** | 4.9 | 17.8 | **6.3** |
| **6.9** | 0.88 | 3.1 | 0.01 | **6.3** | 2.2 | 1.70 | 12.23 | 4.45 | 57.2 | **1.5** | 6.5 | 21.2 | **7.8** |
| **1.4** | 5.55 | 19.5 | 0.06 | **7.7** | 1.5 | 1.74 | 12.02 | 4.92 | 60.2 | **4.8** | 34.8 | 9.2 | **6.9** |
| **6.3** | 0.45 | 2.3 | 0.00 | **5.0** | 1.0 | 0.97 | 7.21 | 3.63 | 65.3 | **2.3** | 34.1 | 21.4 | **7.4** |
| **7.4** | 0.30 | 1.4 | 0.00 | **6.6** | 1.0 | 1.54 | 13.68 | 3.88 | 60.6 | **2.6** | 26.2 | 17.6 | **7.4** |
| **6.3** | 1.94 | 3.1 | 0.06 | **7.3** | 2.3 | 1.77 | 13.45 | 4.09 | 64.6 | **1.7** | 19.6 | 16.1 | **8.5** |
| **1.4** | 5.61 | 48.5 | 1.97 | **2.7** | 0.3 | 0.30 | 3.89 | 4.14 | 70.6 | **4.8** | 26.7 | 5.5 | **4.1** |
| **5.4** | 0.31 | 5.7 | 0.01 | **9.8** | 8.3 | 2.77 | 32.02 | 4.27 | 47.6 | **0.6** | 7.8 | 27.8 | **6.6** |
| **4.8** | 1.31 | 6.1 | 0.00 | **5.6** | 0.6 | 1.33 | 11.93 | 4.54 | 72.4 | **4.3** | 14.3 | 6.3 | **6.5** |
| **8.3** | 0.96 | 3.1 | 0.02 | **4.7** | 2.2 | 1.07 | 8.07 | 3.49 | 73.4 | **4.6** | 18.7 | 4.9 | **7.9** |
| **7.3** | 0.09 | 0.6 | -0.08 | **5.0** | 0.6 | 0.90 | 5.96 | 4.63 | 75.5 | **3.6** | 19.3 | 11.4 | **7.4** |
| **7.1** | 0.00 | 4.8 | -0.01 | **3.0** | 0.2 | 0.54 | 5.39 | 4.11 | 86.5 | **5.4** | 33.1 | 4.5 | **3.9** |
| **7.6** | 0.17 | 1.4 | 0.09 | **4.9** | 5.1 | 0.91 | 9.45 | 3.62 | 68.5 | **5.6** | 37.8 | 5.0 | **6.3** |
| **6.0** | 4.73 | 6.8 | 1.43 | **2.4** | 0.2 | 0.36 | 2.77 | 3.10 | 82.2 | **7.2** | 77.2 | 3.3 | **5.3** |
| **6.6** | 1.10 | 4.1 | 0.03 | **2.9** | 1.1 | 1.05 | 10.50 | 3.43 | 82.6 | **4.3** | 29.9 | 10.1 | **5.2** |
| **5.4** | 1.89 | 7.8 | 0.17 | **5.6** | 3.1 | 1.42 | 10.93 | 3.27 | 57.8 | **1.4** | 12.2 | 25.5 | **8.0** |
| **5.9** | 2.68 | 8.5 | -0.07 | **2.9** | 0.1 | 0.52 | 5.26 | 3.03 | 78.7 | **6.9** | 66.8 | 1.1 | **3.0** |
| **4.0** | 0.62 | 7.4 | 0.00 | **6.7** | 1.2 | 1.58 | 12.86 | 4.37 | 62.7 | **4.3** | 16.4 | 5.8 | **6.9** |
| **4.1** | 1.56 | 9.8 | 0.17 | **7.9** | 16.4 | 1.83 | 17.74 | 4.33 | 57.8 | **1.7** | 21.2 | 23.1 | **8.3** |
| **6.2** | 1.80 | 7.4 | 0.00 | **5.1** | 4.1 | 1.00 | 9.15 | 3.99 | 74.8 | **1.7** | 16.9 | 22.7 | **6.7** |
| **4.9** | 1.25 | 7.5 | 0.01 | **5.9** | 9.7 | 1.19 | 9.08 | 4.08 | 67.1 | **3.8** | 16.2 | 10.3 | **8.8** |
| **6.1** | 3.45 | 11.2 | 0.07 | **3.3** | 0.6 | 0.58 | 4.74 | 4.37 | 87.0 | **3.3** | 27.0 | 14.0 | **7.1** |
| **4.8** | 4.70 | 16.1 | 0.35 | **5.0** | 1.1 | 0.84 | 5.34 | 3.57 | 59.2 | **2.4** | 22.0 | 17.5 | **8.8** |
| **7.7** | 0.31 | 1.5 | 0.09 | **6.1** | 35.3 | 1.25 | 12.03 | 4.11 | 71.4 | **4.0** | 22.9 | 9.5 | **8.9** |
| **8.7** | 0.13 | 2.2 | 0.10 | **4.5** | 2.7 | 1.15 | 11.08 | 3.12 | 69.5 | **6.7** | 55.8 | 3.7 | **5.8** |
| **8.5** | 0.24 | 0.8 | 0.04 | **3.7** | 1.0 | 0.62 | 4.47 | 3.69 | 73.2 | **2.9** | 22.6 | 15.2 | **7.0** |
| **6.8** | 1.50 | 5.8 | 0.02 | **3.2** | 1.6 | 0.50 | 5.70 | 2.86 | 79.9 | **2.1** | 44.8 | 34.8 | **5.4** |
| **6.4** | 1.05 | 4.5 | 1.06 | **8.6** | 7.1 | 2.00 | 15.30 | 4.13 | 80.1 | **5.5** | 32.6 | 3.6 | **9.0** |
| **7.4** | 0.46 | 3.3 | 0.07 | **5.5** | 623.7 | 1.12 | 12.61 | 3.34 | 62.0 | **5.7** | 25.9 | 2.2 | **7.8** |
| **8.5** | 0.00 | 0.0 | 0.02 | **4.2** | 0.4 | 0.72 | 6.55 | 4.22 | 84.3 | **1.5** | 21.3 | 26.3 | **6.3** |
| **5.6** | 0.83 | 6.7 | 0.36 | **5.0** | 1.3 | 0.99 | 10.91 | 4.22 | 61.6 | **1.7** | 15.2 | 21.0 | **5.6** |
| **7.6** | 0.52 | 2.7 | 0.01 | **5.2** | 162.5 | 1.08 | 9.03 | 2.90 | 52.3 | **3.7** | 26.7 | 10.9 | **8.4** |
| **6.2** | 3.00 | 8.5 | 0.38 | **3.8** | 3.5 | 0.92 | 6.92 | 2.75 | 65.0 | **2.1** | 43.9 | 31.1 | **6.8** |
| **9.6** | 0.00 | 0.0 | 0.06 | **3.2** | 0.4 | 0.70 | 4.86 | 3.19 | 76.0 | **6.7** | 79.3 | 7.1 | **6.7** |
| **6.3** | 0.60 | 3.8 | 0.08 | **8.3** | 14.7 | 1.96 | 16.52 | 4.68 | 60.7 | **3.0** | 25.1 | 15.0 | **9.0** |
| **8.9** | 0.65 | 3.6 | 0.00 | **6.3** | 3.2 | 1.59 | 14.19 | 4.08 | 67.5 | **6.2** | 40.2 | 1.9 | **7.0** |
| **5.9** | 1.04 | 4.2 | 0.09 | **9.4** | 88.5 | 1.81 | 15.48 | 3.60 | 51.1 | **2.6** | 9.9 | 15.5 | **10.0** |
| **8.3** | 0.07 | 0.9 | -0.01 | **5.3** | 5.2 | 1.24 | 13.24 | 3.27 | 69.3 | **2.9** | 20.1 | 14.7 | **6.0** |
| **8.7** | 0.00 | 0.0 | 0.00 | **4.8** | 0.4 | 1.08 | 11.28 | 3.94 | 72.8 | **2.2** | 28.5 | 21.0 | **5.8** |
| **6.9** | 0.15 | 0.6 | 0.03 | **6.1** | 28.4 | 1.25 | 7.71 | 4.37 | 60.9 | **5.7** | 29.3 | 4.9 | **8.0** |
| **0.3** | 7.30 | 91.3 | 0.96 | **0.8** | 0.0 | 0.00 | 0.12 | 4.36 | 96.1 | **3.7** | 21.9 | 11.0 | **0.9** |
| **6.7** | 0.53 | 2.2 | 0.00 | **7.3** | 34.6 | 1.55 | 11.18 | 4.38 | 61.7 | **4.0** | 13.8 | 7.4 | **10.0** |
| **9.1** | 0.00 | 0.0 | -0.14 | **7.2** | 3.9 | 1.71 | 13.61 | 4.23 | 65.3 | **5.1** | 32.5 | 6.1 | **8.8** |

| | | | | | | | One | Asset Mix (As a % of Total Assets) | | | | | | Risk- |
|---|---|---|---|---|---|---|---|---|---|---|---|---|---|---|
| | | | | | | Total | Year | Comm- | Cons- | Mort- | | Capital- | Lever- | Based |
| | | | | 2018 | 2017 | Assets | Asset | ercial | umer | gage | Secur- | ization | age | Capital |
| Name | City | State | Rating | Rating | Rating | ($Mil) | Growth | Loans | Loans | Loans | ities | Index | Ratio | Ratio |
| Clare Bank, N.A. | Platteville | WI | **B+** | B+ | B+ | 275.8 | 1.61 | 2.6 | 1.1 | 22.6 | 31.9 | **10.0** | 12.7 | 28.9 |
| ▲ Claremont Savings Bank | Claremont | NH | **B-** | C+ | C+ | 437.2 | 4.80 | 2.2 | 1.2 | 59.6 | 9.6 | **10.0** | 14.5 | 20.7 |
| Clarion County Community Bank | Clarion | PA | **B-** | B- | B- | 175.4 | 9.52 | 8.9 | 2.1 | 33.2 | 13.2 | **5.5** | 9.8 | 11.4 |
| ▲ Clarkson Bank | Clarkson | NE | **B+** | B | B+ | 59.2 | 5.87 | 5.6 | 1.2 | 0.1 | 33.8 | **10.0** | 13.9 | 19.1 |
| Classic Bank, N.A. | Cameron | TX | **B-** | C+ | B- | 436.4 | 18.57 | 2.9 | 1.6 | 18.5 | 15.3 | **7.6** | 9.4 | 13.3 |
| Claxton Bank | Claxton | GA | **C** | C+ | B- | 114.2 | -5.68 | 3.0 | 1.4 | 10.6 | 24.6 | **10.0** | 11.8 | 17.4 |
| Clay City Banking Co. | Clay City | IL | **C** | C+ | C+ | 153.1 | 6.80 | 8.4 | 2.3 | 24.7 | 14.1 | **8.0** | 9.7 | 14.0 |
| Clay County Bank, Inc. | Clay | WV | **A-** | A- | A- | 94.2 | -0.75 | 1.2 | 13.7 | 41.2 | 21.2 | **10.0** | 14.8 | 36.3 |
| Clay County Savings Bank | Liberty | MO | **C+** | C+ | C+ | 103.6 | 0.03 | 2.8 | 0.5 | 28.0 | 4.8 | **9.3** | 10.5 | 16.5 |
| ▲ Clay County State Bank | Louisville | IL | **B** | C+ | B | 75.7 | -0.62 | 10.5 | 8.2 | 18.8 | 21.3 | **10.0** | 15.1 | 23.8 |
| ▲ CLB The Community Bank | Jonesville | LA | **C+** | C | C | 181.9 | 0.78 | 20.6 | 5.2 | 8.6 | 31.4 | **10.0** | 11.0 | 17.9 |
| Clear Lake Bank and Trust Co. | Clear Lake | IA | **B+** | B+ | B+ | 452.0 | 6.34 | 10.5 | 3.9 | 17.2 | 7.4 | **6.4** | 8.4 | 12.2 |
| Clear Mountain Bank | Bruceton Mills | WV | **A-** | B+ | B+ | 648.6 | 7.48 | 8.4 | 4.6 | 32.8 | 17.1 | **10.0** | 12.3 | 17.5 |
| ClearPoint Federal Bank & Trust | Batesville | IN | **U** | U | U | 113.0 | 17.30 | 0.0 | 0.0 | 0.0 | 93.5 | **10.0** | 15.1 | 64.1 |
| Cleo State Bank | Cleo Springs | OK | **C+** | B- | B+ | 86.2 | -1.34 | 13.2 | 4.3 | 0.1 | 50.0 | **10.0** | 18.1 | 43.7 |
| Cleveland State Bank | Cleveland | MS | **A-** | B+ | B- | 230.8 | 1.74 | 9.1 | 4.7 | 16.5 | 31.3 | **10.0** | 11.4 | 19.4 |
| Cleveland State Bank | Cleveland | WI | **B** | B | C+ | 129.2 | 5.55 | 6.0 | 5.6 | 26.0 | 23.1 | **8.2** | 10.8 | 13.5 |
| Clinton Bank | Clinton | KY | **B-** | B- | B | 64.6 | 3.37 | 4.8 | 1.7 | 10.6 | 31.5 | **10.0** | 18.0 | 24.2 |
| Clinton National Bank | Clinton | IA | **B-** | B- | B- | 375.9 | -1.43 | 8.6 | 1.7 | 8.9 | 41.3 | **10.0** | 13.2 | 24.0 |
| ▲ Clinton Savings Bank | Clinton | MA | **B** | C+ | C+ | 585.9 | 1.86 | 3.2 | 1.9 | 35.9 | 17.1 | **10.0** | 11.4 | 17.9 |
| CNB Bank | Carlsbad | NM | **B+** | B+ | B+ | 449.6 | 8.45 | 10.1 | 7.7 | 12.6 | 40.2 | **6.3** | 8.3 | 15.6 |
| CNB Bank | Clearfield | PA | **B** | B | B | 3740.5 | 16.78 | 12.7 | 2.9 | 18.9 | 14.5 | **6.2** | 8.8 | 11.9 |
| ▲ CNB Bank & Trust, N.A. | Carlinville | IL | **C+** | C- | B- | 1333.2 | 35.48 | 10.9 | 2.0 | 8.9 | 17.7 | **6.6** | 8.6 | 12.3 |
| CNB Bank, Inc. | Berkeley Springs | WV | **B-** | B- | B- | 417.2 | 6.67 | 4.1 | 1.2 | 43.9 | 14.3 | **7.6** | 9.4 | 15.1 |
| Coastal Bank & Trust | Jacksonville | NC | **B-** | B- | B- | 111.9 | 1.99 | 6.8 | 0.6 | 16.5 | 12.9 | **10.0** | 16.4 | 21.3 |
| Coastal Carolina National Bank | Myrtle Beach | SC | **B-** | B- | B- | 445.3 | 17.86 | 7.4 | 3.3 | 20.4 | 6.6 | **6.5** | 9.5 | 12.2 |
| Coastal Community Bank | Everett | WA | **A-** | B+ | B | 1128.2 | 18.50 | 8.3 | 0.4 | 9.2 | 2.9 | **8.4** | 11.2 | 13.6 |
| Coastal Heritage Bank | Weymouth | MA | **C** | C | C | 848.4 | 161.38 | 5.3 | 1.9 | 52.1 | 7.4 | **8.2** | 9.8 | 14.6 |
| ▲ Coastal States Bank | Hilton Head Island | SC | **C-** | D | D | 707.5 | 21.37 | 22.7 | 6.1 | 9.1 | 8.7 | **6.8** | 10.3 | 12.4 |
| Coatesville Savings Bank | Coatesville | PA | **C** | C- | C- | 216.9 | 3.18 | 2.9 | 0.1 | 47.7 | 10.5 | **8.8** | 10.2 | 16.2 |
| Coffee County Bank | Manchester | TN | **B** | B- | B+ | 199.1 | 4.08 | 9.1 | 6.5 | 29.0 | 6.9 | **10.0** | 11.8 | 15.5 |
| ▲ Cogent Bank | Orange City | FL | **D-** | E | E- | 287.3 | 119.68 | 25.8 | 0.7 | 10.7 | 20.8 | **10.0** | 14.2 | 17.0 |
| Colchester State Bank | Colchester | IL | **B** | B | B | 68.6 | 6.92 | 3.7 | 3.6 | 7.0 | 57.9 | **10.0** | 15.1 | 33.9 |
| ▲ Coleman County State Bank | Coleman | TX | **B+** | B- | C+ | 124.9 | 8.64 | 9.3 | 2.1 | 12.9 | 7.9 | **8.2** | 9.8 | 14.8 |
| Colfax Banking Co. | Colfax | LA | **B** | B | B | 113.2 | -6.50 | 1.6 | 2.8 | 22.7 | 35.2 | **8.5** | 10.0 | 18.3 |
| Collins State Bank | Collins | WI | **B-** | B- | C+ | 98.4 | 7.27 | 7.1 | 3.7 | 22.8 | 16.8 | **6.8** | 8.8 | 12.9 |
| Collinsville Bank | Collinsville | CT | **C+** | C | C | 169.7 | 3.55 | 8.2 | 2.6 | 42.2 | 7.0 | **7.0** | 9.0 | 12.6 |
| Collinsville Building and Loan Assn. | Collinsville | IL | **C** | C | D+ | 123.0 | 4.37 | 0.0 | 0.0 | 75.6 | 18.9 | **10.0** | 27.2 | 70.7 |
| Colonial Federal Savings Bank | Quincy | MA | **B** | B | B | 315.6 | 6.19 | 0.0 | 0.5 | 47.5 | 31.5 | **10.0** | 14.8 | 29.6 |
| Colonial Savings, F.A. | Fort Worth | TX | **C** | C | D | 1066.0 | 5.42 | 0.9 | 0.3 | 43.0 | 20.4 | **7.7** | 9.5 | 24.0 |
| Colony Bank | Fitzgerald | GA | **B** | B | B | 1511.4 | 20.93 | 5.0 | 1.5 | 12.8 | 23.0 | **8.2** | 9.8 | 14.2 |
| Colorado Bank and Trust Co. of La Junta | La Junta | CO | **B+** | B | B- | 142.3 | 5.90 | 11.6 | 2.9 | 13.7 | 26.7 | **8.5** | 10.0 | 17.6 |
| ▲ Colorado Federal Savings Bank | Greenwood Village | CO | **B** | B- | B- | 2019.7 | 9.30 | 0.7 | 0.0 | 15.0 | 24.3 | **10.0** | 11.1 | 18.8 |
| Colorado National Bank | Denver | CO | **D** | D | D- | 25.2 | -53.01 | 0.0 | 0.0 | 0.0 | 4.8 | **10.0** | 23.8 | 171.7 |
| Columbia Bank | Lake City | FL | **C** | D+ | D+ | 205.9 | 0.39 | 7.6 | 0.7 | 12.0 | 12.8 | **9.1** | 10.9 | 14.2 |
| Columbia Bank | Fair Lawn | NJ | **B** | B | B- | 8177.9 | 22.42 | 6.0 | 0.0 | 29.6 | 17.0 | **8.9** | 10.3 | 14.3 |
| Columbia S&L Assn. | Milwaukee | WI | **E-** | E- | E- | 22.0 | -5.22 | 0.0 | 2.2 | 48.3 | 0.1 | **6.9** | 8.9 | 14.0 |
| Columbia State Bank | Tacoma | WA | **B+** | B+ | B+ | 14072.0 | 7.50 | 15.3 | 0.3 | 2.6 | 26.6 | **8.0** | 10.2 | 13.3 |
| ▲ Columbus Bank and Trust Co. | Columbus | NE | **B-** | C+ | B- | 145.2 | 5.19 | 13.4 | 1.6 | 4.4 | 13.4 | **5.8** | 9.6 | 11.6 |
| Columbus State Bank | Columbus | TX | **B-** | B- | B- | 117.9 | 8.10 | 0.4 | 0.2 | 0.5 | 59.2 | **10.0** | 12.9 | 26.9 |
| Comenity Bank | Wilmington | DE | **D+** | D+ | D+ | 13958.2 | -2.08 | 0.0 | 84.8 | 0.0 | 0.9 | **10.0** | 12.9 | 15.9 |
| Comenity Capital Bank | Draper | UT | **C-** | C- | C- | 9341.9 | 2.03 | 0.1 | 82.8 | 0.0 | 1.0 | **10.0** | 11.9 | 15.7 |
| Comerica Bank | Dallas | TX | **A-** | A- | B+ | 73336.0 | 3.67 | 35.3 | 0.8 | 2.8 | 16.9 | **6.7** | 9.9 | 12.3 |
| Comerica Bank & Trust, N.A. | Ann Arbor | MI | **U** | U | U | 52.8 | 0.96 | 0.0 | 0.0 | 0.0 | 0.0 | **10.0** | 72.7 | 243.5 |
| ▲ Commencement Bank | Tacoma | WA | **A-** | B | B | 388.4 | 8.65 | 21.0 | 0.5 | 4.0 | 3.8 | **10.0** | 12.1 | 15.8 |
| Commerce Bank | Edina | MN | **B-** | B+ | B | 210.3 | -0.79 | 7.8 | 0.1 | 8.0 | 6.7 | **10.0** | 12.5 | 15.8 |
| Commerce Bank | Kansas City | MO | **A** | A- | A- | 25955.5 | 2.25 | 13.2 | 9.5 | 10.1 | 33.0 | **7.8** | 9.6 | 13.2 |
| Commerce Bank | Corinth | MS | **A-** | B+ | A | 129.2 | 10.80 | 14.5 | 5.9 | 29.8 | 17.1 | **10.0** | 11.5 | 18.6 |
| Commerce Bank | Laredo | TX | **A** | A | A | 508.2 | -13.98 | 4.3 | 1.1 | 19.6 | 52.3 | **10.0** | 18.2 | 35.7 |
| Commerce Bank of Arizona, Inc. | Tucson | AZ | **D+** | D | E | 237.9 | 12.60 | 14.5 | 0.1 | 7.4 | 11.0 | **10.0** | 11.1 | 15.0 |

| Asset Quality Index | Adjusted Non-Performing Loans as a % of Total Loans | Adjusted Non-Performing Loans as a % of Capital | Net Charge-Offs Avg Loans | Profitability Index | Net Income ($Mil) | Return on Assets (R.O.A.) | Return on Equity (R.O.E.) | Net Interest Spread | Overhead Efficiency Ratio | Liquidity Index | Liquidity Ratio | Hot Money Ratio | Stability Index |
|---|---|---|---|---|---|---|---|---|---|---|---|---|---|
| **8.5** | 1.58 | 3.3 | 0.00 | **4.9** | 3.3 | 1.23 | 9.78 | 2.76 | 58.7 | **5.0** | 34.0 | 7.3 | **7.9** |
| **7.3** | 0.92 | 4.6 | 0.04 | **3.4** | 3.2 | 0.76 | 5.28 | 3.29 | 85.0 | **1.6** | 17.5 | 23.1 | **7.5** |
| **6.6** | 0.38 | 2.8 | 0.21 | **3.2** | 0.8 | 0.49 | 4.82 | 3.73 | 80.6 | **0.8** | 15.0 | 36.6 | **5.2** |
| **6.5** | 0.53 | 2.1 | -0.38 | **7.0** | 1.0 | 1.76 | 12.66 | 3.67 | 52.6 | **2.3** | 28.8 | 19.6 | **8.2** |
| **5.1** | 0.80 | 5.9 | 0.18 | **4.3** | 3.7 | 0.98 | 10.52 | 3.58 | 75.4 | **1.7** | 14.4 | 20.7 | **5.8** |
| **4.1** | 2.85 | 14.0 | 0.25 | **4.9** | 1.3 | 1.09 | 10.19 | 4.66 | 75.6 | **2.9** | 22.7 | 15.1 | **6.4** |
| **3.0** | 2.37 | 18.8 | 0.03 | **4.0** | 0.9 | 0.65 | 6.54 | 3.69 | 78.9 | **3.3** | 12.5 | 12.5 | **5.0** |
| **8.1** | 0.22 | 2.5 | 0.10 | **7.3** | 1.3 | 1.36 | 9.21 | 4.16 | 62.4 | **3.0** | 33.1 | 17.8 | **8.7** |
| **9.0** | 0.00 | 0.0 | 0.00 | **3.4** | 0.7 | 0.65 | 6.45 | 3.50 | 87.3 | **4.3** | 17.7 | 6.9 | **6.9** |
| **4.5** | 1.95 | 11.0 | 0.17 | **5.2** | 1.0 | 1.31 | 8.63 | 3.42 | 63.9 | **3.7** | 12.1 | 10.2 | **8.0** |
| **3.7** | 3.28 | 17.0 | 0.45 | **4.4** | 1.8 | 1.01 | 9.08 | 4.05 | 71.9 | **3.9** | 30.6 | 12.2 | **6.2** |
| **6.9** | 0.39 | 2.2 | 0.02 | **7.2** | 6.8 | 1.56 | 17.89 | 3.75 | 61.4 | **2.8** | 19.1 | 15.5 | **7.4** |
| **6.4** | 0.95 | 4.3 | 0.15 | **6.9** | 8.5 | 1.33 | 11.20 | 4.07 | 62.5 | **2.0** | 21.7 | 19.7 | **8.2** |
| **10.0** | na | 0.0 | na | **4.2** | 0.8 | 0.83 | 4.84 | 2.37 | 86.9 | **8.6** | 114.7 | 0.8 | **5.9** |
| **2.9** | 16.68 | 21.2 | 0.80 | **3.6** | 0.7 | 0.79 | 4.41 | 3.37 | 72.5 | **4.5** | 59.1 | 15.5 | **6.3** |
| **8.7** | 0.57 | 1.7 | 0.29 | **5.3** | 2.4 | 1.05 | 10.17 | 4.01 | 67.5 | **4.9** | 34.0 | 8.0 | **6.4** |
| **4.6** | 1.75 | 10.4 | 0.01 | **6.2** | 1.6 | 1.26 | 11.73 | 3.91 | 65.6 | **3.8** | 31.4 | 8.0 | **6.4** |
| **4.6** | 3.44 | 11.2 | 0.24 | **4.0** | 0.5 | 0.83 | 4.47 | 3.35 | 70.8 | **2.2** | 12.8 | 17.6 | **7.6** |
| **8.2** | 0.77 | 2.0 | 0.02 | **2.7** | 1.6 | 0.40 | 2.93 | 2.86 | 87.8 | **4.4** | 35.6 | 11.4 | **7.6** |
| **6.2** | 1.45 | 6.8 | -0.01 | **4.0** | 5.2 | 0.90 | 8.23 | 3.26 | 73.9 | **1.6** | 24.3 | 19.9 | **7.6** |
| **6.5** | 0.35 | 2.7 | 0.06 | **8.2** | 8.8 | 2.04 | 25.19 | 4.05 | 50.2 | **6.1** | 40.1 | 3.0 | **6.1** |
| **5.8** | 0.81 | 5.3 | 0.16 | **5.8** | 40.3 | 1.19 | 12.14 | 3.68 | 61.6 | **4.1** | 9.7 | 7.9 | **8.0** |
| **3.4** | 2.36 | 14.0 | 0.09 | **5.6** | 14.1 | 1.07 | 11.04 | 3.69 | 62.4 | **1.7** | 16.4 | 22.3 | **7.8** |
| **6.0** | 0.98 | 5.7 | 0.27 | **3.7** | 2.8 | 0.70 | 8.05 | 3.40 | 78.6 | **2.3** | 14.5 | 17.6 | **4.9** |
| **8.8** | 0.74 | 1.6 | 0.03 | **3.8** | 0.8 | 0.69 | 4.23 | 4.20 | 80.6 | **2.9** | 20.4 | 15.0 | **7.4** |
| **5.6** | 0.73 | 4.3 | 0.07 | **3.9** | 2.9 | 0.70 | 6.63 | 3.71 | 72.7 | **1.4** | 12.5 | 24.8 | **5.7** |
| **7.3** | 0.11 | 0.2 | 0.06 | **6.5** | 14.0 | 1.35 | 12.46 | 4.31 | 60.7 | **4.1** | 14.3 | 6.2 | **8.8** |
| **5.7** | 0.78 | 5.3 | 0.00 | **2.5** | 1.6 | 0.22 | 2.36 | 3.63 | 89.8 | **2.5** | 10.8 | 16.2 | **6.0** |
| **3.7** | 1.15 | 6.5 | 0.17 | **2.5** | 2.7 | 0.40 | 3.40 | 4.19 | 84.3 | **1.6** | 11.5 | 16.5 | **4.5** |
| **3.5** | 2.28 | 15.1 | 0.27 | **2.7** | 0.8 | 0.36 | 3.57 | 3.25 | 78.5 | **1.9** | 14.8 | 18.6 | **5.8** |
| **4.9** | 2.00 | 10.5 | 0.09 | **9.8** | 4.7 | 2.37 | 20.32 | 4.42 | 47.5 | **1.0** | 15.3 | 32.2 | **8.9** |
| **7.3** | 0.52 | 2.4 | -0.12 | **1.0** | 1.1 | 0.55 | 3.23 | 3.55 | 115.6 | **2.9** | 24.2 | 15.5 | **4.7** |
| **6.4** | 3.32 | 7.3 | -0.11 | **4.2** | 0.6 | 0.84 | 5.42 | 3.18 | 66.4 | **3.5** | 45.9 | 18.7 | **6.4** |
| **7.3** | 0.03 | 2.0 | 0.05 | **9.0** | 2.7 | 2.27 | 22.93 | 5.35 | 63.7 | **3.4** | 22.6 | 12.7 | **7.4** |
| **7.9** | 0.05 | 1.4 | 0.00 | **4.8** | 1.3 | 1.18 | 11.85 | 4.02 | 73.8 | **1.4** | 12.2 | 24.6 | **5.9** |
| **7.9** | 0.37 | 1.5 | 0.22 | **5.6** | 1.3 | 1.41 | 15.66 | 4.19 | 67.5 | **4.1** | 28.5 | 10.5 | **5.4** |
| **4.5** | 1.75 | 11.3 | 0.01 | **2.7** | 0.7 | 0.40 | 4.30 | 3.26 | 88.3 | **1.7** | 11.5 | 13.4 | **5.7** |
| **10.0** | 0.00 | 0.0 | 0.03 | **2.3** | 0.5 | 0.38 | 1.37 | 2.42 | 79.9 | **1.8** | 27.9 | 26.4 | **7.4** |
| **9.9** | 0.08 | 0.2 | 0.00 | **3.5** | 1.9 | 0.63 | 4.22 | 2.78 | 73.9 | **2.5** | 37.8 | 25.0 | **7.9** |
| **2.3** | 16.97 | 7.2 | 0.09 | **2.7** | 2.5 | 0.23 | 1.02 | 4.67 | 98.5 | **4.7** | 28.1 | 7.6 | **9.2** |
| **5.7** | 1.53 | 6.6 | 0.17 | **4.7** | 12.3 | 0.87 | 8.36 | 3.73 | 74.2 | **3.5** | 24.3 | 14.5 | **8.0** |
| **5.6** | 0.98 | 2.4 | 0.42 | **9.5** | 2.7 | 1.90 | 20.04 | 4.76 | 58.5 | **4.5** | 22.2 | 6.0 | **6.7** |
| **8.5** | 0.90 | 1.8 | 0.03 | **4.3** | 16.0 | 0.81 | 7.10 | 2.43 | 45.6 | **4.1** | 48.6 | 15.7 | **9.2** |
| **7.4** | 0.00 | 0.0 | 0.00 | **0.0** | -0.3 | -0.93 | -5.02 | 1.58 | 110.6 | **7.8** | 96.6 | 2.8 | **4.8** |
| **2.1** | 4.11 | 15.5 | -0.16 | **2.0** | 0.6 | 0.27 | 2.51 | 3.73 | 93.3 | **3.0** | 13.4 | 13.9 | **5.6** |
| **8.7** | 0.47 | 2.1 | 0.09 | **4.1** | 55.9 | 0.79 | 7.22 | 2.55 | 62.5 | **1.9** | 10.3 | 19.2 | **7.6** |
| **0.3** | 7.35 | 55.5 | 0.30 | **1.1** | -0.1 | -0.28 | -3.04 | 4.64 | 106.6 | **0.6** | 10.1 | 39.3 | **2.9** |
| **5.9** | 0.47 | 1.6 | 0.03 | **7.3** | 197.8 | 1.49 | 9.30 | 4.28 | 58.2 | **6.0** | 28.6 | 2.3 | **10.0** |
| **4.9** | 0.15 | 1.1 | 0.20 | **6.2** | 2.1 | 1.52 | 13.52 | 4.24 | 57.4 | **1.5** | 8.6 | 22.2 | **7.5** |
| **9.8** | 0.00 | 0.0 | 0.00 | **3.8** | 0.8 | 0.79 | 5.66 | 2.61 | 66.6 | **7.1** | 104.4 | 9.7 | **6.7** |
| **0.5** | 1.35 | 20.9 | 6.13 | **10.0** | 451.4 | 3.29 | 24.20 | 21.80 | 50.8 | **0.4** | 17.0 | 73.6 | **9.8** |
| **1.3** | 1.07 | 18.0 | 4.76 | **10.0** | 211.4 | 2.25 | 16.47 | 15.31 | 55.4 | **0.7** | 18.8 | 8.7 | **9.3** |
| **7.1** | 0.54 | 3.0 | 0.21 | **8.8** | 1198.0 | 1.68 | 15.86 | 3.55 | 52.8 | **5.6** | 27.4 | 3.1 | **10.0** |
| **9.3** | na | 0.0 | 0.00 | **10.0** | 22.3 | 34.92 | 37.64 | 2.55 | 58.5 | **4.0** | na | 0.0 | **7.0** |
| **7.0** | 0.89 | 5.2 | 0.02 | **6.5** | 4.8 | 1.31 | 10.63 | 4.25 | 60.3 | **1.6** | 19.8 | 24.1 | **7.2** |
| **3.4** | 4.29 | 28.1 | 0.36 | **4.2** | 2.0 | 0.98 | 7.65 | 3.31 | 62.3 | **0.7** | 15.7 | 16.0 | **8.3** |
| **7.7** | 0.53 | 2.2 | 0.35 | **8.4** | 416.7 | 1.66 | 15.11 | 3.48 | 56.7 | **5.1** | 26.0 | 6.6 | **9.8** |
| **7.1** | 0.45 | 4.3 | 0.25 | **7.6** | 2.1 | 1.68 | 14.50 | 4.28 | 61.5 | **2.0** | 27.6 | 22.0 | **8.4** |
| **8.8** | 0.56 | 1.4 | -0.10 | **8.6** | 8.9 | 1.62 | 9.23 | 3.15 | 43.5 | **3.1** | 63.8 | 36.3 | **9.3** |
| **1.5** | 3.65 | 18.4 | -0.15 | **4.4** | 2.2 | 0.93 | 8.54 | 4.57 | 81.2 | **3.0** | 28.3 | 16.3 | **5.3** |

| Name | City | State | Rating | 2018 Rating | 2017 Rating | Total Assets ($Mil) | One Year Asset Growth | Asset Mix (As a % of Total Assets) Comm-ercial Loans | Cons-umer Loans | Mort-gage Loans | Secur-ities | Capital-ization Index | Lever-age Ratio | Risk-Based Capital Ratio |
|---|---|---|---|---|---|---|---|---|---|---|---|---|---|---|
| Commerce Bank Texas | Stockdale | TX | B | B | B | 54.4 | 5.60 | 15.1 | 0.3 | 16.3 | 19.8 | 10.0 | 13.6 | 22.3 |
| Commerce Community Bank | Oak Grove | LA | B | B- | B- | 65.3 | 1.85 | 18.0 | 1.6 | 10.7 | 25.0 | 8.1 | 9.7 | 14.0 |
| Commerce National Bank & Trust | Winter Park | FL | A- | B | B | 119.2 | 9.06 | 3.4 | 0.8 | 19.4 | 8.7 | 10.0 | 12.4 | 17.5 |
| ▲ Commerce State Bank | West Bend | WI | B- | C+ | C+ | 707.9 | 8.08 | 24.0 | 0.0 | 14.9 | 4.6 | 6.0 | 9.9 | 11.7 |
| CommerceWest Bank | Irvine | CA | B+ | B+ | A- | 883.5 | 10.67 | 10.6 | 0.2 | 0.2 | 7.7 | 6.7 | 9.7 | 12.3 |
| ▲ Commercial & Savings Bank of Millersburg | Millersburg | OH | B+ | B- | B | 818.5 | 11.88 | 12.8 | 2.3 | 17.1 | 15.4 | 8.3 | 9.9 | 15.3 |
| Commercial Bank | Crawford | GA | A | A- | A- | 232.7 | 26.92 | 4.6 | 1.9 | 21.5 | 13.5 | 8.1 | 9.8 | 15.6 |
| Commercial Bank | Parsons | KS | B+ | B+ | B+ | 337.8 | 2.11 | 9.8 | 6.2 | 10.8 | 47.0 | 7.1 | 9.1 | 16.8 |
| Commercial Bank | West Liberty | KY | B- | B | B+ | 156.0 | 11.87 | 4.9 | 6.3 | 30.4 | 15.3 | 10.0 | 12.4 | 20.4 |
| ▲ Commercial Bank | Alma | MI | B- | C | C | 504.4 | -4.24 | 5.3 | 1.7 | 32.3 | 6.2 | 7.4 | 9.3 | 14.2 |
| Commercial Bank | Saint Louis | MO | C | C | C- | 210.2 | 6.52 | 18.0 | 2.0 | 11.5 | 33.0 | 5.8 | 7.8 | 12.4 |
| Commercial Bank | De Kalb | MS | B | B | B | 162.7 | 8.24 | 11.0 | 13.9 | 11.9 | 28.4 | 8.6 | 10.1 | 17.5 |
| Commercial Bank | Nelson | NE | B | B | B | 56.9 | 10.49 | 23.0 | 3.0 | 1.1 | 26.5 | 9.8 | 12.3 | 14.8 |
| Commercial Bank | Honea Path | SC | A- | B+ | B+ | 189.9 | 3.09 | 2.8 | 3.5 | 14.2 | 37.6 | 10.0 | 14.6 | 48.4 |
| ▲ Commercial Bank | Harrogate | TN | B+ | B | B | 1285.1 | 0.37 | 9.3 | 1.3 | 24.0 | 5.2 | 8.3 | 10.1 | 13.6 |
| Commercial Bank | Mason | TX | B- | C+ | C+ | 54.0 | 6.47 | 5.2 | 2.4 | 23.3 | 34.9 | 6.8 | 8.8 | 17.3 |
| ▲ Commercial Bank & Trust Co. | Monticello | AR | B | B- | B | 206.0 | -3.37 | 13.2 | 7.5 | 14.1 | 32.6 | 8.7 | 10.1 | 16.3 |
| Commercial Bank & Trust Co. | Paris | TN | A- | B+ | A | 812.8 | 9.80 | 10.1 | 3.7 | 17.2 | 26.2 | 8.7 | 10.1 | 16.6 |
| Commercial Bank & Trust of PA | Latrobe | PA | B+ | B+ | A- | 419.3 | -0.01 | 2.9 | 0.3 | 26.1 | 36.0 | 10.0 | 13.3 | 21.3 |
| ▲ Commercial Bank of California | Irvine | CA | B | C+ | B- | 1084.4 | 9.90 | 9.1 | 0.9 | 1.6 | 9.0 | 7.3 | 9.9 | 12.7 |
| Commercial Bank of Grayson | Grayson | KY | B | B | B- | 178.8 | 1.59 | 7.5 | 7.7 | 16.4 | 41.6 | 10.0 | 14.6 | 25.6 |
| Commercial Bank of Mott | Mott | ND | A- | B+ | A | 107.9 | 8.34 | 3.8 | 1.7 | 2.4 | 12.1 | 10.0 | 14.9 | 19.4 |
| Commercial Bank of Oak Grove | Oak Grove | MO | B+ | B+ | B+ | 82.6 | 10.40 | 4.6 | 0.8 | 27.4 | 18.4 | 10.0 | 15.6 | 27.6 |
| Commercial Bank of Ozark | Ozark | AL | C | C- | C | 93.9 | -3.54 | 2.7 | 5.2 | 16.9 | 33.3 | 6.7 | 8.7 | 19.3 |
| Commercial Bank of Texas, N.A. | Nacogdoches | TX | B | B- | B | 787.2 | 8.14 | 12.4 | 4.5 | 16.0 | 25.1 | 8.9 | 10.3 | 15.4 |
| Commercial Banking Co. | Valdosta | GA | A- | B+ | B | 235.2 | 0.46 | 6.2 | 1.6 | 30.6 | 8.8 | 10.0 | 14.9 | 23.4 |
| Commercial Capital Bank | Delhi | LA | B- | B- | B- | 167.2 | 14.90 | 6.2 | 2.0 | 17.0 | 4.0 | 10.0 | 11.7 | 15.7 |
| Commercial National Bank of Brady | Brady | TX | A | A- | A | 145.9 | -5.50 | 4.4 | 2.9 | 18.5 | 35.8 | 10.0 | 13.1 | 23.8 |
| Commercial National Bank of Texarkana | Texarkana | TX | B+ | B+ | B | 217.3 | 5.32 | 13.9 | 2.9 | 16.9 | 30.7 | 7.2 | 9.1 | 15.4 |
| Commercial Savings Bank | Carroll | IA | B | B- | B | 195.0 | 0.51 | 8.3 | 2.7 | 29.7 | 6.9 | 6.4 | 8.4 | 12.5 |
| ▼ Commercial State Bank | Republican City | NE | B+ | A- | A | 60.0 | 2.65 | 3.1 | 0.6 | 0.0 | 51.7 | 10.0 | 30.1 | 38.4 |
| Commercial State Bank | Wausa | NE | B- | B- | B- | 132.6 | 6.67 | 19.5 | 5.8 | 3.7 | 3.3 | 7.2 | 10.0 | 12.7 |
| Commercial State Bank | Palmer | TX | C+ | C | C | 81.4 | -2.21 | 11.0 | 3.8 | 9.8 | 30.6 | 6.5 | 8.5 | 18.8 |
| Commercial State Bank of Wagner | Wagner | SD | B- | C+ | B+ | 180.3 | 0.72 | 7.1 | 2.6 | 8.1 | 24.3 | 9.1 | 10.4 | 15.7 |
| Commercial Trust Co. of Fayette | Fayette | MO | B+ | B | B | 134.4 | 11.08 | 2.3 | 5.9 | 43.0 | 7.8 | 8.8 | 10.2 | 18.2 |
| Commodore Bank | Somerset | OH | D+ | D+ | D+ | 76.5 | -6.93 | 4.6 | 6.2 | 35.8 | 27.8 | 6.2 | 8.2 | 15.3 |
| Commonwealth Bank and Trust Co. | Louisville | KY | B- | B- | B- | 1122.1 | 12.64 | 8.2 | 4.2 | 12.9 | 16.1 | 7.1 | 9.6 | 12.5 |
| Commonwealth Business Bank | Los Angeles | CA | A- | A- | B+ | 1162.5 | 0.13 | 10.5 | 0.4 | 1.7 | 8.1 | 10.0 | 12.6 | 16.1 |
| Commonwealth Community Bank, Inc. | Hartford | KY | B- | B | B | 144.1 | 1.18 | 0.2 | 2.7 | 17.2 | 63.1 | 10.0 | 16.5 | 38.3 |
| Commonwealth Cooperative Bank | Hyde Park | MA | B | B | B | 184.0 | 3.62 | 1.2 | 0.1 | 56.2 | 12.6 | 10.0 | 14.9 | 26.0 |
| Commonwealth National Bank | Mobile | AL | D+ | D- | D- | 49.8 | 4.63 | 2.0 | 0.9 | 7.6 | 34.1 | 9.4 | 10.6 | 21.1 |
| ▲ Community 1st Bank Las Vegas | Las Vegas | NM | C+ | C- | D | 146.6 | 2.75 | 2.0 | 0.9 | 10.5 | 36.8 | 8.3 | 9.9 | 22.0 |
| Community Bank | Dunlap | IA | B | B | C+ | 94.6 | 3.85 | 2.5 | 3.5 | 15.9 | 9.5 | 10.0 | 12.6 | 17.5 |
| ▲ Community Bank | Winslow | IL | A- | B+ | B | 223.0 | 5.40 | 6.3 | 1.4 | 20.0 | 31.0 | 10.0 | 14.6 | 25.9 |
| Community Bank | Liberal | KS | B- | C+ | B | 122.3 | 1.27 | 9.3 | 15.7 | 0.1 | 28.9 | 10.0 | 11.8 | 17.9 |
| ▲ Community Bank | Topeka | KS | B+ | B | B | 103.2 | 10.34 | 8.5 | 1.5 | 25.3 | 4.5 | 6.7 | 10.2 | 12.3 |
| Community Bank | Zanesville | OH | B- | C+ | C+ | 449.4 | 2.83 | 6.8 | 6.0 | 37.4 | 12.2 | 9.6 | 10.7 | 17.5 |
| Community Bank | Alva | OK | A- | A- | A- | 109.1 | 5.89 | 5.6 | 1.9 | 5.3 | 52.5 | 10.0 | 11.8 | 18.9 |
| Community Bank | Bristow | OK | A- | B+ | B+ | 87.1 | 1.51 | 5.8 | 4.2 | 31.5 | 11.1 | 6.3 | 8.3 | 14.4 |
| Community Bank | Joseph | OR | B+ | B | B- | 429.3 | 1.59 | 2.2 | 0.3 | 2.6 | 42.5 | 8.3 | 9.9 | 22.5 |
| Community Bank | Carmichaels | PA | B- | B- | B- | 1319.8 | 3.17 | 5.7 | 8.6 | 25.1 | 14.8 | 5.9 | 7.9 | 12.5 |
| Community Bank | Avon | SD | B- | B | B | 53.4 | -0.26 | 10.9 | 6.4 | 6.4 | 37.8 | 10.0 | 15.2 | 27.9 |
| Community Bank | Lexington | TN | B | B | B | 162.6 | 3.98 | 9.0 | 4.0 | 31.0 | 12.1 | 7.4 | 9.3 | 13.8 |
| Community Bank | Bridgeport | TX | B- | C+ | C+ | 99.8 | 0.86 | 14.3 | 2.2 | 18.6 | 10.8 | 9.3 | 10.5 | 15.6 |
| Community Bank | Longview | TX | A | A | A- | 213.5 | -2.77 | 13.8 | 3.2 | 36.7 | 0.0 | 10.0 | 11.2 | 16.3 |
| ▲ Community Bank & Trust - Alabama | Union Springs | AL | D | D- | D- | 48.5 | 2.48 | 7.5 | 5.4 | 12.3 | 40.6 | 6.6 | 8.6 | 21.5 |
| ▼ Community Bank & Trust - West Georgia | LaGrange | GA | E+ | D- | E+ | 73.9 | -15.08 | 6.4 | 1.5 | 19.2 | 12.6 | 0.1 | 3.2 | 6.3 |
| Community Bank & Trust, Waco, Texas | Waco | TX | A- | B+ | A- | 466.5 | 3.59 | 22.0 | 2.5 | 24.4 | 23.7 | 10.0 | 15.3 | 22.2 |
| Community Bank and Trust | Neosho | MO | B- | B- | B- | 310.5 | 0.73 | 7.5 | 1.6 | 16.1 | 13.2 | 6.8 | 8.8 | 18.3 |
| Community Bank and Trust Co. | Muscatine | IA | D+ | C | C | 241.9 | 4.03 | 8.0 | 3.5 | 11.6 | 21.1 | 6.9 | 8.9 | 14.4 |

| Asset Quality Index | Adjusted Non-Performing Loans as a % of Total Loans | Adjusted Non-Performing Loans as a % of Capital | Net Charge-Offs Avg Loans | Profitability Index | Net Income ($Mil) | Return on Assets (R.O.A.) | Return on Equity (R.O.E.) | Net Interest Spread | Overhead Efficiency Ratio | Liquidity Index | Liquidity Ratio | Hot Money Ratio | Stability Index |
|---|---|---|---|---|---|---|---|---|---|---|---|---|---|
| **5.6** | 0.00 | 0.0 | 0.01 | **4.6** | 0.5 | 0.89 | 4.91 | 4.50 | 73.8 | **2.6** | 28.1 | 18.1 | **8.1** |
| **7.5** | 0.60 | 3.1 | 0.04 | **5.5** | 0.7 | 1.10 | 10.76 | 4.07 | 68.3 | **2.1** | 32.9 | 26.6 | **5.7** |
| **7.7** | 0.15 | 0.4 | -0.01 | **6.6** | 1.4 | 1.21 | 9.73 | 3.66 | 78.2 | **1.5** | 24.5 | 26.9 | **9.7** |
| **5.4** | 0.43 | 2.9 | 0.62 | **6.1** | 7.6 | 1.12 | 11.52 | 3.59 | 53.0 | **0.7** | 12.6 | 24.2 | **6.3** |
| **8.7** | 0.12 | 0.1 | 0.01 | **7.0** | 8.2 | 1.39 | 13.11 | 3.84 | 53.2 | **5.8** | 49.1 | 5.8 | **5.1** |
| **5.8** | 1.18 | 5.0 | 0.01 | **6.8** | 10.7 | 1.40 | 13.33 | 3.97 | 57.4 | **4.1** | 20.1 | 8.5 | **7.3** |
| **7.3** | 0.15 | 1.0 | -0.08 | **9.9** | 4.5 | 2.28 | 21.20 | 4.89 | 52.8 | **3.1** | 27.2 | 14.9 | **7.3** |
| **8.3** | 0.25 | 1.2 | 0.05 | **4.7** | 3.9 | 1.17 | 12.53 | 3.26 | 67.4 | **3.5** | 35.4 | 15.9 | **6.3** |
| **7.3** | 0.93 | 3.1 | 0.05 | **3.5** | 1.0 | 0.68 | 4.48 | 4.10 | 81.0 | **2.0** | 25.2 | 20.8 | **7.7** |
| **4.1** | 3.13 | 13.5 | -0.02 | **4.8** | 5.6 | 1.08 | 11.33 | 3.16 | 61.7 | **1.6** | 16.6 | 5.7 | **6.5** |
| **4.8** | 1.36 | 9.9 | -0.19 | **2.9** | 1.0 | 0.46 | 5.84 | 3.40 | 84.6 | **3.7** | 35.9 | 14.9 | **4.1** |
| **6.1** | 0.72 | 4.7 | 0.36 | **5.0** | 1.5 | 0.95 | 9.03 | 4.07 | 69.7 | **2.1** | 28.6 | 22.6 | **6.6** |
| **7.1** | 0.52 | 2.8 | 0.07 | **6.4** | 0.7 | 1.35 | 11.04 | 4.40 | 58.1 | **1.2** | 3.1 | 25.9 | **7.4** |
| **6.9** | 3.09 | 5.8 | 0.13 | **5.4** | 2.5 | 1.31 | 9.07 | 3.19 | 60.2 | **5.8** | 67.3 | 11.8 | **8.4** |
| **5.7** | 1.16 | 8.2 | 0.10 | **6.6** | 16.9 | 1.33 | 13.48 | 3.85 | 54.7 | **1.0** | 9.7 | 22.7 | **9.0** |
| **6.3** | 1.80 | 9.0 | 0.02 | **5.5** | 0.6 | 1.10 | 12.00 | 3.92 | 56.7 | **2.5** | 32.7 | 20.6 | **5.0** |
| **4.8** | 0.99 | 5.8 | 0.15 | **5.1** | 2.3 | 1.09 | 11.15 | 3.55 | 69.5 | **0.7** | 7.7 | 33.8 | **6.8** |
| **7.6** | 0.43 | 1.7 | 0.10 | **7.9** | 13.1 | 1.70 | 14.96 | 3.94 | 61.6 | **4.6** | 35.0 | 10.5 | **9.0** |
| **9.4** | 0.15 | 0.5 | -0.01 | **5.0** | 4.7 | 1.14 | 7.45 | 4.10 | 71.2 | **5.1** | 38.5 | 8.5 | **8.6** |
| **6.5** | 0.33 | 1.8 | 0.10 | **4.7** | 9.2 | 0.91 | 9.08 | 4.26 | 75.0 | **5.5** | 26.2 | 3.8 | **8.0** |
| **6.5** | 1.07 | 4.9 | 0.13 | **4.3** | 1.5 | 0.86 | 5.90 | 3.92 | 76.6 | **6.0** | 44.1 | 4.4 | **7.8** |
| **6.0** | 0.62 | 1.5 | 0.00 | **9.4** | 2.5 | 2.32 | 16.21 | 4.13 | 42.8 | **1.3** | 12.7 | 24.7 | **10.0** |
| **6.3** | 0.97 | 6.4 | 0.00 | **4.2** | 0.6 | 0.74 | 4.76 | 2.96 | 73.6 | **3.9** | 27.7 | 11.4 | **6.5** |
| **3.4** | 2.29 | 15.4 | 0.16 | **3.2** | 0.5 | 0.59 | 6.70 | 3.74 | 83.2 | **4.0** | 25.8 | 10.2 | **3.8** |
| **5.4** | 0.83 | 3.3 | 0.10 | **6.2** | 9.4 | 1.25 | 12.08 | 4.11 | 63.8 | **4.0** | 14.7 | 8.7 | **7.1** |
| **7.3** | 1.18 | 4.1 | 0.00 | **5.9** | 2.8 | 1.21 | 8.17 | 4.53 | 68.0 | **2.6** | 19.7 | 16.5 | **8.1** |
| **4.0** | 3.28 | 18.8 | 0.28 | **8.6** | 3.0 | 1.88 | 14.56 | 4.36 | 57.8 | **1.0** | 27.1 | 39.5 | **8.1** |
| **8.9** | 0.00 | 0.0 | 0.04 | **7.3** | 2.7 | 1.75 | 14.15 | 4.07 | 59.7 | **4.4** | 29.1 | 9.1 | **8.8** |
| **8.6** | 0.04 | 0.5 | 0.10 | **7.3** | 3.8 | 1.78 | 20.54 | 4.33 | 61.2 | **3.1** | 16.3 | 13.4 | **6.7** |
| **7.4** | 0.32 | 3.5 | -0.01 | **5.6** | 2.7 | 1.39 | 16.83 | 3.42 | 57.3 | **1.7** | 20.7 | 22.7 | **5.9** |
| **9.2** | 0.00 | 0.0 | 0.00 | **4.8** | 0.5 | 0.80 | 2.61 | 3.26 | 64.9 | **4.1** | 78.9 | 21.6 | **8.4** |
| **4.8** | 0.48 | 5.1 | 0.14 | **5.5** | 1.7 | 1.32 | 13.47 | 4.05 | 61.9 | **1.2** | 11.5 | 26.0 | **7.1** |
| **4.6** | 1.13 | 6.6 | 1.33 | **5.2** | 1.1 | 1.27 | 14.90 | 4.50 | 65.9 | **4.9** | 38.7 | 9.8 | **4.2** |
| **4.1** | 3.13 | 11.7 | 0.17 | **9.4** | 3.7 | 1.99 | 19.47 | 4.40 | 44.4 | **0.7** | 10.0 | 35.2 | **8.6** |
| **7.2** | 0.29 | 2.1 | 0.07 | **5.3** | 1.7 | 1.33 | 12.59 | 3.34 | 63.6 | **3.1** | 24.2 | 14.2 | **6.4** |
| **4.0** | 1.04 | 14.1 | 0.07 | **1.2** | 0.0 | -0.01 | -0.14 | 3.72 | 100.3 | **5.1** | 29.5 | 4.7 | **3.2** |
| **8.1** | 0.26 | 1.9 | 0.24 | **3.9** | 9.1 | 0.87 | 8.94 | 3.33 | 82.4 | **1.5** | 15.4 | 10.2 | **8.1** |
| **5.8** | 1.00 | 5.3 | 0.08 | **7.3** | 13.9 | 1.20 | 9.93 | 3.94 | 61.5 | **0.7** | 14.5 | 48.0 | **10.0** |
| **9.9** | 0.13 | 1.2 | 0.06 | **3.1** | 0.9 | 0.63 | 4.14 | 2.80 | 80.3 | **4.2** | 76.5 | 23.1 | **7.9** |
| **8.6** | 0.54 | 2.7 | 0.00 | **3.6** | 1.2 | 0.62 | 4.14 | 3.32 | 76.3 | **0.8** | 19.5 | 37.1 | **7.9** |
| **2.0** | 9.52 | 31.3 | -0.58 | **1.0** | 0.0 | 0.06 | 0.65 | 3.69 | 98.0 | **3.6** | 37.9 | 16.1 | **2.2** |
| **7.8** | 0.53 | 1.5 | 0.00 | **4.3** | 1.4 | 0.99 | 9.96 | 3.83 | 75.1 | **5.2** | 42.7 | 9.3 | **3.3** |
| **5.6** | 1.72 | 6.9 | 0.09 | **3.6** | 0.7 | 0.75 | 5.48 | 4.12 | 83.3 | **4.3** | 21.8 | 7.9 | **7.0** |
| **8.9** | 0.32 | 1.7 | 0.19 | **5.6** | 3.1 | 1.44 | 10.15 | 2.92 | 50.5 | **2.8** | 36.3 | 19.9 | **8.1** |
| **2.8** | 3.83 | 13.4 | 0.04 | **5.4** | 1.3 | 1.11 | 9.55 | 4.18 | 66.0 | **1.9** | 27.0 | 24.1 | **7.3** |
| **8.7** | 0.00 | 0.0 | -0.09 | **8.3** | 1.6 | 1.63 | 16.26 | 4.27 | 57.9 | **3.1** | 16.3 | 13.9 | **6.8** |
| **4.3** | 1.98 | 10.2 | 0.03 | **5.3** | 5.2 | 1.14 | 11.50 | 4.16 | 70.4 | **2.8** | 8.7 | 14.2 | **6.2** |
| **8.9** | 0.40 | 1.3 | -0.03 | **5.1** | 1.2 | 1.16 | 9.51 | 3.09 | 61.4 | **1.9** | 39.4 | 39.4 | **8.4** |
| **8.6** | 0.00 | 0.0 | 0.16 | **10.0** | 1.9 | 2.13 | 23.85 | 5.02 | 51.4 | **3.8** | 29.0 | 12.2 | **6.5** |
| **8.5** | 0.41 | 1.6 | 0.03 | **5.1** | 6.3 | 1.49 | 15.15 | 3.91 | 74.3 | **6.4** | 60.3 | 7.1 | **6.4** |
| **5.8** | 0.54 | 2.8 | 0.05 | **4.9** | 14.2 | 1.08 | 10.06 | 3.62 | 68.5 | **3.5** | 10.6 | 11.2 | **8.5** |
| **3.8** | 5.24 | 18.6 | 0.28 | **3.0** | 0.2 | 0.42 | 2.71 | 3.50 | 84.5 | **2.7** | 42.8 | 25.4 | **7.0** |
| **6.9** | 0.12 | 1.3 | 0.10 | **4.5** | 1.3 | 0.79 | 8.34 | 4.04 | 71.3 | **0.7** | 15.0 | 39.2 | **6.0** |
| **7.3** | 0.04 | 0.1 | 0.14 | **4.5** | 0.8 | 0.80 | 7.74 | 4.87 | 71.1 | **3.2** | 25.4 | 14.1 | **5.4** |
| **8.5** | 0.00 | 0.0 | 0.00 | **9.7** | 5.5 | 2.51 | 22.64 | 3.99 | 42.1 | **2.0** | 11.0 | 18.6 | **8.9** |
| **4.4** | 3.06 | 12.4 | -0.03 | **2.9** | 0.3 | 0.55 | 7.32 | 3.58 | 89.7 | **2.8** | 49.8 | 27.6 | **2.3** |
| **1.7** | 3.29 | 46.4 | -0.02 | **0.0** | -0.9 | -1.09 | -31.38 | 4.94 | 126.7 | **5.0** | 28.9 | 5.1 | **0.7** |
| **8.6** | 0.35 | 1.0 | 0.25 | **5.3** | 5.2 | 1.15 | 7.67 | 3.90 | 68.2 | **2.7** | 33.1 | 19.0 | **7.1** |
| **7.7** | 0.55 | 2.1 | 0.07 | **4.4** | 3.5 | 1.13 | 12.19 | 3.48 | 78.2 | **5.8** | 32.8 | 1.8 | **5.5** |
| **3.8** | 0.72 | 3.4 | 1.30 | **1.9** | 0.5 | 0.20 | 1.79 | 3.75 | 78.8 | **4.2** | 40.4 | 14.3 | **4.7** |

| Name | City | State | Rating | 2018 Rating | 2017 Rating | Total Assets ($Mil) | One Year Asset Growth | Asset Mix (As a % of Total Assets) | | | | Capital-ization Index | Lever-age Ratio | Risk-Based Capital Ratio |
|---|---|---|---|---|---|---|---|---|---|---|---|---|---|---|
| | | | | | | | | Comm-ercial Loans | Cons-umer Loans | Mort-gage Loans | Secur-ities | | | |
| Community Bank Delaware | Lewes | DE | B- | B | B | 214.5 | 6.07 | 2.6 | 0.3 | 37.2 | 4.3 | 8.3 | 9.9 | 13.7 |
| ▲ Community Bank Mankato | Vernon Center | MN | C | C | C | 333.4 | 9.42 | 6.3 | 2.0 | 14.7 | 0.3 | 5.5 | 8.6 | 11.4 |
| Community Bank of Cameron | Cameron | WI | B | B- | B | 124.1 | 4.16 | 3.0 | 2.7 | 33.6 | 6.3 | 7.1 | 9.0 | 13.5 |
| ▲ Community Bank of Easton | Easton | IL | A- | B+ | A- | 37.9 | 1.89 | 23.9 | 10.2 | 3.0 | 1.3 | 10.0 | 20.4 | 27.8 |
| ▲ Community Bank of El Dorado Springs | El Dorado Springs | MO | A | B+ | A | 105.4 | 4.27 | 1.9 | 2.1 | 10.7 | 30.2 | 10.0 | 16.4 | 32.9 |
| Community Bank of Elmhurst | Elmhurst | IL | B- | B- | C | 145.8 | 0.04 | 6.7 | 0.1 | 13.2 | 36.9 | 6.7 | 10.5 | 12.3 |
| Community Bank of Georgia | Baxley | GA | C | C+ | B | 138.0 | 51.01 | 5.9 | 1.2 | 9.9 | 7.4 | 7.6 | 9.4 | 13.0 |
| Community Bank of Louisiana | Mansfield | LA | B | B | B | 532.8 | -0.38 | 5.1 | 1.5 | 11.0 | 45.8 | 7.6 | 9.4 | 18.7 |
| Community Bank of Marshall | Marshall | MO | B | B | B- | 176.7 | 8.07 | 3.8 | 2.6 | 11.0 | 38.6 | 10.0 | 11.1 | 18.3 |
| Community Bank of Memphis | Memphis | MO | B- | B- | B- | 43.9 | -7.62 | 3.0 | 3.4 | 15.5 | 22.3 | 10.0 | 12.9 | 24.5 |
| Community Bank of Mississippi | Forest | MS | B- | B- | B- | 3259.7 | 0.64 | 5.9 | 2.7 | 24.2 | 21.9 | 6.4 | 8.4 | 14.6 |
| Community Bank of Missouri | Richmond | MO | B+ | B | B | 53.9 | 2.77 | 5.1 | 1.2 | 20.8 | 3.9 | 10.0 | 14.0 | 19.7 |
| Community Bank of Oelwein | Oelwein | IA | B | B | B | 107.4 | 1.04 | 9.0 | 3.0 | 10.4 | 33.2 | 10.0 | 12.8 | 21.9 |
| Community Bank of Oklahoma | Verden | OK | B- | B- | B- | 41.2 | -5.38 | 17.0 | 6.7 | 4.3 | 10.0 | 10.0 | 14.5 | 17.7 |
| Community Bank of Parkersburg | Parkersburg | WV | B+ | B+ | A- | 255.9 | 4.63 | 2.9 | 7.0 | 57.7 | 11.0 | 9.8 | 10.8 | 17.9 |
| ▲ Community Bank of Pickens County | Jasper | GA | C+ | C- | C- | 366.9 | 3.59 | 5.2 | 2.1 | 15.7 | 9.4 | 10.0 | 11.6 | 16.7 |
| Community Bank of Pleasant Hill | Pleasant Hill | MO | B+ | B+ | B+ | 82.9 | 15.84 | 10.9 | 1.4 | 7.3 | 43.9 | 7.7 | 9.5 | 17.6 |
| Community Bank of Raymore | Raymore | MO | B+ | B+ | B+ | 269.1 | 4.64 | 12.7 | 0.5 | 2.1 | 32.0 | 5.7 | 7.7 | 12.6 |
| Community Bank of Santa Maria | Santa Maria | CA | A- | B+ | B- | 263.3 | 4.85 | 10.6 | 0.3 | 0.3 | 21.5 | 8.4 | 10.2 | 13.7 |
| Community Bank of the Bay | Oakland | CA | B | B- | B | 493.8 | 26.40 | 19.2 | 0.1 | 5.4 | 3.2 | 9.6 | 11.6 | 14.7 |
| Community Bank of the Chesapeake | Waldorf | MD | B- | B- | B | 1796.0 | 6.43 | 5.3 | 0.1 | 16.6 | 11.6 | 7.9 | 10.6 | 13.3 |
| ▲ Community Bank of the Midwest | Great Bend | KS | B | B | B | 175.5 | -0.10 | 12.5 | 2.8 | 7.7 | 8.0 | 6.9 | 10.7 | 12.5 |
| ▲ Community Bank of the South | Merritt Island | FL | A- | C+ | C | 160.2 | 2.60 | 3.6 | 0.7 | 5.4 | 23.0 | 9.1 | 10.4 | 25.2 |
| Community Bank of Trenton | Trenton | IL | B | B- | C+ | 84.5 | 1.29 | 7.0 | 4.5 | 29.7 | 13.1 | 10.0 | 11.9 | 17.2 |
| Community Bank of Wichita, Inc. | Wichita | KS | C+ | B- | B- | 86.7 | 11.51 | 24.4 | 4.7 | 19.7 | 9.2 | 5.8 | 9.0 | 11.6 |
| Community Bank Owatonna | Owatonna | MN | C+ | C+ | C+ | 60.8 | 7.53 | 9.3 | 1.4 | 17.7 | 13.3 | 7.1 | 9.1 | 12.6 |
| Community Bank, N.A. | De Witt | NY | B+ | B+ | B+ | 11210.0 | 7.66 | 5.2 | 11.6 | 24.3 | 27.2 | 6.6 | 8.6 | 14.6 |
| Community Bankers' Bank | Midlothian | VA | C+ | C- | C- | 138.7 | 2.03 | 7.7 | 1.0 | 4.2 | 17.6 | 10.0 | 13.0 | 16.7 |
| Community Banking Co. of Fitzgerald | Fitzgerald | GA | A- | B+ | A- | 162.5 | 2.71 | 6.0 | 9.9 | 24.1 | 10.3 | 10.0 | 12.1 | 17.5 |
| Community Banks of Shelby County | Cowden | IL | C+ | C+ | C | 49.6 | -0.36 | 9.1 | 2.8 | 10.6 | 19.5 | 10.0 | 11.7 | 22.1 |
| Community Commerce Bank | Claremont | CA | B+ | B+ | B | 279.9 | 7.88 | 0.0 | 13.0 | 6.2 | 0.1 | 10.0 | 19.1 | 25.2 |
| Community Development Bank, FSB | Ogema | MN | C+ | B- | B- | 169.9 | 0.21 | 7.6 | 2.6 | 11.4 | 14.7 | 8.0 | 9.6 | 14.6 |
| ▲ Community Federal Savings Bank | New York | NY | C | D | D- | 219.5 | 37.62 | 2.8 | 4.8 | 13.5 | 5.0 | 7.7 | 9.5 | 17.4 |
| Community Financial Bank | Prentice | WI | C+ | C+ | C+ | 44.6 | -4.73 | 5.8 | 1.6 | 32.6 | 0.0 | 9.6 | 10.7 | 17.6 |
| Community Financial Services Bank | Benton | KY | C+ | C+ | C+ | 1238.4 | 5.65 | 13.6 | 10.7 | 19.0 | 10.6 | 6.5 | 9.1 | 12.2 |
| Community First Bank | Kansas City | KS | B+ | B | B | 205.1 | 7.69 | 15.7 | 0.7 | 12.3 | 2.2 | 6.4 | 10.2 | 12.1 |
| ▲ Community First Bank | New Iberia | LA | B | B | B+ | 390.4 | 1.19 | 12.2 | 3.6 | 23.8 | 8.6 | 9.2 | 10.4 | 14.4 |
| Community First Bank | Menahga | MN | A- | A- | A- | 91.1 | 3.15 | 7.9 | 6.0 | 15.9 | 22.0 | 10.0 | 14.7 | 25.7 |
| Community First Bank | Butler | MO | B | B | B- | 179.2 | -0.69 | 10.6 | 3.5 | 19.4 | 5.4 | 6.8 | 8.8 | 12.9 |
| Community First Bank | Maywood | NE | D- | D | D | 118.8 | -8.49 | 5.5 | 2.3 | 6.6 | 17.7 | 7.6 | 10.5 | 13.0 |
| Community First Bank | Walhalla | SC | C | C | C- | 418.3 | 9.57 | 4.0 | 24.2 | 10.2 | 10.8 | 9.1 | 10.6 | 14.2 |
| Community First Bank | Kennewick | WA | B+ | B+ | B+ | 353.5 | 9.05 | 3.7 | 0.9 | 10.6 | 18.8 | 8.0 | 9.6 | 15.7 |
| Community First Bank | Boscobel | WI | B+ | B+ | B | 425.8 | 2.00 | 8.2 | 1.4 | 16.1 | 20.7 | 9.5 | 10.7 | 15.0 |
| Community First Bank | Rosholt | WI | B | B- | C+ | 90.3 | 10.54 | 3.6 | 1.5 | 14.0 | 26.0 | 7.9 | 9.6 | 15.2 |
| Community First Bank of Indiana | Kokomo | IN | B- | B- | B | 330.6 | 15.36 | 13.5 | 1.0 | 9.4 | 1.7 | 7.1 | 11.3 | 12.6 |
| Community First Bank of the Heartland | Mount Vernon | IL | B | B | B+ | 198.4 | 3.00 | 12.0 | 0.4 | 9.9 | 8.0 | 5.8 | 8.7 | 11.6 |
| Community First Bank, N.A. | Forest | OH | C- | C- | C- | 51.4 | -5.50 | 6.4 | 1.7 | 27.3 | 11.0 | 9.0 | 10.4 | 20.1 |
| Community First Banking Co. | West Plains | MO | A- | A- | A | 192.8 | 7.59 | 6.9 | 3.7 | 24.9 | 21.5 | 10.0 | 12.1 | 18.0 |
| Community First National Bank | Manhattan | KS | C+ | C+ | B- | 292.7 | 3.53 | 12.2 | 2.0 | 20.0 | 0.0 | 5.5 | 9.5 | 11.4 |
| ▲ Community National B&T of Texas | Corsicana | TX | A- | B- | B+ | 743.9 | -1.02 | 6.1 | 1.4 | 12.5 | 12.0 | 8.8 | 10.3 | 14.0 |
| ▲ Community National Bank | Seneca | KS | A- | A- | A- | 479.5 | 6.67 | 3.1 | 0.4 | 5.9 | 57.4 | 6.8 | 8.8 | 18.4 |
| Community National Bank | Monett | MO | B+ | B+ | B+ | 154.8 | 27.72 | 3.9 | 3.1 | 16.7 | 8.5 | 6.8 | 8.8 | 14.3 |
| ▼ Community National Bank | Dayton | TN | C | C+ | B- | 272.9 | 15.66 | 4.3 | 1.7 | 17.0 | 11.4 | 9.3 | 10.6 | 17.2 |
| Community National Bank | Hondo | TX | B+ | B | B | 215.7 | 7.35 | 6.3 | 1.9 | 9.7 | 24.1 | 9.5 | 10.7 | 17.2 |
| Community National Bank | Midland | TX | B+ | B | C+ | 1435.2 | 6.17 | 22.2 | 1.2 | 6.0 | 12.7 | 9.0 | 10.4 | 14.9 |
| Community National Bank | Newport | VT | B- | C+ | B- | 737.4 | 2.45 | 12.2 | 0.6 | 22.5 | 5.0 | 7.8 | 9.5 | 14.5 |
| Community National Bank & Trust | Chanute | KS | B- | B- | B- | 1323.3 | 10.10 | 8.5 | 2.7 | 15.8 | 16.8 | 6.7 | 8.7 | 12.3 |
| ▲ Community National Bank in Monmouth | Monmouth | IL | D+ | D+ | C | 41.8 | 9.69 | 5.6 | 6.9 | 16.0 | 16.3 | 10.0 | 15.1 | 26.2 |
| Community National Bank of Okarche | Okarche | OK | A | A | A | 115.7 | -1.10 | 8.1 | 2.5 | 5.4 | 50.7 | 10.0 | 14.0 | 26.5 |
| Community Neighbor Bank | Camden | AL | A- | B+ | A- | 104.1 | 0.44 | 15.2 | 7.7 | 16.6 | 15.0 | 10.0 | 14.7 | 22.4 |

| Asset Quality Index | Adjusted Non-Performing Loans as a % of Total Loans | Adjusted Non-Performing Loans as a % of Capital | Net Charge-Offs Avg Loans | Profitability Index | Net Income ($Mil) | Return on Assets (R.O.A.) | Return on Equity (R.O.E.) | Net Interest Spread | Overhead Efficiency Ratio | Liquidity Index | Liquidity Ratio | Hot Money Ratio | Stability Index |
|---|---|---|---|---|---|---|---|---|---|---|---|---|---|
| **8.2** | 0.07 | 0.4 | 0.01 | **3.7** | 1.3 | 0.62 | 6.31 | 3.23 | 76.0 | **0.6** | 9.1 | 48.7 | **6.1** |
| **3.7** | 1.45 | 12.6 | 0.08 | **5.4** | 3.0 | 0.95 | 11.17 | 3.93 | 64.5 | **1.8** | 16.0 | 20.7 | **5.0** |
| **6.2** | 0.56 | 3.9 | 0.00 | **6.1** | 1.8 | 1.46 | 15.79 | 4.25 | 65.3 | **2.4** | 18.7 | 14.4 | **6.8** |
| **7.5** | 0.00 | 0.0 | 0.00 | **10.0** | 1.0 | 2.79 | 13.75 | 4.72 | 19.8 | **4.0** | 31.2 | 12.2 | **9.3** |
| **7.5** | 1.60 | 3.4 | 0.04 | **6.7** | 1.7 | 1.56 | 9.37 | 3.04 | 51.5 | **4.1** | 56.4 | 18.6 | **10.0** |
| **5.3** | 2.60 | 9.4 | 0.32 | **4.2** | 1.4 | 0.93 | 9.12 | 3.74 | 72.0 | **6.0** | 42.4 | 4.1 | **5.1** |
| **3.3** | 1.90 | 13.7 | -0.14 | **9.0** | 1.7 | 1.54 | 14.29 | 4.78 | 47.0 | **0.8** | 22.2 | 39.9 | **6.0** |
| **7.0** | 1.10 | 5.1 | 0.02 | **6.2** | 7.9 | 1.59 | 17.56 | 3.47 | 58.1 | **2.7** | 29.2 | 17.9 | **5.6** |
| **9.1** | 0.02 | 0.1 | -0.04 | **4.8** | 1.6 | 1.06 | 9.06 | 3.07 | 61.5 | **5.4** | 43.2 | 8.6 | **6.4** |
| **8.1** | 0.00 | 0.0 | 0.02 | **4.9** | 0.5 | 0.99 | 7.26 | 3.46 | 56.9 | **3.8** | 41.1 | 16.4 | **7.0** |
| **6.5** | 0.60 | 5.0 | 0.14 | **4.8** | 29.4 | 0.89 | 10.23 | 3.54 | 70.1 | **1.9** | 20.4 | 22.1 | **7.2** |
| **8.1** | 0.53 | 3.0 | 0.02 | **6.0** | 0.6 | 1.17 | 8.38 | 5.45 | 73.6 | **3.3** | 11.4 | 12.0 | **7.2** |
| **8.4** | 0.00 | 0.4 | 0.12 | **4.5** | 1.1 | 1.02 | 8.19 | 2.84 | 56.0 | **2.2** | 48.9 | 52.3 | **7.2** |
| **5.8** | 2.56 | 7.8 | 0.00 | **6.3** | 0.6 | 1.45 | 10.71 | 5.18 | 73.3 | **2.6** | 20.0 | 16.6 | **7.1** |
| **6.8** | 0.69 | 2.8 | 0.02 | **5.6** | 3.2 | 1.30 | 11.89 | 4.03 | 71.2 | **2.8** | 9.0 | 14.3 | **7.5** |
| **3.0** | 4.28 | 16.1 | 0.12 | **7.7** | 5.5 | 1.54 | 13.40 | 4.07 | 55.8 | **0.8** | 18.9 | 41.1 | **6.5** |
| **7.8** | 0.00 | 0.0 | 0.05 | **4.7** | 0.7 | 0.92 | 9.39 | 3.00 | 73.8 | **7.0** | 57.2 | 0.5 | **6.0** |
| **8.4** | 0.00 | 0.0 | 0.04 | **8.4** | 4.4 | 1.70 | 20.36 | 3.43 | 68.4 | **5.0** | 28.8 | 4.8 | **6.8** |
| **7.4** | 0.33 | 1.3 | -0.01 | **6.3** | 2.9 | 1.14 | 10.48 | 4.63 | 66.3 | **4.7** | 27.3 | 6.2 | **6.4** |
| **6.4** | 0.05 | 0.2 | -0.03 | **4.9** | 4.1 | 0.92 | 7.72 | 4.30 | 65.3 | **2.1** | 18.7 | 18.9 | **6.2** |
| **3.7** | 1.27 | 9.0 | 0.16 | **5.3** | 18.7 | 1.07 | 9.59 | 3.47 | 55.5 | **2.3** | 12.4 | 15.4 | **8.6** |
| **8.5** | 0.07 | 0.4 | 0.82 | **6.3** | 2.5 | 1.46 | 13.83 | 4.01 | 54.0 | **5.0** | 36.9 | 8.5 | **6.8** |
| **8.4** | 0.00 | 0.0 | -0.09 | **6.4** | 2.2 | 1.40 | 13.82 | 3.82 | 55.7 | **6.2** | 61.3 | 8.6 | **6.0** |
| **4.5** | 2.61 | 11.7 | 0.22 | **4.8** | 1.1 | 1.27 | 10.64 | 3.44 | 65.6 | **2.2** | 20.4 | 18.3 | **6.3** |
| **4.7** | 1.13 | 11.0 | 0.00 | **4.7** | 0.7 | 0.84 | 9.13 | 4.64 | 73.4 | **1.0** | 8.4 | 30.1 | **4.3** |
| **7.7** | 0.52 | 1.9 | 0.09 | **3.3** | 0.3 | 0.56 | 6.15 | 3.74 | 81.5 | **1.5** | 26.2 | 23.7 | **4.6** |
| **6.4** | 0.31 | 1.6 | 0.15 | **6.6** | 142.5 | 1.32 | 9.30 | 3.82 | 60.0 | **4.9** | 18.4 | 3.9 | **10.0** |
| **7.5** | 0.00 | 0.0 | 0.15 | **2.7** | 0.6 | 0.46 | 3.44 | 3.02 | 88.3 | **0.7** | 16.5 | 18.6 | **6.7** |
| **6.1** | 1.01 | 5.1 | 0.11 | **7.1** | 2.4 | 1.46 | 11.45 | 4.40 | 57.0 | **1.9** | 15.6 | 19.6 | **8.2** |
| **8.0** | 0.16 | 4.1 | -0.02 | **3.0** | 0.3 | 0.61 | 5.23 | 2.98 | 81.3 | **4.0** | 44.1 | 15.6 | **5.8** |
| **5.9** | 1.29 | 3.0 | -0.06 | **4.6** | 2.0 | 0.72 | 3.73 | 3.33 | 70.6 | **0.6** | 21.2 | 72.0 | **8.6** |
| **4.0** | 1.76 | 8.0 | 0.21 | **3.5** | 0.8 | 0.50 | 3.94 | 3.77 | 79.8 | **3.2** | 25.1 | 14.0 | **6.5** |
| **5.6** | 1.63 | 10.5 | 0.00 | **2.6** | 1.2 | 0.66 | 7.23 | 3.40 | 89.3 | **2.7** | 44.7 | 28.3 | **3.1** |
| **7.6** | 0.73 | 3.2 | 0.11 | **3.3** | 0.3 | 0.59 | 5.75 | 3.13 | 80.7 | **1.4** | 25.8 | 29.4 | **5.8** |
| **1.9** | 3.45 | 25.7 | 0.36 | **3.5** | 7.6 | 0.62 | 6.86 | 3.41 | 67.7 | **0.8** | 11.0 | 24.1 | **7.8** |
| **8.4** | 0.00 | 0.0 | 0.00 | **9.7** | 3.5 | 1.79 | 18.63 | 4.80 | 52.4 | **0.4** | 1.7 | 49.5 | **6.9** |
| **5.2** | 1.10 | 8.1 | 0.07 | **7.2** | 6.7 | 1.67 | 16.71 | 4.53 | 62.3 | **1.6** | 13.8 | 22.3 | **8.4** |
| **8.1** | 0.40 | 1.4 | 0.04 | **6.3** | 1.3 | 1.52 | 9.57 | 4.13 | 65.1 | **4.7** | 45.4 | 10.8 | **9.0** |
| **4.7** | 1.10 | 8.2 | 0.26 | **7.3** | 2.9 | 1.67 | 17.91 | 4.33 | 56.2 | **1.5** | 16.0 | 22.2 | **7.0** |
| **0.0** | 6.46 | 29.2 | 1.28 | **1.5** | -0.9 | -0.76 | -6.05 | 4.43 | 82.5 | **1.3** | 8.1 | 19.9 | **6.9** |
| **4.5** | 0.98 | 3.7 | -0.04 | **2.5** | 1.2 | 0.30 | 2.98 | 3.79 | 90.6 | **1.8** | 16.3 | 20.0 | **5.9** |
| **7.9** | 0.38 | 2.0 | 0.03 | **5.2** | 4.2 | 1.28 | 11.93 | 3.79 | 77.0 | **6.0** | 36.9 | 1.8 | **6.9** |
| **5.1** | 1.55 | 6.8 | 0.03 | **5.8** | 5.8 | 1.38 | 11.56 | 3.96 | 65.1 | **2.8** | 21.2 | 14.0 | **7.6** |
| **8.1** | 0.26 | 1.3 | -0.04 | **4.5** | 0.9 | 1.06 | 9.50 | 4.31 | 75.8 | **6.4** | 43.8 | 1.7 | **6.0** |
| **5.4** | 0.76 | 3.3 | 0.04 | **5.4** | 2.6 | 0.92 | 8.46 | 4.58 | 73.8 | **1.5** | 14.2 | 15.7 | **6.9** |
| **4.2** | 0.88 | 7.4 | 0.29 | **7.3** | 3.5 | 1.76 | 18.64 | 4.49 | 59.1 | **2.3** | 5.6 | 14.1 | **7.6** |
| **9.2** | 0.00 | 0.0 | 0.02 | **2.4** | 0.2 | 0.33 | 3.23 | 3.37 | 87.9 | **6.1** | 43.0 | 3.5 | **4.6** |
| **8.5** | 0.70 | 2.0 | 0.08 | **6.2** | 2.8 | 1.46 | 12.29 | 3.64 | 64.0 | **3.5** | 18.4 | 10.6 | **8.7** |
| **6.4** | 0.46 | 2.7 | 0.13 | **4.6** | 2.9 | 0.98 | 10.64 | 3.32 | 76.0 | **0.8** | 8.4 | 30.8 | **5.8** |
| **6.6** | 0.47 | 1.9 | 0.00 | **7.4** | 11.0 | 1.49 | 12.64 | 4.75 | 61.9 | **3.6** | 14.6 | 11.2 | **8.5** |
| **6.4** | 1.65 | 4.7 | -0.01 | **9.5** | 10.5 | 2.23 | 25.13 | 3.42 | 45.8 | **6.1** | 48.6 | 5.4 | **7.3** |
| **8.7** | 0.09 | 0.5 | 0.01 | **5.5** | 1.7 | 1.28 | 13.58 | 3.83 | 71.2 | **5.2** | 43.6 | 9.8 | **5.7** |
| **2.4** | 4.17 | 28.8 | -0.06 | **4.5** | 2.6 | 1.00 | 9.32 | 4.44 | 79.3 | **2.1** | 20.5 | 19.2 | **7.2** |
| **7.4** | 0.50 | 2.3 | -0.03 | **5.6** | 2.9 | 1.39 | 12.07 | 4.17 | 69.7 | **4.6** | 37.4 | 11.1 | **7.5** |
| **5.8** | 1.12 | 5.3 | 0.23 | **9.0** | 25.0 | 1.80 | 16.54 | 4.42 | 46.7 | **6.3** | 34.3 | 2.7 | **8.2** |
| **4.7** | 0.77 | 5.6 | 0.13 | **6.6** | 9.6 | 1.35 | 12.38 | 4.04 | 60.5 | **3.2** | 8.8 | 10.5 | **7.9** |
| **4.7** | 1.43 | 9.1 | 0.21 | **4.5** | 10.3 | 0.83 | 8.47 | 3.87 | 73.0 | **2.9** | 14.5 | 14.6 | **8.2** |
| **6.1** | 1.00 | 3.9 | 1.80 | **0.6** | -0.1 | -0.17 | -1.06 | 3.88 | 82.6 | **4.3** | 44.4 | 14.3 | **5.1** |
| **8.9** | 0.00 | 0.3 | 0.00 | **7.5** | 2.1 | 1.78 | 13.21 | 3.31 | 46.3 | **0.7** | 9.8 | 40.3 | **9.9** |
| **5.7** | 1.53 | 6.7 | 0.10 | **6.9** | 1.5 | 1.39 | 9.19 | 4.99 | 67.0 | **2.4** | 29.1 | 19.2 | **8.6** |

| Name | City | State | Rating | 2018 Rating | 2017 Rating | Total Assets ($Mil) | One Year Asset Growth | Asset Mix (As a % of Total Assets) Commercial Loans | Consumer Loans | Mortgage Loans | Securities | Capitalization Index | Leverage Ratio | Risk-Based Capital Ratio |
|---|---|---|---|---|---|---|---|---|---|---|---|---|---|---|
| ▲ Community Partners Savings Bank | Salem | IL | **B-** | C | C | 202.1 | 0.51 | 4.5 | 18.8 | 29.3 | 10.7 | **10.0** | 11.4 | 18.4 |
| Community Point Bank | Russellville | MO | **B-** | B- | C+ | 137.0 | 5.96 | 5.5 | 3.2 | 21.7 | 12.6 | **7.3** | 9.2 | 13.7 |
| Community Resource Bank | Northfield | MN | **A-** | A- | B- | 311.6 | -0.90 | 10.2 | 0.9 | 17.5 | 11.7 | **10.0** | 12.8 | 17.1 |
| Community Savings | Caldwell | OH | **D** | D | D | 51.9 | -8.18 | 0.0 | 14.4 | 47.7 | 9.0 | **10.0** | 14.0 | 32.5 |
| Community Savings Bank | Edgewood | IA | **D** | C- | C | 427.1 | -0.13 | 10.5 | 2.2 | 8.7 | 19.6 | **6.7** | 9.1 | 12.2 |
| Community Savings Bank | Chicago | IL | **C** | C | C | 404.9 | 2.70 | 0.0 | 0.0 | 35.0 | 29.5 | **10.0** | 16.3 | 39.2 |
| Community Savings Bank | Bethel | OH | **B-** | B | B | 80.9 | 3.21 | 9.9 | 0.6 | 45.5 | 12.3 | **10.0** | 16.4 | 27.0 |
| Community Shores Bank | Muskegon | MI | **C-** | D+ | D+ | 201.5 | 9.21 | 25.7 | 0.5 | 10.8 | 8.3 | **7.0** | 9.2 | 12.5 |
| Community Spirit Bank | Red Bay | AL | **B** | B | B | 152.6 | 2.89 | 10.4 | 5.1 | 24.5 | 17.2 | **9.2** | 10.5 | 16.7 |
| Community State Bank | Bradley | AR | **C** | C- | D+ | 20.6 | 20.17 | 30.7 | 7.4 | 10.5 | 10.5 | **9.9** | 11.0 | 18.4 |
| Community State Bank | Lamar | CO | **A-** | A- | A- | 132.2 | 13.07 | 13.0 | 2.9 | 5.7 | 8.6 | **10.0** | 13.4 | 17.0 |
| Community State Bank | Starke | FL | **C+** | C | C+ | 130.4 | -3.14 | 7.0 | 2.2 | 14.2 | 27.7 | **6.9** | 8.9 | 18.6 |
| Community State Bank | Ankeny | IA | **B+** | B | B+ | 854.7 | 8.73 | 20.0 | 0.1 | 7.8 | 18.5 | **6.8** | 10.4 | 12.3 |
| Community State Bank | Paton | IA | **B** | B | B+ | 44.6 | -3.23 | 3.8 | 2.1 | 1.8 | 47.9 | **10.0** | 19.8 | 34.2 |
| Community State Bank | Spencer | IA | **B+** | B+ | A- | 211.4 | 1.13 | 13.6 | 1.4 | 5.1 | 39.6 | **7.6** | 9.4 | 18.9 |
| ▲ Community State Bank | Galva | IL | **B-** | C | C | 234.4 | 0.69 | 6.7 | 1.7 | 10.0 | 15.8 | **9.5** | 10.6 | 14.7 |
| Community State Bank | Avilla | IN | **A-** | B+ | A- | 278.5 | 4.94 | 16.8 | 1.5 | 27.8 | 9.3 | **9.5** | 10.7 | 16.1 |
| Community State Bank | Brook | IN | **B-** | C+ | C | 69.2 | 16.23 | 4.7 | 1.3 | 35.5 | 8.1 | **10.0** | 12.9 | 18.9 |
| Community State Bank | Royal Center | IN | **B-** | C+ | C- | 128.6 | 5.69 | 6.0 | 3.4 | 16.4 | 21.8 | **9.6** | 10.7 | 17.6 |
| Community State Bank | Coffeyville | KS | **A** | A- | A- | 156.5 | -3.31 | 10.5 | 1.0 | 6.8 | 32.2 | **10.0** | 11.6 | 17.3 |
| ▲ Community State Bank | Shelbina | MO | **B-** | B- | B- | 81.6 | 11.05 | 5.2 | 11.1 | 26.4 | 23.8 | **7.8** | 9.5 | 15.9 |
| Community State Bank | Hennessey | OK | **C-** | D | D | 68.9 | -2.88 | 10.0 | 3.6 | 5.6 | 46.6 | **5.2** | 7.2 | 18.8 |
| Community State Bank | Poteau | OK | **B-** | B- | B- | 265.3 | -1.03 | 7.9 | 3.5 | 21.6 | 12.3 | **7.8** | 9.5 | 14.1 |
| Community State Bank | Union Grove | WI | **B-** | C+ | C- | 393.5 | 1.21 | 17.1 | 0.5 | 9.6 | 20.7 | **7.2** | 9.8 | 12.7 |
| Community State Bank of Canton | Canton | OK | **B-** | C+ | C+ | 50.1 | 6.64 | 10.9 | 8.5 | 5.5 | 23.8 | **10.0** | 11.3 | 15.6 |
| Community State Bank of Missouri | Bowling Green | MO | **B+** | B+ | B+ | 240.9 | -1.28 | 6.3 | 0.6 | 17.9 | 24.3 | **9.5** | 14.0 | 14.5 |
| Community State Bank of Orbisonia | Orbisonia | PA | **B** | B | B | 329.5 | 0.05 | 3.1 | 8.3 | 60.2 | 6.0 | **10.0** | 11.7 | 19.0 |
| Community State Bank of Rock Falls | Rock Falls | IL | **C-** | C | D+ | 275.4 | 4.35 | 10.1 | 1.7 | 28.2 | 12.0 | **8.6** | 10.1 | 17.0 |
| Community State Bank Of Southwestern In | Poseyville | IN | **B** | B- | B- | 85.3 | 5.54 | 11.8 | 1.9 | 25.1 | 3.3 | **8.7** | 10.1 | 15.8 |
| Community Trust Bank | Irvington | IL | **B-** | B- | B- | 82.8 | -4.06 | 4.6 | 0.7 | 9.8 | 30.0 | **10.0** | 14.4 | 24.9 |
| Community Trust Bank, Inc. | Pikeville | KY | **B** | B- | B- | 4344.7 | 3.95 | 7.4 | 16.9 | 19.7 | 13.5 | **10.0** | 13.3 | 19.1 |
| Community Valley Bank | El Centro | CA | **A-** | B+ | A- | 201.8 | 3.23 | 12.1 | 0.0 | 4.6 | 0.7 | **10.0** | 11.7 | 15.0 |
| ▲ Community West Bank, N.A. | Goleta | CA | **C+** | C- | C+ | 913.7 | 5.18 | 3.6 | 28.2 | 3.3 | 2.8 | **5.5** | 9.1 | 11.4 |
| CommunityBank of Texas, N.A. | Beaumont | TX | **A-** | A- | B+ | 3478.8 | 6.05 | 15.1 | 1.1 | 7.8 | 6.6 | **10.0** | 11.9 | 15.0 |
| Compass Savings Bank | Wilmerding | PA | **D-** | D+ | C- | 49.2 | -21.85 | 0.0 | 0.8 | 70.4 | 9.6 | **7.4** | 9.2 | 19.1 |
| Computershare Trust Co., N.A. | Canton | MA | **U** | U | U | 29.2 | 11.49 | 0.0 | 0.0 | 0.0 | 0.0 | **10.0** | 84.2 | 248.1 |
| Concorde Bank | Blomkest | MN | **C+** | C+ | B- | 56.0 | -2.25 | 7.3 | 2.7 | 20.2 | 2.6 | **9.5** | 10.9 | 14.6 |
| Concordia Bank | Concordia | MO | **B+** | B | B | 69.8 | -5.94 | 4.0 | 1.5 | 22.7 | 9.8 | **9.1** | 11.0 | 14.2 |
| Concordia Bank & Trust Co. | Vidalia | LA | **B** | B | B | 533.4 | 5.31 | 4.3 | 2.2 | 13.1 | 32.7 | **10.0** | 12.1 | 18.8 |
| ▲ Congressional Bank | Bethesda | MD | **C** | C- | B- | 1111.4 | 17.02 | 31.6 | 1.9 | 10.4 | 2.6 | **10.0** | 13.5 | 16.7 |
| Conneaut Savings Bank | Conneaut | OH | **C** | C | C | 77.1 | 2.90 | 1.5 | 0.5 | 49.4 | 21.4 | **10.0** | 14.7 | 31.5 |
| Connect Bank | Star City | AR | **B+** | A- | A- | 96.6 | 3.96 | 11.3 | 1.4 | 17.3 | 23.0 | **10.0** | 15.0 | 23.0 |
| Connecticut Community Bank, N.A. | Norwalk | CT | **C** | C | D | 424.9 | -7.73 | 31.4 | 0.3 | 3.8 | 1.5 | **9.1** | 10.4 | 15.1 |
| Connection Bank | Fort Madison | IA | **B-** | B- | B- | 319.8 | 12.29 | 12.0 | 2.0 | 30.8 | 7.5 | **5.5** | 8.4 | 11.4 |
| Connections Bank | Kirksville | MO | **B** | C+ | B- | 89.4 | 3.47 | 2.5 | 1.0 | 39.5 | 10.1 | **10.0** | 11.2 | 17.1 |
| ConnectOne Bank | Englewood Cliffs | NJ | **C+** | C | C- | 6173.9 | 13.04 | 12.0 | 0.0 | 8.3 | 6.6 | **7.2** | 10.8 | 12.6 |
| Consumers National Bank | Minerva | OH | **B** | B- | C+ | 574.6 | 11.24 | 9.1 | 1.1 | 10.9 | 23.8 | **6.9** | 8.9 | 12.5 |
| Continental Bank | Salt Lake City | UT | **B** | B- | B+ | 151.6 | -8.28 | 71.0 | 0.0 | 0.0 | 7.9 | **10.0** | 16.7 | 20.2 |
| Converse County Bank | Douglas | WY | **B+** | B | B | 684.6 | 13.83 | 7.2 | 4.0 | 4.5 | 59.0 | **6.7** | 8.8 | 26.8 |
| Conway Bank | Conway Springs | KS | **D+** | D+ | C- | 100.2 | 0.16 | 8.2 | 0.9 | 15.6 | 10.4 | **5.4** | 7.4 | 14.1 |
| Conway National Bank | Conway | SC | **B+** | B | B | 1260.9 | 6.13 | 4.8 | 4.0 | 13.2 | 50.8 | **8.1** | 9.7 | 19.7 |
| Cooperative Bank | Roslindale | MA | **C+** | C+ | C+ | 438.3 | 3.98 | 1.9 | 1.0 | 46.1 | 9.7 | **8.2** | 9.8 | 14.6 |
| Cooperative Bank of Cape Cod | Hyannis | MA | **C+** | C+ | C+ | 953.5 | 2.35 | 3.2 | 0.1 | 54.2 | 5.5 | **8.9** | 10.3 | 16.2 |
| Copiah Bank | Hazlehurst | MS | **B-** | B- | B- | 227.3 | 1.15 | 8.2 | 3.1 | 20.1 | 11.3 | **8.4** | 10.0 | 14.2 |
| Corder Bank | Corder | MO | **C** | C- | D+ | 19.6 | 3.81 | 11.4 | 5.3 | 20.3 | 5.1 | **10.0** | 11.4 | 18.5 |
| Core Bank | Omaha | NE | **C+** | B- | B- | 593.8 | 12.00 | 20.3 | 0.3 | 14.9 | 6.9 | **5.3** | 8.4 | 11.2 |
| COREBANK | Waynoka | OK | **C-** | D | D- | 69.1 | 52.72 | 13.6 | 0.4 | 24.2 | 7.4 | **10.0** | 11.7 | 17.5 |
| CoreFirst Bank & Trust | Topeka | KS | **C+** | C+ | C- | 963.2 | 6.26 | 12.0 | 4.3 | 8.4 | 25.2 | **8.0** | 9.6 | 13.7 |
| Corn City State Bank | Deshler | OH | **B+** | B+ | B+ | 67.6 | 3.76 | 0.1 | 2.7 | 28.2 | 44.8 | **10.0** | 14.6 | 35.0 |
| ▲ Corn Growers State Bank | Murdock | NE | **D+** | D- | D- | 25.0 | 0.45 | 3.5 | 8.4 | 9.8 | 15.7 | **6.4** | 8.4 | 18.8 |

| Asset Quality Index | Adjusted Non-Performing Loans as a % of Total Loans | Adjusted Non-Performing Loans as a % of Capital | Net Charge-Offs Avg Loans | Profitability Index | Net Income ($Mil) | Return on Assets (R.O.A.) | Return on Equity (R.O.E.) | Net Interest Spread | Overhead Efficiency Ratio | Liquidity Index | Liquidity Ratio | Hot Money Ratio | Stability Index |
|---|---|---|---|---|---|---|---|---|---|---|---|---|---|
| **3.9** | 1.87 | 10.8 | 0.30 | **3.9** | 1.4 | 0.71 | 6.16 | 4.14 | 73.6 | **2.1** | 16.7 | 18.6 | **5.7** |
| **7.9** | 0.15 | 1.1 | 0.00 | **4.3** | 1.5 | 1.11 | 11.83 | 2.97 | 62.3 | **1.1** | 14.0 | 28.2 | **6.1** |
| **6.0** | 1.48 | 7.6 | -0.10 | **7.6** | 4.3 | 1.38 | 10.33 | 4.19 | 58.9 | **1.6** | 11.6 | 19.6 | **8.4** |
| **5.1** | 2.04 | 9.5 | 0.06 | **0.4** | -0.1 | -0.14 | -1.00 | 4.00 | 105.3 | **4.2** | 24.7 | 8.9 | **5.3** |
| **4.7** | 0.91 | 4.6 | 0.41 | **1.2** | 0.4 | 0.09 | 0.86 | 3.47 | 83.9 | **1.4** | 18.2 | 21.8 | **4.6** |
| **7.4** | 2.77 | 5.5 | -0.04 | **2.4** | 1.1 | 0.29 | 1.75 | 2.79 | 88.5 | **3.1** | 45.5 | 22.1 | **7.4** |
| **9.0** | 0.11 | 0.5 | -0.04 | **3.5** | 0.5 | 0.61 | 3.76 | 3.72 | 82.2 | **2.1** | 18.7 | 19.1 | **7.6** |
| **2.2** | 4.09 | 19.4 | 0.10 | **3.4** | 1.1 | 0.53 | 5.60 | 3.87 | 83.1 | **2.4** | 20.8 | 17.6 | **5.2** |
| **7.1** | 1.06 | 3.3 | 0.18 | **4.2** | 0.9 | 0.59 | 5.41 | 4.43 | 77.3 | **1.4** | 21.7 | 27.8 | **5.4** |
| **4.6** | 1.50 | 7.1 | -0.06 | **5.1** | 0.2 | 1.03 | 7.43 | 4.19 | 68.3 | **1.6** | 31.3 | 27.3 | **4.3** |
| **8.0** | 0.05 | 0.3 | -0.07 | **8.5** | 2.5 | 2.01 | 15.17 | 4.59 | 52.5 | **0.7** | 15.2 | 48.2 | **9.5** |
| **3.7** | 2.10 | 12.2 | 0.18 | **3.6** | 1.0 | 0.79 | 8.87 | 4.27 | 83.9 | **5.5** | 33.0 | 3.8 | **4.4** |
| **7.9** | 0.07 | 0.3 | 0.03 | **6.3** | 10.8 | 1.34 | 11.66 | 4.31 | 63.1 | **3.5** | 21.4 | 12.2 | **8.0** |
| **8.3** | 0.00 | 3.4 | -0.16 | **4.7** | 0.5 | 1.07 | 5.49 | 3.15 | 57.0 | **4.1** | 63.7 | 18.3 | **6.9** |
| **8.5** | 0.03 | 0.1 | 0.03 | **5.6** | 2.8 | 1.35 | 12.32 | 3.49 | 55.1 | **2.7** | 32.1 | 9.9 | **7.3** |
| **4.5** | 1.18 | 7.3 | 0.14 | **6.3** | 3.3 | 1.43 | 13.01 | 4.10 | 58.8 | **0.7** | 8.2 | 25.3 | **7.6** |
| **7.7** | 0.46 | 1.9 | 0.02 | **8.2** | 4.1 | 1.48 | 13.75 | 4.43 | 57.3 | **4.1** | 19.7 | 8.9 | **7.9** |
| **3.5** | 5.48 | 24.3 | 0.06 | **6.2** | 0.8 | 1.25 | 9.90 | 4.05 | 58.6 | **1.0** | 24.0 | 26.8 | **5.4** |
| **4.3** | 2.28 | 10.5 | 0.02 | **4.5** | 1.1 | 0.86 | 7.57 | 4.03 | 75.4 | **4.3** | 17.6 | 6.9 | **6.8** |
| **6.4** | 3.60 | 8.8 | 0.01 | **8.3** | 2.8 | 1.71 | 14.53 | 3.99 | 49.2 | **4.4** | 5.5 | 5.0 | **8.0** |
| **4.1** | 1.36 | 10.3 | 0.22 | **6.6** | 1.0 | 1.31 | 14.42 | 3.49 | 49.6 | **2.7** | 13.0 | 10.6 | **5.9** |
| **3.1** | 4.41 | 17.1 | 1.35 | **5.3** | 0.9 | 1.32 | 19.77 | 4.15 | 64.6 | **6.6** | 48.8 | 1.2 | **3.9** |
| **3.8** | 1.79 | 12.4 | 0.18 | **4.9** | 3.1 | 1.14 | 12.19 | 4.75 | 74.0 | **0.8** | 15.2 | 32.9 | **6.4** |
| **4.9** | 1.69 | 6.2 | -0.03 | **5.8** | 5.5 | 1.39 | 14.89 | 4.17 | 69.6 | **4.3** | 25.7 | 7.7 | **5.9** |
| **6.9** | 0.22 | 4.4 | 0.48 | **6.2** | 0.6 | 1.14 | 10.20 | 4.91 | 72.2 | **2.5** | 5.2 | 15.5 | **6.2** |
| **7.9** | 0.33 | 1.2 | 0.00 | **5.4** | 3.2 | 1.36 | 10.23 | 3.42 | 63.3 | **3.1** | 19.3 | 13.9 | **8.5** |
| **4.8** | 2.10 | 13.4 | 0.09 | **3.8** | 2.1 | 0.62 | 5.36 | 3.93 | 79.2 | **1.6** | 7.1 | 21.0 | **6.6** |
| **2.4** | 3.18 | 20.7 | 0.40 | **4.5** | 2.2 | 0.84 | 8.08 | 3.67 | 61.6 | **2.0** | 21.1 | 19.4 | **5.9** |
| **7.9** | 0.00 | 0.0 | 0.09 | **4.9** | 1.0 | 1.19 | 11.96 | 4.01 | 71.7 | **4.0** | 28.6 | 11.3 | **6.5** |
| **5.5** | 2.99 | 7.1 | 1.61 | **3.8** | 0.6 | 0.73 | 5.25 | 3.84 | 75.6 | **5.9** | 44.1 | 5.1 | **6.7** |
| **3.9** | 2.19 | 9.2 | 0.18 | **6.7** | 60.7 | 1.41 | 9.88 | 3.70 | 58.9 | **2.0** | 9.4 | 17.5 | **10.0** |
| **4.6** | 1.15 | 5.3 | 0.17 | **7.2** | 2.4 | 1.26 | 10.95 | 4.93 | 59.9 | **2.2** | 16.8 | 18.1 | **7.0** |
| **4.0** | 0.60 | 3.8 | -0.02 | **5.3** | 8.2 | 0.94 | 10.73 | 4.06 | 69.7 | **0.7** | 10.0 | 25.1 | **6.3** |
| **6.6** | 0.34 | 1.0 | 0.03 | **7.6** | 51.7 | 1.53 | 10.99 | 4.42 | 57.5 | **3.6** | 18.5 | 7.2 | **10.0** |
| **8.5** | 0.00 | 0.8 | 0.00 | **0.0** | -0.5 | -0.94 | -10.44 | 1.89 | 170.2 | **0.9** | 20.8 | 41.8 | **3.5** |
| **6.5** | na | 0.0 | na | **10.0** | 6.2 | 21.35 | 23.31 | 1.94 | 63.8 | **4.0** | na | 0.0 | **6.6** |
| **3.1** | 2.00 | 14.0 | 0.07 | **5.6** | 0.7 | 1.25 | 11.80 | 4.95 | 69.1 | **2.6** | 21.1 | 16.7 | **7.0** |
| **1.8** | 6.65 | 29.4 | 0.01 | **4.7** | 0.7 | 0.92 | 8.80 | 4.39 | 72.2 | **4.3** | 10.4 | 6.0 | **6.4** |
| **5.8** | 1.28 | 10.2 | 0.09 | **4.5** | 5.8 | 1.13 | 8.95 | 3.46 | 70.6 | **1.5** | 17.2 | 25.5 | **8.1** |
| **2.3** | 3.81 | 17.3 | 0.34 | **6.3** | 7.6 | 0.72 | 5.21 | 5.25 | 78.8 | **1.8** | 24.2 | 15.9 | **9.7** |
| **9.7** | 0.35 | 1.4 | 0.02 | **1.9** | 0.1 | 0.13 | 0.89 | 3.15 | 96.0 | **5.3** | 40.7 | 8.1 | **6.8** |
| **6.2** | 2.30 | 8.5 | 0.10 | **6.3** | 1.2 | 1.28 | 8.30 | 4.51 | 71.4 | **1.9** | 24.6 | 22.0 | **8.9** |
| **2.8** | 1.96 | 12.0 | 0.07 | **2.6** | 1.8 | 0.39 | 3.85 | 4.05 | 92.4 | **3.9** | 19.2 | 9.7 | **4.5** |
| **6.5** | 0.21 | 1.8 | 0.04 | **5.2** | 3.6 | 1.19 | 11.69 | 3.69 | 70.0 | **2.5** | 15.0 | 6.8 | **6.0** |
| **8.2** | 0.29 | 1.8 | 0.05 | **4.6** | 0.8 | 0.88 | 6.91 | 4.28 | 66.5 | **0.6** | 10.7 | 44.3 | **7.3** |
| **3.2** | 1.38 | 7.5 | 0.09 | **6.1** | 79.1 | 1.32 | 10.23 | 3.46 | 46.1 | **0.7** | 9.4 | 19.9 | **9.5** |
| **7.5** | 0.20 | 1.4 | 0.00 | **4.8** | 5.6 | 1.03 | 11.34 | 3.63 | 69.1 | **3.2** | 16.4 | 13.1 | **6.3** |
| **4.2** | 4.47 | 12.0 | 1.35 | **7.0** | 1.9 | 1.20 | 7.07 | 5.80 | 64.4 | **0.4** | 18.2 | 96.1 | **8.5** |
| **9.2** | 0.01 | 0.0 | 0.14 | **6.9** | 11.3 | 1.82 | 19.29 | 2.72 | 43.2 | **3.4** | 53.7 | 23.5 | **6.4** |
| **1.8** | 4.35 | 22.5 | 1.01 | **1.3** | -0.1 | -0.11 | -1.18 | 3.93 | 85.9 | **1.8** | 27.9 | 24.7 | **4.4** |
| **8.7** | 0.56 | 2.4 | 0.09 | **5.4** | 13.7 | 1.12 | 11.31 | 3.17 | 60.2 | **5.0** | 45.8 | 13.9 | **8.0** |
| **6.4** | 0.62 | 3.5 | 0.01 | **3.2** | 2.1 | 0.48 | 4.89 | 3.17 | 79.8 | **1.3** | 12.5 | 19.3 | **6.1** |
| **5.3** | 1.17 | 6.6 | 0.03 | **3.7** | 6.6 | 0.70 | 6.99 | 3.32 | 75.4 | **2.9** | 9.4 | 12.7 | **6.8** |
| **5.4** | 1.00 | 6.3 | 0.09 | **4.5** | 1.9 | 0.82 | 8.38 | 4.17 | 73.9 | **2.4** | 12.7 | 17.0 | **6.2** |
| **3.6** | 0.00 | 29.5 | 0.28 | **5.0** | 0.2 | 1.22 | 10.82 | 4.02 | 66.2 | **4.0** | 32.0 | 10.4 | **4.6** |
| **5.5** | 1.00 | 5.1 | 0.13 | **3.8** | 3.4 | 0.59 | 6.95 | 4.01 | 82.5 | **3.7** | 12.3 | 10.2 | **5.8** |
| **8.5** | 0.02 | 0.1 | -0.01 | **1.5** | 0.2 | 0.35 | 2.51 | 3.58 | 81.1 | **0.9** | 26.2 | 63.9 | **4.0** |
| **3.4** | 2.69 | 16.2 | 0.06 | **6.2** | 14.3 | 1.52 | 16.15 | 3.58 | 66.9 | **4.6** | 11.5 | 4.1 | **6.0** |
| **9.2** | 0.05 | 0.7 | 0.06 | **4.8** | 0.9 | 1.28 | 8.44 | 2.82 | 60.2 | **2.4** | 34.0 | 23.4 | **8.2** |
| **5.3** | 0.77 | 4.7 | -0.01 | **3.3** | 0.1 | 0.55 | 6.89 | 3.77 | 82.8 | **4.9** | 35.8 | 5.6 | **2.3** |

| Name | City | State | Rating | 2018 Rating | 2017 Rating | Total Assets ($Mil) | One Year Asset Growth | Asset Mix (As a % of Total Assets): Comm-ercial Loans | Cons-umer Loans | Mort-gage Loans | Secur-ities | Capital-ization Index | Lever-age Ratio | Risk-Based Capital Ratio |
|---|---|---|---|---|---|---|---|---|---|---|---|---|---|---|
| Cornerstone Bank | Eureka Springs | AR | **B-** | B- | B | 336.8 | 17.19 | 5.7 | 3.6 | 20.0 | 10.3 | **5.5** | 8.0 | 11.4 |
| Cornerstone Bank | Atlanta | GA | **D** | D+ | E | 195.4 | -12.80 | 11.6 | 0.2 | 15.2 | 16.8 | **9.2** | 10.5 | 18.3 |
| Cornerstone Bank | Clarinda | IA | **C-** | C- | C | 41.3 | 6.90 | 5.0 | 6.4 | 34.2 | 6.9 | **10.0** | 13.6 | 27.1 |
| Cornerstone Bank | Overland Park | KS | **B+** | B | B | 238.0 | 9.32 | 17.7 | 0.6 | 18.9 | 8.6 | **7.5** | 9.5 | 12.9 |
| Cornerstone Bank | Worcester | MA | **C** | C | C | 1166.3 | 0.70 | 4.2 | 0.7 | 43.3 | 4.5 | **8.9** | 10.4 | 14.1 |
| Cornerstone Bank | South West City | MO | **B-** | C+ | B- | 139.3 | -1.26 | 11.3 | 9.4 | 27.4 | 12.3 | **10.0** | 14.0 | 22.2 |
| Cornerstone Bank | Fargo | ND | **C** | C | C- | 983.7 | 4.64 | 9.6 | 2.3 | 10.2 | 18.8 | **6.5** | 8.5 | 12.5 |
| Cornerstone Bank | York | NE | **B+** | B+ | B- | 1734.6 | 1.66 | 14.8 | 1.5 | 3.2 | 14.7 | **7.8** | 10.3 | 13.2 |
| ▲ Cornerstone Bank | Mount Laurel | NJ | **D+** | D | D- | 259.4 | 2.87 | 6.0 | 0.0 | 30.1 | 11.9 | **4.7** | 6.7 | 11.0 |
| Cornerstone Bank | Watonga | OK | **C+** | C | C | 219.9 | 6.23 | 5.5 | 3.7 | 8.2 | 45.5 | **6.4** | 8.4 | 16.3 |
| ▼ CornerStone Bank, N.A. | Lexington | VA | **C+** | B | B | 166.5 | 12.04 | 10.3 | 2.5 | 26.7 | 2.7 | **8.8** | 10.2 | 14.1 |
| Cornerstone Community Bank | Red Bluff | CA | **B** | B- | B | 288.3 | 8.26 | 13.4 | 0.4 | 3.7 | 4.6 | **6.9** | 10.1 | 12.5 |
| Cornerstone Community Bank | Grafton | WI | **C+** | C+ | C+ | 215.2 | 7.11 | 8.0 | 0.1 | 10.2 | 0.1 | **5.0** | 9.2 | 11.0 |
| Cornerstone National Bank & Trust Co. | Palatine | IL | **B-** | B- | B+ | 631.3 | 11.08 | 20.4 | 0.5 | 7.5 | 15.7 | **5.3** | 8.5 | 11.2 |
| CornerStone State Bank | Montgomery | MN | **A-** | B+ | B | 174.1 | 1.20 | 7.6 | 4.9 | 22.6 | 24.5 | **10.0** | 11.6 | 17.8 |
| Cornhusker Bank | Lincoln | NE | **B-** | B- | B- | 658.4 | 7.94 | 7.4 | 0.9 | 15.2 | 12.5 | **7.0** | 9.0 | 12.5 |
| ▲ Cortland Savings and Banking Co. | Cortland | OH | **B** | C | B- | 733.8 | 3.19 | 13.6 | 0.5 | 11.5 | 18.6 | **8.3** | 9.9 | 14.1 |
| CorTrust Bank N.A. | Mitchell | SD | **B-** | B- | B- | 1233.9 | 41.52 | 10.8 | 3.2 | 6.8 | 21.6 | **7.7** | 9.4 | 13.8 |
| Corydon State Bank | Corydon | IA | **B+** | B+ | A | 99.5 | -14.43 | 9.7 | 2.8 | 12.4 | 14.9 | **10.0** | 20.7 | 27.0 |
| Cottonport Bank | Cottonport | LA | **B+** | B+ | B | 370.0 | 13.21 | 6.6 | 3.1 | 14.7 | 15.2 | **10.0** | 12.5 | 20.0 |
| Cottonwood Valley Bank | Cedar Point | KS | **C+** | C+ | C+ | 34.2 | 5.48 | 8.7 | 1.7 | 0.6 | 31.6 | **10.0** | 13.4 | 29.1 |
| Coulee Bank | La Crosse | WI | **C+** | B- | B | 386.4 | -0.72 | 15.0 | 1.7 | 9.7 | 17.4 | **6.4** | 9.4 | 12.1 |
| Country Bank for Savings | Ware | MA | **B** | B | B | 1688.0 | 3.83 | 1.5 | 0.5 | 31.7 | 19.5 | **10.0** | 14.6 | 19.5 |
| Country Club Bank | Kansas City | MO | **A-** | A- | B+ | 1489.2 | 4.89 | 18.0 | 0.6 | 8.9 | 21.8 | **8.3** | 9.9 | 14.3 |
| Country Club Trust Co., N.A. | Kansas City | MO | **U** | U | U | 18.2 | -13.29 | 0.0 | 0.0 | 0.0 | 83.2 | **10.0** | 80.6 | 415.8 |
| COUNTRY Trust Bank | Bloomington | IL | **U** | U | U | 30.0 | 5.46 | 0.0 | 0.0 | 0.0 | 65.5 | **10.0** | 98.0 | 128.5 |
| Countryside Bank | Unadilla | NE | **B** | B | B | 80.2 | 5.57 | 5.5 | 5.4 | 17.1 | 19.1 | **10.0** | 17.0 | 28.7 |
| ▲ County Bank | Rehoboth Beach | DE | **B-** | C- | C- | 379.0 | 4.21 | 8.0 | 7.8 | 10.4 | 11.5 | **10.0** | 12.6 | 16.1 |
| County Bank | Sigourney | IA | **C** | C+ | B | 173.6 | 7.53 | 11.9 | 2.2 | 10.8 | 5.4 | **6.6** | 9.7 | 12.2 |
| County Bank | Brunswick | MO | **B-** | B- | B- | 90.8 | -2.09 | 7.5 | 4.5 | 23.9 | 13.4 | **6.1** | 8.1 | 13.8 |
| County National Bank | Hillsdale | MI | **B** | B- | B- | 736.8 | 11.33 | 18.6 | 4.4 | 21.5 | 3.0 | **7.1** | 9.3 | 12.6 |
| County Savings Bank | Essington | PA | **C** | C- | D+ | 84.3 | 2.79 | 0.0 | 0.1 | 37.9 | 10.0 | **5.3** | 7.3 | 22.7 |
| Countybank | Greenwood | SC | **B-** | B- | B- | 437.9 | 6.50 | 5.2 | 1.5 | 23.0 | 26.4 | **6.1** | 8.2 | 13.0 |
| Covenant Bank | Doylestown | PA | **B-** | C | D+ | 515.8 | 7.60 | 9.8 | 0.2 | 14.7 | 4.4 | **8.1** | 10.3 | 13.4 |
| Covington County Bank | Collins | MS | **C+** | C | C | 77.9 | -3.26 | 9.7 | 3.8 | 5.9 | 32.8 | **7.1** | 9.9 | 12.6 |
| Covington S&L Assn. | Covington | OH | **B-** | B- | C | 71.3 | 1.15 | 0.1 | 0.4 | 45.9 | 21.5 | **10.0** | 15.7 | 43.7 |
| Cowboy Bank of Texas | Maypearl | TX | **A-** | A- | B+ | 89.6 | 9.32 | 0.6 | 4.2 | 23.5 | 15.4 | **10.0** | 11.1 | 17.1 |
| ▲ Cowboy State Bank | Ranchester | WY | **D** | D- | C- | 49.4 | 5.37 | 3.8 | 4.3 | 10.2 | 22.6 | **6.4** | 8.4 | 13.4 |
| Crawford County Trust and Savings Bank | Denison | IA | **C+** | C+ | B | 200.0 | 4.13 | 6.1 | 3.4 | 9.3 | 11.1 | **7.9** | 9.7 | 13.2 |
| Credit First N.A. | Brook Park | OH | **U** | U | U | 28.7 | -51.44 | 0.0 | 0.0 | 0.0 | 0.0 | **10.0** | 85.2 | 456.7 |
| Credit One Bank, N.A. | Las Vegas | NV | **U** | U | U | 639.2 | 65.93 | 0.0 | 59.6 | 0.0 | 5.0 | **10.0** | 47.1 | 59.9 |
| Crescent Bank & Trust | New Orleans | LA | **C-** | D | D | 962.2 | -1.67 | 2.7 | 80.3 | 2.2 | 9.0 | **10.0** | 13.9 | 16.8 |
| CresCom Bank | Charleston | SC | **A-** | A- | A- | 4709.7 | 24.25 | 9.2 | 0.6 | 17.3 | 18.7 | **10.0** | 15.4 | 16.9 |
| Crest Savings Bank | Wildwood | NJ | **C+** | C+ | C+ | 462.4 | -1.70 | 0.6 | 4.2 | 59.4 | 1.2 | **6.4** | 8.4 | 13.7 |
| Crews Bank & Trust | Arcadia | FL | **A-** | A- | B+ | 165.0 | 14.91 | 1.1 | 2.4 | 18.2 | 20.7 | **10.0** | 12.3 | 25.1 |
| ▲ Crockett National Bank | San Antonio | TX | **A** | B+ | A- | 660.8 | 2.73 | 3.5 | 0.1 | 29.5 | 2.8 | **10.0** | 12.2 | 16.7 |
| Croghan Colonial Bank | Fremont | OH | **B+** | B+ | B | 873.9 | 3.46 | 7.2 | 10.2 | 10.6 | 18.3 | **8.0** | 11.4 | 13.3 |
| Cross County Bank | Wynne | AR | **B+** | B+ | B+ | 269.7 | 12.08 | 6.4 | 1.1 | 11.2 | 4.0 | **10.0** | 12.4 | 17.4 |
| Cross County Savings Bank | Middle Village | NY | **B** | B | B | 462.7 | 9.95 | 0.0 | 0.0 | 50.1 | 4.8 | **10.0** | 11.2 | 18.7 |
| Cross Keys Bank | Saint Joseph | LA | **B+** | B+ | B+ | 403.6 | 5.43 | 6.4 | 0.9 | 11.2 | 27.6 | **10.0** | 12.0 | 17.4 |
| ▲ Cross River Bank | Fort Lee | NJ | **A-** | B | A- | 2062.6 | 48.58 | 3.2 | 44.3 | 4.5 | 0.5 | **10.0** | 12.0 | 18.5 |
| ▲ CrossFirst Bank | Leawood | KS | **B-** | C | C | 4942.0 | 20.38 | 35.2 | 0.4 | 6.4 | 15.0 | **6.7** | 11.2 | 12.3 |
| ▲ Crossroads Bank | Effingham | IL | **A-** | A- | A- | 177.6 | 6.19 | 13.8 | 1.4 | 9.4 | 24.9 | **10.0** | 14.1 | 18.2 |
| ▲ Crossroads Bank | Wabash | IN | **B** | C+ | C+ | 419.0 | 4.74 | 6.4 | 4.3 | 29.0 | 19.0 | **7.8** | 9.5 | 14.3 |
| ▲ Crossroads Bank | Yoakum | TX | **A** | A- | A- | 219.6 | 8.50 | 10.3 | 7.5 | 22.3 | 32.4 | **10.0** | 11.3 | 21.6 |
| Crowell State Bank | Crowell | TX | **B-** | B- | B- | 41.3 | 3.85 | 12.2 | 7.0 | 7.7 | 20.0 | **8.9** | 10.3 | 17.7 |
| ▼ Crown Bank | Edina | MN | **C-** | B- | B | 195.9 | 4.29 | 43.4 | 1.2 | 1.6 | 7.4 | **7.4** | 10.7 | 12.9 |
| ▲ Crown Bank | Elizabeth | NJ | **C+** | C- | D | 523.2 | 3.69 | 4.1 | 0.1 | 2.6 | 12.5 | **10.0** | 19.5 | 25.7 |
| Crystal Lake Bank & Trust Co., N.A. | Crystal Lake | IL | **B** | B | B- | 1179.2 | 11.25 | 35.1 | 14.9 | 3.1 | 10.9 | **6.5** | 10.2 | 12.1 |
| CTBC Bank Corp. (USA) | Los Angeles | CA | **A-** | A- | B | 3673.7 | 6.36 | 8.2 | 0.0 | 35.9 | 9.8 | **10.0** | 14.4 | 20.9 |

| Asset Quality Index | Adjusted Non-Performing Loans as a % of Total Loans | Adjusted Non-Performing Loans as a % of Capital | Net Charge-Offs Avg Loans | Profitability Index | Net Income ($Mil) | Return on Assets (R.O.A.) | Return on Equity (R.O.E.) | Net Interest Spread | Overhead Efficiency Ratio | Liquidity Index | Liquidity Ratio | Hot Money Ratio | Stability Index |
|---|---|---|---|---|---|---|---|---|---|---|---|---|---|
| **7.5** | 0.39 | 2.8 | 0.02 | **6.2** | 5.0 | 1.59 | 19.68 | 4.17 | 63.2 | **1.0** | 6.3 | 22.7 | **5.7** |
| **1.3** | 11.59 | 38.0 | 0.66 | **0.5** | -1.3 | -0.64 | -6.46 | 3.57 | 108.7 | **1.5** | 24.9 | 27.5 | **3.6** |
| **5.4** | 0.43 | 8.6 | 0.04 | **0.9** | -0.1 | -0.16 | -1.15 | 2.95 | 107.7 | **2.2** | 37.5 | 29.0 | **5.6** |
| **8.5** | 0.00 | 0.0 | 0.10 | **7.1** | 3.8 | 1.69 | 17.62 | 3.55 | 50.8 | **4.1** | 14.2 | 7.9 | **6.6** |
| **7.9** | 0.59 | 3.5 | -0.05 | **2.9** | 5.6 | 0.49 | 4.75 | 3.00 | 82.0 | **1.4** | 8.9 | 19.9 | **7.4** |
| **3.9** | 2.07 | 10.0 | 0.16 | **5.7** | 1.8 | 1.25 | 8.87 | 5.19 | 73.6 | **0.8** | 20.0 | 33.5 | **7.8** |
| **3.2** | 3.69 | 16.7 | 0.21 | **4.9** | 11.0 | 1.16 | 13.22 | 3.75 | 70.0 | **2.5** | 15.8 | 16.5 | **6.3** |
| **6.1** | 0.60 | 7.1 | 0.10 | **6.1** | 22.8 | 1.39 | 13.05 | 3.78 | 66.2 | **1.2** | 14.2 | 23.7 | **9.1** |
| **5.8** | 0.53 | 3.6 | -0.03 | **3.1** | 5.1 | 2.00 | 29.29 | 2.91 | 98.3 | **1.9** | 24.4 | 21.4 | **2.0** |
| **8.9** | 0.05 | 0.2 | 0.14 | **4.0** | 1.7 | 0.78 | 10.05 | 3.50 | 77.5 | **5.3** | 41.8 | 8.5 | **3.7** |
| **3.1** | 2.54 | 15.7 | 0.21 | **3.5** | 0.8 | 0.52 | 4.93 | 3.83 | 83.2 | **0.8** | 11.3 | 34.4 | **6.7** |
| **7.3** | 0.04 | 0.1 | 0.04 | **7.1** | 3.8 | 1.33 | 13.22 | 4.39 | 55.8 | **1.2** | 10.2 | 22.2 | **6.7** |
| **5.2** | 0.79 | 5.0 | 0.00 | **6.3** | 2.4 | 1.17 | 12.83 | 3.97 | 59.9 | **2.0** | 15.6 | 17.2 | **5.8** |
| **5.3** | 0.83 | 6.2 | -0.02 | **5.3** | 5.9 | 0.96 | 10.61 | 3.61 | 69.8 | **3.6** | 24.9 | 11.9 | **6.8** |
| **5.3** | 1.35 | 6.7 | 0.66 | **5.0** | 1.9 | 1.10 | 9.43 | 3.68 | 66.1 | **4.3** | 22.4 | 7.7 | **7.2** |
| **6.9** | 0.57 | 3.3 | 0.05 | **4.5** | 6.1 | 0.99 | 10.92 | 3.70 | 71.8 | **3.4** | 21.1 | 10.7 | **7.1** |
| **5.0** | 1.63 | 7.1 | 0.09 | **5.8** | 8.2 | 1.19 | 12.24 | 3.79 | 63.2 | **2.9** | 15.8 | 10.2 | **6.6** |
| **6.7** | 0.98 | 5.5 | 0.88 | **3.8** | 6.1 | 0.61 | 5.47 | 4.43 | 72.9 | **3.6** | 20.4 | 12.0 | **8.0** |
| **0.6** | 8.59 | 36.0 | 3.69 | **1.9** | -1.5 | -1.40 | -6.70 | 3.83 | 25.5 | **1.1** | 27.7 | 29.9 | **7.0** |
| **6.2** | 1.24 | 5.5 | 0.29 | **5.6** | 4.0 | 1.15 | 8.92 | 4.34 | 68.9 | **2.7** | 30.3 | 18.4 | **6.7** |
| **9.4** | 0.00 | 0.0 | -0.13 | **2.5** | 0.2 | 0.50 | 3.68 | 2.67 | 88.0 | **5.0** | 64.0 | 14.2 | **6.9** |
| **3.0** | 2.67 | 16.2 | 0.29 | **4.0** | 3.6 | 0.91 | 9.90 | 3.35 | 73.7 | **2.7** | 12.5 | 12.0 | **6.3** |
| **6.3** | 1.98 | 8.3 | 0.01 | **4.2** | 13.8 | 0.82 | 5.73 | 3.12 | 68.1 | **2.1** | 21.8 | 15.7 | **9.6** |
| **7.2** | 0.48 | 2.8 | 0.03 | **6.7** | 23.0 | 1.63 | 15.49 | 4.07 | 74.5 | **5.6** | 27.6 | 4.4 | **9.0** |
| **10.0** | na | 0.0 | na | **9.5** | 2.1 | 9.51 | 9.71 | 2.01 | 84.0 | **4.0** | na | 0.0 | **7.0** |
| **10.0** | na | 0.0 | na | **10.0** | 4.5 | 17.11 | 17.03 | 3.69 | 89.3 | **4.0** | na | 0.0 | **7.0** |
| **8.6** | 0.00 | 0.0 | 0.06 | **4.0** | 0.7 | 0.92 | 5.30 | 3.33 | 75.9 | **4.9** | 37.8 | 9.9 | **7.9** |
| **4.4** | 4.15 | 11.5 | -0.04 | **7.8** | 5.4 | 1.48 | 12.13 | 4.59 | 61.0 | **5.0** | 25.9 | 3.8 | **7.1** |
| **3.1** | 1.08 | 8.8 | 0.16 | **6.5** | 2.6 | 1.53 | 15.05 | 4.40 | 62.2 | **2.1** | 9.2 | 17.9 | **7.1** |
| **5.4** | 0.95 | 6.9 | 0.08 | **5.0** | 1.1 | 1.22 | 13.31 | 4.51 | 75.1 | **3.3** | 15.4 | 12.5 | **5.0** |
| **4.7** | 0.92 | 5.7 | 0.04 | **6.8** | 9.6 | 1.36 | 14.21 | 4.28 | 65.0 | **3.7** | 12.5 | 10.2 | **6.9** |
| **8.7** | 0.30 | 0.9 | 0.01 | **2.9** | 0.4 | 0.49 | 6.97 | 3.48 | 81.5 | **6.0** | 52.2 | 6.3 | **3.3** |
| **5.6** | 0.98 | 6.6 | 0.01 | **4.7** | 4.6 | 1.09 | 13.84 | 3.72 | 84.6 | **5.2** | 19.6 | 1.6 | **5.3** |
| **5.0** | 0.68 | 2.3 | 0.26 | **4.8** | 4.9 | 0.99 | 9.61 | 3.65 | 63.6 | **1.2** | 13.8 | 27.5 | **4.7** |
| **5.3** | 1.29 | 5.0 | 0.29 | **3.3** | 0.5 | 0.60 | 6.39 | 3.32 | 79.1 | **1.7** | 29.0 | 28.9 | **5.0** |
| **10.0** | 0.31 | 0.8 | 0.00 | **3.7** | 0.5 | 0.72 | 4.55 | 3.18 | 73.1 | **6.2** | 43.8 | 3.2 | **7.8** |
| **7.3** | 0.28 | 5.8 | 0.01 | **9.4** | 1.9 | 2.22 | 20.96 | 3.88 | 56.1 | **1.4** | 19.6 | 24.0 | **8.1** |
| **4.5** | 1.51 | 6.1 | 0.10 | **2.1** | 0.2 | 0.35 | 4.41 | 4.62 | 88.4 | **3.1** | 31.4 | 16.6 | **2.7** |
| **5.5** | 0.26 | 2.2 | 0.05 | **7.9** | 3.6 | 1.86 | 19.00 | 3.97 | 57.7 | **3.3** | 12.7 | 12.1 | **7.2** |
| **10.0** | na | 0.0 | na | **10.0** | 12.5 | 46.40 | 41.09 | -0.01 | 68.6 | **4.0** | na | 100.0 | **6.7** |
| **5.2** | 0.00 | 3.3 | 7.60 | **10.0** | 219.9 | 47.64 | 103.74 | 15.56 | 68.0 | **2.3** | 55.9 | 99.9 | **8.7** |
| **1.2** | 2.84 | 17.6 | 6.42 | **3.7** | 5.0 | 0.50 | 3.70 | 12.55 | 49.1 | **0.6** | 13.3 | 61.2 | **7.7** |
| **6.0** | 0.97 | 3.8 | 0.02 | **8.2** | 65.0 | 1.67 | 10.06 | 4.07 | 54.7 | **1.8** | 21.5 | 19.8 | **10.0** |
| **7.8** | 0.27 | 1.8 | 0.00 | **2.8** | 1.7 | 0.36 | 4.33 | 3.00 | 83.2 | **3.8** | 4.9 | 9.0 | **4.8** |
| **6.3** | 1.91 | 6.9 | 0.13 | **4.7** | 1.5 | 1.00 | 8.39 | 3.95 | 77.7 | **5.1** | 48.2 | 11.7 | **7.8** |
| **8.2** | 0.05 | 0.5 | 0.00 | **10.0** | 16.6 | 3.55 | 28.66 | 4.10 | 72.8 | **1.2** | 9.1 | 26.8 | **10.0** |
| **5.6** | 0.53 | 2.1 | 0.07 | **6.5** | 11.9 | 1.39 | 10.09 | 4.28 | 63.8 | **4.2** | 5.6 | 5.8 | **9.1** |
| **6.8** | 0.74 | 3.9 | 0.13 | **7.9** | 3.7 | 1.45 | 11.45 | 5.03 | 61.0 | **1.3** | 20.3 | 27.0 | **8.2** |
| **8.5** | 0.54 | 3.6 | 0.00 | **3.3** | 1.9 | 0.42 | 3.73 | 4.03 | 85.2 | **2.7** | 18.5 | 16.0 | **6.6** |
| **6.0** | 2.93 | 9.3 | 0.55 | **4.7** | 3.8 | 1.02 | 8.26 | 3.68 | 68.8 | **2.6** | 37.3 | 22.1 | **7.2** |
| **6.6** | 0.43 | 2.5 | 1.39 | **10.0** | 43.7 | 2.45 | 19.98 | 7.62 | 43.1 | **0.8** | 18.3 | 60.6 | **9.2** |
| **5.7** | 1.32 | 8.2 | 0.31 | **4.1** | 40.9 | 0.91 | 8.11 | 3.34 | 58.6 | **1.4** | 20.5 | 17.9 | **7.8** |
| **8.5** | 0.00 | 0.1 | 0.00 | **6.5** | 2.3 | 1.33 | 9.40 | 3.07 | 47.5 | **3.1** | 32.2 | 17.0 | **8.4** |
| **4.9** | 1.59 | 6.7 | 0.01 | **5.6** | 4.7 | 1.14 | 11.33 | 3.63 | 66.4 | **2.2** | 21.9 | 18.5 | **7.3** |
| **8.0** | 0.53 | 2.3 | 0.09 | **7.8** | 4.0 | 1.95 | 16.66 | 4.17 | 55.6 | **3.7** | 44.8 | 17.7 | **8.0** |
| **5.6** | 0.29 | 2.9 | 0.22 | **8.5** | 0.8 | 2.03 | 19.14 | 4.72 | 59.9 | **1.3** | 22.5 | 29.2 | **6.7** |
| **7.5** | 0.35 | 2.0 | 0.04 | **1.0** | -0.8 | -0.41 | -3.65 | 4.03 | 108.8 | **0.9** | 12.9 | 26.4 | **6.0** |
| **3.6** | 3.42 | 9.6 | 0.07 | **9.7** | 20.7 | 4.04 | 20.73 | 4.82 | 41.6 | **1.4** | 32.3 | 42.2 | **10.0** |
| **7.1** | 0.19 | 1.3 | 0.03 | **7.3** | 16.9 | 1.48 | 15.29 | 3.37 | 41.4 | **1.3** | 11.8 | 19.2 | **7.7** |
| **8.7** | 0.38 | 2.0 | 0.00 | **6.2** | 43.1 | 1.21 | 8.51 | 3.34 | 55.4 | **0.9** | 17.1 | 32.1 | **10.0** |

| Name | City | State | Rating | 2018 Rating | 2017 Rating | Total Assets ($Mil) | One Year Asset Growth | Asset Mix (As a % of Total Assets) Commercial Loans | Consumer Loans | Mortgage Loans | Securities | Capitalization Index | Leverage Ratio | Risk-Based Capital Ratio |
|---|---|---|---|---|---|---|---|---|---|---|---|---|---|---|
| Culbertson Bank | Culbertson | NE | **C** | C- | D+ | 14.2 | -2.35 | 7.3 | 0.7 | 0.1 | 42.9 | **10.0** | 14.3 | 27.4 |
| Cullman Savings Bank | Cullman | AL | **A-** | B+ | A- | 296.6 | 1.48 | 8.9 | 0.9 | 42.9 | 7.9 | **10.0** | 15.9 | 22.4 |
| Cumberland Federal Bank, FSB | Cumberland | WI | **B+** | A- | B | 166.4 | 17.90 | 1.3 | 1.2 | 19.4 | 49.8 | **10.0** | 11.6 | 18.7 |
| Cumberland Security Bank, Inc. | Somerset | KY | **A** | B+ | A | 215.9 | 5.43 | 7.7 | 4.3 | 28.6 | 12.0 | **10.0** | 13.4 | 19.0 |
| Cumberland Valley National B&T Co. | London | KY | **C+** | C+ | C+ | 518.4 | 3.81 | 7.3 | 2.0 | 14.8 | 14.6 | **8.7** | 10.1 | 15.2 |
| Currie State Bank | Currie | MN | **C-** | C- | C- | 87.1 | 5.99 | 6.4 | 1.6 | 6.1 | 0.9 | **6.1** | 10.1 | 11.8 |
| CUSB Bank | Cresco | IA | **B+** | C+ | C+ | 490.9 | 4.12 | 7.7 | 4.7 | 8.3 | 20.2 | **10.0** | 13.7 | 16.8 |
| Custer Federal State Bank | Broken Bow | NE | **B-** | B | B- | 116.2 | -7.79 | 4.8 | 2.4 | 16.0 | 17.5 | **10.0** | 11.4 | 20.1 |
| Customers Bank | Phoenixville | PA | **B-** | B | B | 11511.7 | 17.13 | 13.0 | 10.6 | 4.5 | 5.0 | **7.5** | 10.4 | 12.9 |
| Cypress Bank, SSB | Pittsburg | TX | **B-** | C+ | B- | 190.3 | 1.45 | 7.3 | 7.6 | 32.1 | 23.4 | **9.9** | 10.9 | 19.0 |
| D.A. Davidson Trust Co. | Great Falls | MT | **U** | U | U | 9.9 | 23.08 | 0.0 | 0.0 | 0.0 | 75.3 | **10.0** | 74.8 | 165.2 |
| D.L. Evans Bank | Burley | ID | **A-** | B+ | B+ | 1794.0 | 14.00 | 8.0 | 2.0 | 5.4 | 20.4 | **7.8** | 9.6 | 14.8 |
| Dacotah Bank | Aberdeen | SD | **B-** | B | B | 2689.4 | 4.76 | 11.3 | 2.9 | 3.9 | 9.2 | **9.7** | 11.5 | 14.7 |
| Dairy State Bank | Rice Lake | WI | **B** | B | B- | 517.2 | 5.29 | 10.5 | 1.0 | 8.5 | 47.4 | **10.0** | 12.4 | 23.7 |
| Dakota Community Bank & Trust, N.A. | Hebron | ND | **B+** | B | B+ | 862.6 | 6.48 | 8.6 | 1.4 | 3.5 | 27.9 | **6.0** | 8.0 | 13.8 |
| Dakota Heritage Bank | Hunter | ND | **C+** | B+ | A- | 208.5 | 2.38 | 7.9 | 3.3 | 2.5 | 12.5 | **8.1** | 10.8 | 13.4 |
| ▲ Dakota Prairie Bank | Fort Pierre | SD | **A-** | B+ | B+ | 93.1 | -2.90 | 9.6 | 2.5 | 2.4 | 6.9 | **10.0** | 12.1 | 17.7 |
| ▲ Dakota Western Bank | Bowman | ND | **B+** | B | B+ | 295.8 | 5.40 | 7.8 | 2.8 | 1.3 | 20.9 | **10.0** | 11.0 | 15.3 |
| ▼ Dalhart Federal S&L Assn., SSB | Dalhart | TX | **C** | C+ | C+ | 111.5 | 0.51 | 0.6 | 2.3 | 48.9 | 31.7 | **10.0** | 12.2 | 27.8 |
| ▼ Dallas Capital Bank, N.A. | Dallas | TX | **C-** | C | C | 850.8 | -0.34 | 11.7 | 0.0 | 9.3 | 13.2 | **7.0** | 9.1 | 12.5 |
| Damariscotta Bank & Trust Co. | Damariscotta | ME | **C+** | C | C | 201.4 | 1.60 | 3.4 | 1.1 | 34.8 | 20.8 | **7.9** | 9.6 | 17.4 |
| Danville State Savings Bank | Danville | IA | **B+** | B+ | B+ | 145.6 | 1.85 | 4.0 | 4.5 | 21.9 | 46.9 | **10.0** | 12.8 | 25.5 |
| Dart Bank | Mason | MI | **C+** | B- | B- | 460.7 | 1.44 | 6.2 | 1.0 | 27.5 | 8.5 | **8.2** | 9.8 | 14.5 |
| Davis Trust Co. | Elkins | WV | **B** | B- | B- | 147.2 | 1.20 | 8.1 | 3.9 | 16.9 | 12.7 | **10.0** | 12.7 | 17.0 |
| De Witt Bank & Trust Co. | De Witt | IA | **B** | B | B+ | 183.2 | 11.22 | 8.3 | 2.2 | 9.2 | 21.3 | **5.9** | 10.2 | 11.7 |
| Dean Co-operative Bank | Franklin | MA | **C+** | C+ | C+ | 342.8 | 8.06 | 4.6 | 1.1 | 50.7 | 15.5 | **6.8** | 8.8 | 14.7 |
| ▼ Dearborn Federal Savings Bank | Dearborn | MI | **B** | B+ | B+ | 255.8 | -3.93 | 0.0 | 0.0 | 74.2 | 2.5 | **10.0** | 30.1 | 60.3 |
| Dearborn Savings Bank | Lawrenceburg | IN | **B-** | B | B | 129.2 | 5.17 | 0.5 | 0.4 | 43.2 | 2.1 | **8.5** | 10.0 | 16.7 |
| Decatur County Bank | Decaturville | TN | **C-** | D+ | C | 133.9 | 13.65 | 14.9 | 7.1 | 22.9 | 11.6 | **4.4** | 7.6 | 10.7 |
| Decorah Bank & Trust Co. | Decorah | IA | **A-** | A- | A- | 483.7 | 2.46 | 14.2 | 2.5 | 9.6 | 18.9 | **9.9** | 10.9 | 15.0 |
| Dedham Institution for Savings | Dedham | MA | **B** | B | B | 1543.3 | -1.06 | 2.2 | 0.1 | 41.1 | 17.8 | **10.0** | 12.7 | 17.5 |
| Dedicated Community Bank | Darlington | SC | **C** | C | C | 68.9 | 0.05 | 13.6 | 3.0 | 18.8 | 16.7 | **7.8** | 9.6 | 13.5 |
| ▲ Deerwood Bank | Waite Park | MN | **B** | C+ | B | 719.0 | 0.73 | 17.8 | 1.4 | 14.4 | 6.0 | **5.9** | 8.8 | 11.7 |
| Defiance State Bank | Defiance | IA | **C-** | D+ | C- | 35.4 | 5.14 | 9.6 | 7.3 | 7.9 | 7.8 | **5.2** | 9.3 | 11.1 |
| Del Norte Bank | Del Norte | CO | **B-** | C+ | C+ | 100.0 | 3.68 | 4.8 | 1.1 | 25.6 | 8.3 | **7.1** | 9.0 | 15.5 |
| Delaware National Bank of Delhi | Delhi | NY | **B-** | C+ | C+ | 296.5 | 0.37 | 7.3 | 1.6 | 24.9 | 23.3 | **9.2** | 10.5 | 28.7 |
| Delta Bank | Vidalia | LA | **B-** | B- | B | 309.6 | 4.28 | 5.1 | 2.3 | 19.4 | 16.5 | **6.9** | 8.9 | 13.6 |
| Delta National Bank and Trust Co. | New York | NY | **C** | C | C- | 382.9 | 22.75 | 25.0 | 6.4 | 0.0 | 24.2 | **10.0** | 15.7 | 25.5 |
| DeMotte State Bank | Demotte | IN | **B+** | B | B | 446.3 | 6.90 | 9.5 | 1.0 | 13.4 | 32.8 | **10.0** | 12.3 | 19.9 |
| Denali State Bank | Fairbanks | AK | **B-** | B- | B- | 295.9 | 4.65 | 17.6 | 8.4 | 8.6 | 25.5 | **8.1** | 9.8 | 14.6 |
| Denison State Bank | Holton | KS | **A-** | B+ | A- | 359.0 | 5.04 | 10.7 | 2.0 | 12.1 | 28.7 | **10.0** | 14.4 | 20.4 |
| Denmark State Bank | Denmark | WI | **B** | B | B | 539.7 | 9.32 | 14.6 | 1.8 | 8.8 | 6.6 | **8.5** | 10.2 | 13.8 |
| Denver Savings Bank | Denver | IA | **C** | C+ | B- | 175.4 | -2.46 | 14.1 | 1.4 | 16.0 | 19.4 | **7.6** | 9.5 | 13.0 |
| Department Stores National Bank | Sioux Falls | SD | **B+** | B+ | B+ | 324.2 | 0.05 | 0.0 | 21.9 | 0.0 | 0.0 | **10.0** | 12.2 | 47.4 |
| Depository Trust Co. | New York | NY | **U** | U | U | 3209.4 | 5.85 | 0.0 | 0.0 | 0.0 | 0.0 | **10.0** | 20.1 | 103.9 |
| Desjardins Bank, N.A. | Hallandale Beach | FL | **B-** | B- | C+ | 221.1 | 2.84 | 2.2 | 3.9 | 60.1 | 9.5 | **10.0** | 14.6 | 30.4 |
| Deutsche Bank National Trust Co. | Los Angeles | CA | **U** | U | U | 289.0 | 4.26 | 0.0 | 0.0 | 0.0 | 35.3 | **10.0** | 80.6 | 282.9 |
| Deutsche Bank Trust Co. Americas | New York | NY | **A** | A- | B | 37585.0 | -4.07 | 6.4 | 0.4 | 5.5 | 0.0 | **10.0** | 25.3 | 70.5 |
| Deutsche Bank Trust Co. Delaware | Wilmington | DE | **A+** | A- | B+ | 304.3 | 0.42 | 0.0 | 0.0 | 0.0 | 0.7 | **10.0** | 92.8 | 2631. |
| Deutsche Bank Trust Co., N.A. | New York | NY | **U** | U | U | 158.7 | 13.72 | 0.0 | 0.0 | 0.0 | 66.2 | **10.0** | 86.5 | 511.6 |
| Devon Bank | Chicago | IL | **C** | C- | C | 290.8 | -1.00 | 12.2 | 1.5 | 16.9 | 16.1 | **6.2** | 8.3 | 11.9 |
| Dewey Bank | Dewey | IL | **C-** | D+ | D+ | 22.8 | 0.64 | 8.0 | 1.8 | 8.3 | 28.3 | **6.4** | 8.4 | 12.7 |
| DeWitt Savings Bank | Clinton | IL | **B-** | B | C+ | 112.0 | 2.76 | 0.0 | 22.8 | 30.1 | 29.5 | **10.0** | 13.1 | 24.9 |
| Diamond Bank | Glenwood | AR | **B** | B- | B+ | 642.3 | 6.18 | 6.3 | 2.2 | 19.0 | 21.2 | **8.4** | 9.9 | 16.1 |
| Dickinson County Bank | Enterprise | KS | **E+** | D+ | C | 17.0 | 13.56 | 11.7 | 7.3 | 34.1 | 4.2 | **6.7** | 8.7 | 14.3 |
| Dieterich Bank | Effingham | IL | **B-** | C+ | C+ | 806.2 | 23.05 | 6.3 | 1.7 | 10.0 | 22.3 | **8.2** | 9.8 | 13.5 |
| Dilley State Bank | Dilley | TX | **B+** | B+ | B+ | 137.8 | 9.81 | 1.6 | 0.7 | 0.2 | 52.2 | **10.0** | 16.7 | 56.0 |
| Dime Bank | Norwich | CT | **B-** | C+ | C- | 894.7 | 4.74 | 6.0 | 0.1 | 33.5 | 15.2 | **10.0** | 12.1 | 16.6 |
| Dime Bank | Honesdale | PA | **B-** | C+ | C | 732.1 | 5.40 | 12.8 | 1.6 | 13.5 | 17.4 | **9.5** | 11.3 | 14.6 |
| ▼ Dime Community Bank | Brooklyn | NY | **B-** | B+ | B+ | 6348.5 | 0.55 | 5.3 | 0.0 | 2.3 | 8.7 | **8.1** | 10.2 | 13.4 |

| Asset Quality Index | Adjusted Non-Performing Loans as a % of Total Loans | Adjusted Non-Performing Loans as a % of Capital | Net Charge-Offs Avg Loans | Profitability Index | Net Income ($Mil) | Return on Assets (R.O.A.) | Return on Equity (R.O.E.) | Net Interest Spread | Overhead Efficiency Ratio | Liquidity Index | Liquidity Ratio | Hot Money Ratio | Stability Index |
|---|---|---|---|---|---|---|---|---|---|---|---|---|---|
| **7.5** | 0.00 | 1.0 | 1.84 | **0.4** | -0.1 | -0.49 | -3.29 | 3.81 | 90.8 | **4.5** | 51.8 | 12.6 | **4.7** |
| **8.0** | 1.00 | 2.7 | 0.00 | **6.6** | 3.8 | 1.28 | 8.21 | 3.99 | 61.2 | **0.6** | 7.6 | 33.4 | **8.8** |
| **9.3** | 0.67 | 1.8 | 0.00 | **5.0** | 1.5 | 0.99 | 8.33 | 3.11 | 59.7 | **2.3** | 46.5 | 9.2 | **6.7** |
| **8.4** | 0.09 | 1.1 | 0.10 | **10.0** | 6.5 | 3.00 | 22.12 | 4.86 | 45.9 | **2.9** | 18.2 | 14.8 | **9.7** |
| **4.9** | 1.40 | 8.4 | 0.07 | **3.5** | 3.6 | 0.69 | 6.84 | 3.45 | 79.7 | **1.4** | 20.5 | 28.1 | **7.0** |
| **1.7** | 1.57 | 16.7 | -0.01 | **8.8** | 1.1 | 1.37 | 13.88 | 4.98 | 58.2 | **0.5** | 4.0 | 22.9 | **7.7** |
| **6.0** | 1.36 | 6.7 | 0.10 | **5.9** | 7.0 | 1.45 | 10.09 | 3.49 | 55.8 | **0.9** | 19.6 | 19.6 | **8.3** |
| **5.8** | 1.30 | 9.1 | 0.96 | **2.8** | 0.4 | 0.35 | 3.17 | 3.25 | 82.2 | **1.4** | 31.0 | 35.7 | **6.7** |
| **7.1** | 0.30 | 2.3 | 0.08 | **4.3** | 83.4 | 0.78 | 7.63 | 2.78 | 63.8 | **1.6** | 7.8 | 4.6 | **7.7** |
| **4.7** | 1.14 | 6.4 | 0.07 | **4.4** | 1.6 | 0.83 | 7.60 | 3.94 | 74.7 | **1.6** | 29.8 | 30.3 | **6.5** |
| **9.8** | na | 0.0 | na | **10.0** | 0.9 | 9.38 | 12.73 | 2.83 | 85.4 | **10.0** | 280.3 | 0.0 | **6.0** |
| **7.7** | 0.55 | 2.3 | 0.00 | **7.5** | 22.8 | 1.40 | 14.49 | 4.56 | 62.5 | **4.2** | 24.8 | 11.3 | **8.6** |
| **4.5** | 2.78 | 13.0 | 0.04 | **6.0** | 30.6 | 1.18 | 10.16 | 3.87 | 63.4 | **2.6** | 11.4 | 15.6 | **9.6** |
| **8.2** | 1.45 | 2.7 | 0.01 | **4.1** | 4.3 | 0.89 | 6.83 | 2.79 | 71.6 | **4.9** | 44.4 | 11.4 | **8.0** |
| **7.2** | 0.32 | 2.1 | 0.01 | **7.6** | 15.2 | 1.85 | 21.63 | 3.69 | 57.3 | **4.6** | 33.8 | 7.9 | **7.7** |
| **3.7** | 1.02 | 4.2 | 0.03 | **8.7** | 4.1 | 2.01 | 17.04 | 4.74 | 55.6 | **2.8** | 8.5 | 14.3 | **8.9** |
| **7.1** | 0.25 | 0.7 | 0.00 | **7.0** | 1.4 | 1.53 | 12.84 | 4.57 | 64.2 | **2.0** | 19.6 | 19.3 | **8.2** |
| **5.1** | 1.33 | 7.5 | 0.30 | **8.8** | 5.4 | 1.95 | 17.02 | 4.37 | 46.3 | **1.6** | 17.2 | 17.9 | **8.9** |
| **8.6** | 0.29 | 4.2 | 0.00 | **2.0** | 0.2 | 0.14 | 1.15 | 3.85 | 95.6 | **2.0** | 41.5 | 38.1 | **6.5** |
| **7.7** | 0.19 | 1.3 | 0.94 | **1.9** | 2.0 | 0.23 | 2.16 | 2.64 | 66.6 | **1.2** | 14.0 | 24.2 | **6.9** |
| **4.1** | 2.32 | 14.8 | 0.04 | **3.3** | 1.0 | 0.52 | 5.47 | 3.43 | 85.2 | **3.4** | 30.1 | 14.8 | **5.4** |
| **6.0** | 1.31 | 8.8 | 0.02 | **5.1** | 1.8 | 1.22 | 9.01 | 2.52 | 65.2 | **4.9** | 59.8 | 15.6 | **8.0** |
| **4.2** | 2.50 | 10.4 | 0.74 | **3.9** | 3.3 | 0.70 | 7.77 | 3.96 | 79.1 | **2.9** | 19.4 | 15.1 | **6.3** |
| **4.7** | 5.93 | 20.9 | 0.12 | **5.1** | 1.6 | 1.06 | 10.73 | 4.79 | 73.1 | **4.5** | 22.9 | 6.1 | **5.5** |
| **7.3** | 0.04 | 1.0 | 0.22 | **4.6** | 2.1 | 1.19 | 11.22 | 3.35 | 75.1 | **3.4** | 26.6 | 13.3 | **7.1** |
| **6.3** | 0.88 | 4.7 | 0.06 | **3.5** | 1.9 | 0.58 | 6.73 | 3.59 | 81.2 | **3.4** | 15.7 | 12.2 | **5.1** |
| **8.5** | 2.48 | 4.0 | 0.00 | **3.7** | 1.2 | 0.46 | 1.57 | 2.96 | 78.2 | **3.8** | 26.4 | 11.6 | **7.6** |
| **8.2** | 0.17 | 1.2 | 0.00 | **3.5** | 0.8 | 0.64 | 6.28 | 3.02 | 73.7 | **1.2** | 20.0 | 29.8 | **6.2** |
| **4.7** | 0.42 | 4.0 | 0.06 | **3.8** | 0.8 | 0.64 | 9.35 | 4.80 | 82.7 | **1.5** | 10.8 | 22.0 | **3.7** |
| **6.2** | 0.85 | 4.7 | 0.21 | **7.5** | 8.3 | 1.74 | 14.50 | 3.71 | 56.5 | **3.3** | 22.2 | 13.1 | **9.4** |
| **9.2** | 0.30 | 1.7 | 0.00 | **4.8** | 15.9 | 1.04 | 8.92 | 3.26 | 75.1 | **2.8** | 24.6 | 13.1 | **8.6** |
| **5.1** | 1.58 | 5.8 | 0.09 | **3.6** | 0.4 | 0.58 | 6.41 | 3.93 | 82.6 | **2.5** | 15.2 | 16.8 | **5.3** |
| **5.4** | 0.31 | 2.1 | 0.01 | **7.1** | 8.8 | 1.25 | 11.92 | 4.64 | 63.0 | **4.8** | 15.6 | 3.3 | **8.0** |
| **7.1** | 0.00 | 0.0 | 0.56 | **3.0** | 0.1 | 0.42 | 4.42 | 3.83 | 88.5 | **2.3** | 31.9 | 22.5 | **4.5** |
| **5.6** | 0.22 | 4.3 | 0.01 | **5.4** | 0.9 | 0.86 | 9.83 | 4.52 | 73.2 | **1.2** | 9.5 | 21.7 | **5.5** |
| **6.5** | 0.63 | 3.6 | 0.05 | **4.1** | 2.8 | 0.91 | 9.15 | 3.11 | 65.7 | **2.8** | 20.9 | 15.7 | **5.5** |
| **4.3** | 0.76 | 6.4 | -0.09 | **7.3** | 5.4 | 1.74 | 20.58 | 4.42 | 64.5 | **1.3** | 13.9 | 27.3 | **6.7** |
| **8.5** | 0.00 | 0.0 | 0.00 | **2.3** | 1.1 | 0.34 | 2.08 | 2.15 | 91.3 | **3.8** | 55.6 | 10.7 | **6.5** |
| **5.1** | 2.62 | 11.2 | 0.04 | **4.7** | 4.2 | 0.98 | 8.18 | 3.72 | 69.5 | **4.4** | 32.2 | 10.4 | **6.8** |
| **4.6** | 1.21 | 6.7 | 0.35 | **5.1** | 3.0 | 1.04 | 9.94 | 5.16 | 73.4 | **4.7** | 19.9 | 5.0 | **6.3** |
| **8.2** | 0.61 | 2.1 | -0.12 | **8.1** | 6.6 | 1.87 | 13.24 | 3.82 | 55.2 | **2.4** | 10.2 | 16.8 | **9.4** |
| **8.0** | 0.16 | 0.9 | -0.03 | **4.9** | 5.0 | 0.98 | 9.44 | 3.74 | 71.7 | **3.3** | 17.5 | 11.9 | **7.4** |
| **8.3** | 0.00 | 0.0 | 0.07 | **3.5** | 1.3 | 0.71 | 7.08 | 2.94 | 67.8 | **0.9** | 24.1 | 42.1 | **5.5** |
| **7.2** | 0.57 | 1.9 | 2.89 | **6.2** | 4.6 | 1.20 | 7.28 | 3.16 | 29.6 | **3.3** | 90.7 | 99.9 | **8.3** |
| **10.0** | na | 0.0 | na | **9.5** | 76.5 | 2.25 | 11.23 | 1.54 | 76.8 | **4.0** | 123.2 | 0.0 | **7.0** |
| **8.2** | 0.99 | 3.9 | 0.00 | **3.7** | 1.2 | 0.54 | 3.65 | 4.55 | 86.5 | **4.9** | 24.9 | 4.0 | **7.7** |
| **10.0** | na | 0.0 | na | **9.5** | 7.7 | 2.70 | 3.45 | 2.31 | 94.3 | **4.0** | 364.2 | 0.0 | **7.0** |
| **9.5** | 0.61 | 0.7 | 0.01 | **6.8** | 529.0 | 1.38 | 5.56 | 2.06 | 55.0 | **8.3** | 86.4 | 0.4 | **10.0** |
| **9.2** | 1.37 | 0.0 | 0.14 | **9.5** | 9.0 | 2.92 | 3.09 | 3.05 | 44.9 | **4.0** | na | 95.7 | **9.0** |
| **10.0** | na | 0.0 | na | **9.5** | 4.1 | 2.84 | 3.22 | 2.07 | 92.7 | **4.0** | 355.3 | 0.0 | **7.0** |
| **4.2** | 2.13 | 9.5 | 0.18 | **3.0** | 1.3 | 0.43 | 4.79 | 3.92 | 90.6 | **3.2** | 21.7 | 13.6 | **5.2** |
| **4.1** | 1.10 | 4.3 | 0.26 | **1.0** | 0.0 | 0.02 | 0.14 | 4.13 | 94.6 | **4.3** | 22.5 | 7.1 | **3.7** |
| **6.6** | 1.31 | 5.3 | 0.12 | **3.3** | 0.7 | 0.62 | 4.85 | 3.35 | 76.3 | **2.2** | 34.3 | 23.2 | **7.1** |
| **4.8** | 1.71 | 8.0 | 0.15 | **5.2** | 7.9 | 1.25 | 12.26 | 3.62 | 65.9 | **1.2** | 14.7 | 29.4 | **8.0** |
| **2.1** | 3.34 | 17.9 | -0.03 | **3.4** | 0.1 | 0.40 | 4.42 | 4.09 | 88.8 | **1.4** | 25.5 | 28.4 | **1.7** |
| **4.5** | 1.73 | 10.4 | 0.25 | **4.1** | 6.7 | 0.96 | 10.09 | 3.20 | 62.3 | **3.7** | 21.2 | 11.1 | **5.4** |
| **10.0** | 0.04 | 0.1 | 0.08 | **4.1** | 1.1 | 0.84 | 5.23 | 2.35 | 60.0 | **7.1** | 94.8 | 8.4 | **8.1** |
| **6.4** | 1.70 | 6.9 | 0.02 | **3.0** | 5.1 | 0.59 | 5.08 | 3.07 | 79.6 | **2.4** | 20.8 | 16.4 | **7.3** |
| **4.6** | 2.13 | 9.2 | 0.08 | **5.6** | 8.7 | 1.24 | 10.78 | 4.14 | 66.6 | **1.4** | 6.6 | 22.9 | **7.5** |
| **7.0** | 0.21 | 1.8 | 0.20 | **3.9** | 40.0 | 0.63 | 5.93 | 2.50 | 57.4 | **1.1** | 12.0 | 19.5 | **9.0** |

| Name | City | State | Rating | 2018 Rating | 2017 Rating | Total Assets ($Mil) | One Year Asset Growth | Asset Mix (As a % of Total Assets): Commercial Loans | Consumer Loans | Mortgage Loans | Securities | Capitalization Index | Leverage Ratio | Risk-Based Capital Ratio |
|---|---|---|---|---|---|---|---|---|---|---|---|---|---|---|
| Discover Bank | Greenwood | DE | D+ | C- | C- | 112384.2 | 4.04 | 0.2 | 84.0 | 1.2 | 9.4 | 8.6 | 10.1 | 13.8 |
| Dixon Bank | Dixon | KY | B | B | B | 83.4 | -0.96 | 3.0 | 2.8 | 3.9 | 56.8 | 10.0 | 24.4 | 58.2 |
| ▲ DMB Community Bank | De Forest | WI | A- | B+ | A- | 491.5 | 1.29 | 0.9 | 0.5 | 19.1 | 12.1 | 10.0 | 12.6 | 19.8 |
| DNB National Bank | Clear Lake | SD | C+ | C+ | C+ | 81.9 | 2.01 | 5.5 | 0.9 | 6.4 | 50.4 | 7.2 | 9.1 | 23.1 |
| Dogwood State Bank | Raleigh | NC | D+ | C | C | 347.6 | 28.46 | 17.7 | 0.6 | 13.3 | 10.9 | 10.0 | 23.5 | 27.4 |
| Dollar Bank, Federal Savings Bank | Pittsburgh | PA | B | B | B- | 9043.2 | 6.21 | 7.9 | 3.1 | 53.0 | 12.1 | 10.0 | 12.0 | 19.4 |
| Dolores State Bank | Dolores | CO | A- | B+ | A- | 267.1 | 1.92 | 10.8 | 4.9 | 30.1 | 25.2 | 10.0 | 14.0 | 23.9 |
| Dominion Bank | Grapeland | TX | C | C+ | C+ | 145.1 | 323.64 | 36.6 | 1.5 | 6.5 | 2.3 | 10.0 | 37.2 | 36.7 |
| Donley County State Bank | Clarendon | TX | C+ | C | C | 41.7 | -2.98 | 4.6 | 1.6 | 0.1 | 34.1 | 10.0 | 19.0 | 58.0 |
| ▲ Douglas National Bank | Douglas | GA | A | A- | A | 180.6 | 0.71 | 10.5 | 3.0 | 20.8 | 3.8 | 10.0 | 12.7 | 16.8 |
| ▼ DR Bank | Darien | CT | D- | D- | D | 370.2 | -37.20 | 0.4 | 14.5 | 25.1 | 17.5 | 7.3 | 10.4 | 12.8 |
| Drake Bank | Saint Paul | MN | C+ | B- | A- | 116.6 | -2.31 | 24.0 | 1.1 | 19.7 | 3.0 | 7.9 | 9.6 | 13.6 |
| Drummond Community Bank | Chiefland | FL | A- | A- | A- | 655.3 | 24.69 | 4.8 | 2.5 | 15.8 | 32.1 | 10.0 | 11.5 | 18.8 |
| DSRM National Bank | Albuquerque | NM | U | U | U | 3.9 | 1.94 | 0.0 | 0.0 | 0.0 | 66.8 | 10.0 | 85.0 | 272.4 |
| Du Quoin State Bank | Du Quoin | IL | B+ | B+ | B+ | 108.1 | 3.57 | 3.9 | 1.5 | 14.9 | 69.2 | 7.1 | 9.1 | 25.0 |
| Dubuque Bank and Trust Co. | Dubuque | IA | B+ | B+ | B | 1646.1 | 11.05 | 15.4 | 0.9 | 5.7 | 26.2 | 8.3 | 9.8 | 14.6 |
| ▲ Dundee Bank | Omaha | NE | B- | C- | C- | 297.2 | 5.05 | 12.0 | 0.3 | 22.0 | 9.0 | 8.5 | 10.0 | 13.8 |
| Durand State Bank | Durand | IL | B | B- | B- | 106.1 | 3.63 | 6.5 | 2.2 | 12.7 | 25.3 | 10.0 | 11.2 | 18.2 |
| Durden Banking Co., Inc. | Twin City | GA | A | A- | A- | 177.0 | 0.74 | 5.0 | 5.7 | 29.5 | 26.9 | 10.0 | 17.0 | 28.9 |
| Dysart State Bank | Dysart | IA | D- | E | E | 12.1 | -12.32 | 1.2 | 1.1 | 20.3 | 6.2 | 8.9 | 10.3 | 16.5 |
| E*TRADE Bank | Arlington | VA | B | B | B | 44775.5 | -11.18 | 0.0 | 0.4 | 2.0 | 93.2 | 5.2 | 7.2 | 36.7 |
| E*TRADE Savings Bank | Arlington | VA | B | B | B | 3991.6 | -29.67 | 0.0 | 4.2 | 0.0 | 63.0 | 10.0 | 40.7 | 224.7 |
| Eagle Bank | Everett | MA | B- | C | C- | 460.4 | 2.88 | 10.6 | 0.0 | 29.7 | 14.8 | 10.0 | 12.3 | 15.2 |
| Eagle Bank | Glenwood | MN | A | A | B+ | 154.7 | 3.21 | 9.3 | 3.8 | 13.8 | 14.8 | 10.0 | 14.3 | 22.6 |
| ▲ Eagle Bank | Polson | MT | B+ | C+ | C+ | 70.5 | 6.68 | 15.4 | 3.4 | 10.3 | 18.9 | 10.0 | 11.2 | 15.5 |
| Eagle Bank and Trust Co. | Little Rock | AR | B | B- | B | 397.7 | -1.58 | 3.2 | 0.5 | 24.4 | 34.2 | 10.0 | 13.1 | 23.7 |
| Eagle Community Bank | Maple Grove | MN | D | E | E | 25.2 | 2.22 | 12.1 | 1.8 | 25.3 | 0.4 | 6.3 | 8.4 | 12.9 |
| Eagle Savings Bank | Cincinnati | OH | B- | B | B | 142.8 | 4.15 | 4.2 | 0.0 | 50.9 | 0.0 | 10.0 | 15.4 | 17.2 |
| ▲ Eagle State Bank | Eagle | NE | C- | D+ | C- | 43.9 | 3.92 | 10.6 | 1.2 | 15.4 | 5.7 | 5.8 | 8.7 | 11.6 |
| EagleBank | Bethesda | MD | A | A | A- | 8950.2 | 6.80 | 13.9 | 0.0 | 4.0 | 9.3 | 10.0 | 13.2 | 15.5 |
| Eaglemark Savings Bank | Carson City | NV | A- | A- | A- | 45.7 | 13.17 | 0.0 | 25.7 | 0.0 | 39.4 | 10.0 | 28.2 | 41.7 |
| ▲ Earlham Savings Bank | West Des Moines | IA | C | C+ | C+ | 309.0 | 4.17 | 12.3 | 1.9 | 12.1 | 38.0 | 6.6 | 8.6 | 17.3 |
| East Boston Savings Bank | East Boston | MA | B | B- | B- | 6333.1 | 2.84 | 1.6 | 0.2 | 10.5 | 0.2 | 6.2 | 10.5 | 11.9 |
| East Cambridge Savings Bank | Cambridge | MA | C+ | C+ | C | 1106.8 | 2.70 | 2.3 | 1.0 | 46.8 | 10.3 | 9.8 | 10.8 | 17.0 |
| East West Bank | Pasadena | CA | A- | A- | B+ | 44181.5 | 7.71 | 22.1 | 0.1 | 17.1 | 7.5 | 8.7 | 10.3 | 13.9 |
| East Wisconsin Savings Bank | Kaukauna | WI | D+ | D+ | D+ | 241.3 | -3.66 | 0.0 | 23.3 | 49.0 | 9.6 | 7.3 | 9.2 | 16.1 |
| Eastbank, N.A. | New York | NY | B- | B | B | 175.5 | -7.49 | 0.9 | 0.0 | 11.2 | 20.9 | 10.0 | 19.3 | 29.0 |
| Eastern Bank | Boston | MA | B+ | B | B | 11628.8 | 2.20 | 14.8 | 3.3 | 15.6 | 13.0 | 8.2 | 11.4 | 13.5 |
| Eastern Colorado Bank | Cheyenne Wells | CO | A- | B+ | A- | 456.8 | 14.00 | 7.2 | 0.4 | 9.3 | 16.3 | 9.4 | 10.6 | 14.5 |
| Eastern Connecticut Savings Bank | Norwich | CT | D+ | D | D | 193.1 | 6.67 | 5.4 | 2.8 | 36.6 | 0.2 | 6.1 | 8.1 | 12.2 |
| Eastern International Bank | Los Angeles | CA | B | B | B- | 128.7 | 24.64 | 0.0 | 0.0 | 0.1 | 4.7 | 10.0 | 15.9 | 22.4 |
| Eastern Michigan Bank | Croswell | MI | B | B- | B- | 373.9 | 5.30 | 8.8 | 3.7 | 8.1 | 27.6 | 8.5 | 10.0 | 18.4 |
| Eastern National Bank | Miami | FL | D+ | C- | C | 341.6 | -17.16 | 18.0 | 0.7 | 24.7 | 1.3 | 6.2 | 8.8 | 11.9 |
| Eastern Savings Bank, FSB | Hunt Valley | MD | B | B- | C | 316.8 | -2.15 | 0.0 | 0.0 | 48.9 | 0.0 | 10.0 | 25.3 | 37.5 |
| Easthampton Savings Bank | Easthampton | MA | B- | B- | B- | 1403.0 | 2.34 | 9.2 | 0.5 | 35.0 | 12.0 | 6.7 | 8.7 | 12.6 |
| Eaton Federal Savings Bank | Charlotte | MI | B- | C+ | B- | 375.2 | 11.17 | 1.9 | 1.4 | 40.0 | 26.2 | 10.0 | 14.9 | 23.5 |
| Eclipse Bank, Inc. | Louisville | KY | C+ | C+ | C | 176.6 | 15.31 | 5.8 | 1.6 | 10.5 | 5.2 | 8.2 | 12.5 | 13.5 |
| Edgewater Bank | Saint Joseph | MI | C+ | C- | C- | 186.1 | 9.49 | 12.9 | 0.6 | 29.9 | 4.9 | 6.8 | 8.8 | 12.4 |
| Edison National Bank | Fort Myers | FL | B- | B- | C+ | 322.2 | 6.01 | 2.0 | 2.2 | 23.8 | 7.6 | 6.0 | 8.0 | 19.8 |
| Edmonton State Bank | Edmonton | KY | A- | B+ | A | 546.1 | 3.60 | 6.7 | 7.8 | 18.2 | 10.9 | 10.0 | 14.2 | 20.3 |
| Edon State Bank Co. of Edon, Ohio | Edon | OH | B | B | B | 61.8 | -0.01 | 1.4 | 0.4 | 6.0 | 46.2 | 10.0 | 18.3 | 50.2 |
| Edward Jones Trust Co. | Saint Louis | MO | U | U | U | 99.1 | 14.73 | 0.0 | 0.0 | 0.0 | 0.1 | 10.0 | 98.6 | 357.8 |
| EH National Bank | Beverly Hills | CA | C | C- | C | 250.4 | 21.55 | 6.2 | 0.0 | 1.4 | 5.5 | 10.0 | 13.3 | 16.2 |
| El Dorado Savings Bank, F.S.B. | Placerville | CA | B | B- | B- | 2183.8 | -0.03 | 0.0 | 0.0 | 24.8 | 57.0 | 10.0 | 11.3 | 37.4 |
| Elberfeld State Bank | Elberfeld | IN | B | B | B- | 80.9 | -0.10 | 4.0 | 0.7 | 10.3 | 23.7 | 10.0 | 12.2 | 20.9 |
| Elberton Federal S&L Assn. | Elberton | GA | C- | D+ | C | 24.3 | 2.43 | 0.0 | 1.3 | 74.7 | 15.7 | 10.0 | 20.7 | 43.3 |
| Elderton State Bank | Elderton | PA | B+ | B | B | 298.7 | 7.31 | 11.5 | 1.0 | 12.5 | 5.1 | 10.0 | 11.3 | 16.4 |
| Elgin State Bank | Elgin | IA | D- | D- | D | 24.3 | -3.63 | 4.9 | 2.9 | 15.3 | 30.2 | 5.8 | 7.8 | 16.1 |
| Elizabethton Federal Savings Bank | Elizabethton | TN | A | A- | A- | 292.8 | -3.43 | 0.0 | 0.7 | 34.5 | 41.5 | 10.0 | 41.0 | 109.5 |
| Elk State Bank | Clyde | KS | C+ | C+ | C+ | 96.9 | -0.76 | 6.3 | 1.3 | 11.0 | 30.0 | 8.8 | 10.2 | 18.0 |

| Asset Quality Index | Adjusted Non-Performing Loans as a % of Total Loans | Adjusted Non-Performing Loans as a % of Capital | Net Charge-Offs Avg Loans | Profitability Index | Net Income ($Mil) | Return on Assets (R.O.A.) | Return on Equity (R.O.E.) | Net Interest Spread | Overhead Efficiency Ratio | Liquidity Index | Liquidity Ratio | Hot Money Ratio | Stability Index |
|---|---|---|---|---|---|---|---|---|---|---|---|---|---|
| **1.1** | 3.79 | 20.2 | 3.18 | **10.0** | 2895.0 | 2.65 | 26.02 | 9.13 | 35.4 | **0.9** | 17.1 | 12.3 | **10.0** |
| **7.9** | 5.13 | 4.6 | 1.40 | **3.5** | 0.6 | 0.66 | 2.73 | 2.64 | 70.5 | **4.1** | 87.9 | 25.5 | **7.7** |
| **7.5** | 0.00 | 0.0 | -0.09 | **5.5** | 5.5 | 1.11 | 9.12 | 2.82 | 54.0 | **0.8** | 17.9 | 31.4 | **7.7** |
| **9.5** | 0.00 | 0.0 | 0.00 | **3.8** | 0.7 | 0.88 | 9.78 | 2.95 | 78.1 | **4.5** | 56.6 | 15.3 | **5.2** |
| **7.5** | 0.13 | 0.8 | 0.00 | **0.6** | -2.8 | -0.85 | -4.17 | 3.57 | 126.7 | **1.4** | 19.8 | 22.4 | **7.2** |
| **8.3** | 0.66 | 3.3 | 0.12 | **4.1** | 70.8 | 0.81 | 6.84 | 3.01 | 67.9 | **2.9** | 14.8 | 9.6 | **9.0** |
| **6.5** | 1.36 | 5.6 | 0.04 | **8.3** | 4.7 | 1.81 | 12.56 | 4.43 | 53.1 | **4.8** | 31.7 | 7.9 | **8.5** |
| **7.8** | 0.07 | 0.2 | 0.01 | **1.0** | -2.5 | -4.09 | -13.03 | 3.68 | 205.6 | **1.6** | 34.6 | 41.7 | **6.8** |
| **9.7** | 0.35 | 0.4 | 0.00 | **3.1** | 0.3 | 0.64 | 3.35 | 2.54 | 80.1 | **3.0** | 61.6 | 30.3 | **6.7** |
| **8.2** | 0.59 | 2.2 | -0.01 | **10.0** | 5.8 | 3.14 | 25.38 | 5.11 | 48.3 | **1.4** | 10.2 | 20.9 | **9.3** |
| **6.1** | 0.44 | 2.6 | 0.44 | **0.0** | 115.6 | -0.90 | -8.21 | 2.68 | 117.4 | **1.3** | 31.3 | 45.2 | **4.3** |
| **6.0** | 0.27 | 1.0 | 0.17 | **3.7** | 0.6 | 0.52 | 5.65 | 3.52 | 80.3 | **2.7** | 16.0 | 15.8 | **5.6** |
| **8.0** | 0.83 | 2.5 | 0.04 | **6.3** | 8.0 | 1.28 | 11.13 | 4.54 | 69.8 | **4.9** | 35.8 | 7.3 | **8.1** |
| **9.9** | na | 0.0 | na | **8.0** | 0.1 | 1.52 | 1.80 | 1.38 | 88.3 | **4.0** | na | 100.0 | **5.3** |
| **8.1** | 1.40 | 2.2 | 0.03 | **4.9** | 1.2 | 1.15 | 9.08 | 3.97 | 69.4 | **5.3** | 57.8 | 13.1 | **8.2** |
| **5.8** | 2.34 | 7.5 | 0.22 | **8.1** | 36.2 | 2.26 | 23.02 | 3.11 | 50.9 | **6.7** | 45.1 | 3.6 | **7.6** |
| **4.9** | 0.71 | 4.3 | 0.38 | **5.1** | 3.5 | 1.21 | 13.41 | 3.65 | 64.9 | **0.7** | 13.0 | 34.0 | **5.9** |
| **6.2** | 2.41 | 5.9 | 0.03 | **3.9** | 0.9 | 0.83 | 7.51 | 3.32 | 71.6 | **2.7** | 17.9 | 15.6 | **6.3** |
| **7.9** | 0.51 | 2.5 | 0.18 | **9.0** | 3.7 | 2.10 | 13.14 | 5.02 | 58.8 | **2.6** | 21.4 | 16.5 | **9.6** |
| **9.1** | 0.00 | 0.0 | 0.00 | **3.1** | 0.1 | 0.55 | 5.85 | 3.50 | 84.1 | **5.5** | 29.5 | 0.0 | **3.3** |
| **7.1** | 20.02 | 7.0 | -1.67 | **5.7** | 515.9 | 1.06 | 13.73 | 2.76 | 49.8 | **3.4** | 78.3 | 0.0 | **7.1** |
| **7.8** | 0.27 | 0.0 | 0.01 | **3.4** | 12.1 | 0.26 | 0.71 | 2.50 | 68.6 | **4.5** | 152.5 | 0.0 | **7.3** |
| **8.9** | 0.12 | 0.9 | 0.00 | **3.8** | 3.4 | 0.75 | 6.48 | 3.34 | 84.2 | **1.8** | 20.5 | 20.8 | **6.7** |
| **8.5** | 0.02 | 0.1 | 0.00 | **7.1** | 2.7 | 1.77 | 12.47 | 4.00 | 60.0 | **5.4** | 31.8 | 3.4 | **9.3** |
| **8.3** | 0.07 | 0.4 | 0.10 | **8.5** | 1.2 | 1.69 | 15.64 | 4.78 | 56.1 | **1.0** | 24.8 | 18.5 | **6.6** |
| **7.2** | 1.03 | 6.9 | 0.01 | **4.4** | 4.0 | 0.97 | 7.59 | 3.98 | 86.4 | **3.0** | 26.9 | 11.6 | **7.4** |
| **7.0** | 0.00 | 0.0 | 0.00 | **1.2** | 0.0 | 0.09 | 1.02 | 5.15 | 97.8 | **1.8** | 12.0 | 19.6 | **1.9** |
| **8.4** | 1.00 | 4.3 | 0.02 | **3.6** | 0.8 | 0.59 | 3.82 | 3.57 | 85.2 | **2.2** | 15.2 | 18.2 | **7.4** |
| **6.8** | 0.10 | 0.6 | 0.00 | **4.0** | 0.4 | 1.02 | 11.94 | 3.03 | 65.7 | **1.1** | 12.3 | 29.8 | **3.7** |
| **6.2** | 0.64 | 3.5 | 0.13 | **9.7** | 155.3 | 1.76 | 11.83 | 3.92 | 37.8 | **0.8** | 9.2 | 9.1 | **10.0** |
| **7.2** | 0.00 | 0.0 | 0.00 | **10.0** | 4.0 | 10.62 | 41.04 | 13.79 | 76.3 | **4.3** | 80.6 | 19.7 | **8.9** |
| **8.8** | 0.00 | 0.3 | 0.14 | **3.1** | 1.6 | 0.50 | 5.93 | 3.20 | 79.9 | **5.5** | 46.3 | 8.8 | **4.5** |
| **7.1** | 0.10 | 0.6 | 0.01 | **5.2** | 67.1 | 1.07 | 10.43 | 2.87 | 54.2 | **1.2** | 7.5 | 16.6 | **8.6** |
| **9.1** | 0.19 | 1.4 | 0.00 | **3.3** | 6.2 | 0.55 | 5.47 | 3.01 | 76.3 | **1.4** | 15.9 | 26.1 | **7.8** |
| **7.7** | 0.56 | 2.8 | 0.16 | **8.7** | 689.7 | 1.62 | 14.63 | 3.66 | 42.6 | **1.5** | 18.3 | 19.9 | **10.0** |
| **5.4** | 0.63 | 3.2 | 0.02 | **1.8** | 0.4 | 0.16 | 1.74 | 2.65 | 94.9 | **2.4** | 19.7 | 17.6 | **4.9** |
| **7.9** | 0.00 | 0.0 | 0.00 | **2.7** | 0.6 | 0.32 | 1.79 | 3.34 | 86.1 | **2.2** | 43.3 | 34.2 | **7.6** |
| **6.0** | 0.98 | 3.7 | 0.05 | **5.8** | 135.4 | 1.19 | 8.83 | 3.96 | 69.9 | **5.0** | 9.4 | 1.7 | **10.0** |
| **8.1** | 0.12 | 0.3 | -0.01 | **7.4** | 7.9 | 1.90 | 16.16 | 4.50 | 59.2 | **1.7** | 14.4 | 21.4 | **7.8** |
| **1.7** | 4.26 | 34.8 | 0.06 | **1.6** | 0.1 | 0.03 | 0.33 | 3.52 | 97.9 | **1.4** | 13.2 | 25.2 | **3.9** |
| **7.4** | 0.00 | 0.0 | 0.00 | **3.3** | 0.6 | 0.49 | 2.73 | 3.92 | 83.7 | **1.4** | 32.4 | 43.6 | **7.5** |
| **7.0** | 2.24 | 4.6 | 0.07 | **4.9** | 4.2 | 1.12 | 11.43 | 3.45 | 62.0 | **6.7** | 50.9 | 2.2 | **5.9** |
| **3.3** | 3.18 | 16.1 | 0.67 | **0.0** | -2.9 | -0.77 | -7.86 | 3.35 | 121.2 | **0.7** | 11.4 | 43.5 | **3.8** |
| **4.4** | 5.12 | 16.9 | 0.02 | **5.8** | 3.0 | 0.92 | 3.74 | 5.99 | 84.8 | **3.0** | 24.9 | 14.8 | **8.6** |
| **8.5** | 0.28 | 2.1 | 0.18 | **3.8** | 9.6 | 0.69 | 7.92 | 2.89 | 68.2 | **1.4** | 13.3 | 26.6 | **6.8** |
| **8.0** | 1.17 | 3.3 | 0.01 | **3.2** | 2.1 | 0.58 | 3.84 | 3.42 | 80.1 | **4.3** | 37.0 | 12.2 | **6.9** |
| **3.5** | 2.04 | 9.6 | -0.04 | **4.0** | 1.2 | 0.75 | 5.75 | 3.50 | 74.0 | **0.7** | 13.7 | 33.9 | **6.8** |
| **4.8** | 1.12 | 10.1 | 0.04 | **3.6** | 1.4 | 0.83 | 8.17 | 3.71 | 80.0 | **3.1** | 10.5 | 13.0 | **5.9** |
| **9.5** | 0.00 | 0.0 | 0.00 | **4.4** | 3.6 | 1.13 | 14.22 | 3.33 | 67.9 | **6.6** | 52.0 | 3.1 | **5.0** |
| **7.3** | 0.58 | 3.2 | 0.05 | **8.6** | 11.5 | 2.11 | 14.66 | 4.15 | 55.3 | **3.2** | 21.7 | 13.8 | **10.0** |
| **9.4** | 0.00 | 0.0 | 0.00 | **3.9** | 0.5 | 0.86 | 4.50 | 2.53 | 67.3 | **6.6** | 71.4 | 6.2 | **8.3** |
| **10.0** | na | 0.0 | na | **10.0** | 12.1 | 13.42 | 14.31 | 2.55 | 71.1 | **4.0** | na | 0.0 | **6.7** |
| **3.8** | 2.00 | 6.6 | -0.10 | **1.6** | -0.2 | -0.07 | -0.45 | 3.77 | 105.6 | **0.8** | 20.2 | 44.6 | **6.9** |
| **9.6** | 1.32 | 2.3 | -0.01 | **4.4** | 19.4 | 0.89 | 7.94 | 2.46 | 59.3 | **6.4** | 77.9 | 11.4 | **9.0** |
| **9.2** | 2.89 | 2.0 | 0.20 | **4.1** | 0.6 | 0.79 | 6.61 | 3.63 | 73.6 | **4.7** | 40.0 | 11.6 | **7.0** |
| **9.8** | 0.00 | 0.0 | 0.00 | **1.9** | 0.1 | 0.25 | 1.20 | 3.52 | 98.8 | **1.8** | 22.3 | 21.6 | **5.9** |
| **3.8** | 3.75 | 17.9 | 0.15 | **6.7** | 3.9 | 1.35 | 11.76 | 3.74 | 48.6 | **1.8** | 15.4 | 20.0 | **7.7** |
| **8.9** | 0.03 | 0.2 | 0.01 | **1.4** | 0.0 | 0.01 | 0.17 | 3.40 | 98.8 | **5.2** | 43.4 | 6.2 | **1.5** |
| **9.9** | 0.00 | 0.1 | 0.00 | **6.7** | 4.1 | 1.38 | 3.43 | 3.19 | 41.3 | **4.5** | 87.0 | 22.1 | **8.2** |
| **4.3** | 2.43 | 6.8 | 0.29 | **3.7** | 0.7 | 0.67 | 6.52 | 3.41 | 72.2 | **0.9** | 22.4 | 24.9 | **5.3** |

| Name | City | State | Rating | 2018 Rating | 2017 Rating | Total Assets ($Mil) | One Year Asset Growth | Asset Mix (As a % of Total Assets) Commercial Loans | Consumer Loans | Mortgage Loans | Securities | Capitalization Index | Leverage Ratio | Risk-Based Capital Ratio |
|---|---|---|---|---|---|---|---|---|---|---|---|---|---|---|
| Elkhorn Valley Bank & Trust | Norfolk | NE | B | B | B | 795.1 | 3.83 | 14.3 | 3.6 | 6.0 | 29.9 | 10.0 | 12.9 | 17.2 |
| Elkton Bank & Trust Co. | Elkton | KY | A- | A- | B | 143.7 | 1.45 | 4.3 | 4.5 | 15.6 | 40.4 | 10.0 | 12.9 | 26.4 |
| Elmira Savings Bank | Elmira | NY | C+ | C+ | B- | 607.1 | 2.85 | 4.7 | 6.6 | 53.8 | 3.1 | 6.1 | 8.1 | 12.2 |
| ▲ Elysian Bank | Elysian | MN | B+ | B- | B- | 50.6 | 4.07 | 6.4 | 6.9 | 20.2 | 3.7 | 10.0 | 11.3 | 17.5 |
| Embassy Bank for the Lehigh Valley | Bethlehem | PA | B | B | B | 1176.4 | 6.98 | 4.6 | 0.1 | 51.5 | 7.7 | 6.4 | 8.4 | 13.0 |
| Embassy National Bank | Lawrenceville | GA | A | A | A- | 109.6 | 6.33 | 2.2 | 0.1 | 2.2 | 0.0 | 10.0 | 17.8 | 23.9 |
| ▼ Emerald Bank | Burden | KS | D+ | C- | C- | 17.3 | 1.89 | 4.7 | 8.6 | 36.4 | 7.1 | 9.1 | 10.4 | 20.6 |
| Emigrant Bank | New York | NY | B- | B- | B- | 5953.8 | 2.86 | 32.2 | 0.7 | 15.5 | 9.0 | 10.0 | 18.7 | 18.9 |
| Emigrant Mercantile Bank | New York | NY | U | U | U | 3.4 | -0.09 | 0.0 | 0.0 | 0.0 | 0.0 | 10.0 | 85.0 | 424.1 |
| Empire National Bank | Islandia | NY | C+ | C+ | B- | 978.6 | -0.98 | 9.6 | 0.5 | 8.6 | 22.8 | 7.8 | 9.5 | 15.6 |
| Empire State Bank | Newburgh | NY | C | D+ | C- | 420.9 | 4.48 | 4.7 | 0.0 | 39.8 | 3.8 | 7.4 | 9.3 | 14.9 |
| Emprise Bank | Wichita | KS | B+ | B+ | B+ | 1817.2 | 7.74 | 10.6 | 2.8 | 18.6 | 19.0 | 5.9 | 7.9 | 11.8 |
| Encore Bank | Little Rock | AR | D+ | C- | C- | 318.5 | 97.40 | 17.0 | 0.7 | 16.6 | 10.8 | 10.0 | 17.4 | 19.1 |
| Endeavor Bank | San Diego | CA | D | D | | 125.4 | 43.77 | 27.8 | 2.3 | 10.8 | 0.0 | 10.0 | 14.8 | 15.5 |
| EnerBank USA | Salt Lake City | UT | B+ | A- | B+ | 2705.9 | 34.27 | 0.0 | 93.6 | 0.0 | 1.0 | 5.9 | 10.3 | 11.7 |
| Englewood Bank & Trust | Englewood | FL | A- | A- | B+ | 314.4 | 10.32 | 1.7 | 1.2 | 22.5 | 22.7 | 8.5 | 10.0 | 17.3 |
| ▲ Ennis State Bank | Ennis | TX | B+ | B- | B | 261.1 | 12.84 | 11.7 | 0.7 | 9.3 | 18.9 | 7.9 | 9.6 | 14.4 |
| ▲ Enterprise Bank | Omaha | NE | B- | C+ | B- | 337.5 | 18.24 | 11.2 | 0.8 | 5.3 | 1.3 | 6.8 | 9.8 | 12.4 |
| ▼ Enterprise Bank | Allison Park | PA | D- | D | D- | 307.2 | 5.67 | 10.1 | 0.0 | 4.2 | 0.0 | 5.1 | 9.3 | 11.1 |
| Enterprise Bank & Trust | Clayton | MO | B+ | B+ | B+ | 7293.4 | 29.65 | 32.0 | 0.3 | 4.2 | 18.1 | 6.9 | 10.3 | 12.4 |
| Enterprise Bank and Trust Co. | Lowell | MA | B | B- | B- | 3235.1 | 9.13 | 13.6 | 0.3 | 13.4 | 15.6 | 6.2 | 9.3 | 11.9 |
| Enterprise Bank of South Carolina | Ehrhardt | SC | C- | D | D- | 338.6 | 3.08 | 6.7 | 2.5 | 18.3 | 26.0 | 6.5 | 8.5 | 15.4 |
| ▲ Envision Bank | Stoughton | MA | C | D | D+ | 631.3 | 2.64 | 1.4 | 2.5 | 52.5 | 9.1 | 10.0 | 11.3 | 16.7 |
| Ephrata National Bank | Ephrata | PA | B | B- | C+ | 1171.1 | 6.73 | 4.8 | 0.5 | 23.2 | 26.8 | 8.2 | 9.8 | 14.4 |
| ▲ Equitable Bank | Grand Island | NE | C+ | C | B- | 356.9 | 22.09 | 12.6 | 1.5 | 19.3 | 5.3 | 6.0 | 9.4 | 11.8 |
| ▲ Equitable Bank, S.S.B. | Wauwatosa | WI | D | E | E | 301.4 | -2.72 | 0.6 | 0.1 | 44.3 | 7.1 | 7.2 | 9.2 | 14.7 |
| Equitable S&L Assn. | Sterling | CO | B | B | B | 164.0 | -0.68 | 0.0 | 0.7 | 83.3 | 2.8 | 10.0 | 16.3 | 32.0 |
| Equitable S&L Co. | Cadiz | OH | D+ | D | D+ | 13.7 | 6.85 | 0.0 | 0.5 | 48.6 | 15.8 | 10.0 | 19.8 | 43.9 |
| Equity Bank | Andover | KS | C+ | B- | B | 3946.1 | -2.76 | 14.8 | 1.6 | 15.6 | 23.5 | 6.9 | 8.9 | 12.5 |
| ▲ Ergo Bank | Markesan | WI | B- | C | C+ | 91.2 | 5.08 | 13.5 | 1.1 | 11.2 | 12.3 | 10.0 | 12.7 | 16.9 |
| ▼ Ericson State Bank | Ericson | NE | D+ | B- | B- | 100.9 | -0.40 | 7.0 | 6.4 | 1.0 | 8.9 | 0.0 | 3.4 | 5.6 |
| ESB Bank | Caledonia | MN | C+ | C | D+ | 112.9 | 1.18 | 13.3 | 3.8 | 8.8 | 10.3 | 7.8 | 9.8 | 13.2 |
| ▼ ESB Financial | Emporia | KS | C+ | B- | B | 243.6 | 6.19 | 9.3 | 2.3 | 18.9 | 17.0 | 8.8 | 10.2 | 14.1 |
| ▼ Escambia County Bank | Flomaton | AL | C+ | B- | C+ | 73.3 | 2.07 | 10.2 | 5.9 | 15.2 | 55.9 | 10.0 | 15.7 | 34.6 |
| ▲ Esquire Bank, N.A. | Jericho | NY | A | A- | A- | 790.6 | 20.13 | 31.4 | 6.0 | 6.1 | 18.5 | 10.0 | 13.5 | 17.8 |
| ESSA Bank & Trust | Stroudsburg | PA | C+ | C+ | C+ | 1804.0 | -2.94 | 4.0 | 3.9 | 37.0 | 17.3 | 7.7 | 9.4 | 13.6 |
| ▲ Essex Bank | Richmond | VA | B+ | B | B- | 1431.1 | 2.74 | 12.9 | 0.8 | 11.7 | 15.6 | 8.6 | 11.0 | 13.9 |
| ▼ Essex Savings Bank | Essex | CT | B- | B- | B- | 420.9 | 6.68 | 3.0 | 0.7 | 44.5 | 0.2 | 8.4 | 10.0 | 17.8 |
| ETHIC | Boston | MA | D | D- | D- | 219.3 | -8.72 | 1.4 | 19.5 | 15.9 | 0.0 | 10.0 | 14.7 | 18.2 |
| Eureka Homestead | Metairie | LA | C | C | C- | 106.2 | 8.31 | 0.0 | 0.2 | 69.9 | 5.0 | 10.0 | 17.7 | 39.2 |
| Eureka Savings Bank | La Salle | IL | C+ | C+ | B- | 319.2 | 0.31 | 0.8 | 0.5 | 35.5 | 50.4 | 10.0 | 24.2 | 65.8 |
| EvaBank | Cullman | AL | B- | B- | B | 382.8 | 2.99 | 2.5 | 5.0 | 31.7 | 20.8 | 10.0 | 24.9 | 32.1 |
| ▲ Evangeline Bank and Trust Co. | Ville Platte | LA | B+ | B | B | 583.2 | 7.09 | 7.2 | 3.4 | 27.4 | 16.5 | 10.0 | 18.9 | 27.5 |
| Evans Bank, N.A. | Hamburg | NY | B- | C+ | B- | 1446.6 | 5.37 | 15.4 | 0.1 | 12.4 | 9.0 | 8.1 | 10.2 | 13.4 |
| Evercore Trust Co., N.A. | New York | NY | U | U | U | 23.3 | -0.85 | 0.0 | 0.0 | 0.0 | 86.2 | 10.0 | 99.6 | 513.1 |
| Everence Trust Co. | Goshen | IN | U | U | U | 9.5 | 14.27 | 0.0 | 0.0 | 0.0 | 58.2 | 10.0 | 106. | 262.2 |
| Everett Co-operative Bank | Everett | MA | B+ | B+ | B+ | 518.2 | 4.08 | 0.4 | 0.1 | 39.2 | 8.2 | 10.0 | 13.3 | 19.2 |
| Evergreen Bank Group | Oak Brook | IL | B+ | B | B | 1107.0 | 12.28 | 2.5 | 48.8 | 3.9 | 7.7 | 8.5 | 11.2 | 13.7 |
| Evergreen Federal Bank | Grants Pass | OR | B | B | B | 476.8 | 4.69 | 1.6 | 0.2 | 27.6 | 9.8 | 10.0 | 12.5 | 17.8 |
| Evergreen National Bank | Evergreen | CO | C+ | C+ | C- | 120.3 | 4.94 | 2.9 | 0.6 | 15.5 | 24.6 | 7.5 | 9.3 | 19.8 |
| ▼ EverTrust Bank | Pasadena | CA | B+ | A- | A- | 945.2 | 6.52 | 10.7 | 0.0 | 1.1 | 10.9 | 10.0 | 17.0 | 19.6 |
| ▲ Evolve Bank & Trust | Memphis | TN | B- | C+ | C+ | 451.3 | -4.63 | 20.6 | 0.8 | 20.8 | 2.2 | 6.6 | 8.6 | 12.5 |
| Exchange Bank | Santa Rosa | CA | A | A- | B+ | 2669.8 | 0.67 | 7.2 | 0.8 | 11.0 | 26.9 | 9.1 | 10.4 | 15.8 |
| ▲ Exchange Bank | Milledgeville | GA | A- | A- | A- | 259.4 | 4.00 | 3.4 | 1.2 | 17.6 | 29.3 | 10.0 | 13.8 | 22.6 |
| Exchange Bank | Gibbon | NE | B+ | B+ | B+ | 955.6 | 1.85 | 5.7 | 0.9 | 11.9 | 21.8 | 8.2 | 10.1 | 13.5 |
| Exchange Bank | Skiatook | OK | A- | B+ | B | 104.0 | 5.88 | 9.7 | 1.4 | 12.8 | 30.1 | 10.0 | 12.2 | 20.4 |
| Exchange Bank & Trust | Atchison | KS | A- | B+ | B+ | 444.4 | 2.44 | 5.7 | 15.0 | 15.6 | 21.5 | 9.4 | 10.6 | 17.8 |
| Exchange Bank and Trust Co. | Natchitoches | LA | A- | A- | A- | 144.7 | 5.14 | 4.7 | 1.6 | 23.8 | 48.1 | 7.8 | 9.5 | 22.3 |
| ▼ Exchange Bank and Trust Co. | Perry | OK | B- | A- | A- | 301.6 | 6.93 | 6.3 | 5.1 | 20.6 | 27.3 | 9.3 | 10.6 | 16.3 |
| Exchange Bank of Alabama | Altoona | AL | B+ | A- | B+ | 283.4 | 0.86 | 3.8 | 3.4 | 16.1 | 23.9 | 10.0 | 14.6 | 22.7 |

| Asset Quality Index | Adjusted Non-Performing Loans as a % of Total Loans | Adjusted Non-Performing Loans as a % of Capital | Net Charge-Offs Avg Loans | Profitability Index | Net Income ($Mil) | Return on Assets (R.O.A.) | Return on Equity (R.O.E.) | Net Interest Spread | Overhead Efficiency Ratio | Liquidity Index | Liquidity Ratio | Hot Money Ratio | Stability Index |
|---|---|---|---|---|---|---|---|---|---|---|---|---|---|
| **8.0** | 0.46 | 2.0 | 0.40 | **4.7** | 8.2 | 1.05 | 8.14 | 2.99 | 52.8 | **4.6** | 32.7 | 9.6 | **8.1** |
| **8.9** | 0.69 | 2.1 | 0.22 | **5.8** | 1.7 | 1.21 | 9.21 | 3.88 | 62.3 | **3.3** | 47.0 | 20.4 | **7.6** |
| **4.2** | 0.86 | 6.9 | 0.11 | **3.3** | 3.5 | 0.57 | 5.98 | 3.05 | 77.2 | **1.4** | 5.6 | 23.4 | **6.8** |
| **6.4** | 0.94 | 4.4 | 0.13 | **8.6** | 1.0 | 2.09 | 18.47 | 4.65 | 56.0 | **6.1** | 37.0 | 1.2 | **6.9** |
| **9.1** | 0.27 | 1.3 | 0.00 | **4.7** | 11.2 | 0.99 | 11.99 | 3.09 | 59.7 | **2.2** | 5.3 | 17.2 | **7.2** |
| **7.2** | 0.00 | 0.0 | 0.00 | **10.0** | 2.6 | 2.35 | 14.00 | 5.21 | 63.3 | **1.4** | 28.2 | 30.3 | **10.0** |
| **3.1** | 4.60 | 17.5 | 0.22 | **2.1** | 0.0 | 0.12 | 1.13 | 4.22 | 96.5 | **3.5** | 35.6 | 13.8 | **4.9** |
| **3.2** | 4.10 | 14.9 | 0.28 | **6.3** | 63.5 | 1.12 | 5.33 | 4.38 | 68.8 | **4.6** | 15.5 | 5.3 | **10.0** |
| **10.0** | na | 0.0 | na | **0.5** | 0.0 | -0.12 | -0.14 | 1.78 | 109.8 | **4.0** | na | 0.0 | **6.6** |
| **4.9** | 0.76 | 4.1 | 0.04 | **3.1** | 5.2 | 0.51 | 5.75 | 2.66 | 76.9 | **4.6** | 8.4 | 2.3 | **6.7** |
| **4.8** | 1.11 | 6.7 | 0.04 | **3.1** | 2.0 | 0.50 | 6.54 | 2.99 | 78.0 | **1.1** | 10.4 | 25.2 | **4.2** |
| **6.3** | 0.73 | 5.0 | 0.08 | **7.2** | 30.8 | 1.77 | 18.81 | 4.00 | 61.7 | **4.2** | 20.0 | 6.8 | **9.3** |
| **7.3** | 0.16 | 0.5 | 0.09 | **0.5** | -5.1 | -2.38 | -15.77 | 2.45 | 135.5 | **0.4** | 5.2 | 22.2 | **5.0** |
| **8.4** | 0.00 | 0.0 | 0.00 | **0.0** | -3.3 | -3.27 | -17.57 | 3.76 | 159.2 | **3.2** | 21.8 | 13.7 | **1.5** |
| **5.2** | 0.02 | 3.0 | 1.20 | **10.0** | 48.9 | 2.03 | 19.51 | 6.67 | 39.9 | **0.2** | 5.9 | 8.2 | **8.9** |
| **6.9** | 0.49 | 4.5 | 0.00 | **9.5** | 7.1 | 2.32 | 24.18 | 4.13 | 52.6 | **6.0** | 38.8 | 2.8 | **8.1** |
| **5.7** | 0.89 | 3.6 | -0.02 | **7.7** | 4.5 | 1.88 | 18.92 | 4.62 | 60.2 | **4.3** | 24.7 | 8.3 | **7.0** |
| **7.2** | 0.00 | 0.0 | 0.00 | **4.6** | 2.9 | 0.91 | 9.89 | 2.88 | 62.1 | **0.8** | 21.2 | 42.7 | **5.9** |
| **0.0** | 6.54 | 40.4 | -0.01 | **3.1** | 1.5 | 0.51 | 5.47 | 3.30 | 85.4 | **0.5** | 9.5 | 4.1 | **5.1** |
| **6.2** | 0.49 | 2.9 | 0.13 | **7.9** | 100.2 | 1.46 | 10.84 | 3.94 | 54.6 | **2.5** | 15.8 | 7.0 | **10.0** |
| **5.0** | 1.01 | 5.9 | 0.06 | **5.8** | 35.0 | 1.13 | 11.96 | 3.97 | 65.0 | **4.0** | 2.2 | 7.3 | **8.0** |
| **2.1** | 4.94 | 28.1 | 0.04 | **5.7** | 4.0 | 1.20 | 15.59 | 3.80 | 72.0 | **4.5** | 29.9 | 8.7 | **2.9** |
| **6.1** | 1.01 | 5.6 | 0.03 | **2.3** | 3.4 | 0.54 | 4.84 | 2.90 | 91.2 | **0.7** | 11.5 | 26.7 | **6.1** |
| **8.4** | 0.53 | 3.2 | 0.00 | **4.6** | 11.5 | 1.02 | 10.45 | 3.54 | 70.5 | **5.5** | 27.1 | 4.6 | **8.5** |
| **4.1** | 0.99 | 6.4 | 0.01 | **4.3** | 2.5 | 0.75 | 7.55 | 3.55 | 76.0 | **1.6** | 7.9 | 21.4 | **5.7** |
| **6.1** | 0.43 | 4.3 | 0.01 | **1.7** | 0.8 | 0.27 | 4.06 | 3.53 | 94.5 | **2.3** | 10.6 | 17.0 | **0.8** |
| **9.9** | 0.00 | 0.0 | 0.00 | **3.5** | 1.0 | 0.63 | 3.92 | 3.24 | 78.0 | **2.3** | 17.5 | 17.8 | **8.0** |
| **8.3** | 0.56 | 1.7 | 0.00 | **0.3** | 0.0 | -0.32 | -1.53 | 3.21 | 110.1 | **2.1** | 32.0 | 20.6 | **5.3** |
| **4.1** | 1.50 | 7.7 | 0.67 | **4.3** | 29.0 | 0.73 | 6.14 | 3.55 | 63.4 | **2.1** | 6.5 | 17.6 | **9.0** |
| **3.6** | 3.63 | 10.8 | 0.75 | **3.7** | 0.6 | 0.69 | 5.19 | 4.25 | 75.4 | **2.0** | 22.1 | 14.4 | **7.1** |
| **0.0** | 5.43 | 89.4 | 6.69 | **1.4** | -3.6 | -3.31 | -45.97 | 3.81 | 41.0 | **0.4** | 5.8 | 65.0 | **3.6** |
| **8.1** | 0.00 | 0.0 | 0.00 | **6.8** | 1.8 | 1.62 | 16.32 | 3.87 | 60.0 | **1.4** | 6.8 | 23.9 | **7.9** |
| **2.8** | 3.47 | 20.2 | 0.07 | **4.3** | 2.3 | 0.94 | 9.19 | 3.62 | 72.3 | **4.0** | 21.4 | 9.7 | **6.3** |
| **6.5** | 2.97 | 6.8 | -0.14 | **2.2** | 0.2 | 0.31 | 1.99 | 3.43 | 95.4 | **3.0** | 60.6 | 30.5 | **7.3** |
| **7.9** | 0.26 | 1.4 | 0.10 | **10.0** | 15.4 | 2.15 | 16.68 | 4.85 | 50.4 | **5.4** | 29.6 | 2.6 | **7.9** |
| **5.7** | 1.17 | 6.5 | 0.08 | **3.4** | 12.9 | 0.71 | 7.13 | 2.74 | 69.2 | **1.2** | 8.2 | 12.7 | **7.5** |
| **6.5** | 0.48 | 4.1 | 0.08 | **5.3** | 16.3 | 1.15 | 10.88 | 3.84 | 64.2 | **1.3** | 15.5 | 28.6 | **8.9** |
| **3.7** | 3.17 | 18.4 | 0.00 | **4.1** | 2.8 | 0.69 | 5.49 | 3.55 | 87.6 | **3.6** | 22.2 | 11.5 | **6.9** |
| **3.0** | 0.97 | 3.2 | 0.20 | **0.0** | -9.3 | -4.00 | -31.24 | 3.48 | 208.7 | **1.3** | 12.4 | 27.5 | **5.0** |
| **9.9** | 0.00 | 0.0 | -0.01 | **2.2** | 0.3 | 0.24 | 1.65 | 2.04 | 89.2 | **0.7** | 21.7 | 69.9 | **7.3** |
| **7.3** | 3.27 | 6.3 | 0.02 | **2.6** | 1.1 | 0.34 | 1.44 | 2.63 | 86.7 | **6.2** | 75.6 | 10.9 | **6.5** |
| **3.9** | 6.03 | 14.4 | 0.76 | **10.0** | 9.3 | 2.55 | 9.48 | 6.35 | 42.6 | **1.0** | 26.4 | 40.9 | **9.0** |
| **6.3** | 1.44 | 4.7 | 0.08 | **5.6** | 7.0 | 1.20 | 6.33 | 4.21 | 64.7 | **1.3** | 14.5 | 26.7 | **8.6** |
| **3.9** | 1.52 | 8.4 | -0.03 | **5.8** | 18.2 | 1.27 | 13.29 | 3.78 | 63.7 | **2.5** | 5.2 | 13.3 | **8.6** |
| **10.0** | na | 0.0 | na | **8.1** | 0.4 | 1.63 | 1.66 | 2.68 | 91.8 | **4.0** | na | 0.0 | **6.4** |
| **10.0** | na | 0.0 | na | **8.6** | 0.5 | 6.57 | 6.31 | 3.04 | 95.9 | **5.0** | 454.7 | 100.0 | **5.3** |
| **9.0** | 0.24 | 1.4 | 0.02 | **4.4** | 4.4 | 0.85 | 6.59 | 3.00 | 62.0 | **0.9** | 16.1 | 33.1 | **8.3** |
| **5.7** | 0.12 | 1.5 | 0.54 | **7.8** | 15.5 | 1.48 | 13.77 | 4.71 | 45.7 | **0.8** | 17.3 | 36.8 | **8.5** |
| **7.5** | 0.49 | 1.9 | 0.02 | **4.9** | 4.5 | 0.96 | 7.87 | 4.06 | 67.6 | **4.2** | 16.7 | 7.4 | **7.5** |
| **4.3** | 2.18 | 15.7 | 0.02 | **3.5** | 0.7 | 0.61 | 6.58 | 4.21 | 87.5 | **6.7** | 44.7 | 0.2 | **5.1** |
| **3.5** | 2.62 | 9.4 | 0.00 | **8.7** | 13.7 | 1.52 | 7.49 | 4.04 | 43.9 | **0.7** | 18.7 | 55.7 | **9.4** |
| **4.4** | 1.13 | 7.1 | 0.19 | **5.1** | 4.7 | 0.97 | 10.81 | 4.40 | 88.3 | **1.7** | 9.2 | 18.1 | **6.8** |
| **8.4** | 0.58 | 2.0 | 0.00 | **8.0** | 36.5 | 1.40 | 14.45 | 3.92 | 58.1 | **5.8** | 31.9 | 5.5 | **9.3** |
| **7.5** | 1.08 | 4.1 | 0.05 | **6.1** | 3.2 | 1.25 | 9.13 | 4.21 | 65.5 | **3.8** | 31.9 | 13.4 | **8.3** |
| **4.8** | 0.80 | 13.3 | 0.06 | **7.2** | 17.0 | 1.82 | 17.31 | 3.19 | 45.3 | **0.9** | 20.8 | 38.4 | **9.1** |
| **7.7** | 1.88 | 4.6 | -0.07 | **6.1** | 1.4 | 1.35 | 11.71 | 4.23 | 68.0 | **2.6** | 34.5 | 20.4 | **7.4** |
| **7.7** | 0.08 | 0.6 | 0.03 | **7.1** | 5.9 | 1.40 | 13.30 | 3.76 | 57.2 | **4.5** | 23.7 | 6.4 | **6.5** |
| **6.3** | 0.96 | 4.0 | -0.02 | **8.1** | 3.0 | 1.98 | 19.62 | 3.74 | 50.7 | **3.9** | 17.4 | 9.6 | **8.3** |
| **3.5** | 2.88 | 16.0 | 1.79 | **4.3** | 1.8 | 0.60 | 5.37 | 4.37 | 66.5 | **0.9** | 17.0 | 31.0 | **8.1** |
| **8.6** | 0.12 | 0.6 | 0.03 | **5.0** | 3.0 | 1.07 | 7.56 | 3.67 | 68.6 | **2.7** | 17.4 | 15.7 | **8.4** |

| Name | City | State | Rating | 2018 Rating | 2017 Rating | Total Assets ($Mil) | One Year Asset Growth | Asset Mix (As a % of Total Assets): Comm-ercial Loans | Cons-umer Loans | Mort-gage Loans | Secur-ities | Capital-ization Index | Lever-age Ratio | Risk-Based Capital Ratio |
|---|---|---|---|---|---|---|---|---|---|---|---|---|---|---|
| Exchange Bank of Missouri | Fayette | MO | **B+** | B | B | 219.2 | 6.72 | 6.9 | 1.4 | 10.4 | 7.6 | **8.6** | 11.0 | 13.9 |
| Exchange Bank of Northeast Missouri | Kahoka | MO | **C+** | C | B- | 157.8 | 6.51 | 5.2 | 1.3 | 12.8 | 15.7 | **7.3** | 9.5 | 12.7 |
| Exchange State Bank | Adair | IA | **B** | B | B | 37.2 | 2.93 | 2.1 | 1.8 | 7.8 | 17.3 | **10.0** | 12.5 | 19.8 |
| Exchange State Bank | Collins | IA | **B** | B | B | 113.3 | 0.95 | 8.8 | 0.9 | 12.8 | 6.6 | **8.5** | 10.0 | 14.0 |
| Exchange State Bank | Springville | IA | **B** | B- | B- | 45.9 | 1.39 | 4.5 | 1.1 | 17.5 | 28.5 | **7.8** | 9.5 | 13.2 |
| Exchange State Bank | Lanark | IL | **B** | B | B- | 90.7 | 3.92 | 7.5 | 1.3 | 9.5 | 43.4 | **10.0** | 11.9 | 21.0 |
| Exchange State Bank | Carsonville | MI | **A-** | B+ | A- | 168.6 | 1.79 | 6.5 | 2.4 | 12.1 | 27.7 | **10.0** | 12.4 | 18.8 |
| Exchange State Bank of St. Paul, Kansas | Saint Paul | KS | **B-** | B- | B- | 72.6 | 1.98 | 10.0 | 2.5 | 14.3 | 26.4 | **9.0** | 10.3 | 19.6 |
| ▼ Executive National Bank | Miami | FL | **B-** | B- | B- | 467.4 | 10.47 | 6.4 | 0.0 | 18.3 | 10.1 | **9.9** | 10.9 | 17.5 |
| Extraco Banks, N.A. | Temple | TX | **B** | B- | B- | 1525.1 | 6.70 | 2.4 | 7.2 | 19.6 | 22.8 | **9.0** | 10.4 | 17.4 |
| F & C Bank | Holden | MO | **C+** | B | B+ | 234.2 | 5.43 | 5.6 | 2.3 | 24.2 | 5.5 | **7.9** | 10.5 | 13.3 |
| F & M Bank and Trust Co. | Manchester | GA | **E-** | E- | E- | 68.9 | 1.18 | 4.1 | 2.8 | 15.5 | 3.4 | **0.7** | 5.0 | 7.4 |
| F & M Bank Minnesota | Olivia | MN | **B** | B- | B- | 128.3 | -3.31 | 4.4 | 0.4 | 1.9 | 26.9 | **6.0** | 8.6 | 11.8 |
| ▲ F & M Community Bank, N.A. | Preston | MN | **B** | B | B | 138.9 | 5.17 | 6.7 | 1.5 | 14.4 | 15.3 | **9.8** | 11.3 | 14.8 |
| F&M Bank | Washington | GA | **B+** | B+ | B+ | 276.1 | 4.21 | 3.5 | 3.1 | 17.9 | 33.1 | **10.0** | 17.0 | 27.6 |
| F&M Bank | Falls City | NE | **B+** | B+ | B- | 109.4 | 2.85 | 1.7 | 2.1 | 10.3 | 32.9 | **9.1** | 10.4 | 15.7 |
| F&M Bank | West Point | NE | **B+** | B | B+ | 301.0 | 2.60 | 5.0 | 1.1 | 6.7 | 9.9 | **6.7** | 10.1 | 12.3 |
| ▲ F&M Bank | Edmond | OK | **A-** | B+ | B | 480.9 | 0.53 | 7.2 | 2.1 | 14.4 | 20.8 | **9.1** | 10.4 | 14.8 |
| F&M Bank | Clarksville | TN | **C+** | B- | C+ | 1171.2 | 5.98 | 4.4 | 1.5 | 20.3 | 8.8 | **6.3** | 9.0 | 12.0 |
| F&M Bank and Trust Co. | Hannibal | MO | **B-** | C+ | C- | 133.6 | 4.78 | 4.9 | 2.9 | 36.2 | 11.5 | **7.4** | 9.2 | 14.2 |
| Fahey Banking Co. | Marion | OH | **B+** | B+ | B+ | 279.0 | -1.42 | 1.8 | 0.5 | 7.8 | 16.8 | **10.0** | 16.7 | 21.6 |
| Fairfax State Savings Bank | Fairfax | IA | **B** | B | B | 171.8 | 8.75 | 6.2 | 2.4 | 11.6 | 29.1 | **10.0** | 12.0 | 23.1 |
| Fairfield County Bank | Ridgefield | CT | **B** | B | B | 1563.0 | 5.17 | 8.3 | 0.1 | 21.3 | 19.8 | **10.0** | 13.5 | 16.8 |
| Fairfield Federal S&L Assn. of Lancaster | Lancaster | OH | **C+** | C+ | C | 264.3 | 0.63 | 0.0 | 0.4 | 81.9 | 2.7 | **10.0** | 11.5 | 24.0 |
| Fairfield National Bank | Fairfield | IL | **B+** | B+ | B+ | 545.9 | -3.95 | 22.5 | 2.7 | 12.4 | 29.6 | **10.0** | 12.2 | 22.6 |
| Fairmount State Bank | Fairmount | IN | **C+** | C+ | C+ | 45.5 | 2.33 | 3.1 | 11.6 | 19.2 | 16.3 | **10.0** | 15.0 | 21.4 |
| ▼ Fairport Savings Bank | Fairport | NY | **D+** | C- | C- | 321.8 | -1.48 | 2.2 | 0.0 | 66.8 | 7.3 | **7.0** | 9.0 | 15.3 |
| Fairview S&L Assn. | Fairview | OK | **B+** | B+ | B+ | 46.1 | -1.48 | 3.1 | 2.1 | 30.2 | 1.6 | **10.0** | 19.7 | 30.0 |
| Fairview State Banking Co. | Fairview | IL | **C+** | C+ | C+ | 27.7 | -3.07 | 4.3 | 7.5 | 26.5 | 12.2 | **10.0** | 13.5 | 19.3 |
| Falcon International Bank | Laredo | TX | **A** | A- | A- | 1294.5 | 12.49 | 8.9 | 1.9 | 8.5 | 17.2 | **10.0** | 12.7 | 19.4 |
| Falcon National Bank | Foley | MN | **B** | B | B+ | 573.5 | 21.37 | 28.8 | 0.6 | 7.9 | 8.6 | **7.2** | 9.6 | 12.7 |
| Fall River Five Cents Savings Bank | Fall River | MA | **C** | C | C | 1070.9 | 11.42 | 12.0 | 1.4 | 33.3 | 13.0 | **6.7** | 8.7 | 12.8 |
| Falls City National Bank | Falls City | TX | **B** | B- | B | 423.2 | 3.91 | 2.2 | 3.2 | 9.5 | 42.0 | **10.0** | 12.1 | 33.9 |
| ▲ Family Bank | Pelham | GA | **B+** | B | B- | 104.6 | 4.95 | 5.7 | 7.5 | 49.6 | 5.6 | **10.0** | 12.5 | 19.6 |
| Fannin Bank | Bonham | TX | **B** | B | B- | 110.7 | 11.01 | 9.8 | 3.1 | 19.6 | 27.6 | **6.9** | 8.9 | 14.8 |
| ▲ Farm Bureau Bank, FSB | Sparks | NV | **C-** | D | C- | 785.2 | 2.08 | 6.6 | 69.2 | 0.1 | 2.3 | **7.7** | 10.5 | 13.0 |
| Farmers & Mechanics Bank | Galesburg | IL | **B+** | B- | B | 365.0 | -2.26 | 10.9 | 5.1 | 13.4 | 23.5 | **8.8** | 10.2 | 15.5 |
| Farmers & Merchants Bank | Piedmont | AL | **B+** | B | B | 256.6 | 14.62 | 7.6 | 2.2 | 11.9 | 28.4 | **10.0** | 13.1 | 20.0 |
| Farmers & Merchants Bank | Waterloo | AL | **B+** | B+ | A- | 91.5 | 6.51 | 1.5 | 2.1 | 0.2 | 80.0 | **10.0** | 20.6 | 48.6 |
| Farmers & Merchants Bank | Stuttgart | AR | **B+** | B+ | B+ | 1494.0 | 40.53 | 8.2 | 1.5 | 17.7 | 13.2 | **8.6** | 10.2 | 13.8 |
| Farmers & Merchants Bank | Lodi | CA | **A-** | A- | A- | 3722.9 | 8.26 | 10.1 | 0.4 | 7.4 | 15.3 | **6.8** | 9.9 | 12.3 |
| Farmers & Merchants Bank | Eatonton | GA | **B-** | C+ | C+ | 189.8 | 2.26 | 10.4 | 2.0 | 11.1 | 22.7 | **10.0** | 14.3 | 24.5 |
| Farmers & Merchants Bank | Lakeland | GA | **E-** | E- | E- | 497.1 | 1.85 | 8.4 | 6.0 | 19.5 | 10.8 | **2.9** | 6.2 | 9.9 |
| ▲ Farmers & Merchants Bank | Salisbury | NC | **A-** | B- | C+ | 651.4 | 6.99 | 4.3 | 0.3 | 13.2 | 0.2 | **10.0** | 11.5 | 18.6 |
| Farmers & Merchants Bank | Tolna | ND | **C+** | C | C | 105.3 | -0.24 | 9.3 | 2.8 | 2.4 | 25.3 | **8.0** | 9.7 | 13.6 |
| Farmers & Merchants Bank | Miamisburg | OH | **B+** | B+ | B | 181.3 | 15.58 | 7.7 | 1.4 | 16.0 | 18.7 | **8.5** | 10.0 | 15.0 |
| Farmers & Merchants Bank | Duke | OK | **C+** | C | C | 19.0 | -3.66 | 7.6 | 2.1 | 0.0 | 21.4 | **9.6** | 10.7 | 23.3 |
| Farmers & Merchants Bank | Dyer | TN | **C-** | D+ | D+ | 98.9 | 0.67 | 5.7 | 3.7 | 8.0 | 44.8 | **7.6** | 9.4 | 19.3 |
| Farmers & Merchants Bank | New Castle | VA | **A-** | B+ | B+ | 61.1 | -0.57 | 1.7 | 5.0 | 30.4 | 36.2 | **10.0** | 20.5 | 45.8 |
| Farmers & Merchants Bank | Timberville | VA | **C+** | B- | B | 812.9 | 4.41 | 3.5 | 10.6 | 23.5 | 0.6 | **9.8** | 11.1 | 14.8 |
| Farmers & Merchants Bank | Berlin | WI | **C+** | C | B- | 320.0 | 1.65 | 9.7 | 3.1 | 22.5 | 10.5 | **9.4** | 10.6 | 14.5 |
| ▼ Farmers & Merchants Bank & Trust | Burlington | IA | **C-** | C+ | C+ | 199.5 | 6.38 | 7.4 | 1.8 | 30.5 | 14.3 | **7.5** | 9.3 | 15.4 |
| Farmers & Merchants Bank & Trust | Marinette | WI | **B-** | C+ | C+ | 144.6 | 1.96 | 8.6 | 1.6 | 19.8 | 24.2 | **10.0** | 11.9 | 16.7 |
| Farmers & Merchants Bank of Colby | Colby | KS | **A-** | B+ | A | 258.3 | 13.48 | 10.3 | 0.3 | 0.9 | 23.7 | **10.0** | 13.1 | 15.2 |
| Farmers & Merchants Bank of Hutsonville | Hutsonville | IL | **B** | B | B | 44.1 | 4.33 | 7.4 | 8.3 | 25.6 | 7.4 | **10.0** | 17.8 | 31.4 |
| Farmers & Merchants Bank of Long Beach | Long Beach | CA | **A-** | A- | A- | 7605.6 | 4.07 | 0.7 | 0.3 | 8.3 | 38.3 | **10.0** | 14.0 | 20.6 |
| Farmers & Merchants Bank of Orfordville | Orfordville | WI | **B** | B | B | 60.7 | 11.05 | 3.7 | 5.0 | 25.2 | 14.1 | **10.0** | 13.9 | 23.8 |
| Farmers & Merchants Savings Bank | Lone Tree | IA | **B** | B | B- | 92.6 | 6.23 | 8.0 | 1.4 | 22.6 | 18.0 | **10.0** | 12.5 | 16.0 |
| Farmers & Merchants Savings Bank | Manchester | IA | **B-** | C+ | B | 582.4 | -2.73 | 32.4 | 0.7 | 6.8 | 4.7 | **10.0** | 12.8 | 15.1 |
| Farmers & Merchants State Bank | Winterset | IA | **B+** | B+ | A- | 197.1 | 0.01 | 3.6 | 3.0 | 9.7 | 24.9 | **8.6** | 10.1 | 14.4 |

| Asset Quality Index | Adjusted Non-Performing Loans as a % of Total Loans | Adjusted Non-Performing Loans as a % of Capital | Net Charge-Offs Avg Loans | Profitability Index | Net Income ($Mil) | Return on Assets (R.O.A.) | Return on Equity (R.O.E.) | Net Interest Spread | Overhead Efficiency Ratio | Liquidity Index | Liquidity Ratio | Hot Money Ratio | Stability Index |
|---|---|---|---|---|---|---|---|---|---|---|---|---|---|
| **7.0** | 0.10 | 0.6 | 0.25 | **7.3** | 3.0 | 1.42 | 12.31 | 4.25 | 52.1 | **2.5** | 10.6 | 16.1 | **7.6** |
| **3.9** | 1.20 | 6.2 | 0.64 | **3.7** | 1.0 | 0.67 | 5.92 | 4.04 | 72.1 | **2.9** | 18.4 | 14.9 | **7.2** |
| **7.9** | 0.00 | 0.0 | 0.00 | **5.6** | 0.5 | 1.29 | 8.35 | 3.71 | 64.9 | **4.5** | 41.8 | 12.6 | **8.1** |
| **8.2** | 0.00 | 0.0 | 0.00 | **4.4** | 1.0 | 0.90 | 8.87 | 3.54 | 66.3 | **1.4** | 12.2 | 24.7 | **6.9** |
| **8.8** | 0.23 | 1.3 | 0.00 | **5.4** | 0.5 | 1.17 | 12.52 | 3.75 | 63.7 | **5.3** | 38.4 | 7.7 | **5.6** |
| **7.4** | 0.85 | 3.1 | 0.53 | **4.3** | 1.1 | 1.25 | 9.77 | 3.12 | 72.5 | **2.5** | 37.9 | 22.6 | **7.4** |
| **8.6** | 0.58 | 2.0 | 0.00 | **5.4** | 2.0 | 1.24 | 10.06 | 3.90 | 66.8 | **4.8** | 37.9 | 10.2 | **7.2** |
| **8.3** | 0.39 | 1.9 | 0.00 | **4.2** | 0.6 | 0.83 | 8.04 | 3.60 | 70.8 | **2.7** | 38.2 | 22.3 | **5.3** |
| **7.5** | 0.17 | 1.1 | 0.04 | **4.0** | 2.9 | 0.63 | 5.72 | 3.71 | 78.3 | **3.1** | 19.3 | 13.7 | **6.4** |
| **8.3** | 0.05 | 0.3 | 0.03 | **4.7** | 16.5 | 1.11 | 10.63 | 3.56 | 74.0 | **4.9** | 26.1 | 5.7 | **9.3** |
| **3.9** | 1.71 | 13.9 | 0.01 | **8.7** | 4.7 | 2.10 | 19.99 | 5.06 | 58.4 | **3.3** | 6.9 | 11.5 | **8.4** |
| **1.2** | 5.67 | 47.5 | 0.20 | **1.4** | 0.0 | 0.05 | 1.04 | 4.62 | 98.9 | **1.4** | 17.1 | 26.2 | **0.3** |
| **5.7** | 0.15 | 0.5 | -0.06 | **5.8** | 1.8 | 1.41 | 14.47 | 4.23 | 63.5 | **4.1** | 11.2 | 7.6 | **7.0** |
| **5.6** | 1.69 | 9.9 | 0.00 | **5.0** | 1.7 | 1.23 | 11.03 | 4.17 | 72.9 | **3.6** | 8.8 | 8.7 | **7.8** |
| **7.6** | 0.44 | 1.3 | 0.32 | **5.2** | 2.8 | 1.05 | 6.15 | 4.02 | 68.8 | **2.2** | 29.1 | 20.5 | **7.7** |
| **8.5** | 0.14 | 1.5 | 0.12 | **4.7** | 1.2 | 1.15 | 10.26 | 3.07 | 59.8 | **3.4** | 30.2 | 9.6 | **6.5** |
| **8.3** | 0.03 | 0.1 | 0.02 | **6.6** | 4.4 | 1.57 | 15.22 | 3.67 | 62.8 | **3.0** | 18.2 | 14.3 | **6.9** |
| **8.5** | 0.16 | 1.0 | 0.05 | **7.4** | 8.4 | 1.75 | 17.72 | 4.23 | 61.6 | **2.3** | 13.7 | 17.3 | **7.2** |
| **7.5** | 0.29 | 1.9 | 0.11 | **3.6** | 6.9 | 0.60 | 5.44 | 3.36 | 83.7 | **1.1** | 19.5 | 28.6 | **8.9** |
| **5.7** | 1.15 | 6.9 | 0.03 | **4.6** | 1.1 | 0.88 | 8.48 | 3.59 | 70.3 | **4.0** | 15.2 | 9.0 | **4.9** |
| **7.0** | 0.40 | 1.2 | -0.16 | **4.5** | 3.8 | 1.29 | 8.09 | 3.26 | 67.5 | **0.5** | 6.6 | 38.2 | **7.2** |
| **9.0** | 0.10 | 0.4 | -0.15 | **3.9** | 1.7 | 1.01 | 8.14 | 3.03 | 74.4 | **3.8** | 51.4 | 18.7 | **7.0** |
| **7.0** | 1.49 | 5.5 | 0.14 | **3.8** | 10.4 | 0.68 | 4.92 | 3.70 | 79.7 | **4.4** | 23.1 | 7.1 | **9.5** |
| **7.0** | 0.84 | 7.9 | 0.03 | **3.1** | 1.3 | 0.49 | 4.30 | 3.31 | 81.6 | **1.5** | 7.6 | 22.5 | **5.9** |
| **3.2** | 4.67 | 19.7 | 0.19 | **4.9** | 6.5 | 1.15 | 9.38 | 2.78 | 48.6 | **1.0** | 17.1 | 29.5 | **8.5** |
| **4.8** | 1.89 | 8.4 | 0.84 | **3.1** | 0.2 | 0.42 | 3.02 | 4.32 | 75.0 | **4.3** | 16.9 | 7.0 | **5.7** |
| **8.3** | 0.38 | 3.4 | 0.08 | **1.2** | -0.1 | -0.03 | -0.35 | 2.69 | 99.1 | **0.9** | 10.2 | 31.7 | **5.1** |
| **8.8** | 0.00 | 0.0 | 0.01 | **6.6** | 0.7 | 1.42 | 7.48 | 4.20 | 61.7 | **3.0** | 26.0 | 15.5 | **7.7** |
| **4.3** | 3.02 | 17.0 | 0.42 | **3.6** | 0.2 | 0.54 | 3.89 | 4.42 | 77.5 | **2.0** | 26.5 | 20.9 | **5.1** |
| **7.1** | 1.11 | 3.4 | 0.00 | **8.5** | 20.8 | 1.69 | 13.41 | 4.15 | 57.7 | **2.0** | 25.8 | 28.1 | **10.0** |
| **7.4** | 0.19 | 1.5 | 0.13 | **4.8** | 4.2 | 0.80 | 8.29 | 4.57 | 68.4 | **1.3** | 11.0 | 20.9 | **7.3** |
| **8.1** | 0.44 | 2.8 | 0.00 | **3.1** | 5.4 | 0.52 | 6.05 | 2.92 | 82.9 | **1.6** | 17.2 | 21.6 | **6.2** |
| **6.4** | 3.42 | 7.8 | 0.24 | **9.8** | 9.0 | 2.18 | 19.06 | 3.52 | 23.6 | **5.9** | 57.3 | 9.9 | **7.6** |
| **5.1** | 1.35 | 9.6 | 0.17 | **5.1** | 1.0 | 0.99 | 8.08 | 5.01 | 76.5 | **1.3** | 12.5 | 26.1 | **6.7** |
| **4.9** | 0.97 | 15.0 | 0.11 | **4.6** | 1.0 | 0.91 | 10.13 | 4.55 | 77.6 | **1.9** | 25.8 | 16.8 | **5.9** |
| **2.2** | 0.79 | 6.1 | 0.93 | **3.0** | 3.1 | 0.39 | 3.76 | 4.34 | 74.8 | **0.5** | 12.6 | 33.0 | **5.6** |
| **5.2** | 0.85 | 2.6 | 0.08 | **5.2** | 3.9 | 1.04 | 7.87 | 3.39 | 66.9 | **4.1** | 19.4 | 8.7 | **7.3** |
| **7.7** | 0.45 | 2.7 | 0.18 | **4.7** | 2.3 | 1.01 | 7.50 | 4.30 | 70.2 | **4.6** | 36.5 | 10.9 | **7.0** |
| **9.6** | 4.84 | 1.8 | -0.31 | **3.8** | 0.7 | 0.84 | 3.93 | 2.48 | 62.0 | **3.6** | 85.9 | 31.6 | **6.7** |
| **6.3** | 0.40 | 2.0 | 0.13 | **4.9** | 13.6 | 0.96 | 7.46 | 4.28 | 68.4 | **3.3** | 9.4 | 12.3 | **9.5** |
| **8.4** | 0.45 | 1.4 | 0.02 | **8.9** | 57.7 | 1.66 | 16.44 | 4.32 | 50.7 | **3.5** | 15.3 | 12.1 | **9.9** |
| **3.9** | 5.60 | 13.7 | -1.04 | **4.5** | 1.7 | 0.90 | 6.60 | 4.13 | 82.0 | **3.8** | 30.0 | 12.7 | **5.9** |
| **0.3** | 5.74 | 62.7 | 0.87 | **2.3** | 0.7 | 0.15 | 2.30 | 3.83 | 78.2 | **0.7** | 14.6 | 37.9 | **1.5** |
| **5.6** | 1.92 | 8.0 | -0.01 | **8.2** | 10.3 | 1.64 | 14.36 | 4.40 | 60.6 | **5.4** | 35.4 | 5.6 | **7.7** |
| **4.0** | 1.61 | 4.6 | 0.17 | **3.6** | 0.7 | 0.68 | 6.10 | 3.84 | 75.7 | **2.8** | 28.0 | 16.2 | **7.1** |
| **5.6** | 0.91 | 4.5 | 0.12 | **6.4** | 2.3 | 1.36 | 13.61 | 4.42 | 61.8 | **3.9** | 10.9 | 8.8 | **6.4** |
| **8.8** | 0.00 | 0.0 | 0.00 | **3.5** | 0.2 | 0.77 | 7.06 | 3.35 | 74.4 | **4.5** | 59.7 | 14.3 | **5.1** |
| **5.5** | 2.52 | 5.7 | 0.22 | **1.3** | 0.2 | 0.24 | 2.56 | 3.41 | 97.0 | **5.4** | 43.6 | 7.9 | **3.9** |
| **9.0** | 0.00 | 0.4 | 0.16 | **6.4** | 0.8 | 1.24 | 6.22 | 4.26 | 62.9 | **4.9** | 41.4 | 10.5 | **8.1** |
| **3.8** | 0.91 | 6.4 | 0.61 | **4.0** | 4.5 | 0.59 | 5.26 | 4.28 | 70.4 | **4.0** | 11.1 | 7.7 | **7.9** |
| **3.6** | 2.17 | 13.8 | 0.29 | **4.5** | 2.8 | 0.88 | 8.35 | 3.97 | 65.1 | **0.7** | 13.4 | 26.2 | **6.0** |
| **3.2** | 2.52 | 17.6 | 0.50 | **2.0** | 0.4 | 0.18 | 2.00 | 3.64 | 91.7 | **4.6** | 21.3 | 5.5 | **3.9** |
| **6.1** | 1.59 | 6.4 | -0.01 | **3.5** | 0.8 | 0.55 | 4.68 | 3.90 | 75.9 | **4.0** | 38.1 | 14.2 | **5.8** |
| **8.4** | 0.34 | 1.4 | 0.00 | **8.9** | 3.6 | 1.52 | 10.74 | 3.73 | 38.2 | **0.7** | 17.6 | 33.8 | **9.1** |
| **8.4** | 0.00 | 0.0 | 0.00 | **5.3** | 0.6 | 1.36 | 7.49 | 3.30 | 58.0 | **1.9** | 31.1 | 28.1 | **7.8** |
| **8.9** | 0.17 | 0.6 | 0.00 | **5.4** | 85.6 | 1.14 | 8.12 | 3.44 | 61.0 | **4.3** | 23.0 | 9.8 | **10.0** |
| **5.6** | 1.36 | 3.7 | 0.00 | **3.7** | 0.2 | 1.29 | 9.21 | 3.34 | 42.6 | **3.9** | 44.6 | 15.6 | **7.0** |
| **8.1** | 0.00 | 0.0 | -0.01 | **3.9** | 0.7 | 0.82 | 5.84 | 3.29 | 71.0 | **1.7** | 13.3 | 16.0 | **6.2** |
| **7.0** | 0.85 | 3.6 | 0.28 | **9.0** | 16.2 | 2.74 | 22.91 | 4.03 | 44.0 | **1.7** | 20.0 | 23.3 | **9.6** |
| **8.6** | 0.31 | 1.0 | 0.19 | **5.9** | 2.3 | 1.19 | 11.93 | 3.53 | 56.3 | **3.8** | 28.8 | 12.2 | **6.8** |

| Name | City | State | Rating | 2018 Rating | 2017 Rating | Total Assets ($Mil) | One Year Asset Growth | Asset Mix (As a % of Total Assets) Commercial Loans | Consumer Loans | Mortgage Loans | Securities | Capitalization Index | Leverage Ratio | Risk-Based Capital Ratio |
|---|---|---|---|---|---|---|---|---|---|---|---|---|---|---|
| Farmers & Merchants State Bank | New York Mills | MN | **B** | B | B | 62.5 | 1.29 | 8.7 | 4.4 | 6.7 | 35.8 | **10.0** | 16.1 | 28.4 |
| Farmers & Merchants State Bank | Archbold | OH | **A-** | A- | B+ | 1582.9 | 45.56 | 8.6 | 3.1 | 7.9 | 13.0 | **6.7** | 10.0 | 12.3 |
| Farmers & Merchants State Bank | Waterloo | WI | **B-** | C+ | B- | 179.3 | 7.51 | 1.4 | 1.0 | 16.3 | 8.7 | **9.5** | 11.2 | 14.6 |
| Farmers & Merchants Union Bank | Columbus | WI | **C+** | B- | B | 398.3 | -1.21 | 7.9 | 0.6 | 8.4 | 7.0 | **9.4** | 11.7 | 14.5 |
| ▲ Farmers & Stockmens Bank | Clayton | NM | **B** | B | B | 223.1 | -0.59 | 5.5 | 0.9 | 4.4 | 1.5 | **9.3** | 11.9 | 14.5 |
| Farmers & Traders Bank of Campton | Campton | KY | **B-** | B- | B- | 46.8 | -2.52 | 2.1 | 4.7 | 26.1 | 36.1 | **9.7** | 10.8 | 16.1 |
| Farmers & Traders Savings Bank | Bancroft | IA | **B-** | B- | B- | 58.0 | 1.78 | 2.8 | 1.6 | 4.3 | 31.1 | **9.7** | 10.8 | 17.7 |
| Farmers and Drovers Bank | Council Grove | KS | **A-** | B+ | B+ | 188.8 | 2.94 | 2.8 | 8.4 | 14.3 | 35.8 | **10.0** | 26.8 | 48.6 |
| Farmers and Mechanics FSB | Bloomfield | IN | **C-** | C- | C- | 74.2 | 0.38 | 0.2 | 0.1 | 33.2 | 46.2 | **10.0** | 17.0 | 53.8 |
| Farmers and Merchants Bank | LaFayette | AL | **A-** | B+ | B+ | 171.3 | 3.66 | 12.1 | 5.9 | 9.3 | 48.8 | **10.0** | 13.8 | 22.2 |
| Farmers and Merchants Bank | Sylvania | GA | **B** | B | B- | 123.2 | 7.40 | 1.8 | 2.8 | 10.6 | 32.9 | **10.0** | 15.4 | 38.2 |
| Farmers and Merchants Bank | Boswell | IN | **B** | B | B | 131.1 | 4.57 | 3.8 | 0.8 | 17.1 | 21.7 | **10.0** | 11.2 | 18.5 |
| Farmers and Merchants Bank | Laotto | IN | **A-** | B+ | B+ | 162.6 | 2.51 | 10.0 | 2.8 | 28.0 | 17.1 | **9.8** | 10.9 | 16.5 |
| Farmers and Merchants Bank | Mound City | KS | **D+** | D | D | 38.7 | -2.39 | 15.1 | 6.1 | 34.5 | 12.0 | **5.8** | 7.8 | 13.4 |
| Farmers and Merchants Bank | Upperco | MD | **B-** | C | B- | 443.1 | 6.02 | 6.0 | 0.1 | 9.1 | 12.8 | **8.7** | 10.9 | 13.9 |
| Farmers and Merchants Bank | Baldwyn | MS | **A-** | B+ | A- | 347.4 | 2.04 | 4.8 | 8.3 | 18.6 | 29.2 | **10.0** | 14.7 | 24.1 |
| Farmers and Merchants Bank | Axtell | NE | **D+** | D+ | D | 7.4 | -2.48 | 6.3 | 4.3 | 0.4 | 55.9 | **9.2** | 10.5 | 33.7 |
| Farmers and Merchants Bank | Milford | NE | **B** | B | B- | 722.1 | 7.55 | 1.9 | 3.6 | 3.8 | 50.2 | **10.0** | 11.2 | 15.1 |
| Farmers and Merchants Bank | Milligan | NE | **B** | B- | B | 120.3 | 3.06 | 8.7 | 1.0 | 2.9 | 0.0 | **9.0** | 11.5 | 14.2 |
| Farmers and Merchants Bank | Caldwell | OH | **B-** | C+ | B | 111.9 | 0.76 | 7.2 | 6.4 | 43.1 | 17.7 | **10.0** | 14.3 | 26.2 |
| Farmers and Merchants Bank | Arnett | OK | **B** | B | B | 53.2 | -1.00 | 3.8 | 8.2 | 1.2 | 41.9 | **10.0** | 14.2 | 32.5 |
| Farmers and Merchants Bank | Maysville | OK | **B-** | C+ | B- | 18.3 | -2.77 | 52.2 | 11.5 | 0.3 | 6.1 | **6.5** | 8.5 | 12.3 |
| Farmers and Merchants Bank | Holly Hill | SC | **B+** | B | B- | 425.4 | 11.26 | 1.2 | 1.7 | 6.3 | 23.7 | **10.0** | 13.5 | 46.0 |
| Farmers and Merchants Bank | De Leon | TX | **C+** | C | D+ | 93.4 | 0.55 | 4.5 | 4.7 | 23.0 | 18.4 | **7.7** | 9.5 | 15.8 |
| Farmers and Merchants Bank of Ashland | Ashland | NE | **B** | B | B- | 80.4 | 5.30 | 4.4 | 1.2 | 17.9 | 11.4 | **9.9** | 11.0 | 16.3 |
| Farmers and Merchants Bank of Kendall | Kendall | WI | **C+** | B- | B+ | 73.8 | -1.93 | 4.4 | 2.0 | 8.8 | 0.0 | **10.0** | 15.3 | 18.6 |
| Farmers and Merchants Bank of St. Clair | Saint Clair | MO | **A-** | B+ | B | 206.1 | 7.50 | 7.4 | 1.7 | 26.2 | 14.9 | **10.0** | 13.2 | 20.7 |
| Farmers and Merchants National Bank | Nashville | IL | **A-** | A- | B | 189.6 | 8.66 | 3.7 | 1.1 | 14.8 | 21.5 | **10.0** | 11.9 | 17.9 |
| Farmers and Merchants National Bank | Fairview | OK | **A** | A | A | 120.0 | -2.18 | 3.1 | 2.4 | 9.3 | 47.2 | **10.0** | 12.4 | 25.2 |
| Farmers and Merchants State Bank | Bushnell | IL | **B-** | C+ | C+ | 74.0 | 4.89 | 4.6 | 5.5 | 10.7 | 14.7 | **7.0** | 9.0 | 18.0 |
| ▲ Farmers and Merchants State Bank | Alpha | MN | **C-** | C- | D+ | 49.7 | 3.08 | 3.6 | 2.3 | 8.4 | 1.7 | **10.0** | 11.5 | 17.9 |
| Farmers and Merchants State Bank | Appleton | MN | **B-** | C+ | B+ | 45.8 | -0.56 | 5.4 | 2.3 | 3.2 | 11.9 | **10.0** | 14.2 | 17.5 |
| Farmers and Merchants State Bank | Blooming Prairie | MN | **C+** | C | C- | 89.0 | 8.16 | 8.6 | 1.9 | 12.4 | 0.2 | **6.4** | 8.5 | 13.5 |
| ▲ Farmers and Merchants State Bank | Pierz | MN | **B-** | B- | C+ | 231.2 | 2.86 | 9.2 | 2.2 | 12.2 | 16.5 | **10.0** | 11.0 | 15.8 |
| Farmers and Merchants State Bank | Springfield | MN | **C+** | C+ | B- | 126.2 | 0.64 | 4.3 | 1.6 | 4.9 | 15.2 | **6.6** | 8.7 | 13.4 |
| Farmers and Merchants State Bank | Langdon | ND | **B** | B+ | B+ | 110.8 | 3.09 | 4.4 | 2.4 | 1.1 | 26.7 | **10.0** | 14.9 | 22.6 |
| Farmers and Merchants State Bank | Bloomfield | NE | **B** | B- | B+ | 127.8 | -5.62 | 5.1 | 4.3 | 0.1 | 22.6 | **10.0** | 13.6 | 15.2 |
| ▼ Farmers and Merchants State Bank | Plankinton | SD | **C** | B- | B+ | 113.0 | -0.74 | 7.7 | 4.1 | 7.4 | 6.2 | **7.7** | 11.0 | 13.1 |
| ▼ Farmers and Merchants State Bank | Scotland | SD | **C+** | B- | B- | 29.8 | 5.10 | 5.7 | 10.5 | 1.9 | 36.6 | **10.0** | 11.0 | 20.1 |
| ▲ Farmers and Merchants Trust Co. | Chambersburg | PA | **B+** | C+ | B+ | 1271.1 | 5.03 | 6.2 | 0.5 | 12.0 | 14.8 | **7.9** | 9.6 | 15.9 |
| Farmers and Miners Bank | Pennington Gap | VA | **A-** | B+ | B+ | 133.4 | -1.34 | 3.0 | 7.4 | 20.8 | 20.0 | **10.0** | 14.4 | 31.0 |
| Farmers Bank | Greenwood | AR | **B+** | B+ | B | 219.3 | 6.18 | 6.1 | 5.8 | 28.3 | 22.2 | **10.0** | 18.1 | 30.2 |
| Farmers Bank | Ault | CO | **A** | A | A | 255.8 | 9.45 | 5.5 | 0.5 | 4.9 | 7.8 | **10.0** | 13.2 | 18.7 |
| Farmers Bank | Greensboro | GA | **B-** | B- | B- | 112.3 | 1.19 | 8.7 | 0.7 | 13.5 | 46.7 | **10.0** | 14.7 | 27.6 |
| ▲ Farmers Bank | Buhl | ID | **A** | A- | B+ | 471.3 | 1.78 | 12.1 | 1.9 | 5.3 | 32.1 | **10.0** | 15.0 | 23.3 |
| Farmers Bank | Nicholasville | KY | **B** | B | B | 162.5 | 15.28 | 1.9 | 0.9 | 27.9 | 20.4 | **9.4** | 10.6 | 20.6 |
| ▼ Farmers Bank | Carnegie | OK | **D-** | C- | D+ | 89.9 | -6.77 | 7.5 | 2.5 | 26.0 | 3.3 | **0.0** | 1.7 | 3.6 |
| Farmers Bank | Parsons | TN | **C+** | C+ | C+ | 38.4 | 3.92 | 5.6 | 11.0 | 17.3 | 11.7 | **10.0** | 13.0 | 30.4 |
| Farmers Bank | Portland | TN | **A-** | A- | A- | 697.5 | 4.48 | 5.0 | 1.4 | 16.8 | 23.2 | **10.0** | 12.3 | 16.4 |
| ▲ Farmers Bank | Windsor | VA | **B+** | B | B+ | 476.5 | -0.38 | 10.9 | 1.8 | 8.0 | 30.5 | **8.6** | 10.0 | 14.7 |
| Farmers Bank & Trust | Atwood | KS | **B-** | C+ | B | 112.8 | 7.57 | 5.1 | 1.0 | 2.9 | 30.4 | **7.0** | 9.0 | 16.8 |
| Farmers Bank & Trust | Great Bend | KS | **A** | A | A | 872.8 | 7.06 | 2.0 | 0.2 | 5.3 | 53.2 | **10.0** | 18.2 | 28.4 |
| Farmers Bank & Trust Co. | Magnolia | AR | **B** | B- | B- | 1725.7 | 12.27 | 11.6 | 1.7 | 18.5 | 13.2 | **6.8** | 9.0 | 12.4 |
| ▲ Farmers Bank and Savings Co. | Pomeroy | OH | **B** | B- | B | 334.5 | 3.59 | 4.4 | 5.6 | 36.4 | 15.0 | **8.9** | 10.3 | 16.7 |
| Farmers Bank and Trust Co. | Blytheville | AR | **B** | B | B- | 295.6 | 10.87 | 13.4 | 2.9 | 17.3 | 4.1 | **6.8** | 8.8 | 13.4 |
| Farmers Bank and Trust Co. | Marion | KY | **B+** | B+ | A | 374.3 | 83.59 | 5.2 | 3.2 | 31.7 | 12.6 | **8.1** | 9.7 | 13.8 |
| Farmers Bank and Trust Co. | Princeton | KY | **A** | A | A | 137.1 | 5.27 | 5.5 | 1.4 | 15.9 | 12.7 | **10.0** | 13.7 | 18.9 |
| Farmers Bank of Appomattox | Appomattox | VA | **B+** | B | B+ | 235.8 | 2.53 | 5.8 | 16.7 | 24.0 | 24.2 | **10.0** | 14.7 | 21.7 |
| Farmers Bank of Green City | Green City | MO | **C** | C- | C | 55.1 | 2.37 | 19.7 | 5.1 | 14.1 | 15.5 | **7.6** | 9.4 | 13.0 |
| Farmers Bank of Lincoln | Lincoln | MO | **A-** | A- | A- | 125.6 | 1.74 | 3.2 | 3.3 | 37.3 | 8.6 | **10.0** | 11.3 | 20.0 |

**Arrows denote recent upgrades ▲ or downgrades ▼**

| Asset Quality Index | Adjusted Non-Performing Loans as a % of Total Loans | Adjusted Non-Performing Loans as a % of Capital | Net Charge-Offs Avg Loans | Profitability Index | Net Income ($Mil) | Return on Assets (R.O.A.) | Return on Equity (R.O.E.) | Net Interest Spread | Overhead Efficiency Ratio | Liquidity Index | Liquidity Ratio | Hot Money Ratio | Stability Index |
|---|---|---|---|---|---|---|---|---|---|---|---|---|---|
| 8.7 | 0.00 | 0.0 | -0.04 | 4.2 | 0.6 | 0.92 | 5.83 | 3.51 | 73.6 | 4.2 | 39.3 | 13.7 | 7.0 |
| 7.4 | 0.35 | 1.8 | 0.06 | 6.2 | 17.5 | 1.16 | 9.19 | 3.85 | 64.2 | 3.2 | 11.9 | 12.5 | 9.3 |
| 6.2 | 0.20 | 0.7 | -0.46 | 6.9 | 2.4 | 1.33 | 11.88 | 3.52 | 56.8 | 4.0 | 17.7 | 9.0 | 7.2 |
| 3.9 | 3.30 | 9.4 | 1.08 | 6.4 | 4.3 | 1.09 | 9.62 | 3.70 | 45.8 | 0.8 | 17.8 | 38.5 | 8.1 |
| 6.8 | 0.23 | 1.1 | 0.06 | 9.1 | 4.4 | 2.08 | 16.02 | 4.81 | 72.1 | 4.0 | 21.9 | 9.9 | 9.3 |
| 7.2 | 0.53 | 1.3 | 0.06 | 4.0 | 0.4 | 0.88 | 7.38 | 4.02 | 78.3 | 1.8 | 25.8 | 23.6 | 5.6 |
| 7.4 | 0.09 | 0.8 | 0.00 | 3.6 | 0.4 | 0.75 | 6.89 | 3.14 | 74.4 | 2.6 | 38.5 | 24.6 | 6.3 |
| 8.4 | 0.45 | 0.8 | -0.15 | 5.0 | 2.0 | 1.09 | 4.06 | 3.35 | 59.2 | 2.9 | 31.3 | 17.6 | 8.2 |
| 10.0 | 0.15 | 0.9 | 0.00 | 1.0 | 0.2 | 0.22 | 1.28 | 2.40 | 110.3 | 3.8 | 74.1 | 17.3 | 7.4 |
| 7.5 | 1.83 | 5.5 | 0.07 | 5.6 | 2.0 | 1.21 | 8.54 | 3.88 | 61.8 | 3.2 | 41.9 | 19.6 | 7.9 |
| 8.0 | 2.79 | 4.7 | 0.20 | 4.8 | 1.2 | 1.05 | 6.69 | 3.69 | 65.0 | 4.2 | 49.9 | 16.6 | 7.1 |
| 8.8 | 0.34 | 1.5 | -0.09 | 4.2 | 1.0 | 0.75 | 6.64 | 3.54 | 74.7 | 2.1 | 21.3 | 19.2 | 6.8 |
| 8.6 | 0.04 | 1.6 | 0.01 | 6.0 | 2.3 | 1.46 | 13.64 | 3.90 | 63.6 | 5.5 | 33.0 | 3.3 | 7.2 |
| 2.2 | 4.12 | 22.1 | 0.19 | 5.7 | 0.5 | 1.36 | 18.08 | 4.44 | 67.0 | 1.4 | 8.7 | 24.0 | 4.6 |
| 5.7 | 0.58 | 2.0 | -0.01 | 4.5 | 3.6 | 0.84 | 7.73 | 3.66 | 71.7 | 1.4 | 13.7 | 20.7 | 6.9 |
| 6.2 | 1.75 | 4.7 | 0.14 | 8.6 | 6.0 | 1.75 | 11.67 | 4.99 | 65.0 | 1.9 | 27.1 | 23.9 | 8.7 |
| 9.2 | 0.00 | 0.0 | 0.00 | 1.1 | 0.0 | 0.04 | 0.37 | 3.39 | 103.9 | 5.3 | 54.2 | 4.8 | 4.5 |
| 8.3 | 0.09 | 0.9 | 0.32 | 4.4 | 8.5 | 1.28 | 10.89 | 2.64 | 57.8 | 2.6 | 56.0 | 5.3 | 7.5 |
| 3.0 | 2.35 | 15.2 | -0.02 | 7.9 | 2.1 | 1.80 | 14.71 | 4.17 | 51.7 | 0.6 | 13.7 | 24.6 | 8.6 |
| 3.4 | 3.22 | 16.2 | 0.21 | 6.1 | 1.3 | 1.16 | 8.11 | 4.94 | 64.4 | 3.2 | 19.5 | 13.3 | 8.2 |
| 8.5 | 0.00 | 0.0 | 0.25 | 4.8 | 0.7 | 1.22 | 9.04 | 2.68 | 59.6 | 3.7 | 42.2 | 16.7 | 7.6 |
| 7.5 | 0.00 | 0.1 | 0.01 | 9.0 | 0.4 | 2.30 | 27.46 | 5.65 | 61.4 | 3.9 | 29.5 | 10.4 | 5.1 |
| 6.7 | 6.09 | 8.1 | 0.00 | 4.5 | 3.4 | 0.97 | 7.28 | 3.10 | 64.9 | 6.8 | 72.2 | 7.0 | 5.9 |
| 6.4 | 0.53 | 3.2 | 0.09 | 4.2 | 0.9 | 1.03 | 11.04 | 4.33 | 71.1 | 5.1 | 31.1 | 5.2 | 5.2 |
| 8.7 | 0.00 | 0.0 | 0.00 | 4.1 | 0.6 | 0.75 | 6.84 | 4.35 | 78.7 | 4.4 | 15.5 | 6.4 | 6.5 |
| 2.8 | 5.64 | 17.5 | 0.00 | 10.0 | 1.8 | 2.42 | 15.54 | 4.96 | 48.2 | 1.7 | 11.8 | 20.9 | 9.0 |
| 8.7 | 0.27 | 2.1 | 0.09 | 5.4 | 2.0 | 1.01 | 7.71 | 4.23 | 71.4 | 3.2 | 20.7 | 13.5 | 7.3 |
| 8.3 | 0.59 | 2.7 | 0.04 | 6.2 | 2.8 | 1.53 | 12.40 | 3.92 | 62.8 | 4.4 | 13.2 | 5.8 | 8.1 |
| 9.3 | 0.00 | 0.0 | 0.03 | 7.4 | 2.0 | 1.71 | 13.78 | 3.80 | 56.6 | 3.3 | 28.6 | 14.9 | 9.1 |
| 8.6 | 0.00 | 0.0 | 0.03 | 5.1 | 0.7 | 0.97 | 10.47 | 3.50 | 70.9 | 5.8 | 38.3 | 4.2 | 4.7 |
| 2.8 | 2.60 | 33.3 | 0.84 | 2.0 | 0.1 | 0.19 | 1.73 | 3.22 | 77.2 | 3.0 | 50.3 | 18.0 | 1.5 |
| 4.0 | 1.83 | 8.8 | 0.48 | 8.1 | 0.9 | 1.87 | 13.07 | 4.55 | 50.2 | 3.2 | 18.0 | 7.5 | 8.6 |
| 4.8 | 0.74 | 4.8 | 0.00 | 8.5 | 1.7 | 2.04 | 24.42 | 4.57 | 57.4 | 4.7 | 23.6 | 5.3 | 5.1 |
| 4.3 | 3.95 | 13.3 | 0.05 | 8.8 | 4.4 | 1.99 | 18.63 | 4.50 | 53.3 | 4.1 | 25.8 | 9.9 | 8.5 |
| 5.4 | 0.00 | 0.4 | 0.00 | 4.9 | 1.3 | 1.12 | 13.01 | 3.86 | 68.3 | 2.9 | 13.3 | 12.6 | 5.0 |
| 4.3 | 3.53 | 8.8 | 0.00 | 8.6 | 2.3 | 2.15 | 14.86 | 4.02 | 44.4 | 2.2 | 22.6 | 19.0 | 9.9 |
| 6.9 | 0.38 | 2.0 | 0.01 | 8.8 | 2.4 | 1.79 | 14.20 | 4.43 | 51.7 | 4.4 | 5.6 | 5.1 | 7.9 |
| 2.7 | 2.89 | 20.4 | 1.16 | 8.6 | 2.0 | 1.79 | 16.39 | 4.31 | 45.8 | 0.7 | 10.6 | 17.8 | 8.7 |
| 6.5 | 0.14 | 1.1 | 0.07 | 3.1 | 0.1 | 0.45 | 3.99 | 3.90 | 83.7 | 4.2 | 31.5 | 11.2 | 5.8 |
| 6.0 | 1.35 | 6.0 | 0.07 | 5.5 | 16.4 | 1.30 | 13.36 | 3.84 | 65.7 | 4.9 | 15.1 | 3.2 | 7.6 |
| 6.7 | 1.71 | 4.2 | 0.16 | 6.1 | 1.7 | 1.25 | 8.83 | 5.00 | 71.4 | 3.8 | 51.9 | 19.2 | 7.8 |
| 7.9 | 0.39 | 2.9 | -0.24 | 3.6 | 1.3 | 0.63 | 3.32 | 4.30 | 84.3 | 3.5 | 16.0 | 11.8 | 7.8 |
| 8.4 | 0.09 | 0.5 | 0.07 | 9.9 | 6.1 | 2.50 | 18.19 | 4.64 | 46.2 | 2.2 | 30.5 | 23.0 | 9.7 |
| 6.6 | 0.00 | 12.2 | 0.04 | 2.9 | 0.4 | 0.43 | 2.97 | 3.02 | 81.2 | 3.5 | 17.0 | 11.6 | 6.4 |
| 7.8 | 1.28 | 4.3 | -0.05 | 7.4 | 7.1 | 1.55 | 10.18 | 3.91 | 54.4 | 5.3 | 46.9 | 10.1 | 8.7 |
| 9.2 | 0.04 | 0.2 | -0.01 | 4.7 | 1.4 | 0.92 | 8.41 | 3.54 | 67.5 | 1.7 | 21.9 | 24.0 | 6.6 |
| 0.3 | 6.76 | 273.4 | 7.05 | 0.0 | -6.8 | -6.62 | -118.72 | 3.18 | 111.6 | 0.7 | 23.1 | 67.0 | 1.1 |
| 2.9 | 4.29 | 14.6 | 0.28 | 4.0 | 0.2 | 0.61 | 4.57 | 4.24 | 79.0 | 3.2 | 48.6 | 21.8 | 6.4 |
| 7.8 | 1.07 | 3.7 | 0.02 | 7.3 | 9.5 | 1.40 | 11.74 | 4.19 | 62.2 | 1.4 | 19.8 | 27.6 | 7.9 |
| 6.5 | 0.64 | 1.9 | 0.08 | 5.4 | 5.3 | 1.19 | 9.78 | 3.83 | 74.6 | 2.3 | 26.4 | 18.9 | 7.8 |
| 5.5 | 3.42 | 9.0 | 0.09 | 4.6 | 1.2 | 1.23 | 13.21 | 3.17 | 70.0 | 6.2 | 47.7 | 4.8 | 5.4 |
| 9.3 | 1.44 | 1.6 | -0.16 | 7.9 | 13.9 | 1.64 | 8.59 | 3.46 | 44.5 | 2.0 | 45.7 | 38.5 | 10.0 |
| 4.9 | 0.94 | 7.2 | 0.28 | 6.0 | 19.0 | 1.18 | 11.67 | 3.62 | 57.9 | 1.0 | 10.9 | 32.1 | 9.4 |
| 5.1 | 1.37 | 7.8 | 0.08 | 4.6 | 3.1 | 0.94 | 9.09 | 3.99 | 73.7 | 1.6 | 11.7 | 22.2 | 6.5 |
| 5.1 | 1.01 | 6.7 | 0.20 | 8.7 | 5.6 | 2.01 | 21.37 | 4.00 | 53.5 | 0.9 | 22.9 | 39.2 | 7.3 |
| 6.6 | 0.45 | 4.0 | 0.08 | 4.4 | 2.5 | 0.88 | 8.09 | 3.66 | 75.9 | 1.4 | 9.4 | 24.6 | 7.3 |
| 8.7 | 0.05 | 0.4 | 0.03 | 7.3 | 2.3 | 1.74 | 12.07 | 4.34 | 62.8 | 3.8 | 14.7 | 9.7 | 9.6 |
| 6.3 | 0.90 | 3.8 | 0.07 | 5.1 | 2.6 | 1.11 | 7.96 | 4.13 | 67.9 | 3.4 | 27.4 | 13.6 | 7.7 |
| 4.2 | 1.63 | 11.1 | 0.09 | 3.1 | 0.2 | 0.44 | 4.73 | 3.75 | 75.2 | 0.6 | 11.5 | 43.0 | 5.1 |
| 8.9 | 0.01 | 0.9 | 0.02 | 6.5 | 1.9 | 1.47 | 13.27 | 3.71 | 61.9 | 3.0 | 21.3 | 14.7 | 8.2 |

| Name | City | State | Rating | 2018 Rating | 2017 Rating | Total Assets ($Mil) | One Year Asset Growth | Asset Mix (As a % of Total Assets) Comm-ercial Loans | Cons-umer Loans | Mort-gage Loans | Secur-ities | Capital-ization Index | Lever-age Ratio | Risk-Based Capital Ratio |
|---|---|---|---|---|---|---|---|---|---|---|---|---|---|---|
| Farmers Bank of Lohman | Jefferson City | MO | **B-** | B- | B- | 67.9 | 4.42 | 5.9 | 3.0 | 13.4 | 53.2 | **10.0** | 15.5 | 34.6 |
| Farmers Bank of Milton | Milton | KY | **B** | B | B | 259.6 | 7.81 | 4.5 | 2.8 | 29.3 | 29.0 | **10.0** | 14.5 | 22.5 |
| Farmers Bank of Mt. Pulaski | Mount Pulaski | IL | **C** | C | C | 54.9 | 17.37 | 3.0 | 3.1 | 21.4 | 33.7 | **10.0** | 12.1 | 35.6 |
| Farmers Bank of Northern Missouri | Unionville | MO | **B+** | B+ | B+ | 383.4 | -1.25 | 3.4 | 1.8 | 9.5 | 27.9 | **10.0** | 12.9 | 19.2 |
| Farmers Bank of Osborne, Kansas | Osborne | KS | **B** | B- | B | 67.1 | 0.81 | 1.8 | 1.4 | 2.5 | 19.7 | **10.0** | 12.7 | 18.9 |
| ▲ Farmers Bank of Willards | Willards | MD | **B** | C | C | 389.5 | 3.67 | 8.8 | 2.1 | 36.9 | 6.0 | **10.0** | 11.0 | 15.8 |
| ▲ Farmers Bank, Frankfort, Indiana, Inc. | Frankfort | IN | **B-** | C+ | B- | 611.8 | 8.70 | 9.3 | 2.5 | 6.5 | 22.2 | **8.6** | 11.3 | 13.8 |
| Farmers Building and Savings Bank | Rochester | PA | **B** | B+ | B+ | 102.2 | 9.31 | 0.2 | 0.0 | 42.4 | 26.2 | **10.0** | 20.2 | 53.2 |
| Farmers National Bank | Prophetstown | IL | **A** | A | A | 737.2 | 7.81 | 3.3 | 0.7 | 4.0 | 40.6 | **10.0** | 13.5 | 19.0 |
| Farmers National Bank | Phillipsburg | KS | **A-** | B+ | A | 143.3 | 5.21 | 19.8 | 2.9 | 7.4 | 18.1 | **10.0** | 16.2 | 21.1 |
| Farmers National Bank of Canfield | Canfield | OH | **B+** | B | B | 2432.1 | 5.32 | 8.7 | 8.7 | 15.7 | 17.6 | **6.3** | 9.1 | 12.0 |
| Farmers National Bank of Danville | Danville | KY | **B+** | B+ | B+ | 585.1 | 5.95 | 5.1 | 1.4 | 25.2 | 19.5 | **8.2** | 9.8 | 14.7 |
| ▲ Farmers National Bank of Emlenton | Emlenton | PA | **B-** | C+ | C+ | 909.9 | 1.83 | 4.4 | 1.6 | 45.4 | 13.2 | **6.2** | 8.2 | 13.7 |
| Farmers National Bank of Griggsville | Griggsville | IL | **C** | C | B- | 96.0 | 6.80 | 5.8 | 6.2 | 14.5 | 4.3 | **9.7** | 11.2 | 14.8 |
| ▲ Farmers National Bank of Lebanon | Lebanon | KY | **B** | C+ | C | 101.3 | -0.64 | 6.0 | 2.5 | 8.1 | 35.2 | **10.0** | 12.0 | 19.0 |
| Farmers National Bank of Scottsville | Scottsville | KY | **A-** | B+ | B+ | 255.2 | 1.49 | 6.2 | 1.5 | 19.5 | 19.6 | **10.0** | 15.9 | 22.0 |
| Farmers Savings Bank | Colesburg | IA | **B** | B+ | B+ | 210.1 | 2.37 | 6.9 | 2.6 | 5.4 | 30.1 | **10.0** | 11.9 | 16.8 |
| Farmers Savings Bank | Fostoria | IA | **B** | B | B+ | 137.0 | 4.43 | 8.2 | 2.4 | 21.5 | 15.6 | **10.0** | 14.3 | 20.4 |
| Farmers Savings Bank | Frederika | IA | **B** | B | B | 47.7 | 0.50 | 4.7 | 2.9 | 10.8 | 19.3 | **10.0** | 18.6 | 28.4 |
| Farmers Savings Bank | Marshalltown | IA | **A-** | B+ | B | 115.3 | 7.14 | 5.8 | 1.6 | 11.5 | 20.6 | **10.0** | 14.7 | 21.6 |
| Farmers Savings Bank | Wever | IA | **C** | C+ | B- | 110.7 | -10.07 | 15.3 | 1.8 | 30.6 | 9.4 | **10.0** | 15.6 | 24.0 |
| Farmers Savings Bank | Spencer | OH | **A-** | B+ | A- | 285.6 | 1.89 | 1.7 | 0.5 | 18.3 | 65.0 | **10.0** | 26.2 | 68.0 |
| Farmers Savings Bank | Mineral Point | WI | **B** | B | B+ | 316.6 | 7.17 | 7.2 | 7.0 | 10.8 | 33.3 | **6.9** | 8.9 | 16.1 |
| Farmers Savings Bank & Trust | Traer | IA | **A-** | B+ | B+ | 160.5 | 1.91 | 4.2 | 1.5 | 10.5 | 31.0 | **9.2** | 10.5 | 17.4 |
| Farmers Security Bank | Washburn | ND | **B-** | C- | C+ | 57.7 | 2.45 | 8.3 | 2.4 | 2.1 | 19.0 | **10.0** | 11.6 | 17.1 |
| Farmers State Bank | Dublin | GA | **A-** | B+ | B+ | 124.4 | -1.49 | 7.8 | 7.3 | 18.8 | 19.9 | **10.0** | 15.4 | 20.9 |
| Farmers State Bank | Lincolnton | GA | **A** | A- | A- | 131.1 | 10.97 | 2.9 | 6.9 | 22.5 | 17.1 | **10.0** | 16.5 | 25.6 |
| ▲ Farmers State Bank | Algona | IA | **A-** | B+ | C+ | 112.7 | 2.08 | 11.6 | 1.3 | 16.2 | 15.0 | **10.0** | 11.7 | 16.3 |
| Farmers State Bank | Lake View | IA | **B** | B- | C+ | 36.1 | 7.43 | 7.4 | 5.3 | 13.3 | 27.2 | **10.0** | 12.0 | 34.3 |
| Farmers State Bank | Marcus | IA | **B+** | B+ | A- | 66.3 | -3.71 | 6.0 | 3.5 | 6.1 | 24.7 | **10.0** | 14.4 | 19.7 |
| Farmers State Bank | Marion | IA | **A** | A | A | 848.6 | 6.60 | 7.6 | 1.2 | 8.0 | 11.5 | **10.0** | 13.8 | 19.2 |
| Farmers State Bank | Mason City | IA | **A-** | B+ | A- | 192.2 | 1.50 | 5.4 | 2.0 | 17.4 | 41.4 | **10.0** | 12.7 | 22.5 |
| Farmers State Bank | Waterloo | IA | **B** | B | B | 1168.6 | 10.65 | 9.6 | 8.1 | 18.8 | 10.5 | **7.4** | 9.3 | 12.8 |
| Farmers State Bank | Yale | IA | **B** | B- | B- | 55.5 | 7.85 | 5.5 | 2.4 | 11.9 | 30.4 | **10.0** | 11.4 | 17.6 |
| Farmers State Bank | Elmwood | IL | **C-** | C- | C- | 55.9 | 7.05 | 2.9 | 1.4 | 22.9 | 33.1 | **6.8** | 8.8 | 15.5 |
| Farmers State Bank | Pittsfield | IL | **A-** | B+ | B+ | 260.8 | 1.42 | 1.8 | 1.1 | 4.1 | 14.8 | **10.0** | 13.6 | 16.6 |
| Farmers State Bank | Lagrange | IN | **B+** | B | B | 836.3 | 10.20 | 4.0 | 1.9 | 32.4 | 11.8 | **7.4** | 9.3 | 14.8 |
| ▼ Farmers State Bank | Dwight | KS | **C-** | C- | C+ | 15.7 | -4.65 | 4.6 | 1.3 | 7.9 | 0.0 | **10.0** | 12.1 | 24.0 |
| Farmers State Bank | Fairview | KS | **D+** | D | D | 21.3 | -3.93 | 1.4 | 4.3 | 8.4 | 4.7 | **8.6** | 10.1 | 13.8 |
| ▲ Farmers State Bank | Holton | KS | **B+** | B | B | 58.3 | 1.79 | 4.7 | 1.2 | 24.3 | 22.6 | **10.0** | 13.6 | 22.6 |
| Farmers State Bank | McPherson | KS | **A-** | A- | A- | 122.9 | 6.85 | 7.4 | 4.1 | 18.3 | 37.7 | **8.3** | 9.8 | 15.7 |
| Farmers State Bank | Phillipsburg | KS | **C** | C- | D+ | 36.2 | -1.14 | 6.9 | 10.1 | 11.2 | 24.5 | **9.9** | 10.9 | 16.4 |
| Farmers State Bank | Wathena | KS | **B** | B | B | 63.2 | 3.04 | 7.7 | 4.5 | 15.6 | 50.0 | **10.0** | 16.5 | 34.7 |
| Farmers State Bank | Westmoreland | KS | **B+** | B+ | B+ | 186.5 | 8.19 | 9.0 | 2.4 | 13.7 | 12.5 | **8.7** | 14.2 | 13.9 |
| Farmers State Bank | Booneville | KY | **B-** | B- | B- | 50.1 | -0.57 | 4.2 | 5.7 | 18.7 | 43.2 | **10.0** | 12.6 | 19.8 |
| Farmers State Bank | Cameron | MO | **B-** | B- | B- | 240.1 | 0.78 | 2.8 | 3.0 | 42.3 | 11.5 | **7.4** | 9.2 | 12.9 |
| Farmers State Bank | Victor | MT | **B** | C+ | B- | 436.5 | 10.33 | 5.4 | 3.0 | 14.1 | 24.1 | **8.3** | 9.8 | 14.9 |
| Farmers State Bank | Dodge | NE | **C+** | C+ | C+ | 275.2 | 11.25 | 13.5 | 1.0 | 2.8 | 5.8 | **6.4** | 8.8 | 12.1 |
| Farmers State Bank | New Madison | OH | **B** | B | B | 181.8 | 0.58 | 4.0 | 4.2 | 25.8 | 16.6 | **10.0** | 12.4 | 19.1 |
| Farmers State Bank | West Salem | OH | **C+** | C+ | C+ | 123.3 | 1.41 | 7.3 | 1.6 | 24.2 | 9.7 | **7.3** | 9.2 | 13.9 |
| Farmers State Bank | Quinton | OK | **B-** | C+ | C+ | 115.0 | 9.88 | 8.3 | 10.1 | 17.2 | 26.3 | **6.4** | 8.4 | 13.6 |
| Farmers State Bank | Hosmer | SD | **B-** | B- | B- | 19.6 | 0.51 | 32.6 | 5.8 | 0.0 | 4.4 | **10.0** | 16.8 | 17.3 |
| Farmers State Bank | Parkston | SD | **B** | B | B | 225.3 | -0.79 | 4.9 | 2.9 | 0.0 | 37.4 | **7.2** | 9.1 | 15.5 |
| Farmers State Bank | Mountain City | TN | **B** | B | B | 146.6 | 3.32 | 5.8 | 5.1 | 29.3 | 24.5 | **10.0** | 16.4 | 26.3 |
| Farmers State Bank | Center | TX | **B-** | B- | C+ | 334.1 | 0.00 | 17.4 | 2.2 | 7.5 | 19.0 | **10.0** | 13.5 | 22.1 |
| Farmers State Bank | Groesbeck | TX | **B+** | B+ | B+ | 131.3 | -3.12 | 2.7 | 6.3 | 17.6 | 22.4 | **8.2** | 9.8 | 18.5 |
| Farmers State Bank | Winthrop | WA | **B-** | C+ | C+ | 42.2 | 4.07 | 3.4 | 1.2 | 0.9 | 50.3 | **8.7** | 10.1 | 78.3 |
| Farmers State Bank | Pine Bluffs | WY | **C-** | C+ | C | 27.7 | 9.28 | 5.3 | 1.7 | 7.4 | 1.3 | **5.4** | 7.4 | 15.1 |
| Farmers State Bank & Trust Co. | Mount Sterling | IL | **B-** | C+ | C+ | 94.5 | 2.95 | 12.6 | 3.8 | 17.0 | 18.4 | **7.0** | 9.0 | 12.7 |
| Farmers State Bank & Trust Co. | Church Point | LA | **B-** | B- | B | 112.7 | 4.55 | 10.5 | 2.6 | 10.8 | 25.7 | **10.0** | 11.1 | 16.6 |

| Asset Quality Index | Adjusted Non-Performing Loans as a % of Total Loans | Adjusted Non-Performing Loans as a % of Capital | Net Charge-Offs Avg Loans | Profitability Index | Net Income ($Mil) | Return on Assets (R.O.A.) | Return on Equity (R.O.E.) | Net Interest Spread | Overhead Efficiency Ratio | Liquidity Index | Liquidity Ratio | Hot Money Ratio | Stability Index |
|---|---|---|---|---|---|---|---|---|---|---|---|---|---|
| **9.6** | 0.00 | 0.6 | 0.00 | **3.6** | 0.5 | 0.68 | 4.35 | 2.51 | 68.8 | **5.9** | 77.0 | 11.1 | **7.3** |
| **4.8** | 3.08 | 12.7 | 0.30 | **4.6** | 2.3 | 0.93 | 6.20 | 3.65 | 70.0 | **1.8** | 23.8 | 21.9 | **8.0** |
| **9.4** | 0.11 | 1.0 | -0.27 | **2.2** | 0.2 | 0.36 | 2.86 | 2.82 | 86.5 | **4.5** | 62.4 | 16.2 | **6.0** |
| **7.6** | 0.27 | 1.2 | 0.01 | **6.1** | 4.8 | 1.29 | 9.57 | 3.90 | 57.8 | **4.2** | 26.1 | 9.5 | **7.7** |
| **5.4** | 2.62 | 5.7 | -0.01 | **6.2** | 1.0 | 1.54 | 12.59 | 3.81 | 60.2 | **2.9** | 31.5 | 17.8 | **7.7** |
| **4.5** | 1.79 | 15.3 | 0.34 | **5.8** | 4.2 | 1.08 | 9.84 | 4.46 | 62.1 | **1.6** | 11.0 | 20.9 | **5.9** |
| **5.3** | 0.59 | 3.3 | 0.04 | **7.0** | 8.2 | 1.41 | 12.42 | 4.11 | 62.3 | **3.9** | 22.2 | 10.0 | **8.1** |
| **7.7** | 2.66 | 5.8 | 0.00 | **3.4** | 0.6 | 0.59 | 2.83 | 2.32 | 67.3 | **7.6** | 64.5 | 0.0 | **8.2** |
| **6.4** | 1.29 | 7.3 | 0.13 | **6.9** | 10.1 | 1.44 | 10.01 | 3.45 | 39.2 | **1.6** | 34.3 | 36.7 | **9.9** |
| **7.1** | 0.88 | 3.5 | -0.29 | **6.4** | 1.7 | 1.26 | 6.89 | 3.73 | 57.7 | **2.3** | 14.8 | 16.6 | **8.4** |
| **6.7** | 0.39 | 2.4 | 0.09 | **6.9** | 34.4 | 1.46 | 13.12 | 3.79 | 56.8 | **1.9** | 11.1 | 11.1 | **8.6** |
| **5.3** | 1.30 | 7.1 | 0.15 | **4.7** | 5.6 | 1.02 | 9.02 | 4.11 | 76.9 | **4.6** | 19.5 | 5.0 | **7.0** |
| **5.7** | 0.37 | 3.6 | 0.10 | **4.5** | 8.6 | 0.95 | 10.45 | 3.39 | 65.9 | **2.5** | 12.8 | 16.4 | **6.0** |
| **3.0** | 2.41 | 16.3 | 0.24 | **7.0** | 1.5 | 1.64 | 14.93 | 4.30 | 60.4 | **1.0** | 19.7 | 28.7 | **8.0** |
| **8.8** | 0.04 | 0.2 | -0.03 | **3.9** | 0.8 | 0.81 | 7.40 | 3.79 | 76.7 | **4.3** | 36.2 | 12.2 | **5.2** |
| **8.5** | 0.45 | 2.2 | 0.02 | **5.7** | 2.8 | 1.11 | 6.94 | 4.16 | 69.5 | **2.5** | 16.8 | 16.4 | **8.7** |
| **3.7** | 4.15 | 19.5 | 0.05 | **4.1** | 1.9 | 0.93 | 7.61 | 3.10 | 65.0 | **1.3** | 31.1 | 38.0 | **8.4** |
| **5.2** | 2.04 | 8.6 | 0.09 | **4.9** | 1.3 | 0.98 | 6.83 | 3.39 | 59.8 | **2.5** | 25.1 | 17.4 | **8.2** |
| **8.5** | 0.34 | 1.0 | -0.06 | **4.9** | 0.5 | 1.01 | 5.39 | 3.23 | 55.0 | **5.3** | 48.9 | 9.8 | **6.7** |
| **8.0** | 0.78 | 3.2 | -0.02 | **5.4** | 1.2 | 1.12 | 7.68 | 3.69 | 68.3 | **2.8** | 34.7 | 14.9 | **8.3** |
| **1.8** | 6.68 | 30.0 | 0.06 | **5.0** | 1.2 | 1.07 | 7.21 | 3.92 | 72.4 | **4.0** | 28.0 | 11.1 | **7.6** |
| **6.6** | 6.07 | 6.4 | -0.89 | **6.8** | 4.7 | 1.68 | 6.25 | 3.38 | 48.3 | **4.3** | 86.6 | 25.5 | **9.9** |
| **7.7** | 0.35 | 1.6 | 0.08 | **5.0** | 3.5 | 1.16 | 12.97 | 2.97 | 66.0 | **5.6** | 35.7 | 4.2 | **6.4** |
| **8.8** | 0.00 | 0.0 | 0.00 | **6.5** | 2.4 | 1.48 | 14.85 | 3.64 | 60.1 | **4.9** | 34.2 | 7.8 | **6.7** |
| **5.0** | 2.43 | 6.8 | 0.37 | **4.1** | 0.4 | 0.72 | 6.33 | 4.14 | 68.6 | **4.5** | 28.6 | 8.6 | **5.7** |
| **5.9** | 1.95 | 5.5 | 0.04 | **5.8** | 1.7 | 1.38 | 9.29 | 4.43 | 68.6 | **2.7** | 25.7 | 16.6 | **8.6** |
| **8.0** | 0.21 | 1.1 | 0.14 | **7.9** | 2.3 | 1.87 | 10.88 | 5.79 | 65.9 | **3.2** | 26.0 | 14.5 | **8.5** |
| **8.0** | 0.76 | 3.4 | 0.00 | **6.1** | 1.6 | 1.43 | 12.40 | 3.63 | 62.4 | **4.2** | 26.7 | 9.2 | **7.8** |
| **8.9** | 0.00 | 0.0 | -0.02 | **4.1** | 0.3 | 0.88 | 7.30 | 3.20 | 64.0 | **6.8** | 68.1 | 4.0 | **5.7** |
| **8.2** | 0.05 | 0.2 | 1.29 | **4.7** | 0.7 | 1.02 | 7.13 | 3.49 | 51.8 | **5.0** | 33.4 | 6.7 | **8.6** |
| **8.4** | 0.20 | 1.0 | 0.03 | **6.5** | 12.7 | 1.57 | 11.15 | 3.43 | 57.1 | **3.5** | 21.3 | 12.0 | **9.9** |
| **8.3** | 0.96 | 3.5 | 0.10 | **5.6** | 2.1 | 1.15 | 9.02 | 3.57 | 61.3 | **2.6** | 44.3 | 28.7 | **7.6** |
| **8.0** | 0.01 | 0.1 | 0.04 | **5.7** | 15.3 | 1.39 | 15.42 | 3.19 | 52.3 | **0.8** | 11.4 | 20.0 | **8.5** |
| **7.6** | 1.06 | 2.4 | 0.00 | **5.5** | 0.6 | 1.27 | 10.90 | 3.63 | 61.6 | **3.8** | 50.6 | 17.5 | **6.2** |
| **5.2** | 1.92 | 8.1 | 0.30 | **2.6** | 0.3 | 0.52 | 6.11 | 3.36 | 82.8 | **3.1** | 29.6 | 15.9 | **2.7** |
| **7.1** | 0.37 | 2.8 | 0.01 | **6.1** | 3.8 | 1.50 | 11.13 | 3.90 | 65.2 | **3.7** | 16.2 | 10.5 | **8.4** |
| **7.4** | 0.33 | 1.7 | -0.05 | **7.6** | 12.5 | 1.62 | 16.93 | 4.07 | 56.6 | **4.0** | 22.4 | 8.9 | **6.4** |
| **7.9** | 0.00 | 0.0 | 0.00 | **1.3** | 0.0 | 0.03 | 0.20 | 3.40 | 99.2 | **4.8** | 48.5 | 10.4 | **5.1** |
| **5.5** | 0.32 | 2.1 | -0.09 | **3.2** | 0.1 | 0.52 | 5.31 | 3.73 | 85.9 | **4.4** | 28.2 | 7.2 | **3.8** |
| **8.7** | 0.10 | 0.4 | 0.07 | **6.7** | 0.8 | 1.35 | 10.58 | 4.41 | 63.2 | **1.9** | 21.2 | 20.3 | **7.1** |
| **8.8** | 0.10 | 0.5 | 0.07 | **5.9** | 1.6 | 1.33 | 13.45 | 3.87 | 62.7 | **4.2** | 43.3 | 15.0 | **7.4** |
| **3.6** | 2.24 | 12.3 | 0.11 | **3.9** | 0.3 | 0.74 | 6.75 | 3.79 | 79.3 | **1.1** | 22.2 | 30.6 | **5.3** |
| **8.6** | 0.12 | 0.3 | 0.17 | **3.7** | 0.4 | 0.68 | 4.00 | 3.84 | 83.4 | **6.0** | 57.0 | 7.2 | **7.6** |
| **3.8** | 2.14 | 13.2 | 0.45 | **4.0** | 1.6 | 0.85 | 5.75 | 3.36 | 67.9 | **1.8** | 22.1 | 21.8 | **8.0** |
| **6.3** | 2.01 | 6.3 | 0.06 | **5.3** | 0.7 | 1.30 | 10.51 | 4.18 | 74.0 | **2.7** | 30.3 | 18.4 | **6.6** |
| **7.1** | 0.31 | 2.4 | 0.04 | **4.5** | 2.0 | 0.83 | 8.07 | 4.19 | 75.7 | **3.0** | 17.5 | 14.2 | **6.4** |
| **5.9** | 0.82 | 3.5 | 0.03 | **5.0** | 4.9 | 1.19 | 11.80 | 4.45 | 74.2 | **3.6** | 27.4 | 12.8 | **5.9** |
| **4.3** | 0.96 | 7.1 | 0.01 | **5.2** | 3.1 | 1.17 | 12.33 | 3.69 | 63.6 | **0.8** | 14.5 | 36.1 | **6.1** |
| **8.5** | 0.09 | 1.8 | 0.04 | **4.7** | 1.8 | 0.98 | 8.42 | 3.76 | 70.3 | **1.2** | 13.4 | 28.4 | **7.1** |
| **5.3** | 1.52 | 6.7 | 0.17 | **3.7** | 0.8 | 0.67 | 7.30 | 4.38 | 83.9 | **5.0** | 16.9 | 2.0 | **5.5** |
| **5.5** | 0.77 | 3.2 | 0.44 | **4.5** | 1.0 | 0.88 | 10.68 | 5.05 | 77.4 | **5.1** | 30.0 | 4.7 | **5.0** |
| **7.7** | 0.32 | 1.9 | 0.05 | **7.0** | 0.3 | 1.58 | 9.99 | 5.03 | 67.9 | **1.2** | 22.4 | 30.5 | **5.7** |
| **8.5** | 0.04 | 0.2 | 0.02 | **4.9** | 2.2 | 0.98 | 10.15 | 3.44 | 63.2 | **4.6** | 40.5 | 12.0 | **5.5** |
| **5.2** | 4.21 | 9.4 | 0.24 | **3.9** | 1.0 | 0.67 | 4.28 | 4.31 | 78.3 | **2.7** | 16.2 | 15.4 | **7.5** |
| **4.9** | 2.70 | 10.6 | -0.41 | **3.8** | 2.4 | 0.72 | 5.34 | 3.78 | 80.1 | **4.2** | 42.1 | 14.6 | **6.0** |
| **7.9** | 0.56 | 1.5 | 0.05 | **5.8** | 1.8 | 1.40 | 13.98 | 4.10 | 70.1 | **4.9** | 35.1 | 8.6 | **7.1** |
| **8.6** | 2.87 | 3.1 | 0.18 | **3.7** | 0.3 | 0.72 | 7.22 | 2.81 | 63.3 | **8.1** | 93.0 | 0.0 | **4.7** |
| **8.7** | 0.00 | 0.0 | 0.00 | **0.6** | -0.7 | -2.42 | -26.35 | 4.13 | 162.6 | **5.8** | 46.7 | 6.3 | **3.7** |
| **7.9** | 0.21 | 1.5 | 0.03 | **5.9** | 1.1 | 1.18 | 12.97 | 3.84 | 61.0 | **1.6** | 22.9 | 24.8 | **5.6** |
| **5.6** | 1.38 | 6.9 | 0.05 | **6.7** | 1.7 | 1.52 | 13.39 | 4.98 | 69.4 | **2.7** | 19.5 | 16.1 | **8.3** |

| Name | City | State | Rating | 2018 Rating | 2017 Rating | Total Assets ($Mil) | One Year Asset Growth | Asset Mix (As a % of Total Assets): Comm-ercial Loans | Cons-umer Loans | Mort-gage Loans | Secur-ities | Capital-ization Index | Lever-age Ratio | Risk-Based Capital Ratio |
|---|---|---|---|---|---|---|---|---|---|---|---|---|---|---|
| Farmers State Bank and Trust Co. | Jacksonville | IL | **B-** | C | C | 206.4 | 4.43 | 5.9 | 7.0 | 11.3 | 31.2 | **10.0** | 12.6 | 21.0 |
| Farmers State Bank Hillsboro | Hillsboro | WI | **A** | A- | A- | 170.7 | 0.30 | 2.1 | 1.9 | 9.3 | 42.6 | **10.0** | 19.7 | 35.2 |
| Farmers State Bank of Aliceville, Kansas | Westphalia | KS | **A-** | B+ | A | 150.5 | -0.46 | 5.0 | 6.7 | 17.0 | 18.1 | **10.0** | 15.6 | 25.8 |
| Farmers State Bank of Alto Pass, Ill. | Harrisburg | IL | **C-** | C+ | C- | 238.9 | 4.64 | 15.6 | 1.7 | 15.3 | 8.7 | **5.1** | 8.6 | 11.1 |
| Farmers State Bank of Blue Mound | Blue Mound | KS | **B-** | B- | B- | 44.1 | -1.35 | 7.3 | 3.6 | 1.2 | 7.0 | **10.0** | 18.5 | 23.7 |
| Farmers State Bank of Brush | Brush | CO | **A-** | B+ | A- | 112.2 | 3.91 | 2.8 | 1.3 | 3.2 | 28.1 | **10.0** | 18.9 | 33.7 |
| ▲ Farmers State Bank of Bucklin, Kansas | Bucklin | KS | **C+** | C- | C | 47.7 | 3.69 | 6.4 | 1.0 | 1.4 | 22.8 | **7.8** | 9.6 | 20.4 |
| Farmers State Bank of Calhan | Calhan | CO | **B** | B- | B | 283.9 | 4.28 | 6.4 | 2.5 | 11.9 | 45.5 | **9.2** | 10.4 | 18.8 |
| Farmers State Bank of Canton | Canton | SD | **B-** | B- | B- | 47.2 | -1.30 | 3.1 | 4.6 | 25.1 | 11.3 | **10.0** | 12.3 | 19.0 |
| Farmers State Bank of Emden | Emden | IL | **B-** | B- | C+ | 34.2 | 0.11 | 4.0 | 1.5 | 1.8 | 54.4 | **10.0** | 27.7 | 59.9 |
| Farmers State Bank of Hamel | Hamel | MN | **B** | B- | B- | 129.9 | -1.76 | 3.6 | 0.5 | 12.4 | 37.2 | **10.0** | 11.2 | 26.3 |
| ▲ Farmers State Bank of Hartland | Hartland | MN | **B+** | B- | B- | 169.2 | 10.98 | 9.2 | 1.2 | 2.8 | 18.6 | **9.7** | 10.8 | 15.6 |
| Farmers State Bank of Hoffman | Hoffman | IL | **B** | B | B | 151.0 | 4.93 | 3.7 | 1.4 | 12.5 | 42.7 | **10.0** | 15.8 | 31.3 |
| Farmers State Bank of Hoffman | Hoffman | MN | **B** | B- | B+ | 31.0 | 3.60 | 6.0 | 3.6 | 8.9 | 33.0 | **10.0** | 13.1 | 23.4 |
| Farmers State Bank of Medora | Medora | IL | **C** | C | C+ | 19.9 | -0.11 | 13.0 | 6.2 | 2.2 | 42.2 | **10.0** | 17.0 | 33.1 |
| Farmers State Bank of Munith | Munith | MI | **B-** | B- | B- | 77.5 | -2.79 | 2.8 | 5.6 | 31.3 | 16.9 | **9.4** | 10.6 | 19.4 |
| Farmers State Bank of Newcastle | Newcastle | TX | **B-** | B- | B- | 47.1 | 0.16 | 5.6 | 2.9 | 8.0 | 32.8 | **8.1** | 9.7 | 19.5 |
| Farmers State Bank of Oakley, Kansas | Oakley | KS | **A-** | B+ | A- | 151.6 | 5.61 | 5.6 | 0.5 | 1.0 | 21.4 | **10.0** | 15.4 | 17.8 |
| Farmers State Bank of Trimont | Trimont | MN | **B** | B- | B- | 60.7 | -1.35 | 7.9 | 2.3 | 4.5 | 24.1 | **10.0** | 16.3 | 22.8 |
| Farmers State Bank of Turton | Turton | SD | **B** | B | B | 31.7 | 0.87 | 2.4 | 2.7 | 0.0 | 16.8 | **10.0** | 12.2 | 23.2 |
| Farmers State Bank of Underwood | Underwood | MN | **B-** | C+ | C+ | 73.0 | 2.11 | 14.7 | 4.3 | 15.4 | 6.7 | **8.3** | 9.8 | 14.4 |
| Farmers State Bank of Watkins | Watkins | MN | **B** | B | B | 46.7 | 7.70 | 4.1 | 4.7 | 14.2 | 30.0 | **10.0** | 12.7 | 24.2 |
| Farmers State Bank of Waupaca | Waupaca | WI | **A-** | A- | A | 215.7 | 7.02 | 7.5 | 3.8 | 22.1 | 25.0 | **10.0** | 12.5 | 16.7 |
| Farmers State Bank of Western Illinois | Alpha | IL | **A-** | B+ | B- | 144.3 | 4.23 | 4.1 | 2.4 | 6.4 | 28.7 | **10.0** | 12.4 | 19.7 |
| Farmers State Bank, Allen, Oklahoma | Allen | OK | **B** | B- | C | 40.3 | -7.24 | 17.7 | 13.8 | 16.0 | 8.6 | **10.0** | 13.3 | 17.8 |
| Farmers State Bank, S/B | Bolivar | MO | **C** | C+ | C+ | 65.6 | -3.37 | 1.1 | 2.9 | 30.4 | 8.2 | **7.4** | 9.4 | 12.8 |
| ▲ Farmers Trust & Savings Bank | Earling | IA | **B+** | B | B | 98.1 | 7.30 | 10.4 | 1.5 | 7.7 | 0.9 | **8.0** | 9.6 | 14.3 |
| Farmers Trust & Savings Bank | Williamsburg | IA | **A** | A- | A+ | 154.3 | 13.26 | 6.5 | 3.3 | 13.3 | 39.2 | **10.0** | 23.9 | 36.9 |
| Farmers Trust and Savings Bank | Buffalo Center | IA | **A-** | B+ | A- | 262.3 | 2.95 | 13.0 | 1.0 | 5.7 | 1.0 | **10.0** | 12.8 | 15.9 |
| Farmers Trust and Savings Bank | Spencer | IA | **C+** | C+ | B- | 454.1 | 4.09 | 11.3 | 1.0 | 8.1 | 13.8 | **5.5** | 9.0 | 11.4 |
| ▲ Farmers-Merchants Bank & Trust Co. | Breaux Bridge | LA | **D+** | D | D | 334.9 | 6.56 | 4.8 | 4.9 | 14.9 | 9.3 | **10.0** | 12.3 | 18.0 |
| Farmers-Merchants Bank of Illinois | Paxton | IL | **B** | C+ | C- | 204.1 | 17.74 | 2.0 | 1.3 | 14.4 | 9.4 | **7.7** | 11.7 | 13.1 |
| ▲ Farmington State Bank | Farmington | WA | **C** | C- | C+ | 9.5 | 0.42 | 10.7 | 1.6 | 0.5 | 1.0 | **10.0** | 27.1 | 49.7 |
| Fauquier Bank | Warrenton | VA | **B** | B- | C+ | 721.7 | -1.18 | 3.8 | 1.9 | 31.2 | 11.1 | **7.6** | 9.4 | 13.5 |
| Fayette County National Bank of Fayettevill | Fayetteville | WV | **B+** | B | B | 91.8 | 4.12 | 0.9 | 4.2 | 49.8 | 26.8 | **10.0** | 12.4 | 26.2 |
| Fayette Savings Bank, SSB | La Grange | TX | **B** | B | B | 208.6 | 19.14 | 1.2 | 2.0 | 50.8 | 10.1 | **8.3** | 9.9 | 14.7 |
| Fayetteville Bank | Fayetteville | TX | **B** | B+ | A- | 563.3 | 12.35 | 3.8 | 0.8 | 4.1 | 78.7 | **9.0** | 10.3 | 25.2 |
| FBT Bank & Mortgage | Fordyce | AR | **B+** | B | B+ | 167.0 | 3.15 | 11.4 | 7.5 | 20.3 | 27.7 | **10.0** | 11.8 | 19.1 |
| FCB Banks | Collinsville | IL | **B** | B | B- | 1749.6 | 12.52 | 3.5 | 4.3 | 36.5 | 11.2 | **6.4** | 8.5 | 14.1 |
| FCN Bank, N.A. | Brookville | IN | **B+** | B+ | B | 472.2 | 6.89 | 8.1 | 1.6 | 15.6 | 32.1 | **9.5** | 10.7 | 18.7 |
| FDS Bank | Mason | OH | **A+** | A+ | A+ | 199.3 | 13.62 | 1.0 | 0.6 | 0.0 | 49.1 | **10.0** | 89.0 | 70.9 |
| Federal Savings Bank | Chicago | IL | **A** | A | A | 604.5 | 52.78 | 0.0 | 1.6 | 85.6 | 0.1 | **10.0** | 14.7 | 32.7 |
| Federated Bank | Onarga | IL | **C** | C+ | B- | 99.0 | 9.43 | 5.6 | 2.7 | 11.8 | 29.4 | **6.5** | 8.5 | 19.1 |
| Federation Bank | Washington | IA | **C+** | C+ | B- | 136.9 | 12.41 | 9.7 | 4.0 | 13.4 | 16.5 | **6.0** | 8.8 | 11.8 |
| Feliciana Bank & Trust Co. | Clinton | LA | **B+** | B- | B+ | 128.6 | -1.73 | 9.2 | 2.1 | 32.6 | 12.6 | **10.0** | 11.6 | 17.2 |
| Fidelity Bank | West Memphis | AR | **A-** | B+ | B | 439.9 | 17.00 | 3.3 | 0.8 | 4.5 | 48.6 | **10.0** | 11.5 | 20.7 |
| ▲ Fidelity Bank | West Des Moines | IA | **B-** | C+ | B- | 85.2 | 1.14 | 0.1 | 0.1 | 46.6 | 4.1 | **7.8** | 9.5 | 15.4 |
| Fidelity Bank | New Orleans | LA | **B** | B | B- | 760.1 | -7.75 | 4.0 | 0.7 | 31.0 | 16.0 | **10.0** | 18.2 | 26.9 |
| Fidelity Bank | Edina | MN | **A-** | A | A | 534.0 | 10.95 | 25.3 | 0.6 | 0.0 | 9.6 | **8.7** | 11.0 | 13.9 |
| Fidelity Bank | Fuquay-Varina | NC | **A-** | B+ | B- | 2072.5 | 7.42 | 5.5 | 0.5 | 3.3 | 26.6 | **9.2** | 10.5 | 16.3 |
| Fidelity Bank & Trust | Dubuque | IA | **B** | B+ | B | 1373.9 | 67.74 | 10.1 | 1.7 | 10.3 | 15.9 | **6.4** | 9.0 | 12.0 |
| Fidelity Bank of Texas | Waco | TX | **B+** | B+ | B+ | 91.5 | -0.27 | 1.0 | 1.3 | 22.8 | 1.1 | **10.0** | 18.7 | 46.0 |
| Fidelity Bank, N.A. | Wichita | KS | **B-** | B- | B- | 2411.7 | 6.25 | 9.1 | 3.6 | 16.7 | 11.1 | **6.4** | 9.6 | 12.0 |
| Fidelity Co-operative Bank | Leominster | MA | **C+** | C+ | C+ | 972.8 | 4.04 | 11.7 | 0.2 | 30.9 | 10.9 | **6.4** | 8.6 | 12.1 |
| ▲ Fidelity Deposit and Discount Bank | Dunmore | PA | **A-** | B+ | B | 1013.6 | 3.10 | 7.9 | 10.8 | 23.3 | 18.3 | **8.9** | 10.3 | 15.8 |
| Fidelity Federal S&L Assn. of Delaware | Delaware | OH | **C-** | C- | C- | 107.4 | 1.89 | 0.0 | 1.4 | 33.0 | 39.8 | **10.0** | 21.0 | 48.3 |
| Fidelity Personal Trust Co., FSB | Boston | MA | **U** | U | U | 99.0 | 4.74 | 0.0 | 0.0 | 0.0 | 0.0 | **10.0** | 88.4 | 87.9 |
| Fidelity S&L Assn. of Bucks County | Bristol | PA | **C+** | C | C | 87.8 | 0.53 | 0.0 | 0.2 | 60.6 | 0.6 | **10.0** | 15.6 | 31.7 |
| Fidelity State Bank and Trust Co. | Dodge City | KS | **A-** | B+ | B | 174.0 | 0.86 | 3.5 | 0.3 | 1.4 | 28.9 | **10.0** | 18.9 | 74.5 |
| Fidelity State Bank and Trust Co. | Topeka | KS | **C+** | C | C+ | 130.7 | -4.14 | 10.3 | 19.6 | 8.5 | 28.9 | **7.6** | 9.4 | 14.9 |

| Asset Quality Index | Adjusted Non-Performing Loans as a % of Total Loans | Adjusted Non-Performing Loans as a % of Capital | Net Charge-Offs Avg Loans | Profitability Index | Net Income ($Mil) | Return on Assets (R.O.A.) | Return on Equity (R.O.E.) | Net Interest Spread | Overhead Efficiency Ratio | Liquidity Index | Liquidity Ratio | Hot Money Ratio | Stability Index |
|---|---|---|---|---|---|---|---|---|---|---|---|---|---|
| **5.0** | 2.22 | 8.7 | 0.19 | **4.1** | 2.2 | 1.09 | 9.06 | 3.75 | 68.5 | **5.8** | 37.7 | 3.8 | **5.6** |
| **9.0** | 0.31 | 0.4 | 0.02 | **8.1** | 3.0 | 1.77 | 9.44 | 3.44 | 40.9 | **5.6** | 56.7 | 11.3 | **9.3** |
| **8.1** | 0.00 | 0.2 | 0.00 | **6.6** | 1.8 | 1.23 | 8.04 | 3.52 | 50.8 | **1.3** | 15.0 | 27.4 | **8.8** |
| **1.8** | 2.78 | 26.0 | 0.36 | **4.3** | 2.1 | 0.89 | 10.44 | 4.66 | 75.8 | **2.9** | 13.9 | 14.4 | **4.6** |
| **6.4** | 1.40 | 3.6 | -0.10 | **5.7** | 0.6 | 1.29 | 7.02 | 5.20 | 73.2 | **2.9** | 19.7 | 14.8 | **7.3** |
| **7.7** | 0.01 | 0.0 | 0.00 | **9.3** | 2.0 | 1.86 | 9.80 | 4.28 | 52.2 | **2.0** | 26.8 | 22.1 | **8.6** |
| **8.6** | 0.00 | 0.0 | -0.08 | **3.7** | 0.3 | 0.65 | 5.64 | 3.72 | 77.4 | **5.4** | 44.7 | 8.7 | **5.7** |
| **7.2** | 0.34 | 1.4 | 0.02 | **5.0** | 3.4 | 1.24 | 11.68 | 3.85 | 70.4 | **3.4** | 31.4 | 15.3 | **6.8** |
| **8.6** | 0.27 | 1.5 | 0.24 | **3.0** | 0.2 | 0.44 | 3.57 | 4.15 | 87.3 | **4.2** | 17.2 | 7.7 | **6.0** |
| **9.0** | 1.12 | 2.0 | 0.00 | **3.8** | 0.3 | 0.82 | 2.95 | 2.77 | 63.3 | **3.1** | 48.9 | 22.8 | **7.0** |
| **9.5** | 0.00 | 0.0 | 0.00 | **4.0** | 1.3 | 1.01 | 9.35 | 3.02 | 68.1 | **5.5** | 53.8 | 10.8 | **6.8** |
| **5.4** | 1.27 | 3.6 | 0.05 | **7.6** | 2.9 | 1.82 | 15.63 | 4.21 | 57.0 | **3.2** | 26.8 | 6.0 | **8.2** |
| **9.2** | 0.97 | 2.2 | 0.00 | **3.6** | 1.0 | 0.67 | 4.26 | 3.17 | 74.3 | **4.7** | 43.0 | 12.0 | **8.0** |
| **8.7** | 0.00 | 0.0 | 0.00 | **3.9** | 0.3 | 0.89 | 6.56 | 3.30 | 72.8 | **3.6** | 53.1 | 19.3 | **7.5** |
| **4.3** | 0.00 | 16.4 | 0.55 | **1.6** | 0.0 | -0.04 | -0.24 | 3.56 | 90.5 | **5.3** | 75.5 | 12.9 | **5.8** |
| **4.7** | 2.18 | 11.0 | -0.12 | **4.5** | 0.7 | 0.85 | 8.31 | 4.23 | 78.8 | **5.7** | 36.3 | 3.8 | **6.3** |
| **7.4** | 0.32 | 1.4 | -0.07 | **6.2** | 0.6 | 1.32 | 13.11 | 3.80 | 59.3 | **7.0** | 54.8 | 0.0 | **5.7** |
| **7.3** | 0.00 | 0.0 | -0.03 | **7.7** | 2.2 | 1.52 | 9.44 | 3.63 | 47.8 | **1.0** | 13.2 | 31.6 | **9.3** |
| **7.3** | 0.84 | 2.7 | 0.36 | **5.9** | 0.8 | 1.24 | 7.61 | 3.66 | 55.6 | **1.6** | 34.4 | 23.5 | **7.2** |
| **7.4** | 0.00 | 1.8 | -0.01 | **6.9** | 0.5 | 1.59 | 12.99 | 4.39 | 57.7 | **2.7** | 33.3 | 19.2 | **6.3** |
| **4.5** | 1.06 | 9.5 | 0.06 | **7.6** | 1.3 | 1.79 | 19.07 | 4.89 | 61.8 | **1.3** | 18.7 | 28.0 | **7.1** |
| **7.4** | 0.03 | 2.9 | 0.05 | **6.5** | 0.7 | 1.60 | 12.33 | 4.01 | 62.1 | **6.2** | 49.2 | 3.7 | **7.1** |
| **8.7** | 0.33 | 1.5 | 0.31 | **6.1** | 2.5 | 1.24 | 9.05 | 4.42 | 63.8 | **4.0** | 36.5 | 13.6 | **7.8** |
| **8.7** | 0.30 | 1.9 | 0.21 | **5.2** | 1.8 | 1.31 | 10.18 | 4.14 | 64.9 | **5.1** | 36.5 | 7.7 | **7.3** |
| **5.7** | 0.35 | 6.2 | 0.17 | **6.4** | 0.7 | 1.53 | 12.00 | 5.11 | 69.2 | **1.5** | 12.8 | 23.7 | **8.1** |
| **4.3** | 0.64 | 4.2 | 0.00 | **2.8** | 0.2 | 0.39 | 3.07 | 5.35 | 86.3 | **1.6** | 9.4 | 21.8 | **6.9** |
| **7.3** | 0.00 | 0.5 | -0.03 | **7.6** | 1.7 | 1.82 | 18.71 | 4.30 | 58.0 | **4.1** | 25.3 | 9.8 | **7.0** |
| **8.4** | 0.99 | 1.6 | 0.01 | **9.0** | 3.0 | 2.12 | 8.42 | 4.02 | 47.5 | **6.1** | 52.6 | 7.0 | **9.6** |
| **5.8** | 0.12 | 0.2 | 0.08 | **7.5** | 4.4 | 1.68 | 13.17 | 4.00 | 51.9 | **3.8** | 13.0 | 9.9 | **9.1** |
| **5.3** | 1.00 | 4.3 | 0.14 | **5.4** | 5.7 | 1.27 | 14.38 | 3.22 | 52.4 | **1.6** | 7.5 | 10.5 | **6.1** |
| **2.1** | 5.15 | 19.7 | 0.09 | **5.1** | 3.9 | 1.17 | 9.17 | 4.28 | 72.3 | **2.5** | 24.8 | 17.7 | **8.5** |
| **3.9** | 0.52 | 5.1 | 0.00 | **6.8** | 3.0 | 1.66 | 10.02 | 3.54 | 54.9 | **1.0** | 3.5 | 22.8 | **7.6** |
| **8.8** | 0.00 | 0.0 | 0.00 | **3.6** | 0.1 | 0.87 | 4.03 | 4.24 | 83.0 | **7.2** | 70.3 | 0.0 | **5.7** |
| **7.6** | 0.18 | 0.7 | 0.05 | **4.7** | 7.4 | 1.04 | 10.95 | 3.78 | 71.8 | **4.4** | 16.8 | 6.4 | **6.1** |
| **5.9** | 1.55 | 8.8 | 0.07 | **5.4** | 1.0 | 1.08 | 8.53 | 4.27 | 68.6 | **3.9** | 14.8 | 9.4 | **7.3** |
| **6.1** | 0.42 | 3.7 | 0.00 | **5.5** | 2.5 | 1.35 | 14.95 | 3.31 | 57.8 | **0.6** | 5.2 | 35.0 | **5.6** |
| **10.0** | 0.00 | 0.0 | 0.02 | **3.9** | 5.0 | 0.96 | 8.60 | 2.22 | 59.4 | **2.8** | 57.4 | 42.6 | **7.2** |
| **4.6** | 7.23 | 14.7 | 0.50 | **4.9** | 1.5 | 0.91 | 7.91 | 4.23 | 71.7 | **2.5** | 34.3 | 21.4 | **6.5** |
| **5.8** | 0.94 | 6.9 | 0.00 | **5.6** | 16.3 | 0.97 | 11.31 | 2.70 | 59.2 | **2.9** | 15.2 | 14.7 | **7.6** |
| **6.7** | 0.97 | 2.6 | 0.52 | **5.7** | 5.4 | 1.19 | 10.32 | 3.72 | 62.4 | **4.3** | 39.6 | 13.3 | **7.3** |
| **10.0** | 0.00 | 0.0 | 0.20 | **10.0** | 617.1 | 498.69 | 633.38 | 2.21 | 18.6 | **9.3** | 156.2 | 0.0 | **8.8** |
| **7.2** | 0.64 | 3.3 | -0.52 | **10.0** | 47.2 | 8.04 | 50.39 | 2.33 | 79.5 | **0.2** | 5.0 | 37.7 | **9.0** |
| **7.0** | 0.00 | 0.0 | 0.02 | **3.3** | 0.5 | 0.59 | 4.84 | 3.62 | 86.2 | **5.7** | 49.3 | 7.4 | **6.5** |
| **4.5** | 0.61 | 5.3 | 0.31 | **4.5** | 1.2 | 0.92 | 9.60 | 4.04 | 68.0 | **2.9** | 20.3 | 13.7 | **6.1** |
| **5.9** | 0.95 | 8.1 | 0.08 | **5.5** | 1.6 | 1.26 | 11.36 | 4.18 | 69.2 | **0.7** | 11.5 | 41.2 | **7.8** |
| **8.3** | 0.23 | 0.8 | 0.00 | **6.0** | 6.1 | 1.55 | 12.70 | 3.36 | 57.9 | **1.5** | 20.5 | 26.1 | **7.3** |
| **5.7** | 0.44 | 3.6 | 0.01 | **4.1** | 1.0 | 1.14 | 10.17 | 3.46 | 89.1 | **0.7** | 13.5 | 38.4 | **7.0** |
| **7.8** | 0.96 | 2.3 | 0.04 | **3.7** | 5.0 | 0.62 | 3.47 | 4.85 | 90.2 | **3.6** | 19.9 | 8.5 | **8.0** |
| **6.8** | 0.04 | 0.2 | 0.29 | **8.7** | 11.0 | 2.12 | 12.08 | 5.55 | 55.9 | **4.1** | 1.3 | 0.7 | **10.0** |
| **7.2** | 1.54 | 4.0 | -0.03 | **7.1** | 29.2 | 1.45 | 13.25 | 3.78 | 59.2 | **6.4** | 37.5 | 3.4 | **9.3** |
| **6.6** | 0.42 | 3.0 | -0.03 | **6.8** | 15.6 | 1.48 | 13.06 | 4.38 | 57.6 | **3.5** | 24.9 | 14.8 | **9.5** |
| **6.8** | 2.11 | 5.4 | 0.02 | **4.8** | 0.8 | 0.90 | 4.99 | 3.93 | 74.8 | **6.4** | 63.0 | 5.5 | **7.9** |
| **4.1** | 2.12 | 7.3 | 0.06 | **4.1** | 17.7 | 0.76 | 7.65 | 3.33 | 73.4 | **3.1** | 5.4 | 12.4 | **8.2** |
| **5.1** | 1.75 | 8.6 | 0.01 | **3.4** | 6.1 | 0.63 | 7.40 | 3.45 | 77.1 | **2.2** | 8.2 | 10.6 | **5.8** |
| **6.6** | 0.62 | 3.5 | 0.15 | **6.2** | 12.9 | 1.31 | 12.74 | 3.63 | 60.2 | **4.1** | 14.7 | 8.5 | **9.2** |
| **9.7** | 0.14 | 0.3 | 0.00 | **1.6** | 0.2 | 0.17 | 0.79 | 3.18 | 97.0 | **6.3** | 60.6 | 7.9 | **7.4** |
| **10.0** | na | 0.0 | na | **9.5** | 40.4 | 42.03 | 47.21 | 3.34 | 44.9 | **4.0** | na | 100.0 | **7.0** |
| **7.1** | 1.74 | 7.6 | 0.00 | **2.3** | 0.2 | 0.23 | 1.58 | 3.26 | 90.6 | **3.0** | 32.8 | 17.0 | **6.9** |
| **9.8** | 0.59 | 0.7 | 0.02 | **5.2** | 1.9 | 1.14 | 5.94 | 3.02 | 57.8 | **7.5** | 77.2 | 3.1 | **8.4** |
| **5.2** | 0.32 | 2.0 | 0.16 | **3.4** | 0.9 | 0.63 | 6.81 | 3.25 | 77.6 | **4.9** | 26.8 | 4.5 | **5.6** |

| Name | City | State | Rating | 2018 Rating | 2017 Rating | Total Assets ($Mil) | One Year Asset Growth | Asset Mix (As a % of Total Assets) Commercial Loans | Consumer Loans | Mortgage Loans | Securities | Capitalization Index | Leverage Ratio | Risk-Based Capital Ratio |
|---|---|---|---|---|---|---|---|---|---|---|---|---|---|---|
| Field & Main Bank | Henderson | KY | **C+** | C | C+ | 471.9 | 6.41 | 11.7 | 0.9 | 21.5 | 7.8 | **7.4** | 9.4 | 12.8 |
| Fieldpoint Private Bank & Trust | Greenwich | CT | **B** | B | B- | 919.9 | 1.64 | 3.5 | 8.9 | 33.8 | 12.0 | **10.0** | 12.0 | 17.4 |
| Fifth District Savings Bank | New Orleans | LA | **B-** | B- | B- | 437.1 | 3.07 | 0.0 | 0.3 | 70.3 | 14.8 | **10.0** | 17.5 | 37.0 |
| Fifth Third Bank, N.A. | Cincinnati | OH | **B** | B | B- | 167845.1 | 16.19 | 27.2 | 10.0 | 10.8 | 21.1 | **8.2** | 10.4 | 13.5 |
| Finance Factors, Ltd. | Honolulu | HI | **B** | B- | B- | 589.2 | 1.57 | 0.0 | 1.0 | 29.0 | 18.6 | **10.0** | 11.8 | 17.5 |
| Financial Federal Bank | Memphis | TN | **A-** | B+ | A | 652.1 | 11.01 | 16.9 | 2.9 | 22.8 | 0.0 | **9.6** | 12.5 | 14.6 |
| ▲ Financial Security Bank | Kerkhoven | MN | **C+** | C | C+ | 104.3 | 8.05 | 12.8 | 0.7 | 10.0 | 5.1 | **6.5** | 9.1 | 12.1 |
| FineMark National Bank & Trust | Fort Myers | FL | **B-** | B- | C+ | 2165.2 | 16.73 | 5.0 | 3.8 | 40.5 | 23.4 | **7.8** | 9.5 | 16.5 |
| Finwise Bank | Murray | UT | **A-** | B+ | B+ | 170.9 | 46.98 | 4.7 | 26.5 | 7.0 | 0.3 | **10.0** | 16.2 | 20.5 |
| First & Farmers National Bank, Inc. | Somerset | KY | **B-** | B+ | B+ | 521.9 | 2.15 | 3.6 | 3.1 | 28.6 | 33.7 | **9.7** | 10.8 | 15.8 |
| First & Peoples Bank and Trust Co. | Russell | KY | **B** | B | C | 205.9 | 6.06 | 11.9 | 17.9 | 10.2 | 38.2 | **10.0** | 19.5 | 34.8 |
| First Advantage Bank | Clarksville | TN | **C+** | C+ | B- | 737.2 | 10.92 | 10.2 | 20.9 | 10.9 | 5.3 | **5.4** | 10.2 | 11.3 |
| First American Bank | Fort Dodge | IA | **B** | B- | B | 675.0 | -29.39 | 4.4 | 0.1 | 6.4 | 16.0 | **10.0** | 15.9 | 51.9 |
| First American Bank | Elk Grove Village | IL | **C+** | B- | B | 5300.3 | -0.45 | 9.0 | 1.9 | 6.1 | 54.1 | **5.0** | 7.0 | 13.9 |
| First American Bank | Artesia | NM | **A** | A | A- | 1215.6 | 6.55 | 10.9 | 0.2 | 7.4 | 40.0 | **9.3** | 10.5 | 18.6 |
| First American Bank | Stonewall | OK | **B** | B | B | 31.3 | 2.12 | 13.0 | 11.1 | 21.8 | 6.8 | **10.0** | 12.0 | 18.1 |
| First American Bank and Trust | Vacherie | LA | **A** | A- | A- | 921.7 | 2.40 | 4.2 | 1.6 | 27.3 | 20.0 | **10.0** | 15.0 | 23.2 |
| First American Bank and Trust Co. | Athens | GA | **A-** | A- | B | 551.5 | 3.53 | 2.6 | 0.4 | 17.1 | 15.0 | **10.0** | 11.1 | 18.6 |
| ▼ First American Bank, N.A. | Hudson | WI | **B-** | B | B- | 130.6 | 4.58 | 10.1 | 1.2 | 10.7 | 7.3 | **3.3** | 8.3 | 10.1 |
| First American National Bank | Iuka | MS | **B-** | B- | B- | 274.5 | 4.10 | 4.5 | 5.8 | 25.3 | 28.6 | **10.0** | 11.2 | 19.4 |
| First American State Bank | Greenwood Village | CO | **B-** | B- | C | 263.1 | 8.01 | 2.5 | 0.1 | 38.6 | 13.9 | **7.3** | 9.2 | 15.4 |
| First American Trust, F.S.B. | Santa Ana | CA | **U** | U | U | 3764.2 | -8.40 | 0.0 | 0.0 | 0.0 | 88.2 | **6.6** | 8.6 | 37.8 |
| First Arkansas Bank and Trust | Jacksonville | AR | **B-** | B- | B | 789.8 | 3.77 | 16.7 | 9.7 | 9.2 | 22.8 | **10.0** | 15.1 | 19.6 |
| First Bank | Ketchikan | AK | **B-** | C+ | C+ | 593.9 | 4.79 | 3.7 | 1.4 | 5.1 | 51.1 | **7.7** | 9.4 | 20.7 |
| First Bank | Wadley | AL | **B+** | B+ | B+ | 89.6 | 2.82 | 3.7 | 1.8 | 5.2 | 47.3 | **7.2** | 9.2 | 15.5 |
| First Bank | Clewiston | FL | **B** | B- | B- | 395.4 | 10.83 | 6.4 | 2.0 | 14.6 | 9.2 | **8.0** | 9.7 | 14.1 |
| First Bank | Dalton | GA | **B-** | B- | B- | 408.6 | 11.50 | 11.3 | 1.5 | 15.1 | 14.2 | **6.5** | 9.2 | 12.1 |
| First Bank | Sterling | KS | **B+** | B+ | A- | 148.2 | 6.58 | 4.3 | 0.9 | 11.8 | 30.8 | **10.0** | 14.3 | 22.1 |
| First Bank | Creve Coeur | MO | **B+** | B | B- | 6166.7 | -2.83 | 10.0 | 0.3 | 11.6 | 32.1 | **8.4** | 9.9 | 15.4 |
| First Bank | McComb | MS | **B** | B | B | 561.0 | 3.15 | 9.9 | 1.5 | 25.7 | 6.0 | **9.5** | 10.7 | 15.3 |
| First Bank | Southern Pines | NC | **B+** | B | B | 6144.7 | 4.76 | 5.4 | 0.9 | 18.6 | 14.5 | **9.8** | 11.2 | 14.9 |
| First Bank | Hamilton | NJ | **B** | B | C+ | 2013.4 | 17.66 | 11.9 | 0.2 | 6.6 | 4.7 | **7.3** | 10.3 | 12.8 |
| First Bank | Erick | OK | **A-** | B+ | A- | 72.3 | 0.04 | 18.7 | 4.9 | 10.2 | 5.1 | **10.0** | 12.1 | 16.1 |
| First Bank | Burkburnett | TX | **B-** | B- | B+ | 478.7 | 13.98 | 12.5 | 1.1 | 29.3 | 0.8 | **10.0** | 11.2 | 15.0 |
| ▲ First Bank | Strasburg | VA | **A-** | B+ | B | 799.6 | 6.23 | 6.1 | 1.4 | 24.4 | 17.3 | **8.7** | 10.1 | 14.8 |
| First Bank & Trust | Brookings | SD | **B+** | B+ | B+ | 2069.6 | 5.97 | 11.5 | 2.6 | 6.3 | 15.3 | **7.1** | 9.7 | 12.6 |
| First Bank & Trust | Sioux Falls | SD | **B+** | B+ | B+ | 1024.3 | 4.48 | 20.1 | 1.2 | 5.5 | 13.3 | **8.7** | 10.9 | 13.9 |
| First Bank & Trust | Lubbock | TX | **B+** | B | B | 1137.7 | 2.50 | 13.0 | 1.1 | 11.1 | 28.1 | **8.9** | 10.3 | 14.1 |
| ▲ First Bank & Trust | Seymour | TX | **B-** | C | C | 120.0 | -26.88 | 10.0 | 1.0 | 0.1 | 60.5 | **10.0** | 13.6 | 31.4 |
| ▼ First Bank & Trust Co. | Duncan | OK | **B+** | A- | A- | 560.4 | -4.26 | 5.4 | 2.6 | 26.9 | 8.4 | **10.0** | 16.3 | 22.4 |
| First Bank & Trust Co. | Perry | OK | **A-** | A | A | 150.8 | 3.37 | 5.1 | 7.4 | 16.9 | 28.6 | **10.0** | 13.8 | 19.9 |
| First Bank and Trust | New Orleans | LA | **B-** | B- | B- | 977.5 | 5.82 | 8.7 | 2.2 | 20.7 | 3.6 | **6.8** | 10.0 | 12.4 |
| First Bank and Trust Co. | Minden | NE | **C+** | C+ | C+ | 72.4 | -0.37 | 6.7 | 2.7 | 13.1 | 29.8 | **9.6** | 10.7 | 18.4 |
| First Bank and Trust Co. | Clinton | OK | **B** | B- | B- | 53.9 | -4.84 | 2.3 | 10.7 | 17.6 | 33.4 | **10.0** | 13.4 | 33.7 |
| First Bank and Trust Co. | Lebanon | VA | **A** | A | A | 1946.5 | 7.60 | 7.6 | 3.0 | 15.7 | 1.6 | **10.0** | 11.6 | 16.6 |
| First Bank and Trust Co. of Illinois | Palatine | IL | **C-** | C | B- | 188.2 | 1.73 | 19.4 | 0.0 | 1.4 | 1.1 | **7.7** | 9.4 | 13.8 |
| First Bank and Trust Co. of Murphysboro | Murphysboro | IL | **D** | D+ | C- | 77.3 | -3.39 | 10.9 | 5.2 | 20.5 | 17.1 | **6.8** | 8.8 | 13.3 |
| First Bank and Trust of Childress | Childress | TX | **C+** | C+ | C- | 117.1 | 7.26 | 14.1 | 3.5 | 9.1 | 37.7 | **7.0** | 9.0 | 20.6 |
| First Bank and Trust of Fullerton | Fullerton | NE | **B+** | B | B | 93.4 | 5.72 | 3.6 | 1.1 | 0.3 | 13.4 | **10.0** | 14.6 | 19.0 |
| First Bank and Trust of Memphis | Memphis | TX | **B+** | B | B | 58.2 | -3.63 | 7.7 | 0.4 | 12.8 | 0.0 | **10.0** | 13.6 | 23.2 |
| First Bank Blue Earth | Blue Earth | MN | **A-** | B+ | B+ | 246.4 | 5.30 | 8.0 | 1.6 | 4.1 | 28.0 | **8.3** | 9.8 | 13.8 |
| First Bank Elk River | Elk River | MN | **C+** | C | C+ | 287.9 | 4.94 | 17.3 | 0.7 | 6.2 | 31.6 | **7.7** | 9.5 | 13.7 |
| First Bank Financial Centre | Oconomowoc | WI | **C+** | B- | B- | 1201.8 | 2.28 | 4.8 | 0.1 | 16.7 | 13.5 | **7.0** | 9.4 | 12.5 |
| First Bank Hampton | Hampton | IA | **A-** | B+ | A | 166.0 | 4.72 | 16.9 | 4.3 | 13.7 | 16.0 | **10.0** | 13.0 | 17.2 |
| First Bank Kansas | Salina | KS | **B+** | B | B- | 443.1 | 3.22 | 5.2 | 3.4 | 16.9 | 38.7 | **8.0** | 9.7 | 17.8 |
| First Bank of Alabama | Talladega | AL | **A-** | A- | A- | 578.2 | 8.02 | 9.4 | 1.9 | 12.9 | 22.4 | **10.0** | 12.9 | 19.1 |
| ▲ First Bank of Baldwin | Baldwin | WI | **B-** | C | C | 188.2 | 6.21 | 5.4 | 1.3 | 9.7 | 31.0 | **8.0** | 9.7 | 16.6 |
| First Bank of Bancroft | Bancroft | NE | **B-** | B- | B- | 23.4 | 7.06 | 6.0 | 1.7 | 3.9 | 22.0 | **10.0** | 16.6 | 31.9 |
| First Bank of Beloit | Beloit | KS | **B-** | C+ | C | 82.6 | 6.45 | 7.2 | 1.6 | 13.4 | 23.1 | **10.0** | 13.8 | 21.6 |
| First Bank of Berne | Berne | IN | **B+** | B | A- | 714.3 | 0.41 | 5.0 | 0.9 | 18.8 | 16.5 | **8.7** | 10.2 | 14.8 |

| Asset Quality Index | Adjusted Non-Performing Loans as a % of Total Loans | Adjusted Non-Performing Loans as a % of Capital | Net Charge-Offs Avg Loans | Profitability Index | Net Income ($Mil) | Return on Assets (R.O.A.) | Return on Equity (R.O.E.) | Net Interest Spread | Overhead Efficiency Ratio | Liquidity Index | Liquidity Ratio | Hot Money Ratio | Stability Index |
|---|---|---|---|---|---|---|---|---|---|---|---|---|---|
| **3.9** | 1.08 | 7.9 | 0.19 | **4.6** | 4.4 | 0.97 | 8.65 | 4.04 | 78.2 | **1.2** | 11.0 | 28.5 | **6.2** |
| **5.1** | 1.45 | 9.2 | 0.05 | **3.4** | 4.9 | 0.53 | 4.61 | 2.58 | 81.8 | **1.4** | 7.6 | 23.9 | **7.5** |
| **9.9** | 0.20 | 1.0 | 0.00 | **3.4** | 2.4 | 0.56 | 3.19 | 2.78 | 76.1 | **1.5** | 24.4 | 26.6 | **7.9** |
| **4.8** | 1.28 | 4.7 | 0.35 | **9.2** | 2717.0 | 1.70 | 12.94 | 3.50 | 52.8 | **4.9** | 24.2 | 2.8 | **10.0** |
| **8.8** | 0.08 | 2.2 | -0.04 | **4.5** | 4.8 | 0.84 | 7.07 | 3.74 | 73.0 | **1.1** | 22.8 | 33.4 | **7.9** |
| **6.2** | 0.46 | 3.0 | -0.01 | **6.1** | 8.5 | 1.37 | 10.80 | 2.84 | 56.3 | **0.3** | 4.3 | 70.9 | **10.0** |
| **5.2** | 0.50 | 4.0 | 0.00 | **4.4** | 1.0 | 0.95 | 10.30 | 3.78 | 74.9 | **1.4** | 9.7 | 23.9 | **6.3** |
| **8.9** | 0.13 | 0.9 | 0.01 | **4.3** | 17.7 | 0.89 | 9.58 | 2.50 | 66.7 | **4.5** | 13.2 | 4.9 | **7.5** |
| **6.5** | 0.89 | 3.4 | 2.33 | **10.0** | 10.2 | 7.16 | 42.55 | 14.28 | 44.0 | **0.9** | 24.6 | 34.9 | **9.3** |
| **5.6** | 0.65 | 3.1 | -0.02 | **3.7** | 3.2 | 0.61 | 4.67 | 3.74 | 81.8 | **2.3** | 31.6 | 22.5 | **8.5** |
| **6.9** | 0.53 | 3.2 | 0.28 | **3.5** | 1.3 | 0.64 | 3.54 | 4.00 | 79.0 | **4.4** | 28.7 | 9.1 | **7.6** |
| **3.5** | 0.94 | 6.7 | 0.15 | **4.3** | 4.5 | 0.64 | 6.04 | 4.06 | 78.3 | **1.2** | 7.4 | 26.6 | **6.7** |
| **9.5** | 0.16 | 0.2 | -0.07 | **7.6** | 39.5 | 4.41 | 34.27 | 2.50 | 38.9 | **4.3** | 58.4 | 18.1 | **8.3** |
| **5.7** | 2.13 | 7.6 | 0.36 | **2.0** | 35.5 | 0.72 | 8.72 | 2.66 | 110.3 | **5.5** | 32.3 | 7.8 | **7.1** |
| **8.7** | 0.33 | 1.4 | 0.67 | **8.8** | 26.7 | 2.22 | 21.32 | 4.41 | 53.5 | **5.4** | 28.5 | 6.0 | **10.0** |
| **4.5** | 1.65 | 7.9 | 0.12 | **7.4** | 0.6 | 1.76 | 14.85 | 4.96 | 63.5 | **1.6** | 23.9 | 24.9 | **7.0** |
| **6.8** | 1.72 | 5.4 | 0.03 | **7.5** | 13.9 | 1.52 | 10.38 | 4.27 | 62.6 | **3.3** | 21.7 | 13.3 | **9.9** |
| **8.4** | 0.76 | 2.9 | -0.10 | **6.6** | 7.3 | 1.32 | 12.12 | 3.68 | 61.7 | **4.5** | 21.9 | 6.2 | **8.1** |
| **5.0** | 0.96 | 2.5 | -0.01 | **5.6** | 0.5 | 2.15 | 15.24 | 5.82 | 46.8 | **0.9** | 20.7 | 30.0 | **6.1** |
| **6.5** | 1.22 | 6.0 | 0.21 | **3.3** | 1.7 | 0.61 | 5.34 | 4.31 | 87.4 | **4.2** | 33.5 | 11.9 | **6.3** |
| **9.0** | 0.00 | 0.0 | 0.03 | **3.3** | 1.4 | 0.55 | 6.01 | 3.17 | 75.6 | **0.8** | 22.4 | 47.5 | **4.7** |
| **10.0** | na | 0.0 | na | **8.5** | 65.5 | 1.64 | 19.39 | 2.33 | 24.4 | **8.8** | 109.7 | 0.1 | **7.0** |
| **3.2** | 3.51 | 11.4 | 0.32 | **7.0** | 12.7 | 1.66 | 8.28 | 4.74 | 74.0 | **4.4** | 20.9 | 6.6 | **8.4** |
| **8.7** | 0.01 | 1.3 | 0.01 | **4.2** | 6.0 | 1.04 | 10.85 | 3.34 | 75.8 | **4.3** | 57.8 | 17.9 | **6.5** |
| **8.4** | 0.31 | 1.2 | 0.06 | **6.1** | 1.4 | 1.64 | 15.80 | 4.23 | 70.4 | **5.5** | 59.3 | 10.6 | **6.5** |
| **6.8** | 0.24 | 1.0 | -0.01 | **5.0** | 3.8 | 1.00 | 10.69 | 4.13 | 68.4 | **4.1** | 18.0 | 8.1 | **5.9** |
| **3.6** | 1.05 | 7.2 | 0.25 | **7.2** | 5.5 | 1.38 | 15.61 | 4.41 | 59.0 | **1.6** | 18.3 | 24.2 | **6.6** |
| **9.0** | 0.04 | 0.2 | -0.01 | **4.5** | 1.3 | 0.89 | 6.27 | 3.58 | 70.6 | **2.3** | 32.9 | 21.1 | **8.5** |
| **8.4** | 0.33 | 1.5 | -0.01 | **5.9** | 70.1 | 1.13 | 10.03 | 3.38 | 65.8 | **5.5** | 33.1 | 7.8 | **9.6** |
| **5.9** | 0.65 | 6.8 | 0.04 | **4.2** | 5.1 | 0.91 | 9.18 | 3.51 | 75.1 | **1.2** | 17.1 | 20.1 | **7.7** |
| **5.9** | 0.75 | 2.8 | 0.04 | **8.1** | 95.4 | 1.58 | 11.05 | 4.08 | 56.2 | **3.3** | 16.4 | 11.4 | **9.9** |
| **4.0** | 1.28 | 9.4 | 0.12 | **4.6** | 15.2 | 0.82 | 7.29 | 3.33 | 59.3 | **1.2** | 9.3 | 24.0 | **8.6** |
| **8.1** | 0.05 | 0.3 | -0.19 | **9.7** | 1.8 | 2.43 | 19.79 | 5.53 | 56.1 | **4.2** | 26.1 | 8.3 | **8.0** |
| **4.1** | 1.45 | 11.2 | 0.08 | **9.9** | 9.9 | 2.25 | 20.03 | 5.09 | 69.0 | **2.5** | 18.8 | 16.6 | **8.2** |
| **7.0** | 0.25 | 1.8 | 0.09 | **6.9** | 10.6 | 1.37 | 13.75 | 3.99 | 63.9 | **4.3** | 20.0 | 7.6 | **7.0** |
| **5.0** | 1.05 | 5.9 | 0.01 | **6.9** | 25.2 | 1.28 | 11.44 | 3.81 | 60.9 | **2.1** | 8.5 | 15.6 | **8.5** |
| **4.8** | 1.20 | 7.9 | 0.18 | **8.0** | 14.0 | 1.42 | 11.56 | 4.75 | 63.3 | **2.8** | 14.8 | 12.3 | **8.5** |
| **5.3** | 0.53 | 1.1 | 0.40 | **6.3** | 13.2 | 1.18 | 5.63 | 4.48 | 66.3 | **3.4** | 38.0 | 20.6 | **8.6** |
| **8.2** | 0.12 | 0.2 | 0.04 | **4.9** | 1.6 | 1.09 | 6.90 | 2.45 | 62.6 | **6.7** | 62.5 | 5.7 | **6.0** |
| **3.5** | 4.89 | 21.2 | 0.03 | **8.4** | 11.5 | 1.98 | 13.05 | 4.34 | 56.4 | **3.4** | 12.0 | 11.6 | **10.0** |
| **5.0** | 4.04 | 10.9 | -0.04 | **8.5** | 3.1 | 2.03 | 14.97 | 4.58 | 59.1 | **3.7** | 24.3 | 11.4 | **9.2** |
| **4.3** | 1.16 | 10.3 | -0.04 | **8.0** | 19.1 | 1.97 | 19.93 | 4.46 | 63.4 | **0.9** | 6.2 | 31.5 | **8.0** |
| **5.0** | 3.78 | 8.8 | 0.01 | **3.1** | 0.4 | 0.63 | 5.84 | 3.25 | 82.0 | **4.1** | 32.5 | 11.8 | **5.7** |
| **8.5** | 0.00 | 1.3 | 0.33 | **3.6** | 0.5 | 0.81 | 6.23 | 3.98 | 82.6 | **3.0** | 27.4 | 15.9 | **6.3** |
| **8.1** | 0.20 | 1.7 | 0.01 | **8.0** | 28.8 | 1.53 | 13.29 | 3.94 | 55.6 | **3.7** | 14.1 | 10.8 | **10.0** |
| **7.4** | 0.00 | 0.0 | 0.00 | **0.9** | -0.3 | -0.18 | -1.92 | 4.76 | 105.4 | **0.9** | 22.4 | 36.0 | **4.4** |
| **1.1** | 2.62 | 41.8 | 0.64 | **1.5** | 0.0 | 0.01 | 0.12 | 3.59 | 94.3 | **2.1** | 14.1 | 18.5 | **4.1** |
| **5.9** | 1.13 | 3.1 | -0.03 | **3.6** | 0.9 | 0.81 | 9.60 | 2.70 | 71.2 | **0.7** | 18.0 | 52.0 | **4.7** |
| **7.3** | 0.00 | 0.4 | 0.02 | **4.9** | 0.9 | 1.03 | 7.03 | 3.37 | 60.0 | **1.6** | 20.2 | 18.1 | **8.1** |
| **8.7** | 0.00 | 0.0 | 0.00 | **4.9** | 0.6 | 1.11 | 8.28 | 3.38 | 68.5 | **2.3** | 43.8 | 32.7 | **8.4** |
| **7.6** | 0.28 | 1.8 | -0.23 | **6.7** | 3.8 | 1.65 | 16.02 | 3.41 | 53.2 | **2.6** | 15.0 | 16.2 | **8.4** |
| **7.2** | 0.47 | 2.4 | 0.01 | **3.2** | 2.1 | 0.73 | 7.23 | 3.22 | 81.5 | **3.5** | 22.5 | 10.9 | **5.6** |
| **2.9** | 1.63 | 12.3 | 0.07 | **4.7** | 12.4 | 1.03 | 11.06 | 3.67 | 76.1 | **1.3** | 7.0 | 22.1 | **7.4** |
| **7.2** | 0.92 | 2.5 | 0.63 | **7.2** | 2.5 | 1.55 | 12.16 | 4.03 | 50.3 | **3.0** | 17.8 | 14.2 | **9.3** |
| **7.4** | 0.02 | 3.7 | 0.08 | **7.5** | 7.6 | 1.76 | 18.71 | 3.68 | 66.1 | **4.9** | 37.4 | 9.7 | **7.0** |
| **7.0** | 1.85 | 6.0 | 0.23 | **8.0** | 8.5 | 1.56 | 11.37 | 4.47 | 53.5 | **1.4** | 14.1 | 25.6 | **9.2** |
| **4.2** | 2.11 | 9.1 | -0.01 | **4.8** | 2.2 | 1.18 | 11.40 | 3.93 | 73.5 | **5.4** | 31.0 | 3.6 | **6.6** |
| **6.6** | 1.09 | 8.9 | -0.08 | **5.2** | 0.2 | 1.03 | 5.99 | 3.83 | 67.1 | **5.5** | 51.6 | 7.0 | **5.0** |
| **8.8** | 0.15 | 0.6 | 0.00 | **3.9** | 0.6 | 0.75 | 5.62 | 3.85 | 76.2 | **4.4** | 17.3 | 6.6 | **6.7** |
| **5.8** | 0.58 | 4.0 | 0.04 | **8.9** | 15.2 | 2.15 | 21.02 | 3.83 | 49.5 | **4.8** | 18.5 | 3.5 | **8.7** |

| | | | | | | | | Asset Mix (As a % of Total Assets) | | | | | | |
|---|---|---|---|---|---|---|---|---|---|---|---|---|---|---|
| Name | City | State | Rating | 2018 Rating | 2017 Rating | Total Assets ($Mil) | One Year Asset Growth | Commercial Loans | Consumer Loans | Mortgage Loans | Securities | Capitalization Index | Leverage Ratio | Risk-Based Capital Ratio |
| First Bank of Boaz | Boaz | AL | **A+** | A+ | A+ | 232.9 | 2.04 | 4.9 | 2.2 | 6.0 | 70.6 | **10.0** | 17.9 | 34.6 |
| First Bank of Celeste | Celeste | TX | **C+** | C | C+ | 52.9 | 7.01 | 6.4 | 7.1 | 4.9 | 28.8 | **5.9** | 7.9 | 19.7 |
| First Bank of Coastal Georgia | Pembroke | GA | **B-** | B | B | 129.1 | 5.12 | 2.3 | 0.6 | 9.3 | 65.3 | **10.0** | 13.6 | 33.6 |
| First Bank of Greenwich | Cos Cob | CT | **B-** | B- | B- | 385.2 | 6.93 | 9.1 | 0.2 | 35.0 | 3.9 | **7.9** | 9.6 | 13.4 |
| First Bank of Highland Park | Highland Park | IL | **C+** | C+ | C | 1863.9 | 7.86 | 42.5 | 0.1 | 2.7 | 14.0 | **5.0** | 9.8 | 11.0 |
| First Bank of Linden | Linden | AL | **B** | B+ | B+ | 80.5 | 3.93 | 8.1 | 6.9 | 4.6 | 46.0 | **10.0** | 14.4 | 27.2 |
| First Bank of Manhattan | Manhattan | IL | **B-** | B | B- | 172.7 | 7.36 | 1.3 | 2.2 | 18.7 | 25.1 | **8.3** | 9.9 | 22.3 |
| First Bank of Muleshoe | Muleshoe | TX | **B-** | B- | C+ | 90.7 | -5.43 | 4.4 | 1.2 | 0.2 | 70.7 | **10.0** | 15.6 | 62.4 |
| ▲ First Bank of Ohio | Tiffin | OH | **B+** | B+ | A- | 205.2 | 13.61 | 0.0 | 68.6 | 0.0 | 22.4 | **10.0** | 35.2 | 45.5 |
| First Bank of Okarche | Okarche | OK | **A** | A- | A | 108.1 | 5.30 | 7.9 | 1.9 | 1.3 | 37.0 | **10.0** | 11.4 | 26.9 |
| First Bank of Owasso | Owasso | OK | **A-** | A- | A- | 408.5 | 3.77 | 2.4 | 0.4 | 11.2 | 2.7 | **8.9** | 11.3 | 14.1 |
| First Bank of Pike | Molena | GA | **C-** | C- | C- | 52.0 | 6.56 | 6.8 | 9.8 | 25.1 | 22.2 | **6.4** | 8.4 | 15.3 |
| ▲ First Bank of the Lake | Osage Beach | MO | **C** | C | C | 114.6 | 40.21 | 22.6 | 0.6 | 5.6 | 18.6 | **7.2** | 9.2 | 23.5 |
| ▲ First Bank of the Palm Beaches | West Palm Beach | FL | **B-** | C+ | C- | 191.7 | 5.51 | 1.8 | 0.3 | 25.2 | 0.2 | **7.1** | 9.1 | 13.2 |
| First Bank of Thomas | Thomas | OK | **B+** | B+ | B+ | 44.6 | -4.73 | 2.5 | 0.9 | 10.4 | 23.4 | **10.0** | 15.8 | 31.7 |
| First Bank of Utica | Utica | NE | **C+** | C+ | C+ | 67.7 | 0.16 | 9.9 | 4.0 | 11.2 | 2.3 | **10.0** | 12.5 | 15.9 |
| First Bank Richmond | Richmond | IN | **B-** | C+ | C+ | 983.4 | 16.38 | 8.0 | 1.4 | 13.3 | 22.2 | **10.0** | 14.6 | 19.5 |
| First Bank, Upper Michigan | Gladstone | MI | **D+** | D | D+ | 468.9 | -0.97 | 13.4 | 9.8 | 17.2 | 11.8 | **9.4** | 10.9 | 14.5 |
| First Bankers Trust Co., N.A. | Quincy | IL | **B-** | C+ | B- | 921.6 | 0.45 | 7.3 | 4.8 | 7.0 | 37.5 | **8.1** | 9.7 | 16.2 |
| First Bethany Bank & Trust | Bethany | OK | **B** | B | B | 220.5 | 3.29 | 5.3 | 0.5 | 12.1 | 38.9 | **8.1** | 9.7 | 16.5 |
| First Business Bank | Madison | WI | **B-** | C+ | C+ | 2083.9 | 6.41 | 24.4 | 0.3 | 1.8 | 10.1 | **6.1** | 10.2 | 11.8 |
| First Cahawba Bank | Selma | AL | **B** | B | B | 130.0 | 14.97 | 17.2 | 4.3 | 17.5 | 10.3 | **10.0** | 11.2 | 16.2 |
| First Capital Bank | Laurinburg | NC | **C-** | C+ | C+ | 136.6 | 53.74 | 3.3 | 1.5 | 24.8 | 9.0 | **10.0** | 19.1 | 24.3 |
| First Capital Bank | Germantown | TN | **B-** | B- | B- | 357.7 | 14.06 | 17.8 | 0.8 | 8.8 | 1.4 | **6.1** | 10.5 | 11.8 |
| ▲ First Capital Bank | Quanah | TX | **C** | C- | C- | 65.1 | 9.52 | 16.8 | 7.0 | 14.8 | 0.0 | **6.8** | 8.9 | 12.4 |
| First Carolina Bank | Rocky Mount | NC | **B** | C+ | C | 657.8 | 30.42 | 6.7 | 0.3 | 8.8 | 30.6 | **10.0** | 14.2 | 18.2 |
| First Central Bank | Cambridge | NE | **C-** | C | C+ | 111.3 | 6.22 | 14.0 | 3.8 | 2.9 | 10.5 | **7.7** | 10.3 | 13.1 |
| First Central Bank McCook | McCook | NE | **C-** | C- | C- | 125.8 | 4.63 | 29.6 | 2.4 | 3.6 | 7.7 | **7.1** | 10.4 | 12.6 |
| First Central National Bank of Saint Paris | Saint Paris | OH | **B** | B | B | 95.6 | 1.36 | 3.1 | 2.2 | 13.6 | 24.6 | **10.0** | 17.8 | 29.3 |
| First Central Savings Bank | Glen Cove | NY | **D+** | D+ | C- | 637.1 | 9.07 | 13.0 | 0.0 | 13.3 | 6.9 | **5.6** | 8.7 | 11.5 |
| First Central State Bank | De Witt | IA | **A-** | A- | B+ | 585.1 | 38.07 | 10.4 | 2.3 | 12.0 | 19.8 | **10.0** | 11.7 | 15.4 |
| First Century Bank | Tazewell | TN | **B+** | B+ | B- | 419.7 | 7.68 | 7.4 | 1.4 | 28.2 | 1.6 | **7.5** | 9.3 | 13.2 |
| First Century Bank, N.A. | Gainesville | GA | **B** | B | B | 467.5 | 233.06 | 0.5 | 0.1 | 1.7 | 9.5 | **10.0** | 14.3 | 69.2 |
| ▲ First Chatham Bank | Savannah | GA | **C-** | D- | E- | 378.0 | 4.03 | 7.9 | 0.6 | 7.9 | 7.1 | **6.8** | 8.8 | 13.0 |
| ▼ First Choice Bank | Cerritos | CA | **B+** | B+ | A- | 1690.4 | 4.19 | 14.3 | 0.0 | 11.5 | 1.9 | **8.8** | 12.0 | 14.0 |
| First Choice Bank | Pontotoc | MS | **A-** | B+ | B | 309.0 | 4.35 | 8.6 | 6.3 | 25.2 | 24.4 | **10.0** | 12.9 | 20.5 |
| First Citizens Bank | Luverne | AL | **A-** | A- | A- | 245.9 | 1.00 | 8.8 | 5.1 | 14.4 | 27.7 | **10.0** | 14.0 | 21.4 |
| First Citizens Bank | Mason City | IA | **A-** | A- | A- | 1291.8 | 3.00 | 12.7 | 1.1 | 9.4 | 24.0 | **10.0** | 12.4 | 15.6 |
| First Citizens Bank of Butte | Butte | MT | **B-** | B- | B- | 70.4 | 1.00 | 9.5 | 5.1 | 19.8 | 14.5 | **9.4** | 10.6 | 22.1 |
| ▼ First Citizens Bank of Polson, N.A. | Polson | MT | **E+** | E+ | E- | 16.9 | -8.80 | 4.7 | 3.9 | 15.7 | 9.1 | **2.7** | 4.9 | 10.9 |
| First Citizens Community Bank | Mansfield | PA | **B** | B | B | 1465.4 | 2.51 | 4.0 | 0.7 | 19.3 | 16.4 | **7.4** | 9.2 | 13.3 |
| First Citizens National Bank | Dyersburg | TN | **B+** | B+ | B+ | 1824.2 | 7.10 | 4.4 | 1.5 | 10.6 | 34.4 | **8.6** | 10.1 | 16.2 |
| First Citizens National Bank of Upper Sand | Upper Sandusky | OH | **B-** | B- | B- | 297.9 | 4.81 | 5.6 | 1.1 | 18.2 | 19.0 | **10.0** | 14.0 | 22.5 |
| First Citizens State Bank | Whitewater | WI | **A-** | A- | B+ | 327.2 | 2.76 | 5.3 | 0.8 | 21.4 | 22.4 | **10.0** | 20.1 | 30.1 |
| First Citrus Bank | Tampa | FL | **B-** | C+ | C- | 418.3 | 3.92 | 7.9 | 0.1 | 8.1 | 0.0 | **6.5** | 9.9 | 12.2 |
| First City Bank | Columbus | OH | **C+** | C+ | C+ | 64.6 | -4.87 | 2.1 | 0.2 | 21.8 | 3.1 | **10.0** | 11.6 | 16.4 |
| First City Bank of Florida | Fort Walton Beach | FL | **E-** | E- | E- | 141.4 | -10.47 | 5.4 | 0.7 | 15.6 | 5.8 | **0.0** | 2.4 | 4.7 |
| ▲ First Colony Bank of Florida | Maitland | FL | **B** | B- | B+ | 231.3 | 6.66 | 13.3 | 0.2 | 0.8 | 13.2 | **7.9** | 9.8 | 13.2 |
| First Colorado National Bank | Paonia | CO | **B** | C+ | B | 77.7 | 12.20 | 0.8 | 0.2 | 1.6 | 0.0 | **10.0** | 23.8 | 83.0 |
| ▲ First Columbia Bank & Trust Co. | Bloomsburg | PA | **A-** | B+ | A- | 738.4 | 2.26 | 2.9 | 0.8 | 31.7 | 26.7 | **10.0** | 11.8 | 21.6 |
| First Command Bank | Fort Worth | TX | **A-** | B+ | B | 787.5 | 1.00 | 10.7 | 25.5 | 0.0 | 43.8 | **5.3** | 7.3 | 12.7 |
| ▲ First Commerce Bank | Marysville | KS | **B+** | B- | B+ | 98.7 | -2.23 | 10.6 | 5.2 | 30.9 | 7.0 | **10.0** | 11.7 | 18.9 |
| ▲ First Commerce Bank | Lakewood | NJ | **C+** | C- | C+ | 1007.5 | 4.70 | 5.4 | 0.0 | 23.2 | 12.0 | **10.0** | 14.1 | 19.1 |
| First Commerce Bank | Lewisburg | TN | **B** | B | B+ | 447.5 | 8.72 | 8.2 | 2.9 | 14.5 | 11.6 | **6.9** | 8.9 | 12.9 |
| First Commercial Bank | Jackson | MS | **B** | B | B | 422.3 | 5.16 | 19.2 | 1.3 | 8.5 | 5.1 | **10.0** | 12.7 | 15.2 |
| First Commercial Bank (USA) | Alhambra | CA | **A-** | B+ | A- | 692.1 | 18.30 | 8.0 | 0.0 | 11.2 | 5.1 | **10.0** | 20.4 | 25.9 |
| ▲ First Commercial Bank, N.A. | Seguin | TX | **B** | B | B- | 360.6 | 9.83 | 5.1 | 1.7 | 12.4 | 16.1 | **7.3** | 9.2 | 15.1 |
| First Commonwealth Bank | Indiana | PA | **B+** | B+ | B | 8288.4 | 6.10 | 13.1 | 8.4 | 13.3 | 15.0 | **8.0** | 9.7 | 13.7 |
| First Community Bank | Batesville | AR | **B-** | B- | B- | 1521.1 | 3.37 | 13.1 | 3.9 | 19.8 | 14.8 | **6.9** | 9.5 | 12.4 |
| First Community Bank | Newell | IA | **B** | B- | C+ | 97.6 | 2.64 | 5.5 | 2.3 | 5.4 | 18.7 | **8.0** | 9.7 | 14.1 |

| Asset Quality Index | Adjusted Non-Performing Loans as a % of Total Loans | Adjusted Non-Performing Loans as a % of Capital | Net Charge-Offs Avg Loans | Profitability Index | Net Income ($Mil) | Return on Assets (R.O.A.) | Return on Equity (R.O.E.) | Net Interest Spread | Overhead Efficiency Ratio | Liquidity Index | Liquidity Ratio | Hot Money Ratio | Stability Index |
|---|---|---|---|---|---|---|---|---|---|---|---|---|---|
| **9.6** | 0.05 | 0.2 | 0.01 | **7.8** | 3.6 | 1.52 | 8.30 | 3.58 | 43.4 | **3.9** | 65.9 | 23.3 | **9.5** |
| **8.5** | 0.00 | 0.0 | 0.02 | **4.2** | 0.5 | 1.01 | 12.68 | 3.34 | 75.2 | **5.4** | 59.1 | 11.4 | **4.7** |
| **9.7** | 0.84 | 1.6 | -0.65 | **3.3** | 0.9 | 0.71 | 5.05 | 2.91 | 86.1 | **4.6** | 23.6 | 5.5 | **6.5** |
| **5.2** | 0.94 | 6.1 | 0.00 | **3.2** | 1.6 | 0.41 | 4.17 | 2.85 | 80.4 | **0.6** | 8.3 | 32.2 | **5.8** |
| **5.6** | 1.95 | 8.7 | 0.16 | **3.2** | 9.0 | 0.51 | 5.06 | 2.44 | 67.0 | **0.7** | 13.0 | 29.7 | **8.2** |
| **8.1** | 1.31 | 3.2 | 0.65 | **3.9** | 0.6 | 0.69 | 4.58 | 3.80 | 70.8 | **2.7** | 60.5 | 34.7 | **7.5** |
| **6.0** | 2.49 | 8.7 | 0.05 | **3.4** | 1.3 | 0.77 | 7.50 | 3.44 | 79.3 | **5.0** | 33.3 | 6.8 | **6.9** |
| **9.8** | 0.10 | 0.1 | 0.08 | **3.5** | 0.6 | 0.65 | 4.26 | 3.01 | 76.9 | **7.6** | 92.0 | 3.4 | **7.0** |
| **5.6** | 0.11 | 0.3 | 0.64 | **7.8** | 3.2 | 1.63 | 4.49 | 4.84 | 43.1 | **1.4** | 38.3 | 60.4 | **7.1** |
| **8.6** | 0.74 | 2.2 | 0.15 | **8.8** | 2.3 | 2.10 | 18.19 | 3.64 | 40.8 | **4.8** | 64.6 | 16.3 | **9.0** |
| **7.2** | 0.00 | 0.0 | 0.05 | **9.5** | 9.4 | 2.20 | 20.72 | 3.98 | 45.2 | **0.8** | 7.4 | 19.6 | **9.1** |
| **5.6** | 0.02 | 3.3 | 0.10 | **3.5** | 0.3 | 0.52 | 6.12 | 5.45 | 85.1 | **3.4** | 32.5 | 15.4 | **3.4** |
| **5.7** | 1.15 | 3.4 | 0.65 | **6.7** | 1.6 | 1.59 | 17.22 | 3.72 | 62.5 | **2.2** | 46.5 | 56.5 | **5.9** |
| **7.5** | 0.04 | 0.1 | 0.00 | **4.7** | 1.8 | 0.96 | 11.03 | 4.14 | 70.1 | **2.6** | 23.9 | 17.1 | **4.6** |
| **7.8** | 1.16 | 3.5 | 0.01 | **6.3** | 0.7 | 1.45 | 9.64 | 3.59 | 61.2 | **3.8** | 48.3 | 17.6 | **8.7** |
| **3.9** | 1.59 | 8.4 | 0.01 | **4.2** | 0.5 | 0.75 | 5.89 | 4.08 | 73.1 | **0.9** | 6.6 | 30.6 | **6.8** |
| **7.4** | 0.18 | 2.6 | 0.16 | **1.0** | -7.1 | -0.75 | -6.45 | 3.41 | 122.3 | **1.5** | 17.1 | 16.9 | **7.0** |
| **1.6** | 3.78 | 13.6 | 0.15 | **8.3** | 8.6 | 1.86 | 14.26 | 4.40 | 61.6 | **2.0** | 18.7 | 18.4 | **8.6** |
| **4.1** | 1.55 | 6.6 | 0.70 | **4.3** | 7.9 | 0.87 | 8.62 | 3.11 | 63.0 | **1.9** | 8.2 | 14.3 | **6.5** |
| **8.0** | 0.47 | 2.3 | 0.00 | **4.7** | 2.4 | 1.09 | 11.49 | 3.17 | 66.0 | **2.5** | 24.0 | 15.0 | **6.6** |
| **4.2** | 1.21 | 5.6 | 0.17 | **6.0** | 28.2 | 1.38 | 13.12 | 3.79 | 65.4 | **4.1** | 13.0 | 8.2 | **9.2** |
| **8.4** | 0.22 | 1.2 | 0.01 | **3.9** | 0.8 | 0.68 | 5.87 | 4.43 | 77.7 | **3.8** | 21.4 | 10.6 | **6.6** |
| **7.3** | 1.29 | 3.8 | 0.04 | **0.2** | -1.0 | -0.92 | -4.53 | 4.17 | 113.3 | **1.0** | 18.2 | 33.1 | **6.3** |
| **7.3** | 0.13 | 0.6 | 0.00 | **4.8** | 3.0 | 0.92 | 8.51 | 2.94 | 56.8 | **0.6** | 14.4 | 59.5 | **5.7** |
| **4.7** | 0.65 | 5.3 | 0.42 | **5.0** | 0.6 | 0.90 | 10.05 | 5.38 | 73.9 | **0.8** | 17.6 | 35.2 | **4.3** |
| **7.8** | 0.00 | 0.0 | -0.01 | **4.5** | 5.8 | 1.03 | 9.12 | 2.96 | 52.9 | **1.7** | 37.4 | 35.6 | **7.1** |
| **0.7** | 6.05 | 44.1 | 0.27 | **6.1** | 1.1 | 0.97 | 9.52 | 3.99 | 67.5 | **0.8** | 16.5 | 31.7 | **5.9** |
| **0.3** | 6.60 | 88.3 | 0.49 | **7.4** | 1.6 | 1.29 | 12.44 | 4.77 | 53.5 | **0.6** | 15.8 | 46.3 | **5.7** |
| **8.9** | 0.12 | 0.8 | 0.00 | **3.9** | 0.7 | 0.77 | 4.40 | 3.11 | 71.2 | **4.6** | 47.7 | 13.3 | **7.7** |
| **2.1** | 2.99 | 13.2 | 0.46 | **2.4** | 2.7 | 0.44 | 4.71 | 3.35 | 77.4 | **0.8** | 18.3 | 37.8 | **3.5** |
| **8.1** | 0.75 | 2.6 | 0.08 | **6.1** | 6.6 | 1.18 | 10.12 | 3.29 | 57.3 | **3.2** | 26.7 | 13.8 | **8.1** |
| **8.4** | 0.20 | 1.1 | 0.00 | **7.2** | 5.5 | 1.37 | 13.89 | 4.14 | 60.8 | **1.9** | 11.7 | 13.0 | **6.0** |
| **10.0** | 0.59 | 0.4 | 1.71 | **8.0** | 3.6 | 1.90 | 17.68 | 3.06 | 55.8 | **3.7** | 88.8 | 41.0 | **3.9** |
| **4.8** | 2.93 | 9.8 | 0.06 | **3.2** | 2.3 | 0.63 | 6.14 | 4.40 | 85.5 | **3.9** | 23.1 | 10.2 | **4.9** |
| **5.0** | 0.84 | 3.3 | 0.03 | **9.5** | 28.8 | 1.79 | 10.81 | 5.29 | 49.2 | **2.7** | 13.5 | 8.5 | **9.8** |
| **8.3** | 0.34 | 1.7 | 0.14 | **5.7** | 3.6 | 1.15 | 9.01 | 3.96 | 64.4 | **1.6** | 20.4 | 24.8 | **7.6** |
| **7.1** | 1.11 | 3.9 | 0.09 | **7.5** | 3.7 | 1.49 | 10.75 | 4.53 | 60.6 | **1.7** | 19.5 | 22.7 | **8.0** |
| **7.7** | 0.27 | 1.4 | 0.05 | **6.7** | 20.3 | 1.61 | 12.73 | 3.37 | 54.4 | **2.6** | 13.8 | 16.2 | **10.0** |
| **5.3** | 3.67 | 9.4 | 0.00 | **4.3** | 0.7 | 0.99 | 9.06 | 4.21 | 77.6 | **4.9** | 32.7 | 7.6 | **6.3** |
| **5.6** | 0.06 | 7.5 | 0.37 | **0.0** | -1.2 | -6.42 | -87.18 | 4.23 | 224.8 | **5.9** | 40.3 | 0.6 | **0.4** |
| **4.7** | 1.69 | 8.4 | 0.06 | **6.6** | 20.5 | 1.41 | 13.85 | 3.75 | 55.8 | **3.1** | 6.0 | 11.6 | **9.6** |
| **8.4** | 0.28 | 1.3 | 0.03 | **5.3** | 19.1 | 1.11 | 9.50 | 3.51 | 67.5 | **2.2** | 25.8 | 24.7 | **9.7** |
| **6.1** | 2.36 | 5.7 | -0.01 | **3.5** | 2.1 | 0.71 | 5.00 | 3.90 | 78.6 | **4.1** | 23.0 | 8.8 | **7.0** |
| **9.2** | 0.00 | 0.0 | 0.11 | **6.0** | 4.1 | 1.32 | 6.66 | 3.59 | 60.6 | **4.0** | 41.5 | 15.2 | **8.5** |
| **5.6** | 0.62 | 3.6 | 0.09 | **5.6** | 4.2 | 1.06 | 11.00 | 3.96 | 65.4 | **2.0** | 18.5 | 12.6 | **5.5** |
| **7.6** | 0.00 | 0.0 | 0.00 | **3.1** | 0.3 | 0.51 | 4.50 | 3.59 | 87.7 | **1.5** | 11.9 | 23.3 | **6.6** |
| **0.3** | 16.77 | 175.6 | 0.82 | **0.4** | -0.7 | -0.48 | -19.35 | 4.18 | 113.0 | **4.9** | 20.1 | 3.6 | **0.9** |
| **6.0** | 0.74 | 2.5 | 0.49 | **9.0** | 4.8 | 2.14 | 21.54 | 4.21 | 45.7 | **2.3** | 33.2 | 23.6 | **8.1** |
| **8.1** | 0.00 | 0.0 | 0.48 | **3.5** | 6.4 | -0.47 | -2.34 | 4.47 | 102.1 | **6.6** | 115.2 | 12.3 | **9.1** |
| **6.7** | 1.04 | 4.1 | 0.03 | **5.4** | 8.7 | 1.19 | 9.43 | 3.24 | 60.6 | **3.4** | 9.4 | 11.4 | **8.6** |
| **7.0** | 0.28 | 1.1 | 0.38 | **9.1** | 17.3 | 2.25 | 27.53 | 3.50 | 58.1 | **7.1** | 57.2 | 1.7 | **6.1** |
| **6.9** | 0.52 | 3.0 | -0.04 | **7.5** | 1.8 | 1.75 | 14.48 | 3.99 | 59.3 | **2.7** | 21.3 | 16.0 | **7.9** |
| **2.8** | 2.01 | 9.3 | 0.22 | **5.6** | 9.5 | 0.96 | 6.87 | 3.40 | 62.7 | **1.2** | 21.8 | 36.2 | **10.0** |
| **8.4** | 0.10 | 0.7 | 0.01 | **6.9** | 5.6 | 1.30 | 14.77 | 3.78 | 53.3 | **0.9** | 18.2 | 33.9 | **6.3** |
| **8.2** | 0.18 | 1.1 | 0.03 | **4.9** | 4.4 | 1.11 | 8.39 | 3.57 | 68.5 | **0.8** | 17.6 | 24.7 | **7.9** |
| **7.2** | 0.00 | 0.0 | 0.00 | **7.9** | 7.7 | 1.25 | 5.96 | 3.47 | 48.2 | **0.7** | 15.7 | 47.9 | **9.1** |
| **5.8** | 0.98 | 5.4 | -0.05 | **5.5** | 4.8 | 1.38 | 14.12 | 4.38 | 67.7 | **5.6** | 34.9 | 3.7 | **6.1** |
| **5.9** | 0.51 | 2.6 | 0.18 | **6.9** | 111.7 | 1.39 | 10.68 | 3.79 | 57.3 | **4.3** | 6.5 | 5.6 | **9.8** |
| **5.0** | 1.83 | 10.5 | 0.25 | **5.1** | 14.5 | 0.97 | 10.47 | 3.62 | 67.5 | **0.9** | 16.0 | 34.8 | **7.5** |
| **6.0** | 0.46 | 1.5 | 0.02 | **5.3** | 1.3 | 1.29 | 10.34 | 3.39 | 63.4 | **3.5** | 30.2 | 14.1 | **7.1** |

| Name | City | State | Rating | 2018 Rating | 2017 Rating | Total Assets ($Mil) | One Year Asset Growth | Asset Mix (As a % of Total Assets) | | | | Capital-ization Index | Lever-age Ratio | Risk-Based Capital Ratio |
|---|---|---|---|---|---|---|---|---|---|---|---|---|---|---|
| | | | | | | | | Comm-ercial Loans | Cons-umer Loans | Mort-gage Loans | Secur-ities | | | |
| First Community Bank | Harbor Springs | MI | **B+** | B | B+ | 312.3 | 0.01 | 12.0 | 0.6 | 9.4 | 8.3 | **7.6** | 9.9 | 13.0 |
| First Community Bank | Lester Prairie | MN | **B-** | B- | C+ | 63.1 | 2.30 | 4.3 | 1.5 | 10.1 | 25.4 | **9.5** | 10.7 | 18.3 |
| First Community Bank | Glasgow | MT | **B** | B- | C+ | 302.4 | 4.95 | 4.6 | 1.5 | 9.4 | 23.4 | **10.0** | 11.5 | 16.8 |
| First Community Bank | Beemer | NE | **B-** | C+ | B- | 146.7 | -1.65 | 8.0 | 1.6 | 6.1 | 9.0 | **9.2** | 10.5 | 14.8 |
| First Community Bank | Lexington | SC | **B+** | B+ | B- | 1170.1 | 7.21 | 3.9 | 0.9 | 9.5 | 24.5 | **8.5** | 10.0 | 14.3 |
| First Community Bank | Corpus Christi | TX | **A-** | B+ | B | 428.9 | 1.43 | 12.8 | 2.8 | 16.4 | 16.8 | **10.0** | 12.1 | 17.7 |
| First Community Bank | San Benito | TX | **B** | B | B | 489.2 | 12.66 | 12.6 | 1.1 | 8.5 | 19.8 | **6.7** | 8.7 | 13.5 |
| First Community Bank | Bluefield | VA | **B** | B | B | 2797.0 | 25.05 | 5.0 | 3.9 | 28.2 | 6.1 | **8.5** | 12.6 | 13.8 |
| ▲ First Community Bank | Milton | WI | **A-** | B+ | B+ | 112.1 | 9.04 | 4.3 | 1.2 | 15.4 | 26.8 | **7.1** | 9.9 | 12.6 |
| First Community Bank and Trust | Beecher | IL | **A-** | B+ | B- | 151.4 | 4.40 | 12.3 | 2.1 | 8.3 | 21.4 | **10.0** | 11.9 | 19.2 |
| First Community Bank of Central Alabama | Wetumpka | AL | **B+** | B+ | B+ | 394.6 | 5.64 | 8.3 | 5.2 | 16.4 | 23.5 | **5.7** | 8.1 | 11.6 |
| First Community Bank of Cullman | Cullman | AL | **C+** | C | C+ | 128.8 | 10.13 | 4.4 | 2.6 | 35.3 | 3.5 | **6.3** | 8.3 | 12.4 |
| First Community Bank of East Tennessee | Rogersville | TN | **B** | B- | B- | 162.1 | -6.64 | 7.2 | 2.4 | 24.1 | 12.0 | **10.0** | 12.9 | 18.4 |
| First Community Bank of Hillsboro | Hillsboro | IL | **B** | C+ | B- | 105.5 | 6.10 | 8.8 | 3.2 | 16.9 | 29.3 | **7.5** | 9.3 | 17.4 |
| First Community Bank of Moultrie County | Sullivan | IL | **B** | C+ | C+ | 87.8 | 2.92 | 4.9 | 5.8 | 27.2 | 8.5 | **8.6** | 10.0 | 18.6 |
| First Community Bank of Tennessee | Shelbyville | TN | **B+** | B+ | A- | 570.9 | 20.24 | 5.3 | 0.9 | 36.8 | 12.0 | **8.9** | 11.7 | 14.0 |
| First Community Bank of the Heartland, Inc | Clinton | KY | **B-** | C+ | B- | 262.6 | 11.14 | 3.4 | 3.4 | 12.4 | 21.8 | **5.9** | 7.9 | 12.0 |
| First Community Bank of the Ozarks | Branson | MO | **B+** | B+ | B+ | 127.0 | 18.79 | 3.0 | 1.7 | 21.3 | 12.8 | **9.8** | 10.8 | 15.7 |
| First Community Bank, Xenia-Flora | Xenia | IL | **B** | B- | B | 41.0 | -4.90 | 4.5 | 6.1 | 23.6 | 27.5 | **10.0** | 12.4 | 22.7 |
| ▲ First Community National Bank | Cuba | MO | **C-** | D- | D- | 126.4 | -0.61 | 2.7 | 1.9 | 21.6 | 22.5 | **7.6** | 9.4 | 15.9 |
| First Community Trust, N.A. | Dubuque | IA | **U** | U | U | 12.5 | 57.59 | 0.0 | 0.0 | 0.0 | 39.2 | **10.0** | 89.2 | 59.6 |
| First County Bank | Stamford | CT | **C+** | C+ | C | 1755.4 | 4.81 | 3.8 | 1.0 | 49.6 | 13.9 | **7.7** | 9.5 | 15.3 |
| First Credit Bank | Los Angeles | CA | **B-** | C | C+ | 434.6 | -9.05 | 1.2 | 0.0 | 9.6 | 5.2 | **10.0** | 44.6 | 55.6 |
| First Dakota National Bank | Yankton | SD | **B** | B | B | 1776.9 | 6.33 | 8.1 | 2.0 | 6.8 | 11.8 | **7.2** | 10.2 | 12.6 |
| First Eagle Bank | Chicago | IL | **A** | A | A | 538.1 | 6.21 | 1.6 | 0.0 | 19.4 | 26.7 | **10.0** | 17.1 | 24.4 |
| ▲ First Electronic Bank | Salt Lake City | UT | **A-** | B | B | 52.6 | 38.62 | 16.8 | 18.1 | 0.0 | 0.1 | **10.0** | 25.4 | 74.0 |
| ▲ First Enterprise Bank | Oklahoma City | OK | **B-** | C- | C- | 160.5 | 0.27 | 15.2 | 0.7 | 17.1 | 0.0 | **10.0** | 13.2 | 17.0 |
| First Exchange Bank | White Hall | WV | **C-** | C- | C- | 301.0 | 11.87 | 7.6 | 3.7 | 41.2 | 5.9 | **7.9** | 9.6 | 14.1 |
| ▲ First FarmBank | Greeley | CO | **C+** | C- | C | 257.1 | 4.66 | 5.6 | 0.4 | 9.9 | 17.4 | **7.0** | 9.0 | 12.6 |
| First Farmers & Merchants Bank | Cannon Falls | MN | **B+** | A- | A- | 333.8 | 3.15 | 10.9 | 2.4 | 9.0 | 12.3 | **10.0** | 13.6 | 17.7 |
| ▼ First Farmers & Merchants National Bank | Fairmont | MN | **B** | B+ | B+ | 104.1 | -0.89 | 19.0 | 4.1 | 15.5 | 8.8 | **10.0** | 14.6 | 16.6 |
| First Farmers & Merchants National Bank | Luverne | MN | **B** | B+ | A- | 188.9 | 4.40 | 12.2 | 1.4 | 2.6 | 4.6 | **10.0** | 16.6 | 17.3 |
| ▼ First Farmers & Merchants State Bank | Brownsdale | MN | **B** | B+ | A- | 76.4 | -0.29 | 9.4 | 0.5 | 3.9 | 17.6 | **10.0** | 18.2 | 22.3 |
| First Farmers & Merchants State Bank | Grand Meadow | MN | **B** | B+ | A- | 73.2 | 7.09 | 7.0 | 0.3 | 5.4 | 6.8 | **9.0** | 10.6 | 14.2 |
| First Farmers and Commercial Bank | Pikeville | TN | **B-** | C+ | B | 136.7 | 18.12 | 13.8 | 3.5 | 13.9 | 17.0 | **9.9** | 10.9 | 14.9 |
| First Farmers and Merchants Bank | Columbia | TN | **B+** | B | B- | 1401.8 | 2.69 | 8.6 | 1.0 | 22.2 | 24.8 | **8.2** | 9.8 | 14.7 |
| First Farmers Bank & Trust | Converse | IN | **B-** | B- | B- | 1907.9 | 9.44 | 15.4 | 0.6 | 3.7 | 19.3 | **8.0** | 10.0 | 13.4 |
| First Farmers National Bank of Waurika | Waurika | OK | **B** | B | B+ | 47.4 | 3.48 | 1.3 | 3.4 | 0.7 | 45.8 | **10.0** | 21.0 | 43.0 |
| First Farmers State Bank | Minier | IL | **A-** | A- | A- | 180.8 | 7.26 | 4.3 | 0.3 | 7.7 | 17.3 | **10.0** | 12.4 | 20.9 |
| First Federal Bank | Lake City | FL | **A-** | A- | A- | 2177.6 | 20.20 | 2.1 | 2.7 | 23.9 | 24.9 | **8.9** | 10.2 | 17.5 |
| First Federal Bank | Dunn | NC | **C+** | C | D+ | 187.9 | 2.09 | 6.4 | 0.5 | 35.3 | 19.9 | **10.0** | 11.5 | 19.7 |
| First Federal Bank | Dickson | TN | **A-** | A- | A- | 730.8 | 7.06 | 3.1 | 2.3 | 21.0 | 29.7 | **10.0** | 11.1 | 19.0 |
| ▲ First Federal Bank & Trust | Sheridan | WY | **B** | C+ | C | 333.1 | 7.90 | 7.9 | 1.0 | 25.4 | 24.1 | **10.0** | 16.1 | 20.1 |
| First Federal Bank Littlefield, Texas | Littlefield | TX | **B** | B | B | 50.6 | -1.96 | 10.8 | 10.5 | 16.7 | 0.0 | **10.0** | 19.2 | 24.9 |
| First Federal Bank Of Kansas City | Kansas City | MO | **D+** | C- | C | 791.6 | -3.50 | 0.0 | 2.6 | 67.4 | 13.7 | **10.0** | 14.2 | 28.3 |
| First Federal Bank of Louisiana | Lake Charles | LA | **C+** | C+ | C | 897.2 | 4.89 | 2.9 | 2.0 | 29.0 | 19.1 | **10.0** | 12.5 | 21.1 |
| First Federal Bank of Ohio | Galion | OH | **C+** | C | C- | 239.6 | -0.63 | 0.1 | 1.2 | 28.2 | 32.6 | **10.0** | 15.1 | 35.2 |
| First Federal Bank of the Midwest | Defiance | OH | **B** | B | B | 3439.8 | 9.05 | 15.5 | 1.0 | 10.3 | 8.2 | **6.4** | 10.1 | 12.1 |
| ▲ First Federal Bank of Wisconsin | Waukesha | WI | **B-** | C+ | C- | 291.7 | 11.07 | 5.1 | 0.2 | 19.1 | 16.2 | **10.0** | 19.4 | 24.7 |
| First Federal Bank, A FSB | Tuscaloosa | AL | **C** | C- | C- | 132.3 | 6.31 | 0.3 | 0.3 | 70.7 | 0.7 | **10.0** | 11.1 | 17.7 |
| First Federal Community Bank of Bucyrus | Bucyrus | OH | **C+** | C+ | C+ | 181.9 | 18.26 | 5.0 | 5.0 | 50.8 | 7.0 | **6.4** | 8.4 | 13.0 |
| First Federal Community Bank, N.A. | Dover | OH | **B** | B | B | 451.2 | 14.87 | 8.4 | 2.5 | 26.2 | 3.8 | **6.7** | 8.7 | 12.9 |
| First Federal Community Bank, SSB | Paris | TX | **B** | B | B- | 446.9 | 3.05 | 9.6 | 2.6 | 40.6 | 3.4 | **10.0** | 11.6 | 17.5 |
| First Federal S&L Assn. | Hazard | KY | **C+** | C | B- | 83.3 | 6.10 | 0.0 | 1.4 | 76.1 | 0.2 | **10.0** | 22.4 | 39.9 |
| First Federal S&L Assn. | Morehead | KY | **C+** | C+ | C | 33.6 | -3.10 | 1.9 | 1.6 | 54.9 | 0.0 | **10.0** | 29.6 | 52.9 |
| ▼ First Federal S&L Assn. | Aberdeen | MS | **C+** | B- | B- | 43.5 | 13.00 | 0.0 | 1.6 | 61.9 | 12.4 | **10.0** | 16.8 | 43.4 |
| First Federal S&L Assn. of Bath | Bath | ME | **B** | B | B | 134.8 | 0.56 | 0.8 | 1.2 | 74.6 | 2.3 | **10.0** | 17.4 | 29.9 |
| First Federal S&L Assn. of Centerburg | Centerburg | OH | **C+** | C+ | C+ | 21.7 | -6.11 | 0.0 | 0.4 | 63.5 | 2.9 | **10.0** | 20.5 | 42.8 |
| First Federal S&L Assn. of Central Illinois, | Shelbyville | IL | **B+** | B+ | B+ | 133.7 | 11.84 | 6.6 | 5.2 | 30.5 | 17.7 | **10.0** | 11.2 | 16.2 |
| First Federal S&L Assn. of Delta | Delta | OH | **C+** | C- | C- | 165.0 | 1.79 | 0.3 | 0.2 | 48.5 | 18.7 | **10.0** | 12.7 | 33.3 |

| Asset Quality Index | Adjusted Non-Performing Loans as a % of Total Loans | Adjusted Non-Performing Loans as a % of Capital | Net Charge-Offs Avg Loans | Profitability Index | Net Income ($Mil) | Return on Assets (R.O.A.) | Return on Equity (R.O.E.) | Net Interest Spread | Overhead Efficiency Ratio | Liquidity Index | Liquidity Ratio | Hot Money Ratio | Stability Index |
|---|---|---|---|---|---|---|---|---|---|---|---|---|---|
| 7.3 | 0.07 | 0.8 | 0.01 | 6.9 | 5.0 | 1.63 | 16.55 | 4.62 | 67.2 | 4.3 | 13.2 | 6.1 | 7.5 |
| 9.0 | 0.00 | 0.0 | 0.00 | 4.3 | 0.6 | 0.98 | 9.19 | 3.70 | 73.1 | 4.4 | 39.0 | 12.8 | 5.6 |
| 5.9 | 0.75 | 4.7 | -0.03 | 4.7 | 2.9 | 1.00 | 8.69 | 4.13 | 74.7 | 3.6 | 22.2 | 7.9 | 7.2 |
| 5.5 | 0.58 | 1.7 | 0.01 | 4.3 | 1.2 | 0.82 | 7.58 | 4.18 | 73.2 | 0.9 | 21.3 | 35.9 | 7.1 |
| 6.6 | 0.53 | 2.3 | -0.03 | 5.3 | 11.8 | 1.06 | 9.24 | 3.73 | 69.4 | 4.2 | 18.8 | 8.7 | 9.2 |
| 6.7 | 1.06 | 2.9 | 0.22 | 5.9 | 5.6 | 1.32 | 11.02 | 5.65 | 74.9 | 2.9 | 23.6 | 15.5 | 7.9 |
| 7.4 | 0.69 | 2.8 | 0.04 | 7.0 | 6.5 | 1.42 | 16.06 | 4.61 | 64.4 | 2.3 | 15.9 | 17.8 | 5.8 |
| 4.3 | 1.08 | 4.7 | 0.20 | 9.5 | 39.5 | 1.78 | 12.19 | 4.60 | 56.1 | 4.1 | 15.0 | 8.7 | 10.0 |
| 8.5 | 0.08 | 0.5 | -0.15 | 7.3 | 1.8 | 1.71 | 17.03 | 3.60 | 59.9 | 3.2 | 36.4 | 17.8 | 7.7 |
| 5.7 | 1.92 | 8.9 | -0.04 | 6.7 | 2.0 | 1.32 | 10.36 | 4.56 | 64.5 | 5.2 | 28.3 | 3.9 | 6.1 |
| 6.6 | 0.54 | 2.9 | 0.08 | 9.6 | 8.1 | 2.17 | 27.37 | 4.23 | 51.0 | 2.4 | 25.1 | 17.9 | 6.8 |
| 5.4 | 0.55 | 5.5 | 0.03 | 3.9 | 0.9 | 0.74 | 8.91 | 3.47 | 63.2 | 0.6 | 11.8 | 47.8 | 4.5 |
| 7.0 | 0.52 | 2.6 | -0.06 | 4.6 | 1.6 | 0.89 | 7.32 | 4.20 | 77.9 | 3.9 | 8.2 | 8.2 | 6.8 |
| 6.9 | 0.49 | 2.0 | 0.10 | 5.1 | 1.4 | 1.35 | 14.78 | 3.23 | 59.9 | 3.5 | 15.1 | 11.4 | 6.3 |
| 6.2 | 0.35 | 2.0 | 0.02 | 5.0 | 1.1 | 1.31 | 12.31 | 3.83 | 67.0 | 4.9 | 31.4 | 6.9 | 6.2 |
| 8.0 | 0.18 | 1.2 | -0.01 | 6.2 | 7.0 | 1.39 | 11.23 | 3.43 | 85.3 | 0.6 | 10.2 | 35.2 | 7.3 |
| 5.5 | 1.11 | 3.5 | 0.11 | 4.0 | 2.1 | 0.89 | 9.00 | 3.99 | 79.5 | 1.4 | 15.2 | 22.7 | 5.8 |
| 5.1 | 1.82 | 8.7 | 0.07 | 4.5 | 1.2 | 1.05 | 9.23 | 3.96 | 74.3 | 2.6 | 23.4 | 16.8 | 6.6 |
| 8.2 | 0.45 | 2.8 | 0.00 | 6.2 | 0.6 | 1.44 | 11.98 | 3.74 | 63.2 | 4.7 | 33.2 | 8.8 | 7.7 |
| 4.9 | 2.65 | 9.8 | 0.18 | 2.3 | 0.7 | 0.55 | 6.15 | 4.11 | 106.4 | 4.5 | 39.4 | 12.5 | 3.2 |
| 10.0 | na | 0.0 | na | 9.5 | 1.4 | 13.04 | 14.77 | 1.95 | 67.9 | 4.0 | na | 0.0 | 6.2 |
| 6.1 | 1.70 | 10.6 | 0.02 | 3.0 | 8.6 | 0.51 | 5.76 | 2.92 | 80.1 | 1.4 | 14.5 | 20.6 | 6.8 |
| 4.0 | 7.59 | 10.0 | 0.00 | 10.0 | 24.0 | 5.28 | 11.88 | 6.78 | 8.5 | 2.3 | 51.0 | 45.0 | 9.3 |
| 5.2 | 0.77 | 5.9 | 0.17 | 6.0 | 19.7 | 1.15 | 11.14 | 4.11 | 67.2 | 3.3 | 11.9 | 10.9 | 7.5 |
| 8.9 | 0.08 | 0.2 | 0.01 | 9.8 | 12.8 | 2.48 | 14.25 | 3.94 | 40.5 | 1.4 | 25.9 | 25.0 | 10.0 |
| 7.5 | 0.00 | 0.0 | 0.00 | 10.0 | 2.9 | 6.26 | 20.81 | 13.92 | 74.8 | 3.9 | 87.9 | 11.7 | 9.0 |
| 3.5 | 1.95 | 12.2 | 0.11 | 8.9 | 3.0 | 1.86 | 14.37 | 5.50 | 67.9 | 0.6 | 11.0 | 32.8 | 9.4 |
| 2.2 | 3.26 | 20.6 | 0.18 | 5.8 | 3.9 | 1.39 | 16.52 | 4.11 | 62.5 | 1.7 | 11.7 | 20.7 | 6.5 |
| 5.0 | 0.68 | 5.0 | -0.01 | 4.6 | 2.4 | 0.96 | 11.18 | 4.03 | 69.5 | 1.2 | 14.4 | 28.4 | 5.1 |
| 4.7 | 2.43 | 11.5 | 0.15 | 8.4 | 6.1 | 1.93 | 13.34 | 4.40 | 56.0 | 4.4 | 23.1 | 7.3 | 8.3 |
| 4.2 | 3.55 | 14.1 | 0.17 | 5.0 | 1.2 | 1.18 | 8.14 | 4.18 | 67.1 | 0.8 | 3.6 | 31.7 | 7.7 |
| 3.2 | 2.44 | 11.0 | 0.00 | 8.9 | 3.5 | 1.97 | 11.92 | 4.84 | 53.2 | 1.8 | 9.8 | 19.5 | 8.3 |
| 6.2 | 1.74 | 6.5 | 0.20 | 6.2 | 1.1 | 1.46 | 7.91 | 4.40 | 67.2 | 4.3 | 20.4 | 7.5 | 7.9 |
| 0.0 | 10.07 | 50.0 | 0.17 | 4.8 | 0.7 | 1.06 | 9.71 | 4.29 | 71.0 | 2.3 | 19.7 | 18.2 | 7.0 |
| 3.6 | 1.81 | 8.3 | 0.56 | 4.1 | 0.9 | 0.73 | 6.29 | 4.01 | 69.3 | 0.8 | 14.4 | 34.6 | 5.7 |
| 8.6 | 0.22 | 1.1 | 0.00 | 5.2 | 16.5 | 1.22 | 11.77 | 3.49 | 66.8 | 3.5 | 13.6 | 8.3 | 8.4 |
| 4.3 | 1.93 | 13.4 | 0.27 | 7.9 | 29.6 | 1.61 | 15.08 | 4.07 | 53.7 | 2.9 | 15.0 | 10.6 | 9.8 |
| 8.7 | 0.00 | 0.0 | -0.01 | 5.1 | 0.6 | 1.29 | 6.24 | 3.89 | 65.6 | 2.2 | 29.7 | 22.2 | 7.4 |
| 7.4 | 0.00 | 0.1 | -0.01 | 7.1 | 2.8 | 1.64 | 13.27 | 3.64 | 58.9 | 1.8 | 12.8 | 19.6 | 7.9 |
| 5.9 | 1.24 | 5.1 | 0.02 | 6.0 | 27.2 | 1.34 | 10.95 | 4.17 | 74.4 | 2.9 | 19.8 | 11.0 | 9.9 |
| 6.3 | 1.55 | 8.3 | 0.00 | 2.4 | 0.5 | 0.28 | 2.52 | 3.70 | 91.4 | 1.8 | 23.6 | 22.2 | 6.4 |
| 7.5 | 1.14 | 4.7 | 0.02 | 6.8 | 11.2 | 1.58 | 12.78 | 3.60 | 54.9 | 3.2 | 32.3 | 16.2 | 8.9 |
| 4.8 | 2.48 | 9.8 | -0.13 | 4.1 | 2.7 | 0.93 | 5.98 | 3.23 | 75.5 | 3.4 | 23.4 | 12.8 | 7.4 |
| 7.7 | 0.17 | 0.9 | 0.81 | 4.9 | 0.4 | 0.75 | 3.84 | 5.01 | 73.7 | 0.9 | 19.9 | 34.7 | 7.6 |
| 8.9 | 0.32 | 1.8 | 0.00 | 0.6 | -1.2 | -0.15 | -1.15 | 2.24 | 103.3 | 1.2 | 17.3 | 29.4 | 6.8 |
| 7.7 | 0.83 | 3.3 | 0.02 | 2.9 | 4.3 | 0.48 | 3.88 | 3.07 | 82.1 | 3.2 | 14.9 | 12.9 | 7.3 |
| 9.1 | 1.15 | 3.4 | 0.00 | 2.5 | 0.9 | 0.38 | 2.50 | 3.22 | 87.6 | 6.2 | 60.3 | 8.9 | 7.2 |
| 4.6 | 0.78 | 3.5 | 0.00 | 7.3 | 48.2 | 1.48 | 11.75 | 3.96 | 57.8 | 3.4 | 8.3 | 11.7 | 10.0 |
| 8.2 | 1.18 | 3.1 | 0.03 | 3.5 | 1.8 | 0.69 | 3.58 | 3.55 | 72.3 | 3.4 | 36.0 | 16.9 | 6.8 |
| 6.3 | 1.76 | 7.2 | 0.04 | 5.0 | 1.9 | 1.53 | 14.04 | 3.20 | 86.5 | 0.5 | 7.6 | 50.7 | 5.8 |
| 4.7 | 2.01 | 11.5 | 0.03 | 3.8 | 1.2 | 0.69 | 8.19 | 3.95 | 82.5 | 1.9 | 7.5 | 19.0 | 4.2 |
| 6.4 | 0.36 | 2.4 | 0.02 | 7.3 | 6.1 | 1.48 | 16.27 | 3.93 | 54.3 | 2.4 | 15.2 | 15.3 | 6.1 |
| 6.2 | 0.85 | 6.5 | 0.07 | 4.4 | 3.6 | 0.81 | 7.15 | 3.61 | 70.2 | 1.2 | 13.2 | 28.6 | 6.8 |
| 4.6 | 3.29 | 17.8 | 0.07 | 3.8 | 0.6 | 0.74 | 3.30 | 3.08 | 68.9 | 1.0 | 5.5 | 28.6 | 6.0 |
| 6.0 | 4.29 | 10.0 | 0.00 | 2.6 | 0.1 | 0.27 | 0.92 | 3.69 | 91.1 | 1.7 | 23.4 | 24.7 | 6.8 |
| 9.7 | 0.00 | 0.9 | 0.02 | 2.3 | 0.1 | 0.28 | 1.61 | 1.94 | 79.0 | 1.6 | 35.8 | 49.7 | 6.6 |
| 4.5 | 4.92 | 17.9 | -0.04 | 5.2 | 1.4 | 1.02 | 6.18 | 4.75 | 71.3 | 3.4 | 10.4 | 11.3 | 7.9 |
| 9.8 | 0.00 | 0.0 | 0.00 | 3.5 | 0.1 | 0.57 | 2.94 | 3.51 | 78.1 | 3.0 | 24.7 | 14.8 | 7.6 |
| 5.4 | 1.75 | 9.1 | 1.08 | 4.2 | 0.9 | 0.66 | 5.57 | 3.97 | 69.8 | 1.8 | 20.6 | 21.2 | 6.7 |
| 8.9 | 0.80 | 2.8 | 0.00 | 2.7 | 0.7 | 0.40 | 3.15 | 3.52 | 84.4 | 6.4 | 47.1 | 3.2 | 6.5 |

| Name | City | State | Rating | 2018 Rating | 2017 Rating | Total Assets ($Mil) | One Year Asset Growth | Asset Mix (As a % of Total Assets) Comm-ercial Loans | Cons-umer Loans | Mort-gage Loans | Secur-ities | Capital-ization Index | Lever-age Ratio | Risk-Based Capital Ratio |
|---|---|---|---|---|---|---|---|---|---|---|---|---|---|---|
| First Federal S&L Assn. of Greene County | Waynesburg | PA | **B-** | C+ | C+ | 938.4 | 2.34 | 0.0 | 0.4 | 64.8 | 17.2 | **10.0** | 14.5 | 32.5 |
| First Federal S&L Assn. of Greensburg | Greensburg | IN | **C+** | C | C | 160.3 | 7.15 | 0.6 | 2.1 | 40.9 | 19.3 | **8.2** | 9.8 | 21.9 |
| First Federal S&L Assn. of Lakewood | Lakewood | OH | **C-** | C- | C+ | 1924.1 | -1.83 | 1.8 | 4.0 | 63.5 | 6.5 | **9.3** | 10.5 | 16.7 |
| First Federal S&L Assn. of Lorain | Lorain | OH | **C** | C | C | 439.8 | -0.63 | 0.0 | 0.2 | 56.1 | 19.3 | **10.0** | 15.1 | 32.6 |
| First Federal S&L Assn. of McMinnville | McMinnville | OR | **B** | B | B- | 458.8 | 8.11 | 0.6 | 0.2 | 41.7 | 30.8 | **10.0** | 14.7 | 29.2 |
| First Federal S&L Assn. of Newark | Newark | OH | **C** | C | C | 222.0 | 0.26 | 0.0 | 0.3 | 49.2 | 10.2 | **10.0** | 15.9 | 25.5 |
| First Federal S&L Assn. of Pascagoula-Mo | Pascagoula | MS | **C** | C | C | 310.4 | 1.60 | 0.0 | 0.4 | 79.9 | 9.6 | **7.5** | 9.4 | 20.0 |
| First Federal S&L Assn. of Port Angeles | Port Angeles | WA | **B-** | C+ | C+ | 1295.3 | 4.26 | 1.0 | 9.0 | 25.6 | 23.5 | **10.0** | 12.2 | 18.7 |
| First Federal S&L Assn. of Ravenswood | Ravenswood | WV | **D+** | D | C- | 24.3 | 9.64 | 0.0 | 0.5 | 74.3 | 0.1 | **5.3** | 7.3 | 15.5 |
| First Federal S&L Assn. of San Rafael | San Rafael | CA | **B-** | B- | B- | 201.5 | 4.01 | 0.0 | 0.0 | 1.3 | 0.0 | **10.0** | 20.4 | 26.2 |
| First Federal S&L Assn. of Valdosta | Valdosta | GA | **B-** | C+ | C | 189.2 | 4.89 | 0.0 | 2.4 | 70.3 | 1.5 | **10.0** | 15.3 | 25.2 |
| First Federal S&L Assn. of Van Wert | Van Wert | OH | **C+** | C+ | C+ | 115.5 | 5.72 | 0.0 | 0.4 | 43.7 | 32.8 | **10.0** | 20.3 | 45.1 |
| First Federal S&L Bank | Olathe | KS | **B** | B | C | 97.0 | 6.39 | 0.2 | 0.0 | 76.7 | 0.0 | **10.0** | 11.6 | 22.6 |
| First Federal Savings Bank | Ottawa | IL | **C** | C | C+ | 371.8 | 1.93 | 0.3 | 0.9 | 53.1 | 3.6 | **10.0** | 11.6 | 26.7 |
| First Federal Savings Bank | Evansville | IN | **C** | C | C- | 452.8 | 2.81 | 16.2 | 0.8 | 21.9 | 12.8 | **6.2** | 8.2 | 13.1 |
| First Federal Savings Bank | Huntington | IN | **B-** | B | B+ | 353.9 | 5.90 | 15.7 | 3.5 | 13.5 | 18.0 | **10.0** | 11.2 | 16.0 |
| First Federal Savings Bank | Rochester | IN | **B-** | C | C+ | 437.3 | -1.24 | 1.1 | 0.1 | 65.4 | 0.0 | **8.7** | 10.1 | 18.1 |
| First Federal Savings Bank of Angola | Angola | IN | **B** | B | B | 123.4 | -6.26 | 0.4 | 3.8 | 66.3 | 0.0 | **10.0** | 21.4 | 45.8 |
| First Federal Savings Bank of Kentucky | Frankfort | KY | **C** | C | B- | 246.4 | 1.58 | 0.6 | 0.4 | 63.8 | 0.4 | **10.0** | 12.9 | 21.3 |
| First Federal Savings of Middletown | Middletown | NY | **C+** | C- | C- | 149.4 | -2.15 | 0.0 | 0.0 | 0.6 | 30.3 | **10.0** | 36.9 | 65.0 |
| First Fidelity Bank | Fort Payne | AL | **C+** | C+ | C | 102.9 | 3.98 | 7.4 | 2.6 | 25.4 | 36.3 | **8.0** | 9.7 | 19.8 |
| First Fidelity Bank | Oklahoma City | OK | **B** | B | B- | 1797.2 | 8.38 | 6.6 | 14.6 | 7.0 | 21.7 | **7.1** | 9.1 | 13.2 |
| ▲ First Fidelity Bank | Burke | SD | **B+** | B | A- | 390.8 | 7.81 | 3.9 | 2.4 | 1.7 | 29.3 | **8.3** | 9.9 | 13.6 |
| First Financial Bank | Bessemer | AL | **C+** | B- | C- | 169.0 | 5.67 | 7.3 | 1.9 | 11.6 | 34.1 | **7.2** | 9.1 | 14.8 |
| First Financial Bank | El Dorado | AR | **B+** | B+ | B+ | 1416.9 | 35.66 | 8.0 | 1.9 | 4.9 | 5.0 | **8.6** | 10.1 | 17.4 |
| First Financial Bank | Cincinnati | OH | **B+** | B+ | B | 14434.3 | 3.74 | 15.5 | 0.7 | 9.5 | 20.8 | **7.3** | 9.9 | 12.7 |
| First Financial Bank in Winnebago | Winnebago | MN | **B** | B | B | 48.8 | 5.33 | 12.8 | 2.4 | 7.3 | 16.4 | **10.0** | 14.9 | 18.8 |
| First Financial Bank, N.A. | Terre Haute | IN | **A-** | A- | A- | 3918.5 | 34.02 | 15.3 | 7.8 | 11.1 | 23.6 | **10.0** | 11.9 | 15.9 |
| First Financial Bank, N.A. | Abilene | TX | **A** | A | A- | 8228.2 | 6.82 | 8.2 | 5.0 | 13.5 | 41.1 | **9.8** | 10.8 | 18.3 |
| First Financial Northwest Bank | Renton | WA | **B+** | A- | B+ | 1342.0 | 7.30 | 1.8 | 1.5 | 26.9 | 10.2 | **8.9** | 10.3 | 14.4 |
| First Financial Trust & Asset Mgmt Co. | Abilene | TX | **U** | U | U | 29.5 | 22.00 | 0.0 | 0.0 | 0.0 | 79.5 | **10.0** | 102. | 370.4 |
| First Financial Trust, N.A. | Wellesley | MA | **U** | U | U | 10.4 | 8.39 | 0.0 | 0.0 | 0.0 | 20.6 | **10.0** | 97.1 | 228.3 |
| First Florida Integrity Bank | Naples | FL | **B** | B- | B- | 1575.9 | 8.14 | 10.2 | 0.3 | 10.5 | 15.7 | **6.4** | 9.3 | 12.1 |
| First Foundation Bank | Irvine | CA | **B-** | B- | B | 6298.2 | 7.91 | 6.7 | 0.2 | 13.9 | 16.1 | **5.2** | 8.2 | 11.1 |
| ▲ First Freedom Bank | Lebanon | TN | **B-** | C+ | B- | 488.0 | 2.27 | 18.2 | 3.8 | 10.8 | 0.0 | **5.9** | 10.2 | 11.7 |
| First FSB of Champaign-Urbana | Champaign | IL | **B-** | C+ | C+ | 172.6 | 3.13 | 5.3 | 1.1 | 24.9 | 0.1 | **8.9** | 10.3 | 22.2 |
| First FSB of Lincolnton | Lincolnton | NC | **A-** | B+ | B+ | 382.3 | 0.23 | 0.6 | 0.7 | 64.5 | 5.7 | **10.0** | 16.7 | 30.3 |
| First FSB of Mascoutah | Mascoutah | IL | **C** | C | C- | 113.3 | 7.01 | 1.8 | 1.1 | 40.7 | 29.8 | **10.0** | 12.7 | 24.4 |
| First FSB of Twin Falls | Twin Falls | ID | **A-** | B+ | B | 705.8 | 8.84 | 5.9 | 5.3 | 34.2 | 4.2 | **10.0** | 11.9 | 16.0 |
| First FSB of Washington | Washington | IN | **C-** | C- | D+ | 78.3 | 6.22 | 6.0 | 2.3 | 50.0 | 3.6 | **10.0** | 11.7 | 22.6 |
| First General Bank | Rowland Heights | CA | **A-** | B+ | B+ | 977.3 | 3.18 | 6.4 | 0.0 | 3.3 | 0.8 | **10.0** | 14.2 | 17.8 |
| First Guaranty Bank | Hammond | LA | **B** | B | B | 2112.8 | 16.55 | 12.7 | 1.5 | 13.6 | 20.2 | **7.1** | 10.4 | 12.6 |
| ▲ First Harrison Bank | Corydon | IN | **B+** | B- | B+ | 823.0 | 4.17 | 5.5 | 7.2 | 14.1 | 30.9 | **8.5** | 10.0 | 14.9 |
| First Hawaiian Bank | Honolulu | HI | **B+** | B | B | 20167.6 | -2.55 | 12.1 | 7.5 | 18.1 | 20.2 | **6.7** | 8.7 | 12.7 |
| First Heritage Bank | Shenandoah | IA | **B-** | B- | B | 40.0 | 0.74 | 14.6 | 3.5 | 22.6 | 19.5 | **10.0** | 11.4 | 16.7 |
| First Heritage Bank | Centralia | KS | **B** | B | B | 175.0 | 3.22 | 20.9 | 0.9 | 8.8 | 25.3 | **7.4** | 9.2 | 15.4 |
| First Home Bank | Saint Petersburg | FL | **B+** | A- | A- | 531.2 | 45.90 | 31.7 | 0.2 | 22.4 | 0.0 | **9.2** | 10.5 | 17.8 |
| First Hope Bank, A National Banking Assn. | Hope | NJ | **C** | C | C | 520.8 | 1.11 | 5.5 | 0.3 | 12.2 | 21.7 | **7.6** | 9.4 | 13.6 |
| First Horizon Bank | Memphis | TN | **B-** | B- | B- | 43126.2 | 6.13 | 19.0 | 0.8 | 11.8 | 10.3 | **4.5** | 9.1 | 10.8 |
| First IC Bank | Doraville | GA | **B+** | A | A | 704.8 | 40.76 | 6.8 | 0.0 | 7.6 | 8.5 | **9.9** | 10.9 | 15.1 |
| First Independence Bank | Detroit | MI | **B-** | B- | C+ | 296.0 | 13.96 | 12.2 | 0.0 | 17.1 | 1.5 | **7.0** | 9.0 | 12.5 |
| First Independent Bank | Russell | MN | **C** | C | B | 280.0 | -2.87 | 8.7 | 3.4 | 6.6 | 23.8 | **10.0** | 12.1 | 15.9 |
| First Independent Bank | Aurora | MO | **B** | B | B | 93.7 | 4.22 | 8.0 | 4.0 | 23.3 | 28.8 | **10.0** | 12.1 | 22.5 |
| First International Bank & Trust | Watford City | ND | **B** | B | B | 3466.1 | 17.92 | 14.5 | 3.0 | 10.6 | 12.4 | **6.0** | 8.9 | 11.8 |
| First Internet Bank of Indiana | Fishers | IN | **B-** | B- | B- | 4097.5 | 15.80 | 9.1 | 7.4 | 8.2 | 14.7 | **6.3** | 8.3 | 12.6 |
| First Interstate Bank | Billings | MT | **B+** | B- | B- | 14582.6 | 10.14 | 8.7 | 7.2 | 8.6 | 20.9 | **6.9** | 8.9 | 12.5 |
| ▲ First Iowa State Bank | Albia | IA | **B+** | B+ | B+ | 146.1 | 1.61 | 6.1 | 1.5 | 11.8 | 23.0 | **10.0** | 12.8 | 19.7 |
| First Iowa State Bank | Keosauqua | IA | **B+** | B+ | B+ | 136.8 | 3.15 | 14.7 | 3.1 | 15.3 | 18.9 | **9.3** | 10.5 | 15.5 |
| First Ipswich Bank | Ipswich | MA | **B-** | B- | B- | 466.4 | 10.63 | 6.9 | 0.0 | 16.8 | 11.7 | **6.8** | 8.8 | 14.2 |
| First Jackson Bank, Inc. | Stevenson | AL | **A-** | B+ | B+ | 279.2 | 6.44 | 7.0 | 4.0 | 18.6 | 20.0 | **10.0** | 12.4 | 17.5 |

| Asset Quality Index | Adjusted Non-Performing Loans as a % of Total Loans | Adjusted Non-Performing Loans as a % of Capital | Net Charge-Offs Avg Loans | Profitability Index | Net Income ($Mil) | Return on Assets (R.O.A.) | Return on Equity (R.O.E.) | Net Interest Spread | Overhead Efficiency Ratio | Liquidity Index | Liquidity Ratio | Hot Money Ratio | Stability Index |
|---|---|---|---|---|---|---|---|---|---|---|---|---|---|
| **9.5** | 0.60 | 2.4 | 0.04 | **3.1** | 4.2 | 0.45 | 3.12 | 2.65 | 75.7 | **2.2** | 33.1 | 25.2 | **8.1** |
| **5.6** | 2.31 | 9.3 | 0.06 | **2.7** | 0.6 | 0.40 | 3.77 | 2.99 | 82.3 | **6.4** | 42.6 | 1.8 | **5.8** |
| **8.0** | 0.41 | 2.5 | -0.01 | **2.5** | 6.5 | 0.34 | 3.22 | 2.30 | 86.2 | **1.9** | 9.5 | 13.5 | **7.5** |
| **4.8** | 5.80 | 18.4 | -0.11 | **1.7** | 0.5 | 0.11 | 0.75 | 2.85 | 99.6 | **3.0** | 31.6 | 17.0 | **6.8** |
| **9.6** | 0.67 | 1.5 | 0.00 | **4.1** | 3.4 | 0.77 | 5.23 | 3.45 | 72.5 | **5.0** | 41.0 | 10.4 | **8.1** |
| **6.9** | 2.52 | 8.0 | 0.00 | **2.3** | 0.6 | 0.29 | 1.84 | 3.06 | 89.3 | **1.2** | 17.7 | 29.1 | **7.2** |
| **6.5** | 0.89 | 6.3 | 0.07 | **2.4** | 1.0 | 0.32 | 3.51 | 3.06 | 84.9 | **0.6** | 13.3 | 53.3 | **4.7** |
| **8.2** | 0.59 | 2.2 | 0.07 | **3.6** | 9.3 | 0.75 | 6.46 | 3.19 | 74.1 | **2.0** | 25.3 | 22.2 | **8.8** |
| **9.7** | 0.00 | 0.0 | 0.00 | **2.8** | 0.1 | 0.33 | 3.94 | 3.03 | 73.7 | **0.7** | 12.3 | 36.3 | **3.6** |
| **7.1** | 0.00 | 0.0 | 0.00 | **2.9** | 0.7 | 0.34 | 1.67 | 3.42 | 85.8 | **0.5** | 2.9 | 38.4 | **7.6** |
| **4.9** | 3.41 | 16.2 | 0.09 | **2.3** | 0.4 | 0.22 | 1.40 | 4.29 | 92.3 | **1.8** | 7.6 | 19.2 | **7.0** |
| **10.0** | 0.00 | 0.0 | -0.01 | **3.2** | 0.7 | 0.66 | 3.19 | 3.27 | 77.2 | **4.8** | 44.6 | 12.1 | **7.8** |
| **3.7** | 4.43 | 27.4 | -0.01 | **9.8** | 2.8 | 2.92 | 24.83 | 4.21 | 27.8 | **0.5** | 20.0 | 41.7 | **8.9** |
| **7.0** | 2.02 | 6.5 | -0.02 | **2.3** | 0.8 | 0.21 | 1.82 | 2.59 | 93.8 | **2.6** | 35.6 | 21.3 | **6.4** |
| **7.0** | 0.50 | 3.0 | 0.16 | **2.6** | 2.0 | 0.47 | 4.84 | 3.24 | 84.0 | **2.1** | 20.4 | 8.6 | **5.4** |
| **4.2** | 2.59 | 14.5 | 0.04 | **6.6** | 4.8 | 1.37 | 12.20 | 3.57 | 60.1 | **1.1** | 21.1 | 17.5 | **7.7** |
| **4.0** | 4.64 | 16.0 | 0.04 | **4.7** | 4.5 | 0.99 | 9.58 | 3.91 | 80.5 | **1.5** | 13.0 | 24.6 | **6.2** |
| **9.5** | 0.23 | 1.5 | 0.01 | **3.0** | 0.5 | 0.39 | 1.89 | 3.30 | 82.9 | **3.7** | 32.5 | 13.8 | **7.6** |
| **3.3** | 1.88 | 9.4 | 0.04 | **2.3** | 0.6 | 0.24 | 1.30 | 3.12 | 89.4 | **0.8** | 6.5 | 33.0 | **6.7** |
| **9.9** | 0.22 | 0.3 | 0.00 | **2.7** | 0.7 | 0.46 | 1.25 | 2.95 | 72.8 | **5.7** | 89.3 | 15.0 | **7.3** |
| **7.9** | 0.96 | 4.2 | 0.00 | **3.4** | 0.7 | 0.68 | 7.23 | 3.15 | 75.9 | **3.9** | 51.6 | 18.6 | **5.5** |
| **5.8** | 0.83 | 3.5 | 0.01 | **5.1** | 21.0 | 1.23 | 12.62 | 3.34 | 67.2 | **5.0** | 20.9 | 3.4 | **9.7** |
| **7.4** | 0.08 | 0.8 | 0.05 | **8.1** | 6.3 | 1.72 | 17.14 | 4.15 | 58.0 | **4.2** | 26.4 | 8.4 | **7.5** |
| **6.1** | 0.76 | 3.7 | 0.10 | **2.1** | 0.0 | 0.02 | 0.17 | 4.09 | 96.7 | **5.1** | 26.7 | 3.4 | **5.0** |
| **4.3** | 4.59 | 10.7 | 0.18 | **9.8** | 26.7 | 2.34 | 18.98 | 4.25 | 60.4 | **1.1** | 17.5 | 27.6 | **10.0** |
| **5.2** | 0.64 | 2.3 | 0.33 | **7.5** | 214.4 | 1.52 | 9.82 | 4.08 | 52.4 | **3.1** | 17.6 | 6.9 | **10.0** |
| **7.8** | 0.72 | 1.8 | -0.18 | **5.5** | 0.6 | 1.34 | 9.01 | 3.95 | 64.4 | **3.0** | 19.6 | 14.3 | **7.5** |
| **7.1** | 0.42 | 2.1 | 0.15 | **7.2** | 47.3 | 1.42 | 10.06 | 4.03 | 61.9 | **4.1** | 12.1 | 8.0 | **9.9** |
| **7.2** | 0.58 | 2.2 | 0.04 | **9.4** | 157.6 | 2.01 | 15.13 | 4.07 | 47.9 | **4.9** | 18.7 | 3.5 | **10.0** |
| **7.6** | 0.27 | 1.1 | -0.02 | **4.5** | 11.5 | 0.89 | 8.73 | 3.18 | 67.5 | **0.7** | 11.7 | 33.3 | **9.8** |
| **10.0** | na | 0.0 | na | **10.0** | 13.9 | 54.04 | 53.99 | 4.93 | 40.6 | **4.0** | na | 0.0 | **7.0** |
| **6.5** | na | 0.0 | na | **9.5** | 0.7 | 7.47 | 7.65 | 2.58 | 69.9 | **4.0** | na | 0.0 | **6.3** |
| **7.5** | 0.02 | 0.1 | 0.00 | **5.4** | 16.3 | 1.10 | 11.90 | 3.56 | 59.7 | **3.5** | 11.1 | 11.3 | **7.9** |
| **6.4** | 0.31 | 2.4 | 0.02 | **4.8** | 58.1 | 0.95 | 9.87 | 2.94 | 55.2 | **0.9** | 16.4 | 14.2 | **7.2** |
| **4.7** | 0.78 | 5.8 | 0.11 | **6.0** | 5.8 | 1.21 | 11.61 | 3.91 | 57.8 | **0.8** | 8.0 | 32.3 | **6.6** |
| **3.5** | 3.68 | 19.7 | 0.00 | **5.2** | 1.6 | 0.95 | 9.14 | 3.75 | 75.7 | **6.3** | 45.1 | 3.1 | **5.7** |
| **7.5** | 1.45 | 5.6 | -0.01 | **5.7** | 4.5 | 1.16 | 7.19 | 3.60 | 62.0 | **0.9** | 15.0 | 33.1 | **8.4** |
| **9.5** | 0.03 | 0.2 | 0.05 | **2.5** | 0.4 | 0.41 | 3.29 | 2.47 | 78.0 | **2.0** | 27.4 | 21.9 | **6.7** |
| **8.3** | 0.27 | 1.3 | 0.01 | **6.3** | 8.8 | 1.29 | 10.84 | 4.91 | 72.1 | **4.3** | 14.0 | 6.8 | **7.9** |
| **5.6** | 1.22 | 8.8 | 0.12 | **1.0** | 0.0 | -0.01 | -0.05 | 2.88 | 98.6 | **1.8** | 27.6 | 26.2 | **6.5** |
| **7.0** | 0.19 | 1.0 | -0.01 | **9.8** | 20.8 | 2.15 | 15.67 | 4.36 | 30.8 | **0.4** | 5.9 | 49.2 | **10.0** |
| **6.6** | 1.04 | 5.8 | 0.34 | **4.5** | 16.1 | 0.86 | 8.75 | 3.41 | 64.4 | **1.3** | 14.9 | 28.3 | **7.9** |
| **6.1** | 0.58 | 2.4 | 0.09 | **5.7** | 9.7 | 1.20 | 11.30 | 4.00 | 63.7 | **5.7** | 35.0 | 3.3 | **6.8** |
| **7.1** | 0.16 | 0.9 | 0.19 | **7.5** | 289.7 | 1.42 | 11.07 | 3.20 | 47.2 | **3.8** | 17.7 | 10.6 | **10.0** |
| **8.5** | 0.01 | 0.0 | 0.09 | **4.2** | 0.4 | 0.90 | 7.71 | 4.27 | 76.3 | **3.6** | 17.5 | 11.1 | **6.8** |
| **8.4** | 0.05 | 0.5 | 0.00 | **5.0** | 2.1 | 1.18 | 12.15 | 3.53 | 64.4 | **1.1** | 21.6 | 18.2 | **7.0** |
| **4.6** | 1.05 | 5.6 | 1.24 | **5.7** | 5.5 | 1.21 | 10.27 | 4.25 | 76.9 | **1.6** | 24.0 | 24.9 | **7.8** |
| **4.6** | 0.96 | 5.9 | 0.06 | **3.2** | 2.6 | 0.49 | 5.52 | 3.35 | 85.0 | **4.4** | 15.5 | 6.1 | **5.6** |
| **4.8** | 1.02 | 4.8 | 0.09 | **6.2** | 516.7 | 1.24 | 9.98 | 3.36 | 62.2 | **3.2** | 10.3 | 6.6 | **10.0** |
| **4.8** | 1.38 | 6.1 | -0.14 | **9.6** | 10.8 | 1.71 | 14.49 | 3.96 | 54.2 | **0.9** | 23.7 | 44.2 | **9.9** |
| **4.9** | 1.71 | 12.8 | 0.10 | **5.1** | 1.6 | 1.02 | 12.46 | 4.29 | 84.7 | **1.7** | 19.8 | 17.7 | **4.2** |
| **4.1** | 2.77 | 15.7 | 0.13 | **6.4** | 4.2 | 1.49 | 12.47 | 4.18 | 61.5 | **3.2** | 26.0 | 14.5 | **8.0** |
| **5.8** | 1.51 | 7.0 | 0.01 | **4.6** | 0.8 | 0.89 | 7.50 | 3.68 | 68.2 | **3.6** | 43.1 | 17.4 | **6.5** |
| **5.4** | 1.35 | 6.9 | 0.08 | **6.3** | 47.2 | 1.51 | 16.47 | 4.50 | 69.3 | **3.3** | 11.1 | 11.6 | **8.7** |
| **7.8** | 0.22 | 2.0 | 0.07 | **3.9** | 30.4 | 0.78 | 9.91 | 1.93 | 52.1 | **0.6** | 12.3 | 45.2 | **6.8** |
| **5.3** | 0.53 | 2.6 | 0.16 | **8.0** | 213.7 | 1.51 | 11.84 | 4.01 | 54.6 | **4.4** | 18.6 | 6.9 | **10.0** |
| **6.5** | 0.34 | 4.9 | 0.07 | **7.9** | 2.4 | 1.73 | 12.92 | 4.41 | 54.8 | **3.6** | 33.3 | 14.8 | **8.4** |
| **4.3** | 1.68 | 11.4 | 0.05 | **5.5** | 1.6 | 1.19 | 10.61 | 4.96 | 73.3 | **3.1** | 22.6 | 14.2 | **7.2** |
| **5.8** | 0.42 | 2.9 | 0.33 | **2.3** | 1.4 | 0.32 | 3.29 | 2.96 | 86.5 | **2.5** | 27.3 | 17.8 | **5.9** |
| **8.4** | 0.07 | 0.2 | 0.06 | **7.5** | 4.0 | 1.52 | 12.52 | 3.91 | 47.5 | **0.8** | 19.4 | 41.0 | **7.4** |

| Name | City | State | Rating | 2018 Rating | 2017 Rating | Total Assets ($Mil) | One Year Asset Growth | Asset Mix (As a % of Total Assets) Comm-ercial Loans | Cons-umer Loans | Mort-gage Loans | Secur-ities | Capital-ization Index | Lever-age Ratio | Risk-Based Capital Ratio |
|---|---|---|---|---|---|---|---|---|---|---|---|---|---|---|
| First Kansas Bank | Hoisington | KS | B+ | B | C+ | 193.9 | -1.50 | 3.7 | 1.0 | 10.5 | 54.1 | 6.8 | 8.9 | 25.7 |
| First Kentucky Bank, Inc. | Mayfield | KY | B | B | B | 454.8 | 2.86 | 5.7 | 5.3 | 24.2 | 25.1 | 7.2 | 9.1 | 13.8 |
| First Keystone Community Bank | Berwick | PA | B | B | B | 1005.2 | -0.52 | 6.6 | 0.6 | 21.2 | 27.7 | 7.6 | 9.4 | 14.5 |
| First Liberty Bank | Oklahoma City | OK | B- | B- | B- | 435.6 | 2.98 | 27.7 | 0.2 | 18.1 | 2.3 | 5.8 | 9.5 | 11.6 |
| First Liberty National Bank | Liberty | TX | A- | B+ | B | 351.5 | 14.44 | 6.2 | 5.2 | 17.5 | 22.3 | 10.0 | 11.4 | 19.9 |
| First Merchants Bank | Muncie | IN | A- | A- | B+ | 12430.4 | 25.89 | 17.0 | 1.1 | 9.6 | 21.0 | 7.4 | 10.0 | 12.9 |
| First Metro Bank | Muscle Shoals | AL | A | A | A | 684.4 | 7.42 | 8.6 | 2.5 | 18.2 | 22.2 | 10.0 | 11.6 | 20.6 |
| First Mid Bank & Trust, N.A. | Mattoon | IL | B+ | B+ | B+ | 3808.2 | 12.11 | 13.9 | 2.2 | 7.6 | 19.8 | 9.1 | 10.4 | 14.7 |
| First Midwest Bank | Chicago | IL | B | B | B | 17757.8 | 15.08 | 21.5 | 2.8 | 12.6 | 16.3 | 5.4 | 8.8 | 11.3 |
| ▲ First Midwest Bank of Dexter | Dexter | MO | B- | B- | B | 356.8 | 5.80 | 23.0 | 2.1 | 13.2 | 3.2 | 9.1 | 11.4 | 14.3 |
| ▲ First Midwest Bank of Poplar Bluff | Poplar Bluff | MO | B- | B- | B- | 448.6 | 6.29 | 23.0 | 3.5 | 23.6 | 5.7 | 7.4 | 9.8 | 12.9 |
| ▲ First Midwest Bank of the Ozarks | Piedmont | MO | B- | B- | B | 123.8 | 1.55 | 13.8 | 5.6 | 14.6 | 9.7 | 8.5 | 11.1 | 13.8 |
| First Minnetonka City Bank | Minnetonka | MN | A- | B+ | B+ | 218.7 | -0.83 | 11.6 | 1.6 | 15.0 | 30.2 | 10.0 | 11.4 | 19.5 |
| First Missouri Bank | Brookfield | MO | B- | B- | B | 300.0 | 13.95 | 9.7 | 1.2 | 13.4 | 5.8 | 8.2 | 9.8 | 13.5 |
| First Missouri Bank of SEMO | Kennett | MO | B+ | A- | B+ | 201.3 | 0.18 | 9.2 | 1.7 | 20.8 | 2.4 | 6.5 | 8.5 | 13.8 |
| First Missouri State Bank | Poplar Bluff | MO | B+ | B+ | B+ | 185.4 | 7.59 | 6.8 | 4.3 | 32.6 | 1.2 | 7.6 | 9.4 | 13.5 |
| First Missouri State Bank of Cape County | Cape Girardeau | MO | B- | B- | C+ | 173.2 | 8.15 | 11.1 | 1.8 | 18.7 | 6.3 | 6.2 | 8.5 | 11.9 |
| First Montana Bank, Inc. | Missoula | MT | C+ | B- | B- | 323.0 | 4.77 | 12.9 | 5.3 | 8.7 | 13.2 | 8.1 | 10.7 | 13.4 |
| First Mutual Bank, FSB | Belpre | OH | C- | C- | C | 88.5 | -2.73 | 0.0 | 1.3 | 41.9 | 29.0 | 6.6 | 8.6 | 20.8 |
| First National B&T Co. of Ardmore | Ardmore | OK | B | B | B | 546.2 | 6.91 | 11.3 | 3.5 | 9.3 | 29.3 | 8.4 | 10.0 | 15.3 |
| First National B&T Co. of Bottineau | Bottineau | ND | B- | B- | C+ | 143.8 | -0.37 | 2.5 | 2.6 | 7.0 | 31.8 | 10.0 | 12.4 | 19.9 |
| ▲ First National B&T Co. of Broken Arrow | Broken Arrow | OK | B | C+ | B- | 183.9 | -0.32 | 14.4 | 2.2 | 22.7 | 3.7 | 10.0 | 11.6 | 15.6 |
| First National B&T Co. of Iron Mountain | Iron Mountain | MI | C+ | C+ | C+ | 322.3 | -2.03 | 12.6 | 2.5 | 12.9 | 32.4 | 7.7 | 9.5 | 15.5 |
| ▲ First National B&T Co. of McAlester | McAlester | OK | B | C+ | D+ | 471.0 | 2.31 | 4.3 | 2.2 | 10.2 | 35.2 | 10.0 | 11.6 | 18.3 |
| ▲ First National B&T Co. of Miami | Miami | OK | B | C+ | C+ | 132.9 | 1.15 | 4.8 | 3.5 | 14.9 | 18.5 | 9.3 | 10.5 | 18.6 |
| First National B&T Co. of Newtown | Newtown | PA | B+ | B- | C+ | 951.8 | 1.89 | 0.8 | 0.3 | 13.9 | 47.8 | 8.7 | 10.2 | 23.1 |
| First National B&T Co. of Okmulgee | Okmulgee | OK | B | B+ | B+ | 264.7 | 0.54 | 10.6 | 2.8 | 15.6 | 33.0 | 10.0 | 11.6 | 15.1 |
| First National B&T Co. of Vinita | Vinita | OK | C+ | C | B- | 390.9 | -14.97 | 18.3 | 4.6 | 7.0 | 28.6 | 5.6 | 7.6 | 11.6 |
| ▲ First National B&T Co. of Weatherford | Weatherford | OK | B+ | B+ | B+ | 258.6 | 4.27 | 12.2 | 2.0 | 7.2 | 2.8 | 9.9 | 12.3 | 14.9 |
| First National Bank | Hamilton | AL | A | A- | A- | 295.8 | 2.31 | 5.3 | 8.7 | 11.1 | 37.9 | 10.0 | 18.1 | 34.9 |
| First National Bank | Paragould | AR | A- | A- | A- | 1627.1 | 0.12 | 6.2 | 2.5 | 27.2 | 8.6 | 8.7 | 10.1 | 14.6 |
| First National Bank | Waverly | IA | B+ | A- | B+ | 529.8 | 30.03 | 14.3 | 1.2 | 10.7 | 7.7 | 9.7 | 11.1 | 14.8 |
| First National Bank | Mattoon | IL | C- | C- | C- | 91.4 | 1.08 | 12.5 | 3.6 | 11.3 | 24.0 | 6.9 | 8.9 | 13.0 |
| First National Bank | Cloverdale | IN | C+ | C+ | C+ | 313.6 | 2.69 | 4.3 | 1.4 | 17.7 | 20.5 | 8.8 | 10.2 | 21.5 |
| First National Bank | Arcadia | LA | B- | C- | C+ | 249.0 | 0.65 | 6.8 | 1.3 | 20.0 | 1.5 | 6.4 | 10.0 | 12.0 |
| First National Bank | Damariscotta | ME | B | B | B | 2036.9 | 6.34 | 9.1 | 1.3 | 24.2 | 31.8 | 6.8 | 8.8 | 15.2 |
| First National Bank | Alamogordo | NM | A- | B+ | A | 386.9 | 9.88 | 3.4 | 0.8 | 4.5 | 44.8 | 10.0 | 11.7 | 21.9 |
| First National Bank | Heavener | OK | B+ | B+ | B+ | 83.6 | 4.48 | 3.2 | 3.5 | 17.6 | 11.0 | 6.6 | 8.6 | 15.1 |
| First National Bank | Fort Pierre | SD | A- | A | A | 1330.0 | 33.32 | 7.8 | 14.0 | 7.8 | 8.9 | 10.0 | 18.5 | 24.0 |
| First National Bank | Oldham | SD | A- | A- | B | 323.9 | 5.35 | 5.8 | 14.8 | 7.5 | 14.7 | 10.0 | 13.4 | 18.9 |
| First National Bank | Rotan | TX | C+ | C | C- | 78.4 | -1.44 | 5.9 | 3.3 | 0.3 | 54.4 | 10.0 | 11.5 | 23.3 |
| ▲ First National Bank | Spearman | TX | A- | B+ | B+ | 228.0 | 0.86 | 11.2 | 2.5 | 7.0 | 20.8 | 10.0 | 13.7 | 19.5 |
| ▲ First National Bank | Wichita Falls | TX | B | C+ | B | 527.3 | 10.88 | 7.4 | 1.0 | 30.1 | 2.8 | 7.6 | 10.0 | 13.0 |
| First National Bank | Altavista | VA | B- | B- | B- | 499.4 | 6.37 | 11.5 | 19.9 | 13.5 | 9.0 | 6.8 | 9.7 | 12.4 |
| First National Bank & Trust of Elk City | Elk City | OK | A- | B+ | B+ | 304.6 | 0.56 | 8.6 | 0.7 | 13.2 | 36.4 | 10.0 | 11.3 | 21.0 |
| First National Bank Alaska | Anchorage | AK | A | A | A | 3808.3 | 1.46 | 9.1 | 0.4 | 2.5 | 41.7 | 10.0 | 13.8 | 21.1 |
| First National Bank and Trust | Atmore | AL | B- | B- | B- | 157.7 | 8.05 | 9.8 | 3.3 | 15.1 | 24.5 | 10.0 | 11.7 | 16.7 |
| ▲ First National Bank and Trust | Phillipsburg | KS | B | B- | B+ | 223.7 | 5.89 | 9.2 | 4.8 | 10.8 | 21.0 | 10.0 | 15.6 | 21.0 |
| First National Bank and Trust Co. | Clinton | IL | C+ | B- | B- | 174.9 | 1.80 | 1.3 | 0.3 | 5.5 | 79.6 | 7.5 | 9.4 | 18.9 |
| ▲ First National Bank and Trust Co. | Chickasha | OK | B+ | B- | B | 664.8 | 6.11 | 10.2 | 1.2 | 6.9 | 29.4 | 10.0 | 12.0 | 17.8 |
| First National Bank and Trust Co. | Shawnee | OK | C+ | C | C | 243.6 | -1.71 | 7.0 | 0.9 | 6.4 | 42.2 | 10.0 | 15.1 | 31.2 |
| First National Bank and Trust Co. | Beloit | WI | B- | B- | B- | 1170.1 | 1.45 | 9.5 | 0.9 | 18.1 | 15.3 | 8.2 | 9.9 | 13.5 |
| First National Bank at Darlington | Darlington | WI | B+ | B+ | A- | 156.0 | 3.62 | 4.8 | 2.6 | 7.0 | 8.1 | 10.0 | 15.1 | 21.4 |
| First National Bank at Paris | Paris | AR | B+ | B | B+ | 187.0 | 11.16 | 4.9 | 9.2 | 20.2 | 12.9 | 10.0 | 11.3 | 15.8 |
| First National Bank at Saint James | Saint James | MN | D+ | D | D+ | 30.0 | -3.25 | 4.2 | 4.5 | 22.8 | 5.2 | 6.8 | 8.8 | 13.4 |
| First National Bank Baird | Baird | TX | C+ | C+ | B- | 416.9 | -0.09 | 18.0 | 1.6 | 14.0 | 1.4 | 7.7 | 10.3 | 13.1 |
| First National Bank in Amboy | Amboy | IL | B | B | B | 211.6 | 5.67 | 5.9 | 2.5 | 9.6 | 40.6 | 10.0 | 11.3 | 19.1 |
| First National Bank in Carlyle | Carlyle | IL | B | B | C+ | 202.0 | 7.12 | 5.2 | 1.8 | 7.8 | 27.5 | 10.0 | 11.0 | 18.3 |
| First National Bank in Cimarron | Cimarron | KS | B | B- | B- | 111.3 | 9.27 | 12.3 | 2.6 | 6.2 | 41.1 | 5.7 | 7.7 | 13.0 |
| First National Bank in Cooper | Cooper | TX | B | B- | B- | 45.0 | -3.19 | 4.6 | 6.1 | 21.0 | 15.5 | 10.0 | 14.8 | 48.8 |

| Asset Quality Index | Adjusted Non-Performing Loans as a % of Total Loans | Adjusted Non-Performing Loans as a % of Capital | Net Charge-Offs Avg Loans | Profitability Index | Net Income ($Mil) | Return on Assets (R.O.A.) | Return on Equity (R.O.E.) | Net Interest Spread | Overhead Efficiency Ratio | Liquidity Index | Liquidity Ratio | Hot Money Ratio | Stability Index |
|---|---|---|---|---|---|---|---|---|---|---|---|---|---|
| **9.8** | 0.00 | 0.0 | 0.02 | **5.3** | 2.6 | 1.44 | 15.35 | 3.05 | 54.5 | **4.3** | 23.2 | 7.5 | **6.6** |
| **8.4** | 0.14 | 0.9 | 0.03 | **4.4** | 4.8 | 1.07 | 11.48 | 3.37 | 71.0 | **1.7** | 21.8 | 18.1 | **6.4** |
| **5.1** | 1.98 | 7.1 | 0.03 | **4.2** | 10.0 | 0.99 | 8.83 | 3.17 | 68.1 | **2.8** | 9.8 | 9.7 | **9.1** |
| **8.3** | 0.12 | 0.9 | 0.14 | **4.3** | 3.1 | 0.71 | 7.89 | 3.88 | 65.5 | **0.6** | 6.5 | 36.5 | **6.6** |
| **7.5** | 0.48 | 4.3 | 0.44 | **6.6** | 5.0 | 1.57 | 12.75 | 4.52 | 66.3 | **4.6** | 27.3 | 7.3 | **6.9** |
| **7.0** | 0.19 | 0.8 | 0.04 | **7.9** | 175.2 | 1.58 | 10.97 | 3.77 | 53.7 | **3.6** | 22.4 | 7.4 | **10.0** |
| **8.7** | 0.09 | 0.3 | 0.08 | **8.5** | 10.1 | 1.55 | 13.29 | 3.60 | 48.4 | **1.9** | 22.0 | 21.1 | **8.5** |
| **4.9** | 1.03 | 4.7 | 0.23 | **6.2** | 45.4 | 1.22 | 9.69 | 3.84 | 56.6 | **3.2** | 4.7 | 11.6 | **9.4** |
| **4.7** | 0.65 | 4.4 | 0.31 | **6.9** | 226.4 | 1.34 | 10.07 | 4.00 | 54.4 | **3.3** | 12.2 | 10.5 | **9.5** |
| **5.2** | 1.45 | 10.3 | 0.07 | **6.5** | 4.3 | 1.26 | 11.46 | 3.93 | 60.4 | **1.4** | 12.6 | 25.2 | **6.7** |
| **5.0** | 0.84 | 7.7 | 0.19 | **6.5** | 6.9 | 1.60 | 16.30 | 3.97 | 59.4 | **1.2** | 10.3 | 24.5 | **6.9** |
| **2.3** | 2.23 | 19.1 | 0.24 | **5.4** | 1.3 | 1.06 | 9.60 | 3.98 | 67.2 | **1.1** | 10.6 | 26.4 | **6.7** |
| **9.1** | 0.23 | 1.1 | 0.02 | **5.6** | 3.0 | 1.37 | 12.45 | 3.61 | 62.3 | **5.5** | 43.0 | 7.8 | **7.4** |
| **3.2** | 2.81 | 20.4 | 0.02 | **6.4** | 4.1 | 1.44 | 14.71 | 3.91 | 63.2 | **2.7** | 16.9 | 15.4 | **7.4** |
| **6.2** | 0.75 | 5.5 | 0.60 | **5.8** | 2.7 | 1.34 | 15.06 | 4.00 | 59.4 | **2.9** | 18.9 | 15.0 | **7.1** |
| **4.9** | 0.78 | 6.1 | 0.02 | **6.4** | 2.5 | 1.42 | 13.41 | 4.00 | 64.5 | **0.9** | 11.3 | 30.8 | **7.3** |
| **4.7** | 0.80 | 6.7 | -0.02 | **3.9** | 1.5 | 0.89 | 10.66 | 3.21 | 73.9 | **0.7** | 15.0 | 37.9 | **5.7** |
| **3.3** | 0.94 | 8.0 | 0.13 | **5.7** | 3.2 | 1.03 | 9.44 | 4.66 | 68.6 | **4.4** | 6.6 | 4.7 | **6.7** |
| **3.6** | 1.87 | 6.4 | 0.19 | **1.1** | 0.0 | 0.05 | 0.35 | 3.62 | 99.8 | **5.3** | 49.4 | 10.1 | **5.5** |
| **5.4** | 1.72 | 9.6 | 0.02 | **5.3** | 6.6 | 1.23 | 12.43 | 3.84 | 69.4 | **2.2** | 13.9 | 17.8 | **7.3** |
| **4.2** | 3.56 | 11.1 | -0.46 | **3.8** | 1.0 | 0.68 | 5.52 | 3.32 | 62.3 | **3.7** | 23.6 | 11.1 | **7.0** |
| **6.0** | 2.36 | 7.8 | 0.35 | **6.3** | 2.2 | 1.20 | 10.59 | 4.81 | 65.2 | **4.1** | 13.8 | 7.5 | **7.1** |
| **5.0** | 1.58 | 6.0 | 0.85 | **3.8** | 2.1 | 0.66 | 6.66 | 3.95 | 72.6 | **5.3** | 44.3 | 9.3 | **5.2** |
| **4.1** | 4.20 | 17.5 | 0.06 | **6.1** | 6.8 | 1.44 | 11.93 | 3.48 | 59.1 | **3.2** | 25.3 | 14.3 | **8.6** |
| **6.7** | 0.32 | 3.1 | 0.04 | **5.5** | 1.4 | 1.06 | 11.61 | 4.80 | 70.5 | **4.8** | 15.2 | 3.3 | **5.6** |
| **7.3** | 1.06 | 3.0 | 0.00 | **5.2** | 11.3 | 1.21 | 13.32 | 3.24 | 61.5 | **6.4** | 45.2 | 2.4 | **5.7** |
| **4.1** | 3.46 | 14.6 | 0.11 | **6.2** | 4.0 | 1.49 | 11.99 | 3.75 | 63.0 | **2.2** | 27.4 | 19.7 | **8.5** |
| **1.6** | 5.49 | 39.7 | 3.23 | **1.1** | -4.9 | -1.10 | -12.78 | 3.39 | 74.0 | **1.1** | 11.9 | 19.0 | **5.3** |
| **5.4** | 0.95 | 5.6 | 0.21 | **7.7** | 4.7 | 1.78 | 13.82 | 4.73 | 62.1 | **1.3** | 11.8 | 26.1 | **8.2** |
| **8.5** | 0.09 | 0.2 | 0.21 | **7.2** | 4.8 | 1.68 | 9.60 | 4.09 | 58.9 | **6.1** | 57.8 | 8.6 | **8.8** |
| **7.8** | 0.48 | 3.2 | 0.11 | **5.9** | 20.1 | 1.22 | 11.63 | 3.38 | 56.4 | **0.8** | 10.0 | 33.6 | **8.9** |
| **5.1** | 1.15 | 5.6 | 0.26 | **6.2** | 5.3 | 1.17 | 9.24 | 3.73 | 54.3 | **3.0** | 18.0 | 14.2 | **8.1** |
| **4.3** | 1.53 | 10.0 | 0.11 | **2.9** | 0.5 | 0.58 | 6.66 | 3.22 | 79.8 | **1.7** | 23.8 | 24.5 | **4.8** |
| **6.9** | 1.38 | 4.9 | -0.01 | **3.6** | 2.0 | 0.68 | 6.79 | 3.29 | 75.5 | **6.2** | 52.4 | 5.9 | **5.9** |
| **4.2** | 1.13 | 7.6 | 0.07 | **8.1** | 4.4 | 1.76 | 18.40 | 5.88 | 70.4 | **2.7** | 4.7 | 14.3 | **7.8** |
| **5.7** | 1.37 | 9.6 | 0.07 | **6.0** | 26.1 | 1.32 | 14.97 | 3.08 | 51.8 | **1.4** | 24.6 | 25.0 | **8.0** |
| **6.8** | 1.69 | 3.9 | 0.40 | **6.6** | 5.5 | 1.54 | 12.82 | 3.93 | 63.8 | **6.3** | 48.7 | 4.0 | **8.6** |
| **7.3** | 2.09 | 1.5 | 0.19 | **6.7** | 1.0 | 1.21 | 13.33 | 5.26 | 70.8 | **3.1** | 21.5 | 14.3 | **6.2** |
| **5.4** | 1.14 | 3.5 | 4.28 | **10.0** | 28.5 | 2.49 | 10.76 | 8.46 | 37.9 | **2.8** | 14.8 | 15.2 | **9.3** |
| **5.6** | 1.23 | 4.6 | 4.26 | **6.1** | 2.8 | 0.91 | 6.64 | 8.13 | 53.8 | **3.3** | 14.5 | 12.3 | **6.6** |
| **4.6** | 3.84 | 13.5 | 0.03 | **3.3** | 0.7 | 1.01 | 8.91 | 3.67 | 76.7 | **4.3** | 27.8 | 9.5 | **5.3** |
| **6.4** | 1.51 | 6.8 | 0.33 | **5.9** | 3.6 | 1.65 | 11.96 | 4.07 | 63.4 | **1.0** | 12.6 | 31.6 | **9.0** |
| **5.5** | 0.39 | 3.3 | 0.16 | **5.4** | 6.5 | 1.30 | 13.00 | 4.15 | 70.8 | **1.0** | 3.6 | 28.7 | **7.9** |
| **5.9** | 0.32 | 2.5 | 0.01 | **4.6** | 4.5 | 0.94 | 10.30 | 3.96 | 74.7 | **4.2** | 15.5 | 7.5 | **5.4** |
| **7.0** | 0.48 | 2.0 | -0.10 | **8.1** | 6.1 | 1.97 | 16.83 | 3.83 | 51.5 | **2.3** | 34.1 | 25.2 | **8.8** |
| **7.9** | 1.29 | 2.9 | 0.01 | **7.8** | 55.7 | 1.47 | 10.47 | 3.74 | 53.6 | **4.9** | 13.5 | 3.2 | **10.0** |
| **4.9** | 2.23 | 11.6 | 0.18 | **3.8** | 1.3 | 0.84 | 7.48 | 3.72 | 79.5 | **2.7** | 24.4 | 16.2 | **6.9** |
| **4.2** | 2.37 | 10.7 | 0.22 | **4.7** | 2.4 | 1.08 | 6.93 | 4.08 | 74.2 | **2.1** | 14.9 | 18.6 | **8.6** |
| **9.9** | 0.13 | 0.5 | 0.02 | **3.5** | 3.7 | 2.06 | 21.86 | 3.11 | 92.2 | **2.2** | 45.7 | 40.5 | **5.7** |
| **5.5** | 1.53 | 5.5 | 0.57 | **10.0** | 12.5 | 1.93 | 14.57 | 4.75 | 48.7 | **3.3** | 26.3 | 10.4 | **8.7** |
| **8.0** | 1.04 | 3.6 | 0.11 | **2.4** | 1.1 | 0.41 | 2.73 | 3.49 | 90.8 | **5.6** | 41.7 | 6.7 | **7.2** |
| **7.7** | 0.36 | 2.1 | 0.03 | **4.3** | 9.6 | 0.85 | 7.23 | 3.59 | 78.1 | **4.7** | 25.3 | 8.9 | **9.2** |
| **5.5** | 0.17 | 0.8 | 0.10 | **5.4** | 1.5 | 0.99 | 6.60 | 3.65 | 58.7 | **2.5** | 35.0 | 22.9 | **8.1** |
| **5.2** | 0.34 | 5.3 | 0.15 | **8.5** | 3.4 | 1.89 | 13.59 | 4.73 | 62.8 | **1.1** | 9.9 | 28.8 | **8.6** |
| **3.2** | 1.19 | 16.1 | 0.00 | **3.2** | 0.1 | 0.37 | 4.16 | 4.59 | 90.6 | **1.8** | 24.7 | 23.5 | **3.0** |
| **2.7** | 1.69 | 16.1 | 0.91 | **3.8** | 1.9 | 0.45 | 4.57 | 5.24 | 77.1 | **1.9** | 12.5 | 19.0 | **5.9** |
| **8.7** | 0.26 | 1.1 | 0.03 | **3.4** | 1.4 | 0.68 | 5.79 | 3.47 | 78.9 | **5.2** | 36.3 | 6.9 | **7.0** |
| **8.5** | 0.09 | 0.5 | 0.00 | **4.4** | 1.8 | 0.91 | 8.19 | 3.20 | 64.7 | **3.9** | 22.1 | 9.5 | **6.7** |
| **8.7** | 0.00 | 0.0 | -0.01 | **5.2** | 1.3 | 1.26 | 15.95 | 3.84 | 67.1 | **2.9** | 21.2 | 15.2 | **4.9** |
| **8.1** | 0.00 | 3.8 | 0.00 | **4.7** | 0.5 | 1.06 | 7.35 | 3.39 | 64.1 | **4.7** | 50.6 | 13.2 | **6.4** |

| Name | City | State | Rating | 2018 Rating | 2017 Rating | Total Assets ($Mil) | One Year Asset Growth | Asset Mix (As a % of Total Assets) Comm-ercial Loans | Cons-umer Loans | Mort-gage Loans | Secur-ities | Capital-ization Index | Lever-age Ratio | Risk-Based Capital Ratio |
|---|---|---|---|---|---|---|---|---|---|---|---|---|---|---|
| First National Bank in Creston | Creston | IA | **B+** | B+ | B+ | 249.3 | 1.48 | 7.2 | 2.6 | 11.4 | 21.1 | **9.4** | 10.6 | 15.5 |
| ▼ First National Bank in DeRidder | DeRidder | LA | **B** | B+ | B+ | 324.8 | 28.71 | 6.5 | 2.4 | 23.2 | 16.8 | **8.3** | 9.9 | 18.6 |
| First National Bank in Fairfield | Fairfield | IA | **C+** | C | C+ | 148.0 | 0.27 | 10.5 | 1.0 | 13.4 | 5.5 | **8.3** | 9.8 | 14.7 |
| First National Bank in Falfurrias | Falfurrias | TX | **C+** | C+ | C+ | 78.9 | 0.32 | 7.4 | 3.9 | 1.3 | 56.3 | **8.6** | 10.1 | 38.0 |
| ▲ First National Bank in Frankfort | Frankfort | KS | **B** | B- | B- | 48.3 | 3.61 | 5.2 | 3.3 | 9.6 | 41.1 | **9.2** | 10.5 | 18.8 |
| First National Bank in Fredonia | Fredonia | KS | **A-** | B+ | A- | 95.2 | 0.31 | 6.2 | 7.1 | 10.3 | 52.7 | **10.0** | 17.6 | 38.6 |
| ▲ First National Bank in Howell | Howell | MI | **B** | B- | B- | 431.1 | 5.60 | 6.7 | 12.0 | 11.6 | 7.7 | **9.0** | 12.3 | 14.1 |
| First National Bank in Marlow | Marlow | OK | **C+** | C+ | B- | 57.9 | -3.70 | 7.8 | 9.3 | 16.5 | 15.8 | **8.1** | 9.8 | 14.5 |
| First National Bank in New Bremen | New Bremen | OH | **B+** | B+ | B | 297.9 | 4.30 | 4.8 | 0.8 | 9.6 | 31.2 | **8.9** | 10.3 | 23.6 |
| First National Bank in Okeene | Okeene | OK | **C** | C+ | B | 84.0 | 7.44 | 4.5 | 0.2 | 0.1 | 33.6 | **10.0** | 16.1 | 24.5 |
| ▲ First National Bank in Olney | Olney | IL | **B+** | B+ | B+ | 345.2 | 3.40 | 5.4 | 2.8 | 16.1 | 25.1 | **10.0** | 11.3 | 17.5 |
| First National Bank in Ord | Ord | NE | **B** | C+ | C+ | 130.6 | -4.37 | 4.0 | 2.0 | 10.9 | 36.1 | **7.3** | 9.2 | 17.3 |
| First National Bank in Philip | Philip | SD | **A-** | B+ | A | 291.1 | 8.18 | 4.8 | 0.6 | 0.0 | 14.6 | **10.0** | 12.9 | 19.3 |
| First National Bank in Pinckneyville | Pinckneyville | IL | **A-** | A- | A- | 99.2 | -2.24 | 2.4 | 4.6 | 24.9 | 48.8 | **10.0** | 15.1 | 33.2 |
| First National Bank in Port Lavaca | Port Lavaca | TX | **B** | B | B | 334.9 | 5.38 | 2.9 | 1.8 | 31.3 | 39.7 | **8.3** | 9.9 | 22.9 |
| First National Bank in Sioux Falls | Sioux Falls | SD | **A-** | B | B | 1339.6 | 7.54 | 10.8 | 0.8 | 19.1 | 21.6 | **10.0** | 13.1 | 17.8 |
| First National Bank in Staunton | Staunton | IL | **B+** | B+ | B+ | 549.3 | 1.59 | 6.1 | 4.3 | 24.1 | 19.0 | **10.0** | 12.0 | 16.9 |
| ▼ First National Bank in Taylorville | Taylorville | IL | **A-** | A | A | 193.0 | 0.15 | 8.1 | 2.8 | 9.5 | 49.5 | **10.0** | 17.7 | 36.1 |
| First National Bank in Tigerton | Tigerton | WI | **C+** | C+ | C+ | 22.1 | -4.99 | 0.2 | 2.1 | 29.3 | 27.1 | **10.0** | 14.7 | 41.6 |
| First National Bank in Tremont | Tremont | IL | **B** | B | B- | 122.4 | -1.15 | 7.3 | 1.8 | 22.8 | 24.5 | **10.0** | 12.0 | 20.0 |
| First National Bank in Trinidad | Trinidad | CO | **B-** | C+ | C | 205.8 | -4.10 | 0.9 | 0.9 | 31.2 | 38.8 | **10.0** | 12.2 | 27.1 |
| First National Bank Minnesota | Saint Peter | MN | **C+** | C+ | C+ | 214.8 | 1.74 | 12.0 | 2.9 | 7.5 | 11.8 | **6.5** | 9.2 | 12.2 |
| First National Bank North | Walker | MN | **A** | A- | A- | 564.9 | 4.76 | 5.0 | 7.6 | 23.6 | 20.1 | **9.5** | 10.6 | 18.1 |
| First National Bank Northwest Florida | Panama City | FL | **B+** | B+ | B- | 177.2 | 14.35 | 1.0 | 0.0 | 9.0 | 5.1 | **9.2** | 10.4 | 37.5 |
| First National Bank of Absecon | Absecon | NJ | **C+** | C | C | 147.0 | -2.76 | 4.8 | 0.2 | 27.4 | 36.8 | **10.0** | 11.2 | 23.4 |
| ▲ First National Bank of Albany | Albany | TX | **A-** | B+ | A- | 567.0 | -4.28 | 21.9 | 2.5 | 10.1 | 19.5 | **10.0** | 11.7 | 16.7 |
| First National Bank of Allendale | Allendale | IL | **B** | B- | B+ | 252.9 | 9.04 | 9.1 | 6.4 | 18.7 | 19.4 | **9.6** | 10.7 | 15.7 |
| First National Bank of Alvin | Alvin | TX | **B+** | B+ | B+ | 147.3 | 4.99 | 0.4 | 0.2 | 1.3 | 72.0 | **10.0** | 12.4 | 38.3 |
| First National Bank of America | East Lansing | MI | **B-** | C | C | 2488.0 | 38.34 | 0.2 | 0.3 | 84.5 | 2.1 | **7.7** | 9.4 | 17.6 |
| First National Bank of Anderson | Anderson | TX | **B** | B | B | 180.0 | 5.16 | 11.3 | 4.6 | 13.4 | 12.1 | **9.9** | 11.0 | 17.2 |
| First National Bank of Anson | Anson | TX | **B-** | C+ | C+ | 65.5 | 4.04 | 11.6 | 10.3 | 20.3 | 26.1 | **6.9** | 8.9 | 16.7 |
| First National Bank of Arenzville | Arenzville | IL | **B-** | B- | B- | 86.7 | 3.27 | 10.3 | 4.7 | 13.4 | 15.6 | **8.6** | 10.3 | 13.9 |
| First National Bank of Aspermont | Aspermont | TX | **B+** | B+ | B+ | 60.4 | -11.00 | 2.6 | 3.1 | 6.5 | 65.1 | **10.0** | 17.0 | 49.4 |
| First National Bank of Assumption | Assumption | IL | **C** | C- | C | 21.3 | 2.70 | 4.2 | 3.9 | 7.4 | 28.8 | **9.5** | 10.7 | 27.9 |
| First National Bank of Ava | Ava | IL | **B** | B | B | 65.3 | 4.81 | 4.2 | 3.7 | 18.5 | 43.2 | **10.0** | 12.8 | 21.7 |
| First National Bank of Bagley | Bagley | MN | **C+** | C+ | C+ | 89.0 | 0.96 | 9.0 | 9.1 | 24.2 | 15.2 | **5.9** | 7.9 | 12.8 |
| First National Bank of Ballinger | Ballinger | TX | **B-** | B- | B- | 188.6 | 4.66 | 11.0 | 1.2 | 10.8 | 13.9 | **8.8** | 10.2 | 14.9 |
| ▲ First National Bank of Bangor | Bangor | WI | **A** | B+ | A- | 233.9 | 1.30 | 4.1 | 1.6 | 19.0 | 13.6 | **10.0** | 32.5 | 38.6 |
| First National Bank of Bastrop | Bastrop | TX | **A-** | B+ | A- | 622.1 | 9.35 | 2.1 | 2.0 | 17.0 | 31.6 | **9.6** | 10.7 | 17.5 |
| First National Bank of Beardstown | Beardstown | IL | **A-** | B+ | B+ | 130.8 | 8.78 | 3.9 | 5.9 | 11.4 | 12.8 | **10.0** | 11.8 | 18.4 |
| First National Bank of Bellevue | Bellevue | OH | **C+** | C+ | B- | 227.1 | 2.29 | 15.1 | 1.7 | 6.9 | 11.8 | **6.9** | 10.2 | 12.4 |
| First National Bank of Bellville | Bellville | TX | **B+** | A- | A- | 726.5 | 6.30 | 2.5 | 1.7 | 10.2 | 65.6 | **10.0** | 11.2 | 26.1 |
| First National Bank of Bemidji | Bemidji | MN | **A** | A | A | 670.3 | 2.27 | 12.0 | 12.1 | 13.0 | 36.4 | **10.0** | 14.1 | 19.7 |
| First National Bank of Benton | Benton | LA | **A-** | B+ | B+ | 63.3 | 7.22 | 2.6 | 1.5 | 40.1 | 13.1 | **10.0** | 18.6 | 42.4 |
| First National Bank of Blanchester | Blanchester | OH | **B+** | B+ | B+ | 60.6 | -0.11 | 2.1 | 4.7 | 46.2 | 13.6 | **10.0** | 11.9 | 23.4 |
| First National Bank of Bosque County | Valley Mills | TX | **B+** | B- | B | 119.4 | -1.08 | 12.7 | 6.2 | 30.9 | 5.2 | **10.0** | 11.3 | 17.5 |
| First National Bank of Brookfield | Brookfield | IL | **A-** | B | B- | 212.5 | 14.19 | 0.2 | 7.7 | 17.5 | 6.4 | **9.6** | 10.7 | 16.2 |
| First National Bank of Brooksville | Brooksville | KY | **B-** | B- | C+ | 64.8 | 7.13 | 1.3 | 2.1 | 32.8 | 33.4 | **10.0** | 11.7 | 24.1 |
| First National Bank of Brownstown | Brownstown | IL | **C+** | C | C | 40.4 | 6.18 | 3.9 | 6.9 | 15.1 | 27.5 | **10.0** | 11.0 | 23.8 |
| First National Bank of Brundidge | Brundidge | AL | **B-** | B- | B- | 89.7 | 1.11 | 4.7 | 3.6 | 13.8 | 14.5 | **10.0** | 17.2 | 29.3 |
| First National Bank of Buhl | Mountain Iron | MN | **D** | D- | D- | 26.1 | -0.93 | 6.6 | 10.5 | 43.5 | 0.0 | **6.0** | 8.0 | 15.1 |
| First National Bank of Burleson | Burleson | TX | **A-** | B+ | B+ | 199.0 | -3.53 | 7.9 | 2.6 | 1.8 | 46.0 | **9.1** | 10.4 | 27.9 |
| First National Bank of Carmi | Carmi | IL | **B** | B- | B- | 426.5 | 5.18 | 9.2 | 0.9 | 4.6 | 17.8 | **7.2** | 9.2 | 14.6 |
| First National Bank of Central Texas | Waco | TX | **B+** | B+ | B+ | 878.3 | 3.12 | 17.1 | 1.1 | 13.7 | 5.0 | **6.3** | 9.5 | 12.0 |
| ▲ First National Bank of Chadron | Chadron | NE | **A-** | B | B+ | 128.1 | 2.01 | 3.9 | 1.0 | 0.2 | 32.5 | **10.0** | 14.1 | 20.5 |
| ▲ First National Bank of Chisholm | Chisholm | MN | **C-** | D+ | D | 73.9 | 2.48 | 8.4 | 5.8 | 7.7 | 57.8 | **7.2** | 9.1 | 17.2 |
| First National Bank of Clarksdale | Clarksdale | MS | **B+** | A- | A- | 345.4 | -4.81 | 6.0 | 3.2 | 8.2 | 29.2 | **10.0** | 12.9 | 19.0 |
| First National Bank of Coffee County | Douglas | GA | **B+** | B+ | A- | 234.5 | 20.46 | 4.3 | 0.7 | 13.0 | 2.8 | **7.4** | 9.3 | 15.2 |
| ▲ First National Bank of Cokato | Cokato | MN | **B** | C+ | C+ | 61.0 | -1.73 | 16.2 | 3.1 | 15.1 | 8.1 | **8.0** | 9.7 | 15.6 |
| First National Bank of Coleraine | Coleraine | MN | **C+** | C | C | 86.0 | -6.86 | 3.3 | 3.2 | 15.1 | 42.3 | **6.4** | 8.4 | 19.6 |

| Asset Quality Index | Adjusted Non-Performing Loans as a % of Total Loans | Adjusted Non-Performing Loans as a % of Capital | Net Charge-Offs Avg Loans | Profitability Index | Net Income ($Mil) | Return on Assets (R.O.A.) | Return on Equity (R.O.E.) | Net Interest Spread | Overhead Efficiency Ratio | Liquidity Index | Liquidity Ratio | Hot Money Ratio | Stability Index |
|---|---|---|---|---|---|---|---|---|---|---|---|---|---|
| 8.2 | 0.22 | 1.0 | 0.13 | 7.1 | 3.9 | 1.57 | 15.15 | 3.91 | 70.0 | 3.4 | 20.6 | 12.7 | 8.1 |
| 6.9 | 0.49 | 3.0 | 0.03 | 4.4 | 2.5 | 0.90 | 9.45 | 3.74 | 77.0 | 4.8 | 34.2 | 8.7 | 5.2 |
| 2.1 | 5.20 | 33.1 | 0.33 | 1.5 | 0.5 | 0.32 | 3.31 | 3.48 | 77.9 | 2.8 | 19.8 | 12.5 | 4.3 |
| 6.4 | 2.33 | 4.2 | -0.12 | 3.4 | 0.6 | 0.80 | 7.85 | 2.74 | 75.1 | 5.0 | 37.3 | 8.7 | 4.3 |
| 8.7 | 0.00 | 0.0 | 0.22 | 6.9 | 0.8 | 1.68 | 17.09 | 3.53 | 67.3 | 4.3 | 39.4 | 13.4 | 6.3 |
| 7.7 | 1.22 | 3.0 | 0.25 | 6.3 | 1.3 | 1.45 | 8.09 | 3.63 | 59.3 | 3.7 | 60.4 | 20.2 | 8.4 |
| 5.9 | 0.69 | 3.3 | -0.07 | 7.1 | 6.0 | 1.44 | 12.23 | 4.55 | 67.2 | 4.2 | 11.5 | 6.7 | 7.3 |
| 7.2 | 0.00 | 0.3 | 0.09 | 3.6 | 0.4 | 0.61 | 6.26 | 4.54 | 86.7 | 2.2 | 21.2 | 18.4 | 5.1 |
| 9.0 | 0.34 | 1.2 | -0.02 | 5.7 | 4.2 | 1.43 | 13.66 | 2.93 | 53.0 | 6.0 | 53.6 | 7.8 | 7.0 |
| 8.4 | 0.73 | 2.4 | 1.12 | 6.3 | 1.1 | 1.29 | 7.75 | 3.59 | 53.6 | 2.0 | 34.6 | 29.0 | 4.3 |
| 6.0 | 1.21 | 4.9 | 0.05 | 5.8 | 4.2 | 1.24 | 9.85 | 3.52 | 59.3 | 3.4 | 20.7 | 12.8 | 7.7 |
| 8.8 | 0.18 | 0.9 | -0.01 | 4.4 | 1.4 | 1.10 | 12.24 | 3.34 | 66.4 | 4.0 | 20.3 | 7.8 | 5.5 |
| 7.3 | 0.06 | 0.3 | 0.01 | 8.1 | 4.6 | 1.70 | 12.73 | 3.77 | 49.1 | 2.4 | 26.7 | 7.4 | 9.4 |
| 8.3 | 0.79 | 1.9 | 0.07 | 5.5 | 1.3 | 1.32 | 8.33 | 4.17 | 65.5 | 4.8 | 27.2 | 5.9 | 8.3 |
| 8.3 | 0.53 | 3.2 | 0.01 | 5.1 | 3.5 | 1.07 | 10.64 | 3.06 | 55.6 | 4.1 | 29.9 | 11.2 | 6.4 |
| 5.5 | 1.90 | 10.2 | 0.01 | 6.0 | 15.0 | 1.23 | 9.25 | 3.72 | 69.8 | 3.9 | 10.7 | 5.0 | 9.9 |
| 8.4 | 0.48 | 2.2 | 0.09 | 5.3 | 7.2 | 1.33 | 11.03 | 3.31 | 64.9 | 4.1 | 18.7 | 8.2 | 8.6 |
| 9.0 | 0.10 | 0.2 | 1.27 | 5.2 | 2.3 | 1.16 | 6.48 | 3.33 | 51.1 | 5.1 | 55.2 | 13.4 | 9.6 |
| 9.7 | 0.64 | 0.9 | -0.02 | 2.4 | 0.1 | 0.37 | 2.65 | 3.44 | 88.9 | 4.7 | 41.5 | 9.0 | 6.5 |
| 7.4 | 0.45 | 2.9 | 0.09 | 4.1 | 1.0 | 0.78 | 6.29 | 3.79 | 78.1 | 3.3 | 26.4 | 14.0 | 6.8 |
| 5.6 | 4.28 | 12.4 | 0.08 | 3.3 | 1.4 | 0.64 | 5.28 | 3.82 | 82.3 | 4.9 | 29.8 | 6.3 | 6.9 |
| 4.2 | 1.53 | 9.5 | 0.00 | 6.6 | 3.4 | 1.57 | 14.97 | 4.51 | 67.9 | 3.8 | 12.1 | 9.8 | 6.3 |
| 8.2 | 0.20 | 1.0 | 0.05 | 8.5 | 11.3 | 2.05 | 18.22 | 4.12 | 53.4 | 1.9 | 25.8 | 21.8 | 9.1 |
| 9.4 | 0.30 | 1.0 | 0.00 | 5.3 | 2.4 | 1.33 | 12.81 | 3.12 | 57.9 | 6.0 | 68.9 | 11.2 | 7.2 |
| 8.6 | 0.86 | 3.3 | 0.01 | 3.2 | 0.7 | 0.49 | 4.49 | 3.55 | 83.2 | 6.9 | 54.8 | 2.2 | 5.6 |
| 6.7 | 0.86 | 4.0 | 0.38 | 8.2 | 11.6 | 2.00 | 17.06 | 4.45 | 44.5 | 1.1 | 25.7 | 20.8 | 9.0 |
| 4.7 | 1.42 | 7.8 | 0.05 | 5.2 | 2.6 | 1.11 | 10.22 | 3.74 | 58.7 | 1.9 | 16.4 | 19.6 | 6.2 |
| 10.0 | 0.00 | 0.0 | -0.07 | 5.1 | 1.9 | 1.34 | 10.94 | 2.61 | 52.5 | 4.3 | 65.7 | 19.5 | 7.6 |
| 4.2 | 2.18 | 17.9 | 0.05 | 10.0 | 54.5 | 2.55 | 28.19 | 5.49 | 37.0 | 0.4 | 6.0 | 35.0 | 9.1 |
| 8.1 | 0.23 | 1.4 | 0.10 | 4.6 | 1.6 | 0.89 | 7.96 | 3.93 | 70.4 | 1.4 | 23.5 | 28.6 | 6.4 |
| 7.4 | 0.00 | 1.1 | -0.81 | 8.9 | 1.4 | 2.28 | 24.94 | 5.18 | 58.2 | 4.7 | 17.6 | 4.4 | 5.4 |
| 5.1 | 1.50 | 5.6 | 0.04 | 4.6 | 0.9 | 1.06 | 10.31 | 3.95 | 73.2 | 2.2 | 15.2 | 18.0 | 6.5 |
| 9.5 | 0.00 | 0.0 | 0.04 | 5.4 | 0.9 | 1.41 | 8.32 | 3.11 | 55.9 | 3.5 | 57.3 | 20.7 | 7.8 |
| 8.3 | 1.02 | 2.7 | 0.02 | 3.4 | 0.1 | 0.60 | 5.72 | 3.25 | 77.9 | 5.2 | 57.6 | 10.3 | 4.8 |
| 5.1 | 3.81 | 10.4 | 0.10 | 6.3 | 0.8 | 1.24 | 8.97 | 4.54 | 63.8 | 4.6 | 38.4 | 11.4 | 7.9 |
| 6.4 | 0.37 | 2.9 | 0.00 | 4.2 | 0.9 | 0.94 | 11.52 | 3.93 | 72.0 | 3.8 | 15.7 | 9.9 | 4.7 |
| 3.3 | 2.40 | 13.9 | 0.02 | 7.1 | 3.0 | 1.69 | 16.07 | 4.59 | 60.2 | 1.7 | 20.4 | 23.0 | 6.8 |
| 7.4 | 2.22 | 3.1 | 0.00 | 9.8 | 5.6 | 2.59 | 8.24 | 4.46 | 24.8 | 4.9 | 24.9 | 3.8 | 9.6 |
| 7.5 | 0.35 | 2.2 | 0.04 | 8.0 | 11.0 | 1.83 | 17.07 | 4.10 | 58.5 | 2.5 | 22.2 | 17.0 | 9.1 |
| 8.2 | 0.16 | 1.0 | 0.00 | 5.2 | 1.6 | 1.28 | 10.66 | 4.10 | 69.1 | 4.1 | 24.0 | 8.9 | 7.3 |
| 2.8 | 2.07 | 11.1 | 0.02 | 5.6 | 2.6 | 1.12 | 10.85 | 4.15 | 67.3 | 1.4 | 7.0 | 11.0 | 7.2 |
| 8.5 | 0.02 | 0.7 | 0.03 | 4.8 | 8.5 | 1.20 | 8.44 | 2.58 | 59.3 | 2.5 | 51.2 | 40.4 | 8.4 |
| 6.3 | 1.46 | 3.9 | 0.05 | 7.7 | 12.4 | 1.88 | 12.86 | 3.51 | 51.5 | 2.1 | 28.1 | 21.2 | 10.0 |
| 9.2 | 0.64 | 2.1 | 0.01 | 7.9 | 1.0 | 1.62 | 8.80 | 4.13 | 52.6 | 4.2 | 27.6 | 9.8 | 7.7 |
| 7.5 | 1.24 | 6.6 | 0.08 | 5.0 | 0.6 | 0.99 | 8.35 | 4.08 | 70.2 | 4.6 | 25.9 | 6.2 | 6.4 |
| 5.5 | 1.32 | 10.1 | 0.10 | 5.9 | 1.8 | 1.48 | 13.15 | 4.39 | 65.4 | 3.7 | 19.1 | 10.8 | 7.1 |
| 7.4 | 0.00 | 0.0 | -0.27 | 5.6 | 2.2 | 1.13 | 10.14 | 3.84 | 61.7 | 3.0 | 24.9 | 14.7 | 6.9 |
| 7.5 | 1.32 | 5.5 | 0.11 | 3.8 | 0.5 | 0.76 | 6.38 | 3.86 | 80.5 | 4.4 | 22.8 | 6.9 | 6.3 |
| 6.3 | 0.71 | 5.9 | 0.24 | 3.6 | 0.3 | 0.75 | 6.69 | 3.45 | 71.4 | 4.3 | 43.2 | 14.0 | 5.3 |
| 8.3 | 0.51 | 1.8 | 0.02 | 3.7 | 0.5 | 0.61 | 3.55 | 4.01 | 81.3 | 1.7 | 26.9 | 27.0 | 7.6 |
| 2.3 | 2.49 | 15.6 | 0.06 | 2.2 | 0.1 | 0.39 | 4.19 | 4.46 | 91.1 | 2.3 | 24.8 | 18.3 | 1.7 |
| 9.1 | 0.64 | 1.8 | 0.01 | 6.3 | 3.0 | 1.53 | 14.47 | 3.74 | 56.6 | 7.0 | 64.6 | 4.0 | 6.8 |
| 6.8 | 0.30 | 1.3 | -0.11 | 4.4 | 3.2 | 0.77 | 7.91 | 3.69 | 76.4 | 5.0 | 33.5 | 7.1 | 5.2 |
| 5.4 | 1.20 | 9.8 | 1.36 | 6.5 | 10.9 | 1.27 | 12.91 | 4.27 | 45.2 | 2.4 | 7.7 | 16.3 | 8.5 |
| 8.0 | 0.09 | 0.3 | -0.01 | 5.9 | 1.2 | 0.98 | 6.13 | 4.02 | 65.8 | 3.6 | 33.4 | 14.7 | 8.2 |
| 7.4 | 0.42 | 2.2 | -0.41 | 2.1 | 0.3 | 0.36 | 3.78 | 3.51 | 93.1 | 5.7 | 38.6 | 5.0 | 3.9 |
| 8.4 | 0.70 | 2.1 | 0.31 | 3.6 | 1.4 | 0.39 | 2.87 | 3.60 | 88.8 | 2.4 | 22.5 | 17.7 | 7.8 |
| 8.8 | 0.07 | 0.6 | -0.27 | 5.7 | 2.7 | 1.32 | 14.62 | 5.13 | 69.5 | 5.1 | 34.9 | 6.9 | 5.5 |
| 8.3 | 0.19 | 1.2 | 0.45 | 6.9 | 1.0 | 1.60 | 17.57 | 4.28 | 59.6 | 5.7 | 31.8 | 1.8 | 6.1 |
| 9.3 | 0.00 | 0.0 | 0.00 | 3.3 | 0.5 | 0.62 | 7.40 | 3.01 | 74.9 | 4.8 | 40.1 | 10.8 | 4.0 |

| Name | City | State | Rating | 2018 Rating | 2017 Rating | Total Assets ($Mil) | One Year Asset Growth | Asset Mix (As a % of Total Assets) Comm-ercial Loans | Cons-umer Loans | Mort-gage Loans | Secur-ities | Capital-ization Index | Lever-age Ratio | Risk-Based Capital Ratio |
|---|---|---|---|---|---|---|---|---|---|---|---|---|---|---|
| First National Bank of Decatur County | Bainbridge | GA | **B-** | B- | B- | 194.2 | 2.53 | 11.3 | 3.1 | 20.0 | 10.4 | **7.8** | 9.6 | 13.6 |
| First National Bank of Dennison | Dennison | OH | **B** | B- | B- | 230.4 | 1.75 | 4.0 | 20.5 | 15.3 | 28.5 | **9.0** | 10.3 | 19.2 |
| First National Bank of Dighton | Dighton | KS | **B-** | B | B- | 58.1 | 3.28 | 6.8 | 2.4 | 2.2 | 24.6 | **10.0** | 20.2 | 31.5 |
| First National Bank of Dozier | Dozier | AL | **B-** | B- | B- | 35.0 | 5.89 | 5.5 | 2.3 | 6.0 | 51.7 | **10.0** | 14.8 | 40.0 |
| First National Bank of Dryden | Dryden | NY | **B+** | B+ | B+ | 182.2 | 7.33 | 3.3 | 5.8 | 16.0 | 42.5 | **9.0** | 10.3 | 31.0 |
| First National Bank of Dublin | Dublin | TX | **B+** | B | B+ | 93.0 | 2.73 | 11.2 | 9.3 | 4.4 | 2.4 | **8.4** | 10.9 | 13.7 |
| First National Bank of Eagle Lake | Eagle Lake | TX | **B** | B+ | B+ | 125.2 | 4.41 | 10.3 | 0.5 | 2.5 | 13.7 | **8.9** | 10.3 | 15.2 |
| First National Bank of Eastern Arkansas | Forrest City | AR | **B+** | B+ | B- | 429.8 | 3.11 | 6.1 | 1.9 | 7.1 | 28.5 | **9.3** | 10.5 | 19.0 |
| First National Bank of Eldorado | Eldorado | TX | **A-** | A- | A- | 61.7 | 1.93 | 16.2 | 3.4 | 16.4 | 26.7 | **10.0** | 16.8 | 27.7 |
| First National Bank of Elmer | Elmer | NJ | **C** | D+ | D+ | 285.9 | 1.11 | 5.1 | 0.2 | 28.9 | 4.3 | **7.6** | 9.4 | 13.5 |
| First National Bank of Ely | Ely | NV | **B+** | B | C+ | 105.9 | 5.01 | 4.0 | 0.2 | 1.4 | 83.1 | **9.4** | 10.6 | 30.3 |
| ▲ First National Bank of Evant | Evant | TX | **B+** | B- | B | 99.3 | 1.00 | 8.1 | 7.0 | 36.7 | 11.3 | **8.1** | 9.8 | 16.6 |
| First National Bank of Fairfax | Fairfax | MN | **B+** | B | B | 30.6 | -2.15 | 11.3 | 0.6 | 0.9 | 17.5 | **10.0** | 39.0 | 38.3 |
| First National Bank of Fleming | Fleming | CO | **C** | C- | C- | 22.6 | 0.52 | 4.6 | 1.8 | 4.5 | 9.3 | **10.0** | 13.2 | 28.7 |
| First National Bank of Fletcher | Fletcher | OK | **B+** | B+ | B | 18.8 | 5.63 | 10.7 | 5.7 | 3.4 | 57.4 | **10.0** | 11.3 | 19.9 |
| First National Bank of Floydada | Floydada | TX | **A-** | B+ | A- | 116.4 | 5.64 | 3.7 | 2.2 | 0.2 | 20.6 | **8.9** | 10.3 | 17.6 |
| First National Bank of Fort Smith | Fort Smith | AR | **A-** | A- | B+ | 1353.9 | 0.07 | 12.9 | 1.0 | 12.6 | 14.2 | **9.5** | 11.2 | 14.5 |
| First National Bank of Fort Stockton | Fort Stockton | TX | **B** | B- | B- | 132.0 | 0.81 | 12.9 | 1.7 | 5.1 | 37.7 | **8.9** | 10.3 | 17.4 |
| First National Bank of Frederick | Frederick | SD | **C+** | C+ | B- | 25.3 | 17.26 | 2.1 | 0.2 | 0.0 | 18.5 | **10.0** | 12.1 | 26.3 |
| First National Bank of Germantown | Germantown | OH | **C** | C- | D+ | 66.1 | 11.35 | 7.9 | 4.4 | 31.6 | 21.3 | **6.7** | 8.8 | 15.4 |
| First National Bank of Giddings | Giddings | TX | **B** | B- | B- | 221.9 | 5.71 | 4.6 | 2.0 | 21.3 | 29.0 | **10.0** | 11.8 | 19.9 |
| ▼ First National Bank of Gilbert | Gilbert | MN | **D+** | C- | C | 48.7 | 18.60 | 4.5 | 5.6 | 49.7 | 5.0 | **5.2** | 7.2 | 13.7 |
| ▲ First National Bank of Gillette | Gillette | WY | **B** | B- | B- | 566.9 | 5.90 | 7.1 | 1.7 | 2.5 | 69.4 | **10.0** | 12.3 | 36.3 |
| First National Bank of Gilmer | Gilmer | TX | **B-** | C+ | B- | 469.2 | 24.35 | 9.6 | 5.0 | 18.1 | 16.9 | **8.0** | 9.7 | 15.9 |
| First National Bank of Gordon | Gordon | NE | **B+** | B | B+ | 202.3 | 6.18 | 5.3 | 2.9 | 0.1 | 39.4 | **10.0** | 13.9 | 23.2 |
| First National Bank of Granbury | Granbury | TX | **A-** | A- | A- | 629.4 | 5.13 | 4.2 | 2.9 | 21.0 | 36.3 | **10.0** | 11.5 | 21.9 |
| ▲ First National Bank of Grayson | Grayson | KY | **A-** | B | B+ | 250.6 | -0.47 | 4.2 | 13.8 | 24.4 | 21.9 | **10.0** | 11.8 | 21.5 |
| First National Bank of Griffin | Griffin | GA | **C** | C | D+ | 277.7 | 3.99 | 2.2 | 1.6 | 6.7 | 37.7 | **4.9** | 6.9 | 14.1 |
| First National Bank of Groton | Groton | NY | **A-** | B+ | A- | 182.8 | -0.10 | 8.2 | 9.3 | 25.0 | 36.1 | **10.0** | 14.5 | 28.5 |
| First National Bank of Hartford | Hartford | AL | **B** | B | B- | 121.9 | 4.31 | 5.6 | 5.4 | 24.4 | 25.1 | **10.0** | 14.9 | 24.5 |
| ▲ First National Bank of Harveyville | Harveyville | KS | **C-** | D+ | C- | 13.8 | -3.18 | 10.1 | 6.1 | 25.3 | 0.0 | **9.1** | 10.4 | 17.6 |
| ▲ First National Bank of Hebbronville | Hebbronville | TX | **A-** | A- | A- | 89.1 | -4.73 | 0.9 | 12.7 | 11.1 | 48.4 | **10.0** | 17.8 | 47.0 |
| First National Bank of Henning | Ottertail | MN | **A-** | B+ | A- | 218.0 | 6.13 | 6.1 | 5.6 | 20.2 | 26.9 | **10.0** | 11.9 | 18.2 |
| First National Bank of Hereford | Hereford | TX | **B** | C+ | D+ | 176.6 | 4.42 | 16.8 | 1.2 | 7.6 | 11.4 | **7.1** | 9.7 | 12.6 |
| ▲ First National Bank of Hooker | Hooker | OK | **B** | B+ | A- | 73.1 | -4.64 | 7.3 | 3.1 | 14.1 | 26.9 | **10.0** | 14.7 | 22.0 |
| ▼ First National Bank of Hope | Hope | KS | **D-** | D+ | D+ | 86.6 | 4.01 | 5.3 | 1.6 | 2.8 | 16.8 | **9.7** | 11.3 | 14.7 |
| ▲ First National Bank of Hughes Springs | Hughes Springs | TX | **B** | B+ | A- | 268.0 | -2.60 | 10.8 | 5.4 | 20.2 | 10.4 | **10.0** | 11.9 | 18.7 |
| First National Bank of Hugo | Hugo | CO | **A-** | A- | B+ | 120.3 | 3.08 | 0.9 | 1.9 | 4.7 | 22.0 | **10.0** | 11.1 | 19.6 |
| ▲ First National Bank of Huntsville | Huntsville | TX | **B+** | B | B | 485.9 | 3.39 | 6.0 | 5.4 | 21.0 | 37.8 | **10.0** | 11.9 | 23.8 |
| ▲ First National Bank of Hutchinson | Hutchinson | KS | **A-** | B | B | 782.4 | 8.70 | 11.1 | 1.4 | 7.2 | 16.9 | **10.0** | 12.7 | 16.3 |
| First National Bank of Izard County | Calico Rock | AR | **A** | A | A | 168.5 | 2.83 | 2.4 | 5.5 | 18.0 | 31.8 | **10.0** | 35.0 | 67.5 |
| First National Bank of Jasper | Jasper | TX | **B** | B | B | 242.3 | -6.02 | 3.7 | 4.4 | 8.1 | 60.7 | **10.0** | 13.9 | 46.0 |
| First National Bank of Jeanerette | Jeanerette | LA | **B** | C+ | B- | 280.5 | 7.81 | 8.0 | 2.6 | 26.1 | 7.0 | **9.9** | 10.9 | 15.9 |
| First National Bank of Johnson | Johnson | NE | **C+** | C+ | C | 71.3 | 0.01 | 1.3 | 2.6 | 5.2 | 47.9 | **10.0** | 20.2 | 39.3 |
| First National Bank of Kansas | Burlington | KS | **C+** | C+ | C | 88.4 | 3.05 | 5.9 | 2.0 | 8.7 | 64.7 | **6.5** | 8.6 | 21.6 |
| First National Bank of Kemp | Kemp | TX | **B-** | C+ | C | 96.5 | 10.34 | 15.2 | 1.4 | 18.0 | 19.7 | **8.0** | 9.7 | 17.7 |
| First National Bank of Kentucky | Carrollton | KY | **B+** | B+ | B+ | 121.4 | 0.29 | 2.2 | 2.3 | 36.4 | 17.0 | **10.0** | 11.5 | 19.6 |
| First National Bank of Lacon | Lacon | IL | **C+** | C | C+ | 60.0 | 2.29 | 9.0 | 7.8 | 14.3 | 10.8 | **7.7** | 9.5 | 14.2 |
| First National Bank of Lake Jackson | Lake Jackson | TX | **B** | B | B | 284.2 | 6.49 | 1.4 | 0.5 | 0.1 | 77.2 | **8.0** | 9.7 | 42.3 |
| First National Bank of Las Animas | Las Animas | CO | **A** | A | A | 377.1 | 4.28 | 4.4 | 1.3 | 11.2 | 19.7 | **10.0** | 12.3 | 17.5 |
| First National Bank of Lawrence County | Walnut Ridge | AR | **B+** | B+ | B | 218.3 | 5.68 | 9.0 | 2.3 | 16.0 | 27.2 | **10.0** | 11.3 | 19.3 |
| First National Bank of Le Center | Le Center | MN | **A-** | A- | B+ | 128.9 | 17.26 | 5.7 | 4.5 | 11.5 | 27.0 | **8.1** | 9.8 | 19.9 |
| First National Bank of Lindsay | Lindsay | OK | **B+** | B | B | 66.0 | 10.78 | 27.8 | 3.6 | 14.2 | 13.0 | **10.0** | 11.9 | 16.2 |
| First National Bank of Lipan | Lipan | TX | **C-** | D+ | D | 21.5 | -4.80 | 3.5 | 13.2 | 10.7 | 10.5 | **7.5** | 9.3 | 28.9 |
| First National Bank of Litchfield | Litchfield | IL | **B+** | B+ | B+ | 101.0 | -3.00 | 8.2 | 3.1 | 10.0 | 9.1 | **10.0** | 13.0 | 15.9 |
| First National Bank of Livingston | Livingston | TX | **B+** | B+ | B+ | 379.5 | 0.14 | 2.6 | 3.7 | 17.3 | 43.0 | **10.0** | 14.3 | 44.0 |
| First National Bank of Long Island | Glen Head | NY | **B** | B | B | 4096.8 | -3.39 | 2.5 | 0.1 | 39.6 | 17.0 | **7.6** | 9.4 | 16.1 |
| First National Bank of Louisburg | Louisburg | KS | **A-** | B+ | B | 123.3 | 7.33 | 3.0 | 0.8 | 28.8 | 43.5 | **10.0** | 13.7 | 25.6 |
| First National Bank of Louisiana | Crowley | LA | **A** | A- | A- | 390.3 | 0.84 | 14.3 | 1.2 | 15.1 | 8.3 | **10.0** | 12.8 | 17.3 |
| First National Bank of Manchester | Manchester | KY | **B** | B | B- | 141.2 | 1.71 | 6.4 | 3.2 | 14.0 | 28.3 | **10.0** | 14.5 | 23.8 |

| Asset Quality Index | Adjusted Non-Performing Loans as a % of Total Loans | Adjusted Non-Performing Loans as a % of Capital | Net Charge-Offs Avg Loans | Profitability Index | Net Income ($Mil) | Return on Assets (R.O.A.) | Return on Equity (R.O.E.) | Net Interest Spread | Overhead Efficiency Ratio | Liquidity Index | Liquidity Ratio | Hot Money Ratio | Stability Index |
|---|---|---|---|---|---|---|---|---|---|---|---|---|---|
| **5.7** | 0.73 | 5.3 | 0.05 | **4.4** | 1.7 | 0.93 | 10.08 | 3.71 | 71.1 | **2.1** | 24.1 | 19.4 | **4.7** |
| **6.6** | 0.10 | 2.0 | 0.15 | **4.8** | 2.3 | 0.97 | 9.98 | 4.26 | 70.2 | **4.8** | 32.6 | 8.0 | **6.0** |
| **8.0** | 1.40 | 3.3 | 3.63 | **1.6** | -0.4 | -0.64 | -3.09 | 3.59 | 68.0 | **6.0** | 45.9 | 4.6 | **7.7** |
| **9.6** | 0.00 | 0.0 | -0.03 | **2.5** | 0.1 | 0.40 | 2.64 | 2.99 | 85.9 | **4.1** | 78.5 | 21.7 | **7.1** |
| **6.6** | 1.38 | 4.0 | 0.48 | **4.6** | 1.8 | 0.99 | 9.63 | 3.59 | 63.7 | **6.2** | 40.8 | 2.0 | **7.0** |
| **7.3** | 0.20 | 1.5 | 0.41 | **7.2** | 1.5 | 1.64 | 14.87 | 5.44 | 66.9 | **4.3** | 22.3 | 7.6 | **7.0** |
| **5.6** | 1.51 | 7.7 | 0.61 | **4.9** | 1.3 | 1.08 | 10.05 | 4.57 | 73.3 | **4.8** | 25.8 | 5.4 | **7.0** |
| **7.4** | 0.74 | 3.9 | 0.01 | **5.8** | 5.9 | 1.43 | 13.68 | 3.68 | 62.7 | **3.7** | 36.0 | 15.3 | **7.3** |
| **8.8** | 0.00 | 0.5 | 0.00 | **9.8** | 1.6 | 2.70 | 15.92 | 6.02 | 54.0 | **5.4** | 25.1 | 0.6 | **9.3** |
| **3.0** | 1.75 | 9.7 | 0.02 | **4.2** | 2.1 | 0.75 | 8.14 | 4.10 | 74.5 | **3.5** | 9.6 | 11.1 | **5.7** |
| **8.8** | 6.27 | 2.4 | 0.57 | **4.5** | 1.2 | 1.20 | 10.71 | 3.05 | 56.9 | **7.9** | 75.0 | 0.0 | **5.7** |
| **7.4** | 0.18 | 1.3 | 0.05 | **8.0** | 1.9 | 1.92 | 20.99 | 5.02 | 64.5 | **3.7** | 19.6 | 10.9 | **7.0** |
| **7.8** | 0.36 | 0.1 | 0.18 | **6.9** | 0.5 | 1.78 | 4.62 | 3.70 | 60.4 | **6.7** | 62.8 | 3.9 | **6.9** |
| **6.1** | 7.27 | 1.9 | 0.09 | **4.5** | 0.2 | 0.87 | 6.54 | 4.52 | 73.8 | **0.6** | 11.1 | 43.3 | **4.3** |
| **8.4** | 0.90 | 1.3 | 0.41 | **3.1** | 0.1 | 0.54 | 4.47 | 4.32 | 88.9 | **6.3** | 57.0 | 3.2 | **5.6** |
| **8.5** | 0.00 | 0.0 | -0.33 | **6.8** | 1.8 | 1.63 | 14.43 | 3.45 | 51.3 | **3.3** | 49.2 | 21.7 | **7.9** |
| **6.6** | 0.64 | 3.0 | 0.16 | **9.8** | 25.0 | 1.86 | 14.75 | 4.27 | 50.9 | **4.1** | 14.2 | 8.6 | **9.6** |
| **8.4** | 0.00 | 0.0 | 0.01 | **4.8** | 1.6 | 1.19 | 11.26 | 4.46 | 67.2 | **2.9** | 26.0 | 15.5 | **6.6** |
| **8.9** | 0.00 | 0.2 | 0.00 | **3.4** | 0.1 | 0.53 | 3.84 | 3.70 | 79.1 | **6.4** | 61.2 | 5.2 | **6.8** |
| **5.8** | 0.86 | 5.1 | 0.04 | **4.6** | 0.6 | 0.94 | 11.09 | 3.96 | 70.6 | **4.5** | 24.7 | 6.4 | **3.6** |
| **6.7** | 1.09 | 5.0 | 0.00 | **4.6** | 2.2 | 1.06 | 9.24 | 3.40 | 63.0 | **2.9** | 19.4 | 14.7 | **6.7** |
| **5.7** | 0.01 | 7.2 | 0.01 | **3.0** | 0.2 | 0.39 | 4.94 | 4.12 | 83.3 | **2.7** | 21.2 | 16.3 | **2.9** |
| **5.8** | 6.18 | 8.6 | 0.34 | **4.1** | 5.0 | 0.92 | 7.34 | 2.54 | 62.2 | **4.4** | 70.6 | 19.5 | **7.1** |
| **3.8** | 1.54 | 9.3 | 0.13 | **6.4** | 6.5 | 1.57 | 13.29 | 3.94 | 62.6 | **2.6** | 34.4 | 20.9 | **7.6** |
| **5.6** | 1.73 | 5.1 | 1.74 | **6.9** | 3.3 | 1.68 | 12.11 | 4.38 | 48.1 | **1.5** | 10.3 | 20.8 | **7.6** |
| **8.0** | 0.55 | 3.2 | 0.15 | **5.5** | 7.7 | 1.24 | 10.76 | 3.83 | 63.7 | **5.0** | 44.2 | 11.0 | **7.8** |
| **5.5** | 1.05 | 5.0 | 0.10 | **7.9** | 4.1 | 1.64 | 13.91 | 4.26 | 62.1 | **3.7** | 23.2 | 11.2 | **7.5** |
| **5.9** | 1.17 | 5.4 | 0.10 | **3.7** | 1.9 | 0.68 | 9.09 | 3.71 | 79.1 | **6.4** | 51.8 | 4.4 | **2.6** |
| **6.3** | 1.09 | 6.3 | 0.45 | **7.2** | 2.6 | 1.41 | 9.70 | 4.64 | 57.1 | **3.9** | 15.1 | 9.2 | **7.9** |
| **6.9** | 1.86 | 5.8 | 0.20 | **4.0** | 1.0 | 0.85 | 5.74 | 4.43 | 81.0 | **1.9** | 23.5 | 20.8 | **7.5** |
| **6.5** | 0.95 | 2.9 | 0.00 | **3.0** | 0.1 | 0.40 | 4.16 | 3.64 | 85.0 | **2.0** | 33.5 | 22.0 | **4.5** |
| **8.2** | 1.08 | 1.7 | 0.45 | **6.1** | 1.3 | 1.39 | 7.85 | 3.51 | 63.1 | **2.1** | 44.6 | 38.7 | **8.6** |
| **6.8** | 0.40 | 6.4 | 0.02 | **6.6** | 3.4 | 1.60 | 12.84 | 3.84 | 60.7 | **2.7** | 21.5 | 16.2 | **7.7** |
| **6.0** | 0.79 | 5.1 | 0.07 | **5.7** | 2.6 | 1.59 | 15.85 | 4.41 | 63.5 | **2.6** | 26.1 | 17.2 | **5.3** |
| **5.5** | 1.33 | 5.7 | 1.15 | **5.3** | 0.7 | 0.96 | 6.48 | 4.61 | 61.1 | **2.5** | 20.8 | 17.2 | **8.8** |
| **0.0** | 12.20 | 52.1 | 0.78 | **3.2** | 0.4 | 0.49 | 4.16 | 3.88 | 76.5 | **3.0** | 25.5 | 15.3 | **5.1** |
| **4.9** | 2.39 | 9.0 | 0.68 | **8.2** | 6.3 | 2.31 | 17.76 | 5.52 | 62.0 | **4.0** | 18.6 | 9.3 | **8.9** |
| **7.6** | 0.60 | 4.1 | 0.18 | **6.5** | 1.9 | 1.61 | 12.46 | 4.39 | 61.0 | **5.0** | 29.4 | 5.0 | **8.1** |
| **8.4** | 0.07 | 0.3 | 0.03 | **5.2** | 5.5 | 1.17 | 9.14 | 3.47 | 62.9 | **4.4** | 32.1 | 10.5 | **7.4** |
| **8.5** | 0.19 | 0.7 | 0.05 | **5.8** | 9.3 | 1.27 | 9.99 | 3.58 | 69.4 | **4.5** | 24.5 | 6.7 | **8.2** |
| **8.8** | 1.38 | 1.8 | 0.04 | **6.0** | 2.1 | 1.27 | 3.70 | 4.30 | 63.2 | **4.3** | 61.5 | 18.5 | **8.6** |
| **8.2** | 0.38 | 0.6 | 0.64 | **4.4** | 2.4 | 0.94 | 7.18 | 3.28 | 65.8 | **4.5** | 30.2 | 9.1 | **7.1** |
| **4.3** | 1.07 | 12.4 | 0.07 | **6.5** | 3.9 | 1.49 | 13.47 | 4.83 | 63.3 | **3.0** | 24.4 | 14.7 | **8.0** |
| **8.8** | 0.00 | 0.0 | -0.02 | **3.0** | 0.4 | 0.49 | 2.37 | 2.66 | 78.2 | **6.7** | 66.6 | 4.6 | **6.7** |
| **9.5** | 0.00 | 1.1 | -0.03 | **3.3** | 0.6 | 0.66 | 7.80 | 2.75 | 80.8 | **1.6** | 26.4 | 27.6 | **4.8** |
| **8.3** | 0.00 | 0.0 | 0.08 | **4.3** | 0.8 | 0.91 | 8.01 | 4.19 | 74.4 | **5.0** | 34.4 | 7.3 | **5.9** |
| **7.8** | 0.40 | 1.8 | 0.22 | **4.7** | 1.4 | 1.13 | 9.92 | 3.94 | 73.9 | **1.6** | 19.0 | 23.6 | **7.7** |
| **5.8** | 0.07 | 1.3 | -0.03 | **4.5** | 0.6 | 1.04 | 10.97 | 4.19 | 74.5 | **3.1** | 13.0 | 13.3 | **5.0** |
| **10.0** | 0.00 | 0.0 | -0.43 | **4.4** | 3.0 | 1.11 | 11.86 | 2.16 | 50.1 | **3.5** | 23.0 | 12.5 | **5.8** |
| **8.6** | 0.11 | 0.3 | 0.00 | **10.0** | 9.4 | 2.50 | 20.08 | 4.71 | 47.5 | **3.2** | 18.2 | 13.2 | **9.7** |
| **8.7** | 0.39 | 1.9 | 0.09 | **5.3** | 2.7 | 1.24 | 11.26 | 4.07 | 69.7 | **1.4** | 18.5 | 26.6 | **7.4** |
| **5.9** | 0.82 | 4.1 | -0.02 | **5.7** | 1.8 | 1.38 | 13.52 | 3.13 | 56.6 | **3.8** | 13.8 | 9.8 | **7.7** |
| **7.1** | 0.46 | 2.5 | 0.08 | **6.8** | 0.8 | 1.29 | 10.72 | 4.85 | 56.6 | **1.4** | 10.3 | 23.9 | **6.9** |
| **8.4** | 0.00 | 0.0 | 0.00 | **2.4** | 0.1 | 0.33 | 3.62 | 3.48 | 89.0 | **6.4** | 70.9 | 5.2 | **3.5** |
| **7.1** | 0.06 | 1.1 | 0.01 | **5.6** | 1.4 | 1.35 | 10.79 | 3.91 | 66.3 | **1.6** | 9.2 | 20.7 | **8.1** |
| **9.0** | 0.49 | 1.0 | 0.16 | **5.3** | 5.0 | 1.32 | 8.95 | 3.10 | 71.2 | **6.7** | 58.5 | 4.7 | **8.7** |
| **9.2** | 0.06 | 0.3 | 0.05 | **5.1** | 44.3 | 1.06 | 11.45 | 2.56 | 51.9 | **3.1** | 9.5 | 7.7 | **8.3** |
| **9.7** | 0.03 | 0.1 | 0.00 | **5.4** | 1.7 | 1.40 | 9.93 | 3.32 | 61.5 | **4.1** | 40.1 | 14.7 | **8.6** |
| **8.5** | 0.00 | 0.0 | 0.01 | **8.1** | 7.7 | 1.97 | 15.89 | 4.26 | 56.6 | **4.4** | 16.0 | 5.9 | **9.5** |
| **6.1** | 3.10 | 8.5 | 0.05 | **4.1** | 1.2 | 0.85 | 5.92 | 3.50 | 77.1 | **2.0** | 34.9 | 29.5 | **8.0** |

| Name | City | State | Rating | 2018 Rating | 2017 Rating | Total Assets ($Mil) | One Year Asset Growth | Asset Mix (As a % of Total Assets) Comm-ercial Loans | Cons-umer Loans | Mort-gage Loans | Secur-ities | Capital-ization Index | Lever-age Ratio | Risk-Based Capital Ratio |
|---|---|---|---|---|---|---|---|---|---|---|---|---|---|---|
| First National Bank of Manchester | Manchester | TN | **A-** | B+ | A- | 292.1 | 2.50 | 7.1 | 4.6 | 24.5 | 15.5 | **10.0** | 13.0 | 19.2 |
| First National Bank of Manning | Manning | IA | **B+** | B | B | 65.8 | -0.99 | 4.6 | 1.8 | 8.1 | 14.2 | **10.0** | 18.8 | 30.1 |
| First National Bank of McConnelsville | McConnelsville | OH | **C+** | C+ | C+ | 150.7 | 3.82 | 1.0 | 4.5 | 34.6 | 19.4 | **5.3** | 7.3 | 16.3 |
| First National Bank of McGregor | McGregor | TX | **B+** | C+ | B | 531.2 | 29.32 | 10.0 | 3.2 | 31.6 | 0.0 | **10.0** | 12.1 | 15.4 |
| ▲ First National Bank of McIntosh | McIntosh | MN | **B** | B- | B- | 26.7 | 0.05 | 4.1 | 3.7 | 10.7 | 21.9 | **10.0** | 26.4 | 77.4 |
| ▲ First National Bank of Mertzon | Mertzon | TX | **B-** | C | C- | 485.7 | 9.54 | 3.5 | 0.7 | 1.3 | 54.4 | **5.3** | 7.3 | 40.1 |
| First National Bank of Michigan | Kalamazoo | MI | **B-** | B- | B | 629.2 | 10.01 | 16.2 | 0.3 | 3.9 | 5.9 | **5.9** | 10.0 | 11.7 |
| First National Bank of Middle Tennessee | McMinnville | TN | **A-** | B+ | B+ | 534.3 | 5.42 | 5.7 | 0.4 | 24.9 | 22.0 | **10.0** | 12.4 | 20.5 |
| First National Bank of Milaca | Milaca | MN | **A-** | B | B+ | 213.4 | -1.30 | 13.8 | 5.1 | 17.1 | 20.9 | **10.0** | 11.7 | 21.3 |
| First National Bank of Monterey | Monterey | IN | **B** | B | B | 330.4 | 0.86 | 3.5 | 1.2 | 12.1 | 27.7 | **10.0** | 12.7 | 19.8 |
| First National Bank of Moody | Moody | TX | **B-** | B- | B | 48.2 | 2.35 | 2.9 | 3.2 | 19.0 | 40.8 | **10.0** | 20.8 | 44.0 |
| First National Bank of Moose Lake | Moose Lake | MN | **A-** | B+ | B+ | 111.0 | 3.93 | 5.2 | 3.6 | 22.9 | 14.2 | **10.0** | 13.2 | 17.6 |
| First National Bank of Mount Dora | Mount Dora | FL | **A-** | B+ | A- | 243.5 | 4.10 | 2.8 | 1.7 | 13.2 | 44.9 | **10.0** | 15.4 | 26.1 |
| First National Bank of Muscatine | Muscatine | IA | **B-** | B | B- | 322.0 | 2.58 | 13.3 | 2.4 | 28.6 | 2.7 | **10.0** | 11.7 | 17.2 |
| First National Bank of Nevada | Nevada | MO | **B** | B | B | 98.5 | 0.35 | 4.2 | 1.6 | 13.3 | 35.9 | **10.0** | 15.7 | 26.7 |
| First National Bank of Nokomis | Nokomis | IL | **B** | B | C+ | 152.3 | 4.93 | 2.7 | 2.3 | 13.3 | 27.2 | **10.0** | 11.5 | 18.7 |
| ▲ First National Bank of North Arkansas | Berryville | AR | **B** | C+ | B | 202.9 | -0.45 | 9.4 | 10.8 | 30.5 | 1.1 | **10.0** | 11.2 | 15.9 |
| ▼ First National Bank of Northfield | Northfield | MN | **B** | B+ | B+ | 247.1 | 19.09 | 9.7 | 0.3 | 16.0 | 7.0 | **8.5** | 10.0 | 14.2 |
| First National Bank of Okawville | Okawville | IL | **B** | B | B | 62.4 | -5.53 | 1.5 | 1.5 | 7.8 | 38.6 | **10.0** | 12.8 | 21.3 |
| First National Bank of Oklahoma | Oklahoma City | OK | **B-** | B+ | B+ | 573.8 | 14.76 | 9.9 | 1.7 | 18.4 | 4.3 | **6.3** | 8.6 | 11.9 |
| First National Bank of Omaha | Omaha | NE | **B-** | B- | B- | 22555.0 | 4.50 | 8.4 | 31.9 | 4.4 | 17.4 | **7.2** | 10.3 | 12.7 |
| First National Bank of Oneida | Oneida | TN | **A-** | B+ | B+ | 221.7 | 3.14 | 3.5 | 2.7 | 27.7 | 20.4 | **10.0** | 11.7 | 19.1 |
| First National Bank of Orwell | Orwell | VT | **C-** | D+ | D+ | 72.9 | 1.48 | 4.8 | 2.7 | 63.9 | 0.0 | **7.0** | 9.0 | 15.9 |
| First National Bank of Osakis | Osakis | MN | **B-** | B | B+ | 71.3 | 8.82 | 6.8 | 1.9 | 24.0 | 20.6 | **6.8** | 8.8 | 12.5 |
| First National Bank of Ottawa | Ottawa | IL | **B** | B- | B | 452.1 | 55.68 | 21.1 | 0.8 | 18.9 | 7.8 | **8.8** | 11.3 | 14.0 |
| First National Bank of Pana | Pana | IL | **A-** | B+ | B+ | 190.5 | 8.65 | 6.8 | 1.6 | 17.9 | 15.2 | **10.0** | 11.8 | 17.3 |
| First National Bank of Pandora | Pandora | OH | **C+** | C+ | C+ | 190.3 | 6.55 | 8.4 | 2.6 | 18.6 | 22.5 | **6.4** | 8.4 | 12.2 |
| First National Bank of Pasco | Dade City | FL | **C+** | C | C+ | 183.8 | 5.38 | 11.4 | 3.6 | 12.2 | 18.5 | **10.0** | 12.9 | 18.5 |
| ▼ First National Bank of Pawnee | Pawnee | OK | **B-** | B | B | 60.1 | -0.09 | 2.9 | 2.9 | 6.1 | 36.5 | **10.0** | 14.6 | 27.5 |
| First National Bank of Pennsylvania | Pittsburgh | PA | **B-** | B- | B- | 34531.4 | 4.56 | 14.4 | 6.0 | 15.2 | 19.1 | **5.5** | 8.9 | 11.3 |
| First National Bank of Peterstown | Peterstown | WV | **B** | B | B | 68.2 | 7.85 | 3.6 | 4.4 | 40.5 | 17.6 | **10.0** | 12.0 | 22.7 |
| First National Bank of Picayune | Picayune | MS | **B** | B | B | 202.9 | -2.74 | 5.2 | 6.1 | 28.0 | 20.8 | **10.0** | 15.2 | 23.9 |
| First National Bank of Primghar | Primghar | IA | **B-** | B- | B- | 32.3 | -1.80 | 6.7 | 1.8 | 1.6 | 18.6 | **10.0** | 18.1 | 22.3 |
| ▲ First National Bank of Proctor | Proctor | MN | **C-** | C- | C- | 24.9 | 6.75 | 1.2 | 4.2 | 36.2 | 8.7 | **8.1** | 9.7 | 24.2 |
| First National Bank of Pulaski | Pulaski | TN | **A-** | B+ | B+ | 895.7 | 5.20 | 5.0 | 2.7 | 12.7 | 25.3 | **9.8** | 10.9 | 15.5 |
| ▲ First National Bank of Quitaque | Quitaque | TX | **B** | C | B- | 70.4 | 20.27 | 3.7 | 4.1 | 0.0 | 7.6 | **10.0** | 13.6 | 26.5 |
| First National Bank of Raymond | Raymond | IL | **C+** | B | B | 149.4 | 2.62 | 4.4 | 2.1 | 8.0 | 38.3 | **10.0** | 11.1 | 17.7 |
| First National Bank of River Falls | River Falls | WI | **A-** | B+ | B+ | 276.9 | -0.35 | 5.6 | 1.5 | 12.5 | 33.7 | **10.0** | 11.2 | 20.1 |
| First National Bank of Russell Springs | Russell Springs | KY | **B** | B | B | 234.4 | 10.96 | 4.9 | 1.9 | 9.2 | 31.4 | **10.0** | 12.4 | 21.4 |
| First National Bank of Sandoval | Sandoval | IL | **B** | B- | B- | 56.1 | 14.32 | 5.4 | 9.2 | 35.5 | 18.3 | **10.0** | 11.6 | 18.6 |
| First National Bank of Scotia | Scotia | NY | **C+** | C+ | C+ | 483.1 | 1.84 | 11.3 | 27.1 | 20.3 | 5.6 | **6.5** | 8.7 | 12.1 |
| ▲ First National Bank of Scott City | Scott City | KS | **B** | C | D+ | 129.6 | 5.66 | 9.3 | 5.4 | 5.3 | 24.0 | **10.0** | 12.8 | 16.9 |
| First National Bank of Sedan | Sedan | KS | **C-** | D | D | 54.9 | -5.98 | 8.3 | 2.1 | 11.0 | 25.9 | **10.0** | 12.9 | 22.6 |
| First National Bank of Shiner | Shiner | TX | **B+** | B+ | B+ | 859.2 | 16.10 | 2.1 | 0.7 | 3.9 | 77.3 | **9.3** | 10.6 | 26.6 |
| First National Bank of Sonora | Sonora | TX | **B** | B- | B- | 451.5 | 6.63 | 5.4 | 3.8 | 18.7 | 2.3 | **8.4** | 9.9 | 16.9 |
| First National Bank of South Carolina | Holly Hill | SC | **B** | B | B | 200.5 | 4.15 | 2.2 | 1.6 | 9.7 | 26.9 | **10.0** | 12.9 | 29.2 |
| First National Bank of South Miami | South Miami | FL | **B-** | B- | B- | 853.3 | 17.82 | 2.7 | 0.1 | 11.5 | 9.7 | **8.2** | 9.8 | 16.2 |
| First National Bank of South Padre Island | South Padre Island | TX | **B** | B | B | 55.5 | -3.62 | 2.1 | 0.5 | 37.1 | 8.9 | **10.0** | 11.4 | 24.7 |
| First National Bank of Sparta | Sparta | IL | **A-** | B+ | B | 82.1 | 3.23 | 9.0 | 9.0 | 22.2 | 35.6 | **10.0** | 13.2 | 26.8 |
| First National Bank of Spearville | Spearville | KS | **B** | B | B | 41.2 | 7.58 | 6.5 | 3.9 | 0.0 | 5.7 | **10.0** | 14.6 | 25.1 |
| First National Bank of St. Ignace | Saint Ignace | MI | **C-** | C- | C- | 263.2 | 1.36 | 3.5 | 1.7 | 9.4 | 54.8 | **5.2** | 7.2 | 15.7 |
| First National Bank of Stanton | Stanton | TX | **B+** | B- | B- | 251.1 | 12.40 | 4.8 | 1.1 | 1.7 | 52.6 | **8.1** | 9.7 | 24.7 |
| First National Bank of Steeleville | Steeleville | IL | **B+** | B+ | B+ | 205.9 | 5.09 | 7.0 | 3.9 | 20.7 | 40.0 | **10.0** | 14.7 | 28.1 |
| First National Bank of Sterling City | Sterling City | TX | **C** | C- | C+ | 197.8 | 7.76 | 1.1 | 2.1 | 4.8 | 63.1 | **6.6** | 8.6 | 33.2 |
| First National Bank of Stigler | Stigler | OK | **B** | B | B | 118.0 | 6.73 | 5.5 | 2.3 | 6.0 | 48.7 | **5.9** | 7.9 | 17.3 |
| First National Bank of Sycamore | Sycamore | OH | **C** | C | C+ | 151.1 | 1.51 | 6.5 | 1.6 | 22.8 | 34.0 | **9.3** | 10.6 | 17.8 |
| First National Bank of Syracuse | Syracuse | KS | **B** | B | B+ | 374.5 | 9.73 | 13.2 | 1.8 | 5.8 | 11.0 | **8.0** | 10.3 | 13.3 |
| First National Bank of Tahoka | Tahoka | TX | **C+** | B- | B- | 55.4 | 2.91 | 1.7 | 2.6 | 1.5 | 34.0 | **10.0** | 11.3 | 32.1 |
| First National Bank of Tennessee | Livingston | TN | **A-** | B+ | B | 882.8 | 4.42 | 9.1 | 2.9 | 14.8 | 20.5 | **10.0** | 12.9 | 21.9 |
| First National Bank of Tom Bean | Tom Bean | TX | **D+** | D+ | C- | 120.0 | -7.02 | 16.9 | 12.2 | 26.2 | 11.3 | **7.0** | 9.0 | 14.5 |

| Asset Quality Index | Adjusted Non-Performing Loans as a % of Total Loans | Adjusted Non-Performing Loans as a % of Capital | Net Charge-Offs Avg Loans | Profitability Index | Net Income ($Mil) | Return on Assets (R.O.A.) | Return on Equity (R.O.E.) | Net Interest Spread | Overhead Efficiency Ratio | Liquidity Index | Liquidity Ratio | Hot Money Ratio | Stability Index |
|---|---|---|---|---|---|---|---|---|---|---|---|---|---|
| **7.4** | 0.73 | 4.0 | 0.09 | **8.4** | 4.3 | 1.48 | 11.65 | 4.28 | 52.7 | **1.3** | 12.1 | 25.2 | **8.2** |
| **8.6** | 0.00 | 0.0 | -0.01 | **4.7** | 0.7 | 1.02 | 5.41 | 3.41 | 62.1 | **5.3** | 44.8 | 9.3 | **7.7** |
| **4.3** | 0.43 | 5.1 | 0.03 | **3.5** | 1.0 | 0.66 | 6.01 | 3.29 | 78.1 | **4.7** | 22.6 | 5.3 | **6.6** |
| **8.1** | 0.08 | 2.8 | 0.09 | **5.9** | 4.8 | 1.02 | 8.74 | 4.77 | 66.5 | **0.4** | 11.9 | 45.1 | **6.2** |
| **9.0** | 0.00 | 0.0 | 0.11 | **4.0** | 0.2 | 0.91 | 3.40 | 2.93 | 71.5 | **5.4** | 70.7 | 13.4 | **7.6** |
| **9.8** | 0.00 | 0.0 | -0.17 | **4.8** | 5.0 | 1.09 | 15.29 | 2.26 | 40.7 | **7.2** | 81.3 | 5.6 | **4.0** |
| **5.7** | 0.03 | 0.2 | 0.17 | **5.4** | 6.0 | 1.09 | 11.04 | 3.79 | 62.8 | **1.2** | 19.3 | 20.0 | **7.0** |
| **9.0** | 0.10 | 0.7 | -0.01 | **5.7** | 6.5 | 1.26 | 9.89 | 3.37 | 68.1 | **0.7** | 10.7 | 31.5 | **8.4** |
| **5.8** | 2.02 | 8.9 | 0.66 | **6.4** | 3.2 | 1.48 | 12.47 | 3.98 | 63.5 | **5.4** | 32.5 | 4.1 | **8.6** |
| **8.0** | 0.64 | 2.2 | 0.03 | **4.0** | 2.7 | 0.82 | 6.47 | 3.13 | 68.4 | **3.4** | 28.4 | 12.3 | **7.5** |
| **4.9** | 3.97 | 12.0 | -0.08 | **4.8** | 0.5 | 1.09 | 5.26 | 3.89 | 71.6 | **2.3** | 46.7 | 6.9 | **7.9** |
| **6.4** | 1.24 | 5.5 | 0.00 | **8.0** | 2.1 | 1.90 | 14.45 | 4.39 | 59.8 | **1.2** | 24.9 | 20.1 | **9.3** |
| **6.0** | 4.74 | 7.5 | 0.04 | **6.8** | 3.5 | 1.45 | 8.94 | 3.88 | 70.7 | **6.8** | 58.1 | 3.9 | **8.1** |
| **4.2** | 3.56 | 17.7 | 0.10 | **5.4** | 3.4 | 1.06 | 9.19 | 3.24 | 61.7 | **3.6** | 21.2 | 11.8 | **6.7** |
| **5.2** | 3.10 | 11.9 | 0.06 | **3.6** | 0.6 | 0.63 | 4.13 | 3.53 | 77.1 | **4.9** | 50.4 | 12.0 | **7.9** |
| **7.3** | 1.20 | 3.9 | 0.64 | **4.5** | 1.4 | 0.93 | 7.63 | 3.70 | 67.0 | **4.3** | 37.0 | 12.3 | **7.8** |
| **4.8** | 1.67 | 10.5 | 0.09 | **6.3** | 2.8 | 1.41 | 12.30 | 5.58 | 75.3 | **3.4** | 17.6 | 12.3 | **7.6** |
| **7.6** | 0.00 | 0.0 | 0.01 | **2.8** | 0.4 | 0.53 | 4.96 | 3.27 | 76.4 | **4.2** | 28.5 | 10.2 | **7.5** |
| **9.5** | 0.00 | 0.0 | 0.03 | **3.5** | 0.4 | 0.65 | 5.20 | 3.25 | 77.1 | **6.2** | 59.0 | 6.3 | **6.2** |
| **5.8** | 0.95 | 8.1 | 0.23 | **6.6** | 7.8 | 1.46 | 18.24 | 3.75 | 55.7 | **0.8** | 16.0 | 41.5 | **7.4** |
| **4.6** | 1.16 | 5.5 | 2.00 | **7.4** | 300.5 | 1.40 | 13.13 | 6.44 | 58.2 | **3.2** | 10.1 | 6.6 | **9.0** |
| **6.7** | 0.59 | 3.1 | 0.17 | **5.9** | 3.0 | 1.40 | 11.97 | 4.21 | 62.7 | **1.6** | 11.9 | 21.6 | **7.3** |
| **2.4** | 2.74 | 21.8 | 0.04 | **5.1** | 0.7 | 0.95 | 10.81 | 3.86 | 69.7 | **0.6** | 7.9 | 32.4 | **5.2** |
| **3.5** | 0.76 | 11.5 | 0.00 | **3.7** | 0.4 | 1.27 | 10.05 | 3.23 | 65.9 | **3.9** | 21.1 | 10.1 | **7.0** |
| **3.9** | 1.11 | 8.3 | -0.06 | **4.6** | 2.4 | 0.68 | 5.18 | 4.09 | 76.2 | **2.2** | 4.1 | 14.8 | **6.9** |
| **5.7** | 2.10 | 10.1 | -0.03 | **6.6** | 2.8 | 1.52 | 13.09 | 3.68 | 59.5 | **3.2** | 22.6 | 14.0 | **8.1** |
| **5.2** | 1.47 | 6.6 | 0.05 | **3.9** | 1.4 | 0.75 | 8.71 | 3.86 | 78.1 | **2.3** | 11.2 | 17.3 | **5.0** |
| **6.1** | 1.09 | 5.4 | 0.03 | **3.2** | 0.9 | 0.50 | 4.38 | 4.40 | 81.7 | **3.8** | 23.7 | 10.8 | **6.3** |
| **3.5** | 10.62 | 27.1 | 0.32 | **3.0** | 0.3 | 0.48 | 3.26 | 3.81 | 80.5 | **4.7** | 38.7 | 11.2 | **7.4** |
| **5.2** | 0.48 | 2.4 | 0.12 | **5.6** | 408.8 | 1.23 | 8.55 | 3.25 | 54.9 | **3.3** | 8.6 | 9.8 | **10.0** |
| **5.0** | 2.37 | 12.3 | 0.05 | **3.5** | 0.4 | 0.60 | 4.94 | 3.71 | 78.0 | **3.2** | 30.1 | 15.5 | **6.3** |
| **4.6** | 2.20 | 10.7 | 0.14 | **10.0** | 5.6 | 2.71 | 18.23 | 5.09 | 50.8 | **1.9** | 23.0 | 20.2 | **9.8** |
| **7.4** | 0.00 | 1.7 | 0.00 | **4.5** | 0.3 | 0.84 | 4.74 | 3.80 | 71.4 | **2.1** | 29.2 | 23.2 | **7.2** |
| **8.1** | 0.23 | 3.2 | 0.00 | **2.1** | 0.0 | 0.09 | 0.95 | 3.64 | 96.4 | **5.1** | 45.1 | 7.9 | **4.2** |
| **7.3** | 0.39 | 1.9 | -0.03 | **6.3** | 10.8 | 1.25 | 11.48 | 3.80 | 60.1 | **1.9** | 26.6 | 23.4 | **7.8** |
| **5.3** | 4.18 | 8.4 | 0.01 | **5.7** | 0.8 | 1.19 | 8.37 | 4.12 | 64.8 | **3.1** | 49.5 | 22.8 | **6.9** |
| **7.1** | 0.81 | 3.9 | 1.04 | **3.1** | 0.7 | 0.44 | 4.01 | 3.55 | 70.9 | **3.8** | 43.0 | 16.5 | **6.8** |
| **8.9** | 0.09 | 0.2 | -0.06 | **4.8** | 3.2 | 1.15 | 10.00 | 3.63 | 71.1 | **5.3** | 31.7 | 4.3 | **7.2** |
| **7.9** | 1.33 | 2.9 | 0.02 | **4.3** | 2.1 | 0.94 | 7.36 | 3.71 | 70.5 | **2.0** | 25.3 | 20.5 | **6.4** |
| **6.6** | 0.36 | 3.7 | 0.00 | **5.6** | 0.7 | 1.30 | 11.03 | 4.55 | 65.4 | **2.4** | 17.3 | 17.5 | **6.5** |
| **4.7** | 0.18 | 2.4 | 0.10 | **3.9** | 3.4 | 0.71 | 9.21 | 3.92 | 76.1 | **4.6** | 8.1 | 3.9 | **5.2** |
| **4.9** | 1.72 | 7.8 | 0.68 | **4.8** | 1.1 | 0.93 | 7.14 | 4.04 | 64.5 | **5.1** | 36.0 | 7.6 | **5.7** |
| **8.8** | 0.64 | 2.4 | 1.17 | **0.5** | -0.2 | -0.36 | -2.94 | 3.52 | 98.9 | **3.6** | 26.7 | 12.8 | **4.5** |
| **9.4** | 0.22 | 0.3 | 0.67 | **4.3** | 8.8 | 1.12 | 9.48 | 2.57 | 53.2 | **3.1** | 62.3 | 35.8 | **7.5** |
| **5.1** | 1.43 | 5.3 | 0.08 | **4.7** | 5.1 | 1.19 | 11.25 | 4.33 | 70.8 | **2.1** | 28.1 | 21.2 | **6.7** |
| **7.8** | 1.19 | 3.7 | 0.01 | **4.3** | 1.5 | 0.77 | 6.07 | 3.58 | 75.6 | **6.7** | 58.9 | 5.0 | **7.2** |
| **4.7** | 1.32 | 7.9 | -0.01 | **4.3** | 6.7 | 0.85 | 8.79 | 3.26 | 71.6 | **4.0** | 28.8 | 11.0 | **6.3** |
| **9.5** | 0.55 | 2.4 | 0.02 | **4.5** | 0.6 | 1.01 | 8.42 | 3.99 | 74.7 | **5.7** | 44.6 | 6.7 | **6.8** |
| **7.3** | 0.61 | 3.1 | 0.14 | **7.0** | 1.4 | 1.71 | 12.69 | 4.16 | 62.7 | **5.2** | 32.3 | 5.4 | **7.6** |
| **7.7** | 0.00 | 0.0 | -0.06 | **7.2** | 0.6 | 1.44 | 8.61 | 3.61 | 50.8 | **3.4** | 52.6 | 17.1 | **7.0** |
| **3.1** | 5.03 | 19.4 | 0.03 | **2.5** | 1.1 | 0.41 | 4.81 | 2.85 | 86.7 | **5.1** | 64.8 | 15.1 | **4.6** |
| **9.6** | 0.09 | 0.2 | 0.08 | **7.1** | 3.4 | 1.53 | 15.18 | 3.62 | 46.9 | **7.0** | 61.3 | 3.5 | **5.7** |
| **7.8** | 1.13 | 3.1 | 0.09 | **5.2** | 2.9 | 1.46 | 9.71 | 3.41 | 67.5 | **3.7** | 30.3 | 13.2 | **8.8** |
| **9.4** | 0.48 | 1.1 | 0.13 | **4.1** | 2.0 | 1.07 | 16.10 | 2.60 | 61.0 | **5.9** | 64.1 | 11.1 | **3.0** |
| **8.5** | 0.24 | 1.0 | 0.02 | **7.1** | 2.0 | 1.74 | 21.16 | 3.64 | 55.6 | **5.6** | 49.4 | 9.1 | **5.1** |
| **5.8** | 0.40 | 6.7 | -0.03 | **3.3** | 1.0 | 0.67 | 5.95 | 3.30 | 75.3 | **3.1** | 27.3 | 15.5 | **6.6** |
| **4.3** | 1.36 | 8.9 | 0.31 | **7.9** | 5.1 | 1.49 | 13.07 | 4.56 | 57.0 | **0.6** | 13.7 | 45.1 | **7.9** |
| **7.9** | 1.00 | 2.3 | 0.15 | **3.8** | 0.4 | 0.70 | 6.48 | 4.06 | 80.0 | **4.1** | 72.4 | 19.9 | **5.8** |
| **7.1** | 1.73 | 5.2 | 0.06 | **7.0** | 14.4 | 1.68 | 13.63 | 3.69 | 58.1 | **4.3** | 41.3 | 14.0 | **8.8** |
| **1.2** | 2.06 | 21.9 | 0.02 | **2.8** | 0.6 | 0.49 | 5.48 | 4.37 | 80.7 | **1.0** | 13.4 | 31.4 | **5.2** |

| Name | City | State | Rating | 2018 Rating | 2017 Rating | Total Assets ($Mil) | One Year Asset Growth | Asset Mix (As a % of Total Assets) Comm-ercial Loans | Cons-umer Loans | Mort-gage Loans | Secur-ities | Capital-ization Index | Lever-age Ratio | Risk-Based Capital Ratio |
|---|---|---|---|---|---|---|---|---|---|---|---|---|---|---|
| First National Bank of Trinity | Trinity | TX | **B** | B- | B- | 59.7 | 3.26 | 4.5 | 14.6 | 13.7 | 41.7 | **9.3** | 10.5 | 19.4 |
| First National Bank of Wakefield | Wakefield | MI | **C+** | C | C | 49.5 | 2.97 | 1.9 | 9.5 | 17.9 | 34.0 | **8.0** | 9.7 | 25.9 |
| First National Bank of Waseca | Waseca | MN | **B** | B- | B | 142.1 | 4.73 | 7.9 | 2.4 | 32.4 | 7.5 | **7.1** | 9.0 | 13.1 |
| First National Bank of Waterloo | Waterloo | IL | **C+** | C+ | C+ | 491.8 | 3.62 | 4.1 | 0.5 | 16.1 | 32.2 | **9.1** | 10.4 | 15.3 |
| First National Bank of Wauchula | Wauchula | FL | **C+** | C | C | 72.7 | 2.53 | 7.4 | 3.0 | 31.8 | 12.3 | **10.0** | 11.8 | 18.6 |
| First National Bank of Waverly | Waverly | OH | **C** | C | C | 150.3 | -3.12 | 3.6 | 3.8 | 20.9 | 18.1 | **7.5** | 9.3 | 19.7 |
| First National Bank of Waynesboro | Waynesboro | GA | **A** | A | A | 148.0 | 6.31 | 4.8 | 9.0 | 27.8 | 9.9 | **10.0** | 17.7 | 31.0 |
| First National Bank of Weatherford | Weatherford | TX | **B-** | C+ | B- | 276.6 | 13.23 | 14.3 | 2.0 | 9.8 | 2.6 | **7.3** | 9.4 | 12.7 |
| First National Bank of Williamson | Williamson | WV | **B** | B- | B- | 87.3 | 10.32 | 5.6 | 7.2 | 37.8 | 12.5 | **8.8** | 10.2 | 18.0 |
| ▲ First National Bank of Winnsboro | Winnsboro | TX | **B+** | B | B | 135.3 | -1.34 | 6.5 | 2.2 | 15.9 | 14.7 | **10.0** | 21.2 | 30.4 |
| First National Bank Texas | Killeen | TX | **B+** | B+ | B | 2179.2 | 16.27 | 0.3 | 14.4 | 11.5 | 27.1 | **6.8** | 8.8 | 22.4 |
| First National Bank USA | Boutte | LA | **A-** | B+ | B+ | 129.4 | 3.48 | 3.7 | 1.0 | 23.2 | 2.2 | **10.0** | 13.3 | 21.8 |
| First National Bank, Ames, Iowa | Ames | IA | **A-** | A- | A- | 913.3 | 8.50 | 2.8 | 0.5 | 10.8 | 28.1 | **7.5** | 9.3 | 13.9 |
| ▲ First National Bank, Cortez | Cortez | CO | **B** | B- | B- | 106.2 | -0.54 | 6.2 | 3.7 | 9.9 | 22.0 | **10.0** | 11.0 | 17.8 |
| First National Bankers Bank | Baton Rouge | LA | **B-** | C+ | C+ | 836.8 | -5.55 | 5.3 | 0.0 | 1.5 | 4.6 | **10.0** | 15.4 | 21.9 |
| First National Community Bank | Chatsworth | GA | **B** | B | B | 285.9 | 74.26 | 5.7 | 0.9 | 16.0 | 6.7 | **9.7** | 10.8 | 16.5 |
| First National Community Bank | New Richmond | WI | **C-** | C+ | B- | 216.1 | 6.01 | 5.8 | 3.1 | 16.9 | 24.6 | **7.5** | 9.3 | 14.9 |
| First National Trust Co. | Pittsburgh | PA | **U** | U | U | 33.0 | 20.16 | 0.0 | 0.0 | 0.0 | 0.0 | **10.0** | 87.5 | 145.7 |
| ▲ First Nations Bank | Chicago | IL | **A-** | B+ | A- | 370.6 | 9.84 | 3.1 | 0.7 | 6.4 | 2.4 | **10.0** | 13.1 | 17.9 |
| First NaturalState Bank | McGehee | AR | **B-** | C+ | C+ | 60.7 | 8.10 | 16.7 | 6.5 | 16.9 | 19.8 | **9.1** | 10.4 | 16.1 |
| First Nebraska Bank | Valley | NE | **B+** | B | B | 281.7 | -0.25 | 8.0 | 1.4 | 10.1 | 15.5 | **8.3** | 10.2 | 13.6 |
| First Neighbor Bank, N.A. | Toledo | IL | **B-** | C+ | C+ | 452.8 | 8.71 | 17.7 | 4.8 | 11.9 | 7.0 | **7.5** | 10.8 | 12.9 |
| ▼ First Neighborhood Bank | Spencer | WV | **C+** | B- | B- | 143.4 | 6.60 | 6.2 | 2.4 | 30.3 | 20.4 | **9.7** | 10.8 | 19.0 |
| First New Mexico Bank | Deming | NM | **A** | A | A | 204.3 | -1.41 | 12.0 | 1.9 | 9.7 | 32.5 | **10.0** | 14.7 | 26.1 |
| First New Mexico Bank of Silver City | Silver City | NM | **A** | A | A | 113.8 | 2.38 | 1.7 | 0.9 | 9.8 | 33.6 | **10.0** | 12.6 | 25.3 |
| First New Mexico Bank, Las Cruces | Las Cruces | NM | **A** | A | A | 115.0 | 2.26 | 4.3 | 2.4 | 17.5 | 18.3 | **10.0** | 15.2 | 24.0 |
| First Northeast Bank of Nebraska | Lyons | NE | **A-** | B | B | 297.1 | -4.68 | 4.8 | 1.3 | 2.0 | 30.6 | **10.0** | 14.1 | 15.7 |
| First Northern Bank and Trust Co. | Palmerton | PA | **B** | B- | B- | 720.7 | 2.34 | 5.4 | 0.5 | 30.6 | 18.6 | **10.0** | 14.3 | 20.9 |
| First Northern Bank of Dixon | Dixon | CA | **A-** | B+ | B | 1292.6 | 3.42 | 7.7 | 0.1 | 5.4 | 26.5 | **8.4** | 10.0 | 15.8 |
| ▲ First Northern Bank of Wyoming | Buffalo | WY | **B-** | C+ | B- | 379.9 | 11.58 | 9.0 | 4.0 | 12.9 | 19.6 | **7.1** | 9.1 | 14.4 |
| First Oklahoma Bank | Jenks | OK | **C** | C- | C | 749.9 | 16.93 | 17.7 | 0.4 | 15.4 | 0.1 | **5.1** | 9.2 | 11.1 |
| First Option Bank | Osawatomie | KS | **B** | B | B | 434.9 | 34.77 | 3.6 | 2.3 | 21.2 | 40.0 | **6.9** | 8.9 | 18.9 |
| First Palmetto Bank | Camden | SC | **B+** | B | B | 718.6 | 3.65 | 2.3 | 1.0 | 15.4 | 19.7 | **9.5** | 10.6 | 17.5 |
| First Peoples Bank | Pine Mountain | GA | **A-** | B+ | B+ | 179.5 | 15.65 | 4.0 | 1.4 | 18.8 | 24.4 | **10.0** | 11.5 | 18.1 |
| First Peoples Bank of Tennessee | Jefferson City | TN | **B-** | C+ | C | 157.3 | 5.59 | 10.3 | 1.2 | 9.7 | 15.3 | **7.4** | 9.3 | 12.9 |
| First Piedmont Federal S&L Assn. of Gaffn | Gaffney | SC | **A** | A | A+ | 418.7 | 2.32 | 2.3 | 1.0 | 41.2 | 0.8 | **10.0** | 26.1 | 41.4 |
| First Pioneer National Bank | Wray | CO | **A-** | B+ | A- | 181.5 | 1.27 | 2.3 | 2.9 | 3.4 | 22.5 | **10.0** | 14.5 | 20.8 |
| First Port City Bank | Bainbridge | GA | **B+** | B+ | A- | 251.4 | 23.92 | 9.5 | 1.2 | 16.8 | 9.4 | **6.4** | 8.6 | 12.0 |
| First Premier Bank | Sioux Falls | SD | **A** | A | A | 2041.6 | 15.92 | 6.0 | 38.4 | 2.8 | 12.2 | **10.0** | 14.3 | 22.5 |
| ▲ First Progressive Bank | Brewton | AL | **C** | C+ | C- | 30.1 | -0.53 | 8.2 | 3.9 | 11.4 | 57.5 | **10.0** | 27.8 | 74.1 |
| First Pryority Bank | Pryor | OK | **B** | B | B | 209.1 | 22.17 | 29.6 | 6.4 | 5.0 | 4.7 | **9.5** | 10.6 | 16.1 |
| ▲ First Reliance Bank | Florence | SC | **C+** | C+ | B- | 659.2 | 13.06 | 8.8 | 12.4 | 19.4 | 7.0 | **5.7** | 9.2 | 11.5 |
| First Republic Bank | San Francisco | CA | **B** | B | B+ | 116263.6 | 17.20 | 7.5 | 4.1 | 41.2 | 16.4 | **6.4** | 8.4 | 12.7 |
| First Resource Bank | Lino Lakes | MN | **B-** | B- | B+ | 223.2 | 16.52 | 11.1 | 0.2 | 23.5 | 3.4 | **7.5** | 9.3 | 13.3 |
| ▲ First Resource Bank | Exton | PA | **C+** | C- | C | 336.4 | 11.23 | 7.2 | 0.3 | 21.4 | 11.1 | **6.6** | 8.6 | 13.2 |
| First Robinson Savings Bank, N.A. | Robinson | IL | **B-** | B- | B- | 362.6 | 12.90 | 5.5 | 3.9 | 19.4 | 24.9 | **7.8** | 9.5 | 17.2 |
| First S&L Assn. | Mebane | NC | **C+** | C+ | C+ | 55.9 | 5.30 | 0.0 | 0.0 | 58.0 | 21.0 | **10.0** | 22.6 | 53.1 |
| First Savanna Savings Bank | Savanna | IL | **D-** | D | D- | 11.7 | -2.66 | 0.0 | 10.5 | 56.2 | 10.4 | **6.5** | 8.5 | 16.5 |
| ▼ First Savings Bank | Danville | IL | **C** | B- | B | 36.9 | 7.28 | 0.0 | 0.9 | 29.8 | 57.1 | **10.0** | 24.9 | 85.9 |
| First Savings Bank | Clarksville | IN | **B+** | B- | B- | 1289.7 | 20.36 | 5.4 | 1.2 | 22.6 | 14.0 | **7.0** | 9.3 | 12.5 |
| First Savings Bank | Beresford | SD | **A-** | A- | B+ | 869.7 | 10.87 | 1.9 | 16.3 | 8.4 | 14.2 | **10.0** | 15.5 | 21.0 |
| First Savings Bank of Hegewisch | Chicago | IL | **B** | B | B | 679.4 | 3.18 | 0.0 | 0.1 | 48.0 | 30.8 | **10.0** | 16.1 | 47.6 |
| First Seacoast Bank | Dover | NH | **C** | C | C | 410.2 | 5.87 | 6.0 | 0.5 | 52.4 | 10.9 | **10.0** | 11.4 | 18.5 |
| ▲ First Secure Bank and Trust Co. | Palos Hills | IL | **B-** | C | D+ | 189.4 | 27.13 | 7.0 | 0.1 | 14.8 | 9.6 | **8.0** | 9.7 | 13.4 |
| First Secure Community Bank | Sugar Grove | IL | **C+** | C | C+ | 372.4 | 21.30 | 17.3 | 1.8 | 4.2 | 17.7 | **5.2** | 9.3 | 11.1 |
| First Security Bank | Searcy | AR | **A+** | A+ | A+ | 5828.2 | 10.76 | 6.9 | 0.8 | 5.8 | 42.3 | **10.0** | 18.4 | 23.9 |
| ▲ First Security Bank | Mapleton | IA | **A-** | B+ | A- | 69.6 | 0.46 | 2.9 | 3.2 | 3.4 | 16.3 | **10.0** | 13.0 | 18.3 |
| ▲ First Security Bank | Mackinaw | IL | **D+** | D | D | 83.8 | 7.32 | 6.2 | 0.5 | 16.0 | 4.0 | **7.5** | 9.3 | 13.6 |
| First Security Bank | Overbrook | KS | **C+** | C+ | C+ | 64.8 | 5.74 | 7.2 | 1.7 | 23.8 | 5.4 | **6.0** | 8.0 | 11.9 |
| ▲ First Security Bank | Byron | MN | **C+** | C | C+ | 70.9 | 0.69 | 6.4 | 3.0 | 20.0 | 20.9 | **6.7** | 8.7 | 13.8 |

| Asset Quality Index | Adjusted Non-Performing Loans as a % of Total Loans | Adjusted Non-Performing Loans as a % of Capital | Net Charge-Offs Avg Loans | Profitability Index | Net Income ($Mil) | Return on Assets (R.O.A.) | Return on Equity (R.O.E.) | Net Interest Spread | Overhead Efficiency Ratio | Liquidity Index | Liquidity Ratio | Hot Money Ratio | Stability Index |
|---|---|---|---|---|---|---|---|---|---|---|---|---|---|
| **7.2** | 0.30 | 2.4 | 0.15 | **5.1** | 0.8 | 1.27 | 12.68 | 4.20 | 73.3 | **4.3** | 35.5 | 11.9 | **5.6** |
| **5.6** | 2.36 | 8.0 | 0.14 | **3.1** | 0.3 | 0.55 | 5.81 | 3.88 | 83.4 | **4.7** | 59.7 | 14.9 | **4.2** |
| **5.9** | 0.43 | 3.4 | 0.01 | **7.0** | 2.2 | 1.62 | 16.20 | 4.52 | 66.2 | **3.3** | 12.3 | 11.5 | **7.7** |
| **5.8** | 1.41 | 5.0 | 0.00 | **3.8** | 3.6 | 0.75 | 6.68 | 3.30 | 73.0 | **4.3** | 17.2 | 7.3 | **6.1** |
| **4.2** | 2.88 | 15.6 | -0.36 | **3.4** | 0.4 | 0.54 | 4.74 | 4.91 | 94.0 | **1.5** | 17.5 | 25.5 | **5.6** |
| **4.0** | 2.46 | 15.6 | 0.08 | **3.0** | 0.6 | 0.42 | 4.42 | 3.79 | 89.5 | **4.3** | 20.2 | 7.2 | **5.0** |
| **8.0** | 0.52 | 2.5 | 0.18 | **8.9** | 2.3 | 1.69 | 9.48 | 4.90 | 59.0 | **3.4** | 29.9 | 14.4 | **8.8** |
| **6.0** | 0.41 | 3.4 | 0.14 | **6.7** | 3.6 | 1.38 | 14.13 | 4.93 | 65.1 | **1.6** | 17.8 | 23.9 | **5.7** |
| **5.6** | 0.29 | 4.3 | 0.27 | **3.9** | 0.6 | 0.67 | 6.43 | 4.31 | 81.7 | **1.0** | 15.5 | 32.6 | **5.9** |
| **6.3** | 3.45 | 5.4 | 0.01 | **8.2** | 2.5 | 1.82 | 9.21 | 5.01 | 57.6 | **1.8** | 18.5 | 20.3 | **7.9** |
| **8.2** | 0.14 | 0.3 | 1.80 | **7.7** | 37.9 | 1.88 | 20.80 | 3.68 | 83.4 | **6.9** | 41.6 | 1.0 | **6.8** |
| **5.6** | 1.13 | 8.8 | -0.11 | **5.6** | 1.7 | 1.29 | 9.73 | 4.62 | 72.4 | **1.9** | 21.6 | 20.1 | **8.1** |
| **8.6** | 0.03 | 0.3 | 0.00 | **5.7** | 10.3 | 1.21 | 12.06 | 3.13 | 58.7 | **5.0** | 35.3 | 8.3 | **7.6** |
| **5.5** | 0.69 | 9.0 | 0.43 | **4.7** | 1.1 | 0.97 | 9.25 | 4.16 | 67.4 | **3.9** | 15.2 | 9.4 | **6.4** |
| **4.5** | 2.40 | 8.3 | -0.07 | **3.6** | 6.5 | 0.72 | 4.41 | 3.27 | 80.7 | **5.8** | 30.4 | 0.1 | **7.6** |
| **4.6** | 1.73 | 7.5 | -0.01 | **4.3** | 1.6 | 0.68 | 5.63 | 4.02 | 79.9 | **4.0** | 22.1 | 9.8 | **8.1** |
| **2.2** | 4.59 | 21.0 | 0.35 | **4.2** | 1.7 | 0.82 | 8.87 | 3.92 | 75.3 | **4.6** | 21.9 | 5.3 | **5.8** |
| **6.5** | na | 0.0 | na | **9.5** | 8.9 | 30.96 | 37.17 | 1.61 | 74.9 | **4.0** | 215.6 | 0.0 | **6.3** |
| **7.3** | 0.00 | 0.0 | 0.07 | **6.7** | 4.1 | 1.15 | 8.74 | 3.18 | 50.5 | **0.8** | 19.0 | 45.8 | **8.3** |
| **4.0** | 2.61 | 13.3 | 0.09 | **3.6** | 0.4 | 0.65 | 6.11 | 3.78 | 78.4 | **2.9** | 12.5 | 14.5 | **5.8** |
| **7.2** | 0.74 | 3.3 | -0.01 | **5.1** | 3.5 | 1.23 | 12.09 | 4.15 | 71.7 | **4.2** | 14.2 | 7.1 | **7.0** |
| **4.9** | 0.83 | 4.9 | 0.19 | **4.9** | 3.9 | 0.89 | 7.78 | 3.80 | 66.1 | **1.2** | 9.2 | 22.7 | **7.4** |
| **8.0** | 0.05 | 0.2 | 0.46 | **2.9** | 0.5 | 0.36 | 3.17 | 3.55 | 83.0 | **4.0** | 33.9 | 12.9 | **6.3** |
| **8.6** | 1.13 | 3.4 | 0.13 | **7.5** | 3.2 | 1.58 | 10.97 | 4.23 | 56.7 | **6.6** | 46.8 | 1.5 | **8.7** |
| **9.4** | 0.08 | 0.3 | 0.19 | **8.6** | 1.8 | 1.61 | 13.16 | 4.30 | 54.6 | **7.3** | 61.5 | 1.9 | **8.2** |
| **8.9** | 0.16 | 0.6 | -0.02 | **8.8** | 1.8 | 1.60 | 10.73 | 5.11 | 61.0 | **4.9** | 42.6 | 11.3 | **8.8** |
| **8.4** | 0.00 | 0.0 | -0.05 | **5.3** | 3.4 | 1.13 | 8.30 | 3.43 | 58.3 | **2.5** | 19.0 | 12.7 | **8.5** |
| **7.5** | 0.68 | 3.4 | -0.03 | **4.1** | 5.5 | 0.78 | 5.35 | 3.74 | 74.5 | **3.6** | 13.8 | 11.1 | **7.8** |
| **7.7** | 0.54 | 1.8 | 0.06 | **6.4** | 14.9 | 1.19 | 12.36 | 3.98 | 62.0 | **6.4** | 36.8 | 3.0 | **8.2** |
| **4.3** | 1.24 | 10.1 | 0.12 | **5.5** | 4.6 | 1.26 | 14.12 | 4.22 | 70.9 | **1.4** | 15.0 | 18.6 | **6.4** |
| **5.3** | 0.85 | 4.3 | 0.22 | **3.6** | 4.5 | 0.64 | 7.09 | 3.52 | 74.7 | **0.6** | 14.5 | 57.6 | **5.2** |
| **7.1** | 0.67 | 2.1 | -0.04 | **5.3** | 4.4 | 1.26 | 13.82 | 3.06 | 69.9 | **3.2** | 26.2 | 14.3 | **5.3** |
| **5.3** | 0.70 | 3.3 | 0.00 | **5.4** | 7.8 | 1.08 | 9.60 | 3.27 | 59.1 | **1.9** | 30.0 | 27.0 | **8.1** |
| **7.6** | 1.07 | 4.7 | 0.00 | **6.3** | 1.9 | 1.27 | 11.46 | 5.17 | 65.2 | **4.8** | 24.4 | 4.4 | **5.8** |
| **6.1** | 0.04 | 0.3 | 0.03 | **4.4** | 1.3 | 0.86 | 9.37 | 4.36 | 75.4 | **4.4** | 17.9 | 6.1 | **4.9** |
| **9.3** | 0.51 | 1.1 | 0.00 | **9.7** | 7.2 | 1.73 | 6.30 | 4.70 | 55.6 | **4.9** | 32.5 | 7.6 | **9.2** |
| **7.4** | 0.00 | 0.0 | 0.00 | **6.7** | 2.6 | 1.44 | 9.89 | 3.82 | 53.1 | **1.9** | 14.4 | 19.3 | **8.4** |
| **7.9** | 0.26 | 1.5 | 0.00 | **5.2** | 1.5 | 0.70 | 7.79 | 3.89 | 77.6 | **1.9** | 22.0 | 20.7 | **6.4** |
| **6.8** | 0.37 | 1.4 | 0.31 | **8.1** | 37.7 | 1.90 | 13.23 | 3.70 | 58.8 | **3.3** | 28.1 | 2.9 | **10.0** |
| **8.2** | 4.41 | 4.0 | 0.00 | **2.3** | 0.1 | 0.21 | 0.74 | 2.94 | 83.6 | **6.4** | 98.6 | 11.7 | **6.3** |
| **5.3** | 0.57 | 3.6 | 0.19 | **6.2** | 2.5 | 1.32 | 12.06 | 3.97 | 53.3 | **1.0** | 25.3 | 42.9 | **7.0** |
| **4.1** | 0.92 | 4.2 | 0.10 | **4.7** | 5.5 | 0.89 | 8.40 | 4.10 | 75.8 | **1.7** | 12.4 | 20.4 | **6.7** |
| **8.7** | 0.17 | 1.5 | 0.01 | **4.3** | 930.3 | 0.88 | 10.07 | 2.88 | 64.2 | **3.2** | 15.9 | 10.1 | **7.7** |
| **6.8** | 0.27 | 1.5 | 0.00 | **3.9** | 1.4 | 0.71 | 6.64 | 3.79 | 72.3 | **1.5** | 14.5 | 16.7 | **8.5** |
| **3.8** | 0.88 | 6.3 | 0.10 | **4.2** | 2.3 | 0.76 | 8.73 | 3.82 | 69.4 | **1.1** | 12.4 | 27.6 | **4.5** |
| **3.5** | 2.90 | 16.1 | 0.11 | **5.0** | 3.3 | 0.98 | 10.43 | 3.56 | 68.0 | **4.4** | 22.4 | 6.8 | **5.0** |
| **9.9** | 0.00 | 1.3 | 0.00 | **2.0** | 0.1 | 0.19 | 0.83 | 2.74 | 94.9 | **2.0** | 44.6 | 52.7 | **7.5** |
| **2.6** | 2.21 | 21.3 | 0.01 | **0.0** | -0.4 | -3.25 | -30.54 | 4.10 | 175.7 | **1.3** | 23.5 | 29.4 | **3.3** |
| **10.0** | 0.62 | 0.7 | 0.00 | **1.7** | 0.0 | 0.04 | 0.17 | 2.37 | 99.2 | **4.2** | 91.2 | 25.1 | **5.9** |
| **5.6** | 1.24 | 5.7 | 0.09 | **7.0** | 16.9 | 1.50 | 14.25 | 3.96 | 76.4 | **1.8** | 18.3 | 8.0 | **8.7** |
| **5.6** | 1.27 | 4.3 | 4.38 | **10.0** | 18.3 | 2.19 | 14.11 | 9.00 | 44.0 | **3.6** | 17.1 | 11.4 | **8.8** |
| **9.9** | 0.06 | 0.2 | 0.05 | **3.1** | 2.9 | 0.43 | 2.68 | 2.44 | 76.1 | **3.5** | 55.3 | 24.3 | **8.3** |
| **9.1** | 0.31 | 2.1 | 0.01 | **1.7** | 0.6 | 0.14 | 1.49 | 3.09 | 95.9 | **3.6** | 14.0 | 10.8 | **6.0** |
| **4.7** | 0.81 | 7.4 | -0.03 | **4.2** | 1.2 | 0.76 | 6.70 | 3.35 | 68.6 | **0.9** | 24.5 | 45.1 | **4.9** |
| **5.9** | 0.25 | 2.3 | 0.23 | **3.4** | 1.9 | 0.56 | 5.74 | 3.35 | 73.4 | **1.4** | 31.1 | 34.7 | **5.2** |
| **9.0** | 0.17 | 0.3 | 0.11 | **8.7** | 103.9 | 1.91 | 9.42 | 3.95 | 46.2 | **5.1** | 28.6 | 8.4 | **10.0** |
| **5.9** | 0.00 | 0.0 | 0.00 | **6.4** | 1.0 | 1.40 | 7.88 | 3.95 | 62.4 | **3.4** | 33.5 | 16.0 | **8.3** |
| **1.3** | 2.17 | 15.6 | 0.53 | **3.2** | 0.5 | 0.57 | 5.54 | 3.74 | 74.4 | **1.8** | 14.7 | 20.4 | **5.0** |
| **7.5** | 0.00 | 0.0 | 0.00 | **4.1** | 0.6 | 0.92 | 10.43 | 4.19 | 77.3 | **1.5** | 15.1 | 24.1 | **5.3** |
| **6.9** | 0.35 | 2.4 | 0.19 | **4.7** | 0.8 | 1.14 | 13.47 | 3.80 | 70.8 | **3.3** | 32.0 | 15.7 | **4.6** |

| | | | | | | | One | Asset Mix (As a % of Total Assets) | | | | | | Risk- |
|---|---|---|---|---|---|---|---|---|---|---|---|---|---|---|
| Name | City | State | Rating | 2018 Rating | 2017 Rating | Total Assets ($Mil) | Year Asset Growth | Comm-ercial Loans | Cons-umer Loans | Mort-gage Loans | Secur-ities | Capital-ization Index | Lever-age Ratio | Based Capital Ratio |
| First Security Bank | Union Star | MO | **C** | C- | C- | 32.5 | 5.77 | 3.0 | 10.4 | 32.2 | 27.2 | **6.4** | 8.4 | 16.3 |
| First Security Bank | Batesville | MS | **A-** | B+ | B+ | 580.0 | 6.09 | 6.4 | 3.8 | 18.4 | 22.9 | **9.3** | 10.5 | 17.3 |
| ▼ First Security Bank | Beaver | OK | **D+** | C- | C+ | 117.5 | -2.75 | 8.1 | 2.8 | 7.7 | 5.4 | **6.5** | 10.0 | 12.1 |
| First Security Bank & Trust Co. | Charles City | IA | **C** | C- | C- | 498.5 | -0.21 | 4.8 | 1.4 | 13.4 | 27.9 | **7.8** | 9.6 | 15.6 |
| First Security Bank - Canby | Canby | MN | **B+** | B+ | A | 67.0 | -7.08 | 22.6 | 1.8 | 1.4 | 12.5 | **10.0** | 13.4 | 19.4 |
| First Security Bank - West | Beulah | ND | **A-** | B+ | A- | 61.2 | -9.32 | 17.9 | 1.7 | 0.9 | 19.7 | **10.0** | 12.1 | 19.1 |
| First Security Bank and Trust Co. | Oklahoma City | OK | **C-** | C | C | 55.7 | 14.22 | 15.9 | 3.6 | 35.9 | 3.6 | **5.9** | 8.6 | 11.7 |
| First Security Bank of Deer Lodge | Deer Lodge | MT | **B+** | B+ | B | 40.3 | 2.01 | 12.6 | 6.5 | 30.6 | 0.0 | **8.6** | 10.1 | 17.7 |
| ▲ First Security Bank of Helena | Helena | MT | **B** | C+ | C+ | 57.7 | 9.89 | 16.2 | 2.2 | 20.5 | 4.4 | **10.0** | 12.8 | 19.7 |
| First Security Bank of Nevada | Las Vegas | NV | **A** | A | A- | 229.0 | 13.13 | 4.1 | 0.0 | 1.0 | 2.6 | **10.0** | 19.5 | 29.1 |
| First Security Bank of Roundup | Roundup | MT | **B** | B- | B+ | 66.7 | 4.73 | 8.8 | 4.1 | 4.2 | 34.2 | **10.0** | 11.5 | 20.7 |
| First Security Bank-Hendricks | Hendricks | MN | **B+** | B+ | B+ | 32.7 | 7.96 | 13.6 | 2.2 | 7.3 | 26.4 | **10.0** | 12.1 | 25.4 |
| First Security Bank-Sleepy Eye | Sleepy Eye | MN | **B+** | B+ | A | 196.3 | 3.80 | 8.4 | 1.7 | 7.6 | 22.1 | **10.0** | 13.4 | 20.4 |
| ▲ First Security State Bank | Evansdale | IA | **C+** | C | B- | 101.4 | 1.03 | 31.3 | 30.4 | 5.9 | 4.7 | **9.9** | 11.8 | 14.9 |
| ▲ First Security State Bank | Cranfills Gap | TX | **B** | B- | B- | 117.5 | 2.48 | 3.8 | 3.8 | 22.7 | 41.8 | **5.4** | 7.4 | 16.4 |
| ▲ First Security Trust and Savings Bank | Elmwood Park | IL | **B-** | C | C | 309.8 | -1.56 | 11.7 | 3.8 | 4.6 | 13.9 | **6.9** | 8.9 | 18.1 |
| ▲ First Sentinel Bank | Richlands | VA | **B-** | C+ | B | 286.8 | 9.44 | 4.8 | 35.6 | 20.5 | 0.0 | **7.0** | 9.0 | 12.7 |
| ▼ First Service Bank | Greenbrier | AR | **C+** | B- | B | 364.5 | 18.60 | 9.9 | 1.0 | 22.0 | 3.5 | **5.6** | 9.0 | 11.5 |
| First Shore Federal S&L Assn. | Salisbury | MD | **B** | B | B- | 319.3 | 5.57 | 2.7 | 9.0 | 52.7 | 4.9 | **10.0** | 15.4 | 26.4 |
| First Sound Bank | Seattle | WA | **C-** | C- | C- | 106.9 | -18.96 | 28.5 | 2.1 | 3.3 | 3.0 | **10.0** | 12.1 | 17.7 |
| First Southeast Bank | Harmony | MN | **D+** | D | D | 102.2 | 0.72 | 10.3 | 2.9 | 9.9 | 1.4 | **5.9** | 9.1 | 11.7 |
| First Southern Bank | Florence | AL | **B** | B- | B- | 276.7 | 12.56 | 11.9 | 1.7 | 23.5 | 7.7 | **7.9** | 9.6 | 13.9 |
| First Southern Bank | Patterson | GA | **E** | E- | E- | 126.7 | 24.92 | 7.6 | 2.5 | 10.4 | 15.4 | **10.0** | 14.7 | 21.0 |
| First Southern Bank | Marion | IL | **A-** | A- | A- | 682.9 | 2.41 | 7.7 | 7.5 | 13.5 | 23.6 | **10.0** | 12.5 | 18.1 |
| First Southern Bank | Columbia | MS | **B+** | B | B | 195.8 | 2.80 | 6.1 | 6.1 | 16.6 | 15.0 | **10.0** | 11.4 | 15.9 |
| ▲ First Southern National Bank | Lancaster | KY | **B** | C+ | B- | 895.7 | 6.64 | 6.2 | 2.2 | 26.0 | 15.2 | **7.5** | 9.3 | 15.7 |
| First Southern State Bank | Stevenson | AL | **B+** | B+ | B+ | 555.0 | 41.79 | 5.8 | 5.8 | 19.6 | 27.1 | **8.4** | 9.9 | 16.8 |
| First Southwest Bank | Alamosa | CO | **B-** | C+ | B- | 333.0 | 9.60 | 10.2 | 1.2 | 7.8 | 14.0 | **6.9** | 8.9 | 15.3 |
| First State B&T Co. of Larned | Larned | KS | **A-** | A- | A | 165.9 | 9.23 | 7.4 | 0.7 | 1.6 | 22.4 | **10.0** | 13.9 | 22.3 |
| First State Bank | Crossett | AR | **B-** | B- | B- | 33.9 | 3.46 | 14.5 | 12.0 | 9.3 | 14.8 | **10.0** | 16.7 | 25.2 |
| First State Bank | Lonoke | AR | **C** | C | D+ | 253.6 | -5.41 | 1.7 | 0.5 | 12.7 | 34.5 | **8.3** | 9.8 | 17.5 |
| First State Bank | Russellville | AR | **A-** | A- | A- | 295.3 | 10.38 | 11.7 | 1.0 | 17.3 | 10.2 | **9.9** | 10.9 | 15.7 |
| First State Bank | Wrens | GA | **B** | B- | B- | 159.6 | 7.30 | 12.6 | 2.9 | 29.9 | 11.9 | **7.0** | 9.0 | 13.0 |
| First State Bank | Belmond | IA | **B** | B | B | 97.2 | -5.49 | 9.7 | 3.3 | 10.9 | 37.6 | **10.0** | 12.3 | 23.4 |
| First State Bank | Britt | IA | **A** | A | A | 108.3 | -1.55 | 3.3 | 1.3 | 10.4 | 35.5 | **10.0** | 13.9 | 25.4 |
| First State Bank | Ida Grove | IA | **B** | B | A- | 164.9 | -1.47 | 9.4 | 4.2 | 9.3 | 16.8 | **9.2** | 11.4 | 14.4 |
| ▲ First State Bank | Lynnville | IA | **A-** | B | A- | 195.6 | 4.23 | 7.9 | 2.1 | 12.1 | 11.6 | **10.0** | 13.2 | 16.4 |
| First State Bank | Nashua | IA | **B+** | B+ | B+ | 54.9 | 6.33 | 8.8 | 2.8 | 24.0 | 8.0 | **10.0** | 11.1 | 17.0 |
| First State Bank | Stuart | IA | **B-** | B- | C+ | 106.0 | -2.14 | 7.9 | 2.2 | 8.1 | 34.3 | **9.9** | 10.9 | 20.5 |
| ▲ First State Bank | Sumner | IA | **C+** | C | B- | 95.9 | -9.40 | 7.9 | 3.0 | 13.9 | 32.1 | **10.0** | 12.9 | 21.5 |
| First State Bank | Webster City | IA | **A-** | A- | A- | 486.8 | 8.95 | 11.3 | 0.6 | 8.7 | 9.0 | **10.0** | 14.0 | 16.1 |
| First State Bank | Mendota | IL | **B-** | B- | C+ | 1142.7 | 1.75 | 9.1 | 0.9 | 22.6 | 8.9 | **7.9** | 9.9 | 13.3 |
| First State Bank | Monticello | IL | **B-** | C+ | B- | 272.0 | 3.41 | 5.3 | 1.4 | 9.1 | 28.2 | **6.2** | 8.2 | 13.9 |
| First State Bank | Ness City | KS | **B+** | B+ | B+ | 69.2 | 4.58 | 5.4 | 2.1 | 0.0 | 53.6 | **10.0** | 19.1 | 31.2 |
| First State Bank | Norton | KS | **B-** | B- | B | 452.0 | 1.04 | 9.1 | 2.3 | 2.0 | 40.0 | **9.4** | 10.6 | 16.3 |
| First State Bank | Irvington | KY | **B+** | A- | A- | 208.5 | 2.65 | 2.2 | 4.8 | 33.8 | 18.4 | **10.0** | 11.2 | 15.2 |
| First State Bank | Saint Clair Shores | MI | **B** | B | B | 772.1 | 8.49 | 10.1 | 0.5 | 14.7 | 20.8 | **9.1** | 10.4 | 15.0 |
| First State Bank | Holly Springs | MS | **C** | C+ | C+ | 114.7 | -2.51 | 9.1 | 1.9 | 16.1 | 31.5 | **10.0** | 11.7 | 20.1 |
| First State Bank | Waynesboro | MS | **B+** | B+ | A- | 809.6 | -3.09 | 4.0 | 2.1 | 22.6 | 22.1 | **10.0** | 12.2 | 19.1 |
| First State Bank | Buxton | ND | **B** | B+ | B+ | 255.4 | 38.56 | 15.7 | 1.0 | 10.8 | 5.4 | **7.0** | 10.6 | 12.5 |
| First State Bank | Farnam | NE | **A-** | B+ | A- | 146.4 | -3.87 | 8.3 | 2.5 | 5.4 | 20.7 | **10.0** | 12.4 | 15.8 |
| First State Bank | Gothenburg | NE | **C** | C | B- | 555.6 | 9.83 | 6.0 | 0.8 | 2.1 | 19.9 | **9.2** | 11.6 | 14.3 |
| First State Bank | Hordville | NE | **B-** | C+ | B- | 40.1 | -7.35 | 11.1 | 0.7 | 4.5 | 0.0 | **10.0** | 12.5 | 15.8 |
| ▲ First State Bank | Loomis | NE | **B-** | C+ | B | 148.4 | 3.49 | 7.5 | 2.9 | 5.4 | 9.1 | **8.5** | 11.8 | 13.8 |
| First State Bank | Randolph | NE | **B+** | B+ | B+ | 64.1 | -3.12 | 1.5 | 1.4 | 1.8 | 3.3 | **10.0** | 13.4 | 18.4 |
| First State Bank | Scottsbluff | NE | **A-** | A- | A- | 301.4 | 38.10 | 10.2 | 1.4 | 7.9 | 16.2 | **7.3** | 9.2 | 12.7 |
| First State Bank | Socorro | NM | **B** | B | B | 158.9 | 7.27 | 0.4 | 0.6 | 3.0 | 80.4 | **9.4** | 10.6 | 45.4 |
| First State Bank | Winchester | OH | **B** | B- | B | 494.3 | 6.81 | 2.3 | 10.0 | 19.7 | 23.9 | **8.6** | 10.1 | 15.6 |
| ▼ First State Bank | Anadarko | OK | **B** | A- | A- | 99.8 | -0.97 | 0.9 | 2.6 | 2.6 | 56.8 | **10.0** | 14.0 | 36.9 |
| First State Bank | Boise City | OK | **C+** | C | C+ | 79.2 | 1.65 | 7.6 | 6.1 | 1.5 | 14.3 | **5.8** | 9.9 | 11.6 |

| Asset Quality Index | Adjusted Non-Performing Loans as a % of Total Loans | Adjusted Non-Performing Loans as a % of Capital | Net Charge-Offs / Avg Loans | Profitability Index | Net Income ($Mil) | Return on Assets (R.O.A.) | Return on Equity (R.O.E.) | Net Interest Spread | Overhead Efficiency Ratio | Liquidity Index | Liquidity Ratio | Hot Money Ratio | Stability Index |
|---|---|---|---|---|---|---|---|---|---|---|---|---|---|
| **8.3** | 0.03 | 0.2 | 0.15 | **4.6** | 0.3 | 0.92 | 11.43 | 4.28 | 68.4 | **3.8** | 20.0 | 10.4 | **4.0** |
| **5.9** | 1.39 | 6.7 | 0.10 | **6.6** | 7.9 | 1.36 | 11.94 | 4.43 | 64.9 | **4.2** | 23.0 | 8.3 | **8.3** |
| **0.7** | 3.46 | 35.2 | 0.48 | **7.8** | 2.1 | 1.84 | 18.29 | 4.33 | 48.4 | **0.6** | 9.6 | 45.7 | **6.8** |
| **2.6** | 4.26 | 14.4 | 0.11 | **3.7** | 3.8 | 0.77 | 6.92 | 3.40 | 79.3 | **4.6** | 32.7 | 8.2 | **6.1** |
| **5.2** | 2.13 | 9.4 | 0.01 | **7.3** | 1.1 | 1.70 | 10.67 | 4.17 | 59.0 | **5.0** | 26.7 | 4.3 | **8.3** |
| **8.0** | 0.00 | 0.3 | 0.00 | **6.3** | 1.0 | 1.56 | 11.66 | 3.79 | 57.2 | **5.6** | 28.5 | 1.2 | **8.0** |
| **3.0** | 2.00 | 18.8 | 0.10 | **2.5** | 0.0 | 0.05 | 0.49 | 5.04 | 98.1 | **0.6** | 7.4 | 44.6 | **2.3** |
| **8.3** | 0.00 | 0.0 | 0.00 | **9.6** | 1.0 | 2.52 | 24.35 | 4.65 | 47.7 | **4.2** | 20.6 | 8.1 | **7.0** |
| **5.8** | 0.91 | 3.2 | 0.00 | **5.3** | 0.5 | 0.97 | 6.61 | 4.97 | 65.5 | **3.0** | 24.3 | 15.1 | **7.1** |
| **6.7** | 0.01 | 0.0 | 0.02 | **9.4** | 5.6 | 2.46 | 11.59 | 4.48 | 42.2 | **5.8** | 40.4 | 4.8 | **9.5** |
| **4.8** | 3.12 | 11.6 | 0.33 | **8.6** | 1.2 | 1.92 | 16.12 | 4.49 | 51.8 | **5.3** | 37.2 | 6.7 | **8.2** |
| **9.0** | 0.02 | 0.1 | 0.00 | **7.3** | 0.6 | 1.82 | 15.08 | 3.56 | 53.3 | **5.6** | 53.8 | 9.1 | **8.0** |
| **7.4** | 0.15 | 1.2 | 1.01 | **5.3** | 2.2 | 1.20 | 8.44 | 4.18 | 61.7 | **5.2** | 32.1 | 5.2 | **8.9** |
| **3.3** | 0.96 | 7.0 | 0.17 | **6.6** | 1.5 | 1.51 | 13.46 | 3.76 | 57.7 | **0.9** | 19.4 | 28.3 | **8.0** |
| **8.9** | 0.03 | 0.2 | 0.07 | **5.2** | 1.6 | 1.31 | 17.35 | 3.58 | 69.0 | **5.7** | 52.0 | 9.3 | **4.8** |
| **4.9** | 2.15 | 9.3 | 0.32 | **4.0** | 3.0 | 0.92 | 10.87 | 2.52 | 66.3 | **6.5** | 54.8 | 5.1 | **4.4** |
| **4.1** | 0.67 | 5.1 | 0.73 | **6.2** | 3.2 | 1.14 | 12.84 | 4.56 | 58.0 | **1.1** | 13.1 | 29.9 | **4.9** |
| **5.1** | 1.48 | 6.9 | 0.06 | **4.2** | 2.3 | 0.70 | 7.42 | 4.32 | 81.2 | **0.7** | 6.6 | 20.2 | **5.2** |
| **5.9** | 1.23 | 5.8 | 0.01 | **3.7** | 2.1 | 0.68 | 4.40 | 3.49 | 73.3 | **1.3** | 17.8 | 27.6 | **7.7** |
| **4.2** | 2.02 | 12.5 | -0.03 | **1.6** | 0.0 | 0.04 | 0.30 | 3.59 | 99.1 | **4.1** | 14.8 | 7.9 | **6.3** |
| **2.0** | 1.49 | 10.5 | 0.54 | **4.5** | 1.0 | 0.96 | 10.63 | 4.10 | 71.8 | **1.4** | 9.5 | 17.1 | **6.8** |
| **7.6** | 0.36 | 1.7 | 0.06 | **5.1** | 2.8 | 1.09 | 11.18 | 3.83 | 64.0 | **2.3** | 17.8 | 17.7 | **5.5** |
| **4.1** | 2.68 | 7.4 | 0.72 | **0.2** | -0.7 | -0.61 | -4.33 | 4.67 | 105.7 | **3.9** | 19.2 | 9.8 | **1.7** |
| **5.0** | 1.43 | 8.0 | 0.16 | **7.0** | 9.2 | 1.34 | 9.41 | 3.92 | 54.3 | **2.7** | 17.2 | 15.7 | **9.2** |
| **8.3** | 0.21 | 0.8 | 0.00 | **5.2** | 2.4 | 1.22 | 10.65 | 4.53 | 74.5 | **2.9** | 17.1 | 14.7 | **6.7** |
| **4.7** | 1.19 | 5.5 | 0.04 | **6.2** | 10.9 | 1.25 | 11.46 | 4.53 | 66.3 | **4.0** | 18.2 | 9.0 | **7.6** |
| **7.5** | 0.60 | 1.8 | 0.16 | **5.8** | 5.1 | 1.16 | 12.05 | 3.95 | 60.8 | **2.6** | 31.6 | 19.4 | **6.1** |
| **5.4** | 0.98 | 3.0 | 0.05 | **4.7** | 3.1 | 0.98 | 9.69 | 4.20 | 72.2 | **3.2** | 23.1 | 13.8 | **6.2** |
| **6.7** | 1.60 | 6.6 | 0.17 | **8.0** | 3.4 | 2.19 | 16.42 | 3.49 | 58.6 | **3.8** | 39.1 | 12.0 | **8.9** |
| **6.2** | 1.08 | 6.8 | 0.29 | **4.1** | 0.2 | 0.66 | 3.90 | 5.26 | 81.7 | **2.3** | 35.1 | 24.9 | **6.2** |
| **9.0** | 0.00 | 0.0 | 0.00 | **2.9** | 2.2 | 0.87 | 8.48 | 2.87 | 77.9 | **1.4** | 26.1 | 30.8 | **4.1** |
| **8.6** | 0.13 | 0.8 | 0.00 | **7.0** | 3.7 | 1.26 | 11.48 | 3.93 | 59.1 | **1.8** | 20.0 | 20.0 | **7.5** |
| **5.7** | 1.18 | 9.8 | 0.06 | **7.9** | 2.2 | 1.47 | 17.37 | 5.30 | 61.9 | **1.1** | 16.0 | 28.8 | **5.5** |
| **9.0** | 0.11 | 0.5 | 0.13 | **4.6** | 1.0 | 1.02 | 8.48 | 2.73 | 59.4 | **4.2** | 54.6 | 16.3 | **6.6** |
| **9.0** | 0.00 | 0.0 | 0.00 | **7.4** | 1.6 | 1.45 | 10.59 | 2.97 | 39.7 | **3.8** | 43.5 | 16.9 | **8.9** |
| **4.5** | 0.56 | 6.7 | 0.02 | **6.3** | 2.4 | 1.45 | 12.68 | 3.71 | 57.6 | **1.2** | 22.3 | 31.8 | **8.0** |
| **6.4** | 0.46 | 3.2 | 0.38 | **8.6** | 3.7 | 1.95 | 14.23 | 4.35 | 50.9 | **2.2** | 14.6 | 14.1 | **9.6** |
| **8.5** | 0.00 | 0.0 | -0.01 | **7.1** | 0.7 | 1.38 | 12.27 | 3.40 | 49.5 | **1.3** | 26.1 | 31.9 | **7.0** |
| **8.7** | 0.00 | 0.5 | -0.06 | **3.3** | 0.6 | 0.55 | 5.17 | 3.20 | 77.7 | **5.4** | 42.9 | 8.3 | **6.7** |
| **6.1** | 1.52 | 5.3 | 1.12 | **2.9** | 0.5 | 0.43 | 3.22 | 3.31 | 69.4 | **4.5** | 44.5 | 13.5 | **5.3** |
| **8.1** | 0.01 | 0.4 | 0.00 | **6.6** | 6.0 | 1.30 | 9.31 | 3.31 | 63.6 | **1.3** | 12.3 | 24.4 | **8.7** |
| **6.4** | 0.60 | 5.1 | 0.02 | **4.4** | 9.9 | 0.88 | 8.57 | 3.32 | 70.9 | **1.1** | 7.7 | 24.6 | **8.0** |
| **5.2** | 1.32 | 6.2 | 0.00 | **6.1** | 3.9 | 1.46 | 16.75 | 3.65 | 65.9 | **2.8** | 23.6 | 16.0 | **6.2** |
| **7.6** | 2.22 | 2.2 | 0.25 | **7.4** | 1.3 | 2.00 | 10.85 | 3.57 | 53.4 | **5.0** | 44.1 | 10.9 | **8.0** |
| **3.9** | 2.22 | 9.8 | 0.54 | **5.8** | 5.8 | 1.33 | 11.48 | 3.65 | 57.2 | **0.9** | 21.6 | 25.1 | **7.6** |
| **6.2** | 2.56 | 10.3 | 0.02 | **6.1** | 2.5 | 1.21 | 10.92 | 4.15 | 63.7 | **2.9** | 6.6 | 5.8 | **7.8** |
| **5.8** | 1.02 | 3.7 | -0.07 | **5.1** | 8.1 | 1.05 | 10.11 | 3.75 | 68.5 | **3.0** | 24.6 | 15.2 | **7.6** |
| **5.8** | 1.64 | 7.0 | 0.04 | **2.7** | 0.8 | 0.68 | 6.10 | 3.41 | 92.2 | **2.4** | 16.4 | 17.2 | **6.7** |
| **5.5** | 1.23 | 9.1 | 0.13 | **4.9** | 8.3 | 1.02 | 7.72 | 3.41 | 61.6 | **1.6** | 14.8 | 23.3 | **8.7** |
| **7.2** | 0.34 | 2.5 | 0.00 | **6.0** | 2.7 | 1.30 | 12.37 | 4.55 | 69.5 | **1.2** | 4.7 | 19.5 | **7.9** |
| **6.3** | 0.99 | 4.4 | 0.01 | **6.7** | 2.3 | 1.61 | 12.58 | 3.33 | 58.8 | **1.0** | 19.5 | 33.6 | **9.2** |
| **2.1** | 3.36 | 17.5 | 0.09 | **7.6** | 8.4 | 1.60 | 13.02 | 3.67 | 49.6 | **1.7** | 17.1 | 17.5 | **8.3** |
| **7.1** | 0.00 | 0.0 | 0.00 | **3.8** | 0.2 | 0.59 | 4.84 | 3.63 | 68.4 | **3.8** | 21.9 | 10.6 | **6.2** |
| **6.2** | 0.00 | 0.1 | 0.02 | **8.6** | 2.4 | 1.69 | 12.38 | 4.41 | 53.2 | **1.1** | 9.0 | 21.1 | **8.8** |
| **7.2** | 0.20 | 1.0 | 0.00 | **7.7** | 1.2 | 1.79 | 13.51 | 3.80 | 50.4 | **1.6** | 22.7 | 20.3 | **9.3** |
| **8.1** | 0.26 | 1.5 | -0.24 | **10.0** | 6.3 | 2.25 | 23.07 | 4.70 | 56.2 | **2.4** | 32.2 | 21.0 | **8.4** |
| **10.0** | 2.03 | 0.7 | 0.70 | **4.1** | 1.3 | 0.81 | 7.81 | 3.37 | 69.4 | **7.0** | 62.2 | 3.7 | **6.4** |
| **5.0** | 0.95 | 5.3 | 0.19 | **5.0** | 5.4 | 1.09 | 10.47 | 3.72 | 67.3 | **3.0** | 17.1 | 11.7 | **6.7** |
| **8.9** | 1.76 | 3.5 | 6.61 | **1.4** | -1.3 | -1.31 | -8.99 | 3.38 | 67.2 | **5.5** | 44.4 | 7.7 | **7.4** |
| **4.4** | 0.48 | 5.0 | 0.30 | **7.0** | 1.2 | 1.53 | 18.07 | 4.31 | 59.8 | **0.5** | 2.7 | 40.9 | **6.2** |

| Name | City | State | Rating | 2018 Rating | 2017 Rating | Total Assets ($Mil) | One Year Asset Growth | Asset Mix (As a % of Total Assets) Commercial Loans | Consumer Loans | Mortgage Loans | Securities | Capitalization Index | Leverage Ratio | Risk-Based Capital Ratio |
|---|---|---|---|---|---|---|---|---|---|---|---|---|---|---|
| First State Bank | Elmore City | OK | C+ | C- | C- | 13.7 | 1.83 | 20.1 | 2.6 | 30.5 | 0.0 | **10.0** | 14.4 | 25.9 |
| First State Bank | Noble | OK | C+ | C+ | C+ | 43.6 | -3.32 | 2.3 | 5.1 | 19.4 | 33.8 | **10.0** | 12.0 | 30.5 |
| First State Bank | Oklahoma City | OK | C+ | C | C | 353.7 | 5.96 | 16.9 | 0.6 | 14.1 | 2.8 | **5.6** | 9.1 | 11.4 |
| ▼ First State Bank | Tahlequah | OK | C- | C+ | C- | 62.2 | -0.39 | 11.3 | 2.2 | 14.4 | 21.7 | **10.0** | 12.4 | 17.9 |
| First State Bank | Valliant | OK | C- | D | C- | 67.6 | -0.08 | 8.3 | 4.6 | 28.7 | 10.9 | **7.2** | 9.1 | 13.5 |
| First State Bank | Watonga | OK | B+ | B+ | B+ | 72.9 | -11.56 | 14.0 | 3.3 | 2.3 | 34.6 | **9.9** | 11.0 | 19.8 |
| First State Bank | Abernathy | TX | C+ | C+ | C+ | 41.3 | -1.40 | 6.9 | 9.5 | 0.3 | 12.1 | **7.5** | 9.4 | 15.8 |
| First State Bank | Abilene | TX | C | D+ | D | 43.9 | 12.76 | 5.5 | 1.3 | 2.6 | 10.2 | **5.8** | 7.8 | 26.5 |
| First State Bank | Athens | TX | A- | A- | A- | 467.0 | -0.80 | 5.4 | 3.2 | 31.1 | 27.0 | **10.0** | 11.8 | 21.0 |
| First State Bank | Chico | TX | C+ | C+ | C- | 185.0 | 2.54 | 4.9 | 2.0 | 13.6 | 30.7 | **10.0** | 11.7 | 18.2 |
| ▲ First State Bank | Clute | TX | B- | B | B- | 201.4 | 5.83 | 12.0 | 8.1 | 17.9 | 22.6 | **7.8** | 9.5 | 16.0 |
| First State Bank | Columbus | TX | B- | B- | B- | 145.9 | 2.49 | 1.7 | 3.8 | 3.6 | 54.4 | **10.0** | 14.5 | 33.2 |
| First State Bank | Gainesville | TX | B+ | B+ | B+ | 1148.0 | 5.71 | 7.4 | 1.4 | 10.8 | 33.7 | **7.7** | 9.5 | 14.7 |
| First State Bank | Graham | TX | B+ | B+ | A- | 150.3 | -1.75 | 16.4 | 1.8 | 12.4 | 15.4 | **7.5** | 9.4 | 15.9 |
| First State Bank | Junction | TX | C+ | C- | C+ | 59.8 | 16.33 | 4.2 | 2.6 | 10.5 | 28.7 | **6.7** | 8.7 | 12.5 |
| First State Bank | Louise | TX | A- | B+ | B+ | 518.8 | 7.37 | 10.2 | 0.8 | 9.3 | 18.9 | **7.2** | 9.2 | 13.1 |
| First State Bank | Rice | TX | B- | B- | C | 151.2 | -1.40 | 13.7 | 2.8 | 10.5 | 25.3 | **10.0** | 12.5 | 20.6 |
| First State Bank | Shallowater | TX | B- | B+ | A- | 95.2 | -15.23 | 7.7 | 1.6 | 3.5 | 11.6 | **10.0** | 18.1 | 26.3 |
| First State Bank | Spearman | TX | B | B- | B- | 145.0 | -1.72 | 6.5 | 0.7 | 5.3 | 8.7 | **8.1** | 9.7 | 14.5 |
| First State Bank | Stratford | TX | A- | A- | A- | 244.2 | -0.26 | 7.0 | 1.4 | 5.6 | 31.3 | **10.0** | 12.2 | 16.6 |
| First State Bank | New London | WI | B- | B- | B- | 299.9 | -3.18 | 3.9 | 5.0 | 12.5 | 34.5 | **9.2** | 10.5 | 16.0 |
| First State Bank | Barboursville | WV | E- | E- | E- | 152.4 | -1.77 | 10.6 | 2.1 | 25.7 | 6.7 | **0.0** | 1.3 | 3.0 |
| ▲ First State Bank & Trust | Williston | ND | A- | B | B- | 465.4 | 2.87 | 5.4 | 1.1 | 2.6 | 57.2 | **10.0** | 13.1 | 27.2 |
| First State Bank & Trust Co. | Fremont | NE | B+ | B- | B- | 258.8 | 2.21 | 19.2 | 2.0 | 21.2 | 8.9 | **7.5** | 9.4 | 13.3 |
| ▲ First State Bank and Trust | Tonganoxie | KS | B- | C+ | C+ | 296.4 | 6.36 | 5.8 | 2.4 | 15.6 | 19.8 | **6.3** | 8.3 | 12.9 |
| First State Bank and Trust | Bayport | MN | B | B- | B- | 279.5 | 9.15 | 6.0 | 5.3 | 31.5 | 18.7 | **6.6** | 8.6 | 15.4 |
| First State Bank and Trust Co. | Carthage | TX | A- | A- | A | 492.4 | 0.41 | 2.1 | 5.2 | 18.8 | 57.3 | **10.0** | 15.8 | 36.3 |
| First State Bank and Trust Co., Inc. | Caruthersville | MO | A- | A- | A- | 384.2 | 1.92 | 7.3 | 3.4 | 15.1 | 19.4 | **10.0** | 12.7 | 17.5 |
| ▼ First State Bank in Temple | Temple | OK | C+ | C+ | C+ | 23.9 | -4.11 | 4.7 | 4.0 | 3.1 | 34.5 | **10.0** | 20.2 | 30.1 |
| First State Bank Minnesota | Le Roy | MN | B | B- | B- | 70.7 | 2.97 | 7.5 | 1.9 | 5.0 | 6.2 | **10.0** | 11.5 | 17.9 |
| ▲ First State Bank Nebraska | Lincoln | NE | B | B- | B | 608.4 | 7.93 | 11.3 | 1.2 | 12.6 | 10.4 | **6.5** | 9.0 | 12.1 |
| First State Bank of Bedias | Bedias | TX | A | A | A | 160.3 | 1.08 | 12.2 | 4.7 | 10.1 | 22.4 | **10.0** | 17.0 | 28.1 |
| First State Bank of Beecher City | Beecher City | IL | B+ | B | B | 71.4 | -2.10 | 6.8 | 12.5 | 20.9 | 4.9 | **10.0** | 13.9 | 19.7 |
| First State Bank of Ben Wheeler, Texas | Ben Wheeler | TX | A- | A- | A | 153.4 | 5.25 | 6.9 | 3.9 | 20.7 | 39.5 | **10.0** | 13.8 | 25.4 |
| First State Bank of Bigfork | Bigfork | MN | D+ | D | D | 81.6 | 3.90 | 9.5 | 11.3 | 36.4 | 1.4 | **9.8** | 10.9 | 15.1 |
| ▲ First State Bank of Blakely | Blakely | GA | A- | B+ | A | 509.2 | 4.44 | 7.3 | 2.5 | 14.2 | 12.0 | **10.0** | 14.5 | 22.7 |
| ▲ First State Bank of Bloomington | Bloomington | IL | C+ | C+ | B- | 119.5 | 3.94 | 7.0 | 2.0 | 26.4 | 16.3 | **7.1** | 9.1 | 15.5 |
| First State Bank of Brownsboro | Brownsboro | TX | B- | C+ | B | 110.8 | 7.23 | 6.3 | 7.8 | 19.3 | 36.5 | **9.1** | 10.4 | 18.5 |
| First State Bank of Burnet | Burnet | TX | A- | A- | B+ | 247.9 | 0.66 | 4.2 | 1.6 | 8.1 | 59.4 | **10.0** | 13.6 | 29.7 |
| First State Bank of Campbell Hill | Campbell Hill | IL | B+ | B | B- | 114.6 | 3.25 | 6.3 | 3.9 | 28.7 | 16.6 | **10.0** | 11.4 | 20.4 |
| First State Bank of Cando | Cando | ND | C+ | C+ | C+ | 63.7 | 5.46 | 3.9 | 5.7 | 4.0 | 30.2 | **7.6** | 9.4 | 16.4 |
| First State Bank of Claremont | Groton | SD | B- | B- | C+ | 58.7 | -0.99 | 6.4 | 1.0 | 0.0 | 19.5 | **10.0** | 11.9 | 22.5 |
| First State Bank of Decatur | Decatur | MI | B | B | B | 51.1 | -5.60 | 14.0 | 4.0 | 41.1 | 30.5 | **10.0** | 21.5 | 46.6 |
| ▲ First State Bank of DeKalb County | Fort Payne | AL | B- | C+ | B | 200.7 | 10.09 | 7.7 | 6.2 | 19.5 | 19.7 | **9.7** | 11.0 | 14.7 |
| First State Bank of DeQueen | De Queen | AR | B+ | B+ | B+ | 275.2 | 12.23 | 8.8 | 3.7 | 14.2 | 15.9 | **8.2** | 9.8 | 13.8 |
| ▲ First State Bank of Dongola | Dongola | IL | C+ | C | C- | 24.6 | 0.77 | 5.3 | 11.8 | 30.7 | 7.4 | **10.0** | 11.2 | 20.0 |
| First State Bank of Forrest | Forrest | IL | C- | C- | C | 227.3 | 6.71 | 14.7 | 5.3 | 32.3 | 9.2 | **6.3** | 8.3 | 12.6 |
| First State Bank of Forsyth | Forsyth | MT | B | B- | B | 122.1 | 0.05 | 4.7 | 3.7 | 9.7 | 36.0 | **10.0** | 12.1 | 20.3 |
| First State Bank of Fountain | Fountain | MN | D | D+ | D+ | 32.1 | -3.84 | 4.5 | 1.3 | 10.8 | 37.8 | **8.9** | 10.3 | 18.2 |
| ▲ First State Bank of Golva | Golva | ND | A- | B+ | B+ | 78.1 | -0.51 | 4.9 | 2.6 | 3.8 | 38.5 | **9.0** | 10.4 | 15.4 |
| First State Bank of Grove City | Grove City | MN | B- | B | B- | 29.7 | 19.17 | 8.5 | 3.5 | 20.3 | 0.8 | **9.7** | 10.8 | 21.5 |
| First State Bank of Harvey | Harvey | ND | B | B- | B- | 82.4 | -1.79 | 3.2 | 2.5 | 5.8 | 49.9 | **9.1** | 10.4 | 22.2 |
| ▲ First State Bank of Healy | Healy | KS | B- | C | C- | 83.1 | 7.70 | 10.8 | 1.0 | 1.2 | 28.9 | **10.0** | 20.9 | 28.5 |
| First State Bank of Kiester | Kiester | MN | D+ | D | C- | 23.8 | 21.68 | 13.1 | 2.4 | 9.1 | 1.1 | **9.7** | 10.8 | 17.3 |
| First State Bank of Le Center | Le Center | MN | B+ | B | B+ | 86.9 | 2.94 | 12.2 | 6.8 | 18.5 | 15.0 | **10.0** | 11.1 | 17.5 |
| First State Bank of Livingston | Livingston | TX | B | B | B | 344.7 | 1.80 | 1.7 | 3.0 | 4.5 | 44.0 | **10.0** | 15.3 | 36.6 |
| First State Bank of Malta | Malta | MT | D | D+ | B- | 138.6 | -0.91 | 2.9 | 1.8 | 0.0 | 24.1 | **10.0** | 16.0 | 20.3 |
| ▲ First State Bank of Middlebury | Middlebury | IN | B+ | B- | B | 593.3 | 5.11 | 14.0 | 2.0 | 22.9 | 17.6 | **10.0** | 11.5 | 16.5 |
| First State Bank of Newcastle | Newcastle | WY | B | B | B | 154.2 | 8.84 | 5.9 | 2.4 | 7.8 | 54.0 | **10.0** | 13.4 | 38.5 |
| ▲ First State Bank of Odem | Odem | TX | A | A- | A- | 149.4 | 4.56 | 11.5 | 1.7 | 5.4 | 31.2 | **10.0** | 12.1 | 23.7 |

| Asset Quality Index | Adjusted Non-Performing Loans as a % of Total Loans | Adjusted Non-Performing Loans as a % of Capital | Net Charge-Offs Avg Loans | Profitability Index | Net Income ($Mil) | Return on Assets (R.O.A.) | Return on Equity (R.O.E.) | Net Interest Spread | Overhead Efficiency Ratio | Liquidity Index | Liquidity Ratio | Hot Money Ratio | Stability Index |
|---|---|---|---|---|---|---|---|---|---|---|---|---|---|
| **6.7** | 0.66 | 2.8 | 0.00 | **7.1** | 0.4 | 2.50 | 18.72 | 3.45 | 90.7 | **5.4** | 34.6 | 2.5 | **5.7** |
| **6.2** | 2.63 | 7.5 | 0.06 | **3.4** | 0.3 | 0.58 | 5.26 | 4.25 | 86.8 | **5.4** | 33.0 | 4.0 | **5.1** |
| **7.1** | 0.03 | 0.1 | 0.03 | **4.4** | 2.9 | 0.84 | 8.95 | 3.48 | 71.3 | **0.7** | 11.7 | 41.2 | **5.7** |
| **4.9** | 3.99 | 9.1 | 0.04 | **1.4** | 0.1 | 0.15 | 1.11 | 3.48 | 94.5 | **2.2** | 30.4 | 22.9 | **6.3** |
| **4.3** | 1.47 | 10.8 | -0.07 | **3.6** | 0.5 | 0.69 | 8.09 | 4.69 | 85.3 | **1.2** | 10.9 | 28.2 | **4.9** |
| **7.4** | 0.73 | 1.6 | 0.44 | **8.7** | 1.6 | 2.06 | 20.08 | 4.58 | 52.9 | **4.6** | 41.6 | 12.1 | **7.5** |
| **4.6** | 1.49 | 8.0 | 0.38 | **5.1** | 0.5 | 1.22 | 11.78 | 6.12 | 76.6 | **1.7** | 14.0 | 21.4 | **4.3** |
| **8.7** | 0.00 | 0.0 | 0.00 | **3.8** | 0.3 | 0.71 | 7.72 | 3.48 | 73.4 | **6.2** | 68.7 | 8.2 | **3.1** |
| **6.5** | 1.75 | 9.1 | 0.27 | **6.1** | 5.5 | 1.16 | 10.45 | 3.88 | 60.7 | **3.8** | 13.7 | 10.1 | **7.5** |
| **5.9** | 1.60 | 6.2 | -0.09 | **2.9** | 1.2 | 0.68 | 5.96 | 3.09 | 88.9 | **1.9** | 30.7 | 26.8 | **5.9** |
| **6.7** | 0.69 | 4.8 | 0.29 | **7.3** | 3.5 | 1.78 | 18.84 | 4.41 | 61.2 | **4.2** | 27.4 | 9.7 | **6.3** |
| **9.4** | 0.02 | 0.0 | 0.13 | **3.1** | 1.1 | 0.75 | 5.38 | 2.51 | 72.0 | **3.0** | 60.7 | 35.3 | **7.3** |
| **6.9** | 0.77 | 4.7 | 0.01 | **5.0** | 12.8 | 1.14 | 12.20 | 3.99 | 74.8 | **5.6** | 31.4 | 6.6 | **8.7** |
| **8.8** | 0.05 | 0.7 | 0.04 | **6.7** | 2.4 | 1.62 | 16.96 | 3.95 | 63.9 | **3.0** | 39.7 | 20.4 | **7.2** |
| **6.4** | 1.16 | 5.9 | 0.09 | **5.6** | 0.8 | 1.57 | 16.58 | 4.44 | 70.1 | **4.3** | 30.6 | 10.6 | **4.7** |
| **8.4** | 0.14 | 0.6 | 0.05 | **9.7** | 11.8 | 2.40 | 25.72 | 5.35 | 56.1 | **4.8** | 29.3 | 6.7 | **7.6** |
| **6.9** | 0.39 | 1.6 | 0.19 | **3.5** | 0.9 | 0.61 | 4.55 | 4.32 | 84.9 | **3.1** | 21.8 | 14.1 | **7.3** |
| **2.6** | 4.72 | 14.6 | 0.15 | **9.7** | 2.2 | 2.21 | 11.96 | 5.14 | 57.1 | **2.0** | 18.9 | 19.6 | **9.3** |
| **8.5** | 0.13 | 1.0 | 0.00 | **7.0** | 2.7 | 1.85 | 22.63 | 3.97 | 61.5 | **1.4** | 23.9 | 28.5 | **5.3** |
| **8.5** | 0.00 | 0.0 | 0.00 | **7.2** | 4.2 | 1.71 | 14.48 | 3.64 | 56.8 | **2.6** | 33.9 | 19.8 | **8.6** |
| **4.2** | 4.01 | 12.3 | -0.03 | **4.4** | 2.7 | 0.89 | 7.06 | 3.31 | 67.3 | **4.3** | 32.7 | 9.1 | **6.7** |
| **0.0** | 19.75 | 523.8 | -0.01 | **0.0** | -3.7 | -2.39 | -100.16 | 3.04 | 160.6 | **0.9** | 17.5 | 30.1 | **0.3** |
| **6.4** | 2.76 | 6.5 | 0.37 | **7.6** | 7.9 | 1.72 | 12.61 | 3.48 | 47.6 | **5.6** | 51.5 | 9.7 | **9.2** |
| **6.4** | 0.22 | 1.8 | 0.01 | **7.9** | 4.7 | 1.87 | 19.78 | 4.55 | 60.9 | **3.6** | 18.4 | 11.4 | **7.0** |
| **7.5** | 0.64 | 2.4 | 0.01 | **4.1** | 2.3 | 0.77 | 9.00 | 3.99 | 80.3 | **4.0** | 11.9 | 8.4 | **5.6** |
| **8.6** | 0.10 | 0.3 | 0.02 | **5.6** | 3.6 | 1.36 | 15.10 | 3.89 | 73.7 | **4.2** | 27.0 | 9.9 | **6.0** |
| **8.4** | 1.55 | 3.8 | 0.13 | **5.5** | 5.6 | 1.11 | 6.88 | 2.95 | 56.6 | **1.5** | 33.4 | 38.4 | **9.1** |
| **8.4** | 0.24 | 1.7 | 0.09 | **6.9** | 6.1 | 1.65 | 12.96 | 4.27 | 64.9 | **2.9** | 15.7 | 14.8 | **8.5** |
| **7.1** | 0.08 | 0.2 | 0.12 | **3.4** | 0.2 | 0.64 | 3.21 | 4.43 | 83.2 | **1.3** | 10.1 | 25.2 | **6.4** |
| **3.5** | 3.96 | 15.7 | -0.01 | **6.4** | 1.0 | 1.52 | 13.33 | 3.99 | 61.4 | **5.4** | 28.6 | 2.3 | **7.4** |
| **7.1** | 0.17 | 1.0 | 0.10 | **5.3** | 8.1 | 1.37 | 13.55 | 3.46 | 58.6 | **1.9** | 9.7 | 19.1 | **8.1** |
| **8.2** | 0.23 | 2.3 | 0.09 | **8.5** | 3.3 | 2.09 | 12.91 | 4.25 | 48.7 | **2.5** | 41.6 | 28.8 | **9.7** |
| **4.9** | 1.12 | 8.4 | 0.24 | **9.5** | 1.6 | 2.20 | 12.72 | 4.38 | 51.5 | **3.0** | 16.5 | 14.0 | **9.0** |
| **8.6** | 0.00 | 0.0 | 0.39 | **6.9** | 2.6 | 1.74 | 12.76 | 3.41 | 57.1 | **1.7** | 31.6 | 30.5 | **9.2** |
| **1.0** | 4.26 | 30.4 | 0.23 | **4.5** | 0.7 | 0.85 | 7.89 | 4.34 | 71.4 | **1.6** | 13.7 | 19.9 | **6.3** |
| **5.4** | 2.47 | 9.2 | 0.34 | **7.4** | 7.0 | 1.38 | 9.35 | 4.24 | 54.1 | **0.9** | 20.9 | 27.2 | **9.4** |
| **4.4** | 1.09 | 9.8 | 0.02 | **5.3** | 1.5 | 1.30 | 13.59 | 3.90 | 73.5 | **3.7** | 21.7 | 11.0 | **6.3** |
| **5.7** | 0.99 | 4.3 | 0.08 | **4.4** | 1.0 | 0.99 | 9.64 | 3.96 | 76.7 | **3.6** | 25.9 | 12.1 | **6.1** |
| **9.4** | 0.42 | 0.7 | 0.04 | **5.1** | 3.0 | 1.20 | 8.97 | 3.71 | 64.9 | **5.9** | 66.6 | 11.1 | **8.3** |
| **5.6** | 1.15 | 7.4 | 0.01 | **5.9** | 1.4 | 1.18 | 10.62 | 3.91 | 61.0 | **4.4** | 24.1 | 7.0 | **6.7** |
| **6.9** | 0.88 | 4.4 | -0.01 | **3.8** | 0.5 | 0.77 | 7.75 | 3.61 | 72.4 | **3.0** | 32.7 | 17.5 | **5.5** |
| **5.3** | 3.43 | 7.3 | 1.48 | **4.0** | 0.5 | 0.78 | 6.43 | 3.92 | 76.0 | **5.0** | 44.1 | 10.6 | **5.8** |
| **7.4** | 1.12 | 1.8 | 0.12 | **4.0** | 0.4 | 0.84 | 3.97 | 3.87 | 75.3 | **4.1** | 46.3 | 15.7 | **7.1** |
| **3.9** | 0.87 | 10.5 | 0.27 | **6.1** | 2.3 | 1.23 | 10.17 | 4.93 | 61.8 | **2.9** | 28.9 | 17.1 | **6.3** |
| **5.1** | 0.70 | 5.0 | 0.34 | **5.7** | 3.4 | 1.29 | 13.33 | 3.88 | 65.1 | **0.7** | 13.2 | 18.8 | **6.9** |
| **5.9** | 1.56 | 4.3 | -0.01 | **4.8** | 0.3 | 1.09 | 9.73 | 4.55 | 77.9 | **4.5** | 35.1 | 8.5 | **5.1** |
| **2.0** | 1.90 | 20.3 | 0.52 | **2.8** | 0.9 | 0.42 | 4.95 | 2.81 | 69.8 | **1.3** | 14.4 | 25.9 | **5.3** |
| **4.4** | 4.17 | 14.0 | 0.32 | **6.7** | 1.5 | 1.24 | 9.73 | 3.76 | 50.6 | **4.5** | 46.5 | 14.1 | **8.2** |
| **9.0** | 0.00 | 0.0 | 0.00 | **1.1** | 0.0 | 0.02 | 0.21 | 2.96 | 104.6 | **4.2** | 48.7 | 15.5 | **4.9** |
| **6.9** | 1.17 | 2.4 | 0.00 | **8.7** | 1.7 | 2.22 | 21.08 | 4.41 | 49.4 | **5.1** | 30.3 | 5.3 | **8.5** |
| **6.2** | 0.37 | 1.1 | -0.03 | **5.0** | 0.2 | 1.04 | 5.63 | 3.60 | 59.2 | **4.6** | 47.0 | 13.3 | **8.1** |
| **8.0** | 0.00 | 2.3 | -0.04 | **4.6** | 1.0 | 1.18 | 10.72 | 3.19 | 66.6 | **6.3** | 60.6 | 5.7 | **6.8** |
| **3.7** | 6.25 | 11.2 | -0.14 | **5.6** | 1.0 | 1.32 | 6.17 | 3.87 | 69.4 | **1.8** | 29.8 | 26.0 | **7.0** |
| **8.6** | 0.16 | 0.8 | 0.24 | **3.9** | 0.2 | 1.07 | 9.07 | 3.94 | 75.1 | **5.4** | 44.1 | 5.4 | **1.5** |
| **5.3** | 1.89 | 8.9 | 0.27 | **8.6** | 1.8 | 2.15 | 19.51 | 4.42 | 54.4 | **3.1** | 20.3 | 14.3 | **8.1** |
| **8.1** | 0.61 | 2.0 | 0.03 | **4.5** | 3.6 | 1.06 | 6.62 | 3.49 | 70.4 | **4.9** | 39.7 | 10.5 | **8.1** |
| **0.0** | 24.90 | 83.6 | 2.74 | **2.3** | -0.8 | -0.55 | -3.26 | 2.80 | 58.0 | **3.1** | 25.5 | 14.9 | **8.3** |
| **5.3** | 1.71 | 10.7 | 0.02 | **6.7** | 8.4 | 1.46 | 12.72 | 4.30 | 65.0 | **1.8** | 20.9 | 20.4 | **8.2** |
| **9.0** | 1.58 | 2.3 | 0.13 | **3.3** | 1.0 | 0.67 | 4.71 | 2.66 | 74.0 | **3.6** | 60.3 | 26.6 | **7.6** |
| **8.8** | 0.00 | 0.0 | 0.18 | **7.5** | 2.1 | 1.46 | 12.09 | 5.01 | 63.3 | **5.7** | 39.0 | 4.8 | **7.3** |

| Name | City | State | Rating | 2018 Rating | 2017 Rating | Total Assets ($Mil) | One Year Asset Growth | Asset Mix (As a % of Total Assets) Commercial Loans | Consumer Loans | Mortgage Loans | Securities | Capital-ization Index | Lever-age Ratio | Risk-Based Capital Ratio |
|---|---|---|---|---|---|---|---|---|---|---|---|---|---|---|
| First State Bank of Olmsted | Olmsted | IL | B- | B- | B- | 53.9 | 4.03 | 13.1 | 3.7 | 29.5 | 18.9 | 10.0 | 13.2 | 21.5 |
| ▲ First State Bank of Paint Rock | Paint Rock | TX | A- | B | B | 112.4 | 9.65 | 7.0 | 3.9 | 3.8 | 32.8 | 10.0 | 12.9 | 22.5 |
| First State Bank of Porter | Porter | IN | B+ | A- | A- | 142.7 | 1.47 | 1.2 | 0.3 | 23.0 | 31.3 | 10.0 | 16.2 | 27.6 |
| ▲ First State Bank of Purdy | Monett | MO | B- | C | C+ | 154.9 | -4.15 | 15.5 | 1.0 | 9.6 | 6.7 | 6.7 | 9.2 | 12.3 |
| First State Bank of Randolph County | Cuthbert | GA | D+ | C- | C+ | 79.2 | -0.13 | 8.3 | 3.4 | 4.4 | 46.9 | 8.1 | 9.7 | 18.3 |
| First State Bank of Ransom | Ransom | KS | B | B | B+ | 40.2 | -8.30 | 9.0 | 1.5 | 1.1 | 49.2 | 10.0 | 23.5 | 45.2 |
| First State Bank of Red Wing | Red Wing | MN | D+ | D+ | D+ | 79.0 | -0.68 | 3.9 | 3.7 | 11.2 | 38.8 | 6.9 | 8.9 | 27.8 |
| First State Bank of Roscoe | Roscoe | SD | A- | B+ | A- | 117.3 | 11.43 | 6.7 | 0.5 | 0.2 | 3.3 | 10.0 | 11.6 | 16.5 |
| First State Bank of Rosemount | Rosemount | MN | D- | D- | D- | 72.2 | 0.01 | 5.7 | 8.5 | 17.9 | 22.0 | 4.9 | 6.9 | 11.4 |
| First State Bank of San Diego | San Diego | TX | C+ | C+ | C+ | 67.7 | 3.06 | 13.6 | 3.9 | 3.2 | 37.1 | 7.3 | 9.2 | 22.9 |
| First State Bank of Sauk Centre | Sauk Centre | MN | A- | B+ | B+ | 109.6 | -1.38 | 10.0 | 4.8 | 17.7 | 14.2 | 10.0 | 12.8 | 20.1 |
| First State Bank of Shelby | Shelby | MT | A | A | A | 127.9 | -3.04 | 4.4 | 0.7 | 0.0 | 72.8 | 10.0 | 22.7 | 67.0 |
| First State Bank of St. Charles, Missouri | Saint Charles | MO | A- | A- | A- | 383.9 | 8.74 | 10.4 | 0.1 | 44.5 | 12.6 | 10.0 | 13.6 | 17.0 |
| First State Bank of St. Peter | Saint Peter | IL | B+ | B+ | A- | 28.1 | -8.15 | 0.9 | 4.7 | 3.8 | 59.8 | 10.0 | 17.1 | 39.1 |
| First State Bank of Swanville | Swanville | MN | C+ | C+ | D+ | 24.0 | -7.15 | 16.0 | 3.3 | 16.4 | 1.9 | 10.0 | 16.0 | 24.4 |
| First State Bank of Texas | Orange | TX | B- | B- | C- | 178.5 | 8.79 | 17.0 | 10.2 | 14.1 | 10.2 | 10.0 | 11.4 | 15.6 |
| First State Bank of the Florida Keys | Key West | FL | B | B- | B | 943.1 | -1.84 | 5.7 | 0.8 | 19.2 | 28.0 | 6.9 | 8.9 | 17.0 |
| First State Bank of the South, Inc. | Sulligent | AL | B+ | B+ | B+ | 107.9 | 6.92 | 7.5 | 7.8 | 12.2 | 35.3 | 10.0 | 15.6 | 24.7 |
| First State Bank of the Southeast, Inc. | Middlesboro | KY | C+ | B- | C+ | 354.2 | 2.05 | 9.3 | 3.1 | 27.2 | 10.3 | 7.1 | 9.1 | 12.9 |
| First State Bank of Uvalde | Uvalde | TX | B+ | B | B | 1770.2 | 2.08 | 2.6 | 0.6 | 4.7 | 50.3 | 7.5 | 9.3 | 28.8 |
| First State Bank of Van Orin | Van Orin | IL | C | C- | C- | 40.4 | -1.35 | 3.6 | 1.6 | 2.1 | 35.9 | 8.0 | 9.7 | 24.0 |
| First State Bank of Warren | Warren | AR | B- | C+ | C | 110.5 | 0.37 | 12.2 | 2.2 | 5.5 | 51.9 | 10.0 | 11.2 | 22.0 |
| First State Bank of Wyoming | Wyoming | MN | A- | B+ | B+ | 180.2 | -4.16 | 4.6 | 1.9 | 14.7 | 51.3 | 10.0 | 17.8 | 40.2 |
| First State Bank Shannon-Polo | Shannon | IL | C+ | C+ | B | 170.3 | 8.18 | 8.6 | 2.8 | 8.8 | 27.3 | 6.7 | 9.4 | 12.3 |
| ▲ First State Bank Southwest | Worthington | MN | A | A- | A | 299.7 | 11.61 | 7.7 | 2.7 | 3.2 | 29.1 | 10.0 | 11.8 | 18.7 |
| First State Bank, Pond Creek, Oklahoma | Pond Creek | OK | B | B- | C | 47.0 | -3.10 | 16.7 | 3.8 | 19.4 | 14.2 | 10.0 | 11.1 | 20.8 |
| First State Community Bank | Farmington | MO | B+ | B | B | 2622.8 | 6.39 | 6.1 | 2.1 | 21.4 | 11.4 | 7.0 | 10.6 | 12.5 |
| ▼ First Summit Bank | Ryan | OK | C | C+ | C | 27.2 | 1.40 | 10.7 | 3.8 | 7.6 | 0.0 | 10.0 | 13.1 | 18.1 |
| First Texas Bank | Georgetown | TX | B+ | B- | C+ | 655.7 | -1.79 | 2.7 | 1.1 | 2.9 | 56.2 | 6.8 | 8.8 | 17.7 |
| First Texas Bank | Killeen | TX | B | B- | C+ | 298.0 | 1.11 | 1.0 | 0.4 | 11.7 | 46.1 | 10.0 | 11.1 | 21.7 |
| ▲ First Texas Bank | Lampasas | TX | A- | B- | B- | 141.9 | 3.20 | 2.7 | 1.4 | 15.1 | 41.1 | 10.0 | 11.6 | 20.7 |
| First Texoma National Bank | Durant | OK | A- | B+ | B | 185.5 | 5.05 | 6.1 | 5.5 | 28.8 | 11.2 | 9.6 | 10.7 | 15.7 |
| First Tri-County Bank | Swanton | NE | C | C | C+ | 53.6 | 1.84 | 9.4 | 5.0 | 19.6 | 2.7 | 7.9 | 10.3 | 13.3 |
| ▼ First Trust and Savings Bank | Coralville | IA | C- | C+ | C | 49.2 | -10.03 | 4.0 | 1.6 | 3.0 | 67.2 | 10.0 | 12.6 | 30.7 |
| First Trust and Savings Bank | Wheatland | IA | B- | B- | C+ | 190.0 | 4.54 | 13.3 | 3.4 | 5.1 | 4.2 | 6.7 | 10.4 | 12.3 |
| First Trust and Savings Bank of Watseka | Watseka | IL | A | A | A | 254.5 | 2.66 | 8.4 | 1.2 | 5.6 | 34.2 | 10.0 | 15.7 | 27.3 |
| First Trust Bank of Illinois | Kankakee | IL | B | B | B+ | 306.1 | 26.22 | 12.5 | 1.1 | 7.2 | 38.2 | 8.9 | 11.5 | 14.1 |
| ▲ First United Bank | Park River | ND | C+ | C- | C+ | 261.8 | 4.40 | 5.2 | 2.0 | 3.9 | 18.6 | 9.3 | 10.5 | 14.4 |
| First United Bank | Dimmitt | TX | A- | A- | A- | 1370.0 | 4.13 | 13.1 | 0.4 | 7.3 | 22.5 | 9.6 | 10.7 | 14.7 |
| First United Bank & Trust | Oakland | MD | B | B- | B- | 1423.5 | 4.30 | 8.2 | 2.5 | 26.1 | 15.4 | 10.0 | 11.0 | 15.6 |
| First United Bank and Trust Co. | Madisonville | KY | A- | A- | A | 339.6 | 0.17 | 9.1 | 2.6 | 25.1 | 14.5 | 10.0 | 12.4 | 16.6 |
| First United Bank and Trust Co. | Durant | OK | B | B | B+ | 8090.9 | 15.42 | 7.6 | 2.2 | 21.1 | 15.4 | 6.0 | 9.2 | 11.7 |
| First United National Bank | Fryburg | PA | B | B | B | 261.0 | 1.51 | 4.2 | 6.6 | 44.6 | 21.6 | 7.8 | 9.5 | 18.7 |
| First US Bank | Birmingham | AL | B- | C+ | B- | 788.5 | -0.39 | 7.4 | 14.7 | 11.2 | 13.7 | 7.9 | 9.6 | 13.8 |
| ▲ First Utah Bank | Salt Lake City | UT | B- | C | B | 425.7 | 12.34 | 13.4 | 1.1 | 2.3 | 5.0 | 9.5 | 11.2 | 14.6 |
| First Vision Bank of Tennessee | Tullahoma | TN | B+ | B+ | A- | 277.3 | 11.05 | 6.5 | 2.8 | 19.9 | 6.0 | 8.9 | 10.3 | 15.1 |
| First Volunteer Bank | Chattanooga | TN | A- | B+ | B- | 997.5 | 1.11 | 7.1 | 2.3 | 14.3 | 2.9 | 10.0 | 12.6 | 16.7 |
| First Western Bank | Booneville | AR | B- | C+ | C+ | 462.2 | 8.84 | 2.2 | 1.0 | 34.7 | 6.1 | 6.5 | 8.5 | 12.3 |
| ▼ First Western Bank & Trust | Minot | ND | B- | B+ | B+ | 1089.6 | -2.05 | 17.0 | 3.1 | 4.0 | 19.2 | 5.9 | 9.6 | 11.7 |
| First Western Federal Savings Bank | Rapid City | SD | A- | A- | A- | 61.4 | 6.82 | 0.0 | 0.2 | 85.1 | 0.0 | 10.0 | 14.2 | 27.8 |
| First Western Trust Bank | Denver | CO | C+ | C+ | C | 1241.3 | 15.79 | 15.7 | 6.8 | 30.3 | 4.8 | 5.7 | 8.1 | 11.5 |
| First Westroads Bank, Inc. | Omaha | NE | A | A | A- | 270.1 | 1.38 | 11.0 | 0.2 | 9.0 | 12.6 | 10.0 | 12.9 | 17.3 |
| ▲ First Whitney Bank and Trust | Atlantic | IA | B+ | B+ | A- | 231.7 | 2.50 | 17.1 | 1.3 | 5.3 | 22.1 | 5.5 | 11.5 | 11.4 |
| First, A National Banking Assn. | Hattiesburg | MS | B+ | A- | B | 3934.6 | 31.27 | 8.4 | 1.1 | 15.4 | 19.5 | 10.0 | 11.8 | 15.6 |
| First-Citizens Bank & Trust Co. | Raleigh | NC | B+ | B+ | B+ | 39787.7 | 12.82 | 8.9 | 4.5 | 14.1 | 17.7 | 6.9 | 9.4 | 12.5 |
| First-Lockhart National Bank | Lockhart | TX | B | B | B | 304.0 | 11.41 | 1.8 | 0.6 | 20.3 | 16.4 | 7.7 | 9.4 | 15.4 |
| Firstar Bank | Sallisaw | OK | B- | C+ | B- | 713.5 | 21.73 | 17.6 | 2.8 | 19.8 | 5.5 | 4.8 | 8.3 | 10.9 |
| FirstBank | Lakewood | CO | A- | A- | A- | 19904.3 | 7.53 | 1.0 | 0.4 | 31.8 | 32.6 | 6.5 | 8.5 | 16.7 |
| FirstBank | Antlers | OK | B | B- | B | 322.2 | -4.02 | 8.3 | 11.2 | 32.4 | 0.7 | 7.4 | 9.3 | 13.6 |
| FirstBank | Nashville | TN | B+ | B+ | B+ | 6120.1 | 19.22 | 16.9 | 3.6 | 15.9 | 11.3 | 6.4 | 9.9 | 12.1 |

| Asset Quality Index | Adjusted Non-Performing Loans as a % of Total Loans | Adjusted Non-Performing Loans as a % of Capital | Net Charge-Offs Avg Loans | Profitability Index | Net Income ($Mil) | Return on Assets (R.O.A.) | Return on Equity (R.O.E.) | Net Interest Spread | Overhead Efficiency Ratio | Liquidity Index | Liquidity Ratio | Hot Money Ratio | Stability Index |
|---|---|---|---|---|---|---|---|---|---|---|---|---|---|
| **5.0** | 0.00 | 12.6 | 0.00 | **4.7** | 0.5 | 0.92 | 7.24 | 4.00 | 70.4 | **2.9** | 15.2 | 14.7 | **7.0** |
| **5.7** | 4.36 | 10.9 | 0.01 | **8.2** | 2.2 | 2.06 | 16.41 | 4.17 | 51.4 | **4.4** | 49.3 | 15.1 | **7.8** |
| **8.2** | 1.44 | 2.7 | 0.22 | **5.0** | 1.5 | 1.08 | 6.51 | 3.99 | 68.0 | **2.5** | 37.7 | 25.0 | **8.3** |
| **4.2** | 1.87 | 11.9 | 0.06 | **4.7** | 1.8 | 1.11 | 13.07 | 4.15 | 73.9 | **3.4** | 14.6 | 8.7 | **5.7** |
| **1.2** | 9.14 | 34.2 | 0.01 | **2.7** | 0.4 | 0.53 | 5.78 | 3.33 | 84.9 | **5.3** | 48.9 | 9.8 | **4.7** |
| **8.9** | 0.20 | 0.4 | -0.16 | **5.4** | 0.5 | 1.25 | 5.39 | 3.34 | 57.4 | **5.7** | 63.6 | 10.6 | **6.0** |
| **9.1** | 0.03 | 0.1 | -0.27 | **1.5** | 0.1 | 0.10 | 1.10 | 2.17 | 96.6 | **3.5** | 59.1 | 21.4 | **4.2** |
| **7.3** | 0.01 | 0.1 | 0.06 | **6.0** | 1.4 | 1.31 | 10.46 | 3.68 | 54.9 | **2.5** | 25.3 | 17.6 | **8.7** |
| **4.1** | 1.97 | 13.1 | 0.08 | **2.9** | 0.3 | 0.43 | 6.28 | 3.51 | 82.1 | **5.0** | 29.9 | 5.4 | **1.8** |
| **6.4** | 0.70 | 4.5 | 0.00 | **4.9** | 0.7 | 1.15 | 12.25 | 3.54 | 70.6 | **4.9** | 47.3 | 11.6 | **5.0** |
| **8.0** | 0.00 | 0.0 | 0.06 | **7.3** | 2.0 | 1.77 | 12.92 | 3.86 | 52.4 | **2.3** | 16.6 | 17.4 | **8.4** |
| **9.9** | 1.61 | 1.1 | 0.49 | **5.9** | 1.7 | 1.30 | 5.77 | 3.29 | 54.6 | **6.7** | 104.3 | 11.7 | **9.1** |
| **6.4** | 1.04 | 4.8 | -0.02 | **8.5** | 6.4 | 1.70 | 12.89 | 3.77 | 80.1 | **2.2** | 16.6 | 18.3 | **8.1** |
| **9.2** | 0.00 | 0.2 | 0.01 | **6.9** | 0.4 | 1.37 | 8.28 | 3.75 | 51.9 | **6.5** | 76.9 | 8.1 | **7.6** |
| **6.1** | 1.87 | 4.0 | -0.01 | **3.7** | 0.2 | 0.73 | 4.62 | 4.71 | 86.3 | **4.1** | 31.5 | 10.0 | **5.8** |
| **6.5** | 0.27 | 1.2 | 0.30 | **3.3** | 1.3 | 0.72 | 5.27 | 4.48 | 75.5 | **2.6** | 16.9 | 15.9 | **7.4** |
| **5.4** | 1.38 | 5.9 | 0.02 | **5.5** | 12.3 | 1.28 | 14.85 | 3.54 | 67.0 | **4.6** | 20.8 | 5.4 | **7.0** |
| **8.2** | 0.31 | 1.1 | 0.16 | **4.0** | 0.8 | 0.77 | 4.82 | 3.89 | 77.5 | **3.3** | 51.5 | 24.4 | **8.0** |
| **3.4** | 1.99 | 15.5 | 0.42 | **2.1** | 0.1 | 0.03 | 0.37 | 3.66 | 93.0 | **1.3** | 12.9 | 22.8 | **4.6** |
| **9.7** | 0.24 | 0.9 | 0.02 | **5.5** | 21.9 | 1.24 | 13.48 | 2.31 | 37.1 | **3.1** | 58.8 | 50.8 | **7.9** |
| **5.7** | 1.43 | 3.6 | 0.05 | **2.5** | 0.2 | 0.41 | 3.97 | 2.73 | 80.5 | **5.5** | 64.7 | 11.5 | **4.7** |
| **7.8** | 0.85 | 2.4 | 0.07 | **3.1** | 0.6 | 0.57 | 5.24 | 2.96 | 81.6 | **3.6** | 39.4 | 16.9 | **5.9** |
| **7.6** | 2.99 | 4.3 | 0.02 | **5.2** | 2.1 | 1.14 | 6.44 | 3.18 | 60.1 | **6.4** | 64.4 | 8.4 | **8.0** |
| **3.3** | 0.96 | 5.2 | 1.12 | **2.7** | 0.6 | 0.38 | 3.65 | 3.37 | 70.4 | **3.2** | 21.3 | 13.6 | **6.6** |
| **8.5** | 0.32 | 1.1 | 0.00 | **8.0** | 4.8 | 1.86 | 16.17 | 3.95 | 59.4 | **4.7** | 33.1 | 9.0 | **8.2** |
| **8.2** | 0.24 | 1.9 | -0.27 | **5.7** | 0.7 | 1.34 | 11.65 | 4.94 | 72.3 | **3.3** | 25.5 | 13.6 | **5.4** |
| **7.0** | 0.49 | 2.9 | 0.08 | **7.4** | 39.7 | 1.56 | 13.23 | 3.87 | 60.0 | **2.2** | 6.6 | 14.0 | **10.0** |
| **6.6** | 0.53 | 4.6 | -0.04 | **2.0** | 0.0 | 0.08 | 0.58 | 4.63 | 98.0 | **1.5** | 18.3 | 25.2 | **6.4** |
| **9.4** | 0.00 | 0.0 | 0.00 | **5.9** | 8.5 | 1.31 | 14.98 | 3.11 | 52.3 | **6.9** | 65.4 | 4.7 | **6.3** |
| **9.5** | 1.18 | 2.3 | 0.01 | **3.9** | 2.6 | 0.88 | 7.96 | 3.44 | 70.1 | **7.1** | 59.1 | 2.6 | **7.4** |
| **9.3** | 0.21 | 1.2 | -0.43 | **7.1** | 2.1 | 1.53 | 13.10 | 3.79 | 58.9 | **6.6** | 53.9 | 3.9 | **7.8** |
| **7.5** | 0.37 | 2.0 | 0.14 | **5.6** | 2.0 | 1.10 | 9.55 | 4.63 | 72.4 | **2.3** | 15.1 | 17.3 | **7.3** |
| **6.7** | 0.00 | 0.0 | 0.14 | **2.6** | 0.1 | 0.22 | 1.97 | 4.02 | 85.9 | **4.1** | 8.4 | 6.9 | **5.8** |
| **6.8** | 3.79 | 7.0 | 0.45 | **1.5** | 0.1 | 0.14 | 1.16 | 2.83 | 101.4 | **2.5** | 36.5 | 22.5 | **5.4** |
| **4.3** | 0.57 | 4.5 | 0.30 | **5.8** | 2.5 | 1.32 | 12.88 | 3.78 | 57.9 | **1.2** | 6.5 | 24.9 | **7.6** |
| **8.6** | 1.11 | 2.2 | 0.14 | **7.0** | 3.4 | 1.35 | 8.50 | 3.04 | 48.0 | **4.3** | 31.8 | 11.0 | **8.8** |
| **4.6** | 2.63 | 10.7 | 0.01 | **4.7** | 2.4 | 1.00 | 8.93 | 3.05 | 58.1 | **3.9** | 32.5 | 13.2 | **6.3** |
| **3.9** | 0.87 | 5.1 | 0.01 | **7.8** | 4.8 | 1.88 | 17.52 | 4.40 | 53.4 | **2.1** | 16.5 | 7.9 | **8.3** |
| **8.2** | 0.16 | 0.5 | 0.01 | **8.0** | 26.6 | 1.97 | 18.37 | 4.04 | 54.6 | **1.2** | 9.0 | 27.9 | **10.0** |
| **6.2** | 1.40 | 8.7 | -0.02 | **4.7** | 13.7 | 0.97 | 9.70 | 3.71 | 70.4 | **1.6** | 9.8 | 13.7 | **8.3** |
| **8.1** | 0.53 | 2.5 | 0.11 | **5.8** | 4.2 | 1.30 | 10.36 | 4.03 | 69.3 | **3.9** | 9.7 | 8.6 | **8.8** |
| **5.4** | 0.94 | 5.2 | 0.14 | **5.6** | 59.5 | 0.79 | 7.70 | 4.00 | 67.5 | **1.3** | 9.9 | 22.6 | **9.0** |
| **6.4** | 0.63 | 3.8 | 0.09 | **4.5** | 2.3 | 0.86 | 8.99 | 3.57 | 70.9 | **4.5** | 31.1 | 9.1 | **5.9** |
| **5.2** | 0.70 | 4.2 | 0.38 | **4.2** | 5.5 | 0.70 | 6.66 | 5.19 | 76.8 | **1.9** | 17.6 | 18.5 | **6.2** |
| **4.2** | 1.99 | 4.8 | 0.07 | **7.8** | 5.5 | 1.32 | 11.33 | 5.09 | 68.7 | **1.3** | 17.4 | 28.2 | **8.5** |
| **6.5** | 0.18 | 1.7 | 0.08 | **6.3** | 3.1 | 1.16 | 11.60 | 3.82 | 63.7 | **0.9** | 17.1 | 33.6 | **6.6** |
| **5.7** | 0.50 | 3.3 | 0.04 | **10.0** | 20.1 | 2.01 | 16.38 | 5.22 | 55.1 | **3.6** | 13.1 | 10.8 | **9.6** |
| **7.6** | 0.32 | 1.9 | 0.01 | **4.3** | 3.5 | 0.80 | 9.23 | 3.85 | 74.2 | **1.2** | 10.3 | 27.2 | **5.1** |
| **4.7** | 2.00 | 10.2 | 0.11 | **4.8** | 10.6 | 0.97 | 8.51 | 3.35 | 64.7 | **1.5** | 19.7 | 19.7 | **8.0** |
| **9.2** | 0.33 | 1.5 | 0.00 | **9.5** | 1.3 | 2.15 | 14.84 | 5.01 | 55.5 | **0.4** | 6.5 | 67.9 | **8.0** |
| **4.1** | 1.18 | 8.0 | 0.02 | **3.9** | 9.6 | 0.82 | 8.91 | 3.08 | 81.5 | **2.9** | 11.8 | 12.0 | **7.3** |
| **7.3** | 0.16 | 0.8 | -0.01 | **8.0** | 4.4 | 1.61 | 12.54 | 4.03 | 54.7 | **4.7** | 18.9 | 4.6 | **9.8** |
| **8.3** | 0.00 | 0.0 | 0.00 | **9.4** | 4.6 | 2.12 | 19.07 | 3.70 | 38.5 | **2.5** | 25.4 | 17.8 | **8.6** |
| **4.3** | 1.73 | 7.1 | 0.00 | **7.2** | 51.1 | 1.48 | 9.58 | 4.14 | 54.1 | **3.1** | 14.7 | 13.8 | **9.6** |
| **6.2** | 0.78 | 4.8 | 0.11 | **6.2** | 452.7 | 1.22 | 12.81 | 3.78 | 67.1 | **4.4** | 13.2 | 5.8 | **8.6** |
| **8.9** | 0.00 | 0.0 | 0.01 | **4.4** | 2.3 | 0.84 | 8.81 | 3.66 | 74.1 | **3.1** | 23.6 | 14.2 | **6.0** |
| **3.5** | 1.36 | 9.5 | 0.07 | **7.6** | 8.5 | 1.33 | 12.61 | 4.57 | 65.2 | **1.5** | 11.4 | 19.9 | **7.9** |
| **9.6** | 0.14 | 1.4 | 0.03 | **8.5** | 301.0 | 1.58 | 18.02 | 3.64 | 50.1 | **6.0** | 36.4 | 5.2 | **8.7** |
| **6.3** | 0.08 | 1.8 | 0.23 | **7.0** | 5.1 | 1.56 | 16.86 | 5.99 | 74.2 | **0.7** | 12.0 | 42.7 | **7.0** |
| **5.5** | 0.60 | 3.5 | 0.11 | **8.5** | 85.8 | 1.49 | 11.70 | 4.37 | 67.1 | **2.6** | 10.3 | 15.6 | **10.0** |

| Name | City | State | Rating | 2018 Rating | 2017 Rating | Total Assets ($Mil) | One Year Asset Growth | Asset Mix (As a % of Total Assets) Commercial Loans | Consumer Loans | Mortgage Loans | Securities | Capitalization Index | Leverage Ratio | Risk-Based Capital Ratio |
|---|---|---|---|---|---|---|---|---|---|---|---|---|---|---|
| ▲ FirstBank of Nebraska | Wahoo | NE | **B+** | B- | B+ | 282.4 | 4.69 | 5.1 | 1.0 | 7.7 | 31.1 | **9.2** | 10.5 | 14.3 |
| FirstBank Puerto Rico | San Juan | PR | **C-** | D+ | D | 12597.4 | 2.99 | 9.0 | 14.7 | 23.4 | 17.7 | **10.0** | 17.3 | 24.7 |
| FirstBank Southwest | Amarillo | TX | **B+** | B | B- | 1036.7 | 3.99 | 17.7 | 3.5 | 9.0 | 26.9 | **7.5** | 9.4 | 13.9 |
| FirstCapital Bank of Texas, N.A. | Midland | TX | **B-** | C+ | B | 1732.4 | 54.33 | 16.4 | 0.8 | 14.7 | 6.2 | **8.0** | 10.9 | 13.3 |
| FirsTier Bank | Kimball | NE | **A-** | B+ | A | 432.9 | 23.94 | 33.7 | 1.7 | 3.2 | 5.9 | **9.7** | 13.4 | 14.8 |
| FirstOak Bank | Independence | KS | **A-** | B+ | A- | 186.1 | 3.15 | 12.0 | 1.3 | 14.4 | 7.3 | **8.7** | 10.1 | 14.4 |
| Firstrust Savings Bank | Conshohocken | PA | **B+** | B+ | B | 3722.5 | 7.64 | 22.2 | 4.8 | 14.0 | 7.6 | **7.3** | 10.3 | 12.8 |
| FirstState Bank | Lineville | AL | **A-** | B+ | A- | 252.3 | 11.28 | 3.0 | 4.6 | 10.7 | 38.2 | **10.0** | 12.0 | 18.7 |
| Fisher National Bank | Fisher | IL | **A-** | B+ | A- | 130.7 | 6.09 | 4.2 | 2.5 | 38.8 | 11.5 | **10.0** | 13.5 | 21.3 |
| ▼ Five Points Bank | Grand Island | NE | **A-** | A | A | 1284.5 | 16.27 | 16.8 | 1.2 | 6.1 | 24.3 | **8.4** | 10.5 | 13.7 |
| ▼ Five Points Bank of Hastings | Hastings | NE | **A-** | A | A | 382.2 | 17.84 | 8.3 | 0.4 | 4.3 | 24.8 | **10.0** | 12.9 | 19.3 |
| ▲ Five Star Bank | Rancho Cordova | CA | **B+** | B | B+ | 1479.8 | 16.33 | 7.2 | 0.6 | 2.1 | 5.8 | **5.3** | 9.3 | 11.3 |
| Five Star Bank | Warsaw | NY | **B** | B | B | 4346.6 | 1.74 | 10.5 | 19.9 | 14.0 | 18.0 | **7.0** | 9.7 | 12.5 |
| ▲ Flagler Bank | West Palm Beach | FL | **B+** | B- | B | 333.0 | 11.49 | 15.9 | 0.0 | 9.3 | 17.0 | **8.4** | 9.9 | 14.9 |
| Flagship Bank | Clearwater | FL | **B** | B- | B- | 155.0 | 34.60 | 10.8 | 0.2 | 3.9 | 2.9 | **10.0** | 19.7 | 23.2 |
| ▲ Flagship Bank Minnesota | Wayzata | MN | **B** | C+ | C+ | 239.2 | 5.82 | 8.0 | 0.4 | 25.6 | 3.2 | **7.6** | 10.1 | 13.0 |
| Flagstar Bank, FSB | Troy | MI | **B+** | B+ | A- | 23234.5 | 25.82 | 4.7 | 3.1 | 39.3 | 11.7 | **5.7** | 7.7 | 11.7 |
| Flanagan State Bank | Flanagan | IL | **B-** | C+ | B- | 191.1 | 1.98 | 4.5 | 2.3 | 25.3 | 22.8 | **8.7** | 10.1 | 14.7 |
| Flatirons Bank | Boulder | CO | **B** | B+ | B+ | 191.9 | 10.33 | 10.1 | 0.3 | 31.9 | 29.6 | **8.3** | 9.9 | 17.1 |
| ▼ Flatwater Bank | Gothenburg | NE | **C** | B+ | A- | 217.1 | 10.59 | 13.9 | 2.0 | 4.2 | 20.3 | **7.2** | 9.6 | 12.6 |
| Fleetwood Bank | Fleetwood | PA | **C+** | C+ | C | 260.2 | 0.37 | 2.8 | 0.2 | 40.4 | 18.3 | **8.2** | 9.8 | 17.0 |
| Flint Community Bank | Albany | GA | **C** | C | B- | 261.0 | 16.91 | 7.2 | 1.3 | 27.0 | 1.8 | **5.4** | 8.0 | 11.3 |
| Flint Hills Bank | Eskridge | KS | **A-** | B+ | A- | 130.8 | 2.85 | 5.3 | 3.3 | 13.2 | 37.6 | **10.0** | 12.7 | 24.6 |
| Flora Bank & Trust | Flora | IL | **B-** | B- | B- | 71.5 | 2.21 | 7.8 | 9.8 | 21.3 | 8.2 | **10.0** | 12.2 | 20.5 |
| Florence Bank | Florence | MA | **B** | B | B | 1451.2 | 7.66 | 2.5 | 0.0 | 43.3 | 21.1 | **10.0** | 11.3 | 17.7 |
| Florida Business Bank | Melbourne | FL | **A-** | B+ | A- | 145.0 | 7.25 | 7.5 | 0.1 | 1.3 | 14.7 | **10.0** | 11.6 | 15.4 |
| ▲ Florida Capital Bank, N.A. | Jacksonville | FL | **C** | C- | C- | 496.4 | 21.81 | 6.3 | 0.0 | 31.5 | 4.0 | **6.1** | 8.1 | 12.3 |
| Flushing Bank | Uniondale | NY | **B** | B+ | B+ | 7017.6 | 2.69 | 10.4 | 0.0 | 10.8 | 11.7 | **8.0** | 9.7 | 13.4 |
| ▲ FMB Bank | Wright City | MO | **D+** | D+ | D | 36.9 | 0.95 | 8.5 | 3.9 | 17.5 | 29.9 | **8.4** | 9.9 | 16.0 |
| ▲ FMS Bank | Fort Morgan | CO | **C+** | B- | B+ | 197.2 | 7.08 | 14.7 | 14.1 | 11.2 | 13.8 | **5.8** | 10.4 | 11.6 |
| ▲ FNB Bank | Scottsboro | AL | **B-** | C+ | B+ | 674.3 | 4.28 | 8.7 | 2.4 | 15.7 | 16.1 | **10.0** | 11.0 | 16.1 |
| FNB Bank | Fontanelle | IA | **B+** | B+ | A- | 206.0 | 0.93 | 4.8 | 1.0 | 8.3 | 7.6 | **10.0** | 13.5 | 17.2 |
| FNB Bank | Goodland | KS | **B+** | B+ | B+ | 195.4 | 4.42 | 3.6 | 1.1 | 1.6 | 25.2 | **10.0** | 13.0 | 17.7 |
| FNB Bank, Inc. | Mayfield | KY | **B-** | C+ | B | 516.6 | 1.93 | 8.7 | 11.3 | 19.8 | 18.5 | **6.5** | 8.5 | 12.4 |
| FNB Bank, Inc. | Romney | WV | **B** | B- | B- | 203.8 | 5.03 | 8.4 | 3.7 | 29.3 | 13.4 | **9.2** | 10.4 | 14.6 |
| FNB Community Bank | Vandalia | IL | **A-** | B+ | A- | 355.6 | 5.42 | 4.3 | 1.1 | 14.7 | 30.2 | **10.0** | 12.6 | 20.0 |
| ▼ FNB Community Bank | Midwest City | OK | **C+** | B- | C+ | 454.5 | -5.00 | 5.5 | 4.1 | 6.7 | 36.8 | **9.3** | 10.5 | 18.7 |
| FNB Coweta | Coweta | OK | **C+** | C+ | C+ | 77.2 | 1.23 | 7.7 | 2.1 | 13.0 | 38.3 | **8.8** | 10.2 | 22.4 |
| FNB Oxford Bank | Oxford | MS | **B+** | A- | A- | 367.3 | 18.71 | 6.6 | 1.2 | 18.5 | 34.1 | **9.7** | 10.8 | 16.5 |
| ▲ FNB South | Alma | GA | **A** | B+ | A | 412.0 | 10.80 | 7.5 | 5.5 | 16.2 | 7.9 | **10.0** | 16.2 | 23.6 |
| FNB Washington | Washington | KS | **B+** | B+ | B+ | 71.5 | -15.09 | 0.6 | 2.0 | 13.2 | 33.3 | **10.0** | 27.9 | 55.9 |
| FNBC Bank | Ash Flat | AR | **C** | C | B- | 529.5 | 14.10 | 8.2 | 4.8 | 14.9 | 24.7 | **8.5** | 10.0 | 14.9 |
| FNBC Bank and Trust | La Grange | IL | **B** | B- | B- | 531.2 | 0.79 | 3.1 | 0.4 | 16.1 | 31.5 | **8.5** | 10.0 | 18.1 |
| FNBT Bank | Fort Walton Beach | FL | **A-** | B | B | 455.5 | 4.43 | 3.4 | 0.8 | 10.7 | 1.4 | **9.9** | 10.9 | 19.7 |
| FNCB Bank | Dunmore | PA | **B** | B- | C+ | 1191.1 | -3.12 | 12.4 | 10.4 | 14.4 | 22.9 | **9.0** | 10.4 | 14.8 |
| ▼ FNNB Bank | Newton | IA | **D+** | C | C- | 78.4 | -5.07 | 8.8 | 0.9 | 9.9 | 26.8 | **6.8** | 8.8 | 14.2 |
| Focus Bank | Charleston | MO | **B+** | B- | B- | 772.9 | 4.67 | 7.7 | 1.9 | 24.6 | 6.9 | **9.5** | 10.7 | 14.7 |
| Forcht Bank, N.A. | Lexington | KY | **B-** | B- | B | 1209.0 | -2.56 | 4.0 | 1.9 | 29.9 | 17.4 | **8.7** | 10.1 | 15.8 |
| Ford County State Bank | Spearville | KS | **C+** | B- | B- | 40.6 | 3.76 | 16.5 | 1.5 | 2.4 | 5.1 | **10.0** | 13.1 | 19.3 |
| Foresight Bank | Plainview | MN | **B-** | C | B- | 262.5 | 6.80 | 5.4 | 1.8 | 26.8 | 14.2 | **7.7** | 9.5 | 13.7 |
| Forest Park National Bank and Trust Co. | Forest Park | IL | **B-** | B- | C+ | 242.3 | 4.90 | 4.4 | 0.3 | 19.8 | 6.4 | **6.5** | 8.6 | 12.3 |
| Forreston State Bank | Forreston | IL | **B+** | B+ | B+ | 218.5 | 1.10 | 5.1 | 0.3 | 6.6 | 25.8 | **6.8** | 8.8 | 12.6 |
| Fort Davis State Bank | Fort Davis | TX | **C+** | C+ | C+ | 91.8 | 6.94 | 10.8 | 4.1 | 5.5 | 27.9 | **7.6** | 9.4 | 18.2 |
| Fort Hood National Bank | Fort Hood | TX | **B+** | B | B | 293.5 | 4.87 | 0.0 | 15.7 | 15.6 | 35.3 | **6.9** | 8.9 | 46.1 |
| Fort Jennings State Bank | Fort Jennings | OH | **B** | B | A- | 191.5 | 8.57 | 10.3 | 3.6 | 23.1 | 2.7 | **9.9** | 10.9 | 15.9 |
| Forte Bank | Hartford | WI | **B** | B | B | 236.9 | 13.62 | 9.2 | 0.5 | 17.8 | 11.2 | **10.0** | 11.2 | 15.8 |
| Fortifi Bank | Berlin | WI | **C+** | C | B- | 456.7 | 8.77 | 13.9 | 1.7 | 15.1 | 11.6 | **5.6** | 9.7 | 11.4 |
| Fortis Private Bank | Denver | CO | **C-** | D+ | D+ | 875.4 | 19.39 | 4.6 | 8.8 | 29.7 | 17.3 | **6.8** | 8.8 | 12.4 |
| Fortress Bank | Peoria | IL | **C** | C | C | 474.0 | 10.28 | 14.9 | 1.5 | 14.7 | 12.7 | **5.5** | 8.7 | 11.4 |
| FortuneBank | Arnold | MO | **C-** | C- | D | 199.2 | 2.95 | 16.2 | 0.3 | 15.9 | 4.7 | **5.0** | 8.6 | 11.0 |

| Asset Quality Index | Adjusted Non-Performing Loans as a % of Total Loans | Adjusted Non-Performing Loans as a % of Capital | Net Charge-Offs Avg Loans | Profitability Index | Net Income ($Mil) | Return on Assets (R.O.A.) | Return on Equity (R.O.E.) | Net Interest Spread | Overhead Efficiency Ratio | Liquidity Index | Liquidity Ratio | Hot Money Ratio | Stability Index |
|---|---|---|---|---|---|---|---|---|---|---|---|---|---|
| **5.9** | 0.52 | 3.1 | 0.15 | **8.4** | 5.7 | 2.06 | 19.54 | 3.94 | 42.1 | **1.6** | 17.7 | 11.3 | **8.0** |
| **1.9** | 6.69 | 18.2 | 0.91 | **7.2** | 174.0 | 1.40 | 7.62 | 4.97 | 56.6 | **1.5** | 18.7 | 20.6 | **9.4** |
| **7.6** | 0.41 | 2.6 | 0.08 | **5.5** | 13.6 | 1.34 | 14.04 | 3.62 | 66.8 | **2.2** | 21.5 | 19.6 | **8.5** |
| **4.5** | 1.48 | 5.5 | 0.13 | **7.4** | 20.8 | 1.50 | 12.89 | 5.39 | 61.6 | **1.1** | 16.8 | 31.2 | **9.5** |
| **7.9** | 0.13 | 0.8 | 0.01 | **8.9** | 7.6 | 2.00 | 14.36 | 4.52 | 53.1 | **0.8** | 14.5 | 39.5 | **9.5** |
| **8.2** | 0.00 | 0.0 | 0.15 | **9.0** | 3.7 | 2.05 | 19.12 | 5.20 | 57.4 | **2.8** | 21.4 | 15.5 | **7.7** |
| **7.1** | 0.48 | 2.6 | 0.06 | **6.2** | 49.0 | 1.42 | 13.43 | 4.19 | 68.3 | **2.5** | 10.6 | 12.4 | **10.0** |
| **7.4** | 0.90 | 3.6 | 0.23 | **5.5** | 2.8 | 1.15 | 9.25 | 4.11 | 65.9 | **2.0** | 32.6 | 27.8 | **7.3** |
| **7.2** | 1.20 | 4.4 | 0.05 | **8.3** | 2.5 | 1.96 | 14.80 | 4.01 | 56.0 | **2.2** | 19.8 | 18.5 | **9.4** |
| **7.9** | 0.01 | 3.3 | 0.21 | **6.2** | 16.4 | 1.40 | 12.37 | 3.32 | 54.0 | **3.4** | 17.5 | 12.5 | **9.5** |
| **8.8** | 0.01 | 0.0 | -0.01 | **5.3** | 3.7 | 1.16 | 9.25 | 3.06 | 55.7 | **5.8** | 40.1 | 4.7 | **8.1** |
| **7.2** | 0.11 | 0.7 | 0.21 | **9.7** | 31.8 | 2.33 | 26.28 | 4.13 | 36.1 | **4.4** | 18.4 | 7.2 | **9.1** |
| **6.9** | 0.27 | 1.7 | 0.37 | **5.5** | 53.7 | 1.26 | 12.70 | 3.37 | 55.4 | **1.1** | 3.2 | 22.7 | **8.1** |
| **7.5** | 0.16 | 0.9 | 0.17 | **7.1** | 5.2 | 1.62 | 17.01 | 3.35 | 47.1 | **0.8** | 21.6 | 45.1 | **7.2** |
| **6.6** | 0.00 | 0.0 | 0.00 | **4.0** | 0.0 | 0.09 | 0.63 | 4.82 | 86.6 | **2.8** | 43.1 | 24.9 | **7.2** |
| **6.1** | 0.41 | 1.8 | -0.04 | **6.0** | 2.7 | 1.15 | 11.04 | 4.30 | 62.8 | **1.6** | 6.3 | 20.3 | **5.6** |
| **6.9** | 3.00 | 2.7 | 0.25 | **5.6** | 241.2 | 1.17 | 12.45 | 3.15 | 74.3 | **2.6** | 10.8 | 11.7 | **7.8** |
| **4.4** | 1.64 | 8.4 | 0.20 | **6.4** | 3.2 | 1.71 | 16.70 | 3.63 | 85.7 | **3.3** | 23.7 | 13.1 | **5.7** |
| **9.0** | 0.48 | 1.3 | 0.00 | **4.6** | 1.9 | 1.06 | 10.51 | 3.66 | 73.4 | **2.3** | 36.8 | 22.3 | **6.6** |
| **2.5** | 2.32 | 20.4 | 0.32 | **6.0** | 2.7 | 1.29 | 11.82 | 4.11 | 62.1 | **0.6** | 7.6 | 20.1 | **8.3** |
| **8.4** | 0.27 | 1.8 | -0.02 | **3.9** | 2.0 | 0.77 | 8.25 | 3.68 | 76.1 | **4.5** | 25.3 | 7.0 | **5.5** |
| **2.6** | 2.03 | 18.3 | 0.08 | **5.9** | 3.3 | 1.38 | 16.37 | 3.83 | 62.4 | **1.7** | 16.1 | 19.1 | **5.3** |
| **8.8** | 0.07 | 0.3 | 0.00 | **6.3** | 2.0 | 1.56 | 12.50 | 3.18 | 55.9 | **2.1** | 24.6 | 19.5 | **8.1** |
| **6.7** | 0.82 | 3.5 | -0.03 | **3.7** | 0.4 | 0.60 | 4.96 | 3.88 | 79.0 | **4.0** | 27.8 | 10.9 | **6.1** |
| **9.4** | 0.21 | 1.3 | 0.07 | **4.6** | 11.0 | 0.80 | 7.24 | 3.50 | 72.0 | **4.2** | 28.7 | 13.3 | **8.6** |
| **7.4** | 0.00 | 0.0 | 0.06 | **6.7** | 1.7 | 1.18 | 8.80 | 3.92 | 61.0 | **1.7** | 24.7 | 24.5 | **8.9** |
| **4.8** | 1.63 | 6.1 | 0.06 | **5.2** | 7.1 | 1.59 | 17.83 | 3.22 | 79.9 | **0.6** | 9.4 | 18.8 | **5.0** |
| **6.8** | 0.33 | 2.4 | 0.04 | **3.9** | 50.1 | 0.72 | 7.46 | 2.61 | 62.3 | **1.5** | 10.5 | 15.9 | **8.3** |
| **3.9** | 5.61 | 13.8 | 0.15 | **2.6** | 0.2 | 0.39 | 4.14 | 3.61 | 88.1 | **2.8** | 22.6 | 15.5 | **4.7** |
| **4.5** | 0.77 | 4.9 | 0.82 | **5.8** | 2.2 | 1.15 | 11.02 | 5.34 | 70.5 | **1.5** | 13.1 | 23.4 | **6.6** |
| **4.2** | 1.42 | 7.4 | 0.55 | **5.9** | 7.7 | 1.16 | 9.32 | 4.52 | 65.1 | **2.9** | 12.5 | 14.5 | **7.9** |
| **4.1** | 0.99 | 4.8 | 0.04 | **5.9** | 2.7 | 1.31 | 8.53 | 3.99 | 65.5 | **2.9** | 13.9 | 14.3 | **9.2** |
| **6.6** | 0.45 | 1.1 | 0.05 | **4.7** | 2.0 | 1.09 | 8.13 | 4.23 | 74.4 | **3.4** | 10.4 | 11.4 | **8.1** |
| **5.0** | 0.85 | 3.2 | 0.07 | **4.3** | 4.1 | 0.81 | 7.92 | 3.52 | 73.9 | **1.7** | 9.2 | 12.4 | **7.7** |
| **5.1** | 1.56 | 6.3 | 0.03 | **5.5** | 2.2 | 1.11 | 10.66 | 4.05 | 65.2 | **1.5** | 18.4 | 26.2 | **6.3** |
| **6.6** | 0.48 | 4.5 | 0.03 | **6.2** | 4.3 | 1.25 | 9.02 | 3.82 | 60.7 | **3.9** | 26.2 | 10.8 | **8.2** |
| **8.0** | 0.40 | 1.9 | 0.87 | **2.9** | 2.8 | 0.56 | 5.56 | 3.44 | 72.8 | **4.6** | 25.0 | 5.9 | **6.9** |
| **8.7** | 0.24 | 1.1 | 0.02 | **3.8** | 0.6 | 0.81 | 8.27 | 3.63 | 77.7 | **4.6** | 39.5 | 11.9 | **5.3** |
| **8.2** | 0.39 | 1.4 | 0.02 | **5.0** | 3.9 | 1.12 | 9.63 | 3.25 | 64.3 | **1.9** | 22.2 | 13.2 | **7.1** |
| **8.3** | 0.02 | 0.2 | 0.40 | **10.0** | 10.2 | 2.66 | 16.39 | 5.26 | 45.9 | **3.2** | 21.1 | 13.5 | **8.3** |
| **8.1** | 2.53 | 2.4 | 0.00 | **6.0** | 0.9 | 1.25 | 4.70 | 3.24 | 50.7 | **3.8** | 26.2 | 11.4 | **7.8** |
| **3.1** | 1.69 | 10.2 | 0.29 | **5.3** | 6.6 | 1.33 | 13.95 | 4.05 | 63.3 | **1.7** | 20.9 | 23.3 | **6.9** |
| **5.9** | 1.71 | 7.0 | -0.01 | **5.3** | 6.6 | 1.26 | 12.02 | 3.50 | 70.7 | **5.8** | 38.0 | 4.1 | **7.3** |
| **7.9** | 1.31 | 2.4 | -0.25 | **6.5** | 7.6 | 1.70 | 15.59 | 3.17 | 65.1 | **6.6** | 60.2 | 5.8 | **7.4** |
| **4.9** | 2.01 | 8.9 | 0.16 | **4.4** | 11.7 | 0.98 | 9.01 | 3.31 | 68.4 | **3.6** | 6.0 | 10.2 | **9.6** |
| **8.7** | 0.03 | 0.2 | 0.67 | **1.4** | -0.1 | -0.09 | -1.03 | 3.56 | 92.7 | **5.1** | 36.8 | 7.6 | **4.1** |
| **5.6** | 0.90 | 7.1 | 0.19 | **5.5** | 9.8 | 1.29 | 11.86 | 3.51 | 66.2 | **0.7** | 12.4 | 33.4 | **7.9** |
| **6.2** | 0.98 | 3.1 | 0.04 | **3.4** | 7.6 | 0.61 | 4.79 | 3.87 | 83.8 | **3.8** | 13.5 | 10.0 | **9.2** |
| **4.3** | 3.50 | 13.7 | 0.30 | **4.4** | 0.0 | 0.08 | 0.54 | 4.59 | 50.2 | **4.3** | 35.6 | 12.2 | **7.8** |
| **2.4** | 5.73 | 22.4 | -0.05 | **6.0** | 3.5 | 1.39 | 13.96 | 3.50 | 62.4 | **0.9** | 23.8 | 32.0 | **7.9** |
| **4.9** | 0.67 | 5.1 | -0.04 | **5.1** | 2.7 | 1.11 | 12.89 | 4.70 | 75.5 | **4.1** | 13.1 | 7.9 | **5.7** |
| **6.8** | 0.79 | 2.8 | 0.03 | **4.4** | 2.4 | 1.08 | 9.67 | 3.02 | 66.3 | **1.0** | 25.5 | 29.4 | **6.3** |
| **5.9** | 0.48 | 2.9 | 0.16 | **3.6** | 0.7 | 0.76 | 7.84 | 4.31 | 82.3 | **5.8** | 46.9 | 6.2 | **5.1** |
| **8.7** | 0.12 | 0.0 | 0.24 | **4.4** | 2.9 | 1.06 | 11.62 | 2.95 | 81.3 | **7.0** | 61.2 | 3.4 | **6.3** |
| **5.0** | 0.87 | 5.4 | 0.08 | **5.9** | 2.0 | 1.09 | 9.75 | 4.51 | 64.5 | **1.8** | 16.7 | 20.0 | **7.2** |
| **8.7** | 0.07 | 0.4 | -0.01 | **4.5** | 1.9 | 0.83 | 7.25 | 3.82 | 72.6 | **4.0** | 22.6 | 9.9 | **6.4** |
| **4.3** | 1.08 | 7.3 | 0.08 | **4.1** | 2.9 | 0.69 | 7.01 | 4.22 | 78.3 | **1.5** | 16.1 | 18.6 | **5.2** |
| **8.5** | 0.06 | 0.8 | 0.00 | **2.5** | 3.5 | 0.45 | 5.00 | 2.76 | 78.5 | **1.8** | 25.5 | 13.6 | **4.6** |
| **3.6** | 0.83 | 9.7 | 0.00 | **4.1** | 3.6 | 0.83 | 7.88 | 3.44 | 69.0 | **0.7** | 13.0 | 29.4 | **6.3** |
| **2.7** | 0.86 | 7.4 | 0.40 | **3.7** | 1.3 | 0.69 | 7.48 | 3.75 | 82.9 | **0.7** | 10.4 | 30.3 | **4.3** |

| Name | City | State | Rating | 2018 Rating | 2017 Rating | Total Assets ($Mil) | One Year Asset Growth | Comm-ercial Loans | Cons-umer Loans | Mort-gage Loans | Secur-ities | Capital-ization Index | Lever-age Ratio | Risk-Based Capital Ratio |
|---|---|---|---|---|---|---|---|---|---|---|---|---|---|---|
| | | | | | | | | Asset Mix (As a % of Total Assets) | | | | | | |
| Forward Bank | Marshfield | WI | C+ | B- | B- | 593.8 | 29.25 | 11.8 | 2.5 | 16.3 | 9.3 | **5.4** | 8.4 | 11.3 |
| Foundation One Bank | Omaha | NE | C+ | C+ | B- | 110.4 | 5.00 | 25.5 | 3.3 | 24.7 | 8.2 | **10.0** | 11.6 | 15.7 |
| Fountain Trust Co. | Covington | IN | A- | B+ | B+ | 406.9 | 10.07 | 5.3 | 1.1 | 22.2 | 24.3 | **10.0** | 11.6 | 21.1 |
| Four Corners Community Bank | Farmington | NM | C- | C- | B- | 365.0 | 3.91 | 11.3 | 0.7 | 6.7 | 15.3 | **10.0** | 12.0 | 16.3 |
| Four County Bank | Allentown | GA | B+ | B | B | 72.3 | 1.24 | 10.1 | 9.2 | 21.3 | 15.9 | **10.0** | 15.0 | 21.8 |
| Fowler State Bank | Fowler | CO | B | B | B | 87.4 | 2.51 | 3.4 | 1.0 | 4.7 | 32.5 | **10.0** | 14.7 | 25.7 |
| Fowler State Bank | Fowler | IN | A- | A- | A- | 167.3 | 0.20 | 7.8 | 5.2 | 9.3 | 46.2 | **10.0** | 13.7 | 20.9 |
| Fowler State Bank | Fowler | KS | D+ | D+ | D+ | 82.4 | -5.74 | 13.0 | 2.2 | 3.3 | 23.7 | **7.2** | 9.2 | 15.4 |
| Fox Valley Savings Bank | Fond du Lac | WI | B | B | B- | 340.5 | -2.27 | 2.1 | 0.9 | 29.0 | 39.4 | **10.0** | 15.1 | 21.4 |
| Foxboro Federal Savings | Foxborough | MA | B- | B- | C+ | 164.7 | -0.52 | 0.0 | 0.9 | 64.9 | 12.5 | **10.0** | 17.0 | 35.4 |
| Frandsen Bank & Trust | Lonsdale | MN | B | B | B | 1708.3 | 0.08 | 9.7 | 2.1 | 16.1 | 19.6 | **6.3** | 8.9 | 11.9 |
| Franklin Bank | Pilesgrove | NJ | C+ | C+ | C- | 260.3 | 1.10 | 4.6 | 1.6 | 44.3 | 13.7 | **8.5** | 10.0 | 17.9 |
| Franklin Bank & Trust Co. | Franklin | KY | A- | B+ | B+ | 551.5 | 7.11 | 21.6 | 1.0 | 15.2 | 1.0 | **10.0** | 12.4 | 15.7 |
| Franklin Savings Bank | Farmington | ME | B+ | B+ | A- | 457.1 | 9.09 | 8.0 | 3.2 | 38.0 | 3.6 | **10.0** | 24.9 | 31.3 |
| Franklin Savings Bank | Franklin | NH | C+ | C+ | C+ | 527.9 | 8.84 | 5.1 | 0.3 | 26.5 | 20.2 | **9.1** | 10.4 | 15.9 |
| Franklin State Bank | Franklin | MN | B- | B | B | 33.2 | 8.43 | 3.8 | 3.9 | 9.8 | 11.7 | **10.0** | 14.9 | 27.0 |
| Franklin State Bank & Trust Co. | Winnsboro | LA | B+ | B | C+ | 179.2 | 6.36 | 3.2 | 4.9 | 16.7 | 13.8 | **7.9** | 9.6 | 18.5 |
| Franklin Synergy Bank | Franklin | TN | B | B+ | B+ | 3904.3 | -7.97 | 14.8 | 0.1 | 12.8 | 16.7 | **9.8** | 12.1 | 14.8 |
| Frazer Bank | Altus | OK | C- | C+ | B | 288.9 | -6.18 | 12.7 | 0.9 | 9.1 | 25.9 | **8.2** | 9.8 | 14.5 |
| Frederick Community Bank | Cissna Park | IL | B+ | B | B- | 147.0 | 1.46 | 8.6 | 2.0 | 6.8 | 31.1 | **8.7** | 10.1 | 17.8 |
| Fredonia Valley Bank | Fredonia | KY | B+ | B+ | B+ | 84.5 | -2.26 | 4.3 | 3.2 | 41.7 | 16.4 | **10.0** | 17.4 | 28.3 |
| Freedom Bank | Saint Petersburg | FL | B- | B- | C+ | 338.9 | 24.93 | 18.1 | 0.9 | 2.1 | 1.6 | **4.6** | 8.9 | 10.8 |
| ▲ Freedom Bank | Huntingburg | IN | A- | A- | A- | 447.1 | 6.50 | 4.8 | 4.0 | 39.2 | 1.5 | **8.5** | 10.5 | 13.7 |
| Freedom Bank | Overland Park | KS | C+ | B- | B- | 174.8 | -8.65 | 13.5 | 0.0 | 6.2 | 16.2 | **7.7** | 12.9 | 13.1 |
| ▲ Freedom Bank | Columbia Falls | MT | C+ | C+ | B | 81.3 | 2.75 | 22.2 | 1.7 | 15.4 | 0.0 | **9.9** | 11.0 | 15.0 |
| Freedom Bank | Maywood | NJ | B- | B- | B | 468.6 | 10.42 | 2.1 | 0.0 | 20.2 | 0.3 | **8.9** | 10.8 | 14.1 |
| ▼ Freedom Bank | Freer | TX | C | C- | C | 48.2 | 11.53 | 13.4 | 4.6 | 8.6 | 11.4 | **9.7** | 10.8 | 15.9 |
| Freedom Bank of Southern Missouri | Cassville | MO | B | B+ | B+ | 292.2 | 3.73 | 9.5 | 3.0 | 19.3 | 5.3 | **8.7** | 10.1 | 14.2 |
| Freedom Bank of Virginia | Fairfax | VA | B- | C+ | B- | 500.4 | 4.51 | 15.4 | 4.2 | 14.4 | 10.0 | **10.0** | 12.8 | 16.2 |
| Freedom Bank, Inc. | Belington | WV | C- | D+ | D+ | 166.0 | 2.89 | 9.7 | 9.6 | 39.8 | 8.1 | **9.8** | 10.9 | 17.3 |
| Freedom Financial Bank | West Des Moines | IA | B | B | B+ | 195.8 | -0.02 | 9.1 | 0.1 | 11.0 | 2.3 | **6.6** | 10.0 | 12.2 |
| Freedom National Bank | Greenville | RI | C | C | C- | 124.9 | 1.35 | 13.3 | 0.2 | 15.1 | 7.5 | **9.0** | 10.4 | 14.1 |
| FreedomBank | Elkader | IA | C+ | B | B+ | 412.4 | 55.69 | 7.3 | 2.4 | 15.3 | 9.8 | **5.6** | 8.8 | 11.5 |
| Freehold Bank | Freehold | NJ | C+ | C+ | C+ | 293.2 | -1.44 | 0.5 | 0.0 | 20.4 | 48.5 | **10.0** | 13.2 | 22.5 |
| Freeland State Bank | Freeland | MI | C- | C- | C- | 51.1 | 0.97 | 0.0 | 0.6 | 10.0 | 46.5 | **10.0** | 18.6 | 133.1 |
| Freeport State Bank | Freeport | MN | B | B- | B | 118.2 | 2.13 | 9.0 | 2.7 | 9.1 | 15.4 | **9.2** | 10.4 | 14.4 |
| Fremont Bank | Fremont | CA | B+ | B+ | B+ | 4377.7 | 10.90 | 6.7 | 0.1 | 32.9 | 8.8 | **5.0** | 7.6 | 11.0 |
| Fresno First Bank | Fresno | CA | B+ | B- | B | 538.3 | 15.23 | 24.4 | 0.0 | 1.6 | 20.3 | **7.5** | 9.4 | 16.1 |
| Friend Bank | Slocomb | AL | B | B- | B | 134.2 | 4.55 | 6.4 | 4.2 | 21.9 | 11.1 | **7.7** | 9.4 | 16.7 |
| Friendly Hills Bank | Whittier | CA | B | B- | C+ | 158.9 | 3.85 | 4.3 | 0.0 | 11.2 | 20.6 | **10.0** | 11.7 | 18.3 |
| Friendship State Bank | Friendship | IN | A- | B+ | B+ | 388.7 | 4.17 | 1.9 | 2.9 | 44.0 | 12.4 | **8.3** | 9.9 | 17.4 |
| Frontier Bank | Lamar | CO | A- | A | A | 318.3 | 3.33 | 1.6 | 0.7 | 9.3 | 43.5 | **9.2** | 10.4 | 18.7 |
| Frontier Bank | Omaha | NE | C+ | C+ | C+ | 893.9 | 10.88 | 10.9 | 1.5 | 16.6 | 7.3 | **4.7** | 9.2 | 10.9 |
| ▲ Frontier Bank | Sioux Falls | SD | B- | C+ | C+ | 217.2 | -0.06 | 4.8 | 1.0 | 14.1 | 22.7 | **6.9** | 8.9 | 12.7 |
| Frontier Bank of Texas | Elgin | TX | B+ | A- | A- | 362.7 | 37.78 | 6.7 | 1.7 | 21.0 | 4.0 | **8.1** | 10.6 | 13.4 |
| Frontier Community Bank | Waynesboro | VA | C+ | C+ | C+ | 135.3 | 9.45 | 9.9 | 1.6 | 29.7 | 0.4 | **8.6** | 10.1 | 15.7 |
| Frontier State Bank | Oklahoma City | OK | C | C | D+ | 561.6 | -7.03 | 10.9 | 0.4 | 16.5 | 14.4 | **10.0** | 13.1 | 17.9 |
| Frost Bank | San Antonio | TX | A- | B+ | B+ | 34105.3 | 5.41 | 17.1 | 1.5 | 2.8 | 38.9 | **7.2** | 9.2 | 13.4 |
| ▲ Frost State Bank | Frost | MN | C- | C | C+ | 54.2 | 6.76 | 11.2 | 3.5 | 1.6 | 1.0 | **10.0** | 12.7 | 16.1 |
| FSNB, N.A. | Lawton | OK | A | A | A | 391.9 | 2.23 | 1.9 | 2.0 | 12.4 | 32.5 | **10.0** | 15.7 | 35.4 |
| Fulton Bank, N.A. | Lancaster | PA | B | B | B | 21768.0 | 73.33 | 11.6 | 2.2 | 14.5 | 13.2 | **6.5** | 9.8 | 12.2 |
| ▲ Fulton Savings Bank | Fulton | NY | A | B+ | B+ | 379.3 | 1.98 | 0.4 | 1.0 | 28.1 | 31.9 | **10.0** | 28.6 | 57.0 |
| FVCbank | Fairfax | VA | B+ | B | B | 1534.0 | 13.72 | 6.6 | 1.4 | 7.5 | 9.2 | **8.1** | 12.2 | 13.4 |
| G.W. Jones Exchange Bank | Marcellus | MI | C+ | C+ | C- | 61.5 | 2.64 | 2.5 | 1.5 | 16.1 | 20.3 | **10.0** | 11.6 | 26.5 |
| Galion Building and Loan Bank | Galion | OH | C | C | C | 62.3 | 1.35 | 0.8 | 1.8 | 66.8 | 13.0 | **10.0** | 11.9 | 26.5 |
| ▲ Garden Plain State Bank | Wichita | KS | A | B+ | B+ | 99.4 | 3.35 | 6.8 | 1.9 | 12.6 | 39.7 | **10.0** | 15.5 | 22.8 |
| ▲ Garfield County Bank | Jordan | MT | D | D | D | 94.9 | 2.91 | 3.7 | 2.2 | 2.4 | 7.2 | **10.0** | 12.8 | 16.5 |
| Garrett State Bank | Garrett | IN | B | B- | B+ | 259.8 | 8.58 | 4.3 | 2.5 | 49.6 | 18.5 | **9.3** | 10.6 | 19.7 |
| ▲ Garrison State Bank and Trust | Garrison | ND | B | C+ | B- | 146.7 | 2.53 | 4.6 | 3.9 | 2.4 | 20.5 | **10.0** | 12.1 | 18.4 |
| Gary State Bank | Gary | MN | B- | B- | B- | 14.4 | 2.77 | 9.1 | 5.7 | 1.1 | 0.0 | **10.0** | 14.2 | 20.8 |

| Asset Quality Index | Adjusted Non-Performing Loans as a % of Total Loans | Adjusted Non-Performing Loans as a % of Capital | Net Charge-Offs Avg Loans | Profitability Index | Net Income ($Mil) | Return on Assets (R.O.A.) | Return on Equity (R.O.E.) | Net Interest Spread | Overhead Efficiency Ratio | Liquidity Index | Liquidity Ratio | Hot Money Ratio | Stability Index |
|---|---|---|---|---|---|---|---|---|---|---|---|---|---|
| **5.1** | 0.80 | 4.5 | 0.02 | **3.6** | 3.3 | 0.61 | 5.66 | 4.06 | 80.3 | **3.1** | 17.4 | 13.8 | **6.5** |
| **7.4** | 0.36 | 3.7 | 0.13 | **2.5** | 0.2 | 0.21 | 1.72 | 3.31 | 84.3 | **0.8** | 16.7 | 40.1 | **6.3** |
| **7.1** | 0.60 | 4.0 | 0.05 | **6.5** | 5.4 | 1.43 | 11.15 | 4.37 | 65.1 | **5.4** | 42.3 | 8.1 | **7.6** |
| **1.0** | 5.92 | 26.3 | 0.73 | **6.6** | 4.7 | 1.28 | 10.66 | 4.35 | 61.4 | **1.8** | 16.7 | 20.0 | **9.0** |
| **7.5** | 0.26 | 1.3 | -0.05 | **8.2** | 1.4 | 1.94 | 13.50 | 4.49 | 56.6 | **0.9** | 22.5 | 36.7 | **8.9** |
| **6.9** | 0.80 | 2.8 | 0.86 | **4.2** | 0.7 | 0.86 | 5.84 | 3.27 | 67.2 | **2.5** | 47.0 | 30.9 | **7.7** |
| **8.0** | 0.69 | 2.1 | 0.15 | **5.9** | 2.4 | 1.44 | 9.75 | 4.36 | 71.0 | **6.2** | 46.3 | 3.9 | **8.7** |
| **0.3** | 12.76 | 52.9 | 1.61 | **0.7** | -0.7 | -0.88 | -9.29 | 3.45 | 92.6 | **2.1** | 34.0 | 25.0 | **4.5** |
| **7.5** | 1.93 | 5.2 | 0.14 | **3.8** | 2.6 | 0.74 | 5.03 | 2.80 | 72.8 | **3.7** | 39.2 | 16.1 | **7.4** |
| **10.0** | 0.00 | 0.0 | 0.00 | **3.7** | 1.3 | 0.79 | 4.66 | 3.18 | 72.7 | **3.6** | 31.4 | 14.0 | **8.0** |
| **6.1** | 0.55 | 2.6 | 0.01 | **6.8** | 28.2 | 1.66 | 13.52 | 4.34 | 65.8 | **4.9** | 11.2 | 2.6 | **9.2** |
| **7.1** | 0.52 | 2.9 | 0.02 | **3.5** | 1.3 | 0.49 | 4.98 | 3.60 | 82.6 | **4.1** | 21.7 | 9.0 | **5.1** |
| **8.2** | 0.31 | 1.8 | 0.56 | **6.7** | 7.3 | 1.36 | 11.25 | 3.87 | 54.1 | **0.9** | 12.6 | 33.5 | **8.1** |
| **7.1** | 1.25 | 4.5 | 0.06 | **5.2** | 4.0 | 0.93 | 3.89 | 4.57 | 75.7 | **2.7** | 6.3 | 10.1 | **8.1** |
| **6.1** | 1.13 | 5.1 | 0.00 | **3.4** | 3.0 | 0.58 | 5.62 | 3.30 | 80.4 | **2.7** | 23.8 | 16.3 | **7.0** |
| **5.9** | 2.77 | 9.2 | 0.11 | **4.0** | 0.2 | 0.67 | 4.32 | 3.21 | 67.6 | **3.8** | 45.6 | 16.8 | **7.6** |
| **6.8** | 0.61 | 3.5 | 0.13 | **6.6** | 2.6 | 1.55 | 15.95 | 4.42 | 64.9 | **1.6** | 29.5 | 30.2 | **5.6** |
| **8.5** | 0.10 | 0.7 | 0.35 | **4.4** | 36.3 | 0.90 | 8.03 | 3.03 | 57.7 | **1.2** | 17.3 | 11.9 | **8.7** |
| **5.0** | 2.18 | 8.4 | 0.92 | **1.8** | 0.4 | 0.14 | 1.54 | 3.51 | 85.2 | **1.0** | 11.6 | 27.4 | **3.8** |
| **8.9** | 0.05 | 0.3 | 0.03 | **5.7** | 2.1 | 1.44 | 13.88 | 3.29 | 60.9 | **4.4** | 32.0 | 10.5 | **6.1** |
| **4.4** | 5.71 | 18.7 | 0.11 | **6.4** | 1.0 | 1.23 | 7.02 | 4.41 | 66.7 | **5.0** | 29.5 | 5.3 | **8.2** |
| **6.2** | 0.36 | 2.7 | 0.00 | **7.4** | 4.5 | 1.47 | 16.59 | 4.18 | 60.2 | **1.6** | 19.3 | 21.4 | **5.7** |
| **7.1** | 0.16 | 1.6 | 0.05 | **9.2** | 9.5 | 2.17 | 20.77 | 3.34 | 43.6 | **2.4** | 11.6 | 16.6 | **8.9** |
| **6.6** | 0.51 | 1.5 | -0.13 | **3.6** | 1.3 | 0.70 | 6.68 | 3.02 | 76.9 | **4.7** | 8.0 | 3.2 | **6.1** |
| **3.6** | 1.23 | 8.6 | 0.02 | **8.8** | 1.4 | 1.69 | 16.02 | 5.39 | 60.6 | **1.1** | 10.9 | 29.8 | **8.6** |
| **7.5** | 0.00 | 0.0 | 0.01 | **4.6** | 3.6 | 0.78 | 7.54 | 3.30 | 65.9 | **0.6** | 11.4 | 46.6 | **6.6** |
| **6.4** | 0.09 | 1.1 | -0.02 | **2.3** | 0.2 | 0.42 | 2.65 | 3.89 | 90.5 | **2.3** | 33.7 | 23.9 | **5.2** |
| **5.3** | 0.87 | 4.7 | 0.11 | **6.1** | 4.2 | 1.43 | 14.34 | 3.82 | 59.3 | **1.2** | 10.8 | 26.5 | **7.0** |
| **4.5** | 0.42 | 9.1 | 0.16 | **3.4** | 2.7 | 0.55 | 4.39 | 3.54 | 84.8 | **0.8** | 17.3 | 36.9 | **7.1** |
| **1.8** | 4.58 | 22.3 | 0.19 | **4.8** | 1.4 | 0.88 | 8.29 | 4.05 | 68.0 | **3.9** | 18.3 | 9.7 | **5.9** |
| **7.4** | 0.00 | 0.0 | 0.00 | **5.1** | 2.2 | 1.17 | 11.62 | 3.06 | 58.5 | **0.6** | 12.9 | 40.6 | **7.5** |
| **3.8** | 1.86 | 9.4 | 0.23 | **2.8** | 0.4 | 0.36 | 3.55 | 3.86 | 84.1 | **1.1** | 4.9 | 16.4 | **5.7** |
| **3.9** | 0.56 | 2.6 | 0.07 | **6.3** | 5.5 | 1.47 | 12.77 | 3.80 | 58.5 | **1.8** | 14.5 | 16.7 | **7.5** |
| **9.2** | 0.08 | 0.1 | 0.00 | **2.5** | 0.8 | 0.26 | 1.96 | 1.76 | 80.2 | **2.2** | 35.0 | 27.2 | **6.7** |
| **8.0** | 13.40 | 5.0 | -0.39 | **1.5** | 0.1 | 0.18 | 0.98 | 2.38 | 96.2 | **7.7** | 106.5 | 5.0 | **6.6** |
| **6.7** | 0.98 | 4.1 | -0.03 | **5.1** | 1.1 | 0.94 | 9.26 | 4.56 | 73.2 | **1.8** | 21.0 | 15.6 | **6.4** |
| **7.9** | 0.51 | 3.1 | -0.04 | **5.4** | 50.9 | 1.21 | 15.44 | 3.96 | 74.7 | **4.6** | 14.2 | 5.1 | **8.1** |
| **6.8** | 0.16 | 0.9 | 0.05 | **9.6** | 9.2 | 1.89 | 20.15 | 4.78 | 49.1 | **4.6** | 27.8 | 7.0 | **6.4** |
| **5.4** | 0.67 | 3.8 | 0.00 | **7.5** | 2.3 | 1.70 | 17.48 | 4.72 | 57.8 | **3.1** | 29.7 | 16.0 | **6.4** |
| **8.9** | 0.36 | 1.6 | 0.34 | **4.0** | 1.1 | 0.70 | 6.05 | 3.78 | 73.3 | **5.7** | 40.6 | 5.7 | **7.1** |
| **8.2** | 0.26 | 1.8 | 0.05 | **7.3** | 5.4 | 1.43 | 13.32 | 4.52 | 65.7 | **2.5** | 22.3 | 17.4 | **6.8** |
| **9.1** | 0.03 | 0.1 | 0.00 | **8.0** | 5.8 | 1.88 | 17.16 | 3.59 | 51.5 | **3.7** | 30.4 | 13.6 | **8.7** |
| **3.3** | 1.60 | 11.1 | 0.29 | **5.0** | 9.8 | 1.17 | 10.49 | 3.21 | 54.6 | **1.0** | 11.8 | 20.9 | **7.7** |
| **5.8** | 1.17 | 4.9 | 0.03 | **4.1** | 1.9 | 0.85 | 9.33 | 3.59 | 75.8 | **1.3** | 18.4 | 13.4 | **6.1** |
| **8.1** | 0.14 | 1.2 | 0.21 | **4.7** | 2.7 | 0.83 | 7.42 | 4.13 | 70.6 | **0.7** | 15.4 | 38.6 | **6.8** |
| **8.7** | 0.00 | 0.0 | 0.00 | **3.7** | 1.0 | 0.76 | 7.59 | 3.09 | 73.1 | **0.8** | 17.9 | 37.2 | **6.3** |
| **3.4** | 4.49 | 20.8 | 0.61 | **2.6** | 3.6 | 0.59 | 4.99 | 2.46 | 69.1 | **0.7** | 19.0 | 60.5 | **5.3** |
| **7.3** | 0.73 | 2.8 | 0.23 | **6.6** | 453.5 | 1.42 | 12.26 | 3.67 | 60.1 | **6.8** | 43.7 | 2.8 | **10.0** |
| **2.3** | 2.98 | 16.9 | 0.79 | **6.6** | 0.6 | 1.18 | 9.32 | 3.60 | 36.7 | **0.7** | 19.9 | 61.1 | **7.1** |
| **9.6** | 0.04 | 0.2 | 2.36 | **10.0** | 16.0 | 4.16 | 26.02 | 3.83 | 70.8 | **7.1** | 59.3 | 2.2 | **9.1** |
| **5.0** | 1.15 | 6.8 | 0.11 | **6.4** | 248.2 | 1.38 | 12.70 | 3.96 | 63.3 | **4.0** | 16.0 | 7.6 | **9.4** |
| **9.8** | 1.38 | 2.4 | 0.09 | **6.5** | 6.5 | 1.72 | 6.09 | 4.37 | 68.7 | **7.3** | 78.8 | 4.5 | **8.1** |
| **5.7** | 0.76 | 5.2 | 0.05 | **6.3** | 18.1 | 1.25 | 9.76 | 3.61 | 52.9 | **1.2** | 12.1 | 21.9 | **9.3** |
| **9.0** | 0.62 | 3.4 | -0.01 | **3.2** | 0.4 | 0.59 | 5.13 | 4.18 | 85.4 | **6.8** | 60.8 | 2.5 | **5.8** |
| **6.8** | 1.17 | 9.2 | -0.02 | **1.9** | 0.1 | 0.18 | 1.51 | 3.31 | 93.4 | **3.4** | 25.0 | 13.1 | **5.6** |
| **8.6** | 0.00 | 0.0 | 0.66 | **7.7** | 1.5 | 1.57 | 10.13 | 3.56 | 57.9 | **4.9** | 59.5 | 13.7 | **7.5** |
| **0.4** | 6.22 | 34.4 | 1.45 | **5.2** | 0.9 | 1.00 | 8.14 | 3.93 | 54.6 | **1.0** | 26.0 | 46.7 | **7.0** |
| **5.2** | 1.68 | 9.7 | 0.07 | **7.0** | 4.1 | 1.68 | 15.43 | 3.79 | 56.7 | **2.6** | 28.6 | 10.8 | **7.8** |
| **3.6** | 0.05 | 8.5 | 0.11 | **5.8** | 1.6 | 1.08 | 8.91 | 4.09 | 61.5 | **3.8** | 27.6 | 12.0 | **7.1** |
| **6.9** | 0.00 | 1.1 | -0.06 | **8.1** | 0.3 | 1.88 | 13.45 | 4.84 | 65.5 | **5.1** | 25.4 | 2.5 | **6.3** |

| Name | City | State | Rating | 2018 Rating | 2017 Rating | Total Assets ($Mil) | One Year Asset Growth | Asset Mix (As a % of Total Assets) Comm-ercial Loans | Cons-umer Loans | Mort-gage Loans | Secur-ities | Capital-ization Index | Lever-age Ratio | Risk-Based Capital Ratio |
|---|---|---|---|---|---|---|---|---|---|---|---|---|---|---|
| Gate City Bank | Fargo | ND | B | B | B | 2380.3 | 6.68 | 2.5 | 28.6 | 48.0 | 3.6 | 10.0 | 11.4 | 16.5 |
| Gates Banking and Trust Co. | Gates | TN | B | B+ | B+ | 47.3 | -1.96 | 10.6 | 0.6 | 2.9 | 57.6 | 8.8 | 10.2 | 20.1 |
| ▲ Gateway Bank | Rison | AR | B- | B- | C+ | 76.5 | 4.48 | 11.8 | 3.4 | 34.6 | 4.5 | 10.0 | 11.7 | 17.1 |
| Gateway Bank | Mendota Heights | MN | A- | A- | A- | 196.3 | 8.06 | 25.0 | 2.4 | 13.6 | 1.2 | 8.0 | 9.7 | 13.5 |
| ▲ Gateway Bank, F.S.B. | Oakland | CA | D | E | E- | 128.6 | 17.52 | 3.1 | 0.0 | 48.5 | 2.8 | 10.0 | 12.9 | 27.2 |
| Gateway Commercial Bank | Mesa | AZ | A- | A- | B+ | 135.8 | 11.60 | 14.4 | 0.3 | 2.1 | 26.4 | 10.0 | 12.8 | 18.2 |
| GBC International Bank | Los Angeles | CA | B- | B- | B | 608.6 | 13.47 | 10.9 | 0.0 | 0.4 | 3.9 | 9.4 | 10.8 | 14.5 |
| Geddes Federal S&L Assn. | Syracuse | NY | B- | B | B+ | 558.8 | 3.86 | 0.0 | 0.1 | 86.1 | 6.2 | 10.0 | 16.2 | 29.4 |
| Generations Bank | Rogers | AR | B | B- | B- | 527.4 | 1.19 | 6.7 | 2.7 | 24.1 | 12.3 | 7.6 | 9.5 | 13.0 |
| Generations Bank | Exeter | NE | C- | C- | D+ | 37.8 | -0.32 | 10.9 | 2.4 | 9.4 | 14.5 | 8.3 | 11.3 | 13.6 |
| Generations Bank | Seneca Falls | NY | D+ | D | D+ | 347.8 | 9.21 | 3.7 | 15.3 | 40.7 | 9.4 | 6.1 | 8.1 | 12.9 |
| ▲ Genesee Regional Bank | Rochester | NY | A- | B- | B | 574.7 | -1.20 | 22.3 | 0.8 | 11.0 | 14.6 | 10.0 | 11.3 | 16.8 |
| Genoa Banking Co. | Genoa | OH | C+ | C+ | C+ | 406.2 | 7.83 | 4.3 | 4.8 | 26.7 | 14.4 | 6.3 | 8.3 | 13.0 |
| Genoa Community Bank | Genoa | NE | B | C+ | B- | 64.0 | 3.09 | 3.4 | 1.1 | 3.9 | 8.9 | 10.0 | 11.6 | 17.0 |
| ▲ Geo. D. Warthen Bank | Sandersville | GA | B- | C+ | C- | 181.0 | 2.76 | 8.6 | 8.5 | 23.5 | 17.4 | 7.7 | 9.5 | 15.9 |
| Georgia Banking Co. | Sandy Springs | GA | C+ | B | C+ | 474.8 | 35.64 | 2.9 | 6.4 | 66.1 | 3.6 | 6.0 | 8.0 | 14.1 |
| ▲ Georgia Community Bank | Dawson | GA | B | B | B- | 331.5 | 97.11 | 6.3 | 3.5 | 25.6 | 15.5 | 10.0 | 12.2 | 21.8 |
| ▲ Georgia Primary Bank | Atlanta | GA | C+ | C- | D | 207.7 | 6.86 | 11.3 | 0.4 | 5.7 | 14.0 | 9.6 | 11.8 | 14.7 |
| Gerber State Bank | Argenta | IL | B- | B- | B- | 75.9 | -3.49 | 8.1 | 1.3 | 11.7 | 46.0 | 10.0 | 12.5 | 23.6 |
| German American Bank | Jasper | IN | A- | A- | A- | 4385.5 | 11.82 | 10.6 | 1.1 | 12.4 | 19.4 | 7.4 | 10.3 | 12.8 |
| German-American State Bank | German Valley | IL | B | B | B- | 249.4 | 1.34 | 14.6 | 4.8 | 6.3 | 21.0 | 8.1 | 10.1 | 13.4 |
| ▲ Germantown Trust & Savings Bank | Breese | IL | A | A- | A | 394.2 | 4.73 | 1.5 | 1.0 | 15.2 | 42.0 | 10.0 | 13.1 | 23.1 |
| Gibraltar Bank | Parsippany | NJ | C | C- | D | 104.4 | 0.67 | 0.0 | 0.0 | 60.0 | 7.8 | 10.0 | 11.2 | 20.1 |
| Gibsland Bank & Trust Co. | Gibsland | LA | C | D+ | D | 465.9 | 9.58 | 13.6 | 2.5 | 13.0 | 14.3 | 8.5 | 11.0 | 13.8 |
| ▲ Gifford State Bank | Gifford | IL | C- | D+ | C- | 156.0 | 1.55 | 6.4 | 4.2 | 29.5 | 1.9 | 8.2 | 9.9 | 13.5 |
| Gilmer National Bank | Gilmer | TX | B | B- | B+ | 225.5 | 7.11 | 8.4 | 10.4 | 19.4 | 13.0 | 10.0 | 14.1 | 21.4 |
| Glacier Bank | Kalispell | MT | A- | A- | A- | 13673.0 | 12.97 | 7.3 | 1.3 | 9.1 | 20.6 | 9.6 | 11.5 | 14.6 |
| Glasford State Bank | Glasford | IL | B- | C+ | C+ | 46.4 | 23.86 | 0.6 | 10.1 | 24.6 | 21.7 | 6.3 | 8.3 | 18.8 |
| Glen Burnie Mutual Savings Bank | Glen Burnie | MD | C- | C- | C- | 100.1 | 2.61 | 0.0 | 0.0 | 75.6 | 2.0 | 5.7 | 7.7 | 17.4 |
| Glen Rock Savings Bank | Glen Rock | NJ | D+ | D+ | D | 271.5 | 2.23 | 1.0 | 0.0 | 48.8 | 19.2 | 10.0 | 11.9 | 24.2 |
| Glenmede Trust Co., N.A. | Philadelphia | PA | U | U | U | 89.7 | -4.82 | 0.0 | 0.0 | 0.0 | 11.0 | 10.0 | 63.1 | 102.8 |
| Glennville Bank | Glennville | GA | A- | B+ | A- | 260.1 | 8.94 | 3.5 | 3.8 | 21.8 | 25.1 | 10.0 | 11.6 | 18.5 |
| Glens Falls National Bank and Trust Co. | Glens Falls | NY | B+ | B+ | B+ | 2564.3 | 4.90 | 2.7 | 26.9 | 23.7 | 20.7 | 7.8 | 9.5 | 14.5 |
| Glenview State Bank | Glenview | IL | B | B | B- | 1298.8 | 3.93 | 4.1 | 16.7 | 8.8 | 54.9 | 9.8 | 10.9 | 18.3 |
| Glenwood State Bank | Glenwood | IA | B- | C | C- | 226.3 | 27.74 | 4.8 | 2.3 | 11.0 | 34.5 | 9.3 | 10.5 | 22.4 |
| Glenwood State Bank | Glenwood | MN | C+ | C | C- | 315.4 | 6.42 | 18.5 | 1.8 | 15.1 | 0.1 | 5.2 | 9.4 | 11.1 |
| Global Bank | New York | NY | C+ | C | C | 202.5 | 18.87 | 1.0 | 0.0 | 24.6 | 1.9 | 10.0 | 12.6 | 15.2 |
| GN Bank | Chicago | IL | D- | D | D- | 137.4 | -1.37 | 1.4 | 1.3 | 18.7 | 37.1 | 6.0 | 8.0 | 19.1 |
| ▲ GNB Bank | Grundy Center | IA | B+ | B | B | 549.8 | -2.14 | 20.7 | 1.0 | 5.3 | 12.0 | 9.7 | 12.2 | 14.8 |
| GNBank, N.A. | Girard | KS | B- | C | C+ | 737.8 | 15.02 | 13.0 | 2.0 | 9.4 | 22.5 | 9.0 | 10.3 | 14.5 |
| ▲ Gogebic Range Bank | Ironwood | MI | B- | C | B | 123.4 | 0.87 | 16.5 | 6.3 | 11.2 | 27.3 | 8.8 | 10.2 | 16.3 |
| Gold Coast Bank | Chicago | IL | A- | B+ | A | 379.8 | 0.18 | 4.1 | 0.4 | 21.1 | 0.0 | 10.0 | 12.2 | 19.4 |
| Gold Coast Bank | Islandia | NY | B- | B- | C+ | 559.8 | 0.63 | 1.6 | 0.2 | 21.7 | 11.5 | 9.3 | 10.5 | 15.2 |
| Golden Bank, N.A. | Houston | TX | A- | A- | A- | 1022.6 | 13.06 | 2.2 | 0.1 | 9.6 | 10.5 | 10.0 | 13.2 | 17.1 |
| ▲ Golden Belt Bank, FSA | Ellis | KS | B+ | B+ | B+ | 236.8 | 0.78 | 9.0 | 3.0 | 34.2 | 12.6 | 10.0 | 12.1 | 15.6 |
| Golden Pacific Bank, N.A. | Sacramento | CA | C | C- | C | 134.3 | 4.51 | 13.3 | 0.9 | 5.6 | 1.3 | 8.5 | 10.0 | 16.3 |
| ▲ Golden State Bank | Glendale | CA | C+ | B- | C- | 350.1 | 13.81 | 12.4 | 0.1 | 1.7 | 0.0 | 6.7 | 9.3 | 12.3 |
| Golden Valley Bank | Chico | CA | B+ | B+ | B+ | 357.0 | 23.58 | 5.7 | 0.1 | 7.3 | 36.9 | 6.4 | 8.4 | 13.9 |
| ▼ Goldman Sachs Bank USA | New York | NY | B | A- | A- | 228836.0 | 19.49 | 6.7 | 4.3 | 5.0 | 3.2 | 8.0 | 13.2 | 13.3 |
| Goldman Sachs Trust Co., N.A. | New York | NY | U | U | U | 79.1 | 12.61 | 0.0 | 0.0 | 0.0 | 31.6 | 10.0 | 76.9 | 241.6 |
| ▲ Goldwater Bank, N.A. | Phoenix | AZ | C | C- | D+ | 187.5 | 29.36 | 2.1 | 0.2 | 67.6 | 2.1 | 9.5 | 10.7 | 21.7 |
| Goodfield State Bank | Goodfield | IL | A- | B+ | A | 134.4 | 10.13 | 13.5 | 1.9 | 20.7 | 11.7 | 10.0 | 13.2 | 17.7 |
| ▲ Goose River Bank | Mayville | ND | B | C+ | B | 127.5 | 4.81 | 18.7 | 3.3 | 0.9 | 9.9 | 8.1 | 10.7 | 13.5 |
| ▲ Goppert Financial Bank | Lathrop | MO | B | B- | C+ | 180.0 | 0.44 | 7.8 | 0.7 | 9.8 | 32.3 | 9.5 | 10.7 | 18.3 |
| Goppert State Service Bank | Garnett | KS | B | B | C+ | 192.5 | 9.26 | 15.7 | 5.2 | 14.8 | 14.5 | 9.6 | 10.8 | 15.2 |
| Gorham Savings Bank | Gorham | ME | C+ | C+ | C+ | 1256.7 | 5.28 | 9.9 | 0.3 | 18.2 | 14.2 | 7.7 | 10.1 | 13.1 |
| Gorham State Bank | Gorham | KS | C+ | B- | B- | 28.9 | -3.38 | 9.2 | 3.7 | 12.5 | 2.2 | 10.0 | 12.2 | 20.8 |
| ▼ Gouverneur S&L Assn. | Gouverneur | NY | B- | B+ | B+ | 125.6 | -3.81 | 1.4 | 2.1 | 58.9 | 13.2 | 10.0 | 22.9 | 37.8 |
| ▼ Graham S&L, SSB | Graham | TX | B | B+ | B+ | 137.8 | 7.00 | 2.8 | 2.0 | 45.0 | 7.4 | 10.0 | 11.3 | 20.9 |
| ▲ Grand Bank | Tulsa | OK | B- | B- | B+ | 391.3 | 9.58 | 15.2 | 0.2 | 11.9 | 11.3 | 7.8 | 10.2 | 13.2 |

| Asset Quality Index | Adjusted Non-Performing Loans as a % of Total Loans | Adjusted Non-Performing Loans as a % of Capital | Net Charge-Offs Avg Loans | Profitability Index | Net Income ($Mil) | Return on Assets (R.O.A.) | Return on Equity (R.O.E.) | Net Interest Spread | Overhead Efficiency Ratio | Liquidity Index | Liquidity Ratio | Hot Money Ratio | Stability Index |
|---|---|---|---|---|---|---|---|---|---|---|---|---|---|
| **6.8** | 0.24 | 2.2 | 0.11 | **4.3** | 20.0 | 0.87 | 7.79 | 3.26 | 75.8 | **4.4** | 9.2 | 5.5 | **8.6** |
| **9.4** | 0.34 | 0.5 | 0.00 | **3.7** | 0.4 | 0.76 | 6.94 | 2.88 | 69.5 | **0.9** | 24.0 | 50.6 | **6.6** |
| **5.3** | 2.44 | 15.1 | -0.11 | **3.5** | 0.5 | 0.69 | 6.01 | 3.87 | 77.1 | **0.5** | 10.0 | 44.8 | **5.3** |
| **8.3** | 0.11 | 0.4 | 0.01 | **6.3** | 2.8 | 1.49 | 15.75 | 3.79 | 59.6 | **1.6** | 23.0 | 20.7 | **7.7** |
| **4.4** | 4.89 | 12.7 | 0.00 | **0.0** | -0.4 | -0.34 | -2.40 | 3.47 | 116.8 | **2.4** | 33.5 | 22.0 | **4.1** |
| **8.8** | 0.00 | 0.0 | -0.03 | **5.4** | 1.3 | 1.07 | 7.93 | 3.58 | 57.0 | **3.8** | 34.3 | 14.4 | **6.9** |
| **7.1** | 0.05 | 0.0 | 0.00 | **4.3** | 5.3 | 0.92 | 8.40 | 3.46 | 66.6 | **0.8** | 16.9 | 46.1 | **7.1** |
| **9.9** | 0.41 | 2.2 | 0.01 | **3.2** | 2.6 | 0.47 | 2.86 | 2.10 | 69.7 | **0.7** | 10.8 | 39.3 | **8.7** |
| **5.9** | 0.60 | 4.4 | 0.02 | **5.2** | 5.6 | 1.06 | 11.32 | 3.79 | 66.0 | **0.6** | 9.9 | 37.5 | **6.2** |
| **3.1** | 2.86 | 11.3 | 0.02 | **4.1** | 0.3 | 0.71 | 5.77 | 4.22 | 75.8 | **2.1** | 11.7 | 11.8 | **6.0** |
| **1.4** | 3.42 | 23.6 | 0.10 | **1.4** | 0.1 | 0.03 | 0.34 | 3.53 | 100.6 | **1.1** | 8.6 | 28.9 | **3.2** |
| **7.6** | 0.19 | 0.8 | 0.07 | **7.1** | 8.6 | 1.45 | 13.48 | 3.87 | 58.4 | **1.6** | 19.0 | 17.4 | **7.5** |
| **8.4** | 0.04 | 0.9 | 0.04 | **3.7** | 2.5 | 0.64 | 7.80 | 3.79 | 78.9 | **1.5** | 15.5 | 18.4 | **4.8** |
| **7.1** | 1.64 | 1.2 | 0.57 | **5.5** | 0.8 | 1.24 | 10.55 | 3.64 | 71.6 | **1.1** | 27.1 | 35.1 | **8.1** |
| **4.3** | 1.97 | 11.3 | 0.15 | **4.2** | 1.4 | 0.79 | 8.58 | 4.73 | 77.5 | **4.7** | 26.5 | 5.9 | **4.5** |
| **4.1** | 0.98 | 11.8 | 0.26 | **3.8** | 2.5 | 0.54 | 6.05 | 3.30 | 80.7 | **0.5** | 3.2 | 38.2 | **5.7** |
| **4.9** | 2.83 | 12.7 | 0.32 | **7.2** | 4.0 | 1.88 | 19.92 | 6.38 | 67.9 | **1.4** | 24.8 | 29.2 | **5.4** |
| **5.7** | 0.08 | 0.5 | -0.01 | **4.5** | 1.7 | 0.86 | 7.10 | 3.88 | 72.1 | **1.0** | 25.1 | 40.8 | **6.5** |
| **5.8** | 2.47 | 6.2 | 0.07 | **3.6** | 0.6 | 0.78 | 6.46 | 3.17 | 72.7 | **4.6** | 31.0 | 8.7 | **6.6** |
| **6.9** | 0.45 | 2.3 | 0.17 | **7.3** | 61.7 | 1.50 | 11.81 | 4.01 | 58.6 | **4.0** | 18.7 | 9.1 | **10.0** |
| **5.6** | 0.62 | 3.5 | 0.04 | **6.2** | 2.8 | 1.14 | 11.11 | 3.59 | 60.5 | **1.7** | 13.7 | 20.5 | **7.2** |
| **8.3** | 0.41 | 3.9 | 0.55 | **7.7** | 7.2 | 1.85 | 13.90 | 2.95 | 35.3 | **3.3** | 39.8 | 18.6 | **9.4** |
| **9.6** | 0.15 | 1.0 | 0.00 | **2.1** | 0.2 | 0.19 | 1.60 | 2.86 | 92.0 | **1.1** | 17.4 | 30.6 | **6.3** |
| **3.2** | 2.84 | 10.9 | 1.30 | **4.0** | 2.6 | 0.60 | 5.71 | 4.45 | 65.1 | **0.9** | 19.7 | 33.2 | **4.5** |
| **3.1** | 1.61 | 11.2 | 1.70 | **3.5** | 1.0 | 0.62 | 6.16 | 4.18 | 68.3 | **3.0** | 14.9 | 14.0 | **5.5** |
| **4.4** | 1.82 | 10.2 | 0.33 | **5.6** | 2.5 | 1.12 | 7.97 | 3.77 | 57.8 | **1.6** | 31.9 | 33.4 | **7.6** |
| **6.6** | 0.67 | 2.2 | 0.08 | **8.8** | 225.8 | 1.77 | 12.35 | 4.47 | 57.6 | **4.5** | 14.3 | 5.3 | **10.0** |
| **4.0** | 0.00 | 12.0 | 0.32 | **3.7** | 0.3 | 0.69 | 7.76 | 3.64 | 77.9 | **6.2** | 44.4 | 2.9 | **4.8** |
| **5.5** | 1.05 | 15.5 | 0.00 | **2.1** | 0.3 | 0.30 | 3.90 | 1.05 | 71.2 | **5.5** | 24.4 | 0.0 | **4.0** |
| **6.4** | 1.54 | 8.3 | 0.07 | **0.9** | 0.1 | 0.02 | 0.19 | 2.40 | 100.5 | **1.7** | 15.6 | 21.9 | **5.9** |
| **10.0** | na | 0.0 | na | **9.5** | 34.5 | 34.00 | 65.93 | 2.83 | 79.7 | **4.0** | 83.2 | 0.0 | **7.0** |
| **6.1** | 1.27 | 6.3 | 0.20 | **7.0** | 3.3 | 1.32 | 10.85 | 4.42 | 63.7 | **1.4** | 23.6 | 28.1 | **7.5** |
| **6.8** | 0.20 | 1.5 | 0.05 | **5.9** | 29.7 | 1.21 | 12.46 | 3.10 | 60.5 | **3.5** | 9.6 | 4.9 | **8.4** |
| **7.9** | 0.03 | 0.1 | 0.01 | **4.6** | 14.5 | 1.14 | 9.94 | 2.61 | 63.9 | **6.3** | 55.9 | 9.1 | **9.4** |
| **8.8** | 0.00 | 0.3 | 0.02 | **3.9** | 1.7 | 0.78 | 7.66 | 3.17 | 71.7 | **6.4** | 55.2 | 5.8 | **5.1** |
| **4.1** | 1.12 | 8.5 | 0.02 | **6.9** | 4.7 | 1.53 | 16.49 | 4.02 | 62.1 | **1.9** | 3.8 | 17.0 | **7.8** |
| **7.5** | 0.00 | 0.0 | 0.00 | **3.2** | 0.9 | 0.49 | 3.84 | 3.74 | 83.6 | **0.5** | 4.2 | 46.7 | **6.3** |
| **1.7** | 14.18 | 39.1 | 0.50 | **0.0** | -1.5 | -1.06 | -12.38 | 2.70 | 135.4 | **2.9** | 39.6 | 18.8 | **1.9** |
| **6.3** | 1.02 | 4.6 | 1.21 | **5.8** | 6.5 | 1.18 | 8.95 | 4.18 | 58.6 | **0.7** | 12.1 | 25.8 | **9.7** |
| **3.1** | 2.06 | 10.8 | 0.04 | **5.3** | 7.1 | 1.02 | 8.34 | 4.00 | 68.8 | **3.0** | 12.7 | 11.6 | **8.0** |
| **4.5** | 1.56 | 7.6 | 0.23 | **6.3** | 1.5 | 1.19 | 10.96 | 4.65 | 64.4 | **4.4** | 36.2 | 11.6 | **6.5** |
| **8.2** | 0.65 | 3.1 | 0.27 | **7.6** | 4.8 | 1.25 | 10.06 | 3.74 | 60.2 | **1.3** | 31.6 | 44.1 | **8.8** |
| **6.3** | 0.60 | 4.3 | -0.02 | **3.5** | 3.6 | 0.62 | 6.01 | 2.63 | 68.5 | **0.7** | 11.4 | 32.1 | **6.5** |
| **7.4** | 0.17 | 0.9 | 0.00 | **8.3** | 15.2 | 1.58 | 11.95 | 3.90 | 49.0 | **1.8** | 28.7 | 45.2 | **9.9** |
| **5.6** | 1.00 | 6.6 | 0.03 | **8.0** | 4.7 | 1.94 | 14.67 | 3.94 | 56.8 | **3.7** | 8.9 | 9.9 | **9.4** |
| **3.4** | 1.05 | 5.2 | 0.18 | **3.2** | 0.3 | 0.26 | 2.09 | 4.83 | 89.1 | **2.9** | 16.3 | 14.6 | **6.8** |
| **4.7** | 0.23 | 8.0 | -0.03 | **3.9** | 1.7 | 0.51 | 4.87 | 3.98 | 76.4 | **1.4** | 27.6 | 31.3 | **6.5** |
| **9.0** | 0.05 | 0.3 | 0.00 | **5.2** | 4.0 | 1.19 | 14.60 | 3.46 | 61.8 | **5.8** | 50.2 | 8.2 | **4.9** |
| **8.7** | 0.60 | 1.7 | 0.55 | **4.3** | 1616.0 | 0.79 | 5.67 | 1.48 | 48.1 | **3.4** | 67.3 | 11.7 | **10.0** |
| **10.0** | na | 0.0 | na | **9.5** | 37.9 | 46.99 | 64.59 | 2.20 | 49.4 | **4.0** | 256.3 | 0.0 | **6.3** |
| **8.0** | 0.80 | 2.1 | -0.04 | **5.9** | 8.8 | 5.34 | 59.12 | 2.96 | 88.2 | **0.4** | 6.3 | 66.0 | **3.0** |
| **7.4** | 0.26 | 1.8 | 0.18 | **9.4** | 2.7 | 2.15 | 16.49 | 3.97 | 54.7 | **1.9** | 23.6 | 21.4 | **9.0** |
| **6.8** | 0.14 | 0.9 | -0.03 | **6.6** | 2.0 | 1.70 | 16.06 | 4.75 | 67.2 | **3.3** | 15.6 | 12.8 | **7.2** |
| **8.4** | 0.04 | 0.7 | 0.14 | **4.3** | 1.4 | 0.79 | 7.67 | 3.70 | 71.7 | **4.3** | 22.9 | 7.8 | **5.7** |
| **8.1** | 0.04 | 0.6 | -0.03 | **5.3** | 2.0 | 1.07 | 10.02 | 3.84 | 64.5 | **2.6** | 12.9 | 16.0 | **6.8** |
| **6.1** | 1.20 | 8.6 | 0.00 | **3.4** | 8.0 | 0.66 | 6.93 | 3.41 | 77.6 | **1.2** | 4.6 | 7.8 | **7.6** |
| **3.7** | 5.78 | 26.9 | 0.00 | **4.5** | 0.2 | 0.73 | 6.13 | 3.70 | 66.3 | **5.7** | 41.4 | 5.4 | **6.5** |
| **7.0** | 2.00 | 5.7 | 0.16 | **2.5** | 0.1 | 0.06 | 0.26 | 4.54 | 102.1 | **4.4** | 16.0 | 6.3 | **7.9** |
| **8.5** | 0.65 | 3.9 | 0.03 | **3.8** | 1.2 | 0.87 | 7.44 | 3.48 | 74.1 | **1.1** | 26.3 | 35.5 | **7.9** |
| **4.1** | 1.34 | 7.5 | 0.07 | **6.7** | 5.0 | 1.33 | 12.51 | 3.96 | 54.6 | **0.8** | 17.1 | 37.9 | **7.4** |

| | | | | | | | | Asset Mix (As a % of Total Assets) | | | | | | |
|---|---|---|---|---|---|---|---|---|---|---|---|---|---|---|
| Name | City | State | Rating | 2018 Rating | 2017 Rating | Total Assets ($Mil) | One Year Asset Growth | Comm-ercial Loans | Cons-umer Loans | Mort-gage Loans | Secur-ities | Capital-ization Index | Lever-age Ratio | Risk-Based Capital Ratio |
| Grand Bank for Savings, FSB | Hattiesburg | MS | **B+** | B+ | B+ | 84.5 | 0.20 | 0.0 | 0.5 | 75.8 | 0.0 | **10.0** | 12.1 | 27.9 |
| Grand Marais State Bank | Grand Marais | MN | **B** | B- | B | 90.2 | 2.49 | 9.6 | 1.9 | 30.3 | 34.7 | **5.8** | 7.8 | 15.4 |
| Grand Rapids State Bank | Grand Rapids | MN | **B-** | B- | C+ | 224.5 | -2.61 | 11.7 | 4.0 | 10.0 | 20.8 | **8.7** | 10.1 | 14.2 |
| ▲ Grand Ridge National Bank | Grand Ridge | IL | **A** | A- | A- | 221.6 | 10.52 | 8.2 | 0.0 | 10.0 | 0.2 | **10.0** | 12.0 | 15.7 |
| Grand River Bank | Grandville | MI | **C+** | C+ | C+ | 321.2 | 21.60 | 8.1 | 0.1 | 15.2 | 1.8 | **6.8** | 10.5 | 12.3 |
| Grand Rivers Community Bank | Grand Chain | IL | **E-** | E- | E | 29.6 | -18.15 | 9.3 | 1.2 | 14.9 | 4.1 | **1.0** | 4.4 | 8.0 |
| ▲ Grand Savings Bank | Grove | OK | **B+** | B- | B | 541.5 | 13.37 | 6.8 | 7.7 | 21.0 | 6.2 | **7.7** | 9.4 | 13.6 |
| Grand Timber Bank | McGregor | MN | **B-** | C+ | C+ | 44.3 | 2.34 | 8.6 | 8.6 | 31.0 | 14.4 | **10.0** | 15.1 | 21.8 |
| Grand Valley Bank | Heber City | UT | **B+** | B+ | B | 437.3 | 12.14 | 1.3 | 0.4 | 7.5 | 49.1 | **7.8** | 9.5 | 18.3 |
| GrandSouth Bank | Greenville | SC | **B** | B | B+ | 911.5 | 17.49 | 22.3 | 4.5 | 11.1 | 8.1 | **7.2** | 10.1 | 12.7 |
| Grandview Bank | Grandview | TX | **A-** | B+ | B+ | 258.8 | 27.49 | 13.3 | 6.2 | 14.7 | 19.9 | **8.1** | 9.8 | 15.7 |
| Granger National Bank | Granger | TX | **B** | B- | B- | 32.8 | 2.04 | 1.7 | 2.4 | 5.0 | 56.0 | **10.0** | 17.2 | 40.9 |
| Granite Community Bank | Cold Spring | MN | **C+** | C | C+ | 117.0 | 3.53 | 6.5 | 2.6 | 8.2 | 7.6 | **4.1** | 8.9 | 10.6 |
| ▲ Granite Falls Bank | Granite Falls | MN | **A-** | B- | B | 139.1 | -0.26 | 4.7 | 0.6 | 1.9 | 41.9 | **9.9** | 11.0 | 16.5 |
| Granite Mountain Bank, Inc. | Philipsburg | MT | **B** | B- | B- | 85.9 | 11.05 | 11.0 | 2.3 | 14.7 | 10.6 | **6.8** | 8.8 | 19.9 |
| Grant County Bank | Ulysses | KS | **B-** | C+ | C+ | 238.5 | 1.40 | 8.4 | 1.8 | 21.3 | 28.6 | **10.0** | 14.4 | 24.1 |
| Grant County Bank | Medford | OK | **C** | C | C+ | 55.4 | -6.94 | 4.8 | 6.4 | 1.6 | 36.2 | **10.0** | 16.1 | 34.1 |
| ▲ Grant County Bank | Petersburg | WV | **B** | B- | B | 260.4 | 0.17 | 7.2 | 3.0 | 29.8 | 6.9 | **10.0** | 13.9 | 19.2 |
| ▲ Grant County State Bank | Swayzee | IN | **B** | C+ | B | 196.4 | 10.85 | 8.3 | 6.4 | 38.9 | 0.0 | **10.0** | 11.7 | 18.6 |
| Grant County State Bank | Carson | ND | **A-** | A- | A- | 36.9 | -6.48 | 1.5 | 0.1 | 0.0 | 0.0 | **10.0** | 12.4 | 18.9 |
| Granville National Bank | Granville | IL | **B-** | B- | C | 90.4 | 3.91 | 3.2 | 5.0 | 23.8 | 37.7 | **9.8** | 10.9 | 28.0 |
| Gratz Bank | Gratz | PA | **B** | B | B | 372.3 | 11.29 | 5.6 | 0.6 | 27.3 | 20.0 | **6.5** | 8.5 | 14.1 |
| Great American Bank | Lawrence | KS | **B** | B- | B+ | 214.8 | 4.02 | 7.2 | 0.5 | 24.3 | 0.9 | **8.2** | 10.4 | 13.5 |
| Great Midwest Bank, S.S.B. | Brookfield | WI | **B+** | B | B | 847.8 | 7.41 | 0.0 | 0.1 | 67.1 | 6.2 | **10.0** | 15.3 | 22.2 |
| Great Nations Bank | Norman | OK | **B-** | B- | B- | 65.8 | 0.28 | 24.9 | 0.8 | 10.9 | 1.8 | **10.0** | 13.8 | 16.3 |
| ▼ Great North Bank | Florence | WI | **D+** | C- | C+ | 145.8 | -3.68 | 23.7 | 2.4 | 13.2 | 24.9 | **6.7** | 8.7 | 12.9 |
| ▲ Great Plains Bank | Eureka | SD | **D+** | D- | D | 115.6 | 5.21 | 10.9 | 1.0 | 3.9 | 5.7 | **10.0** | 13.3 | 15.7 |
| Great Plains National Bank | Hollis | OK | **B** | B+ | B+ | 814.4 | 5.78 | 21.0 | 3.7 | 18.4 | 7.3 | **8.3** | 10.4 | 13.6 |
| Great Plains State Bank | Petersburg | NE | **C** | C | C+ | 277.1 | 41.73 | 14.0 | 0.5 | 0.1 | 6.9 | **8.6** | 10.6 | 13.8 |
| Great Rivers Bank | Barry | IL | **C+** | C+ | C- | 136.7 | 30.47 | 8.3 | 2.1 | 7.2 | 9.3 | **9.3** | 10.8 | 14.4 |
| Great Southern Bank | Springfield | MO | **A-** | B+ | B- | 5015.0 | 7.18 | 4.9 | 4.0 | 11.8 | 7.5 | **8.8** | 12.3 | 14.0 |
| Great Southern Bank | Meridian | MS | **B** | B | B | 294.0 | -0.03 | 4.8 | 11.3 | 12.7 | 48.3 | **7.7** | 9.5 | 21.6 |
| Great Western Bank | Sioux Falls | SD | **C+** | C+ | C+ | 12848.1 | 2.22 | 10.8 | 0.4 | 4.3 | 14.8 | **6.7** | 10.0 | 12.3 |
| Greater Community Bank | Rome | GA | **B+** | B | B- | 225.4 | 20.05 | 12.7 | 8.2 | 11.2 | 2.6 | **8.0** | 10.4 | 13.4 |
| Greater State Bank | McAllen | TX | **C** | C | C | 89.3 | 15.45 | 10.3 | 1.3 | 13.9 | 6.8 | **7.3** | 9.2 | 15.8 |
| ▲ Green Belt Bank & Trust | Iowa Falls | IA | **C** | C- | C | 494.7 | 6.21 | 9.0 | 2.0 | 6.4 | 11.9 | **5.3** | 9.0 | 11.3 |
| ▲ Green Dot Bank | Provo | UT | **A+** | A | A | 1595.1 | 7.05 | 1.0 | 1.1 | 0.1 | 17.4 | **10.0** | 13.9 | 83.4 |
| Greene County Commercial Bank | Catskill | NY | **U** | U | U | 593.5 | 37.02 | 0.0 | 0.0 | 0.0 | 88.3 | **6.4** | 8.4 | 43.1 |
| Greeneville Federal Bank, FSB | Greeneville | TN | **B-** | B | B+ | 149.8 | -5.79 | 9.9 | 1.3 | 27.7 | 1.0 | **10.0** | 15.1 | 21.8 |
| Greenfield Banking Co. | Greenfield | IN | **A-** | A- | B | 619.7 | 7.90 | 3.7 | 0.8 | 6.9 | 21.6 | **9.7** | 10.8 | 17.4 |
| ▼ Greenfield Banking Co. | Greenfield | TN | **D** | C- | C+ | 66.2 | 9.71 | 15.1 | 8.9 | 18.0 | 5.6 | **4.4** | 9.3 | 10.7 |
| Greenfield Co-operative Bank | Greenfield | MA | **B** | B | C+ | 663.6 | 8.63 | 5.0 | 0.5 | 40.2 | 21.1 | **10.0** | 11.9 | 22.0 |
| Greenfield Savings Bank | Greenfield | MA | **B** | B | B | 869.5 | 1.54 | 4.0 | 0.1 | 55.0 | 10.2 | **10.0** | 12.2 | 20.4 |
| Greenleaf Wayside Bank | Greenleaf | WI | **B** | B | C+ | 101.5 | 7.12 | 4.0 | 1.0 | 20.9 | 29.3 | **8.6** | 10.1 | 17.4 |
| ▼ Greenville Federal | Greenville | OH | **C** | C+ | B- | 198.5 | 9.60 | 8.4 | 0.8 | 49.3 | 0.8 | **9.5** | 10.7 | 15.7 |
| Greenville National Bank | Greenville | OH | **B+** | B+ | B+ | 484.8 | 7.54 | 3.6 | 11.5 | 20.6 | 15.2 | **9.0** | 10.4 | 16.3 |
| Greenville Savings Bank | Greenville | PA | **B** | B | B | 246.2 | 2.15 | 0.8 | 0.8 | 59.7 | 12.2 | **10.0** | 14.4 | 25.9 |
| Greenwoods State Bank | Lake Mills | WI | **C-** | C | B- | 313.7 | 74.86 | 8.8 | 1.3 | 16.9 | 4.5 | **5.5** | 9.0 | 11.4 |
| Grinnell State Bank | Grinnell | IA | **B** | B | B+ | 325.5 | 4.33 | 5.0 | 0.4 | 5.2 | 13.5 | **10.0** | 12.7 | 16.3 |
| ▼ Grove Bank & Trust | Miami | FL | **B-** | B+ | B+ | 716.8 | 9.19 | 7.3 | 0.5 | 3.5 | 36.8 | **10.0** | 16.2 | 28.3 |
| Grundy Bank | Morris | IL | **B** | B- | B+ | 275.2 | 1.42 | 6.7 | 0.6 | 19.6 | 10.9 | **7.7** | 9.4 | 16.4 |
| Grundy National Bank | Grundy | VA | **C** | C- | C- | 304.9 | -0.38 | 7.0 | 5.2 | 8.0 | 34.8 | **10.0** | 22.3 | 38.1 |
| GSL Savings Bank | Guttenberg | NJ | **D+** | D+ | C- | 112.1 | 7.37 | 1.7 | 0.0 | 57.9 | 1.8 | **9.3** | 10.5 | 17.1 |
| Guadalupe Bank | Kerrville | TX | **B+** | B | B | 172.5 | 8.12 | 5.3 | 1.4 | 26.7 | 0.3 | **7.0** | 9.0 | 15.6 |
| Guaranty Bank | Springfield | MO | **C** | C | C | 1010.1 | 4.72 | 10.6 | 0.5 | 12.0 | 11.7 | **7.9** | 10.5 | 13.3 |
| Guaranty Bank & Trust Co. of Delhi | Delhi | LA | **B+** | B+ | A- | 296.8 | 17.00 | 3.9 | 1.9 | 29.2 | 4.7 | **5.9** | 7.9 | 13.0 |
| Guaranty Bank & Trust, N.A. | Mount Pleasant | TX | **B+** | B | B | 2318.5 | 2.28 | 8.5 | 2.3 | 17.8 | 16.1 | **7.7** | 10.1 | 13.1 |
| Guaranty Bank and Trust Co. | New Roads | LA | **A-** | B+ | A- | 216.5 | 6.43 | 2.8 | 2.1 | 31.9 | 14.0 | **10.0** | 13.5 | 20.7 |
| Guaranty Bank and Trust Co. | Belzoni | MS | **B** | B- | B | 1040.6 | 25.22 | 13.0 | 1.1 | 9.8 | 14.8 | **6.8** | 9.6 | 12.4 |
| Guaranty State Bank and Trust Co. | Beloit | KS | **C+** | C | C- | 298.6 | 7.24 | 6.8 | 1.0 | 7.6 | 7.2 | **10.0** | 12.9 | 16.4 |

| Asset Quality Index | Adjusted Non-Performing Loans as a % of Total Loans | Adjusted Non-Performing Loans as a % of Capital | Net Charge-Offs Avg Loans | Profitability Index | Net Income ($Mil) | Return on Assets (R.O.A.) | Return on Equity (R.O.E.) | Net Interest Spread | Overhead Efficiency Ratio | Liquidity Index | Liquidity Ratio | Hot Money Ratio | Stability Index |
|---|---|---|---|---|---|---|---|---|---|---|---|---|---|
| **6.9** | 1.61 | 8.6 | 0.03 | **4.2** | 0.6 | 0.74 | 5.84 | 6.06 | 88.8 | **0.6** | 16.7 | 44.7 | **6.7** |
| **9.0** | 0.00 | 0.0 | 0.05 | **6.6** | 1.4 | 1.59 | 20.53 | 3.80 | 60.2 | **4.4** | 9.4 | 5.1 | **5.6** |
| **8.4** | 0.00 | 0.0 | 0.08 | **4.8** | 2.7 | 1.20 | 11.88 | 3.98 | 73.2 | **4.5** | 14.7 | 5.4 | **6.3** |
| **7.2** | 0.15 | 0.8 | 0.18 | **10.0** | 4.0 | 1.89 | 15.42 | 5.57 | 53.6 | **1.2** | 18.6 | 29.5 | **8.7** |
| **7.3** | 0.00 | 0.0 | 0.00 | **3.4** | 1.8 | 0.60 | 5.94 | 3.00 | 73.7 | **0.7** | 9.3 | 26.1 | **6.0** |
| **1.1** | 3.84 | 33.0 | 0.70 | **1.1** | -0.6 | -1.78 | -25.98 | 3.67 | 150.6 | **1.3** | 27.7 | 33.4 | **0.3** |
| **6.7** | 0.49 | 2.9 | 0.02 | **7.6** | 8.9 | 1.79 | 19.05 | 4.41 | 62.9 | **1.3** | 17.6 | 27.0 | **7.5** |
| **3.5** | 4.68 | 17.8 | 0.08 | **8.7** | 0.9 | 2.24 | 15.23 | 4.78 | 60.3 | **4.7** | 22.7 | 5.1 | **8.6** |
| **7.8** | 0.26 | 1.8 | -0.02 | **6.0** | 5.1 | 1.21 | 11.69 | 3.88 | 61.5 | **5.4** | 49.1 | 10.4 | **6.4** |
| **7.0** | 0.44 | 2.6 | 0.24 | **5.1** | 8.9 | 1.04 | 10.41 | 5.10 | 66.6 | **1.1** | 15.2 | 30.6 | **6.2** |
| **8.2** | 0.15 | 1.0 | 0.06 | **8.3** | 4.0 | 1.77 | 18.25 | 4.41 | 50.1 | **3.7** | 32.3 | 13.8 | **6.2** |
| **7.9** | 1.04 | 2.2 | 0.06 | **3.8** | 0.2 | 0.75 | 4.18 | 3.59 | 78.0 | **5.4** | 80.5 | 14.5 | **7.3** |
| **4.9** | 0.76 | 3.6 | 0.12 | **5.6** | 1.3 | 1.10 | 12.77 | 3.96 | 67.5 | **1.1** | 10.0 | 27.0 | **5.7** |
| **7.8** | 0.34 | 0.7 | -0.08 | **7.4** | 2.4 | 1.74 | 14.53 | 4.04 | 52.2 | **4.2** | 19.6 | 7.6 | **7.7** |
| **8.8** | 0.00 | 0.0 | 0.00 | **5.2** | 0.9 | 1.10 | 12.00 | 4.48 | 68.3 | **6.1** | 43.7 | 3.3 | **4.9** |
| **3.7** | 4.29 | 16.7 | 0.30 | **6.0** | 3.5 | 1.50 | 10.12 | 3.54 | 63.0 | **1.4** | 21.3 | 26.6 | **8.4** |
| **5.5** | 2.22 | 10.0 | 0.46 | **2.0** | 0.1 | 0.24 | 1.55 | 2.68 | 86.3 | **2.2** | 45.6 | 35.4 | **4.8** |
| **4.2** | 2.48 | 15.9 | 0.09 | **5.8** | 2.7 | 1.04 | 7.99 | 4.57 | 69.3 | **2.0** | 11.7 | 18.6 | **7.2** |
| **4.5** | 2.25 | 13.6 | 0.45 | **9.7** | 4.9 | 2.57 | 22.18 | 4.26 | 30.1 | **0.8** | 19.0 | 40.8 | **8.6** |
| **7.3** | 0.00 | 0.0 | 0.00 | **8.5** | 0.7 | 1.92 | 15.08 | 4.97 | 60.6 | **3.8** | 32.6 | 13.4 | **7.0** |
| **7.1** | 0.50 | 1.8 | 0.20 | **3.5** | 0.6 | 0.67 | 5.68 | 2.85 | 70.9 | **6.0** | 51.4 | 6.2 | **6.4** |
| **6.9** | 0.39 | 2.4 | -0.01 | **5.4** | 3.8 | 1.08 | 11.52 | 3.50 | 60.7 | **3.6** | 25.3 | 11.9 | **5.6** |
| **5.4** | 0.00 | 0.0 | 0.01 | **8.2** | 4.0 | 1.90 | 14.21 | 4.70 | 58.0 | **1.0** | 6.3 | 29.7 | **9.5** |
| **6.4** | 1.65 | 7.5 | 0.00 | **4.6** | 8.0 | 0.97 | 6.38 | 2.61 | 63.5 | **0.4** | 9.2 | 43.3 | **8.5** |
| **8.2** | 0.10 | 0.6 | 0.04 | **2.7** | 0.2 | 0.33 | 2.39 | 3.56 | 89.7 | **0.4** | 8.7 | 64.9 | **7.3** |
| **2.8** | 2.65 | 14.6 | -0.02 | **1.4** | 0.5 | 0.35 | 3.87 | 3.42 | 89.0 | **1.2** | 32.6 | 48.5 | **4.5** |
| **1.0** | 3.88 | 22.5 | 0.06 | **8.3** | 2.2 | 1.96 | 15.16 | 4.35 | 44.1 | **0.7** | 13.2 | 33.4 | **8.9** |
| **4.1** | 1.12 | 7.0 | 0.31 | **9.4** | 15.5 | 1.94 | 19.24 | 5.76 | 72.3 | **1.3** | 11.0 | 26.3 | **9.2** |
| **5.2** | 0.58 | 3.9 | 0.00 | **2.8** | 0.8 | 0.31 | 2.87 | 2.88 | 69.7 | **0.6** | 13.4 | 23.8 | **5.8** |
| **4.3** | 0.96 | 5.7 | 0.34 | **3.2** | 0.8 | 0.68 | 5.36 | 3.59 | 72.9 | **3.3** | 23.8 | 13.2 | **6.2** |
| **6.8** | 0.28 | 1.6 | 0.10 | **8.1** | 79.7 | 1.64 | 12.81 | 4.09 | 52.1 | **0.7** | 10.3 | 30.3 | **10.0** |
| **6.6** | 0.36 | 2.7 | 0.39 | **4.5** | 2.7 | 0.91 | 9.79 | 4.43 | 76.1 | **5.4** | 56.9 | 12.4 | **5.0** |
| **3.2** | 1.97 | 8.7 | 0.38 | **7.8** | 177.3 | 1.39 | 9.26 | 3.76 | 44.1 | **3.4** | 11.0 | 8.3 | **10.0** |
| **7.1** | 0.19 | 1.3 | 0.15 | **5.5** | 2.8 | 1.32 | 13.20 | 4.49 | 67.3 | **1.9** | 18.2 | 18.2 | **6.3** |
| **5.2** | 1.01 | 6.4 | 0.39 | **3.1** | 0.3 | 0.37 | 3.97 | 4.53 | 88.4 | **1.3** | 29.0 | 34.2 | **4.2** |
| **4.3** | 0.45 | 3.1 | 0.48 | **5.8** | 7.1 | 1.42 | 15.26 | 3.47 | 53.4 | **1.6** | 12.0 | 20.6 | **6.6** |
| **9.9** | 7.00 | 1.2 | 8.62 | **10.0** | 50.2 | 3.12 | 23.86 | 2.88 | 14.9 | **3.8** | 102.3 | 0.2 | **9.4** |
| **10.0** | na | 0.0 | na | **7.7** | 7.6 | 1.45 | 15.88 | 2.46 | 10.0 | **5.3** | 14.3 | 0.2 | **7.0** |
| **4.5** | 3.30 | 17.4 | -0.01 | **3.6** | 0.8 | 0.52 | 3.58 | 3.96 | 83.8 | **1.2** | 15.0 | 26.7 | **7.7** |
| **5.5** | 1.69 | 7.8 | 0.09 | **6.8** | 7.7 | 1.37 | 13.34 | 3.82 | 58.6 | **6.8** | 50.6 | 1.6 | **7.0** |
| **2.5** | 2.11 | 14.0 | 0.13 | **3.8** | 0.6 | 0.88 | 9.22 | 4.20 | 70.2 | **0.8** | 18.2 | 41.0 | **2.3** |
| **7.5** | 1.00 | 4.5 | 0.06 | **3.8** | 4.6 | 0.72 | 6.07 | 3.00 | 70.1 | **2.7** | 31.6 | 18.6 | **7.1** |
| **7.9** | 0.68 | 4.5 | 0.04 | **4.3** | 7.2 | 0.84 | 7.07 | 3.43 | 72.7 | **1.3** | 13.1 | 23.8 | **7.8** |
| **9.0** | 0.00 | 0.0 | -0.03 | **4.8** | 1.1 | 1.14 | 11.48 | 3.60 | 71.1 | **5.9** | 42.1 | 4.2 | **6.3** |
| **7.9** | 0.41 | 2.9 | 0.01 | **2.4** | 0.5 | 0.28 | 2.52 | 3.24 | 90.0 | **0.8** | 15.4 | 36.7 | **6.0** |
| **5.1** | 0.74 | 4.5 | 0.14 | **6.4** | 6.4 | 1.35 | 12.70 | 3.68 | 57.0 | **3.4** | 18.2 | 12.1 | **7.0** |
| **8.0** | 0.56 | 4.4 | 0.12 | **3.7** | 1.5 | 0.62 | 4.36 | 2.85 | 71.5 | **1.8** | 24.1 | 21.9 | **7.5** |
| **2.9** | 1.40 | 6.3 | 0.01 | **4.2** | 2.0 | 0.78 | 6.88 | 4.28 | 78.9 | **1.6** | 11.3 | 17.5 | **6.5** |
| **4.9** | 1.11 | 8.2 | -0.01 | **5.6** | 3.8 | 1.17 | 9.31 | 3.70 | 61.5 | **3.8** | 14.9 | 9.8 | **6.6** |
| **9.2** | 0.20 | 0.4 | 0.01 | **2.7** | 2.0 | 0.30 | 1.74 | 2.83 | 90.7 | **6.0** | 48.3 | 6.0 | **8.8** |
| **5.4** | 1.74 | 5.1 | 0.01 | **9.4** | 6.3 | 2.31 | 20.77 | 4.35 | 53.1 | **4.8** | 21.7 | 4.3 | **8.4** |
| **5.0** | 3.95 | 8.2 | 0.29 | **2.5** | 1.4 | 0.44 | 2.00 | 2.92 | 80.4 | **3.1** | 48.8 | 25.5 | **6.5** |
| **9.3** | 0.04 | 0.3 | 0.00 | **1.6** | 0.2 | 0.15 | 1.34 | 2.74 | 93.2 | **0.8** | 14.8 | 36.4 | **6.2** |
| **8.9** | 0.01 | 0.4 | 0.10 | **6.5** | 2.3 | 1.35 | 15.31 | 4.45 | 66.4 | **4.8** | 32.2 | 8.1 | **6.4** |
| **4.8** | 1.37 | 8.6 | 0.08 | **5.8** | 11.5 | 1.17 | 10.69 | 3.63 | 65.1 | **3.3** | 22.8 | 15.0 | **9.2** |
| **7.2** | 0.47 | 5.2 | 0.05 | **9.8** | 5.9 | 2.18 | 26.33 | 4.76 | 60.8 | **1.8** | 28.5 | 25.7 | **6.1** |
| **7.6** | 1.08 | 2.8 | -0.02 | **5.7** | 28.1 | 1.21 | 10.70 | 3.77 | 62.9 | **1.8** | 9.0 | 19.6 | **9.1** |
| **7.6** | 0.24 | 2.9 | 0.05 | **7.8** | 3.2 | 1.51 | 11.55 | 4.77 | 59.3 | **3.0** | 9.1 | 13.5 | **8.1** |
| **5.5** | 1.29 | 6.8 | -0.09 | **7.6** | 16.3 | 1.81 | 17.80 | 4.20 | 61.9 | **1.7** | 11.0 | 21.1 | **8.9** |
| **2.6** | 3.28 | 17.4 | 0.22 | **5.4** | 2.9 | 1.02 | 7.83 | 4.02 | 62.8 | **2.1** | 21.2 | 10.9 | **6.6** |

| Name | City | State | Rating | 2018 Rating | 2017 Rating | Total Assets ($Mil) | One Year Asset Growth | Asset Mix (As a % of Total Assets) Comm-ercial Loans | Cons-umer Loans | Mort-gage Loans | Secur-ities | Capital-ization Index | Lever-age Ratio | Risk-Based Capital Ratio |
|---|---|---|---|---|---|---|---|---|---|---|---|---|---|---|
| Guardian Bank | Valdosta | GA | **B+** | B | B+ | 429.2 | 4.94 | 9.6 | 1.7 | 14.6 | 25.7 | **9.0** | 10.3 | 17.2 |
| Guardian Savings Bank | Granite City | IL | **D** | D+ | C | 35.9 | -9.93 | 0.0 | 0.4 | 23.1 | 47.8 | **10.0** | 19.9 | 92.5 |
| ▲ Guardian Savings Bank, F.S.B. | West Chester | OH | **B+** | B | B- | 997.6 | 6.89 | 0.0 | 0.0 | 64.2 | 0.0 | **9.8** | 10.8 | 24.0 |
| Guilford Savings Bank | Guilford | CT | **B** | B- | B- | 838.2 | 6.49 | 3.0 | 0.7 | 38.2 | 11.5 | **10.0** | 12.1 | 17.2 |
| ▲ Gulf Coast Bank | Abbeville | LA | **A-** | B | B+ | 369.3 | -1.74 | 5.0 | 9.2 | 17.4 | 10.7 | **10.0** | 14.5 | 21.7 |
| Gulf Coast Bank and Trust Co. | New Orleans | LA | **B-** | C+ | C+ | 1820.6 | 7.00 | 26.1 | 1.6 | 15.8 | 10.8 | **6.7** | 9.0 | 12.3 |
| Gunnison Bank and Trust Co. | Gunnison | CO | **A-** | B | B | 122.9 | 25.24 | 1.8 | 0.3 | 24.3 | 3.4 | **7.9** | 9.6 | 15.3 |
| Gunnison S&L Assn. | Gunnison | CO | **B-** | C+ | C- | 100.3 | -0.73 | 0.0 | 0.9 | 49.1 | 0.5 | **10.0** | 13.2 | 35.1 |
| ▲ Guthrie County State Bank | Panora | IA | **B-** | C+ | B- | 118.1 | -7.69 | 6.2 | 3.6 | 18.8 | 18.5 | **10.0** | 11.9 | 17.1 |
| H. F. Gehant Banking Co. | West Brooklyn | IL | **B+** | B | B | 58.7 | 1.64 | 4.8 | 2.7 | 14.5 | 8.5 | **10.0** | 15.9 | 21.4 |
| Habib American Bank | New York | NY | **B+** | B+ | B+ | 1896.5 | 16.81 | 2.6 | 0.5 | 7.2 | 5.5 | **6.4** | 8.4 | 17.1 |
| Haddon Savings Bank | Haddon Heights | NJ | **C** | C | C | 326.9 | -1.27 | 4.7 | 0.0 | 27.6 | 52.5 | **9.1** | 10.4 | 22.2 |
| ▲ Halstead Bank | Halstead | KS | **B** | B- | C+ | 118.2 | -0.27 | 9.5 | 7.8 | 17.8 | 7.3 | **8.1** | 10.0 | 13.4 |
| ▲ Hamilton Bank | Hamilton | MO | **B** | C+ | B- | 79.1 | 2.37 | 3.9 | 3.1 | 18.2 | 27.3 | **8.8** | 10.2 | 14.0 |
| ▲ Hamler State Bank | Hamler | OH | **A-** | B+ | B+ | 85.8 | 5.39 | 6.6 | 1.1 | 16.5 | 22.1 | **10.0** | 16.4 | 24.3 |
| Hamlin Bank and Trust Co. | Smethport | PA | **A-** | B+ | A | 388.8 | -2.54 | 1.1 | 4.6 | 51.2 | 26.0 | **10.0** | 19.7 | 27.2 |
| Hancock Bank and Trust Co. | Hawesville | KY | **B-** | C+ | C | 288.9 | 0.51 | 6.6 | 1.4 | 24.6 | 6.3 | **10.0** | 11.0 | 15.8 |
| Hancock County Savings Bank, FSB | Chester | WV | **B** | B | B | 373.2 | 1.85 | 0.2 | 3.0 | 75.5 | 9.6 | **10.0** | 18.7 | 37.0 |
| Hancock Whitney Bank | Gulfport | MS | **B-** | C+ | C+ | 30597.2 | 8.44 | 22.5 | 3.4 | 11.3 | 20.6 | **5.7** | 9.0 | 11.5 |
| Hanmi Bank | Los Angeles | CA | **B+** | A- | A- | 5530.7 | 0.74 | 17.6 | 0.1 | 7.4 | 11.5 | **9.6** | 11.6 | 14.6 |
| Hanover Community Bank | Garden City Park | NY | **B+** | B+ | B- | 861.6 | 32.24 | 0.9 | 0.1 | 53.5 | 1.5 | **8.7** | 10.1 | 19.7 |
| Happy State Bank | Amarillo | TX | **A-** | A- | B+ | 3824.4 | 11.03 | 14.4 | 0.8 | 9.6 | 17.2 | **10.0** | 14.6 | 18.2 |
| Harbor Bank of Maryland | Baltimore | MD | **D-** | D- | D- | 311.3 | 10.26 | 9.3 | 0.9 | 15.6 | 9.8 | **4.6** | 6.6 | 11.4 |
| HarborOne Bank | Brockton | MA | **C+** | C | C | 3928.0 | 7.42 | 5.0 | 11.1 | 27.8 | 6.8 | **10.0** | 12.2 | 15.1 |
| Hardin County Bank | Savannah | TN | **C+** | C+ | C | 502.1 | 1.58 | 28.2 | 3.8 | 16.2 | 10.0 | **5.7** | 9.2 | 11.5 |
| ▲ Hardin County Savings Bank | Eldora | IA | **B** | B- | B- | 229.1 | 7.19 | 7.5 | 1.5 | 9.2 | 33.3 | **7.4** | 9.2 | 13.2 |
| Harford Bank | Aberdeen | MD | **B-** | C | C | 377.3 | 3.49 | 3.9 | 2.4 | 17.6 | 11.2 | **10.0** | 11.2 | 16.0 |
| ▲ Harleysville Bank | Harleysville | PA | **B** | B- | B- | 785.6 | 1.65 | 1.0 | 0.1 | 45.7 | 16.2 | **8.3** | 9.9 | 15.2 |
| Harrison Building and Loan Assn. | Harrison | OH | **B** | B- | B- | 227.2 | 2.44 | 2.2 | 0.1 | 36.4 | 35.6 | **10.0** | 15.5 | 32.0 |
| Harrison County Bank | Lost Creek | WV | **B** | B | B | 117.2 | 4.62 | 0.8 | 5.6 | 27.8 | 41.0 | **10.0** | 11.0 | 22.8 |
| Hart County Bank and Trust Co. | Munfordville | KY | **B** | B | B | 27.3 | 7.54 | 17.9 | 1.6 | 1.3 | 24.8 | **10.0** | 23.2 | 30.2 |
| Hartsburg State Bank | Hartsburg | IL | **C+** | C | C | 16.1 | -2.90 | 6.1 | 1.4 | 4.8 | 27.2 | **10.0** | 13.4 | 19.3 |
| Harvard State Bank | Harvard | IL | **B-** | B- | B- | 259.8 | 13.39 | 5.5 | 1.2 | 19.7 | 30.5 | **7.4** | 9.3 | 16.3 |
| Harvest Bank | Kimball | MN | **B-** | B | B- | 152.3 | 5.24 | 8.7 | 3.0 | 17.6 | 15.0 | **7.8** | 9.5 | 13.9 |
| Harwood State Bank | Harwood | ND | **C** | C- | C- | 41.6 | 1.45 | 10.5 | 2.9 | 1.9 | 3.9 | **7.9** | 9.6 | 15.1 |
| Haskell National Bank | Haskell | TX | **B** | B- | B- | 71.3 | 2.32 | 4.8 | 4.2 | 12.1 | 39.0 | **10.0** | 12.5 | 29.8 |
| Hatboro Federal Savings, FA | Hatboro | PA | **B** | B | B- | 517.3 | 3.54 | 0.0 | 0.0 | 67.1 | 15.8 | **10.0** | 23.1 | 44.7 |
| Hatch Bank | San Marcos | CA | **C+** | B | B+ | 68.5 | 4.15 | 0.0 | 49.7 | 34.7 | 0.0 | **10.0** | 39.6 | 46.2 |
| Havana National Bank | Havana | IL | **D+** | C- | B- | 256.2 | 6.95 | 7.4 | 1.4 | 8.0 | 17.5 | **9.8** | 11.0 | 14.8 |
| Haven Savings Bank | Hoboken | NJ | **C-** | C- | C | 995.7 | -2.05 | 0.5 | 0.0 | 58.0 | 10.1 | **8.9** | 10.3 | 17.7 |
| Haverford Trust Co. | Radnor | PA | **A** | A | A | 171.2 | 33.12 | 0.8 | 36.1 | 0.5 | 40.5 | **8.6** | 15.5 | 13.8 |
| Haverhill Bank | Haverhill | MA | **C+** | C | C | 415.9 | 5.49 | 10.7 | 0.2 | 44.6 | 16.3 | **9.6** | 10.7 | 16.9 |
| Haviland State Bank | Haviland | KS | **B** | B | B | 40.7 | 4.25 | 6.4 | 1.3 | 1.1 | 21.0 | **10.0** | 14.3 | 20.2 |
| Hawaii National Bank | Honolulu | HI | **C+** | C | C- | 665.0 | 4.06 | 20.5 | 0.4 | 17.5 | 15.9 | **8.0** | 9.7 | 14.3 |
| ▲ Hawthorn Bank | Jefferson City | MO | **A-** | B | B | 1483.7 | 0.67 | 10.0 | 2.2 | 15.0 | 11.7 | **9.3** | 11.2 | 14.4 |
| Headwaters State Bank | Land O'Lakes | WI | **B+** | B+ | B+ | 67.1 | -3.87 | 2.3 | 2.6 | 33.6 | 23.4 | **10.0** | 15.3 | 30.4 |
| Heartland Bank | Somers | IA | **A-** | B+ | A | 160.1 | 4.72 | 14.5 | 1.3 | 7.8 | 15.4 | **10.0** | 13.3 | 15.8 |
| ▲ Heartland Bank | Geneva | NE | **C+** | C+ | C+ | 619.9 | 40.17 | 5.3 | 1.2 | 2.2 | 16.7 | **7.6** | 10.0 | 13.0 |
| Heartland Bank | Whitehall | OH | **A-** | B+ | B | 1112.5 | 6.44 | 7.1 | 0.8 | 18.6 | 12.6 | **9.4** | 10.9 | 14.5 |
| Heartland Bank and Trust Co. | Bloomington | IL | **A-** | A- | A- | 2909.7 | 1.93 | 9.8 | 0.6 | 8.3 | 18.9 | **8.8** | 10.3 | 14.0 |
| Heartland National Bank | Sebring | FL | **A-** | B+ | B | 411.3 | 8.14 | 2.2 | 1.7 | 9.9 | 23.2 | **8.1** | 9.7 | 21.4 |
| ▲ Heartland State Bank | Edgeley | ND | **B-** | C+ | C+ | 60.4 | -5.61 | 2.6 | 2.4 | 0.8 | 21.1 | **10.0** | 11.1 | 16.9 |
| ▲ Heartland State Bank | Redfield | SD | **B-** | B | A- | 89.0 | 2.09 | 9.2 | 1.7 | 0.1 | 7.1 | **7.7** | 11.0 | 13.1 |
| Heartland Tri-State Bank | Elkhart | KS | **B-** | C+ | B | 122.0 | 30.27 | 3.0 | 2.7 | 3.0 | 30.2 | **7.6** | 9.4 | 16.5 |
| Hebron Savings Bank | Hebron | MD | **C-** | D+ | D+ | 604.4 | 1.70 | 7.5 | 0.8 | 25.5 | 5.5 | **7.0** | 9.7 | 12.5 |
| Helm Bank USA | Miami | FL | **B** | B | C+ | 841.7 | 8.39 | 0.6 | 1.5 | 59.9 | 27.2 | **10.0** | 11.8 | 28.8 |
| Henderson Federal Savings Bank | Henderson | TX | **B** | B | B+ | 106.1 | -0.69 | 2.6 | 4.3 | 55.0 | 10.5 | **10.0** | 22.3 | 45.2 |
| Henderson State Bank | Henderson | NE | **C-** | C- | D+ | 266.2 | -0.75 | 10.0 | 0.5 | 0.2 | 18.3 | **8.9** | 11.2 | 14.1 |
| ▼ Hendricks County Bank and Trust Co. | Brownsburg | IN | **C+** | B- | B- | 168.8 | 5.91 | 5.9 | 1.9 | 18.0 | 27.2 | **10.0** | 11.4 | 16.9 |
| Henry County Bank | Napoleon | OH | **C** | C | C | 286.2 | 3.08 | 3.3 | 4.1 | 11.7 | 45.6 | **8.4** | 9.9 | 20.1 |

| Asset Quality Index | Adjusted Non-Performing Loans as a % of Total Loans | Adjusted Non-Performing Loans as a % of Capital | Net Charge-Offs / Avg Loans | Profitability Index | Net Income ($Mil) | Return on Assets (R.O.A.) | Return on Equity (R.O.E.) | Net Interest Spread | Overhead Efficiency Ratio | Liquidity Index | Liquidity Ratio | Hot Money Ratio | Stability Index |
|---|---|---|---|---|---|---|---|---|---|---|---|---|---|
| **3.9** | 1.92 | 15.3 | 0.16 | **6.0** | 6.1 | 1.44 | 14.27 | 3.57 | 60.2 | **1.7** | 20.0 | 22.3 | **7.5** |
| **9.8** | 1.75 | 2.5 | 0.02 | **0.0** | -0.6 | -1.50 | -7.65 | 2.20 | 161.0 | **4.0** | 78.8 | 23.2 | **6.5** |
| **5.9** | 0.83 | 3.8 | -0.04 | **7.9** | 18.7 | 1.92 | 15.85 | 2.59 | 46.4 | **1.5** | 25.1 | 28.2 | **10.0** |
| **7.6** | 0.78 | 4.1 | 0.03 | **3.8** | 6.3 | 0.77 | 6.35 | 3.12 | 79.5 | **2.7** | 19.7 | 16.1 | **8.0** |
| **5.8** | 1.16 | 5.0 | 0.12 | **6.2** | 4.4 | 1.17 | 8.45 | 4.73 | 73.6 | **4.6** | 28.4 | 7.3 | **7.7** |
| **4.1** | 1.70 | 14.9 | 0.23 | **7.3** | 27.1 | 1.53 | 16.73 | 7.62 | 76.4 | **1.9** | 19.7 | 16.4 | **8.7** |
| **8.9** | 0.09 | 0.3 | -0.01 | **9.1** | 1.9 | 1.70 | 17.89 | 5.19 | 63.1 | **3.7** | 27.2 | 9.2 | **6.5** |
| **9.8** | 0.37 | 1.7 | 0.00 | **3.4** | 0.7 | 0.68 | 5.50 | 3.15 | 73.2 | **3.1** | 45.5 | 23.1 | **6.6** |
| **8.2** | 0.49 | 2.0 | 0.00 | **3.7** | 0.9 | 0.71 | 6.20 | 3.99 | 81.3 | **3.9** | 13.0 | 9.3 | **6.4** |
| **8.2** | 0.34 | 1.1 | 0.08 | **5.1** | 0.7 | 1.20 | 7.54 | 3.78 | 66.7 | **1.5** | 25.8 | 28.2 | **8.3** |
| **8.8** | 0.18 | 1.0 | 0.03 | **7.0** | 21.8 | 1.22 | 14.36 | 2.11 | 48.7 | **2.8** | 48.4 | 49.7 | **7.6** |
| **8.5** | 0.78 | 2.7 | 0.29 | **2.4** | 0.8 | 0.25 | 2.53 | 1.87 | 80.7 | **2.9** | 50.6 | 15.8 | **5.1** |
| **7.2** | 0.26 | 1.9 | 0.06 | **5.2** | 1.4 | 1.17 | 12.34 | 4.30 | 70.4 | **1.9** | 9.6 | 10.5 | **5.6** |
| **5.0** | 0.32 | 7.5 | 0.16 | **6.6** | 1.3 | 1.58 | 15.58 | 4.32 | 64.2 | **3.5** | 24.5 | 12.6 | **6.9** |
| **8.7** | 0.03 | 0.1 | 0.00 | **5.5** | 1.2 | 1.40 | 8.83 | 3.32 | 56.4 | **2.3** | 26.8 | 19.2 | **8.6** |
| **6.9** | 0.70 | 4.8 | 0.52 | **7.6** | 9.0 | 2.28 | 10.26 | 3.95 | 57.2 | **4.8** | 40.3 | 11.0 | **7.9** |
| **5.2** | 1.37 | 6.0 | -0.04 | **3.6** | 2.2 | 0.75 | 6.65 | 3.85 | 82.6 | **2.7** | 10.7 | 15.3 | **6.0** |
| **8.7** | 0.98 | 3.1 | 0.03 | **4.8** | 3.4 | 0.91 | 4.94 | 3.51 | 69.5 | **3.2** | 15.2 | 12.8 | **7.9** |
| **4.0** | 1.41 | 7.7 | 0.23 | **5.4** | 337.0 | 1.16 | 10.17 | 3.46 | 62.9 | **3.8** | 12.9 | 9.4 | **9.7** |
| **4.6** | 1.40 | 8.8 | 0.02 | **5.4** | 41.3 | 0.76 | 6.23 | 3.53 | 57.2 | **0.9** | 14.9 | 29.7 | **10.0** |
| **9.0** | 0.21 | 1.4 | 0.00 | **6.4** | 8.2 | 2.52 | 25.70 | 7.73 | 60.9 | **0.7** | 13.5 | 39.3 | **7.5** |
| **5.9** | 1.66 | 6.8 | 0.30 | **5.6** | 47.6 | 1.34 | 8.80 | 4.40 | 65.6 | **1.8** | 13.4 | 7.1 | **9.6** |
| **2.2** | 4.07 | 27.6 | 0.12 | **0.2** | -2.5 | -0.83 | -11.76 | 3.36 | 115.9 | **1.6** | 26.8 | 27.7 | **2.0** |
| **4.3** | 1.37 | 6.6 | 0.04 | **3.2** | 21.0 | 0.57 | 4.85 | 3.21 | 82.7 | **2.2** | 10.1 | 15.0 | **8.1** |
| **3.9** | 1.65 | 12.0 | 0.08 | **5.6** | 5.4 | 1.07 | 11.61 | 3.77 | 64.4 | **0.6** | 4.7 | 28.5 | **5.6** |
| **8.6** | 0.17 | 1.1 | -0.04 | **5.0** | 2.7 | 1.27 | 14.37 | 3.01 | 60.0 | **2.1** | 28.0 | 21.7 | **5.5** |
| **3.7** | 1.75 | 11.0 | 0.00 | **4.7** | 3.3 | 0.88 | 7.98 | 3.82 | 69.7 | **2.0** | 16.7 | 17.9 | **6.9** |
| **5.2** | 1.30 | 9.0 | 0.04 | **5.3** | 8.6 | 1.10 | 11.48 | 3.20 | 55.1 | **3.9** | 17.3 | 9.8 | **6.5** |
| **6.5** | 2.15 | 9.0 | 0.00 | **4.0** | 1.7 | 0.74 | 4.62 | 4.07 | 75.4 | **4.5** | 47.6 | 14.5 | **7.3** |
| **8.1** | 0.00 | 1.9 | -0.07 | **4.7** | 1.2 | 1.02 | 9.40 | 3.75 | 70.6 | **5.9** | 50.5 | 7.8 | **6.3** |
| **8.5** | 0.00 | 0.0 | -0.08 | **5.7** | 0.4 | 1.37 | 5.80 | 3.99 | 65.5 | **5.5** | 43.5 | 7.2 | **7.9** |
| **8.7** | 0.00 | 0.7 | -0.43 | **4.1** | 0.1 | 0.92 | 7.11 | 3.51 | 74.5 | **1.7** | 25.4 | 23.0 | **6.1** |
| **3.4** | 3.14 | 17.6 | 0.34 | **3.2** | 1.7 | 0.67 | 6.43 | 3.27 | 78.5 | **2.8** | 23.8 | 16.0 | **5.0** |
| **2.8** | 3.75 | 22.1 | -0.01 | **6.4** | 2.2 | 1.53 | 15.95 | 4.10 | 62.7 | **4.6** | 19.4 | 5.1 | **6.3** |
| **7.0** | 0.14 | 0.4 | -0.01 | **3.7** | 0.2 | 0.58 | 6.15 | 3.60 | 78.1 | **3.4** | 42.0 | 18.5 | **4.7** |
| **9.0** | 0.05 | 0.1 | 0.08 | **3.7** | 0.5 | 0.67 | 5.36 | 3.56 | 83.2 | **5.6** | 57.1 | 9.8 | **6.6** |
| **6.6** | 3.88 | 8.6 | -0.02 | **4.4** | 4.8 | 0.93 | 4.09 | 2.87 | 58.5 | **1.3** | 24.9 | 30.4 | **8.7** |
| **5.7** | 0.00 | 0.2 | 1.00 | **0.9** | -0.4 | -0.58 | -1.38 | 3.03 | 94.2 | **0.5** | 24.1 | 97.7 | **6.6** |
| **1.9** | 1.51 | 18.4 | 0.60 | **5.8** | 2.8 | 1.10 | 9.92 | 3.65 | 53.5 | **2.7** | 11.4 | 14.9 | **7.2** |
| **6.3** | 0.62 | 4.8 | 0.02 | **2.0** | 1.2 | 0.12 | 1.14 | 2.14 | 92.7 | **0.6** | 12.8 | 42.3 | **7.6** |
| **6.8** | 0.00 | 0.0 | 0.00 | **9.5** | 7.9 | 5.51 | 30.90 | 1.46 | 82.7 | **2.8** | 65.1 | 83.4 | **9.5** |
| **8.0** | 0.24 | 1.5 | 0.07 | **3.3** | 2.3 | 0.57 | 5.23 | 3.27 | 79.2 | **1.5** | 24.5 | 27.1 | **6.4** |
| **7.3** | 0.00 | 0.0 | 0.00 | **5.9** | 0.5 | 1.19 | 8.34 | 4.27 | 63.2 | **3.6** | 14.8 | 10.9 | **8.1** |
| **6.2** | 1.03 | 6.8 | 0.02 | **3.5** | 3.7 | 0.58 | 5.84 | 4.17 | 84.2 | **4.7** | 26.3 | 6.2 | **5.8** |
| **7.1** | 0.62 | 3.4 | 0.03 | **6.1** | 18.8 | 1.28 | 12.02 | 3.64 | 60.2 | **2.0** | 9.0 | 15.3 | **8.8** |
| **7.2** | 1.02 | 3.8 | 0.21 | **5.9** | 1.0 | 1.43 | 9.51 | 4.03 | 66.0 | **5.0** | 46.2 | 11.2 | **8.4** |
| **6.1** | 0.17 | 0.9 | -0.05 | **9.1** | 3.3 | 2.17 | 15.88 | 4.58 | 54.0 | **1.3** | 8.0 | 20.8 | **9.6** |
| **4.4** | 0.89 | 4.0 | 0.01 | **7.8** | 9.0 | 1.47 | 12.08 | 4.03 | 56.2 | **3.6** | 18.7 | 11.2 | **8.6** |
| **8.5** | 0.24 | 1.7 | 0.03 | **6.1** | 13.6 | 1.23 | 11.34 | 3.93 | 61.1 | **1.7** | 10.2 | 19.6 | **9.1** |
| **5.9** | 0.97 | 5.3 | 0.09 | **9.6** | 64.1 | 2.23 | 19.10 | 4.56 | 52.8 | **5.2** | 23.0 | 4.2 | **9.5** |
| **9.2** | 0.10 | 0.4 | -0.04 | **6.3** | 5.2 | 1.30 | 13.53 | 3.28 | 52.1 | **6.3** | 60.2 | 8.4 | **6.2** |
| **6.1** | 0.01 | 0.0 | 0.09 | **4.4** | 0.6 | 0.98 | 7.82 | 3.91 | 75.0 | **1.8** | 17.5 | 17.2 | **6.7** |
| **6.9** | 0.00 | 0.0 | 0.68 | **8.9** | 1.5 | 1.74 | 14.76 | 5.31 | 57.1 | **1.4** | 14.6 | 18.0 | **8.8** |
| **5.0** | 0.50 | 7.5 | 0.05 | **4.4** | 0.9 | 0.84 | 8.44 | 3.70 | 72.9 | **2.7** | 22.3 | 16.1 | **6.0** |
| **2.3** | 3.60 | 21.0 | 0.25 | **4.8** | 5.6 | 0.93 | 9.77 | 3.87 | 63.8 | **1.5** | 8.3 | 21.6 | **6.3** |
| **6.2** | 2.78 | 10.8 | 0.00 | **4.2** | 6.7 | 0.80 | 6.87 | 3.68 | 76.0 | **2.8** | 41.4 | 24.7 | **8.0** |
| **5.7** | 2.40 | 7.5 | 0.35 | **4.8** | 1.0 | 0.96 | 4.37 | 3.74 | 60.6 | **0.8** | 18.7 | 43.7 | **8.1** |
| **4.5** | 0.25 | 2.4 | 1.86 | **4.7** | 1.8 | 0.66 | 5.95 | 3.65 | 45.9 | **0.5** | 15.2 | 52.6 | **7.9** |
| **7.6** | 1.05 | 5.2 | 0.01 | **2.2** | 0.1 | 0.08 | 0.68 | 3.86 | 93.7 | **3.5** | 29.2 | 13.9 | **6.3** |
| **5.2** | 3.74 | 9.4 | 0.05 | **2.9** | 1.3 | 0.46 | 4.59 | 3.05 | 83.7 | **1.1** | 27.7 | 31.4 | **4.5** |

| Name | City | State | Rating | 2018 Rating | 2017 Rating | Total Assets ($Mil) | One Year Asset Growth | Asset Mix (As a % of Total Assets) Comm-ercial Loans | Cons-umer Loans | Mort-gage Loans | Secur-ities | Capital-ization Index | Lever-age Ratio | Risk-Based Capital Ratio |
|---|---|---|---|---|---|---|---|---|---|---|---|---|---|---|
| Heritage Bank | Marion | IA | C- | D+ | D+ | 34.5 | -3.39 | 6.0 | 2.2 | 21.1 | 35.9 | 9.8 | 10.8 | 24.5 |
| Heritage Bank | Topeka | KS | C | C- | C+ | 64.3 | 6.10 | 10.9 | 1.3 | 21.2 | 5.0 | 8.5 | 10.2 | 13.8 |
| Heritage Bank | Wood River | NE | A | B+ | A | 519.9 | -1.26 | 4.3 | 1.0 | 3.3 | 50.7 | 10.0 | 15.9 | 27.2 |
| Heritage Bank | Olympia | WA | B+ | B | B | 5550.7 | 4.45 | 9.5 | 5.4 | 4.5 | 17.2 | 6.7 | 10.2 | 12.3 |
| Heritage Bank & Trust | Columbia | TN | B- | C+ | B- | 184.8 | 15.62 | 5.9 | 1.8 | 27.1 | 12.4 | 6.2 | 8.8 | 11.9 |
| ▼ Heritage Bank Minnesota | West Concord | MN | C+ | B- | C+ | 57.3 | 6.99 | 7.1 | 7.3 | 36.2 | 7.9 | 8.6 | 10.1 | 15.2 |
| Heritage Bank of Commerce | San Jose | CA | A- | A- | A- | 4108.1 | 32.72 | 14.2 | 0.5 | 2.5 | 18.8 | 8.7 | 10.2 | 13.9 |
| ▲ Heritage Bank of Schaumburg | Schaumburg | IL | B- | C | C- | 133.5 | -8.94 | 3.2 | 0.0 | 9.9 | 14.8 | 7.6 | 9.4 | 23.0 |
| Heritage Bank of St. Tammany | Covington | LA | B- | B- | C+ | 131.4 | 9.93 | 1.8 | 0.2 | 51.8 | 5.0 | 10.0 | 14.6 | 25.1 |
| Heritage Bank of the Ozarks | Lebanon | MO | B- | B- | B- | 163.4 | 12.16 | 4.9 | 3.1 | 17.1 | 16.4 | 6.9 | 8.9 | 12.9 |
| Heritage Bank, Inc. | Burlington | KY | C+ | C+ | B- | 975.7 | 8.61 | 9.3 | 0.6 | 9.3 | 15.3 | 6.0 | 8.6 | 11.8 |
| ▲ Heritage Bank, N.A. | Spicer | MN | C | C- | C+ | 403.1 | -7.30 | 7.9 | 2.8 | 15.8 | 12.7 | 8.1 | 9.7 | 14.4 |
| Heritage Community Bank | Chamois | MO | B- | B- | B | 146.2 | 2.67 | 12.1 | 1.6 | 26.3 | 4.6 | 7.6 | 9.7 | 13.0 |
| Heritage Community Bank | Greeneville | TN | B- | B- | C+ | 121.0 | 14.46 | 5.9 | 4.8 | 36.7 | 2.9 | 8.0 | 9.7 | 15.3 |
| Heritage First Bank | Rome | GA | B- | B- | B- | 147.7 | 10.65 | 10.0 | 4.4 | 17.7 | 8.3 | 8.5 | 11.0 | 13.7 |
| Heritage Southeast Bank | Jonesboro | GA | C+ | B- | B- | 1336.8 | 160.56 | 11.4 | 1.3 | 9.2 | 9.4 | 5.0 | 8.7 | 11.0 |
| Heritage State Bank | Lawrenceville | IL | C- | C- | B | 79.9 | -13.53 | 3.5 | 0.0 | 0.6 | 0.0 | 9.5 | 12.0 | 14.6 |
| Herring Bank | Amarillo | TX | C+ | B- | B | 445.4 | 8.83 | 10.0 | 5.7 | 8.3 | 10.1 | 8.1 | 9.9 | 13.4 |
| Hershey State Bank | Hershey | NE | B+ | B+ | A- | 77.4 | 1.76 | 12.0 | 7.3 | 18.6 | 5.1 | 10.0 | 13.4 | 18.0 |
| Hertford Savings Bank, SSB | Hertford | NC | C | C | C | 13.0 | -0.68 | 0.0 | 3.3 | 58.8 | 0.1 | 10.0 | 16.7 | 28.8 |
| Hiawatha Bank and Trust Co. | Hiawatha | IA | B | B- | B- | 53.2 | -0.07 | 7.1 | 1.7 | 35.4 | 0.5 | 10.0 | 12.2 | 17.1 |
| Hiawatha National Bank | Hager City | WI | C | C | C | 228.2 | 8.47 | 14.6 | 1.2 | 11.2 | 10.0 | 7.7 | 9.6 | 13.1 |
| Hibernia Bank | New Orleans | LA | B- | C | C | 203.1 | 4.65 | 1.4 | 0.1 | 46.5 | 3.6 | 10.0 | 13.4 | 21.3 |
| Hickory Point Bank and Trust | Decatur | IL | B | B- | B- | 635.0 | -1.68 | 9.6 | 0.9 | 6.5 | 17.9 | 8.7 | 10.6 | 14.0 |
| ▲ Hicksville Bank | Hicksville | OH | B | B- | B- | 119.6 | 6.08 | 5.6 | 1.6 | 17.6 | 31.6 | 10.0 | 13.1 | 21.7 |
| High Country Bank | Salida | CO | A- | A- | A- | 292.7 | 9.42 | 9.4 | 0.8 | 27.3 | 10.3 | 6.8 | 9.6 | 12.4 |
| High Plains Bank | Flagler | CO | A- | A- | A- | 193.8 | 9.60 | 6.3 | 1.2 | 15.4 | 6.4 | 9.0 | 10.3 | 14.2 |
| ▲ High Plains Bank | Keyes | OK | B | B- | B+ | 142.1 | 49.29 | 7.0 | 2.8 | 7.2 | 10.4 | 9.9 | 11.3 | 14.9 |
| Highland Bank | Saint Michael | MN | B | B- | B- | 518.8 | 0.61 | 19.3 | 0.4 | 6.5 | 27.0 | 9.0 | 10.4 | 14.2 |
| Highland Federal S&L Assn. | Crossville | TN | C+ | C | C- | 61.5 | 1.89 | 0.0 | 0.1 | 33.9 | 1.5 | 10.0 | 22.8 | 49.7 |
| ▲ Highland State Bank | Highland | WI | B | C+ | C+ | 34.2 | -0.77 | 3.0 | 6.1 | 27.0 | 6.2 | 10.0 | 11.4 | 26.9 |
| Highlands Community Bank | Covington | VA | B+ | B | B+ | 152.7 | 6.32 | 5.4 | 15.0 | 20.4 | 31.6 | 10.0 | 13.1 | 19.9 |
| Highpoint Community Bank | Hastings | MI | C+ | C+ | C+ | 324.6 | 1.83 | 3.5 | 3.6 | 29.4 | 15.9 | 8.4 | 9.9 | 17.5 |
| Hill Bank & Trust Co. | Weimar | TX | B | B | B | 143.3 | 3.62 | 1.2 | 0.8 | 3.2 | 83.8 | 10.0 | 16.8 | 26.5 |
| Hill-Dodge Banking Co. | Warsaw | IL | B- | B- | B- | 43.8 | -2.20 | 13.7 | 3.6 | 4.1 | 4.0 | 10.0 | 14.2 | 22.8 |
| Hills Bank and Trust Co. | Hills | IA | A | A | A | 3299.6 | 8.49 | 6.7 | 1.0 | 30.1 | 10.8 | 10.0 | 12.8 | 18.2 |
| Hillsboro Bank | Plant City | FL | A | A | A | 153.5 | 6.62 | 6.3 | 1.2 | 21.2 | 19.5 | 10.0 | 13.7 | 25.2 |
| ▲ Hillsboro State Bank | Hillsboro | KS | C- | D | D | 17.3 | -9.76 | 8.8 | 1.7 | 14.4 | 8.4 | 8.6 | 10.0 | 17.9 |
| Hilltop National Bank | Casper | WY | A- | B+ | B+ | 778.2 | -3.92 | 4.3 | 2.3 | 12.1 | 49.6 | 10.0 | 12.2 | 29.8 |
| ▲ Hingham Institution for Savings | Hingham | MA | A- | B+ | B+ | 2590.4 | 7.55 | 0.0 | 0.0 | 39.5 | 0.0 | 8.3 | 9.8 | 13.6 |
| Hinsdale Bank & Trust Co., N.A. | Hinsdale | IL | B | B | B- | 3306.8 | 34.51 | 27.5 | 9.6 | 6.3 | 12.5 | 7.1 | 11.1 | 12.6 |
| HNB First Bank | Headland | AL | A- | B+ | B | 163.6 | 9.49 | 10.0 | 2.9 | 15.9 | 10.0 | 8.4 | 9.9 | 14.3 |
| ▲ HNB National Bank | Hannibal | MO | A | B+ | A | 517.7 | 10.20 | 5.4 | 1.6 | 17.0 | 6.4 | 10.0 | 13.5 | 18.8 |
| Hocking Valley Bank | Athens | OH | B | B | B- | 268.3 | 2.63 | 5.6 | 1.0 | 30.7 | 18.5 | 9.6 | 10.8 | 18.2 |
| ▲ Hodge Bank & Trust Co. | Hodge | LA | B | B- | B+ | 71.4 | 3.23 | 13.3 | 9.2 | 29.5 | 11.9 | 10.0 | 19.1 | 33.1 |
| Holcomb Bank | Rochelle | IL | C+ | C | C- | 191.7 | 3.32 | 14.2 | 2.0 | 14.3 | 15.8 | 9.1 | 10.4 | 14.5 |
| Holladay Bank & Trust | Salt Lake City | UT | A- | A- | A- | 57.0 | -5.16 | 5.3 | 4.1 | 12.4 | 3.3 | 10.0 | 16.7 | 28.2 |
| Holmes County Bank & Trust Co. | Lexington | MS | B | B- | C | 120.1 | 2.84 | 9.2 | 2.6 | 7.1 | 37.9 | 10.0 | 13.0 | 27.5 |
| Home Bank and Trust Co. | Eureka | KS | B- | C+ | C+ | 111.7 | 7.10 | 11.8 | 3.3 | 33.6 | 4.0 | 5.1 | 8.1 | 11.1 |
| ▲ Home Bank of California | San Diego | CA | A | B+ | A | 177.4 | 8.35 | 0.6 | 0.0 | 26.8 | 0.0 | 10.0 | 13.9 | 18.5 |
| Home Bank SB | Martinsville | IN | B- | B- | B- | 329.9 | 10.04 | 3.2 | 1.0 | 31.1 | 23.7 | 10.0 | 12.0 | 20.6 |
| Home Bank, N.A. | Lafayette | LA | B | B- | B | 2195.9 | 2.13 | 7.4 | 2.1 | 20.6 | 12.1 | 10.0 | 11.2 | 15.3 |
| Home Banking Co. | Selmer | TN | C+ | C+ | C+ | 91.2 | -0.82 | 7.9 | 6.7 | 12.1 | 39.9 | 10.0 | 11.1 | 18.9 |
| Home Exchange Bank | Jamesport | MO | A- | A | A | 170.4 | 3.05 | 3.2 | 0.4 | 3.2 | 47.5 | 9.8 | 10.9 | 22.4 |
| Home Federal Bank | Shreveport | LA | B+ | B+ | B+ | 455.8 | 7.00 | 7.8 | 0.1 | 28.6 | 16.8 | 10.0 | 11.1 | 17.5 |
| Home Federal Bank Corp. | Middlesboro | KY | B | B | B | 389.9 | 2.24 | 3.5 | 1.9 | 41.9 | 17.5 | 10.0 | 11.6 | 18.5 |
| Home Federal Bank of Hollywood | Hallandale Beach | FL | D | D | D | 56.0 | 6.71 | 6.4 | 0.0 | 50.6 | 4.1 | 10.0 | 11.7 | 19.9 |
| Home Federal Bank of Tennessee | Knoxville | TN | B | B | B | 2259.9 | 4.99 | 1.9 | 0.4 | 19.9 | 46.8 | 10.0 | 18.8 | 33.7 |
| Home Federal S&L Assn. | Bamberg | SC | C+ | C+ | B- | 42.0 | 5.60 | 0.0 | 3.7 | 62.6 | 2.0 | 10.0 | 12.7 | 23.3 |
| Home Federal S&L Assn. of Grand Island | Grand Island | NE | B- | C+ | B- | 292.1 | 3.58 | 10.5 | 4.5 | 12.8 | 24.0 | 10.0 | 12.5 | 17.8 |

**Arrows denote recent upgrades ▲ or downgrades ▼**

| Asset Quality Index | Adjusted Non-Performing Loans as a % of Total Loans | Adjusted Non-Performing Loans as a % of Capital | Net Charge-Offs Avg Loans | Profitability Index | Net Income ($Mil) | Return on Assets (R.O.A.) | Return on Equity (R.O.E.) | Net Interest Spread | Overhead Efficiency Ratio | Liquidity Index | Liquidity Ratio | Hot Money Ratio | Stability Index |
|---|---|---|---|---|---|---|---|---|---|---|---|---|---|
| **7.1** | 0.67 | 3.1 | 0.16 | **2.1** | 0.1 | 0.22 | 2.22 | 3.75 | 92.5 | **5.6** | 49.2 | 7.9 | **4.7** |
| **5.7** | 0.75 | 2.8 | 0.10 | **2.9** | 0.3 | 0.50 | 4.87 | 3.88 | 86.0 | **1.0** | 17.7 | 33.3 | **4.6** |
| **8.9** | 0.17 | 0.5 | 0.03 | **9.2** | 10.0 | 1.93 | 12.66 | 3.42 | 39.0 | **5.2** | 31.0 | 2.9 | **10.0** |
| **4.7** | 1.56 | 5.9 | 0.09 | **6.3** | 72.2 | 1.34 | 9.08 | 4.27 | 61.0 | **4.3** | 20.0 | 7.7 | **9.8** |
| **6.0** | 0.45 | 3.5 | -0.33 | **4.4** | 1.7 | 0.97 | 11.11 | 3.81 | 77.3 | **1.4** | 16.3 | 23.2 | **5.5** |
| **6.8** | 0.54 | 3.5 | 0.17 | **3.0** | 0.3 | 0.46 | 4.45 | 4.44 | 87.4 | **4.3** | 8.2 | 5.7 | **5.6** |
| **6.5** | 0.36 | 1.5 | 0.27 | **7.2** | 44.3 | 1.31 | 10.38 | 4.37 | 57.0 | **6.1** | 34.0 | 4.3 | **9.9** |
| **4.3** | 0.76 | 2.7 | -0.01 | **4.4** | 1.6 | 1.15 | 8.05 | 3.32 | 62.3 | **5.6** | 40.7 | 6.5 | **7.6** |
| **8.5** | 0.73 | 3.8 | 0.01 | **3.3** | 0.7 | 0.58 | 3.93 | 3.37 | 79.8 | **0.8** | 16.8 | 37.7 | **7.3** |
| **6.5** | 0.45 | 3.6 | 0.07 | **5.0** | 1.4 | 0.92 | 10.67 | 4.17 | 71.4 | **0.8** | 17.9 | 25.5 | **5.7** |
| **4.0** | 1.75 | 7.1 | 0.03 | **4.9** | 9.3 | 1.03 | 11.28 | 3.75 | 68.9 | **3.3** | 19.2 | 12.7 | **5.8** |
| **3.4** | 1.48 | 8.1 | 0.27 | **7.2** | 10.2 | 2.37 | 25.11 | 4.11 | 61.3 | **1.8** | 16.5 | 11.7 | **5.5** |
| **4.8** | 1.10 | 10.1 | 0.01 | **4.9** | 1.6 | 1.07 | 11.23 | 3.95 | 71.5 | **1.2** | 7.4 | 27.0 | **5.8** |
| **7.3** | 0.20 | 1.4 | 0.00 | **4.0** | 0.9 | 0.79 | 8.13 | 3.93 | 79.9 | **0.9** | 12.6 | 32.2 | **5.8** |
| **4.3** | 1.62 | 10.8 | 0.21 | **4.7** | 1.4 | 1.03 | 9.41 | 5.19 | 76.4 | **1.6** | 15.2 | 22.9 | **6.0** |
| **5.2** | 1.63 | 6.4 | 0.07 | **3.2** | 2.6 | 0.32 | 2.94 | 4.47 | 86.8 | **2.1** | 15.4 | 19.0 | **8.0** |
| **0.6** | 3.97 | 23.6 | 2.91 | **1.1** | -1.3 | -1.48 | -13.26 | 4.34 | 63.4 | **3.5** | 11.9 | 11.0 | **6.8** |
| **5.1** | 1.00 | 5.1 | 0.18 | **3.3** | 2.5 | 0.58 | 6.24 | 4.25 | 88.7 | **2.9** | 19.8 | 15.1 | **5.9** |
| **5.6** | 2.05 | 3.3 | -0.02 | **6.7** | 0.5 | 1.58 | 9.05 | 5.61 | 56.8 | **0.5** | 10.7 | 48.9 | **8.3** |
| **5.7** | 1.94 | 11.0 | 0.00 | **2.7** | 0.0 | 0.14 | 0.83 | 3.90 | 91.1 | **1.5** | 17.9 | 24.7 | **6.6** |
| **7.9** | 0.00 | 0.0 | 0.04 | **6.3** | 0.6 | 1.16 | 9.83 | 4.02 | 61.6 | **0.5** | 2.2 | 12.7 | **7.0** |
| **2.3** | 6.19 | 24.1 | 0.03 | **3.4** | 1.5 | 0.69 | 6.68 | 3.67 | 78.0 | **0.9** | 9.5 | 13.7 | **5.3** |
| **7.1** | 0.42 | 1.9 | 0.00 | **3.2** | 0.3 | 0.16 | 0.95 | 3.33 | 90.3 | **0.7** | 14.4 | 41.5 | **7.3** |
| **5.8** | 0.87 | 4.7 | 0.00 | **5.0** | 6.5 | 1.02 | 9.62 | 3.59 | 70.6 | **3.7** | 11.0 | 10.1 | **7.1** |
| **5.7** | 1.92 | 7.9 | -0.01 | **4.1** | 1.0 | 0.81 | 6.05 | 3.88 | 75.3 | **3.9** | 23.8 | 10.5 | **7.2** |
| **7.1** | 0.00 | 0.0 | 0.00 | **9.3** | 4.8 | 1.72 | 18.44 | 5.64 | 61.6 | **4.2** | 8.4 | 6.3 | **6.8** |
| **8.1** | 0.13 | 0.8 | 0.00 | **6.8** | 2.9 | 1.57 | 15.48 | 5.17 | 66.7 | **3.0** | 15.4 | 12.7 | **7.9** |
| **5.5** | 0.59 | 3.3 | 0.59 | **6.5** | 1.8 | 1.35 | 12.09 | 4.38 | 59.2 | **0.8** | 20.4 | 42.1 | **8.1** |
| **5.5** | 1.06 | 6.0 | 0.05 | **4.6** | 5.4 | 1.03 | 9.54 | 4.02 | 73.5 | **3.5** | 25.9 | 6.2 | **7.9** |
| **9.8** | 0.10 | 0.8 | 0.00 | **3.2** | 0.3 | 0.53 | 2.32 | 3.80 | 84.2 | **5.0** | 49.5 | 11.5 | **7.1** |
| **8.1** | 0.22 | 0.9 | -0.03 | **4.6** | 0.4 | 1.10 | 9.97 | 3.74 | 71.2 | **5.7** | 49.7 | 7.7 | **5.8** |
| **5.0** | 1.56 | 7.9 | 0.18 | **5.4** | 1.6 | 1.10 | 8.18 | 4.25 | 68.1 | **2.5** | 40.8 | 27.9 | **7.6** |
| **8.0** | 0.43 | 1.4 | 0.01 | **3.8** | 2.3 | 0.73 | 7.24 | 3.68 | 80.9 | **5.1** | 27.9 | 3.8 | **5.7** |
| **9.7** | 0.00 | 0.0 | 0.00 | **4.8** | 1.6 | 1.15 | 6.65 | 2.44 | 52.4 | **4.9** | 95.9 | 20.0 | **8.5** |
| **5.5** | 1.39 | 5.2 | 2.15 | **3.1** | 0.2 | 0.49 | 3.21 | 3.90 | 60.7 | **6.0** | 51.2 | 6.1 | **6.9** |
| **7.7** | 0.71 | 3.3 | 0.04 | **6.9** | 45.8 | 1.41 | 11.30 | 3.12 | 54.6 | **2.9** | 20.4 | 11.3 | **10.0** |
| **9.1** | 0.24 | 0.6 | 0.01 | **8.3** | 2.3 | 1.57 | 11.44 | 4.13 | 50.6 | **4.5** | 49.5 | 14.8 | **9.0** |
| **6.7** | 10.41 | 6.4 | 0.01 | **2.6** | 0.1 | 0.37 | 3.86 | 3.25 | 86.7 | **6.0** | 50.5 | 3.6 | **3.8** |
| **9.4** | 1.16 | 2.1 | 0.02 | **5.5** | 10.8 | 1.41 | 11.76 | 3.08 | 65.1 | **6.4** | 61.4 | 7.6 | **8.1** |
| **7.8** | 0.31 | 2.4 | 0.00 | **8.1** | 38.9 | 1.55 | 16.94 | 2.70 | 30.3 | **0.7** | 12.8 | 32.8 | **8.2** |
| **5.3** | 0.42 | 4.1 | 0.17 | **8.1** | 38.5 | 1.45 | 11.18 | 3.61 | 47.2 | **1.7** | 16.4 | 15.8 | **8.6** |
| **8.3** | 0.08 | 0.6 | -0.02 | **6.2** | 2.3 | 1.46 | 14.40 | 3.92 | 64.0 | **1.6** | 17.4 | 23.1 | **6.8** |
| **7.6** | 0.75 | 2.7 | -0.01 | **10.0** | 12.9 | 2.64 | 19.34 | 4.46 | 50.2 | **3.3** | 19.9 | 13.1 | **9.5** |
| **7.8** | 0.33 | 2.6 | 0.08 | **5.0** | 2.9 | 1.06 | 9.95 | 3.63 | 66.8 | **3.9** | 17.2 | 9.6 | **6.8** |
| **4.4** | 3.80 | 11.1 | 0.55 | **10.0** | 2.0 | 2.85 | 15.24 | 5.12 | 43.0 | **1.9** | 28.3 | 25.4 | **8.9** |
| **4.6** | 1.72 | 8.7 | 0.12 | **3.5** | 1.2 | 0.65 | 6.33 | 3.77 | 78.4 | **2.1** | 20.6 | 19.2 | **5.0** |
| **7.6** | 0.68 | 1.2 | -0.04 | **8.2** | 0.8 | 1.36 | 8.25 | 5.15 | 64.8 | **2.6** | 36.6 | 21.9 | **7.9** |
| **4.5** | 7.68 | 17.5 | 0.64 | **4.4** | 1.5 | 1.25 | 9.79 | 3.35 | 69.1 | **3.2** | 32.9 | 16.8 | **6.7** |
| **8.2** | 0.00 | 0.0 | 0.03 | **5.7** | 1.4 | 1.38 | 17.22 | 4.21 | 71.1 | **1.4** | 11.8 | 24.8 | **5.5** |
| **7.6** | 0.00 | 0.0 | 0.00 | **10.0** | 4.8 | 2.74 | 19.62 | 4.80 | 40.7 | **0.5** | 8.8 | 57.4 | **10.0** |
| **6.4** | 1.00 | 5.5 | 0.14 | **3.6** | 2.1 | 0.67 | 5.32 | 3.65 | 83.0 | **4.7** | 38.4 | 11.1 | **7.0** |
| **4.1** | 1.55 | 8.6 | 0.09 | **6.5** | 28.1 | 1.28 | 9.35 | 4.31 | 63.2 | **3.3** | 7.8 | 11.9 | **10.0** |
| **7.5** | 0.92 | 3.9 | 0.01 | **2.8** | 0.3 | 0.30 | 2.74 | 3.76 | 87.9 | **3.7** | 48.9 | 18.0 | **5.7** |
| **9.2** | 0.00 | 0.0 | 0.00 | **5.9** | 2.3 | 1.36 | 12.44 | 2.64 | 46.0 | **2.0** | 43.4 | 12.7 | **9.5** |
| **6.2** | 1.99 | 9.0 | 0.41 | **5.4** | 4.5 | 1.00 | 8.92 | 3.60 | 62.1 | **1.3** | 22.1 | 26.3 | **7.1** |
| **8.4** | 0.82 | 3.2 | 0.02 | **4.2** | 2.9 | 0.76 | 6.71 | 3.67 | 75.9 | **1.6** | 16.9 | 24.2 | **7.0** |
| **7.4** | 1.35 | 7.8 | 0.00 | **0.0** | -0.8 | -1.52 | -11.50 | 3.45 | 138.6 | **0.6** | 17.3 | 70.2 | **6.4** |
| **9.1** | 0.25 | 0.6 | 0.00 | **3.3** | 11.8 | 0.54 | 2.90 | 2.48 | 76.9 | **4.4** | 53.3 | 18.2 | **9.2** |
| **7.0** | 0.71 | 3.7 | 0.14 | **3.0** | 0.2 | 0.42 | 3.27 | 3.60 | 86.4 | **0.6** | 16.0 | 57.1 | **5.9** |
| **7.2** | 0.71 | 4.3 | 0.00 | **3.6** | 2.0 | 0.67 | 5.57 | 3.80 | 82.0 | **4.2** | 22.2 | 8.3 | **7.1** |

| Name | City | State | Rating | 2018 Rating | 2017 Rating | Total Assets ($Mil) | One Year Asset Growth | Asset Mix (As a % of Total Assets): Commercial Loans | Consumer Loans | Mortgage Loans | Securities | Capitalization Index | Leverage Ratio | Risk-Based Capital Ratio |
|---|---|---|---|---|---|---|---|---|---|---|---|---|---|---|
| Home Federal S&L Assn. of Niles Ohio | Niles | OH | C+ | C | C | 99.8 | 1.06 | 2.7 | 3.1 | 35.5 | 22.5 | 10.0 | 12.5 | 19.9 |
| Home Federal Savings Bank | Rochester | MN | A- | B+ | B+ | 777.1 | 9.26 | 7.2 | 2.9 | 18.0 | 13.9 | 9.4 | 10.9 | 14.5 |
| Home Loan Investment Bank, F.S.B. | Warwick | RI | D+ | D | D | 346.2 | 14.63 | 0.0 | 31.2 | 41.6 | 0.4 | 7.7 | 9.7 | 13.1 |
| Home Loan Savings Bank | Coshocton | OH | B | B+ | A- | 224.3 | 6.39 | 13.5 | 2.7 | 40.4 | 1.8 | 10.0 | 12.0 | 16.6 |
| Home Loan State Bank | Grand Junction | CO | C+ | C | C | 131.8 | 7.18 | 14.2 | 2.8 | 3.1 | 36.4 | 6.2 | 8.2 | 13.5 |
| Home National Bank | Racine | OH | C- | C- | C- | 71.9 | 10.34 | 4.0 | 11.2 | 33.8 | 25.9 | 10.0 | 12.5 | 21.6 |
| Home National Bank of Thorntown | Thorntown | IN | B- | B- | B- | 116.6 | 8.34 | 14.3 | 2.4 | 14.6 | 42.0 | 7.9 | 9.6 | 17.0 |
| Home S&L Assn. of Carroll County, F.A. | Norborne | MO | C+ | C+ | C+ | 86.5 | -0.47 | 0.8 | 3.3 | 47.3 | 9.0 | 10.0 | 20.5 | 39.2 |
| Home S&L Co. of Kenton, Ohio | Kenton | OH | B | B | B- | 129.4 | -2.09 | 6.1 | 0.7 | 21.7 | 18.3 | 10.0 | 27.6 | 41.9 |
| Home Savings Bank | Chanute | KS | B- | B- | C+ | 77.0 | 4.48 | 6.9 | 4.7 | 31.7 | 31.7 | 10.0 | 18.7 | 33.2 |
| Home Savings Bank | Salt Lake City | UT | A- | B+ | A- | 125.1 | -0.45 | 0.0 | 0.0 | 31.0 | 1.5 | 10.0 | 14.3 | 20.7 |
| Home Savings Bank | Madison | WI | D+ | D | D | 160.9 | 12.34 | 1.2 | 0.3 | 41.9 | 0.9 | 7.9 | 9.6 | 15.7 |
| Home Savings Bank of Wapakoneta | Wapakoneta | OH | B- | B- | B- | 36.8 | -2.56 | 0.0 | 0.2 | 64.1 | 15.2 | 10.0 | 13.1 | 21.3 |
| Home Savings Bank, FSB | Ludlow | KY | D | D+ | D+ | 26.0 | 0.22 | 0.0 | 0.0 | 38.3 | 5.8 | 10.0 | 14.1 | 35.7 |
| Home State Bank | Jefferson | IA | B- | C+ | B | 276.3 | 8.49 | 14.5 | 1.3 | 3.6 | 7.9 | 5.4 | 8.3 | 11.3 |
| Home State Bank | Royal | IA | B+ | B+ | A- | 47.3 | 3.12 | 0.4 | 0.5 | 2.4 | 30.7 | 10.0 | 29.8 | 39.9 |
| Home State Bank | Litchfield | MN | B+ | B+ | B+ | 152.7 | -0.52 | 11.0 | 2.6 | 8.8 | 27.7 | 10.0 | 11.2 | 15.4 |
| Home State Bank, N.A. | Crystal Lake | IL | B | B- | B- | 615.0 | 5.10 | 6.6 | 0.7 | 20.5 | 20.3 | 10.0 | 12.7 | 19.4 |
| Home Trust & Savings Bank | Osage | IA | B+ | B+ | A- | 238.8 | -2.44 | 5.3 | 1.7 | 16.9 | 24.7 | 9.2 | 10.4 | 16.2 |
| HOMEBANK | Palmyra | MO | B- | B- | B | 422.0 | 5.60 | 16.5 | 1.9 | 10.9 | 7.9 | 6.3 | 9.7 | 12.0 |
| ▼ HomeBank of Arkansas | Portland | AR | D+ | C | C+ | 67.8 | -4.10 | 12.2 | 3.5 | 26.4 | 2.3 | 9.3 | 10.5 | 16.0 |
| HomeBank Texas | Seagoville | TX | A- | B+ | B | 201.4 | 6.52 | 10.4 | 1.0 | 28.5 | 5.6 | 9.7 | 10.8 | 16.2 |
| Homeland Community Bank | McMinnville | TN | C+ | C | C- | 152.9 | 2.43 | 7.0 | 3.4 | 23.8 | 18.0 | 7.2 | 9.1 | 14.1 |
| Homeland Federal Savings Bank | Columbia | LA | B- | C+ | B | 343.3 | 15.33 | 8.7 | 9.5 | 30.4 | 4.1 | 8.6 | 10.2 | 13.9 |
| HomePride Bank | Mansfield | MO | D- | D- | D- | 99.4 | 2.74 | 2.9 | 2.1 | 52.6 | 6.4 | 6.5 | 8.5 | 15.1 |
| ▲ Homestead Bank | Cozad | NE | B+ | B | B+ | 270.2 | 3.64 | 6.0 | 1.0 | 1.0 | 22.6 | 10.0 | 16.2 | 23.2 |
| Homestead Savings Bank | Albion | MI | D- | E- | E- | 65.8 | 2.15 | 2.4 | 1.6 | 50.4 | 5.6 | 5.3 | 7.3 | 13.6 |
| HomeStreet Bank | Seattle | WA | C+ | B- | B | 6771.3 | -3.30 | 5.4 | 0.2 | 17.5 | 13.9 | 9.2 | 10.6 | 14.4 |
| Hometown Bank | Oxford | MA | B- | B- | B- | 1018.6 | 29.12 | 6.8 | 0.4 | 25.8 | 17.3 | 9.4 | 10.6 | 15.5 |
| HomeTown Bank | Redwood Falls | MN | A- | B+ | A- | 353.7 | 11.01 | 11.2 | 2.4 | 18.8 | 19.8 | 8.9 | 10.2 | 15.4 |
| Hometown Bank | Kent | OH | C- | C- | C- | 206.8 | 1.64 | 9.3 | 1.2 | 32.0 | 5.1 | 5.4 | 8.3 | 11.3 |
| ▲ Hometown Bank | Fond du Lac | WI | A- | B+ | A | 490.3 | 55.54 | 21.5 | 0.4 | 11.1 | 4.2 | 9.9 | 12.0 | 14.9 |
| HomeTown Bank of Alabama | Oneonta | AL | A- | A- | A | 397.8 | 10.18 | 4.4 | 9.7 | 38.2 | 18.7 | 10.0 | 14.3 | 24.1 |
| Hometown Bank of Corbin, Inc. | Corbin | KY | B- | C+ | C+ | 178.6 | 8.96 | 4.6 | 3.2 | 26.5 | 22.7 | 7.1 | 9.1 | 14.4 |
| Hometown Bank of Pennsylvania | Bedford | PA | B- | B- | B- | 219.3 | 24.54 | 11.1 | 0.7 | 29.5 | 5.5 | 6.4 | 8.4 | 12.5 |
| HomeTown Bank, N.A. | Galveston | TX | A- | B+ | B+ | 626.9 | 5.65 | 6.5 | 1.7 | 16.3 | 23.9 | 10.0 | 12.4 | 18.2 |
| Hometown Community Bank | Cyrus | MN | C+ | C | D+ | 63.5 | 1.94 | 7.3 | 2.1 | 18.9 | 3.5 | 8.3 | 10.2 | 13.6 |
| Hometown National Bank | LaSalle | IL | B+ | B+ | A- | 223.2 | -2.03 | 16.3 | 0.5 | 6.8 | 20.6 | 10.0 | 11.7 | 15.8 |
| ▲ HomeTrust Bank | Asheville | NC | B- | B- | C | 3468.4 | 1.73 | 12.2 | 4.5 | 14.6 | 11.5 | 6.7 | 10.3 | 12.3 |
| Homewood Federal Savings Bank | Baltimore | MD | B- | B- | B | 60.6 | 9.71 | 0.1 | 2.8 | 58.9 | 4.5 | 10.0 | 26.9 | 47.3 |
| Hondo National Bank | Hondo | TX | B+ | B+ | B+ | 271.7 | 5.55 | 11.0 | 2.5 | 15.1 | 20.2 | 8.4 | 10.0 | 13.7 |
| Honesdale National Bank | Honesdale | PA | A- | A- | A | 705.4 | 6.92 | 10.4 | 3.8 | 24.8 | 17.2 | 10.0 | 14.7 | 19.5 |
| Honor Bank | Honor | MI | B- | C+ | C+ | 242.9 | 2.88 | 11.6 | 2.5 | 12.8 | 8.7 | 6.8 | 9.5 | 12.3 |
| Hoosier Heartland State Bank | Crawfordsville | IN | B- | B- | B- | 203.3 | 2.18 | 3.7 | 4.8 | 10.9 | 29.3 | 6.6 | 8.6 | 13.5 |
| Hopeton State Bank | Hopeton | OK | D+ | C | C- | 25.9 | -6.03 | 5.3 | 4.1 | 0.0 | 40.7 | 9.1 | 10.4 | 16.7 |
| Horatio State Bank | Horatio | AR | B | B- | B+ | 225.7 | 8.03 | 6.2 | 20.0 | 28.4 | 9.6 | 10.0 | 11.8 | 17.7 |
| ▼ Horicon Bank | Horicon | WI | C- | C+ | B- | 883.5 | 16.90 | 11.8 | 0.9 | 14.0 | 3.1 | 6.0 | 9.9 | 11.7 |
| Horizon Bank | Michigan City | IN | B+ | B+ | B+ | 5236.4 | 23.46 | 7.5 | 7.5 | 15.9 | 20.2 | 7.2 | 9.5 | 12.7 |
| Horizon Bank | Waverly | NE | A- | B+ | A | 354.5 | 18.88 | 7.0 | 0.2 | 10.2 | 6.8 | 9.7 | 14.0 | 14.7 |
| Horizon Bank, SSB | Austin | TX | B+ | B+ | B+ | 1243.7 | 25.54 | 19.4 | 0.1 | 9.2 | 9.3 | 5.6 | 8.0 | 11.4 |
| Horizon Community Bank | Lake Havasu City | AZ | B- | B- | B- | 341.4 | 14.89 | 16.4 | 0.3 | 7.9 | 8.2 | 6.9 | 8.9 | 12.7 |
| ▲ Horizon Financial Bank | Munich | ND | B+ | B+ | B+ | 147.3 | -1.45 | 4.1 | 1.7 | 4.5 | 10.2 | 10.0 | 12.6 | 17.8 |
| Houghton State Bank | Red Oak | IA | B | B- | B+ | 178.8 | -1.04 | 5.4 | 0.8 | 5.4 | 11.1 | 10.0 | 11.0 | 15.7 |
| Howard Bank | Baltimore | MD | C+ | C+ | B- | 2374.5 | 4.78 | 15.4 | 2.0 | 19.9 | 9.4 | 7.4 | 10.4 | 12.9 |
| ▲ Howard State Bank | Howard | KS | B+ | B- | C+ | 54.6 | -3.52 | 2.8 | 2.5 | 4.6 | 30.1 | 10.0 | 11.8 | 22.2 |
| Hoyne Savings Bank | Chicago | IL | C- | D+ | D | 445.4 | -0.39 | 0.0 | 0.0 | 30.6 | 37.7 | 10.0 | 16.7 | 39.8 |
| HSBC Bank USA, N.A. | McLean | VA | C | C | C+ | 172887.7 | 1.81 | 14.9 | 1.0 | 10.4 | 28.4 | 10.0 | 12.0 | 19.2 |
| HSBC Trust Co. (Delaware), N.A. | Wilmington | DE | U | U | U | 56.0 | -0.50 | 0.0 | 0.0 | 0.0 | 0.0 | 0.0 | 97.4 | 0.0 |
| Huntingdon Savings Bank | Huntingdon | PA | C | C+ | C+ | 16.2 | -1.57 | 0.0 | 0.0 | 77.6 | 0.0 | 10.0 | 21.5 | 47.2 |
| Huntingdon Valley Bank | Doylestown | PA | C- | C- | C | 351.8 | 11.73 | 4.2 | 1.8 | 70.7 | 4.7 | 6.5 | 8.5 | 14.7 |

| Asset Quality Index | Adjusted Non-Performing Loans as a % of Total Loans | Adjusted Non-Performing Loans as a % of Capital | Net Charge-Offs Avg Loans | Profitability Index | Net Income ($Mil) | Return on Assets (R.O.A.) | Return on Equity (R.O.E.) | Net Interest Spread | Overhead Efficiency Ratio | Liquidity Index | Liquidity Ratio | Hot Money Ratio | Stability Index |
|---|---|---|---|---|---|---|---|---|---|---|---|---|---|
| **7.3** | 0.62 | 4.3 | 0.02 | **2.8** | 0.5 | 0.49 | 3.91 | 2.39 | 79.5 | **0.7** | 11.4 | 41.8 | **6.4** |
| **6.8** | 0.36 | 2.3 | -0.18 | **6.3** | 8.6 | 1.17 | 10.38 | 3.95 | 70.3 | **4.0** | 16.7 | 9.0 | **8.4** |
| **0.5** | 4.70 | 24.6 | 0.52 | **6.4** | 4.6 | 1.43 | 15.68 | 4.57 | 68.5 | **0.6** | 12.5 | 53.6 | **5.6** |
| **4.4** | 2.49 | 15.3 | 0.37 | **9.5** | 3.8 | 1.73 | 14.51 | 4.56 | 49.5 | **2.0** | 7.4 | 17.4 | **8.5** |
| **2.3** | 10.78 | 32.9 | 0.08 | **4.7** | 1.2 | 0.95 | 11.86 | 4.13 | 69.0 | **4.6** | 20.6 | 5.7 | **4.6** |
| **1.7** | 5.84 | 27.1 | 0.48 | **4.9** | 0.8 | 1.13 | 8.68 | 5.10 | 71.7 | **1.5** | 12.4 | 23.1 | **7.0** |
| **4.2** | 2.84 | 11.8 | 0.03 | **4.0** | 0.8 | 0.70 | 7.23 | 3.64 | 76.5 | **3.1** | 25.7 | 14.8 | **5.8** |
| **6.7** | 1.90 | 5.6 | -0.02 | **1.7** | 0.1 | 0.10 | 0.48 | 2.68 | 95.4 | **2.7** | 38.3 | 23.4 | **6.9** |
| **8.8** | 0.98 | 2.1 | 0.05 | **4.0** | 1.0 | 0.80 | 2.99 | 3.20 | 65.7 | **1.9** | 35.3 | 23.0 | **7.9** |
| **8.9** | 0.09 | 0.3 | 0.01 | **3.8** | 0.6 | 0.78 | 4.04 | 3.52 | 78.9 | **1.5** | 28.9 | 25.4 | **7.4** |
| **7.8** | 0.29 | 0.8 | 0.00 | **6.9** | 1.6 | 1.23 | 8.54 | 3.76 | 59.2 | **0.6** | 18.7 | 54.8 | **8.5** |
| **7.2** | 0.73 | 4.4 | 0.01 | **1.9** | 0.5 | 0.34 | 3.79 | 3.21 | 89.2 | **1.3** | 15.5 | 20.2 | **4.1** |
| **9.9** | 0.00 | 0.0 | 0.00 | **2.7** | 0.1 | 0.24 | 1.82 | 3.61 | 89.8 | **3.5** | 21.4 | 12.2 | **7.3** |
| **3.7** | 6.30 | 21.7 | 0.00 | **0.0** | -0.2 | -0.65 | -4.31 | 2.43 | 125.0 | **2.4** | 53.5 | 32.8 | **6.2** |
| **4.7** | 1.06 | 7.5 | 0.06 | **6.4** | 3.8 | 1.44 | 16.57 | 3.83 | 62.3 | **1.3** | 20.0 | 14.2 | **6.0** |
| **7.5** | 0.09 | 1.6 | 0.07 | **7.8** | 0.9 | 1.87 | 6.44 | 3.93 | 46.7 | **5.6** | 54.3 | 9.0 | **7.0** |
| **8.7** | 0.03 | 0.1 | 0.11 | **4.7** | 1.7 | 1.13 | 10.21 | 3.96 | 76.1 | **4.5** | 22.1 | 5.9 | **7.8** |
| **6.3** | 1.03 | 5.0 | 0.20 | **4.3** | 6.1 | 1.02 | 7.97 | 3.99 | 79.8 | **3.7** | 25.7 | 11.5 | **7.4** |
| **5.4** | 0.23 | 7.6 | 0.00 | **5.6** | 3.4 | 1.39 | 13.64 | 2.64 | 44.8 | **3.1** | 29.4 | 16.1 | **6.6** |
| **5.4** | 0.50 | 3.9 | 0.04 | **5.0** | 4.7 | 1.16 | 12.07 | 4.03 | 72.0 | **3.3** | 15.5 | 12.7 | **6.5** |
| **4.7** | 1.37 | 8.8 | 0.02 | **0.4** | -1.0 | -1.36 | -12.52 | 4.09 | 150.3 | **0.8** | 18.1 | 47.0 | **5.9** |
| **8.6** | 0.05 | 0.5 | 0.00 | **8.9** | 4.2 | 2.11 | 19.35 | 4.73 | 54.3 | **2.1** | 21.8 | 17.6 | **7.6** |
| **4.2** | 2.00 | 13.6 | 0.02 | **4.6** | 1.4 | 0.94 | 10.51 | 3.46 | 69.4 | **1.8** | 24.1 | 21.9 | **5.0** |
| **4.4** | 1.45 | 9.4 | 0.69 | **6.0** | 4.3 | 1.35 | 13.55 | 4.41 | 64.2 | **0.6** | 10.6 | 46.4 | **7.3** |
| **3.6** | 1.67 | 12.1 | 0.17 | **0.4** | -0.2 | -0.19 | -2.24 | 4.28 | 100.2 | **1.0** | 12.1 | 31.6 | **2.6** |
| **5.0** | 0.89 | 5.0 | -0.12 | **8.0** | 4.2 | 1.62 | 10.11 | 4.39 | 55.8 | **4.4** | 21.7 | 7.1 | **8.7** |
| **2.8** | 3.03 | 19.6 | 0.02 | **2.5** | 0.4 | 0.65 | 9.58 | 4.00 | 94.7 | **4.6** | 21.0 | 5.3 | **2.1** |
| **4.9** | 1.20 | 4.7 | -0.01 | **3.7** | 23.4 | 0.66 | 6.01 | 3.10 | 78.4 | **1.7** | 13.1 | 16.6 | **8.6** |
| **5.6** | 1.29 | 6.3 | 0.02 | **4.2** | 6.9 | 0.83 | 8.01 | 3.43 | 70.0 | **2.2** | 17.5 | 18.6 | **7.4** |
| **6.9** | 0.58 | 3.1 | -0.01 | **7.7** | 4.9 | 1.48 | 13.19 | 4.36 | 60.0 | **4.6** | 23.8 | 5.8 | **7.6** |
| **2.2** | 2.23 | 21.1 | 0.02 | **3.1** | 1.0 | 0.47 | 5.65 | 3.72 | 88.8 | **1.0** | 10.6 | 30.0 | **3.6** |
| **6.2** | 0.41 | 1.8 | 0.02 | **8.6** | 6.8 | 1.40 | 11.18 | 4.33 | 58.3 | **4.2** | 13.5 | 6.8 | **9.4** |
| **7.5** | 0.87 | 3.9 | 0.35 | **8.4** | 5.6 | 1.49 | 10.31 | 4.50 | 58.7 | **2.1** | 17.1 | 18.7 | **8.9** |
| **6.2** | 0.47 | 3.2 | 0.07 | **5.1** | 2.0 | 1.12 | 12.48 | 4.08 | 74.0 | **3.3** | 21.5 | 13.3 | **5.3** |
| **6.2** | 0.82 | 5.4 | -0.02 | **3.8** | 1.5 | 0.75 | 8.63 | 3.28 | 72.8 | **1.8** | 24.3 | 22.7 | **4.6** |
| **8.7** | 0.32 | 1.5 | 0.11 | **7.1** | 8.6 | 1.43 | 11.63 | 4.12 | 56.0 | **2.0** | 26.1 | 20.8 | **8.7** |
| **6.4** | 0.48 | 4.7 | 0.17 | **4.1** | 0.5 | 0.84 | 7.56 | 3.73 | 72.8 | **1.6** | 13.1 | 21.9 | **5.1** |
| **5.6** | 2.57 | 10.9 | 0.06 | **5.2** | 2.2 | 1.00 | 8.51 | 3.72 | 76.1 | **3.9** | 24.8 | 9.4 | **7.7** |
| **6.0** | 1.08 | 5.3 | 0.21 | **4.1** | 29.5 | 0.84 | 7.57 | 3.33 | 68.5 | **1.9** | 14.7 | 13.3 | **9.2** |
| **8.4** | 1.13 | 1.7 | 0.07 | **3.9** | 0.4 | 0.69 | 2.53 | 3.25 | 70.4 | **1.6** | 35.6 | 52.5 | **7.2** |
| **5.2** | 2.38 | 14.6 | 0.52 | **3.9** | 1.7 | 0.65 | 6.31 | 4.15 | 73.0 | **2.1** | 22.6 | 19.5 | **6.8** |
| **7.8** | 0.52 | 3.5 | 0.38 | **6.3** | 9.0 | 1.31 | 8.76 | 4.17 | 62.1 | **2.9** | 16.5 | 14.9 | **9.4** |
| **5.2** | 0.50 | 3.6 | 0.09 | **5.0** | 2.6 | 1.07 | 11.67 | 4.23 | 72.3 | **3.4** | 15.6 | 10.1 | **5.6** |
| **4.9** | 1.75 | 7.5 | 0.06 | **4.1** | 2.0 | 0.94 | 10.84 | 4.12 | 78.3 | **4.4** | 23.2 | 6.8 | **5.7** |
| **7.0** | 0.00 | 0.0 | 0.08 | **1.9** | 0.1 | 0.43 | 3.69 | 3.87 | 100.8 | **2.6** | 58.0 | 37.5 | **5.6** |
| **4.8** | 0.95 | 7.6 | 0.36 | **8.9** | 3.3 | 1.53 | 13.23 | 4.41 | 47.0 | **0.6** | 12.0 | 46.2 | **8.0** |
| **2.2** | 3.78 | 25.2 | 0.00 | **6.2** | 11.8 | 1.50 | 14.34 | 4.20 | 64.5 | **3.2** | 10.5 | 9.2 | **7.7** |
| **6.0** | 0.57 | 2.9 | 0.06 | **6.7** | 69.6 | 1.42 | 11.14 | 3.79 | 58.7 | **2.7** | 19.8 | 16.3 | **9.4** |
| **7.3** | 0.00 | 0.0 | 0.00 | **9.8** | 6.9 | 2.12 | 15.68 | 4.18 | 40.3 | **1.5** | 13.6 | 23.7 | **9.2** |
| **8.3** | 0.00 | 0.0 | 0.20 | **9.2** | 19.6 | 1.74 | 21.04 | 4.64 | 57.7 | **5.0** | 25.5 | 6.3 | **8.6** |
| **6.1** | 0.91 | 3.5 | 0.03 | **4.8** | 3.1 | 0.94 | 10.51 | 4.46 | 74.9 | **2.6** | 21.9 | 16.5 | **5.7** |
| **6.5** | 0.71 | 3.2 | -0.05 | **5.3** | 1.5 | 1.04 | 8.25 | 4.12 | 65.8 | **1.7** | 11.9 | 15.7 | **7.4** |
| **4.2** | 1.03 | 3.0 | 0.02 | **6.4** | 2.3 | 1.27 | 9.41 | 3.89 | 56.4 | **2.9** | 13.7 | 14.2 | **7.9** |
| **4.3** | 1.08 | 5.4 | 0.21 | **3.8** | 18.8 | 0.83 | 5.77 | 3.60 | 69.2 | **0.9** | 15.8 | 22.3 | **7.6** |
| **7.9** | 0.33 | 1.2 | 0.49 | **5.3** | 0.7 | 1.32 | 11.48 | 3.85 | 65.4 | **6.1** | 44.4 | 3.5 | **6.1** |
| **9.6** | 0.84 | 1.9 | 0.06 | **1.5** | 0.7 | 0.16 | 0.93 | 2.39 | 94.5 | **3.5** | 59.4 | 26.7 | **6.1** |
| **7.4** | 1.72 | 4.2 | 0.14 | **2.4** | 341.0 | 0.19 | 1.55 | 1.41 | 83.8 | **3.3** | 60.0 | 22.3 | **8.9** |
| **10.0** | na | 0.0 | na | **9.3** | 1.3 | 2.34 | 2.41 | 2.27 | 33.5 | **4.0** | na | 0.0 | **6.4** |
| **6.7** | 2.41 | 8.9 | 0.00 | **3.7** | 0.1 | 0.61 | 2.90 | 3.12 | 71.7 | **1.0** | 18.9 | 31.9 | **7.9** |
| **5.5** | 1.26 | 11.9 | 0.12 | **2.4** | 1.0 | 0.31 | 3.69 | 2.59 | 87.1 | **2.3** | 10.1 | 9.2 | **3.6** |

| Name | City | State | Rating | 2018 Rating | 2017 Rating | Total Assets ($Mil) | One Year Asset Growth | Asset Mix (As a % of Total Assets) Commercial Loans | Consumer Loans | Mortgage Loans | Securities | Capitalization Index | Leverage Ratio | Risk-Based Capital Ratio |
|---|---|---|---|---|---|---|---|---|---|---|---|---|---|---|
| Huntington Federal Savings Bank | Huntington | WV | C+ | B- | B | 544.6 | 1.69 | 0.0 | 0.2 | 34.6 | 52.5 | **10.0** | 16.7 | 49.8 |
| Huntington National Bank | Columbus | OH | B- | B- | B- | 108739.4 | 0.06 | 20.8 | 16.5 | 12.2 | 21.5 | **8.3** | 10.0 | 13.6 |
| Huron Community Bank | East Tawas | MI | B | B | B | 221.8 | 3.63 | 9.9 | 1.3 | 11.2 | 15.7 | **10.0** | 12.0 | 18.0 |
| ▲ Huron National Bank | Rogers City | MI | B- | C | C+ | 62.5 | -1.21 | 2.3 | 4.4 | 37.0 | 5.5 | **10.0** | 15.6 | 24.0 |
| Huron Valley State Bank | Milford | MI | B | B | B- | 155.7 | 3.20 | 11.0 | 0.6 | 5.5 | 1.1 | **7.8** | 10.4 | 13.1 |
| Hustisford State Bank | Hustisford | WI | B+ | B+ | B+ | 56.0 | 4.54 | 4.3 | 1.8 | 50.9 | 8.2 | **10.0** | 18.6 | 28.9 |
| Hyden Citizens Bank | Hyden | KY | B- | B- | B- | 123.5 | -4.47 | 11.2 | 4.1 | 23.2 | 29.9 | **8.2** | 9.8 | 15.0 |
| Hyperion Bank | Philadelphia | PA | D+ | D | D- | 177.3 | 61.79 | 8.6 | 0.2 | 35.4 | 1.1 | **10.0** | 12.3 | 17.7 |
| IBERIABANK | Lafayette | LA | B | B- | B- | 31614.9 | 2.85 | 14.6 | 1.8 | 18.2 | 13.0 | **6.0** | 9.7 | 11.8 |
| Idabel National Bank | Idabel | OK | B+ | B+ | A- | 131.8 | 6.54 | 4.2 | 6.3 | 19.3 | 39.2 | **9.0** | 10.4 | 19.7 |
| ▲ Idaho First Bank | McCall | ID | C+ | C- | D+ | 220.1 | 7.96 | 17.5 | 3.0 | 13.3 | 9.7 | **10.0** | 12.1 | 15.6 |
| Idaho Trust Bank | Boise | ID | C | C | B- | 156.1 | 22.92 | 12.0 | 3.6 | 1.0 | 0.3 | **7.8** | 9.5 | 13.6 |
| Illini State Bank | Oglesby | IL | B | B- | B- | 124.4 | 2.25 | 6.6 | 1.0 | 10.2 | 27.5 | **10.0** | 13.0 | 20.8 |
| Illinois Bank & Trust | Rockford | IL | B+ | B+ | B | 1301.2 | 61.65 | 18.6 | 1.4 | 9.1 | 24.3 | **4.1** | 10.3 | 10.5 |
| Impact Bank | Wellington | KS | B- | B- | B- | 140.4 | -0.59 | 11.5 | 2.2 | 3.4 | 26.9 | **9.1** | 10.4 | 16.4 |
| ▲ INB, N.A. | Springfield | IL | B- | C+ | C+ | 1156.2 | 27.19 | 10.9 | 0.1 | 11.0 | 8.6 | **6.7** | 8.7 | 12.5 |
| InBank | Raton | NM | C+ | B | B+ | 393.6 | 10.41 | 8.8 | 1.6 | 7.1 | 25.7 | **7.6** | 12.5 | 13.0 |
| Incommons Bank, N.A. | Mexia | TX | B- | B- | B- | 179.6 | 5.90 | 9.3 | 4.3 | 23.9 | 18.6 | **6.9** | 8.9 | 13.8 |
| IncredibleBank | Wausau | WI | B- | B- | B- | 1399.9 | 3.14 | 23.0 | 5.0 | 8.0 | 14.6 | **4.7** | 8.5 | 10.9 |
| Independence Bank | Havre | MT | A- | B+ | A- | 803.6 | 8.40 | 5.3 | 2.1 | 6.8 | 8.0 | **10.0** | 13.3 | 16.1 |
| Independence Bank | Independence | OH | B | B | B | 174.8 | -6.03 | 23.4 | 0.5 | 5.2 | 16.9 | **10.0** | 13.8 | 21.2 |
| Independence Bank | East Greenwich | RI | B | B | B | 65.4 | 2.53 | 84.0 | 0.3 | 3.0 | 0.0 | **10.0** | 27.0 | 41.4 |
| Independence Bank of Kentucky | Owensboro | KY | B+ | B+ | A- | 2596.5 | 10.07 | 4.3 | 0.4 | 13.0 | 42.3 | **6.1** | 8.1 | 13.0 |
| Independence State Bank | Independence | WI | D | D | D | 69.5 | -0.90 | 10.3 | 1.1 | 9.5 | 11.3 | **6.5** | 8.5 | 12.1 |
| Independent Bank | Grand Rapids | MI | B- | B- | C+ | 3563.7 | 6.18 | 8.8 | 12.6 | 26.8 | 14.6 | **7.6** | 9.5 | 13.0 |
| ▲ Independent Bank | Memphis | TN | B- | C+ | B- | 1110.6 | 4.56 | 8.7 | 44.1 | 1.1 | 0.6 | **6.2** | 11.3 | 11.9 |
| Independent Bank | McKinney | TX | B+ | B+ | B+ | 14953.3 | 51.93 | 9.4 | 0.2 | 9.9 | 7.3 | **6.5** | 10.7 | 12.1 |
| Independent Farmers Bank | Maysville | MO | B | B | B | 129.3 | 6.22 | 5.7 | 3.5 | 10.3 | 39.4 | **7.6** | 9.4 | 16.8 |
| Industrial & Commerc. Bank of China (USA | New York | NY | B | B | B- | 2899.5 | 0.45 | 25.9 | 0.0 | 8.3 | 0.5 | **10.0** | 13.8 | 16.0 |
| ▲ Industrial Bank | Washington | DC | C- | D+ | D+ | 530.8 | 22.66 | 5.8 | 0.2 | 19.3 | 16.4 | **6.3** | 8.3 | 12.4 |
| ▼ Industry State Bank | Industry | TX | B+ | A- | A | 863.3 | 10.33 | 4.8 | 1.2 | 4.5 | 69.0 | **9.3** | 10.5 | 22.7 |
| Inez Deposit Bank | Inez | KY | C+ | C | C | 142.1 | 0.18 | 2.5 | 2.8 | 24.7 | 41.3 | **10.0** | 13.5 | 39.4 |
| Infinity Bank | Santa Ana | CA | D | D | | 116.6 | 65.34 | 41.8 | 0.9 | 1.5 | 23.8 | **10.0** | 24.1 | 29.6 |
| InFirst Bank | Indiana | PA | B- | B- | B- | 420.2 | 4.26 | 6.5 | 0.7 | 52.7 | 8.8 | **8.4** | 9.9 | 14.6 |
| Inland Bank and Trust | Oak Brook | IL | B | B | B | 1123.5 | 1.45 | 8.6 | 0.1 | 12.1 | 19.7 | **10.0** | 12.6 | 15.8 |
| InsBank | Nashville | TN | B | B- | C+ | 551.6 | 6.62 | 23.1 | 1.6 | 6.1 | 3.8 | **7.9** | 11.7 | 13.3 |
| ▲ INSOUTH Bank | Brownsville | TN | B | B- | B- | 331.5 | 2.54 | 16.9 | 2.9 | 16.3 | 10.5 | **7.7** | 10.0 | 13.1 |
| ▲ Institution for Savings | Newburyport | MA | A- | C+ | C+ | 3717.3 | 7.11 | 0.2 | 0.3 | 59.5 | 5.7 | **9.1** | 10.9 | 14.2 |
| ▲ Integrity Bank & Trust | Monument | CO | B | B- | B- | 207.2 | 2.54 | 3.7 | 0.7 | 17.0 | 11.0 | **7.1** | 9.1 | 13.1 |
| Integrity Bank Plus | Wabasso | MN | C+ | C+ | B- | 66.4 | 9.03 | 2.7 | 1.5 | 7.7 | 14.3 | **10.0** | 11.4 | 18.2 |
| Interamerican Bank, A FSB | Miami | FL | C | C- | D+ | 201.4 | -0.25 | 0.3 | 0.6 | 27.0 | 0.0 | **10.0** | 14.2 | 19.9 |
| Interaudi Bank | New York | NY | B+ | B | B- | 2119.7 | 5.08 | 5.6 | 0.2 | 17.4 | 22.7 | **6.5** | 8.5 | 22.7 |
| ▼ InterBank | Oklahoma City | OK | C- | C+ | B- | 3461.2 | -2.82 | 16.2 | 0.6 | 6.3 | 0.0 | **4.9** | 9.7 | 10.9 |
| ▲ Intercity State Bank | Schofield | WI | A | B+ | A- | 199.3 | 5.61 | 10.3 | 1.2 | 19.7 | 10.5 | **10.0** | 22.1 | 30.6 |
| ▼ Intercredit Bank, N.A. | Miami | FL | D+ | C | C+ | 362.3 | -0.42 | 10.5 | 2.8 | 28.5 | 12.9 | **9.1** | 10.4 | 15.0 |
| International Bank of Amherst | Amherst | WI | A- | A- | A- | 74.1 | 1.35 | 5.5 | 0.9 | 10.2 | 30.9 | **10.0** | 14.3 | 30.7 |
| International Bank of Chicago | Chicago | IL | B- | C | C+ | 677.9 | 6.45 | 6.0 | 0.0 | 20.7 | 23.5 | **10.0** | 11.5 | 19.8 |
| International Bank of Commerce | Brownsville | TX | A | A | A | 1074.9 | 5.74 | 14.5 | 0.5 | 3.1 | 28.6 | **10.0** | 17.4 | 23.6 |
| International Bank of Commerce | Laredo | TX | A | A | A | 8724.9 | 3.02 | 9.5 | 0.7 | 10.1 | 27.1 | **10.0** | 15.2 | 18.9 |
| International Bank of Commerce | Zapata | TX | A | A | A | 384.3 | -10.47 | 4.5 | 1.5 | 22.3 | 46.3 | **10.0** | 19.1 | 37.6 |
| International Bank of Commerce Oklahoma | Oklahoma City | OK | A- | A- | A- | 1367.0 | -10.61 | 20.6 | 0.2 | 1.4 | 19.7 | **10.0** | 14.8 | 17.4 |
| International City Bank | Long Beach | CA | B+ | A- | A- | 366.8 | 35.56 | 1.2 | 0.0 | 2.4 | 53.1 | **6.5** | 8.5 | 19.9 |
| International Finance Bank | Miami | FL | C+ | C+ | C+ | 780.1 | 12.65 | 30.7 | 1.6 | 20.7 | 10.1 | **4.0** | 6.7 | 10.5 |
| ▲ Interstate Bank | Perryton | TX | B | C+ | B- | 194.2 | -1.60 | 15.2 | 1.8 | 11.7 | 31.2 | **8.7** | 10.1 | 17.1 |
| Interstate Federal S&L Assn. of McGregor | McGregor | IA | C- | C | C | 8.2 | 3.86 | 0.0 | 0.4 | 74.7 | 0.0 | **10.0** | 21.6 | 44.1 |
| Intracoastal Bank | Palm Coast | FL | B | B | B+ | 344.3 | 5.52 | 7.5 | 0.2 | 1.8 | 22.0 | **6.3** | 9.1 | 12.0 |
| INTRUST Bank, N.A. | Wichita | KS | B | B | B | 5665.4 | 8.92 | 23.2 | 4.3 | 3.8 | 28.3 | **4.7** | 8.3 | 10.9 |
| Investar Bank, N.A. | Baton Rouge | LA | B | B | B | 2146.2 | 20.29 | 14.9 | 1.4 | 13.8 | 12.8 | **7.6** | 10.8 | 13.0 |
| Investment Savings Bank | Altoona | PA | C+ | C+ | C+ | 101.7 | -0.69 | 0.5 | 0.8 | 39.7 | 41.0 | **10.0** | 21.4 | 41.6 |
| Investors Bank | Short Hills | NJ | B | B+ | B+ | 26708.5 | 1.68 | 3.8 | 1.4 | 20.4 | 14.5 | **6.2** | 8.2 | 12.2 |

| Asset Quality Index | Adjusted Non-Performing Loans as a % of Total Loans | Adjusted Non-Performing Loans as a % of Capital | Net Charge-Offs Avg Loans | Profitability Index | Net Income ($Mil) | Return on Assets (R.O.A.) | Return on Equity (R.O.E.) | Net Interest Spread | Overhead Efficiency Ratio | Liquidity Index | Liquidity Ratio | Hot Money Ratio | Stability Index |
|---|---|---|---|---|---|---|---|---|---|---|---|---|---|
| **9.7** | 0.84 | 2.1 | 0.03 | **2.2** | 0.9 | 0.17 | 1.05 | 2.08 | 89.0 | **3.5** | 68.6 | 31.1 | **8.4** |
| **4.3** | 1.46 | 6.3 | 0.35 | **6.9** | 1592.4 | 1.49 | 13.37 | 3.41 | 53.3 | **4.8** | 22.1 | 2.8 | **9.9** |
| **7.6** | 0.95 | 3.9 | 0.40 | **4.3** | 1.9 | 0.85 | 7.25 | 4.00 | 69.1 | **4.2** | 24.6 | 8.5 | **7.1** |
| **4.6** | 4.32 | 12.0 | 0.60 | **3.6** | 0.3 | 0.54 | 3.52 | 3.93 | 72.1 | **4.2** | 45.2 | 14.8 | **6.7** |
| **5.1** | 1.02 | 6.1 | 0.31 | **6.0** | 1.9 | 1.19 | 11.67 | 4.16 | 64.4 | **1.6** | 11.9 | 17.8 | **7.2** |
| **5.6** | 4.57 | 10.7 | 0.00 | **6.1** | 0.6 | 1.08 | 5.58 | 4.45 | 65.6 | **2.9** | 15.0 | 9.6 | **7.7** |
| **6.6** | 0.58 | 3.3 | 0.11 | **4.3** | 1.2 | 0.98 | 10.06 | 4.06 | 75.6 | **1.7** | 14.4 | 21.1 | **5.9** |
| **5.6** | 1.93 | 9.5 | 0.00 | **0.5** | -0.1 | -0.08 | -0.62 | 3.42 | 90.5 | **0.7** | 16.4 | 47.7 | **4.7** |
| **5.1** | 0.83 | 3.9 | 0.13 | **5.9** | 389.6 | 1.25 | 9.45 | 3.46 | 54.7 | **2.8** | 10.6 | 10.0 | **10.0** |
| **5.9** | 0.58 | 3.6 | 0.16 | **8.3** | 2.6 | 2.05 | 20.86 | 3.97 | 52.3 | **1.1** | 25.0 | 33.7 | **8.0** |
| **8.1** | 0.09 | 0.5 | 0.19 | **3.2** | 1.0 | 0.47 | 4.89 | 3.89 | 81.8 | **1.6** | 18.2 | 21.6 | **5.9** |
| **8.5** | 0.13 | 0.6 | -0.06 | **2.9** | 0.9 | 0.64 | 4.46 | 3.87 | 89.4 | **5.0** | 34.8 | 7.6 | **7.1** |
| **7.3** | 0.32 | 1.4 | 0.00 | **4.2** | 1.3 | 1.08 | 6.72 | 3.31 | 62.4 | **2.3** | 21.9 | 5.3 | **8.1** |
| **7.6** | 0.32 | 3.0 | 0.04 | **4.7** | 8.4 | 0.96 | 10.55 | 3.49 | 70.3 | **4.2** | 23.4 | 9.4 | **7.0** |
| **4.9** | 2.52 | 12.8 | 0.01 | **4.1** | 1.3 | 0.97 | 8.87 | 3.64 | 75.2 | **2.3** | 21.6 | 18.1 | **6.8** |
| **4.7** | 0.81 | 5.9 | 0.32 | **4.3** | 11.0 | 1.01 | 11.29 | 3.34 | 74.3 | **2.5** | 18.8 | 3.4 | **7.7** |
| **4.1** | 2.49 | 6.2 | 0.00 | **1.3** | -1.3 | -0.34 | -2.17 | 4.28 | 105.7 | **1.8** | 18.1 | 20.5 | **6.3** |
| **5.7** | 0.47 | 5.2 | 0.07 | **4.0** | 1.3 | 0.75 | 8.04 | 4.49 | 80.1 | **3.6** | 10.7 | 10.5 | **5.5** |
| **4.5** | 1.60 | 8.0 | 0.12 | **6.6** | 21.6 | 1.58 | 16.71 | 4.05 | 66.1 | **1.9** | 18.7 | 8.6 | **8.9** |
| **6.6** | 1.40 | 3.7 | 0.04 | **9.8** | 14.5 | 1.87 | 14.40 | 4.48 | 42.1 | **0.6** | 9.6 | 19.6 | **10.0** |
| **7.2** | 1.37 | 3.9 | 0.17 | **4.2** | 1.6 | 0.87 | 6.84 | 3.38 | 66.0 | **0.8** | 19.7 | 46.0 | **7.0** |
| **4.3** | 3.42 | 5.1 | 6.58 | **10.0** | 2.8 | 4.32 | 15.43 | 7.84 | 41.8 | **1.1** | 28.5 | 52.8 | **8.2** |
| **8.6** | 0.28 | 1.7 | 0.08 | **5.0** | 28.1 | 1.12 | 13.66 | 3.25 | 66.2 | **2.4** | 12.3 | 6.0 | **8.0** |
| **2.2** | 2.73 | 17.3 | 0.00 | **2.7** | 0.3 | 0.43 | 4.65 | 3.67 | 85.8 | **2.3** | 21.5 | 18.2 | **3.9** |
| **4.3** | 2.03 | 8.3 | -0.02 | **6.7** | 48.0 | 1.40 | 13.56 | 3.88 | 64.8 | **3.3** | 18.0 | 7.3 | **9.3** |
| **4.5** | 0.47 | 3.9 | 0.44 | **6.6** | 13.8 | 1.32 | 10.57 | 4.68 | 63.6 | **1.2** | 3.8 | 14.5 | **9.0** |
| **5.8** | 0.19 | 1.2 | 0.07 | **8.3** | 238.3 | 1.64 | 9.82 | 4.07 | 46.7 | **2.1** | 8.8 | 11.7 | **10.0** |
| **5.9** | 0.86 | 3.8 | 0.59 | **6.2** | 1.6 | 1.28 | 12.70 | 4.47 | 59.3 | **3.1** | 21.4 | 14.3 | **6.1** |
| **6.3** | 0.91 | 2.5 | 0.00 | **4.8** | 26.9 | 0.93 | 6.27 | 3.01 | 60.6 | **0.6** | 9.6 | 39.4 | **9.2** |
| **2.3** | 2.50 | 21.1 | 0.26 | **4.7** | 4.9 | 1.14 | 13.27 | 4.41 | 77.2 | **2.7** | 24.8 | 16.2 | **3.7** |
| **9.3** | 0.24 | 0.5 | 0.02 | **6.1** | 12.6 | 1.55 | 12.81 | 2.57 | 58.5 | **2.9** | 59.0 | 40.1 | **8.2** |
| **6.2** | 1.74 | 10.2 | 0.20 | **2.8** | 0.7 | 0.49 | 3.78 | 3.10 | 83.2 | **4.1** | 47.7 | 16.5 | **6.4** |
| **8.9** | 0.00 | 0.0 | 0.00 | **0.0** | -1.9 | -2.08 | -7.27 | 3.61 | 140.9 | **6.6** | 41.3 | 0.0 | **1.5** |
| **5.2** | 1.17 | 10.3 | 0.08 | **3.6** | 2.0 | 0.49 | 4.91 | 3.58 | 78.2 | **1.3** | 9.2 | 23.9 | **6.2** |
| **4.9** | 1.51 | 6.6 | 0.01 | **4.1** | 8.8 | 0.80 | 6.45 | 3.20 | 78.0 | **2.5** | 18.2 | 16.2 | **8.1** |
| **5.3** | 0.67 | 4.6 | 0.04 | **4.9** | 5.4 | 1.04 | 9.24 | 3.25 | 56.4 | **0.6** | 11.0 | 54.2 | **7.0** |
| **4.6** | 1.36 | 10.1 | 0.09 | **6.7** | 4.2 | 1.28 | 12.82 | 4.66 | 68.3 | **2.6** | 4.4 | 15.1 | **6.2** |
| **9.5** | 0.11 | 0.9 | 0.00 | **6.0** | 71.2 | 1.99 | 18.90 | 1.98 | 70.4 | **0.9** | 19.5 | 40.0 | **8.9** |
| **6.1** | 0.28 | 2.1 | 0.03 | **5.7** | 2.3 | 1.11 | 13.03 | 4.56 | 69.1 | **4.2** | 12.0 | 7.3 | **5.7** |
| **3.2** | 7.92 | 21.2 | -0.74 | **7.2** | 1.0 | 1.69 | 13.48 | 4.89 | 71.0 | **3.9** | 29.8 | 11.9 | **7.6** |
| **2.1** | 5.17 | 19.3 | -0.28 | **4.4** | 1.7 | 0.87 | 6.29 | 4.66 | 82.8 | **1.9** | 16.8 | 19.6 | **7.5** |
| **9.6** | 0.40 | 1.9 | 0.00 | **6.4** | 24.5 | 1.22 | 14.86 | 2.64 | 45.4 | **3.2** | 62.4 | 43.5 | **7.0** |
| **0.0** | 4.76 | 32.9 | 1.08 | **7.7** | 54.8 | 1.54 | 12.04 | 4.29 | 43.1 | **3.8** | 11.1 | 9.9 | **10.0** |
| **6.7** | 1.93 | 6.1 | 0.00 | **9.2** | 3.1 | 1.63 | 7.54 | 3.56 | 43.9 | **4.4** | 36.2 | 11.9 | **9.1** |
| **6.5** | 0.88 | 6.2 | 0.00 | **1.1** | 0.2 | 0.05 | 0.50 | 2.95 | 99.7 | **0.8** | 15.4 | 33.5 | **6.5** |
| **9.1** | 0.01 | 0.1 | 0.00 | **6.8** | 1.2 | 1.66 | 11.94 | 3.90 | 59.4 | **6.2** | 51.5 | 4.9 | **8.4** |
| **2.3** | 5.07 | 25.3 | 0.22 | **6.1** | 8.8 | 1.37 | 11.07 | 3.59 | 60.8 | **1.6** | 34.2 | 30.3 | **8.7** |
| **7.8** | 0.08 | 0.3 | 0.14 | **9.8** | 23.7 | 2.23 | 12.75 | 4.33 | 43.7 | **3.0** | 34.4 | 23.6 | **9.4** |
| **7.0** | 0.14 | 4.1 | 0.12 | **9.5** | 165.6 | 1.94 | 11.35 | 4.36 | 51.7 | **3.8** | 29.5 | 15.8 | **9.5** |
| **7.8** | 1.04 | 2.1 | 0.70 | **5.2** | 4.4 | 1.09 | 5.88 | 3.41 | 68.8 | **2.6** | 34.8 | 21.4 | **8.4** |
| **5.8** | 0.13 | 0.4 | 1.49 | **4.6** | 12.2 | 0.83 | 5.29 | 4.10 | 66.1 | **4.3** | 6.5 | 5.6 | **7.0** |
| **9.6** | 0.04 | 0.0 | -0.07 | **3.3** | 0.0 | 0.00 | 0.01 | 2.41 | 108.6 | **3.3** | 49.5 | 18.7 | **7.9** |
| **7.1** | 0.23 | 1.2 | 0.00 | **4.5** | 5.6 | 0.78 | 11.01 | 3.52 | 68.1 | **1.1** | 22.0 | 32.9 | **5.1** |
| **5.1** | 1.59 | 5.8 | 0.06 | **6.7** | 3.3 | 1.68 | 16.12 | 4.01 | 60.1 | **3.4** | 42.0 | 18.3 | **6.9** |
| **9.9** | 0.62 | 1.1 | 0.00 | **1.4** | 0.0 | -0.05 | -0.23 | 3.03 | 101.7 | **2.4** | 22.9 | 17.2 | **7.4** |
| **6.6** | 0.81 | 2.8 | 0.07 | **7.8** | 6.3 | 1.88 | 20.31 | 4.01 | 50.7 | **2.7** | 27.1 | 17.2 | **7.4** |
| **7.5** | 0.63 | 3.5 | 0.30 | **5.8** | 73.9 | 1.41 | 18.08 | 3.49 | 63.0 | **2.3** | 16.3 | 17.0 | **7.7** |
| **6.3** | 0.35 | 2.4 | 0.04 | **4.7** | 18.5 | 0.94 | 8.04 | 3.61 | 65.8 | **1.3** | 12.2 | 27.5 | **8.7** |
| **9.9** | 0.60 | 1.3 | 0.00 | **2.7** | 0.4 | 0.34 | 1.59 | 2.90 | 85.4 | **3.9** | 57.1 | 19.6 | **7.6** |
| **5.8** | 0.50 | 4.1 | 0.03 | **4.3** | 194.1 | 0.73 | 7.42 | 2.53 | 59.3 | **2.3** | 12.6 | 8.9 | **8.4** |

| Name | City | State | Rating | 2018 Rating | 2017 Rating | Total Assets ($Mil) | One Year Asset Growth | Asset Mix (As a % of Total Assets): Commercial Loans | Consumer Loans | Mortgage Loans | Securities | Capitalization Index | Leverage Ratio | Risk-Based Capital Ratio |
|---|---|---|---|---|---|---|---|---|---|---|---|---|---|---|
| Investors Community Bank | Chillicothe | MO | **B+** | B+ | B+ | 70.6 | 0.83 | 1.7 | 4.0 | 21.1 | 55.2 | **10.0** | 13.5 | 33.2 |
| Investors Community Bank | Manitowoc | WI | **B-** | B- | B- | 1370.4 | -9.49 | 5.5 | 0.0 | 1.4 | 11.6 | **10.0** | 14.7 | 18.7 |
| Inwood National Bank | Dallas | TX | **A-** | A- | A- | 3038.1 | 7.84 | 3.5 | 0.2 | 11.4 | 33.0 | **8.6** | 10.1 | 14.6 |
| Ion Bank | Naugatuck | CT | **B-** | C+ | C+ | 1362.1 | 4.98 | 10.2 | 13.1 | 28.1 | 5.2 | **8.4** | 10.5 | 13.7 |
| Iowa Falls State Bank | Iowa Falls | IA | **B-** | B- | B+ | 135.3 | 1.27 | 13.0 | 2.2 | 13.9 | 26.4 | **9.2** | 11.7 | 14.3 |
| Iowa Prairie Bank | Brunsville | IA | **D** | D+ | C- | 61.7 | -18.15 | 9.3 | 2.8 | 0.9 | 46.0 | **5.6** | 7.6 | 13.3 |
| Iowa Savings Bank | Carroll | IA | **B** | B | B | 204.5 | 4.45 | 12.2 | 0.6 | 5.6 | 13.1 | **7.0** | 9.5 | 12.5 |
| Iowa State Bank | Algona | IA | **A-** | A- | A- | 325.2 | 0.81 | 9.8 | 1.6 | 9.6 | 21.2 | **10.0** | 12.0 | 18.0 |
| ▼ Iowa State Bank | Clarksville | IA | **D-** | D+ | C- | 376.4 | 2.68 | 10.0 | 0.8 | 2.8 | 14.2 | **6.6** | 8.6 | 12.5 |
| Iowa State Bank | Des Moines | IA | **A** | A | A+ | 396.9 | 3.29 | 4.6 | 0.3 | 11.9 | 38.7 | **10.0** | 17.0 | 27.7 |
| Iowa State Bank | Hull | IA | **A-** | B+ | A | 645.7 | 4.22 | 6.0 | 1.2 | 3.9 | 12.5 | **10.0** | 13.9 | 15.1 |
| Iowa State Bank | Sac City | IA | **A-** | B+ | A- | 133.8 | 4.81 | 8.3 | 5.0 | 20.7 | 5.9 | **10.0** | 12.4 | 17.0 |
| Iowa State Bank and Trust Co. | Fairfield | IA | **B** | B | B | 135.9 | 2.26 | 8.8 | 1.7 | 21.1 | 8.2 | **9.1** | 10.5 | 14.3 |
| Iowa State Savings Bank | Creston | IA | **C** | C- | C- | 215.4 | 6.26 | 2.8 | 1.5 | 11.7 | 16.3 | **7.8** | 9.5 | 14.2 |
| Iowa Trust & Savings Bank | Emmetsburg | IA | **B+** | B+ | B+ | 320.6 | 35.87 | 3.4 | 0.5 | 9.1 | 18.9 | **7.2** | 10.3 | 12.6 |
| ▲ Iowa Trust and Savings Bank | Centerville | IA | **A** | B+ | A- | 173.9 | -1.96 | 4.5 | 2.0 | 6.5 | 53.2 | **10.0** | 11.1 | 18.3 |
| Ipava State Bank | Ipava | IL | **B+** | B+ | B+ | 141.9 | 2.36 | 7.4 | 3.7 | 23.4 | 15.9 | **6.7** | 8.7 | 14.4 |
| Ipswich State Bank | Ipswich | SD | **B** | B | B | 55.8 | -0.81 | 5.0 | 1.0 | 0.0 | 17.2 | **10.0** | 15.9 | 24.3 |
| Ireland Bank | Malad City | ID | **B+** | B- | B- | 249.6 | 6.58 | 15.4 | 1.1 | 3.5 | 25.1 | **9.8** | 10.8 | 19.1 |
| Iron Workers Savings Bank | Aston | PA | **C** | C | C | 180.2 | 2.38 | 0.5 | 0.0 | 45.3 | 9.6 | **8.5** | 10.0 | 16.7 |
| Iroquois Farmers State Bank | Iroquois | IL | **B-** | B- | B- | 111.1 | 2.85 | 2.5 | 3.4 | 13.0 | 13.4 | **7.3** | 9.2 | 14.5 |
| ▲ Iroquois Federal S&L Assn. | Watseka | IL | **B-** | B- | B- | 678.2 | 2.10 | 8.6 | 1.1 | 18.9 | 21.7 | **10.0** | 11.5 | 16.5 |
| Isabella Bank | Mount Pleasant | MI | **B-** | B- | B | 1763.4 | -1.17 | 8.3 | 4.0 | 17.3 | 24.4 | **6.5** | 8.5 | 12.5 |
| Islanders Bank | Friday Harbor | WA | **A-** | B+ | B+ | 297.8 | 7.42 | 5.7 | 1.0 | 16.3 | 20.0 | **10.0** | 11.7 | 19.4 |
| Israel Discount Bank of New York | New York | NY | **B+** | B+ | C+ | 9777.0 | 5.94 | 28.8 | 0.2 | 0.8 | 24.5 | **9.8** | 10.8 | 15.1 |
| Itasca Bank & Trust Co. | Itasca | IL | **B+** | B- | B- | 566.4 | 4.39 | 22.2 | 0.2 | 13.5 | 21.5 | **8.2** | 9.8 | 13.9 |
| ITS Bank | Johnston | IA | **U** | U | U | 8.1 | 6.56 | 0.0 | 0.0 | 0.0 | 38.5 | **10.0** | 93.4 | 467.9 |
| Iuka State Bank | Salem | IL | **C** | D+ | C | 101.3 | 7.32 | 10.7 | 11.3 | 12.6 | 6.9 | **7.4** | 9.7 | 12.8 |
| Ixonia Bank | Ixonia | WI | **B-** | C+ | C+ | 389.5 | 7.00 | 22.2 | 0.2 | 4.0 | 24.3 | **9.4** | 10.9 | 14.5 |
| Jacksboro National Bank | Jacksboro | TX | **B+** | B+ | B+ | 235.5 | -2.02 | 7.1 | 3.1 | 9.9 | 47.2 | **10.0** | 12.7 | 24.1 |
| Jackson County Bank | Seymour | IN | **B-** | B- | B- | 589.6 | 3.83 | 4.1 | 1.1 | 22.0 | 14.9 | **7.4** | 9.3 | 12.8 |
| ▲ Jackson County Bank | McKee | KY | **A** | A- | A | 137.1 | 1.22 | 1.6 | 10.3 | 20.3 | 38.6 | **10.0** | 27.1 | 51.4 |
| Jackson County Bank | Black River Falls | WI | **D-** | C- | B- | 201.0 | -7.00 | 0.7 | 1.2 | 12.5 | 31.1 | **8.1** | 9.7 | 18.3 |
| Jackson Federal S&L Assn. | Jackson | MN | **C** | C | C+ | 37.2 | -3.50 | 5.4 | 3.8 | 28.7 | 38.5 | **10.0** | 24.1 | 40.4 |
| Jackson Parish Bank | Jonesboro | LA | **B-** | B- | C+ | 83.8 | 1.63 | 3.9 | 3.8 | 10.1 | 46.1 | **10.0** | 15.4 | 42.9 |
| Jackson Savings Bank, SSB | Sylva | NC | **B-** | C+ | C | 33.4 | 2.86 | 0.0 | 0.6 | 63.5 | 0.0 | **10.0** | 20.8 | 43.3 |
| James Polk Stone Community Bank | Portales | NM | **A-** | B+ | A- | 229.8 | 4.32 | 6.4 | 4.8 | 22.8 | 28.2 | **10.0** | 11.5 | 22.7 |
| Janesville State Bank | Janesville | MN | **B+** | B+ | A- | 75.3 | 7.60 | 3.2 | 2.6 | 20.0 | 9.5 | **10.0** | 13.3 | 17.1 |
| ▼ Jarrettsville Federal S&L Assn. | Jarrettsville | MD | **C+** | B- | B- | 130.1 | 6.92 | 0.8 | 0.0 | 57.2 | 8.4 | **10.0** | 13.8 | 29.6 |
| JD Bank | Jennings | LA | **B+** | B | B- | 881.9 | 2.23 | 8.1 | 3.9 | 18.6 | 19.3 | **10.0** | 11.1 | 16.3 |
| Jeff Bank | Jeffersonville | NY | **B+** | B | B+ | 506.0 | 0.85 | 6.0 | 0.7 | 22.2 | 19.3 | **10.0** | 11.8 | 19.8 |
| ▲ Jefferson Bank | Greenville | MS | **A-** | B+ | A- | 124.8 | -4.05 | 9.3 | 0.3 | 3.7 | 19.7 | **10.0** | 17.6 | 21.9 |
| Jefferson Bank | San Antonio | TX | **B+** | B+ | B+ | 1954.1 | 2.55 | 6.8 | 1.4 | 24.0 | 15.2 | **8.2** | 9.8 | 13.5 |
| Jefferson Bank and Trust Co. | Saint Louis | MO | **B** | B | B- | 617.6 | -0.38 | 11.8 | 1.1 | 4.9 | 20.0 | **9.3** | 12.0 | 14.4 |
| Jefferson Bank of Missouri | Jefferson City | MO | **B+** | B+ | B | 644.7 | 9.62 | 7.7 | 22.5 | 18.6 | 21.2 | **7.2** | 9.1 | 12.9 |
| ▲ Jefferson Security Bank | Shepherdstown | WV | **B-** | C+ | C+ | 324.4 | 4.41 | 1.6 | 1.2 | 35.8 | 26.8 | **7.8** | 9.5 | 16.3 |
| Jersey Shore State Bank | Williamsport | PA | **B-** | B- | B- | 1231.3 | -1.90 | 3.0 | 12.0 | 21.4 | 9.6 | **5.1** | 8.2 | 11.1 |
| Jersey State Bank | Jerseyville | IL | **B+** | B+ | B+ | 146.5 | 0.63 | 6.1 | 0.7 | 8.1 | 46.5 | **10.0** | 14.1 | 26.2 |
| Jewett City Savings Bank | Jewett City | CT | **B** | B- | C+ | 295.0 | 3.94 | 9.4 | 2.0 | 38.4 | 6.0 | **10.0** | 16.2 | 23.7 |
| Jim Thorpe Neighborhood Bank | Jim Thorpe | PA | **C+** | C+ | C+ | 198.1 | 3.83 | 1.4 | 0.7 | 24.1 | 34.6 | **7.9** | 9.6 | 20.2 |
| John Deere Financial, F.S.B. | Madison | WI | **A-** | A- | A- | 2832.2 | -5.64 | 5.1 | 16.8 | 0.0 | 0.0 | **10.0** | 17.5 | 22.1 |
| John Marshall Bank | Reston | VA | **B+** | B+ | B+ | 1581.0 | 13.40 | 4.8 | 0.0 | 11.1 | 7.8 | **8.3** | 11.9 | 13.5 |
| Johnson Bank | Racine | WI | **A-** | A- | B | 5209.9 | 4.53 | 18.4 | 1.8 | 18.6 | 11.6 | **10.0** | 12.3 | 16.5 |
| ▲ Johnson City Bank | Johnson City | TX | **A-** | A- | A- | 118.5 | 0.28 | 6.9 | 8.7 | 23.3 | 7.2 | **10.0** | 12.3 | 24.9 |
| Johnson County Bank | Mountain City | TN | **B** | B | B+ | 122.6 | 2.88 | 3.6 | 4.5 | 33.6 | 31.5 | **10.0** | 15.6 | 30.4 |
| Johnson State Bank | Johnson | KS | **B** | B | B+ | 86.9 | 5.05 | 4.4 | 1.6 | 3.8 | 37.5 | **10.0** | 16.0 | 28.8 |
| Jonah Bank of Wyoming | Casper | WY | **B** | B- | B+ | 342.4 | 4.37 | 18.4 | 0.5 | 9.5 | 8.8 | **8.2** | 10.5 | 13.5 |
| ▲ Jones Bank | Seward | NE | **B+** | B- | B+ | 321.8 | 37.43 | 10.7 | 1.3 | 8.1 | 30.7 | **10.0** | 11.5 | 17.4 |
| Jonesboro State Bank | Jonesboro | LA | **A-** | A | A | 315.2 | 13.00 | 0.9 | 1.0 | 4.4 | 86.3 | **10.0** | 11.9 | 40.9 |
| ▲ Jonesburg State Bank | Jonesburg | MO | **B** | B- | B- | 100.4 | 5.76 | 5.5 | 2.1 | 22.7 | 2.3 | **6.3** | 8.4 | 15.1 |

| Asset Quality Index | Adjusted Non-Performing Loans as a % of Total Loans | Adjusted Non-Performing Loans as a % of Capital | Net Charge-Offs Avg Loans | Profitability Index | Net Income ($Mil) | Return on Assets (R.O.A.) | Return on Equity (R.O.E.) | Net Interest Spread | Overhead Efficiency Ratio | Liquidity Index | Liquidity Ratio | Hot Money Ratio | Stability Index |
|---|---|---|---|---|---|---|---|---|---|---|---|---|---|
| **8.7** | 0.16 | 0.4 | 0.09 | **4.0** | 0.7 | 0.93 | 6.80 | 3.33 | 72.9 | **5.5** | 58.1 | 10.7 | **8.0** |
| **3.2** | 5.08 | 15.8 | 0.15 | **6.3** | 19.4 | 1.34 | 9.88 | 3.18 | 55.5 | **1.0** | 20.8 | 28.6 | **9.7** |
| **7.5** | 0.03 | 0.2 | -0.01 | **8.2** | 54.6 | 1.90 | 17.42 | 3.30 | 44.1 | **4.4** | 29.5 | 12.6 | **10.0** |
| **4.6** | 1.60 | 10.5 | 0.10 | **3.6** | 9.5 | 0.71 | 7.70 | 3.43 | 78.6 | **2.7** | 12.6 | 8.3 | **7.3** |
| **4.4** | 1.79 | 9.6 | 0.64 | **6.1** | 2.0 | 1.44 | 12.20 | 3.65 | 61.1 | **3.6** | 33.6 | 14.9 | **7.4** |
| **4.6** | 0.74 | 3.9 | 0.02 | **1.3** | 0.1 | 0.13 | 1.78 | 3.37 | 96.1 | **3.7** | 13.8 | 10.2 | **1.1** |
| **7.2** | 0.57 | 2.0 | 0.01 | **6.8** | 3.3 | 1.66 | 17.62 | 3.47 | 61.5 | **3.6** | 19.1 | 8.4 | **6.7** |
| **5.6** | 3.38 | 11.1 | 0.00 | **5.7** | 3.9 | 1.19 | 9.45 | 4.05 | 61.8 | **2.8** | 16.8 | 15.1 | **8.1** |
| **0.0** | 9.61 | 63.4 | 1.18 | **3.0** | 1.8 | 0.47 | 5.41 | 2.91 | 45.0 | **1.1** | 27.9 | 32.8 | **4.2** |
| **9.3** | 0.40 | 0.5 | -0.02 | **6.6** | 5.7 | 1.50 | 8.45 | 3.31 | 64.8 | **6.0** | 53.7 | 7.8 | **10.0** |
| **7.2** | 0.17 | 1.3 | 0.04 | **7.1** | 9.3 | 1.53 | 10.76 | 3.30 | 52.0 | **3.4** | 16.4 | 12.0 | **9.5** |
| **7.6** | 0.03 | 0.4 | 0.04 | **8.5** | 2.5 | 1.94 | 14.81 | 3.72 | 47.5 | **2.9** | 17.2 | 14.5 | **9.5** |
| **7.1** | 1.18 | 4.1 | 0.00 | **4.8** | 1.3 | 0.97 | 9.85 | 3.55 | 64.3 | **1.7** | 19.9 | 23.3 | **6.2** |
| **4.2** | 0.44 | 2.4 | 0.14 | **3.3** | 1.3 | 0.64 | 6.67 | 3.95 | 76.8 | **2.8** | 18.1 | 15.5 | **6.5** |
| **8.1** | 0.00 | 0.0 | -0.02 | **7.8** | 5.0 | 1.80 | 15.98 | 4.23 | 55.9 | **0.8** | 13.2 | 28.3 | **7.0** |
| **9.0** | 0.00 | 0.0 | 0.03 | **6.5** | 2.7 | 1.55 | 14.38 | 3.49 | 55.8 | **4.6** | 42.0 | 12.4 | **7.9** |
| **8.6** | 0.01 | 0.6 | 0.09 | **6.3** | 2.2 | 1.56 | 17.92 | 4.20 | 66.8 | **2.9** | 14.1 | 14.5 | **6.4** |
| **7.6** | 0.01 | 0.0 | 0.01 | **5.4** | 0.7 | 1.20 | 7.50 | 3.68 | 62.8 | **1.8** | 30.1 | 27.8 | **8.2** |
| **6.0** | 1.19 | 3.5 | -0.03 | **5.5** | 2.7 | 1.11 | 10.19 | 5.16 | 73.0 | **5.3** | 32.8 | 5.1 | **6.8** |
| **9.2** | 0.16 | 1.1 | 0.00 | **2.4** | 0.4 | 0.24 | 2.43 | 3.16 | 90.2 | **1.9** | 22.5 | 20.9 | **5.2** |
| **5.5** | 0.32 | 4.9 | 0.38 | **4.0** | 1.1 | 0.95 | 10.13 | 3.44 | 66.0 | **4.0** | 26.5 | 10.7 | **5.6** |
| **8.6** | 0.29 | 1.4 | 0.01 | **3.4** | 4.0 | 0.59 | 5.26 | 2.69 | 75.3 | **1.0** | 15.7 | 28.0 | **7.4** |
| **4.9** | 2.31 | 10.3 | 0.04 | **4.4** | 17.2 | 0.98 | 11.38 | 3.05 | 68.1 | **1.9** | 18.2 | 18.8 | **7.8** |
| **5.8** | 2.14 | 6.6 | 0.06 | **8.6** | 4.9 | 1.72 | 14.71 | 4.32 | 52.1 | **5.8** | 37.3 | 3.3 | **8.6** |
| **8.2** | 0.29 | 1.0 | -0.01 | **4.9** | 100.4 | 1.05 | 9.92 | 2.80 | 59.6 | **1.7** | 28.0 | 27.9 | **8.7** |
| **5.6** | 1.51 | 7.3 | -0.02 | **6.8** | 7.1 | 1.27 | 12.91 | 4.14 | 59.8 | **1.7** | 20.6 | 23.3 | **7.1** |
| **10.0** | na | 0.0 | na | **10.0** | 0.5 | 5.88 | 6.34 | 7.02 | 20.2 | **4.0** | na | 100.0 | **5.8** |
| **3.5** | 1.42 | 11.7 | 0.26 | **4.5** | 1.1 | 1.11 | 11.35 | 4.50 | 64.2 | **1.3** | 16.2 | 22.7 | **4.3** |
| **8.3** | 0.29 | 1.4 | 0.21 | **3.9** | 2.4 | 0.66 | 5.47 | 3.59 | 76.2 | **2.7** | 35.9 | 13.7 | **6.1** |
| **7.1** | 1.15 | 3.7 | 0.10 | **4.8** | 2.7 | 1.13 | 9.07 | 3.82 | 74.1 | **3.5** | 33.1 | 15.2 | **7.1** |
| **4.8** | 1.63 | 6.9 | 0.07 | **4.3** | 5.4 | 0.91 | 9.22 | 3.33 | 74.1 | **3.3** | 21.0 | 13.2 | **6.7** |
| **8.2** | 0.82 | 2.2 | 0.25 | **7.2** | 2.0 | 1.45 | 5.26 | 4.22 | 57.7 | **4.6** | 52.6 | 14.9 | **8.4** |
| **2.7** | 12.59 | 23.6 | 3.84 | **0.3** | -0.6 | -0.28 | -2.93 | 2.72 | 90.5 | **2.5** | 44.2 | 12.5 | **3.6** |
| **7.9** | 0.59 | 1.1 | 0.00 | **1.9** | 0.1 | 0.18 | 0.74 | 3.41 | 89.7 | **3.8** | 35.9 | 14.9 | **6.4** |
| **8.1** | 1.01 | 3.2 | 0.37 | **3.9** | 0.7 | 1.00 | 6.78 | 3.23 | 70.1 | **6.4** | 58.3 | 4.9 | **6.3** |
| **7.0** | 0.76 | 5.2 | 0.00 | **2.8** | 0.2 | 0.45 | 2.18 | 3.37 | 82.0 | **1.4** | 31.5 | 41.2 | **6.9** |
| **6.0** | 1.77 | 7.1 | 0.12 | **6.8** | 3.6 | 1.59 | 14.18 | 4.88 | 68.8 | **5.6** | 30.5 | 1.7 | **7.8** |
| **7.5** | 0.00 | 0.0 | 0.00 | **7.6** | 1.3 | 1.81 | 13.87 | 3.92 | 54.5 | **2.8** | 6.4 | 14.3 | **8.6** |
| **8.8** | 0.67 | 3.5 | 0.03 | **2.4** | 0.3 | 0.25 | 1.78 | 2.52 | 86.4 | **2.1** | 33.4 | 27.1 | **7.5** |
| **5.0** | 2.30 | 10.2 | 0.08 | **5.7** | 9.8 | 1.13 | 9.90 | 4.68 | 73.4 | **4.2** | 26.6 | 9.5 | **7.5** |
| **4.3** | 3.48 | 18.2 | 0.29 | **5.9** | 6.4 | 1.23 | 11.33 | 4.40 | 63.3 | **5.0** | 29.5 | 5.1 | **7.9** |
| **8.5** | 0.29 | 0.9 | 2.42 | **6.2** | 1.5 | 1.21 | 6.62 | 4.83 | 58.0 | **0.8** | 26.0 | 46.5 | **8.8** |
| **8.4** | 0.35 | 2.7 | 0.01 | **5.4** | 24.3 | 1.28 | 14.79 | 3.69 | 70.3 | **2.7** | 26.8 | 20.3 | **8.3** |
| **7.4** | 0.03 | 0.4 | 0.00 | **5.1** | 6.8 | 1.09 | 9.28 | 2.96 | 52.7 | **1.0** | 11.2 | 26.4 | **8.0** |
| **4.4** | 0.68 | 4.5 | 0.13 | **9.7** | 11.5 | 1.84 | 19.79 | 4.09 | 48.3 | **3.6** | 19.9 | 10.1 | **7.8** |
| **4.3** | 2.51 | 15.5 | 0.05 | **4.1** | 2.8 | 0.89 | 10.85 | 3.43 | 69.6 | **4.2** | 13.3 | 7.0 | **4.8** |
| **4.3** | 1.26 | 10.1 | 0.45 | **4.8** | 13.2 | 1.07 | 13.73 | 3.16 | 60.0 | **1.2** | 7.9 | 18.8 | **7.0** |
| **7.7** | 3.00 | 5.4 | 0.00 | **4.3** | 1.5 | 0.98 | 6.81 | 3.29 | 68.1 | **5.4** | 40.0 | 7.7 | **8.0** |
| **5.7** | 2.46 | 8.5 | 0.32 | **3.8** | 2.1 | 0.71 | 4.26 | 4.06 | 77.9 | **4.1** | 16.5 | 8.4 | **7.2** |
| **8.0** | 0.45 | 1.7 | 0.04 | **3.1** | 1.2 | 0.64 | 6.37 | 3.16 | 80.3 | **3.0** | 25.0 | 14.9 | **5.5** |
| **5.8** | 0.20 | 0.9 | 0.96 | **10.0** | 130.0 | 3.84 | 22.13 | 6.22 | 31.5 | **0.0** | 0.4 | 99.1 | **9.7** |
| **7.4** | 0.07 | 0.2 | 0.01 | **5.8** | 17.4 | 1.18 | 9.94 | 3.51 | 55.0 | **0.8** | 12.2 | 31.9 | **9.0** |
| **7.8** | 0.47 | 2.5 | 0.08 | **6.0** | 58.4 | 1.14 | 8.96 | 3.73 | 68.7 | **4.5** | 13.8 | 5.3 | **10.0** |
| **7.7** | 1.27 | 3.3 | 0.17 | **5.4** | 1.5 | 1.26 | 10.35 | 3.93 | 67.7 | **2.6** | 41.6 | 27.9 | **7.8** |
| **5.3** | 3.87 | 9.9 | 0.08 | **4.4** | 0.9 | 0.75 | 4.70 | 3.72 | 77.5 | **2.2** | 37.4 | 29.1 | **8.0** |
| **3.7** | 4.60 | 19.9 | 0.29 | **5.6** | 1.0 | 1.31 | 8.17 | 3.77 | 63.2 | **4.5** | 45.3 | 13.6 | **8.1** |
| **5.1** | 0.82 | 5.5 | 0.00 | **7.4** | 4.9 | 1.49 | 14.24 | 4.17 | 61.5 | **4.4** | 17.0 | 6.1 | **7.3** |
| **7.6** | 0.25 | 1.1 | 0.27 | **6.6** | 4.2 | 1.52 | 13.64 | 4.64 | 60.9 | **3.5** | 20.3 | 12.3 | **7.5** |
| **9.1** | 4.88 | 3.1 | 0.12 | **5.4** | 5.4 | 1.94 | 13.25 | 2.54 | 75.3 | **2.9** | 76.5 | 62.7 | **8.8** |
| **8.0** | 0.66 | 2.4 | 0.01 | **6.7** | 1.6 | 1.60 | 19.91 | 4.09 | 63.7 | **3.6** | 29.5 | 13.3 | **6.3** |

| Name | City | State | Rating | 2018 Rating | 2017 Rating | Total Assets ($Mil) | One Year Asset Growth | Asset Mix (As a % of Total Assets) Commercial Loans | Consumer Loans | Mortgage Loans | Securities | Capitalization Index | Leverage Ratio | Risk-Based Capital Ratio |
|---|---|---|---|---|---|---|---|---|---|---|---|---|---|---|
| ▲ Jonestown Bank and Trust Co. | Jonestown | PA | **C+** | C | C | 628.0 | 6.68 | 3.5 | 24.8 | 18.9 | 5.7 | **7.1** | 9.1 | 12.6 |
| JPMorgan Chase Bank, Dearborn | Dearborn | MI | **U** | U | B | 61.2 | 0.54 | 0.0 | 0.0 | 0.0 | 0.0 | **10.0** | 99.7 | 511.1 |
| JPMorgan Chase Bank, N.A. | Columbus | OH | **B+** | B+ | B | 2337646.0 | 5.35 | 7.3 | 9.1 | 9.3 | 17.1 | **6.8** | 8.8 | 15.4 |
| Junction National Bank | Junction | TX | **B** | B+ | B+ | 68.2 | 8.00 | 4.1 | 2.7 | 6.0 | 60.0 | **7.9** | 9.6 | 31.1 |
| Juniata Valley Bank | Mifflintown | PA | **B-** | B- | B- | 669.4 | 7.28 | 7.6 | 1.3 | 20.8 | 31.4 | **7.9** | 9.6 | 15.9 |
| Kahoka State Bank | Kahoka | MO | **B-** | C+ | C | 52.2 | 6.29 | 5.0 | 5.0 | 23.3 | 29.9 | **9.4** | 10.6 | 18.2 |
| Kalamazoo County State Bank | Schoolcraft | MI | **C+** | C | C | 96.0 | -1.38 | 3.4 | 15.7 | 11.9 | 43.1 | **10.0** | 12.3 | 23.3 |
| ▲ Kansas State Bank | Ottawa | KS | **B+** | B- | B- | 155.7 | 1.19 | 7.4 | 1.6 | 12.9 | 54.2 | **8.0** | 9.7 | 20.7 |
| Kansas State Bank Overbrook Kansas | Overbrook | KS | **B+** | B+ | B+ | 66.6 | 7.67 | 8.8 | 3.1 | 6.8 | 43.7 | **10.0** | 13.4 | 21.9 |
| KansasLand Bank | Quinter | KS | **C-** | C+ | C | 52.8 | -1.18 | 5.1 | 1.9 | 10.6 | 21.5 | **7.7** | 9.5 | 15.8 |
| Kanza Bank | Kingman | KS | **B-** | B- | B- | 236.6 | 3.83 | 9.4 | 0.8 | 22.2 | 18.2 | **8.4** | 9.9 | 14.7 |
| ▲ Karnes County National Bank | Karnes City | TX | **B** | C | C+ | 424.9 | 2.72 | 1.7 | 0.8 | 2.9 | 73.8 | **9.7** | 10.8 | 35.9 |
| Katahdin Trust Co. | Patten | ME | **B-** | B- | C+ | 850.7 | 5.95 | 19.7 | 0.9 | 18.6 | 11.8 | **8.0** | 9.7 | 13.8 |
| Kaw Valley Bank | Topeka | KS | **B-** | C+ | C | 312.7 | 2.07 | 15.3 | 2.6 | 20.0 | 5.2 | **9.9** | 10.9 | 15.0 |
| ▲ Kaw Valley State Bank | Eudora | KS | **B-** | C | C- | 51.3 | 4.62 | 5.8 | 5.5 | 19.8 | 41.8 | **7.8** | 9.5 | 19.6 |
| ▼ Kaw Valley State Bank and Trust Co. | Wamego | KS | **A-** | A | A | 191.7 | 10.13 | 7.1 | 1.9 | 14.0 | 32.7 | **10.0** | 12.0 | 21.2 |
| Kearney Trust Co. | Kearney | MO | **A-** | A- | A- | 208.3 | 13.66 | 5.5 | 3.7 | 16.1 | 22.9 | **9.2** | 10.4 | 17.3 |
| Kearny Bank | Fairfield | NJ | **B-** | B- | C+ | 6589.0 | -1.43 | 1.0 | 0.1 | 20.9 | 21.6 | **10.0** | 12.0 | 21.1 |
| Kearny County Bank | Lakin | KS | **A-** | B+ | A | 218.7 | 7.79 | 14.4 | 1.7 | 12.8 | 17.4 | **10.0** | 16.9 | 23.0 |
| KEB Hana Bank USA, N.A. | New York | NY | **D** | D | D | 243.1 | 7.33 | 0.0 | 0.0 | 1.4 | 27.1 | **10.0** | 15.8 | 28.1 |
| Kendall State Bank | Valley Falls | KS | **C-** | C | C+ | 39.7 | 9.76 | 4.9 | 2.2 | 13.3 | 0.2 | **9.4** | 10.6 | 15.5 |
| Kennebec Federal S&L Assn. of Waterville | Waterville | ME | **C** | C- | C | 96.0 | -1.22 | 0.0 | 0.1 | 77.5 | 2.5 | **6.9** | 8.9 | 15.4 |
| ▲ Kennebec Savings Bank | Augusta | ME | **A-** | B+ | B+ | 1161.1 | 8.80 | 3.7 | 0.3 | 56.8 | 7.5 | **10.0** | 13.6 | 17.2 |
| Kennebunk Savings Bank | Kennebunk | ME | **B** | B | B | 1326.7 | 6.11 | 3.0 | 0.1 | 27.1 | 8.4 | **10.0** | 11.7 | 15.7 |
| ▲ Kennett Trust Bank | Kennett | MO | **B** | C+ | C+ | 106.7 | -10.07 | 9.7 | 3.1 | 33.5 | 20.9 | **10.0** | 11.5 | 19.3 |
| Kensington Bank | Kensington | MN | **C-** | C+ | B | 277.6 | -1.71 | 9.4 | 1.1 | 8.4 | 8.1 | **5.5** | 8.9 | 11.4 |
| Kentland Bank | Kentland | IN | **A** | A- | A- | 301.0 | -2.33 | 11.2 | 1.5 | 8.5 | 29.6 | **10.0** | 14.2 | 19.1 |
| Kentland Federal S&L Assn. | Kentland | IN | **D** | D | D | 4.1 | -4.79 | 0.6 | 0.0 | 91.5 | 1.7 | **10.0** | 13.4 | 28.1 |
| Kentucky Bank | Paris | KY | **B+** | B+ | B | 1107.7 | 2.23 | 4.6 | 2.1 | 21.2 | 24.0 | **7.5** | 9.3 | 14.7 |
| Kentucky Farmers Bank Corp. | Ashland | KY | **A** | A | A | 208.1 | 16.61 | 3.9 | 5.6 | 25.8 | 32.9 | **10.0** | 20.9 | 32.9 |
| ▲ Kerndt Brothers Savings Bank | Lansing | IA | **B-** | C+ | B | 290.0 | 2.49 | 10.5 | 0.9 | 8.1 | 21.8 | **9.2** | 10.5 | 14.4 |
| Key Community Bank | Inver Grove Heights | MN | **C+** | C+ | C | 52.3 | 5.44 | 7.5 | 5.6 | 7.4 | 0.5 | **9.3** | 10.5 | 18.8 |
| Key National Trust Co. of Delaware | Wilmington | DE | **U** | U | U | 4.7 | 7.87 | 0.0 | 0.0 | 0.0 | 0.0 | **10.0** | 98.1 | 445.0 |
| KeyBank N.A. | Cleveland | OH | **B** | B | B | 143390.3 | 3.92 | 26.4 | 7.1 | 7.7 | 22.3 | **7.2** | 9.9 | 12.7 |
| KeySavings Bank | Wisconsin Rapids | WI | **C-** | C- | C- | 80.8 | 5.60 | 0.9 | 1.2 | 44.1 | 24.2 | **10.0** | 14.2 | 31.7 |
| Keystone Bank, N.A. | Austin | TX | **C** | C | C+ | 201.1 | 167.28 | 6.0 | 1.0 | 14.2 | 10.1 | **10.0** | 11.4 | 17.3 |
| Keystone Savings Bank | Keystone | IA | **B-** | B | B+ | 145.4 | 2.60 | 7.8 | 2.1 | 19.6 | 25.5 | **6.7** | 9.7 | 12.3 |
| Killbuck Savings Bank Co. | Killbuck | OH | **A-** | A- | B+ | 565.6 | 8.61 | 9.7 | 1.2 | 20.7 | 26.0 | **9.2** | 10.5 | 15.1 |
| ▲ Kindred State Bank | Kindred | ND | **C** | D+ | D+ | 31.1 | -0.90 | 4.4 | 7.7 | 4.1 | 5.7 | **6.8** | 8.8 | 17.2 |
| Kingston National Bank | Kingston | OH | **B** | B | B | 373.2 | 6.35 | 8.5 | 2.0 | 20.9 | 22.0 | **6.4** | 8.4 | 12.7 |
| Kingstree Federal S&L Assn. | Kingstree | SC | **C+** | C+ | C+ | 34.6 | 10.41 | 0.7 | 0.4 | 40.8 | 14.5 | **10.0** | 16.4 | 36.1 |
| Kinmundy Bank | Kinmundy | IL | **B** | B- | B+ | 48.7 | 2.46 | 7.7 | 17.7 | 28.1 | 14.0 | **9.7** | 10.8 | 17.5 |
| ▲ Kirkpatrick Bank | Edmond | OK | **B+** | B- | B | 818.6 | 1.90 | 7.1 | 1.0 | 5.9 | 15.4 | **10.0** | 11.7 | 15.7 |
| Kirkwood Bank and Trust Co. | Bismarck | ND | **B** | B- | B- | 246.2 | 3.63 | 11.6 | 3.8 | 9.7 | 13.1 | **7.9** | 9.8 | 13.3 |
| Kirkwood Bank of Nevada | Las Vegas | NV | **B+** | B | B | 139.0 | 61.29 | 4.2 | 0.0 | 2.5 | 0.0 | **10.0** | 12.7 | 18.6 |
| Kish Bank | Belleville | PA | **C+** | C+ | C+ | 916.9 | 8.06 | 10.9 | 0.8 | 24.5 | 15.1 | **6.1** | 8.7 | 11.8 |
| Kitsap Bank | Port Orchard | WA | **A-** | B | B | 1168.1 | 2.81 | 9.1 | 0.4 | 8.8 | 22.2 | **7.3** | 9.2 | 12.7 |
| ▲ Kleberg Bank, N.A. | Kingsville | TX | **B-** | C | B- | 572.4 | 8.34 | 9.0 | 14.7 | 11.6 | 20.5 | **7.2** | 9.2 | 14.3 |
| KodaBank | Drayton | ND | **B** | C+ | B- | 154.6 | 4.96 | 10.5 | 6.9 | 10.2 | 12.5 | **10.0** | 12.2 | 16.5 |
| ▲ Kress National Bank | Kress | TX | **B** | B- | B- | 44.8 | 1.76 | 7.4 | 2.9 | 0.5 | 24.7 | **10.0** | 12.4 | 30.8 |
| ▲ KS Bank, Inc. | Smithfield | NC | **B-** | B- | B- | 403.4 | 0.81 | 3.1 | 0.4 | 23.0 | 16.7 | **8.1** | 9.7 | 14.0 |
| KS StateBank | Manhattan | KS | **A-** | A- | A- | 2142.2 | 5.56 | 13.0 | 0.4 | 16.6 | 15.5 | **7.7** | 9.5 | 14.2 |
| La Monte Community Bank | La Monte | MO | **B+** | B+ | B+ | 30.5 | 2.91 | 3.4 | 2.2 | 16.6 | 23.0 | **10.0** | 11.3 | 18.7 |
| Labette Bank | Altamont | KS | **B+** | B+ | B | 399.2 | -1.10 | 2.5 | 2.7 | 25.5 | 18.5 | **10.0** | 12.2 | 19.0 |
| Ladysmith Federal S&L Assn. | Ladysmith | WI | **B-** | C | C- | 55.9 | 8.25 | 12.1 | 6.2 | 49.1 | 8.9 | **9.8** | 10.9 | 20.4 |
| ▲ Lafayette State Bank | Mayo | FL | **E+** | E- | E- | 109.2 | 9.55 | 6.6 | 2.8 | 15.0 | 7.2 | **6.1** | 8.1 | 13.6 |
| ▲ Lake Area Bank | Lindstrom | MN | **B** | B | B- | 359.3 | 7.30 | 8.2 | 0.1 | 20.7 | 18.6 | **6.9** | 10.3 | 12.4 |
| ▲ Lake Bank | Two Harbors | MN | **B** | C | D+ | 130.9 | -2.61 | 5.9 | 1.4 | 36.0 | 21.6 | **9.0** | 10.3 | 16.9 |
| Lake Central Bank | Annandale | MN | **A** | A- | A- | 158.4 | 4.44 | 7.1 | 0.6 | 16.3 | 36.1 | **10.0** | 13.0 | 17.7 |
| Lake City Bank | Warsaw | IN | **A-** | A- | A- | 4934.3 | 1.55 | 28.9 | 2.0 | 3.8 | 12.3 | **8.9** | 11.4 | 14.0 |

| Asset Quality Index | Adjusted Non-Performing Loans as a % of Total Loans | Adjusted Non-Performing Loans as a % of Capital | Net Charge-Offs Avg Loans | Profitability Index | Net Income ($Mil) | Return on Assets (R.O.A.) | Return on Equity (R.O.E.) | Net Interest Spread | Overhead Efficiency Ratio | Liquidity Index | Liquidity Ratio | Hot Money Ratio | Stability Index |
|---|---|---|---|---|---|---|---|---|---|---|---|---|---|
| **3.4** | 0.89 | 6.0 | 0.14 | **4.4** | 5.4 | 0.87 | 9.63 | 3.63 | 70.1 | **2.3** | 8.7 | 16.7 | **6.2** |
| **10.0** | na | 0.0 | 0.00 | **9.0** | 1.8 | 2.82 | 3.00 | 2.85 | 0.1 | **4.0** | na | 100.0 | **7.0** |
| **6.5** | 1.00 | 3.5 | 0.60 | **6.2** | 31339.0 | 1.34 | 13.21 | 2.78 | 57.5 | **6.6** | 54.2 | 4.9 | **9.3** |
| **9.6** | 0.43 | 0.9 | 0.08 | **5.6** | 1.0 | 1.42 | 14.94 | 3.04 | 59.4 | **4.9** | 72.3 | 15.9 | **5.6** |
| **5.2** | 0.86 | 4.7 | -0.12 | **4.2** | 5.9 | 0.92 | 8.45 | 3.57 | 79.1 | **4.7** | 29.4 | 7.6 | **6.9** |
| **7.6** | 0.75 | 3.3 | 0.12 | **3.6** | 0.3 | 0.58 | 5.36 | 3.53 | 71.8 | **1.7** | 29.9 | 28.9 | **5.4** |
| **8.1** | 0.02 | 0.6 | -0.01 | **2.5** | 0.3 | 0.26 | 2.23 | 3.59 | 89.1 | **6.2** | 58.6 | 5.8 | **5.8** |
| **9.3** | 0.26 | 1.1 | 0.03 | **6.1** | 2.3 | 1.58 | 17.56 | 3.21 | 57.4 | **3.3** | 6.4 | 11.5 | **5.4** |
| **6.4** | 2.28 | 5.2 | -0.07 | **6.1** | 0.8 | 1.26 | 9.22 | 4.01 | 61.4 | **3.0** | 45.2 | 21.9 | **8.2** |
| **1.5** | 9.68 | 37.3 | 2.58 | **0.3** | -1.0 | -1.85 | -19.19 | 3.64 | 88.0 | **0.9** | 11.6 | 33.1 | **5.7** |
| **7.9** | 0.15 | 0.7 | 0.25 | **3.6** | 1.6 | 0.71 | 6.80 | 3.86 | 75.9 | **2.5** | 11.5 | 16.3 | **6.6** |
| **6.4** | 8.38 | 7.1 | -1.43 | **4.7** | 5.1 | 1.23 | 12.62 | 2.98 | 61.5 | **7.0** | 77.1 | 6.2 | **5.1** |
| **5.0** | 0.73 | 4.9 | 0.00 | **4.9** | 8.7 | 1.06 | 10.56 | 3.70 | 66.7 | **0.6** | 10.7 | 16.7 | **6.6** |
| **3.5** | 4.02 | 15.1 | -0.14 | **6.4** | 4.2 | 1.35 | 12.22 | 4.67 | 57.0 | **0.8** | 12.1 | 32.9 | **7.3** |
| **6.2** | 0.92 | 4.0 | 0.08 | **5.4** | 0.7 | 1.26 | 13.31 | 4.10 | 68.4 | **4.9** | 29.1 | 5.9 | **6.2** |
| **6.2** | 2.33 | 11.1 | 0.02 | **7.0** | 3.1 | 1.72 | 14.31 | 3.44 | 58.1 | **2.3** | 30.4 | 20.3 | **8.0** |
| **8.7** | 0.05 | 0.3 | 0.08 | **5.9** | 2.8 | 1.41 | 13.32 | 3.70 | 61.6 | **4.7** | 36.1 | 10.2 | **7.2** |
| **6.2** | 0.61 | 2.4 | 0.02 | **3.5** | 42.3 | 0.64 | 4.24 | 2.49 | 66.1 | **1.6** | 20.4 | 24.7 | **8.8** |
| **6.4** | 1.05 | 5.8 | -0.16 | **9.2** | 4.7 | 2.32 | 13.07 | 4.64 | 54.3 | **2.4** | 17.3 | 15.3 | **9.9** |
| **7.5** | 1.32 | 2.9 | -0.05 | **0.0** | -5.4 | -2.36 | -13.51 | 2.87 | 176.3 | **6.5** | 55.4 | 5.2 | **5.5** |
| **7.8** | 0.29 | 1.4 | 1.40 | **0.7** | -0.4 | -1.19 | -11.98 | 4.58 | 112.7 | **3.4** | 34.4 | 16.0 | **4.9** |
| **6.5** | 0.91 | 8.7 | 0.01 | **2.6** | 0.4 | 0.40 | 4.63 | 3.46 | 85.7 | **0.9** | 8.0 | 28.8 | **4.4** |
| **8.9** | 0.49 | 2.9 | 0.00 | **6.9** | 17.7 | 1.62 | 12.15 | 3.23 | 67.3 | **3.0** | 14.8 | 6.3 | **9.9** |
| **7.7** | 0.64 | 3.8 | 0.04 | **4.4** | 10.3 | 0.82 | 7.44 | 3.88 | 76.3 | **5.0** | 11.7 | 1.2 | **9.0** |
| **8.5** | 0.05 | 1.7 | 0.17 | **4.0** | 0.8 | 0.74 | 6.64 | 3.70 | 75.3 | **1.1** | 26.5 | 25.4 | **5.7** |
| **2.6** | 2.06 | 14.5 | 0.01 | **3.2** | 1.0 | 0.35 | 3.27 | 4.06 | 88.0 | **3.3** | 18.3 | 12.9 | **6.0** |
| **8.7** | 0.35 | 2.0 | 0.15 | **7.7** | 4.7 | 1.53 | 10.56 | 4.48 | 57.3 | **2.7** | 33.6 | 19.2 | **9.1** |
| **5.0** | 1.44 | 9.4 | 0.00 | **0.4** | 0.0 | -0.61 | -4.52 | 3.76 | 116.4 | **1.1** | 7.7 | 27.6 | **6.6** |
| **7.5** | 0.41 | 3.6 | 0.13 | **5.3** | 12.6 | 1.15 | 11.02 | 3.67 | 71.0 | **1.5** | 9.8 | 16.8 | **9.2** |
| **6.4** | 1.51 | 8.4 | 0.14 | **8.4** | 3.3 | 1.72 | 7.39 | 4.73 | 63.5 | **4.5** | 50.6 | 14.7 | **9.1** |
| **4.2** | 1.86 | 7.5 | 0.11 | **4.4** | 2.7 | 0.96 | 8.03 | 3.68 | 72.0 | **3.5** | 28.3 | 13.7 | **7.3** |
| **8.6** | 0.05 | 0.3 | 0.00 | **3.7** | 0.4 | 0.87 | 8.25 | 3.87 | 77.8 | **6.0** | 46.0 | 4.7 | **5.5** |
| **10.0** | na | 0.0 | na | **10.0** | 0.3 | 7.14 | 7.37 | 6.40 | 52.8 | **4.0** | na | 0.0 | **7.0** |
| **5.2** | 0.92 | 5.1 | 0.45 | **6.2** | 1898.4 | 1.33 | 11.55 | 3.14 | 55.6 | **4.7** | 21.1 | 5.5 | **10.0** |
| **8.4** | 0.84 | 3.2 | 0.03 | **1.3** | 0.1 | 0.06 | 0.41 | 2.57 | 101.7 | **4.5** | 47.7 | 13.7 | **6.6** |
| **8.1** | 0.16 | 0.6 | 0.01 | **1.5** | -0.1 | -0.06 | -0.29 | 4.63 | 94.7 | **3.2** | 40.6 | 18.9 | **6.2** |
| **6.5** | 0.47 | 2.8 | 0.30 | **3.9** | 1.1 | 0.80 | 7.25 | 4.24 | 73.6 | **3.4** | 26.5 | 13.5 | **6.4** |
| **8.8** | 0.07 | 0.3 | 0.11 | **6.8** | 7.6 | 1.39 | 12.38 | 3.93 | 57.2 | **3.7** | 23.8 | 11.2 | **8.0** |
| **7.5** | 0.28 | 1.5 | 0.05 | **3.8** | 0.3 | 1.08 | 12.73 | 3.44 | 72.3 | **6.3** | 45.7 | 2.9 | **3.2** |
| **8.6** | 0.12 | 0.8 | 0.02 | **4.1** | 3.1 | 0.84 | 9.95 | 3.34 | 69.8 | **1.4** | 14.6 | 26.3 | **5.4** |
| **5.0** | 3.67 | 14.4 | 0.00 | **2.5** | 0.2 | 0.46 | 2.76 | 2.74 | 84.7 | **1.3** | 30.1 | 37.5 | **7.1** |
| **4.4** | 0.02 | 3.4 | 0.20 | **10.0** | 1.0 | 2.05 | 15.34 | 5.01 | 41.6 | **3.9** | 16.6 | 9.7 | **8.6** |
| **6.3** | 0.23 | 1.3 | 0.41 | **6.8** | 13.4 | 1.67 | 14.79 | 3.90 | 55.4 | **4.3** | 20.2 | 7.5 | **8.3** |
| **7.2** | 0.14 | 0.4 | 0.07 | **5.1** | 2.5 | 1.03 | 10.58 | 3.62 | 68.7 | **3.7** | 17.4 | 10.8 | **6.2** |
| **7.5** | 0.00 | 0.0 | 0.00 | **5.1** | 0.7 | 1.16 | 7.50 | 4.32 | 64.0 | **3.4** | 51.6 | 23.3 | **8.2** |
| **8.0** | 0.16 | 0.8 | -0.07 | **3.9** | 7.8 | 0.88 | 10.20 | 3.46 | 75.3 | **1.6** | 9.0 | 21.5 | **6.2** |
| **7.2** | 0.04 | 0.2 | 0.01 | **6.0** | 15.9 | 1.38 | 12.13 | 4.59 | 70.0 | **5.9** | 27.6 | 2.7 | **9.5** |
| **4.2** | 0.81 | 3.5 | 0.16 | **4.7** | 6.0 | 1.11 | 9.16 | 3.96 | 73.1 | **2.9** | 20.3 | 14.4 | **7.8** |
| **4.2** | 3.32 | 12.1 | 0.26 | **10.0** | 3.4 | 2.30 | 17.68 | 4.56 | 42.9 | **1.6** | 11.7 | 21.4 | **8.3** |
| **8.8** | 0.61 | 1.7 | 0.60 | **4.4** | 0.4 | 0.95 | 8.31 | 3.66 | 70.8 | **3.6** | 64.6 | 23.6 | **6.0** |
| **4.7** | 1.07 | 5.1 | -0.01 | **5.4** | 4.2 | 1.07 | 11.09 | 3.69 | 67.9 | **1.6** | 16.0 | 20.2 | **6.4** |
| **7.6** | 0.34 | 3.5 | 0.37 | **6.7** | 33.2 | 1.62 | 17.37 | 3.13 | 51.0 | **1.1** | 21.8 | 38.6 | **9.3** |
| **7.4** | 0.00 | 0.0 | -0.01 | **3.6** | 0.2 | 0.58 | 5.47 | 3.57 | 78.2 | **3.6** | 8.7 | 10.4 | **6.3** |
| **8.2** | 0.53 | 2.2 | 0.00 | **5.2** | 4.3 | 1.07 | 9.07 | 3.90 | 69.8 | **2.7** | 10.3 | 14.9 | **7.4** |
| **5.0** | 1.60 | 6.1 | 0.67 | **3.4** | 0.3 | 0.59 | 5.37 | 3.90 | 77.5 | **1.2** | 24.4 | 31.2 | **5.2** |
| **1.7** | 7.24 | 44.4 | -0.38 | **3.7** | 0.9 | 0.84 | 10.96 | 4.52 | 84.8 | **4.8** | 28.4 | 5.9 | **1.0** |
| **4.6** | 1.99 | 8.0 | 0.10 | **6.3** | 5.2 | 1.54 | 14.04 | 4.03 | 76.4 | **1.8** | 21.7 | 18.2 | **7.3** |
| **8.5** | 0.22 | 1.5 | 0.00 | **6.6** | 1.6 | 1.22 | 12.35 | 3.77 | 62.7 | **1.3** | 12.3 | 24.4 | **6.3** |
| **6.8** | 2.12 | 5.5 | 0.00 | **9.1** | 3.8 | 2.46 | 18.15 | 4.05 | 53.4 | **5.5** | 31.7 | 3.0 | **8.5** |
| **7.4** | 0.60 | 3.4 | 0.03 | **9.3** | 90.2 | 1.83 | 15.82 | 3.43 | 42.5 | **1.7** | 14.8 | 21.4 | **10.0** |

| | | | | | | | | Asset Mix (As a % of Total Assets) | | | | | | |
|---|---|---|---|---|---|---|---|---|---|---|---|---|---|---|
| Name | City | State | Rating | 2018 Rating | 2017 Rating | Total Assets ($Mil) | One Year Asset Growth | Comm-ercial Loans | Cons-umer Loans | Mort-gage Loans | Secur-ities | Capital-ization Index | Lever-age Ratio | Risk-Based Capital Ratio |
| Lake City Federal Bank | Lake City | MN | **B** | C | D+ | 71.2 | -0.10 | 0.6 | 2.9 | 48.4 | 16.5 | **10.0** | 13.3 | 23.1 |
| ▲ Lake Community Bank | Long Lake | MN | **B+** | B | B+ | 121.2 | 1.59 | 4.3 | 0.6 | 8.3 | 12.8 | **10.0** | 13.2 | 17.5 |
| Lake Country Community Bank | Morristown | MN | **C** | C- | D | 28.1 | 3.59 | 9.2 | 1.2 | 16.7 | 38.6 | **7.4** | 9.3 | 20.4 |
| ▲ Lake Elmo Bank | Lake Elmo | MN | **A-** | B | B | 376.1 | 2.17 | 6.2 | 2.6 | 26.4 | 16.5 | **8.6** | 10.0 | 15.6 |
| Lake Forest Bank & Trust Co., N.A. | Lake Forest | IL | **B+** | B+ | B+ | 4533.0 | 19.42 | 46.5 | 7.4 | 2.4 | 11.8 | **6.3** | 9.9 | 12.0 |
| ▲ Lake Region Bank | New London | MN | **B-** | B- | C+ | 118.5 | 4.47 | 15.7 | 3.9 | 9.2 | 31.7 | **7.8** | 9.5 | 18.2 |
| Lake Shore Savings Bank | Dunkirk | NY | **B** | B | B | 610.9 | 11.94 | 3.4 | 0.2 | 27.0 | 11.6 | **10.0** | 13.0 | 18.0 |
| Lake-Osceola State Bank | Baldwin | MI | **C+** | C+ | C+ | 287.5 | 8.35 | 5.6 | 19.1 | 20.0 | 6.7 | **7.4** | 9.3 | 13.6 |
| Lakeland Bank | Oak Ridge | NJ | **B+** | B+ | B | 6706.4 | 15.69 | 6.2 | 0.2 | 9.3 | 13.1 | **7.2** | 10.2 | 12.7 |
| Lakeside Bank | Chicago | IL | **A-** | A- | A | 1867.1 | 11.23 | 5.3 | 0.0 | 8.4 | 2.6 | **9.3** | 12.0 | 14.4 |
| Lakeside Bank | Lake Charles | LA | **B-** | B- | B- | 216.1 | 8.64 | 8.0 | 2.6 | 17.1 | 14.7 | **10.0** | 11.9 | 18.0 |
| ▼ Lakeside Bank | Rockwall | TX | **C+** | C+ | C | 110.3 | 76.54 | 1.5 | 1.0 | 6.0 | 0.0 | **10.0** | 28.1 | 63.9 |
| Lakeside Bank of Salina | Salina | OK | **B** | B | B | 38.8 | 17.76 | 19.1 | 19.1 | 24.0 | 11.6 | **10.0** | 12.9 | 19.6 |
| Lakeside State Bank | Oologah | OK | **C** | C | C+ | 66.3 | -8.47 | 8.5 | 10.3 | 17.5 | 25.7 | **8.0** | 9.7 | 18.8 |
| Lakestone Bank & Trust | Lapeer | MI | **B+** | B+ | B+ | 669.2 | 8.61 | 8.7 | 1.8 | 16.8 | 27.5 | **9.2** | 10.4 | 16.6 |
| Lakeview Bank | Lakeville | MN | **B** | B | B- | 100.0 | 9.78 | 18.0 | 0.2 | 31.7 | 7.9 | **7.8** | 9.5 | 13.7 |
| ▲ Lamar Bank and Trust Co. | Lamar | MO | **A-** | B+ | A | 172.2 | 7.30 | 11.9 | 2.7 | 17.4 | 9.7 | **9.1** | 10.7 | 14.2 |
| ▲ Lamar National Bank | Paris | TX | **C+** | C+ | B | 184.5 | 14.57 | 5.4 | 2.5 | 32.1 | 13.7 | **10.0** | 12.0 | 19.3 |
| ▼ Lamesa National Bank | Lamesa | TX | **B-** | B | B- | 386.3 | 10.26 | 1.6 | 0.2 | 0.0 | 52.4 | **7.6** | 9.4 | 20.5 |
| ▲ Lamont Bank of St. John | Saint John | WA | **B+** | B | B | 52.5 | 6.59 | 6.6 | 9.9 | 0.1 | 47.8 | **10.0** | 14.0 | 23.2 |
| Landmark Bank | Clinton | LA | **C+** | C | D+ | 141.8 | 7.63 | 7.6 | 2.8 | 29.1 | 15.8 | **8.7** | 10.2 | 15.6 |
| Landmark Bank | Columbia | MO | **B+** | B+ | B+ | 3556.1 | 13.55 | 6.7 | 1.8 | 15.3 | 25.7 | **6.8** | 8.8 | 13.9 |
| Landmark Community Bank | Pittston | PA | **D+** | D+ | D+ | 326.8 | -2.61 | 9.3 | 8.4 | 12.3 | 18.2 | **8.2** | 9.8 | 13.9 |
| Landmark Community Bank | Collierville | TN | **B** | B | B | 941.5 | -2.70 | 5.8 | 0.7 | 48.5 | 12.7 | **8.0** | 9.7 | 16.1 |
| Landmark National Bank | Manhattan | KS | **B** | B+ | B+ | 995.3 | 1.28 | 11.1 | 0.2 | 15.5 | 36.3 | **9.6** | 10.7 | 17.0 |
| Laona State Bank | Laona | WI | **B-** | B | B | 210.6 | 12.92 | 6.2 | 3.7 | 26.6 | 29.9 | **10.0** | 11.0 | 21.0 |
| LaSalle State Bank | La Salle | IL | **C+** | C+ | C+ | 135.9 | -4.65 | 7.1 | 1.6 | 11.7 | 37.1 | **8.6** | 10.0 | 18.6 |
| Latimer State Bank | Wilburton | OK | **B** | B- | B- | 70.2 | 1.83 | 8.3 | 3.6 | 5.1 | 12.8 | **10.0** | 20.0 | 58.0 |
| ▲ Lauderdale County Bank | Halls | TN | **B-** | C+ | C+ | 51.7 | 3.02 | 18.4 | 6.7 | 14.5 | 28.2 | **10.0** | 11.1 | 21.1 |
| Laurens State Bank | Laurens | IA | **B+** | B+ | B+ | 72.0 | 1.37 | 4.4 | 2.1 | 7.0 | 32.1 | **10.0** | 12.0 | 25.9 |
| Lawrenceburg Federal Bank | Lawrenceburg | TN | **B** | B | B+ | 71.9 | 9.49 | 0.0 | 3.0 | 77.1 | 0.0 | **10.0** | 21.2 | 38.4 |
| ▲ LCA Bank Corp. | Park City | UT | **A** | A | A | 157.7 | -9.19 | 1.4 | 0.0 | 0.0 | 0.8 | **10.0** | 15.7 | 18.2 |
| LCNB National Bank | Lebanon | OH | **B** | B | B | 1636.4 | 0.13 | 4.8 | 1.6 | 17.9 | 12.6 | **7.0** | 10.1 | 12.5 |
| Lea County State Bank | Hobbs | NM | **A-** | B | B | 362.4 | 8.26 | 15.1 | 4.4 | 0.7 | 62.6 | **9.2** | 10.4 | 21.9 |
| Lead Bank | Garden City | MO | **C** | C+ | C | 353.9 | 30.63 | 11.2 | 21.9 | 10.6 | 0.6 | **6.9** | 8.9 | 14.0 |
| Leader Bank, N.A. | Arlington | MA | **A** | A | A | 1583.3 | 17.44 | 1.4 | 0.0 | 43.9 | 4.5 | **10.0** | 11.6 | 15.8 |
| ▲ Leaders Bank | Oak Brook | IL | **C+** | C- | D | 355.9 | 13.97 | 16.2 | 1.0 | 5.8 | 6.3 | **10.0** | 11.5 | 16.8 |
| ▲ Ledyard National Bank | Norwich | VT | **B+** | B | B | 499.3 | 2.33 | 8.0 | 2.5 | 24.8 | 27.2 | **8.1** | 9.8 | 15.9 |
| ▲ Lee Bank | Lee | MA | **C+** | C | C | 407.6 | 8.33 | 3.8 | 0.2 | 38.7 | 8.6 | **7.5** | 9.3 | 13.6 |
| ▲ Lee Bank and Trust Co. | Pennington Gap | VA | **B+** | B | B | 149.8 | -0.87 | 13.2 | 3.6 | 23.0 | 9.9 | **10.0** | 16.9 | 27.9 |
| Lee County Bank | Fort Madison | IA | **A-** | A- | A- | 199.7 | 11.94 | 8.6 | 4.3 | 43.8 | 0.9 | **10.0** | 12.4 | 18.7 |
| Legacy Bank | Wiley | CO | **B+** | B+ | B+ | 368.9 | 16.25 | 11.4 | 0.6 | 9.6 | 15.2 | **10.0** | 14.2 | 17.6 |
| Legacy Bank | Altoona | IA | **C** | C- | D+ | 117.6 | 8.59 | 15.9 | 2.4 | 21.7 | 11.3 | **5.5** | 7.5 | 13.0 |
| Legacy Bank | Wichita | KS | **C+** | C | B- | 468.1 | 5.51 | 9.1 | 0.5 | 18.8 | 11.0 | **9.4** | 11.0 | 14.5 |
| Legacy Bank | Hinton | OK | **B-** | B- | B- | 463.8 | 0.10 | 11.4 | 1.2 | 12.4 | 17.8 | **6.7** | 8.8 | 12.6 |
| Legacy Bank & Trust Co. | Rogersville | MO | **B** | B | B- | 302.6 | 20.06 | 13.5 | 2.0 | 24.1 | 1.6 | **6.1** | 9.4 | 11.9 |
| ▲ Legacy Bank of Florida | Boca Raton | FL | **B** | C+ | C+ | 454.6 | 6.45 | 13.4 | 0.2 | 12.3 | 7.3 | **7.2** | 11.1 | 12.7 |
| Legacy National Bank | Springdale | AR | **B-** | C+ | B+ | 547.2 | 4.55 | 9.3 | 1.0 | 17.3 | 3.4 | **7.3** | 9.7 | 12.8 |
| ▲ Legacy State Bank | Loganville | GA | **C-** | D | E | 109.0 | 10.58 | 7.2 | 0.1 | 7.7 | 11.4 | **8.6** | 10.6 | 13.9 |
| Legacy Trust Co., N.A. | Houston | TX | **U** | U | U | 32.4 | 12.35 | 0.0 | 0.0 | 0.0 | 79.7 | **10.0** | 90.1 | 120.5 |
| Legence Bank | Eldorado | IL | **B** | B | B+ | 483.5 | 1.84 | 18.1 | 5.6 | 4.4 | 18.6 | **7.9** | 9.6 | 13.9 |
| ▲ Legend Bank, N.A. | Bowie | TX | **B+** | B | B+ | 758.7 | 9.23 | 11.8 | 0.9 | 13.3 | 22.5 | **8.5** | 10.0 | 14.5 |
| Legends Bank | Linn | MO | **A-** | B+ | A- | 394.1 | 4.87 | 5.1 | 7.7 | 20.3 | 18.9 | **10.0** | 14.3 | 21.6 |
| ▲ Legends Bank | Clarksville | TN | **B+** | B | B | 495.6 | 0.73 | 9.6 | 0.9 | 8.7 | 16.6 | **7.9** | 10.1 | 13.3 |
| ▲ Leighton State Bank | Pella | IA | **A-** | B+ | A- | 186.8 | 1.19 | 11.4 | 1.3 | 16.3 | 10.0 | **10.0** | 11.3 | 15.3 |
| Lemont National Bank | Lemont | IL | **D+** | D+ | D+ | 53.3 | -3.93 | 0.0 | 0.0 | 9.1 | 58.7 | **4.5** | 6.5 | 24.6 |
| Lena State Bank | Lena | IL | **B+** | B | B- | 91.3 | 4.01 | 17.1 | 0.4 | 2.8 | 28.3 | **10.0** | 11.7 | 17.1 |
| Level One Bank | Farmington Hills | MI | **B** | B | B- | 1582.4 | 11.94 | 23.6 | 0.1 | 11.9 | 11.4 | **7.9** | 11.0 | 13.3 |
| ▲ Lewis & Clark Bank | Oregon City | OR | **B+** | B- | B+ | 282.2 | 41.45 | 6.6 | 0.0 | 7.3 | 6.0 | **10.0** | 11.9 | 15.9 |
| Lewisburg Banking Co. | Lewisburg | KY | **B+** | B | A- | 137.6 | 13.59 | 6.1 | 5.0 | 26.4 | 25.6 | **9.2** | 10.5 | 17.2 |

**Arrows denote recent upgrades ▲ or downgrades ▼**

| Asset Quality Index | Adjusted Non-Performing Loans as a % of Total Loans | Adjusted Non-Performing Loans as a % of Capital | Net Charge-Offs Avg Loans | Profitability Index | Net Income ($Mil) | Return on Assets (R.O.A.) | Return on Equity (R.O.E.) | Net Interest Spread | Overhead Efficiency Ratio | Liquidity Index | Liquidity Ratio | Hot Money Ratio | Stability Index |
|---|---|---|---|---|---|---|---|---|---|---|---|---|---|
| **7.9** | 0.78 | 3.9 | -0.01 | **5.3** | 0.7 | 1.04 | 8.24 | 3.51 | 76.1 | **2.7** | 26.1 | 17.1 | **6.7** |
| **7.5** | 0.35 | 1.8 | -0.01 | **6.4** | 1.5 | 1.21 | 9.32 | 4.03 | 59.2 | **3.5** | 25.4 | 12.8 | **7.6** |
| **4.4** | 5.97 | 12.8 | -0.14 | **2.6** | 0.1 | 0.40 | 4.00 | 3.35 | 83.9 | **5.8** | 61.5 | 9.3 | **4.4** |
| **6.6** | 0.45 | 2.5 | -0.04 | **7.4** | 6.8 | 1.82 | 18.50 | 4.03 | 59.2 | **4.4** | 18.5 | 6.4 | **6.8** |
| **5.4** | 0.64 | 4.1 | 0.69 | **9.8** | 89.6 | 2.16 | 20.54 | 3.72 | 42.7 | **2.4** | 19.3 | 7.7 | **8.6** |
| **3.9** | 4.48 | 15.1 | 0.05 | **5.0** | 1.4 | 1.22 | 11.99 | 4.61 | 79.5 | **6.8** | 53.3 | 2.6 | **5.6** |
| **7.5** | 0.77 | 4.4 | 0.02 | **4.0** | 4.2 | 0.74 | 5.42 | 3.59 | 73.1 | **2.1** | 16.3 | 18.6 | **8.2** |
| **3.4** | 1.55 | 8.5 | 0.21 | **5.3** | 3.1 | 1.14 | 12.10 | 4.18 | 68.9 | **2.7** | 19.2 | 13.5 | **5.8** |
| **5.9** | 0.51 | 3.2 | 0.00 | **6.0** | 75.1 | 1.19 | 9.75 | 3.42 | 55.4 | **3.5** | 10.1 | 10.2 | **9.5** |
| **6.3** | 0.44 | 2.9 | 0.02 | **7.3** | 28.7 | 1.63 | 13.98 | 3.67 | 56.8 | **0.9** | 14.0 | 18.2 | **10.0** |
| **8.6** | 0.08 | 0.4 | 0.06 | **3.5** | 1.1 | 0.54 | 4.37 | 3.70 | 79.8 | **1.8** | 25.4 | 22.7 | **7.2** |
| **7.5** | 0.39 | 0.2 | 0.04 | **0.8** | -0.7 | -2.65 | -16.92 | 3.79 | 179.2 | **7.7** | 102.8 | 5.4 | **6.3** |
| **3.5** | 3.65 | 12.1 | 0.35 | **8.0** | 0.5 | 1.40 | 10.88 | 5.70 | 62.0 | **1.8** | 13.2 | 20.1 | **6.8** |
| **5.7** | 1.48 | 5.5 | 0.07 | **3.1** | 0.2 | 0.33 | 3.75 | 4.45 | 87.7 | **3.7** | 23.2 | 11.5 | **4.5** |
| **7.7** | 0.35 | 1.8 | -0.04 | **5.7** | 7.9 | 1.21 | 12.13 | 3.80 | 67.3 | **5.6** | 34.8 | 3.6 | **6.9** |
| **5.2** | 0.68 | 8.0 | 0.03 | **6.8** | 1.2 | 1.18 | 12.61 | 4.45 | 65.2 | **2.6** | 13.8 | 13.3 | **6.8** |
| **6.4** | 0.43 | 2.9 | 0.02 | **7.7** | 2.7 | 1.67 | 15.58 | 4.00 | 61.4 | **4.1** | 14.6 | 8.2 | **8.3** |
| **4.3** | 2.81 | 16.3 | 0.09 | **5.0** | 1.9 | 1.15 | 10.66 | 4.65 | 75.5 | **3.7** | 26.4 | 12.0 | **7.1** |
| **6.5** | 0.96 | 3.7 | 2.67 | **3.1** | 2.8 | 0.78 | 7.88 | 2.21 | 44.1 | **4.0** | 61.7 | 21.3 | **3.8** |
| **8.0** | 1.55 | 2.6 | 1.07 | **7.0** | 0.7 | 1.43 | 10.81 | 3.77 | 44.0 | **6.8** | 48.0 | 0.0 | **6.8** |
| **3.7** | 2.01 | 15.5 | 0.20 | **3.1** | 0.7 | 0.49 | 4.75 | 4.45 | 82.9 | **2.7** | 25.2 | 11.9 | **5.9** |
| **7.3** | 0.43 | 1.7 | 0.11 | **2.4** | -0.5 | -0.08 | -0.95 | 4.14 | 98.0 | **1.2** | 21.3 | 21.5 | **8.1** |
| **5.1** | 0.39 | 2.5 | 0.08 | **1.8** | 1.1 | 0.32 | 3.39 | 3.24 | 91.3 | **2.9** | 11.5 | 14.1 | **4.1** |
| **6.1** | 0.80 | 5.4 | 0.08 | **4.7** | 9.1 | 0.94 | 10.23 | 2.50 | 53.4 | **0.8** | 17.6 | 31.7 | **6.4** |
| **4.9** | 1.59 | 5.3 | 0.13 | **5.0** | 11.3 | 1.14 | 9.41 | 3.59 | 68.7 | **3.0** | 15.5 | 10.3 | **8.8** |
| **3.6** | 4.79 | 19.8 | -0.17 | **3.3** | 1.0 | 0.53 | 4.45 | 3.20 | 76.2 | **3.9** | 43.4 | 16.2 | **6.6** |
| **7.2** | 0.66 | 2.3 | 0.01 | **3.9** | 1.3 | 0.95 | 10.10 | 3.18 | 73.6 | **3.5** | 16.4 | 11.5 | **5.7** |
| **7.3** | 3.39 | 4.8 | 0.15 | **4.1** | 0.7 | 0.99 | 4.90 | 2.75 | 57.6 | **3.5** | 87.6 | 34.5 | **6.8** |
| **5.5** | 1.91 | 6.6 | 0.36 | **3.5** | 0.3 | 0.53 | 4.69 | 3.94 | 81.4 | **2.3** | 42.5 | 32.3 | **5.4** |
| **9.1** | 0.00 | 0.0 | 0.02 | **5.7** | 0.9 | 1.37 | 11.59 | 3.14 | 60.0 | **5.7** | 58.9 | 9.4 | **7.2** |
| **5.9** | 0.86 | 13.1 | 0.02 | **4.0** | 0.4 | 0.55 | 2.49 | 3.51 | 76.3 | **0.7** | 13.7 | 39.9 | **7.6** |
| **8.9** | 0.44 | 2.3 | 1.34 | **10.0** | 3.3 | 2.02 | 13.20 | 6.84 | 45.9 | **0.3** | 12.5 | 0.0 | **8.3** |
| **4.8** | 0.79 | 2.9 | 0.02 | **5.5** | 18.9 | 1.15 | 8.60 | 3.69 | 65.3 | **3.3** | 7.2 | 11.7 | **9.9** |
| **7.8** | 0.00 | 0.0 | -0.75 | **6.2** | 8.4 | 2.44 | 22.53 | 3.57 | 66.4 | **5.2** | 58.9 | 7.6 | **6.0** |
| **2.9** | 0.78 | 9.5 | 0.86 | **5.7** | 3.8 | 1.18 | 13.53 | 14.64 | 87.7 | **0.7** | 8.9 | 12.7 | **5.2** |
| **8.2** | 0.57 | 3.1 | 0.05 | **9.6** | 28.9 | 1.99 | 17.06 | 3.16 | 47.0 | **1.5** | 8.7 | 18.0 | **10.0** |
| **4.4** | 1.75 | 6.6 | -0.02 | **3.7** | 3.3 | 0.96 | 7.78 | 3.34 | 69.5 | **1.1** | 27.3 | 44.3 | **5.3** |
| **6.0** | 0.69 | 2.9 | 0.00 | **5.3** | 6.0 | 1.20 | 12.37 | 3.60 | 75.9 | **4.9** | 28.3 | 5.5 | **7.2** |
| **4.9** | 1.53 | 9.2 | 0.04 | **3.7** | 3.2 | 0.82 | 9.67 | 3.42 | 80.5 | **2.9** | 14.7 | 8.8 | **5.7** |
| **6.9** | 0.45 | 4.3 | 0.14 | **5.2** | 1.5 | 1.03 | 6.70 | 4.09 | 68.6 | **1.5** | 20.1 | 26.6 | **7.1** |
| **8.6** | 0.05 | 0.3 | 0.06 | **7.0** | 3.0 | 1.66 | 13.73 | 3.76 | 54.6 | **5.0** | 17.6 | 2.5 | **7.9** |
| **3.9** | 3.32 | 13.6 | 0.09 | **8.6** | 6.8 | 1.97 | 12.21 | 4.48 | 50.4 | **1.4** | 15.7 | 26.1 | **9.4** |
| **2.6** | 2.06 | 18.4 | 0.12 | **4.0** | 1.0 | 0.87 | 11.49 | 4.10 | 81.5 | **5.3** | 32.1 | 4.6 | **4.6** |
| **3.4** | 2.58 | 16.6 | 0.24 | **6.2** | 6.0 | 1.31 | 11.52 | 4.11 | 57.5 | **2.0** | 10.3 | 15.7 | **6.0** |
| **7.8** | 0.56 | 2.2 | 0.08 | **4.1** | 3.5 | 0.76 | 8.72 | 4.77 | 86.0 | **4.7** | 21.1 | 4.5 | **4.7** |
| **7.9** | 0.18 | 1.0 | 0.05 | **7.9** | 3.8 | 1.38 | 12.74 | 4.53 | 60.2 | **1.6** | 3.5 | 14.6 | **7.0** |
| **7.3** | 0.21 | 0.4 | 0.01 | **4.8** | 4.5 | 0.99 | 9.18 | 3.22 | 62.9 | **0.8** | 9.1 | 33.5 | **6.7** |
| **4.0** | 1.98 | 13.8 | -0.06 | **6.0** | 6.3 | 1.17 | 12.45 | 3.92 | 59.6 | **1.7** | 10.4 | 17.7 | **7.1** |
| **7.5** | 0.00 | 0.0 | 0.00 | **4.7** | 1.3 | 1.25 | 12.22 | 3.81 | 62.6 | **1.5** | 14.6 | 25.0 | **4.9** |
| **10.0** | na | 0.0 | na | **9.5** | 3.0 | 9.88 | 10.86 | 2.60 | 76.6 | **4.0** | na | 0.0 | **6.7** |
| **5.4** | 0.73 | 2.8 | 0.05 | **6.1** | 7.2 | 1.53 | 13.39 | 5.41 | 73.4 | **3.6** | 15.4 | 10.9 | **7.2** |
| **6.0** | 0.60 | 2.7 | -0.03 | **6.9** | 11.8 | 1.62 | 14.70 | 4.55 | 66.1 | **2.6** | 12.8 | 15.7 | **8.4** |
| **7.3** | 0.26 | 3.0 | 0.11 | **8.7** | 6.4 | 1.66 | 11.90 | 4.15 | 50.0 | **2.1** | 5.3 | 17.4 | **8.6** |
| **7.2** | 0.07 | 1.4 | 0.07 | **5.4** | 5.5 | 1.11 | 11.27 | 3.89 | 65.8 | **1.8** | 11.9 | 9.6 | **7.2** |
| **7.8** | 0.26 | 1.7 | 0.14 | **6.1** | 2.6 | 1.37 | 10.99 | 3.52 | 67.3 | **2.2** | 18.6 | 18.1 | **8.8** |
| **9.8** | 0.00 | 0.0 | 0.00 | **2.4** | 0.2 | 0.31 | 4.41 | 3.29 | 87.5 | **7.6** | 83.6 | 1.6 | **2.9** |
| **8.4** | 0.40 | 0.9 | 0.00 | **6.4** | 1.0 | 1.15 | 9.42 | 3.21 | 55.5 | **1.4** | 23.3 | 27.3 | **8.2** |
| **5.2** | 0.92 | 5.7 | 0.02 | **5.5** | 17.1 | 1.14 | 10.16 | 3.70 | 67.6 | **1.1** | 18.2 | 27.5 | **8.7** |
| **6.3** | 0.34 | 1.2 | 0.00 | **5.2** | 2.4 | 0.93 | 7.70 | 4.45 | 69.8 | **3.0** | 25.4 | 15.2 | **7.2** |
| **4.4** | 2.32 | 10.6 | 0.00 | **7.8** | 2.3 | 1.79 | 17.17 | 4.24 | 60.0 | **2.7** | 19.6 | 15.8 | **8.2** |

| | Name | City | State | Rating | 2018 Rating | 2017 Rating | Total Assets ($Mil) | One Year Asset Growth | Comm-ercial Loans | Cons-umer Loans | Mort-gage Loans | Secur-ities | Capital-ization Index | Lever-age Ratio | Risk-Based Capital Ratio |
|---|---|---|---|---|---|---|---|---|---|---|---|---|---|---|---|
| | Liberty Bank | Geraldine | AL | **B** | B | B | 148.5 | 7.69 | 4.7 | 6.7 | 18.2 | 28.6 | **10.0** | 11.3 | 16.4 |
| | Liberty Bank | South San Francisco | CA | **B** | B- | C+ | 277.2 | 8.21 | 5.4 | 0.4 | 1.7 | 18.5 | **8.9** | 12.6 | 14.1 |
| | Liberty Bank | Middletown | CT | **A-** | B | B | 5814.1 | 14.15 | 11.9 | 0.2 | 18.8 | 14.4 | **10.0** | 13.4 | 16.0 |
| ▲ | Liberty Bank | Liberty | IL | **B+** | B- | B- | 99.6 | 2.76 | 5.3 | 6.5 | 17.8 | 14.4 | **10.0** | 12.5 | 18.6 |
| | Liberty Bank | Ironton | OH | **B-** | B- | B- | 50.7 | -3.89 | 2.9 | 4.8 | 46.2 | 10.8 | **10.0** | 16.9 | 29.4 |
| | Liberty Bank and Trust Co. | New Orleans | LA | **B-** | C+ | C+ | 601.6 | 1.52 | 4.3 | 4.6 | 24.8 | 28.9 | **7.5** | 9.3 | 15.6 |
| | Liberty Bank for Savings | Chicago | IL | **C+** | C+ | C+ | 844.9 | 2.44 | 0.0 | 0.0 | 52.3 | 39.3 | **10.0** | 23.5 | 55.6 |
| | Liberty Bank Minnesota | Saint Cloud | MN | **A** | A | A | 218.7 | 3.60 | 0.1 | 3.0 | 35.0 | 21.0 | **10.0** | 12.6 | 25.8 |
| | Liberty Bank, Inc. | Salt Lake City | UT | **E+** | E+ | E | 9.3 | 2.78 | 2.7 | 29.3 | 12.1 | 10.9 | **10.0** | 12.6 | 23.3 |
| ▼ | Liberty Bay Bank | Poulsbo | WA | **C-** | C | C- | 128.2 | 11.04 | 5.8 | 0.2 | 10.9 | 9.7 | **7.5** | 9.4 | 15.7 |
| | Liberty Capital Bank | Addison | TX | **A-** | B+ | A- | 284.5 | 1.14 | 10.0 | 0.1 | 12.1 | 0.0 | **7.7** | 9.9 | 13.1 |
| | Liberty First Bank | Monroe | GA | **B+** | B+ | B+ | 139.7 | 6.13 | 4.1 | 0.6 | 14.8 | 29.9 | **10.0** | 11.7 | 18.4 |
| ▲ | Liberty National Bank | Sioux City | IA | **B+** | B | B | 438.0 | 7.63 | 11.9 | 0.6 | 12.7 | 15.0 | **8.2** | 9.8 | 13.5 |
| | Liberty National Bank | Ada | OH | **B+** | B | B- | 337.5 | -0.42 | 8.5 | 0.2 | 12.9 | 13.3 | **10.0** | 13.3 | 18.1 |
| | Liberty National Bank | Lawton | OK | **A-** | A- | A- | 596.4 | 8.15 | 12.0 | 1.5 | 10.5 | 12.6 | **9.8** | 10.9 | 16.5 |
| | Liberty National Bank in Paris | Paris | TX | **A-** | A- | B+ | 287.9 | 1.62 | 5.3 | 7.3 | 29.1 | 31.2 | **10.0** | 16.4 | 28.3 |
| ▼ | Liberty Savings Assn., FSA | Fort Scott | KS | **C** | C+ | C | 31.1 | -3.22 | 0.3 | 3.5 | 20.9 | 60.2 | **10.0** | 20.9 | 84.3 |
| | Liberty Savings Bank, F.S.B. | Wilmington | OH | **B-** | B- | B | 700.8 | 10.36 | 0.1 | 2.4 | 64.9 | 25.6 | **6.9** | 8.9 | 20.8 |
| | Liberty State Bank | Powers Lake | ND | **A-** | A- | A- | 93.3 | 4.56 | 2.3 | 2.6 | 7.9 | 44.9 | **10.0** | 12.2 | 24.8 |
| | Liberty Trust & Savings Bank | Durant | IA | **A** | A | A | 151.1 | -0.41 | 6.5 | 2.0 | 9.6 | 31.7 | **10.0** | 20.3 | 34.2 |
| | Libertyville Bank & Trust Co., N.A. | Libertyville | IL | **B** | B | B | 1687.7 | 11.13 | 31.1 | 12.0 | 4.7 | 13.3 | **5.9** | 10.0 | 11.7 |
| | Libertyville Savings Bank | Fairfield | IA | **B-** | C+ | B | 344.5 | -0.05 | 7.9 | 1.5 | 11.7 | 26.0 | **9.7** | 10.8 | 16.2 |
| | Lifestore Bank | West Jefferson | NC | **B** | B | C+ | 312.6 | 8.53 | 3.5 | 0.8 | 28.9 | 20.4 | **10.0** | 11.1 | 18.2 |
| | Limestone Bank, Inc. | Louisville | KY | **C** | C- | D | 1239.5 | 16.33 | 11.7 | 3.9 | 14.9 | 16.9 | **6.4** | 10.0 | 12.1 |
| | Lincoln 1st Bank | Lincoln Park | NJ | **D** | D | D | 308.2 | -9.26 | 3.2 | 0.1 | 40.9 | 28.2 | **5.0** | 7.0 | 13.3 |
| | Lincoln FSB of Nebraska | Lincoln | NE | **C+** | C- | C- | 307.6 | -3.38 | 0.0 | 0.0 | 54.9 | 15.3 | **10.0** | 13.7 | 25.2 |
| | Lincoln National Bank | Hodgenville | KY | **A-** | B+ | A- | 317.1 | 9.61 | 3.8 | 5.4 | 40.8 | 9.9 | **10.0** | 13.1 | 21.4 |
| ▲ | Lincoln Savings Bank | Reinbeck | IA | **B** | B | C+ | 1372.0 | 9.62 | 11.9 | 0.8 | 11.5 | 9.2 | **7.1** | 9.7 | 12.5 |
| | Lincoln State Bank | Hankinson | ND | **B** | C+ | C | 77.5 | 2.81 | 8.1 | 5.8 | 3.4 | 38.9 | **9.2** | 10.4 | 16.5 |
| | LincolnWay Community Bank | New Lenox | IL | **C** | C+ | B- | 236.7 | 12.83 | 9.8 | 0.0 | 13.7 | 1.9 | **9.3** | 11.7 | 14.4 |
| | Lindell Bank & Trust Co. | Saint Louis | MO | **A** | A- | A | 518.0 | -3.37 | 6.5 | 0.5 | 16.2 | 36.2 | **10.0** | 19.6 | 39.5 |
| | LINKBANK | Camp Hill | PA | **E** | E- | E- | 233.5 | 179.04 | 14.6 | 0.3 | 14.9 | 20.1 | **10.0** | 14.1 | 18.3 |
| | Lisle Savings Bank | Lisle | IL | **A-** | B | B | 504.8 | -0.80 | 0.3 | 0.0 | 43.1 | 36.3 | **10.0** | 24.8 | 58.1 |
| | Litchfield Bancorp | Litchfield | CT | **C+** | C | C | 256.2 | 0.99 | 5.6 | 1.7 | 37.4 | 12.7 | **6.4** | 8.4 | 13.9 |
| | Litchfield National Bank | Litchfield | IL | **C+** | C+ | C+ | 110.1 | 8.63 | 2.2 | 5.4 | 17.5 | 25.2 | **6.9** | 8.9 | 15.4 |
| | Little Horn State Bank | Hardin | MT | **B-** | B- | C+ | 104.3 | 9.36 | 7.0 | 2.4 | 10.9 | 3.8 | **6.3** | 9.4 | 12.0 |
| | Live Oak Banking Co. | Wilmington | NC | **A-** | A- | A- | 4791.4 | 32.52 | 25.7 | 0.0 | 0.7 | 11.3 | **8.0** | 9.7 | 14.9 |
| ▲ | Llano National Bank | Llano | TX | **A-** | B | B | 189.6 | 4.79 | 2.8 | 3.9 | 18.9 | 33.2 | **10.0** | 12.7 | 22.8 |
| | LNB Community Bank | Lynnville | IN | **C+** | C+ | C+ | 124.4 | 7.44 | 5.9 | 3.3 | 46.3 | 8.1 | **9.3** | 10.6 | 16.9 |
| | Logan Bank & Trust Co. | Logan | WV | **B-** | B- | C+ | 265.8 | 3.20 | 9.3 | 3.9 | 21.5 | 44.0 | **8.1** | 9.8 | 21.8 |
| | Logan County Bank | Scranton | AR | **B+** | B+ | B | 83.6 | 3.08 | 3.5 | 7.5 | 21.8 | 53.6 | **10.0** | 20.7 | 48.8 |
| | Logan State Bank | Logan | IA | **C-** | D+ | C+ | 68.2 | 10.22 | 4.6 | 2.9 | 8.5 | 1.6 | **5.0** | 7.0 | 11.6 |
| | Logansport Savings Bank | Logansport | IN | **A-** | A- | A- | 188.2 | 8.60 | 11.1 | 0.9 | 17.7 | 24.6 | **10.0** | 11.7 | 17.3 |
| | Lone Star Bank | Houston | TX | **B-** | B- | B- | 141.7 | 9.67 | 6.2 | 0.2 | 21.5 | 0.0 | **9.7** | 11.2 | 14.8 |
| | Lone Star Capital Bank, N.A. | San Antonio | TX | **B-** | B- | C | 251.1 | 3.17 | 11.5 | 1.1 | 20.2 | 13.4 | **10.0** | 11.2 | 15.6 |
| | Lone Star National Bank | McAllen | TX | **B+** | B+ | B- | 2418.9 | 9.47 | 3.5 | 1.0 | 8.5 | 30.1 | **10.0** | 11.9 | 20.0 |
| | Lone Star State Bank of West Texas | Lubbock | TX | **C+** | C | C | 1019.2 | 12.03 | 21.0 | 0.5 | 4.1 | 8.6 | **10.0** | 11.4 | 15.2 |
| ▼ | Longview Bank | Ogden | IL | **C** | C+ | B- | 228.1 | 18.12 | 9.1 | 1.2 | 11.7 | 8.4 | **6.5** | 8.5 | 13.1 |
| | Longview Bank & Trust | Chrisman | IL | **C** | C- | C+ | 184.0 | 6.24 | 8.0 | 0.8 | 6.7 | 2.3 | **6.5** | 8.5 | 12.4 |
| | Loomis Federal S&L Assn. | Chicago | IL | **C-** | C- | C- | 61.6 | -8.08 | 2.0 | 0.0 | 34.3 | 15.2 | **10.0** | 28.6 | 116.9 |
| | Lorraine State Bank | Lorraine | KS | **C+** | C+ | C+ | 22.8 | -2.27 | 3.9 | 8.4 | 10.3 | 13.0 | **10.0** | 17.6 | 21.6 |
| | Lovelady State Bank | Lovelady | TX | **B-** | C | C | 45.1 | -6.50 | 9.8 | 11.2 | 12.5 | 15.6 | **10.0** | 11.3 | 20.7 |
| ▲ | Lowell Five Cent Savings Bank | Tewksbury | MA | **A-** | B | B+ | 1190.6 | 5.58 | 4.9 | 0.2 | 25.7 | 8.8 | **10.0** | 13.3 | 17.3 |
| ▲ | Lowry State Bank | Lowry | MN | **C+** | C | D+ | 52.2 | 2.57 | 15.1 | 5.7 | 25.8 | 0.1 | **5.9** | 8.7 | 11.7 |
| | Luana Savings Bank | Luana | IA | **B+** | B+ | B+ | 1523.4 | 28.50 | 1.2 | 1.2 | 24.2 | 11.5 | **5.2** | 8.1 | 11.2 |
| | Lumbee Guaranty Bank | Pembroke | NC | **B** | B- | B- | 343.8 | 2.07 | 2.5 | 2.2 | 14.6 | 29.1 | **10.0** | 12.3 | 19.8 |
| | Lusitania Savings Bank | Newark | NJ | **B+** | B+ | B+ | 332.9 | 5.59 | 0.0 | 0.5 | 39.1 | 18.2 | **10.0** | 15.2 | 39.4 |
| ▲ | Lusk State Bank | Lusk | WY | **A-** | B+ | A- | 54.3 | 1.14 | 2.0 | 3.1 | 0.4 | 12.6 | **10.0** | 14.7 | 20.2 |
| | Luther Burbank Savings | Santa Rosa | CA | **B** | B+ | B+ | 7043.2 | 1.56 | 0.0 | 0.0 | 28.7 | 9.0 | **9.4** | 10.6 | 19.9 |
| | Luzerne Bank | Luzerne | PA | **C+** | C+ | C+ | 453.1 | 3.22 | 9.1 | 5.7 | 15.3 | 6.7 | **5.4** | 8.7 | 11.3 |

| Asset Quality Index | Adjusted Non-Performing Loans as a % of Total Loans | Adjusted Non-Performing Loans as a % of Capital | Net Charge-Offs Avg Loans | Profitability Index | Net Income ($Mil) | Return on Assets (R.O.A.) | Return on Equity (R.O.E.) | Net Interest Spread | Overhead Efficiency Ratio | Liquidity Index | Liquidity Ratio | Hot Money Ratio | Stability Index |
|---|---|---|---|---|---|---|---|---|---|---|---|---|---|
| **7.0** | 0.56 | 6.1 | 0.19 | **4.0** | 1.2 | 0.81 | 7.08 | 4.45 | 76.4 | **2.4** | 36.2 | 25.7 | **6.6** |
| **5.1** | 1.22 | 3.5 | 0.00 | **3.5** | 1.4 | 0.52 | 3.86 | 3.93 | 82.2 | **3.7** | 21.6 | 11.2 | **7.5** |
| **8.4** | 0.31 | 1.4 | 0.03 | **5.6** | 65.3 | 1.23 | 8.43 | 3.07 | 70.5 | **3.7** | 25.0 | 14.1 | **10.0** |
| **5.7** | 0.92 | 6.4 | 0.00 | **6.4** | 1.2 | 1.25 | 9.89 | 4.14 | 60.0 | **3.4** | 22.7 | 12.5 | **7.0** |
| **6.1** | 2.79 | 10.4 | 0.06 | **3.2** | 0.3 | 0.51 | 3.09 | 4.19 | 85.3 | **4.2** | 21.7 | 8.5 | **7.1** |
| **4.3** | 3.19 | 12.1 | 0.30 | **4.2** | 5.7 | 0.94 | 10.10 | 4.24 | 78.7 | **2.5** | 11.3 | 13.0 | **5.5** |
| **10.0** | 0.70 | 1.5 | 0.00 | **2.8** | 3.2 | 0.39 | 1.62 | 2.45 | 80.9 | **4.0** | 53.0 | 18.1 | **8.2** |
| **8.3** | 0.00 | 0.0 | 0.02 | **6.5** | 2.7 | 1.26 | 9.50 | 3.38 | 74.9 | **6.4** | 46.1 | 2.5 | **9.3** |
| **3.2** | 2.19 | 5.1 | -0.14 | **0.0** | -0.5 | -5.49 | -54.95 | 3.08 | 136.7 | **1.4** | 41.5 | 61.1 | **4.2** |
| **5.5** | 0.79 | 5.3 | 0.00 | **2.1** | 0.2 | 0.13 | 1.32 | 3.65 | 94.2 | **3.6** | 26.7 | 12.4 | **4.9** |
| **8.6** | 0.00 | 0.0 | 0.00 | **7.6** | 4.8 | 1.77 | 18.45 | 3.89 | 51.8 | **4.8** | 26.9 | 5.4 | **7.7** |
| **8.0** | 0.95 | 2.3 | 0.00 | **4.6** | 1.5 | 1.09 | 9.77 | 3.96 | 73.3 | **3.0** | 39.8 | 20.1 | **7.2** |
| **7.8** | 0.00 | 0.0 | 0.23 | **6.4** | 5.4 | 1.26 | 10.58 | 3.91 | 57.7 | **1.3** | 19.5 | 25.9 | **7.8** |
| **6.9** | 0.76 | 3.7 | 0.05 | **5.5** | 3.9 | 1.12 | 8.52 | 4.15 | 65.6 | **1.4** | 9.3 | 18.0 | **7.4** |
| **6.2** | 0.51 | 2.7 | 0.09 | **7.3** | 9.0 | 1.60 | 13.92 | 4.56 | 63.6 | **2.3** | 18.6 | 17.9 | **9.7** |
| **8.6** | 0.45 | 1.8 | 0.15 | **6.0** | 3.7 | 1.27 | 7.59 | 3.53 | 57.1 | **3.5** | 27.5 | 13.2 | **8.5** |
| **9.8** | 0.00 | 0.0 | 0.00 | **1.8** | 0.1 | 0.17 | 0.85 | 2.87 | 93.5 | **4.3** | 88.7 | 23.3 | **6.5** |
| **5.6** | 1.81 | 7.4 | -0.43 | **4.3** | 7.2 | 1.10 | 11.57 | 2.32 | 81.6 | **1.2** | 28.4 | 40.9 | **6.4** |
| **8.9** | 0.00 | 0.0 | 0.07 | **8.3** | 1.7 | 1.80 | 14.09 | 3.65 | 47.6 | **2.7** | 36.3 | 20.2 | **9.2** |
| **8.7** | 0.00 | 0.0 | 0.01 | **8.5** | 2.9 | 1.99 | 9.59 | 3.59 | 46.7 | **5.6** | 52.7 | 4.1 | **8.8** |
| **6.3** | 0.48 | 3.4 | 0.04 | **6.8** | 22.9 | 1.43 | 14.26 | 3.32 | 43.2 | **1.6** | 10.3 | 14.1 | **8.1** |
| **4.7** | 1.93 | 7.8 | 0.04 | **5.1** | 4.1 | 1.18 | 9.62 | 3.91 | 68.9 | **5.1** | 36.2 | 7.9 | **7.8** |
| **7.5** | 0.67 | 3.4 | 0.03 | **4.9** | 3.2 | 1.09 | 9.79 | 3.61 | 69.8 | **2.5** | 35.0 | 22.4 | **6.5** |
| **8.2** | 0.22 | 1.1 | 0.06 | **5.0** | 11.4 | 1.03 | 9.01 | 3.56 | 67.6 | **1.5** | 14.8 | 25.8 | **7.6** |
| **6.6** | 0.68 | 4.6 | 0.00 | **0.3** | -1.4 | -0.41 | -6.03 | 1.89 | 132.8 | **0.6** | 7.1 | 33.8 | **2.3** |
| **7.2** | 0.74 | 3.6 | 0.00 | **3.1** | 2.0 | 0.62 | 4.58 | 2.53 | 79.2 | **1.3** | 21.1 | 28.6 | **7.3** |
| **8.1** | 0.37 | 1.9 | 0.06 | **6.6** | 4.2 | 1.37 | 10.32 | 4.35 | 61.7 | **2.1** | 16.9 | 18.6 | **8.0** |
| **4.9** | 1.85 | 9.3 | 0.26 | **5.7** | 13.6 | 1.05 | 9.28 | 3.73 | 69.0 | **0.7** | 13.5 | 29.4 | **9.2** |
| **6.2** | 0.40 | 1.9 | -0.09 | **5.6** | 1.1 | 1.42 | 14.04 | 3.89 | 64.1 | **3.6** | 12.7 | 10.6 | **5.8** |
| **1.4** | 3.24 | 21.1 | 0.00 | **6.8** | 2.5 | 1.15 | 9.81 | 4.63 | 66.8 | **1.0** | 19.5 | 33.0 | **7.3** |
| **8.4** | 0.56 | 1.6 | -0.35 | **8.5** | 11.1 | 2.11 | 10.90 | 4.04 | 57.2 | **5.1** | 33.5 | 6.3 | **10.0** |
| **8.5** | 0.11 | 2.8 | -0.04 | **0.0** | -7.0 | -4.92 | -21.03 | 2.99 | 225.0 | **1.2** | 28.8 | 42.2 | **4.9** |
| **6.9** | 4.70 | 7.0 | -0.06 | **5.4** | 7.1 | 1.39 | 5.79 | 2.51 | 54.7 | **3.5** | 56.2 | 25.3 | **8.7** |
| **5.9** | 0.71 | 5.5 | -0.01 | **2.5** | 0.8 | 0.30 | 3.69 | 3.37 | 88.8 | **2.7** | 20.0 | 14.5 | **5.0** |
| **3.8** | 0.98 | 16.1 | 0.07 | **4.3** | 0.9 | 0.83 | 9.40 | 3.64 | 73.1 | **2.8** | 37.6 | 20.8 | **5.4** |
| **4.7** | 0.76 | 6.5 | 0.00 | **5.8** | 1.0 | 1.02 | 10.37 | 5.07 | 69.7 | **1.7** | 12.6 | 20.2 | **6.7** |
| **5.8** | 2.89 | 6.0 | 0.12 | **5.4** | 25.4 | 0.60 | 5.53 | 3.95 | 74.9 | **0.7** | 17.8 | 38.5 | **9.8** |
| **6.8** | 0.86 | 3.7 | -0.04 | **6.7** | 2.7 | 1.47 | 11.57 | 4.51 | 63.6 | **4.5** | 44.8 | 13.8 | **8.3** |
| **7.0** | 0.36 | 3.2 | 0.00 | **3.9** | 1.0 | 0.84 | 8.00 | 3.66 | 80.9 | **5.0** | 22.5 | 3.2 | **6.3** |
| **9.1** | 0.18 | 0.7 | 0.07 | **4.5** | 2.5 | 0.95 | 10.15 | 3.13 | 64.0 | **3.9** | 40.6 | 15.5 | **5.8** |
| **8.7** | 0.59 | 2.5 | 0.07 | **4.4** | 0.8 | 0.93 | 4.65 | 2.93 | 60.4 | **3.1** | 50.5 | 23.1 | **7.4** |
| **7.1** | 0.00 | 0.0 | 0.08 | **4.7** | 0.7 | 1.08 | 15.31 | 3.88 | 67.7 | **1.1** | 12.0 | 11.8 | **3.9** |
| **7.9** | 1.02 | 3.0 | -0.02 | **6.2** | 2.3 | 1.23 | 9.79 | 3.64 | 63.8 | **4.2** | 27.8 | 10.1 | **8.3** |
| **6.4** | 0.41 | 2.7 | 0.06 | **4.3** | 1.1 | 0.81 | 6.59 | 4.03 | 72.3 | **0.7** | 12.6 | 45.7 | **7.4** |
| **7.4** | 0.57 | 2.2 | 0.00 | **3.3** | 1.2 | 0.50 | 3.57 | 4.06 | 85.2 | **1.8** | 20.3 | 18.7 | **7.6** |
| **5.3** | 2.75 | 10.1 | 0.00 | **5.1** | 25.1 | 1.13 | 9.12 | 3.56 | 71.1 | **2.1** | 20.7 | 20.1 | **9.5** |
| **5.5** | 1.02 | 5.4 | 0.29 | **7.6** | 17.7 | 1.89 | 15.16 | 3.85 | 50.1 | **2.4** | 29.5 | 27.7 | **9.2** |
| **2.5** | 2.84 | 21.1 | 0.02 | **6.3** | 2.3 | 1.15 | 12.45 | 3.66 | 56.4 | **1.7** | 21.1 | 22.9 | **4.8** |
| **3.6** | 0.55 | 4.8 | -0.08 | **6.4** | 2.3 | 1.28 | 14.41 | 3.68 | 55.3 | **2.1** | 24.5 | 19.5 | **4.6** |
| **6.6** | 8.02 | 8.5 | 0.63 | **0.0** | -0.6 | -0.91 | -3.20 | 2.92 | 138.6 | **6.9** | 85.4 | 6.5 | **6.3** |
| **6.8** | 0.00 | 0.0 | -0.08 | **5.8** | 0.3 | 1.15 | 6.54 | 3.73 | 61.7 | **2.5** | 22.0 | 16.8 | **5.0** |
| **6.5** | 0.75 | 3.1 | 0.18 | **5.5** | 0.6 | 1.29 | 11.40 | 5.18 | 72.4 | **3.9** | 44.6 | 16.3 | **5.3** |
| **8.2** | 0.77 | 3.4 | 0.07 | **5.4** | 12.1 | 1.04 | 8.23 | 3.76 | 71.0 | **3.2** | 17.7 | 13.6 | **8.9** |
| **5.2** | 0.54 | 4.2 | 0.11 | **9.4** | 1.1 | 2.17 | 23.17 | 4.86 | 53.0 | **2.8** | 7.0 | 14.4 | **6.5** |
| **8.5** | 0.07 | 0.4 | 0.00 | **6.7** | 19.8 | 1.45 | 16.67 | 2.62 | 38.1 | **0.5** | 11.4 | 10.4 | **8.6** |
| **4.7** | 4.17 | 14.7 | 0.02 | **4.4** | 3.0 | 0.88 | 7.52 | 4.11 | 77.1 | **3.5** | 24.3 | 12.6 | **6.8** |
| **9.4** | 0.80 | 2.4 | 0.01 | **4.3** | 2.5 | 0.76 | 4.99 | 2.62 | 59.1 | **3.7** | 55.6 | 20.9 | **7.9** |
| **7.9** | 0.00 | 0.0 | 0.00 | **8.5** | 1.1 | 2.07 | 14.87 | 4.25 | 57.2 | **4.6** | 38.2 | 5.8 | **9.2** |
| **7.6** | 0.12 | 0.9 | -0.01 | **4.4** | 55.2 | 0.78 | 7.50 | 1.99 | 43.6 | **0.6** | 11.7 | 49.7 | **9.0** |
| **3.9** | 1.03 | 5.4 | 0.03 | **4.4** | 4.0 | 0.88 | 7.61 | 3.56 | 66.9 | **2.7** | 13.7 | 14.9 | **7.1** |

| Name | City | State | Rating | 2018 Rating | 2017 Rating | Total Assets ($Mil) | One Year Asset Growth | Asset Mix (As a % of Total Assets) Commercial Loans | Consumer Loans | Mortgage Loans | Securities | Capitalization Index | Leverage Ratio | Risk-Based Capital Ratio |
|---|---|---|---|---|---|---|---|---|---|---|---|---|---|---|
| Lyndon State Bank | Lyndon | KS | **C** | C | C- | 73.9 | 6.19 | 5.3 | 3.5 | 34.6 | 12.3 | **9.2** | 10.5 | 16.2 |
| Lyon County State Bank | Emporia | KS | **B** | B | C+ | 140.8 | 3.21 | 2.8 | 1.9 | 17.9 | 48.9 | **7.1** | 9.1 | 22.6 |
| Lyons Federal Bank | Lyons | KS | **B** | B | B- | 121.4 | 2.10 | 3.9 | 3.1 | 21.8 | 2.6 | **10.0** | 13.4 | 19.2 |
| Lyons National Bank | Lyons | NY | **B** | B | B | 1163.6 | 7.57 | 9.0 | 2.8 | 26.9 | 17.8 | **6.4** | 8.4 | 12.3 |
| Lytle State Bank of Lytle, Texas | Lytle | TX | **B+** | B+ | B+ | 90.0 | 2.27 | 6.3 | 20.1 | 3.9 | 43.5 | **10.0** | 16.9 | 33.4 |
| ▲ M C Bank & Trust Co. | Morgan City | LA | **B-** | B | B+ | 307.2 | 0.69 | 6.5 | 1.9 | 11.0 | 20.3 | **10.0** | 23.1 | 31.8 |
| ▼ M.Y. Safra Bank, FSB | New York | NY | **D+** | D | D | 439.1 | 12.17 | 0.7 | 10.9 | 20.4 | 32.2 | **10.0** | 11.4 | 23.5 |
| M1 Bank | Macks Creek | MO | **B-** | B- | C- | 298.1 | 58.11 | 43.9 | 0.3 | 1.8 | 0.0 | **5.6** | 10.5 | 11.4 |
| Mabrey Bank | Bixby | OK | **B-** | B- | B- | 1173.3 | 1.75 | 19.8 | 1.7 | 19.1 | 18.4 | **6.2** | 8.5 | 11.9 |
| Macatawa Bank | Holland | MI | **A** | A | A- | 2068.0 | 4.79 | 21.7 | 0.3 | 10.9 | 15.0 | **10.0** | 11.2 | 15.3 |
| ▲ Machias Savings Bank | Machias | ME | **B+** | B | B | 1525.9 | 1.81 | 16.6 | 1.0 | 25.2 | 6.4 | **10.0** | 12.9 | 16.1 |
| Macon Bank and Trust Co. | Lafayette | TN | **B** | B | B | 426.7 | 8.11 | 2.2 | 4.6 | 11.9 | 43.8 | **10.0** | 12.7 | 22.8 |
| Macon-Atlanta State Bank | Macon | MO | **B** | C+ | C- | 287.8 | 3.91 | 5.0 | 2.6 | 7.4 | 33.1 | **8.9** | 10.3 | 17.0 |
| Madison Bank of Maryland | Forest Hill | MD | **C** | C- | D+ | 139.4 | -7.09 | 1.5 | 0.0 | 52.5 | 18.1 | **10.0** | 18.8 | 35.0 |
| Madison County Bank | Madison | NE | **A-** | B+ | A | 429.5 | 4.42 | 0.8 | 1.4 | 14.8 | 16.6 | **10.0** | 17.2 | 20.3 |
| Madison County Community Bank | Madison | FL | **B-** | C+ | C+ | 122.4 | -1.68 | 5.5 | 1.7 | 9.5 | 33.3 | **7.9** | 9.6 | 18.0 |
| Madison Valley Bank | Ennis | MT | **B** | B- | B | 181.7 | 8.48 | 4.5 | 4.7 | 18.8 | 29.4 | **7.0** | 9.0 | 15.2 |
| Magnolia Bank | Magnolia | KY | **A-** | B+ | A- | 313.3 | 16.72 | 3.9 | 0.8 | 35.0 | 7.8 | **8.2** | 9.8 | 17.1 |
| Magnolia State Bank | Bay Springs | MS | **B-** | B- | B- | 339.3 | 3.06 | 6.6 | 4.3 | 24.8 | 7.9 | **8.3** | 9.9 | 13.9 |
| Magyar Bank | New Brunswick | NJ | **C** | C | C- | 640.9 | -0.41 | 7.8 | 0.8 | 30.3 | 7.5 | **7.0** | 9.0 | 13.0 |
| Mahopac Bank | Brewster | NY | **B** | B | B | 1338.2 | -1.98 | 11.0 | 2.0 | 19.1 | 21.1 | **6.9** | 8.9 | 13.0 |
| Main Bank | Albuquerque | NM | **B+** | B | A- | 166.9 | 16.26 | 6.8 | 0.1 | 6.8 | 3.0 | **7.1** | 9.1 | 13.7 |
| ▲ Main Street Bank | Marlborough | MA | **C+** | C | C | 1016.2 | -1.50 | 4.1 | 1.3 | 32.7 | 10.4 | **10.0** | 11.7 | 15.3 |
| ▲ Main Street Bank | Bingham Farms | MI | **B-** | B- | B | 276.6 | 8.39 | 13.2 | 0.4 | 32.8 | 1.7 | **6.9** | 9.0 | 12.4 |
| ▲ Main Street Bank Corp. | Wheeling | WV | **C+** | C | C- | 472.5 | 4.22 | 11.7 | 3.6 | 38.9 | 7.3 | **8.5** | 10.0 | 15.1 |
| Maine Community Bank | Biddeford | ME | **B** | B- | B- | 517.0 | 4.16 | 4.5 | 0.4 | 42.3 | 5.7 | **9.9** | 11.3 | 14.9 |
| Mainstreet Bank | Cook | NE | **B-** | B- | B- | 96.1 | -0.92 | 4.0 | 2.4 | 12.3 | 23.0 | **9.1** | 10.4 | 15.1 |
| MainStreet Bank | Fairfax | VA | **B+** | C+ | C+ | 1277.2 | 16.10 | 9.5 | 5.9 | 9.5 | 9.1 | **8.2** | 12.1 | 13.5 |
| Mainstreet Community Bank of Florida | Deland | FL | **C+** | C+ | B- | 488.4 | 18.76 | 8.7 | 0.7 | 8.4 | 10.1 | **5.3** | 8.6 | 11.3 |
| Malaga Bank F.S.B. | Palos Verdes Estates | CA | **A-** | B+ | A | 1247.5 | 14.78 | 0.1 | 0.0 | 8.5 | 0.0 | **10.0** | 12.7 | 22.9 |
| Malvern Bank | Malvern | IA | **C** | C- | C | 141.1 | -2.25 | 23.2 | 15.2 | 15.7 | 0.6 | **7.9** | 9.8 | 13.2 |
| Malvern Bank, N.A. | Paoli | PA | **B** | B | B | 1259.6 | 11.71 | 8.6 | 0.2 | 21.8 | 3.5 | **10.0** | 12.8 | 16.5 |
| Malvern National Bank | Malvern | AR | **C** | C | C- | 573.8 | 8.14 | 6.1 | 0.8 | 7.4 | 34.8 | **8.2** | 9.8 | 14.5 |
| Manasquan Bank | Manasquan | NJ | **B** | B | B | 1774.5 | 32.51 | 8.8 | 0.1 | 33.2 | 4.2 | **7.5** | 9.7 | 12.9 |
| Manhattan Bank | Manhattan | MT | **B+** | B+ | B- | 180.3 | 4.18 | 4.7 | 2.4 | 15.9 | 31.0 | **7.7** | 9.5 | 15.6 |
| Mansfield Co-operative Bank | Mansfield | MA | **C+** | C+ | C+ | 519.1 | -0.13 | 4.0 | 0.0 | 34.3 | 9.0 | **9.6** | 10.7 | 15.7 |
| Manson State Bank | Manson | IA | **B-** | B- | B- | 33.3 | -2.99 | 9.2 | 1.3 | 7.2 | 36.7 | **10.0** | 12.2 | 20.6 |
| Manufacturers and Traders Trust Co. | Buffalo | NY | **C+** | C+ | C+ | 119432.1 | -0.17 | 16.0 | 9.1 | 13.4 | 7.5 | **6.3** | 9.1 | 12.0 |
| Manufacturers Bank | Los Angeles | CA | **B** | B | C+ | 4387.0 | 56.52 | 20.8 | 0.0 | 0.3 | 14.3 | **6.5** | 8.5 | 13.9 |
| Manufacturers Bank & Trust Co. | Forest City | IA | **A-** | A- | A- | 370.7 | 6.79 | 13.1 | 2.2 | 11.3 | 18.0 | **9.9** | 13.5 | 14.9 |
| Maple Bank | Champlin | MN | **D+** | C | D+ | 69.1 | 29.11 | 21.7 | 0.3 | 7.4 | 1.5 | **5.9** | 9.7 | 11.7 |
| Maple City Savings Bank, FSB | Hornell | NY | **C-** | C- | C | 86.6 | 9.01 | 4.2 | 1.1 | 65.0 | 1.2 | **6.6** | 8.6 | 14.2 |
| MapleMark Bank | Dallas | TX | **D** | D | D | 604.6 | 96.33 | 34.8 | 0.5 | 7.7 | 13.2 | **10.0** | 12.5 | 15.0 |
| Maquoketa State Bank | Maquoketa | IA | **A-** | A- | A- | 343.2 | 4.18 | 8.4 | 2.8 | 5.6 | 32.1 | **10.0** | 16.6 | 20.7 |
| Marathon Bank | Wausau | WI | **B-** | B- | B- | 148.2 | -2.41 | 5.0 | 0.3 | 31.2 | 11.6 | **10.0** | 13.5 | 17.5 |
| Marblehead Bank | Marblehead | MA | **C** | C- | D+ | 217.7 | 2.33 | 1.9 | 0.3 | 48.6 | 6.7 | **7.8** | 9.5 | 14.5 |
| Marblehead Bank | Marblehead | OH | **C** | C | C | 48.8 | 2.83 | 1.5 | 7.5 | 25.4 | 56.2 | **9.2** | 10.4 | 28.2 |
| ▲ Maries County Bank | Vienna | MO | **A-** | B+ | B | 469.3 | -0.60 | 3.4 | 7.9 | 14.6 | 31.4 | **10.0** | 15.9 | 23.5 |
| Marine Bank | Springfield | IL | **C** | C- | C+ | 639.7 | -1.59 | 6.2 | 0.4 | 7.1 | 11.0 | **8.2** | 11.0 | 13.5 |
| Marine Bank & Trust Co. | Vero Beach | FL | **B-** | C+ | C+ | 286.2 | 6.13 | 6.5 | 0.2 | 39.8 | 8.2 | **6.9** | 8.9 | 14.0 |
| Mariner's Bank | Edgewater | NJ | **C** | C- | C | 404.3 | 3.75 | 9.0 | 2.6 | 14.2 | 1.2 | **7.5** | 9.5 | 12.9 |
| ▼ Marion Bank and Trust Co. | Marion | AL | **B-** | B | B | 283.3 | 6.27 | 7.1 | 2.5 | 10.9 | 29.7 | **9.9** | 10.9 | 17.7 |
| Marion Center Bank | Indiana | PA | **C** | C | C | 318.9 | 4.24 | 10.9 | 4.3 | 27.3 | 17.6 | **5.6** | 7.6 | 11.9 |
| ▼ Marion County State Bank | Pella | IA | **B** | B+ | A | 470.5 | 52.02 | 14.5 | 2.2 | 11.4 | 23.9 | **7.3** | 10.0 | 12.7 |
| Marion National Bank | Marion | KS | **C+** | C | C | 27.5 | 26.24 | 4.1 | 0.7 | 6.0 | 27.7 | **10.0** | 13.7 | 27.8 |
| Marion State Bank | Marion | LA | **B** | B | B- | 174.8 | 4.96 | 9.6 | 3.6 | 19.6 | 13.2 | **10.0** | 11.5 | 15.9 |
| Marion State Bank | Marion | TX | **A-** | B+ | A- | 113.4 | 9.27 | 9.7 | 7.9 | 0.1 | 39.9 | **10.0** | 13.9 | 23.9 |
| Marlin Business Bank | Salt Lake City | UT | **A-** | A- | A | 1058.2 | 10.45 | 52.8 | 0.0 | 0.0 | 0.7 | **10.0** | 13.9 | 16.7 |
| Marquette Bank | Orland Park | IL | **C+** | B- | C+ | 1619.7 | 5.84 | 1.1 | 0.0 | 15.0 | 14.1 | **6.8** | 8.8 | 14.1 |
| ▼ Marquette Farmers State Bank | Marquette | KS | **C-** | C | B- | 29.0 | -3.11 | 6.8 | 5.0 | 12.8 | 19.7 | **10.0** | 15.9 | 27.4 |

| Asset Quality Index | Adjusted Non-Performing Loans as a % of Total Loans | Adjusted Non-Performing Loans as a % of Capital | Net Charge-Offs Avg Loans | Profitability Index | Net Income ($Mil) | Return on Assets (R.O.A.) | Return on Equity (R.O.E.) | Net Interest Spread | Overhead Efficiency Ratio | Liquidity Index | Liquidity Ratio | Hot Money Ratio | Stability Index |
|---|---|---|---|---|---|---|---|---|---|---|---|---|---|
| **6.5** | 0.10 | 5.4 | 0.00 | **3.3** | 0.4 | 0.60 | 5.45 | 4.44 | 86.6 | **3.2** | 15.3 | 12.8 | **5.6** |
| **9.5** | 0.00 | 0.0 | 0.02 | **4.8** | 1.7 | 1.24 | 13.51 | 3.56 | 71.5 | **6.5** | 50.4 | 3.3 | **6.6** |
| **7.9** | 0.70 | 2.8 | 0.00 | **3.9** | 1.0 | 0.85 | 6.40 | 3.44 | 73.0 | **1.9** | 19.8 | 20.1 | **7.5** |
| **7.7** | 0.60 | 3.5 | 0.10 | **5.1** | 11.5 | 1.02 | 12.71 | 3.57 | 67.1 | **2.5** | 14.7 | 16.5 | **7.4** |
| **7.0** | 1.72 | 3.6 | 0.49 | **5.1** | 1.0 | 1.15 | 6.86 | 4.00 | 67.1 | **4.7** | 48.6 | 12.7 | **7.1** |
| **4.9** | 3.88 | 3.6 | 0.26 | **5.5** | 3.6 | 1.17 | 5.11 | 4.40 | 62.3 | **2.4** | 32.1 | 20.8 | **7.9** |
| **8.3** | 0.02 | 0.1 | 0.44 | **0.1** | -1.8 | -0.40 | -3.58 | 2.20 | 104.9 | **1.6** | 35.3 | 34.1 | **6.0** |
| **8.3** | 0.03 | 0.5 | 0.00 | **4.4** | 2.1 | 0.85 | 8.89 | 3.72 | 50.3 | **0.9** | 21.8 | 32.3 | **5.7** |
| **8.0** | 0.44 | 3.2 | 0.19 | **4.7** | 11.0 | 0.94 | 11.45 | 3.87 | 71.8 | **1.1** | 11.7 | 19.6 | **7.5** |
| **7.8** | 0.98 | 2.8 | -0.06 | **8.5** | 34.4 | 1.71 | 14.60 | 3.53 | 50.9 | **5.9** | 31.6 | 4.5 | **9.9** |
| **5.0** | 2.20 | 9.2 | 0.14 | **5.4** | 16.6 | 1.13 | 8.72 | 4.34 | 72.5 | **2.5** | 11.0 | 9.5 | **9.4** |
| **8.4** | 0.15 | 1.7 | 0.02 | **3.6** | 3.0 | 0.74 | 5.82 | 3.13 | 78.1 | **2.4** | 46.2 | 34.3 | **7.2** |
| **4.7** | 1.66 | 8.8 | -0.01 | **4.8** | 3.3 | 1.20 | 11.18 | 3.37 | 67.3 | **2.6** | 21.1 | 16.4 | **6.1** |
| **7.4** | 2.70 | 5.1 | -0.29 | **1.8** | 0.2 | 0.15 | 0.83 | 2.63 | 99.7 | **1.2** | 26.9 | 33.7 | **6.9** |
| **6.9** | 0.66 | 2.6 | 0.00 | **6.8** | 5.8 | 1.39 | 7.96 | 3.34 | 55.6 | **4.7** | 17.4 | 4.0 | **9.0** |
| **5.3** | 1.24 | 5.1 | 0.00 | **4.6** | 1.2 | 0.98 | 10.98 | 3.84 | 64.4 | **3.7** | 37.5 | 15.6 | **4.8** |
| **6.7** | 0.44 | 2.6 | -0.06 | **5.3** | 2.1 | 1.23 | 14.07 | 4.14 | 69.5 | **5.3** | 39.0 | 7.7 | **5.8** |
| **8.3** | 0.11 | 0.9 | -0.01 | **8.4** | 8.6 | 3.06 | 30.62 | 3.01 | 86.8 | **0.6** | 11.5 | 35.6 | **7.6** |
| **6.4** | 0.37 | 3.8 | 0.07 | **4.3** | 3.5 | 1.02 | 10.44 | 4.00 | 74.5 | **1.8** | 15.8 | 20.1 | **6.2** |
| **4.5** | 1.67 | 11.8 | 0.00 | **3.3** | 3.0 | 0.47 | 5.53 | 3.54 | 78.2 | **2.3** | 11.3 | 16.1 | **4.9** |
| **6.1** | 0.89 | 4.8 | 0.03 | **5.7** | 15.4 | 1.14 | 11.40 | 3.51 | 61.3 | **4.3** | 12.1 | 6.7 | **7.9** |
| **7.6** | 0.00 | 0.0 | 0.00 | **8.9** | 3.2 | 2.02 | 22.08 | 4.05 | 47.1 | **2.1** | 28.4 | 21.9 | **7.5** |
| **6.3** | 1.25 | 5.8 | 0.05 | **2.9** | 5.3 | 0.51 | 4.29 | 3.47 | 79.9 | **2.5** | 16.7 | 14.8 | **8.3** |
| **6.7** | 0.62 | 2.4 | 0.08 | **4.1** | 2.1 | 0.76 | 8.69 | 3.68 | 85.4 | **0.5** | 4.8 | 37.9 | **5.6** |
| **3.4** | 2.13 | 15.1 | 0.23 | **6.3** | 5.3 | 1.16 | 12.03 | 3.96 | 57.7 | **1.1** | 16.8 | 21.5 | **6.4** |
| **8.6** | 0.24 | 1.3 | 0.00 | **5.1** | 5.6 | 1.10 | 10.40 | 3.34 | 71.8 | **1.6** | 10.2 | 13.4 | **7.0** |
| **8.6** | 0.04 | 0.3 | 0.03 | **3.3** | 0.5 | 0.56 | 5.27 | 4.10 | 84.1 | **2.2** | 19.8 | 18.6 | **6.4** |
| **6.9** | 0.00 | 0.0 | 0.09 | **6.0** | 14.8 | 1.26 | 10.49 | 3.64 | 55.9 | **0.6** | 15.9 | 48.6 | **8.8** |
| **4.7** | 0.77 | 4.9 | -0.03 | **5.4** | 5.8 | 1.31 | 15.82 | 4.33 | 66.8 | **4.0** | 22.8 | 7.9 | **5.6** |
| **7.3** | 0.05 | 0.3 | 0.00 | **8.0** | 16.0 | 1.38 | 10.55 | 2.97 | 33.5 | **0.9** | 7.4 | 32.2 | **10.0** |
| **2.6** | 1.07 | 12.5 | 0.45 | **4.1** | 1.2 | 0.84 | 8.81 | 3.75 | 69.7 | **0.8** | 14.8 | 28.3 | **5.7** |
| **5.5** | 1.43 | 4.9 | 0.01 | **4.5** | 11.4 | 0.95 | 7.61 | 2.61 | 53.1 | **1.8** | 17.7 | 18.8 | **9.0** |
| **7.4** | 0.41 | 2.0 | 0.04 | **2.9** | 3.3 | 0.61 | 6.09 | 3.22 | 81.4 | **1.4** | 15.9 | 23.4 | **6.3** |
| **7.5** | 0.43 | 3.1 | 0.03 | **4.1** | 12.0 | 0.75 | 7.86 | 3.39 | 68.2 | **1.8** | 13.6 | 20.4 | **7.8** |
| **8.1** | 0.02 | 2.2 | 0.00 | **5.4** | 2.3 | 1.30 | 14.18 | 4.08 | 67.1 | **5.2** | 33.6 | 5.8 | **6.9** |
| **7.1** | 0.35 | 2.5 | 0.05 | **3.3** | 2.7 | 0.52 | 4.93 | 3.15 | 79.8 | **1.8** | 16.1 | 20.4 | **7.2** |
| **5.7** | 3.73 | 12.9 | 0.05 | **4.0** | 0.3 | 0.88 | 6.87 | 3.60 | 64.7 | **5.9** | 53.0 | 7.0 | **6.8** |
| **3.5** | 1.30 | 7.4 | 0.16 | **9.0** | 1961.2 | 1.65 | 12.98 | 3.85 | 52.5 | **4.5** | 15.6 | 2.8 | **10.0** |
| **8.6** | 0.26 | 0.6 | 0.04 | **4.0** | 30.1 | 0.68 | 8.13 | 2.16 | 55.6 | **3.9** | 51.0 | 12.2 | **7.9** |
| **7.6** | 0.13 | 1.4 | 0.06 | **8.1** | 7.2 | 2.02 | 15.30 | 3.84 | 56.9 | **2.0** | 20.9 | 18.8 | **9.0** |
| **3.2** | 2.23 | 11.0 | -0.01 | **1.3** | -0.1 | -0.17 | -1.39 | 4.28 | 89.9 | **0.8** | 18.4 | 6.3 | **5.6** |
| **4.2** | 1.65 | 14.5 | 0.23 | **3.1** | 0.6 | 0.72 | 7.45 | 3.92 | 77.8 | **1.2** | 5.4 | 17.7 | **3.8** |
| **8.2** | 0.00 | 0.0 | 0.00 | **0.0** | -3.6 | -0.79 | -4.83 | 2.80 | 121.9 | **1.1** | 20.6 | 32.0 | **5.9** |
| **7.8** | 0.89 | 2.7 | 0.00 | **6.3** | 4.6 | 1.34 | 7.70 | 3.46 | 59.3 | **4.8** | 35.1 | 9.4 | **9.2** |
| **8.2** | 1.06 | 3.4 | -0.04 | **2.9** | 1.4 | 0.89 | 6.85 | 3.30 | 90.6 | **1.8** | 24.7 | 18.6 | **6.5** |
| **6.4** | 0.51 | 6.2 | 0.01 | **2.7** | 0.8 | 0.36 | 4.01 | 3.79 | 88.0 | **4.3** | 10.3 | 6.3 | **5.0** |
| **8.8** | 0.37 | 1.3 | 0.00 | **2.9** | 0.3 | 0.53 | 5.14 | 3.11 | 84.4 | **5.4** | 52.0 | 10.1 | **5.3** |
| **7.2** | 1.13 | 3.4 | 0.12 | **5.3** | 5.1 | 1.09 | 6.88 | 4.03 | 67.2 | **3.0** | 18.8 | 14.3 | **8.0** |
| **3.3** | 1.42 | 8.0 | 0.38 | **4.9** | 7.7 | 1.20 | 10.73 | 3.47 | 70.2 | **2.5** | 15.7 | 10.4 | **8.0** |
| **8.3** | 0.38 | 1.7 | -0.01 | **4.0** | 1.8 | 0.65 | 7.40 | 3.93 | 76.9 | **3.8** | 11.2 | 9.8 | **5.1** |
| **2.9** | 1.56 | 11.4 | -0.01 | **3.6** | 3.4 | 0.85 | 9.46 | 3.30 | 73.2 | **1.7** | 13.9 | 21.5 | **5.2** |
| **3.5** | 3.84 | 16.9 | 0.09 | **4.1** | 2.7 | 0.97 | 8.31 | 3.39 | 69.3 | **1.2** | 26.8 | 34.4 | **6.5** |
| **4.0** | 1.59 | 12.2 | 0.33 | **3.8** | 2.2 | 0.69 | 9.22 | 3.54 | 74.6 | **1.8** | 19.1 | 20.9 | **4.1** |
| **4.2** | 1.09 | 7.1 | 0.16 | **9.3** | 6.9 | 2.05 | 20.72 | 4.72 | 55.6 | **4.8** | 31.0 | 7.1 | **8.2** |
| **8.0** | 0.00 | 0.0 | -0.02 | **5.3** | 0.3 | 1.37 | 8.14 | 3.16 | 61.0 | **5.6** | 63.3 | 10.8 | **6.5** |
| **6.5** | 0.86 | 4.2 | 0.17 | **3.8** | 1.2 | 0.66 | 5.87 | 4.41 | 78.6 | **2.0** | 17.5 | 19.3 | **6.6** |
| **7.1** | 0.67 | 2.2 | 0.58 | **6.3** | 1.5 | 1.40 | 10.26 | 3.53 | 59.7 | **2.1** | 33.0 | 26.3 | **9.0** |
| **7.7** | 0.56 | 3.2 | 2.07 | **7.7** | 14.8 | 1.40 | 10.15 | 8.27 | 60.8 | **0.3** | 13.5 | 49.6 | **9.5** |
| **3.1** | 2.00 | 10.8 | 0.07 | **4.2** | 11.2 | 0.71 | 6.43 | 3.58 | 75.4 | **3.8** | 12.7 | 10.2 | **8.3** |
| **2.6** | 6.78 | 22.5 | 0.26 | **1.5** | 0.1 | 0.32 | 2.03 | 3.39 | 88.7 | **2.8** | 51.7 | 29.0 | **5.2** |

| | | | | | | | | Asset Mix (As a % of Total Assets) | | | | | | |
|---|---|---|---|---|---|---|---|---|---|---|---|---|---|---|
| Name | City | State | Rating | 2018 Rating | 2017 Rating | Total Assets ($Mil) | One Year Asset Growth | Comm-ercial Loans | Cons-umer Loans | Mort-gage Loans | Secur-ities | Capital-ization Index | Lever-age Ratio | Risk-Based Capital Ratio |
| ▼ Marquette Savings Bank | Erie | PA | B | B+ | B+ | 938.6 | 9.00 | 3.8 | 0.2 | 41.2 | 31.9 | **10.0** | 17.7 | 34.3 |
| Marquis Bank | Coral Gables | FL | B | B- | B | 646.0 | -2.46 | 11.0 | 0.7 | 4.7 | 4.7 | **7.3** | 9.8 | 12.8 |
| Mars Bank | Mars | PA | C | C | C- | 407.7 | 2.71 | 2.4 | 0.1 | 36.9 | 24.8 | **7.2** | 9.1 | 16.0 |
| Marseilles Bank | Marseilles | IL | B- | B | B | 62.2 | 7.72 | 0.9 | 10.3 | 29.3 | 47.1 | **8.7** | 10.1 | 20.7 |
| Marshall County State Bank | Newfolden | MN | B | B | B | 32.9 | -1.66 | 1.9 | 3.7 | 9.7 | 36.4 | **10.0** | 18.4 | 97.9 |
| Martha's Vineyard Savings Bank | Edgartown | MA | B+ | B+ | B+ | 845.6 | 0.85 | 1.7 | 0.3 | 47.4 | 7.6 | **10.0** | 13.0 | 20.3 |
| Martinsville First Savings Bank | Martinsville | VA | C+ | C+ | C+ | 38.9 | -1.92 | 0.0 | 0.4 | 49.3 | 17.1 | **10.0** | 17.3 | 42.6 |
| Mascoma Bank | Lebanon | NH | C+ | C+ | C+ | 1935.6 | 9.62 | 6.1 | 0.4 | 41.7 | 9.5 | **7.4** | 9.3 | 13.4 |
| Mason Bank | Mason | TX | A | A- | A- | 120.7 | 0.59 | 5.2 | 4.7 | 9.7 | 61.1 | **10.0** | 18.0 | 43.2 |
| Mason City National Bank | Mason City | IL | B+ | B | B | 68.1 | -2.33 | 0.9 | 1.4 | 11.4 | 47.4 | **10.0** | 17.8 | 39.1 |
| Maspeth Federal S&L Assn. | Maspeth | NY | A- | A- | A- | 1963.0 | 4.25 | 0.0 | 0.0 | 48.8 | 1.6 | **10.0** | 32.8 | 44.2 |
| Massena S&L | Massena | NY | B | B | B | 166.2 | 3.66 | 1.5 | 7.9 | 75.5 | 0.0 | **10.0** | 13.3 | 21.1 |
| MassMutual Trust Co., FSB | Enfield | CT | U | U | U | 86.6 | 1.18 | 0.0 | 0.0 | 0.0 | 85.0 | **10.0** | 32.4 | 41.0 |
| Mauch Chunk Trust Co. | Jim Thorpe | PA | C+ | C+ | C+ | 439.9 | 0.40 | 4.9 | 4.9 | 21.7 | 43.0 | **7.2** | 9.1 | 15.4 |
| Maxwell State Bank | Maxwell | IA | B+ | B+ | A | 27.7 | -3.03 | 2.0 | 0.4 | 3.9 | 35.6 | **10.0** | 18.9 | 49.2 |
| Maynard Savings Bank | Maynard | IA | A- | B+ | B | 60.9 | -0.09 | 5.3 | 5.3 | 23.2 | 13.5 | **10.0** | 15.2 | 24.8 |
| Mayville Savings Bank | Mayville | WI | B- | B- | C+ | 67.3 | 8.24 | 6.0 | 1.2 | 51.0 | 5.6 | **9.8** | 10.9 | 20.1 |
| Mayville State Bank | Mayville | MI | B- | C+ | C+ | 86.4 | -2.67 | 1.1 | 4.2 | 31.6 | 24.3 | **10.0** | 11.2 | 24.1 |
| mBank | Manistique | MI | B | B- | B- | 1316.6 | 0.12 | 15.5 | 1.6 | 17.1 | 8.2 | **7.7** | 10.0 | 13.1 |
| MCBank | Goldthwaite | TX | C | C+ | B- | 325.2 | 3.15 | 4.9 | 2.6 | 12.8 | 49.5 | **7.9** | 9.6 | 19.8 |
| McClain Bank | Purcell | OK | A- | A- | A- | 231.2 | 1.50 | 8.6 | 1.8 | 21.7 | 5.3 | **10.0** | 11.3 | 16.6 |
| McClave State Bank | McClave | CO | B | B- | B- | 45.5 | 7.89 | 12.3 | 1.9 | 4.8 | 10.2 | **10.0** | 13.0 | 15.2 |
| McCurtain County National Bank | Broken Bow | OK | A- | B+ | A- | 264.6 | 3.87 | 2.8 | 6.3 | 30.4 | 10.3 | **10.0** | 13.0 | 27.0 |
| ▲ McFarland State Bank | McFarland | WI | A- | B+ | A- | 527.8 | 7.16 | 6.7 | 0.1 | 15.9 | 10.7 | **9.8** | 11.9 | 14.9 |
| McGehee Bank | McGehee | AR | A- | A- | A- | 132.4 | 7.34 | 12.9 | 1.1 | 2.8 | 18.9 | **10.0** | 13.3 | 17.4 |
| ▲ McHenry Savings Bank | McHenry | IL | E+ | E | E- | 226.9 | 12.50 | 3.0 | 21.3 | 26.4 | 22.1 | **7.6** | 9.4 | 15.7 |
| McIntosh County Bank | Ashley | ND | C | C- | C | 85.0 | -1.45 | 4.4 | 2.2 | 0.2 | 21.6 | **10.0** | 12.0 | 15.8 |
| McKenzie Banking Co. | McKenzie | TN | B- | B+ | A- | 132.2 | 2.64 | 10.4 | 6.6 | 21.9 | 10.0 | **10.0** | 13.8 | 25.2 |
| MCNB Bank and Trust Co. | Welch | WV | C+ | C- | C- | 301.4 | 2.46 | 5.9 | 1.1 | 16.0 | 13.7 | **10.0** | 11.4 | 16.6 |
| MCS Bank | Lewistown | PA | C+ | C+ | C+ | 147.1 | 2.54 | 9.8 | 7.7 | 37.7 | 5.0 | **10.0** | 13.3 | 18.2 |
| Meade County Bank | Brandenburg | KY | B+ | B+ | B+ | 212.1 | 5.73 | 1.6 | 3.3 | 39.1 | 16.1 | **7.9** | 9.7 | 13.3 |
| ▲ Meadows Bank | Las Vegas | NV | B+ | B- | B+ | 961.2 | 11.94 | 16.2 | 0.0 | 3.5 | 1.7 | **9.3** | 12.3 | 14.4 |
| Mechanics and Farmers Bank | Durham | NC | C- | D | D- | 265.3 | 3.23 | 7.6 | 0.4 | 6.1 | 16.5 | **6.2** | 8.3 | 12.3 |
| Mechanics Bank | Walnut Creek | CA | B- | B | B- | 17204.2 | 185.21 | 3.3 | 12.5 | 11.4 | 26.0 | **6.4** | 8.5 | 13.7 |
| Mechanics Bank | Water Valley | MS | B | B- | C+ | 230.3 | 3.35 | 8.9 | 2.2 | 27.4 | 17.7 | **9.6** | 10.7 | 16.6 |
| Mechanics Bank | Mansfield | OH | B- | C+ | C+ | 562.9 | 6.50 | 1.4 | 1.3 | 68.8 | 9.3 | **6.3** | 8.3 | 16.6 |
| Mechanics Cooperative Bank | Taunton | MA | B+ | B- | B- | 605.3 | 5.26 | 5.7 | 0.9 | 29.9 | 12.3 | **9.1** | 10.4 | 15.7 |
| Medallion Bank | Salt Lake City | UT | C+ | C- | D | 1198.6 | 17.06 | 9.0 | 80.9 | 0.0 | 4.1 | **10.0** | 19.6 | 21.3 |
| ▲ Mediapolis Savings Bank | Mediapolis | IA | C+ | D+ | C- | 174.0 | 1.96 | 7.0 | 1.8 | 19.9 | 8.1 | **8.5** | 10.4 | 13.7 |
| Mega Bank | San Gabriel | CA | B | B | B | 390.0 | 5.96 | 8.1 | 0.0 | 18.3 | 8.2 | **10.0** | 11.9 | 18.0 |
| ▼ Melrose Bank | Melrose | MA | C | C+ | C+ | 336.8 | 5.62 | 0.4 | 0.0 | 59.1 | 6.1 | **7.3** | 9.2 | 13.9 |
| ▼ Melvin Savings Bank | Melvin | IA | B- | B | B | 73.9 | 2.35 | 3.5 | 1.6 | 2.9 | 39.6 | **10.0** | 17.1 | 32.1 |
| MEMBERS Trust Co. | Tampa | FL | U | U | U | 40.5 | 5.80 | 0.0 | 0.0 | 0.0 | 67.7 | **10.0** | 88.3 | 556.8 |
| Menard Bank | Menard | TX | B- | B- | B- | 43.2 | 17.70 | 3.5 | 1.0 | 7.7 | 52.7 | **10.0** | 12.0 | 26.6 |
| Mer Rouge State Bank | Mer Rouge | LA | C+ | C+ | C+ | 39.9 | 0.45 | 16.4 | 0.8 | 3.8 | 6.6 | **10.0** | 12.5 | 18.1 |
| Meramec Valley Bank | Ellisville | MO | C | C- | C- | 123.5 | 4.97 | 12.7 | 1.2 | 20.0 | 10.8 | **4.4** | 8.5 | 10.7 |
| Mercantile Bank of Louisiana, Missouri | Louisiana | MO | A- | A- | B+ | 108.3 | -0.14 | 1.6 | 1.5 | 14.1 | 12.6 | **10.0** | 21.1 | 29.1 |
| Mercantile Bank of Michigan | Grand Rapids | MI | A- | A- | B+ | 3615.0 | 8.09 | 21.3 | 0.6 | 10.2 | 9.3 | **7.6** | 11.2 | 13.0 |
| ▼ Mercer County State Bank | Sandy Lake | PA | C+ | B- | B | 426.9 | 5.63 | 6.6 | 0.9 | 21.6 | 30.5 | **7.4** | 9.3 | 16.2 |
| Mercer Savings Bank | Celina | OH | C+ | C+ | C- | 133.9 | 2.46 | 0.8 | 0.7 | 57.1 | 2.9 | **8.3** | 9.9 | 15.4 |
| Merchants & Citizens Bank | McRae | GA | B- | B- | B- | 104.2 | -2.50 | 2.4 | 3.1 | 14.8 | 47.9 | **10.0** | 15.5 | 35.1 |
| Merchants & Farmers Bank | Eutaw | AL | C+ | B- | C+ | 77.5 | 16.46 | 10.8 | 9.4 | 12.5 | 17.1 | **8.6** | 10.1 | 15.5 |
| ▲ Merchants & Farmers Bank | Holly Springs | MS | B | C | B- | 102.9 | 1.64 | 6.1 | 4.4 | 10.6 | 42.5 | **10.0** | 11.2 | 20.6 |
| ▲ Merchants & Farmers Bank & Trust Co. | Leesville | LA | B | B- | B- | 408.2 | -1.83 | 3.8 | 1.0 | 26.5 | 31.4 | **10.0** | 11.5 | 20.0 |
| Merchants & Marine Bank | Pascagoula | MS | B- | B | B | 576.8 | 3.23 | 6.2 | 5.0 | 13.7 | 29.6 | **10.0** | 13.3 | 21.0 |
| ▼ Merchants & Planters Bank | Clarendon | AR | C- | C+ | C+ | 39.9 | -11.30 | 12.0 | 1.8 | 1.6 | 60.3 | **10.0** | 13.1 | 29.7 |
| ▲ Merchants & Planters Bank | Newport | AR | C+ | C+ | B- | 272.3 | 3.04 | 8.4 | 4.1 | 9.7 | 17.7 | **10.0** | 11.1 | 15.5 |
| ▲ Merchants and Farmers Bank | Dumas | AR | B- | B- | B- | 152.2 | 8.95 | 13.4 | 3.1 | 12.2 | 8.0 | **7.6** | 9.7 | 13.0 |
| Merchants and Farmers Bank of Salisbury | Salisbury | MO | C+ | C | C | 104.6 | 1.88 | 2.8 | 2.2 | 13.6 | 30.9 | **7.3** | 9.2 | 15.7 |
| Merchants and Manufacturers Bank | Joliet | IL | C+ | C+ | C+ | 274.1 | 3.64 | 26.0 | 37.8 | 6.6 | 3.0 | **4.4** | 8.3 | 10.7 |

| Asset Quality Index | Adjusted Non-Performing Loans as a % of Total Loans | Adjusted Non-Performing Loans as a % of Capital | Net Charge-Offs Avg Loans | Profitability Index | Net Income ($Mil) | Return on Assets (R.O.A.) | Return on Equity (R.O.E.) | Net Interest Spread | Overhead Efficiency Ratio | Liquidity Index | Liquidity Ratio | Hot Money Ratio | Stability Index |
|---|---|---|---|---|---|---|---|---|---|---|---|---|---|
| 8.9 | 0.85 | 2.7 | 0.04 | 3.7 | 6.3 | 0.70 | 3.86 | 3.14 | 73.3 | 3.4 | 40.5 | 18.1 | 8.7 |
| 7.4 | 0.02 | 0.2 | -0.01 | 6.1 | 8.2 | 1.23 | 12.90 | 3.49 | 55.0 | 0.8 | 16.5 | 36.8 | 7.0 |
| 9.5 | 0.02 | 0.2 | 0.00 | 2.9 | 1.9 | 0.47 | 5.15 | 2.95 | 83.7 | 4.0 | 19.5 | 9.5 | 5.3 |
| 6.2 | 0.41 | 5.6 | 0.14 | 4.1 | 0.6 | 0.92 | 9.36 | 2.66 | 65.3 | 2.5 | 41.5 | 28.6 | 6.1 |
| 9.3 | 0.06 | 2.0 | 0.00 | 4.2 | 0.3 | 0.98 | 5.42 | 2.49 | 61.8 | 7.2 | 77.0 | 3.0 | 7.7 |
| 8.0 | 0.75 | 4.6 | 0.01 | 4.8 | 7.6 | 0.91 | 7.29 | 3.55 | 67.7 | 4.0 | 12.1 | 4.0 | 8.1 |
| 3.0 | 9.05 | 24.2 | 0.33 | 2.7 | 0.2 | 0.38 | 2.23 | 2.90 | 86.1 | 2.8 | 53.4 | 29.1 | 7.4 |
| 8.6 | 0.37 | 1.9 | 0.02 | 3.7 | 13.2 | 0.72 | 7.59 | 3.48 | 78.0 | 2.8 | 11.8 | 13.9 | 7.9 |
| 9.0 | 0.42 | 0.9 | -0.14 | 6.5 | 1.9 | 1.56 | 8.68 | 3.52 | 57.2 | 5.0 | 73.7 | 16.6 | 9.2 |
| 9.2 | 0.53 | 1.0 | 0.01 | 5.3 | 1.0 | 1.38 | 7.65 | 3.10 | 55.6 | 5.3 | 61.4 | 11.9 | 8.1 |
| 6.4 | 2.14 | 5.7 | 0.00 | 7.0 | 22.8 | 1.18 | 3.60 | 3.60 | 56.0 | 1.7 | 10.7 | 20.6 | 10.0 |
| 4.0 | 3.32 | 17.7 | 0.16 | 3.6 | 1.0 | 0.61 | 4.67 | 3.43 | 71.2 | 0.8 | 3.6 | 32.0 | 7.0 |
| 10.0 | na | 0.0 | na | 9.5 | 3.1 | 3.65 | 10.97 | 1.57 | 87.8 | 3.9 | 133.9 | 100.0 | 7.0 |
| 5.8 | 2.82 | 7.9 | 0.37 | 2.7 | 2.4 | 0.53 | 6.02 | 2.83 | 81.4 | 3.4 | 27.3 | 11.0 | 5.0 |
| 9.5 | 0.00 | 0.0 | 0.00 | 5.1 | 0.3 | 1.20 | 6.23 | 3.00 | 51.4 | 5.7 | 93.3 | 13.7 | 7.8 |
| 7.8 | 0.09 | 3.3 | 0.38 | 4.5 | 0.4 | 0.69 | 4.41 | 3.56 | 57.3 | 4.1 | 35.4 | 13.0 | 7.2 |
| 5.3 | 1.44 | 7.3 | -0.03 | 3.7 | 0.4 | 0.66 | 6.12 | 3.30 | 70.5 | 2.9 | 23.9 | 15.2 | 5.7 |
| 8.9 | 1.25 | 2.7 | 0.01 | 3.7 | 0.6 | 0.71 | 6.43 | 3.41 | 78.6 | 6.2 | 52.2 | 4.6 | 6.0 |
| 5.5 | 1.07 | 5.1 | 0.02 | 5.8 | 15.1 | 1.13 | 9.82 | 4.54 | 67.5 | 2.9 | 11.8 | 8.8 | 8.3 |
| 3.3 | 3.72 | 13.8 | 0.32 | 4.8 | 3.6 | 1.14 | 10.94 | 4.00 | 69.6 | 5.5 | 47.3 | 9.2 | 6.6 |
| 5.4 | 3.16 | 19.1 | 0.12 | 7.7 | 3.3 | 1.44 | 12.31 | 4.46 | 62.3 | 4.3 | 22.2 | 7.4 | 7.3 |
| 6.2 | 0.86 | 4.4 | 0.46 | 7.4 | 0.5 | 1.16 | 8.89 | 5.16 | 60.3 | 0.5 | 10.9 | 44.5 | 7.9 |
| 6.7 | 1.43 | 5.4 | 0.05 | 7.7 | 3.8 | 1.47 | 11.27 | 3.75 | 51.8 | 4.0 | 46.7 | 16.5 | 8.0 |
| 7.4 | 0.02 | 0.1 | 0.00 | 6.7 | 7.5 | 1.48 | 13.21 | 3.71 | 67.8 | 1.3 | 11.1 | 15.8 | 8.9 |
| 6.3 | 1.33 | 3.2 | 0.04 | 7.6 | 2.3 | 1.82 | 12.88 | 4.45 | 55.9 | 2.8 | 11.0 | 14.6 | 8.9 |
| 2.6 | 2.02 | 12.4 | 0.10 | 0.9 | 0.2 | 0.08 | 0.83 | 3.25 | 96.8 | 1.2 | 22.5 | 23.6 | 0.8 |
| 2.6 | 4.03 | 11.6 | 0.62 | 6.9 | 1.4 | 1.66 | 13.47 | 4.23 | 55.2 | 3.6 | 14.8 | 11.1 | 8.9 |
| 3.6 | 4.93 | 18.9 | 0.24 | 9.8 | 2.7 | 2.08 | 14.49 | 6.51 | 64.9 | 5.0 | 46.3 | 11.4 | 9.2 |
| 3.3 | 5.22 | 23.6 | 0.20 | 3.9 | 2.3 | 0.77 | 6.93 | 3.76 | 74.3 | 3.3 | 19.8 | 12.8 | 6.3 |
| 4.7 | 1.60 | 9.9 | 0.66 | 2.5 | 0.4 | 0.29 | 2.13 | 3.30 | 81.7 | 1.0 | 9.3 | 24.2 | 6.7 |
| 8.2 | 0.01 | 0.1 | 0.01 | 5.4 | 2.4 | 1.16 | 12.27 | 3.64 | 63.5 | 2.3 | 11.8 | 17.0 | 6.1 |
| 6.7 | 0.71 | 1.5 | 0.01 | 10.0 | 18.4 | 2.02 | 17.03 | 4.90 | 48.9 | 1.7 | 14.9 | 21.7 | 9.2 |
| 3.0 | 2.46 | 11.5 | -0.04 | 2.8 | 1.2 | 0.43 | 5.51 | 3.57 | 88.1 | 0.9 | 17.0 | 32.2 | 3.1 |
| 5.5 | 0.71 | 3.7 | 0.38 | 3.6 | 57.7 | 0.59 | 4.12 | 4.21 | 73.6 | 4.5 | 22.9 | 7.6 | 9.1 |
| 4.6 | 1.42 | 9.2 | 0.12 | 4.6 | 2.1 | 0.92 | 8.34 | 3.79 | 75.5 | 1.3 | 18.8 | 27.6 | 6.1 |
| 6.3 | 0.78 | 5.4 | 0.02 | 4.0 | 4.4 | 0.80 | 9.89 | 3.37 | 74.3 | 3.4 | 12.4 | 11.8 | 5.7 |
| 8.3 | 0.15 | 0.7 | 0.00 | 5.7 | 6.4 | 1.08 | 10.88 | 3.67 | 62.0 | 1.0 | 8.6 | 24.6 | 6.9 |
| 2.8 | 1.69 | 5.1 | 4.25 | 8.4 | 23.0 | 2.09 | 12.77 | 9.56 | 32.8 | 0.3 | 10.2 | 0.0 | 7.7 |
| 3.4 | 1.56 | 10.7 | 0.43 | 4.5 | 1.8 | 1.04 | 10.08 | 3.29 | 61.2 | 1.7 | 15.7 | 22.3 | 6.8 |
| 7.6 | 0.00 | 0.0 | -0.03 | 3.5 | 2.0 | 0.56 | 4.59 | 2.76 | 80.6 | 0.9 | 25.8 | 53.9 | 6.8 |
| 9.5 | 0.06 | 0.5 | 0.00 | 2.4 | 0.8 | 0.23 | 2.34 | 2.26 | 85.6 | 0.7 | 12.6 | 36.8 | 5.5 |
| 6.9 | 2.72 | 5.1 | 0.00 | 2.8 | 0.3 | 0.44 | 2.49 | 2.76 | 80.6 | 6.2 | 73.2 | 9.5 | 7.6 |
| 9.3 | na | 0.0 | na | 8.4 | 0.4 | 1.02 | 1.09 | 2.63 | 96.4 | 4.0 | na | 0.0 | 7.0 |
| 9.7 | 0.00 | 0.0 | 0.00 | 3.6 | 0.3 | 0.86 | 6.57 | 3.46 | 77.2 | 3.1 | 49.8 | 23.9 | 6.3 |
| 7.0 | 0.27 | 0.9 | -0.01 | 4.0 | 0.3 | 0.64 | 4.86 | 4.69 | 72.5 | 3.1 | 45.9 | 21.8 | 5.0 |
| 8.5 | 0.00 | 0.0 | 0.00 | 3.0 | 0.8 | 0.63 | 7.51 | 3.48 | 82.5 | 2.6 | 13.0 | 14.6 | 4.9 |
| 6.5 | 6.10 | 8.9 | -0.02 | 6.4 | 2.1 | 1.90 | 8.82 | 3.98 | 62.4 | 3.7 | 30.8 | 13.6 | 9.1 |
| 7.5 | 0.49 | 1.8 | 0.01 | 7.6 | 55.6 | 1.57 | 13.26 | 3.86 | 54.6 | 2.3 | 10.9 | 11.9 | 10.0 |
| 3.2 | 3.18 | 18.3 | 0.01 | 4.4 | 3.8 | 0.90 | 8.90 | 3.59 | 71.6 | 3.2 | 25.7 | 14.5 | 6.4 |
| 6.4 | 0.47 | 3.9 | 0.01 | 3.5 | 0.8 | 0.58 | 5.93 | 3.52 | 77.9 | 3.6 | 10.1 | 10.7 | 5.5 |
| 7.1 | 0.93 | 2.5 | -0.22 | 3.4 | 0.9 | 0.82 | 4.70 | 3.44 | 78.6 | 2.9 | 39.4 | 21.2 | 7.6 |
| 3.5 | 2.27 | 12.7 | 0.41 | 4.9 | 0.7 | 1.00 | 9.33 | 5.09 | 77.1 | 1.8 | 25.2 | 23.0 | 4.6 |
| 4.6 | 4.46 | 15.9 | 0.40 | 4.1 | 0.9 | 0.83 | 7.38 | 3.73 | 80.9 | 2.7 | 36.4 | 20.5 | 6.3 |
| 6.3 | 1.39 | 5.6 | 0.04 | 4.1 | 3.4 | 0.82 | 6.98 | 3.63 | 74.8 | 2.3 | 24.6 | 14.0 | 6.7 |
| 5.6 | 2.10 | 8.0 | 0.19 | 3.8 | 4.4 | 0.75 | 6.00 | 3.47 | 74.9 | 2.8 | 18.6 | 15.4 | 7.5 |
| 7.2 | 2.40 | 3.9 | 2.82 | 1.1 | -0.1 | -0.15 | -1.14 | 3.06 | 89.5 | 5.7 | 56.7 | 8.9 | 5.4 |
| 4.6 | 2.25 | 11.4 | 0.27 | 4.2 | 2.4 | 0.92 | 8.31 | 4.14 | 79.5 | 1.8 | 16.1 | 19.6 | 6.3 |
| 4.2 | 1.24 | 12.7 | 0.08 | 4.8 | 1.3 | 0.86 | 9.16 | 4.54 | 73.7 | 1.5 | 12.5 | 24.1 | 6.4 |
| 8.9 | 0.00 | 0.0 | 0.00 | 3.4 | 0.7 | 0.68 | 7.30 | 3.60 | 81.5 | 3.4 | 14.6 | 11.8 | 5.5 |
| 6.7 | 0.00 | 0.0 | -0.02 | 4.7 | 2.3 | 0.86 | 10.46 | 4.46 | 74.5 | 1.8 | 4.8 | 11.6 | 5.5 |

| | Name | City | State | Rating | 2018 Rating | 2017 Rating | Total Assets ($Mil) | One Year Asset Growth | Asset Mix (As a % of Total Assets) Commercial Loans | Consumer Loans | Mortgage Loans | Securities | Capitalization Index | Leverage Ratio | Risk-Based Capital Ratio |
|---|---|---|---|---|---|---|---|---|---|---|---|---|---|---|---|
| | Merchants and Planters Bank | Raymond | MS | **B** | C | C- | 91.1 | -0.34 | 6.7 | 1.5 | 14.8 | 21.9 | **9.0** | 10.4 | 16.4 |
| | Merchants Bank | Rugby | ND | **B** | C+ | B | 168.8 | 3.91 | 8.2 | 1.8 | 3.5 | 23.3 | **5.7** | 8.8 | 11.5 |
| ▲ | Merchants Bank of Alabama | Cullman | AL | **B+** | B- | B- | 295.7 | 4.10 | 7.8 | 4.2 | 21.0 | 25.2 | **9.1** | 10.4 | 17.9 |
| | Merchants Bank of Bangor | Bangor | PA | **B** | B- | C+ | 400.9 | 1.25 | 3.8 | 0.9 | 22.8 | 34.7 | **7.6** | 9.4 | 16.1 |
| ▲ | Merchants Bank of Commerce | Redding | CA | **B+** | B | B | 1478.0 | 13.11 | 9.3 | 2.2 | 6.8 | 19.4 | **10.0** | 11.6 | 15.5 |
| | Merchants Bank of Indiana | Carmel | IN | **B+** | A | A | 6167.5 | 66.23 | 6.0 | 0.2 | 1.1 | 4.4 | **6.3** | 9.7 | 12.0 |
| | Merchants Bank, N.A. | Winona | MN | **B** | B | B+ | 1864.1 | 5.53 | 20.9 | 2.4 | 12.4 | 6.8 | **5.8** | 10.1 | 11.6 |
| ▲ | Merchants Commercial Bank | Saint Thomas | VI | **C** | C- | D- | 295.5 | 22.64 | 3.6 | 0.4 | 12.1 | 47.3 | **6.2** | 8.2 | 22.2 |
| | Merchants National Bank | Hillsboro | OH | **B-** | B- | B | 933.5 | 26.71 | 5.6 | 3.3 | 32.4 | 2.7 | **5.7** | 8.7 | 11.5 |
| | Merchants State Bank | Freeman | SD | **B-** | C+ | B- | 175.6 | -0.51 | 5.8 | 1.6 | 2.1 | 13.6 | **10.0** | 13.4 | 16.5 |
| | Meredith Village Savings Bank | Meredith | NH | **B** | B | B | 985.3 | 1.02 | 4.9 | 6.9 | 47.0 | 5.6 | **10.0** | 11.3 | 17.8 |
| | Merit Bank | Huntsville | AL | **C** | C+ | C+ | 83.4 | 189.62 | 2.9 | 4.0 | 7.9 | 15.8 | **10.0** | 25.4 | 48.6 |
| | Merrick Bank Corp. | South Jordan | UT | **C** | C | C | 3965.3 | 1.91 | 0.0 | 97.1 | 0.0 | 3.2 | **10.0** | 21.9 | 24.6 |
| | Merrimack County Savings Bank | Concord | NH | **B-** | B- | B- | 938.4 | 4.75 | 11.3 | 7.4 | 31.7 | 8.5 | **8.2** | 9.8 | 13.7 |
| | MetaBank | Sioux Falls | SD | **B+** | B+ | B+ | 6192.2 | 0.38 | 30.3 | 5.6 | 3.7 | 21.6 | **7.5** | 9.7 | 12.9 |
| | Metairie Bank and Trust Co. | Metairie | LA | **B-** | B- | B- | 394.5 | 2.37 | 4.1 | 1.2 | 35.4 | 11.5 | **8.7** | 10.2 | 15.6 |
| | Metamora State Bank | Metamora | OH | **C** | C | C+ | 82.9 | 11.39 | 5.3 | 1.2 | 20.6 | 16.2 | **6.6** | 8.7 | 13.9 |
| | Methuen Co-operative Bank | Methuen | MA | **C** | C- | D+ | 89.5 | -4.07 | 0.6 | 1.5 | 46.7 | 14.7 | **9.9** | 10.9 | 24.6 |
| | Metro Bank | Pell City | AL | **A-** | B+ | A- | 763.5 | 5.96 | 8.4 | 2.0 | 10.4 | 28.0 | **10.0** | 15.6 | 22.1 |
| | Metro Bank | Louisville | KY | **D** | D+ | D+ | 26.3 | 0.47 | 2.3 | 0.2 | 4.4 | 23.8 | **10.0** | 18.2 | 30.5 |
| | Metro City Bank | Doraville | GA | **A** | A | A | 1636.0 | 13.94 | 3.3 | 0.1 | 45.1 | 1.0 | **10.0** | 11.7 | 20.4 |
| | Metro Phoenix Bank | Phoenix | AZ | **A-** | B+ | A- | 243.3 | 22.12 | 18.8 | 0.0 | 5.9 | 1.0 | **10.0** | 14.6 | 21.9 |
| | Metropolitan Bank | Oakland | CA | **B** | B- | B+ | 181.4 | 2.97 | 2.5 | 0.1 | 22.2 | 6.9 | **10.0** | 12.5 | 20.3 |
| | Metropolitan Capital Bank & Trust | Chicago | IL | **D+** | D- | D+ | 225.0 | -10.83 | 52.4 | 0.2 | 3.5 | 6.2 | **8.1** | 9.7 | 14.8 |
| | Metropolitan Commercial Bank | New York | NY | **A-** | A- | B | 3355.2 | 53.86 | 13.4 | 2.1 | 4.5 | 7.1 | **7.3** | 10.1 | 12.7 |
| | Metz Banking Co. | Nevada | MO | **B+** | B+ | B+ | 74.6 | 1.91 | 7.5 | 1.2 | 13.0 | 16.0 | **10.0** | 12.0 | 18.5 |
| | Miami Savings Bank | Miamitown | OH | **A-** | B+ | B | 129.5 | 2.45 | 4.4 | 0.3 | 36.2 | 7.3 | **10.0** | 16.6 | 28.1 |
| | Mid America Bank | Jefferson City | MO | **A-** | B+ | A- | 480.1 | 2.44 | 12.1 | 1.8 | 19.8 | 5.4 | **9.2** | 10.5 | 15.1 |
| | Mid Penn Bank | Millersburg | PA | **B-** | B- | C+ | 2230.8 | 7.37 | 12.2 | 0.3 | 17.2 | 7.8 | **6.2** | 8.5 | 11.9 |
| | Mid-America Bank | Baldwin City | KS | **B-** | B- | B | 243.9 | 27.09 | 3.8 | 1.0 | 38.9 | 1.6 | **5.5** | 9.4 | 11.4 |
| | Mid-Central Federal Savings Bank | Wadena | MN | **B-** | B- | B- | 116.5 | 2.12 | 2.9 | 16.5 | 52.3 | 0.9 | **7.9** | 9.6 | 16.5 |
| | Mid-Missouri Bank | Springfield | MO | **B** | B | B | 652.4 | 3.58 | 5.9 | 1.1 | 19.8 | 4.8 | **7.3** | 9.2 | 13.0 |
| | MidAmerica National Bank | Canton | IL | **B-** | B- | B | 423.5 | 2.54 | 6.4 | 7.2 | 11.5 | 27.9 | **10.0** | 11.3 | 16.5 |
| | MidCoast Community Bank | Wilmington | DE | **C** | C | D+ | 266.0 | 10.06 | 6.2 | 0.0 | 19.6 | 3.6 | **6.8** | 9.9 | 12.4 |
| ▲ | MidCountry Bank | Minneapolis | MN | **B-** | C+ | B | 762.3 | -3.05 | 9.3 | 0.2 | 13.8 | 6.2 | **10.0** | 12.9 | 15.6 |
| | Middlefield Banking Co. | Middlefield | OH | **B** | B- | B- | 1181.9 | -5.33 | 7.2 | 1.2 | 20.0 | 9.0 | **7.4** | 10.4 | 12.8 |
| | Middlesex Federal Savings, F.A. | Somerville | MA | **C** | C- | C- | 446.3 | 8.19 | 1.9 | 0.0 | 33.5 | 8.0 | **8.4** | 9.9 | 14.3 |
| | Middlesex Savings Bank | Natick | MA | **B** | B | B | 4954.1 | 2.40 | 7.5 | 0.2 | 24.4 | 26.5 | **10.0** | 13.1 | 17.6 |
| | Middletown State Bank | Middletown | IL | **B-** | B | B+ | 37.8 | -1.18 | 3.2 | 1.4 | 31.1 | 10.7 | **7.8** | 9.5 | 14.8 |
| | Middletown Valley Bank | Middletown | MD | **B-** | B- | B- | 513.4 | 17.86 | 19.5 | 0.4 | 19.5 | 8.3 | **10.0** | 11.8 | 15.6 |
| | MidFirst Bank | Oklahoma City | OK | **B** | B | B | 22986.3 | 33.40 | 7.0 | 0.6 | 35.3 | 13.3 | **6.7** | 8.7 | 15.5 |
| | Midland Community Bank | Kincaid | IL | **B+** | B | B | 64.9 | 19.57 | 10.2 | 2.5 | 37.4 | 25.5 | **9.2** | 10.9 | 14.3 |
| | Midland Federal S&L Assn. | Bridgeview | IL | **D+** | D+ | D+ | 115.9 | 1.32 | 0.1 | 0.4 | 31.5 | 39.7 | **7.6** | 9.4 | 35.1 |
| | Midland States Bank | Effingham | IL | **B-** | B- | B- | 6073.8 | 7.89 | 13.6 | 11.1 | 9.4 | 10.7 | **7.9** | 10.5 | 13.2 |
| | MidSouth Bank | Dothan | AL | **B+** | B+ | B | 426.5 | 1.67 | 9.9 | 0.7 | 9.3 | 11.9 | **10.0** | 12.2 | 16.6 |
| ▲ | Midstates Bank, N.A. | Council Bluffs | IA | **B-** | C+ | C | 608.3 | 51.69 | 4.5 | 0.8 | 8.5 | 33.6 | **6.1** | 8.1 | 13.0 |
| ▼ | Midwest Bank | Monmouth | IL | **C+** | B- | B- | 522.4 | 1.77 | 9.4 | 2.6 | 7.8 | 26.8 | **7.6** | 9.4 | 15.3 |
| ▲ | Midwest Bank | Detroit Lakes | MN | **B+** | B | B+ | 527.5 | 12.97 | 17.7 | 1.9 | 14.7 | 5.0 | **6.3** | 9.7 | 12.0 |
| | Midwest Bank N.A. | Pierce | NE | **B+** | B+ | A- | 804.3 | 5.79 | 8.7 | 1.9 | 2.7 | 17.6 | **7.8** | 9.6 | 13.1 |
| | Midwest BankCentre | Saint Louis | MO | **C+** | B- | B- | 2050.5 | 5.35 | 14.8 | 2.6 | 17.1 | 16.9 | **6.0** | 9.2 | 11.8 |
| | Midwest Community Bank | Freeport | IL | **B-** | B- | B- | 244.4 | 9.60 | 1.9 | 0.2 | 28.9 | 0.7 | **9.8** | 10.9 | 15.2 |
| | Midwest Heritage Bank, FSB | West Des Moines | IA | **A** | A | A | 285.8 | 5.04 | 5.6 | 15.9 | 24.9 | 9.8 | **10.0** | 13.3 | 18.0 |
| | Midwest Independent Bank | Jefferson City | MO | **B+** | B+ | B | 284.7 | -4.47 | 1.9 | 0.0 | 1.3 | 12.0 | **10.0** | 12.9 | 22.0 |
| ▲ | Midwest Regional Bank | Festus | MO | **C** | C | C | 749.8 | 13.34 | 16.9 | 0.3 | 6.2 | 3.8 | **5.8** | 9.0 | 11.6 |
| | MidWestOne Bank | Iowa City | IA | **B** | B | B | 4645.4 | 41.45 | 12.5 | 1.5 | 9.4 | 16.9 | **6.1** | 10.1 | 11.8 |
| | Mifflinburg Bank & Trust Co. | Mifflinburg | PA | **B** | B- | B | 458.6 | 5.26 | 10.6 | 2.9 | 18.1 | 18.9 | **8.2** | 9.8 | 14.2 |
| | Milford Bank | Milford | CT | **C+** | C | C | 449.7 | 1.77 | 8.1 | 3.9 | 41.2 | 4.6 | **9.9** | 10.9 | 15.9 |
| | Milford Building and Loan Assn., SB | Milford | IL | **D+** | C- | C- | 30.0 | 1.70 | 0.0 | 0.1 | 59.3 | 0.0 | **7.0** | 9.0 | 19.4 |
| | Milford Federal Bank | Milford | MA | **C+** | C+ | C+ | 413.9 | 6.09 | 0.1 | 1.2 | 76.0 | 3.6 | **10.0** | 12.0 | 19.9 |
| | Millbury National Bank | Millbury | MA | **C** | C | C | 100.5 | 13.70 | 6.3 | 0.9 | 27.8 | 14.4 | **8.9** | 10.3 | 15.4 |

| Asset Quality Index | Adjusted Non-Performing Loans as a % of Total Loans | Adjusted Non-Performing Loans as a % of Capital | Net Charge-Offs Avg Loans | Profitability Index | Net Income ($Mil) | Return on Assets (R.O.A.) | Return on Equity (R.O.E.) | Net Interest Spread | Overhead Efficiency Ratio | Liquidity Index | Liquidity Ratio | Hot Money Ratio | Stability Index |
|---|---|---|---|---|---|---|---|---|---|---|---|---|---|
| **8.3** | 0.27 | 1.4 | -0.03 | **4.7** | 0.9 | 1.03 | 9.78 | 4.18 | 74.7 | **4.4** | 25.6 | 7.6 | **5.5** |
| **6.9** | 0.00 | 0.0 | 0.08 | **7.2** | 2.4 | 1.42 | 14.72 | 4.42 | 53.1 | **2.9** | 6.2 | 13.3 | **6.1** |
| **5.4** | 1.37 | 5.5 | 0.14 | **6.0** | 3.7 | 1.26 | 12.37 | 4.06 | 65.1 | **3.7** | 34.1 | 14.7 | **6.3** |
| **6.3** | 0.90 | 4.5 | 0.01 | **4.4** | 3.6 | 0.89 | 9.81 | 3.58 | 71.3 | **4.8** | 24.5 | 4.9 | **5.3** |
| **5.4** | 1.00 | 4.0 | 0.01 | **6.3** | 17.3 | 1.19 | 9.63 | 4.07 | 61.6 | **4.3** | 22.1 | 9.5 | **9.5** |
| **7.7** | 0.09 | 0.7 | 0.02 | **8.8** | 78.8 | 1.55 | 14.70 | 2.49 | 34.4 | **0.8** | 14.1 | 2.5 | **9.6** |
| **4.5** | 1.38 | 7.9 | 0.09 | **6.7** | 22.4 | 1.25 | 10.52 | 4.38 | 63.2 | **2.8** | 4.7 | 13.9 | **9.1** |
| **3.0** | 5.66 | 18.5 | 0.60 | **8.6** | 4.6 | 1.85 | 22.23 | 4.42 | 45.5 | **7.3** | 63.2 | 1.6 | **3.9** |
| **4.5** | 0.82 | 6.8 | 0.04 | **6.3** | 10.2 | 1.16 | 11.97 | 4.08 | 64.7 | **2.2** | 5.9 | 14.1 | **7.2** |
| **3.8** | 1.25 | 10.4 | 0.16 | **7.7** | 3.0 | 1.75 | 13.35 | 4.40 | 54.3 | **3.0** | 4.7 | 12.2 | **8.9** |
| **6.7** | 0.97 | 5.4 | 0.02 | **4.5** | 7.9 | 0.81 | 7.29 | 3.62 | 72.6 | **2.7** | 2.6 | 14.1 | **6.8** |
| **5.5** | 1.99 | 2.9 | 0.15 | **0.5** | -1.5 | -3.11 | -10.77 | 3.74 | 182.7 | **7.3** | 74.6 | 2.2 | **6.4** |
| **1.7** | 2.49 | 14.6 | 11.25 | **10.0** | 213.5 | 5.48 | 25.96 | 20.23 | 25.8 | **0.5** | 11.9 | 16.6 | **9.5** |
| **6.6** | 0.37 | 2.3 | 0.06 | **3.9** | 6.0 | 0.66 | 6.55 | 3.56 | 73.1 | **3.6** | 1.9 | 9.5 | **6.6** |
| **5.6** | 0.59 | 2.8 | 1.11 | **7.7** | 107.6 | 1.78 | 12.40 | 5.26 | 67.7 | **0.5** | 6.5 | 2.8 | **8.6** |
| **8.6** | 0.25 | 1.5 | 0.05 | **4.7** | 3.9 | 0.98 | 9.93 | 4.31 | 73.0 | **4.3** | 16.3 | 7.0 | **6.3** |
| **5.5** | 1.47 | 5.8 | 0.01 | **2.9** | 0.3 | 0.32 | 3.49 | 3.61 | 90.4 | **2.4** | 26.7 | 18.1 | **4.4** |
| **7.3** | 0.85 | 4.1 | 0.00 | **2.7** | 0.4 | 0.42 | 3.99 | 3.01 | 82.2 | **4.5** | 46.4 | 13.8 | **5.8** |
| **7.2** | 0.77 | 3.4 | 0.14 | **8.3** | 12.2 | 1.63 | 10.56 | 4.15 | 53.4 | **2.7** | 35.6 | 20.6 | **9.0** |
| **6.8** | 2.26 | 4.9 | -0.14 | **0.0** | -0.6 | -2.11 | -11.14 | 2.52 | 168.6 | **1.9** | 51.6 | 87.3 | **7.1** |
| **6.4** | 1.17 | 6.5 | -0.02 | **9.8** | 44.8 | 2.88 | 24.57 | 4.14 | 39.5 | **1.1** | 21.4 | 37.8 | **10.0** |
| **8.4** | 0.05 | 0.2 | -0.04 | **7.0** | 2.2 | 0.99 | 6.60 | 5.03 | 74.0 | **3.9** | 34.3 | 13.6 | **7.2** |
| **5.8** | 1.12 | 3.1 | -0.19 | **7.8** | 2.6 | 1.45 | 12.32 | 3.88 | 55.9 | **1.8** | 20.2 | 22.0 | **8.9** |
| **5.2** | 2.37 | 11.2 | -0.34 | **3.7** | 1.5 | 0.64 | 7.16 | 5.58 | 89.2 | **1.6** | 36.3 | 29.0 | **4.5** |
| **6.9** | 0.21 | 1.4 | -0.13 | **6.9** | 32.9 | 1.16 | 10.19 | 3.52 | 52.8 | **3.7** | 16.8 | 3.7 | **8.0** |
| **8.7** | 0.13 | 0.7 | -0.01 | **5.5** | 0.9 | 1.21 | 9.79 | 3.65 | 67.0 | **2.2** | 30.4 | 21.6 | **8.1** |
| **8.2** | 0.85 | 3.7 | 0.04 | **5.3** | 1.4 | 1.12 | 6.84 | 3.49 | 61.2 | **1.3** | 22.7 | 29.9 | **8.4** |
| **5.5** | 1.21 | 6.1 | 0.07 | **7.3** | 8.2 | 1.67 | 15.85 | 3.81 | 54.3 | **3.5** | 14.4 | 11.5 | **9.3** |
| **5.3** | 0.68 | 4.4 | 0.02 | **4.5** | 19.7 | 0.91 | 7.94 | 3.62 | 71.3 | **2.7** | 8.4 | 14.2 | **8.0** |
| **7.3** | 0.00 | 0.9 | 0.20 | **6.7** | 2.9 | 1.34 | 13.54 | 4.06 | 61.8 | **0.9** | 22.0 | 38.4 | **6.6** |
| **5.9** | 0.36 | 3.3 | 0.13 | **4.1** | 1.0 | 0.89 | 9.57 | 3.70 | 79.3 | **2.5** | 9.6 | 16.0 | **5.6** |
| **4.9** | 1.20 | 8.7 | 0.03 | **6.0** | 7.4 | 1.12 | 12.25 | 3.96 | 69.5 | **1.8** | 13.8 | 12.3 | **6.9** |
| **5.7** | 1.31 | 4.4 | 0.13 | **6.0** | 5.2 | 1.23 | 9.61 | 4.03 | 62.6 | **4.0** | 16.4 | 8.8 | **7.7** |
| **6.5** | 0.01 | 0.1 | 0.24 | **2.5** | 1.0 | 0.37 | 3.61 | 2.94 | 80.6 | **0.7** | 10.9 | 29.1 | **4.0** |
| **3.7** | 2.21 | 8.2 | 0.07 | **4.3** | 8.5 | 0.76 | 5.76 | 4.39 | 74.0 | **1.9** | 14.5 | 15.2 | **8.4** |
| **5.4** | 1.18 | 6.9 | 0.15 | **6.1** | 15.2 | 1.27 | 11.29 | 3.73 | 58.6 | **1.4** | 7.9 | 24.0 | **9.0** |
| **6.9** | 0.17 | 1.2 | 0.00 | **2.6** | 1.4 | 0.33 | 3.58 | 2.80 | 92.9 | **0.7** | 14.7 | 32.4 | **5.2** |
| **8.8** | 0.25 | 1.1 | 0.03 | **4.3** | 42.3 | 0.87 | 6.62 | 2.97 | 69.0 | **3.5** | 35.2 | 18.7 | **9.7** |
| **7.4** | 0.00 | 3.9 | 0.03 | **8.0** | 0.7 | 1.98 | 20.58 | 3.46 | 38.5 | **1.4** | 21.3 | 28.3 | **5.7** |
| **7.4** | 0.43 | 2.4 | 0.03 | **3.6** | 2.7 | 0.57 | 5.87 | 3.71 | 75.6 | **2.6** | 13.6 | 14.8 | **5.9** |
| **6.0** | 0.27 | 1.8 | 0.01 | **6.6** | 295.3 | 1.56 | 17.04 | 3.33 | 58.7 | **3.5** | 23.5 | 10.4 | **9.1** |
| **8.0** | 0.00 | 1.3 | 0.06 | **7.4** | 0.8 | 1.37 | 12.21 | 3.43 | 53.4 | **1.4** | 24.3 | 29.2 | **6.3** |
| **5.4** | 3.88 | 12.7 | 0.02 | **1.4** | 0.0 | 0.03 | 0.33 | 2.71 | 99.1 | **6.0** | 68.3 | 10.9 | **4.6** |
| **4.3** | 0.94 | 5.0 | 0.23 | **5.5** | 64.5 | 1.13 | 8.28 | 3.99 | 63.3 | **3.9** | 12.8 | 8.2 | **8.9** |
| **8.8** | 0.42 | 1.1 | 0.00 | **3.8** | 3.1 | 0.76 | 6.17 | 3.86 | 78.5 | **3.6** | 27.2 | 12.7 | **7.4** |
| **4.3** | 2.00 | 9.0 | 0.02 | **4.6** | 5.1 | 1.00 | 9.62 | 3.80 | 67.7 | **4.6** | 37.2 | 11.3 | **7.7** |
| **1.4** | 4.30 | 18.9 | 0.29 | **4.2** | 4.4 | 0.85 | 6.94 | 3.51 | 72.0 | **2.4** | 13.2 | 11.4 | **7.5** |
| **5.4** | 0.97 | 6.1 | 0.00 | **9.7** | 11.3 | 2.31 | 24.10 | 4.49 | 44.2 | **2.0** | 14.7 | 19.2 | **8.3** |
| **8.0** | 0.12 | 0.8 | 0.01 | **7.3** | 11.3 | 1.46 | 15.05 | 3.67 | 54.4 | **1.3** | 11.3 | 26.9 | **7.8** |
| **7.8** | 0.34 | 2.0 | 0.02 | **3.4** | 11.8 | 0.60 | 5.88 | 2.91 | 77.8 | **2.2** | 9.3 | 17.2 | **8.3** |
| **6.1** | 0.65 | 2.9 | -0.08 | **8.1** | 6.2 | 3.08 | 28.14 | 3.65 | 79.4 | **1.6** | 6.0 | 15.8 | **6.8** |
| **6.6** | 0.49 | 1.3 | 0.19 | **9.6** | 5.5 | 1.97 | 14.85 | 3.79 | 68.5 | **4.4** | 19.5 | 6.6 | **9.0** |
| **8.8** | 0.00 | 0.0 | -0.08 | **4.1** | 2.0 | 0.71 | 5.10 | 2.86 | 78.5 | **4.5** | 49.8 | 9.5 | **7.9** |
| **4.5** | 0.65 | 4.8 | 0.72 | **3.6** | 4.0 | 0.60 | 6.31 | 3.12 | 68.5 | **1.8** | 20.8 | 22.0 | **5.3** |
| **4.9** | 1.33 | 6.9 | 0.23 | **5.2** | 48.6 | 1.13 | 9.94 | 3.87 | 64.6 | **3.1** | 14.7 | 13.6 | **8.8** |
| **4.5** | 2.20 | 10.2 | 0.04 | **5.3** | 5.1 | 1.14 | 11.50 | 3.26 | 61.4 | **2.7** | 12.8 | 14.8 | **6.7** |
| **6.1** | 0.64 | 3.7 | 0.01 | **2.7** | 1.3 | 0.28 | 2.69 | 3.51 | 90.7 | **3.8** | 8.5 | 9.2 | **5.9** |
| **3.4** | 0.58 | 30.3 | 0.20 | **3.0** | 0.1 | 0.37 | 4.22 | 2.42 | 72.1 | **1.5** | 33.2 | 38.8 | **4.6** |
| **7.7** | 0.57 | 3.9 | 0.00 | **2.7** | 1.5 | 0.37 | 3.08 | 2.92 | 85.5 | **2.1** | 7.9 | 18.0 | **6.6** |
| **3.2** | 2.03 | 24.5 | 0.10 | **3.4** | 0.5 | 0.49 | 4.97 | 4.22 | 80.5 | **0.7** | 15.0 | 48.8 | **5.1** |

| Name | City | State | Rating | 2018 Rating | 2017 Rating | Total Assets ($Mil) | One Year Asset Growth | Asset Mix (As a % of Total Assets) Comm-ercial Loans | Cons-umer Loans | Mort-gage Loans | Secur-ities | Capital-ization Index | Lever-age Ratio | Risk-Based Capital Ratio |
|---|---|---|---|---|---|---|---|---|---|---|---|---|---|---|
| ▲ Milledgeville State Bank | Milledgeville | IL | **A-** | A- | A | 147.1 | 3.36 | 14.1 | 0.7 | 5.7 | 22.8 | **10.0** | 11.2 | 16.2 |
| ▲ Millennial Bank | Leeds | AL | **D** | E | E- | 78.1 | 15.87 | 11.9 | 0.9 | 11.7 | 16.1 | **9.4** | 11.8 | 14.5 |
| Millennium Bank | Des Plaines | IL | **A-** | A- | B+ | 153.6 | 31.46 | 6.8 | 0.1 | 4.8 | 0.0 | **10.0** | 12.6 | 17.1 |
| Millennium Bank | Ooltewah | TN | **B-** | B | B+ | 206.1 | 10.62 | 11.4 | 0.6 | 15.3 | 6.1 | **8.3** | 11.1 | 13.6 |
| Millington Bank | Millington | NJ | **B-** | B- | C+ | 593.0 | 1.46 | 10.8 | 0.1 | 23.8 | 6.0 | **7.0** | 10.7 | 12.5 |
| Millville Savings Bank | Millville | NJ | **C+** | C | C | 132.5 | 1.31 | 0.0 | 0.0 | 22.7 | 41.7 | **10.0** | 14.4 | 30.7 |
| Milton Savings Bank | Milton | PA | **B** | B | B | 63.3 | 0.00 | 0.0 | 1.7 | 58.7 | 14.8 | **10.0** | 25.0 | 66.3 |
| ▲ Minden Exchange Bank & Trust Co. | Minden | NE | **A** | A- | A- | 139.7 | -2.39 | 5.8 | 2.9 | 1.3 | 24.5 | **10.0** | 20.9 | 27.8 |
| Mineola Community Bank, SSB | Mineola | TX | **C+** | C+ | C+ | 267.7 | 6.35 | 1.5 | 1.5 | 47.7 | 18.7 | **10.0** | 11.4 | 21.1 |
| Miners and Merchants Bank | Thomas | WV | **B-** | B- | B- | 54.8 | -1.18 | 0.2 | 1.9 | 23.2 | 47.8 | **10.0** | 16.6 | 47.4 |
| Miners Exchange Bank | Coeburn | VA | **B-** | B- | B- | 84.7 | -4.15 | 1.3 | 6.4 | 36.2 | 16.4 | **10.0** | 12.6 | 24.1 |
| Miners National Bank of Eveleth | Eveleth | MN | **C+** | C- | C | 69.7 | 2.47 | 2.3 | 5.4 | 25.6 | 23.6 | **6.1** | 8.1 | 18.8 |
| Miners State Bank | Iron River | MI | **B** | B- | C+ | 136.3 | 8.53 | 12.0 | 0.4 | 4.4 | 18.5 | **7.6** | 10.2 | 13.0 |
| Minnesota Bank & Trust | Edina | MN | **B** | B | B | 718.8 | 7.84 | 19.7 | 2.4 | 6.2 | 23.1 | **8.2** | 10.5 | 13.5 |
| Minnesota First Credit and Savings, Inc. | Rochester | MN | **C+** | C+ | B- | 26.5 | -0.09 | 1.5 | 35.1 | 50.7 | 0.0 | **10.0** | 15.6 | 23.4 |
| ▲ Minnesota Lakes Bank | Delano | MN | **B-** | C+ | C+ | 104.3 | 1.52 | 13.6 | 2.1 | 8.8 | 13.7 | **7.5** | 9.3 | 13.2 |
| Minnesota National Bank | Sauk Centre | MN | **B+** | B | B | 214.3 | 4.57 | 12.1 | 2.8 | 14.9 | 20.6 | **8.5** | 10.0 | 15.7 |
| MinnStar Bank N.A. | Lake Crystal | MN | **B-** | B- | C+ | 142.7 | -0.22 | 8.8 | 0.5 | 20.2 | 1.8 | **7.9** | 9.6 | 13.4 |
| Minnwest Bank | Redwood Falls | MN | **B+** | B | B | 2068.9 | 4.10 | 5.3 | 0.8 | 2.9 | 6.3 | **8.8** | 11.1 | 14.0 |
| Minster Bank | Minster | OH | **B+** | B+ | B+ | 517.9 | 5.65 | 5.6 | 0.5 | 7.7 | 24.2 | **6.1** | 8.1 | 15.1 |
| MINT National Bank | Kingwood | TX | **B-** | C+ | B+ | 247.0 | 19.36 | 5.4 | 0.6 | 10.6 | 0.0 | **10.0** | 12.2 | 16.5 |
| Mission Bank | Kingman | AZ | **B-** | B- | C+ | 122.0 | 6.21 | 4.5 | 0.7 | 3.4 | 34.5 | **7.0** | 9.0 | 16.2 |
| Mission Bank | Bakersfield | CA | **B+** | B | B | 847.2 | 23.44 | 11.6 | 0.0 | 3.7 | 8.3 | **6.3** | 9.6 | 12.0 |
| Mission National Bank | San Francisco | CA | **B+** | B | B- | 250.0 | 0.68 | 1.9 | 0.1 | 28.2 | 0.0 | **10.0** | 13.4 | 21.4 |
| ▲ Mission Valley Bank | Sun Valley | CA | **A-** | B+ | A | 355.1 | 1.49 | 24.1 | 0.4 | 0.9 | 4.9 | **10.0** | 11.7 | 15.5 |
| Mississippi River Bank | Belle Chasse | LA | **A-** | B+ | A- | 106.2 | -5.42 | 16.6 | 1.0 | 8.7 | 17.4 | **10.0** | 14.7 | 32.9 |
| Missouri Bank | Warrenton | MO | **A-** | A- | A- | 246.7 | 6.79 | 4.5 | 0.7 | 16.3 | 21.0 | **10.0** | 12.7 | 16.4 |
| Missouri Bank II | Sedalia | MO | **A-** | A- | A- | 101.6 | 5.55 | 1.1 | 1.6 | 30.1 | 14.1 | **9.4** | 10.6 | 16.5 |
| Mitchell Bank | Milwaukee | WI | **C+** | C- | C- | 47.2 | 0.84 | 7.2 | 0.1 | 11.0 | 0.0 | **10.0** | 17.1 | 61.2 |
| Mizuho Bank (USA) | New York | NY | **B** | B | B- | 6701.3 | 15.00 | 33.5 | 0.0 | 0.0 | 0.0 | **10.0** | 23.4 | 21.9 |
| MNB Bank | McCook | NE | **C+** | C | C+ | 350.2 | -1.07 | 4.3 | 0.8 | 6.3 | 26.2 | **10.0** | 15.5 | 19.8 |
| Modern Bank, N.A. | New York | NY | **C** | C+ | C+ | 791.8 | 2.90 | 42.7 | 0.0 | 4.5 | 18.1 | **7.7** | 10.2 | 13.1 |
| ▲ Monona Bank | Monona | WI | **B-** | C+ | B- | 960.9 | 5.04 | 9.8 | 0.6 | 12.1 | 7.9 | **6.3** | 10.0 | 12.0 |
| Monroe Federal S&L Assn. | Tipp City | OH | **C** | C | C | 108.9 | 12.01 | 6.6 | 0.8 | 28.3 | 12.1 | **10.0** | 11.4 | 18.2 |
| Monroe Savings Bank | Williamstown | NJ | **B-** | C+ | C+ | 93.1 | -0.32 | 0.5 | 11.4 | 50.5 | 13.6 | **10.0** | 14.0 | 27.2 |
| Monson Savings Bank | Monson | MA | **B-** | B- | B- | 433.0 | 2.63 | 8.8 | 0.7 | 29.9 | 9.6 | **7.7** | 9.5 | 14.0 |
| Montecito Bank & Trust | Santa Barbara | CA | **B+** | B+ | B+ | 1608.5 | 7.83 | 7.3 | 1.2 | 13.5 | 27.3 | **9.4** | 10.6 | 14.9 |
| Monterey County Bank | Monterey | CA | **C-** | D+ | C+ | 167.2 | 2.47 | 15.5 | 0.1 | 7.3 | 23.2 | **9.3** | 11.2 | 14.4 |
| Montezuma State Bank | Montezuma | IA | **B-** | C+ | B- | 38.1 | 6.92 | 11.4 | 9.6 | 11.5 | 27.7 | **10.0** | 13.9 | 22.6 |
| Montgomery Bank | Sikeston | MO | **C+** | C+ | C+ | 916.0 | 0.64 | 14.7 | 0.6 | 22.5 | 6.4 | **5.9** | 8.8 | 11.6 |
| Monticello Banking Co. | Monticello | KY | **B** | B | B | 766.2 | 4.08 | 5.6 | 3.4 | 21.8 | 12.8 | **8.0** | 10.4 | 13.3 |
| Montrose Savings Bank | Montrose | MO | **B** | B | B | 41.7 | -0.73 | 6.5 | 3.9 | 15.6 | 21.4 | **10.0** | 15.0 | 24.4 |
| Moody National Bank | Galveston | TX | **A-** | A- | B | 1188.9 | 18.87 | 6.5 | 0.8 | 7.1 | 23.3 | **10.0** | 14.4 | 19.1 |
| Morgan Stanley Bank, N.A. | Salt Lake City | UT | **A** | A | A | 146645.0 | -2.12 | 5.1 | 5.6 | 0.2 | 36.8 | **10.0** | 11.3 | 18.9 |
| Morgan Stanley Private Bank, N.A. | New York | NY | **A** | A | A | 83036.0 | 10.47 | 4.7 | 12.7 | 36.2 | 18.1 | **8.3** | 9.9 | 25.0 |
| ▲ Morganton Savings Bank, S.S.B. | Morganton | NC | **B+** | B- | C | 94.9 | 5.79 | 0.3 | 0.1 | 28.7 | 8.6 | **10.0** | 27.2 | 33.8 |
| Morgantown Bank & Trust Co., Inc. | Morgantown | KY | **B-** | B- | B- | 207.0 | 6.79 | 5.0 | 4.2 | 38.5 | 17.0 | **6.8** | 8.8 | 14.5 |
| ▲ Morris Bank | Dublin | GA | **C+** | C- | C+ | 999.6 | 33.34 | 7.8 | 2.8 | 15.0 | 12.9 | **8.2** | 10.4 | 13.5 |
| ▲ Morris County National Bank | Naples | TX | **C** | C | B- | 89.9 | -5.92 | 6.6 | 7.5 | 17.3 | 26.2 | **9.9** | 11.0 | 16.5 |
| Morris Plan Co. of Terre Haute, Inc. | Terre Haute | IN | **A-** | A- | A- | 96.4 | 25.83 | 0.2 | 91.0 | 2.5 | 3.6 | **10.0** | 27.4 | 29.4 |
| Morton Community Bank | Morton | IL | **B** | B | B | 4048.8 | 7.77 | 11.3 | 2.2 | 9.3 | 21.6 | **7.4** | 9.6 | 12.9 |
| Mound City Bank | Platteville | WI | **C+** | B- | B | 384.0 | 5.25 | 2.0 | 0.6 | 18.4 | 11.8 | **9.9** | 10.9 | 16.3 |
| Mount Vernon Bank | Mount Vernon | GA | **B** | B+ | A- | 129.8 | -1.42 | 3.8 | 2.4 | 13.9 | 24.2 | **10.0** | 11.8 | 20.3 |
| Mount Vernon Bank and Trust Co. | Mount Vernon | IA | **A-** | A- | A | 130.7 | 0.68 | 6.0 | 4.0 | 32.4 | 17.9 | **10.0** | 14.2 | 22.3 |
| Mountain Commerce Bank | Knoxville | TN | **B+** | B+ | B | 906.7 | 6.79 | 8.4 | 1.2 | 21.7 | 5.2 | **8.5** | 11.5 | 13.8 |
| ▲ Mountain Valley Bank | Walden | CO | **B** | B- | B- | 237.7 | 21.72 | 9.5 | 1.5 | 17.7 | 10.9 | **7.9** | 9.6 | 14.2 |
| ▲ Mountain Valley Bank | Dunlap | TN | **C+** | C- | C | 110.7 | 6.65 | 3.7 | 7.7 | 41.9 | 16.1 | **7.2** | 9.2 | 15.7 |
| Mountain Valley Bank, N.A. | Elkins | WV | **A-** | B | B | 143.7 | 3.53 | 6.7 | 2.0 | 29.6 | 23.7 | **10.0** | 14.4 | 26.5 |
| Mountain View Bank of Commerce | Westminster | CO | **C** | C | C | 132.5 | 18.23 | 9.4 | 0.0 | 7.0 | 0.0 | **5.5** | 9.0 | 11.4 |
| MountainOne Bank | North Adams | MA | **B** | B- | B- | 892.7 | 0.35 | 11.4 | 1.0 | 25.8 | 10.8 | **10.0** | 12.3 | 15.6 |

| Asset Quality Index | Adjusted Non-Performing Loans as a % of Total Loans | Adjusted Non-Performing Loans as a % of Capital | Net Charge-Offs / Avg Loans | Profitability Index | Net Income ($Mil) | Return on Assets (R.O.A.) | Return on Equity (R.O.E.) | Net Interest Spread | Overhead Efficiency Ratio | Liquidity Index | Liquidity Ratio | Hot Money Ratio | Stability Index |
|---|---|---|---|---|---|---|---|---|---|---|---|---|---|
| 8.4 | 0.07 | 0.3 | 0.26 | 5.9 | 2.0 | 1.39 | 12.25 | 3.36 | 51.2 | 1.1 | 30.6 | 47.7 | 8.7 |
| 7.3 | 0.00 | 0.0 | 0.01 | 1.9 | 0.3 | 0.42 | 3.36 | 5.35 | 89.5 | 1.9 | 18.4 | 20.1 | 2.8 |
| 6.8 | 0.28 | 3.1 | 0.04 | 9.8 | 3.6 | 2.67 | 23.12 | 3.98 | 58.6 | 0.6 | 21.5 | 62.1 | 8.0 |
| 6.0 | 0.43 | 2.4 | 0.00 | 4.8 | 1.7 | 0.94 | 8.34 | 4.49 | 78.1 | 1.0 | 23.8 | 29.2 | 6.5 |
| 3.4 | 2.15 | 10.5 | -0.01 | 4.2 | 4.5 | 0.78 | 7.35 | 3.16 | 66.5 | 1.2 | 9.7 | 21.7 | 7.4 |
| 9.3 | 1.54 | 2.7 | 0.00 | 2.7 | 0.5 | 0.40 | 2.87 | 3.08 | 82.7 | 6.7 | 65.6 | 6.0 | 7.0 |
| 9.8 | 0.00 | 1.4 | 0.00 | 4.3 | 0.5 | 0.82 | 3.37 | 3.40 | 68.2 | 5.7 | 47.7 | 7.0 | 7.6 |
| 7.2 | 0.00 | 0.2 | 0.00 | 8.3 | 2.7 | 1.88 | 9.71 | 3.76 | 49.3 | 4.5 | 8.4 | 4.3 | 8.9 |
| 7.8 | 0.68 | 5.9 | 0.02 | 2.7 | 1.1 | 0.41 | 3.49 | 3.10 | 84.8 | 2.3 | 30.8 | 21.3 | 7.0 |
| 7.7 | 2.16 | 3.8 | 0.01 | 3.2 | 0.3 | 0.56 | 3.45 | 2.85 | 81.1 | 6.9 | 76.9 | 5.4 | 7.3 |
| 6.7 | 2.23 | 6.3 | 0.38 | 2.6 | 0.1 | 0.16 | 1.28 | 5.12 | 92.9 | 4.3 | 32.1 | 10.9 | 6.0 |
| 9.1 | 0.00 | 0.0 | 0.00 | 3.3 | 0.4 | 0.58 | 6.59 | 4.44 | 82.2 | 5.1 | 34.3 | 6.7 | 3.9 |
| 6.3 | 0.04 | 0.2 | -0.01 | 4.6 | 1.4 | 1.05 | 10.34 | 4.21 | 72.3 | 2.4 | 17.8 | 16.5 | 6.1 |
| 2.9 | 1.64 | 5.6 | 0.09 | 6.4 | 8.8 | 1.32 | 8.30 | 4.45 | 59.7 | 4.8 | 31.1 | 7.1 | 7.6 |
| 6.8 | 0.12 | 0.6 | 0.06 | 3.1 | 0.1 | 0.32 | 2.08 | 5.31 | 93.2 | 1.9 | 12.1 | 13.2 | 6.6 |
| 6.8 | 0.12 | 1.7 | 0.07 | 3.4 | 0.7 | 0.65 | 5.47 | 4.72 | 84.9 | 4.9 | 18.0 | 3.0 | 6.3 |
| 7.2 | 0.38 | 1.6 | 0.02 | 5.4 | 2.7 | 1.34 | 11.32 | 3.85 | 67.8 | 3.9 | 24.3 | 10.6 | 7.2 |
| 7.7 | 0.10 | 0.8 | 0.11 | 4.3 | 1.2 | 0.95 | 10.04 | 4.11 | 75.2 | 3.1 | 19.7 | 13.8 | 5.3 |
| 5.7 | 1.44 | 5.8 | 0.11 | 5.9 | 21.7 | 1.09 | 9.64 | 3.92 | 59.1 | 1.6 | 16.3 | 11.0 | 9.5 |
| 8.7 | 0.31 | 1.6 | 0.02 | 6.3 | 6.9 | 1.38 | 15.84 | 3.41 | 57.9 | 5.3 | 37.4 | 6.9 | 6.3 |
| 5.7 | 0.43 | 2.5 | 0.45 | 9.1 | 3.8 | 1.64 | 13.76 | 3.80 | 56.3 | 0.8 | 23.5 | 54.3 | 8.2 |
| 7.0 | 0.49 | 2.5 | -0.02 | 4.5 | 1.2 | 0.97 | 10.68 | 4.36 | 75.0 | 6.3 | 49.7 | 4.8 | 5.6 |
| 7.3 | 0.14 | 1.1 | 0.01 | 9.5 | 12.6 | 1.65 | 17.49 | 4.74 | 51.1 | 4.4 | 19.2 | 6.4 | 6.8 |
| 8.0 | 0.00 | 0.0 | -0.11 | 5.2 | 2.5 | 1.01 | 7.95 | 3.69 | 75.8 | 1.1 | 27.4 | 35.1 | 7.3 |
| 6.6 | 0.43 | 1.8 | 0.25 | 6.9 | 4.2 | 1.21 | 9.53 | 4.83 | 67.2 | 4.6 | 23.6 | 5.8 | 8.3 |
| 4.1 | 5.26 | 16.7 | 0.25 | 10.0 | 3.0 | 2.67 | 19.17 | 5.30 | 54.9 | 5.7 | 47.1 | 7.7 | 9.1 |
| 8.5 | 0.00 | 0.0 | 0.05 | 6.7 | 3.4 | 1.53 | 12.28 | 4.05 | 59.5 | 4.2 | 21.2 | 8.0 | 8.1 |
| 7.2 | 0.54 | 2.3 | 0.00 | 4.9 | 1.2 | 1.19 | 11.10 | 3.49 | 67.4 | 1.5 | 12.1 | 22.9 | 8.2 |
| 6.7 | 9.77 | 8.0 | -0.01 | 2.8 | 0.2 | 0.43 | 2.46 | 3.48 | 85.0 | 7.7 | 82.0 | 0.9 | 7.0 |
| 8.0 | 0.00 | 0.0 | 0.13 | 4.7 | 57.3 | 0.93 | 4.03 | 1.71 | 82.9 | 0.7 | 17.6 | 17.5 | 8.9 |
| 3.1 | 3.55 | 14.1 | 0.00 | 5.4 | 4.0 | 1.14 | 7.45 | 3.75 | 62.0 | 2.1 | 17.7 | 18.7 | 6.4 |
| 7.4 | 0.00 | 0.0 | 0.00 | 2.7 | 3.0 | 0.39 | 3.57 | 2.09 | 79.1 | 0.2 | 3.3 | 83.9 | 6.9 |
| 5.5 | 0.24 | 1.6 | 0.00 | 5.0 | 9.5 | 1.03 | 9.06 | 3.55 | 63.2 | 1.8 | 14.0 | 12.4 | 7.2 |
| 7.4 | 0.73 | 3.5 | -0.01 | 2.0 | 0.2 | 0.18 | 1.50 | 3.34 | 94.5 | 2.1 | 25.8 | 18.3 | 6.1 |
| 6.3 | 1.67 | 5.1 | 0.00 | 3.6 | 0.6 | 0.63 | 4.62 | 3.23 | 70.7 | 1.8 | 27.5 | 25.6 | 6.8 |
| 6.9 | 0.54 | 2.7 | 0.02 | 4.5 | 3.5 | 0.82 | 8.86 | 3.66 | 71.2 | 1.8 | 16.7 | 19.5 | 5.9 |
| 6.7 | 1.03 | 5.0 | 0.00 | 4.3 | 10.2 | 0.66 | 6.02 | 3.86 | 78.2 | 5.7 | 32.5 | 6.0 | 9.7 |
| 2.4 | 4.31 | 20.3 | 0.15 | 3.0 | 1.7 | 1.03 | 10.11 | 4.39 | 89.0 | 3.5 | 24.1 | 12.5 | 4.4 |
| 4.5 | 2.51 | 9.3 | 0.00 | 5.7 | 0.5 | 1.22 | 8.67 | 3.64 | 59.2 | 5.2 | 36.8 | 7.2 | 6.3 |
| 6.0 | 0.92 | 6.5 | 0.11 | 4.5 | 9.5 | 1.04 | 11.80 | 3.61 | 69.2 | 3.3 | 8.8 | 11.7 | 6.0 |
| 6.4 | 0.60 | 4.2 | 0.13 | 4.8 | 7.6 | 1.01 | 9.27 | 3.96 | 69.4 | 1.2 | 7.4 | 27.1 | 7.6 |
| 7.1 | 0.92 | 3.7 | -0.04 | 7.1 | 0.8 | 1.76 | 11.81 | 4.28 | 54.3 | 4.4 | 31.2 | 9.9 | 7.0 |
| 6.7 | 0.48 | 2.1 | 0.19 | 7.3 | 16.0 | 1.44 | 9.79 | 3.85 | 60.0 | 3.0 | 22.9 | 16.5 | 10.0 |
| 7.9 | 0.84 | 3.4 | 0.01 | 9.5 | 2932.0 | 2.07 | 18.22 | 2.28 | 13.1 | 3.5 | 53.3 | 0.0 | 9.5 |
| 8.0 | 0.15 | 1.2 | 0.00 | 7.8 | 1185.0 | 1.55 | 15.12 | 2.44 | 24.1 | 1.9 | 24.9 | 0.0 | 8.6 |
| 7.7 | 0.77 | 2.0 | -0.88 | 6.0 | 1.3 | 1.34 | 5.11 | 4.66 | 64.6 | 2.6 | 19.9 | 16.4 | 6.9 |
| 7.2 | 0.29 | 3.2 | 0.02 | 3.6 | 1.2 | 0.59 | 6.65 | 3.62 | 84.4 | 1.7 | 14.2 | 21.4 | 5.4 |
| 3.9 | 2.04 | 10.7 | 0.21 | 8.7 | 14.8 | 1.63 | 14.43 | 4.65 | 58.0 | 2.6 | 21.9 | 16.3 | 8.7 |
| 3.3 | 2.71 | 14.7 | 0.70 | 3.1 | 0.4 | 0.44 | 4.39 | 4.13 | 79.1 | 1.6 | 15.6 | 23.8 | 5.2 |
| 4.9 | 0.98 | 3.0 | 2.38 | 10.0 | 3.2 | 3.72 | 12.98 | 11.88 | 34.0 | 0.3 | 2.6 | 61.4 | 8.7 |
| 4.9 | 1.25 | 8.0 | 0.21 | 6.2 | 57.7 | 1.49 | 14.02 | 3.03 | 47.7 | 1.8 | 15.2 | 13.0 | 10.0 |
| 3.8 | 4.20 | 16.5 | 0.49 | 5.5 | 4.1 | 1.11 | 10.18 | 3.24 | 59.9 | 1.8 | 21.9 | 19.9 | 7.2 |
| 3.8 | 4.00 | 18.1 | 0.01 | 5.8 | 1.8 | 1.38 | 12.02 | 4.09 | 69.8 | 2.8 | 36.6 | 20.0 | 7.6 |
| 8.7 | 0.03 | 1.9 | 0.01 | 5.3 | 1.4 | 1.08 | 7.84 | 3.28 | 59.1 | 3.5 | 27.8 | 11.8 | 8.3 |
| 7.2 | 0.21 | 1.5 | 0.04 | 7.9 | 13.0 | 1.49 | 13.45 | 3.54 | 47.2 | 1.2 | 6.6 | 26.6 | 7.3 |
| 5.1 | 1.86 | 8.2 | 0.04 | 5.2 | 2.2 | 1.00 | 9.82 | 3.93 | 69.2 | 1.6 | 22.3 | 23.3 | 6.4 |
| 3.5 | 1.64 | 10.5 | 0.16 | 3.6 | 0.6 | 0.58 | 6.36 | 4.72 | 79.6 | 1.5 | 8.7 | 19.5 | 4.3 |
| 8.9 | 0.00 | 1.6 | 0.04 | 5.3 | 1.6 | 1.12 | 8.36 | 4.30 | 69.1 | 4.8 | 25.9 | 5.3 | 7.6 |
| 6.0 | 0.11 | 1.0 | 0.05 | 3.0 | 0.5 | 0.40 | 4.18 | 3.61 | 85.2 | 0.7 | 14.6 | 43.3 | 4.9 |
| 6.5 | 0.81 | 3.5 | 0.26 | 4.6 | 8.0 | 0.89 | 7.35 | 3.63 | 71.2 | 0.8 | 15.7 | 24.8 | 7.6 |

| Name | City | State | Rating | 2018 Rating | 2017 Rating | Total Assets ($Mil) | One Year Asset Growth | Comm-ercial Loans | Cons-umer Loans | Mort-gage Loans | Secur-ities | Capital-ization Index | Lever-age Ratio | Risk-Based Capital Ratio |
|---|---|---|---|---|---|---|---|---|---|---|---|---|---|---|
| | | | | | | | | Asset Mix (As a % of Total Assets) | | | | | | |
| Movement Bank | Danville | VA | **D** | E | E | 50.4 | 22.16 | 6.3 | 2.0 | 13.4 | 13.4 | **10.0** | 15.6 | 22.5 |
| MRV Banks | Sainte Genevieve | MO | **B** | B- | B- | 526.8 | 10.09 | 18.4 | 0.3 | 6.0 | 1.0 | **5.7** | 8.8 | 11.5 |
| Mt. McKinley Bank | Fairbanks | AK | **A-** | B+ | A- | 467.4 | 8.41 | 7.0 | 0.2 | 4.2 | 48.2 | **10.0** | 20.2 | 38.0 |
| Mt. Victory State Bank | Mount Victory | OH | **C** | C | C | 18.6 | 11.30 | 4.5 | 7.8 | 17.0 | 22.1 | **9.4** | 10.6 | 22.6 |
| ▲ Muenster State Bank | Muenster | TX | **A** | A- | A | 171.7 | -0.01 | 2.8 | 2.1 | 8.9 | 62.8 | **10.0** | 15.1 | 36.1 |
| MUFG Union Bank, N.A. | New York | NY | **C+** | B | B- | 133193.8 | 1.84 | 12.0 | 3.5 | 27.2 | 20.3 | **9.5** | 10.7 | 15.1 |
| Muncy Bank and Trust Co. | Muncy | PA | **B** | B | B+ | 489.4 | 6.47 | 4.9 | 2.2 | 43.1 | 15.0 | **8.3** | 9.9 | 15.8 |
| Municipal Trust and Savings Bank | Bourbonnais | IL | **A** | A- | A | 313.0 | 4.36 | 0.8 | 0.5 | 21.9 | 8.2 | **10.0** | 14.9 | 31.8 |
| Murphy Bank | Fresno | CA | **B+** | B+ | A- | 307.6 | 5.46 | 25.6 | 17.9 | 14.0 | 0.0 | **9.5** | 10.9 | 14.6 |
| ▲ Murphy-Wall State Bank and Trust Co. | Pinckneyville | IL | **B-** | B- | B- | 129.7 | 6.44 | 7.2 | 2.1 | 18.7 | 30.5 | **10.0** | 11.4 | 19.9 |
| Murray Bank | Murray | KY | **B** | B | B | 313.8 | 1.60 | 7.0 | 3.3 | 26.2 | 16.6 | **8.0** | 9.6 | 15.2 |
| ▲ Mutual Federal Bank | Chicago | IL | **C** | C- | C+ | 70.8 | -1.20 | 0.0 | 0.0 | 50.8 | 1.8 | **10.0** | 19.5 | 21.3 |
| Mutual S&L Assn. | Metairie | LA | **B-** | B- | B | 49.1 | -0.14 | 0.0 | 0.3 | 82.3 | 0.0 | **10.0** | 27.2 | 51.2 |
| ▲ Mutual Savings Assn. | Leavenworth | KS | **A-** | B | B | 208.7 | -2.45 | 5.0 | 1.3 | 36.1 | 24.4 | **10.0** | 31.2 | 52.4 |
| Mutual Savings Bank | Franklin | IN | **B-** | B- | B- | 175.9 | 10.60 | 3.4 | 1.9 | 22.2 | 20.9 | **7.9** | 9.8 | 13.3 |
| Mutual Savings Bank | Hartsville | SC | **C-** | C- | D+ | 52.0 | 20.45 | 6.2 | 5.7 | 25.2 | 5.6 | **10.0** | 25.7 | 41.2 |
| ▲ MutualBank | Muncie | IN | **B** | B- | B- | 2058.9 | 0.73 | 6.7 | 13.9 | 23.7 | 18.7 | **8.4** | 9.9 | 13.9 |
| MutualOne Bank | Framingham | MA | **A-** | B+ | A- | 942.6 | 6.20 | 20.8 | 0.8 | 16.3 | 5.9 | **10.0** | 17.8 | 20.2 |
| MVB Bank, Inc. | Fairmont | WV | **B+** | B | B | 1939.9 | 10.99 | 18.8 | 0.2 | 14.4 | 12.1 | **7.4** | 9.9 | 12.8 |
| Nano Banc | Irvine | CA | **C+** | C+ | B | 815.4 | 55.99 | 36.5 | 0.0 | 4.3 | 0.9 | **5.5** | 9.4 | 11.4 |
| Nantahala Bank & Trust Co. | Franklin | NC | **E+** | E- | E- | 156.8 | 2.41 | 3.7 | 1.1 | 24.3 | 11.3 | **6.1** | 8.2 | 11.8 |
| ▲ Napoleon State Bank | Napoleon | IN | **A-** | B+ | A- | 278.2 | 12.92 | 8.4 | 7.3 | 21.3 | 7.3 | **10.0** | 11.0 | 15.1 |
| Nashville Savings Bank | Nashville | IL | **B** | B | B | 64.9 | 5.04 | 7.5 | 2.6 | 24.9 | 14.3 | **10.0** | 13.2 | 20.1 |
| Natbank, N.A. | Hollywood | FL | **B** | B- | B- | 193.8 | 13.86 | 0.6 | 1.5 | 70.9 | 1.4 | **10.0** | 16.3 | 30.3 |
| National Advisors Trust Co. | Kansas City | MO | **U** | U | U | 13.0 | 12.31 | 0.0 | 0.0 | 0.0 | 11.6 | **10.0** | 90.6 | 254.2 |
| National Bank & Trust | La Grange | TX | **B-** | B- | B- | 201.1 | -18.47 | 1.0 | 4.5 | 27.3 | 50.3 | **10.0** | 12.7 | 30.4 |
| National Bank of Adams County | West Union | OH | **B** | B- | C+ | 84.7 | 3.16 | 1.5 | 3.1 | 25.4 | 19.8 | **10.0** | 11.5 | 27.0 |
| National Bank of Andrews | Andrews | TX | **C+** | B- | B+ | 214.9 | -0.56 | 23.9 | 2.7 | 8.3 | 16.0 | **8.4** | 9.9 | 13.8 |
| National Bank of Blacksburg | Blacksburg | VA | **A** | A | A | 1318.6 | 5.22 | 3.3 | 2.6 | 12.5 | 33.0 | **10.0** | 14.2 | 23.1 |
| ▲ National Bank of Commerce | Superior | WI | **B** | B | B+ | 994.6 | 62.73 | 15.4 | 2.1 | 15.0 | 11.0 | **7.9** | 12.4 | 13.3 |
| National Bank of Coxsackie | Coxsackie | NY | **C** | C | C | 325.4 | 10.45 | 3.1 | 2.9 | 32.5 | 32.9 | **6.4** | 8.5 | 16.6 |
| National Bank of Indianapolis | Indianapolis | IN | **B** | B | B- | 2276.1 | 5.64 | 14.4 | 1.5 | 11.5 | 17.0 | **6.0** | 8.0 | 12.5 |
| National Bank of Malvern | Malvern | PA | **B+** | B | B+ | 156.5 | 6.97 | 0.9 | 0.3 | 20.3 | 18.4 | **10.0** | 15.3 | 21.8 |
| National Bank of Middlebury | Middlebury | VT | **B** | B- | C+ | 389.9 | 5.28 | 5.5 | 2.4 | 35.0 | 19.3 | **7.4** | 9.3 | 15.8 |
| National Bank of New York City | Flushing | NY | **B** | B+ | A- | 232.7 | 0.69 | 1.0 | 0.0 | 19.1 | 2.0 | **10.0** | 17.9 | 22.7 |
| National Bank of St. Anne | Saint Anne | IL | **B-** | B- | C+ | 85.0 | 44.24 | 5.3 | 4.2 | 12.8 | 2.1 | **8.4** | 9.9 | 14.5 |
| National Bank of Texas at Fort Worth | Fort Worth | TX | **B-** | B | B | 295.6 | 5.31 | 18.1 | 5.0 | 27.0 | 9.7 | **10.0** | 11.4 | 18.8 |
| National Capital Bank of Washington | Washington | DC | **B-** | B | B+ | 523.3 | 12.16 | 5.7 | 0.2 | 31.4 | 19.0 | **7.7** | 9.4 | 15.7 |
| National Cooperative Bank, N.A. | Hillsboro | OH | **B-** | B | B | 2695.7 | 13.32 | 19.5 | 1.0 | 19.7 | 7.0 | **9.4** | 11.2 | 14.5 |
| National Exchange Bank and Trust | Fond du Lac | WI | **A** | A | A | 1903.7 | -2.15 | 12.2 | 1.0 | 6.5 | 28.1 | **10.0** | 20.5 | 25.8 |
| National Grand Bank of Marblehead | Marblehead | MA | **A-** | A- | A- | 339.9 | 3.35 | 1.0 | 0.5 | 68.2 | 17.4 | **10.0** | 11.5 | 22.0 |
| National Iron Bank | Salisbury | CT | **C** | C | C | 137.4 | 12.54 | 0.9 | 0.7 | 56.4 | 15.9 | **6.0** | 8.0 | 16.5 |
| ▲ National United | Gatesville | TX | **B** | B | B- | 646.0 | 6.95 | 5.0 | 6.9 | 13.2 | 19.5 | **10.0** | 11.0 | 15.0 |
| Nationwide Trust Co., FSB | Columbus | OH | **U** | U | C- | 195.4 | -24.52 | 0.0 | 0.0 | 0.0 | 59.9 | **10.0** | 15.1 | 36.6 |
| Native American Bank, N.A. | Denver | CO | **C-** | C- | C | 132.9 | 17.26 | 56.5 | 0.4 | 0.6 | 6.8 | **8.4** | 10.0 | 26.3 |
| NBC Oklahoma | Oklahoma City | OK | **B-** | C+ | C+ | 684.4 | -5.72 | 20.5 | 0.8 | 11.1 | 8.6 | **6.1** | 8.6 | 11.9 |
| NBH Bank | Greenwood Village | CO | **B** | B | C+ | 5893.8 | 4.03 | 23.9 | 0.4 | 12.9 | 13.9 | **6.0** | 9.1 | 11.8 |
| NBKC Bank | Kansas City | MO | **B+** | B+ | A | 833.4 | 21.77 | 3.1 | 2.1 | 38.4 | 16.9 | **8.4** | 11.8 | 13.7 |
| ▲ NBT Bank, N.A. | Norwich | NY | **B+** | B | B | 9642.9 | 1.59 | 9.9 | 18.6 | 17.0 | 16.8 | **7.3** | 9.6 | 12.7 |
| Nebraska Bank of Commerce | Lincoln | NE | **C** | C | C | 151.0 | 4.18 | 15.0 | 0.8 | 16.9 | 3.3 | **6.4** | 9.0 | 12.1 |
| Nebraska State Bank | Bristow | NE | **C** | C | C+ | 17.7 | -2.30 | 11.0 | 2.5 | 1.4 | 0.0 | **10.0** | 15.2 | 25.6 |
| Nebraska State Bank | Lynch | NE | **C** | C- | D+ | 16.3 | 15.26 | 6.1 | 2.0 | 2.1 | 0.0 | **10.0** | 13.6 | 24.4 |
| Nebraska State Bank | Oshkosh | NE | **A-** | B+ | A- | 49.7 | -4.64 | 0.7 | 0.0 | 0.0 | 0.0 | **10.0** | 18.2 | 22.4 |
| Nebraska State Bank and Trust Co. | Broken Bow | NE | **B** | B | B+ | 243.8 | 1.27 | 9.3 | 3.3 | 9.5 | 6.7 | **6.6** | 10.0 | 12.2 |
| NebraskaLand National Bank | North Platte | NE | **B** | B | B | 752.7 | 6.89 | 12.4 | 0.7 | 6.4 | 28.3 | **10.0** | 12.1 | 17.8 |
| Needham Bank | Needham | MA | **B-** | B- | B- | 2453.2 | 12.83 | 3.1 | 0.4 | 42.2 | 7.8 | **9.8** | 12.1 | 14.8 |
| Neffs National Bank | Neffs | PA | **A-** | A- | A | 375.7 | 1.43 | 1.7 | 2.6 | 22.0 | 49.3 | **10.0** | 18.7 | 37.0 |
| Neighborhood National Bank | San Diego | CA | **D** | D+ | C- | 67.4 | 3.48 | 15.6 | 0.0 | 8.3 | 0.2 | **10.0** | 17.2 | 29.0 |
| Neighborhood National Bank | Mora | MN | **A-** | B+ | B+ | 221.7 | 0.11 | 12.4 | 3.8 | 18.2 | 28.0 | **10.0** | 11.5 | 17.3 |
| Neighbors Bank | Clarence | MO | **C-** | C+ | C- | 31.6 | 17.13 | 1.7 | 1.0 | 25.5 | 11.3 | **10.0** | 14.0 | 26.2 |

| Asset Quality Index | Adjusted Non-Performing Loans as a % of Total Loans | Adjusted Non-Performing Loans as a % of Capital | Net Charge-Offs Avg Loans | Profitability Index | Net Income ($Mil) | Return on Assets (R.O.A.) | Return on Equity (R.O.E.) | Net Interest Spread | Overhead Efficiency Ratio | Liquidity Index | Liquidity Ratio | Hot Money Ratio | Stability Index |
|---|---|---|---|---|---|---|---|---|---|---|---|---|---|
| **5.4** | 2.13 | 9.0 | 0.38 | **0.2** | -0.3 | -0.70 | -4.68 | 5.52 | 104.8 | **5.1** | 33.1 | 5.9 | **4.0** |
| **8.7** | 0.00 | 0.0 | 0.03 | **7.5** | 5.9 | 1.52 | 16.63 | 3.90 | 44.8 | **4.1** | 37.6 | 12.7 | **4.7** |
| **8.7** | 1.24 | 2.1 | 0.22 | **5.4** | 5.0 | 1.11 | 5.42 | 3.96 | 65.0 | **6.5** | 61.2 | 7.1 | **8.3** |
| **8.1** | 0.00 | 0.5 | 0.07 | **2.6** | 0.1 | 0.41 | 3.82 | 3.40 | 83.3 | **4.1** | 39.8 | 12.1 | **4.2** |
| **7.3** | 2.64 | 4.8 | 0.44 | **6.3** | 2.6 | 1.59 | 10.14 | 3.18 | 51.7 | **5.8** | 62.5 | 11.3 | **9.6** |
| **6.2** | 0.94 | 4.8 | 0.17 | **1.4** | -746.3 | -0.57 | -4.92 | 2.46 | 106.5 | **3.7** | 30.6 | 12.1 | **9.7** |
| **6.2** | 1.06 | 6.0 | 0.03 | **5.2** | 5.4 | 1.12 | 11.29 | 3.70 | 66.1 | **1.2** | 9.7 | 22.6 | **6.6** |
| **8.2** | 0.73 | 2.5 | 0.00 | **9.5** | 6.8 | 2.18 | 13.25 | 3.53 | 39.1 | **3.2** | 46.4 | 16.3 | **9.6** |
| **5.8** | 0.10 | 2.1 | 0.06 | **8.4** | 5.3 | 1.72 | 16.13 | 4.11 | 52.2 | **0.4** | 14.6 | 74.0 | **8.3** |
| **3.4** | 4.56 | 20.9 | 0.11 | **3.8** | 0.9 | 0.72 | 5.97 | 4.03 | 77.8 | **3.1** | 14.5 | 8.9 | **6.6** |
| **6.4** | 0.45 | 3.0 | 0.17 | **5.4** | 4.2 | 1.35 | 14.36 | 3.31 | 60.9 | **1.8** | 17.0 | 21.3 | **6.4** |
| **4.0** | 5.13 | 19.5 | 0.35 | **3.0** | 0.3 | 0.48 | 2.52 | 4.45 | 94.4 | **1.7** | 16.0 | 21.8 | **7.4** |
| **9.7** | 0.27 | 0.9 | 0.00 | **3.1** | 0.2 | 0.42 | 1.57 | 2.72 | 82.0 | **0.5** | 6.8 | 58.4 | **7.9** |
| **6.5** | 3.14 | 5.3 | -0.20 | **7.5** | 3.3 | 1.55 | 5.08 | 4.15 | 58.2 | **2.7** | 36.2 | 18.5 | **7.7** |
| **8.7** | 0.00 | 0.1 | -0.01 | **3.9** | 1.1 | 0.64 | 6.37 | 3.68 | 79.1 | **2.5** | 25.6 | 17.7 | **5.4** |
| **8.4** | 0.39 | 1.1 | 0.00 | **1.5** | 0.1 | 0.16 | 0.56 | 3.57 | 95.7 | **0.7** | 19.1 | 32.4 | **5.0** |
| **5.9** | 0.55 | 3.1 | 0.13 | **5.0** | 24.5 | 1.19 | 10.86 | 3.48 | 68.3 | **2.0** | 22.9 | 17.0 | **8.9** |
| **5.6** | 1.27 | 4.1 | 0.03 | **9.4** | 16.3 | 1.71 | 10.01 | 3.78 | 46.7 | **0.8** | 16.3 | 39.1 | **9.0** |
| **6.3** | 0.79 | 3.9 | 0.07 | **8.2** | 32.7 | 1.77 | 16.21 | 3.60 | 71.8 | **2.7** | 13.0 | 11.3 | **8.8** |
| **6.6** | 0.03 | 0.5 | 0.00 | **3.2** | 2.4 | 0.36 | 3.23 | 4.74 | 83.7 | **5.2** | 9.9 | 0.1 | **7.5** |
| **3.7** | 1.53 | 12.2 | 0.06 | **1.5** | -0.1 | -0.08 | -1.08 | 3.80 | 100.9 | **2.4** | 19.3 | 17.6 | **2.1** |
| **6.9** | 0.35 | 3.9 | 0.35 | **6.3** | 2.9 | 1.09 | 9.73 | 4.17 | 62.7 | **2.1** | 17.5 | 18.9 | **7.4** |
| **6.5** | 0.00 | 7.9 | 0.00 | **5.5** | 0.7 | 1.08 | 8.23 | 3.21 | 57.2 | **1.5** | 14.4 | 24.9 | **7.1** |
| **9.5** | 0.22 | 1.0 | 0.00 | **3.9** | 1.2 | 0.66 | 3.82 | 4.22 | 80.2 | **2.3** | 26.1 | 13.9 | **7.4** |
| **8.8** | na | 0.0 | na | **10.0** | 2.2 | 19.60 | 22.18 | 2.89 | 82.5 | **4.0** | na | 100.0 | **6.2** |
| **9.3** | 0.11 | 0.7 | 0.15 | **3.8** | 1.8 | 0.78 | 7.09 | 2.25 | 65.0 | **2.4** | 32.2 | 21.7 | **6.5** |
| **4.6** | 1.10 | 18.2 | 0.00 | **6.4** | 1.4 | 1.63 | 13.91 | 3.81 | 55.5 | **4.9** | 36.5 | 8.9 | **6.9** |
| **1.8** | 4.15 | 23.9 | -0.06 | **10.0** | 6.1 | 2.82 | 26.58 | 4.92 | 58.5 | **4.6** | 25.8 | 6.7 | **8.0** |
| **8.3** | 0.69 | 2.4 | 0.09 | **6.4** | 18.0 | 1.43 | 9.87 | 3.29 | 55.0 | **5.3** | 26.5 | 5.5 | **10.0** |
| **5.0** | 0.68 | 4.2 | 0.01 | **7.4** | 11.7 | 1.72 | 14.36 | 4.23 | 61.0 | **1.5** | 10.6 | 13.4 | **9.2** |
| **7.3** | 0.67 | 3.5 | 0.02 | **3.2** | 1.8 | 0.59 | 6.62 | 3.17 | 77.0 | **4.7** | 6.8 | 3.2 | **4.1** |
| **7.7** | 0.46 | 2.5 | -0.01 | **5.4** | 24.9 | 1.15 | 13.76 | 3.26 | 63.3 | **5.4** | 27.7 | 5.6 | **7.4** |
| **5.3** | 2.42 | 10.7 | 0.00 | **5.5** | 1.8 | 1.16 | 7.50 | 3.62 | 61.4 | **2.7** | 23.0 | 15.7 | **7.9** |
| **6.7** | 0.89 | 5.7 | 0.08 | **4.6** | 3.6 | 0.95 | 10.17 | 3.83 | 70.8 | **4.6** | 15.6 | 4.7 | **5.5** |
| **7.5** | 0.00 | 0.0 | 0.00 | **4.0** | 1.8 | 0.76 | 4.30 | 2.69 | 72.5 | **0.5** | 15.1 | 55.7 | **8.3** |
| **6.7** | 0.25 | 2.2 | 0.00 | **5.0** | 0.6 | 0.83 | 6.80 | 3.69 | 70.8 | **1.4** | 32.4 | 40.4 | **6.8** |
| **8.4** | 0.37 | 2.1 | 0.26 | **3.5** | 1.7 | 0.59 | 5.31 | 3.90 | 78.6 | **2.2** | 28.9 | 20.9 | **6.8** |
| **8.5** | 0.47 | 1.9 | 0.00 | **3.4** | 2.6 | 0.51 | 5.43 | 3.49 | 80.1 | **3.8** | 20.4 | 10.5 | **5.6** |
| **6.9** | 0.62 | 3.3 | -0.02 | **4.0** | 23.9 | 0.91 | 8.25 | 3.11 | 76.4 | **3.8** | 23.8 | 10.5 | **8.5** |
| **7.6** | 1.93 | 3.6 | 0.01 | **9.0** | 32.2 | 1.69 | 8.16 | 3.94 | 51.8 | **6.0** | 29.7 | 3.4 | **10.0** |
| **9.8** | 0.68 | 2.1 | -0.01 | **5.4** | 3.4 | 1.01 | 8.57 | 3.18 | 61.5 | **3.2** | 21.9 | 13.5 | **7.3** |
| **9.7** | 0.00 | 0.0 | 0.01 | **3.0** | 0.8 | 0.56 | 7.07 | 3.09 | 81.9 | **3.4** | 25.0 | 13.2 | **4.2** |
| **5.3** | 0.82 | 4.1 | 0.03 | **4.6** | 6.2 | 0.99 | 9.28 | 4.19 | 69.7 | **4.0** | 27.6 | 10.9 | **6.8** |
| **10.0** | na | 0.0 | na | **7.0** | 20.5 | 9.57 | 37.73 | -1.01 | 90.3 | **8.2** | 87.1 | 0.0 | **5.3** |
| **2.8** | 3.52 | 15.0 | 0.06 | **2.3** | 0.2 | 0.17 | 1.53 | 4.32 | 95.3 | **0.2** | 6.3 | 69.1 | **6.5** |
| **4.6** | 1.19 | 8.5 | 0.20 | **4.2** | 7.0 | 1.01 | 12.14 | 3.94 | 72.8 | **2.8** | 19.2 | 15.2 | **5.6** |
| **6.2** | 0.63 | 3.4 | 0.19 | **6.6** | 83.9 | 1.44 | 13.33 | 3.94 | 61.3 | **3.8** | 8.5 | 9.7 | **8.6** |
| **5.8** | 1.25 | 4.6 | 0.03 | **8.6** | 50.2 | 6.76 | 53.01 | 2.54 | 67.7 | **1.0** | 23.7 | 34.0 | **9.4** |
| **5.9** | 0.54 | 2.5 | 0.36 | **6.1** | 116.4 | 1.22 | 10.55 | 3.63 | 58.8 | **4.0** | 5.8 | 4.5 | **9.2** |
| **7.3** | 0.02 | 0.2 | 0.00 | **3.1** | 0.8 | 0.52 | 5.84 | 2.97 | 77.5 | **0.9** | 12.9 | 33.3 | **5.4** |
| **6.3** | 0.00 | 0.0 | 0.00 | **4.2** | 0.1 | 0.72 | 4.77 | 4.09 | 77.0 | **1.6** | 42.7 | 25.8 | **6.5** |
| **5.6** | 0.00 | 9.7 | -0.10 | **3.4** | 0.1 | 0.63 | 4.31 | 3.63 | 76.9 | **4.8** | 57.7 | 8.9 | **5.4** |
| **7.3** | 0.00 | 0.0 | 0.00 | **10.0** | 2.0 | 4.08 | 24.13 | 5.03 | 39.1 | **2.2** | 20.2 | 18.6 | **9.3** |
| **6.5** | 0.25 | 2.0 | 0.01 | **6.9** | 4.2 | 1.72 | 16.84 | 3.91 | 55.4 | **1.1** | 13.0 | 17.2 | **6.3** |
| **8.7** | 0.02 | 0.0 | 0.00 | **4.1** | 6.7 | 0.92 | 7.83 | 3.30 | 70.2 | **0.9** | 5.0 | 22.0 | **8.0** |
| **6.7** | 0.85 | 5.2 | 0.00 | **3.8** | 16.0 | 0.70 | 5.65 | 2.92 | 66.8 | **0.8** | 14.4 | 35.1 | **8.7** |
| **8.8** | 1.26 | 2.3 | 0.00 | **5.6** | 5.0 | 1.34 | 7.31 | 3.01 | 53.5 | **4.0** | 55.6 | 19.0 | **8.7** |
| **8.6** | 0.51 | 1.1 | -0.05 | **0.0** | -2.3 | -3.53 | -21.31 | 4.56 | 147.5 | **2.6** | 38.4 | 24.8 | **6.5** |
| **7.4** | 1.01 | 5.0 | 0.00 | **5.4** | 3.0 | 1.37 | 11.68 | 4.06 | 70.8 | **4.0** | 22.4 | 9.7 | **7.4** |
| **9.0** | 0.10 | 0.4 | 0.07 | **1.8** | 0.1 | 0.18 | 1.25 | 3.00 | 98.3 | **6.3** | 41.6 | 1.9 | **6.5** |

| Name | City | State | Rating | 2018 Rating | 2017 Rating | Total Assets ($Mil) | One Year Asset Growth | Asset Mix (As a % of Total Assets) Comm-ercial Loans | Cons-umer Loans | Mort-gage Loans | Secur-ities | Capital-ization Index | Lever-age Ratio | Risk-Based Capital Ratio |
|---|---|---|---|---|---|---|---|---|---|---|---|---|---|---|
| Nekoosa Port Edwards State Bank | Nekoosa | WI | A- | B+ | B+ | 231.4 | 12.75 | 2.4 | 2.2 | 30.2 | 17.6 | 10.0 | 14.1 | 27.4 |
| Nelsonville Home & Savings Bank | Nelsonville | OH | B- | B- | B- | 31.1 | 4.33 | 0.0 | 3.0 | 52.8 | 3.2 | 10.0 | 12.4 | 28.4 |
| Neuberger Berman Trust Co. of Delaware | Wilmington | DE | U | U | U | 6.9 | 1.43 | 0.0 | 0.0 | 0.0 | 0.0 | 10.0 | 92.3 | 221.9 |
| Neuberger Berman Trust Co., N.A. | New York | NY | U | U | U | 29.8 | 9.30 | 0.0 | 0.0 | 0.0 | 0.0 | 10.0 | 45.7 | 124.5 |
| Nevada Bank and Trust Co. | Caliente | NV | C+ | C+ | C+ | 148.0 | 15.96 | 5.1 | 4.7 | 3.2 | 50.0 | 8.6 | 10.1 | 21.6 |
| New Albin Savings Bank | New Albin | IA | A | A | A+ | 253.3 | 6.03 | 2.7 | 1.0 | 11.2 | 68.5 | 10.0 | 17.3 | 55.4 |
| ▲ New Buffalo Savings Bank | New Buffalo | MI | C+ | C- | C | 116.8 | -2.23 | 1.1 | 0.1 | 21.4 | 0.0 | 10.0 | 13.3 | 18.7 |
| New Carlisle Federal Savings Bank | New Carlisle | OH | C+ | C+ | C+ | 133.2 | 9.00 | 8.9 | 1.6 | 38.1 | 1.9 | 8.0 | 9.8 | 13.4 |
| New Century Bank | Belleville | KS | B | B+ | B+ | 60.8 | 8.90 | 1.9 | 3.1 | 33.8 | 0.0 | 7.0 | 9.6 | 12.5 |
| New Covenant Trust Co., N.A. | Jeffersonville | IN | U | U | U | 6.7 | 1.15 | 0.0 | 0.0 | 0.0 | 21.6 | 10.0 | 91.6 | 298.5 |
| New Era Bank | Fredericktown | MO | A- | A- | A- | 356.1 | 4.34 | 5.0 | 1.3 | 26.4 | 16.1 | 9.2 | 10.4 | 15.7 |
| New Foundation Savings Bank | Cincinnati | OH | C+ | C | C+ | 19.5 | 5.37 | 4.4 | 0.3 | 62.6 | 1.7 | 10.0 | 11.3 | 20.6 |
| ▲ New Frontier Bank | Saint Charles | MO | B- | C | D+ | 103.6 | 24.22 | 8.4 | 0.2 | 7.2 | 17.6 | 4.9 | 8.5 | 10.9 |
| ▲ New Haven Bank | New Haven | CT | C+ | C | C- | 147.7 | 5.13 | 3.3 | 4.9 | 40.7 | 3.9 | 9.0 | 10.3 | 15.6 |
| New Horizon Bank, N.A. | Powhatan | VA | C+ | C+ | C+ | 88.7 | 5.59 | 8.2 | 1.7 | 15.0 | 6.7 | 8.6 | 10.6 | 13.9 |
| New Market Bank | Elko New Market | MN | C+ | C+ | C | 115.3 | 2.32 | 9.1 | 0.9 | 10.7 | 23.8 | 6.1 | 8.1 | 13.1 |
| New Mexico Bank & Trust | Albuquerque | NM | A- | A- | B | 1763.0 | 18.12 | 11.8 | 0.4 | 5.1 | 27.7 | 6.8 | 9.1 | 12.3 |
| New Millennium Bank | Fort Lee | NJ | C+ | C | C | 389.7 | -5.85 | 13.5 | 0.0 | 14.4 | 0.8 | 6.9 | 8.9 | 12.9 |
| New OMNI Bank, N.A. | Alhambra | CA | A- | A- | A- | 460.3 | 2.81 | 0.4 | 0.2 | 35.1 | 7.4 | 10.0 | 14.5 | 24.1 |
| New Peoples Bank, Inc. | Honaker | VA | C | C- | C | 705.2 | 3.56 | 7.7 | 3.3 | 32.7 | 7.2 | 7.7 | 9.4 | 14.8 |
| New Republic Savings Bank | Roanoke Rapids | NC | C- | C | B- | 64.4 | -1.26 | 4.0 | 0.5 | 48.9 | 0.0 | 8.6 | 10.1 | 15.8 |
| New Tripoli Bank | New Tripoli | PA | B | B+ | A- | 500.4 | 4.21 | 5.2 | 0.4 | 47.0 | 16.3 | 10.0 | 11.1 | 17.0 |
| ▲ New Washington State Bank | New Washington | IN | B+ | B- | B | 343.5 | 4.06 | 11.6 | 11.4 | 15.2 | 11.3 | 8.7 | 10.3 | 13.9 |
| New York Community Bank | Westbury | NY | B | B+ | B | 53617.3 | 3.36 | 3.3 | 0.0 | 0.7 | 10.9 | 7.4 | 9.6 | 12.8 |
| NewBank | Flushing | NY | A- | B+ | A | 451.4 | 7.86 | 21.0 | 0.0 | 0.2 | 0.0 | 10.0 | 11.3 | 20.6 |
| Newburyport Five Cents Savings Bank | Newburyport | MA | C+ | B- | B | 1032.0 | 17.95 | 5.2 | 3.0 | 31.3 | 11.6 | 10.0 | 12.4 | 16.7 |
| Newfield National Bank | Newfield | NJ | C+ | C | C | 701.0 | 5.05 | 7.3 | 0.2 | 19.1 | 24.7 | 7.5 | 9.4 | 17.4 |
| NewFirst National Bank | El Campo | TX | B | B | B | 745.5 | 4.65 | 9.3 | 0.6 | 8.6 | 5.4 | 10.0 | 11.4 | 16.0 |
| Newport Federal Bank | Newport | TN | B | B | B | 211.7 | 2.88 | 0.1 | 1.0 | 39.2 | 37.3 | 10.0 | 11.1 | 24.9 |
| Newton Federal Bank | Covington | GA | C+ | B- | B- | 319.2 | 3.28 | 9.0 | 9.9 | 35.7 | 1.2 | 10.0 | 19.7 | 28.6 |
| Newtown Savings Bank | Newtown | CT | C+ | C+ | C+ | 1334.1 | 1.20 | 5.8 | 2.0 | 43.8 | 11.3 | 6.5 | 8.5 | 13.3 |
| NexBank SSB | Dallas | TX | B+ | A- | B+ | 9768.0 | 17.62 | 4.4 | 0.1 | 39.3 | 16.7 | 6.0 | 8.0 | 13.2 |
| NexTier Bank, N.A. | Butler | PA | B+ | B | B | 1401.0 | 11.45 | 7.2 | 8.8 | 25.0 | 7.9 | 6.1 | 9.7 | 11.8 |
| Nicolet National Bank | Green Bay | WI | B+ | B+ | B+ | 3570.4 | 15.34 | 20.8 | 0.9 | 12.9 | 12.6 | 4.5 | 9.8 | 10.8 |
| Ninnescah Valley Bank | Cunningham | KS | B | B | B | 32.0 | 3.06 | 3.3 | 1.9 | 4.8 | 55.8 | 10.0 | 11.9 | 22.8 |
| Noah Bank | Elkins Park | PA | C- | C | B- | 390.4 | -8.62 | 9.8 | 0.0 | 0.5 | 1.1 | 5.2 | 7.2 | 14.2 |
| ▼ NobleBank & Trust | Anniston | AL | B- | B- | B- | 267.3 | 3.79 | 12.3 | 1.8 | 13.8 | 22.6 | 8.4 | 9.9 | 14.1 |
| ▲ Nodaway Valley Bank | Maryville | MO | A | A- | A | 932.2 | 5.68 | 5.8 | 0.9 | 6.4 | 18.6 | 10.0 | 12.8 | 18.5 |
| Nokomis Savings Bank | Nokomis | IL | C | C+ | B- | 29.7 | 11.67 | 11.1 | 4.0 | 16.6 | 28.5 | 10.0 | 16.9 | 26.9 |
| ▲ Normangee State Bank | Normangee | TX | B- | C+ | C | 117.6 | 0.63 | 5.4 | 11.4 | 27.5 | 30.1 | 10.0 | 16.4 | 29.8 |
| North Adams State Bank | Ursa | IL | B- | B- | B- | 38.3 | 1.78 | 14.8 | 5.3 | 15.6 | 16.1 | 10.0 | 15.0 | 23.4 |
| ▲ North Alabama Bank | Hazel Green | AL | B- | C+ | B- | 118.0 | 16.55 | 4.0 | 1.7 | 11.8 | 5.8 | 7.9 | 9.9 | 13.2 |
| North American Banking Co. | Roseville | MN | A- | B+ | B+ | 667.3 | 14.54 | 10.7 | 0.2 | 5.9 | 13.9 | 7.0 | 9.0 | 13.5 |
| North American Savings Bank, F.S.B. | Kansas City | MO | A- | A- | A- | 2503.8 | 14.59 | 0.5 | 0.1 | 73.2 | 5.2 | 9.7 | 10.8 | 15.3 |
| North Arundel Savings Bank | Pasadena | MD | C | C | C | 43.9 | 2.89 | 0.0 | 2.7 | 56.8 | 2.6 | 10.0 | 13.3 | 28.0 |
| North Brookfield Savings Bank | North Brookfield | MA | B- | B- | B- | 323.5 | 3.00 | 0.6 | 2.1 | 49.9 | 15.9 | 10.0 | 11.8 | 21.8 |
| North Cambridge Co-operative Bank | Cambridge | MA | C+ | C+ | C+ | 93.3 | 4.60 | 0.0 | 0.2 | 53.6 | 15.4 | 10.0 | 22.0 | 50.2 |
| North Central Bank | Hennepin | IL | B | B | B | 121.3 | 0.42 | 7.5 | 4.5 | 20.2 | 27.8 | 10.0 | 12.5 | 16.8 |
| North Country Savings Bank | Canton | NY | B- | B- | B- | 266.2 | 3.36 | 0.1 | 2.5 | 73.4 | 0.7 | 10.0 | 15.8 | 24.8 |
| North County Savings Bank | Red Bud | IL | C+ | C+ | C+ | 53.7 | 3.75 | 0.0 | 3.6 | 41.7 | 15.3 | 7.0 | 9.0 | 25.6 |
| North Dallas Bank & Trust Co. | Dallas | TX | B | B | C+ | 1307.8 | 0.29 | 3.8 | 0.6 | 18.8 | 38.1 | 10.0 | 12.2 | 27.3 |
| North Easton Savings Bank | South Easton | MA | C | C | C | 1135.7 | 104.70 | 4.3 | 3.0 | 42.6 | 12.8 | 6.5 | 8.5 | 13.6 |
| North Georgia National Bank | Calhoun | GA | B- | B- | C+ | 134.4 | -7.20 | 5.9 | 1.1 | 15.8 | 25.5 | 10.0 | 11.9 | 20.1 |
| North Salem State Bank | North Salem | IN | B | B- | B- | 385.3 | 12.59 | 6.7 | 3.9 | 17.0 | 7.4 | 7.1 | 9.1 | 12.7 |
| North Shore Bank of Commerce | Duluth | MN | B | B | B- | 286.7 | 3.68 | 3.0 | 0.8 | 31.8 | 11.7 | 6.9 | 8.9 | 15.5 |
| North Shore Bank, a Co-operative Bank | Peabody | MA | B- | C+ | C+ | 1386.7 | 59.30 | 9.0 | 0.2 | 26.2 | 9.9 | 8.7 | 10.1 | 14.3 |
| North Shore Bank, FSB | Brookfield | WI | B | B- | B- | 2048.2 | 0.82 | 1.5 | 20.9 | 16.2 | 7.7 | 10.0 | 11.9 | 16.6 |
| North Shore Trust and Savings | Waukegan | IL | C | C | C | 235.4 | 4.84 | 0.1 | 0.1 | 36.8 | 29.1 | 10.0 | 19.4 | 58.4 |
| North Side Bank and Trust Co. | Cincinnati | OH | A- | B+ | A- | 754.6 | 11.28 | 19.2 | 1.0 | 11.2 | 15.8 | 8.7 | 12.2 | 13.9 |
| North Side Federal S&L Assn. of Chicago | Chicago | IL | D+ | D | D | 41.0 | 0.45 | 0.0 | 0.0 | 42.5 | 16.2 | 10.0 | 11.0 | 24.7 |

| Asset Quality Index | Adjusted Non-Performing Loans as a % of Total Loans | Adjusted Non-Performing Loans as a % of Capital | Net Charge-Offs Avg Loans | Profitability Index | Net Income ($Mil) | Return on Assets (R.O.A.) | Return on Equity (R.O.E.) | Net Interest Spread | Overhead Efficiency Ratio | Liquidity Index | Liquidity Ratio | Hot Money Ratio | Stability Index |
|---|---|---|---|---|---|---|---|---|---|---|---|---|---|
| **7.7** | 1.64 | 3.9 | 0.14 | **6.1** | 3.3 | 1.56 | 10.86 | 2.98 | 46.1 | **3.0** | 49.0 | 26.1 | **7.8** |
| **9.2** | 0.00 | 0.0 | 0.00 | **4.9** | 0.3 | 0.91 | 7.53 | 3.59 | 60.3 | **2.3** | 29.9 | 20.8 | **6.6** |
| **10.0** | na | 0.0 | na | **10.0** | 0.2 | 3.35 | 3.41 | 80.23 | 96.9 | **4.0** | 371.6 | 0.0 | **5.8** |
| **10.0** | na | 0.0 | na | **10.0** | 1.3 | 4.92 | 11.25 | 83.33 | 95.9 | **4.0** | 111.0 | 0.0 | **7.0** |
| **8.8** | 0.23 | 0.7 | -0.02 | **4.0** | 1.2 | 0.84 | 8.16 | 3.74 | 74.1 | **7.3** | 59.1 | 0.9 | **6.1** |
| **9.7** | 0.05 | 0.1 | 0.04 | **5.9** | 3.2 | 1.30 | 7.11 | 2.46 | 33.5 | **4.2** | 77.7 | 23.4 | **9.4** |
| **4.0** | 2.63 | 6.7 | 0.00 | **3.5** | 0.9 | 0.70 | 5.46 | 3.15 | 86.2 | **0.9** | 18.9 | 26.0 | **6.7** |
| **6.3** | 0.58 | 4.6 | 0.01 | **4.0** | 0.9 | 0.72 | 7.27 | 3.60 | 78.2 | **1.2** | 10.1 | 27.3 | **5.7** |
| **5.1** | 1.13 | 9.0 | 0.13 | **8.2** | 1.0 | 1.63 | 17.07 | 5.44 | 68.0 | **0.6** | 12.1 | 51.7 | **7.3** |
| **10.0** | na | 0.0 | na | **10.0** | 0.3 | 4.97 | 5.55 | 1.98 | 89.1 | **4.0** | na | 0.0 | **5.8** |
| **8.4** | 0.04 | 0.2 | 0.02 | **8.4** | 7.2 | 2.04 | 18.29 | 3.41 | 48.5 | **3.6** | 17.5 | 9.5 | **8.6** |
| **9.4** | 0.65 | 3.0 | -0.06 | **3.5** | 0.0 | 0.61 | 5.29 | 3.57 | 95.3 | **1.8** | 17.6 | 20.6 | **6.0** |
| **1.6** | 2.12 | 13.5 | -0.02 | **3.9** | 1.0 | 1.04 | 10.78 | 4.36 | 68.5 | **3.3** | 20.9 | 13.2 | **5.7** |
| **8.5** | 0.02 | 0.1 | 0.01 | **4.2** | 3.2 | 2.22 | 21.45 | 2.84 | 81.8 | **0.5** | 11.3 | 49.5 | **5.5** |
| **5.7** | 0.48 | 3.5 | 0.06 | **3.5** | 0.4 | 0.46 | 4.43 | 4.32 | 84.1 | **0.9** | 16.2 | 31.3 | **6.3** |
| **4.7** | 2.50 | 12.0 | 0.00 | **4.0** | 0.8 | 0.65 | 8.09 | 4.72 | 80.5 | **5.6** | 29.1 | 1.3 | **4.4** |
| **8.3** | 0.21 | 1.3 | 0.01 | **9.4** | 28.2 | 1.81 | 17.65 | 4.19 | 51.7 | **5.6** | 27.6 | 4.6 | **7.8** |
| **3.2** | 1.60 | 10.2 | 0.04 | **4.7** | 3.9 | 0.89 | 10.41 | 3.14 | 63.7 | **0.7** | 15.5 | 55.3 | **5.4** |
| **9.0** | 0.00 | 0.0 | 0.00 | **5.8** | 4.9 | 1.06 | 7.28 | 3.93 | 62.1 | **0.5** | 13.9 | 72.7 | **8.3** |
| **4.5** | 1.51 | 9.1 | 0.36 | **2.9** | 2.8 | 0.40 | 4.17 | 3.95 | 83.7 | **1.9** | 14.8 | 19.5 | **6.1** |
| **6.6** | 0.47 | 3.3 | 0.02 | **1.8** | 0.0 | -0.07 | -0.64 | 3.82 | 102.1 | **0.4** | 6.8 | 64.4 | **5.4** |
| **7.2** | 0.90 | 5.3 | -0.03 | **4.5** | 4.8 | 0.98 | 8.70 | 3.22 | 65.3 | **1.5** | 4.9 | 21.7 | **7.4** |
| **5.4** | 0.65 | 2.9 | 0.06 | **7.0** | 5.5 | 1.62 | 15.93 | 4.52 | 66.7 | **4.7** | 19.9 | 4.4 | **7.8** |
| **6.1** | 0.15 | 0.9 | 0.05 | **4.7** | 429.9 | 0.83 | 6.03 | 2.10 | 46.8 | **0.7** | 11.3 | 24.8 | **10.0** |
| **8.0** | 0.16 | 1.1 | 1.71 | **6.2** | 3.6 | 0.84 | 7.33 | 3.65 | 52.9 | **2.4** | 49.9 | 42.4 | **7.6** |
| **8.7** | 0.19 | 1.2 | 0.00 | **2.4** | 3.4 | 0.35 | 2.66 | 3.07 | 86.9 | **2.0** | 15.4 | 16.5 | **9.0** |
| **5.8** | 0.90 | 4.8 | 0.24 | **3.4** | 4.9 | 0.71 | 7.58 | 3.46 | 74.1 | **5.3** | 31.7 | 4.7 | **5.9** |
| **6.3** | 0.76 | 4.7 | 0.34 | **10.0** | 20.1 | 2.80 | 23.87 | 4.96 | 49.8 | **5.1** | 27.7 | 3.8 | **9.1** |
| **8.6** | 0.80 | 3.2 | 0.10 | **3.8** | 1.5 | 0.72 | 6.63 | 2.84 | 69.0 | **1.2** | 26.5 | 33.2 | **6.4** |
| **6.6** | 1.72 | 5.2 | -0.02 | **2.4** | 0.8 | 0.27 | 1.36 | 4.12 | 93.7 | **1.5** | 18.9 | 25.1 | **7.2** |
| **5.3** | 1.90 | 12.6 | 0.19 | **3.4** | 7.4 | 0.56 | 6.98 | 3.24 | 77.8 | **3.1** | 15.9 | 13.8 | **6.6** |
| **8.8** | 0.24 | 2.4 | 0.03 | **5.2** | 74.5 | 0.86 | 11.29 | 2.04 | 39.4 | **5.1** | 17.9 | 2.4 | **6.8** |
| **5.7** | 0.61 | 4.8 | 0.00 | **6.5** | 19.0 | 1.44 | 13.40 | 4.05 | 59.3 | **3.8** | 5.1 | 9.1 | **9.2** |
| **6.4** | 0.56 | 2.8 | 0.02 | **8.9** | 54.7 | 1.75 | 13.42 | 4.29 | 56.2 | **3.7** | 15.7 | 9.4 | **9.8** |
| **8.1** | 0.63 | 2.3 | 0.00 | **4.6** | 0.4 | 1.09 | 8.61 | 4.00 | 69.2 | **4.3** | 55.0 | 15.8 | **7.1** |
| **2.2** | 2.43 | 14.4 | 2.41 | **0.9** | -17.1 | -3.99 | -39.61 | 3.19 | 124.5 | **0.8** | 23.5 | 55.3 | **3.8** |
| **5.0** | 1.73 | 9.8 | 0.46 | **3.2** | 1.3 | 0.50 | 5.00 | 4.19 | 72.2 | **2.2** | 26.7 | 19.6 | **6.3** |
| **8.1** | 0.09 | 0.3 | 0.11 | **8.5** | 18.7 | 2.06 | 14.89 | 4.10 | 57.2 | **4.3** | 26.5 | 8.7 | **10.0** |
| **8.2** | 0.41 | 1.5 | 0.09 | **2.1** | 0.1 | 0.21 | 1.22 | 2.90 | 89.3 | **3.0** | 40.4 | 20.4 | **6.3** |
| **4.4** | 4.36 | 12.8 | 1.98 | **3.9** | 0.7 | 0.58 | 3.56 | 4.74 | 57.0 | **2.3** | 30.5 | 20.7 | **7.2** |
| **8.0** | 0.13 | 2.2 | 0.11 | **4.5** | 0.3 | 0.85 | 5.55 | 4.21 | 70.7 | **3.3** | 30.4 | 15.2 | **6.9** |
| **4.9** | 0.83 | 2.7 | -0.02 | **5.9** | 1.2 | 1.09 | 8.74 | 5.58 | 70.1 | **1.2** | 21.0 | 26.0 | **6.9** |
| **7.0** | 0.52 | 3.3 | 0.11 | **9.1** | 12.6 | 2.24 | 24.15 | 3.62 | 50.9 | **3.6** | 40.9 | 13.1 | **7.3** |
| **6.3** | 1.13 | 7.0 | -0.06 | **9.8** | 50.4 | 2.09 | 19.66 | 3.71 | 57.1 | **0.7** | 7.8 | 32.0 | **10.0** |
| **6.6** | 0.74 | 2.0 | 0.18 | **2.6** | 0.1 | 0.15 | 1.16 | 3.94 | 91.2 | **1.3** | 29.8 | 37.1 | **6.3** |
| **8.4** | 0.66 | 3.3 | 0.01 | **2.7** | 1.1 | 0.35 | 2.97 | 3.07 | 88.1 | **3.0** | 23.2 | 14.6 | **6.7** |
| **9.5** | 0.70 | 2.1 | 0.00 | **3.0** | 0.4 | 0.47 | 1.99 | 2.87 | 77.1 | **2.8** | 50.3 | 28.3 | **7.6** |
| **5.8** | 1.65 | 4.9 | 0.01 | **4.9** | 1.4 | 1.15 | 8.22 | 3.50 | 69.8 | **4.2** | 33.0 | 11.6 | **8.6** |
| **7.8** | 0.65 | 4.4 | 0.14 | **2.9** | 0.9 | 0.35 | 2.68 | 4.05 | 88.0 | **4.4** | 6.1 | 4.8 | **6.9** |
| **9.6** | 0.00 | 0.0 | 0.00 | **2.8** | 0.2 | 0.37 | 4.21 | 2.62 | 82.8 | **2.8** | 50.5 | 28.1 | **4.2** |
| **9.3** | 0.05 | 0.2 | -0.04 | **3.7** | 9.2 | 0.71 | 5.83 | 2.65 | 69.3 | **6.0** | 52.4 | 10.4 | **9.3** |
| **7.0** | 0.94 | 5.4 | 0.02 | **2.8** | 3.4 | 0.37 | 3.84 | 3.57 | 87.5 | **3.4** | 18.8 | 12.7 | **6.2** |
| **7.8** | 1.27 | 3.3 | 0.12 | **3.5** | 0.6 | 0.50 | 4.32 | 3.95 | 83.3 | **4.0** | 15.8 | 9.1 | **6.3** |
| **6.4** | 0.73 | 3.5 | -0.02 | **6.3** | 4.6 | 1.29 | 14.79 | 4.31 | 61.8 | **1.8** | 18.0 | 19.6 | **5.7** |
| **7.2** | 0.46 | 2.1 | 0.00 | **6.8** | 4.6 | 1.65 | 18.67 | 4.77 | 74.7 | **4.8** | 21.4 | 4.1 | **5.4** |
| **7.2** | 0.46 | 3.2 | 0.00 | **4.2** | 7.1 | 0.71 | 6.86 | 3.65 | 72.2 | **2.0** | 14.4 | 19.5 | **7.7** |
| **6.1** | 0.49 | 2.4 | 0.00 | **3.9** | 12.4 | 0.61 | 4.88 | 3.62 | 80.2 | **3.7** | 15.9 | 11.1 | **8.9** |
| **9.8** | 1.99 | 2.2 | -0.03 | **2.0** | 0.5 | 0.20 | 1.04 | 2.54 | 91.9 | **4.7** | 63.8 | 17.1 | **7.0** |
| **8.6** | 0.11 | 0.8 | -0.07 | **7.2** | 10.4 | 1.51 | 11.99 | 3.40 | 51.7 | **2.4** | 22.7 | 17.8 | **8.2** |
| **3.3** | 6.61 | 32.1 | 0.00 | **0.7** | -0.1 | -0.17 | -1.75 | 3.73 | 106.4 | **5.3** | 39.2 | 7.8 | **5.0** |

| Name | City | State | Rating | 2018 Rating | 2017 Rating | Total Assets ($Mil) | One Year Asset Growth | Asset Mix (As a % of Total Assets): Commercial Loans | Consumer Loans | Mortgage Loans | Securities | Capitalization Index | Leverage Ratio | Risk-Based Capital Ratio |
|---|---|---|---|---|---|---|---|---|---|---|---|---|---|---|
| North Star Bank | Roseville | MN | **B+** | B | B- | 295.4 | 4.33 | 18.1 | 2.4 | 4.4 | 17.1 | **8.9** | 10.7 | 14.1 |
| North State Bank | Raleigh | NC | **B** | B- | B- | 933.4 | 4.25 | 9.2 | 0.4 | 21.8 | 3.1 | **5.9** | 8.9 | 11.7 |
| North Valley Bank | Thornton | CO | **A** | A | A | 179.6 | 5.89 | 1.0 | 0.1 | 40.7 | 0.0 | **10.0** | 12.2 | 17.8 |
| North Valley Bank | Zanesville | OH | **B-** | B- | C+ | 230.5 | 9.48 | 6.0 | 3.9 | 19.1 | 16.2 | **8.7** | 10.2 | 14.2 |
| Northbrook Bank & Trust Co., N.A. | Northbrook | IL | **B** | B | B- | 2863.1 | 12.55 | 26.1 | 8.4 | 3.8 | 16.4 | **7.0** | 9.8 | 12.5 |
| Northeast Bank | Lewiston | ME | **C+** | | | 1208.0 | 1.21 | 1.2 | 0.2 | 6.9 | 6.0 | **10.0** | 14.3 | 18.5 |
| Northeast Bank | Minneapolis | MN | **A-** | A- | A- | 515.4 | 8.99 | 20.8 | 0.2 | 8.4 | 15.2 | **8.2** | 10.7 | 13.5 |
| ▲ NorthEast Community Bank | White Plains | NY | **B** | B- | B | 946.1 | 9.92 | 8.3 | 0.0 | 1.0 | 1.0 | **9.5** | 12.7 | 14.6 |
| Northeast Georgia Bank | Lavonia | GA | **A-** | A- | B | 477.6 | 0.51 | 4.6 | 6.0 | 6.5 | 21.2 | **10.0** | 12.4 | 22.2 |
| Northeast Missouri State Bank | Kirksville | MO | **A-** | A- | A- | 109.8 | 6.05 | 2.2 | 3.6 | 11.0 | 41.5 | **10.0** | 13.7 | 25.8 |
| Northeast Security Bank | Sumner | IA | **A-** | A- | A- | 282.2 | 2.42 | 6.3 | 0.6 | 10.0 | 28.6 | **10.0** | 12.3 | 17.8 |
| ▲ Northern Bank & Trust Co. | Woburn | MA | **B+** | B- | B+ | 2234.0 | 3.32 | 34.1 | 0.0 | 11.6 | 2.2 | **9.4** | 12.3 | 14.5 |
| Northern California National Bank | Chico | CA | **B+** | B | B- | 274.9 | 12.27 | 4.2 | 0.3 | 6.8 | 23.4 | **7.5** | 9.3 | 20.6 |
| Northern Interstate Bank, N.A. | Norway | MI | **B** | B- | B | 153.9 | -2.10 | 6.6 | 4.0 | 26.9 | 27.8 | **10.0** | 11.7 | 21.6 |
| ▲ Northern Sky Bank | Crookston | MN | **B-** | C+ | B- | 81.9 | 11.13 | 8.4 | 1.7 | 14.1 | 14.7 | **8.8** | 10.2 | 18.3 |
| ▲ Northern State Bank | Ashland | WI | **B+** | B- | B- | 241.9 | 1.92 | 7.1 | 1.2 | 28.7 | 20.1 | **8.0** | 9.7 | 16.7 |
| Northern State Bank of Gonvick | Gonvick | MN | **B** | B- | C+ | 38.5 | -2.63 | 2.9 | 4.6 | 5.7 | 32.1 | **10.0** | 18.7 | 103.3 |
| Northern State Bank of Thief River Falls | Thief River Falls | MN | **B+** | B- | B- | 365.5 | 12.95 | 3.4 | 4.1 | 10.5 | 13.3 | **9.0** | 10.3 | 27.4 |
| Northern State Bank of Virginia | Virginia | MN | **B-** | C | C | 76.5 | 6.28 | 13.3 | 2.8 | 30.3 | 7.0 | **6.9** | 8.9 | 14.1 |
| Northern Trust Co. | Chicago | IL | **B+** | B | B | 135885.4 | 3.18 | 3.0 | 0.2 | 4.0 | 37.4 | **5.3** | 7.3 | 14.0 |
| Northfield Bank | Woodbridge | NJ | **B** | B | B | 5059.5 | 14.74 | 1.2 | 0.0 | 6.6 | 22.7 | **10.0** | 12.3 | 15.7 |
| Northfield Savings Bank | Berlin | VT | **B-** | B- | B- | 1059.0 | 2.49 | 7.6 | 0.2 | 44.4 | 13.8 | **10.0** | 11.8 | 17.5 |
| Northmark Bank | North Andover | MA | **A-** | B+ | B+ | 358.8 | -3.63 | 6.5 | 0.6 | 42.0 | 7.5 | **10.0** | 13.2 | 20.5 |
| Northpointe Bank | Grand Rapids | MI | **B** | B | C | 2186.1 | 70.83 | 0.4 | 0.0 | 56.0 | 0.1 | **6.3** | 8.3 | 15.0 |
| Northrim Bank | Anchorage | AK | **B** | B | B | 1631.8 | 9.85 | 22.0 | 0.4 | 6.5 | 16.9 | **7.9** | 10.4 | 13.3 |
| Northside Community Bank | Gurnee | IL | **B** | B- | B | 243.6 | 8.66 | 4.7 | 0.6 | 7.4 | 0.7 | **10.0** | 22.6 | 25.2 |
| NorthStar Bank | Estherville | IA | **A-** | B+ | A- | 192.2 | 0.85 | 5.9 | 1.1 | 13.4 | 9.0 | **10.0** | 11.2 | 16.6 |
| Northstar Bank | Bad Axe | MI | **C+** | C- | C- | 650.2 | 3.45 | 11.0 | 1.7 | 10.7 | 8.6 | **6.7** | 9.3 | 12.3 |
| Northumberland National Bank | Northumberland | PA | **C+** | C+ | C+ | 537.9 | 0.69 | 12.2 | 0.9 | 36.5 | 23.8 | **9.1** | 10.4 | 17.5 |
| ▲ Northview Bank | Sandstone | MN | **B** | C+ | B | 327.0 | 3.08 | 6.5 | 4.0 | 22.9 | 14.5 | **10.0** | 12.3 | 17.0 |
| ▲ Northway Bank | Berlin | NH | **B** | C+ | C+ | 912.7 | -1.03 | 4.0 | 1.6 | 20.2 | 19.8 | **10.0** | 11.1 | 17.7 |
| Northwest Bank | Spencer | IA | **B+** | B+ | B+ | 1688.8 | 5.12 | 15.7 | 1.7 | 14.5 | 8.5 | **6.0** | 9.6 | 11.7 |
| Northwest Bank | Boise | ID | **A-** | A- | A- | 882.3 | 30.35 | 38.8 | 0.0 | 0.2 | 5.4 | **8.8** | 11.1 | 14.0 |
| Northwest Bank | Warren | PA | **B** | B | B- | 10624.8 | 9.52 | 6.0 | 10.8 | 36.1 | 7.9 | **8.6** | 10.5 | 13.9 |
| ▲ Northwest Bank & Trust Co. | Davenport | IA | **B-** | B- | B | 167.3 | 0.85 | 13.2 | 0.7 | 12.3 | 5.2 | **8.9** | 10.4 | 14.0 |
| Northwest Bank of Rockford | Rockford | IL | **B** | B- | C+ | 295.0 | 6.83 | 19.0 | 3.4 | 11.3 | 14.2 | **7.1** | 9.3 | 12.6 |
| Northwest Community Bank | Winsted | CT | **B-** | B- | C+ | 417.9 | 2.05 | 3.6 | 2.3 | 46.3 | 15.7 | **10.0** | 11.8 | 19.6 |
| Northwestern Bank | Orange City | IA | **A-** | B+ | A- | 218.7 | 0.18 | 5.0 | 1.0 | 8.6 | 9.5 | **10.0** | 13.8 | 16.3 |
| Northwestern Bank | Chippewa Falls | WI | **A** | A- | A- | 455.7 | 1.17 | 20.0 | 0.8 | 7.3 | 15.7 | **9.3** | 10.9 | 14.4 |
| Northwestern Bank, N.A. | Dilworth | MN | **C+** | C+ | C+ | 152.8 | 11.39 | 14.8 | 3.4 | 8.6 | 9.7 | **7.4** | 9.7 | 12.9 |
| Northwestern Mutual Wealth Mgmt Co. | Milwaukee | WI | **U** | U | U | 339.8 | 27.57 | 0.0 | 0.0 | 0.0 | 97.0 | **10.0** | 63.1 | 264.2 |
| Northwoods Bank of Minnesota | Park Rapids | MN | **B-** | B- | B | 119.2 | -1.07 | 5.1 | 1.9 | 19.8 | 33.6 | **9.6** | 10.7 | 19.0 |
| Norway Savings Bank | Norway | ME | **A** | B+ | B | 1237.2 | 2.48 | 5.6 | 6.2 | 31.8 | 5.2 | **10.0** | 15.2 | 17.6 |
| Norwood Co-operative Bank | Norwood | MA | **B** | B | B- | 588.8 | 9.79 | 2.2 | 0.0 | 37.8 | 10.2 | **10.0** | 13.7 | 19.8 |
| NSB Bank | Mason City | IA | **A-** | A- | A- | 211.3 | 3.72 | 21.2 | 1.3 | 6.3 | 12.5 | **7.9** | 10.9 | 13.3 |
| NVE Bank | Englewood | NJ | **B** | B | B- | 674.4 | 1.85 | 0.2 | 0.1 | 37.0 | 11.9 | **10.0** | 15.9 | 27.3 |
| NXT Bank | Central City | IA | **B-** | B- | C+ | 272.6 | 6.02 | 9.5 | 0.4 | 11.4 | 9.0 | **9.7** | 11.1 | 14.8 |
| O'Bannon Banking Co. | Buffalo | MO | **B-** | B- | B- | 216.8 | 3.83 | 8.4 | 1.9 | 23.7 | 10.2 | **7.1** | 9.3 | 12.6 |
| ▲ Oak Bank | Fitchburg | WI | **B** | B+ | A- | 321.4 | 0.46 | 12.6 | 0.7 | 13.8 | 12.0 | **9.5** | 10.7 | 14.7 |
| Oak Valley Community Bank | Oakdale | CA | **B+** | B+ | B | 1147.7 | 4.91 | 5.1 | 0.1 | 2.5 | 16.6 | **6.8** | 9.5 | 12.3 |
| Oak View National Bank | Warrenton | VA | **B-** | C+ | C+ | 263.7 | 10.73 | 8.3 | 1.0 | 34.4 | 1.0 | **7.5** | 9.4 | 14.9 |
| Oakdale State Bank | Oakdale | IL | **C+** | C+ | C+ | 20.8 | -1.75 | 6.6 | 4.0 | 25.6 | 2.0 | **10.0** | 12.3 | 18.4 |
| OakStar Bank | Springfield | MO | **B-** | C+ | B | 995.8 | 6.08 | 15.8 | 1.6 | 21.4 | 1.8 | **7.7** | 10.1 | 13.1 |
| Oakwood Bank | Dallas | TX | **D** | D+ | C- | 384.1 | 45.14 | 30.6 | 0.3 | 8.5 | 1.0 | **7.5** | 10.5 | 12.9 |
| Oakwood Bank | Pigeon Falls | WI | **C** | C+ | B | 90.8 | 7.08 | 4.7 | 0.4 | 10.7 | 1.8 | **5.1** | 8.8 | 11.0 |
| Oakworth Capital Bank | Birmingham | AL | **A-** | A- | A- | 717.8 | 16.93 | 31.0 | 2.0 | 2.2 | 8.5 | **7.8** | 11.0 | 13.2 |
| Ocean Bank | Miami | FL | **B+** | B+ | B | 4314.2 | 11.32 | 7.2 | 0.6 | 4.2 | 11.3 | **9.2** | 10.8 | 14.4 |
| OceanFirst Bank, N.A. | Toms River | NJ | **B** | B | B- | 8253.8 | 9.80 | 4.0 | 1.2 | 32.2 | 11.2 | **8.0** | 10.0 | 13.3 |
| Oconee Federal S&L Assn. | Seneca | SC | **B+** | B+ | A- | 504.6 | -2.05 | 0.8 | 1.2 | 57.7 | 16.5 | **10.0** | 16.0 | 30.4 |
| Oconee State Bank | Watkinsville | GA | **C+** | C+ | C+ | 399.5 | 14.21 | 5.3 | 1.1 | 7.0 | 24.8 | **7.5** | 9.4 | 13.1 |

| Asset Quality Index | Adjusted Non-Performing Loans as a % of Total Loans | Adjusted Non-Performing Loans as a % of Capital | Net Charge-Offs Avg Loans | Profitability Index | Net Income ($Mil) | Return on Assets (R.O.A.) | Return on Equity (R.O.E.) | Net Interest Spread | Overhead Efficiency Ratio | Liquidity Index | Liquidity Ratio | Hot Money Ratio | Stability Index |
|---|---|---|---|---|---|---|---|---|---|---|---|---|---|
| **7.4** | 0.79 | 2.1 | -0.01 | **6.2** | 4.4 | 1.54 | 14.92 | 3.98 | 60.5 | **4.0** | 29.4 | 11.4 | **6.8** |
| **5.7** | 0.17 | 5.3 | -0.01 | **6.1** | 13.9 | 1.49 | 17.26 | 4.25 | 70.8 | **4.7** | 11.9 | 3.4 | **6.9** |
| **8.8** | 0.00 | 0.1 | 0.00 | **10.0** | 5.0 | 2.84 | 23.69 | 5.56 | 49.3 | **3.4** | 8.7 | 11.3 | **9.2** |
| **6.5** | 0.40 | 2.6 | 0.08 | **3.6** | 1.4 | 0.67 | 6.32 | 4.08 | 83.3 | **3.6** | 17.9 | 9.9 | **5.8** |
| **5.4** | 0.92 | 5.8 | 0.06 | **8.8** | 40.9 | 1.56 | 15.42 | 3.37 | 42.5 | **2.8** | 28.9 | 12.6 | **8.0** |
| **2.7** | 3.47 | 15.8 | 0.07 | **10.0** | 20.9 | 1.79 | 12.89 | 5.69 | 56.8 | **0.6** | 8.8 | 44.6 | **10.0** |
| **6.6** | 0.31 | 1.2 | -0.02 | **7.4** | 9.1 | 1.83 | 17.24 | 4.42 | 61.0 | **4.5** | 11.1 | 4.8 | **8.9** |
| **5.8** | 0.53 | 2.9 | 0.04 | **7.3** | 12.4 | 1.30 | 10.03 | 4.39 | 59.4 | **0.8** | 17.4 | 43.0 | **9.2** |
| **8.1** | 0.55 | 2.2 | 0.05 | **7.1** | 8.4 | 1.80 | 16.38 | 3.70 | 55.9 | **4.4** | 35.7 | 11.7 | **7.7** |
| **8.1** | 0.65 | 1.9 | 0.01 | **6.0** | 1.6 | 1.47 | 9.56 | 3.34 | 55.2 | **3.4** | 43.0 | 18.6 | **9.1** |
| **8.4** | 0.01 | 0.0 | 0.00 | **5.4** | 3.0 | 1.09 | 8.41 | 3.31 | 60.1 | **3.4** | 26.7 | 13.5 | **7.7** |
| **5.7** | 0.69 | 3.1 | 0.18 | **9.6** | 37.1 | 1.73 | 15.15 | 4.48 | 43.3 | **0.8** | 10.0 | 22.6 | **9.8** |
| **8.9** | 0.44 | 1.8 | -0.01 | **5.3** | 2.9 | 1.11 | 12.04 | 3.22 | 51.0 | **3.8** | 39.8 | 12.0 | **5.1** |
| **6.1** | 2.07 | 7.5 | 0.04 | **4.2** | 1.3 | 0.83 | 7.11 | 3.96 | 75.1 | **5.2** | 39.3 | 8.2 | **6.7** |
| **7.9** | 0.00 | 0.0 | 0.00 | **4.8** | 0.6 | 1.55 | 12.32 | 4.17 | 41.8 | **4.2** | 37.7 | 13.1 | **6.3** |
| **6.5** | 0.66 | 2.7 | 0.07 | **6.6** | 3.8 | 1.60 | 16.74 | 3.70 | 58.0 | **4.6** | 21.6 | 5.3 | **6.3** |
| **8.8** | 1.38 | 1.4 | -0.02 | **4.0** | 0.4 | 1.02 | 5.62 | 2.55 | 59.3 | **7.3** | 89.2 | 4.6 | **7.0** |
| **7.4** | 0.33 | 2.2 | -0.02 | **5.0** | 4.6 | 1.32 | 13.17 | 2.80 | 55.5 | **6.8** | 59.3 | 4.6 | **6.1** |
| **8.1** | 0.02 | 0.1 | -0.02 | **5.6** | 1.0 | 1.31 | 11.62 | 4.82 | 71.1 | **2.2** | 15.5 | 17.9 | **5.9** |
| **9.4** | 0.35 | 1.1 | 0.00 | **6.0** | 1464.2 | 1.25 | 15.03 | 1.57 | 67.7 | **7.1** | 48.7 | 2.3 | **6.5** |
| **6.4** | 0.67 | 3.1 | -0.04 | **4.4** | 40.0 | 0.85 | 6.36 | 2.51 | 58.4 | **1.7** | 12.9 | 14.0 | **9.6** |
| **8.5** | 0.26 | 1.6 | 0.02 | **3.4** | 6.6 | 0.64 | 5.43 | 3.11 | 77.0 | **1.8** | 10.1 | 19.9 | **8.8** |
| **8.9** | 0.00 | 0.0 | 0.00 | **5.7** | 3.8 | 1.05 | 8.28 | 3.97 | 63.7 | **1.1** | 11.2 | 30.1 | **7.9** |
| **5.5** | 0.73 | 7.1 | -0.01 | **9.2** | 31.0 | 1.71 | 20.73 | 2.47 | 79.5 | **1.0** | 15.9 | 23.5 | **8.9** |
| **4.9** | 1.48 | 7.3 | -0.07 | **7.3** | 20.7 | 1.35 | 11.28 | 4.86 | 74.7 | **4.6** | 23.4 | 8.5 | **10.0** |
| **6.9** | 0.00 | 0.0 | -2.29 | **8.8** | 5.9 | 2.49 | 10.70 | 3.99 | 63.2 | **1.3** | 11.9 | 24.2 | **8.3** |
| **7.1** | 0.00 | 3.4 | 0.02 | **6.3** | 2.6 | 1.39 | 10.34 | 3.34 | 58.8 | **3.2** | 23.1 | 13.6 | **8.9** |
| **3.4** | 2.45 | 8.9 | -0.02 | **6.7** | 9.7 | 1.52 | 14.68 | 4.38 | 65.2 | **3.0** | 19.3 | 12.7 | **8.1** |
| **6.7** | 0.64 | 3.9 | 0.02 | **3.3** | 3.4 | 0.64 | 6.34 | 3.20 | 78.4 | **2.7** | 14.1 | 15.3 | **6.6** |
| **5.4** | 1.17 | 5.9 | 0.05 | **8.3** | 6.2 | 1.94 | 15.23 | 4.84 | 63.6 | **3.2** | 15.7 | 10.9 | **8.8** |
| **7.4** | 0.76 | 3.4 | 0.02 | **4.3** | 9.2 | 1.00 | 8.83 | 3.49 | 81.0 | **4.0** | 8.8 | 7.6 | **6.8** |
| **7.9** | 0.28 | 2.0 | 0.16 | **6.5** | 24.4 | 1.48 | 15.15 | 3.66 | 63.7 | **1.9** | 10.0 | 17.5 | **8.8** |
| **6.3** | 1.07 | 4.8 | 0.05 | **8.6** | 10.9 | 1.43 | 12.16 | 4.74 | 56.0 | **2.2** | 32.7 | 15.0 | **8.7** |
| **4.6** | 1.02 | 5.7 | 0.23 | **5.7** | 115.1 | 1.09 | 8.60 | 4.01 | 64.6 | **4.4** | 9.7 | 5.9 | **9.5** |
| **4.1** | 2.64 | 13.5 | 1.38 | **6.3** | 2.3 | 1.42 | 13.75 | 4.50 | 67.2 | **4.3** | 23.0 | 7.4 | **6.8** |
| **3.8** | 0.85 | 5.0 | 0.93 | **3.1** | 1.0 | 0.35 | 3.64 | 3.78 | 78.5 | **1.6** | 17.3 | 23.0 | **6.3** |
| **8.7** | 0.68 | 3.2 | -0.01 | **4.3** | 3.9 | 0.94 | 8.07 | 2.91 | 73.9 | **2.3** | 23.9 | 16.5 | **6.5** |
| **4.1** | 2.20 | 6.6 | -0.05 | **9.8** | 4.5 | 2.06 | 13.75 | 4.01 | 41.2 | **2.7** | 15.4 | 13.1 | **9.2** |
| **8.3** | 0.03 | 0.1 | 0.35 | **8.4** | 9.1 | 2.02 | 17.93 | 3.98 | 49.5 | **4.6** | 19.6 | 5.5 | **9.1** |
| **5.2** | 0.43 | 2.9 | 0.09 | **3.7** | 0.9 | 0.61 | 5.63 | 4.93 | 87.1 | **2.4** | 16.7 | 8.7 | **6.3** |
| **10.0** | na | 0.0 | na | **10.0** | 79.9 | 23.56 | 40.78 | 1.88 | 88.4 | **5.0** | 320.8 | 100.0 | **6.5** |
| **5.0** | 1.73 | 6.6 | 0.04 | **4.7** | 1.3 | 1.10 | 10.09 | 3.96 | 72.1 | **3.4** | 24.3 | 12.8 | **6.8** |
| **8.1** | 0.20 | 0.9 | 0.03 | **7.3** | 20.6 | 1.69 | 11.10 | 4.28 | 73.3 | **4.1** | 10.7 | 7.7 | **10.0** |
| **8.5** | 0.25 | 1.0 | 0.00 | **4.3** | 4.6 | 0.82 | 5.99 | 3.27 | 65.5 | **0.7** | 12.8 | 29.1 | **9.0** |
| **7.2** | 0.37 | 2.0 | -0.01 | **9.2** | 4.2 | 2.03 | 18.28 | 4.15 | 49.7 | **3.4** | 4.2 | 10.8 | **8.6** |
| **7.5** | 0.96 | 4.1 | 0.01 | **4.1** | 4.9 | 0.74 | 4.56 | 3.16 | 68.8 | **3.6** | 18.4 | 11.5 | **8.8** |
| **7.1** | 0.04 | 0.2 | 0.00 | **4.0** | 2.1 | 0.79 | 6.73 | 2.88 | 65.9 | **1.2** | 14.1 | 28.0 | **6.9** |
| **5.1** | 0.96 | 8.6 | 0.00 | **5.5** | 2.4 | 1.11 | 12.51 | 4.14 | 64.4 | **1.5** | 12.1 | 23.3 | **5.8** |
| **5.9** | 0.32 | 2.0 | 0.17 | **7.4** | 4.5 | 1.42 | 12.74 | 3.83 | 54.9 | **2.6** | 22.9 | 11.4 | **7.5** |
| **7.5** | 0.15 | 0.9 | 0.01 | **6.2** | 13.1 | 1.21 | 12.37 | 4.15 | 61.1 | **5.2** | 21.0 | 2.7 | **8.3** |
| **8.9** | 0.01 | 0.1 | 0.00 | **4.2** | 2.1 | 0.82 | 8.85 | 3.53 | 73.6 | **1.4** | 19.9 | 26.8 | **5.2** |
| **6.1** | 1.20 | 6.6 | 0.05 | **7.1** | 0.3 | 1.29 | 10.49 | 4.83 | 61.5 | **2.6** | 27.2 | 16.9 | **5.0** |
| **4.3** | 1.83 | 7.8 | 0.15 | **4.5** | 8.9 | 0.91 | 8.13 | 3.75 | 73.9 | **2.0** | 3.3 | 15.5 | **7.9** |
| **8.2** | 0.00 | 0.0 | 0.03 | **0.8** | 0.5 | 0.15 | 1.40 | 3.08 | 86.7 | **2.2** | 21.7 | 18.5 | **5.5** |
| **1.3** | 3.41 | 9.2 | 0.00 | **4.8** | 0.9 | 1.08 | 7.69 | 3.92 | 66.3 | **0.8** | 16.7 | 36.3 | **7.7** |
| **8.2** | 0.00 | 0.0 | 0.02 | **6.5** | 8.0 | 1.26 | 10.93 | 3.68 | 64.5 | **1.9** | 24.5 | 21.3 | **7.9** |
| **5.6** | 1.01 | 4.1 | -0.10 | **4.7** | 34.8 | 0.83 | 7.37 | 3.66 | 72.4 | **1.3** | 21.2 | 31.9 | **9.4** |
| **5.7** | 0.67 | 2.8 | 0.02 | **5.4** | 93.1 | 1.16 | 7.81 | 3.69 | 62.4 | **4.1** | 8.1 | 7.2 | **9.2** |
| **7.3** | 0.98 | 4.0 | 0.00 | **4.2** | 4.3 | 0.83 | 5.21 | 3.11 | 68.8 | **1.6** | 21.0 | 24.2 | **9.1** |
| **3.6** | 2.53 | 16.9 | 0.00 | **5.0** | 3.8 | 1.09 | 11.71 | 3.83 | 70.9 | **4.0** | 20.4 | 7.8 | **5.0** |

| Name | City | State | Rating | 2018 Rating | 2017 Rating | Total Assets ($Mil) | One Year Asset Growth | Asset Mix (As a % of Total Assets) Comm-ercial Loans | Cons-umer Loans | Mort-gage Loans | Secur-ities | Capital-ization Index | Lever-age Ratio | Risk-Based Capital Ratio |
|---|---|---|---|---|---|---|---|---|---|---|---|---|---|---|
| Odin State Bank | Odin | MN | D | D | D+ | 45.7 | -4.42 | 9.8 | 7.3 | 12.5 | 10.1 | 9.4 | 10.6 | 14.5 |
| Ohana Pacific Bank | Honolulu | HI | B | B | B | 183.8 | 14.49 | 8.2 | 0.4 | 14.3 | 1.1 | 10.0 | 11.4 | 16.7 |
| ▲ Ohio Valley Bank Co. | Gallipolis | OH | B | C+ | C+ | 998.2 | -1.65 | 6.2 | 11.0 | 30.7 | 11.8 | 10.0 | 11.3 | 17.0 |
| Ohnward Bank & Trust | Cascade | IA | A- | A- | B+ | 295.3 | 5.43 | 10.0 | 2.3 | 7.8 | 14.7 | 10.0 | 12.5 | 15.5 |
| Oklahoma Bank and Trust Co. | Clinton | OK | A- | B+ | A- | 168.1 | 1.28 | 3.1 | 0.8 | 8.4 | 49.7 | 10.0 | 15.1 | 35.1 |
| Oklahoma Capital Bank | Tulsa | OK | B | B | C+ | 175.9 | 1.92 | 20.3 | 1.4 | 11.2 | 6.3 | 10.0 | 16.4 | 22.6 |
| Oklahoma Heritage Bank | Stratford | OK | C+ | C- | D | 82.1 | 1.24 | 8.9 | 5.6 | 30.4 | 13.3 | 9.2 | 10.5 | 17.3 |
| Oklahoma State Bank | Buffalo | OK | B+ | B | B+ | 56.0 | -1.16 | 8.0 | 10.9 | 5.1 | 24.3 | 9.1 | 10.4 | 14.5 |
| ▼ Oklahoma State Bank | Guthrie | OK | D+ | C- | C- | 146.4 | 4.93 | 24.7 | 0.7 | 12.9 | 1.4 | 9.5 | 11.1 | 14.6 |
| Oklahoma State Bank | Vinita | OK | A- | B | B- | 154.8 | -0.75 | 9.5 | 2.4 | 23.1 | 8.9 | 10.0 | 12.1 | 17.6 |
| Old Dominion National Bank | North Garden | VA | D | D | D | 441.6 | 61.81 | 18.5 | 0.1 | 10.8 | 2.9 | 10.0 | 21.4 | 21.8 |
| Old Exchange National Bank of Okawville | Okawville | IL | B+ | B- | B- | 75.0 | 5.90 | 1.0 | 0.5 | 7.3 | 37.8 | 10.0 | 11.2 | 21.5 |
| Old Fort Banking Co. | Old Fort | OH | B | B | B | 566.3 | 6.28 | 10.4 | 0.6 | 14.8 | 27.2 | 6.2 | 8.2 | 13.3 |
| Old Mission Bank | Sault Sainte Marie | MI | B | B | B | 118.7 | 0.80 | 7.2 | 3.2 | 10.0 | 41.8 | 10.0 | 11.5 | 20.2 |
| Old Missouri Bank | Springfield | MO | C+ | C | C+ | 530.9 | 14.14 | 12.3 | 1.6 | 15.5 | 5.4 | 6.1 | 9.4 | 11.9 |
| Old National Bank | Evansville | IN | B- | B- | C+ | 20311.5 | 3.45 | 11.0 | 5.3 | 13.1 | 26.3 | 7.9 | 9.6 | 13.5 |
| Old Plank Trail Community Bank, N.A. | Mokena | IL | B | B | B- | 1614.3 | 2.47 | 32.5 | 15.4 | 2.1 | 14.5 | 5.8 | 9.7 | 11.6 |
| Old Point National Bank of Phoebus | Hampton | VA | C+ | C- | C | 1048.2 | 1.50 | 6.9 | 13.1 | 12.7 | 13.3 | 7.4 | 9.7 | 12.9 |
| Old Point Trust & Financial Services, N.A. | Newport News | VA | U | U | U | 6.7 | 7.53 | 0.0 | 0.0 | 0.0 | 87.0 | 10.0 | 93.0 | 394.3 |
| Old Second National Bank | Aurora | IL | A- | A- | A- | 2632.9 | -1.07 | 16.2 | 0.2 | 8.3 | 18.4 | 10.0 | 12.5 | 15.2 |
| Olpe State Bank | Olpe | KS | B | B- | B- | 39.2 | -6.78 | 4.7 | 2.4 | 20.0 | 20.1 | 10.0 | 15.3 | 30.7 |
| Olympia Federal S&L Assn. | Olympia | WA | B- | B- | B- | 710.5 | 7.18 | 0.3 | 0.5 | 67.1 | 6.0 | 10.0 | 14.7 | 24.1 |
| OmniBank | Bay Springs | MS | D+ | D- | D- | 48.8 | 8.92 | 7.6 | 7.2 | 22.5 | 9.3 | 7.4 | 9.2 | 15.4 |
| ONB Bank | Rochester | MN | B | B | B | 116.7 | 20.10 | 11.7 | 1.2 | 16.8 | 4.6 | 8.2 | 10.7 | 13.5 |
| One American Bank | Sioux Falls | SD | C | C | C | 119.7 | 30.89 | 9.8 | 10.7 | 29.1 | 1.2 | 7.9 | 9.6 | 13.4 |
| One Florida Bank | Orlando | FL | C | B- | C | 419.2 | 710.80 | 21.6 | 0.2 | 6.5 | 0.1 | 10.0 | 27.5 | 31.9 |
| One South Bank | Blakely | GA | C+ | C+ | C | 146.4 | 9.86 | 4.2 | 1.3 | 13.4 | 0.6 | 9.0 | 10.3 | 17.2 |
| ▲ One World Bank | Dallas | TX | B | C+ | C+ | 106.7 | 6.93 | 3.5 | 0.1 | 1.5 | 3.7 | 10.0 | 13.5 | 21.2 |
| OneUnited Bank | Boston | MA | D | D- | D- | 654.1 | -0.33 | 0.0 | 0.4 | 4.3 | 13.9 | 3.8 | 5.8 | 11.5 |
| ▲ Oostburg State Bank | Oostburg | WI | B+ | B | B | 245.5 | 7.97 | 15.6 | 0.8 | 17.8 | 20.1 | 10.0 | 12.9 | 17.3 |
| Open Bank | Los Angeles | CA | A- | B+ | A- | 1179.4 | 12.95 | 9.3 | 0.2 | 10.2 | 4.8 | 10.0 | 12.0 | 15.0 |
| ▲ Opportunity Bank of Montana | Helena | MT | B | B | B | 1039.1 | 23.16 | 7.0 | 1.8 | 14.8 | 11.7 | 10.0 | 11.1 | 15.2 |
| OptimumBank | Plantation | FL | C- | C | D+ | 126.6 | 27.53 | 3.6 | 3.9 | 22.4 | 9.0 | 6.4 | 8.7 | 12.0 |
| Optum Bank, Inc. | Salt Lake City | UT | A+ | A | A | 10826.7 | 17.01 | 2.3 | 0.0 | 0.0 | 77.7 | 10.0 | 11.3 | 23.2 |
| ▲ Optus Bank | Columbia | SC | C | D | D- | 78.1 | 20.11 | 21.9 | 0.5 | 10.1 | 10.9 | 8.7 | 10.2 | 18.1 |
| Opus Bank | Irvine | CA | B- | C+ | C | 7992.4 | 11.30 | 7.3 | 0.0 | 0.6 | 13.0 | 8.1 | 9.7 | 15.1 |
| Orange Bank & Trust Co. | Middletown | NY | B- | C+ | C- | 1219.0 | 15.41 | 18.2 | 0.2 | 8.1 | 20.9 | 7.6 | 9.4 | 13.8 |
| Oregon Coast Bank | Newport | OR | A- | B+ | B+ | 256.7 | 9.06 | 3.9 | 1.3 | 11.2 | 39.9 | 10.0 | 11.7 | 17.3 |
| ▲ Oregon Community Bank | Oregon | WI | A | B+ | A- | 620.0 | 33.84 | 6.0 | 0.4 | 14.6 | 4.8 | 8.7 | 12.7 | 13.9 |
| Oregon Pacific Banking Co. | Florence | OR | B+ | B | B | 364.1 | 17.66 | 17.2 | 0.3 | 10.4 | 7.6 | 10.0 | 11.1 | 15.0 |
| Oriental Bank | San Juan | PR | C- | D+ | D+ | 9253.7 | 41.72 | 9.6 | 21.2 | 27.3 | 11.6 | 6.8 | 8.9 | 13.2 |
| Origin Bank | Choudrant | LA | B | B- | C | 5294.1 | 10.52 | 22.6 | 0.4 | 10.2 | 10.0 | 6.8 | 10.6 | 12.4 |
| Ormsby State Bank | Ormsby | MN | B+ | B+ | B+ | 26.8 | 0.79 | 3.7 | 6.9 | 2.0 | 26.5 | 10.0 | 15.7 | 31.4 |
| Orrstown Bank | Shippensburg | PA | B- | B- | C+ | 2381.6 | 23.25 | 7.3 | 2.1 | 20.1 | 20.6 | 7.6 | 9.4 | 13.4 |
| Osgood State Bank | Osgood | OH | B+ | B | B | 268.3 | 4.90 | 27.9 | 2.0 | 9.0 | 21.8 | 7.6 | 10.1 | 13.0 |
| Ossian State Bank | Ossian | IN | B | C+ | C+ | 111.6 | -0.13 | 6.4 | 1.1 | 5.9 | 13.4 | 8.8 | 10.2 | 16.3 |
| Ottawa Savings Bank | Ottawa | IL | B | B | B | 300.3 | 2.60 | 7.4 | 11.7 | 44.1 | 8.2 | 10.0 | 15.0 | 22.2 |
| Ottoville Bank Co. | Ottoville | OH | A- | A- | A- | 77.2 | -5.04 | 6.4 | 0.5 | 13.5 | 27.2 | 10.0 | 21.7 | 34.8 |
| Our Community Bank | Spencer | IN | C+ | C | B- | 72.7 | 0.43 | 0.0 | 0.7 | 61.0 | 11.5 | 10.0 | 11.6 | 22.1 |
| ▲ Owen County State Bank | Spencer | IN | B | B- | B | 232.5 | 4.77 | 6.1 | 3.5 | 31.2 | 13.8 | 7.7 | 9.5 | 16.0 |
| Owingsville Banking Co. | Owingsville | KY | C- | D+ | C- | 70.1 | 0.12 | 1.5 | 5.5 | 36.8 | 20.4 | 8.4 | 9.9 | 16.6 |
| ▲ Oxford Bank | Oxford | MI | B | C+ | C | 505.3 | 10.48 | 13.9 | 0.9 | 7.7 | 13.3 | 7.5 | 9.4 | 13.8 |
| ▲ Oxford Bank & Trust | Oak Brook | IL | C+ | C- | C- | 614.7 | 9.61 | 2.5 | 13.6 | 5.4 | 28.2 | 7.9 | 9.6 | 14.1 |
| Oxford University Bank | Oxford | MS | B | B | B- | 168.6 | 8.41 | 6.4 | 4.5 | 32.6 | 14.9 | 8.8 | 10.2 | 15.6 |
| Ozark Bank | Ozark | MO | B | B- | B- | 282.0 | 3.07 | 4.6 | 0.7 | 21.7 | 20.9 | 8.5 | 10.0 | 15.5 |
| Ozarks Federal S&L Assn. | Farmington | MO | B- | B- | B- | 247.8 | -0.06 | 0.0 | 0.2 | 67.4 | 5.6 | 10.0 | 14.9 | 22.0 |
| ▲ Ozona National Bank | Ozona | TX | B | B | B- | 266.6 | 4.43 | 4.5 | 1.0 | 12.9 | 32.3 | 10.0 | 11.2 | 23.9 |
| Pacific Alliance Bank | Rosemead | CA | B+ | B+ | B+ | 269.1 | 0.57 | 12.5 | 0.0 | 14.0 | 10.3 | 10.0 | 14.2 | 18.1 |
| Pacific City Bank | Los Angeles | CA | A | A | A- | 1746.3 | 2.91 | 13.0 | 1.3 | 14.8 | 6.8 | 10.0 | 13.1 | 16.7 |
| ▲ Pacific Coast Bankers' Bank | Walnut Creek | CA | A- | B+ | B | 723.4 | 0.48 | 2.6 | 0.0 | 0.1 | 15.0 | 10.0 | 11.3 | 20.4 |

| Asset Quality Index | Adjusted Non-Performing Loans as a % of Total Loans | Adjusted Non-Performing Loans as a % of Capital | Net Charge-Offs Avg Loans | Profitability Index | Net Income ($Mil) | Return on Assets (R.O.A.) | Return on Equity (R.O.E.) | Net Interest Spread | Overhead Efficiency Ratio | Liquidity Index | Liquidity Ratio | Hot Money Ratio | Stability Index |
|---|---|---|---|---|---|---|---|---|---|---|---|---|---|
| **0.4** | 2.88 | 27.7 | 0.91 | **3.5** | 0.3 | 0.61 | 5.74 | 3.99 | 63.1 | **1.1** | 17.9 | 24.5 | **4.8** |
| **8.7** | 0.07 | 0.7 | 0.00 | **4.7** | 1.6 | 0.92 | 8.22 | 3.40 | 62.4 | **0.9** | 23.9 | 40.4 | **7.0** |
| **4.2** | 2.34 | 11.1 | 0.17 | **4.6** | 9.0 | 0.88 | 7.55 | 4.28 | 76.4 | **2.3** | 10.4 | 11.9 | **8.1** |
| **8.1** | 0.10 | 0.4 | 0.01 | **5.7** | 3.3 | 1.13 | 8.98 | 3.52 | 59.6 | **1.5** | 20.5 | 22.0 | **8.6** |
| **8.7** | 0.61 | 2.8 | 0.03 | **5.8** | 2.3 | 1.44 | 9.44 | 3.07 | 54.9 | **1.9** | 25.1 | 21.4 | **8.8** |
| **7.2** | 0.23 | 4.8 | 0.02 | **4.2** | 1.3 | 0.74 | 4.42 | 3.65 | 71.6 | **0.9** | 22.1 | 39.8 | **5.7** |
| **4.0** | 1.31 | 8.0 | 0.31 | **3.1** | 0.5 | 0.54 | 5.22 | 4.58 | 82.1 | **0.8** | 17.3 | 41.4 | **4.4** |
| **7.6** | 0.00 | 0.5 | 0.03 | **10.0** | 1.4 | 2.64 | 25.10 | 5.32 | 53.6 | **2.0** | 6.7 | 18.0 | **7.0** |
| **3.5** | 1.23 | 8.0 | 0.27 | **1.4** | 0.3 | 0.19 | 1.46 | 3.44 | 92.6 | **0.8** | 13.1 | 34.2 | **5.0** |
| **7.7** | 0.66 | 2.0 | 0.26 | **7.4** | 2.4 | 1.61 | 13.53 | 4.54 | 65.3 | **0.7** | 14.9 | 36.3 | **8.9** |
| **7.1** | 0.47 | 2.0 | 0.06 | **0.0** | -0.9 | -0.29 | -1.51 | 3.41 | 106.8 | **1.5** | 23.2 | 27.2 | **4.8** |
| **9.2** | 0.59 | 0.4 | 0.00 | **5.1** | 0.9 | 1.29 | 11.02 | 3.23 | 58.5 | **4.2** | 60.9 | 17.3 | **6.9** |
| **8.4** | 0.36 | 1.3 | 0.01 | **6.3** | 9.0 | 1.63 | 20.27 | 3.42 | 59.2 | **4.1** | 23.1 | 8.8 | **6.4** |
| **5.3** | 2.73 | 9.8 | 0.00 | **4.0** | 1.0 | 0.86 | 7.47 | 3.82 | 79.3 | **4.6** | 49.0 | 14.4 | **7.0** |
| **4.4** | 1.12 | 7.8 | 0.22 | **4.7** | 4.6 | 0.91 | 9.56 | 3.60 | 60.9 | **0.6** | 6.7 | 43.4 | **6.5** |
| **4.3** | 1.13 | 4.0 | 0.05 | **6.1** | 255.0 | 1.28 | 8.80 | 3.61 | 61.0 | **4.4** | 20.7 | 7.0 | **10.0** |
| **6.4** | 0.38 | 2.9 | 0.04 | **5.1** | 16.8 | 1.04 | 10.12 | 3.33 | 63.6 | **3.2** | 11.6 | 11.6 | **8.3** |
| **4.6** | 0.92 | 6.2 | 0.10 | **3.6** | 7.8 | 0.75 | 7.66 | 3.63 | 79.3 | **3.0** | 16.5 | 14.4 | **7.3** |
| **10.0** | na | 0.0 | na | **9.8** | 0.7 | 10.25 | 10.87 | 2.12 | 83.2 | **4.0** | na | 0.0 | **5.0** |
| **6.0** | 0.84 | 5.0 | 0.04 | **9.0** | 46.6 | 1.79 | 13.74 | 4.15 | 55.8 | **3.7** | 9.4 | 9.9 | **10.0** |
| **8.4** | 1.03 | 3.3 | 0.00 | **4.6** | 0.5 | 1.17 | 7.92 | 3.18 | 64.3 | **3.6** | 41.9 | 17.4 | **6.9** |
| **8.8** | 0.51 | 2.8 | 0.00 | **3.5** | 3.9 | 0.56 | 3.81 | 3.56 | 79.3 | **1.5** | 11.1 | 22.9 | **8.4** |
| **4.5** | 1.17 | 7.0 | -0.44 | **1.9** | 0.2 | 0.34 | 3.52 | 4.74 | 94.8 | **4.3** | 28.4 | 9.4 | **4.0** |
| **7.9** | 0.00 | 0.0 | 0.05 | **5.2** | 1.3 | 1.20 | 10.38 | 4.04 | 69.9 | **1.4** | 18.6 | 27.1 | **7.0** |
| **3.7** | 0.59 | 3.3 | 3.58 | **3.2** | 0.6 | 0.54 | 3.95 | 7.31 | 87.3 | **0.8** | 7.9 | 17.2 | **5.6** |
| **7.1** | 0.15 | 0.4 | 0.01 | **0.8** | -5.5 | -2.27 | -6.60 | 2.80 | 158.0 | **4.1** | 37.6 | 13.9 | **7.3** |
| **4.5** | 1.49 | 8.7 | 0.52 | **3.2** | 0.9 | 0.65 | 6.34 | 4.46 | 78.5 | **1.6** | 23.8 | 25.8 | **5.6** |
| **5.1** | 1.26 | 5.0 | -0.13 | **4.9** | 1.3 | 1.17 | 8.90 | 3.57 | 76.7 | **2.0** | 42.2 | 45.0 | **8.1** |
| **3.1** | 1.23 | 11.1 | -0.02 | **0.5** | -0.6 | -0.10 | -1.42 | 1.79 | 121.2 | **0.7** | 16.4 | 51.6 | **3.2** |
| **6.9** | 1.33 | 4.3 | -0.03 | **5.9** | 2.9 | 1.23 | 8.81 | 3.98 | 66.1 | **3.3** | 25.3 | 11.3 | **7.8** |
| **7.1** | 0.16 | 0.6 | 0.07 | **8.6** | 17.5 | 1.58 | 13.09 | 4.19 | 56.6 | **0.8** | 14.0 | 33.3 | **9.6** |
| **6.3** | 0.45 | 3.9 | 0.08 | **6.8** | 13.7 | 1.38 | 10.96 | 4.52 | 68.0 | **1.8** | 13.1 | 16.7 | **9.0** |
| **3.3** | 1.65 | 9.9 | 0.18 | **2.0** | -0.3 | -0.22 | -2.28 | 3.20 | 111.2 | **1.7** | 17.1 | 22.2 | **6.0** |
| **8.6** | 0.11 | 0.1 | 0.00 | **9.8** | 295.5 | 2.83 | 21.13 | 2.88 | 30.0 | **8.5** | 98.5 | 0.0 | **10.0** |
| **4.7** | 2.38 | 6.9 | -0.23 | **3.3** | 0.5 | 0.79 | 7.75 | 4.02 | 83.8 | **1.0** | 26.8 | 54.4 | **3.0** |
| **5.4** | 0.10 | 0.5 | 0.16 | **4.4** | 61.8 | 0.80 | 5.80 | 2.91 | 68.4 | **3.9** | 20.1 | 10.4 | **7.8** |
| **5.4** | 1.01 | 4.8 | 0.07 | **4.6** | 11.3 | 0.96 | 11.18 | 3.92 | 66.8 | **4.4** | 13.2 | 5.9 | **7.1** |
| **6.4** | 0.99 | 8.2 | 0.45 | **5.5** | 3.4 | 1.38 | 12.06 | 3.79 | 65.2 | **4.1** | 39.1 | 14.0 | **7.8** |
| **6.9** | 0.22 | 1.1 | 0.00 | **9.7** | 10.0 | 1.94 | 13.87 | 4.00 | 43.7 | **3.9** | 15.1 | 8.0 | **9.4** |
| **5.7** | 0.98 | 4.0 | -0.07 | **5.4** | 3.8 | 1.09 | 9.67 | 4.47 | 72.1 | **4.8** | 14.2 | 3.4 | **6.3** |
| **0.9** | 3.12 | 20.7 | 1.63 | **5.3** | 56.1 | 0.78 | 5.54 | 5.42 | 56.3 | **1.8** | 17.9 | 18.8 | **8.3** |
| **5.8** | 0.80 | 5.3 | 0.15 | **5.1** | 54.7 | 1.08 | 9.96 | 3.66 | 63.0 | **2.1** | 11.3 | 14.6 | **8.3** |
| **8.3** | 1.77 | 2.3 | -0.03 | **4.8** | 0.3 | 1.22 | 7.87 | 3.00 | 60.6 | **3.5** | 63.7 | 19.1 | **8.2** |
| **6.8** | 0.70 | 5.2 | 0.02 | **4.3** | 21.5 | 0.97 | 9.96 | 3.52 | 77.1 | **3.2** | 18.1 | 12.6 | **8.2** |
| **8.1** | 0.27 | 1.0 | -0.01 | **4.8** | 2.7 | 1.04 | 9.82 | 4.10 | 66.7 | **3.3** | 20.1 | 12.8 | **6.4** |
| **6.2** | 0.89 | 5.2 | -0.01 | **5.0** | 1.3 | 1.21 | 12.33 | 3.67 | 69.7 | **6.1** | 45.4 | 4.8 | **6.2** |
| **6.3** | 0.96 | 4.7 | 0.12 | **4.1** | 2.0 | 0.67 | 4.37 | 3.61 | 71.2 | **1.4** | 14.2 | 26.1 | **7.3** |
| **8.9** | 0.00 | 0.0 | 0.06 | **6.1** | 1.1 | 1.33 | 6.21 | 3.89 | 55.2 | **2.6** | 25.3 | 17.0 | **8.2** |
| **5.9** | 0.72 | 4.9 | 0.12 | **3.4** | 0.5 | 0.67 | 5.78 | 4.02 | 83.7 | **1.7** | 16.3 | 21.1 | **5.6** |
| **6.0** | 0.33 | 2.6 | 0.11 | **4.7** | 2.1 | 0.89 | 9.30 | 3.90 | 71.9 | **3.3** | 27.4 | 14.3 | **6.2** |
| **4.8** | 1.21 | 12.1 | 0.41 | **3.2** | 0.3 | 0.45 | 6.72 | 4.31 | 82.0 | **1.4** | 20.4 | 28.3 | **2.4** |
| **4.8** | 1.57 | 6.4 | -0.05 | **5.6** | 5.4 | 1.15 | 12.19 | 4.16 | 68.5 | **4.6** | 24.7 | 6.2 | **6.0** |
| **3.8** | 0.98 | 5.5 | -0.04 | **4.9** | 7.2 | 1.24 | 12.57 | 4.28 | 71.3 | **2.8** | 23.2 | 14.3 | **6.6** |
| **6.7** | 0.28 | 3.8 | 0.09 | **4.7** | 1.5 | 0.91 | 8.89 | 3.69 | 65.8 | **1.0** | 21.9 | 34.8 | **6.1** |
| **9.0** | 0.00 | 0.1 | -0.03 | **4.6** | 2.7 | 1.10 | 10.62 | 3.57 | 69.4 | **3.0** | 12.8 | 13.8 | **5.7** |
| **7.2** | 1.29 | 6.3 | 0.01 | **3.0** | 1.1 | 0.45 | 3.20 | 2.78 | 80.7 | **1.5** | 7.8 | 22.4 | **7.4** |
| **7.6** | 1.64 | 3.1 | -0.19 | **6.0** | 3.9 | 1.47 | 13.26 | 4.38 | 72.4 | **6.3** | 52.2 | 5.3 | **7.4** |
| **7.5** | 0.00 | 0.0 | 0.00 | **5.0** | 2.3 | 0.83 | 6.13 | 2.98 | 66.3 | **0.6** | 19.0 | 65.4 | **8.6** |
| **7.2** | 0.22 | 1.3 | 0.22 | **8.7** | 24.7 | 1.44 | 11.28 | 4.11 | 51.8 | **0.7** | 10.8 | 39.2 | **10.0** |
| **9.2** | 0.00 | 0.0 | -0.01 | **6.7** | 11.9 | 1.39 | 14.43 | 2.30 | 70.6 | **5.2** | 25.0 | 2.0 | **7.9** |

| Name | City | State | Rating | 2018 Rating | 2017 Rating | Total Assets ($Mil) | One Year Asset Growth | Asset Mix (As a % of Total Assets) Commercial Loans | Consumer Loans | Mortgage Loans | Securities | Capitalization Index | Leverage Ratio | Risk-Based Capital Ratio |
|---|---|---|---|---|---|---|---|---|---|---|---|---|---|---|
| Pacific Crest Savings Bank | Lynnwood | WA | **B+** | B- | B | 244.8 | 10.58 | 0.0 | 0.1 | 18.1 | 8.5 | **10.0** | 11.4 | 18.0 |
| Pacific Enterprise Bank | Irvine | CA | **B** | B+ | B+ | 488.2 | -2.40 | 14.9 | 0.0 | 3.6 | 0.0 | **10.0** | 11.0 | 15.2 |
| Pacific Mercantile Bank | Costa Mesa | CA | **B-** | B | C | 1415.0 | 4.88 | 28.8 | 6.6 | 2.6 | 2.0 | **8.6** | 11.0 | 13.8 |
| Pacific National Bank | Miami | FL | **B-** | B- | B | 623.0 | 34.86 | 7.7 | 0.2 | 13.2 | 16.6 | **10.0** | 11.8 | 17.0 |
| Pacific Premier Bank | Irvine | CA | **A-** | A- | A- | 11778.1 | 2.54 | 14.6 | 0.4 | 2.1 | 12.0 | **8.6** | 12.4 | 13.8 |
| ▲ Pacific Valley Bank | Salinas | CA | **B** | C+ | B- | 351.0 | 9.46 | 9.2 | 0.5 | 3.8 | 0.0 | **9.2** | 10.7 | 14.4 |
| Pacific West Bank | West Linn | OR | **C** | C+ | C+ | 125.4 | 35.73 | 7.2 | 0.1 | 10.9 | 8.3 | **10.0** | 27.9 | 36.6 |
| Pacific Western Bank | Beverly Hills | CA | **B+** | B | B- | 26732.4 | 4.01 | 15.6 | 1.6 | 0.4 | 14.2 | **6.0** | 11.0 | 11.7 |
| Paducah Bank and Trust Co. | Paducah | KY | **A-** | A | A | 715.0 | 10.07 | 11.8 | 1.3 | 22.2 | 14.4 | **9.9** | 10.9 | 14.9 |
| ▲ Palmetto State Bank | Hampton | SC | **A** | B+ | A | 547.1 | 0.18 | 4.6 | 2.7 | 8.3 | 54.9 | **10.0** | 12.8 | 21.9 |
| Palo Savings Bank | Palo | IA | **B** | B+ | A- | 39.5 | 20.24 | 1.7 | 3.0 | 26.6 | 29.5 | **10.0** | 11.9 | 27.9 |
| Pan American Bank & Trust | Melrose Park | IL | **C** | C | C | 367.1 | 3.15 | 7.1 | 0.2 | 20.6 | 13.5 | **7.2** | 9.3 | 12.7 |
| Panola National Bank | Carthage | TX | **B-** | B- | C+ | 113.4 | 0.17 | 3.0 | 5.6 | 30.2 | 41.6 | **10.0** | 11.1 | 25.0 |
| Paper City Savings Assn. | Wisconsin Rapids | WI | **B+** | B | B | 168.6 | 9.89 | 0.0 | 2.7 | 52.2 | 0.5 | **10.0** | 14.1 | 20.6 |
| Paradise Bank | Boca Raton | FL | **A** | A | A | 333.1 | 11.21 | 8.1 | 0.4 | 11.7 | 10.4 | **9.2** | 10.4 | 16.7 |
| ▲ Paragon Bank | Memphis | TN | **B** | B- | C+ | 404.2 | 0.69 | 16.4 | 4.1 | 17.8 | 12.4 | **10.0** | 11.1 | 15.4 |
| ▲ Paramount Bank | Saint Louis | MO | **C-** | C- | D- | 104.3 | 189.02 | 1.3 | 2.7 | 62.4 | 0.0 | **6.9** | 8.9 | 18.7 |
| Park Bank | Holmen | WI | **B-** | B- | B- | 58.4 | 5.03 | 6.2 | 4.0 | 24.3 | 21.7 | **10.0** | 15.8 | 27.3 |
| ▲ Park Bank | Madison | WI | **B-** | B- | B- | 1065.0 | 9.44 | 11.9 | 0.6 | 16.5 | 9.5 | **7.4** | 10.9 | 12.8 |
| ▲ Park Bank | Milwaukee | WI | **A-** | A- | A- | 1128.7 | 12.04 | 24.4 | 0.8 | 1.1 | 12.4 | **9.9** | 11.1 | 14.9 |
| Park National Bank | Newark | OH | **C+** | C+ | C+ | 8528.9 | 10.00 | 9.6 | 16.7 | 17.9 | 14.2 | **6.6** | 8.6 | 12.3 |
| ▲ Park Ridge Community Bank | Park Ridge | IL | **A** | A- | A | 313.6 | 0.68 | 1.7 | 0.0 | 12.1 | 22.3 | **10.0** | 14.5 | 21.6 |
| ▲ Park State Bank | Duluth | MN | **B** | B- | B | 142.4 | 4.29 | 25.8 | 2.3 | 24.3 | 2.2 | **10.0** | 11.2 | 15.2 |
| Park State Bank & Trust | Woodland Park | CO | **B-** | C+ | C+ | 102.7 | 2.54 | 1.0 | 1.1 | 24.0 | 10.3 | **9.7** | 10.8 | 15.2 |
| ▲ Parke Bank | Sewell | NJ | **A** | A- | B- | 1680.8 | 14.57 | 1.5 | 0.8 | 37.7 | 1.7 | **10.0** | 11.9 | 16.7 |
| Parkside Financial Bank & Trust | Clayton | MO | **B+** | B | B | 589.5 | 15.82 | 36.6 | 0.1 | 2.5 | 5.7 | **7.6** | 10.5 | 13.0 |
| Parkway Bank and Trust Co. | Harwood Heights | IL | **B-** | B- | B | 2638.6 | -2.44 | 9.8 | 0.1 | 1.6 | 8.7 | **9.3** | 11.8 | 14.4 |
| Partners Bank | Helena | AR | **C+** | C+ | B- | 206.4 | 26.10 | 19.3 | 0.8 | 4.9 | 24.9 | **10.0** | 13.3 | 17.6 |
| Partners Bank | Spencer | WI | **B+** | B | B | 215.9 | -0.26 | 12.5 | 2.0 | 15.9 | 23.2 | **10.0** | 13.8 | 19.9 |
| Partners Bank of California | Mission Viejo | CA | **B** | B | B- | 307.8 | 19.34 | 12.5 | 0.0 | 8.8 | 1.8 | **9.6** | 11.7 | 14.6 |
| ▲ Partners Bank of New England | Sanford | ME | **B+** | B- | B- | 618.6 | 6.55 | 5.8 | 0.7 | 39.6 | 1.8 | **10.0** | 12.6 | 17.1 |
| Passumpsic Bank | Saint Johnsbury | VT | **C** | C- | C- | 658.4 | 1.21 | 4.3 | 10.9 | 38.1 | 6.3 | **10.0** | 11.1 | 16.4 |
| Pataskala Banking Co. | Pataskala | OH | **D** | D | D | 35.0 | 6.97 | 3.3 | 4.8 | 24.5 | 17.9 | **5.5** | 7.5 | 14.2 |
| Pathfinder Bank | Oswego | NY | **U** | U | | 1090.0 | 17.14 | 14.0 | 7.5 | 23.2 | 21.6 | **6.2** | 8.2 | 12.3 |
| Pathway Bank | Cairo | NE | **C-** | C- | C+ | 170.5 | 2.46 | 6.2 | 1.3 | 4.8 | 9.6 | **8.0** | 10.8 | 13.4 |
| Patriot Bank | Millington | TN | **B** | B | B | 364.6 | 8.62 | 2.8 | 1.8 | 10.3 | 44.4 | **7.0** | 9.0 | 13.4 |
| Patriot Bank, N.A. | Stamford | CT | **D+** | D+ | C+ | 981.1 | 3.07 | 17.7 | 5.7 | 20.2 | 4.9 | **6.1** | 9.4 | 11.8 |
| Patriot Community Bank | Woburn | MA | **B+** | B+ | B+ | 180.2 | 3.97 | 3.7 | 0.0 | 15.5 | 0.0 | **10.0** | 14.3 | 22.5 |
| ▲ Patriots Bank | Garnett | KS | **B** | C+ | C+ | 127.6 | 3.98 | 5.7 | 2.4 | 15.7 | 14.7 | **8.7** | 10.2 | 13.9 |
| ▼ Patterson State Bank | Patterson | LA | **B-** | B | B | 272.5 | 0.15 | 3.4 | 1.8 | 35.4 | 20.9 | **8.5** | 10.0 | 18.5 |
| Pauls Valley National Bank | Pauls Valley | OK | **B-** | C+ | B- | 244.0 | 0.94 | 16.5 | 10.1 | 4.6 | 28.4 | **9.7** | 10.8 | 15.7 |
| Pavillion Bank | Richardson | TX | **B** | B | B | 74.2 | -3.13 | 7.2 | 1.3 | 19.7 | 12.4 | **10.0** | 13.6 | 20.2 |
| Payne County Bank | Perkins | OK | **A** | A | A | 180.2 | 8.94 | 8.8 | 6.0 | 23.2 | 24.2 | **10.0** | 18.3 | 28.0 |
| PBK Bank, Inc. | Stanford | KY | **B+** | B+ | B+ | 118.6 | 1.62 | 3.1 | 5.6 | 24.5 | 7.3 | **10.0** | 13.5 | 21.8 |
| PCSB Bank | Clarinda | IA | **C+** | B- | B- | 260.5 | 7.08 | 9.2 | 3.5 | 8.3 | 20.7 | **9.2** | 10.5 | 15.0 |
| PCSB Bank | Yorktown Heights | NY | **B-** | B- | C+ | 1646.4 | 5.89 | 4.5 | 0.0 | 16.0 | 20.4 | **10.0** | 13.0 | 17.7 |
| Peach State Bank & Trust | Gainesville | GA | **B+** | B | B- | 266.3 | 19.53 | 9.2 | 3.1 | 14.1 | 12.8 | **9.7** | 10.8 | 16.2 |
| Peapack-Gladstone Bank | Bedminster | NJ | **B+** | B+ | B | 5178.0 | 12.22 | 16.5 | 0.8 | 11.4 | 7.6 | **8.5** | 10.6 | 13.8 |
| Pearland State Bank | Pearland | TX | **A-** | B+ | B+ | 193.5 | 3.39 | 3.0 | 0.6 | 4.0 | 67.5 | **10.0** | 11.9 | 33.0 |
| Pecos County State Bank | Fort Stockton | TX | **B** | B | B | 268.7 | 4.38 | 5.4 | 4.5 | 9.3 | 52.6 | **6.7** | 8.7 | 20.9 |
| Pedestal Bank | Houma | LA | **A-** | B | B | 1243.6 | 1.68 | 19.3 | 2.4 | 15.0 | 21.7 | **10.0** | 11.7 | 16.9 |
| ▲ Pee Dee Federal Savings Bank | Marion | SC | **C** | D+ | D | 34.7 | -4.23 | 11.7 | 6.3 | 6.5 | 50.1 | **10.0** | 18.5 | 45.6 |
| ▲ Pegasus Bank | Dallas | TX | **A-** | B- | B- | 742.7 | 16.21 | 23.1 | 3.2 | 9.5 | 4.5 | **6.6** | 8.6 | 14.2 |
| Pendleton Community Bank, Inc. | Franklin | WV | **B** | B | B+ | 442.2 | 43.77 | 8.0 | 4.3 | 26.6 | 15.3 | **6.9** | 8.9 | 13.5 |
| Penn Community Bank | Doylestown | PA | **B-** | B- | B- | 2340.1 | 8.40 | 3.4 | 0.2 | 34.9 | 21.3 | **10.0** | 12.1 | 17.0 |
| PennCrest BANK | Altoona | PA | **B-** | B- | B- | 183.3 | 0.33 | 0.2 | 7.6 | 54.0 | 22.2 | **10.0** | 16.1 | 28.6 |
| Pennian Bank | Mifflintown | PA | **B-** | B | B- | 541.8 | 6.08 | 9.4 | 0.3 | 22.7 | 26.0 | **8.1** | 9.7 | 17.9 |
| Pennsville National Bank | Pennsville | NJ | **C** | C | C | 200.4 | 0.22 | 1.7 | 1.0 | 16.6 | 64.3 | **6.9** | 8.9 | 17.6 |
| Pentucket Bank | Haverhill | MA | **B-** | C+ | C+ | 808.8 | 7.30 | 9.6 | 0.2 | 39.9 | 9.9 | **10.0** | 12.1 | 16.0 |
| ▲ People's B&T Co. of Clinton County | Albany | KY | **B-** | C | C | 41.5 | 8.17 | 11.8 | 23.3 | 27.7 | 1.7 | **8.3** | 9.8 | 14.0 |

| Asset Quality Index | Adjusted Non-Performing Loans as a % of Total Loans | Adjusted Non-Performing Loans as a % of Capital | Net Charge-Offs Avg Loans | Profitability Index | Net Income ($Mil) | Return on Assets (R.O.A.) | Return on Equity (R.O.E.) | Net Interest Spread | Overhead Efficiency Ratio | Liquidity Index | Liquidity Ratio | Hot Money Ratio | Stability Index |
|---|---|---|---|---|---|---|---|---|---|---|---|---|---|
| **5.7** | 1.47 | 7.6 | 0.01 | **5.6** | 3.1 | 1.36 | 11.76 | 3.34 | 57.9 | **1.6** | 34.3 | 30.8 | **7.6** |
| **7.2** | 0.30 | 2.1 | 0.02 | **4.4** | 3.4 | 0.70 | 6.59 | 5.20 | 81.2 | **0.8** | 21.9 | 39.6 | **7.1** |
| **4.9** | 1.39 | 9.0 | 0.82 | **3.5** | 7.4 | 0.52 | 4.72 | 3.66 | 65.2 | **1.9** | 19.3 | 21.0 | **8.3** |
| **8.7** | 0.00 | 0.0 | 0.00 | **2.9** | 2.1 | 0.40 | 3.11 | 2.95 | 77.9 | **1.3** | 29.7 | 37.5 | **7.5** |
| **5.8** | 0.13 | 0.5 | 0.09 | **8.0** | 171.6 | 1.49 | 7.98 | 4.52 | 52.0 | **3.9** | 16.9 | 8.9 | **9.9** |
| **5.3** | 0.39 | 2.5 | -0.01 | **4.7** | 2.7 | 0.84 | 7.81 | 3.92 | 69.6 | **3.8** | 23.9 | 10.6 | **7.1** |
| **8.9** | 0.08 | 0.2 | 0.00 | **0.1** | -0.9 | -0.91 | -2.64 | 3.91 | 125.2 | **4.0** | 45.2 | 16.2 | **6.9** |
| **6.1** | 0.55 | 1.5 | 0.09 | **10.0** | 488.3 | 1.88 | 9.52 | 4.68 | 42.6 | **3.1** | 18.4 | 5.5 | **10.0** |
| **6.4** | 0.51 | 2.8 | 0.15 | **6.5** | 10.8 | 1.57 | 13.66 | 3.64 | 63.2 | **1.3** | 11.7 | 11.6 | **9.1** |
| **7.7** | 1.80 | 3.7 | 0.84 | **6.9** | 7.5 | 1.35 | 8.33 | 3.42 | 52.2 | **5.7** | 57.3 | 10.9 | **9.4** |
| **8.5** | 0.34 | 3.6 | 0.00 | **4.3** | 0.3 | 0.81 | 6.43 | 3.42 | 73.0 | **2.9** | 51.3 | 27.0 | **7.9** |
| **6.4** | 0.19 | 1.3 | 0.23 | **3.2** | 2.8 | 0.75 | 8.32 | 3.60 | 81.3 | **0.9** | 20.3 | 33.6 | **5.3** |
| **8.9** | 0.83 | 2.1 | 0.06 | **3.8** | 0.8 | 0.72 | 6.55 | 3.56 | 82.6 | **5.2** | 49.5 | 11.2 | **6.6** |
| **6.4** | 1.42 | 6.1 | 0.08 | **5.0** | 1.7 | 1.01 | 7.10 | 3.39 | 66.8 | **1.6** | 15.6 | 22.8 | **7.7** |
| **7.6** | 0.00 | 0.2 | 0.38 | **9.4** | 6.8 | 2.11 | 19.19 | 4.89 | 62.1 | **5.2** | 34.5 | 6.2 | **7.8** |
| **8.0** | 1.73 | 1.5 | 0.48 | **4.4** | 3.2 | 0.78 | 7.21 | 3.65 | 73.5 | **1.7** | 15.1 | 10.2 | **6.8** |
| **8.8** | 0.00 | 0.0 | 0.00 | **2.5** | 0.3 | 0.36 | 3.03 | 2.02 | 96.9 | **0.4** | 10.6 | 40.1 | **5.2** |
| **5.9** | 7.32 | 7.4 | 0.62 | **4.3** | 0.4 | 0.77 | 4.82 | 4.89 | 78.5 | **5.0** | 19.3 | 2.7 | **5.9** |
| **4.6** | 1.56 | 11.1 | 0.00 | **5.1** | 10.0 | 0.98 | 9.34 | 3.48 | 65.4 | **4.5** | 12.4 | 4.8 | **9.3** |
| **7.0** | 0.63 | 3.6 | 0.47 | **8.1** | 18.5 | 1.85 | 16.36 | 3.62 | 49.7 | **5.1** | 38.7 | 11.8 | **9.5** |
| **3.4** | 1.69 | 10.7 | 0.04 | **6.8** | 113.6 | 1.35 | 13.77 | 3.84 | 61.7 | **3.9** | 10.2 | 8.4 | **8.8** |
| **7.9** | 0.28 | 1.2 | 0.00 | **9.7** | 7.5 | 2.37 | 16.66 | 4.26 | 41.1 | **3.6** | 21.7 | 11.6 | **9.9** |
| **7.5** | 0.18 | 1.2 | 0.00 | **9.9** | 2.6 | 1.90 | 14.54 | 5.57 | 54.0 | **2.7** | 11.1 | 14.9 | **6.3** |
| **4.2** | 2.45 | 12.3 | 0.00 | **5.1** | 1.2 | 1.16 | 11.45 | 4.85 | 79.9 | **5.4** | 27.4 | 2.1 | **6.0** |
| **6.5** | 1.56 | 5.9 | 0.00 | **9.8** | 30.7 | 2.00 | 17.46 | 3.79 | 28.8 | **0.8** | 14.7 | 37.0 | **10.0** |
| **6.9** | 0.63 | 3.9 | 0.74 | **8.0** | 7.8 | 1.53 | 14.17 | 3.69 | 53.0 | **1.8** | 22.9 | 5.7 | **7.6** |
| **3.5** | 3.34 | 13.5 | 0.03 | **6.0** | 29.4 | 1.13 | 9.82 | 2.93 | 50.7 | **1.1** | 14.6 | 25.4 | **9.4** |
| **8.6** | 0.26 | 1.0 | 0.03 | **3.1** | 1.0 | 0.52 | 3.69 | 3.85 | 87.4 | **1.1** | 8.7 | 28.6 | **6.6** |
| **6.7** | 1.45 | 5.6 | 0.22 | **5.4** | 2.4 | 1.12 | 7.56 | 3.58 | 68.3 | **2.0** | 24.7 | 17.8 | **7.2** |
| **7.0** | 0.24 | 1.6 | -0.03 | **4.8** | 2.1 | 0.80 | 6.76 | 4.26 | 69.1 | **3.8** | 24.6 | 6.3 | **6.7** |
| **8.8** | 0.23 | 1.3 | 0.04 | **5.4** | 6.5 | 1.12 | 9.37 | 3.87 | 79.3 | **2.9** | 11.7 | 11.7 | **7.5** |
| **4.1** | 1.57 | 8.3 | 0.30 | **5.4** | 9.4 | 1.41 | 11.29 | 3.62 | 75.5 | **1.7** | 8.3 | 8.2 | **7.4** |
| **4.7** | 2.43 | 10.6 | 0.01 | **2.9** | 0.1 | 0.41 | 5.50 | 4.58 | 90.4 | **6.2** | 42.6 | 2.8 | **2.3** |
| **6.5** | 0.93 | 6.3 | 0.09 | **3.1** | 5.1 | 0.51 | 6.41 | 3.12 | 75.6 | **0.7** | 14.1 | 35.1 | **6.0** |
| **0.8** | 3.35 | 22.4 | -0.08 | **3.8** | 1.1 | 0.60 | 5.51 | 3.48 | 81.2 | **1.7** | 15.7 | 22.2 | **7.4** |
| **6.6** | 1.04 | 4.3 | 0.09 | **5.1** | 4.1 | 1.16 | 12.07 | 3.15 | 70.2 | **0.6** | 4.9 | 37.1 | **5.7** |
| **1.7** | 2.44 | 22.8 | 0.31 | **1.7** | -0.1 | -0.01 | -0.14 | 3.03 | 88.3 | **0.5** | 9.9 | 26.3 | **6.8** |
| **6.0** | 2.65 | 8.2 | 0.00 | **5.5** | 2.0 | 1.11 | 7.96 | 3.20 | 63.5 | **1.2** | 29.2 | 46.3 | **8.1** |
| **4.8** | 2.64 | 8.7 | 0.01 | **4.9** | 1.4 | 1.09 | 10.95 | 4.45 | 74.4 | **1.7** | 9.0 | 20.0 | **7.0** |
| **5.3** | 1.46 | 9.3 | 0.32 | **3.7** | 1.6 | 0.70 | 6.80 | 3.79 | 77.2 | **3.2** | 26.2 | 14.4 | **5.5** |
| **4.3** | 1.45 | 7.7 | 0.07 | **4.3** | 2.1 | 0.86 | 7.98 | 4.01 | 75.0 | **2.3** | 33.8 | 24.3 | **6.4** |
| **5.4** | 4.09 | 17.9 | 0.04 | **6.4** | 1.0 | 1.32 | 9.85 | 4.88 | 63.1 | **2.2** | 32.5 | 25.1 | **6.6** |
| **8.5** | 0.40 | 1.6 | 0.16 | **7.4** | 3.0 | 1.77 | 9.40 | 4.44 | 60.0 | **2.6** | 34.8 | 20.1 | **9.6** |
| **5.2** | 2.12 | 8.3 | 0.02 | **10.0** | 2.5 | 2.07 | 15.41 | 5.54 | 59.4 | **4.1** | 17.8 | 8.6 | **8.7** |
| **4.6** | 1.58 | 7.3 | 0.50 | **3.3** | 1.4 | 0.58 | 5.44 | 3.27 | 72.5 | **4.7** | 33.9 | 9.0 | **6.0** |
| **7.3** | 0.49 | 1.8 | 0.02 | **3.4** | 8.8 | 0.55 | 4.16 | 2.93 | 72.7 | **1.4** | 16.8 | 21.6 | **8.4** |
| **8.4** | 0.00 | 0.0 | 0.11 | **5.1** | 2.6 | 1.04 | 10.06 | 4.46 | 70.1 | **4.2** | 21.6 | 8.2 | **6.1** |
| **5.0** | 0.71 | 4.9 | -0.03 | **5.5** | 51.9 | 1.08 | 9.26 | 2.69 | 57.9 | **2.3** | 5.1 | 11.4 | **8.9** |
| **9.8** | 0.00 | 1.2 | 0.04 | **6.1** | 3.0 | 1.58 | 13.58 | 2.85 | 48.3 | **3.8** | 70.6 | 26.4 | **7.8** |
| **8.1** | 0.14 | 2.3 | 0.05 | **6.1** | 4.1 | 1.52 | 17.86 | 3.80 | 63.2 | **3.8** | 10.5 | 9.6 | **5.7** |
| **6.2** | 0.48 | 2.9 | 0.28 | **8.1** | 22.4 | 1.80 | 14.23 | 4.55 | 61.6 | **2.2** | 23.3 | 21.8 | **10.0** |
| **7.6** | 2.51 | 3.9 | 0.40 | **2.8** | 0.2 | 0.50 | 2.80 | 4.01 | 86.1 | **5.3** | 83.7 | 15.1 | **5.3** |
| **8.1** | 0.27 | 1.9 | 0.05 | **3.6** | 2.5 | 0.38 | 5.04 | 3.51 | 84.3 | **5.7** | 42.6 | 6.1 | **6.5** |
| **3.4** | 2.70 | 15.0 | 0.09 | **6.3** | 4.3 | 1.22 | 10.17 | 4.42 | 65.2 | **3.1** | 14.0 | 13.3 | **6.0** |
| **8.8** | 0.44 | 1.7 | 0.02 | **3.1** | 10.2 | 0.45 | 3.58 | 2.96 | 79.9 | **2.3** | 19.3 | 14.0 | **8.3** |
| **8.9** | 0.27 | 2.1 | 0.09 | **2.8** | 0.8 | 0.42 | 2.64 | 3.20 | 83.6 | **4.6** | 30.8 | 8.3 | **7.5** |
| **7.4** | 0.33 | 2.1 | 0.09 | **3.5** | 3.6 | 0.69 | 6.90 | 3.09 | 75.1 | **2.4** | 17.9 | 17.1 | **7.1** |
| **5.0** | 1.91 | 5.6 | 0.14 | **3.2** | 1.1 | 0.56 | 6.18 | 2.90 | 78.1 | **7.2** | 66.2 | 3.2 | **4.5** |
| **7.7** | 1.02 | 5.6 | 0.00 | **3.6** | 5.3 | 0.68 | 5.67 | 2.91 | 90.8 | **1.3** | 13.2 | 27.5 | **7.6** |
| **3.1** | 0.85 | 7.7 | 0.17 | **4.7** | 0.3 | 0.83 | 8.56 | 4.95 | 78.3 | **0.6** | 13.1 | 56.2 | **5.1** |

| Name | City | State | Rating | 2018 Rating | 2017 Rating | Total Assets ($Mil) | One Year Asset Growth | Asset Mix (As a % of Total Assets) Commercial Loans | Consumer Loans | Mortgage Loans | Securities | Capitalization Index | Leverage Ratio | Risk-Based Capital Ratio |
|---|---|---|---|---|---|---|---|---|---|---|---|---|---|---|
| ▲ People's B&T Co. of Pickett County | Byrdstown | TN | **B-** | C | C | 124.2 | 5.67 | 17.5 | 10.0 | 23.1 | 10.1 | **10.0** | 12.6 | 19.1 |
| ▲ People's Bank of Commerce | Medford | OR | **B** | B- | B- | 370.2 | 5.90 | 9.2 | 1.2 | 9.5 | 7.5 | **7.2** | 10.4 | 12.7 |
| People's Bank of Seneca | Seneca | MO | **B-** | B- | B- | 238.5 | 22.18 | 18.2 | 1.4 | 29.8 | 5.8 | **6.7** | 9.0 | 12.3 |
| People's United Bank, N.A. | Bridgeport | CT | **B** | B | B- | 58343.5 | 22.57 | 16.3 | 0.9 | 19.4 | 13.0 | **6.5** | 9.3 | 12.1 |
| PeopleFirst Bank | Joliet | IL | **B** | C+ | C+ | 136.2 | -2.27 | 6.7 | 0.1 | 7.1 | 4.4 | **10.0** | 12.9 | 17.5 |
| Peoples B&T Co. of Madison County | Berea | KY | **B** | B | B- | 404.3 | 1.00 | 2.5 | 2.9 | 21.6 | 25.4 | **10.0** | 12.8 | 20.7 |
| Peoples B&T Co. of Pointe Coupee Parish | New Roads | LA | **B** | B- | B+ | 324.4 | 19.31 | 5.0 | 1.5 | 35.8 | 2.0 | **10.0** | 13.4 | 20.3 |
| Peoples Bank | Magnolia | AR | **C+** | C+ | B- | 207.4 | -5.59 | 2.6 | 21.8 | 42.9 | 9.4 | **8.9** | 10.3 | 18.2 |
| Peoples Bank | Sheridan | AR | **A** | A | A | 168.5 | 8.61 | 9.8 | 2.9 | 8.6 | 27.6 | **10.0** | 14.1 | 23.7 |
| ▲ Peoples Bank | Eatonton | GA | **E+** | E | E- | 134.3 | 11.94 | 1.2 | 4.1 | 23.7 | 13.5 | **4.5** | 6.5 | 11.4 |
| Peoples Bank | Lyons | GA | **B-** | B- | C+ | 111.4 | 22.86 | 5.4 | 1.7 | 15.6 | 2.1 | **7.4** | 9.3 | 16.4 |
| Peoples Bank | Willacoochee | GA | **B** | B | B | 75.9 | -1.41 | 3.4 | 4.4 | 14.6 | 19.6 | **10.0** | 14.2 | 23.3 |
| Peoples Bank | Clive | IA | **C-** | C | B- | 341.2 | 2.49 | 4.8 | 1.1 | 12.7 | 21.7 | **5.9** | 8.6 | 11.7 |
| Peoples Bank | Rock Valley | IA | **C** | C- | C- | 638.8 | 9.35 | 10.8 | 1.5 | 4.7 | 6.6 | **8.4** | 11.6 | 13.6 |
| ▲ Peoples Bank | Brownstown | IN | **B-** | C+ | C+ | 203.8 | -3.82 | 2.3 | 5.9 | 20.3 | 51.6 | **9.3** | 10.5 | 23.5 |
| Peoples Bank | Coldwater | KS | **B+** | B | B | 51.8 | 0.09 | 4.9 | 1.4 | 8.6 | 37.4 | **10.0** | 12.7 | 20.2 |
| Peoples Bank | Pratt | KS | **C+** | B- | C+ | 369.3 | 2.45 | 7.0 | 1.3 | 8.5 | 24.3 | **10.0** | 11.9 | 19.3 |
| Peoples Bank | Lebanon | KY | **B-** | B- | B- | 64.6 | 17.94 | 7.7 | 3.7 | 5.7 | 23.7 | **9.1** | 10.6 | 14.2 |
| Peoples Bank | Marion | KY | **D+** | C- | D+ | 73.8 | 17.82 | 35.2 | 5.9 | 7.9 | 4.1 | **4.4** | 8.9 | 10.7 |
| Peoples Bank | Taylorsville | KY | **B+** | B | B+ | 109.8 | 3.08 | 2.3 | 2.6 | 22.8 | 21.7 | **10.0** | 12.3 | 21.4 |
| Peoples Bank | Chatham | LA | **D+** | C- | C- | 89.2 | 0.91 | 14.5 | 8.4 | 26.3 | 2.0 | **7.9** | 10.1 | 13.3 |
| ▲ Peoples Bank | Chestertown | MD | **B-** | B- | C | 249.2 | 1.07 | 3.7 | 0.4 | 33.9 | 6.0 | **9.0** | 10.3 | 16.5 |
| Peoples Bank | Cuba | MO | **B+** | B+ | B+ | 215.1 | 0.51 | 3.4 | 2.8 | 36.2 | 17.3 | **9.5** | 10.6 | 16.5 |
| Peoples Bank | Mendenhall | MS | **C-** | C | C- | 309.3 | 4.03 | 12.1 | 4.1 | 17.3 | 11.1 | **8.5** | 10.0 | 14.6 |
| Peoples Bank | Ripley | MS | **B** | B+ | B+ | 417.0 | 0.72 | 12.3 | 7.2 | 17.1 | 46.7 | **9.2** | 10.5 | 21.6 |
| Peoples Bank | Newton | NC | **A** | A- | A- | 1153.5 | 5.65 | 7.7 | 0.7 | 16.9 | 17.0 | **10.0** | 11.6 | 15.8 |
| Peoples Bank | Gambier | OH | **C** | C | C | 59.2 | 9.43 | 2.8 | 4.0 | 41.7 | 20.7 | **8.2** | 9.8 | 19.4 |
| Peoples Bank | Marietta | OH | **B** | B | B- | 4352.7 | 9.19 | 14.3 | 11.3 | 15.4 | 22.2 | **8.1** | 9.8 | 14.6 |
| Peoples Bank | Tulsa | OK | **B** | B- | B- | 96.1 | -12.07 | 23.1 | 7.2 | 14.6 | 0.0 | **10.0** | 13.1 | 15.9 |
| Peoples Bank | Iva | SC | **B** | B | B | 296.5 | 7.88 | 2.4 | 2.4 | 16.5 | 30.1 | **10.0** | 12.0 | 19.6 |
| ▲ Peoples Bank | Clifton | TN | **C-** | D+ | C+ | 206.4 | -3.54 | 26.4 | 7.6 | 13.8 | 6.3 | **7.5** | 9.5 | 13.0 |
| Peoples Bank | Sardis | TN | **A-** | B+ | B+ | 89.5 | 0.30 | 3.8 | 4.8 | 27.4 | 11.8 | **8.0** | 9.7 | 14.2 |
| Peoples Bank | Lubbock | TX | **A-** | A- | B+ | 570.8 | 15.12 | 8.8 | 2.4 | 8.1 | 14.8 | **8.7** | 10.1 | 14.4 |
| Peoples Bank | Paris | TX | **B-** | B- | B | 153.5 | -0.26 | 7.0 | 1.0 | 29.2 | 17.7 | **6.9** | 8.9 | 15.9 |
| Peoples Bank | Bellingham | WA | **A-** | A- | B+ | 1979.6 | 14.31 | 4.6 | 7.2 | 8.8 | 5.3 | **10.0** | 11.4 | 15.2 |
| Peoples Bank & Trust | Buford | GA | **B** | B | B- | 336.7 | 6.27 | 3.8 | 0.9 | 10.7 | 34.7 | **9.1** | 10.4 | 19.0 |
| Peoples Bank & Trust | Pana | IL | **C-** | C+ | B | 424.5 | 0.24 | 10.4 | 0.3 | 4.1 | 20.4 | **8.3** | 9.9 | 14.1 |
| ▲ Peoples Bank & Trust Co. | Owenton | KY | **B+** | B | B+ | 52.5 | -3.19 | 3.3 | 2.9 | 34.0 | 14.3 | **10.0** | 14.5 | 22.3 |
| Peoples Bank & Trust Co. | Troy | MO | **B-** | C+ | C+ | 485.3 | 6.12 | 10.8 | 0.5 | 8.5 | 29.1 | **8.4** | 9.9 | 14.3 |
| Peoples Bank & Trust Co. | Ryan | OK | **B-** | B | B | 48.3 | 21.13 | 12.5 | 0.3 | 4.3 | 2.4 | **10.0** | 13.0 | 17.5 |
| Peoples Bank & Trust Co. | Manchester | TN | **A-** | B+ | B- | 100.3 | -0.67 | 7.7 | 5.3 | 31.2 | 11.5 | **10.0** | 12.7 | 19.2 |
| Peoples Bank & Trust Co. of Hazard | Hazard | KY | **E** | E+ | D- | 236.8 | -4.89 | 15.9 | 2.3 | 21.9 | 10.7 | **3.7** | 5.7 | 10.4 |
| Peoples Bank and Trust Co. | McPherson | KS | **B+** | B+ | B+ | 643.7 | 31.97 | 16.5 | 2.6 | 4.6 | 31.2 | **9.2** | 11.8 | 14.3 |
| Peoples Bank Co. | Coldwater | OH | **A** | A- | A | 513.5 | -0.74 | 3.9 | 2.2 | 15.1 | 37.4 | **9.9** | 10.9 | 19.4 |
| Peoples Bank Midwest | Hayward | WI | **B** | B+ | A | 401.8 | 7.51 | 8.3 | 0.3 | 10.7 | 11.4 | **5.3** | 10.1 | 11.2 |
| ▲ Peoples Bank MT. Washington | Mount Washington | KY | **A-** | B | B | 85.7 | 1.45 | 5.5 | 0.3 | 7.1 | 15.3 | **10.0** | 12.7 | 17.9 |
| Peoples Bank of Alabama | Cullman | AL | **B-** | B- | B- | 825.0 | 4.90 | 14.9 | 2.4 | 9.6 | 9.1 | **7.8** | 9.7 | 13.2 |
| Peoples Bank of Altenburg | Altenburg | MO | **B-** | C+ | C+ | 63.5 | 3.74 | 6.4 | 1.8 | 33.4 | 15.1 | **9.3** | 10.5 | 16.1 |
| Peoples Bank of Deer Lodge | Deer Lodge | MT | **C-** | C- | C+ | 37.7 | -1.57 | 10.3 | 4.6 | 15.6 | 24.3 | **6.7** | 8.7 | 15.3 |
| Peoples Bank of East Tennessee | Madisonville | TN | **A-** | B+ | B | 224.8 | 4.13 | 5.2 | 3.6 | 30.7 | 16.1 | **10.0** | 11.2 | 17.0 |
| Peoples Bank of Georgia | Talbotton | GA | **B-** | C+ | C+ | 88.7 | 4.89 | 8.0 | 9.4 | 30.3 | 14.7 | **9.9** | 10.9 | 16.8 |
| Peoples Bank of Graceville | Graceville | FL | **A-** | A- | A- | 99.1 | -0.42 | 2.9 | 1.7 | 13.4 | 48.6 | **10.0** | 11.1 | 40.2 |
| Peoples Bank of Greensboro | Greensboro | AL | **B-** | B- | B- | 91.0 | 5.08 | 7.6 | 8.5 | 13.9 | 34.4 | **7.5** | 9.3 | 15.9 |
| ▲ Peoples Bank of Kankakee County | Bourbonnais | IL | **C+** | C | B- | 230.4 | 14.26 | 5.6 | 3.0 | 9.8 | 40.6 | **6.0** | 8.0 | 14.0 |
| Peoples Bank of Kentucky, Inc. | Flemingsburg | KY | **B** | B- | B | 324.5 | 2.16 | 6.8 | 7.1 | 18.4 | 6.8 | **10.0** | 11.8 | 15.2 |
| Peoples Bank of Macon | Macon | IL | **C+** | C+ | C+ | 20.0 | -1.11 | 10.4 | 6.8 | 5.9 | 45.0 | **10.0** | 13.6 | 31.2 |
| Peoples Bank of Middle Tennessee | Shelbyville | TN | **A-** | A- | B+ | 153.7 | 2.09 | 4.1 | 5.2 | 17.7 | 20.9 | **10.0** | 12.5 | 18.3 |
| Peoples Bank of Moniteau County | Jamestown | MO | **C-** | D+ | D- | 59.4 | 2.40 | 2.6 | 4.2 | 19.8 | 27.6 | **7.2** | 9.1 | 14.1 |
| Peoples Bank of Red Level | Red Level | AL | **C** | C | C | 14.9 | -2.10 | 0.9 | 20.3 | 12.3 | 35.7 | **10.0** | 12.6 | 26.5 |
| Peoples Bank of the South | La Follette | TN | **C** | C | C+ | 153.7 | 4.70 | 1.8 | 1.8 | 35.5 | 0.1 | **10.0** | 13.8 | 20.0 |

| Asset Quality Index | Adjusted Non-Performing Loans as a % of Total Loans | Adjusted Non-Performing Loans as a % of Capital | Net Charge-Offs Avg Loans | Profitability Index | Net Income ($Mil) | Return on Assets (R.O.A.) | Return on Equity (R.O.E.) | Net Interest Spread | Overhead Efficiency Ratio | Liquidity Index | Liquidity Ratio | Hot Money Ratio | Stability Index |
|---|---|---|---|---|---|---|---|---|---|---|---|---|---|
| 3.6 | 3.23 | 15.0 | 0.52 | 6.3 | 1.4 | 1.15 | 8.77 | 5.04 | 64.9 | 0.8 | 18.5 | 38.4 | 6.8 |
| 6.0 | 0.60 | 1.5 | 0.00 | 6.1 | 4.1 | 1.13 | 10.74 | 4.51 | 72.0 | 4.6 | 11.7 | 4.1 | 6.7 |
| 5.1 | 0.88 | 5.2 | 0.26 | 7.5 | 2.9 | 1.37 | 14.59 | 4.49 | 51.7 | 0.6 | 6.0 | 27.0 | 5.3 |
| 4.9 | 0.75 | 3.4 | 0.06 | 5.0 | 543.5 | 1.06 | 7.88 | 3.21 | 61.8 | 2.0 | 9.3 | 10.3 | 10.0 |
| 5.2 | 1.96 | 8.5 | -0.14 | 4.8 | 1.3 | 0.93 | 7.65 | 3.77 | 71.6 | 1.2 | 20.4 | 23.0 | 6.7 |
| 4.8 | 3.24 | 8.5 | 0.13 | 6.6 | 5.9 | 1.47 | 10.24 | 4.11 | 61.5 | 4.1 | 15.7 | 8.3 | 7.9 |
| 5.0 | 2.13 | 10.6 | 0.09 | 9.7 | 5.4 | 1.79 | 13.23 | 4.35 | 49.3 | 0.8 | 17.8 | 37.2 | 9.1 |
| 3.2 | 1.90 | 11.7 | 0.87 | 5.3 | 2.5 | 1.19 | 11.67 | 4.10 | 60.6 | 0.8 | 22.1 | 30.9 | 5.8 |
| 8.8 | 0.07 | 0.2 | 0.09 | 9.3 | 2.8 | 1.77 | 12.23 | 3.97 | 43.3 | 3.9 | 23.6 | 10.2 | 9.3 |
| 1.7 | 5.42 | 38.9 | 0.04 | 3.1 | 0.7 | 0.52 | 8.14 | 4.34 | 86.7 | 4.6 | 27.9 | 7.1 | 1.4 |
| 5.4 | 0.60 | 4.3 | 0.09 | 6.3 | 1.2 | 1.23 | 13.18 | 4.81 | 66.6 | 2.0 | 26.0 | 20.8 | 5.7 |
| 8.4 | 0.76 | 3.1 | 0.00 | 5.0 | 0.9 | 1.18 | 8.86 | 3.72 | 72.6 | 1.7 | 23.7 | 23.5 | 7.6 |
| 2.5 | 2.01 | 9.7 | 0.00 | 3.4 | 2.7 | 0.81 | 6.10 | 3.90 | 75.9 | 1.6 | 16.9 | 23.1 | 3.7 |
| 2.8 | 1.38 | 8.7 | -0.02 | 8.8 | 11.9 | 2.03 | 15.79 | 4.08 | 50.6 | 1.7 | 13.5 | 16.7 | 9.9 |
| 7.5 | 0.47 | 1.7 | 0.03 | 4.0 | 1.9 | 0.88 | 8.36 | 3.21 | 70.9 | 6.3 | 63.0 | 8.5 | 5.5 |
| 8.4 | 0.18 | 0.7 | 0.00 | 3.9 | 0.5 | 0.94 | 6.90 | 3.40 | 72.4 | 1.0 | 23.2 | 24.4 | 7.1 |
| 2.8 | 4.55 | 18.5 | 1.99 | 5.9 | 4.8 | 1.36 | 9.50 | 4.53 | 61.0 | 1.7 | 21.8 | 24.2 | 8.1 |
| 8.5 | 0.00 | 0.0 | 0.01 | 3.9 | 0.4 | 0.71 | 6.92 | 3.81 | 79.2 | 3.5 | 33.2 | 15.0 | 5.3 |
| 3.6 | 1.58 | 12.5 | 0.18 | 4.9 | 0.6 | 0.80 | 8.82 | 4.49 | 73.4 | 0.9 | 10.0 | 32.4 | 4.6 |
| 5.1 | 3.37 | 11.6 | -0.04 | 5.7 | 1.5 | 1.44 | 11.43 | 4.33 | 69.7 | 3.8 | 20.3 | 10.7 | 8.0 |
| 1.3 | 2.62 | 31.2 | 0.30 | 4.2 | 0.7 | 0.75 | 8.03 | 4.06 | 68.5 | 0.3 | 10.0 | 64.5 | 5.0 |
| 4.4 | 2.20 | 11.1 | -0.18 | 5.1 | 2.6 | 1.05 | 9.42 | 3.93 | 80.5 | 4.3 | 20.2 | 7.1 | 6.9 |
| 5.5 | 1.56 | 8.0 | 0.11 | 8.0 | 3.9 | 1.86 | 17.43 | 4.29 | 60.4 | 3.4 | 8.8 | 11.3 | 8.0 |
| 1.7 | 5.05 | 30.1 | 0.44 | 10.0 | 7.9 | 2.54 | 25.65 | 5.37 | 63.1 | 1.1 | 16.3 | 31.1 | 7.5 |
| 7.8 | 0.60 | 2.4 | 1.13 | 4.3 | 3.9 | 0.92 | 8.40 | 3.24 | 63.8 | 2.9 | 45.3 | 25.7 | 6.6 |
| 8.5 | 0.42 | 2.3 | 0.08 | 6.6 | 15.2 | 1.33 | 10.56 | 4.53 | 70.0 | 4.4 | 18.1 | 6.6 | 9.9 |
| 8.8 | 0.22 | 1.4 | 0.04 | 3.2 | 0.3 | 0.53 | 5.14 | 4.13 | 83.7 | 3.0 | 26.0 | 15.5 | 5.0 |
| 4.6 | 0.95 | 4.4 | 0.04 | 6.7 | 58.9 | 1.40 | 10.77 | 3.71 | 64.2 | 2.2 | 13.1 | 11.9 | 9.4 |
| 6.7 | 0.35 | 1.5 | 0.36 | 5.4 | 1.3 | 1.22 | 7.34 | 5.48 | 59.9 | 1.4 | 4.8 | 23.1 | 7.5 |
| 6.5 | 2.01 | 5.7 | 0.02 | 4.7 | 3.1 | 1.07 | 8.31 | 3.58 | 72.7 | 3.4 | 40.3 | 18.0 | 7.3 |
| 2.9 | 1.71 | 7.7 | 0.45 | 4.9 | 1.9 | 0.91 | 10.17 | 4.58 | 64.5 | 0.6 | 12.4 | 35.9 | 5.3 |
| 5.8 | 0.68 | 4.4 | 0.07 | 4.6 | 0.8 | 0.88 | 9.20 | 4.33 | 72.9 | 1.6 | 18.7 | 24.1 | 6.1 |
| 8.2 | 0.09 | 0.5 | 0.01 | 6.9 | 7.5 | 1.42 | 13.35 | 4.12 | 62.4 | 2.4 | 28.6 | 19.2 | 7.3 |
| 7.3 | 0.38 | 2.6 | 0.11 | 6.0 | 2.5 | 1.61 | 19.61 | 3.46 | 71.5 | 1.4 | 14.7 | 13.1 | 6.1 |
| 6.9 | 0.41 | 1.6 | 0.00 | 6.6 | 23.4 | 1.28 | 11.00 | 4.01 | 66.5 | 3.5 | 22.2 | 13.5 | 9.4 |
| 9.2 | 0.08 | 0.3 | -0.19 | 4.8 | 3.3 | 1.01 | 9.79 | 3.71 | 71.4 | 2.6 | 43.6 | 29.1 | 6.4 |
| 1.8 | 3.50 | 21.6 | 1.55 | 6.3 | 5.5 | 1.34 | 13.08 | 4.41 | 51.3 | 2.1 | 28.3 | 18.4 | 7.4 |
| 6.8 | 0.75 | 2.6 | -0.02 | 5.8 | 0.8 | 1.57 | 11.07 | 4.60 | 77.3 | 4.0 | 17.8 | 8.9 | 8.4 |
| 5.1 | 1.73 | 7.1 | -0.16 | 5.2 | 6.1 | 1.33 | 12.83 | 3.58 | 71.8 | 4.4 | 19.1 | 6.4 | 7.1 |
| 3.7 | 3.91 | 20.5 | 0.00 | 6.6 | 0.4 | 0.98 | 7.63 | 4.71 | 77.3 | 1.5 | 35.1 | 51.4 | 8.2 |
| 8.1 | 0.04 | 2.9 | 0.02 | 6.4 | 1.3 | 1.31 | 10.98 | 4.62 | 66.1 | 2.9 | 15.8 | 14.6 | 7.7 |
| 0.3 | 5.95 | 65.5 | 0.89 | 0.2 | -0.3 | -0.11 | -1.73 | 3.49 | 90.7 | 1.4 | 23.7 | 28.2 | 0.9 |
| 6.3 | 0.88 | 2.6 | 0.02 | 5.1 | 6.2 | 1.10 | 8.40 | 3.70 | 66.6 | 2.9 | 14.4 | 14.1 | 8.1 |
| 8.9 | 0.02 | 0.2 | 0.02 | 8.3 | 9.6 | 1.76 | 15.97 | 3.25 | 41.4 | 5.1 | 38.2 | 8.3 | 8.8 |
| 5.8 | 0.03 | 0.1 | -0.01 | 6.4 | 1.9 | 2.09 | 10.83 | 4.09 | 46.2 | 3.2 | 10.4 | 11.7 | 8.2 |
| 6.1 | 2.48 | 6.3 | -0.01 | 6.5 | 1.3 | 1.55 | 12.02 | 4.79 | 72.0 | 5.0 | 28.5 | 5.2 | 8.7 |
| 4.5 | 1.75 | 7.5 | 0.00 | 6.6 | 13.3 | 1.64 | 16.85 | 4.51 | 70.7 | 4.2 | 20.0 | 7.9 | 7.1 |
| 6.9 | 0.41 | 2.5 | -0.40 | 6.7 | 1.1 | 1.75 | 17.28 | 4.09 | 66.5 | 4.3 | 21.1 | 7.5 | 6.3 |
| 3.8 | 1.78 | 14.8 | 0.47 | 4.3 | 0.2 | 0.49 | 5.62 | 4.31 | 69.7 | 5.6 | 33.5 | 3.3 | 4.6 |
| 6.9 | 1.14 | 5.8 | 0.06 | 6.0 | 2.8 | 1.27 | 11.12 | 5.07 | 69.4 | 3.6 | 20.2 | 11.7 | 6.6 |
| 3.9 | 1.32 | 12.3 | 0.43 | 5.0 | 0.8 | 0.94 | 8.83 | 5.51 | 72.9 | 1.3 | 10.5 | 22.9 | 5.7 |
| 8.4 | 1.68 | 3.0 | 0.06 | 5.2 | 1.3 | 1.27 | 10.81 | 2.85 | 57.7 | 4.1 | 63.1 | 18.3 | 7.7 |
| 5.3 | 1.14 | 6.4 | 0.00 | 4.9 | 1.0 | 1.14 | 12.58 | 3.78 | 70.1 | 2.6 | 34.9 | 21.3 | 5.6 |
| 3.5 | 2.80 | 14.1 | 0.00 | 4.1 | 2.0 | 0.96 | 11.47 | 3.11 | 74.7 | 4.5 | 36.5 | 11.2 | 4.0 |
| 4.6 | 1.29 | 8.1 | 0.10 | 5.8 | 3.7 | 1.16 | 9.70 | 4.19 | 63.2 | 1.0 | 6.4 | 30.1 | 7.5 |
| 8.6 | 0.00 | 0.0 | 0.00 | 3.4 | 0.1 | 0.64 | 4.66 | 2.82 | 72.7 | 4.4 | 33.3 | 8.6 | 6.4 |
| 7.5 | 0.56 | 3.0 | 0.10 | 6.4 | 1.7 | 1.14 | 9.53 | 3.88 | 60.2 | 1.0 | 20.0 | 25.5 | 7.8 |
| 2.2 | 3.33 | 18.9 | 0.56 | 2.6 | 0.3 | 0.47 | 5.20 | 3.16 | 76.9 | 4.3 | 35.7 | 11.8 | 3.4 |
| 3.7 | 5.78 | 17.4 | 0.87 | 5.3 | 0.2 | 1.01 | 7.76 | 5.51 | 66.2 | 6.6 | 65.8 | 2.5 | 5.0 |
| 2.7 | 3.31 | 19.3 | -0.19 | 9.3 | 2.9 | 1.94 | 13.97 | 4.83 | 60.8 | 1.3 | 12.5 | 27.3 | 9.7 |

| Name | City | State | Rating | 2018 Rating | 2017 Rating | Total Assets ($Mil) | One Year Asset Growth | Asset Mix (As a % of Total Assets) Commercial Loans | Consumer Loans | Mortgage Loans | Securities | Capitalization Index | Leverage Ratio | Risk-Based Capital Ratio |
|---|---|---|---|---|---|---|---|---|---|---|---|---|---|---|
| ▲ Peoples Bank of Wyaconda | Kahoka | MO | **B+** | B | B | 100.6 | -0.31 | 3.7 | 4.2 | 18.7 | 26.3 | **10.0** | 11.2 | 17.6 |
| Peoples Bank SB | Munster | IN | **B-** | B | B | 1326.5 | 21.28 | 8.0 | 0.8 | 23.6 | 20.9 | **6.3** | 8.3 | 12.5 |
| ▲ Peoples Bank, Biloxi, Mississippi | Biloxi | MS | **C** | C- | C- | 592.0 | -3.57 | 6.3 | 0.8 | 9.2 | 42.1 | **10.0** | 14.7 | 25.5 |
| Peoples Community Bank | Greenville | MO | **A-** | B+ | A- | 489.2 | 4.29 | 3.7 | 6.4 | 35.2 | 21.8 | **10.0** | 17.8 | 25.5 |
| ▲ Peoples Community Bank | Mazomanie | WI | **A-** | B+ | B+ | 300.8 | 6.90 | 3.7 | 1.3 | 8.4 | 21.9 | **10.0** | 11.9 | 19.0 |
| Peoples Community Bank SB | Monticello | IN | **C+** | C- | C+ | 28.9 | 1.93 | 0.3 | 1.5 | 72.1 | 3.5 | **10.0** | 45.2 | 83.5 |
| Peoples Exchange Bank | Monroeville | AL | **B** | B- | B- | 69.9 | 11.07 | 17.1 | 7.1 | 16.4 | 18.6 | **10.0** | 14.7 | 20.3 |
| Peoples Exchange Bank | Winchester | KY | **B** | B- | B- | 416.8 | 5.26 | 3.9 | 1.4 | 30.6 | 4.4 | **7.5** | 9.4 | 14.2 |
| Peoples Federal S&L Assn. | Sidney | OH | **B-** | B- | B- | 115.8 | 3.07 | 2.6 | 1.3 | 47.9 | 7.0 | **10.0** | 13.2 | 25.1 |
| Peoples First Savings Bank | Mason | OH | **C** | B- | C- | 70.8 | 1.04 | 0.0 | 0.3 | 44.6 | 1.3 | **10.0** | 11.4 | 19.2 |
| Peoples Independent Bank | Boaz | AL | **B** | B | B+ | 303.7 | 1.33 | 7.3 | 1.6 | 8.7 | 36.4 | **8.4** | 9.9 | 15.4 |
| Peoples National Bank of Checotah | Checotah | OK | **A-** | A- | B+ | 137.5 | -0.84 | 0.9 | 11.4 | 10.3 | 45.3 | **10.0** | 17.4 | 44.0 |
| Peoples National Bank of Kewanee | Kewanee | IL | **B+** | B+ | A- | 369.3 | 4.84 | 4.0 | 1.3 | 7.1 | 37.3 | **10.0** | 12.7 | 21.7 |
| Peoples National Bank, N.A. | Mount Vernon | IL | **C+** | B- | B- | 1209.7 | -0.01 | 13.9 | 0.4 | 5.4 | 4.3 | **5.5** | 9.6 | 11.4 |
| Peoples S&L Co. | Bucyrus | OH | **C+** | B- | B- | 140.1 | 2.16 | 0.0 | 1.0 | 35.4 | 40.6 | **10.0** | 20.9 | 64.5 |
| Peoples S&L Co. | West Liberty | OH | **B-** | B- | B- | 51.2 | 1.91 | 1.7 | 2.5 | 59.5 | 6.3 | **10.0** | 14.6 | 24.0 |
| Peoples Savings Bank | Crawfordsville | IA | **B** | B- | B- | 35.4 | 1.06 | 9.8 | 1.0 | 9.2 | 49.6 | **9.4** | 10.6 | 14.7 |
| Peoples Savings Bank | Indianola | IA | **B** | B | B | 326.0 | 12.89 | 14.8 | 0.8 | 8.1 | 25.3 | **6.9** | 8.9 | 13.9 |
| Peoples Savings Bank | Montezuma | IA | **B-** | B- | B- | 40.7 | 6.83 | 9.3 | 7.0 | 13.3 | 33.5 | **10.0** | 11.2 | 20.4 |
| Peoples Savings Bank | Wellsburg | IA | **C** | C | C+ | 96.3 | -2.65 | 12.9 | 2.2 | 6.2 | 20.3 | **8.0** | 9.7 | 13.6 |
| Peoples Savings Bank | New Matamoras | OH | **B** | B | B | 62.0 | -4.44 | 3.8 | 4.1 | 28.4 | 50.1 | **10.0** | 12.0 | 36.2 |
| Peoples Savings Bank | Urbana | OH | **C** | C | C | 124.2 | 2.61 | 1.4 | 1.9 | 58.4 | 1.2 | **9.0** | 10.3 | 17.0 |
| Peoples Savings Bank of Rhineland | Rhineland | MO | **B-** | B- | B- | 288.7 | 6.02 | 11.2 | 1.7 | 22.3 | 6.5 | **8.2** | 10.5 | 13.5 |
| Peoples Security Bank and Trust Co. | Scranton | PA | **B+** | B | B | 2477.0 | 8.37 | 13.4 | 4.1 | 14.0 | 13.7 | **7.4** | 10.0 | 12.8 |
| Peoples State Bank | Ellettsville | IN | **B** | B | B+ | 306.7 | 6.78 | 4.4 | 0.9 | 8.2 | 42.7 | **8.8** | 10.2 | 17.1 |
| ▼ Peoples State Bank | Cherryvale | KS | **C-** | C- | C+ | 17.3 | 2.41 | 17.5 | 4.2 | 15.1 | 1.7 | **10.0** | 26.2 | 30.2 |
| ▲ Peoples State Bank | Manhattan | KS | **C+** | C+ | B- | 257.2 | 13.82 | 10.5 | 1.4 | 11.1 | 3.2 | **8.2** | 10.7 | 13.5 |
| Peoples State Bank | Fairmount | ND | **D+** | D+ | D+ | 28.6 | 0.07 | 14.8 | 2.9 | 5.4 | 25.7 | **5.6** | 7.6 | 12.6 |
| Peoples State Bank | Westhope | ND | **B+** | B+ | B+ | 63.3 | -6.71 | 1.4 | 3.1 | 0.4 | 16.8 | **10.0** | 14.5 | 21.6 |
| Peoples State Bank | New Lexington | OH | **B-** | C+ | C+ | 135.9 | 7.52 | 4.0 | 9.8 | 40.5 | 9.2 | **7.9** | 9.6 | 14.4 |
| Peoples State Bank | Blair | OK | **B-** | C+ | C+ | 17.3 | 8.07 | 34.6 | 8.1 | 2.7 | 5.7 | **7.3** | 9.2 | 13.8 |
| Peoples State Bank | Rocksprings | TX | **A-** | B+ | A- | 83.1 | 5.18 | 1.3 | 1.5 | 12.3 | 40.8 | **10.0** | 13.0 | 22.6 |
| Peoples State Bank | Shepherd | TX | **B-** | B- | B- | 130.2 | 5.58 | 3.3 | 3.7 | 5.4 | 41.0 | **8.2** | 9.8 | 22.7 |
| Peoples State Bank | Prairie Du Chien | WI | **C** | C+ | B | 801.2 | 1.89 | 8.4 | 0.6 | 8.2 | 27.0 | **8.9** | 10.2 | 15.9 |
| Peoples State Bank | Wausau | WI | **B+** | B | B | 974.0 | 6.33 | 10.4 | 0.5 | 15.9 | 17.6 | **8.8** | 10.2 | 14.1 |
| Peoples State Bank of Colfax | Colfax | IL | **B+** | B | B | 34.3 | 3.96 | 8.9 | 6.9 | 18.4 | 11.1 | **10.0** | 11.9 | 21.6 |
| Peoples State Bank of Hallettsville | Hallettsville | TX | **B-** | B- | B- | 281.5 | 2.72 | 1.0 | 1.5 | 11.1 | 38.0 | **10.0** | 11.5 | 39.6 |
| Peoples State Bank of Munising | Munising | MI | **A-** | B+ | B+ | 141.6 | -0.92 | 9.6 | 5.8 | 13.6 | 22.7 | **10.0** | 12.0 | 17.2 |
| Peoples State Bank of Newton, Illinois | Newton | IL | **B-** | B- | B+ | 461.8 | 1.22 | 11.6 | 2.1 | 11.7 | 23.4 | **8.6** | 10.2 | 13.9 |
| Peoples State Bank of Plainview | Plainview | MN | **B-** | B- | B | 285.1 | 6.23 | 9.0 | 3.2 | 15.1 | 24.5 | **6.8** | 8.8 | 14.1 |
| Peoples State Bank of Velva | Velva | ND | **C-** | C | C+ | 117.6 | 0.74 | 12.1 | 2.7 | 7.2 | 7.3 | **8.0** | 9.8 | 13.3 |
| ▲ Peoples State Bank of Wells | Wells | MN | **B-** | C | B | 58.3 | 5.01 | 4.5 | 1.5 | 10.2 | 4.9 | **10.0** | 11.0 | 15.1 |
| Peoples Trust & Savings Bank | Boonville | IN | **B** | B | B | 190.0 | 0.46 | 3.4 | 0.8 | 34.3 | 26.9 | **10.0** | 16.0 | 24.0 |
| Peoples Trust and Savings Bank | Riverside | IA | **B** | B- | B- | 27.7 | -5.19 | 3.7 | 0.7 | 12.8 | 39.6 | **10.0** | 12.3 | 17.6 |
| Peoples Trust Co. of St. Albans | Saint Albans | VT | **B** | B- | B- | 267.7 | 0.27 | 3.1 | 2.0 | 25.8 | 19.6 | **10.0** | 12.3 | 19.7 |
| PeoplesBank | Holyoke | MA | **B-** | B- | C+ | 2943.8 | 2.66 | 9.1 | 0.4 | 30.6 | 12.5 | **7.4** | 9.4 | 12.8 |
| PeoplesBank, A Codorus Valley Co. | York | PA | **B+** | B+ | B | 1883.1 | 4.40 | 12.9 | 0.6 | 12.8 | 8.5 | **9.0** | 10.4 | 14.1 |
| PeoplesSouth Bank | Colquitt | GA | **B** | B- | B | 809.0 | -1.53 | 4.0 | 3.4 | 15.1 | 25.3 | **7.8** | 9.5 | 15.0 |
| PeoplesTrust Bank | Hamilton | AL | **B-** | B- | B- | 103.7 | 2.74 | 18.5 | 6.7 | 13.2 | 17.8 | **10.0** | 12.3 | 15.3 |
| Perennial Bank | Darwin | MN | **B** | B- | B- | 107.6 | -0.48 | 3.3 | 4.5 | 12.5 | 38.3 | **7.7** | 9.4 | 25.4 |
| Perpetual Federal Savings Bank | Urbana | OH | **A** | A- | A- | 395.3 | 1.30 | 2.3 | 1.0 | 49.4 | 0.3 | **10.0** | 19.4 | 35.3 |
| Perryton National Bank | Perryton | TX | **A-** | B+ | B+ | 182.4 | 5.80 | 8.6 | 4.6 | 5.2 | 54.6 | **10.0** | 14.0 | 33.8 |
| Persons Banking Co. | Forsyth | GA | **D+** | D | E+ | 316.6 | 2.48 | 3.3 | 1.5 | 15.7 | 20.2 | **4.8** | 6.8 | 11.7 |
| Peru Federal Savings Bank | Peru | IL | **B-** | B- | B- | 152.9 | 3.17 | 3.2 | 1.8 | 33.0 | 33.6 | **10.0** | 14.0 | 28.3 |
| Peshtigo National Bank | Peshtigo | WI | **B-** | B | B+ | 214.6 | 7.10 | 5.7 | 2.0 | 16.4 | 30.7 | **9.9** | 10.9 | 21.0 |
| Petefish, Skiles & Co. | Virginia | IL | **A-** | B+ | A- | 193.8 | 3.43 | 4.1 | 8.5 | 11.6 | 23.4 | **10.0** | 11.7 | 16.3 |
| Petit Jean State Bank | Morrilton | AR | **A-** | B+ | A- | 191.5 | 4.24 | 11.6 | 2.0 | 12.9 | 27.8 | **10.0** | 14.8 | 29.2 |
| Phelps County Bank | Rolla | MO | **B** | B | B | 374.9 | 3.59 | 3.0 | 1.5 | 31.5 | 25.9 | **5.9** | 7.9 | 15.5 |
| ▲ Phenix-Girard Bank | Phenix City | AL | **B+** | B | B | 196.4 | 6.43 | 1.1 | 0.5 | 9.8 | 50.2 | **10.0** | 16.0 | 29.6 |
| Philadelphia Trust Co. | Philadelphia | PA | **B+** | B+ | B+ | 23.4 | 11.38 | 3.1 | 7.4 | 1.9 | 6.4 | **10.0** | 71.8 | 143.8 |

| Asset Quality Index | Adjusted Non-Performing Loans as a % of Total Loans | Adjusted Non-Performing Loans as a % of Capital | Net Charge-Offs Avg Loans | Profitability Index | Net Income ($Mil) | Return on Assets (R.O.A.) | Return on Equity (R.O.E.) | Net Interest Spread | Overhead Efficiency Ratio | Liquidity Index | Liquidity Ratio | Hot Money Ratio | Stability Index |
|---|---|---|---|---|---|---|---|---|---|---|---|---|---|
| **8.5** | 0.00 | 0.4 | 0.00 | **5.1** | 0.9 | 0.96 | 8.96 | 3.51 | 62.4 | **2.0** | 13.6 | 18.8 | **7.1** |
| **5.8** | 0.89 | 5.8 | 0.18 | **4.3** | 11.5 | 0.90 | 9.36 | 3.76 | 71.2 | **3.2** | 21.7 | 14.9 | **7.8** |
| **5.6** | 3.83 | 10.2 | 0.42 | **2.0** | 1.9 | 0.31 | 2.18 | 3.25 | 92.5 | **3.0** | 10.8 | 13.6 | **6.7** |
| **6.7** | 0.80 | 2.9 | 0.16 | **10.0** | 14.8 | 3.02 | 17.28 | 4.91 | 41.0 | **1.9** | 20.4 | 20.8 | **9.6** |
| **6.5** | 1.55 | 3.4 | -0.16 | **5.8** | 3.2 | 1.11 | 8.43 | 3.54 | 66.1 | **3.8** | 17.7 | 10.1 | **7.5** |
| **9.3** | 1.31 | 2.5 | 0.00 | **2.8** | 0.2 | 0.60 | 1.34 | 3.87 | 84.1 | **5.6** | 26.1 | 0.0 | **5.5** |
| **5.8** | 1.24 | 5.1 | 0.06 | **4.8** | 0.7 | 0.98 | 6.67 | 5.18 | 75.2 | **2.9** | 20.1 | 12.3 | **6.9** |
| **7.7** | 0.24 | 2.0 | 0.05 | **4.9** | 4.4 | 1.06 | 11.54 | 3.79 | 71.1 | **1.6** | 13.9 | 22.4 | **6.3** |
| **7.2** | 0.98 | 5.1 | -0.03 | **4.0** | 0.8 | 0.73 | 5.51 | 3.75 | 77.1 | **4.1** | 25.4 | 9.5 | **7.3** |
| **9.3** | 0.00 | 0.0 | 0.06 | **2.5** | 0.3 | 0.38 | 3.45 | 3.30 | 85.7 | **1.4** | 18.7 | 26.3 | **6.5** |
| **8.6** | 0.38 | 1.1 | 0.12 | **5.0** | 4.2 | 1.39 | 12.40 | 4.02 | 71.6 | **5.5** | 46.0 | 8.7 | **6.3** |
| **8.5** | 0.48 | 0.8 | 0.07 | **5.5** | 1.9 | 1.35 | 7.96 | 3.31 | 64.1 | **5.3** | 60.5 | 13.4 | **8.6** |
| **5.6** | 3.78 | 8.5 | 0.05 | **5.3** | 3.3 | 0.93 | 6.35 | 4.57 | 63.8 | **4.8** | 45.9 | 12.4 | **8.0** |
| **4.0** | 2.39 | 16.2 | 0.50 | **4.4** | 11.3 | 0.96 | 10.02 | 4.19 | 71.1 | **2.6** | 6.0 | 15.1 | **8.3** |
| **8.4** | 0.50 | 6.3 | 0.11 | **2.3** | 0.4 | 0.29 | 1.36 | 3.30 | 89.3 | **5.3** | 71.5 | 15.0 | **7.7** |
| **9.2** | 0.00 | 0.0 | -0.02 | **3.1** | 0.2 | 0.38 | 2.57 | 3.71 | 88.0 | **2.9** | 13.9 | 14.2 | **7.2** |
| **9.4** | 0.00 | 0.0 | 0.00 | **5.3** | 0.5 | 1.46 | 14.52 | 3.35 | 60.7 | **6.3** | 61.0 | 5.8 | **6.4** |
| **6.8** | 0.80 | 4.5 | 0.49 | **4.4** | 2.6 | 0.87 | 8.64 | 3.58 | 60.8 | **2.6** | 25.0 | 13.7 | **6.1** |
| **6.6** | 1.48 | 6.0 | 0.52 | **3.7** | 0.3 | 0.64 | 5.43 | 3.79 | 72.8 | **6.1** | 55.9 | 6.5 | **5.6** |
| **2.0** | 3.34 | 19.8 | 0.51 | **3.4** | 0.7 | 0.75 | 7.90 | 3.48 | 76.4 | **1.4** | 24.1 | 28.3 | **4.1** |
| **7.5** | 1.57 | 4.7 | 0.09 | **4.6** | 0.6 | 0.99 | 7.88 | 3.95 | 70.1 | **6.5** | 53.9 | 2.9 | **6.7** |
| **3.2** | 2.32 | 22.6 | 0.05 | **3.2** | 0.6 | 0.46 | 5.30 | 4.08 | 83.9 | **1.4** | 10.7 | 24.4 | **4.0** |
| **5.1** | 0.78 | 5.5 | 0.03 | **4.7** | 2.6 | 0.96 | 10.76 | 4.05 | 67.3 | **3.7** | 13.9 | 10.4 | **5.6** |
| **6.4** | 0.48 | 2.7 | 0.14 | **5.4** | 27.6 | 1.18 | 9.67 | 3.59 | 61.9 | **2.9** | 9.6 | 13.0 | **9.9** |
| **8.8** | 0.09 | 0.4 | 0.06 | **4.4** | 3.2 | 1.09 | 10.48 | 3.26 | 73.8 | **4.8** | 44.2 | 11.9 | **6.9** |
| **1.5** | 9.46 | 33.7 | 0.05 | **9.0** | 0.3 | 1.84 | 6.90 | 5.18 | 61.9 | **1.3** | 9.9 | 25.3 | **7.8** |
| **4.6** | 0.85 | 5.8 | 0.14 | **3.6** | 0.9 | 0.36 | 3.36 | 5.13 | 86.1 | **0.8** | 17.7 | 35.4 | **5.7** |
| **6.2** | 0.76 | 5.7 | 0.00 | **3.3** | 0.2 | 0.55 | 7.36 | 3.99 | 81.3 | **5.3** | 30.3 | 3.6 | **2.6** |
| **7.5** | 0.00 | 0.0 | -0.02 | **6.1** | 1.0 | 1.52 | 10.85 | 4.15 | 61.5 | **4.7** | 41.6 | 11.7 | **7.9** |
| **4.1** | 1.69 | 10.2 | 0.03 | **4.5** | 1.1 | 0.88 | 8.62 | 4.53 | 76.0 | **3.1** | 10.9 | 13.3 | **5.8** |
| **7.8** | 0.00 | 0.0 | 0.03 | **6.9** | 0.3 | 1.63 | 16.94 | 5.63 | 73.7 | **5.3** | 40.2 | 4.7 | **5.4** |
| **9.4** | 0.00 | 0.0 | -0.01 | **6.6** | 1.4 | 1.68 | 13.56 | 3.06 | 43.5 | **5.0** | 47.8 | 11.1 | **8.2** |
| **8.1** | 0.48 | 1.7 | 0.02 | **3.9** | 1.0 | 0.77 | 8.53 | 3.34 | 76.1 | **3.5** | 41.8 | 17.8 | **5.7** |
| **1.5** | 5.88 | 27.9 | 0.45 | **4.4** | 7.4 | 0.94 | 8.59 | 3.43 | 60.7 | **2.4** | 26.9 | 18.6 | **8.1** |
| **6.0** | 0.68 | 4.3 | 0.02 | **6.5** | 11.8 | 1.29 | 12.51 | 3.74 | 58.7 | **3.3** | 15.6 | 8.7 | **7.3** |
| **8.3** | 0.00 | 0.0 | 0.03 | **7.7** | 0.5 | 1.49 | 12.05 | 4.26 | 54.8 | **4.8** | 33.3 | 8.3 | **7.0** |
| **7.8** | 0.55 | 1.4 | 0.01 | **3.8** | 2.4 | 0.87 | 7.31 | 2.36 | 57.0 | **3.0** | 62.1 | 35.5 | **6.8** |
| **6.1** | 1.24 | 4.5 | 0.03 | **6.9** | 2.1 | 1.47 | 11.25 | 4.29 | 61.1 | **2.9** | 18.5 | 14.7 | **8.2** |
| **4.6** | 1.20 | 6.8 | 0.32 | **5.9** | 5.2 | 1.13 | 10.23 | 3.68 | 57.4 | **3.0** | 15.1 | 12.6 | **7.2** |
| **5.8** | 0.87 | 4.6 | 0.04 | **5.9** | 3.8 | 1.40 | 14.75 | 3.62 | 63.7 | **2.6** | 24.5 | 15.1 | **6.7** |
| **1.6** | 8.49 | 41.3 | 0.06 | **5.2** | 1.4 | 1.23 | 12.67 | 4.31 | 67.8 | **1.5** | 16.6 | 25.1 | **5.4** |
| **5.8** | 0.29 | 3.8 | -0.92 | **6.9** | 0.9 | 1.70 | 13.71 | 4.05 | 65.7 | **1.7** | 17.3 | 22.9 | **6.2** |
| **9.2** | 0.60 | 1.9 | 0.02 | **3.6** | 1.4 | 0.75 | 4.49 | 3.39 | 78.1 | **2.4** | 34.3 | 22.8 | **8.2** |
| **5.8** | 2.78 | 10.1 | -0.07 | **2.6** | 0.2 | 0.67 | 5.64 | 2.86 | 83.7 | **5.6** | 46.8 | 7.7 | **5.4** |
| **5.1** | 3.10 | 12.7 | 0.02 | **3.9** | 2.2 | 0.79 | 6.35 | 4.07 | 82.9 | **4.1** | 25.9 | 9.8 | **7.1** |
| **7.4** | 0.38 | 2.7 | 0.06 | **3.9** | 25.2 | 0.87 | 8.84 | 3.03 | 69.6 | **3.4** | 10.3 | 8.1 | **7.7** |
| **4.7** | 1.74 | 11.3 | 0.04 | **5.5** | 19.4 | 1.05 | 10.07 | 3.69 | 65.4 | **2.6** | 9.7 | 15.0 | **9.3** |
| **5.1** | 1.26 | 6.5 | 0.01 | **7.2** | 12.1 | 1.47 | 16.34 | 4.06 | 56.3 | **3.4** | 28.9 | 14.3 | **6.7** |
| **5.2** | 1.60 | 8.2 | 0.01 | **6.8** | 1.4 | 1.34 | 10.87 | 4.10 | 58.5 | **1.1** | 20.6 | 32.0 | **7.4** |
| **8.5** | 0.00 | 0.6 | 0.06 | **4.4** | 1.2 | 1.11 | 11.98 | 3.19 | 65.8 | **7.3** | 61.5 | 1.9 | **5.2** |
| **8.6** | 0.76 | 2.7 | -0.05 | **8.1** | 6.0 | 1.54 | 8.05 | 2.90 | 34.9 | **0.8** | 18.7 | 42.1 | **8.8** |
| **7.1** | 1.86 | 4.0 | 0.01 | **6.4** | 3.0 | 1.65 | 12.16 | 3.15 | 48.9 | **4.7** | 61.4 | 16.6 | **8.8** |
| **6.5** | 1.00 | 2.1 | 0.76 | **1.9** | 0.5 | 0.16 | 2.35 | 4.29 | 91.1 | **3.6** | 22.3 | 11.7 | **1.2** |
| **7.9** | 1.29 | 3.4 | -0.21 | **3.3** | 1.0 | 0.64 | 4.60 | 2.88 | 78.5 | **3.4** | 40.6 | 18.1 | **7.2** |
| **7.6** | 0.65 | 1.7 | -0.05 | **4.1** | 1.8 | 0.88 | 7.57 | 3.63 | 77.5 | **4.5** | 35.4 | 8.0 | **7.1** |
| **7.3** | 0.39 | 1.8 | 0.09 | **6.2** | 2.7 | 1.40 | 10.50 | 3.93 | 65.9 | **3.7** | 15.7 | 10.4 | **8.5** |
| **7.1** | 2.13 | 4.8 | 0.26 | **7.7** | 2.8 | 1.52 | 10.45 | 3.77 | 45.7 | **2.5** | 37.0 | 24.1 | **8.4** |
| **7.6** | 0.26 | 2.2 | 0.07 | **6.6** | 5.8 | 1.61 | 21.08 | 3.65 | 64.9 | **4.9** | 20.1 | 3.3 | **4.9** |
| **9.1** | 1.54 | 2.0 | 0.10 | **5.2** | 2.6 | 1.33 | 8.52 | 3.34 | 63.5 | **5.5** | 35.4 | 4.7 | **8.0** |
| **8.8** | 0.00 | 0.0 | 0.00 | **9.5** | 1.4 | 6.33 | 8.82 | 1.65 | 77.7 | **5.2** | 199.5 | 69.4 | **7.0** |

| Name | City | State | Rating | 2018 Rating | 2017 Rating | Total Assets ($Mil) | One Year Asset Growth | Asset Mix (As a % of Total Assets) Commercial Loans | Consumer Loans | Mortgage Loans | Securities | Capitalization Index | Leverage Ratio | Risk-Based Capital Ratio |
|---|---|---|---|---|---|---|---|---|---|---|---|---|---|---|
| Philo Exchange Bank | Philo | IL | **B+** | B | B | 105.3 | 8.92 | 2.1 | 1.6 | 8.4 | 23.1 | **10.0** | 11.4 | 16.0 |
| Phoenixville Federal Bank and Trust | Phoenixville | PA | **B-** | B- | C | 463.4 | 4.55 | 3.3 | 0.0 | 43.1 | 11.6 | **10.0** | 12.5 | 18.2 |
| Pickens S&L Assn., FA | Pickens | SC | **B-** | B- | C+ | 100.8 | 8.98 | 0.7 | 1.1 | 38.4 | 30.3 | **10.0** | 11.2 | 22.9 |
| ▲ Piedmont Bank | Peachtree Corners | GA | **B** | C+ | B- | 1045.2 | 6.59 | 13.3 | 1.0 | 5.9 | 5.4 | **7.9** | 10.8 | 13.2 |
| Piedmont Federal Savings Bank | Winston-Salem | NC | **C+** | C+ | C+ | 871.4 | -3.54 | 0.0 | 0.0 | 57.6 | 29.5 | **10.0** | 26.2 | 70.0 |
| Piggott State Bank | Piggott | AR | **B** | B | B+ | 90.1 | 7.21 | 7.8 | 4.1 | 18.5 | 34.3 | **7.2** | 9.1 | 18.0 |
| Pike National Bank | McComb | MS | **B+** | B+ | B+ | 253.9 | 2.93 | 6.8 | 4.0 | 17.7 | 20.6 | **10.0** | 13.7 | 22.2 |
| Pikes Peak National Bank | Colorado Springs | CO | **B-** | C+ | B- | 92.1 | -2.43 | 4.0 | 0.4 | 4.1 | 0.0 | **10.0** | 14.3 | 36.9 |
| Pilgrim Bank | Pittsburg | TX | **B** | B- | B- | 548.1 | -4.54 | 5.1 | 1.0 | 11.4 | 24.9 | **10.0** | 11.9 | 17.6 |
| Pilot Bank | Tampa | FL | **C** | C- | C- | 430.4 | 19.34 | 29.9 | 19.0 | 4.8 | 11.1 | **6.6** | 9.6 | 12.2 |
| Pilot Grove Savings Bank | Pilot Grove | IA | **A-** | A- | B+ | 619.6 | 7.05 | 7.9 | 3.4 | 29.6 | 4.3 | **8.5** | 10.0 | 14.0 |
| ▲ Pine Country Bank | Little Falls | MN | **B+** | B- | B | 182.6 | 5.51 | 9.3 | 0.7 | 6.6 | 16.1 | **8.0** | 10.0 | 13.4 |
| Pine Island Bank | Pine Island | MN | **B+** | B+ | B | 109.3 | 4.96 | 4.7 | 1.3 | 30.4 | 9.0 | **8.3** | 9.9 | 14.4 |
| Pine River State Bank | Pine River | MN | **B-** | C+ | C+ | 123.1 | 6.42 | 6.3 | 2.0 | 19.5 | 16.9 | **7.0** | 9.0 | 15.9 |
| Pineland Bank | Alma | GA | **B** | B- | C+ | 288.3 | 5.29 | 5.6 | 2.3 | 10.4 | 7.3 | **9.9** | 11.0 | 16.2 |
| ▲ Pineries Bank | Stevens Point | WI | **B+** | B | B | 104.5 | 6.33 | 2.0 | 2.2 | 34.4 | 7.3 | **8.6** | 10.0 | 19.2 |
| Pinnacle Bank | Jasper | AL | **A-** | A- | B+ | 230.3 | 4.28 | 14.0 | 2.3 | 6.5 | 44.1 | **10.0** | 12.6 | 19.8 |
| ▲ Pinnacle Bank | Gilroy | CA | **A-** | B | B | 419.9 | 16.67 | 8.2 | 0.2 | 5.8 | 0.3 | **10.0** | 12.9 | 15.2 |
| Pinnacle Bank | Elberton | GA | **B+** | B+ | B | 1030.7 | 8.83 | 7.0 | 2.1 | 6.4 | 12.1 | **6.6** | 9.7 | 12.2 |
| ▲ Pinnacle Bank | Marshalltown | IA | **A** | B+ | A | 215.1 | 8.08 | 16.8 | 2.4 | 6.4 | 23.4 | **10.0** | 15.8 | 20.4 |
| Pinnacle Bank | Lincoln | NE | **A-** | A- | A- | 5333.8 | 12.78 | 6.8 | 1.3 | 9.5 | 12.4 | **7.7** | 10.3 | 13.1 |
| Pinnacle Bank | Nashville | TN | **B+** | B+ | B+ | 27665.8 | 11.09 | 21.6 | 1.1 | 7.6 | 13.5 | **6.6** | 10.5 | 12.2 |
| ▲ Pinnacle Bank | Fort Worth | TX | **A-** | B+ | B+ | 1486.2 | 10.96 | 7.1 | 1.4 | 12.8 | 23.6 | **8.0** | 9.7 | 14.6 |
| Pinnacle Bank - Wyoming | Torrington | WY | **A-** | B+ | B+ | 972.1 | 12.42 | 5.5 | 1.8 | 13.9 | 19.9 | **8.3** | 9.8 | 13.8 |
| Pinnacle Bank, Inc. | Vanceburg | KY | **B-** | B- | B- | 51.3 | 4.97 | 4.1 | 4.7 | 35.3 | 9.2 | **10.0** | 14.5 | 20.2 |
| Pioneer Bank | Sioux City | IA | **B** | B | B | 186.0 | 1.73 | 12.0 | 0.8 | 25.8 | 6.7 | **7.4** | 9.6 | 12.8 |
| Pioneer Bank | Mapleton | MN | **C** | C+ | B | 658.2 | 44.93 | 10.6 | 1.5 | 10.4 | 12.8 | **7.6** | 9.4 | 14.5 |
| Pioneer Bank | Roswell | NM | **B-** | B- | C+ | 812.9 | -0.86 | 4.2 | 2.0 | 19.9 | 43.1 | **8.3** | 9.9 | 19.3 |
| Pioneer Bank | Albany | NY | **B** | B+ | B- | 1390.1 | 8.02 | 12.5 | 0.1 | 26.5 | 6.6 | **10.0** | 12.4 | 16.8 |
| ▲ Pioneer Bank | Stanley | VA | **B** | C- | D+ | 228.4 | 9.27 | 4.7 | 11.9 | 27.5 | 4.4 | **10.0** | 11.7 | 15.7 |
| Pioneer Bank | Auburndale | WI | **B-** | B | B- | 161.2 | 0.34 | 5.8 | 0.7 | 10.6 | 4.8 | **4.2** | 8.7 | 10.6 |
| Pioneer Bank & Trust | Spearfish | SD | **A** | A | A- | 694.7 | 4.16 | 9.7 | 1.6 | 5.6 | 34.9 | **10.0** | 11.2 | 18.3 |
| Pioneer Bank, SSB | Austin | TX | **C+** | C | C+ | 1691.1 | 8.86 | 6.5 | 1.6 | 16.4 | 18.5 | **6.0** | 8.0 | 12.0 |
| Pioneer Commercial Bank | Albany | NY | **U** | U | U | 282.8 | 18.23 | 0.0 | 0.0 | 0.0 | 3.4 | **6.2** | 8.2 | 48.7 |
| Pioneer Community Bank, Inc. | Iaeger | WV | **B** | B | B | 113.9 | 2.66 | 14.4 | 3.2 | 53.6 | 4.4 | **10.0** | 14.4 | 25.3 |
| Pioneer Federal S&L Assn. | Dillon | MT | **B-** | B | B | 89.4 | -0.19 | 4.4 | 1.8 | 56.8 | 21.9 | **10.0** | 18.8 | 37.5 |
| ▼ Pioneer Savings Bank | Cleveland | OH | **C** | C+ | C | 41.1 | 8.85 | 0.0 | 0.4 | 39.4 | 31.4 | **10.0** | 16.3 | 35.4 |
| Pioneer State Bank | Earlville | IL | **C** | C | B- | 106.9 | 0.97 | 7.0 | 1.0 | 14.3 | 8.8 | **10.0** | 12.4 | 17.6 |
| Pioneer Trust Bank, N.A. | Salem | OR | **A** | A | A+ | 539.2 | 7.54 | 12.6 | 0.4 | 6.9 | 19.4 | **10.0** | 12.6 | 18.7 |
| Piqua State Bank | Piqua | KS | **B** | C+ | C | 26.6 | -6.92 | 7.3 | 2.9 | 10.8 | 28.1 | **10.0** | 12.2 | 23.4 |
| Piscataqua Savings Bank | Portsmouth | NH | **B-** | B- | B- | 295.7 | 6.98 | 0.0 | 0.4 | 57.0 | 21.3 | **10.0** | 15.9 | 26.6 |
| Pitney Bowes Bank, Inc. | Salt Lake City | UT | **A-** | B+ | B+ | 747.6 | 4.99 | 30.8 | 0.0 | 0.0 | 48.4 | **8.7** | 10.1 | 19.2 |
| Pittsfield Co-operative Bank | Pittsfield | MA | **B** | B | C+ | 321.8 | 4.73 | 4.3 | 0.6 | 43.9 | 12.3 | **10.0** | 13.6 | 19.6 |
| Plains Commerce Bank | Hoven | SD | **C** | D+ | D+ | 707.3 | 7.79 | 8.5 | 0.8 | 10.8 | 7.1 | **10.0** | 12.6 | 16.1 |
| Plains State Bank | Plains | KS | **C** | C | D+ | 208.0 | 0.25 | 11.5 | 1.2 | 18.4 | 22.1 | **8.1** | 10.2 | 13.4 |
| ▲ Plains State Bank | Humble | TX | **C** | C- | C | 605.9 | 27.12 | 12.9 | 0.4 | 5.0 | 8.5 | **9.1** | 10.4 | 14.2 |
| PlainsCapital Bank | Dallas | TX | **A-** | A- | A | 11335.5 | 12.17 | 9.9 | 0.4 | 24.8 | 11.5 | **9.0** | 11.6 | 14.1 |
| Planters and Citizens Bank | Camilla | GA | **B-** | B- | C | 101.0 | -8.36 | 5.1 | 2.3 | 3.9 | 38.1 | **10.0** | 12.0 | 20.4 |
| Planters Bank & Trust Co. | Indianola | MS | **B** | B | B | 1098.2 | 4.86 | 8.5 | 2.1 | 14.4 | 34.4 | **8.2** | 9.8 | 16.5 |
| Planters Bank, Inc. | Hopkinsville | KY | **B+** | B+ | B+ | 1163.0 | 8.44 | 7.3 | 0.9 | 13.3 | 19.2 | **7.5** | 10.9 | 13.0 |
| Planters First Bank | Hawkinsville | GA | **B-** | C+ | C- | 310.6 | -6.91 | 7.2 | 1.6 | 10.0 | 11.0 | **8.1** | 10.4 | 13.4 |
| Plaquemine Bank and Trust Co. | Plaquemine | LA | **B-** | B- | B- | 168.2 | 7.80 | 8.9 | 3.0 | 11.0 | 30.0 | **10.0** | 11.8 | 20.2 |
| Platinum Bank | Oakdale | MN | **B** | B | C+ | 278.8 | 9.52 | 35.4 | 1.8 | 9.5 | 3.9 | **6.4** | 8.4 | 12.5 |
| Platte Valley Bank | North Bend | NE | **A-** | B+ | B+ | 87.5 | 0.00 | 9.2 | 3.7 | 3.6 | 17.4 | **10.0** | 13.6 | 21.7 |
| Platte Valley Bank | Scottsbluff | NE | **B-** | C+ | B | 729.8 | 9.12 | 13.8 | 6.5 | 20.9 | 8.2 | **6.9** | 9.2 | 12.5 |
| ▲ Platte Valley Bank | Torrington | WY | **B** | C+ | B | 453.0 | 6.50 | 26.8 | 4.9 | 14.1 | 5.3 | **7.9** | 10.5 | 13.3 |
| ▼ Platte Valley Bank of Missouri | Platte City | MO | **B+** | A- | A- | 703.1 | 26.76 | 5.4 | 0.8 | 12.8 | 11.9 | **6.8** | 10.4 | 12.4 |
| Plattsmouth State Bank | Plattsmouth | NE | **C+** | C+ | C | 96.1 | -0.39 | 5.3 | 0.7 | 5.2 | 49.1 | **8.2** | 9.8 | 14.5 |
| Pleasants County Bank | Saint Marys | WV | **C** | B- | C+ | 64.1 | -4.79 | 4.7 | 7.4 | 25.5 | 19.2 | **10.0** | 11.0 | 19.4 |
| ▲ Plumas Bank | Quincy | CA | **B** | B | B | 864.5 | 4.94 | 5.4 | 11.2 | 1.6 | 18.4 | **9.0** | 10.4 | 14.2 |

| Asset Quality Index | Adjusted Non-Performing Loans as a % of Total Loans | Adjusted Non-Performing Loans as a % of Capital | Net Charge-Offs Avg Loans | Profitability Index | Net Income ($Mil) | Return on Assets (R.O.A.) | Return on Equity (R.O.E.) | Net Interest Spread | Overhead Efficiency Ratio | Liquidity Index | Liquidity Ratio | Hot Money Ratio | Stability Index |
|---|---|---|---|---|---|---|---|---|---|---|---|---|---|
| **7.5** | 0.47 | 3.4 | 0.00 | **5.5** | 1.3 | 1.37 | 11.17 | 3.60 | 61.4 | **4.0** | 19.1 | 8.9 | **7.7** |
| **8.1** | 0.27 | 1.6 | 0.01 | **3.6** | 3.6 | 0.80 | 6.49 | 3.44 | 72.4 | **3.1** | 14.8 | 13.5 | **7.0** |
| **8.7** | 0.39 | 3.3 | 0.00 | **3.2** | 0.6 | 0.59 | 4.97 | 3.48 | 82.2 | **3.6** | 45.5 | 18.5 | **6.6** |
| **6.7** | 0.30 | 1.9 | 0.00 | **8.3** | 16.2 | 1.62 | 14.39 | 4.47 | 51.0 | **0.9** | 10.9 | 32.8 | **9.5** |
| **10.0** | 0.09 | 0.2 | 0.01 | **2.2** | 1.9 | 0.21 | 0.82 | 2.34 | 88.5 | **2.5** | 49.9 | 33.5 | **8.2** |
| **8.4** | 0.00 | 0.0 | 0.13 | **5.2** | 1.1 | 1.27 | 13.18 | 3.83 | 68.2 | **3.8** | 39.5 | 16.0 | **6.3** |
| **5.9** | 2.39 | 8.1 | 0.09 | **6.0** | 3.1 | 1.21 | 8.91 | 4.40 | 69.8 | **1.8** | 22.3 | 22.6 | **7.7** |
| **6.5** | 2.23 | 5.0 | -0.01 | **5.1** | 1.0 | 1.04 | 7.24 | 5.25 | 73.0 | **6.9** | 66.1 | 3.3 | **8.6** |
| **8.2** | 0.04 | 0.2 | 0.12 | **4.5** | 6.1 | 1.08 | 8.34 | 3.52 | 69.0 | **2.3** | 20.3 | 18.2 | **8.1** |
| **4.0** | 1.09 | 4.4 | 0.00 | **3.2** | 2.3 | 0.57 | 5.60 | 3.25 | 74.9 | **1.1** | 15.5 | 19.8 | **5.4** |
| **5.8** | 0.36 | 3.7 | 0.02 | **8.5** | 11.3 | 1.88 | 16.82 | 3.60 | 50.6 | **3.5** | 11.7 | 11.2 | **8.8** |
| **4.7** | 1.82 | 8.0 | 0.04 | **6.3** | 2.2 | 1.26 | 12.67 | 4.47 | 63.3 | **3.4** | 16.6 | 9.5 | **6.1** |
| **6.0** | 0.77 | 5.5 | 0.00 | **8.3** | 2.1 | 2.07 | 18.48 | 3.94 | 46.3 | **0.7** | 5.9 | 23.6 | **7.7** |
| **5.3** | 1.24 | 5.2 | -0.14 | **4.5** | 1.3 | 1.09 | 12.27 | 4.25 | 73.7 | **5.3** | 36.6 | 6.6 | **5.1** |
| **5.1** | 1.32 | 7.3 | 0.09 | **4.6** | 2.2 | 0.78 | 7.01 | 4.99 | 78.3 | **3.4** | 21.4 | 12.8 | **5.3** |
| **8.7** | 0.31 | 1.7 | -0.01 | **5.5** | 1.4 | 1.34 | 13.20 | 3.27 | 60.2 | **2.8** | 39.5 | 23.1 | **7.3** |
| **8.8** | 0.15 | 0.5 | 0.06 | **6.2** | 3.0 | 1.32 | 9.96 | 4.01 | 59.8 | **2.3** | 23.9 | 18.5 | **8.0** |
| **7.0** | 0.04 | 0.2 | 0.02 | **8.4** | 5.6 | 1.42 | 11.16 | 5.46 | 63.3 | **2.8** | 17.6 | 15.2 | **7.4** |
| **7.2** | 0.15 | 0.6 | 0.11 | **7.1** | 12.7 | 1.31 | 11.53 | 4.57 | 64.0 | **5.3** | 29.0 | 7.6 | **9.1** |
| **7.8** | 0.40 | 1.4 | 0.00 | **9.9** | 3.7 | 1.87 | 11.10 | 4.19 | 42.0 | **5.3** | 31.9 | 1.5 | **9.2** |
| **8.1** | 0.16 | 1.4 | 0.03 | **7.5** | 72.7 | 1.45 | 13.65 | 3.55 | 55.2 | **3.4** | 12.7 | 12.2 | **9.0** |
| **6.1** | 0.33 | 1.3 | 0.09 | **7.9** | 408.3 | 1.55 | 9.37 | 3.49 | 46.7 | **2.1** | 14.0 | 10.2 | **10.0** |
| **6.8** | 0.04 | 2.0 | 0.00 | **5.8** | 16.4 | 1.15 | 8.36 | 4.03 | 62.9 | **3.7** | 28.4 | 15.7 | **9.0** |
| **6.4** | 0.27 | 1.8 | 0.03 | **8.2** | 14.7 | 1.60 | 16.49 | 3.92 | 53.6 | **1.8** | 20.7 | 22.3 | **8.4** |
| **5.2** | 1.19 | 6.6 | 0.38 | **4.7** | 0.4 | 0.87 | 5.24 | 4.87 | 73.0 | **0.8** | 14.2 | 31.8 | **7.5** |
| **8.4** | 0.16 | 1.3 | 0.14 | **4.5** | 1.9 | 1.07 | 11.48 | 3.41 | 67.0 | **1.7** | 8.3 | 19.8 | **6.6** |
| **3.0** | 2.80 | 14.4 | 0.76 | **5.2** | 5.9 | 1.06 | 10.36 | 4.34 | 66.9 | **2.8** | 24.1 | 15.9 | **7.8** |
| **8.1** | 1.15 | 1.6 | 0.22 | **4.0** | 8.0 | 0.95 | 10.32 | 2.81 | 71.3 | **4.7** | 33.8 | 9.6 | **6.2** |
| **6.2** | 0.99 | 5.9 | 1.51 | **3.6** | 4.4 | 0.32 | 3.02 | 4.01 | 64.6 | **4.5** | 11.9 | 5.4 | **8.2** |
| **4.3** | 1.41 | 8.9 | 0.16 | **5.4** | 2.4 | 1.09 | 9.26 | 4.67 | 73.8 | **2.1** | 14.0 | 13.9 | **7.0** |
| **4.4** | 1.95 | 6.6 | 0.00 | **3.2** | 0.6 | 0.35 | 3.22 | 4.41 | 88.0 | **3.6** | 18.1 | 11.2 | **6.1** |
| **8.8** | 0.18 | 0.9 | 0.09 | **7.8** | 10.8 | 1.61 | 14.15 | 3.54 | 50.6 | **4.8** | 34.3 | 8.8 | **8.2** |
| **7.0** | 0.76 | 4.5 | 0.08 | **3.5** | 10.3 | 0.63 | 7.03 | 2.76 | 72.9 | **2.1** | 31.7 | 36.1 | **6.9** |
| **10.0** | na | 0.0 | na | **5.2** | 3.4 | 1.07 | 13.90 | 1.63 | 11.1 | **8.6** | 106.4 | 0.0 | **4.0** |
| **6.2** | 1.21 | 7.1 | 0.77 | **3.5** | 0.4 | 0.38 | 2.64 | 4.70 | 89.8 | **3.4** | 15.5 | 12.1 | **7.4** |
| **9.6** | 0.05 | 0.2 | 0.01 | **1.7** | -0.1 | -0.12 | -0.62 | 3.80 | 106.6 | **3.3** | 35.0 | 17.0 | **7.6** |
| **8.0** | 0.87 | 4.9 | -0.10 | **1.7** | 0.1 | 0.19 | 1.08 | 2.83 | 94.8 | **2.1** | 46.1 | 52.3 | **7.1** |
| **5.1** | 2.61 | 9.9 | 0.43 | **2.4** | 0.3 | 0.32 | 2.58 | 4.21 | 86.4 | **3.7** | 18.1 | 10.9 | **6.4** |
| **8.6** | 0.00 | 0.0 | -0.01 | **9.8** | 13.4 | 2.59 | 20.39 | 4.14 | 32.1 | **6.0** | 38.7 | 2.9 | **9.5** |
| **9.1** | 0.00 | 0.0 | 0.03 | **5.5** | 0.4 | 1.39 | 12.53 | 4.37 | 72.5 | **6.5** | 57.5 | 3.8 | **5.9** |
| **10.0** | 0.22 | 0.9 | 0.00 | **2.6** | 1.0 | 0.36 | 2.37 | 2.32 | 85.9 | **2.4** | 34.5 | 22.9 | **7.7** |
| **6.5** | 1.43 | 3.8 | 1.82 | **10.0** | 62.6 | 8.56 | 85.82 | 10.14 | 4.1 | **7.8** | 70.2 | 0.0 | **7.4** |
| **6.7** | 1.27 | 4.0 | 0.00 | **3.9** | 2.3 | 0.73 | 4.59 | 3.53 | 74.0 | **1.9** | 23.2 | 19.3 | **7.7** |
| **2.3** | 3.68 | 19.3 | -0.02 | **7.0** | 10.7 | 1.59 | 11.41 | 4.25 | 77.4 | **0.9** | 17.8 | 30.5 | **10.0** |
| **6.3** | 0.55 | 3.2 | 0.12 | **3.0** | 1.2 | 0.56 | 4.75 | 3.56 | 80.8 | **1.5** | 10.5 | 20.3 | **6.8** |
| **3.6** | 1.54 | 6.1 | 0.02 | **7.6** | 7.5 | 1.38 | 13.08 | 4.12 | 58.8 | **0.9** | 22.6 | 33.5 | **7.9** |
| **6.7** | 0.42 | 2.5 | 0.07 | **9.3** | 185.6 | 1.85 | 12.77 | 3.99 | 75.5 | **2.9** | 11.8 | 14.1 | **10.0** |
| **9.1** | 0.06 | 0.1 | 0.16 | **3.5** | 0.6 | 0.62 | 5.36 | 3.69 | 78.7 | **6.8** | 56.5 | 3.4 | **6.0** |
| **5.8** | 1.70 | 7.4 | 0.21 | **5.2** | 12.0 | 1.10 | 10.58 | 3.46 | 64.2 | **2.9** | 31.5 | 22.1 | **8.2** |
| **7.1** | 1.04 | 4.4 | -0.01 | **6.4** | 15.1 | 1.36 | 12.72 | 3.49 | 54.2 | **1.6** | 6.6 | 15.6 | **10.0** |
| **4.4** | 1.70 | 9.3 | 0.01 | **4.6** | 3.3 | 1.04 | 10.29 | 4.50 | 79.5 | **3.7** | 15.3 | 10.5 | **6.5** |
| **5.5** | 2.73 | 9.6 | 0.10 | **3.8** | 1.0 | 0.66 | 5.70 | 3.85 | 74.4 | **2.7** | 30.8 | 18.3 | **6.1** |
| **7.7** | 1.21 | 1.2 | 0.23 | **6.7** | 3.8 | 1.46 | 16.35 | 3.96 | 59.0 | **4.6** | 14.9 | 4.3 | **6.2** |
| **8.3** | 0.06 | 1.7 | 0.07 | **5.7** | 1.0 | 1.17 | 8.37 | 3.76 | 58.9 | **6.2** | 44.2 | 3.1 | **7.7** |
| **4.4** | 0.89 | 6.9 | 0.06 | **5.8** | 7.9 | 1.12 | 11.66 | 3.81 | 60.3 | **1.4** | 12.6 | 24.1 | **7.3** |
| **5.0** | 0.65 | 4.3 | 0.53 | **9.4** | 8.8 | 1.98 | 19.27 | 5.58 | 50.1 | **0.7** | 11.6 | 31.9 | **7.7** |
| **7.6** | 0.13 | 0.5 | 0.02 | **4.9** | 4.1 | 0.67 | 6.13 | 4.36 | 86.0 | **3.8** | 18.4 | 10.5 | **8.0** |
| **9.2** | 0.00 | 0.0 | -0.08 | **4.0** | 1.7 | 1.75 | 19.53 | 3.38 | 86.7 | **3.8** | 45.3 | 16.8 | **5.2** |
| **4.8** | 0.30 | 11.4 | 0.03 | **3.7** | 0.4 | 0.62 | 5.76 | 3.72 | 78.4 | **4.5** | 37.0 | 11.3 | **5.9** |
| **6.5** | 0.47 | 2.5 | 0.21 | **10.0** | 16.1 | 1.89 | 18.66 | 4.86 | 49.0 | **5.0** | 15.8 | 2.0 | **7.7** |

| Name | City | State | Rating | 2018 Rating | 2017 Rating | Total Assets ($Mil) | One Year Asset Growth | Asset Mix (As a % of Total Assets) Commercial Loans | Consumer Loans | Mortgage Loans | Securities | Capitalization Index | Leverage Ratio | Risk-Based Capital Ratio |
|---|---|---|---|---|---|---|---|---|---|---|---|---|---|---|
| Plus International Bank | Miami | FL | **C-** | D+ | D+ | 72.6 | -6.13 | 22.9 | 0.0 | 29.3 | 15.3 | **10.0** | 18.6 | 31.8 |
| PNB Community Bank | Niceville | FL | **B-** | C | C- | 105.0 | 6.42 | 4.4 | 0.9 | 27.9 | 27.9 | **10.0** | 11.3 | 21.0 |
| PNC Bank, N.A. | Wilmington | DE | **B-** | B- | B- | 397703.3 | 7.34 | 23.5 | 7.9 | 8.5 | 21.9 | **6.3** | 8.3 | 12.1 |
| Poca Valley Bank, Inc. | Walton | WV | **B-** | C+ | B- | 377.2 | 1.27 | 11.7 | 7.1 | 35.6 | 10.3 | **7.1** | 9.0 | 14.2 |
| Pocahontas State Bank | Pocahontas | IA | **B+** | B+ | A | 101.8 | 3.07 | 5.7 | 0.4 | 4.0 | 43.6 | **10.0** | 27.9 | 47.3 |
| ▲ Pointbank | Pilot Point | TX | **B+** | B | B | 553.5 | 1.46 | 11.7 | 2.4 | 9.2 | 30.2 | **10.0** | 11.2 | 18.4 |
| Points West Community Bank | Windsor | CO | **A-** | B+ | B+ | 259.9 | 3.01 | 6.4 | 0.6 | 6.3 | 25.3 | **8.3** | 9.8 | 15.0 |
| POINTWEST Bank | West | TX | **B** | B- | B- | 103.6 | 1.12 | 1.4 | 7.9 | 23.9 | 24.9 | **9.2** | 10.5 | 23.4 |
| Ponce Bank | Bronx | NY | **C+** | C+ | C+ | 1051.7 | -0.62 | 1.0 | 0.1 | 37.2 | 2.1 | **10.0** | 12.9 | 18.6 |
| Pony Express Bank | Liberty | MO | **B** | B | B+ | 176.3 | 2.92 | 13.1 | 2.5 | 16.4 | 6.6 | **10.0** | 11.2 | 15.3 |
| ▼ Poplar Grove State Bank | Poplar Grove | IL | **A-** | A | A | 78.2 | -6.40 | 4.7 | 0.7 | 8.3 | 46.6 | **8.2** | 9.8 | 23.2 |
| Poppy Bank | Santa Rosa | CA | **A** | A | B+ | 2533.9 | 30.67 | 5.0 | 0.0 | 7.5 | 9.1 | **10.0** | 11.0 | 16.7 |
| Popular Bank | New York | NY | **C+** | C | C+ | 10055.9 | 7.19 | 2.7 | 3.1 | 10.7 | 14.2 | **10.0** | 12.3 | 17.0 |
| Port Austin State Bank | Port Austin | MI | **B+** | B+ | B+ | 52.6 | -0.59 | 3.1 | 4.0 | 39.6 | 11.5 | **10.0** | 18.4 | 30.0 |
| Port Richmond Savings | Philadelphia | PA | **A-** | B | B | 81.7 | 7.63 | 6.1 | 0.0 | 64.0 | 0.0 | **10.0** | 18.3 | 31.0 |
| ▲ Port Washington State Bank | Port Washington | WI | **B** | B- | B- | 637.4 | 5.88 | 7.0 | 2.8 | 15.8 | 20.0 | **7.8** | 9.5 | 13.6 |
| Portage Community Bank | Ravenna | OH | **B** | B | B | 356.8 | 5.11 | 6.1 | 1.1 | 31.0 | 17.5 | **10.0** | 11.9 | 17.6 |
| Portage County Bank | Almond | WI | **B-** | B | B- | 177.4 | 6.31 | 7.1 | 0.7 | 14.8 | 10.5 | **9.5** | 10.7 | 17.1 |
| Potter State Bank of Potter | Potter | NE | **B** | B- | B- | 41.9 | 6.26 | 12.3 | 2.4 | 1.3 | 22.0 | **10.0** | 14.5 | 23.4 |
| ▲ Powell State Bank | Powell | TX | **C-** | D | C- | 29.5 | -35.87 | 11.8 | 13.8 | 5.2 | 34.0 | **9.2** | 10.5 | 22.1 |
| Powell Valley National Bank | Jonesville | VA | **B** | B+ | B+ | 303.3 | 2.01 | 5.0 | 4.2 | 27.7 | 11.5 | **10.0** | 13.1 | 19.4 |
| Prairie Bank of Kansas | Stafford | KS | **C** | C+ | C- | 103.7 | -2.39 | 5.2 | 1.8 | 5.9 | 27.5 | **7.8** | 9.5 | 15.1 |
| ▼ Prairie Community Bank | Marengo | IL | **C** | C- | D+ | 124.3 | 8.13 | 13.8 | 1.3 | 18.9 | 5.4 | **8.6** | 10.1 | 14.8 |
| Prairie State Bank & Trust | Springfield | IL | **A-** | A- | A- | 684.7 | -3.58 | 8.8 | 0.8 | 16.1 | 20.8 | **10.0** | 11.6 | 16.9 |
| ▲ Prairie Sun Bank | Milan | MN | **C-** | D | D | 50.3 | 45.75 | 7.8 | 4.3 | 3.3 | 8.7 | **5.8** | 9.2 | 11.6 |
| Preferred Bank | Los Angeles | CA | **B+** | B+ | A- | 4630.2 | 9.77 | 23.5 | 0.0 | 10.0 | 5.4 | **8.4** | 10.3 | 13.7 |
| Preferred Bank | Casey | IL | **C-** | C- | C | 60.4 | 4.56 | 19.2 | 4.7 | 18.0 | 17.8 | **7.6** | 9.4 | 13.5 |
| Preferred Bank | Rothville | MO | **B-** | B- | B | 113.8 | 7.40 | 3.8 | 2.3 | 11.1 | 48.8 | **5.9** | 7.9 | 21.0 |
| Premier Bank | Dubuque | IA | **B** | B | B | 332.5 | 1.72 | 11.8 | 1.1 | 16.4 | 21.7 | **6.8** | 8.8 | 12.6 |
| ▲ Premier Bank | Rock Valley | IA | **C+** | C | C+ | 564.3 | 2.16 | 9.2 | 1.7 | 5.6 | 10.0 | **8.1** | 10.4 | 13.4 |
| ▲ Premier Bank | Maplewood | MN | **B-** | C+ | C+ | 861.2 | 8.10 | 8.3 | 0.4 | 5.3 | 8.7 | **8.1** | 10.3 | 13.4 |
| Premier Bank | Omaha | NE | **B+** | B | B | 309.4 | 14.27 | 12.9 | 0.3 | 7.0 | 8.4 | **6.3** | 10.9 | 12.0 |
| Premier Bank Minnesota | Farmington | MN | **B** | B | B | 266.5 | 10.80 | 11.5 | 0.3 | 5.9 | 8.4 | **7.5** | 10.1 | 12.9 |
| Premier Bank of Arkansas | Marion | AR | **A-** | A- | B+ | 164.1 | 3.14 | 10.0 | 1.5 | 18.3 | 7.8 | **10.0** | 14.1 | 20.8 |
| Premier Bank of the South | Cullman | AL | **B** | B | B | 207.3 | 7.34 | 9.8 | 5.9 | 28.5 | 15.1 | **7.5** | 9.4 | 15.8 |
| Premier Bank Rochester | Rochester | MN | **B-** | C+ | B | 235.4 | 12.20 | 7.2 | 0.1 | 10.1 | 6.0 | **6.3** | 9.5 | 12.0 |
| Premier Bank, Inc. | Huntington | WV | **B** | B- | B- | 1221.1 | -1.47 | 7.3 | 1.2 | 19.7 | 15.8 | **10.0** | 11.3 | 15.8 |
| ▲ Premier Community Bank | Marion | WI | **B-** | C+ | C+ | 315.8 | 4.06 | 5.0 | 2.6 | 12.1 | 13.8 | **7.9** | 10.1 | 13.2 |
| Premier Valley Bank | Fresno | CA | **A-** | B+ | B+ | 903.2 | 6.30 | 14.5 | 0.3 | 3.0 | 26.5 | **7.9** | 10.4 | 13.2 |
| ▲ PremierBank | Fort Atkinson | WI | **B** | C+ | B | 422.8 | -2.12 | 7.8 | 1.2 | 15.5 | 27.3 | **9.5** | 10.7 | 16.9 |
| Prescott State Bank | Prescott | KS | **B-** | B- | B- | 12.9 | -2.34 | 9.3 | 3.4 | 14.3 | 10.2 | **10.0** | 16.7 | 29.9 |
| Presidential Bank, FSB | Bethesda | MD | **B** | B- | C | 617.2 | 15.86 | 4.7 | 2.7 | 31.1 | 5.5 | **9.4** | 10.6 | 16.2 |
| Primary Bank | Bedford | NH | **C+** | C | D | 299.2 | 46.04 | 19.1 | 0.0 | 5.1 | 0.6 | **7.3** | 10.6 | 12.7 |
| Prime Alliance Bank | Woods Cross | UT | **B-** | C+ | C | 499.3 | 18.61 | 35.6 | 0.0 | 0.4 | 8.7 | **7.3** | 11.2 | 12.8 |
| Prime Bank | Edmond | OK | **A-** | A | A | 286.0 | 6.74 | 18.5 | 0.4 | 17.1 | 0.0 | **10.0** | 12.9 | 15.6 |
| Prime Meridian Bank | Tallahassee | FL | **B+** | B+ | B | 500.8 | 24.69 | 13.8 | 1.5 | 19.7 | 12.3 | **7.5** | 9.3 | 14.5 |
| Prime Security Bank | Karlstad | MN | **B-** | C | B- | 86.6 | 7.95 | 9.2 | 0.5 | 14.8 | 1.0 | **7.1** | 9.4 | 12.6 |
| Primebank | Le Mars | IA | **B** | B+ | A- | 499.6 | 9.77 | 11.3 | 1.3 | 15.2 | 9.9 | **9.4** | 11.6 | 14.5 |
| ▲ PrimeSouth Bank | Waycross | GA | **B** | B | B+ | 685.7 | 19.30 | 10.7 | 3.1 | 26.7 | 10.3 | **9.2** | 10.5 | 14.8 |
| Princeville State Bank | Princeville | IL | **C** | C- | C+ | 85.9 | 7.39 | 8.0 | 3.6 | 5.0 | 39.7 | **6.9** | 8.9 | 14.9 |
| Principal Bank | Des Moines | IA | **B+** | B+ | B+ | 3833.4 | 23.88 | 0.0 | 0.0 | 28.3 | 67.5 | **5.1** | 7.1 | 15.3 |
| ▲ PrinsBank | Prinsburg | MN | **A-** | B+ | A | 146.6 | 5.61 | 3.2 | 0.6 | 2.9 | 4.0 | **10.0** | 17.2 | 22.9 |
| Priority Bank | Fayetteville | AR | **B-** | C+ | C | 92.8 | 10.31 | 3.4 | 1.3 | 70.8 | 0.2 | **6.7** | 8.7 | 14.4 |
| PriorityOne Bank | Magee | MS | **B** | B+ | B+ | 696.7 | 7.38 | 9.1 | 3.9 | 16.2 | 12.2 | **9.7** | 10.8 | 15.2 |
| Private Trust Co., N.A. | Cleveland | OH | **U** | U | U | 21.0 | 6.80 | 0.0 | 0.0 | 0.0 | 56.8 | **10.0** | 84.1 | 693.4 |
| ▲ Produce State Bank | Hollandale | MN | **B+** | B- | C+ | 60.3 | -5.64 | 18.7 | 5.1 | 5.4 | 8.8 | **10.0** | 11.0 | 16.3 |
| Professional Bank | Coral Gables | FL | **C+** | C+ | C+ | 1052.5 | 44.25 | 11.2 | 0.8 | 30.2 | 2.7 | **6.7** | 8.7 | 13.6 |
| Profile Bank | Rochester | NH | **C** | C | C | 220.2 | 6.54 | 2.8 | 1.6 | 29.5 | 17.4 | **10.0** | 12.4 | 20.7 |
| ▲ Profinium, Inc. | Truman | MN | **B** | C+ | B- | 383.9 | 2.64 | 10.2 | 0.7 | 10.1 | 16.1 | **8.1** | 9.8 | 13.5 |
| Progress Bank and Trust | Huntsville | AL | **B** | B | B | 1208.5 | 3.15 | 18.3 | 2.0 | 11.5 | 4.6 | **7.5** | 11.8 | 12.9 |

| Asset Quality Index | Adjusted Non-Performing Loans as a % of Total Loans | Adjusted Non-Performing Loans as a % of Capital | Net Charge-Offs Avg Loans | Profitability Index | Net Income ($Mil) | Return on Assets (R.O.A.) | Return on Equity (R.O.E.) | Net Interest Spread | Overhead Efficiency Ratio | Liquidity Index | Liquidity Ratio | Hot Money Ratio | Stability Index |
|---|---|---|---|---|---|---|---|---|---|---|---|---|---|
| **4.3** | 7.20 | 19.6 | 0.00 | **1.5** | 0.0 | 0.02 | 0.11 | 3.86 | 102.3 | **1.2** | 31.6 | 61.5 | **7.1** |
| **6.4** | 2.16 | 6.8 | 0.18 | **3.4** | 0.6 | 0.57 | 5.18 | 4.33 | 84.6 | **4.5** | 35.9 | 11.0 | **6.2** |
| **4.6** | 1.07 | 5.5 | 0.27 | **5.3** | 4386.8 | 1.15 | 10.81 | 2.90 | 63.1 | **5.9** | 31.1 | 2.5 | **9.6** |
| **4.9** | 0.97 | 5.7 | 0.14 | **4.2** | 3.0 | 0.81 | 8.67 | 4.37 | 77.7 | **3.0** | 18.2 | 14.6 | **5.4** |
| **8.4** | 0.00 | 0.0 | 0.00 | **9.4** | 1.9 | 1.95 | 6.76 | 3.53 | 28.6 | **4.5** | 79.2 | 18.4 | **7.0** |
| **8.7** | 0.24 | 1.0 | 0.05 | **5.1** | 6.6 | 1.20 | 11.01 | 4.07 | 73.2 | **4.6** | 24.2 | 5.7 | **8.2** |
| **7.8** | 0.52 | 1.4 | -0.05 | **9.0** | 5.0 | 1.96 | 18.39 | 4.49 | 56.1 | **3.0** | 17.3 | 14.2 | **9.4** |
| **8.9** | 0.00 | 0.0 | 0.07 | **5.1** | 1.3 | 1.27 | 12.89 | 3.67 | 72.2 | **6.1** | 57.3 | 8.5 | **5.2** |
| **4.6** | 1.90 | 10.1 | 0.06 | **1.2** | -3.0 | -0.29 | -2.24 | 3.75 | 107.7 | **0.6** | 5.4 | 27.0 | **8.9** |
| **7.1** | 0.56 | 3.4 | -0.01 | **9.7** | 4.2 | 2.37 | 18.94 | 5.05 | 52.7 | **3.3** | 15.1 | 7.7 | **9.0** |
| **7.5** | 0.00 | 0.9 | 0.00 | **5.9** | 1.1 | 1.32 | 5.23 | 3.77 | 64.9 | **6.1** | 53.3 | 5.4 | **8.5** |
| **7.2** | 0.85 | 2.1 | -0.09 | **9.7** | 47.5 | 2.17 | 19.85 | 3.52 | 35.7 | **1.3** | 22.3 | 32.5 | **10.0** |
| **4.0** | 0.51 | 2.7 | 0.68 | **3.4** | 55.3 | 0.57 | 3.12 | 3.32 | 67.4 | **1.6** | 18.9 | 19.7 | **7.2** |
| **8.4** | 0.06 | 2.3 | 0.00 | **6.1** | 0.8 | 1.52 | 8.30 | 3.98 | 59.0 | **3.6** | 24.6 | 11.8 | **8.1** |
| **8.5** | 0.37 | 3.0 | 0.00 | **5.9** | 0.9 | 1.18 | 6.37 | 4.49 | 72.3 | **2.2** | 3.7 | 16.9 | **7.7** |
| **6.7** | 0.68 | 2.8 | 0.05 | **4.7** | 5.7 | 0.96 | 10.30 | 3.40 | 67.8 | **3.8** | 12.0 | 9.3 | **5.8** |
| **6.9** | 1.47 | 7.9 | 0.01 | **4.3** | 3.0 | 0.87 | 7.28 | 3.45 | 72.5 | **2.3** | 13.6 | 17.2 | **7.1** |
| **7.9** | 0.25 | 1.1 | 0.00 | **3.6** | 1.2 | 0.74 | 6.56 | 3.81 | 80.7 | **2.4** | 40.4 | 17.7 | **6.6** |
| **8.6** | 0.00 | 1.4 | -0.07 | **4.7** | 0.4 | 1.00 | 6.95 | 4.19 | 71.3 | **3.9** | 58.8 | 18.7 | **7.0** |
| **4.3** | 2.20 | 8.7 | 0.21 | **2.9** | 0.1 | 0.33 | 3.75 | 3.83 | 85.4 | **5.0** | 32.0 | 6.7 | **3.9** |
| **6.4** | 0.97 | 4.8 | 0.09 | **4.1** | 2.4 | 0.81 | 6.01 | 3.86 | 79.9 | **1.5** | 14.8 | 23.9 | **8.3** |
| **4.5** | 1.71 | 8.7 | 0.04 | **2.9** | 0.5 | 0.49 | 5.03 | 3.48 | 79.2 | **1.9** | 18.2 | 20.1 | **4.7** |
| **1.6** | 6.35 | 28.7 | 0.40 | **2.0** | -0.8 | -0.65 | -5.73 | 3.80 | 73.7 | **1.5** | 20.0 | 26.3 | **6.8** |
| **8.1** | 0.30 | 1.8 | 0.13 | **6.3** | 10.3 | 1.46 | 12.92 | 3.77 | 62.7 | **3.6** | 10.8 | 10.3 | **9.0** |
| **3.1** | 0.55 | 6.3 | 0.02 | **6.0** | 0.7 | 1.56 | 15.34 | 5.13 | 65.7 | **3.5** | 15.3 | 11.5 | **4.9** |
| **5.7** | 0.06 | 0.4 | -0.01 | **9.7** | 78.4 | 1.82 | 17.55 | 3.92 | 32.7 | **0.8** | 12.5 | 35.2 | **9.3** |
| **2.4** | 0.90 | 25.6 | 0.18 | **1.7** | 0.1 | 0.11 | 1.17 | 3.12 | 96.0 | **1.2** | 13.7 | 28.7 | **4.2** |
| **9.3** | 0.17 | 0.7 | 0.01 | **4.4** | 1.2 | 1.07 | 13.43 | 3.28 | 68.9 | **6.5** | 55.2 | 5.1 | **4.9** |
| **7.7** | 0.77 | 2.8 | 0.03 | **4.3** | 3.6 | 1.08 | 12.15 | 2.93 | 68.8 | **3.1** | 18.5 | 6.5 | **6.2** |
| **4.0** | 1.30 | 5.4 | 0.09 | **9.0** | 11.5 | 2.05 | 18.12 | 3.63 | 37.2 | **0.6** | 12.5 | 38.7 | **9.1** |
| **4.4** | 1.03 | 5.2 | 0.68 | **9.6** | 14.4 | 1.77 | 17.27 | 4.07 | 40.9 | **3.1** | 15.7 | 13.5 | **8.5** |
| **7.3** | 0.00 | 0.0 | -0.01 | **7.2** | 4.3 | 1.46 | 13.19 | 4.16 | 57.2 | **2.6** | 18.3 | 15.1 | **6.9** |
| **4.5** | 0.94 | 4.4 | 0.48 | **8.0** | 4.8 | 1.89 | 19.12 | 4.26 | 57.0 | **2.9** | 14.4 | 14.7 | **8.1** |
| **7.5** | 0.21 | 5.2 | 0.11 | **5.6** | 1.7 | 1.05 | 7.24 | 4.32 | 63.5 | **2.4** | 19.3 | 17.4 | **8.2** |
| **7.9** | 0.66 | 2.3 | 0.63 | **5.6** | 2.4 | 1.20 | 13.09 | 4.51 | 70.1 | **3.2** | 16.9 | 13.1 | **5.9** |
| **5.5** | 0.39 | 2.4 | 0.55 | **5.7** | 2.8 | 1.23 | 12.58 | 3.90 | 57.2 | **1.6** | 15.9 | 23.4 | **7.6** |
| **4.1** | 1.44 | 7.9 | 0.13 | **8.5** | 20.5 | 1.66 | 11.80 | 4.45 | 49.9 | **3.3** | 14.5 | 12.6 | **8.8** |
| **4.3** | 3.00 | 11.0 | 0.03 | **4.6** | 2.8 | 0.90 | 9.02 | 3.92 | 74.5 | **4.2** | 25.9 | 7.6 | **6.3** |
| **6.3** | 0.70 | 1.0 | 0.19 | **7.0** | 11.8 | 1.36 | 8.26 | 4.55 | 57.7 | **5.3** | 35.1 | 5.8 | **8.6** |
| **4.8** | 1.95 | 5.5 | 0.12 | **5.3** | 4.6 | 1.10 | 9.00 | 3.50 | 68.9 | **4.6** | 24.5 | 6.0 | **7.2** |
| **8.6** | 0.00 | 0.0 | 0.00 | **3.7** | 0.1 | 0.61 | 3.72 | 3.89 | 81.7 | **2.5** | 44.1 | 23.2 | **6.3** |
| **5.0** | 1.52 | 7.1 | 0.05 | **4.6** | 4.6 | 0.82 | 7.45 | 4.19 | 83.2 | **3.4** | 8.3 | 11.4 | **6.8** |
| **4.4** | 1.70 | 10.3 | 0.00 | **3.5** | 2.3 | 0.95 | 8.33 | 3.46 | 66.1 | **0.9** | 22.4 | 31.0 | **4.3** |
| **4.4** | 1.45 | 8.3 | 0.71 | **10.0** | 11.0 | 2.42 | 22.81 | 4.59 | 28.1 | **0.5** | 15.3 | 73.4 | **7.9** |
| **5.4** | 0.90 | 5.9 | 0.01 | **9.8** | 7.1 | 2.55 | 19.98 | 4.24 | 39.7 | **0.7** | 12.7 | 36.5 | **9.5** |
| **6.7** | 0.92 | 5.6 | 0.12 | **4.8** | 3.9 | 0.86 | 9.56 | 3.64 | 63.5 | **3.6** | 27.6 | 12.9 | **5.8** |
| **7.4** | 0.00 | 0.0 | 0.00 | **5.4** | 1.0 | 1.23 | 13.33 | 4.37 | 71.0 | **1.4** | 11.9 | 16.3 | **5.9** |
| **4.3** | 0.40 | 9.3 | -0.03 | **7.3** | 7.8 | 1.69 | 14.41 | 3.49 | 52.8 | **1.3** | 14.7 | 24.6 | **8.8** |
| **6.2** | 0.40 | 2.2 | 0.20 | **7.6** | 9.4 | 1.46 | 12.79 | 4.51 | 61.5 | **1.7** | 7.6 | 19.8 | **8.4** |
| **2.4** | 5.11 | 18.9 | 0.10 | **3.1** | 0.5 | 0.58 | 6.37 | 3.72 | 80.2 | **2.1** | 34.6 | 16.1 | **4.6** |
| **9.2** | 0.74 | 2.3 | -0.28 | **7.9** | 43.1 | 1.27 | 17.14 | 2.04 | 26.7 | **4.4** | 76.4 | 6.1 | **6.5** |
| **7.0** | 0.20 | 3.1 | 0.83 | **10.0** | 4.8 | 3.53 | 21.52 | 5.51 | 42.4 | **3.2** | 33.6 | 17.0 | **8.7** |
| **3.7** | 1.85 | 17.6 | -0.02 | **8.4** | 2.0 | 2.37 | 26.09 | 4.18 | 71.8 | **0.6** | 7.6 | 41.7 | **6.2** |
| **4.9** | 0.93 | 6.5 | 0.42 | **6.5** | 9.9 | 1.47 | 13.59 | 4.21 | 67.9 | **1.7** | 12.8 | 19.1 | **8.8** |
| **6.9** | na | 0.0 | na | **10.0** | 4.1 | 18.27 | 20.11 | 1.89 | 53.9 | **4.0** | na | 0.0 | **6.1** |
| **8.2** | 0.08 | 0.5 | -0.03 | **7.3** | 1.1 | 1.79 | 16.46 | 3.97 | 57.8 | **4.9** | 30.2 | 6.5 | **6.0** |
| **8.6** | 0.33 | 2.6 | 0.00 | **2.9** | 3.4 | 0.39 | 4.69 | 3.29 | 83.9 | **3.9** | 22.2 | 11.4 | **5.5** |
| **7.5** | 1.72 | 5.5 | 0.01 | **2.4** | 0.6 | 0.28 | 2.30 | 3.32 | 89.8 | **3.2** | 32.2 | 16.6 | **6.3** |
| **5.1** | 0.72 | 3.5 | -0.09 | **4.8** | 3.3 | 0.86 | 8.03 | 3.56 | 70.0 | **3.4** | 11.2 | 10.2 | **6.6** |
| **7.7** | 0.39 | 2.0 | 0.11 | **4.8** | 11.6 | 0.99 | 7.73 | 3.48 | 65.1 | **1.6** | 14.0 | 24.0 | **9.0** |

| Name | City | State | Rating | 2018 Rating | 2017 Rating | Total Assets ($Mil) | One Year Asset Growth | Asset Mix (As a % of Total Assets) Commercial Loans | Consumer Loans | Mortgage Loans | Securities | Capitalization Index | Leverage Ratio | Risk-Based Capital Ratio |
|---|---|---|---|---|---|---|---|---|---|---|---|---|---|---|
| Progressive Bank | Monroe | LA | **B** | B | B | 585.3 | 3.89 | 11.9 | 0.9 | 15.1 | 9.8 | **7.6** | 10.5 | 13.0 |
| Progressive National Bank | Mansfield | LA | **C+** | D+ | D+ | 75.0 | 23.61 | 4.5 | 2.9 | 23.6 | 17.9 | **6.2** | 8.2 | 16.4 |
| Progressive Ozark Bank | Salem | MO | **A-** | A- | A- | 115.9 | -0.14 | 5.0 | 6.1 | 50.5 | 5.2 | **9.8** | 10.9 | 16.9 |
| Progressive Savings Bank | Jamestown | TN | **B-** | B- | B- | 295.3 | -1.24 | 4.7 | 2.2 | 23.1 | 10.0 | **8.8** | 10.2 | 14.8 |
| ProGrowth Bank | Nicollet | MN | **B** | C+ | C | 148.7 | 4.39 | 5.6 | 1.0 | 11.6 | 18.0 | **8.7** | 10.1 | 17.7 |
| PromiseOne Bank | Duluth | GA | **A-** | B+ | A- | 450.4 | 16.19 | 8.6 | 0.0 | 1.8 | 11.7 | **10.0** | 12.7 | 18.9 |
| Prospect Bank | Paris | IL | **B-** | B- | B | 559.6 | 8.30 | 12.3 | 0.5 | 8.4 | 32.7 | **7.5** | 9.3 | 13.9 |
| Prosperity Bank | El Campo | TX | **A-** | A- | B+ | 32184.4 | 41.85 | 8.6 | 0.5 | 13.2 | 26.7 | **7.5** | 10.6 | 12.9 |
| Providence Bank | Columbia | MO | **B** | B | B | 1070.1 | 4.80 | 21.4 | 3.2 | 7.7 | 14.8 | **10.0** | 13.6 | 15.9 |
| ▲ Providence Bank | Rocky Mount | NC | **A-** | B | B+ | 479.4 | 5.97 | 5.7 | 0.4 | 10.0 | 4.1 | **10.0** | 12.6 | 15.5 |
| ▲ Providence Bank & Trust | South Holland | IL | **B+** | B | B | 1020.3 | 61.92 | 13.8 | 0.0 | 5.9 | 12.7 | **10.0** | 11.4 | 15.3 |
| Providence Bank of Texas | Southlake | TX | **B** | B- | B | 151.9 | 1.33 | 3.7 | 0.6 | 13.7 | 0.0 | **10.0** | 13.7 | 17.9 |
| Provident Bank | Amesbury | MA | **B+** | B+ | B | 1120.9 | 15.10 | 40.2 | 1.1 | 5.0 | 3.7 | **10.0** | 15.2 | 17.6 |
| Provident Bank | Iselin | NJ | **B-** | B- | B- | 9807.7 | 0.84 | 7.4 | 0.2 | 13.6 | 14.7 | **7.4** | 9.8 | 12.8 |
| ▲ Provident Savings Bank, F.S.B. | Riverside | CA | **C+** | C+ | C | 1107.4 | -1.76 | 0.1 | 0.0 | 31.6 | 7.5 | **8.9** | 10.2 | 17.7 |
| Provident State Bank, Inc. | Preston | MD | **B-** | C+ | C+ | 462.7 | 8.38 | 3.4 | 0.6 | 20.7 | 12.2 | **8.6** | 10.1 | 13.9 |
| Prudential Bank | Philadelphia | PA | **B-** | B | C+ | 1295.4 | 16.16 | 1.5 | 0.1 | 19.6 | 46.5 | **9.1** | 10.4 | 19.2 |
| Prudential Bank & Trust, FSB | Hartford | CT | **U** | U | U | 20.8 | 5.07 | 0.0 | 0.0 | 0.0 | 92.1 | **10.0** | 78.5 | 232.7 |
| PS Bank | Wyalusing | PA | **B** | B | B | 401.4 | 8.16 | 9.3 | 0.6 | 21.1 | 27.0 | **7.5** | 9.3 | 15.2 |
| Pueblo Bank and Trust Co. | Pueblo | CO | **B+** | A- | B+ | 434.0 | 2.42 | 5.0 | 0.2 | 5.5 | 27.2 | **10.0** | 12.1 | 18.2 |
| Pulaski Savings Bank | Chicago | IL | **D** | D- | D- | 46.4 | 2.80 | 0.0 | 0.6 | 73.6 | 11.4 | **5.5** | 7.5 | 17.4 |
| Putnam 1st Mercantile Bank | Cookeville | TN | **A-** | B+ | B+ | 127.2 | 5.44 | 16.3 | 2.8 | 21.7 | 13.3 | **10.0** | 11.6 | 17.3 |
| Putnam Bank | Putnam | CT | **B-** | B- | C+ | 523.6 | 1.85 | 1.6 | 0.2 | 39.4 | 16.1 | **10.0** | 12.9 | 19.7 |
| Putnam County Bank | Hurricane | WV | **B-** | C+ | B- | 589.7 | 0.25 | 2.9 | 0.8 | 35.0 | 27.5 | **10.0** | 15.8 | 33.5 |
| Putnam County National Bank of Carmel | Carmel | NY | **B** | B- | D+ | 156.5 | -5.02 | 1.7 | 0.3 | 24.1 | 15.5 | **10.0** | 21.9 | 54.7 |
| ▲ Putnam County State Bank | Unionville | MO | **B** | B+ | A- | 224.7 | 6.93 | 11.4 | 1.7 | 7.6 | 2.5 | **10.0** | 13.2 | 15.9 |
| PyraMax Bank, FSB | Greenfield | WI | **D+** | D | C- | 425.7 | -11.06 | 7.8 | 0.2 | 19.0 | 16.4 | **9.0** | 10.7 | 14.1 |
| QNB Bank | Quakertown | PA | **B-** | B- | B- | 1212.6 | 4.03 | 13.6 | 0.5 | 14.0 | 28.8 | **6.9** | 8.9 | 12.9 |
| ▲ Quad City Bank and Trust Co. | Bettendorf | IA | **B+** | B | B | 1702.0 | 3.77 | 23.6 | 0.7 | 8.5 | 13.0 | **6.1** | 9.9 | 11.8 |
| Quail Creek Bank, N.A. | Oklahoma City | OK | **C-** | C | B- | 691.6 | 0.46 | 3.2 | 1.0 | 22.1 | 14.0 | **7.9** | 9.6 | 15.1 |
| Quaint Oak Bank | Southampton | PA | **B** | C+ | C+ | 300.5 | 11.08 | 13.1 | 0.0 | 18.7 | 2.5 | **9.0** | 10.4 | 14.4 |
| Quantum National Bank | Suwanee | GA | **A** | A | A- | 512.7 | 4.66 | 3.6 | 0.0 | 11.1 | 2.8 | **10.0** | 11.6 | 15.2 |
| Quarry City S&L Assn. | Warrensburg | MO | **C+** | B- | B- | 59.0 | 8.52 | 0.4 | 1.3 | 29.9 | 0.0 | **10.0** | 15.5 | 21.8 |
| Queensborough National Bank & Trust Co. | Louisville | GA | **C-** | C | C+ | 1220.7 | 4.20 | 6.1 | 1.1 | 11.8 | 19.3 | **8.2** | 9.8 | 14.8 |
| ▲ Queenstown Bank of Maryland | Queenstown | MD | **A-** | B+ | B+ | 473.1 | 1.74 | 3.0 | 1.5 | 36.6 | 3.2 | **10.0** | 13.9 | 19.3 |
| Quoin Financial Bank | Miller | SD | **A-** | A- | A- | 174.7 | 1.85 | 12.5 | 1.6 | 5.8 | 12.8 | **10.0** | 11.7 | 15.2 |
| ▲ Quontic Bank | New York | NY | **B** | B | B+ | 394.7 | 8.42 | 0.6 | 0.0 | 52.8 | 1.7 | **8.6** | 10.0 | 21.0 |
| R Bank | Round Rock | TX | **B-** | C+ | C+ | 553.6 | 13.63 | 18.0 | 0.6 | 16.2 | 12.9 | **9.8** | 11.1 | 14.9 |
| ▲ Rabun County Bank | Clayton | GA | **B+** | B | C | 188.3 | 6.84 | 2.6 | 5.0 | 29.3 | 2.2 | **10.0** | 12.7 | 22.0 |
| Raccoon Valley Bank | Perry | IA | **C+** | C+ | B- | 304.9 | 8.60 | 11.7 | 0.6 | 7.3 | 20.4 | **5.0** | 7.9 | 11.0 |
| Radius Bank | Boston | MA | **C+** | C+ | C- | 1390.3 | 10.50 | 6.0 | 22.0 | 14.7 | 16.7 | **6.2** | 8.7 | 11.9 |
| ▲ Ramsey National Bank | Devils Lake | ND | **A** | A- | A | 255.6 | 1.27 | 12.9 | 0.9 | 8.3 | 16.5 | **10.0** | 13.2 | 18.6 |
| ▲ Randall State Bank | Randall | MN | **B-** | C+ | B | 46.5 | 1.05 | 6.5 | 2.3 | 23.4 | 3.4 | **10.0** | 12.0 | 18.6 |
| ▲ Range Bank, N.A. | Marquette | MI | **B-** | C+ | B- | 370.8 | -3.08 | 12.7 | 0.9 | 14.6 | 22.7 | **8.2** | 9.8 | 14.7 |
| Raritan State Bank | Raritan | IL | **C+** | C+ | C+ | 184.0 | 6.21 | 9.4 | 5.6 | 26.3 | 19.3 | **10.0** | 11.7 | 17.6 |
| Raymond Federal Bank | Raymond | WA | **C-** | D+ | C | 59.5 | 1.39 | 0.0 | 0.4 | 75.6 | 8.7 | **9.7** | 10.8 | 23.7 |
| Raymond James Bank, N.A. | Saint Petersburg | FL | **A-** | A- | A- | 26468.6 | 5.28 | 30.6 | 10.7 | 17.8 | 12.2 | **6.8** | 8.8 | 14.5 |
| Raymond James Trust, N.A. | Saint Petersburg | FL | **U** | U | U | 36.4 | 13.41 | 0.0 | 0.0 | 0.0 | 3.3 | **10.0** | 99.2 | 248.4 |
| Rayne Building and Loan Assn. | Rayne | LA | **B-** | B | B | 53.5 | -5.35 | 6.7 | 1.2 | 25.3 | 37.9 | **10.0** | 28.2 | 62.2 |
| Rayne State Bank & Trust Co. | Rayne | LA | **A** | A- | A- | 382.6 | 1.87 | 10.8 | 0.5 | 19.3 | 19.8 | **10.0** | 13.0 | 19.8 |
| ▲ RBC Bank (Georgia), N.A. | Raleigh | NC | **A-** | B+ | B- | 4528.7 | -8.54 | 0.0 | 4.1 | 27.5 | 61.2 | **8.3** | 9.9 | 30.6 |
| RCB Bank | Claremore | OK | **B** | B | B | 3176.4 | 12.40 | 4.7 | 5.4 | 8.6 | 23.6 | **7.1** | 9.1 | 13.3 |
| Reading Cooperative Bank | Reading | MA | **B-** | B- | B- | 597.5 | 4.74 | 3.1 | 0.1 | 47.1 | 16.0 | **6.9** | 8.9 | 15.2 |
| Readlyn Savings Bank | Readlyn | IA | **A-** | A- | A- | 77.5 | 3.92 | 8.5 | 1.5 | 21.3 | 20.3 | **10.0** | 16.0 | 21.8 |
| ReconTrust Co., N.A. | Simi Valley | CA | **U** | U | U | 350.1 | -2.60 | 0.0 | 0.0 | 0.0 | 0.0 | **10.0** | 99.2 | 457.2 |
| Red River Bank | Alexandria | LA | **A-** | A- | B | 1988.2 | 6.89 | 12.4 | 1.5 | 20.3 | 16.9 | **10.0** | 11.5 | 16.2 |
| Red River State Bank | Halstad | MN | **B** | B+ | B+ | 91.9 | -2.48 | 38.5 | 11.2 | 7.9 | 6.0 | **7.7** | 9.5 | 14.3 |
| Red Rock Bank | Sanborn | MN | **A-** | B | B | 42.9 | 7.66 | 8.6 | 2.4 | 11.4 | 4.8 | **6.1** | 8.1 | 14.9 |
| Redstone Bank | Centennial | CO | **A-** | B+ | A- | 159.8 | -1.12 | 5.9 | 0.0 | 17.0 | 18.9 | **10.0** | 13.2 | 20.0 |
| ▲ Redwood Capital Bank | Eureka | CA | **B+** | B | B | 368.3 | -0.09 | 8.6 | 0.3 | 7.1 | 8.3 | **7.6** | 9.4 | 13.9 |

| Asset Quality Index | Adjusted Non-Performing Loans as a % of Total Loans | Adjusted Non-Performing Loans as a % of Capital | Net Charge-Offs Avg Loans | Profitability Index | Net Income ($Mil) | Return on Assets (R.O.A.) | Return on Equity (R.O.E.) | Net Interest Spread | Overhead Efficiency Ratio | Liquidity Index | Liquidity Ratio | Hot Money Ratio | Stability Index |
|---|---|---|---|---|---|---|---|---|---|---|---|---|---|
| **8.2** | 0.18 | 1.2 | 0.05 | **4.2** | 3.8 | 0.65 | 6.08 | 3.84 | 79.2 | **2.5** | 15.8 | 16.6 | **7.6** |
| **8.7** | 0.09 | 0.8 | 0.04 | **5.0** | 0.9 | 1.30 | 16.47 | 3.97 | 73.4 | **2.6** | 31.4 | 19.1 | **4.2** |
| **6.5** | 0.55 | 3.3 | 0.03 | **7.5** | 1.8 | 1.58 | 14.10 | 4.62 | 71.7 | **4.7** | 7.8 | 2.8 | **8.5** |
| **5.1** | 0.64 | 8.2 | 0.17 | **3.4** | 1.5 | 0.50 | 4.85 | 4.08 | 87.6 | **1.9** | 22.0 | 21.2 | **6.0** |
| **7.2** | 0.31 | 1.1 | 0.08 | **4.9** | 1.1 | 0.91 | 9.20 | 4.35 | 71.2 | **5.5** | 34.1 | 4.1 | **4.6** |
| **6.2** | 3.10 | 4.1 | 0.07 | **9.8** | 11.5 | 2.74 | 20.90 | 4.25 | 52.9 | **1.1** | 29.4 | 47.1 | **8.8** |
| **5.6** | 1.67 | 7.5 | -0.15 | **4.2** | 5.1 | 0.96 | 10.14 | 2.86 | 70.7 | **0.9** | 24.5 | 22.6 | **7.0** |
| **6.8** | 0.29 | 0.9 | 0.03 | **7.2** | 348.7 | 1.45 | 8.04 | 3.33 | 46.0 | **3.7** | 12.3 | 10.4 | **10.0** |
| **5.8** | 0.80 | 3.4 | 0.38 | **4.0** | 9.0 | 0.87 | 5.75 | 3.57 | 72.5 | **1.1** | 7.8 | 24.5 | **8.8** |
| **7.1** | 0.07 | 0.4 | 0.06 | **7.8** | 7.4 | 1.55 | 13.09 | 3.94 | 45.6 | **0.8** | 14.2 | 34.1 | **7.8** |
| **5.6** | 0.97 | 4.1 | -0.14 | **8.4** | 31.7 | 3.02 | 27.14 | 4.65 | 52.6 | **3.4** | 22.0 | 12.5 | **9.5** |
| **5.3** | 1.60 | 5.4 | 0.00 | **4.2** | 1.1 | 0.74 | 5.56 | 4.02 | 76.6 | **0.9** | 22.4 | 34.6 | **7.8** |
| **6.3** | 0.78 | 3.7 | 0.35 | **5.3** | 10.7 | 1.03 | 8.31 | 4.43 | 58.6 | **3.9** | 7.4 | 3.3 | **9.7** |
| **4.4** | 1.11 | 4.2 | 0.18 | **5.6** | 112.3 | 1.14 | 8.33 | 3.35 | 55.6 | **3.9** | 8.2 | 6.1 | **9.9** |
| **4.6** | 1.71 | 8.2 | -0.01 | **3.7** | 6.5 | 0.59 | 5.70 | 3.63 | 80.8 | **3.3** | 4.9 | 11.6 | **8.0** |
| **6.0** | 0.60 | 4.2 | 0.09 | **4.5** | 3.8 | 0.84 | 8.79 | 3.73 | 72.0 | **2.5** | 9.2 | 16.0 | **5.5** |
| **5.6** | 2.33 | 9.5 | -0.02 | **3.7** | 10.4 | 0.86 | 7.82 | 2.19 | 58.2 | **2.2** | 37.3 | 33.7 | **9.2** |
| **9.4** | na | 0.0 | na | **10.0** | 5.4 | 23.26 | 26.55 | 2.60 | 22.5 | **4.0** | na | 100.0 | **7.0** |
| **6.8** | 0.39 | 3.0 | 0.06 | **5.6** | 4.6 | 1.18 | 12.84 | 3.33 | 60.7 | **1.8** | 24.2 | 18.2 | **6.3** |
| **8.8** | 0.73 | 1.8 | -0.13 | **5.3** | 5.1 | 1.20 | 10.33 | 4.05 | 74.9 | **5.6** | 34.2 | 3.2 | **8.1** |
| **5.6** | 2.28 | 14.0 | 0.00 | **0.7** | 0.1 | 0.13 | 1.72 | 2.48 | 94.5 | **4.0** | 16.8 | 8.8 | **1.8** |
| **7.5** | 0.06 | 1.9 | 0.21 | **6.6** | 1.9 | 1.49 | 13.00 | 3.96 | 55.7 | **0.9** | 20.4 | 39.5 | **7.3** |
| **6.5** | 1.05 | 5.1 | 0.00 | **3.9** | 4.1 | 0.77 | 5.74 | 3.00 | 69.1 | **2.2** | 17.5 | 15.0 | **8.1** |
| **5.0** | 4.71 | 12.9 | 0.32 | **3.8** | 4.7 | 0.79 | 5.23 | 2.93 | 59.9 | **1.5** | 33.5 | 40.5 | **6.4** |
| **5.4** | 6.71 | 10.9 | 0.00 | **4.0** | 1.3 | 0.82 | 3.83 | 3.47 | 72.2 | **5.9** | 42.9 | 5.1 | **6.2** |
| **5.9** | 0.20 | 5.4 | 0.08 | **9.5** | 3.7 | 1.71 | 12.92 | 3.63 | 36.2 | **0.7** | 16.6 | 49.6 | **8.7** |
| **5.9** | 0.78 | 4.3 | 0.07 | **1.5** | 1.1 | 0.24 | 2.36 | 2.82 | 97.8 | **1.6** | 21.4 | 15.9 | **5.0** |
| **5.4** | 2.00 | 11.9 | 0.03 | **4.3** | 10.7 | 0.89 | 10.29 | 3.16 | 66.4 | **3.6** | 14.4 | 11.1 | **7.6** |
| **6.6** | 0.50 | 3.5 | 0.25 | **6.1** | 21.6 | 1.28 | 13.33 | 3.34 | 55.6 | **4.7** | 17.6 | 4.9 | **7.9** |
| **3.2** | 2.11 | 13.8 | 0.16 | **7.5** | 11.0 | 1.61 | 16.64 | 3.84 | 53.5 | **2.6** | 28.1 | 17.9 | **8.7** |
| **6.0** | 0.13 | 1.3 | 0.02 | **5.1** | 2.9 | 1.04 | 9.82 | 3.36 | 69.6 | **0.7** | 11.9 | 45.1 | **5.8** |
| **7.3** | 0.00 | 0.0 | 0.00 | **10.0** | 15.1 | 3.08 | 27.10 | 5.21 | 43.5 | **2.5** | 13.8 | 11.9 | **9.3** |
| **5.2** | 1.97 | 9.3 | 0.00 | **3.3** | 0.3 | 0.51 | 3.21 | 3.81 | 85.8 | **2.4** | 21.0 | 17.4 | **7.2** |
| **2.1** | 3.75 | 26.6 | 0.13 | **5.9** | 14.6 | 1.22 | 12.40 | 4.06 | 69.6 | **3.4** | 18.9 | 12.7 | **8.9** |
| **5.5** | 2.09 | 9.6 | 0.05 | **8.8** | 7.5 | 1.62 | 11.76 | 4.27 | 50.1 | **1.7** | 12.6 | 20.8 | **8.2** |
| **7.8** | 0.55 | 2.6 | 0.00 | **6.9** | 2.2 | 1.28 | 10.89 | 4.62 | 63.2 | **1.3** | 8.8 | 23.5 | **7.5** |
| **6.0** | 0.60 | 5.1 | 0.04 | **6.2** | 5.1 | 1.32 | 13.24 | 3.50 | 83.6 | **0.8** | 20.7 | 44.2 | **6.8** |
| **8.1** | 0.03 | 0.2 | 0.10 | **4.1** | 3.7 | 0.71 | 6.43 | 3.99 | 76.1 | **0.9** | 12.9 | 31.3 | **7.2** |
| **7.0** | 0.82 | 3.3 | -0.31 | **6.0** | 2.2 | 1.21 | 9.01 | 4.26 | 67.0 | **4.8** | 33.1 | 8.1 | **8.7** |
| **7.7** | 0.39 | 1.6 | 0.00 | **5.3** | 3.5 | 1.24 | 15.70 | 3.58 | 65.0 | **1.7** | 19.8 | 23.0 | **5.2** |
| **3.8** | 1.19 | 8.7 | 0.38 | **2.8** | 6.2 | 0.47 | 5.09 | 3.01 | 78.2 | **1.4** | 11.0 | 7.6 | **7.2** |
| **8.1** | 0.01 | 0.0 | -0.13 | **8.3** | 5.3 | 2.07 | 15.57 | 3.94 | 56.3 | **3.0** | 9.1 | 11.1 | **9.5** |
| **3.6** | 3.16 | 14.6 | 0.03 | **8.7** | 0.9 | 1.92 | 16.59 | 5.20 | 61.5 | **2.9** | 26.7 | 16.3 | **8.2** |
| **4.3** | 2.48 | 11.4 | 0.02 | **4.1** | 2.9 | 0.79 | 7.84 | 3.77 | 74.7 | **4.7** | 31.6 | 8.5 | **5.9** |
| **1.7** | 6.22 | 29.3 | 0.13 | **4.3** | 1.4 | 0.81 | 6.94 | 3.46 | 64.4 | **1.6** | 21.5 | 24.3 | **6.9** |
| **8.7** | 0.57 | 2.0 | 0.00 | **2.2** | 0.2 | 0.25 | 2.35 | 3.75 | 91.3 | **1.6** | 19.0 | 24.7 | **5.8** |
| **7.6** | 0.23 | 1.7 | 0.03 | **8.7** | 418.6 | 1.66 | 19.10 | 3.35 | 36.8 | **4.6** | 19.5 | 1.6 | **9.2** |
| **10.0** | na | 0.0 | na | **10.0** | 7.5 | 23.73 | 27.25 | 2.49 | 82.4 | **4.0** | 488.1 | 0.0 | **7.0** |
| **9.0** | 0.79 | 2.9 | 0.00 | **3.2** | 0.3 | 0.60 | 2.09 | 3.58 | 83.3 | **2.7** | 66.6 | 56.6 | **7.2** |
| **8.7** | 0.14 | 0.4 | -0.01 | **7.2** | 6.5 | 1.73 | 13.23 | 4.38 | 61.2 | **4.5** | 20.7 | 6.4 | **9.2** |
| **9.8** | 0.24 | 1.0 | 0.21 | **7.6** | 74.6 | 1.57 | 18.43 | 2.71 | 38.1 | **7.8** | 72.3 | 1.6 | **7.1** |
| **6.7** | 0.31 | 1.7 | 0.07 | **5.3** | 40.1 | 1.31 | 12.94 | 3.61 | 67.0 | **3.2** | 14.0 | 11.9 | **9.0** |
| **7.7** | 0.14 | 1.7 | 0.24 | **3.4** | 3.6 | 0.61 | 6.80 | 3.31 | 73.7 | **1.5** | 19.9 | 12.9 | **5.6** |
| **8.6** | 0.01 | 0.3 | 0.03 | **8.1** | 1.3 | 1.79 | 11.24 | 3.51 | 44.1 | **1.3** | 27.9 | 33.7 | **8.0** |
| **10.0** | na | 0.0 | na | **1.9** | -9.7 | -2.74 | -2.75 | 6.00 | 192.7 | **4.0** | na | 0.0 | **7.0** |
| **7.9** | 0.49 | 2.6 | 0.03 | **6.3** | 25.4 | 1.33 | 12.05 | 3.57 | 59.5 | **3.6** | 21.7 | 12.7 | **9.5** |
| **6.5** | 0.23 | 1.8 | 0.23 | **5.7** | 1.3 | 1.39 | 13.98 | 4.40 | 64.1 | **0.7** | 13.0 | 33.9 | **6.7** |
| **7.1** | 0.00 | 1.4 | 0.00 | **4.8** | 0.5 | 1.18 | 10.49 | 3.69 | 65.3 | **5.3** | 45.9 | 9.6 | **6.3** |
| **7.8** | 0.00 | 0.0 | 0.00 | **5.4** | 1.4 | 0.91 | 5.63 | 5.01 | 59.3 | **2.0** | 32.2 | 26.8 | **7.8** |
| **7.1** | 0.18 | 0.8 | -0.24 | **7.3** | 4.9 | 1.33 | 14.67 | 4.20 | 61.3 | **3.8** | 14.2 | 9.8 | **6.5** |

| Name | City | State | Rating | 2018 Rating | 2017 Rating | Total Assets ($Mil) | One Year Asset Growth | Asset Mix (As a % of Total Assets) Commercial Loans | Consumer Loans | Mortgage Loans | Securities | Capitalization Index | Leverage Ratio | Risk-Based Capital Ratio |
|---|---|---|---|---|---|---|---|---|---|---|---|---|---|---|
| Regal Bank | Livingston | NJ | **C** | C | C | 511.5 | -1.70 | 1.2 | 0.1 | 2.6 | 8.3 | **8.2** | 9.8 | 15.3 |
| Regent Bank | Tulsa | OK | **C+** | C+ | C | 672.4 | 15.78 | 24.5 | 0.5 | 13.2 | 2.0 | **5.3** | 10.1 | 11.2 |
| ▲ Regional Missouri Bank | Marceline | MO | **C** | C | C | 374.3 | 53.33 | 5.9 | 2.0 | 17.3 | 14.9 | **9.7** | 12.1 | 14.8 |
| Regions Bank | Birmingham | AL | **B** | B- | C+ | 125641.0 | 0.74 | 19.7 | 6.1 | 14.1 | 19.1 | **7.5** | 10.2 | 12.9 |
| Reliabank Dakota | Estelline | SD | **B-** | B- | B | 471.2 | 20.26 | 14.1 | 1.8 | 6.4 | 23.5 | **5.9** | 9.0 | 11.7 |
| Reliance Bank | Faribault | MN | **B-** | B | B | 155.7 | 8.48 | 22.0 | 1.2 | 12.8 | 12.7 | **8.7** | 10.1 | 13.9 |
| Reliance Savings Bank | Altoona | PA | **C+** | C+ | C+ | 556.1 | 4.63 | 3.9 | 1.5 | 25.7 | 21.4 | **8.8** | 10.2 | 14.3 |
| ▼ Reliance State Bank | Story City | IA | **B+** | A- | A- | 230.0 | 1.66 | 6.7 | 1.1 | 11.1 | 24.0 | **7.6** | 10.0 | 13.0 |
| Reliant Bank | Brentwood | TN | **B** | B+ | B+ | 1897.6 | 10.17 | 12.4 | 0.9 | 13.5 | 13.7 | **7.4** | 10.3 | 12.8 |
| Relyance Bank, N.A. | Pine Bluff | AR | **B** | C+ | B | 860.1 | 4.18 | 7.9 | 1.1 | 10.6 | 11.7 | **9.6** | 12.1 | 14.6 |
| Renasant Bank | Tupelo | MS | **A-** | A- | B+ | 13387.5 | 3.66 | 10.0 | 2.3 | 18.2 | 9.6 | **8.0** | 11.0 | 13.4 |
| ▲ Republic Bank & Trust | Norman | OK | **B-** | C+ | C+ | 697.0 | 25.41 | 6.5 | 1.2 | 12.8 | 29.9 | **10.0** | 11.7 | 16.4 |
| Republic Bank & Trust Co. | Louisville | KY | **A-** | A- | A- | 5611.1 | 7.28 | 7.4 | 4.5 | 21.9 | 9.5 | **9.9** | 12.1 | 14.9 |
| Republic Bank of Arizona | Phoenix | AZ | **B+** | B+ | B+ | 107.9 | 3.64 | 8.0 | 0.1 | 9.5 | 23.1 | **10.0** | 15.0 | 22.8 |
| Republic Bank of Chicago | Oak Brook | IL | **B+** | B | B | 2016.4 | -2.01 | 20.6 | 0.1 | 6.8 | 11.6 | **8.3** | 11.1 | 13.6 |
| Republic Banking Co. | Republic | OH | **B-** | B- | B- | 51.0 | 6.70 | 5.1 | 9.4 | 40.0 | 6.0 | **10.0** | 15.2 | 22.7 |
| Republic First Bank | Philadelphia | PA | **D+** | C | C- | 3332.5 | 21.38 | 4.4 | 0.1 | 10.8 | 35.8 | **5.5** | 7.5 | 11.9 |
| ▲ Resource Bank | Covington | LA | **B** | C+ | B- | 752.3 | 0.77 | 3.4 | 1.0 | 22.9 | 6.0 | **9.7** | 12.1 | 14.8 |
| Resource Bank, N.A. | DeKalb | IL | **C** | C+ | C+ | 528.4 | 11.64 | 4.8 | 0.7 | 14.5 | 32.1 | **6.8** | 8.9 | 14.1 |
| Revere Bank | Rockville | MD | **B+** | B+ | B- | 2851.2 | 16.13 | 12.2 | 0.0 | 11.9 | 6.5 | **7.7** | 9.5 | 13.2 |
| Reynolds State Bank | Reynolds | IL | **A** | A | A+ | 106.0 | 5.25 | 2.9 | 0.1 | 0.8 | 68.4 | **10.0** | 18.3 | 55.1 |
| Rhinebeck Bank | Poughkeepsie | NY | **C** | D+ | C | 973.8 | 10.38 | 12.0 | 35.5 | 6.8 | 11.8 | **7.4** | 10.8 | 12.8 |
| Richland County Bank | Richland Center | WI | **B** | B- | B- | 101.9 | 2.43 | 4.6 | 3.3 | 11.0 | 42.6 | **10.0** | 18.3 | 34.7 |
| Richland State Bank | Bruce | SD | **B+** | B+ | A- | 36.5 | -1.76 | 5.7 | 9.8 | 2.2 | 37.4 | **9.3** | 10.5 | 18.8 |
| Richton Bank & Trust Co. | Richton | MS | **B** | B | B | 55.7 | -1.66 | 17.4 | 3.3 | 9.5 | 30.7 | **10.0** | 16.8 | 32.4 |
| Richwood Banking Co., Inc. | Richwood | OH | **B-** | B- | B | 732.6 | 3.70 | 4.9 | 0.6 | 20.8 | 20.0 | **7.7** | 9.5 | 13.2 |
| Riddell National Bank | Brazil | IN | **C+** | C | C | 238.7 | 10.31 | 10.9 | 5.7 | 34.9 | 10.7 | **6.9** | 9.0 | 12.5 |
| Ridgewood Savings Bank | Ridgewood | NY | **B** | C+ | C+ | 5814.1 | 5.05 | 0.0 | 0.1 | 35.0 | 20.1 | **10.0** | 12.9 | 21.1 |
| Riley State Bank of Riley, Kansas | Riley | KS | **B** | B | B | 89.5 | 2.86 | 10.7 | 4.5 | 7.0 | 24.5 | **9.7** | 10.8 | 16.7 |
| Rio Bank | McAllen | TX | **B-** | C+ | B- | 545.0 | 4.41 | 12.0 | 1.4 | 8.5 | 21.8 | **7.8** | 9.6 | 14.2 |
| Rio Grande S&L Assn. | Monte Vista | CO | **C+** | C+ | C+ | 111.2 | 6.32 | 1.5 | 2.7 | 56.3 | 6.5 | **10.0** | 11.0 | 18.1 |
| River Bank | La Crosse | WI | **B** | B- | B | 526.9 | 7.34 | 6.4 | 0.3 | 11.3 | 6.5 | **7.7** | 10.7 | 13.1 |
| ▲ River Bank & Trust | Prattville | AL | **A-** | B+ | B | 1364.1 | 27.44 | 10.0 | 3.0 | 16.5 | 22.2 | **9.2** | 11.0 | 14.4 |
| River City Bank | Sacramento | CA | **B+** | B+ | B+ | 2544.7 | 15.33 | 3.9 | 0.0 | 5.6 | 19.9 | **6.7** | 9.5 | 12.3 |
| River City Bank | Rome | GA | **A-** | B | C+ | 161.9 | -3.11 | 6.6 | 1.8 | 13.5 | 21.6 | **10.0** | 11.6 | 17.8 |
| River City Bank, Inc. | Louisville | KY | **B+** | A- | A- | 310.4 | -9.99 | 0.4 | 0.4 | 29.9 | 15.3 | **10.0** | 13.9 | 18.5 |
| River Falls State Bank | River Falls | WI | **B+** | B- | B- | 94.8 | 3.32 | 1.1 | 2.9 | 33.1 | 13.4 | **10.0** | 13.9 | 23.2 |
| River Valley Community Bank | Yuba City | CA | **B** | B- | B- | 442.3 | 17.33 | 5.8 | 0.0 | 2.5 | 39.5 | **6.2** | 8.2 | 12.5 |
| RiverBank | Pocahontas | AR | **B-** | C+ | B | 105.6 | 10.66 | 7.1 | 1.3 | 9.5 | 5.6 | **8.9** | 10.3 | 18.1 |
| RiverBank | Spokane | WA | **C+** | C | C | 147.3 | 5.87 | 9.5 | 0.2 | 8.9 | 1.7 | **8.9** | 10.3 | 14.3 |
| ▲ RiverHills Bank | Vicksburg | MS | **B+** | B- | B | 327.6 | 3.66 | 7.6 | 1.6 | 11.3 | 33.0 | **10.0** | 11.0 | 20.5 |
| ▲ RiverHills Bank | Milford | OH | **B-** | C+ | B- | 182.6 | 11.55 | 7.4 | 0.2 | 7.9 | 20.7 | **7.1** | 10.9 | 12.6 |
| Riverland Bank | Jordan | MN | **C+** | C+ | C+ | 145.2 | 1.79 | 18.2 | 0.9 | 21.6 | 1.0 | **10.0** | 13.0 | 15.9 |
| ▲ Rivers Edge Bank | Marion | SD | **C** | C | C | 211.9 | 3.16 | 5.7 | 2.5 | 6.5 | 2.4 | **6.7** | 8.7 | 12.7 |
| ▲ Riverside Bank | Sparkman | AR | **B** | B- | B- | 60.4 | -3.55 | 16.0 | 7.1 | 50.7 | 2.0 | **7.4** | 9.2 | 13.2 |
| Riverview Bank | Marysville | PA | **C** | C | D | 1080.1 | -5.05 | 7.2 | 0.8 | 15.2 | 8.5 | **6.8** | 9.1 | 12.4 |
| Riverview Community Bank | Vancouver | WA | **A** | A- | B | 1183.3 | 2.89 | 5.9 | 0.4 | 8.3 | 13.2 | **10.0** | 12.1 | 17.7 |
| Riverwind Bank | Augusta | AR | **B** | B- | B- | 104.9 | 0.92 | 15.2 | 3.0 | 15.3 | 16.8 | **9.7** | 10.8 | 16.8 |
| RiverWood Bank | Baxter | MN | **C+** | C | C+ | 445.3 | 6.47 | 11.0 | 6.0 | 13.9 | 14.5 | **6.6** | 8.6 | 12.3 |
| RNB State Bank | Rawlins | WY | **C+** | C+ | C+ | 178.8 | 0.49 | 9.1 | 1.9 | 5.4 | 20.5 | **8.3** | 9.9 | 15.8 |
| Roanoke Rapids Savings Bank, SSB | Roanoke Rapids | NC | **C+** | C- | D+ | 72.7 | -4.42 | 0.7 | 1.8 | 35.4 | 13.9 | **10.0** | 24.5 | 46.5 |
| Robert Lee State Bank | Robert Lee | TX | **B-** | C+ | C+ | 46.0 | 11.51 | 4.3 | 5.5 | 16.7 | 42.3 | **10.0** | 13.3 | 29.6 |
| Robertson Banking Co. | Demopolis | AL | **A-** | A- | A- | 327.9 | 7.69 | 6.9 | 1.5 | 19.0 | 8.5 | **8.3** | 10.0 | 13.6 |
| Rochelle State Bank | Rochelle | GA | **C+** | B- | B- | 29.4 | 8.35 | 4.2 | 5.5 | 0.5 | 38.7 | **10.0** | 16.9 | 36.5 |
| Rochester State Bank | Rochester | IL | **C** | C | C- | 98.3 | 8.07 | 1.7 | 1.7 | 10.3 | 68.3 | **8.8** | 10.2 | 18.3 |
| Rock Canyon Bank | Provo | UT | **B+** | B+ | B | 507.4 | 21.88 | 9.8 | 0.2 | 5.8 | 0.0 | **7.1** | 10.3 | 12.6 |
| Rockefeller Trust Co., N.A. | New York | NY | **U** | U | U | 15.7 | 14.46 | 0.0 | 0.0 | 0.0 | 81.8 | **10.0** | 86.4 | 358.1 |
| Rockhold Bank | Bainbridge | OH | **D-** | D | D+ | 40.1 | 4.49 | 5.5 | 0.9 | 50.2 | 0.0 | **6.4** | 8.4 | 13.6 |
| Rockland Savings Bank, FSB | Rockland | ME | **C+** | D+ | D | 87.0 | 14.73 | 7.6 | 1.7 | 49.4 | 0.1 | **10.0** | 11.5 | 17.9 |
| Rockland Trust Co. | Rockland | MA | **B+** | B+ | B+ | 11397.6 | 28.78 | 12.4 | 0.2 | 21.2 | 10.4 | **8.8** | 11.1 | 14.0 |

| Asset Quality Index | Adjusted Non-Performing Loans as a % of Total Loans | Adjusted Non-Performing Loans as a % of Capital | Net Charge-Offs Avg Loans | Profitability Index | Net Income ($Mil) | Return on Assets (R.O.A.) | Return on Equity (R.O.E.) | Net Interest Spread | Overhead Efficiency Ratio | Liquidity Index | Liquidity Ratio | Hot Money Ratio | Stability Index |
|---|---|---|---|---|---|---|---|---|---|---|---|---|---|
| **7.1** | 0.00 | 0.0 | 0.00 | **2.6** | 1.5 | 0.30 | 3.02 | 2.89 | 85.3 | **1.1** | 19.0 | 32.3 | **6.6** |
| **5.5** | 0.91 | 6.5 | 0.11 | **4.6** | 5.0 | 0.82 | 8.00 | 3.75 | 66.6 | **0.7** | 10.9 | 34.9 | **6.3** |
| **5.6** | 0.58 | 2.7 | 0.07 | **8.0** | 4.9 | 1.80 | 17.45 | 4.33 | 58.8 | **3.4** | 21.1 | 10.8 | **8.4** |
| **4.8** | 1.14 | 4.8 | 0.43 | **7.2** | 1785.0 | 1.44 | 10.95 | 3.56 | 55.8 | **4.9** | 18.8 | 3.7 | **10.0** |
| **6.1** | 0.62 | 4.4 | 0.40 | **5.5** | 4.9 | 1.13 | 11.98 | 3.91 | 66.0 | **2.9** | 26.4 | 16.1 | **7.1** |
| **4.6** | 1.51 | 10.5 | 0.85 | **4.5** | 1.4 | 0.91 | 9.20 | 3.70 | 62.4 | **1.7** | 19.8 | 21.0 | **7.6** |
| **5.0** | 2.16 | 7.5 | 0.52 | **3.5** | 3.6 | 0.66 | 6.24 | 3.05 | 71.7 | **2.5** | 9.4 | 13.7 | **7.2** |
| **4.8** | 1.72 | 9.8 | 0.01 | **6.5** | 2.8 | 1.24 | 9.00 | 3.29 | 51.7 | **4.2** | 20.6 | 7.9 | **8.4** |
| **7.4** | 0.32 | 1.7 | -0.04 | **4.3** | 19.8 | 0.79 | 6.26 | 3.54 | 73.9 | **0.7** | 15.3 | 40.6 | **9.4** |
| **5.2** | 0.80 | 4.0 | 0.17 | **5.4** | 9.0 | 1.07 | 8.17 | 3.74 | 67.3 | **1.9** | 4.1 | 18.4 | **8.0** |
| **6.4** | 0.39 | 1.7 | 0.04 | **7.3** | 179.3 | 1.39 | 7.81 | 4.15 | 60.9 | **3.2** | 11.3 | 13.0 | **10.0** |
| **4.1** | 3.93 | 16.2 | 0.13 | **6.2** | 7.4 | 1.31 | 11.55 | 4.48 | 67.2 | **5.0** | 49.0 | 12.4 | **7.2** |
| **6.5** | 0.98 | 4.6 | 0.61 | **7.9** | 91.0 | 1.63 | 13.67 | 4.50 | 55.4 | **2.9** | 14.1 | 8.5 | **9.6** |
| **7.8** | 0.85 | 2.0 | 0.10 | **3.8** | 0.5 | 0.42 | 2.86 | 4.02 | 87.6 | **1.7** | 36.6 | 35.3 | **7.5** |
| **5.7** | 1.25 | 7.0 | 0.08 | **7.7** | 28.7 | 1.44 | 13.48 | 3.99 | 55.2 | **2.7** | 21.6 | 16.1 | **9.2** |
| **3.4** | 3.49 | 19.9 | 0.01 | **8.1** | 0.8 | 1.67 | 10.72 | 4.31 | 50.7 | **2.4** | 11.3 | 16.7 | **7.5** |
| **6.6** | 1.06 | 6.1 | 0.08 | **1.4** | -0.3 | -0.01 | -0.12 | 2.91 | 99.9 | **4.5** | 16.4 | 6.2 | **5.1** |
| **5.6** | 0.54 | 2.0 | 0.00 | **6.4** | 9.4 | 1.26 | 10.65 | 4.48 | 64.1 | **3.1** | 9.9 | 13.2 | **8.3** |
| **2.9** | 4.35 | 21.1 | 0.03 | **4.3** | 4.8 | 0.95 | 10.07 | 3.86 | 78.7 | **4.1** | 24.2 | 9.1 | **6.5** |
| **7.1** | 0.16 | 0.9 | 0.02 | **6.3** | 31.7 | 1.19 | 11.11 | 3.57 | 49.8 | **1.3** | 10.4 | 24.2 | **8.5** |
| **10.0** | 0.00 | 0.3 | -0.95 | **5.7** | 1.1 | 1.09 | 4.47 | 2.49 | 36.4 | **7.4** | 90.7 | 5.7 | **9.4** |
| **3.3** | 1.12 | 8.3 | 0.43 | **4.2** | 6.8 | 0.74 | 7.21 | 3.76 | 71.3 | **2.3** | 11.7 | 16.9 | **5.3** |
| **9.0** | 0.02 | 0.0 | 0.02 | **4.8** | 1.2 | 1.24 | 6.71 | 3.48 | 65.2 | **5.9** | 58.2 | 10.1 | **7.9** |
| **7.9** | 0.00 | 0.0 | 0.10 | **7.4** | 0.7 | 1.98 | 15.22 | 4.01 | 66.0 | **4.6** | 65.9 | 16.1 | **7.0** |
| **8.6** | 0.00 | 1.6 | 0.18 | **4.6** | 0.6 | 1.05 | 6.39 | 4.24 | 78.7 | **5.5** | 49.9 | 9.2 | **7.6** |
| **5.7** | 0.72 | 4.7 | 0.01 | **4.3** | 6.2 | 0.85 | 8.22 | 3.76 | 71.2 | **1.9** | 10.1 | 19.1 | **6.7** |
| **3.9** | 1.71 | 13.7 | 0.12 | **4.5** | 1.9 | 0.82 | 9.55 | 3.78 | 72.1 | **1.2** | 17.4 | 26.9 | **4.4** |
| **6.8** | 0.73 | 3.8 | 0.00 | **4.0** | 44.8 | 0.79 | 5.91 | 2.28 | 73.1 | **2.6** | 28.7 | 24.2 | **9.1** |
| **7.1** | 0.00 | 0.0 | 0.30 | **4.1** | 0.8 | 0.90 | 8.20 | 3.48 | 69.6 | **1.8** | 10.7 | 19.4 | **6.9** |
| **4.4** | 1.17 | 7.7 | 0.04 | **6.1** | 6.6 | 1.20 | 11.29 | 4.98 | 71.0 | **3.6** | 19.8 | 11.2 | **6.5** |
| **5.1** | 1.65 | 11.7 | 0.01 | **2.3** | 0.2 | 0.22 | 1.94 | 4.05 | 92.5 | **1.6** | 12.4 | 22.9 | **6.1** |
| **4.4** | 0.75 | 4.1 | 0.02 | **7.3** | 7.8 | 1.53 | 13.63 | 3.19 | 45.8 | **0.9** | 5.9 | 30.8 | **8.8** |
| **7.1** | 0.58 | 2.2 | 0.11 | **6.3** | 14.2 | 1.24 | 10.26 | 4.08 | 59.4 | **3.5** | 22.2 | 13.6 | **8.9** |
| **7.5** | 0.00 | 0.0 | -0.03 | **6.0** | 25.3 | 1.07 | 11.33 | 2.72 | 38.9 | **4.4** | 11.2 | 5.8 | **8.8** |
| **8.8** | 0.00 | 0.0 | -0.16 | **5.8** | 1.7 | 1.04 | 9.03 | 4.44 | 67.6 | **4.0** | 30.4 | 11.6 | **6.4** |
| **6.6** | 1.72 | 6.3 | 0.74 | **4.3** | 2.3 | 0.72 | 5.42 | 3.99 | 75.5 | **2.2** | 22.8 | 18.9 | **8.2** |
| **8.9** | 0.38 | 1.8 | -0.01 | **4.6** | 1.0 | 1.12 | 7.63 | 3.75 | 69.1 | **5.2** | 29.3 | 3.6 | **7.8** |
| **9.1** | 0.15 | 0.4 | -0.01 | **5.2** | 4.4 | 1.08 | 12.51 | 3.25 | 56.1 | **3.7** | 39.1 | 16.2 | **5.0** |
| **4.0** | 1.97 | 8.3 | 0.03 | **9.4** | 1.6 | 1.53 | 14.66 | 4.30 | 41.2 | **0.7** | 18.3 | 51.8 | **7.6** |
| **7.1** | 0.45 | 1.5 | -0.01 | **3.3** | 0.8 | 0.59 | 5.69 | 4.30 | 85.8 | **1.8** | 27.7 | 26.3 | **5.9** |
| **6.5** | 0.88 | 5.6 | 0.02 | **6.3** | 5.3 | 1.62 | 15.17 | 3.37 | 55.8 | **2.2** | 30.2 | 22.2 | **7.5** |
| **6.3** | 0.13 | 0.9 | 0.02 | **7.6** | 2.7 | 1.62 | 15.54 | 5.29 | 69.7 | **1.5** | 13.9 | 4.5 | **6.6** |
| **6.8** | 0.28 | 1.8 | 0.00 | **3.0** | 1.0 | 0.73 | 5.61 | 4.00 | 79.4 | **0.6** | 10.9 | 48.2 | **6.0** |
| **3.5** | 0.88 | 4.3 | 0.01 | **5.2** | 2.5 | 1.22 | 11.56 | 3.86 | 63.2 | **3.8** | 19.5 | 9.0 | **7.1** |
| **7.3** | 0.20 | 1.8 | -0.02 | **9.8** | 1.4 | 2.34 | 26.77 | 3.97 | 54.1 | **0.6** | 8.0 | 44.5 | **6.3** |
| **7.2** | 0.27 | 1.8 | 0.14 | **2.8** | 4.9 | 0.44 | 4.01 | 4.12 | 83.7 | **3.4** | 8.2 | 11.4 | **7.7** |
| **6.4** | 0.63 | 2.0 | 0.01 | **8.3** | 18.2 | 1.57 | 11.44 | 4.52 | 60.8 | **4.3** | 20.8 | 8.8 | **10.0** |
| **6.3** | 0.67 | 3.7 | 0.30 | **3.9** | 0.7 | 0.67 | 6.40 | 4.01 | 73.3 | **1.9** | 28.9 | 25.7 | **5.9** |
| **4.3** | 0.74 | 5.4 | 0.02 | **5.0** | 4.0 | 0.94 | 10.54 | 3.78 | 67.3 | **1.8** | 15.4 | 17.3 | **5.7** |
| **7.3** | 0.60 | 2.7 | 0.01 | **3.6** | 1.3 | 0.76 | 7.58 | 4.09 | 83.8 | **4.0** | 22.1 | 8.7 | **5.8** |
| **8.6** | 0.69 | 1.3 | 0.00 | **2.3** | 0.3 | 0.36 | 1.45 | 3.79 | 87.3 | **3.2** | 30.5 | 15.7 | **6.3** |
| **8.9** | 0.55 | 2.2 | -0.05 | **3.1** | 0.2 | 0.53 | 3.78 | 3.61 | 86.8 | **1.6** | 27.7 | 28.0 | **5.9** |
| **8.5** | 0.18 | 1.0 | 0.01 | **7.3** | 5.4 | 1.68 | 16.13 | 4.25 | 58.6 | **1.5** | 15.7 | 22.9 | **7.8** |
| **5.5** | 10.89 | 17.2 | 0.08 | **1.2** | -0.2 | -0.75 | -4.16 | 3.55 | 86.0 | **3.0** | 61.4 | 31.2 | **6.5** |
| **8.1** | 0.62 | 2.5 | 0.00 | **3.1** | 0.7 | 0.73 | 6.99 | 3.21 | 74.4 | **7.5** | 77.6 | 1.0 | **5.1** |
| **6.9** | 0.24 | 1.5 | 0.17 | **9.5** | 7.3 | 1.62 | 15.05 | 6.43 | 68.4 | **1.6** | 18.4 | 17.2 | **7.3** |
| **10.0** | na | 0.0 | na | **10.0** | 1.2 | 8.28 | 9.45 | 2.02 | 85.1 | **4.0** | na | 0.0 | **6.5** |
| **3.1** | 2.26 | 19.9 | 0.06 | **0.1** | -0.2 | -0.56 | -5.94 | 3.98 | 112.4 | **0.8** | 9.6 | 26.8 | **2.6** |
| **8.2** | 0.80 | 3.0 | 0.00 | **2.7** | 0.3 | 0.41 | 3.27 | 3.89 | 93.6 | **0.9** | 22.0 | 33.7 | **5.0** |
| **5.5** | 0.73 | 3.2 | 0.03 | **8.2** | 171.1 | 1.58 | 11.16 | 4.14 | 55.0 | **3.8** | 10.6 | 7.1 | **10.0** |

| Name | City | State | Rating | 2018 Rating | 2017 Rating | Total Assets ($Mil) | One Year Asset Growth | Asset Mix (As a % of Total Assets) Comm-ercial Loans | Cons-umer Loans | Mort-gage Loans | Secur-ities | Capital-ization Index | Lever-age Ratio | Risk-Based Capital Ratio |
|---|---|---|---|---|---|---|---|---|---|---|---|---|---|---|
| ▲ Rockwood Bank | Eureka | MO | **A-** | B | B | 243.2 | 2.07 | 4.9 | 1.0 | 20.9 | 0.0 | **10.0** | 15.1 | 20.1 |
| Rocky Mountain Bank | Billings | MT | **B** | B | B | 533.1 | 8.70 | 12.6 | 2.1 | 8.4 | 26.6 | **7.3** | 9.2 | 13.8 |
| Rocky Mountain Bank | Jackson | WY | **B+** | B+ | B+ | 315.1 | -0.88 | 6.2 | 13.8 | 22.9 | 5.5 | **10.0** | 11.8 | 16.6 |
| Rocky Mountain Bank & Trust | Florence | CO | **C+** | C- | D+ | 73.9 | 6.95 | 18.2 | 1.1 | 16.6 | 23.2 | **8.5** | 10.0 | 17.4 |
| ▼ Rolette State Bank | Rolette | ND | **D-** | D | D | 38.5 | -3.16 | 14.4 | 2.3 | 2.8 | 9.9 | **8.1** | 9.8 | 13.4 |
| Rolling Hills Bank & Trust | Atlantic | IA | **D+** | C | B- | 318.4 | 9.22 | 5.8 | 0.7 | 3.6 | 0.7 | **7.3** | 10.1 | 12.7 |
| Rollstone Bank & Trust | Fitchburg | MA | **C+** | B- | C+ | 694.7 | 5.11 | 5.1 | 0.1 | 21.0 | 21.6 | **9.9** | 10.9 | 16.4 |
| Rondout Savings Bank | Kingston | NY | **C** | C+ | C+ | 383.4 | 0.22 | 6.4 | 0.3 | 49.4 | 11.6 | **10.0** | 11.0 | 17.8 |
| Root River State Bank | Chatfield | MN | **C+** | C+ | C+ | 69.7 | 1.39 | 6.1 | 1.0 | 9.3 | 34.9 | **10.0** | 12.3 | 22.3 |
| Roscoe State Bank | Roscoe | TX | **A-** | B+ | B | 169.9 | 5.48 | 4.0 | 1.6 | 12.9 | 47.4 | **9.2** | 10.5 | 19.4 |
| Rosedale Federal S&L Assn. | Baltimore | MD | **B** | B | B+ | 973.4 | 2.05 | 0.0 | 0.0 | 44.0 | 11.5 | **10.0** | 25.4 | 42.3 |
| Roselle Bank | Roselle | NJ | **D** | D | D | 434.5 | 5.93 | 1.2 | 0.0 | 37.7 | 43.4 | **10.0** | 12.8 | 34.6 |
| Round Top State Bank | Round Top | TX | **A-** | A- | A- | 604.8 | 7.96 | 2.9 | 2.2 | 25.3 | 27.6 | **10.0** | 11.6 | 19.4 |
| ▲ Roundbank | Waseca | MN | **B** | B | B | 325.1 | 5.51 | 9.2 | 1.2 | 23.1 | 21.1 | **10.0** | 11.4 | 15.8 |
| Rowley Savings Bank | Rowley | IA | **C-** | D | D | 16.2 | 2.55 | 5.8 | 4.7 | 8.2 | 0.0 | **7.2** | 9.1 | 45.9 |
| Roxboro Savings Bank, SSB | Roxboro | NC | **B+** | B+ | B+ | 225.9 | 1.05 | 0.6 | 0.4 | 27.7 | 37.7 | **10.0** | 21.7 | 47.3 |
| Royal Bank | Elroy | WI | **B+** | B | B+ | 468.0 | 5.69 | 7.5 | 4.5 | 16.1 | 16.8 | **8.8** | 10.2 | 15.1 |
| ▲ Royal Banks of Missouri | Saint Louis | MO | **B-** | C | C- | 697.2 | -0.77 | 10.1 | 0.9 | 5.6 | 6.2 | **10.0** | 15.4 | 16.2 |
| Royal Business Bank | Los Angeles | CA | **A** | A | A | 2783.3 | -6.29 | 5.7 | 0.0 | 40.4 | 4.8 | **10.0** | 15.2 | 21.9 |
| Royal Savings Bank | Chicago | IL | **B+** | B+ | B+ | 404.8 | -0.49 | 1.8 | 0.4 | 30.7 | 9.7 | **9.0** | 10.3 | 16.8 |
| RSI Bank | Rahway | NJ | **B-** | B- | B- | 548.0 | 0.20 | 2.0 | 0.1 | 40.8 | 23.6 | **10.0** | 16.0 | 28.6 |
| RSNB Bank | Rock Springs | WY | **A** | A- | A- | 368.8 | 3.40 | 3.1 | 0.8 | 4.0 | 58.8 | **10.0** | 11.8 | 24.0 |
| Rushford State Bank (Inc.) | Rushford | MN | **C-** | D+ | C- | 58.2 | 8.22 | 4.2 | 3.2 | 16.6 | 7.1 | **6.4** | 8.4 | 13.4 |
| Rushville State Bank | Rushville | IL | **A-** | B+ | A- | 104.4 | 4.96 | 5.5 | 2.0 | 3.9 | 44.5 | **10.0** | 14.2 | 26.6 |
| S&T Bank | Indiana | PA | **B** | B+ | B- | 8748.0 | 20.94 | 15.9 | 0.9 | 13.5 | 8.9 | **7.4** | 10.1 | 12.8 |
| ▲ Sabal Palm Bank | Sarasota | FL | **B-** | C+ | C+ | 253.8 | 19.02 | 4.3 | 0.6 | 23.9 | 6.6 | **7.3** | 9.2 | 14.1 |
| ▲ Sabine State Bank and Trust Co. | Many | LA | **B+** | B | B | 953.7 | 6.16 | 11.4 | 1.8 | 10.3 | 9.6 | **6.3** | 10.0 | 12.0 |
| Saco & Biddeford Savings Institution | Saco | ME | **B** | B | B | 1031.6 | 4.31 | 1.5 | 0.6 | 54.4 | 10.4 | **10.0** | 11.8 | 18.5 |
| Sacramento Deposit Bank | Sacramento | KY | **A-** | B+ | A- | 110.9 | 5.44 | 4.9 | 5.1 | 20.2 | 24.0 | **10.0** | 11.1 | 17.0 |
| Safra National Bank of New York | New York | NY | **B+** | B+ | B | 8296.3 | 1.36 | 10.5 | 0.0 | 0.1 | 46.7 | **6.6** | 8.6 | 19.8 |
| ▲ Sage Capital Bank | Gonzales | TX | **B+** | B | B | 420.0 | 3.57 | 4.6 | 0.6 | 10.5 | 15.1 | **9.6** | 10.7 | 15.5 |
| Sainte Marie State Bank | Sainte Marie | IL | **D** | D+ | C | 16.7 | -14.16 | 4.7 | 1.2 | 0.8 | 4.9 | **10.0** | 23.1 | 26.7 |
| Saints Avenue Bank | New London | MO | **C-** | D+ | D+ | 105.0 | 18.59 | 16.1 | 11.9 | 15.8 | 9.0 | **4.5** | 8.4 | 10.8 |
| Salem Co-operative Bank | Salem | NH | **C** | C+ | C+ | 453.8 | 3.35 | 2.1 | 0.0 | 61.2 | 14.5 | **10.0** | 14.9 | 26.0 |
| Salem Five Cents Savings Bank | Salem | MA | **A-** | B | B | 5155.5 | 2.89 | 10.7 | 2.2 | 29.8 | 17.4 | **9.5** | 10.7 | 15.3 |
| ▲ Salisbury Bank and Trust Co. | Lakeville | CT | **B** | B- | B- | 1112.5 | -0.80 | 14.4 | 0.6 | 31.2 | 8.3 | **7.4** | 9.6 | 12.8 |
| Sallie Mae Bank | Salt Lake City | UT | **D+** | D+ | D+ | 32598.5 | 22.62 | 0.0 | 77.0 | 0.0 | 1.5 | **8.1** | 10.2 | 13.4 |
| Salyersville National Bank | Salyersville | KY | **B** | B+ | B+ | 110.5 | -1.41 | 3.1 | 2.6 | 17.3 | 33.5 | **10.0** | 15.2 | 28.5 |
| Samson Banking Co., Inc. | Samson | AL | **A-** | B+ | B | 81.1 | 4.15 | 4.1 | 5.9 | 17.9 | 46.5 | **10.0** | 14.0 | 29.7 |
| San Luis Valley Federal Bank | Alamosa | CO | **B** | B | B | 291.7 | 5.86 | 3.4 | 1.8 | 40.7 | 15.3 | **10.0** | 16.9 | 24.1 |
| Sanborn Savings Bank | Sanborn | IA | **C+** | C+ | B | 69.3 | 5.61 | 5.0 | 3.2 | 14.4 | 10.6 | **7.6** | 9.4 | 14.8 |
| Sandhills Bank | North Myrtle Beach | SC | **C** | C | C | 193.0 | 11.44 | 4.3 | 1.9 | 36.1 | 10.0 | **7.1** | 9.1 | 14.2 |
| Sandhills State Bank | Bassett | NE | **C+** | C | B- | 298.0 | 23.27 | 8.6 | 0.8 | 1.0 | 15.2 | **6.1** | 8.6 | 11.8 |
| Sandy Spring Bank | Olney | MD | **B-** | B | B+ | 8616.4 | 4.70 | 7.3 | 0.3 | 17.5 | 12.3 | **8.1** | 10.9 | 13.4 |
| Sanger Bank | Sanger | TX | **A** | A | A | 146.1 | 10.04 | 8.7 | 2.0 | 12.2 | 18.5 | **10.0** | 15.0 | 27.2 |
| Sanibel Captiva Community Bank | Sanibel | FL | **B-** | B- | B- | 450.9 | 0.65 | 3.8 | 2.0 | 44.6 | 1.7 | **5.5** | 7.8 | 11.4 |
| Santa Anna National Bank | Santa Anna | TX | **B+** | B+ | A- | 53.9 | 9.07 | 18.1 | 7.7 | 1.2 | 39.8 | **9.4** | 10.6 | 17.6 |
| Santa Cruz County Bank | Santa Cruz | CA | **A** | A- | B+ | 1071.0 | 61.68 | 8.7 | 0.2 | 5.1 | 6.3 | **10.0** | 11.9 | 16.3 |
| Santander Bank, N.A. | Boston | MA | **C+** | C+ | C+ | 84670.9 | 9.62 | 17.9 | 9.2 | 9.9 | 17.6 | **10.0** | 12.8 | 16.8 |
| Saratoga National Bank and Trust Co. | Saratoga Springs | NY | **B+** | B+ | B+ | 643.0 | 18.58 | 4.2 | 19.0 | 26.1 | 12.1 | **7.9** | 9.6 | 13.6 |
| Sargent County Bank | Forman | ND | **A-** | A- | A- | 192.6 | 2.85 | 1.9 | 2.1 | 0.6 | 43.9 | **8.1** | 9.8 | 14.7 |
| Sauk Valley Bank & Trust Co. | Sterling | IL | **B-** | B- | B- | 451.4 | 4.70 | 15.4 | 0.4 | 7.9 | 22.3 | **8.3** | 10.0 | 13.6 |
| Savanna-Thomson State Bank | Savanna | IL | **B** | B | B | 101.2 | 6.47 | 10.3 | 0.4 | 6.7 | 22.6 | **10.0** | 11.3 | 17.9 |
| Savannah Bank, N.A. | Savannah | NY | **B-** | B- | B- | 143.4 | 0.22 | 8.0 | 0.7 | 23.3 | 41.9 | **6.9** | 8.9 | 19.6 |
| Savers Co-operative Bank | Southbridge | MA | **B-** | B- | B- | 594.4 | 4.24 | 4.1 | 4.8 | 35.4 | 9.5 | **9.9** | 10.9 | 15.1 |
| SaviBank | Burlington | WA | **C+** | C+ | C+ | 312.3 | 16.76 | 11.7 | 6.8 | 11.1 | 3.1 | **5.9** | 10.0 | 11.7 |
| Savings Bank | Primghar | IA | **A-** | B | C+ | 223.5 | 7.30 | 12.7 | 2.1 | 6.4 | 13.3 | **9.6** | 12.2 | 14.6 |
| ▲ Savings Bank | Wakefield | MA | **B-** | C+ | C+ | 613.7 | 1.62 | 1.3 | 0.1 | 54.1 | 8.1 | **10.0** | 12.4 | 21.1 |
| Savings Bank | Circleville | OH | **B-** | B- | B- | 352.4 | 3.28 | 9.0 | 3.8 | 38.1 | 25.3 | **10.0** | 11.3 | 20.7 |
| Savings Bank of Danbury | Danbury | CT | **A-** | B+ | B+ | 1117.1 | 3.45 | 5.3 | 0.1 | 43.9 | 7.1 | **10.0** | 12.6 | 17.5 |

| Asset Quality Index | Adjusted Non-Performing Loans as a % of Total Loans | Adjusted Non-Performing Loans as a % of Capital | Net Charge-Offs Avg Loans | Profitability Index | Net Income ($Mil) | Return on Assets (R.O.A.) | Return on Equity (R.O.E.) | Net Interest Spread | Overhead Efficiency Ratio | Liquidity Index | Liquidity Ratio | Hot Money Ratio | Stability Index |
|---|---|---|---|---|---|---|---|---|---|---|---|---|---|
| **6.7** | 0.96 | 4.2 | -0.23 | **8.4** | 5.2 | 2.16 | 14.58 | 4.72 | 56.7 | **4.2** | 18.8 | 7.8 | **7.6** |
| **4.6** | 3.16 | 9.1 | 0.20 | **4.9** | 3.8 | 0.75 | 7.25 | 4.24 | 71.1 | **4.0** | 26.7 | 10.7 | **7.5** |
| **6.9** | 0.59 | 3.9 | 1.24 | **5.2** | 3.2 | 1.04 | 8.40 | 4.30 | 52.9 | **4.0** | 16.2 | 6.7 | **7.0** |
| **6.5** | 0.31 | 1.6 | 0.07 | **6.4** | 1.3 | 1.78 | 17.65 | 4.59 | 73.3 | **5.2** | 32.4 | 5.6 | **4.1** |
| **0.0** | 9.37 | 37.6 | 0.17 | **3.8** | 0.2 | 0.61 | 6.30 | 4.93 | 87.0 | **1.6** | 7.6 | 14.4 | **5.0** |
| **1.5** | 2.24 | 13.4 | -0.01 | **5.7** | 3.2 | 1.04 | 8.65 | 3.75 | 58.6 | **2.5** | 18.3 | 16.1 | **7.7** |
| **6.4** | 1.11 | 4.6 | 0.11 | **3.0** | 3.7 | 0.53 | 4.89 | 2.56 | 88.6 | **1.4** | 26.7 | 17.0 | **7.5** |
| **5.7** | 1.19 | 5.8 | 0.02 | **2.9** | 1.6 | 0.41 | 4.10 | 3.13 | 85.2 | **1.4** | 6.5 | 23.7 | **6.1** |
| **9.0** | 0.00 | 0.0 | -0.01 | **2.8** | 0.3 | 0.43 | 3.46 | 3.23 | 83.9 | **5.3** | 40.8 | 8.3 | **6.2** |
| **9.0** | 0.23 | 0.6 | 0.07 | **5.6** | 2.3 | 1.40 | 12.70 | 4.03 | 68.7 | **3.0** | 40.9 | 20.3 | **7.5** |
| **4.9** | 6.22 | 13.3 | -0.05 | **3.7** | 6.2 | 0.64 | 2.54 | 2.92 | 71.6 | **2.2** | 30.1 | 22.6 | **8.9** |
| **9.9** | 1.22 | 2.0 | 0.00 | **0.0** | -3.7 | -0.86 | -6.05 | 1.34 | 161.5 | **2.6** | 50.6 | 33.6 | **6.2** |
| **8.8** | 0.11 | 1.0 | 0.01 | **6.2** | 7.6 | 1.31 | 11.49 | 3.22 | 52.8 | **1.8** | 29.9 | 27.6 | **8.3** |
| **5.5** | 1.48 | 6.9 | -0.17 | **7.2** | 5.6 | 1.76 | 15.22 | 3.95 | 70.4 | **1.8** | 20.6 | 16.9 | **8.2** |
| **9.3** | 0.00 | 0.1 | -0.16 | **4.0** | 0.2 | 0.96 | 10.73 | 3.39 | 72.0 | **7.2** | 85.4 | 2.8 | **3.7** |
| **7.7** | 2.32 | 4.5 | 0.00 | **4.8** | 2.5 | 1.10 | 5.38 | 3.40 | 62.2 | **3.0** | 50.9 | 27.6 | **8.3** |
| **5.6** | 1.17 | 5.0 | 0.04 | **6.6** | 5.8 | 1.30 | 12.17 | 4.23 | 60.4 | **3.9** | 22.7 | 10.2 | **7.2** |
| **4.9** | 0.94 | 4.7 | 0.20 | **5.3** | 7.0 | 1.00 | 6.31 | 3.54 | 58.1 | **0.7** | 11.5 | 36.6 | **8.3** |
| **7.9** | 0.53 | 1.0 | 0.04 | **9.5** | 45.3 | 1.60 | 9.91 | 3.56 | 46.1 | **0.7** | 10.8 | 43.6 | **10.0** |
| **6.9** | 0.54 | 2.9 | 0.05 | **5.5** | 4.0 | 0.99 | 8.42 | 3.82 | 61.2 | **1.0** | 19.2 | 24.7 | **7.6** |
| **6.8** | 2.01 | 6.8 | -0.07 | **3.1** | 2.4 | 0.44 | 2.78 | 2.80 | 78.8 | **3.6** | 32.9 | 14.4 | **8.3** |
| **9.5** | 0.20 | 0.5 | 0.04 | **7.1** | 6.3 | 1.74 | 14.72 | 3.52 | 54.4 | **5.5** | 44.3 | 8.2 | **8.0** |
| **3.5** | 2.77 | 14.5 | 0.12 | **3.7** | 0.4 | 0.72 | 8.52 | 4.43 | 81.0 | **2.1** | 21.1 | 19.0 | **4.1** |
| **6.2** | 2.32 | 7.4 | 0.00 | **6.1** | 1.6 | 1.52 | 10.79 | 3.49 | 55.6 | **4.9** | 40.7 | 10.6 | **8.7** |
| **4.3** | 1.26 | 6.0 | 0.22 | **6.6** | 102.2 | 1.34 | 10.42 | 3.57 | 54.8 | **2.6** | 9.2 | 10.7 | **10.0** |
| **8.9** | 0.00 | 0.0 | -0.08 | **4.3** | 1.8 | 0.76 | 8.35 | 3.87 | 72.6 | **3.4** | 24.9 | 13.2 | **5.2** |
| **7.2** | 0.39 | 2.0 | 0.09 | **7.8** | 17.2 | 1.79 | 18.14 | 4.59 | 66.9 | **4.4** | 11.4 | 5.6 | **8.2** |
| **6.6** | 0.97 | 6.3 | 0.00 | **3.6** | 7.0 | 0.69 | 6.07 | 2.75 | 82.4 | **0.8** | 11.9 | 26.1 | **8.6** |
| **7.8** | 0.19 | 1.5 | 0.28 | **7.6** | 1.9 | 1.77 | 14.76 | 4.37 | 57.1 | **2.6** | 35.8 | 22.1 | **8.3** |
| **9.2** | 0.00 | 0.0 | 0.00 | **5.5** | 79.0 | 0.99 | 8.68 | 1.70 | 56.5 | **1.3** | 25.8 | 12.2 | **9.0** |
| **8.3** | 0.12 | 0.6 | 0.03 | **5.3** | 4.2 | 1.04 | 9.11 | 4.15 | 69.9 | **2.3** | 20.6 | 17.8 | **7.2** |
| **7.3** | 0.00 | 0.0 | 1.49 | **0.0** | -0.1 | -0.76 | -3.47 | 2.67 | 122.3 | **2.4** | 17.3 | 16.9 | **4.9** |
| **6.6** | 0.29 | 2.5 | 0.10 | **2.5** | 0.4 | 0.41 | 4.86 | 3.99 | 85.7 | **2.6** | 11.5 | 10.5 | **3.8** |
| **9.2** | 0.54 | 2.5 | 0.00 | **2.2** | 0.9 | 0.19 | 1.30 | 2.61 | 90.7 | **1.3** | 17.9 | 24.5 | **7.6** |
| **7.5** | 0.62 | 3.5 | 0.01 | **5.8** | 63.1 | 1.23 | 11.69 | 2.94 | 56.8 | **2.5** | 16.7 | 14.9 | **9.0** |
| **6.2** | 0.68 | 3.7 | -0.01 | **4.9** | 11.9 | 1.07 | 10.27 | 3.31 | 64.8 | **3.9** | 3.3 | 8.1 | **8.9** |
| **0.7** | 5.64 | 21.8 | 1.05 | **10.0** | 598.6 | 2.03 | 19.68 | 5.83 | 32.0 | **0.8** | 20.2 | 9.1 | **9.9** |
| **8.2** | 0.44 | 1.5 | 0.94 | **3.6** | 0.7 | 0.63 | 4.17 | 3.80 | 70.4 | **1.3** | 19.6 | 28.3 | **8.2** |
| **8.5** | 0.00 | 0.0 | 0.12 | **6.3** | 1.2 | 1.49 | 10.86 | 3.72 | 61.4 | **4.5** | 54.6 | 15.1 | **8.0** |
| **7.8** | 1.06 | 3.9 | 0.00 | **4.4** | 2.2 | 0.79 | 4.72 | 4.09 | 75.6 | **4.1** | 29.8 | 11.2 | **7.9** |
| **4.9** | 1.05 | 5.0 | 0.35 | **4.3** | 0.7 | 0.99 | 9.85 | 3.41 | 63.8 | **2.5** | 22.5 | 17.4 | **4.9** |
| **7.6** | 0.21 | 1.7 | 0.01 | **3.2** | 0.7 | 0.39 | 3.73 | 3.60 | 87.4 | **0.9** | 15.8 | 33.2 | **5.6** |
| **4.4** | 0.12 | 2.6 | -0.01 | **4.6** | 2.9 | 0.99 | 8.79 | 4.04 | 71.2 | **1.8** | 12.1 | 17.1 | **6.4** |
| **4.1** | 0.79 | 3.7 | 0.03 | **7.2** | 119.3 | 1.43 | 10.58 | 3.50 | 52.4 | **1.7** | 10.6 | 16.5 | **10.0** |
| **9.0** | 0.00 | 0.0 | 0.00 | **5.8** | 1.6 | 1.17 | 7.83 | 3.85 | 65.7 | **3.2** | 43.8 | 20.4 | **8.3** |
| **4.5** | 1.58 | 14.6 | 0.00 | **9.8** | 7.7 | 1.76 | 23.98 | 4.76 | 55.0 | **4.1** | 11.4 | 7.3 | **5.5** |
| **8.1** | 0.09 | 0.4 | 0.10 | **8.2** | 0.9 | 1.65 | 14.23 | 4.86 | 59.4 | **2.8** | 36.4 | 19.8 | **7.0** |
| **7.0** | 0.00 | 0.5 | 0.00 | **9.5** | 12.3 | 1.56 | 14.70 | 4.72 | 53.3 | **3.1** | 22.1 | 15.3 | **9.4** |
| **5.1** | 0.94 | 3.3 | 0.40 | **2.5** | 245.4 | 0.31 | 1.80 | 3.00 | 82.1 | **3.9** | 21.2 | 3.8 | **8.2** |
| **7.4** | 0.06 | 0.4 | 0.04 | **6.9** | 8.2 | 1.40 | 14.33 | 3.21 | 46.6 | **2.6** | 14.1 | 16.0 | **7.3** |
| **8.4** | 0.00 | 0.0 | 0.03 | **6.4** | 2.9 | 1.55 | 12.64 | 3.76 | 53.9 | **4.5** | 36.3 | 11.4 | **7.7** |
| **3.5** | 2.01 | 13.8 | 0.02 | **4.4** | 3.6 | 0.83 | 8.97 | 3.57 | 69.1 | **1.8** | 16.8 | 13.1 | **5.7** |
| **6.5** | 1.06 | 4.2 | 0.14 | **3.8** | 0.8 | 0.88 | 6.00 | 3.41 | 70.3 | **5.4** | 26.8 | 1.8 | **7.5** |
| **7.6** | 0.70 | 3.4 | 0.01 | **3.3** | 1.0 | 0.68 | 7.76 | 3.19 | 77.7 | **1.8** | 20.3 | 21.7 | **5.6** |
| **5.4** | 0.91 | 4.7 | 0.04 | **3.6** | 3.9 | 0.67 | 6.12 | 3.20 | 74.2 | **1.8** | 16.6 | 19.4 | **7.1** |
| **5.8** | 0.41 | 1.8 | 0.03 | **3.6** | 1.5 | 0.52 | 4.83 | 4.32 | 81.7 | **1.0** | 11.0 | 24.7 | **6.9** |
| **7.0** | 0.00 | 0.0 | 0.00 | **8.0** | 4.0 | 1.87 | 15.45 | 3.43 | 40.9 | **1.7** | 10.2 | 20.7 | **8.8** |
| **8.7** | 0.37 | 2.2 | 0.00 | **4.0** | 4.7 | 0.78 | 6.19 | 3.08 | 85.0 | **1.6** | 17.0 | 22.9 | **7.7** |
| **6.5** | 1.44 | 5.9 | 0.06 | **3.6** | 2.3 | 0.67 | 5.83 | 3.31 | 77.5 | **3.1** | 19.2 | 13.8 | **6.5** |
| **5.8** | 1.81 | 10.3 | 0.08 | **5.3** | 11.8 | 1.10 | 9.05 | 3.60 | 65.2 | **1.2** | 10.6 | 22.5 | **9.4** |

| Name | City | State | Rating | 2018 Rating | 2017 Rating | Total Assets ($Mil) | One Year Asset Growth | Asset Mix (As a % of Total Assets) Comm-ercial Loans | Cons-umer Loans | Mort-gage Loans | Secur-ities | Capital-ization Index | Lever-age Ratio | Risk-Based Capital Ratio |
|---|---|---|---|---|---|---|---|---|---|---|---|---|---|---|
| Savings Bank of Mendocino County | Ukiah | CA | A | A | A- | 1104.1 | -0.38 | 3.3 | 0.5 | 5.4 | 45.5 | 10.0 | 16.9 | 28.6 |
| Savings Bank of Walpole | Walpole | NH | B- | C+ | C- | 447.1 | 8.86 | 7.1 | 0.3 | 38.3 | 19.5 | 6.0 | 8.0 | 14.5 |
| ▲ Savoy Bank | New York | NY | C | D+ | C | 382.7 | 9.49 | 8.8 | 0.0 | 13.2 | 0.7 | 9.0 | 10.6 | 14.2 |
| ▼ Sawyer Savings Bank | Saugerties | NY | D+ | C- | C- | 255.1 | 3.57 | 3.5 | 0.1 | 46.5 | 22.2 | 8.6 | 10.0 | 19.5 |
| SB One Bank | Paramus | NJ | C+ | C+ | B | 2002.7 | 11.65 | 6.2 | 0.1 | 16.9 | 10.8 | 6.7 | 10.2 | 12.3 |
| Schaumburg Bank & Trust Co., N.A. | Schaumburg | IL | B | B | B- | 1214.0 | 5.09 | 29.7 | 14.0 | 3.0 | 16.4 | 6.4 | 9.8 | 12.0 |
| Schertz Bank & Trust | Schertz | TX | A- | B+ | B+ | 416.1 | 1.87 | 5.1 | 0.5 | 5.0 | 2.6 | 9.7 | 13.0 | 14.7 |
| Schuyler Savings Bank | Kearny | NJ | C | C | C | 120.2 | 0.01 | 0.0 | 0.1 | 57.6 | 16.4 | 10.0 | 16.1 | 34.8 |
| ▲ Scott State Bank | Bethany | IL | B | B- | B- | 172.7 | 6.12 | 8.9 | 3.0 | 12.6 | 30.5 | 10.0 | 14.4 | 26.0 |
| Scottsburg Building and Loan Assn. | Scottsburg | IN | C+ | C+ | C+ | 86.6 | -5.12 | 1.2 | 0.1 | 45.1 | 36.1 | 10.0 | 15.1 | 33.8 |
| Scribner Bank | Scribner | NE | A- | B+ | A- | 67.9 | 4.27 | 8.3 | 1.0 | 2.9 | 11.0 | 10.0 | 15.2 | 20.9 |
| ▲ Seacoast Commerce Bank | San Diego | CA | B- | B | B+ | 1131.3 | 8.73 | 1.8 | 0.0 | 1.2 | 0.0 | 6.9 | 8.9 | 14.9 |
| Seacoast National Bank | Stuart | FL | B+ | B+ | B- | 7108.4 | 5.34 | 10.3 | 2.9 | 17.4 | 17.0 | 9.6 | 11.4 | 14.7 |
| Seamen's Bank | Provincetown | MA | C+ | C | C | 377.6 | -1.81 | 2.7 | 0.1 | 46.4 | 16.9 | 10.0 | 11.3 | 18.0 |
| Seaside National Bank & Trust | Orlando | FL | B- | B- | C+ | 1874.3 | -0.47 | 35.3 | 2.0 | 8.6 | 22.4 | 6.9 | 8.9 | 12.6 |
| Seattle Bank | Seattle | WA | B | B- | C+ | 715.4 | 13.43 | 9.2 | 1.1 | 9.2 | 0.5 | 8.2 | 9.8 | 17.2 |
| Sebree Deposit Bank | Sebree | KY | D+ | D+ | D+ | 21.3 | -0.11 | 4.8 | 7.7 | 33.7 | 17.4 | 10.0 | 11.5 | 21.4 |
| Second Federal S&L Assn. of Philadelphia | Philadelphia | PA | D | D | D | 15.5 | 27.80 | 0.0 | 0.0 | 54.4 | 15.7 | 10.0 | 39.2 | 69.2 |
| Securian Trust Co., N.A. | Saint Paul | MN | U | U | U | 15.2 | 4.29 | 0.0 | 0.0 | 0.0 | 88.4 | 10.0 | 92.4 | 102.5 |
| ▲ Security Bank | Stephens | AR | B+ | B | B- | 69.0 | 2.62 | 5.0 | 5.6 | 55.1 | 6.2 | 8.5 | 10.0 | 16.7 |
| ▲ Security Bank | Laurel | NE | A- | B- | A- | 220.9 | -3.07 | 8.2 | 2.4 | 3.3 | 21.5 | 10.0 | 12.2 | 16.4 |
| Security Bank | Tulsa | OK | B- | B+ | A- | 584.7 | 7.40 | 27.6 | 1.1 | 8.6 | 3.6 | 9.5 | 11.9 | 14.5 |
| Security Bank | Dyersburg | TN | B- | B | B | 199.4 | 3.02 | 6.5 | 1.7 | 5.4 | 55.4 | 9.1 | 10.4 | 18.3 |
| ▲ Security Bank | Midland | TX | A- | B | C+ | 934.8 | 7.22 | 21.4 | 0.5 | 2.4 | 8.6 | 10.0 | 11.5 | 19.5 |
| Security Bank | New Auburn | WI | B | C+ | B | 118.3 | 14.73 | 7.0 | 1.3 | 14.5 | 9.3 | 10.0 | 12.9 | 16.1 |
| Security Bank & Trust Co. | Glencoe | MN | B+ | B+ | B+ | 581.5 | 12.57 | 6.9 | 0.6 | 5.6 | 24.4 | 8.1 | 9.7 | 16.4 |
| Security Bank and Trust Co. | Maysville | KY | B+ | B+ | B+ | 52.7 | -4.14 | 4.3 | 1.7 | 17.0 | 39.7 | 10.0 | 19.6 | 37.9 |
| Security Bank and Trust Co. | Miami | OK | B- | B- | B | 90.2 | 0.27 | 7.5 | 4.1 | 28.9 | 14.4 | 8.0 | 9.7 | 14.1 |
| Security Bank and Trust Co. | Paris | TN | B+ | B+ | A- | 468.6 | 10.38 | 22.2 | 1.8 | 15.0 | 13.8 | 6.1 | 9.4 | 11.9 |
| Security Bank Minnesota | Albert Lea | MN | B+ | B+ | B+ | 135.7 | 3.61 | 55.7 | 3.5 | 3.4 | 7.9 | 7.4 | 10.4 | 12.8 |
| ▲ Security Bank of Crawford | Crawford | TX | C+ | C | C | 77.6 | 21.93 | 5.0 | 3.1 | 38.2 | 0.0 | 7.2 | 9.1 | 16.0 |
| Security Bank of Kansas City | Kansas City | KS | A- | A- | A- | 3017.8 | 0.45 | 6.2 | 0.4 | 2.1 | 32.9 | 10.0 | 14.6 | 21.3 |
| Security Bank of Pulaski County | Waynesville | MO | C+ | C+ | C+ | 119.5 | 6.99 | 6.2 | 3.9 | 18.6 | 25.9 | 6.7 | 8.7 | 13.3 |
| Security Bank of Southwest Missouri | Cassville | MO | B+ | B | B | 78.8 | -0.90 | 5.8 | 5.7 | 32.9 | 18.0 | 10.0 | 12.1 | 29.2 |
| Security Bank of the Ozarks | Eminence | MO | C+ | C | C+ | 95.4 | -2.27 | 7.9 | 7.1 | 13.4 | 11.5 | 6.7 | 8.7 | 12.3 |
| ▲ Security Bank USA | Bemidji | MN | B+ | B- | B- | 156.4 | 6.61 | 17.2 | 4.7 | 19.4 | 5.6 | 7.6 | 9.4 | 14.7 |
| Security Bank, s.b. | Springfield | IL | C | C- | D+ | 184.1 | 24.57 | 6.4 | 3.4 | 20.8 | 11.3 | 7.2 | 9.2 | 18.0 |
| Security Federal Bank | Aiken | SC | B- | B- | B- | 962.7 | 5.49 | 2.2 | 2.4 | 9.9 | 45.1 | 9.0 | 10.4 | 19.4 |
| Security Federal Bank | Elizabethton | TN | B- | B- | B+ | 62.2 | -8.63 | 3.0 | 1.9 | 35.7 | 15.7 | 10.0 | 16.0 | 26.7 |
| Security Federal Savings Bank | Jasper | AL | C+ | C | C | 34.8 | -8.27 | 0.0 | 9.1 | 33.7 | 15.8 | 10.0 | 13.4 | 26.7 |
| Security Federal Savings Bank | Logansport | IN | B- | B- | B- | 293.8 | 14.16 | 4.1 | 1.0 | 29.4 | 8.1 | 10.0 | 11.3 | 17.5 |
| Security Financial Bank | Durand | WI | B- | B | B | 501.3 | 1.91 | 14.7 | 0.2 | 8.0 | 16.6 | 6.6 | 9.4 | 12.2 |
| ▲ Security First Bank | Lincoln | NE | C+ | C+ | B- | 1151.0 | 17.08 | 5.4 | 10.3 | 7.9 | 17.5 | 5.9 | 8.6 | 11.7 |
| Security First Bank of North Dakota | Center | ND | A- | B+ | A- | 185.3 | 1.26 | 9.8 | 2.1 | 8.3 | 4.4 | 10.0 | 14.6 | 16.9 |
| Security First National Bank of Hugo | Hugo | OK | A- | B+ | B+ | 118.0 | 5.46 | 2.7 | 1.8 | 24.8 | 8.2 | 6.2 | 8.2 | 12.3 |
| Security FSB of McMinnville | McMinnville | TN | A- | B+ | B | 224.3 | 5.10 | 14.9 | 6.1 | 24.8 | 16.0 | 10.0 | 11.0 | 15.3 |
| Security National Bank | Witt | IL | B | B- | B- | 81.2 | 4.06 | 9.0 | 2.9 | 21.3 | 13.7 | 9.2 | 10.5 | 16.1 |
| Security National Bank of Enid | Enid | OK | B+ | B+ | B+ | 324.6 | -0.59 | 3.2 | 1.4 | 20.1 | 35.7 | 6.8 | 8.8 | 14.9 |
| Security National Bank of Omaha | Omaha | NE | A | A- | A- | 878.1 | -8.74 | 20.6 | 3.4 | 6.8 | 22.2 | 10.0 | 11.6 | 15.2 |
| Security National Bank of Sioux City, Iowa | Sioux City | IA | A- | B+ | A- | 1036.0 | 3.99 | 5.5 | 1.6 | 14.1 | 26.1 | 10.0 | 11.3 | 18.2 |
| ▲ Security National Bank of South Dakota | Dakota Dunes | SD | A | A- | A- | 206.3 | 6.98 | 3.9 | 2.1 | 11.5 | 23.2 | 10.0 | 11.0 | 20.2 |
| Security National Trust Co. | Wheeling | WV | U | U | U | 5.5 | 1.89 | 0.0 | 0.0 | 0.0 | 73.5 | 10.0 | 110. | 126.3 |
| ▲ Security Savings Bank | Gowrie | IA | A- | B+ | B+ | 132.7 | 3.38 | 4.1 | 2.2 | 12.3 | 23.9 | 10.0 | 11.4 | 15.4 |
| Security Savings Bank | Monmouth | IL | B- | C+ | C | 199.0 | 1.45 | 2.6 | 6.3 | 11.8 | 15.8 | 10.0 | 11.2 | 16.5 |
| Security Savings Bank | Canton | SD | C+ | B- | B | 444.6 | 88.62 | 4.1 | 1.0 | 5.8 | 9.2 | 7.1 | 9.0 | 13.3 |
| Security State Bank | McRae | GA | A- | B+ | A- | 46.5 | -3.51 | 12.8 | 2.6 | 5.7 | 30.5 | 10.0 | 16.0 | 34.4 |
| ▲ Security State Bank | Algona | IA | A- | B+ | A- | 100.9 | -0.29 | 11.3 | 1.1 | 2.6 | 2.3 | 10.0 | 17.6 | 21.9 |
| Security State Bank | Radcliffe | IA | C- | C- | C+ | 96.2 | -2.14 | 6.8 | 1.8 | 15.4 | 18.6 | 7.3 | 9.2 | 18.3 |
| ▲ Security State Bank | Sutherland | IA | B+ | B- | B | 228.1 | 62.94 | 7.7 | 2.1 | 4.5 | 0.3 | 7.7 | 10.6 | 13.1 |
| Security State Bank | Waverly | IA | A- | B+ | B+ | 88.1 | 6.49 | 1.0 | 2.3 | 10.7 | 37.1 | 10.0 | 12.1 | 20.6 |

| Asset Quality Index | Adjusted Non-Performing Loans as a % of Total Loans | Adjusted Non-Performing Loans as a % of Capital | Net Charge-Offs Avg Loans | Profitability Index | Net Income ($Mil) | Return on Assets (R.O.A.) | Return on Equity (R.O.E.) | Net Interest Spread | Overhead Efficiency Ratio | Liquidity Index | Liquidity Ratio | Hot Money Ratio | Stability Index |
|---|---|---|---|---|---|---|---|---|---|---|---|---|---|
| **9.1** | 0.61 | 1.1 | 0.01 | **7.3** | 15.0 | 1.36 | 8.23 | 3.85 | 53.6 | **6.7** | 49.0 | 4.9 | **10.0** |
| **5.8** | 1.01 | 6.3 | 0.03 | **3.5** | 3.0 | 0.69 | 8.56 | 3.36 | 76.4 | **4.7** | 26.0 | 5.7 | **5.8** |
| **3.0** | 0.70 | 5.0 | 0.73 | **8.0** | 5.3 | 1.44 | 14.01 | 4.58 | 53.4 | **0.5** | 13.4 | 60.6 | **7.7** |
| **5.9** | 1.80 | 8.1 | 0.42 | **1.4** | 0.1 | 0.04 | 0.39 | 2.67 | 93.3 | **1.0** | 27.2 | 30.2 | **5.7** |
| **3.9** | 0.95 | 6.3 | 0.07 | **5.8** | 23.8 | 1.26 | 11.01 | 3.43 | 56.3 | **0.9** | 14.4 | 15.6 | **8.0** |
| **6.7** | 0.30 | 2.2 | 0.18 | **5.4** | 12.7 | 1.05 | 9.78 | 3.11 | 55.5 | **1.4** | 15.1 | 23.0 | **8.5** |
| **6.6** | 0.52 | 2.2 | 0.01 | **7.7** | 6.1 | 1.50 | 11.99 | 3.97 | 49.4 | **0.7** | 12.0 | 38.6 | **8.0** |
| **7.8** | 1.40 | 3.9 | -0.01 | **2.2** | 0.3 | 0.28 | 1.72 | 2.65 | 87.8 | **1.3** | 28.4 | 33.8 | **7.3** |
| **8.8** | 0.26 | 1.7 | -0.07 | **4.1** | 1.7 | 1.01 | 6.86 | 3.42 | 73.0 | **5.3** | 38.5 | 7.5 | **7.5** |
| **10.0** | 0.41 | 1.3 | 0.01 | **2.6** | 0.3 | 0.35 | 2.41 | 2.58 | 83.9 | **1.4** | 33.4 | 47.2 | **7.1** |
| **7.2** | 0.23 | 1.4 | 0.05 | **9.4** | 1.2 | 1.86 | 12.45 | 4.37 | 64.9 | **4.9** | 25.3 | 4.0 | **9.0** |
| **5.9** | 0.90 | 1.5 | 0.03 | **7.7** | 14.8 | 1.36 | 11.70 | 6.10 | 68.2 | **5.0** | 9.6 | 1.8 | **9.3** |
| **5.9** | 0.73 | 3.1 | 0.17 | **7.4** | 101.5 | 1.49 | 10.64 | 3.97 | 53.1 | **2.5** | 17.3 | 8.6 | **9.6** |
| **3.0** | 4.91 | 23.6 | 0.00 | **3.1** | 2.1 | 0.54 | 4.87 | 3.37 | 78.7 | **2.2** | 25.0 | 19.3 | **6.4** |
| **7.3** | 0.56 | 4.1 | 0.31 | **4.2** | 15.5 | 0.83 | 9.65 | 2.79 | 59.1 | **1.1** | 19.3 | 18.6 | **7.4** |
| **5.8** | 1.91 | 5.2 | 0.05 | **5.0** | 6.7 | 1.04 | 10.11 | 3.84 | 60.0 | **0.7** | 17.2 | 42.7 | **7.7** |
| **8.6** | 0.00 | 0.0 | 0.05 | **0.8** | 0.0 | -0.19 | -1.58 | 3.63 | 106.2 | **1.4** | 25.3 | 27.8 | **4.9** |
| **10.0** | 0.00 | 0.0 | 0.00 | **0.0** | -0.2 | -1.45 | -3.16 | 3.68 | 135.8 | **2.2** | 57.3 | 45.2 | **6.0** |
| **10.0** | na | 0.0 | na | **9.5** | 0.3 | 1.79 | 1.94 | 3.18 | 93.8 | **4.0** | na | 0.0 | **6.7** |
| **6.9** | 0.13 | 0.9 | 0.13 | **5.3** | 0.7 | 0.99 | 10.42 | 4.00 | 62.8 | **0.5** | 9.5 | 50.3 | **6.0** |
| **6.7** | 0.37 | 0.9 | 0.45 | **6.4** | 3.3 | 1.45 | 12.05 | 4.52 | 66.3 | **3.9** | 23.5 | 7.9 | **8.5** |
| **4.6** | 1.22 | 8.4 | 0.64 | **9.0** | 11.1 | 1.95 | 16.18 | 3.83 | 42.2 | **0.8** | 18.2 | 36.7 | **9.7** |
| **6.3** | 2.12 | 4.4 | 0.00 | **4.0** | 1.8 | 0.92 | 8.11 | 3.19 | 77.3 | **1.9** | 29.1 | 25.8 | **7.1** |
| **7.8** | 0.14 | 0.6 | 0.02 | **9.3** | 22.3 | 2.53 | 18.32 | 5.17 | 58.6 | **5.8** | 37.4 | 3.9 | **9.6** |
| **3.8** | 3.09 | 18.3 | 0.00 | **6.9** | 1.3 | 1.26 | 9.49 | 3.86 | 59.9 | **1.6** | 22.3 | 14.8 | **7.2** |
| **5.7** | 1.34 | 5.2 | 0.11 | **6.3** | 8.0 | 1.49 | 14.99 | 3.14 | 60.4 | **3.9** | 24.8 | 10.3 | **8.2** |
| **9.0** | 0.21 | 0.6 | -0.05 | **6.1** | 0.8 | 1.52 | 7.69 | 3.72 | 60.0 | **4.6** | 35.7 | 10.6 | **8.2** |
| **4.6** | 1.05 | 7.4 | 0.43 | **3.7** | 0.6 | 0.69 | 6.94 | 3.94 | 75.7 | **1.3** | 11.8 | 25.8 | **6.7** |
| **8.4** | 0.04 | 0.3 | 0.02 | **7.0** | 6.5 | 1.44 | 14.96 | 3.72 | 60.2 | **1.6** | 12.5 | 15.8 | **7.4** |
| **7.6** | 0.03 | 0.2 | 0.19 | **7.0** | 1.9 | 1.45 | 13.50 | 4.51 | 65.0 | **1.5** | 9.4 | 22.5 | **7.0** |
| **7.3** | 0.26 | 1.9 | -0.31 | **4.3** | 0.6 | 0.80 | 8.95 | 3.90 | 67.1 | **1.1** | 30.4 | 51.3 | **3.5** |
| **6.4** | 2.05 | 3.9 | 0.14 | **7.1** | 42.7 | 1.40 | 8.56 | 3.54 | 51.1 | **5.4** | 36.5 | 9.6 | **9.6** |
| **5.4** | 0.86 | 5.2 | 0.03 | **3.7** | 0.8 | 0.72 | 7.95 | 4.25 | 80.5 | **1.7** | 13.8 | 17.3 | **4.8** |
| **4.3** | 0.49 | 13.5 | 0.13 | **9.8** | 1.8 | 2.22 | 17.65 | 4.52 | 56.6 | **2.7** | 20.9 | 15.8 | **8.5** |
| **5.5** | 0.37 | 2.5 | 0.01 | **4.8** | 1.0 | 1.08 | 11.37 | 5.03 | 74.4 | **2.5** | 14.0 | 16.5 | **5.2** |
| **5.4** | 0.66 | 4.2 | -0.02 | **7.3** | 2.8 | 1.79 | 19.40 | 4.45 | 64.6 | **4.1** | 13.0 | 7.8 | **7.0** |
| **2.4** | 3.50 | 21.6 | 0.10 | **2.7** | 0.5 | 0.32 | 3.22 | 3.49 | 82.9 | **6.2** | 48.0 | 4.8 | **4.4** |
| **6.1** | 0.90 | 3.3 | 0.07 | **4.1** | 8.5 | 0.89 | 8.76 | 3.35 | 74.0 | **2.7** | 30.0 | 13.8 | **7.3** |
| **5.4** | 1.66 | 10.4 | -0.02 | **2.7** | 0.3 | 0.37 | 2.46 | 3.27 | 88.9 | **0.8** | 15.8 | 35.4 | **6.6** |
| **8.9** | 0.00 | 1.0 | 0.33 | **2.8** | 0.1 | 0.35 | 2.76 | 3.53 | 89.1 | **2.3** | 42.9 | 32.0 | **5.7** |
| **6.5** | 1.17 | 4.8 | 0.11 | **3.4** | 1.6 | 0.58 | 4.83 | 3.84 | 83.6 | **3.6** | 21.6 | 11.9 | **6.0** |
| **4.6** | 1.34 | 8.0 | 0.01 | **6.0** | 7.3 | 1.48 | 13.79 | 3.92 | 60.6 | **4.1** | 21.4 | 7.9 | **7.8** |
| **4.0** | 0.94 | 6.2 | 1.01 | **4.3** | 8.6 | 0.80 | 8.10 | 3.63 | 63.7 | **1.9** | 20.8 | 20.6 | **8.1** |
| **7.7** | 0.44 | 1.2 | -0.07 | **7.9** | 3.6 | 1.99 | 13.80 | 4.90 | 62.8 | **3.7** | 9.5 | 10.0 | **9.3** |
| **4.8** | 2.40 | 19.4 | -0.01 | **10.0** | 2.6 | 2.24 | 24.42 | 5.85 | 52.2 | **1.9** | 10.9 | 19.2 | **6.8** |
| **7.4** | 0.09 | 0.6 | 0.02 | **5.9** | 2.6 | 1.18 | 11.00 | 3.84 | 62.5 | **1.7** | 12.5 | 21.2 | **6.8** |
| **4.9** | 2.00 | 7.5 | 0.22 | **3.9** | 0.5 | 0.59 | 5.52 | 3.82 | 75.4 | **3.1** | 27.6 | 15.5 | **6.0** |
| **6.8** | 0.42 | 3.0 | 0.16 | **6.6** | 5.5 | 1.67 | 17.76 | 3.27 | 52.0 | **4.5** | 19.7 | 6.2 | **7.6** |
| **8.4** | 0.08 | 0.4 | 0.00 | **6.2** | 11.4 | 1.25 | 10.81 | 3.71 | 66.4 | **4.8** | 20.0 | 4.1 | **8.6** |
| **6.4** | 1.76 | 6.2 | -0.01 | **7.7** | 15.6 | 1.57 | 13.51 | 3.16 | 58.1 | **4.1** | 22.6 | 9.1 | **9.4** |
| **8.7** | 0.03 | 0.1 | 0.00 | **8.4** | 2.9 | 1.53 | 12.98 | 2.66 | 55.3 | **2.6** | 35.2 | 18.1 | **8.8** |
| **10.0** | na | 0.0 | na | **9.5** | 1.3 | 26.14 | 22.15 | 2.17 | 76.5 | **4.0** | na | 0.0 | **5.7** |
| **8.3** | 0.61 | 2.7 | 0.23 | **5.9** | 1.8 | 1.43 | 12.90 | 3.36 | 61.6 | **2.2** | 22.8 | 18.8 | **7.8** |
| **5.9** | 0.42 | 2.5 | 0.08 | **3.4** | 1.1 | 0.57 | 5.12 | 2.99 | 75.0 | **1.8** | 19.6 | 20.6 | **6.3** |
| **4.5** | 0.50 | 5.9 | 0.02 | **3.7** | 3.5 | 0.77 | 8.39 | 3.10 | 73.5 | **1.7** | 15.6 | 21.7 | **5.8** |
| **8.9** | 0.00 | 0.0 | -0.06 | **6.8** | 0.7 | 1.61 | 10.44 | 4.65 | 66.7 | **5.7** | 55.1 | 8.8 | **7.8** |
| **6.8** | 0.66 | 3.9 | 0.02 | **8.2** | 1.6 | 1.61 | 9.43 | 4.36 | 48.4 | **2.6** | 24.1 | 17.0 | **8.7** |
| **2.7** | 2.85 | 17.7 | 0.00 | **2.4** | 0.3 | 0.30 | 3.11 | 2.68 | 87.5 | **3.9** | 37.9 | 14.7 | **4.9** |
| **6.6** | 0.04 | 0.4 | 0.04 | **10.0** | 4.7 | 2.59 | 26.42 | 4.98 | 41.3 | **1.4** | 8.1 | 12.2 | **7.9** |
| **9.0** | 0.00 | 1.2 | 0.14 | **4.7** | 0.9 | 1.07 | 8.79 | 3.02 | 60.2 | **6.1** | 49.7 | 4.9 | **6.7** |

| Name | City | State | Rating | 2018 Rating | 2017 Rating | Total Assets ($Mil) | One Year Asset Growth | Asset Mix (As a % of Total Assets): Commercial Loans | Consumer Loans | Mortgage Loans | Securities | Capitalization Index | Leverage Ratio | Risk-Based Capital Ratio |
|---|---|---|---|---|---|---|---|---|---|---|---|---|---|---|
| Security State Bank | Scott City | KS | **A-** | B+ | A- | 304.2 | 6.51 | 12.0 | 2.2 | 2.4 | 20.9 | **10.0** | 15.0 | 18.3 |
| Security State Bank | Wellington | KS | **C+** | C | C- | 50.9 | -9.05 | 4.0 | 0.7 | 7.6 | 49.8 | **10.0** | 14.1 | 27.2 |
| Security State Bank | Cheyenne | OK | **A-** | A- | A | 167.9 | -3.50 | 5.5 | 3.5 | 20.5 | 27.7 | **10.0** | 14.3 | 20.6 |
| Security State Bank | Alexandria | SD | **B** | B- | B | 84.1 | 6.02 | 7.5 | 3.8 | 2.1 | 30.1 | **8.3** | 9.9 | 16.3 |
| ▲ Security State Bank | Emery | SD | **B+** | B | B | 51.9 | 7.23 | 18.1 | 2.8 | 0.0 | 1.4 | **10.0** | 14.0 | 29.8 |
| ▲ Security State Bank | Tyndall | SD | **B** | C+ | B- | 219.4 | -5.62 | 10.4 | 0.7 | 2.4 | 8.0 | **8.0** | 10.3 | 13.4 |
| Security State Bank | Farwell | TX | **A-** | A- | A- | 185.7 | 16.98 | 17.2 | 0.5 | 9.1 | 19.2 | **10.0** | 12.3 | 18.9 |
| Security State Bank | Pearsall | TX | **A-** | B | B+ | 662.3 | 6.52 | 3.2 | 0.8 | 2.0 | 30.2 | **10.0** | 12.5 | 17.8 |
| Security State Bank | Winters | TX | **B-** | C+ | C+ | 61.7 | -3.07 | 8.4 | 8.4 | 8.8 | 28.4 | **7.4** | 9.3 | 17.9 |
| Security State Bank | Centralia | WA | **A** | A- | A- | 487.0 | 7.25 | 5.4 | 1.3 | 5.0 | 2.7 | **10.0** | 13.4 | 29.4 |
| Security State Bank | Iron River | WI | **B-** | C | C | 103.8 | 8.89 | 17.1 | 1.5 | 11.6 | 18.4 | **10.0** | 18.3 | 24.6 |
| Security State Bank | Basin | WY | **B** | B+ | B+ | 367.2 | 6.61 | 5.3 | 3.1 | 8.5 | 30.9 | **10.0** | 11.3 | 19.4 |
| Security State Bank & Trust | Fredericksburg | TX | **A** | A | A- | 1172.7 | 14.12 | 9.4 | 1.9 | 9.8 | 19.5 | **10.0** | 13.2 | 15.6 |
| Security State Bank of Aitkin | Aitkin | MN | **A-** | B+ | A- | 99.7 | 0.58 | 18.2 | 2.3 | 11.1 | 22.6 | **10.0** | 12.6 | 20.3 |
| Security State Bank of Fergus Falls | Fergus Falls | MN | **B+** | B- | B- | 124.8 | -1.45 | 6.6 | 0.3 | 6.4 | 23.0 | **8.2** | 10.5 | 13.5 |
| Security State Bank of Hibbing | Hibbing | MN | **B** | C+ | C+ | 137.4 | -0.97 | 13.8 | 1.6 | 11.7 | 19.2 | **9.7** | 10.8 | 22.2 |
| Security State Bank of Kenyon | Kenyon | MN | **D-** | D- | D | 56.5 | -1.73 | 5.7 | 1.5 | 16.2 | 2.1 | **9.0** | 11.8 | 14.2 |
| Security State Bank of Marine | Marine On Saint Croi | MN | **A-** | B+ | B+ | 145.1 | 1.23 | 4.2 | 2.0 | 37.8 | 3.8 | **10.0** | 11.1 | 18.8 |
| Security State Bank of Oklahoma | Wewoka | OK | **C** | C | B- | 263.2 | 5.37 | 16.4 | 10.6 | 16.4 | 12.4 | **10.0** | 11.6 | 15.3 |
| Security State Bank of Oklee | Oklee | MN | **B+** | B | B | 32.7 | -2.38 | 3.4 | 5.5 | 13.7 | 24.5 | **10.0** | 17.8 | 48.8 |
| Security State Bank of Wanamingo | Wanamingo | MN | **B+** | B | B | 71.3 | 4.53 | 5.8 | 1.2 | 3.1 | 17.6 | **10.0** | 12.1 | 19.6 |
| ▼ Security State Bank of Warroad | Warroad | MN | **D** | D+ | D+ | 101.9 | 6.93 | 14.1 | 13.1 | 2.5 | 30.7 | **10.0** | 16.8 | 23.3 |
| ▲ Security State Bank, Wishek, North Dakota | Wishek | ND | **B+** | B | B- | 75.5 | 4.67 | 6.7 | 2.7 | 0.7 | 36.0 | **9.2** | 10.5 | 21.4 |
| Security Trust & Savings Bank | Storm Lake | IA | **B-** | B- | C+ | 228.5 | -0.37 | 4.4 | 1.0 | 7.8 | 42.2 | **8.9** | 10.3 | 21.7 |
| SEI Private Trust Co. | Oaks | PA | **U** | U | U | 187.3 | 9.51 | 0.0 | 0.0 | 0.0 | 56.0 | **10.0** | 92.4 | 273.9 |
| Seiling State Bank | Seiling | OK | **B** | B- | C+ | 112.3 | -5.13 | 10.9 | 2.8 | 9.5 | 23.0 | **7.4** | 9.3 | 14.4 |
| Select Bank | Forest | VA | **B-** | B- | B- | 255.3 | 15.36 | 31.2 | 2.1 | 26.4 | 0.5 | **8.1** | 9.8 | 18.0 |
| Select Bank & Trust Co. | Dunn | NC | **B** | B | B- | 1274.0 | 1.29 | 4.1 | 0.4 | 12.0 | 5.7 | **10.0** | 13.6 | 15.7 |
| ▲ Senath State Bank | Senath | MO | **A** | A- | A- | 83.7 | 2.18 | 6.2 | 7.4 | 27.2 | 6.2 | **10.0** | 16.1 | 30.6 |
| SENB Bank | Moline | IL | **B-** | B- | B- | 297.2 | 32.20 | 12.4 | 1.1 | 18.3 | 20.2 | **7.5** | 9.3 | 13.1 |
| Seneca Savings | Baldwinsville | NY | **C** | C | C | 210.3 | 7.62 | 8.0 | 0.3 | 48.1 | 13.3 | **8.7** | 10.1 | 16.3 |
| ▲ Sentry Bank | Saint Joseph | MN | **B-** | C+ | B | 237.9 | 4.41 | 9.3 | 3.0 | 14.6 | 18.6 | **7.4** | 9.2 | 13.4 |
| ServisFirst Bank | Birmingham | AL | **A-** | A- | B+ | 8946.4 | 11.73 | 29.0 | 0.7 | 5.1 | 8.5 | **6.7** | 9.8 | 12.3 |
| Settlers Bank | Marietta | OH | **A-** | B+ | B+ | 128.6 | 4.76 | 4.2 | 3.8 | 40.9 | 4.6 | **10.0** | 13.1 | 22.6 |
| ▼ Settlers bank | Windsor | WI | **C+** | B- | B- | 310.2 | 10.05 | 23.3 | 1.4 | 14.5 | 2.9 | **6.0** | 9.4 | 11.8 |
| Severn Savings Bank, FSB | Annapolis | MD | **A-** | B+ | B | 823.6 | -15.15 | 4.0 | 0.3 | 32.2 | 4.7 | **10.0** | 13.4 | 19.6 |
| Sevier County Bank | Sevierville | TN | **E-** | E- | E- | 332.6 | 9.27 | 7.0 | 0.8 | 12.6 | 9.6 | **7.5** | 9.3 | 15.0 |
| Sewickley Savings Bank | Sewickley | PA | **B-** | B- | B- | 314.5 | -0.34 | 1.8 | 0.1 | 6.0 | 64.9 | **10.0** | 29.1 | 64.4 |
| Seymour Bank | Seymour | MO | **B** | B | B | 163.0 | 19.69 | 2.6 | 5.2 | 18.0 | 26.3 | **10.0** | 13.6 | 17.4 |
| Shamrock Bank, N.A. | Coalgate | OK | **A-** | A- | A- | 315.8 | 3.70 | 6.9 | 4.3 | 17.4 | 22.0 | **10.0** | 11.6 | 16.9 |
| Sharon Bank | Springfield | PA | **D+** | D+ | C- | 173.2 | 5.23 | 2.7 | 0.2 | 31.4 | 25.1 | **8.4** | 9.9 | 13.7 |
| ▲ Shelby County State Bank | Harlan | IA | **B-** | C+ | B | 269.2 | 3.00 | 3.4 | 1.3 | 5.5 | 16.7 | **10.0** | 11.3 | 15.8 |
| Shelby County State Bank | Shelbyville | IL | **B+** | B | B | 247.4 | -1.63 | 7.8 | 2.7 | 17.2 | 15.2 | **8.8** | 10.3 | 14.0 |
| Shelby Savings Bank, SSB | Center | TX | **A-** | B+ | A- | 302.9 | 2.32 | 11.5 | 4.8 | 14.8 | 10.3 | **10.0** | 12.6 | 16.9 |
| Shelby State Bank | Shelby | MI | **B-** | B- | B- | 277.5 | 13.01 | 4.7 | 1.3 | 13.0 | 24.8 | **6.5** | 8.5 | 12.3 |
| Shell Lake State Bank | Shell Lake | WI | **A-** | A | A | 213.2 | -0.13 | 3.4 | 3.4 | 27.8 | 38.2 | **10.0** | 16.7 | 31.0 |
| ▲ Sherburne State Bank | Becker | MN | **B** | C+ | B | 131.4 | 8.53 | 10.1 | 1.7 | 14.1 | 12.4 | **5.5** | 8.4 | 11.4 |
| Sherwood Community Bank | Creighton | MO | **C+** | C | C | 46.9 | -0.60 | 5.0 | 1.3 | 28.1 | 17.2 | **8.4** | 9.9 | 18.8 |
| Sherwood State Bank | Sherwood | OH | **C+** | C | C+ | 73.4 | 5.71 | 7.1 | 5.9 | 34.2 | 16.2 | **10.0** | 11.3 | 17.6 |
| Shinhan Bank America | New York | NY | **C** | C+ | B+ | 1627.7 | 14.39 | 15.4 | 0.2 | 14.1 | 4.1 | **10.0** | 13.3 | 18.3 |
| Shore United Bank | Easton | MD | **B+** | B+ | B+ | 1559.0 | 5.50 | 6.0 | 1.1 | 22.8 | 8.4 | **8.6** | 10.6 | 13.9 |
| Sibley State Bank | Sibley | IA | **B** | C | D+ | 79.4 | -1.02 | 2.3 | 1.6 | 3.6 | 6.9 | **10.0** | 12.8 | 16.1 |
| Sicily Island State Bank | Sicily Island | LA | **B-** | B- | B | 65.7 | 10.99 | 8.7 | 4.4 | 29.3 | 6.2 | **10.0** | 13.0 | 20.7 |
| ▼ Sidney Federal S&L Assn. | Sidney | NE | **E+** | D- | E+ | 18.4 | 8.09 | 10.8 | 2.4 | 57.7 | 13.7 | **6.6** | 8.6 | 13.0 |
| Sidney State Bank | Sidney | MI | **C** | C | B- | 81.8 | 9.39 | 4.8 | 4.6 | 49.5 | 6.5 | **6.4** | 8.4 | 14.2 |
| Signature Bank | Rosemont | IL | **A-** | B+ | B- | 914.1 | 4.44 | 38.2 | 0.1 | 2.7 | 10.8 | **7.6** | 10.3 | 13.0 |
| Signature Bank | New York | NY | **B+** | B+ | B+ | 50621.2 | 6.88 | 18.3 | 0.4 | 1.0 | 17.9 | **7.9** | 9.6 | 13.3 |
| Signature Bank of Arkansas | Fayetteville | AR | **B** | B | B | 701.5 | 14.38 | 10.4 | 3.5 | 16.6 | 8.1 | **8.4** | 11.6 | 13.6 |
| ▲ Signature Bank of Georgia | Sandy Springs | GA | **C-** | D | D | 156.7 | 30.97 | 8.0 | 0.2 | 3.0 | 16.8 | **10.0** | 12.7 | 19.4 |
| Signature Bank, N.A. | Toledo | OH | **A-** | B+ | B | 984.6 | 7.76 | 25.2 | 0.7 | 9.1 | 2.0 | **8.2** | 10.7 | 13.5 |

| Asset Quality Index | Adjusted Non-Performing Loans as a % of Total Loans | Adjusted Non-Performing Loans as a % of Capital | Net Charge-Offs Avg Loans | Profitability Index | Net Income ($Mil) | Return on Assets (R.O.A.) | Return on Equity (R.O.E.) | Net Interest Spread | Overhead Efficiency Ratio | Liquidity Index | Liquidity Ratio | Hot Money Ratio | Stability Index |
|---|---|---|---|---|---|---|---|---|---|---|---|---|---|
| **7.2** | 0.00 | 0.0 | -0.01 | **7.5** | 4.5 | 1.51 | 10.04 | 3.49 | 46.4 | **0.6** | 12.4 | 45.5 | **8.7** |
| **5.6** | 1.76 | 10.4 | 0.04 | **2.7** | 0.3 | 0.52 | 3.93 | 3.37 | 85.2 | **6.0** | 44.1 | 4.2 | **5.0** |
| **6.2** | 0.73 | 3.7 | 0.52 | **9.7** | 4.0 | 2.35 | 15.74 | 4.33 | 47.8 | **0.9** | 10.5 | 32.5 | **9.5** |
| **6.6** | 0.25 | 1.4 | 0.04 | **4.1** | 0.7 | 0.89 | 8.31 | 3.48 | 68.7 | **2.2** | 32.2 | 24.9 | **6.7** |
| **8.7** | 0.00 | 0.0 | 0.00 | **5.1** | 0.5 | 1.08 | 7.74 | 3.34 | 56.4 | **5.2** | 68.4 | 13.6 | **7.3** |
| **5.3** | 0.89 | 5.2 | -0.18 | **7.5** | 4.2 | 1.83 | 19.20 | 4.18 | 51.4 | **0.9** | 15.7 | 24.5 | **6.4** |
| **8.7** | 0.00 | 0.0 | -0.03 | **8.3** | 3.0 | 1.95 | 14.71 | 4.12 | 55.2 | **2.0** | 30.7 | 26.1 | **7.7** |
| **8.5** | 0.92 | 2.0 | 0.00 | **6.0** | 7.8 | 1.24 | 9.57 | 3.17 | 53.4 | **1.0** | 19.5 | 33.0 | **8.5** |
| **8.2** | 0.05 | 1.6 | 0.23 | **5.3** | 0.8 | 1.33 | 14.60 | 4.27 | 67.7 | **4.6** | 26.6 | 6.5 | **4.6** |
| **8.7** | 0.70 | 2.3 | -0.02 | **9.1** | 13.6 | 2.88 | 21.65 | 4.00 | 46.1 | **6.8** | 62.5 | 5.4 | **9.2** |
| **3.7** | 5.02 | 15.7 | 0.00 | **5.8** | 1.3 | 1.27 | 6.84 | 4.18 | 64.6 | **1.7** | 29.8 | 26.5 | **6.7** |
| **5.6** | 1.42 | 5.3 | 0.51 | **3.9** | 2.2 | 0.64 | 5.60 | 3.53 | 69.1 | **2.4** | 41.5 | 28.9 | **6.8** |
| **6.4** | 1.06 | 5.2 | 0.01 | **8.2** | 20.9 | 1.94 | 14.68 | 4.69 | 61.7 | **3.5** | 21.4 | 13.1 | **10.0** |
| **7.8** | 0.37 | 1.4 | 0.20 | **6.7** | 1.7 | 1.66 | 13.42 | 4.37 | 58.6 | **4.6** | 20.8 | 5.4 | **8.0** |
| **6.4** | 1.28 | 1.5 | 0.01 | **5.7** | 1.8 | 1.44 | 12.99 | 4.21 | 65.8 | **3.7** | 8.9 | 9.0 | **7.0** |
| **4.8** | 3.29 | 10.2 | 0.22 | **5.0** | 1.3 | 0.98 | 9.76 | 4.14 | 63.6 | **5.4** | 43.7 | 8.7 | **5.3** |
| **0.0** | 10.84 | 101.4 | -0.14 | **2.7** | 0.2 | 0.37 | 3.19 | 4.26 | 85.6 | **3.1** | 10.3 | 12.8 | **6.0** |
| **8.4** | 0.56 | 1.9 | 0.04 | **8.9** | 3.0 | 2.13 | 20.09 | 4.65 | 55.6 | **3.7** | 27.9 | 12.6 | **8.6** |
| **4.2** | 1.80 | 11.0 | 0.19 | **9.3** | 4.8 | 1.90 | 17.10 | 4.82 | 49.5 | **0.7** | 9.1 | 30.6 | **6.9** |
| **8.3** | 0.00 | 0.3 | 0.24 | **6.8** | 0.6 | 1.73 | 10.13 | 2.89 | 55.6 | **6.7** | 62.3 | 3.4 | **7.8** |
| **8.6** | 0.00 | 0.0 | 0.01 | **6.4** | 1.0 | 1.58 | 13.06 | 3.91 | 60.1 | **5.0** | 42.6 | 10.6 | **7.3** |
| **4.6** | 2.20 | 7.4 | 3.43 | **0.0** | -0.7 | -0.72 | -4.21 | 3.93 | 73.4 | **4.8** | 39.1 | 10.7 | **5.4** |
| **8.8** | 0.00 | 0.1 | 0.11 | **6.2** | 1.2 | 1.64 | 12.73 | 3.39 | 64.1 | **5.9** | 57.5 | 8.1 | **6.1** |
| **8.8** | 0.16 | 0.5 | -0.05 | **3.3** | 1.4 | 0.62 | 5.37 | 2.52 | 70.5 | **5.4** | 57.1 | 12.1 | **6.4** |
| **10.0** | na | 0.0 | na | **10.0** | 86.8 | 47.69 | 53.09 | 2.81 | 56.2 | **4.0** | na | 100.0 | **7.0** |
| **8.4** | 0.13 | 0.8 | 0.05 | **4.9** | 1.5 | 1.27 | 13.69 | 4.23 | 67.9 | **1.0** | 8.2 | 30.1 | **5.6** |
| **5.3** | 0.79 | 5.8 | 0.01 | **4.0** | 1.7 | 0.72 | 7.83 | 3.17 | 72.1 | **0.6** | 8.0 | 42.6 | **5.2** |
| **4.4** | 1.19 | 5.1 | 0.08 | **5.7** | 14.5 | 1.14 | 7.64 | 4.14 | 64.0 | **0.8** | 12.3 | 31.6 | **9.8** |
| **7.9** | 0.00 | 3.5 | 0.00 | **9.0** | 1.8 | 2.21 | 14.48 | 4.25 | 52.1 | **6.3** | 44.6 | 2.6 | **9.5** |
| **7.5** | 0.18 | 2.5 | 0.06 | **3.9** | 2.6 | 0.90 | 9.53 | 4.24 | 74.5 | **2.9** | 14.5 | 14.4 | **5.6** |
| **5.3** | 1.70 | 12.1 | 0.14 | **3.2** | 1.3 | 0.62 | 7.12 | 3.20 | 74.5 | **0.6** | 10.3 | 34.2 | **4.5** |
| **5.7** | 0.13 | 0.7 | -0.06 | **7.2** | 3.0 | 1.35 | 11.53 | 3.74 | 47.7 | **2.0** | 31.9 | 24.7 | **6.7** |
| **7.1** | 0.41 | 3.7 | 0.32 | **9.5** | 152.2 | 1.76 | 18.08 | 3.58 | 32.2 | **4.0** | 12.4 | 8.6 | **9.2** |
| **6.5** | 1.13 | 5.7 | 0.01 | **7.2** | 1.8 | 1.43 | 10.79 | 4.05 | 55.2 | **2.6** | 22.7 | 16.8 | **8.4** |
| **4.1** | 1.51 | 12.1 | 0.06 | **2.1** | 0.5 | 0.16 | 1.57 | 3.38 | 77.1 | **0.6** | 9.2 | 43.4 | **5.5** |
| **6.2** | 1.99 | 6.9 | 0.06 | **5.5** | 9.2 | 1.03 | 7.73 | 3.62 | 70.0 | **2.0** | 19.1 | 19.1 | **8.6** |
| **6.9** | 0.56 | 2.0 | 0.02 | **0.0** | -2.1 | -0.66 | -9.34 | 3.61 | 129.0 | **1.6** | 19.3 | 24.5 | **2.2** |
| **10.0** | 0.06 | 0.0 | 0.00 | **3.4** | 2.1 | 0.66 | 2.32 | 1.83 | 59.2 | **4.2** | 106.2 | 33.1 | **8.0** |
| **8.6** | 0.00 | 1.2 | -0.27 | **4.3** | 1.2 | 0.87 | 6.61 | 3.99 | 80.8 | **4.1** | 39.4 | 13.7 | **6.9** |
| **8.4** | 0.31 | 1.7 | 0.01 | **6.2** | 4.6 | 1.47 | 12.08 | 4.47 | 67.2 | **2.3** | 28.9 | 19.8 | **7.5** |
| **8.5** | 0.33 | 1.8 | 0.00 | **1.1** | 0.0 | 0.01 | 0.05 | 2.77 | 97.1 | **2.1** | 31.3 | 24.6 | **4.8** |
| **6.3** | 0.70 | 2.4 | 0.09 | **6.7** | 3.6 | 1.35 | 10.99 | 3.75 | 53.9 | **4.5** | 26.2 | 7.1 | **7.7** |
| **8.3** | 0.00 | 0.0 | 0.00 | **5.8** | 3.6 | 1.41 | 14.17 | 3.64 | 62.8 | **3.7** | 12.2 | 10.4 | **7.1** |
| **8.1** | 0.31 | 2.5 | 0.10 | **5.6** | 4.3 | 1.41 | 10.84 | 4.26 | 70.9 | **1.7** | 21.0 | 23.3 | **7.9** |
| **4.7** | 2.81 | 11.4 | 0.02 | **3.9** | 1.9 | 0.72 | 8.08 | 4.02 | 83.1 | **4.7** | 27.1 | 6.5 | **4.9** |
| **8.8** | 0.94 | 2.4 | -0.15 | **5.7** | 3.0 | 1.42 | 8.53 | 3.38 | 65.2 | **4.4** | 33.6 | 8.9 | **8.6** |
| **5.4** | 0.87 | 3.9 | 0.05 | **9.0** | 2.1 | 1.65 | 20.54 | 4.47 | 55.1 | **3.4** | 23.1 | 12.7 | **6.3** |
| **5.9** | 0.09 | 6.1 | 0.01 | **3.1** | 0.2 | 0.50 | 5.00 | 4.17 | 88.7 | **4.8** | 28.5 | 6.2 | **5.3** |
| **4.0** | 1.89 | 11.6 | 0.21 | **3.6** | 0.5 | 0.67 | 6.06 | 4.43 | 78.6 | **3.7** | 15.3 | 10.4 | **5.7** |
| **7.3** | 0.20 | 1.1 | -0.04 | **2.0** | 1.6 | 0.11 | 0.76 | 3.32 | 96.1 | **0.9** | 17.0 | 36.5 | **8.4** |
| **4.9** | 1.20 | 7.3 | 0.04 | **6.0** | 16.6 | 1.11 | 9.73 | 3.51 | 61.6 | **3.9** | 11.5 | 9.5 | **8.9** |
| **5.2** | 1.30 | 5.9 | 0.02 | **6.5** | 1.0 | 1.31 | 10.80 | 3.55 | 55.7 | **1.3** | 12.3 | 26.9 | **7.2** |
| **3.6** | 5.64 | 21.2 | 0.30 | **4.2** | 0.6 | 0.90 | 7.16 | 4.44 | 74.3 | **0.8** | 21.4 | 47.0 | **7.2** |
| **6.3** | 0.89 | 8.7 | 0.02 | **0.0** | -0.3 | -1.95 | -20.84 | 3.38 | 146.5 | **2.3** | 9.2 | 16.6 | **1.4** |
| **4.8** | 1.78 | 10.8 | 0.05 | **3.9** | 0.6 | 0.70 | 8.28 | 4.23 | 77.2 | **3.3** | 16.4 | 12.8 | **4.5** |
| **8.2** | 0.30 | 0.8 | -0.04 | **9.6** | 16.1 | 1.87 | 18.22 | 4.48 | 46.7 | **4.4** | 24.2 | 4.6 | **6.3** |
| **6.9** | 0.31 | 1.8 | 0.01 | **5.8** | 588.9 | 1.20 | 12.70 | 2.77 | 40.0 | **4.4** | 15.6 | 5.6 | **8.3** |
| **6.4** | 0.37 | 2.6 | 0.14 | **4.8** | 5.7 | 0.89 | 7.68 | 4.03 | 71.6 | **0.7** | 13.9 | 27.7 | **7.2** |
| **6.3** | 3.62 | 4.5 | -0.01 | **1.5** | 0.4 | 0.26 | 1.92 | 3.96 | 92.5 | **5.4** | 39.0 | 7.0 | **4.5** |
| **8.2** | 0.04 | 0.3 | 0.00 | **7.2** | 13.2 | 1.40 | 13.22 | 3.56 | 50.6 | **2.9** | 21.3 | 13.2 | **8.1** |

| Name | City | State | Rating | 2018 Rating | 2017 Rating | Total Assets ($Mil) | One Year Asset Growth | Asset Mix (As a % of Total Assets): Commercial Loans | Consumer Loans | Mortgage Loans | Securities | Capitalization Index | Leverage Ratio | Risk-Based Capital Ratio |
|---|---|---|---|---|---|---|---|---|---|---|---|---|---|---|
| Silex Banking Co. | Silex | MO | B+ | B+ | B | 72.0 | -1.81 | 4.4 | 0.6 | 10.5 | 39.8 | 10.0 | 16.1 | 32.2 |
| Silicon Valley Bank | Santa Clara | CA | A- | B+ | B | 69942.9 | 24.59 | 16.3 | 0.3 | 4.5 | 40.1 | 5.3 | 7.3 | 12.0 |
| Silver Lake Bank | Topeka | KS | B+ | B | B | 293.8 | 9.35 | 12.0 | 1.3 | 20.7 | 15.5 | 10.0 | 11.2 | 15.2 |
| Silvergate Bank | La Jolla | CA | A- | B+ | B | 2127.2 | 6.37 | 0.7 | 0.0 | 27.3 | 42.2 | 9.3 | 10.5 | 25.2 |
| Simmesport State Bank | Simmesport | LA | B- | C+ | B- | 106.8 | 25.89 | 5.3 | 15.0 | 38.3 | 3.5 | 10.0 | 12.6 | 20.7 |
| Simmons Bank | Pine Bluff | AR | B+ | B | B- | 17659.3 | 6.91 | 12.6 | 2.0 | 10.2 | 13.7 | 7.4 | 10.7 | 12.9 |
| Simply Bank | Spring City | TN | C+ | C- | C- | 361.1 | 6.66 | 10.4 | 1.6 | 19.6 | 7.7 | 7.4 | 9.7 | 12.9 |
| Siouxland Bank | South Sioux City | NE | C+ | C | C | 59.0 | 13.67 | 8.8 | 2.6 | 16.1 | 0.0 | 8.6 | 10.0 | 21.0 |
| SJN Bank of Kansas | Saint John | KS | B | B+ | B+ | 181.7 | 23.33 | 9.2 | 1.8 | 4.1 | 33.2 | 6.3 | 8.3 | 13.3 |
| Skowhegan Savings Bank | Skowhegan | ME | B+ | B | B | 606.3 | 2.21 | 6.9 | 9.1 | 34.5 | 12.9 | 10.0 | 15.3 | 22.2 |
| Skyline National Bank | Independence | VA | B- | C+ | B- | 705.5 | 3.74 | 4.1 | 1.0 | 25.5 | 4.7 | 8.2 | 10.8 | 13.5 |
| Sloan State Bank | Sloan | IA | B+ | B+ | A- | 56.8 | -0.38 | 3.9 | 7.8 | 16.2 | 33.3 | 10.0 | 11.7 | 21.1 |
| ▲ Slovenian S&L Assn. of Canonsburg | Strabane | PA | A- | B+ | A- | 438.1 | 8.88 | 0.0 | 0.3 | 34.8 | 51.2 | 10.0 | 15.2 | 21.7 |
| Slovenian S&L Assn. of Franklin-Conemau | Conemaugh | PA | C+ | C+ | C+ | 149.6 | 7.33 | 0.0 | 2.2 | 48.1 | 31.4 | 10.0 | 11.7 | 19.0 |
| Smackover State Bank | Smackover | AR | B | B | B | 183.1 | -1.70 | 2.6 | 4.4 | 19.7 | 42.3 | 10.0 | 12.9 | 29.1 |
| ▲ Small Business Bank | Lenexa | KS | C+ | C | C- | 60.2 | -6.75 | 23.5 | 8.9 | 14.8 | 12.2 | 10.0 | 15.4 | 23.3 |
| SmartBank | Pigeon Forge | TN | B | B | B- | 2449.0 | 7.47 | 13.0 | 0.4 | 13.7 | 7.3 | 8.0 | 11.4 | 13.3 |
| SNB Bank, N.A. | Shattuck | OK | C+ | C | C+ | 127.4 | 12.11 | 15.2 | 12.5 | 2.1 | 11.0 | 6.8 | 8.8 | 13.5 |
| Solera National Bank | Lakewood | CO | A- | B+ | B | 282.1 | 28.10 | 7.9 | 5.7 | 9.5 | 12.5 | 10.0 | 14.2 | 18.1 |
| Solomon State Bank | Solomon | KS | A- | A- | A | 204.9 | 3.37 | 3.1 | 1.6 | 46.9 | 6.2 | 10.0 | 16.7 | 32.1 |
| Solon State Bank | Solon | IA | A- | A- | A- | 96.2 | -1.30 | 21.8 | 2.1 | 12.0 | 32.0 | 10.0 | 23.9 | 26.3 |
| Solutions North Bank | Stockton | KS | B+ | B+ | B+ | 248.6 | 2.58 | 6.7 | 2.1 | 5.4 | 19.5 | 10.0 | 11.5 | 16.6 |
| Solvay Bank | Solvay | NY | B | B | B | 934.6 | 2.92 | 8.5 | 9.5 | 28.0 | 30.0 | 8.2 | 9.8 | 17.5 |
| Somerset Savings Bank, SLA | Bound Brook | NJ | B- | C+ | C+ | 587.9 | 3.96 | 0.0 | 0.0 | 55.5 | 26.0 | 10.0 | 20.8 | 47.3 |
| Somerset Trust Co. | Somerset | PA | B- | B- | B- | 1335.5 | 8.57 | 18.9 | 3.4 | 13.7 | 22.5 | 5.8 | 9.0 | 11.6 |
| Somerville Bank | Somerville | OH | B- | C+ | C | 198.1 | 9.27 | 5.0 | 1.2 | 17.9 | 15.2 | 9.1 | 10.4 | 15.9 |
| Sonabank | Glen Allen | VA | A- | B+ | B+ | 2723.9 | 0.62 | 6.5 | 1.0 | 22.2 | 8.7 | 10.0 | 12.1 | 15.3 |
| Sooner State Bank | Tuttle | OK | A | A- | A | 261.0 | 26.35 | 3.2 | 2.1 | 19.0 | 18.7 | 8.7 | 10.1 | 16.2 |
| Sound Banking Co. | Lakewood | WA | B+ | B- | B- | 54.7 | -10.61 | 8.6 | 0.6 | 22.8 | 0.0 | 7.1 | 9.1 | 15.6 |
| ▲ Sound Community Bank | Seattle | WA | B- | C+ | B | 719.9 | 0.44 | 2.8 | 10.2 | 27.3 | 1.3 | 7.7 | 10.2 | 13.0 |
| South Atlantic Bank | Myrtle Beach | SC | B- | C+ | C+ | 714.4 | 14.21 | 5.6 | 0.9 | 24.1 | 10.7 | 6.2 | 9.1 | 11.9 |
| South Central Bank, Inc. | Glasgow | KY | B+ | B | B | 1275.1 | 6.69 | 6.8 | 1.7 | 14.9 | 14.5 | 9.7 | 10.8 | 15.1 |
| South Central State Bank | Campbell | NE | A- | B+ | B+ | 134.2 | -5.23 | 2.5 | 0.9 | 0.6 | 19.9 | 10.0 | 12.4 | 15.2 |
| South Coast Bank & Trust | Brunswick | GA | B | B | B | 145.4 | 11.75 | 4.7 | 0.9 | 21.9 | 7.1 | 8.7 | 10.2 | 13.9 |
| South Georgia Bank | Glennville | GA | A | A | A- | 163.4 | 2.41 | 3.2 | 4.4 | 18.4 | 19.0 | 10.0 | 12.6 | 21.1 |
| South Georgia Banking Co. | Tifton | GA | A- | B+ | A- | 474.0 | 1.23 | 4.7 | 1.9 | 10.9 | 15.3 | 10.0 | 12.2 | 20.3 |
| ▲ South Lafourche Bank & Trust Co. | Larose | LA | C- | D | D- | 140.6 | -3.30 | 11.4 | 4.4 | 40.6 | 8.2 | 10.0 | 13.7 | 23.3 |
| South Louisiana Bank | Houma | LA | A- | B+ | A | 485.7 | 5.79 | 18.4 | 1.9 | 9.6 | 12.2 | 10.0 | 14.4 | 21.8 |
| ▲ South Ottumwa Savings Bank | Ottumwa | IA | A- | B+ | B+ | 410.6 | -2.74 | 5.5 | 1.0 | 17.6 | 34.8 | 10.0 | 13.5 | 22.6 |
| ▲ South Porte Bank | Marion | IL | B- | C | C | 104.3 | 1.13 | 6.2 | 2.3 | 26.4 | 8.5 | 7.8 | 9.5 | 13.7 |
| South Shore Bank | South Weymouth | MA | C+ | C+ | C+ | 1566.4 | 10.45 | 10.3 | 0.4 | 23.3 | 15.7 | 8.6 | 10.1 | 14.7 |
| South State Bank | Columbia | SC | A- | A- | B+ | 15917.4 | 8.48 | 6.8 | 4.2 | 18.8 | 12.3 | 7.1 | 9.6 | 12.6 |
| South Story Bank & Trust | Slater | IA | B | C+ | B- | 242.2 | 20.80 | 11.0 | 0.9 | 15.5 | 7.2 | 9.3 | 12.6 | 14.4 |
| SouthCrest Bank, N.A. | Atlanta | GA | B | B- | B- | 553.5 | 0.84 | 6.4 | 0.4 | 11.8 | 24.7 | 8.0 | 9.6 | 14.2 |
| SouthEast Bank | Farragut | TN | B | B | C+ | 1751.5 | 40.77 | 6.7 | 54.7 | 6.5 | 0.0 | 7.5 | 9.4 | 13.4 |
| Southeast First National Bank | Summerville | GA | C | C+ | C | 60.4 | 3.44 | 0.5 | 2.4 | 13.2 | 52.1 | 10.0 | 11.8 | 34.2 |
| Southeastern Bank | Darien | GA | A | A- | A- | 455.3 | 8.61 | 4.9 | 1.9 | 13.1 | 25.2 | 10.0 | 12.0 | 20.0 |
| Southern Bancorp Bank | Arkadelphia | AR | B- | B- | B- | 1496.0 | 7.80 | 9.2 | 2.6 | 17.0 | 12.5 | 7.1 | 9.0 | 14.1 |
| Southern Bank | Sardis | GA | B- | B- | B- | 79.1 | 2.87 | 0.6 | 8.3 | 29.6 | 22.5 | 10.0 | 12.3 | 23.5 |
| Southern Bank | Poplar Bluff | MO | B+ | B+ | B+ | 2298.8 | 4.61 | 11.0 | 1.4 | 16.8 | 7.7 | 7.6 | 10.6 | 13.0 |
| Southern Bank & Trust | Clarkesville | GA | B- | C+ | B- | 230.7 | 19.14 | 6.0 | 4.2 | 19.9 | 8.7 | 6.9 | 8.9 | 12.6 |
| Southern Bank and Trust Co. | Mount Olive | NC | A- | A- | B | 2925.5 | 11.49 | 6.8 | 0.9 | 11.5 | 27.3 | 8.0 | 9.6 | 13.4 |
| Southern Bank Co. | Gadsden | AL | C | C- | D- | 98.8 | -2.82 | 14.8 | 1.9 | 8.0 | 17.1 | 9.8 | 10.9 | 18.1 |
| Southern Bank of Tennessee | Mount Juliet | TN | B+ | B+ | B- | 300.8 | 6.42 | 6.7 | 1.4 | 21.1 | 8.9 | 10.0 | 13.1 | 16.8 |
| Southern First Bank | Greenville | SC | B+ | B+ | B+ | 2267.5 | 19.25 | 10.4 | 1.1 | 24.7 | 3.0 | 8.0 | 10.8 | 13.3 |
| Southern Heritage Bank | Jonesville | LA | A- | B+ | A- | 305.5 | -0.07 | 8.8 | 5.1 | 29.7 | 19.4 | 10.0 | 11.6 | 19.1 |
| Southern Hills Community Bank | Leesburg | OH | C | C- | C- | 160.7 | 3.91 | 2.9 | 3.4 | 43.6 | 1.8 | 10.0 | 15.2 | 25.4 |
| Southern Illinois Bank | Johnston City | IL | B+ | B+ | A- | 113.7 | 6.42 | 7.9 | 1.6 | 16.6 | 23.7 | 10.0 | 12.6 | 18.7 |
| Southern Independent Bank | Opp | AL | B+ | B | B | 252.7 | 6.71 | 15.1 | 2.9 | 14.5 | 31.9 | 10.0 | 11.3 | 18.9 |
| Southern Michigan Bank & Trust | Coldwater | MI | B | B | B | 806.6 | 9.62 | 13.1 | 0.5 | 7.5 | 15.3 | 7.8 | 9.7 | 13.1 |

| Asset Quality Index | Adjusted Non-Performing Loans as a % of Total Loans | Adjusted Non-Performing Loans as a % of Capital | Net Charge-Offs Avg Loans | Profitability Index | Net Income ($Mil) | Return on Assets (R.O.A.) | Return on Equity (R.O.E.) | Net Interest Spread | Overhead Efficiency Ratio | Liquidity Index | Liquidity Ratio | Hot Money Ratio | Stability Index |
|---|---|---|---|---|---|---|---|---|---|---|---|---|---|
| **9.0** | 0.00 | 0.2 | -0.02 | **5.0** | 0.7 | 1.00 | 6.12 | 3.54 | 65.1 | **6.0** | 56.3 | 7.0 | **8.0** |
| **8.7** | 0.39 | 2.2 | 0.24 | **9.2** | 1036.6 | 1.68 | 21.43 | 3.54 | 45.5 | **7.4** | 48.1 | 0.1 | **7.0** |
| **5.2** | 3.09 | 10.3 | 0.00 | **5.2** | 3.1 | 1.05 | 9.34 | 3.64 | 61.9 | **1.4** | 11.1 | 25.0 | **7.1** |
| **9.0** | 0.61 | 2.2 | 0.01 | **6.7** | 27.3 | 1.31 | 12.43 | 3.54 | 57.8 | **4.6** | 54.4 | 0.1 | **7.9** |
| **3.3** | 3.07 | 18.2 | 0.19 | **5.7** | 1.0 | 1.05 | 7.58 | 4.76 | 66.8 | **0.8** | 19.6 | 51.7 | **6.8** |
| **5.2** | 0.68 | 2.8 | 0.25 | **7.6** | 258.9 | 1.50 | 9.87 | 3.94 | 56.2 | **2.5** | 13.1 | 11.4 | **9.2** |
| **3.7** | 1.74 | 6.5 | -0.01 | **5.2** | 4.3 | 1.19 | 12.58 | 4.46 | 74.6 | **1.5** | 9.9 | 23.6 | **7.6** |
| **8.5** | 0.00 | 0.0 | 0.20 | **3.6** | 0.5 | 0.82 | 8.09 | 3.12 | 66.8 | **3.3** | 47.9 | 19.8 | **4.3** |
| **6.8** | 0.53 | 4.1 | 0.26 | **5.3** | 1.8 | 1.09 | 11.74 | 4.37 | 69.0 | **3.3** | 20.8 | 13.3 | **5.9** |
| **5.7** | 1.21 | 4.9 | 0.06 | **5.2** | 6.5 | 1.09 | 7.10 | 3.70 | 75.3 | **4.0** | 16.5 | 9.2 | **8.6** |
| **4.5** | 1.43 | 7.8 | 0.05 | **5.3** | 7.2 | 1.06 | 9.34 | 4.51 | 70.8 | **2.4** | 9.8 | 16.7 | **6.5** |
| **5.9** | 0.74 | 6.1 | 0.05 | **8.0** | 1.1 | 1.85 | 15.19 | 3.76 | 48.4 | **5.5** | 38.4 | 6.1 | **8.0** |
| **6.0** | 2.61 | 10.2 | 0.09 | **6.2** | 5.3 | 1.26 | 8.41 | 2.64 | 37.9 | **3.0** | 65.5 | 52.6 | **8.6** |
| **7.7** | 0.01 | 5.8 | 0.07 | **2.3** | 0.4 | 0.26 | 2.26 | 2.82 | 88.1 | **2.9** | 48.9 | 28.2 | **6.4** |
| **9.1** | 0.26 | 0.8 | 0.03 | **4.2** | 1.7 | 0.90 | 6.88 | 2.76 | 64.6 | **2.2** | 38.5 | 30.0 | **7.5** |
| **6.2** | 1.85 | 3.9 | 0.17 | **2.7** | 0.2 | 0.30 | 2.05 | 3.59 | 93.7 | **3.5** | 18.8 | 12.0 | **6.2** |
| **6.5** | 0.15 | 1.1 | 0.03 | **5.3** | 25.6 | 1.10 | 7.94 | 4.08 | 63.5 | **1.3** | 12.8 | 15.3 | **9.2** |
| **5.6** | 0.46 | 3.6 | 0.15 | **4.2** | 1.1 | 0.92 | 10.24 | 3.65 | 72.8 | **0.7** | 15.5 | 35.1 | **4.5** |
| **7.1** | 0.01 | 0.1 | 0.02 | **6.7** | 3.6 | 1.46 | 9.85 | 3.88 | 49.0 | **3.2** | 17.6 | 13.1 | **7.9** |
| **6.7** | 1.86 | 6.3 | -0.09 | **6.2** | 2.9 | 1.42 | 8.43 | 3.23 | 47.0 | **1.6** | 25.9 | 25.8 | **7.1** |
| **5.5** | 2.42 | 5.6 | 0.06 | **10.0** | 2.7 | 2.74 | 11.12 | 5.21 | 49.7 | **5.6** | 46.3 | 7.5 | **8.7** |
| **8.1** | 0.00 | 2.2 | 0.03 | **4.6** | 2.2 | 0.87 | 7.69 | 3.68 | 67.1 | **1.7** | 20.5 | 22.8 | **7.1** |
| **6.9** | 0.48 | 2.2 | 0.05 | **4.5** | 8.8 | 0.94 | 10.06 | 2.85 | 62.8 | **2.3** | 19.1 | 17.8 | **6.4** |
| **10.0** | 0.07 | 0.2 | 0.00 | **3.3** | 3.1 | 0.53 | 2.64 | 2.48 | 71.8 | **4.7** | 47.3 | 13.5 | **8.4** |
| **5.4** | 1.34 | 7.8 | 0.20 | **4.1** | 11.6 | 0.90 | 10.58 | 4.45 | 79.3 | **2.9** | 17.8 | 11.9 | **7.4** |
| **6.1** | 0.51 | 4.4 | 0.00 | **4.1** | 1.9 | 1.03 | 9.54 | 3.39 | 69.2 | **1.8** | 25.9 | 23.2 | **6.6** |
| **7.4** | 0.44 | 1.2 | 0.11 | **6.4** | 36.5 | 1.34 | 8.92 | 3.54 | 56.0 | **1.1** | 6.6 | 23.3 | **9.4** |
| **8.3** | 0.34 | 1.8 | 0.04 | **7.5** | 3.9 | 1.76 | 15.22 | 4.48 | 62.7 | **3.7** | 24.0 | 11.5 | **7.3** |
| **8.8** | 0.00 | 0.0 | 0.00 | **8.3** | 1.1 | 1.84 | 19.02 | 5.10 | 63.8 | **1.7** | 25.3 | 24.4 | **6.3** |
| **4.6** | 1.05 | 6.9 | 0.00 | **5.3** | 7.3 | 1.04 | 10.18 | 4.12 | 71.0 | **1.2** | 10.1 | 26.2 | **7.3** |
| **8.2** | 0.17 | 1.0 | 0.00 | **4.4** | 6.5 | 0.93 | 9.38 | 4.18 | 73.3 | **2.1** | 13.9 | 17.4 | **6.1** |
| **6.0** | 1.20 | 5.4 | 0.02 | **5.4** | 14.1 | 1.18 | 10.70 | 3.57 | 66.3 | **2.4** | 14.1 | 17.3 | **8.3** |
| **7.2** | 0.01 | 0.0 | 0.00 | **6.0** | 1.8 | 1.34 | 11.08 | 3.80 | 56.4 | **2.9** | 20.8 | 14.1 | **7.6** |
| **6.8** | 0.12 | 2.4 | 0.01 | **5.0** | 1.6 | 1.19 | 11.52 | 4.03 | 69.2 | **1.4** | 15.9 | 25.4 | **6.8** |
| **8.4** | 0.24 | 1.5 | -0.30 | **9.9** | 3.8 | 2.37 | 18.87 | 4.93 | 55.8 | **1.5** | 29.0 | 31.8 | **9.4** |
| **7.2** | 0.54 | 3.6 | 0.13 | **5.9** | 5.5 | 1.22 | 8.61 | 4.02 | 64.1 | **4.5** | 40.7 | 12.9 | **8.1** |
| **3.0** | 3.11 | 15.5 | 0.66 | **2.3** | 0.6 | 0.40 | 3.02 | 3.98 | 79.6 | **1.8** | 19.6 | 21.8 | **5.4** |
| **6.3** | 1.20 | 4.6 | 0.16 | **8.4** | 7.8 | 1.61 | 11.02 | 4.55 | 58.2 | **2.0** | 27.5 | 22.3 | **8.5** |
| **8.4** | 0.65 | 2.0 | 0.02 | **6.0** | 6.0 | 1.47 | 10.40 | 3.10 | 58.5 | **2.8** | 39.4 | 21.7 | **8.6** |
| **5.3** | 0.42 | 4.0 | 0.02 | **4.5** | 1.0 | 0.93 | 9.87 | 3.20 | 60.2 | **0.7** | 12.7 | 43.2 | **5.2** |
| **6.4** | 0.79 | 4.9 | 0.00 | **3.9** | 11.3 | 0.77 | 7.17 | 3.37 | 68.0 | **3.7** | 19.6 | 11.0 | **8.1** |
| **6.1** | 0.31 | 1.8 | 0.05 | **6.4** | 194.5 | 1.26 | 7.91 | 3.83 | 61.9 | **4.3** | 14.3 | 6.9 | **9.9** |
| **5.2** | 0.28 | 1.6 | 0.00 | **3.5** | 0.3 | 0.64 | 6.19 | 4.41 | 51.8 | **1.3** | 6.9 | 16.4 | **6.4** |
| **5.2** | 1.28 | 7.3 | 0.01 | **4.8** | 5.0 | 0.94 | 9.22 | 3.88 | 71.9 | **4.1** | 23.0 | 9.3 | **6.0** |
| **4.4** | 0.25 | 3.5 | 0.11 | **6.3** | 20.7 | 1.27 | 14.25 | 3.72 | 58.3 | **0.5** | 4.5 | 26.6 | **7.5** |
| **9.3** | 0.12 | 0.5 | 0.02 | **1.9** | 0.1 | 0.15 | 1.27 | 2.62 | 95.5 | **2.2** | 47.2 | 42.1 | **5.5** |
| **8.2** | 0.85 | 3.3 | -0.45 | **7.9** | 6.7 | 1.57 | 12.23 | 4.28 | 60.8 | **5.1** | 27.6 | 3.8 | **7.4** |
| **4.6** | 1.58 | 6.9 | 0.30 | **4.7** | 13.8 | 0.98 | 8.53 | 3.81 | 63.5 | **2.0** | 19.1 | 15.6 | **9.1** |
| **5.4** | 2.19 | 9.6 | 0.34 | **2.7** | 0.3 | 0.37 | 3.05 | 4.38 | 87.3 | **2.1** | 26.9 | 21.0 | **6.0** |
| **5.2** | 1.30 | 6.6 | 0.03 | **7.1** | 31.6 | 1.43 | 13.49 | 3.80 | 56.0 | **1.4** | 4.4 | 21.5 | **9.1** |
| **4.8** | 1.02 | 6.3 | 0.01 | **6.7** | 2.8 | 1.30 | 14.56 | 4.54 | 64.1 | **1.4** | 15.8 | 26.4 | **5.8** |
| **7.1** | 0.57 | 3.5 | 0.01 | **6.6** | 38.0 | 1.38 | 13.42 | 3.83 | 64.8 | **4.5** | 18.5 | 6.1 | **8.5** |
| **4.2** | 2.03 | 9.4 | 0.34 | **3.0** | 0.4 | 0.43 | 3.69 | 4.91 | 86.6 | **1.5** | 30.4 | 32.4 | **4.6** |
| **8.5** | 0.00 | 0.1 | 0.00 | **5.1** | 3.2 | 1.13 | 8.35 | 3.89 | 72.1 | **1.0** | 22.2 | 34.6 | **7.9** |
| **7.1** | 0.61 | 3.8 | 0.08 | **6.8** | 28.8 | 1.39 | 14.05 | 3.55 | 54.8 | **2.7** | 9.7 | 11.6 | **8.4** |
| **6.1** | 0.91 | 5.9 | 0.10 | **6.8** | 4.8 | 1.59 | 13.61 | 4.70 | 68.2 | **2.5** | 18.6 | 16.9 | **8.3** |
| **5.3** | 3.31 | 11.0 | 0.21 | **1.9** | 0.2 | 0.15 | 0.94 | 4.37 | 94.9 | **2.3** | 25.6 | 18.5 | **6.3** |
| **7.0** | 0.15 | 3.4 | 0.38 | **4.8** | 1.1 | 0.94 | 7.49 | 3.90 | 65.3 | **4.2** | 17.3 | 7.9 | **7.4** |
| **8.3** | 1.21 | 3.3 | 0.05 | **4.8** | 2.5 | 1.03 | 8.70 | 3.22 | 62.8 | **2.1** | 42.0 | 36.3 | **6.4** |
| **6.0** | 0.87 | 2.3 | 0.03 | **5.6** | 9.0 | 1.14 | 10.13 | 3.74 | 68.3 | **2.8** | 22.2 | 14.9 | **8.0** |

| Name | City | State | Rating | 2018 Rating | 2017 Rating | Total Assets ($Mil) | One Year Asset Growth | Comm-ercial Loans | Cons-umer Loans | Mort-gage Loans | Secur-ities | Capital-ization Index | Lever-age Ratio | Risk-Based Capital Ratio |
|---|---|---|---|---|---|---|---|---|---|---|---|---|---|---|
| Southern States Bank | Anniston | AL | **B-** | B+ | B+ | 1095.5 | 23.36 | 11.9 | 1.1 | 8.7 | 5.5 | **8.1** | 10.8 | 13.4 |
| SouthernTrust Bank | Goreville | IL | **C** | C | C- | 58.7 | 4.97 | 4.5 | 1.5 | 19.1 | 31.2 | **8.2** | 9.8 | 22.3 |
| SouthFirst Bank | Sylacauga | AL | **D+** | C+ | C+ | 76.9 | -6.61 | 3.4 | 0.6 | 39.9 | 13.5 | **10.0** | 12.6 | 21.9 |
| SouthPoint Bank | Birmingham | AL | **B-** | B- | B | 410.1 | 12.33 | 18.7 | 1.0 | 10.7 | 9.1 | **4.9** | 9.4 | 11.0 |
| Southside Bank | Tyler | TX | **A-** | A- | A- | 6743.5 | 10.23 | 5.2 | 1.5 | 11.6 | 37.0 | **10.0** | 11.6 | 18.2 |
| SouthStar Bank, S.S.B. | Moulton | TX | **A-** | A- | A- | 815.9 | 20.43 | 2.3 | 0.5 | 23.2 | 10.0 | **10.0** | 11.4 | 15.3 |
| SouthTrust Bank, N.A. | George West | TX | **B-** | B- | C- | 406.7 | 7.86 | 3.4 | 1.1 | 4.2 | 24.2 | **9.5** | 10.7 | 19.8 |
| Southwest Bank | Odessa | TX | **B+** | B+ | B+ | 456.3 | 9.25 | 30.3 | 0.7 | 5.9 | 12.5 | **6.1** | 8.1 | 12.2 |
| Southwest Bank of Weatherford | Weatherford | OK | **B+** | B+ | B+ | 68.5 | -5.66 | 3.6 | 4.1 | 15.7 | 23.8 | **10.0** | 12.7 | 22.2 |
| ▲ Southwest Capital Bank | Albuquerque | NM | **C** | C | B- | 338.6 | -11.38 | 12.9 | 0.2 | 7.0 | 12.8 | **9.7** | 10.8 | 16.5 |
| ▲ Southwest Georgia Bank | Moultrie | GA | **B** | B- | B- | 554.3 | 3.92 | 7.4 | 0.7 | 18.3 | 17.0 | **6.6** | 8.6 | 13.1 |
| Southwest Missouri Bank | Carthage | MO | **B** | B | B | 795.9 | 6.07 | 8.4 | 7.4 | 20.0 | 31.0 | **7.6** | 9.4 | 16.1 |
| Southwest National Bank | Wichita | KS | **B-** | B- | B | 461.7 | 1.18 | 9.2 | 37.8 | 5.7 | 8.6 | **6.0** | 9.6 | 11.7 |
| Southwestern National Bank | Houston | TX | **B+** | B | B | 590.5 | 39.59 | 1.9 | 0.0 | 2.1 | 5.9 | **10.0** | 12.8 | 15.3 |
| Southwind Bank | Natoma | KS | **B** | B- | B | 131.7 | 7.27 | 5.3 | 3.2 | 11.2 | 47.1 | **8.9** | 10.3 | 17.3 |
| Spectra Bank | Fort Worth | TX | **C** | B- | B | 68.5 | -2.63 | 16.7 | 1.4 | 2.5 | 2.9 | **6.5** | 8.7 | 12.1 |
| Spencer County Bank | Santa Claus | IN | **B** | B- | B- | 109.0 | 2.77 | 5.8 | 5.5 | 30.2 | 25.3 | **10.0** | 13.2 | 19.9 |
| Spencer Savings Bank, SLA | Elmwood Park | NJ | **B-** | B- | B- | 3041.8 | 3.19 | 0.9 | 0.2 | 24.8 | 13.5 | **10.0** | 11.2 | 16.4 |
| Spirit of Texas Bank, SSB | Conroe | TX | **B+** | B | B | 2384.7 | 62.68 | 11.0 | 0.7 | 15.7 | 4.1 | **9.2** | 11.3 | 14.4 |
| ▲ SpiritBank | Tulsa | OK | **C** | C | C- | 631.9 | -4.78 | 15.8 | 1.6 | 9.6 | 10.6 | **7.9** | 11.1 | 13.2 |
| Spiro State Bank | Spiro | OK | **C+** | C | C- | 51.4 | 2.51 | 4.1 | 3.9 | 9.7 | 46.1 | **10.0** | 12.4 | 35.2 |
| Spratt Savings Bank | Chester | SC | **C+** | C+ | C+ | 130.4 | 10.19 | 1.4 | 0.4 | 12.7 | 48.9 | **10.0** | 22.8 | 67.9 |
| Spring Bank | Bronx | NY | **B+** | B+ | A- | 193.6 | 6.36 | 8.4 | 0.8 | 12.2 | 19.5 | **10.0** | 13.0 | 20.3 |
| ▲ Spring Bank | Brookfield | WI | **B-** | C | C+ | 317.1 | 9.17 | 12.7 | 0.1 | 13.2 | 4.5 | **9.5** | 11.5 | 14.6 |
| Spring Hill State Bank | Longview | TX | **B+** | B- | B | 195.0 | -5.05 | 6.5 | 5.0 | 47.9 | 3.4 | **10.0** | 12.2 | 24.1 |
| ▲ Spring Valley Bank | Wyoming | OH | **A-** | A- | A- | 82.0 | 7.62 | 0.3 | 0.1 | 44.9 | 0.1 | **10.0** | 41.9 | 42.0 |
| Spring Valley City Bank | Spring Valley | IL | **B+** | B+ | B+ | 190.2 | 4.11 | 11.0 | 3.5 | 17.0 | 38.5 | **10.0** | 14.5 | 29.2 |
| ▲ Springfield First Community Bank | Springfield | MO | **B+** | B- | B | 748.8 | 18.31 | 12.5 | 0.6 | 9.7 | 4.6 | **7.3** | 10.5 | 12.7 |
| Springfield State Bank | Springfield | KY | **A-** | B+ | B+ | 326.6 | 3.47 | 3.8 | 2.3 | 27.0 | 38.3 | **10.0** | 15.8 | 25.0 |
| Springfield State Bank | Springfield | NE | **B+** | B | B | 56.3 | 9.68 | 3.3 | 3.8 | 8.1 | 17.7 | **9.3** | 10.5 | 27.0 |
| Springs Valley Bank & Trust Co. | Jasper | IN | **B-** | B- | B- | 452.6 | 12.84 | 5.3 | 2.9 | 20.6 | 12.8 | **9.2** | 10.5 | 14.6 |
| Spur Security Bank | Spur | TX | **C+** | C+ | C+ | 46.2 | 2.08 | 2.3 | 3.3 | 0.9 | 65.1 | **10.0** | 12.0 | 37.2 |
| SSB Bank | Pittsburgh | PA | **C** | C | C | 202.6 | 7.34 | 11.8 | 1.0 | 32.1 | 4.9 | **5.7** | 8.6 | 11.5 |
| SSB Community Bank | Strasburg | OH | **C+** | C+ | C+ | 105.5 | 15.98 | 11.1 | 1.3 | 33.0 | 0.0 | **5.0** | 7.8 | 11.0 |
| St. Ansgar State Bank | Saint Ansgar | IA | **A-** | A- | B | 124.0 | 3.36 | 7.1 | 1.8 | 8.4 | 20.4 | **10.0** | 11.9 | 16.6 |
| St. Charles Bank & Trust Co., N.A. | Saint Charles | IL | **B** | B | B- | 1525.7 | 31.34 | 24.4 | 16.9 | 4.4 | 9.9 | **6.0** | 10.2 | 11.7 |
| ▲ St. Clair County State Bank | Osceola | MO | **A** | A- | A- | 146.9 | 4.30 | 6.4 | 3.7 | 19.3 | 9.6 | **10.0** | 14.2 | 18.9 |
| St. Clair State Bank (Inc.) | Saint Clair | MN | **B+** | B+ | A- | 97.7 | 4.74 | 8.1 | 6.0 | 12.2 | 1.4 | **8.2** | 10.4 | 13.5 |
| St. Henry Bank | Saint Henry | OH | **A** | A | A+ | 309.8 | -3.01 | 6.3 | 0.8 | 14.5 | 17.7 | **10.0** | 15.7 | 20.9 |
| St. Johns Bank and Trust Co. | Saint Louis | MO | **C+** | C+ | C- | 290.5 | 0.93 | 5.7 | 0.5 | 7.9 | 16.0 | **8.4** | 9.9 | 15.0 |
| St. Landry Bank and Trust Co. | Opelousas | LA | **C+** | B | B- | 274.0 | -1.87 | 5.0 | 0.8 | 4.3 | 57.4 | **8.1** | 9.7 | 28.0 |
| St. Landry Homestead FSB | Opelousas | LA | **B** | B | B | 218.6 | -1.34 | 1.3 | 2.5 | 51.5 | 12.5 | **10.0** | 23.1 | 41.1 |
| St. Louis Bank | Town And Country | MO | **C** | C | C | 463.5 | 6.21 | 15.1 | 0.2 | 5.6 | 11.2 | **5.8** | 9.1 | 11.6 |
| St. Martin National Bank | Saint Martin | MN | **B** | B | B | 23.2 | 4.77 | 4.0 | 3.4 | 22.3 | 16.7 | **10.0** | 15.0 | 30.7 |
| ▲ Stafford Savings Bank | Stafford Springs | CT | **A-** | B- | B | 303.8 | 9.43 | 0.0 | 0.4 | 19.2 | 13.7 | **10.0** | 43.6 | 32.9 |
| Standard Bank, PaSB | Monroeville | PA | **B** | B | B- | 983.6 | 1.26 | 4.4 | 0.1 | 41.7 | 16.4 | **10.0** | 11.5 | 17.6 |
| Standing Stone Bank | Lancaster | OH | **C+** | C | C- | 102.0 | -3.05 | 8.6 | 18.6 | 22.4 | 13.9 | **7.1** | 9.0 | 13.6 |
| Stanley Bank | Overland Park | KS | **A-** | B+ | A- | 120.9 | 8.11 | 32.5 | 2.5 | 4.1 | 0.0 | **10.0** | 18.0 | 31.7 |
| Stanton State Bank | Stanton | NE | **C+** | C | C | 44.9 | 0.80 | 13.0 | 3.7 | 16.3 | 28.0 | **8.2** | 9.8 | 17.6 |
| ▼ Star Bank | Maple Lake | MN | **C** | B- | B+ | 291.4 | 0.33 | 6.3 | 2.4 | 9.8 | 1.6 | **6.9** | 10.0 | 12.4 |
| STAR Financial Bank | Fort Wayne | IN | **B+** | B | B | 2089.5 | 4.34 | 19.8 | 1.7 | 10.1 | 17.1 | **8.1** | 10.5 | 13.5 |
| Starion Bank | Bismarck | ND | **B+** | A- | A- | 1376.4 | 1.08 | 11.0 | 2.1 | 8.1 | 26.3 | **9.8** | 10.9 | 15.2 |
| State Bank | La Junta | CO | **B** | B | B | 105.3 | -0.69 | 1.7 | 2.6 | 9.5 | 20.7 | **10.0** | 14.9 | 22.1 |
| ▲ State Bank | Spencer | IA | **C+** | C | C | 69.1 | 2.67 | 7.4 | 3.3 | 17.9 | 12.2 | **6.6** | 8.6 | 13.4 |
| State Bank | Spirit Lake | IA | **C+** | B- | B- | 70.4 | -6.68 | 5.9 | 1.0 | 13.6 | 30.4 | **10.0** | 12.4 | 23.7 |
| State Bank | Freeport | IL | **B+** | B | B- | 271.4 | 2.70 | 16.3 | 0.2 | 4.6 | 25.9 | **9.5** | 10.7 | 14.8 |
| State Bank | Wonder Lake | IL | **C** | C | C- | 225.3 | -3.91 | 7.1 | 0.6 | 25.2 | 17.2 | **8.9** | 10.3 | 15.4 |
| State Bank | Fenton | MI | **B+** | B | B- | 1033.9 | 11.62 | 6.7 | 0.8 | 29.3 | 5.1 | **7.8** | 10.5 | 13.2 |
| State Bank | Richmond | MO | **B** | B | B | 32.9 | -0.19 | 4.0 | 3.3 | 24.1 | 28.8 | **6.9** | 8.9 | 22.4 |
| State Bank | Green River | WY | **D-** | D+ | D+ | 29.1 | -4.71 | 5.5 | 1.6 | 8.9 | 1.7 | **10.0** | 12.3 | 25.1 |

| Asset Quality Index | Adjusted Non-Performing Loans as a % of Total Loans | Adjusted Non-Performing Loans as a % of Capital | Net Charge-Offs Avg Loans | Profitability Index | Net Income ($Mil) | Return on Assets (R.O.A.) | Return on Equity (R.O.E.) | Net Interest Spread | Overhead Efficiency Ratio | Liquidity Index | Liquidity Ratio | Hot Money Ratio | Stability Index |
|---|---|---|---|---|---|---|---|---|---|---|---|---|---|
| **4.2** | 1.90 | 10.2 | 0.57 | **4.1** | 6.1 | 0.62 | 5.29 | 3.89 | 65.6 | **1.3** | 15.7 | 25.1 | **9.3** |
| **4.7** | 2.74 | 11.5 | -0.02 | **3.7** | 0.4 | 0.64 | 6.65 | 3.55 | 80.9 | **3.8** | 40.7 | 16.1 | **4.3** |
| **5.2** | 2.32 | 11.4 | 0.40 | **1.5** | 0.0 | -0.02 | -0.14 | 3.98 | 100.6 | **2.2** | 26.7 | 19.4 | **5.7** |
| **5.9** | 0.12 | 1.6 | 0.06 | **6.8** | 5.2 | 1.33 | 14.37 | 3.89 | 67.1 | **0.6** | 6.9 | 30.2 | **6.4** |
| **6.9** | 0.41 | 1.0 | 0.21 | **6.0** | 83.5 | 1.31 | 9.08 | 3.20 | 52.8 | **2.3** | 26.2 | 17.3 | **9.6** |
| **8.5** | 0.22 | 2.1 | -0.10 | **5.8** | 8.7 | 1.15 | 9.77 | 4.72 | 71.0 | **1.6** | 11.5 | 20.7 | **7.1** |
| **5.5** | 1.16 | 3.7 | 0.12 | **3.7** | 3.0 | 0.75 | 6.82 | 3.95 | 79.3 | **3.4** | 31.5 | 15.1 | **6.5** |
| **6.9** | 0.55 | 4.2 | 0.43 | **7.9** | 7.6 | 1.75 | 20.58 | 5.12 | 67.1 | **4.6** | 32.8 | 9.4 | **6.4** |
| **4.8** | 3.36 | 13.8 | -0.02 | **4.8** | 0.7 | 0.89 | 7.20 | 3.77 | 72.1 | **3.8** | 40.3 | 15.9 | **7.4** |
| **3.4** | 4.50 | 15.9 | 1.43 | **3.5** | 1.4 | 0.39 | 3.98 | 4.72 | 74.6 | **4.2** | 28.9 | 10.5 | **7.0** |
| **8.0** | 0.06 | 0.5 | 0.18 | **4.8** | 5.5 | 1.01 | 12.33 | 4.06 | 70.6 | **3.3** | 12.6 | 12.1 | **5.7** |
| **6.0** | 1.09 | 4.2 | 0.11 | **4.5** | 7.1 | 0.95 | 10.25 | 3.93 | 73.8 | **4.0** | 23.4 | 9.8 | **5.8** |
| **5.7** | 0.43 | 2.1 | 0.22 | **5.3** | 5.4 | 1.19 | 12.37 | 3.74 | 67.0 | **1.3** | 13.5 | 13.4 | **6.0** |
| **7.5** | 0.03 | 0.2 | 0.01 | **4.7** | 4.4 | 0.89 | 6.77 | 3.62 | 67.3 | **0.9** | 21.7 | 37.0 | **8.5** |
| **6.4** | 0.65 | 3.0 | 0.02 | **5.2** | 1.4 | 1.11 | 10.50 | 3.52 | 59.7 | **5.1** | 41.6 | 10.1 | **6.3** |
| **4.1** | 3.18 | 14.9 | 2.63 | **1.2** | -1.9 | -2.58 | -27.49 | 5.32 | 93.9 | **2.7** | 20.8 | 16.2 | **6.1** |
| **5.6** | 2.19 | 10.5 | 0.04 | **4.0** | 0.8 | 0.79 | 6.15 | 3.46 | 75.0 | **2.9** | 33.0 | 18.2 | **6.8** |
| **5.8** | 1.20 | 6.1 | 0.13 | **3.4** | 17.0 | 0.56 | 5.05 | 2.60 | 66.1 | **1.6** | 15.9 | 24.8 | **8.3** |
| **7.0** | 0.38 | 1.9 | 0.17 | **5.8** | 24.7 | 1.31 | 10.22 | 4.52 | 67.1 | **1.4** | 18.0 | 28.8 | **9.3** |
| **3.2** | 2.05 | 7.8 | -0.18 | **3.0** | 3.6 | 0.57 | 5.01 | 3.46 | 90.3 | **0.7** | 14.8 | 39.6 | **6.6** |
| **9.5** | 0.28 | 0.7 | 0.04 | **2.2** | 0.2 | 0.33 | 2.54 | 3.43 | 92.1 | **6.4** | 64.5 | 6.4 | **6.2** |
| **9.9** | 0.85 | 1.0 | 0.00 | **2.8** | 0.5 | 0.41 | 1.73 | 2.72 | 78.6 | **5.3** | 86.5 | 16.6 | **7.2** |
| **4.3** | 1.86 | 9.9 | -0.39 | **8.9** | 3.2 | 1.65 | 13.01 | 4.72 | 64.8 | **0.8** | 18.4 | 36.5 | **8.0** |
| **4.1** | 0.89 | 5.8 | 0.08 | **7.3** | 4.1 | 1.36 | 11.78 | 3.41 | 45.8 | **0.8** | 16.3 | 43.4 | **8.0** |
| **6.2** | 0.42 | 7.6 | 0.10 | **5.8** | 2.4 | 1.19 | 10.37 | 3.81 | 60.7 | **1.7** | 21.3 | 22.7 | **7.2** |
| **7.6** | 0.92 | 1.7 | 0.05 | **10.0** | 3.8 | 4.82 | 11.67 | 6.52 | 25.0 | **0.7** | 12.8 | 47.1 | **9.4** |
| **7.6** | 0.98 | 3.2 | 0.03 | **4.5** | 1.7 | 0.92 | 6.16 | 3.06 | 65.0 | **3.7** | 43.9 | 17.7 | **8.1** |
| **6.8** | 0.07 | 0.2 | 0.01 | **6.6** | 8.2 | 1.32 | 7.36 | 3.80 | 50.3 | **1.8** | 19.5 | 15.8 | **8.4** |
| **8.8** | 0.61 | 3.0 | 0.13 | **5.1** | 3.8 | 1.18 | 7.76 | 3.34 | 64.3 | **2.0** | 32.9 | 27.2 | **8.2** |
| **8.8** | 0.00 | 0.0 | -0.01 | **5.5** | 0.8 | 1.38 | 12.97 | 3.40 | 57.8 | **6.8** | 56.6 | 1.6 | **7.2** |
| **4.9** | 1.66 | 8.1 | 0.13 | **4.2** | 3.8 | 0.88 | 8.10 | 3.55 | 75.0 | **1.5** | 19.5 | 16.5 | **6.3** |
| **9.5** | 0.00 | 0.1 | 0.01 | **2.6** | 0.3 | 0.67 | 5.85 | 2.67 | 89.3 | **3.0** | 71.2 | 35.7 | **5.2** |
| **2.4** | 3.06 | 24.8 | 0.07 | **2.3** | 0.5 | 0.23 | 2.63 | 2.41 | 86.9 | **0.6** | 18.5 | 51.8 | **4.4** |
| **3.0** | 2.49 | 20.3 | 0.00 | **5.5** | 1.3 | 1.33 | 17.31 | 3.73 | 67.3 | **1.4** | 14.5 | 26.3 | **4.9** |
| **8.5** | 0.00 | 0.0 | -0.02 | **5.6** | 1.6 | 1.37 | 11.52 | 3.48 | 58.5 | **5.0** | 32.3 | 6.8 | **7.2** |
| **5.7** | 0.34 | 2.8 | 0.60 | **3.9** | 8.3 | 0.64 | 5.70 | 3.29 | 59.9 | **1.4** | 11.9 | 18.2 | **8.4** |
| **7.9** | 0.05 | 2.0 | 0.04 | **8.3** | 2.3 | 1.61 | 11.62 | 4.20 | 49.7 | **2.2** | 15.4 | 18.0 | **8.8** |
| **8.0** | 0.02 | 0.2 | 0.03 | **7.9** | 1.7 | 1.83 | 16.76 | 3.72 | 49.7 | **1.7** | 25.5 | 24.4 | **9.0** |
| **8.8** | 0.00 | 0.0 | 0.00 | **9.7** | 7.2 | 2.40 | 15.57 | 4.04 | 41.1 | **4.5** | 29.1 | 8.4 | **10.0** |
| **7.5** | 0.02 | 0.1 | 0.05 | **3.8** | 2.1 | 0.71 | 7.14 | 4.07 | 74.8 | **4.9** | 16.9 | 3.0 | **5.7** |
| **4.4** | 2.53 | 17.0 | 4.12 | **0.9** | -4.8 | -1.65 | -15.39 | 2.73 | 57.3 | **5.9** | 52.0 | 8.2 | **6.7** |
| **5.3** | 6.36 | 11.7 | 0.08 | **3.5** | 1.3 | 0.60 | 2.67 | 3.36 | 77.4 | **1.2** | 19.0 | 29.5 | **7.5** |
| **3.7** | 1.04 | 7.5 | 0.16 | **3.0** | 2.2 | 0.48 | 5.22 | 2.88 | 75.0 | **0.5** | 11.0 | 42.1 | **4.7** |
| **8.9** | 0.00 | 0.0 | 0.00 | **7.0** | 0.4 | 1.65 | 10.89 | 3.64 | 65.7 | **6.0** | 52.6 | 3.7 | **6.3** |
| **10.0** | 1.03 | 0.5 | 0.00 | **7.4** | 19.1 | 6.54 | 15.91 | 2.61 | 68.5 | **7.7** | 131.4 | 8.4 | **8.8** |
| **7.7** | 0.54 | 2.3 | 0.04 | **4.3** | 8.8 | 0.90 | 6.38 | 3.14 | 64.5 | **2.8** | 19.9 | 15.3 | **8.1** |
| **5.4** | 0.37 | 2.9 | 0.13 | **3.7** | 0.8 | 0.72 | 8.47 | 3.74 | 78.7 | **1.0** | 21.9 | 8.0 | **4.6** |
| **8.3** | 0.05 | 0.2 | 0.16 | **5.7** | 1.2 | 1.00 | 5.42 | 4.18 | 74.7 | **5.6** | 45.7 | 7.7 | **7.8** |
| **6.5** | 0.01 | 0.1 | 0.00 | **2.6** | 0.2 | 0.35 | 3.49 | 3.23 | 86.7 | **4.9** | 20.2 | 3.6 | **5.0** |
| **1.5** | 4.34 | 31.5 | 0.01 | **7.4** | 4.5 | 1.58 | 15.95 | 4.65 | 67.3 | **4.0** | 18.9 | 9.4 | **8.1** |
| **5.7** | 0.92 | 4.8 | 0.17 | **5.9** | 24.7 | 1.20 | 11.01 | 3.87 | 66.4 | **4.7** | 17.2 | 4.0 | **8.8** |
| **5.3** | 1.94 | 9.5 | 0.01 | **5.7** | 18.8 | 1.36 | 12.40 | 3.47 | 60.8 | **1.9** | 16.9 | 17.3 | **10.0** |
| **6.7** | 1.14 | 4.2 | 0.12 | **5.9** | 1.2 | 1.17 | 7.97 | 4.78 | 67.8 | **4.2** | 20.6 | 8.4 | **8.4** |
| **8.5** | 0.13 | 1.0 | 0.00 | **3.9** | 0.5 | 0.80 | 9.18 | 3.60 | 78.4 | **2.0** | 25.6 | 20.1 | **4.1** |
| **3.7** | 9.03 | 27.8 | 1.88 | **2.2** | 0.2 | 0.29 | 2.33 | 3.08 | 69.5 | **3.0** | 46.6 | 23.0 | **5.2** |
| **6.3** | 0.67 | 3.2 | 0.15 | **7.9** | 4.0 | 1.53 | 14.15 | 3.49 | 46.9 | **1.8** | 16.5 | 20.1 | **7.8** |
| **3.5** | 2.22 | 11.9 | 0.07 | **2.9** | 0.7 | 0.32 | 2.71 | 4.11 | 90.9 | **4.5** | 18.1 | 5.9 | **6.7** |
| **8.4** | 0.14 | 1.3 | 0.00 | **6.7** | 12.6 | 1.32 | 12.44 | 3.94 | 61.0 | **1.8** | 9.6 | 16.5 | **7.9** |
| **4.7** | 2.02 | 10.2 | 0.00 | **5.3** | 0.4 | 1.28 | 14.63 | 3.75 | 69.4 | **6.4** | 46.2 | 1.8 | **5.7** |
| **8.3** | 0.08 | 0.2 | 0.35 | **0.0** | -0.9 | -3.23 | -24.73 | 3.92 | 316.1 | **5.2** | 55.2 | 11.4 | **5.1** |

| Name | City | State | Rating | 2018 Rating | 2017 Rating | Total Assets ($Mil) | One Year Asset Growth | Asset Mix (As a % of Total Assets) Commercial Loans | Consumer Loans | Mortgage Loans | Securities | Capitalization Index | Leverage Ratio | Risk-Based Capital Ratio |
|---|---|---|---|---|---|---|---|---|---|---|---|---|---|---|
| State Bank & Trust | Winfield | AL | B- | B- | C+ | 245.9 | 3.41 | 1.9 | 7.7 | 13.7 | 60.2 | 9.7 | 10.8 | 22.8 |
| State Bank & Trust Co. | Nevada | IA | A- | B+ | B+ | 159.3 | -2.29 | 11.1 | 0.6 | 12.4 | 23.8 | 7.8 | 9.5 | 13.5 |
| ▲ State Bank & Trust Co. | Golden Meadow | LA | C+ | D+ | D- | 115.0 | -0.99 | 20.5 | 4.3 | 18.7 | 12.9 | 10.0 | 12.1 | 18.6 |
| State Bank & Trust Co. | Ridgeland | MS | B- | B- | B- | 1150.8 | -2.37 | 5.1 | 1.9 | 16.9 | 9.2 | 6.4 | 9.3 | 12.1 |
| State Bank & Trust of Kenmare | Kenmare | ND | B- | C | C+ | 129.2 | -6.43 | 13.4 | 2.8 | 7.9 | 29.1 | 8.8 | 10.2 | 16.2 |
| State Bank and Trust Co. | Defiance | OH | B+ | B+ | B- | 1029.7 | 4.54 | 13.0 | 1.3 | 21.8 | 9.8 | 8.1 | 11.4 | 13.4 |
| State Bank Financial | La Crosse | WI | B | B | C+ | 364.8 | 5.44 | 8.8 | 0.4 | 7.4 | 29.7 | 9.3 | 10.5 | 15.3 |
| State Bank Northwest | Spokane Valley | WA | B- | C+ | C | 152.1 | 8.12 | 13.8 | 0.1 | 10.3 | 3.1 | 10.0 | 12.5 | 18.2 |
| ▲ State Bank of Arcadia | Arcadia | WI | B | B- | B- | 178.9 | -0.91 | 4.1 | 1.7 | 18.6 | 16.2 | 10.0 | 11.3 | 24.3 |
| State Bank of Arizona | Lake Havasu City | AZ | B | B | B- | 677.6 | 3.41 | 5.1 | 1.2 | 6.2 | 22.4 | 9.7 | 10.8 | 14.9 |
| State Bank of Belle Plaine | Belle Plaine | MN | B- | B- | B- | 130.4 | 3.74 | 2.3 | 1.3 | 12.7 | 42.9 | 8.4 | 9.9 | 19.0 |
| ▲ State Bank of Bellingham | Bellingham | MN | C | C | B | 47.8 | -15.11 | 3.0 | 0.7 | 0.0 | 18.3 | 10.0 | 12.4 | 16.8 |
| State Bank of Bement | Bement | IL | B- | B- | B- | 105.5 | -1.88 | 19.9 | 13.7 | 8.1 | 17.4 | 10.0 | 11.7 | 15.4 |
| State Bank of Bern | Bern | KS | A- | B+ | A- | 96.1 | 2.23 | 2.6 | 2.3 | 1.1 | 37.6 | 10.0 | 16.4 | 24.7 |
| ▲ State Bank of Bottineau | Bottineau | ND | B- | C+ | B- | 77.8 | 0.01 | 5.2 | 2.4 | 19.5 | 1.3 | 7.6 | 10.1 | 13.0 |
| State Bank of Brooks | Corning | IA | C | C | C | 18.7 | 8.29 | 2.5 | 4.9 | 10.6 | 31.6 | 10.0 | 11.7 | 41.1 |
| State Bank of Burnettsville | Burnettsville | IN | D- | D+ | D- | 42.6 | 15.81 | 4.6 | 6.2 | 21.4 | 23.4 | 9.0 | 10.3 | 20.5 |
| State Bank of Burrton | Burrton | KS | C | C- | C- | 9.9 | -2.70 | 17.6 | 4.7 | 19.3 | 24.0 | 10.0 | 11.7 | 25.9 |
| State Bank of Bussey | Bussey | IA | C | C- | C- | 43.3 | -6.31 | 7.0 | 2.0 | 31.1 | 2.9 | 7.3 | 9.2 | 14.5 |
| ▲ State Bank of Canton | Canton | KS | B | C+ | C+ | 28.8 | 0.30 | 15.4 | 1.4 | 2.2 | 24.3 | 10.0 | 20.5 | 43.2 |
| State Bank of Cerro Gordo | Cerro Gordo | IL | B- | B- | B- | 29.9 | 0.72 | 15.7 | 5.2 | 11.8 | 31.8 | 10.0 | 12.4 | 22.5 |
| State Bank of Ceylon | Ceylon | MN | D+ | D+ | D | 12.7 | 7.81 | 3.1 | 3.4 | 27.3 | 12.3 | 10.0 | 13.6 | 17.9 |
| State Bank of Chandler | Chandler | MN | B- | B- | B | 46.2 | 3.27 | 3.6 | 3.5 | 3.4 | 9.1 | 10.0 | 12.9 | 19.0 |
| ▲ State Bank of Cherry | Cherry | IL | A- | A- | A- | 89.7 | 5.01 | 6.8 | 4.2 | 13.1 | 17.5 | 10.0 | 14.1 | 19.9 |
| State Bank of Chilton | Chilton | WI | B | B | B- | 327.1 | 12.14 | 8.1 | 0.8 | 12.1 | 6.2 | 10.0 | 11.5 | 16.1 |
| State Bank of Cochran | Cochran | GA | B+ | B | B | 217.5 | -0.53 | 4.4 | 7.1 | 16.9 | 11.0 | 10.0 | 17.3 | 32.3 |
| State Bank of Cold Spring | Cold Spring | MN | C+ | C+ | C+ | 64.5 | -0.26 | 3.3 | 5.0 | 26.6 | 15.5 | 7.8 | 9.5 | 18.2 |
| ▲ State Bank of Colon | Colon | NE | D+ | D | D+ | 17.7 | 1.68 | 2.3 | 0.5 | 0.5 | 7.7 | 7.5 | 9.3 | 17.2 |
| ▲ State Bank of Cross Plains | Cross Plains | WI | C+ | C | D+ | 1322.2 | 33.83 | 10.9 | 1.1 | 15.3 | 11.5 | 6.9 | 10.3 | 12.4 |
| State Bank of Danvers | Benson | MN | B+ | B | B- | 50.4 | -0.59 | 4.0 | 0.7 | 0.3 | 35.4 | 10.0 | 12.7 | 22.0 |
| State Bank of Davis | Davis | IL | B+ | B | C+ | 152.2 | 0.03 | 16.5 | 0.9 | 3.3 | 37.1 | 9.8 | 10.9 | 18.1 |
| State Bank of De Kalb | De Kalb | TX | B+ | B+ | A | 266.3 | 5.96 | 15.5 | 1.5 | 16.9 | 0.0 | 8.7 | 10.3 | 13.9 |
| State Bank of Downs | Downs | KS | C+ | C- | C+ | 96.0 | 8.77 | 15.1 | 1.5 | 24.4 | 5.4 | 10.0 | 12.8 | 18.7 |
| ▲ State Bank of Eagle Butte | Eagle Butte | SD | C- | D+ | C- | 66.5 | 2.67 | 6.2 | 22.3 | 3.1 | 45.7 | 7.6 | 9.4 | 16.3 |
| State Bank of Easton | Easton | MN | C- | D+ | C- | 20.3 | -1.78 | 11.7 | 4.7 | 3.1 | 6.7 | 10.0 | 13.3 | 19.9 |
| State Bank of Fairmont | Fairmont | MN | C+ | B- | C | 116.7 | 7.02 | 21.3 | 4.8 | 4.0 | 13.6 | 9.2 | 10.5 | 14.3 |
| State Bank of Faribault | Faribault | MN | B | B- | B | 214.9 | 2.91 | 7.8 | 3.1 | 16.6 | 21.1 | 9.7 | 10.8 | 15.1 |
| State Bank of Geneva | Geneva | IL | C- | D+ | D- | 82.7 | 2.66 | 5.5 | 1.0 | 11.6 | 13.9 | 7.9 | 9.6 | 16.4 |
| State Bank of Graymont | Graymont | IL | B | B | B | 210.8 | 4.78 | 6.0 | 1.9 | 8.0 | 17.5 | 10.0 | 12.3 | 17.3 |
| State Bank of Herscher | Herscher | IL | B+ | B | C+ | 145.2 | -0.32 | 12.7 | 0.2 | 6.7 | 37.7 | 10.0 | 12.5 | 20.6 |
| State Bank of India (California) | Los Angeles | CA | B+ | B | C | 867.3 | 15.49 | 22.8 | 0.0 | 0.0 | 10.6 | 10.0 | 16.7 | 20.2 |
| State Bank of Industry | Industry | IL | B | B | B | 55.1 | 0.06 | 7.1 | 3.7 | 16.9 | 15.3 | 10.0 | 14.9 | 22.6 |
| State Bank of Jeffers | Jeffers | MN | B | B- | B- | 28.5 | 2.08 | 8.0 | 2.9 | 1.7 | 18.1 | 10.0 | 12.9 | 15.7 |
| State Bank of Lake Park | Lake Park | MN | C+ | C | C | 38.3 | 3.27 | 8.6 | 6.6 | 29.6 | 8.7 | 8.7 | 10.2 | 18.8 |
| State Bank of Lakota | Lakota | ND | B- | C+ | C+ | 52.4 | 4.83 | 8.1 | 5.0 | 11.0 | 15.6 | 7.8 | 9.6 | 14.7 |
| State Bank of Lincoln | Lincoln | IL | A- | B+ | A- | 334.3 | -15.24 | 6.6 | 0.3 | 3.8 | 40.0 | 8.2 | 9.8 | 17.6 |
| State Bank of Lismore | Lismore | MN | C | C | C+ | 64.1 | 4.02 | 6.9 | 2.5 | 0.0 | 0.1 | 6.4 | 10.4 | 12.1 |
| State Bank of Lizton | Lizton | IN | B+ | B | B | 504.1 | 1.44 | 8.8 | 0.9 | 7.8 | 13.9 | 8.9 | 10.7 | 14.1 |
| State Bank of Medora | Medora | IN | B | B | B | 93.2 | 6.24 | 1.3 | 4.4 | 16.1 | 58.1 | 10.0 | 14.4 | 33.2 |
| State Bank of Missouri | Concordia | MO | B | B | B- | 100.0 | -0.28 | 6.2 | 1.8 | 24.9 | 28.2 | 6.6 | 8.6 | 18.4 |
| ▼ State Bank of Nauvoo | Nauvoo | IL | D | C- | C- | 32.7 | 7.17 | 8.0 | 8.9 | 30.3 | 0.0 | 6.3 | 8.3 | 15.0 |
| State Bank of New Richland | New Richland | MN | C | C- | C- | 119.3 | 7.40 | 3.7 | 1.6 | 17.1 | 11.1 | 5.6 | 8.7 | 11.5 |
| ▲ State Bank of Newburg | Newburg | WI | A- | B | B | 192.2 | 6.43 | 2.1 | 0.7 | 30.5 | 10.0 | 10.0 | 19.3 | 28.1 |
| State Bank of Odell | Odell | NE | C | C | C | 27.1 | 3.17 | 3.6 | 10.0 | 3.1 | 3.0 | 8.6 | 10.1 | 18.7 |
| State Bank of Pearl City | Pearl City | IL | B- | C | B- | 56.3 | 0.63 | 2.5 | 43.5 | 7.0 | 15.0 | 10.0 | 11.9 | 20.0 |
| State Bank of Reeseville | Reeseville | WI | B- | B- | B | 102.9 | 15.91 | 7.1 | 2.0 | 10.6 | 50.1 | 7.8 | 9.5 | 18.3 |
| State Bank of Saunemin | Saunemin | IL | B- | B- | B- | 37.2 | 2.79 | 11.0 | 2.4 | 3.4 | 26.8 | 10.0 | 11.5 | 16.0 |
| State Bank of Schaller | Schaller | IA | B | B | B+ | 33.7 | 7.59 | 4.6 | 2.1 | 4.0 | 43.2 | 10.0 | 13.9 | 27.0 |
| State Bank of Scotia | Scotia | NE | B- | B- | B | 46.7 | 10.79 | 5.0 | 2.2 | 8.0 | 5.8 | 10.0 | 22.2 | 28.9 |
| State Bank of Southern Utah | Cedar City | UT | A | A | A | 1259.1 | 16.49 | 6.8 | 3.0 | 3.3 | 22.9 | 10.0 | 13.2 | 18.7 |

| Asset Quality Index | Adjusted Non-Performing Loans as a % of Total Loans | Adjusted Non-Performing Loans as a % of Capital | Net Charge-Offs Avg Loans | Profitability Index | Net Income ($Mil) | Return on Assets (R.O.A.) | Return on Equity (R.O.E.) | Net Interest Spread | Overhead Efficiency Ratio | Liquidity Index | Liquidity Ratio | Hot Money Ratio | Stability Index |
|---|---|---|---|---|---|---|---|---|---|---|---|---|---|
| **5.0** | 2.04 | 7.4 | 0.28 | **3.7** | 2.0 | 0.82 | 7.74 | 2.80 | 71.4 | **2.6** | 53.6 | 50.0 | **5.8** |
| **4.8** | 1.25 | 7.4 | 0.37 | **6.6** | 2.1 | 1.28 | 11.23 | 3.28 | 45.0 | **4.0** | 19.9 | 6.8 | **7.7** |
| **2.7** | 2.84 | 14.6 | 0.51 | **3.3** | 0.8 | 0.70 | 5.99 | 3.89 | 79.0 | **1.7** | 18.4 | 22.2 | **5.7** |
| **6.0** | 0.40 | 2.3 | 0.13 | **4.7** | 11.1 | 0.95 | 8.65 | 3.74 | 68.9 | **1.6** | 10.5 | 21.9 | **8.7** |
| **4.4** | 1.62 | 4.4 | 0.01 | **3.9** | 1.4 | 0.98 | 9.92 | 3.26 | 69.0 | **2.8** | 32.2 | 18.6 | **5.9** |
| **7.1** | 0.48 | 2.5 | 0.03 | **6.5** | 12.5 | 1.22 | 9.55 | 3.75 | 69.0 | **1.8** | 7.9 | 19.1 | **10.0** |
| **6.8** | 2.00 | 3.6 | 0.01 | **4.8** | 4.2 | 1.23 | 11.01 | 3.21 | 68.8 | **4.4** | 25.2 | 7.3 | **6.8** |
| **6.9** | 0.73 | 0.5 | 0.10 | **6.9** | 2.4 | 1.68 | 14.10 | 5.31 | 70.3 | **3.9** | 31.6 | 12.8 | **7.8** |
| **8.3** | 1.51 | 2.3 | 0.03 | **4.4** | 1.8 | 1.06 | 8.36 | 2.75 | 66.8 | **5.6** | 44.2 | 7.5 | **7.2** |
| **4.4** | 1.21 | 4.2 | -0.07 | **6.3** | 8.2 | 1.21 | 10.73 | 3.89 | 63.9 | **4.3** | 31.3 | 10.5 | **7.6** |
| **7.4** | 0.00 | 0.0 | 0.00 | **2.9** | 0.3 | 1.02 | 9.27 | 3.09 | 66.8 | **5.1** | 36.3 | 7.8 | **6.1** |
| **4.4** | 0.00 | 0.0 | 0.04 | **7.2** | 0.9 | 1.79 | 15.13 | 3.43 | 53.5 | **0.9** | 23.8 | 34.1 | **8.1** |
| **6.3** | 0.13 | 2.7 | 0.07 | **2.8** | 0.5 | 0.43 | 3.68 | 3.38 | 85.0 | **3.2** | 18.2 | 13.3 | **6.5** |
| **8.4** | 0.83 | 1.4 | 0.20 | **6.3** | 1.2 | 1.26 | 7.40 | 3.71 | 52.0 | **3.4** | 48.3 | 19.4 | **8.3** |
| **8.2** | 0.00 | 0.0 | -0.08 | **5.5** | 1.0 | 1.29 | 13.10 | 4.63 | 67.5 | **2.8** | 13.7 | 14.8 | **6.7** |
| **5.6** | 0.82 | 11.5 | 0.24 | **2.4** | 0.1 | 0.34 | 2.84 | 2.58 | 83.1 | **7.2** | 84.9 | 3.1 | **5.3** |
| **6.4** | 0.37 | 1.7 | 1.24 | **3.3** | 0.3 | 0.69 | 6.49 | 3.88 | 78.4 | **2.8** | 38.3 | 20.9 | **3.5** |
| **8.9** | 0.00 | 0.0 | 0.25 | **2.1** | 0.0 | 0.27 | 2.37 | 3.99 | 93.2 | **2.8** | 26.8 | 15.7 | **5.2** |
| **7.0** | 0.52 | 3.1 | 0.06 | **3.2** | 0.3 | 0.58 | 6.58 | 4.16 | 85.0 | **3.3** | 17.6 | 12.7 | **4.3** |
| **8.3** | 1.94 | 3.3 | 0.00 | **5.6** | 0.5 | 1.56 | 7.58 | 3.18 | 79.2 | **7.3** | 72.6 | 1.8 | **6.6** |
| **8.1** | 0.00 | 0.6 | 0.16 | **3.4** | 0.2 | 0.62 | 4.34 | 3.51 | 79.1 | **5.6** | 45.4 | 7.4 | **5.9** |
| **5.3** | 1.96 | 8.1 | 0.06 | **0.9** | -0.1 | -0.44 | -3.42 | 4.94 | 113.5 | **1.8** | 29.5 | 22.5 | **4.2** |
| **6.8** | 0.29 | 2.4 | 0.00 | **5.3** | 0.5 | 1.04 | 8.14 | 4.09 | 65.0 | **4.1** | 29.9 | 11.2 | **7.0** |
| **7.8** | 0.71 | 3.3 | -0.01 | **6.3** | 1.3 | 1.45 | 10.22 | 3.85 | 56.7 | **3.3** | 33.9 | 16.6 | **8.6** |
| **4.3** | 2.83 | 13.7 | -0.06 | **7.3** | 5.2 | 1.81 | 15.22 | 3.83 | 53.7 | **3.3** | 25.7 | 13.7 | **7.2** |
| **5.2** | 3.92 | 10.2 | 0.02 | **9.8** | 5.2 | 2.45 | 14.88 | 4.66 | 52.9 | **4.3** | 39.8 | 13.2 | **9.4** |
| **4.2** | 2.79 | 14.0 | -0.01 | **4.3** | 0.7 | 1.07 | 11.23 | 3.40 | 69.7 | **4.9** | 33.2 | 7.7 | **5.0** |
| **7.3** | 0.28 | 1.3 | 0.00 | **1.4** | 0.0 | 0.21 | 2.36 | 2.39 | 91.2 | **2.1** | 44.2 | 19.0 | **4.2** |
| **7.1** | 0.55 | 3.2 | 0.04 | **5.1** | 11.4 | 0.93 | 8.34 | 3.52 | 66.7 | **4.4** | 13.8 | 6.6 | **9.1** |
| **8.9** | 0.05 | 0.2 | -0.34 | **8.5** | 1.1 | 2.26 | 18.08 | 3.90 | 49.6 | **5.0** | 32.3 | 6.7 | **7.8** |
| **4.7** | 2.97 | 8.8 | 0.02 | **6.5** | 2.0 | 1.30 | 11.13 | 3.11 | 48.8 | **1.7** | 25.2 | 25.1 | **7.9** |
| **4.7** | 0.78 | 6.3 | 0.10 | **8.3** | 5.0 | 1.88 | 18.22 | 4.41 | 61.6 | **2.3** | 13.6 | 17.2 | **8.7** |
| **3.1** | 4.57 | 18.9 | -0.13 | **7.1** | 1.6 | 1.76 | 13.48 | 4.19 | 60.7 | **3.9** | 21.5 | 9.9 | **7.5** |
| **2.3** | 1.67 | 7.9 | 3.29 | **3.2** | 0.2 | 0.37 | 3.94 | 5.82 | 66.2 | **1.2** | 8.9 | 26.5 | **4.2** |
| **4.8** | 2.45 | 10.2 | 0.39 | **3.3** | 0.2 | 0.90 | 7.16 | 3.50 | 76.2 | **2.7** | 38.9 | 18.6 | **3.5** |
| **3.1** | 2.92 | 14.6 | 0.05 | **4.0** | 1.0 | 0.85 | 8.02 | 3.75 | 71.1 | **2.3** | 22.8 | 18.1 | **6.2** |
| **7.9** | 0.23 | 0.9 | 0.02 | **5.1** | 2.6 | 1.23 | 11.22 | 4.35 | 76.1 | **3.8** | 17.5 | 10.1 | **7.1** |
| **6.7** | 1.06 | 3.5 | 0.20 | **2.4** | 0.3 | 0.37 | 3.88 | 3.70 | 91.2 | **2.3** | 30.2 | 20.6 | **4.6** |
| **7.7** | 0.73 | 3.1 | 0.00 | **4.5** | 1.9 | 0.92 | 7.50 | 3.19 | 62.9 | **3.6** | 24.4 | 12.0 | **7.3** |
| **5.4** | 1.88 | 5.4 | 0.18 | **5.9** | 1.8 | 1.21 | 9.02 | 3.72 | 70.9 | **4.1** | 24.6 | 9.5 | **7.3** |
| **7.1** | 0.04 | 0.0 | -0.05 | **5.8** | 8.3 | 1.03 | 5.95 | 3.52 | 59.6 | **0.7** | 16.1 | 44.1 | **7.8** |
| **8.4** | 0.08 | 2.0 | 0.07 | **5.5** | 0.8 | 1.44 | 9.83 | 3.35 | 57.1 | **1.1** | 27.3 | 42.0 | **7.5** |
| **8.3** | 0.00 | 0.0 | -0.02 | **3.9** | 0.2 | 0.68 | 5.29 | 3.42 | 72.1 | **5.8** | 49.5 | 6.9 | **6.4** |
| **3.6** | 3.42 | 15.1 | 0.00 | **5.2** | 0.5 | 1.32 | 12.20 | 4.50 | 70.8 | **3.6** | 34.7 | 15.1 | **5.4** |
| **7.0** | 0.04 | 0.2 | 0.04 | **5.7** | 0.7 | 1.39 | 13.37 | 4.08 | 64.2 | **2.0** | 14.7 | 19.0 | **5.0** |
| **8.6** | 0.32 | 1.2 | -0.16 | **6.4** | 4.6 | 1.32 | 12.60 | 3.54 | 61.3 | **4.5** | 29.7 | 8.9 | **8.0** |
| **3.6** | 0.92 | 7.8 | 0.27 | **5.2** | 0.7 | 1.18 | 11.39 | 4.37 | 62.5 | **1.0** | 12.3 | 30.7 | **6.6** |
| **6.1** | 0.54 | 3.1 | 0.06 | **5.7** | 6.5 | 1.28 | 12.09 | 3.96 | 63.3 | **2.6** | 14.7 | 16.0 | **7.4** |
| **8.2** | 1.25 | 2.5 | 0.02 | **3.7** | 0.7 | 0.74 | 5.00 | 2.70 | 68.7 | **3.7** | 70.6 | 25.3 | **7.5** |
| **6.7** | 0.66 | 3.7 | 0.01 | **5.9** | 1.4 | 1.43 | 16.01 | 3.54 | 64.0 | **4.6** | 26.8 | 7.2 | **6.2** |
| **1.1** | 4.39 | 31.6 | 1.80 | **2.3** | 0.0 | 0.07 | 0.81 | 3.97 | 65.3 | **5.1** | 33.4 | 6.4 | **4.1** |
| **3.2** | 1.14 | 11.8 | -0.01 | **9.5** | 2.5 | 2.22 | 23.88 | 3.74 | 42.9 | **0.7** | 10.9 | 19.4 | **7.4** |
| **5.7** | 5.43 | 11.2 | 0.00 | **8.7** | 3.0 | 1.65 | 8.52 | 3.78 | 43.5 | **1.1** | 27.1 | 27.8 | **9.2** |
| **5.0** | 0.88 | 4.2 | -0.25 | **2.8** | 0.1 | 0.42 | 4.14 | 3.93 | 87.1 | **6.7** | 58.2 | 2.7 | **4.4** |
| **6.7** | 0.27 | 1.5 | 0.32 | **3.6** | 0.4 | 0.71 | 6.05 | 3.51 | 79.2 | **2.3** | 30.2 | 20.7 | **5.3** |
| **9.0** | 0.09 | 0.2 | 0.05 | **3.6** | 0.8 | 0.77 | 7.34 | 3.07 | 72.8 | **2.9** | 59.8 | 11.3 | **6.0** |
| **8.5** | 0.00 | 0.0 | 0.00 | **3.3** | 0.3 | 0.71 | 6.20 | 3.11 | 65.7 | **4.9** | 44.4 | 11.1 | **6.7** |
| **7.5** | 0.00 | 1.1 | 0.01 | **6.7** | 0.5 | 1.53 | 10.27 | 3.16 | 56.5 | **4.8** | 35.9 | 9.4 | **7.7** |
| **6.5** | 0.89 | 3.0 | 0.24 | **6.6** | 0.6 | 1.24 | 5.46 | 3.96 | 52.7 | **1.1** | 26.8 | 36.1 | **6.3** |
| **7.4** | 0.96 | 3.5 | 0.25 | **9.4** | 20.4 | 1.69 | 12.74 | 4.47 | 51.6 | **4.5** | 30.9 | 12.7 | **10.0** |

| Name | City | State | Rating | 2018 Rating | 2017 Rating | Total Assets ($Mil) | One Year Asset Growth | Asset Mix (As a % of Total Assets) Commercial Loans | Consumer Loans | Mortgage Loans | Securities | Capitalization Index | Leverage Ratio | Risk-Based Capital Ratio |
|---|---|---|---|---|---|---|---|---|---|---|---|---|---|---|
| ▲ State Bank of Southwest Missouri | Springfield | MO | B- | C+ | C+ | 133.7 | 14.20 | 4.1 | 5.4 | 33.1 | 7.6 | 5.2 | 7.2 | 11.7 |
| State Bank of Spring Hill | Spring Hill | KS | C+ | C | C | 45.7 | 11.38 | 3.7 | 1.0 | 4.9 | 44.8 | 7.7 | 9.4 | 25.0 |
| State Bank of St. Jacob | Saint Jacob | IL | B+ | B+ | B+ | 66.7 | 4.54 | 5.8 | 9.8 | 14.6 | 29.0 | 10.0 | 16.0 | 31.7 |
| State Bank of Table Rock | Table Rock | NE | C- | D+ | D+ | 95.8 | 10.85 | 9.5 | 3.2 | 10.0 | 1.7 | 6.3 | 8.3 | 12.0 |
| ▲ State Bank of Taunton | Taunton | MN | B- | D+ | C | 48.2 | 0.90 | 5.3 | 0.4 | 5.1 | 13.8 | 10.0 | 11.2 | 15.0 |
| State Bank of Texas | Dallas | TX | B+ | B+ | A | 853.1 | -7.21 | 0.8 | 0.7 | 6.4 | 7.1 | 10.0 | 17.9 | 20.1 |
| State Bank of the Lakes, N.A. | Antioch | IL | B | B | B | 1338.4 | 9.90 | 29.0 | 20.9 | 3.0 | 14.6 | 5.7 | 9.5 | 11.5 |
| State Bank of Toledo | Toledo | IA | D | D+ | C- | 115.3 | -1.72 | 4.2 | 4.8 | 28.7 | 0.0 | 6.2 | 9.2 | 11.9 |
| State Bank of Toulon | Toulon | IL | B- | B- | B+ | 225.8 | -0.35 | 7.6 | 1.4 | 6.2 | 23.6 | 8.6 | 10.6 | 13.8 |
| State Bank of Wapello | Wapello | IA | B | B- | B- | 37.4 | -0.46 | 1.8 | 5.1 | 11.2 | 18.8 | 10.0 | 14.3 | 28.9 |
| State Bank of Waterloo | Waterloo | IL | C | C | D+ | 195.7 | 19.68 | 3.4 | 1.0 | 16.1 | 16.7 | 5.8 | 8.3 | 11.6 |
| ▲ State Bank of Wheaton | Wheaton | MN | A- | B+ | A- | 88.4 | 3.53 | 4.9 | 0.7 | 0.9 | 0.8 | 10.0 | 24.4 | 31.7 |
| ▲ State Bank of Whittington | Benton | IL | B | C+ | B- | 134.2 | 5.70 | 8.7 | 15.5 | 15.9 | 24.2 | 9.4 | 10.6 | 15.7 |
| State Bank of Wynnewood | Wynnewood | OK | B+ | A- | A | 95.5 | 0.57 | 7.8 | 1.8 | 9.3 | 45.2 | 10.0 | 14.8 | 22.6 |
| State Central Bank | Bonaparte | IA | D+ | D+ | D- | 42.1 | 10.72 | 18.0 | 2.1 | 12.5 | 28.1 | 8.1 | 9.8 | 14.5 |
| State Exchange Bank | Mankato | KS | B- | C+ | C+ | 37.5 | 0.82 | 3.7 | 3.5 | 5.5 | 38.0 | 10.0 | 12.9 | 21.1 |
| ▲ State Exchange Bank | Lamont | OK | D+ | D- | D | 66.2 | 1.83 | 13.9 | 0.9 | 5.0 | 4.7 | 10.0 | 12.2 | 15.2 |
| ▲ State Farm Bank, FSB | Bloomington | IL | C+ | C- | C- | 16424.8 | -3.01 | 0.9 | 37.6 | 18.9 | 38.1 | 10.0 | 12.0 | 20.7 |
| State National Bank of Big Spring | Big Spring | TX | A- | B | C+ | 425.8 | 8.56 | 3.8 | 0.6 | 1.3 | 55.4 | 9.3 | 10.5 | 31.2 |
| State National Bank of Groom | Groom | TX | C | C | C- | 38.6 | 7.64 | 8.7 | 1.6 | 3.9 | 10.5 | 9.5 | 10.6 | 15.7 |
| State Nebraska Bank & Trust | Wayne | NE | A- | B+ | B+ | 160.3 | 0.41 | 12.3 | 2.2 | 10.8 | 28.9 | 10.0 | 13.4 | 19.2 |
| ▼ State Savings Bank | Creston | IA | B- | B+ | B- | 125.3 | 5.93 | 11.0 | 5.2 | 20.2 | 0.1 | 7.2 | 9.6 | 12.7 |
| State Savings Bank | Rake | IA | D- | D- | D- | 77.0 | 1.28 | 10.3 | 0.7 | 0.7 | 2.4 | 8.2 | 11.4 | 13.5 |
| State Savings Bank | West Des Moines | IA | B+ | B+ | A- | 155.3 | 10.88 | 8.7 | 0.6 | 16.4 | 0.4 | 7.5 | 9.9 | 12.9 |
| State Savings Bank | Frankfort | MI | D+ | C- | D | 219.9 | 2.14 | 8.4 | 0.9 | 27.9 | 3.2 | 9.4 | 10.7 | 14.5 |
| State Savings Bank of Manistique | Manistique | MI | B | B | B- | 122.6 | -0.81 | 7.5 | 5.1 | 17.2 | 43.4 | 10.0 | 12.0 | 19.0 |
| State Street B&T Co. of California, N.A. | Los Angeles | CA | U | U | U | 16.0 | 1.28 | 0.0 | 0.0 | 0.0 | 0.0 | 10.0 | 99.4 | 354.2 |
| ▲ State Street Bank and Trust Co. | Quincy | IL | B | B- | B- | 234.6 | 5.91 | 3.4 | 24.3 | 24.9 | 14.4 | 7.2 | 9.3 | 12.6 |
| State Street Bank and Trust Co. | Boston | MA | B+ | B+ | B | 242148.0 | 0.05 | 1.8 | 0.0 | 0.0 | 39.5 | 5.7 | 7.7 | 17.8 |
| State Street Bank and Trust Co., N.A. | New York | NY | U | U | U | 34.7 | 2.49 | 0.0 | 0.0 | 0.0 | 0.0 | 10.0 | 99.3 | 326.3 |
| Stearns Bank Holdingford N.A. | Holdingford | MN | A- | A- | A- | 103.0 | 19.63 | 77.0 | 0.2 | 0.8 | 2.6 | 10.0 | 16.1 | 20.1 |
| Stearns Bank N.A. | Saint Cloud | MN | A- | A- | A- | 2275.4 | 9.93 | 66.0 | 0.1 | 1.1 | 0.8 | 10.0 | 20.0 | 21.0 |
| Stearns Bank Upsala N.A. | Upsala | MN | A- | A- | A- | 81.9 | 19.36 | 73.6 | 0.2 | 0.8 | 4.1 | 10.0 | 14.4 | 19.8 |
| ▲ Stephenson National Bank and Trust | Marinette | WI | B | C+ | B- | 530.6 | 1.89 | 13.2 | 3.2 | 13.9 | 25.0 | 8.1 | 9.8 | 14.4 |
| Sterling Bank | Poplar Bluff | MO | A- | A- | A- | 1243.0 | -0.07 | 36.1 | 0.6 | 3.9 | 4.5 | 9.8 | 10.8 | 15.0 |
| Sterling Bank | Barron | WI | B | B | B+ | 248.9 | 3.75 | 4.3 | 0.4 | 11.9 | 21.8 | 6.6 | 8.6 | 13.1 |
| ▲ Sterling Bank and Trust, FSB | Southfield | MI | A | A- | A- | 3241.2 | 1.34 | 0.1 | 0.0 | 76.6 | 4.5 | 9.3 | 10.5 | 18.9 |
| Sterling Federal Bank, F.S.B. | Sterling | IL | D+ | C- | C- | 452.1 | -1.58 | 4.0 | 0.5 | 28.4 | 37.3 | 6.5 | 8.5 | 16.2 |
| Sterling National Bank | Montebello | NY | B | B | B | 30566.5 | -2.44 | 17.7 | 0.0 | 7.5 | 16.8 | 8.2 | 10.1 | 13.5 |
| Sterling State Bank | Austin | MN | C+ | C+ | C | 352.8 | 0.45 | 8.8 | 1.2 | 9.5 | 33.2 | 7.2 | 9.1 | 16.1 |
| Steuben Trust Co. | Hornell | NY | A- | B+ | A- | 559.6 | 1.51 | 3.6 | 3.7 | 14.6 | 33.0 | 10.0 | 12.2 | 19.8 |
| Stifel Bank | Clayton | MO | B | B | B+ | 2260.4 | 27.68 | 13.5 | 21.5 | 1.2 | 37.4 | 5.1 | 7.1 | 18.0 |
| Stifel Bank and Trust | Saint Louis | MO | B+ | B+ | B+ | 14144.7 | -12.20 | 24.9 | 7.1 | 24.0 | 33.4 | 5.1 | 7.1 | 13.3 |
| Stifel Trust Co. Delaware, N.A. | Wilmington | DE | U | U | U | 14.8 | 13.24 | 0.0 | 0.0 | 0.0 | 6.2 | 10.0 | 87.9 | 352.6 |
| Stifel Trust Co., N.A. | Saint Louis | MO | U | U | U | 625.7 | 3413.3 | 0.0 | 0.0 | 0.0 | 80.6 | 5.3 | 7.3 | 33.4 |
| ▲ Stillman BancCorp, N.A. | Stillman Valley | IL | B | B- | C+ | 469.0 | 7.70 | 3.6 | 1.3 | 7.7 | 55.2 | 6.8 | 8.8 | 19.8 |
| Stock Exchange Bank | Caldwell | KS | C+ | C | C | 53.3 | -0.76 | 4.4 | 3.7 | 44.2 | 11.4 | 7.7 | 9.5 | 15.6 |
| Stock Exchange Bank | Woodward | OK | A | A- | A- | 241.3 | -4.09 | 5.8 | 4.3 | 7.2 | 39.9 | 10.0 | 16.7 | 25.9 |
| Stock Growers Bank | Napoleon | ND | A- | A- | A- | 71.1 | 1.52 | 2.1 | 3.3 | 2.9 | 31.8 | 9.4 | 10.6 | 14.9 |
| Stock Yards Bank & Trust Co. | Louisville | KY | A | A | A | 3720.0 | 12.69 | 22.1 | 1.3 | 9.7 | 12.7 | 6.6 | 10.7 | 12.2 |
| Stockgrowers State Bank | Ashland | KS | B+ | B | B | 141.4 | 6.85 | 8.3 | 0.9 | 1.5 | 29.8 | 10.0 | 14.1 | 18.9 |
| Stockgrowers State Bank | Maple Hill | KS | B+ | B+ | A- | 87.0 | 1.81 | 8.0 | 1.3 | 14.4 | 35.5 | 10.0 | 11.7 | 18.6 |
| Stockman Bank of Montana | Miles City | MT | A- | A- | A- | 3986.0 | 9.24 | 3.6 | 0.7 | 5.8 | 23.1 | 8.7 | 10.2 | 14.3 |
| ▲ Stockmans Bank | Altus | OK | C+ | C- | C | 283.1 | 14.97 | 3.9 | 0.6 | 8.7 | 2.9 | 6.3 | 9.6 | 12.0 |
| Stockmens Bank | Colorado Springs | CO | B | B- | B | 353.5 | 2.56 | 11.3 | 0.7 | 18.5 | 11.3 | 8.0 | 9.7 | 14.0 |
| Stockmens Bank | Cascade | MT | B- | B- | B- | 39.8 | 15.30 | 3.9 | 2.0 | 4.9 | 10.0 | 10.0 | 11.3 | 26.5 |
| Stockmens National Bank in Cotulla | Cotulla | TX | B+ | B+ | B- | 116.2 | 18.25 | 2.2 | 3.0 | 2.9 | 32.0 | 10.0 | 12.3 | 36.9 |
| Stone Bank | Mountain View | AR | C+ | C | B- | 476.7 | 28.27 | 11.0 | 0.7 | 7.2 | 10.8 | 9.7 | 10.8 | 15.6 |
| StonehamBank | Stoneham | MA | C+ | C+ | B- | 606.4 | 0.95 | 12.8 | 0.2 | 35.7 | 10.6 | 9.0 | 10.3 | 15.1 |
| Stoughton Co-operative Bank | Stoughton | MA | C- | C- | C- | 118.5 | 2.69 | 0.4 | 2.1 | 63.7 | 18.4 | 6.7 | 8.7 | 16.4 |

| Asset Quality Index | Adjusted Non-Performing Loans as a % of Total Loans | Adjusted Non-Performing Loans as a % of Capital | Net Charge-Offs Avg Loans | Profitability Index | Net Income ($Mil) | Return on Assets (R.O.A.) | Return on Equity (R.O.E.) | Net Interest Spread | Overhead Efficiency Ratio | Liquidity Index | Liquidity Ratio | Hot Money Ratio | Stability Index |
|---|---|---|---|---|---|---|---|---|---|---|---|---|---|
| 6.8 | 0.34 | 2.9 | -0.01 | 5.7 | 1.5 | 1.17 | 16.21 | 3.52 | 73.1 | 4.0 | 22.2 | 9.7 | 4.8 |
| 8.3 | 0.00 | 0.0 | 1.46 | 3.4 | 0.3 | 0.57 | 5.94 | 3.41 | 69.7 | 6.1 | 50.2 | 4.9 | 4.7 |
| 7.9 | 1.40 | 3.4 | 0.13 | 5.8 | 0.9 | 1.35 | 8.27 | 3.39 | 54.9 | 5.4 | 57.9 | 10.9 | 7.7 |
| 3.3 | 1.30 | 7.8 | -0.02 | 3.5 | 0.6 | 0.70 | 8.36 | 3.68 | 79.3 | 2.3 | 19.8 | 17.9 | 4.5 |
| 8.5 | 0.00 | 0.0 | -0.06 | 4.2 | 0.6 | 1.15 | 11.06 | 3.95 | 77.4 | 3.0 | 20.6 | 14.5 | 5.1 |
| 4.7 | 1.12 | 4.8 | 0.28 | 10.0 | 40.4 | 4.67 | 28.41 | 6.17 | 23.7 | 0.8 | 20.3 | 47.6 | 10.0 |
| 4.5 | 1.10 | 6.1 | 0.16 | 4.7 | 11.4 | 0.90 | 6.73 | 3.28 | 53.7 | 2.0 | 11.5 | 15.8 | 8.6 |
| 0.7 | 5.74 | 47.3 | 0.03 | 6.3 | 1.6 | 1.42 | 15.41 | 4.29 | 63.6 | 1.4 | 8.8 | 15.4 | 7.1 |
| 5.2 | 0.88 | 5.2 | 0.27 | 4.0 | 2.2 | 0.96 | 8.36 | 3.64 | 67.6 | 2.7 | 17.9 | 15.9 | 6.3 |
| 9.0 | 0.08 | 0.2 | 0.15 | 4.4 | 0.4 | 1.07 | 7.57 | 3.10 | 65.4 | 7.1 | 59.4 | 0.0 | 6.6 |
| 5.9 | 1.30 | 4.9 | -0.08 | 2.8 | 0.8 | 0.44 | 4.99 | 3.22 | 84.7 | 2.7 | 23.2 | 16.3 | 4.1 |
| 7.3 | 0.74 | 2.2 | 0.21 | 10.0 | 2.4 | 2.90 | 11.96 | 4.51 | 36.3 | 2.7 | 35.9 | 19.9 | 9.8 |
| 4.8 | 0.29 | 4.9 | 0.22 | 5.2 | 1.7 | 1.27 | 11.96 | 4.45 | 69.3 | 4.9 | 27.7 | 5.1 | 6.1 |
| 8.2 | 0.86 | 2.3 | 0.00 | 5.0 | 1.3 | 1.39 | 8.97 | 3.47 | 64.2 | 1.7 | 35.4 | 32.7 | 8.2 |
| 0.3 | 35.90 | 82.4 | 6.47 | 0.5 | -0.4 | -0.98 | -7.45 | 3.69 | 81.6 | 6.3 | 37.7 | 0.3 | 5.1 |
| 8.1 | 0.73 | 2.5 | 0.04 | 4.0 | 0.3 | 0.89 | 6.74 | 3.60 | 75.1 | 5.1 | 35.4 | 7.3 | 5.9 |
| 1.0 | 8.43 | 27.0 | 0.45 | 6.6 | 1.0 | 1.59 | 13.64 | 4.34 | 58.0 | 0.8 | 21.5 | 44.8 | 5.9 |
| 4.1 | 1.72 | 7.3 | 1.08 | 2.8 | 60.4 | 0.37 | 3.18 | 2.91 | 68.3 | 1.7 | 31.5 | 25.7 | 7.2 |
| 9.8 | 0.06 | 0.1 | -0.19 | 6.1 | 6.4 | 1.64 | 15.12 | 2.87 | 43.3 | 7.4 | 83.1 | 4.3 | 6.6 |
| 3.8 | 2.54 | 9.7 | 0.02 | 3.1 | 0.2 | 0.39 | 3.64 | 4.18 | 91.4 | 4.4 | 25.1 | 7.2 | 5.2 |
| 6.4 | 0.74 | 6.0 | 0.14 | 7.0 | 2.2 | 1.43 | 10.99 | 3.64 | 49.5 | 4.3 | 13.7 | 6.3 | 8.4 |
| 3.4 | 2.12 | 13.9 | 0.11 | 8.1 | 2.1 | 1.71 | 17.64 | 3.96 | 53.8 | 1.6 | 9.6 | 21.0 | 8.1 |
| 0.0 | 6.36 | 36.3 | 0.61 | 3.6 | 0.4 | 0.55 | 4.90 | 3.13 | 40.0 | 0.7 | 19.3 | 55.9 | 5.0 |
| 6.9 | 0.40 | 3.1 | 0.03 | 6.7 | 2.1 | 1.43 | 14.62 | 3.86 | 62.9 | 3.9 | 12.2 | 9.1 | 7.8 |
| 5.2 | 1.12 | 5.5 | -0.01 | 1.7 | 0.1 | 0.04 | 0.32 | 4.16 | 99.9 | 4.3 | 16.6 | 6.9 | 5.5 |
| 6.2 | 1.73 | 4.7 | 0.06 | 4.1 | 1.1 | 0.87 | 7.31 | 3.73 | 70.6 | 5.6 | 49.1 | 9.0 | 6.5 |
| 10.0 | na | 0.0 | na | 7.3 | 0.2 | 1.32 | 1.34 | 1.03 | 91.7 | 4.0 | na | 0.0 | 7.0 |
| 6.9 | 0.07 | 1.5 | 0.07 | 6.3 | 3.5 | 1.55 | 16.89 | 3.99 | 67.1 | 3.9 | 21.8 | 9.9 | 6.2 |
| 8.4 | 0.00 | 0.0 | 0.01 | 5.2 | 2371.0 | 1.08 | 9.04 | 1.76 | 74.0 | 3.3 | 57.3 | 30.1 | 9.3 |
| 10.0 | na | 0.0 | na | 9.5 | 0.9 | 2.64 | 2.70 | 1.02 | 93.2 | 4.0 | na | 0.0 | 7.0 |
| 7.5 | 0.73 | 2.3 | 0.44 | 5.9 | 1.2 | 1.23 | 7.40 | 3.28 | 25.9 | 0.6 | 20.0 | 50.4 | 8.0 |
| 5.5 | 3.10 | 6.1 | 0.81 | 10.0 | 52.2 | 2.45 | 12.16 | 6.63 | 48.6 | 0.5 | 6.0 | 11.0 | 9.5 |
| 6.9 | 0.97 | 2.8 | 0.62 | 5.8 | 0.9 | 1.16 | 7.48 | 3.09 | 27.7 | 0.6 | 21.5 | 52.7 | 8.2 |
| 4.9 | 1.28 | 6.7 | 0.12 | 5.2 | 6.3 | 1.20 | 11.70 | 3.55 | 71.0 | 3.5 | 17.9 | 10.8 | 7.9 |
| 7.5 | 0.44 | 2.6 | 0.06 | 6.6 | 15.3 | 1.23 | 10.39 | 3.75 | 49.2 | 1.1 | 20.2 | 18.3 | 9.4 |
| 7.0 | 0.43 | 2.6 | 0.00 | 6.9 | 4.0 | 1.64 | 18.54 | 3.77 | 57.7 | 2.9 | 31.9 | 17.8 | 6.7 |
| 9.0 | 0.45 | 3.3 | 0.00 | 9.8 | 60.9 | 1.85 | 18.71 | 3.91 | 39.2 | 1.1 | 8.0 | 27.9 | 9.3 |
| 4.9 | 2.78 | 8.7 | 0.19 | 1.0 | -0.4 | -0.08 | -0.86 | 2.95 | 99.1 | 2.8 | 40.0 | 22.3 | 4.5 |
| 4.5 | 1.06 | 4.3 | 0.17 | 7.4 | 448.3 | 1.49 | 9.88 | 3.53 | 41.9 | 2.9 | 12.2 | 6.4 | 10.0 |
| 8.8 | 0.07 | 0.6 | 0.16 | 2.8 | 1.6 | 0.45 | 5.05 | 3.31 | 88.1 | 4.3 | 17.4 | 6.8 | 5.3 |
| 7.9 | 0.31 | 1.4 | 0.05 | 6.3 | 7.2 | 1.27 | 11.17 | 3.74 | 62.9 | 1.6 | 14.8 | 21.0 | 8.2 |
| 7.1 | 0.02 | 0.1 | 0.02 | 5.8 | 27.0 | 1.34 | 20.06 | 3.17 | 39.5 | 6.1 | 38.7 | 3.4 | 6.0 |
| 8.3 | 0.16 | 1.3 | 0.00 | 9.3 | 258.3 | 1.77 | 24.31 | 3.14 | 23.2 | 4.7 | 25.8 | 1.2 | 6.6 |
| 10.0 | na | 0.0 | na | 10.0 | 1.1 | 7.75 | 8.92 | 2.12 | 72.0 | 4.0 | na | 0.0 | 7.0 |
| 10.0 | na | 0.0 | na | 6.9 | 3.2 | 1.07 | 11.82 | 1.62 | 71.6 | 8.6 | 104.8 | 0.1 | 7.0 |
| 9.3 | 0.00 | 0.2 | -0.04 | 4.6 | 5.3 | 1.19 | 12.80 | 2.83 | 67.8 | 3.7 | 48.1 | 18.4 | 5.8 |
| 5.1 | 2.04 | 16.2 | -0.01 | 4.7 | 0.5 | 0.93 | 10.28 | 4.48 | 71.8 | 0.9 | 14.6 | 33.1 | 5.0 |
| 8.8 | 0.15 | 0.4 | 0.15 | 6.9 | 3.6 | 1.43 | 9.12 | 3.66 | 55.4 | 4.7 | 28.9 | 6.9 | 8.6 |
| 8.8 | 0.00 | 0.0 | 0.00 | 7.2 | 1.1 | 1.68 | 11.52 | 3.86 | 53.0 | 4.9 | 42.2 | 10.8 | 7.9 |
| 8.0 | 0.40 | 2.5 | -0.01 | 9.5 | 66.3 | 1.95 | 17.74 | 3.81 | 54.0 | 4.1 | 9.5 | 6.5 | 9.9 |
| 7.4 | 0.08 | 0.3 | 0.19 | 5.1 | 1.6 | 1.19 | 8.09 | 3.61 | 71.9 | 1.3 | 27.3 | 27.8 | 7.7 |
| 7.8 | 0.35 | 4.2 | 0.01 | 5.8 | 1.2 | 1.38 | 11.32 | 3.85 | 58.8 | 3.1 | 19.3 | 14.2 | 7.2 |
| 7.0 | 0.91 | 4.8 | 0.02 | 8.3 | 73.6 | 1.97 | 18.86 | 3.95 | 51.8 | 3.5 | 21.1 | 11.6 | 10.0 |
| 3.8 | 0.67 | 6.7 | 0.02 | 6.7 | 3.8 | 1.51 | 15.59 | 4.86 | 68.8 | 0.7 | 11.5 | 36.2 | 6.4 |
| 7.6 | 0.29 | 2.0 | 0.03 | 5.2 | 3.7 | 1.03 | 10.59 | 3.84 | 57.5 | 3.3 | 10.7 | 11.9 | 6.2 |
| 8.3 | 0.78 | 4.2 | -0.01 | 3.1 | 0.2 | 0.56 | 4.58 | 3.14 | 82.3 | 4.9 | 74.7 | 16.0 | 6.0 |
| 9.7 | 0.00 | 0.0 | 0.01 | 5.1 | 1.3 | 1.30 | 11.13 | 2.60 | 54.7 | 5.2 | 65.4 | 14.7 | 6.2 |
| 3.8 | 3.16 | 14.4 | 0.40 | 4.2 | 3.4 | 0.82 | 7.21 | 3.32 | 69.0 | 0.7 | 17.7 | 42.1 | 6.5 |
| 6.8 | 0.10 | 0.6 | 0.00 | 3.8 | 4.1 | 0.68 | 6.79 | 3.27 | 82.6 | 1.5 | 7.0 | 19.8 | 7.0 |
| 7.8 | 0.45 | 3.6 | 0.00 | 2.1 | 0.3 | 0.26 | 3.14 | 2.53 | 90.0 | 1.0 | 23.1 | 33.7 | 4.5 |

| Name | City | State | Rating | 2018 Rating | 2017 Rating | Total Assets ($Mil) | One Year Asset Growth | Asset Mix (As a % of Total Assets) Comm-ercial Loans | Cons-umer Loans | Mort-gage Loans | Secur-ities | Capital-ization Index | Lever-age Ratio | Risk-Based Capital Ratio |
|---|---|---|---|---|---|---|---|---|---|---|---|---|---|---|
| Strasburg State Bank | Strasburg | ND | **C+** | C+ | B- | 70.8 | 12.38 | 3.2 | 0.5 | 0.0 | 15.4 | **6.6** | 8.6 | 12.3 |
| Streator Home Savings Bank | Streator | IL | **B-** | B- | B- | 160.8 | -3.72 | 0.0 | 1.3 | 23.4 | 66.7 | **10.0** | 26.0 | 93.4 |
| ▲ Stride Bank, N.A. | Enid | OK | **C+** | C- | D+ | 699.5 | 5.27 | 28.4 | 2.1 | 5.9 | 10.0 | **4.4** | 9.4 | 10.7 |
| ▲ Stroud National Bank | Stroud | OK | **B-** | C+ | C+ | 74.1 | -5.55 | 7.4 | 5.6 | 22.3 | 27.1 | **10.0** | 12.5 | 21.9 |
| Sturdy Savings Bank | Cape May Court Hou | NJ | **C+** | C+ | C+ | 845.9 | 0.60 | 2.8 | 0.1 | 28.4 | 25.8 | **7.6** | 9.4 | 15.4 |
| Sturgis Bank & Trust Co. | Sturgis | MI | **B-** | C+ | C+ | 473.4 | 9.75 | 7.6 | 1.3 | 25.5 | 11.8 | **6.4** | 8.4 | 12.7 |
| Success Bank | Bloomfield | IA | **B-** | C+ | B | 200.4 | 3.23 | 6.8 | 1.8 | 14.7 | 5.0 | **10.0** | 11.7 | 15.3 |
| Sugar River Bank | Newport | NH | **B-** | B- | C+ | 307.4 | 2.77 | 4.8 | 2.6 | 49.1 | 18.2 | **10.0** | 14.5 | 24.5 |
| Sullivan Bank | Sullivan | MO | **B-** | B- | B- | 527.9 | 6.64 | 9.9 | 2.2 | 31.9 | 7.4 | **7.9** | 9.6 | 14.3 |
| Sumitomo Mitsui Trust Bank (U.S.A.) Ltd. | Hoboken | NJ | **B+** | B- | C+ | 2708.7 | 2.13 | 0.0 | 0.0 | 0.0 | 0.0 | **10.0** | 11.2 | 27.0 |
| Summit Bank | Oakland | CA | **A-** | B+ | A- | 258.1 | -3.28 | 12.9 | 0.2 | 1.4 | 0.2 | **10.0** | 13.4 | 17.2 |
| Summit Bank | Eugene | OR | **B-** | B- | B+ | 507.4 | 21.83 | 24.2 | 0.3 | 2.0 | 0.9 | **5.1** | 9.4 | 11.1 |
| Summit Community Bank, Inc. | Moorefield | WV | **B+** | B | B | 2401.9 | 9.53 | 8.2 | 1.5 | 17.8 | 11.5 | **7.3** | 10.6 | 12.7 |
| ▲ Summit National Bank | Hulett | WY | **C** | D+ | D+ | 80.1 | 5.17 | 4.6 | 3.0 | 5.4 | 12.3 | **8.1** | 9.8 | 15.2 |
| Summit State Bank | Santa Rosa | CA | **B** | B+ | B+ | 696.0 | 11.87 | 7.9 | 0.0 | 7.4 | 8.9 | **6.8** | 9.3 | 12.4 |
| Sumner Bank & Trust | Gallatin | TN | **B** | B- | B- | 195.7 | 16.57 | 4.4 | 0.8 | 18.1 | 11.3 | **7.5** | 9.3 | 14.1 |
| Suncrest Bank | West Sacramento | CA | **B+** | B+ | B+ | 984.9 | 6.05 | 4.5 | 0.0 | 4.2 | 19.8 | **9.7** | 10.9 | 14.8 |
| Sundance State Bank | Sundance | WY | **B-** | C | B | 193.7 | 1.55 | 12.8 | 3.6 | 8.8 | 30.6 | **9.6** | 10.8 | 16.4 |
| Sundown State Bank | Sundown | TX | **B+** | B | B+ | 173.7 | 11.32 | 13.4 | 0.7 | 0.7 | 10.1 | **9.2** | 10.5 | 14.4 |
| Sunflower Bank, N.A. | Denver | CO | **C** | C | C- | 4172.7 | 8.22 | 19.1 | 0.5 | 16.0 | 14.5 | **6.7** | 9.8 | 12.3 |
| ▲ SunMark Community Bank | Hawkinsville | GA | **B+** | B+ | B+ | 281.6 | 4.51 | 6.8 | 2.6 | 18.8 | 8.5 | **10.0** | 11.7 | 17.6 |
| Sunnyside Federal S&L Assn. of Irvington | Irvington | NY | **D+** | D+ | D+ | 87.7 | 9.56 | 1.4 | 6.9 | 25.2 | 43.8 | **10.0** | 13.4 | 26.8 |
| Sunrise Bank | Cocoa Beach | FL | **A-** | B+ | B+ | 253.0 | 14.36 | 4.6 | 0.9 | 7.4 | 15.1 | **10.0** | 11.4 | 16.1 |
| Sunrise Bank Dakota | Onida | SD | **D+** | D+ | C | 54.2 | -5.45 | 6.0 | 1.2 | 4.4 | 11.1 | **10.0** | 12.7 | 21.0 |
| ▲ Sunrise Banks, N.A. | Saint Paul | MN | **B** | B | C+ | 1179.9 | 4.68 | 6.8 | 4.0 | 10.1 | 12.7 | **6.8** | 8.8 | 13.9 |
| Sunset Bank & Savings | Waukesha | WI | **C+** | C+ | C- | 130.6 | 2.75 | 5.4 | 0.9 | 37.7 | 8.5 | **9.6** | 10.7 | 17.8 |
| SunSouth Bank | Dothan | AL | **E** | E | E- | 111.7 | -6.40 | 30.6 | 0.4 | 10.6 | 33.6 | **5.0** | 7.0 | 17.2 |
| Sunstate Bank | Miami | FL | **B** | C+ | C | 451.8 | 7.90 | 0.8 | 0.5 | 27.9 | 7.8 | **7.9** | 9.6 | 15.2 |
| Sunwest Bank | Irvine | CA | **B+** | B+ | A- | 1435.4 | 7.64 | 12.3 | 2.4 | 3.3 | 5.0 | **9.0** | 13.2 | 14.1 |
| Superior National Bank & Trust Co. | Hancock | MI | **A-** | B+ | B+ | 572.6 | 2.65 | 5.8 | 8.1 | 21.5 | 34.2 | **10.0** | 13.0 | 25.3 |
| Superior Savings Bank | Superior | WI | **B** | B- | B- | 68.5 | 2.45 | 7.1 | 0.8 | 46.9 | 3.7 | **10.0** | 19.4 | 37.5 |
| Surety Bank | Deland | FL | **B-** | B- | B | 123.3 | -1.53 | 2.7 | 0.2 | 7.6 | 15.9 | **10.0** | 11.4 | 19.7 |
| Surrey Bank & Trust | Mount Airy | NC | **A-** | B+ | A | 329.5 | 6.59 | 23.5 | 1.2 | 7.1 | 2.4 | **10.0** | 14.1 | 21.5 |
| Susquehanna Community Bank | West Milton | PA | **B+** | B+ | B+ | 453.9 | 8.07 | 4.9 | 3.6 | 8.7 | 37.2 | **7.8** | 9.9 | 13.2 |
| Sutton Bank | Attica | OH | **B** | B | B+ | 643.0 | 22.41 | 8.4 | 1.0 | 4.7 | 20.3 | **8.8** | 10.2 | 19.0 |
| ▲ Swedish-American State Bank | Courtland | KS | **C+** | C- | D | 40.3 | -4.10 | 6.1 | 2.9 | 11.0 | 16.4 | **10.0** | 13.2 | 17.4 |
| Sweet Water State Bank | Sweet Water | AL | **B-** | C+ | C | 99.9 | -1.17 | 14.0 | 4.6 | 8.1 | 14.6 | **10.0** | 11.6 | 16.0 |
| Sycamore Bank | Senatobia | MS | **B** | B | B | 227.3 | 2.54 | 6.0 | 3.0 | 21.9 | 13.0 | **8.6** | 10.1 | 15.1 |
| Synchrony Bank | Draper | UT | **C** | C | C | 91281.0 | -0.55 | 1.2 | 83.1 | 0.0 | 7.0 | **10.0** | 11.9 | 15.6 |
| ▲ Synergy Bank | Houma | LA | **B** | C+ | D+ | 556.8 | 8.23 | 13.9 | 2.0 | 12.6 | 26.2 | **10.0** | 11.4 | 18.6 |
| Synovus Bank | Columbus | GA | **B+** | B+ | B+ | 48103.4 | 47.64 | 17.7 | 5.4 | 12.8 | 14.1 | **6.0** | 9.9 | 11.8 |
| Synovus Trust Co., N.A. | Columbus | GA | **U** | U | U | 101.5 | 6.55 | 0.0 | 0.0 | 0.0 | 19.6 | **10.0** | 95.1 | 127.0 |
| Systematic Savings Bank | Springfield | MO | **D** | D | D | 37.7 | 0.19 | 3.0 | 0.5 | 50.2 | 5.6 | **10.0** | 13.3 | 24.3 |
| ▲ T Bank, N.A. | Dallas | TX | **B+** | B- | B+ | 358.8 | 17.31 | 35.7 | 1.0 | 1.5 | 5.3 | **10.0** | 11.1 | 15.7 |
| Table Grove State Bank | Table Grove | IL | **B** | B- | B- | 45.6 | 1.00 | 1.5 | 9.3 | 1.6 | 24.0 | **10.0** | 12.4 | 17.7 |
| Table Rock Community Bank | Kimberling City | MO | **B-** | C+ | C+ | 86.8 | 2.62 | 4.2 | 5.9 | 32.2 | 9.9 | **7.7** | 9.5 | 14.4 |
| ▲ Talbot State Bank | Woodland | GA | **C-** | D | D | 56.6 | -7.88 | 0.0 | 0.4 | 46.7 | 26.2 | **10.0** | 11.6 | 32.4 |
| Tampa State Bank | Tampa | KS | **C+** | C+ | B | 57.3 | 0.30 | 10.1 | 2.7 | 17.9 | 26.6 | **9.0** | 10.4 | 14.8 |
| ▼ Tarboro Savings Bank, SSB | Tarboro | NC | **C+** | B- | B | 49.6 | 4.28 | 0.0 | 0.1 | 59.1 | 0.1 | **10.0** | 14.3 | 25.0 |
| Taylor County Bank | Campbellsville | KY | **A-** | B+ | A | 177.5 | -0.98 | 12.4 | 4.8 | 22.6 | 18.3 | **10.0** | 15.0 | 21.6 |
| Taylorsville Savings Bank, SSB | Taylorsville | NC | **B-** | C+ | C+ | 108.4 | 4.88 | 1.1 | 1.0 | 54.2 | 5.0 | **9.9** | 10.9 | 18.9 |
| TBK Bank, SSB | Dallas | TX | **B** | B- | B- | 5037.6 | 11.33 | 35.9 | 0.4 | 3.0 | 4.9 | **6.3** | 10.9 | 12.0 |
| TC Federal Bank | Thomasville | GA | **C+** | C+ | B | 321.8 | 8.26 | 2.4 | 0.4 | 34.2 | 6.9 | **10.0** | 12.6 | 18.9 |
| TCF National Bank | Sioux Falls | SD | **B+** | B | B- | 46627.4 | 96.67 | 22.0 | 3.3 | 14.3 | 14.7 | **6.7** | 9.1 | 12.3 |
| ▲ TCM Bank, N.A. | Tampa | FL | **B-** | C+ | B | 327.1 | 9.10 | 21.1 | 66.8 | 0.0 | 0.9 | **10.0** | 16.4 | 18.0 |
| TD Bank USA, N.A. | Wilmington | DE | **B-** | C+ | C+ | 17800.5 | -16.25 | 1.6 | 59.5 | 0.0 | 21.5 | **10.0** | 16.9 | 26.3 |
| TD Bank, N.A. | Wilmington | DE | **B-** | C+ | C+ | 320472.0 | 5.88 | 10.2 | 9.4 | 8.9 | 39.5 | **6.9** | 9.0 | 15.6 |
| Tecumseh Federal Bank | Tecumseh | NE | **B** | B | B- | 50.7 | 0.79 | 2.4 | 1.6 | 39.3 | 13.4 | **10.0** | 21.1 | 44.7 |
| Tejas Bank | Monahans | TX | **A-** | B+ | B+ | 190.4 | 7.67 | 19.7 | 2.6 | 2.0 | 21.5 | **8.2** | 9.8 | 16.2 |
| Templeton Savings Bank | Templeton | IA | **A-** | A- | A- | 127.2 | 3.31 | 10.9 | 2.8 | 15.5 | 10.5 | **10.0** | 14.3 | 20.2 |

| Asset Quality Index | Adjusted Non-Performing Loans as a % of Total Loans | Adjusted Non-Performing Loans as a % of Capital | Net Charge-Offs Avg Loans | Profitability Index | Net Income ($Mil) | Return on Assets (R.O.A.) | Return on Equity (R.O.E.) | Net Interest Spread | Overhead Efficiency Ratio | Liquidity Index | Liquidity Ratio | Hot Money Ratio | Stability Index |
|---|---|---|---|---|---|---|---|---|---|---|---|---|---|
| **6.2** | 0.00 | 0.0 | 0.00 | **4.3** | 0.6 | 0.95 | 10.91 | 3.41 | 65.0 | **3.9** | 39.1 | 15.2 | **4.5** |
| **9.7** | 2.01 | 1.7 | 0.11 | **2.6** | 0.7 | 0.42 | 1.69 | 2.14 | 80.1 | **4.7** | 94.8 | 22.2 | **7.6** |
| **3.3** | 1.70 | 13.4 | 0.33 | **5.6** | 8.1 | 1.20 | 12.81 | 4.82 | 74.9 | **2.5** | 7.0 | 6.5 | **6.6** |
| **4.9** | 2.70 | 11.7 | 0.21 | **3.6** | 0.5 | 0.66 | 5.43 | 4.51 | 84.4 | **4.1** | 26.1 | 9.9 | **5.8** |
| **7.1** | 0.72 | 4.3 | 0.07 | **3.1** | 3.1 | 0.36 | 3.58 | 3.61 | 85.5 | **5.2** | 22.8 | 2.0 | **6.4** |
| **4.3** | 1.71 | 7.6 | 0.02 | **5.4** | 5.4 | 1.19 | 12.62 | 3.99 | 68.5 | **2.9** | 14.2 | 10.0 | **5.9** |
| **6.0** | 0.65 | 3.8 | 0.15 | **8.1** | 3.5 | 1.78 | 15.39 | 4.83 | 57.8 | **1.8** | 10.3 | 16.5 | **8.6** |
| **7.4** | 0.97 | 4.6 | 0.21 | **3.5** | 1.7 | 0.55 | 3.92 | 3.65 | 80.9 | **3.1** | 23.2 | 14.3 | **7.5** |
| **4.0** | 1.72 | 12.1 | 0.21 | **5.6** | 6.2 | 1.19 | 12.41 | 3.77 | 60.3 | **1.6** | 8.2 | 21.6 | **7.0** |
| **10.0** | 0.00 | 0.0 | 0.00 | **4.5** | 26.4 | 0.92 | 7.98 | 0.84 | 71.6 | **8.8** | 112.2 | 0.0 | **9.1** |
| **6.5** | 0.12 | 0.3 | 0.00 | **8.3** | 3.8 | 1.49 | 11.71 | 5.25 | 59.5 | **4.6** | 30.3 | 8.5 | **8.1** |
| **5.8** | 0.23 | 1.5 | 0.39 | **7.3** | 5.6 | 1.24 | 12.87 | 5.40 | 58.8 | **3.7** | 11.0 | 10.0 | **6.4** |
| **6.1** | 0.64 | 4.2 | 0.08 | **6.5** | 32.3 | 1.42 | 12.82 | 3.70 | 55.6 | **1.8** | 11.8 | 12.4 | **9.1** |
| **2.9** | 1.63 | 11.8 | 0.22 | **3.8** | 0.5 | 0.70 | 7.18 | 3.89 | 80.3 | **3.7** | 21.3 | 10.9 | **6.3** |
| **5.5** | 0.50 | 2.2 | -0.01 | **5.3** | 6.5 | 1.00 | 10.00 | 3.65 | 62.1 | **1.0** | 15.1 | 28.1 | **6.9** |
| **8.9** | 0.06 | 0.4 | 0.03 | **5.2** | 1.9 | 1.04 | 11.49 | 3.95 | 65.4 | **4.5** | 30.5 | 9.2 | **5.1** |
| **5.8** | 0.78 | 3.4 | 0.15 | **6.9** | 11.9 | 1.25 | 8.42 | 4.45 | 53.6 | **4.6** | 29.5 | 7.8 | **8.5** |
| **3.5** | 2.75 | 13.3 | 0.65 | **5.5** | 2.1 | 1.14 | 9.95 | 3.96 | 53.8 | **2.6** | 30.3 | 18.7 | **6.5** |
| **8.5** | 0.00 | 0.0 | -0.01 | **6.8** | 2.3 | 1.42 | 13.17 | 4.76 | 61.8 | **3.1** | 33.9 | 17.6 | **6.0** |
| **6.2** | 0.41 | 2.9 | 0.13 | **3.3** | 24.6 | 0.62 | 5.38 | 3.63 | 84.0 | **3.1** | 6.5 | 7.3 | **7.8** |
| **6.7** | 0.66 | 3.7 | 0.33 | **6.1** | 4.0 | 1.48 | 13.19 | 4.72 | 72.7 | **3.6** | 21.3 | 11.6 | **7.5** |
| **8.2** | 1.44 | 3.8 | 0.17 | **0.2** | -0.4 | -0.42 | -3.39 | 2.56 | 117.1 | **3.0** | 45.9 | 22.4 | **5.8** |
| **7.6** | 0.14 | 0.8 | 0.00 | **5.4** | 3.1 | 1.32 | 11.73 | 4.01 | 67.5 | **1.5** | 29.7 | 29.6 | **7.6** |
| **0.7** | 15.56 | 39.0 | 0.57 | **2.0** | 0.2 | 0.40 | 3.27 | 3.05 | 87.8 | **2.3** | 26.3 | 15.2 | **5.2** |
| **8.0** | 0.20 | 1.0 | 0.33 | **4.8** | 11.5 | 1.03 | 11.71 | 4.67 | 83.1 | **1.6** | 27.8 | 1.7 | **8.3** |
| **6.1** | 0.78 | 3.6 | 0.12 | **2.3** | 0.3 | 0.25 | 2.08 | 3.23 | 90.4 | **1.2** | 17.9 | 29.3 | **6.4** |
| **6.2** | 0.42 | 2.6 | 0.06 | **1.5** | 0.1 | 0.12 | 1.87 | 2.59 | 102.3 | **1.6** | 31.5 | 32.2 | **0.4** |
| **7.7** | 0.15 | 0.5 | -0.16 | **5.6** | 6.9 | 1.56 | 14.20 | 3.30 | 61.1 | **2.3** | 47.6 | 49.5 | **6.5** |
| **4.7** | 0.76 | 4.4 | -0.09 | **9.4** | 22.0 | 1.64 | 13.07 | 4.44 | 51.6 | **4.2** | 12.9 | 3.5 | **10.0** |
| **6.1** | 2.49 | 5.6 | -0.06 | **5.9** | 7.0 | 1.23 | 9.58 | 3.75 | 65.3 | **4.2** | 46.7 | 15.5 | **8.2** |
| **6.4** | 3.48 | 7.0 | 0.00 | **5.1** | 0.6 | 0.93 | 4.79 | 3.85 | 69.7 | **5.2** | 35.5 | 6.6 | **7.0** |
| **5.0** | 3.31 | 9.9 | -0.03 | **7.3** | 2.1 | 1.70 | 15.08 | 4.07 | 70.4 | **3.5** | 40.7 | 17.5 | **7.8** |
| **7.7** | 0.80 | 1.3 | 0.08 | **8.8** | 5.0 | 1.57 | 10.69 | 4.57 | 57.3 | **2.9** | 26.2 | 13.4 | **9.2** |
| **6.9** | 0.27 | 4.3 | 0.02 | **4.8** | 5.0 | 1.08 | 11.02 | 3.20 | 68.3 | **4.3** | 26.0 | 8.4 | **7.0** |
| **5.2** | 1.89 | 5.8 | 0.97 | **9.8** | 17.4 | 3.11 | 30.03 | 3.93 | 46.8 | **4.4** | 42.5 | 1.2 | **7.9** |
| **3.2** | 0.33 | 15.1 | 0.34 | **6.5** | 0.7 | 1.75 | 14.28 | 4.56 | 65.4 | **1.4** | 4.5 | 23.4 | **4.7** |
| **4.5** | 2.50 | 14.7 | 0.24 | **4.2** | 0.8 | 0.82 | 7.23 | 5.34 | 77.2 | **1.5** | 23.5 | 26.6 | **6.4** |
| **5.6** | 1.15 | 4.3 | 0.02 | **5.1** | 2.4 | 1.05 | 10.60 | 4.27 | 71.3 | **3.6** | 13.7 | 10.3 | **5.9** |
| **1.8** | 0.91 | 12.2 | 5.89 | **10.0** | 3228.0 | 3.53 | 26.37 | 12.16 | 33.6 | **0.9** | 20.5 | 32.7 | **10.0** |
| **5.1** | 2.77 | 9.1 | 0.05 | **6.4** | 7.5 | 1.38 | 11.84 | 4.02 | 59.6 | **2.3** | 31.1 | 21.9 | **7.2** |
| **6.7** | 0.62 | 3.0 | 0.16 | **7.1** | 584.1 | 1.25 | 11.79 | 3.74 | 53.6 | **1.7** | 14.9 | 13.5 | **9.6** |
| **6.6** | na | 0.0 | na | **9.5** | 9.3 | 9.55 | 10.01 | 1.63 | 76.0 | **4.0** | na | 0.0 | **7.0** |
| **7.1** | 0.00 | 0.0 | 0.13 | **0.2** | -0.1 | -0.24 | -1.77 | 3.48 | 106.5 | **0.7** | 24.6 | 56.5 | **5.4** |
| **5.8** | 1.99 | 2.1 | 0.37 | **7.4** | 4.9 | 1.49 | 10.59 | 4.20 | 71.7 | **0.4** | 7.4 | 61.1 | **8.6** |
| **6.8** | 0.05 | 0.7 | 0.04 | **6.1** | 0.7 | 1.53 | 12.70 | 4.20 | 70.0 | **4.6** | 23.1 | 5.5 | **6.9** |
| **5.2** | 0.93 | 6.0 | 0.03 | **6.1** | 1.0 | 1.12 | 12.14 | 4.80 | 70.7 | **3.1** | 12.0 | 13.2 | **5.5** |
| **5.1** | 4.43 | 14.3 | 0.03 | **2.1** | 0.8 | 1.42 | 12.27 | 3.82 | 106.7 | **2.1** | 47.4 | 43.3 | **5.1** |
| **5.6** | 0.66 | 3.9 | 0.12 | **3.2** | 0.4 | 0.63 | 6.13 | 3.32 | 84.7 | **1.6** | 16.3 | 23.8 | **6.3** |
| **7.1** | 0.00 | 6.5 | 0.26 | **1.8** | 0.0 | 0.09 | 0.61 | 3.43 | 92.7 | **0.8** | 19.2 | 43.1 | **7.8** |
| **6.0** | 1.06 | 5.9 | 0.08 | **9.0** | 3.8 | 2.07 | 14.06 | 4.72 | 58.2 | **3.0** | 17.4 | 14.0 | **9.6** |
| **4.4** | 3.37 | 15.2 | 0.07 | **4.1** | 0.7 | 0.67 | 6.84 | 4.19 | 77.9 | **1.5** | 17.4 | 20.5 | **5.7** |
| **4.6** | 0.85 | 5.0 | 0.17 | **7.8** | 67.3 | 1.42 | 9.74 | 6.07 | 68.6 | **1.0** | 9.2 | 21.8 | **10.0** |
| **7.1** | 1.25 | 6.8 | 0.05 | **2.7** | 1.2 | 0.39 | 3.05 | 3.30 | 85.9 | **1.8** | 19.3 | 21.4 | **6.4** |
| **5.5** | 0.56 | 3.6 | 0.43 | **5.3** | 359.7 | 1.11 | 10.24 | 4.21 | 71.8 | **2.7** | 18.2 | 11.1 | **9.2** |
| **3.7** | 0.19 | 4.5 | 2.98 | **6.9** | 4.1 | 1.32 | 7.55 | 7.52 | 71.5 | **0.2** | 11.7 | 99.9 | **6.9** |
| **3.1** | 1.01 | 7.3 | 5.16 | **7.7** | 288.2 | 1.61 | 10.25 | 10.84 | 59.7 | **2.4** | 44.3 | 0.0 | **7.5** |
| **5.1** | 0.89 | 3.2 | 0.41 | **4.0** | 2682.1 | 0.88 | 6.73 | 2.50 | 56.3 | **2.8** | 47.2 | 1.8 | **9.0** |
| **9.0** | 0.62 | 2.4 | -0.03 | **3.6** | 0.3 | 0.58 | 2.76 | 3.52 | 82.2 | **3.5** | 45.6 | 18.7 | **7.3** |
| **8.1** | 0.00 | 0.6 | 0.14 | **9.4** | 4.8 | 2.68 | 23.93 | 4.37 | 44.6 | **5.3** | 33.7 | 5.1 | **8.1** |
| **7.8** | 0.04 | 0.6 | 0.03 | **6.9** | 1.7 | 1.34 | 8.57 | 3.86 | 53.7 | **2.7** | 22.7 | 16.5 | **8.7** |

| Name | City | State | Rating | 2018 Rating | 2017 Rating | Total Assets ($Mil) | One Year Asset Growth | Asset Mix (As a % of Total Assets) Comm-ercial Loans | Cons-umer Loans | Mort-gage Loans | Secur-ities | Capital-ization Index | Lever-age Ratio | Risk-Based Capital Ratio |
|---|---|---|---|---|---|---|---|---|---|---|---|---|---|---|
| Tempo Bank | Trenton | IL | **C-** | C- | C | 99.0 | 2.61 | 0.0 | 1.2 | 82.0 | 0.0 | **10.0** | 11.2 | 21.3 |
| Tennessee Bank & Trust | Nashville | TN | **D** | D+ | | 254.0 | -1.66 | 28.7 | 0.2 | 7.8 | 0.0 | **5.2** | 8.8 | 11.1 |
| Tennessee State Bank | Pigeon Forge | TN | **A-** | B | C+ | 677.8 | 6.68 | 1.3 | 3.8 | 17.5 | 18.1 | **10.0** | 11.0 | 16.3 |
| ▲ Tensas State Bank | Newellton | LA | **B+** | B | B+ | 159.4 | 5.26 | 12.7 | 1.2 | 11.3 | 30.8 | **10.0** | 12.7 | 20.6 |
| Terrabank, N.A. | Miami | FL | **C+** | C+ | C+ | 449.8 | 14.59 | 4.9 | 0.6 | 17.1 | 23.9 | **7.1** | 9.1 | 14.9 |
| Terre Haute Savings Bank | Terre Haute | IN | **C** | C | C | 350.4 | 2.71 | 9.3 | 1.3 | 26.4 | 22.0 | **7.6** | 9.4 | 13.8 |
| Territorial Savings Bank | Honolulu | HI | **B+** | B+ | A- | 2086.3 | 0.83 | 0.4 | 0.0 | 73.7 | 18.2 | **9.9** | 10.9 | 23.6 |
| Teutopolis State Bank | Teutopolis | IL | **A** | A | A | 261.0 | 10.65 | 5.3 | 2.3 | 9.5 | 26.4 | **10.0** | 13.0 | 20.4 |
| Texan Bank, N.A. | Houston | TX | **C** | C | D+ | 342.4 | 14.60 | 9.9 | 0.3 | 4.5 | 1.1 | **9.0** | 12.0 | 14.2 |
| Texana Bank, N.A. | Linden | TX | **C-** | D+ | D | 217.6 | 3.21 | 25.5 | 1.9 | 24.2 | 7.6 | **6.1** | 8.5 | 11.8 |
| Texas Advantage Community Bank, N.A. | Alvin | TX | **B-** | B- | C | 126.3 | 16.51 | 19.2 | 2.5 | 5.0 | 8.7 | **7.5** | 9.3 | 16.1 |
| Texas Bank | Henderson | TX | **B-** | B | B | 492.8 | -0.75 | 7.3 | 5.0 | 16.1 | 26.8 | **9.6** | 10.7 | 16.2 |
| Texas Bank and Trust Co. | Longview | TX | **A-** | B+ | B+ | 2669.1 | 5.58 | 14.5 | 1.9 | 21.3 | 5.2 | **10.0** | 11.7 | 15.7 |
| ▲ Texas Bank Financial | Weatherford | TX | **B+** | B+ | A- | 441.8 | 26.79 | 0.9 | 0.2 | 65.1 | 0.4 | **8.5** | 10.0 | 16.9 |
| Texas Brand Bank | Dallas | TX | **B+** | B+ | B+ | 228.7 | 12.36 | 12.1 | 0.4 | 6.2 | 1.9 | **9.8** | 12.9 | 14.8 |
| Texas Capital Bank, N.A. | Dallas | TX | **B-** | B- | B- | 32529.3 | 15.16 | 23.3 | 0.2 | 9.3 | 0.7 | **4.8** | 8.2 | 10.9 |
| Texas Champion Bank | Corpus Christi | TX | **C-** | D+ | D | 312.3 | -2.31 | 6.5 | 1.1 | 4.9 | 8.0 | **10.0** | 12.0 | 16.5 |
| Texas Citizens Bank, N.A. | Pasadena | TX | **C-** | C- | C | 516.8 | -7.07 | 16.2 | 2.3 | 7.6 | 0.2 | **8.1** | 10.1 | 13.4 |
| Texas Community Bank | Laredo | TX | **A** | A- | B+ | 1475.8 | 2.49 | 10.3 | 1.1 | 11.3 | 26.1 | **10.0** | 11.1 | 19.9 |
| Texas Exchange Bank, SSB | Crowley | TX | **A** | A | A | 953.9 | 25.29 | 27.7 | 0.0 | 0.0 | 49.0 | **10.0** | 15.3 | 27.7 |
| Texas Financial Bank | Eden | TX | **A-** | B+ | B+ | 105.9 | 2.33 | 2.4 | 1.0 | 0.3 | 37.0 | **9.6** | 10.7 | 22.8 |
| ▲ Texas First Bank | Texas City | TX | **A-** | A- | A- | 1472.5 | 35.04 | 7.9 | 0.6 | 10.1 | 29.0 | **9.1** | 10.4 | 16.5 |
| Texas Gulf Bank, N.A. | Houston | TX | **B-** | B+ | B+ | 663.1 | 10.80 | 10.2 | 0.7 | 16.0 | 28.8 | **8.6** | 10.0 | 15.3 |
| Texas Heritage Bank | Boerne | TX | **B** | B- | B | 150.4 | 1.95 | 6.2 | 1.6 | 19.7 | 1.8 | **7.5** | 9.4 | 13.7 |
| Texas Heritage National Bank | Daingerfield | TX | **B** | B | B+ | 146.4 | 9.10 | 4.9 | 4.5 | 20.2 | 9.5 | **9.3** | 10.8 | 14.4 |
| Texas Hill Country Bank | Bandera | TX | **B** | B | B | 169.9 | 12.87 | 14.8 | 1.2 | 15.3 | 2.0 | **7.1** | 9.8 | 12.6 |
| Texas National Bank | Mercedes | TX | **B** | B | B | 330.0 | 8.69 | 11.9 | 1.5 | 17.5 | 19.2 | **7.6** | 9.4 | 14.1 |
| Texas National Bank | Sweetwater | TX | **C+** | C+ | C+ | 145.3 | 7.56 | 5.4 | 1.5 | 5.9 | 54.6 | **8.3** | 9.9 | 22.9 |
| Texas National Bank of Jacksonville | Jacksonville | TX | **B** | B- | B- | 561.8 | 5.69 | 12.5 | 3.2 | 28.8 | 3.1 | **8.9** | 10.3 | 14.9 |
| Texas Regional Bank | Harlingen | TX | **B-** | C+ | C+ | 1020.1 | 14.50 | 9.8 | 1.0 | 8.2 | 27.8 | **8.6** | 10.0 | 14.1 |
| Texas Republic Bank, N.A. | Frisco | TX | **A-** | B+ | A- | 304.5 | 18.74 | 8.9 | 0.3 | 35.2 | 0.0 | **10.0** | 11.3 | 15.9 |
| Texas Security Bank | Dallas | TX | **A-** | A- | A- | 560.5 | 17.75 | 16.9 | 0.2 | 10.4 | 15.3 | **10.0** | 13.2 | 16.3 |
| Texas State Bank | San Angelo | TX | **A** | A- | B+ | 287.6 | 6.29 | 7.4 | 1.0 | 12.6 | 30.2 | **10.0** | 11.8 | 20.9 |
| ▲ TexasBank | Brownwood | TX | **A** | B+ | A+ | 495.3 | 1.75 | 4.1 | 1.4 | 15.1 | 9.6 | **10.0** | 13.6 | 19.5 |
| Texico State Bank | Texico | IL | **D-** | D- | D- | 8.3 | 5.27 | 1.6 | 2.0 | 26.3 | 0.0 | **6.4** | 8.4 | 21.8 |
| TexStar National Bank | Universal City | TX | **B+** | B | B | 283.0 | 8.78 | 11.0 | 0.5 | 7.8 | 6.5 | **9.9** | 10.9 | 15.2 |
| Thayer County Bank | Hebron | NE | **C** | C- | C | 65.0 | 2.21 | 17.4 | 3.0 | 16.3 | 21.0 | **10.0** | 11.3 | 23.0 |
| The Bank | Oberlin | KS | **D+** | C- | C- | 360.1 | 0.00 | 2.9 | 0.3 | 0.5 | 11.3 | **10.0** | 13.5 | 21.2 |
| The Bank | Jennings | LA | **A-** | B+ | B+ | 245.4 | 5.75 | 11.5 | 12.8 | 28.8 | 5.3 | **10.0** | 11.8 | 16.2 |
| ▲ The Bank of Soperton | Soperton | GA | **B** | C+ | B- | 92.9 | 17.53 | 19.0 | 7.9 | 24.5 | 5.0 | **9.0** | 10.3 | 15.5 |
| The Bankers Bank | Oklahoma City | OK | **B-** | B- | C+ | 309.3 | 6.32 | 5.7 | 0.3 | 1.9 | 0.0 | **10.0** | 13.2 | 19.1 |
| Think Mutual Bank | Rochester | MN | **B+** | B+ | B | 1669.8 | 1.38 | 1.2 | 14.2 | 43.9 | 23.3 | **10.0** | 16.9 | 29.3 |
| Third Coast Bank, SSB | Humble | TX | **C** | C- | C+ | 926.5 | 9.58 | 23.2 | 0.4 | 7.0 | 0.1 | **6.2** | 8.9 | 11.9 |
| Third Federal S&L Assn. of Cleveland | Cleveland | OH | **B-** | B- | B- | 14789.9 | 4.11 | 0.0 | 0.0 | 78.7 | 3.8 | **8.8** | 10.2 | 18.8 |
| Thomaston Savings Bank | Thomaston | CT | **C+** | C+ | C+ | 1110.7 | 6.19 | 6.8 | 1.6 | 27.6 | 22.5 | **10.0** | 11.5 | 16.7 |
| Thomasville National Bank | Thomasville | GA | **A-** | A- | B+ | 955.4 | 8.68 | 14.5 | 1.7 | 23.6 | 8.3 | **7.1** | 9.0 | 12.6 |
| Three Rivers Bank of Montana | Kalispell | MT | **B+** | A- | A- | 169.4 | 6.02 | 14.5 | 3.0 | 9.8 | 9.8 | **10.0** | 11.6 | 15.6 |
| Thrivent Trust Co. | Appleton | WI | **U** | U | U | 73.7 | 10.01 | 0.0 | 0.0 | 0.0 | 34.1 | **10.0** | 38.4 | 133.3 |
| Thumb Bank & Trust | Pigeon | MI | **C+** | C+ | C | 274.3 | 4.65 | 7.6 | 1.2 | 7.1 | 20.9 | **6.9** | 8.9 | 12.8 |
| TIAA, FSB | Jacksonville | FL | **C+** | B- | C+ | 41950.7 | 13.69 | 2.1 | 0.0 | 42.0 | 6.3 | **5.6** | 7.6 | 12.7 |
| TIB The Independent BankersBank, N.A. | Farmers Branch | TX | **B** | B- | B- | 2712.8 | 7.95 | 4.6 | 3.1 | 1.0 | 12.4 | **8.0** | 9.6 | 16.9 |
| ▲ Tilden Bank | Tilden | NE | **C+** | C | C+ | 83.7 | 1.96 | 3.8 | 2.6 | 1.6 | 14.9 | **8.7** | 10.4 | 13.9 |
| Timberland Bank | Hoquiam | WA | **A** | A | A- | 1268.0 | 5.88 | 5.8 | 0.3 | 11.6 | 6.2 | **10.0** | 12.7 | 19.1 |
| Timberline Bank | Grand Junction | CO | **B-** | B- | B- | 320.2 | 14.82 | 13.9 | 1.4 | 10.5 | 15.1 | **7.0** | 9.1 | 12.5 |
| Timberwood Bank | Tomah | WI | **A-** | A- | A- | 190.9 | 3.32 | 8.7 | 0.6 | 8.8 | 20.4 | **10.0** | 11.0 | 16.5 |
| ▼ Time Federal Savings Bank | Medford | WI | **C+** | B+ | B+ | 808.2 | 38.90 | 3.7 | 0.1 | 46.7 | 18.3 | **10.0** | 14.0 | 26.3 |
| Tioga Franklin Savings Bank | Philadelphia | PA | **C** | B- | B- | 43.9 | 6.93 | 1.7 | 0.5 | 58.0 | 4.1 | **10.0** | 11.1 | 18.6 |
| Tioga State Bank | Spencer | NY | **A-** | B+ | B+ | 488.0 | 0.88 | 11.0 | 1.6 | 24.8 | 24.8 | **10.0** | 12.4 | 20.0 |
| Tipton Latham Bank, N.A. | Tipton | MO | **B** | B | B+ | 140.7 | 4.94 | 7.9 | 3.0 | 20.7 | 21.4 | **9.8** | 10.9 | 16.3 |
| Titan Bank, N.A. | Mineral Wells | TX | **A-** | A- | A- | 180.1 | 70.91 | 4.0 | 0.1 | 21.7 | 10.7 | **8.1** | 9.7 | 19.0 |

| Asset Quality Index | Adjusted Non-Performing Loans as a % of Total Loans | Adjusted Non-Performing Loans as a % of Capital | Net Charge-Offs Avg Loans | Profitability Index | Net Income ($Mil) | Return on Assets (R.O.A.) | Return on Equity (R.O.E.) | Net Interest Spread | Overhead Efficiency Ratio | Liquidity Index | Liquidity Ratio | Hot Money Ratio | Stability Index |
|---|---|---|---|---|---|---|---|---|---|---|---|---|---|
| **5.7** | 1.96 | 14.6 | 0.00 | **1.7** | 0.1 | 0.09 | 0.83 | 2.59 | 94.1 | **1.2** | 11.2 | 27.3 | **5.8** |
| **3.2** | 3.10 | 16.8 | 0.80 | **0.5** | -0.9 | -0.35 | -4.04 | 3.59 | 93.2 | **1.3** | 15.3 | 27.6 | **1.9** |
| **6.1** | 1.08 | 5.9 | 0.30 | **6.2** | 8.2 | 1.27 | 11.12 | 4.10 | 70.6 | **4.2** | 21.2 | 6.9 | **6.3** |
| **5.1** | 2.83 | 11.1 | 0.34 | **5.2** | 1.9 | 1.26 | 9.54 | 3.61 | 64.9 | **2.3** | 36.4 | 26.6 | **8.1** |
| **8.8** | 0.02 | 0.1 | 0.01 | **3.3** | 2.3 | 0.56 | 6.16 | 3.49 | 79.6 | **2.5** | 32.7 | 19.5 | **4.9** |
| **5.7** | 0.64 | 5.7 | 0.05 | **2.7** | 1.5 | 0.44 | 4.56 | 3.46 | 87.8 | **2.7** | 22.9 | 16.3 | **5.1** |
| **9.9** | 0.08 | 0.5 | 0.00 | **5.0** | 22.5 | 1.08 | 10.13 | 2.93 | 58.8 | **1.7** | 12.2 | 22.0 | **8.7** |
| **8.8** | 0.00 | 0.1 | 0.02 | **6.9** | 3.4 | 1.40 | 10.33 | 3.32 | 45.0 | **5.3** | 38.3 | 7.3 | **7.8** |
| **3.6** | 0.59 | 6.1 | 0.44 | **2.8** | 0.8 | 0.25 | 2.00 | 4.09 | 84.3 | **0.8** | 14.7 | 38.6 | **5.7** |
| **6.2** | 0.20 | 2.7 | 0.09 | **2.6** | 1.1 | 0.52 | 6.17 | 3.97 | 85.7 | **0.6** | 9.5 | 30.8 | **4.0** |
| **8.0** | 0.00 | 1.3 | -0.01 | **4.5** | 1.1 | 0.92 | 9.50 | 4.04 | 71.4 | **1.9** | 35.2 | 32.1 | **5.4** |
| **6.0** | 0.94 | 6.5 | 0.08 | **4.4** | 5.0 | 1.02 | 9.77 | 4.10 | 74.3 | **1.9** | 26.7 | 23.9 | **6.4** |
| **6.7** | 0.70 | 3.4 | 0.06 | **7.7** | 40.3 | 1.55 | 12.88 | 3.82 | 55.2 | **3.1** | 19.4 | 14.5 | **10.0** |
| **6.3** | 0.50 | 5.0 | 0.00 | **10.0** | 9.3 | 2.36 | 25.06 | 4.75 | 60.4 | **0.7** | 15.1 | 44.1 | **7.7** |
| **7.3** | 0.00 | 0.0 | -0.03 | **5.0** | 2.0 | 0.95 | 7.36 | 4.37 | 69.8 | **0.8** | 18.5 | 39.3 | **7.2** |
| **6.0** | 0.83 | 8.0 | 0.28 | **5.5** | 334.2 | 1.09 | 12.49 | 3.29 | 52.9 | **2.6** | 15.9 | 1.9 | **8.2** |
| **4.5** | 2.13 | 11.0 | -0.22 | **3.4** | 1.3 | 0.41 | 3.35 | 4.75 | 96.9 | **4.2** | 20.5 | 8.0 | **6.1** |
| **3.2** | 1.76 | 11.6 | 0.70 | **2.6** | 1.4 | 0.26 | 2.84 | 4.55 | 80.1 | **2.1** | 19.1 | 17.4 | **5.0** |
| **8.8** | 0.18 | 0.5 | 0.04 | **7.5** | 21.6 | 1.50 | 13.97 | 3.67 | 53.7 | **2.6** | 29.9 | 25.1 | **9.4** |
| **9.0** | 0.00 | 0.0 | 0.00 | **8.2** | 24.8 | 3.04 | 22.64 | 2.48 | 18.9 | **2.2** | 52.5 | 35.5 | **9.2** |
| **9.3** | 0.01 | 0.0 | 0.00 | **6.0** | 1.4 | 1.29 | 12.78 | 3.42 | 62.0 | **4.5** | 43.4 | 13.6 | **7.2** |
| **6.1** | 1.42 | 5.0 | 0.05 | **7.1** | 20.2 | 1.73 | 16.42 | 4.26 | 58.7 | **5.3** | 36.5 | 10.2 | **9.8** |
| **7.2** | 0.17 | 0.7 | 0.01 | **5.8** | 9.2 | 1.45 | 13.52 | 3.93 | 64.3 | **3.8** | 28.6 | 12.0 | **7.7** |
| **7.4** | 0.06 | 0.5 | 0.03 | **5.8** | 2.2 | 1.49 | 16.05 | 4.43 | 68.9 | **1.9** | 18.9 | 19.8 | **6.9** |
| **3.8** | 1.86 | 14.7 | -0.01 | **5.0** | 1.6 | 1.15 | 10.40 | 4.05 | 71.2 | **1.5** | 21.0 | 26.6 | **7.3** |
| **8.5** | 0.00 | 0.0 | 0.00 | **4.7** | 1.4 | 0.91 | 9.42 | 4.11 | 70.5 | **1.4** | 21.4 | 28.5 | **5.6** |
| **6.8** | 0.43 | 2.9 | -0.05 | **5.8** | 3.3 | 1.13 | 12.18 | 5.08 | 74.6 | **1.1** | 13.5 | 29.4 | **5.9** |
| **9.3** | 0.18 | 0.4 | -0.01 | **3.4** | 1.0 | 0.72 | 7.05 | 2.99 | 77.2 | **5.8** | 51.4 | 8.6 | **6.0** |
| **5.2** | 1.08 | 8.4 | 0.38 | **5.7** | 6.2 | 1.12 | 11.12 | 3.87 | 58.6 | **0.6** | 8.7 | 46.6 | **7.4** |
| **7.4** | 1.01 | 3.3 | 0.04 | **4.1** | 8.3 | 0.86 | 7.87 | 4.19 | 77.7 | **3.3** | 27.9 | 17.2 | **7.1** |
| **7.3** | 0.00 | 3.2 | 0.03 | **9.2** | 4.8 | 1.67 | 14.69 | 4.88 | 55.8 | **0.8** | 13.8 | 35.7 | **7.6** |
| **8.5** | 0.12 | 0.3 | -0.07 | **7.4** | 7.5 | 1.53 | 11.99 | 3.96 | 53.2 | **1.8** | 30.0 | 12.6 | **6.2** |
| **9.2** | 0.00 | 0.0 | 0.00 | **6.7** | 4.6 | 1.68 | 13.86 | 3.85 | 62.5 | **5.9** | 40.1 | 4.4 | **8.2** |
| **7.0** | 0.08 | 0.3 | 0.02 | **10.0** | 12.5 | 2.51 | 18.48 | 4.62 | 53.3 | **3.7** | 25.9 | 11.6 | **9.8** |
| **6.8** | 1.03 | 4.5 | 0.00 | **1.6** | 0.0 | 0.03 | 0.29 | 3.69 | 99.3 | **7.0** | 66.2 | 0.0 | **1.0** |
| **7.3** | 0.08 | 0.5 | 0.10 | **5.4** | 3.6 | 1.32 | 11.66 | 4.14 | 65.4 | **0.8** | 17.7 | 28.3 | **7.7** |
| **2.6** | 4.31 | 22.8 | 0.07 | **4.5** | 0.6 | 0.86 | 7.79 | 3.55 | 68.1 | **1.8** | 15.2 | 20.7 | **5.1** |
| **0.7** | 10.88 | 31.3 | -0.01 | **9.0** | 7.3 | 2.12 | 15.89 | 4.11 | 48.3 | **3.5** | 33.1 | 9.0 | **9.6** |
| **7.5** | 0.15 | 2.5 | 0.38 | **8.2** | 3.6 | 1.50 | 12.84 | 5.49 | 61.3 | **2.2** | 18.1 | 18.2 | **7.3** |
| **5.3** | 0.63 | 3.1 | 0.07 | **7.8** | 1.5 | 1.69 | 18.11 | 5.37 | 65.4 | **1.0** | 17.7 | 33.2 | **7.8** |
| **5.8** | 1.92 | 8.4 | 0.31 | **3.5** | 1.9 | 0.65 | 5.19 | 2.74 | 87.6 | **2.5** | 42.4 | 11.2 | **7.0** |
| **8.1** | 0.07 | 0.3 | 0.06 | **4.3** | 13.6 | 0.82 | 4.98 | 3.11 | 71.5 | **6.3** | 35.3 | 3.0 | **9.8** |
| **4.1** | 0.54 | 4.9 | 0.06 | **3.6** | 4.4 | 0.51 | 5.60 | 4.19 | 80.2 | **0.7** | 11.5 | 34.2 | **5.7** |
| **7.2** | 1.18 | 7.4 | -0.05 | **3.5** | 78.7 | 0.55 | 5.40 | 1.82 | 66.4 | **0.6** | 6.2 | 30.8 | **7.7** |
| **6.1** | 1.91 | 8.8 | 0.08 | **2.9** | 5.7 | 0.52 | 4.98 | 3.18 | 82.8 | **2.5** | 26.6 | 21.4 | **7.7** |
| **7.1** | 0.38 | 2.8 | 0.02 | **9.8** | 18.8 | 1.97 | 21.13 | 3.68 | 46.1 | **2.9** | 8.8 | 11.5 | **9.0** |
| **3.1** | 1.57 | 13.8 | 0.25 | **6.2** | 2.0 | 1.23 | 10.53 | 5.25 | 66.3 | **2.6** | 16.9 | 16.1 | **7.6** |
| **6.5** | na | 0.0 | na | **0.0** | -1.3 | -1.76 | -3.32 | -0.62 | 102.4 | **4.1** | 144.7 | 100.0 | **1.5** |
| **5.4** | 1.05 | 6.3 | 0.50 | **3.8** | 2.0 | 0.76 | 8.19 | 3.78 | 80.3 | **2.4** | 28.0 | 18.8 | **5.7** |
| **4.5** | 0.98 | 6.2 | 0.07 | **3.2** | 197.9 | 0.50 | 5.12 | 2.27 | 75.2 | **0.7** | 9.9 | 24.1 | **7.7** |
| **8.5** | 0.14 | 0.8 | 0.20 | **4.3** | 23.6 | 0.93 | 8.82 | 1.90 | 77.5 | **4.2** | 43.9 | 8.4 | **8.1** |
| **3.8** | 2.13 | 6.8 | -0.08 | **7.2** | 1.3 | 1.50 | 13.42 | 4.25 | 60.5 | **4.4** | 10.0 | 5.3 | **6.9** |
| **6.8** | 0.64 | 2.5 | -0.02 | **10.0** | 25.4 | 2.05 | 15.49 | 4.51 | 52.7 | **4.2** | 20.6 | 8.4 | **10.0** |
| **5.9** | 1.15 | 7.4 | 0.06 | **4.0** | 1.7 | 0.55 | 6.31 | 4.55 | 83.3 | **4.9** | 21.0 | 3.5 | **5.3** |
| **5.2** | 2.99 | 11.4 | -0.03 | **6.6** | 2.4 | 1.28 | 10.24 | 3.53 | 57.6 | **2.0** | 30.2 | 19.6 | **8.4** |
| **8.8** | 0.71 | 1.8 | 0.01 | **2.5** | 2.0 | 0.32 | 1.48 | 2.21 | 85.0 | **2.2** | 28.2 | 20.8 | **8.1** |
| **5.7** | 2.81 | 9.3 | 0.00 | **2.1** | 0.1 | 0.11 | 0.96 | 4.16 | 90.6 | **0.5** | 12.1 | 52.4 | **6.1** |
| **7.8** | 1.08 | 4.3 | 0.07 | **5.8** | 6.2 | 1.29 | 11.03 | 4.10 | 65.2 | **2.6** | 15.2 | 11.7 | **7.3** |
| **5.6** | 1.32 | 5.9 | 0.05 | **4.1** | 1.5 | 1.08 | 10.07 | 2.94 | 65.7 | **1.4** | 31.2 | 40.2 | **6.7** |
| **7.7** | 0.05 | 0.4 | 0.02 | **8.6** | 3.0 | 1.86 | 19.00 | 4.04 | 58.1 | **5.0** | 34.0 | 3.9 | **7.0** |

| Name | City | State | Rating | 2018 Rating | 2017 Rating | Total Assets ($Mil) | One Year Asset Growth | Asset Mix (As a % of Total Assets): Comm-ercial Loans | Cons-umer Loans | Mort-gage Loans | Secur-ities | Capital-ization Index | Lever-age Ratio | Risk-Based Capital Ratio |
|---|---|---|---|---|---|---|---|---|---|---|---|---|---|---|
| ▼ Titonka Savings Bank | Titonka | IA | **C+** | B- | C+ | 185.9 | 2.51 | 3.8 | 1.6 | 9.7 | 36.5 | **10.0** | 11.3 | 20.3 |
| TNB Bank | Tuscola | IL | **C+** | C | C | 87.3 | 7.20 | 4.2 | 1.6 | 8.0 | 16.1 | **10.0** | 12.7 | 21.3 |
| TNBANK | Oak Ridge | TN | **C** | C | C- | 231.4 | 3.95 | 4.3 | 1.4 | 20.5 | 11.8 | **5.5** | 9.1 | 11.4 |
| Today's Bank | Huntsville | AR | **C+** | C | D+ | 266.5 | 11.96 | 8.8 | 1.5 | 15.8 | 18.9 | **7.5** | 9.3 | 13.0 |
| Tolleson Private Bank | Dallas | TX | **A-** | B | B | 552.3 | 7.05 | 14.0 | 4.6 | 38.7 | 14.9 | **7.2** | 9.1 | 15.3 |
| Tomahawk Community Bank, SSB | Tomahawk | WI | **B** | B- | B- | 151.4 | 5.84 | 9.2 | 5.1 | 36.9 | 6.6 | **10.0** | 13.3 | 18.3 |
| Tompkins State Bank | Avon | IL | **B-** | B- | B- | 221.8 | 5.57 | 8.5 | 1.5 | 8.0 | 25.0 | **7.4** | 9.2 | 13.7 |
| Tompkins Trust Co. | Ithaca | NY | **B+** | B+ | B+ | 2063.7 | -2.25 | 4.8 | 1.6 | 26.6 | 24.4 | **7.2** | 9.2 | 14.1 |
| Torrington Savings Bank | Torrington | CT | **B** | B- | B- | 829.5 | 1.13 | 0.4 | 0.2 | 56.4 | 18.5 | **10.0** | 20.1 | 39.7 |
| Touchmark National Bank | Alpharetta | GA | **B** | B- | A- | 407.6 | 0.49 | 15.8 | 0.2 | 2.1 | 5.7 | **10.0** | 12.3 | 22.2 |
| ▲ Touchstone Bank | Prince George | VA | **B-** | C+ | B- | 468.1 | 9.81 | 6.4 | 1.0 | 23.5 | 12.9 | **7.9** | 9.6 | 14.2 |
| Towanda State Bank | Towanda | KS | **E+** | E+ | E+ | 10.3 | 0.35 | 0.7 | 8.1 | 55.8 | 14.1 | **4.4** | 6.4 | 13.1 |
| Tower Community Bank | Jasper | TN | **C+** | C- | D+ | 215.8 | 7.71 | 4.8 | 3.4 | 16.1 | 9.1 | **5.9** | 9.2 | 11.7 |
| Town & Country Bank | Salem | MO | **A-** | A- | A- | 526.3 | 4.75 | 2.5 | 3.5 | 34.5 | 16.7 | **10.0** | 11.5 | 18.1 |
| Town & Country Bank | Ravenna | NE | **A-** | A- | A- | 164.7 | -0.42 | 4.0 | 1.7 | 2.9 | 26.7 | **10.0** | 13.0 | 16.7 |
| Town & Country Bank | Las Vegas | NV | **B+** | B+ | A- | 173.7 | 0.56 | 3.7 | 0.0 | 3.5 | 0.1 | **10.0** | 12.7 | 18.0 |
| Town & Country Bank and Trust Co. | Bardstown | KY | **A** | A- | B+ | 311.2 | 2.22 | 4.5 | 1.1 | 23.2 | 18.3 | **10.0** | 12.5 | 17.0 |
| Town and Country Bank | Springfield | IL | **B-** | B- | B- | 810.2 | 4.11 | 10.6 | 0.6 | 16.3 | 17.7 | **7.6** | 9.7 | 13.0 |
| Town and Country Bank Midwest | Quincy | IL | **A-** | B+ | A- | 192.1 | 15.01 | 17.5 | 1.1 | 14.1 | 6.7 | **9.5** | 10.7 | 15.6 |
| Town Bank, N.A. | Hartland | WI | **B** | B | B | 2416.9 | 12.56 | 21.6 | 20.0 | 6.0 | 13.4 | **5.6** | 9.3 | 11.5 |
| ▲ Town Center Bank | New Lenox | IL | **C+** | C | C- | 106.8 | 2.84 | 11.8 | 2.3 | 1.7 | 15.8 | **7.1** | 11.0 | 12.6 |
| ▲ Town-Country National Bank | Camden | AL | **A-** | B | A- | 111.4 | 3.03 | 15.7 | 13.8 | 13.8 | 26.6 | **10.0** | 18.6 | 27.5 |
| TowneBank | Portsmouth | VA | **A-** | A- | A- | 11947.8 | 7.03 | 10.3 | 2.6 | 13.5 | 12.4 | **8.4** | 10.0 | 14.6 |
| Toyota Financial Savings Bank | Henderson | NV | **C** | C+ | B- | 1047.8 | 1.84 | 0.0 | 0.1 | 83.1 | 0.8 | **10.0** | 16.4 | 32.7 |
| TPNB Bank | Paris | MO | **B+** | B+ | B+ | 86.1 | 5.03 | 3.0 | 1.0 | 9.2 | 35.4 | **10.0** | 15.1 | 24.1 |
| Traders & Farmers Bank | Haleyville | AL | **B** | B | B | 366.4 | 2.15 | 3.8 | 4.4 | 19.0 | 47.6 | **10.0** | 16.3 | 29.4 |
| Tradition Capital Bank | Wayzata | MN | **C+** | B- | B | 911.7 | 16.89 | 11.2 | 0.8 | 12.6 | 12.9 | **5.8** | 9.8 | 11.6 |
| Traditional Bank, Inc. | Mount Sterling | KY | **A-** | A- | A- | 1663.1 | 9.21 | 5.4 | 0.4 | 23.5 | 24.6 | **8.6** | 10.0 | 14.4 |
| ▲ Traditions Bank | Cullman | AL | **B+** | B | B | 377.0 | 7.05 | 15.1 | 8.0 | 31.6 | 6.3 | **9.5** | 10.7 | 15.0 |
| Traditions First Bank | Erin | TN | **B-** | B- | B | 155.9 | 7.90 | 3.8 | 1.6 | 19.4 | 24.0 | **6.9** | 8.9 | 14.0 |
| ▲ TrailWest Bank | Lolo | MT | **B+** | B | B+ | 677.7 | 18.50 | 9.1 | 2.2 | 29.1 | 3.3 | **7.5** | 9.3 | 13.7 |
| TransPecos Banks, SSB | Pecos | TX | **C+** | B- | B | 232.7 | 3.86 | 26.4 | 2.1 | 17.1 | 16.3 | **6.1** | 8.2 | 11.9 |
| Transportation Alliance Bank, Inc. | Ogden | UT | **C** | C+ | B | 827.0 | 11.85 | 68.5 | 2.7 | 0.0 | 9.7 | **8.4** | 11.7 | 13.7 |
| Treynor State Bank | Treynor | IA | **D** | D+ | D- | 370.9 | -4.88 | 5.2 | 0.7 | 2.7 | 54.2 | **7.1** | 9.1 | 13.5 |
| Tri City National Bank | Oak Creek | WI | **A-** | B+ | B | 1467.1 | 4.37 | 2.4 | 0.3 | 11.0 | 26.1 | **10.0** | 11.6 | 18.0 |
| Tri Counties Bank | Chico | CA | **A** | A- | A- | 6469.4 | 1.87 | 3.9 | 1.3 | 8.4 | 20.6 | **10.0** | 11.5 | 15.0 |
| Tri Valley Bank | Talmage | NE | **C** | C | C | 51.9 | 9.41 | 9.2 | 1.2 | 11.6 | 2.5 | **4.4** | 8.1 | 10.7 |
| Tri-County Bank | Brown City | MI | **A-** | A- | A- | 319.4 | 7.35 | 7.7 | 1.4 | 9.3 | 12.5 | **10.0** | 12.4 | 16.5 |
| Tri-County Bank | Stuart | NE | **B-** | C+ | B- | 143.6 | 12.94 | 9.9 | 2.5 | 15.1 | 18.0 | **6.4** | 9.0 | 12.1 |
| Tri-County Bank & Trust Co. | Roachdale | IN | **B** | B | B | 205.3 | 3.81 | 3.6 | 4.4 | 14.6 | 42.5 | **10.0** | 12.1 | 25.8 |
| ▲ Tri-County Trust Co. | Glasgow | MO | **B-** | B | B | 58.3 | 0.71 | 6.0 | 6.5 | 25.6 | 23.0 | **10.0** | 12.3 | 15.8 |
| Tri-State Bank of Memphis | Memphis | TN | **C-** | C- | D+ | 85.6 | 3.95 | 7.6 | 3.4 | 8.8 | 20.2 | **9.4** | 10.6 | 17.2 |
| Tri-Valley Bank | Randolph | IA | **B-** | C+ | C | 60.9 | 4.92 | 6.8 | 1.6 | 11.5 | 25.1 | **10.0** | 12.0 | 18.3 |
| Triad Bank | Frontenac | MO | **C+** | C | B- | 382.9 | 6.17 | 15.0 | 0.3 | 16.4 | 6.4 | **6.1** | 9.6 | 11.9 |
| Triad Bank, N.A. | Tulsa | OK | **B** | B- | B+ | 153.3 | -2.86 | 13.5 | 3.0 | 37.0 | 0.0 | **9.8** | 10.9 | 19.8 |
| TriCentury Bank | De Soto | KS | **A-** | B+ | B | 102.5 | -0.90 | 12.4 | 1.0 | 19.4 | 0.0 | **10.0** | 11.9 | 16.9 |
| Trinity Bank, N.A. | Fort Worth | TX | **A-** | A | A | 309.1 | 20.17 | 31.7 | 0.2 | 5.1 | 22.9 | **10.0** | 11.9 | 21.1 |
| TriStar Bank | Dickson | TN | **C+** | C | B- | 308.1 | 2.59 | 5.6 | 9.7 | 21.4 | 14.6 | **5.6** | 8.4 | 11.4 |
| TriState Capital Bank | Pittsburgh | PA | **B-** | B- | B- | 7687.0 | 29.25 | 33.9 | 25.6 | 0.5 | 5.8 | **5.2** | 7.2 | 11.6 |
| Triumph Bank | Memphis | TN | **C+** | B- | B- | 837.1 | 6.26 | 19.5 | 0.8 | 20.1 | 17.9 | **6.3** | 8.8 | 12.0 |
| Triumph State Bank | Trimont | MN | **C+** | C+ | C+ | 74.4 | 12.14 | 8.4 | 4.0 | 1.7 | 11.4 | **8.2** | 9.8 | 14.3 |
| Troy Bank & Trust Co. | Troy | AL | **B+** | B+ | B | 898.9 | 2.62 | 11.1 | 2.8 | 16.0 | 24.1 | **10.0** | 11.1 | 17.1 |
| TruBank | Indianola | IA | **B-** | B | B | 312.1 | 2.02 | 6.6 | 0.9 | 11.2 | 17.7 | **9.4** | 10.6 | 14.9 |
| Truist Bank | Winston-Salem | NC | **B+** | B+ | B | 461256.0 | 110.55 | 15.9 | 11.4 | 13.2 | 16.2 | **6.3** | 14.5 | 12.0 |
| TruPoint Bank | Grundy | VA | **B-** | C | C- | 458.2 | 5.23 | 15.9 | 4.3 | 17.2 | 16.6 | **8.3** | 9.9 | 15.6 |
| ▲ Trust Bank | Lenox | GA | **C** | C | C | 38.1 | -2.19 | 3.9 | 6.9 | 18.1 | 5.3 | **8.9** | 10.3 | 16.9 |
| Trust Co. of Toledo, N.A. | Holland | OH | **U** | U | U | 4.3 | -4.00 | 0.0 | 0.0 | 0.0 | 70.4 | **10.0** | 68.2 | 474.7 |
| ▲ TrustBank | Olney | IL | **B+** | B+ | A- | 236.3 | 0.88 | 7.8 | 2.6 | 16.9 | 9.1 | **8.9** | 10.8 | 14.0 |
| ▲ TrustCo Bank | Glenville | NY | **A-** | B+ | B | 5220.3 | 5.26 | 0.4 | 0.2 | 69.0 | 11.4 | **8.5** | 10.0 | 19.7 |
| Trustmark National Bank | Jackson | MS | **B+** | B | B | 13495.9 | 1.60 | 11.0 | 1.3 | 12.7 | 17.4 | **7.7** | 10.4 | 13.1 |

| Asset Quality Index | Adjusted Non-Performing Loans as a % of Total Loans | Adjusted Non-Performing Loans as a % of Capital | Net Charge-Offs Avg Loans | Profitability Index | Net Income ($Mil) | Return on Assets (R.O.A.) | Return on Equity (R.O.E.) | Net Interest Spread | Overhead Efficiency Ratio | Liquidity Index | Liquidity Ratio | Hot Money Ratio | Stability Index |
|---|---|---|---|---|---|---|---|---|---|---|---|---|---|
| **6.9** | 3.27 | 7.5 | 1.01 | **1.8** | 0.2 | 0.12 | 1.09 | 2.87 | 78.5 | **3.6** | 45.4 | 18.3 | **6.5** |
| **8.5** | 0.42 | 2.1 | 0.01 | **2.2** | 0.2 | 0.23 | 1.77 | 3.32 | 84.0 | **3.0** | 41.9 | 21.0 | **6.8** |
| **4.2** | 1.97 | 13.5 | 0.00 | **3.6** | 1.2 | 0.52 | 5.98 | 3.76 | 81.8 | **1.4** | 13.1 | 25.1 | **5.3** |
| **4.8** | 0.80 | 5.4 | 0.01 | **4.3** | 2.5 | 1.05 | 11.47 | 4.20 | 77.7 | **1.1** | 26.5 | 38.9 | **5.0** |
| **8.0** | 0.01 | 0.1 | 0.02 | **9.2** | 14.2 | 2.60 | 28.40 | 3.03 | 44.4 | **4.7** | 23.4 | 5.3 | **7.7** |
| **7.5** | 0.48 | 2.4 | 0.03 | **4.4** | 1.2 | 0.86 | 6.38 | 4.21 | 75.7 | **4.3** | 16.8 | 7.2 | **7.0** |
| **6.2** | 0.18 | 1.3 | 0.05 | **4.2** | 2.0 | 0.94 | 8.79 | 3.45 | 71.1 | **2.5** | 14.6 | 13.0 | **6.7** |
| **7.6** | 0.87 | 6.9 | 0.07 | **8.1** | 31.7 | 1.54 | 20.90 | 3.20 | 68.5 | **4.0** | 3.5 | 6.7 | **6.9** |
| **9.7** | 0.70 | 2.0 | 0.04 | **4.5** | 8.2 | 0.99 | 4.91 | 2.62 | 75.3 | **2.9** | 37.1 | 19.3 | **8.4** |
| **4.8** | 1.86 | 5.8 | 0.25 | **6.4** | 5.3 | 1.27 | 10.66 | 2.78 | 51.1 | **0.6** | 14.7 | 59.1 | **7.7** |
| **5.7** | 0.65 | 4.0 | 0.01 | **4.0** | 3.3 | 0.72 | 7.13 | 4.17 | 80.1 | **2.7** | 19.8 | 15.8 | **4.8** |
| **0.3** | 4.26 | 67.4 | 0.97 | **0.0** | -0.2 | -2.04 | -27.42 | 4.09 | 123.5 | **3.6** | 14.9 | 10.9 | **1.8** |
| **6.5** | 0.10 | 2.2 | 0.07 | **3.6** | 1.1 | 0.58 | 5.94 | 4.11 | 83.2 | **1.4** | 12.3 | 22.6 | **4.5** |
| **7.5** | 0.55 | 3.1 | 0.03 | **6.7** | 8.3 | 1.60 | 12.82 | 4.10 | 63.9 | **3.1** | 10.6 | 13.0 | **9.2** |
| **7.3** | 0.12 | 0.6 | 0.00 | **7.8** | 2.6 | 1.57 | 12.32 | 4.12 | 52.1 | **2.8** | 22.2 | 15.5 | **8.3** |
| **4.0** | 4.89 | 12.3 | -0.02 | **9.0** | 3.2 | 1.88 | 14.32 | 4.29 | 55.1 | **4.8** | 33.0 | 8.2 | **8.3** |
| **8.4** | 0.74 | 3.1 | -0.01 | **5.7** | 3.6 | 1.15 | 9.19 | 4.13 | 71.6 | **4.8** | 21.9 | 4.5 | **8.6** |
| **5.8** | 0.52 | 3.1 | 0.22 | **5.0** | 8.3 | 1.03 | 10.13 | 3.62 | 66.7 | **1.9** | 15.4 | 15.1 | **6.6** |
| **5.7** | 0.15 | 7.1 | 0.03 | **9.2** | 4.1 | 2.15 | 19.59 | 4.16 | 53.8 | **2.8** | 31.5 | 18.0 | **7.9** |
| **6.5** | 0.17 | 1.1 | 0.08 | **4.6** | 19.4 | 0.86 | 6.99 | 3.16 | 63.5 | **4.0** | 18.7 | 7.4 | **8.5** |
| **5.7** | 0.30 | 1.6 | 0.05 | **3.9** | 2.2 | 2.20 | 18.26 | 3.71 | 92.6 | **1.3** | 12.6 | 27.1 | **7.2** |
| **5.8** | 1.50 | 5.0 | 0.32 | **9.3** | 2.3 | 2.13 | 11.54 | 5.30 | 56.4 | **1.6** | 34.1 | 34.8 | **9.4** |
| **7.1** | 0.36 | 1.5 | 0.04 | **6.4** | 138.8 | 1.24 | 9.04 | 3.52 | 71.5 | **2.1** | 15.1 | 14.3 | **9.9** |
| **9.9** | 0.46 | 1.6 | -0.01 | **2.1** | 1.4 | 0.14 | 0.82 | 1.18 | 81.4 | **0.5** | 11.7 | 38.2 | **8.5** |
| **6.1** | 3.19 | 9.7 | 0.05 | **4.6** | 0.8 | 0.91 | 6.09 | 3.29 | 66.3 | **4.0** | 32.7 | 12.7 | **8.0** |
| **8.5** | 0.72 | 3.1 | 0.12 | **4.0** | 2.8 | 0.77 | 4.93 | 3.82 | 72.8 | **3.0** | 47.1 | 24.9 | **7.7** |
| **7.0** | 0.12 | 0.6 | 0.04 | **3.8** | 6.9 | 0.84 | 9.33 | 3.42 | 66.2 | **1.5** | 17.6 | 13.5 | **6.7** |
| **7.8** | 0.52 | 3.2 | 0.06 | **6.5** | 24.4 | 1.54 | 15.09 | 3.31 | 53.8 | **1.6** | 14.6 | 17.3 | **10.0** |
| **5.6** | 0.69 | 4.2 | 0.61 | **6.7** | 4.7 | 1.29 | 12.45 | 5.85 | 64.3 | **1.2** | 13.9 | 18.6 | **6.2** |
| **8.7** | 0.00 | 1.3 | 0.00 | **4.3** | 1.3 | 0.83 | 9.01 | 3.64 | 73.6 | **1.7** | 27.0 | 26.8 | **6.0** |
| **7.3** | 0.20 | 1.6 | 0.03 | **6.2** | 9.1 | 1.42 | 15.49 | 3.73 | 59.4 | **2.2** | 18.0 | 15.6 | **7.9** |
| **4.9** | 0.09 | 7.7 | 2.01 | **3.7** | 1.4 | 0.60 | 6.76 | 5.21 | 68.6 | **1.3** | 13.9 | 5.6 | **4.8** |
| **3.2** | 1.56 | 9.1 | 2.49 | **4.3** | 3.8 | 0.51 | 3.76 | 7.67 | 66.8 | **0.8** | 21.3 | 37.8 | **9.1** |
| **4.4** | 2.11 | 6.4 | 0.62 | **0.6** | 2.2 | 0.59 | 6.22 | 3.10 | 123.2 | **2.3** | 47.6 | 29.2 | **3.5** |
| **5.4** | 1.98 | 6.2 | -0.01 | **6.1** | 18.7 | 1.30 | 11.45 | 3.92 | 67.8 | **5.7** | 24.2 | 1.7 | **9.2** |
| **5.6** | 0.50 | 1.9 | 0.01 | **7.9** | 95.0 | 1.48 | 10.27 | 4.50 | 58.9 | **4.8** | 20.7 | 5.3 | **10.0** |
| **8.2** | 0.00 | 0.0 | 0.00 | **7.9** | 0.8 | 1.70 | 19.41 | 3.55 | 49.4 | **0.8** | 16.3 | 34.6 | **4.3** |
| **7.2** | 0.76 | 4.2 | 0.02 | **8.3** | 5.1 | 1.63 | 13.62 | 4.66 | 57.7 | **3.9** | 16.6 | 9.3 | **7.9** |
| **7.4** | 0.24 | 0.9 | 0.02 | **5.0** | 1.4 | 1.03 | 11.38 | 4.43 | 69.9 | **3.5** | 20.4 | 11.8 | **5.5** |
| **7.0** | 1.88 | 6.1 | 0.63 | **4.3** | 2.0 | 0.94 | 7.61 | 3.36 | 66.5 | **5.9** | 61.1 | 10.5 | **7.3** |
| **5.3** | 1.46 | 6.8 | 0.46 | **4.9** | 0.7 | 1.20 | 9.72 | 4.02 | 67.9 | **0.8** | 21.8 | 38.3 | **7.6** |
| **2.0** | 9.38 | 22.0 | -0.02 | **2.9** | 0.4 | 0.45 | 3.42 | 3.98 | 86.9 | **3.1** | 23.2 | 14.1 | **5.7** |
| **7.5** | 0.30 | 0.9 | 0.03 | **3.6** | 0.4 | 0.61 | 4.99 | 4.09 | 81.0 | **2.6** | 28.4 | 16.8 | **5.7** |
| **4.5** | 1.21 | 4.8 | -0.01 | **5.5** | 4.0 | 1.07 | 11.46 | 3.72 | 58.8 | **1.5** | 11.7 | 5.9 | **6.1** |
| **3.9** | 0.87 | 6.9 | 0.68 | **6.7** | 2.6 | 1.55 | 13.58 | 4.94 | 63.2 | **4.5** | 5.4 | 3.8 | **8.4** |
| **8.6** | 0.00 | 0.0 | -0.01 | **6.6** | 1.3 | 1.29 | 11.17 | 3.63 | 54.2 | **1.9** | 21.1 | 21.0 | **6.1** |
| **8.6** | 0.25 | 1.1 | 0.28 | **7.2** | 4.0 | 1.48 | 11.49 | 3.81 | 46.2 | **4.9** | 51.1 | 13.1 | **8.0** |
| **6.2** | 0.26 | 2.6 | 0.02 | **4.2** | 2.3 | 0.77 | 9.28 | 3.90 | 74.7 | **1.2** | 10.8 | 27.7 | **5.1** |
| **6.8** | 0.00 | 0.0 | -0.03 | **4.2** | 58.5 | 0.88 | 12.42 | 1.99 | 54.5 | **1.3** | 11.8 | 16.4 | **5.4** |
| **4.3** | 1.52 | 11.4 | 0.05 | **4.1** | 6.5 | 0.82 | 8.86 | 2.77 | 71.7 | **0.8** | 20.0 | 35.3 | **6.2** |
| **4.5** | 1.24 | 5.1 | 0.11 | **4.8** | 0.7 | 0.88 | 8.84 | 4.08 | 68.1 | **4.5** | 31.9 | 10.0 | **5.3** |
| **6.0** | 1.98 | 7.6 | 0.19 | **5.4** | 9.5 | 1.03 | 8.88 | 3.57 | 66.0 | **1.8** | 21.6 | 22.3 | **7.8** |
| **7.7** | 0.36 | 2.0 | 0.00 | **4.5** | 2.8 | 0.92 | 8.00 | 3.68 | 69.6 | **1.4** | 13.1 | 26.0 | **6.7** |
| **6.1** | 0.29 | 1.6 | 0.22 | **7.0** | 3387.0 | 1.42 | 10.12 | 3.32 | 60.5 | **4.6** | 22.6 | 5.2 | **10.0** |
| **7.7** | 0.31 | 2.1 | -0.01 | **4.2** | 3.9 | 0.87 | 9.01 | 3.53 | 72.7 | **3.2** | 10.9 | 12.4 | **4.7** |
| **2.9** | 2.17 | 12.2 | -0.35 | **4.6** | 0.3 | 0.67 | 6.29 | 5.89 | 94.7 | **2.3** | 25.4 | 18.5 | **5.6** |
| **10.0** | na | 0.0 | na | **9.5** | 1.7 | 34.55 | 39.66 | 2.32 | 79.6 | **4.0** | na | 0.0 | **5.7** |
| **5.8** | 0.63 | 4.4 | 0.04 | **7.0** | 4.1 | 1.69 | 15.04 | 4.16 | 68.7 | **4.0** | 5.6 | 7.2 | **8.3** |
| **7.9** | 0.79 | 4.7 | 0.02 | **6.1** | 60.4 | 1.18 | 12.11 | 3.10 | 55.7 | **2.8** | 17.8 | 15.7 | **8.8** |
| **6.0** | 0.59 | 3.0 | 0.07 | **5.3** | 153.3 | 1.14 | 9.21 | 3.59 | 69.3 | **4.1** | 8.0 | 7.1 | **9.7** |

| Name | City | State | Rating | 2018 Rating | 2017 Rating | Total Assets ($Mil) | One Year Asset Growth | Asset Mix (As a % of Total Assets) Comm-ercial Loans | Cons-umer Loans | Mort-gage Loans | Secur-ities | Capital-ization Index | Lever-age Ratio | Risk-Based Capital Ratio |
|---|---|---|---|---|---|---|---|---|---|---|---|---|---|---|
| TrustTexas Bank, SSB | Cuero | TX | **B-** | B- | B- | 346.5 | 3.75 | 4.5 | 1.0 | 26.8 | 34.2 | **10.0** | 12.3 | 22.9 |
| Truxton Trust Co. | Nashville | TN | **A** | A | A- | 532.9 | 10.69 | 7.4 | 4.8 | 14.2 | 21.8 | **9.4** | 11.3 | 14.5 |
| TSB Bank | Lomira | WI | **A-** | B+ | B+ | 143.1 | 0.99 | 8.7 | 1.0 | 17.3 | 12.5 | **10.0** | 12.5 | 15.6 |
| Tucumcari Federal S&L Assn. | Tucumcari | NM | **C+** | C+ | C+ | 33.7 | 2.12 | 0.0 | 0.7 | 53.0 | 19.5 | **10.0** | 15.2 | 34.3 |
| ▲ Turbotville National Bank | Turbotville | PA | **B+** | B+ | A | 150.4 | 5.70 | 6.0 | 1.7 | 28.1 | 17.5 | **10.0** | 16.6 | 23.6 |
| Turtle Mountain State Bank | Belcourt | ND | **C** | D+ | D+ | 35.8 | 7.14 | 25.4 | 6.1 | 3.8 | 7.9 | **8.3** | 9.9 | 37.0 |
| Tustin Community Bank | Tustin | CA | **B** | B+ | B+ | 74.5 | -2.22 | 3.5 | 43.8 | 5.7 | 0.0 | **10.0** | 14.6 | 18.7 |
| Twin City Bank | Longview | WA | **B-** | C+ | C | 52.0 | 2.13 | 13.6 | 0.2 | 17.3 | 0.0 | **9.3** | 10.5 | 15.8 |
| ▲ Twin River Bank | Lewiston | ID | **B+** | B- | B- | 105.8 | 5.77 | 14.4 | 3.4 | 11.9 | 3.3 | **6.8** | 8.8 | 16.0 |
| Twin Valley Bank | West Alexandria | OH | **C+** | C+ | B- | 81.1 | 20.58 | 11.1 | 2.5 | 18.5 | 18.8 | **7.6** | 9.4 | 13.5 |
| Two Rivers Bank | Blair | NE | **B+** | B | B | 141.7 | 0.94 | 6.2 | 1.7 | 15.3 | 27.3 | **10.0** | 13.3 | 20.2 |
| Two Rivers Bank & Trust | Burlington | IA | **B-** | B- | C+ | 852.5 | 2.72 | 17.2 | 1.2 | 18.2 | 10.0 | **5.9** | 9.4 | 11.7 |
| U.S. Bank N.A. | Minneapolis | MN | **B** | B- | B- | 486004.2 | 5.77 | 16.2 | 12.0 | 16.0 | 24.9 | **6.4** | 8.4 | 12.3 |
| U.S. Bank Trust Co., N.A. | Portland | OR | **U** | U | U | 19.1 | 5.07 | 0.0 | 0.0 | 0.0 | 0.0 | **10.0** | 101. | 498.8 |
| U.S. Bank Trust N.A. | Wilmington | DE | **U** | U | U | 659.2 | 3.86 | 0.0 | 0.0 | 0.0 | 0.0 | **10.0** | 98.5 | 492.6 |
| U.S. Bank Trust N.A. SD | Sioux Falls | SD | **U** | U | U | 103.9 | 9.58 | 0.0 | 0.0 | 0.0 | 0.0 | **10.0** | 99.9 | 406.4 |
| U.S. Century Bank | Doral | FL | **B-** | B- | C+ | 1312.3 | 13.59 | 4.4 | 0.1 | 20.6 | 13.9 | **7.2** | 9.2 | 12.8 |
| UBank | Jellico | TN | **B** | B | B | 66.8 | 3.10 | 6.2 | 9.0 | 18.6 | 14.7 | **10.0** | 14.0 | 20.9 |
| UBank | Huntington | TX | **B+** | B- | B- | 245.5 | -3.19 | 12.8 | 2.7 | 20.8 | 7.5 | **10.0** | 11.0 | 15.4 |
| UBS Bank USA | Salt Lake City | UT | **A** | A | A- | 63780.7 | 7.44 | 8.6 | 36.2 | 27.1 | 9.1 | **9.4** | 10.6 | 35.7 |
| Uinta Bank | Mountain View | WY | **B-** | B- | B- | 220.1 | 14.49 | 10.8 | 0.6 | 1.6 | 62.1 | **6.0** | 8.0 | 20.8 |
| ▲ Ulster Savings Bank | Kingston | NY | **C+** | C- | C- | 956.4 | 6.71 | 4.2 | 2.6 | 45.6 | 7.1 | **10.0** | 11.0 | 15.9 |
| Ultima Bank Minnesota | Winger | MN | **C+** | C | C | 188.7 | 6.80 | 11.5 | 1.5 | 6.3 | 0.0 | **7.2** | 10.1 | 12.7 |
| UMB Bank & Trust, N.A. | Saint Louis | MO | **U** | U | U | 3.0 | 0.20 | 0.0 | 0.0 | 0.0 | 0.0 | **10.0** | 100. | 103.0 |
| UMB Bank, N.A. | Kansas City | MO | **B-** | B- | B- | 26357.6 | 13.92 | 23.0 | 1.4 | 3.6 | 32.4 | **6.2** | 8.6 | 11.9 |
| Umpqua Bank | Roseburg | OR | **B+** | B+ | B+ | 28816.7 | 7.11 | 11.6 | 1.4 | 14.9 | 9.8 | **7.9** | 10.2 | 13.3 |
| UNB Bank | Mount Carmel | PA | **C-** | D+ | D+ | 145.8 | 3.36 | 2.3 | 1.2 | 45.1 | 25.4 | **8.1** | 9.7 | 22.9 |
| UniBank | Lynnwood | WA | **A-** | B+ | B+ | 347.4 | 13.96 | 5.2 | 0.0 | 0.0 | 13.9 | **10.0** | 15.3 | 19.1 |
| UniBank for Savings | Whitinsville | MA | **B-** | B- | B- | 1767.7 | 0.27 | 4.0 | 24.5 | 25.3 | 13.9 | **6.8** | 8.8 | 13.0 |
| ▼ UNICO Bank | Mineral Point | MO | **C** | C+ | B+ | 338.3 | 12.44 | 5.6 | 3.6 | 29.5 | 11.9 | **5.9** | 7.9 | 12.2 |
| Unified Bank | Martins Ferry | OH | **B+** | B | B | 684.9 | 15.65 | 14.8 | 1.4 | 13.4 | 27.6 | **8.6** | 10.1 | 13.8 |
| Unified Trust Co., N.A. | Lexington | KY | **U** | U | U | 19.5 | 9.72 | 0.0 | 0.0 | 0.0 | 26.8 | **10.0** | 61.5 | 53.7 |
| Union Bank | Lake Odessa | MI | **C** | C | C | 207.0 | 10.55 | 9.2 | 0.9 | 8.2 | 7.1 | **5.1** | 9.1 | 11.1 |
| Union Bank | Greenville | NC | **B** | B | B | 821.6 | 10.23 | 5.7 | 0.5 | 16.0 | 20.0 | **6.9** | 8.9 | 13.5 |
| Union Bank | Halliday | ND | **C+** | C+ | C+ | 159.6 | 3.99 | 4.3 | 5.6 | 11.6 | 17.3 | **8.6** | 10.0 | 14.9 |
| ▼ Union Bank | Jamestown | TN | **C+** | B- | B- | 196.7 | 0.39 | 7.0 | 4.7 | 20.4 | 24.2 | **10.0** | 12.6 | 23.1 |
| Union Bank | Morrisville | VT | **B** | B | B | 872.3 | 8.41 | 5.5 | 0.4 | 21.6 | 10.1 | **6.1** | 8.1 | 13.0 |
| ▲ Union Bank & Trust Co. | Monticello | AR | **B-** | C- | D+ | 208.0 | -1.50 | 15.4 | 5.2 | 19.0 | 15.6 | **9.8** | 10.9 | 14.9 |
| ▲ Union Bank & Trust Co. | Livingston | TN | **B+** | B- | B | 85.8 | 4.57 | 7.6 | 6.0 | 28.5 | 19.4 | **10.0** | 12.2 | 20.9 |
| Union Bank and Trust Co. | Minneapolis | MN | **B-** | B- | B- | 153.8 | 2.25 | 7.8 | 0.6 | 0.1 | 23.2 | **7.3** | 9.2 | 22.3 |
| ▲ Union Bank and Trust Co. | Lincoln | NE | **A-** | B+ | B+ | 4583.4 | 10.45 | 15.1 | 14.2 | 3.2 | 12.9 | **8.7** | 11.0 | 13.9 |
| Union Bank Co. | Columbus Grove | OH | **B** | B- | B- | 878.0 | 5.90 | 7.0 | 1.1 | 16.9 | 20.9 | **7.5** | 9.3 | 13.3 |
| Union Bank of Blair | Blair | WI | **C** | C | C- | 105.6 | -2.67 | 15.5 | 2.3 | 11.0 | 7.7 | **10.0** | 14.8 | 20.5 |
| ▲ Union Bank of Mena | Mena | AR | **B+** | B | B+ | 266.9 | 3.06 | 5.2 | 12.8 | 30.8 | 25.0 | **9.0** | 10.4 | 18.9 |
| Union Bank, Inc. | Middlebourne | WV | **B+** | B | B | 263.1 | 2.18 | 5.9 | 2.8 | 17.3 | 42.1 | **7.9** | 9.6 | 20.5 |
| Union Banking Co. | West Mansfield | OH | **B+** | B+ | B+ | 56.8 | 0.50 | 0.2 | 0.3 | 5.3 | 85.2 | **10.0** | 11.0 | 43.3 |
| Union County Savings Bank | Elizabeth | NJ | **C+** | B- | B- | 1789.7 | 1.73 | 0.0 | 0.1 | 5.3 | 75.5 | **10.0** | 13.9 | 52.7 |
| Union Federal S&L Assn. | Kewanee | IL | **B-** | B- | B- | 151.3 | 1.99 | 2.2 | 0.1 | 47.1 | 10.8 | **10.0** | 14.7 | 25.7 |
| Union National Bank | Elgin | IL | **B+** | A- | B+ | 307.5 | 5.52 | 9.7 | 0.0 | 2.9 | 1.5 | **10.0** | 12.1 | 18.5 |
| ▲ Union S&L Assn. | Connersville | IN | **B-** | C+ | C+ | 168.0 | 3.20 | 1.4 | 12.9 | 42.7 | 0.3 | **9.0** | 10.3 | 15.6 |
| Union Savings Bank | Danbury | CT | **B+** | B | B- | 2276.6 | 5.42 | 3.3 | 0.2 | 29.0 | 10.2 | **10.0** | 12.6 | 17.6 |
| UNION Savings BANK | Freeport | IL | **C** | C | C- | 154.5 | -0.29 | 5.7 | 3.1 | 31.9 | 19.4 | **9.2** | 10.5 | 16.9 |
| Union Savings Bank | Cincinnati | OH | **A-** | B+ | B | 3079.6 | 11.95 | 0.4 | 0.8 | 68.2 | 0.2 | **8.1** | 9.7 | 16.1 |
| Union State Bank | Pell City | AL | **D+** | D- | D- | 211.9 | -2.32 | 4.5 | 1.4 | 5.5 | 25.9 | **5.7** | 7.7 | 13.3 |
| Union State Bank | Greenfield | IA | **C-** | C- | B | 81.8 | 6.68 | 3.6 | 1.6 | 18.1 | 10.3 | **8.4** | 10.2 | 13.7 |
| Union State Bank | Winterset | IA | **C+** | C+ | C+ | 92.9 | 3.11 | 5.1 | 2.4 | 29.2 | 15.5 | **6.7** | 8.7 | 14.9 |
| Union State Bank | Arkansas City | KS | **B** | B | B | 337.4 | 4.18 | 7.3 | 2.6 | 16.1 | 16.0 | **7.6** | 9.4 | 13.7 |
| Union State Bank | Clay Center | KS | **B-** | B- | C+ | 146.7 | 1.34 | 2.6 | 0.9 | 11.1 | 45.8 | **10.0** | 11.4 | 19.4 |
| Union State Bank | Olsburg | KS | **C+** | B | B | 32.0 | -1.45 | 12.2 | 4.4 | 3.9 | 16.5 | **10.0** | 13.1 | 27.0 |
| Union State Bank | Uniontown | KS | **C** | D+ | D+ | 49.9 | -1.39 | 7.1 | 4.5 | 26.6 | 11.2 | **6.5** | 8.6 | 12.8 |

| Asset Quality Index | Adjusted Non-Performing Loans as a % of Total Loans | Adjusted Non-Performing Loans as a % of Capital | Net Charge-Offs Avg Loans | Profitability Index | Net Income ($Mil) | Return on Assets (R.O.A.) | Return on Equity (R.O.E.) | Net Interest Spread | Overhead Efficiency Ratio | Liquidity Index | Liquidity Ratio | Hot Money Ratio | Stability Index |
|---|---|---|---|---|---|---|---|---|---|---|---|---|---|
| **7.8** | 0.16 | 0.7 | 0.13 | **2.9** | 2.3 | 0.69 | 5.72 | 3.56 | 92.2 | **4.4** | 43.8 | 13.8 | **7.0** |
| **8.5** | 0.19 | 0.6 | 0.00 | **8.7** | 8.9 | 1.78 | 15.94 | 3.32 | 58.5 | **5.1** | 30.9 | 2.8 | **8.2** |
| **5.8** | 2.10 | 12.7 | -0.03 | **6.4** | 1.7 | 1.20 | 10.12 | 3.76 | 58.8 | **1.3** | 16.2 | 20.2 | **7.3** |
| **6.6** | 2.06 | 10.8 | -0.02 | **2.3** | 0.1 | 0.23 | 1.53 | 3.59 | 90.2 | **0.7** | 14.8 | 46.8 | **6.5** |
| **5.1** | 2.93 | 10.1 | 0.06 | **6.6** | 2.1 | 1.44 | 8.61 | 3.49 | 47.1 | **2.4** | 31.1 | 19.9 | **8.7** |
| **5.7** | 5.84 | 3.5 | 0.41 | **5.5** | 0.5 | 1.48 | 15.65 | 3.80 | 69.9 | **4.2** | 62.7 | 17.8 | **4.0** |
| **6.7** | 0.06 | 0.3 | 0.84 | **4.9** | 0.7 | 0.93 | 6.54 | 6.19 | 73.6 | **0.8** | 19.3 | 49.3 | **6.8** |
| **6.4** | 0.96 | 0.0 | 0.00 | **4.8** | 0.5 | 0.95 | 9.21 | 5.08 | 78.9 | **3.0** | 10.4 | 13.8 | **6.1** |
| **7.6** | 0.00 | 1.2 | 0.00 | **7.7** | 2.0 | 1.94 | 22.73 | 4.59 | 56.7 | **5.5** | 40.1 | 6.8 | **5.5** |
| **6.2** | 0.39 | 2.7 | 0.52 | **3.2** | 0.5 | 0.64 | 6.46 | 3.96 | 78.8 | **2.8** | 13.7 | 15.0 | **4.7** |
| **8.7** | 0.11 | 1.3 | 0.03 | **4.8** | 1.8 | 1.25 | 9.45 | 3.79 | 71.1 | **1.8** | 19.2 | 12.5 | **7.4** |
| **5.1** | 1.19 | 7.1 | 0.10 | **4.7** | 7.3 | 0.88 | 8.72 | 3.57 | 71.9 | **4.2** | 9.1 | 6.7 | **6.9** |
| **4.8** | 1.12 | 4.9 | 0.49 | **7.5** | 6975.7 | 1.50 | 14.38 | 3.14 | 55.1 | **4.6** | 31.6 | 3.8 | **9.9** |
| **10.0** | na | 0.0 | na | **10.0** | 0.9 | 4.87 | 4.85 | 6.67 | 17.2 | **4.0** | na | 0.0 | **6.3** |
| **9.2** | na | 0.0 | na | **9.8** | 25.2 | 3.89 | 3.97 | 2.32 | 22.1 | **4.0** | na | 0.0 | **7.0** |
| **10.0** | na | 0.0 | na | **9.5** | 9.2 | 9.24 | 9.37 | 2.24 | 20.7 | **4.0** | na | 0.0 | **7.0** |
| **8.6** | 0.44 | 1.4 | -0.12 | **3.9** | 10.4 | 0.84 | 6.73 | 3.34 | 69.3 | **1.8** | 18.8 | 22.2 | **9.0** |
| **6.9** | 0.14 | 1.7 | 0.27 | **5.1** | 0.7 | 1.06 | 7.54 | 4.76 | 74.1 | **1.0** | 18.2 | 32.5 | **7.0** |
| **6.0** | 1.04 | 4.5 | 0.30 | **4.7** | 2.0 | 0.82 | 7.22 | 4.83 | 82.1 | **3.6** | 10.8 | 10.7 | **7.1** |
| **6.8** | 0.06 | 0.5 | 0.00 | **9.4** | 1001.4 | 1.74 | 15.38 | 2.79 | 16.3 | **3.3** | 24.5 | 0.0 | **9.9** |
| **7.0** | 0.00 | 1.4 | 0.03 | **4.4** | 2.0 | 0.95 | 11.39 | 2.46 | 54.0 | **1.8** | 38.1 | 28.7 | **4.8** |
| **4.1** | 2.37 | 12.4 | 0.06 | **4.1** | 6.8 | 0.75 | 6.69 | 3.50 | 79.6 | **2.0** | 11.1 | 15.8 | **6.3** |
| **5.2** | 0.34 | 2.4 | 0.05 | **9.9** | 4.1 | 2.26 | 21.82 | 5.09 | 55.0 | **0.7** | 3.3 | 31.2 | **8.0** |
| **10.0** | na | 0.0 | na | **2.7** | 0.0 | 0.73 | 0.73 | 5.56 | 99.9 | **4.0** | 0.0 | 0.0 | **7.0** |
| **8.1** | 0.42 | 2.4 | 0.27 | **4.6** | 263.7 | 1.12 | 12.17 | 3.31 | 67.7 | **5.1** | 25.5 | 3.9 | **7.1** |
| **6.3** | 0.20 | 1.5 | 0.28 | **6.8** | 370.9 | 1.33 | 8.27 | 3.84 | 58.9 | **2.6** | 14.2 | 11.5 | **10.0** |
| **9.4** | 0.01 | 0.3 | 0.01 | **2.1** | 0.4 | 0.28 | 2.94 | 2.59 | 87.4 | **3.1** | 25.5 | 14.5 | **5.4** |
| **7.1** | 0.29 | 1.4 | -0.03 | **9.0** | 5.9 | 1.85 | 12.56 | 4.23 | 53.6 | **1.2** | 23.2 | 29.3 | **8.5** |
| **4.4** | 1.25 | 9.1 | 0.40 | **3.3** | 9.8 | 0.54 | 6.34 | 3.01 | 71.6 | **4.0** | 14.7 | 8.8 | **7.1** |
| **1.9** | 3.27 | 23.8 | 0.16 | **3.0** | 1.6 | 0.49 | 5.61 | 3.47 | 85.3 | **1.5** | 16.1 | 25.2 | **4.8** |
| **7.0** | 0.33 | 2.2 | 0.17 | **7.0** | 9.6 | 1.51 | 14.36 | 3.85 | 54.3 | **4.3** | 25.7 | 8.3 | **6.9** |
| **10.0** | na | 0.0 | na | **10.0** | 5.9 | 42.61 | 53.62 | 2.09 | 82.4 | **4.0** | 74.8 | 0.0 | **6.5** |
| **1.5** | 5.09 | 25.3 | -0.18 | **4.0** | 1.4 | 0.74 | 7.47 | 4.45 | 81.5 | **4.4** | 16.8 | 6.0 | **5.1** |
| **6.9** | 0.11 | 1.6 | 0.00 | **4.6** | 7.2 | 0.92 | 8.68 | 3.81 | 69.0 | **1.6** | 22.5 | 17.1 | **6.6** |
| **5.7** | 0.81 | 4.4 | 0.12 | **3.7** | 0.9 | 0.60 | 5.70 | 4.02 | 78.4 | **4.3** | 19.2 | 7.0 | **6.0** |
| **3.1** | 8.11 | 22.5 | 0.51 | **2.3** | 0.4 | 0.20 | 1.60 | 3.57 | 89.7 | **1.7** | 34.4 | 34.7 | **5.8** |
| **5.4** | 0.66 | 5.7 | 0.06 | **6.6** | 11.1 | 1.36 | 16.22 | 4.02 | 66.4 | **3.6** | 18.3 | 9.8 | **6.2** |
| **5.2** | 1.19 | 5.6 | 0.03 | **7.2** | 3.7 | 1.74 | 16.75 | 3.97 | 60.4 | **1.1** | 15.8 | 27.3 | **7.1** |
| **5.2** | 1.74 | 8.0 | 0.50 | **10.0** | 1.8 | 2.20 | 16.59 | 5.74 | 51.1 | **3.4** | 25.8 | 13.5 | **8.6** |
| **9.4** | 0.00 | 0.0 | 0.00 | **4.2** | 1.2 | 0.83 | 9.18 | 3.11 | 79.0 | **7.7** | 72.4 | 0.8 | **5.1** |
| **6.0** | 0.47 | 3.2 | 0.09 | **8.1** | 64.0 | 1.48 | 13.49 | 3.55 | 60.2 | **1.5** | 14.6 | 14.9 | **9.9** |
| **6.3** | 0.44 | 1.6 | -0.01 | **5.5** | 10.0 | 1.16 | 9.31 | 3.93 | 70.9 | **3.4** | 24.3 | 12.1 | **8.6** |
| **1.5** | 9.22 | 28.1 | 0.49 | **6.2** | 1.2 | 1.13 | 7.66 | 3.69 | 52.9 | **0.9** | 18.5 | 24.1 | **6.3** |
| **5.9** | 0.72 | 3.3 | 0.17 | **8.9** | 5.4 | 2.04 | 19.52 | 4.44 | 57.2 | **2.5** | 20.7 | 17.3 | **8.1** |
| **6.4** | 0.77 | 2.6 | 0.01 | **6.8** | 4.4 | 1.70 | 13.88 | 3.88 | 54.9 | **5.5** | 33.9 | 4.0 | **8.2** |
| **10.0** | 0.23 | 0.7 | 0.00 | **3.9** | 0.5 | 0.87 | 6.63 | 2.98 | 64.1 | **1.4** | 18.0 | 26.6 | **8.1** |
| **9.4** | 0.94 | 0.2 | 0.00 | **2.2** | 3.7 | 0.21 | 1.49 | 0.71 | 59.0 | **4.0** | 107.9 | 63.1 | **9.2** |
| **6.8** | 1.31 | 4.6 | 0.05 | **3.4** | 0.8 | 0.53 | 3.58 | 3.44 | 77.7 | **3.3** | 23.8 | 13.1 | **7.6** |
| **7.1** | 0.38 | 2.0 | -0.02 | **4.5** | 2.7 | 0.87 | 7.17 | 2.91 | 61.1 | **0.6** | 11.3 | 48.6 | **7.6** |
| **4.0** | 1.67 | 9.6 | 0.06 | **4.4** | 1.4 | 0.83 | 8.12 | 3.71 | 72.6 | **1.2** | 10.6 | 27.2 | **6.1** |
| **6.0** | 1.28 | 6.3 | 0.06 | **4.9** | 22.2 | 1.01 | 8.21 | 3.59 | 68.9 | **4.1** | 10.4 | 7.6 | **9.3** |
| **5.5** | 0.68 | 5.0 | 0.13 | **2.8** | 0.6 | 0.37 | 3.66 | 3.41 | 88.1 | **4.4** | 28.2 | 8.6 | **5.1** |
| **6.6** | 0.71 | 3.9 | -0.06 | **8.6** | 59.2 | 2.05 | 18.72 | 2.77 | 49.4 | **0.9** | 9.6 | 33.2 | **10.0** |
| **3.9** | 3.19 | 14.2 | -0.09 | **2.8** | 1.2 | 0.59 | 8.19 | 3.59 | 89.1 | **5.2** | 31.1 | 4.9 | **1.9** |
| **2.2** | 0.35 | 1.8 | -0.01 | **6.1** | 1.1 | 1.38 | 8.83 | 4.55 | 65.2 | **0.8** | 10.4 | 29.7 | **8.7** |
| **7.6** | 0.00 | 0.0 | 0.03 | **4.1** | 1.0 | 1.04 | 12.06 | 3.85 | 80.1 | **2.6** | 20.2 | 16.3 | **4.9** |
| **7.5** | 0.03 | 0.1 | 0.04 | **4.0** | 2.7 | 0.81 | 6.72 | 3.63 | 77.9 | **2.0** | 20.1 | 19.5 | **7.7** |
| **5.2** | 4.73 | 11.5 | -0.02 | **3.5** | 1.0 | 0.66 | 5.70 | 2.87 | 70.3 | **1.3** | 11.3 | 20.9 | **6.2** |
| **3.7** | 17.82 | 26.8 | 1.98 | **1.0** | -0.5 | -1.41 | -9.63 | 3.07 | 70.5 | **5.5** | 46.1 | 7.9 | **6.8** |
| **5.7** | 0.62 | 4.9 | 0.18 | **4.5** | 0.5 | 0.91 | 10.60 | 5.14 | 77.6 | **3.3** | 12.8 | 12.1 | **4.3** |

| Name | City | State | Rating | 2018 Rating | 2017 Rating | Total Assets ($Mil) | One Year Asset Growth | Asset Mix (As a % of Total Assets) Comm-ercial Loans | Cons-umer Loans | Mort-gage Loans | Secur-ities | Capital-ization Index | Lever-age Ratio | Risk-Based Capital Ratio |
|---|---|---|---|---|---|---|---|---|---|---|---|---|---|---|
| ▲ Union State Bank of Browns Valley | Browns Valley | MN | B- | C+ | B- | 23.8 | 5.20 | 7.1 | 1.9 | 0.6 | 8.0 | 10.0 | 11.5 | 18.9 |
| Union State Bank of Everest | Everest | KS | B- | C+ | B | 308.9 | -1.90 | 6.4 | 2.7 | 18.2 | 24.5 | 9.4 | 10.6 | 15.9 |
| Union State Bank of Fargo | Fargo | ND | B- | B- | B- | 109.9 | 0.92 | 9.3 | 5.1 | 23.9 | 5.3 | 8.8 | 10.2 | 14.0 |
| ▼ Union State Bank of Hazen | Hazen | ND | C | B- | B+ | 153.6 | 6.69 | 4.5 | 5.1 | 13.2 | 26.8 | 8.2 | 9.8 | 14.9 |
| Union State Bank of West Salem | West Salem | WI | B- | B- | C+ | 89.6 | 1.16 | 6.5 | 4.9 | 24.7 | 16.1 | 10.0 | 11.7 | 16.3 |
| ▲ Unison Bank | Jamestown | ND | B | B+ | B+ | 336.9 | 10.92 | 2.5 | 9.4 | 19.7 | 14.2 | 8.6 | 10.1 | 13.9 |
| United Bank | Atmore | AL | B | B- | B- | 711.5 | 11.55 | 17.6 | 2.9 | 10.8 | 19.5 | 7.9 | 9.6 | 14.2 |
| United Bank | Springdale | AR | B+ | B+ | B+ | 202.2 | 3.88 | 9.5 | 1.4 | 33.5 | 2.0 | 10.0 | 11.9 | 15.9 |
| United Bank | Zebulon | GA | A | A | A- | 1510.8 | 8.72 | 3.7 | 2.3 | 11.5 | 26.2 | 8.4 | 10.0 | 18.8 |
| United Bank | Vienna | VA | B | B | B | 19644.6 | 2.06 | 8.0 | 5.9 | 18.6 | 12.3 | 8.8 | 11.3 | 14.0 |
| United Bank & Trust | Marysville | KS | A- | A- | A- | 628.8 | 0.20 | 7.0 | 1.7 | 8.0 | 13.3 | 10.0 | 11.8 | 15.8 |
| ▼ United Bank & Trust N.A. | Marshalltown | IA | B+ | A- | A- | 100.5 | -7.20 | 4.5 | 0.8 | 9.1 | 32.9 | 8.2 | 9.8 | 14.3 |
| United Bank and Trust Co. | Hampton | IA | A | A- | A- | 170.5 | 5.89 | 4.9 | 3.3 | 11.5 | 28.3 | 10.0 | 15.1 | 24.8 |
| United Bank of El Paso del Norte | El Paso | TX | C | C+ | B- | 236.1 | -3.89 | 17.3 | 0.5 | 3.2 | 8.0 | 9.5 | 11.8 | 14.6 |
| United Bank of Iowa | Ida Grove | IA | A- | A- | B+ | 1742.6 | 10.62 | 3.7 | 3.0 | 7.0 | 19.1 | 8.9 | 10.3 | 14.1 |
| ▲ United Bank of Michigan | Grand Rapids | MI | C+ | C- | C | 695.2 | 5.15 | 3.7 | 1.3 | 10.7 | 0.5 | 7.1 | 10.3 | 12.6 |
| United Bank of Philadelphia | Philadelphia | PA | E- | E- | E- | 49.4 | -1.75 | 10.0 | 1.3 | 8.0 | 8.5 | 3.7 | 5.7 | 11.9 |
| United Bank of Union | Union | MO | C | C- | C- | 370.7 | -0.52 | 13.9 | 0.9 | 16.9 | 16.6 | 8.6 | 10.7 | 13.9 |
| United Bankers' Bank | Bloomington | MN | B- | B- | B- | 788.0 | -13.72 | 9.5 | 0.5 | 1.2 | 0.7 | 10.0 | 12.7 | 15.2 |
| United Business Bank | Walnut Creek | CA | A- | B+ | B+ | 1992.8 | 34.85 | 7.9 | 0.1 | 6.9 | 6.0 | 9.7 | 11.0 | 14.8 |
| United Citizens Bank & Trust Co. | Campbellsburg | KY | B+ | B | B | 111.8 | 2.29 | 1.8 | 1.7 | 23.7 | 15.3 | 10.0 | 12.9 | 21.6 |
| United Citizens Bank of Southern Kentucky | Columbia | KY | A- | B+ | A- | 173.7 | 8.71 | 9.9 | 5.6 | 32.2 | 7.4 | 10.0 | 12.2 | 16.8 |
| United Community Bank | Blairsville | GA | A- | A- | B+ | 12887.1 | 2.70 | 14.8 | 1.0 | 11.1 | 19.9 | 10.0 | 11.6 | 15.5 |
| ▲ United Community Bank | Milford | IA | B | B- | B | 210.0 | -7.41 | 7.8 | 1.3 | 12.0 | 1.5 | 6.9 | 9.6 | 12.4 |
| United Community Bank | Chatham | IL | B- | B | B | 2663.2 | 28.19 | 10.7 | 1.9 | 9.4 | 25.5 | 6.5 | 8.5 | 12.9 |
| ▲ United Community Bank | Raceland | LA | C+ | C- | D+ | 535.0 | -0.97 | 19.9 | 0.6 | 11.1 | 3.4 | 10.0 | 15.0 | 18.6 |
| United Community Bank | Perham | MN | B+ | B | B | 259.8 | 6.19 | 12.5 | 3.4 | 10.2 | 28.0 | 10.0 | 11.1 | 17.9 |
| ▲ United Community Bank of North Dakota | Leeds | ND | B | B- | B+ | 355.8 | -7.97 | 16.2 | 1.6 | 4.4 | 12.0 | 10.0 | 11.7 | 16.0 |
| ▲ United Community Bank of W Kentucky | Morganfield | KY | A | A- | A | 272.9 | 4.13 | 11.6 | 5.6 | 17.5 | 24.5 | 10.0 | 13.8 | 20.6 |
| United Cumberland Bank | Whitley City | KY | B- | C+ | B | 297.6 | 3.60 | 7.9 | 11.3 | 27.6 | 19.5 | 10.0 | 13.4 | 23.5 |
| ▲ United Farmers State Bank | Adams | MN | B | B+ | A | 160.1 | 4.17 | 5.8 | 1.0 | 4.4 | 3.4 | 7.6 | 11.3 | 13.0 |
| United Fidelity Bank, FSB | Evansville | IN | B+ | B+ | B+ | 968.8 | 21.36 | 1.0 | 0.1 | 9.1 | 59.1 | 6.7 | 8.7 | 26.8 |
| United Midwest Savings Bank, N.A. | De Graff | OH | C- | D+ | D | 293.5 | 5.40 | 23.5 | 17.7 | 11.4 | 0.1 | 9.3 | 10.6 | 16.5 |
| United Minnesota Bank | New London | MN | C | D+ | C | 33.4 | 8.65 | 11.7 | 9.9 | 27.8 | 3.3 | 5.2 | 7.2 | 11.9 |
| United Mississippi Bank | Natchez | MS | C+ | C+ | B- | 350.1 | -2.11 | 9.5 | 3.6 | 13.5 | 16.5 | 9.0 | 10.5 | 14.1 |
| United National Bank | Cairo | GA | B | B | B | 216.5 | -3.66 | 13.8 | 3.7 | 15.0 | 6.2 | 10.0 | 14.7 | 20.1 |
| United Orient Bank | New York | NY | B | B | B | 82.9 | -9.10 | 1.3 | 0.0 | 20.9 | 2.4 | 10.0 | 16.5 | 24.0 |
| United Pacific Bank | City of Industry | CA | B | B | B | 149.4 | 6.91 | 2.1 | 0.0 | 0.3 | 0.2 | 10.0 | 16.8 | 21.9 |
| ▲ United Prairie Bank | Mountain Lake | MN | C+ | C+ | B- | 616.3 | 2.82 | 12.4 | 0.7 | 5.1 | 12.3 | 5.9 | 9.8 | 11.7 |
| United Republic Bank | Elkhorn | NE | D+ | C- | C+ | 136.2 | 4.88 | 8.5 | 0.3 | 12.4 | 8.3 | 6.3 | 10.7 | 12.0 |
| United Roosevelt Savings Bank | Carteret | NJ | C- | D+ | D+ | 146.9 | 15.08 | 7.6 | 0.1 | 51.3 | 4.9 | 10.0 | 11.6 | 19.3 |
| United Savings Bank | Philadelphia | PA | B- | B- | B- | 356.8 | 2.71 | 0.3 | 0.0 | 29.0 | 25.5 | 10.0 | 16.8 | 35.9 |
| United Security Bank | Fresno | CA | B+ | B+ | B+ | 955.8 | 2.55 | 7.5 | 7.3 | 5.3 | 8.0 | 10.0 | 12.8 | 17.8 |
| United Security Bank | Auxvasse | MO | B+ | B+ | A- | 61.5 | -3.10 | 5.7 | 7.2 | 34.3 | 27.3 | 10.0 | 14.6 | 21.7 |
| United Southern Bank | Umatilla | FL | B | B- | B- | 550.0 | 5.49 | 2.5 | 1.2 | 13.8 | 30.3 | 8.6 | 10.1 | 16.2 |
| ▲ United Southern Bank | Hopkinsville | KY | B+ | B- | C+ | 219.3 | -1.86 | 6.0 | 2.6 | 23.9 | 15.6 | 10.0 | 12.6 | 17.2 |
| United Southwest Bank | Cottonwood | MN | C | C- | C- | 50.8 | 5.94 | 2.5 | 1.9 | 0.3 | 31.0 | 6.4 | 8.4 | 16.4 |
| ▲ United State Bank | Lewistown | MO | B | B- | C+ | 181.1 | 6.33 | 5.6 | 1.4 | 7.5 | 8.2 | 7.1 | 9.6 | 12.6 |
| United Texas Bank | Dallas | TX | B- | B- | B- | 663.6 | 44.68 | 16.9 | 0.2 | 8.3 | 9.8 | 6.6 | 8.6 | 12.4 |
| ▲ United Trust Bank | Palos Heights | IL | E+ | E | E- | 26.2 | -0.69 | 0.0 | 0.6 | 28.0 | 0.3 | 8.9 | 10.3 | 15.8 |
| ▲ United Valley Bank | Cavalier | ND | B- | B- | B | 365.0 | 0.59 | 13.8 | 2.7 | 8.0 | 15.0 | 7.7 | 9.5 | 13.1 |
| Unity Bank | Clinton | NJ | A- | B+ | B | 1712.4 | 9.00 | 4.8 | 0.1 | 29.6 | 3.8 | 7.1 | 10.2 | 12.6 |
| Unity Bank | Augusta | WI | D+ | C- | C+ | 527.2 | 193.03 | 7.6 | 2.5 | 13.3 | 6.1 | 6.4 | 8.8 | 12.0 |
| Unity National Bank of Houston | Houston | TX | D- | D- | D+ | 106.1 | 12.98 | 13.0 | 0.6 | 14.6 | 7.0 | 8.2 | 9.8 | 13.8 |
| Universal Bank | West Covina | CA | C+ | B | B | 417.2 | 9.23 | 0.6 | 0.0 | 4.0 | 3.7 | 10.0 | 14.4 | 22.9 |
| University Bank | Ann Arbor | MI | B+ | B+ | B+ | 357.4 | 45.04 | 0.5 | 0.1 | 40.2 | 3.1 | 6.1 | 8.2 | 14.6 |
| ▲ University National Bank of Lawrence | Lawrence | KS | B | C+ | C+ | 77.7 | 1.83 | 4.4 | 0.8 | 44.4 | 2.8 | 7.5 | 9.3 | 15.8 |
| Univest Bank and Trust Co. | Souderton | PA | B | B | B | 5361.4 | 7.98 | 15.4 | 0.6 | 14.7 | 8.2 | 5.9 | 9.9 | 11.7 |
| Upper Peninsula State Bank | Escanaba | MI | A- | A- | A- | 218.6 | 7.98 | 5.2 | 5.3 | 15.6 | 16.5 | 10.0 | 17.2 | 23.5 |
| Upstate National Bank | Ogdensburg | NY | C | C+ | B- | 164.7 | 17.83 | 4.1 | 0.1 | 28.8 | 9.0 | 7.3 | 9.2 | 13.0 |

| Asset Quality Index | Adjusted Non-Performing Loans as a % of Total Loans | Adjusted Non-Performing Loans as a % of Capital | Net Charge-Offs Avg Loans | Profitability Index | Net Income ($Mil) | Return on Assets (R.O.A.) | Return on Equity (R.O.E.) | Net Interest Spread | Overhead Efficiency Ratio | Liquidity Index | Liquidity Ratio | Hot Money Ratio | Stability Index |
|---|---|---|---|---|---|---|---|---|---|---|---|---|---|
| **8.9** | 0.00 | 0.0 | 0.06 | **5.1** | 0.3 | 1.28 | 11.41 | 3.16 | 57.4 | **5.5** | 63.1 | 9.6 | **6.0** |
| **4.5** | 1.46 | 7.0 | -0.02 | **5.5** | 3.9 | 1.24 | 11.11 | 4.01 | 72.0 | **3.8** | 14.2 | 9.7 | **7.6** |
| **5.2** | 0.75 | 2.1 | -0.06 | **4.4** | 0.7 | 0.64 | 4.70 | 4.26 | 74.1 | **2.6** | 22.3 | 16.3 | **6.4** |
| **2.4** | 3.95 | 19.2 | 0.85 | **4.5** | 1.3 | 0.91 | 8.84 | 4.06 | 68.7 | **4.5** | 28.2 | 8.2 | **6.5** |
| **4.5** | 2.52 | 14.1 | 0.08 | **3.4** | 0.4 | 0.49 | 4.18 | 3.81 | 76.1 | **4.3** | 28.5 | 8.5 | **5.9** |
| **6.8** | 0.60 | 1.8 | 0.00 | **7.6** | 4.7 | 1.49 | 12.99 | 4.31 | 55.4 | **1.6** | 14.8 | 16.1 | **7.7** |
| **5.6** | 0.69 | 3.8 | 0.18 | **6.9** | 9.2 | 1.36 | 14.96 | 4.12 | 60.9 | **3.6** | 28.2 | 11.4 | **6.3** |
| **6.1** | 1.39 | 6.8 | 0.02 | **4.8** | 2.1 | 1.08 | 9.00 | 3.71 | 74.8 | **0.8** | 16.8 | 32.0 | **8.2** |
| **7.4** | 1.03 | 4.6 | -0.01 | **9.6** | 34.4 | 2.41 | 22.97 | 3.99 | 55.4 | **6.1** | 36.3 | 4.6 | **10.0** |
| **4.5** | 0.86 | 3.5 | 0.15 | **7.2** | 268.6 | 1.38 | 7.64 | 3.45 | 51.6 | **3.3** | 10.7 | 11.5 | **9.8** |
| **7.9** | 0.12 | 0.7 | 0.00 | **6.8** | 8.4 | 1.37 | 10.95 | 3.62 | 52.5 | **1.9** | 11.9 | 17.3 | **8.9** |
| **8.8** | 0.13 | 0.7 | -0.01 | **4.4** | 0.9 | 0.88 | 6.78 | 2.98 | 68.6 | **5.0** | 37.2 | 8.9 | **7.8** |
| **8.6** | 0.33 | 0.6 | 0.06 | **6.7** | 2.6 | 1.60 | 10.48 | 3.44 | 48.9 | **4.8** | 48.6 | 13.3 | **9.1** |
| **3.4** | 1.66 | 9.1 | 0.13 | **6.1** | 3.0 | 1.25 | 10.97 | 5.37 | 63.3 | **2.2** | 11.8 | 16.5 | **7.1** |
| **5.6** | 0.83 | 3.9 | 0.05 | **7.0** | 26.1 | 1.58 | 13.88 | 3.24 | 53.4 | **1.8** | 22.4 | 26.6 | **10.0** |
| **4.7** | 0.78 | 3.0 | 0.16 | **5.1** | 7.0 | 1.03 | 10.38 | 3.95 | 70.1 | **3.9** | 12.1 | 7.8 | **7.2** |
| **0.3** | 12.36 | 84.0 | 0.02 | **0.0** | -1.5 | -3.01 | -57.73 | 4.88 | 163.2 | **5.4** | 35.8 | 5.3 | **0.0** |
| **2.8** | 2.94 | 15.9 | 0.12 | **6.3** | 5.7 | 1.51 | 14.43 | 3.63 | 59.1 | **1.5** | 8.0 | 22.4 | **7.4** |
| **7.1** | 0.54 | 2.2 | 0.02 | **3.4** | 4.7 | 0.56 | 4.53 | 2.98 | 80.9 | **0.9** | 20.6 | 1.3 | **7.5** |
| **6.6** | 0.53 | 2.3 | 0.00 | **5.6** | 17.7 | 1.01 | 8.11 | 4.19 | 66.0 | **3.2** | 24.1 | 15.9 | **9.1** |
| **4.4** | 5.27 | 16.7 | 0.00 | **6.5** | 1.5 | 1.38 | 10.93 | 4.41 | 62.9 | **4.4** | 27.2 | 8.6 | **7.7** |
| **7.1** | 0.76 | 3.4 | 0.08 | **7.5** | 2.4 | 1.46 | 12.12 | 4.18 | 59.0 | **0.8** | 12.7 | 34.0 | **7.9** |
| **6.7** | 0.91 | 3.0 | 0.14 | **7.8** | 190.5 | 1.51 | 11.30 | 4.13 | 54.5 | **3.8** | 19.4 | 9.3 | **10.0** |
| **5.0** | 1.25 | 4.4 | 0.00 | **6.4** | 3.1 | 1.41 | 13.51 | 4.11 | 60.7 | **3.3** | 8.4 | 12.1 | **7.8** |
| **4.8** | 1.90 | 9.8 | 0.30 | **5.2** | 27.2 | 1.11 | 12.00 | 3.34 | 63.6 | **3.9** | 20.2 | 7.8 | **8.0** |
| **3.0** | 2.59 | 10.8 | 0.28 | **6.5** | 10.0 | 1.85 | 13.23 | 4.73 | 54.1 | **2.9** | 17.8 | 14.7 | **6.9** |
| **6.8** | 1.37 | 5.3 | 0.02 | **5.1** | 3.0 | 1.18 | 10.43 | 3.86 | 69.6 | **3.1** | 32.1 | 16.6 | **7.3** |
| **6.4** | 0.73 | 2.1 | 1.67 | **5.5** | 3.6 | 0.98 | 8.46 | 4.28 | 47.4 | **3.1** | 17.0 | 13.8 | **7.3** |
| **8.3** | 0.36 | 1.6 | 0.09 | **8.4** | 4.4 | 1.64 | 11.74 | 4.03 | 55.8 | **1.9** | 20.4 | 14.2 | **9.3** |
| **3.9** | 2.83 | 10.2 | 0.29 | **8.3** | 5.5 | 1.85 | 14.15 | 4.71 | 60.5 | **1.8** | 19.6 | 21.9 | **8.5** |
| **5.3** | 0.83 | 5.4 | 0.26 | **8.6** | 2.9 | 1.86 | 15.58 | 4.17 | 48.1 | **3.3** | 14.4 | 11.0 | **9.2** |
| **6.3** | 3.50 | 4.4 | 0.09 | **6.0** | 12.5 | 1.39 | 11.36 | 2.31 | 64.7 | **5.6** | 43.9 | 7.0 | **7.8** |
| **2.3** | 3.53 | 14.3 | 1.50 | **9.6** | 5.1 | 1.69 | 16.43 | 4.66 | 68.1 | **0.8** | 20.4 | 48.1 | **7.3** |
| **6.8** | 0.00 | 0.0 | 0.20 | **3.7** | 0.2 | 0.53 | 6.86 | 4.54 | 86.4 | **4.5** | 24.2 | 6.8 | **3.3** |
| **3.9** | 0.84 | 4.7 | 0.17 | **3.9** | 2.6 | 0.74 | 6.99 | 4.44 | 83.6 | **2.8** | 13.7 | 14.2 | **6.6** |
| **3.7** | 3.85 | 18.4 | 0.13 | **7.9** | 3.1 | 1.44 | 10.14 | 4.77 | 54.6 | **1.3** | 5.6 | 22.5 | **8.0** |
| **7.6** | 0.00 | 0.0 | 0.00 | **3.9** | 0.5 | 0.54 | 3.45 | 5.67 | 88.2 | **2.8** | 21.1 | 15.6 | **7.2** |
| **7.3** | 0.04 | 0.2 | 0.00 | **3.7** | 1.0 | 0.68 | 3.94 | 3.45 | 77.7 | **0.9** | 25.2 | 48.5 | **8.4** |
| **3.8** | 1.20 | 6.3 | 0.02 | **5.8** | 8.9 | 1.49 | 13.73 | 4.45 | 69.0 | **1.7** | 12.9 | 16.6 | **7.6** |
| **6.4** | 0.00 | 0.1 | -0.01 | **2.7** | 0.7 | 0.49 | 3.52 | 3.45 | 73.1 | **0.6** | 15.1 | 47.8 | **2.9** |
| **9.0** | 0.39 | 2.9 | 0.00 | **1.6** | 0.2 | 0.14 | 1.45 | 2.54 | 89.9 | **1.9** | 16.5 | 19.5 | **4.7** |
| **9.9** | 0.00 | 0.0 | 0.00 | **3.9** | 3.0 | 0.82 | 4.77 | 2.84 | 62.1 | **3.2** | 43.3 | 19.9 | **8.0** |
| **4.4** | 2.29 | 9.9 | 0.09 | **9.1** | 14.9 | 1.55 | 12.21 | 4.27 | 50.0 | **4.8** | 28.1 | 6.0 | **9.5** |
| **8.5** | 0.00 | 0.0 | 0.01 | **5.1** | 0.8 | 1.21 | 8.66 | 4.11 | 70.8 | **2.1** | 23.9 | 19.6 | **8.3** |
| **5.1** | 1.90 | 8.5 | -0.10 | **5.3** | 5.6 | 1.05 | 10.88 | 3.96 | 69.4 | **6.3** | 40.4 | 1.8 | **7.2** |
| **5.1** | 2.04 | 10.5 | -0.32 | **6.7** | 3.7 | 1.67 | 14.29 | 4.22 | 73.1 | **2.3** | 17.6 | 17.7 | **6.7** |
| **6.3** | 0.61 | 7.7 | 0.00 | **2.6** | 0.2 | 0.37 | 4.19 | 3.46 | 80.2 | **6.8** | 56.5 | 1.6 | **4.0** |
| **4.6** | 0.51 | 3.4 | 0.02 | **6.7** | 2.8 | 1.52 | 16.22 | 3.77 | 55.6 | **1.5** | 16.1 | 19.9 | **7.1** |
| **8.6** | 0.00 | 0.0 | 0.00 | **3.9** | 4.5 | 0.78 | 8.05 | 2.44 | 56.0 | **1.9** | 40.3 | 46.2 | **5.3** |
| **4.5** | 2.25 | 14.1 | 0.00 | **0.0** | -1.3 | -4.97 | -38.70 | 4.22 | 243.0 | **1.7** | 18.8 | 22.1 | **3.3** |
| **4.4** | 1.47 | 7.3 | 0.18 | **4.8** | 3.8 | 1.06 | 9.45 | 4.26 | 70.0 | **3.4** | 8.4 | 11.5 | **7.4** |
| **6.2** | 0.45 | 3.9 | 0.09 | **7.6** | 22.5 | 1.47 | 14.78 | 4.06 | 53.6 | **1.7** | 13.9 | 16.7 | **8.4** |
| **1.7** | 2.53 | 25.6 | 0.05 | **4.1** | 4.4 | 0.87 | 10.50 | 4.44 | 77.9 | **1.0** | 10.8 | 24.0 | **6.3** |
| **2.6** | 2.24 | 12.8 | 0.39 | **0.1** | -0.7 | -0.65 | -7.16 | 3.69 | 106.6 | **0.7** | 19.2 | 50.3 | **4.1** |
| **7.4** | 0.70 | 2.1 | -0.04 | **3.7** | 2.5 | 0.61 | 4.26 | 2.75 | 77.3 | **1.0** | 21.1 | 34.5 | **8.5** |
| **5.0** | 1.81 | 5.2 | 0.02 | **8.4** | 3.8 | 1.56 | 15.46 | 5.55 | 92.3 | **6.0** | 33.7 | 0.5 | **5.7** |
| **7.6** | 0.52 | 3.9 | -0.16 | **5.9** | 1.1 | 1.45 | 15.08 | 4.06 | 70.5 | **3.2** | 14.6 | 12.7 | **5.8** |
| **5.1** | 0.89 | 5.3 | 0.06 | **6.6** | 70.5 | 1.35 | 10.63 | 3.71 | 60.4 | **3.5** | 4.5 | 6.6 | **9.2** |
| **7.7** | 0.84 | 3.3 | 0.02 | **7.6** | 3.2 | 1.55 | 9.39 | 4.12 | 59.9 | **2.3** | 32.2 | 11.3 | **8.3** |
| **7.7** | 0.00 | 0.0 | 0.00 | **3.2** | 1.3 | 0.89 | 7.92 | 3.00 | 74.7 | **0.4** | 15.1 | 70.0 | **6.8** |

| Name | City | State | Rating | 2018 Rating | 2017 Rating | Total Assets ($Mil) | One Year Asset Growth | Asset Mix (As a % of Total Assets) Commercial Loans | Consumer Loans | Mortgage Loans | Securities | Capitalization Index | Leverage Ratio | Risk-Based Capital Ratio |
|---|---|---|---|---|---|---|---|---|---|---|---|---|---|---|
| ▲ US Metro Bank | Garden Grove | CA | **A-** | B+ | A- | 542.3 | 39.45 | 10.3 | 0.0 | 0.5 | 0.0 | **9.8** | 10.9 | 14.9 |
| USAA Federal Savings Bank | San Antonio | TX | **C+** | C+ | C+ | 88795.6 | 8.81 | 0.0 | 48.3 | 4.7 | 35.4 | **7.9** | 9.6 | 16.5 |
| USAA Savings Bank | Las Vegas | NV | **U** | U | U | 1784.2 | 6.57 | 0.0 | 0.0 | 0.0 | 16.7 | **10.0** | 18.5 | 153.5 |
| USNY Bank | Geneva | NY | **B-** | B- | B+ | 439.8 | 8.47 | 13.4 | 0.7 | 10.6 | 4.5 | **7.2** | 10.6 | 12.7 |
| Utah Independent Bank | Salina | UT | **A-** | B+ | A- | 88.1 | 9.12 | 17.0 | 5.6 | 13.3 | 14.4 | **10.0** | 14.9 | 20.0 |
| Uwharrie Bank | Albemarle | NC | **C+** | C+ | C+ | 654.6 | 3.89 | 6.4 | 2.0 | 11.3 | 15.6 | **6.5** | 8.6 | 13.6 |
| ▲ Valley Bank of Commerce | Roswell | NM | **A** | A- | B+ | 187.6 | 0.36 | 18.5 | 0.5 | 5.5 | 0.1 | **9.6** | 10.7 | 24.1 |
| Valley Bank of Kalispell | Kalispell | MT | **B** | C+ | B | 138.4 | 15.25 | 14.6 | 4.8 | 17.4 | 13.3 | **8.7** | 10.2 | 14.4 |
| ▲ Valley Bank of Nevada | North Las Vegas | NV | **D+** | D | D | 148.6 | 10.48 | 12.2 | 0.3 | 1.0 | 2.0 | **7.1** | 9.1 | 13.6 |
| ▼ Valley Bank of Ronan | Ronan | MT | **D+** | C+ | B | 105.9 | -0.95 | 14.5 | 5.5 | 13.0 | 7.0 | **9.4** | 10.6 | 18.5 |
| ▼ Valley Central Bank | Liberty Township | OH | **C-** | C | C+ | 152.1 | 35.24 | 2.5 | 0.5 | 51.2 | 3.1 | **10.0** | 22.6 | 33.6 |
| Valley Exchange Bank | Lennox | SD | **B** | B | C+ | 67.1 | -0.86 | 2.9 | 1.4 | 1.0 | 11.2 | **10.0** | 11.8 | 34.3 |
| ▼ Valley National Bank | Wayne | NJ | **C+** | B- | B- | 37441.6 | 17.63 | 11.3 | 6.0 | 11.9 | 10.5 | **5.9** | 9.3 | 11.7 |
| Valley Premier Bank | Hawley | MN | **B** | B | B | 110.1 | -2.23 | 13.7 | 3.5 | 11.7 | 31.2 | **8.8** | 10.2 | 17.4 |
| Valley Republic Bank | Bakersfield | CA | **B+** | B- | B- | 938.7 | 20.38 | 12.3 | 0.2 | 3.8 | 17.7 | **7.7** | 10.4 | 13.1 |
| Valley State Bank | Russellville | AL | **B** | B | B- | 126.8 | 7.85 | 7.4 | 2.9 | 20.0 | 36.9 | **10.0** | 17.6 | 34.7 |
| Valley State Bank | Belle Plaine | KS | **B** | B | B | 137.6 | 9.21 | 8.1 | 10.1 | 17.0 | 21.6 | **10.0** | 13.3 | 21.9 |
| Valley State Bank | Syracuse | KS | **B-** | B- | C+ | 160.4 | 13.60 | 10.6 | 5.0 | 13.9 | 9.8 | **5.7** | 9.5 | 11.5 |
| Valliance Bank | Oklahoma City | OK | **C** | C | C+ | 453.9 | 7.57 | 20.1 | 0.3 | 11.2 | 7.4 | **4.5** | 9.1 | 10.8 |
| Valor Bank | Edmond | OK | **B** | B | C | 100.1 | 20.68 | 3.7 | 0.1 | 42.9 | 0.5 | **6.6** | 8.6 | 12.8 |
| ▲ ValueBank Texas | Corpus Christi | TX | **A** | B+ | B+ | 237.6 | -1.90 | 3.9 | 0.5 | 13.6 | 17.6 | **10.0** | 11.2 | 20.0 |
| Van Wert Federal Savings Bank | Van Wert | OH | **C+** | C+ | C+ | 117.8 | 4.18 | 0.0 | 0.7 | 47.0 | 14.8 | **10.0** | 21.1 | 48.2 |
| Vanguard National Trust Co., N.A. | Malvern | PA | **U** | U | U | 81.6 | -13.77 | 0.0 | 0.0 | 0.0 | 70.2 | **10.0** | 78.8 | 331.9 |
| Vantage Bank | Alexandria | MN | **C-** | D+ | D+ | 34.8 | 20.90 | 7.2 | 5.7 | 33.7 | 0.0 | **4.3** | 8.4 | 10.6 |
| ▲ Vantage Bank Texas | San Antonio | TX | **B** | | B- | 2173.7 | 13.42 | 11.7 | 0.4 | 4.8 | 5.7 | **10.0** | 13.3 | 15.0 |
| Vast Bank, N.A. | Tulsa | OK | **B-** | B- | C+ | 681.3 | 9.02 | 20.4 | 1.4 | 9.9 | 1.0 | **7.6** | 10.2 | 13.0 |
| VCC Bank | Richmond | VA | **D** | D | C- | 222.2 | 14.47 | 9.6 | 0.0 | 9.3 | 9.7 | **9.3** | 10.5 | 14.5 |
| VeraBank, N.A. | Henderson | TX | **B** | B | B | 2408.1 | 4.31 | 8.5 | 3.7 | 16.4 | 21.2 | **6.8** | 8.8 | 14.5 |
| Vergas State Bank | Vergas | MN | **B-** | B- | B- | 51.0 | 6.98 | 3.0 | 2.5 | 9.9 | 14.4 | **10.0** | 15.2 | 40.0 |
| Veritex Community Bank | Dallas | TX | **B** | B | B+ | 7951.3 | 147.86 | 20.3 | 0.2 | 6.5 | 12.6 | **6.9** | 11.1 | 12.4 |
| Vermilion Bank & Trust Co. | Kaplan | LA | **B-** | C+ | B- | 128.6 | 0.66 | 5.9 | 4.3 | 18.3 | 16.5 | **9.2** | 10.5 | 17.4 |
| Vermilion Valley Bank | Piper City | IL | **A-** | B+ | A | 134.2 | 5.81 | 3.2 | 1.4 | 10.4 | 19.0 | **10.0** | 16.4 | 24.2 |
| Vermillion State Bank | Vermillion | MN | **A+** | A+ | A+ | 597.8 | 7.36 | 15.4 | 1.4 | 12.0 | 39.8 | **10.0** | 16.0 | 28.0 |
| Vermont State Bank | Vermont | IL | **D** | D | D | 29.4 | 2.95 | 7.4 | 21.4 | 32.5 | 9.2 | **10.0** | 12.3 | 18.4 |
| Versailles S&L Co. | Versailles | OH | **B** | B- | C+ | 54.9 | 2.22 | 1.9 | 2.2 | 55.6 | 0.1 | **10.0** | 21.1 | 37.7 |
| Verus Bank of Commerce | Fort Collins | CO | **A-** | B+ | A | 274.9 | 6.22 | 2.8 | 0.0 | 8.8 | 0.0 | **9.3** | 12.3 | 14.4 |
| Victor State Bank | Victor | IA | **A-** | A- | A | 35.7 | 2.22 | 9.9 | 1.8 | 7.6 | 43.7 | **10.0** | 11.5 | 22.3 |
| Victory Bank | Limerick | PA | **B-** | C | C | 279.4 | 11.03 | 13.3 | 3.6 | 12.8 | 4.0 | **5.4** | 9.6 | 11.3 |
| Victory Community Bank | Fort Mitchell | KY | **A-** | B+ | A- | 181.1 | 0.50 | 0.0 | 0.3 | 63.1 | 5.9 | **10.0** | 15.1 | 27.9 |
| Victory State Bank | Staten Island | NY | **B** | B | B- | 371.0 | -1.64 | 5.8 | 0.1 | 5.2 | 41.1 | **8.7** | 10.1 | 20.4 |
| Vidalia Federal Savings Bank | Vidalia | GA | **C+** | B- | B- | 199.0 | -5.31 | 0.0 | 1.9 | 27.7 | 47.4 | **10.0** | 16.1 | 56.4 |
| ▲ Viking Bank | Alexandria | MN | **B** | B- | B- | 224.4 | 25.53 | 9.4 | 2.2 | 19.5 | 3.3 | **7.7** | 10.0 | 13.1 |
| Villa Grove State Bank | Villa Grove | IL | **B+** | B+ | B+ | 73.9 | 6.66 | 7.4 | 2.6 | 43.1 | 14.3 | **10.0** | 11.5 | 22.3 |
| ▲ Village Bank | Saint Libory | IL | **B** | B- | B- | 91.4 | 2.53 | 5.5 | 6.3 | 21.7 | 20.0 | **7.6** | 9.4 | 19.4 |
| Village Bank | Auburndale | MA | **B** | B | B | 1287.9 | 7.65 | 3.2 | 0.3 | 42.9 | 11.2 | **9.8** | 10.9 | 17.1 |
| Village Bank | Saint Francis | MN | **C+** | C | D+ | 302.2 | 2.16 | 14.2 | 1.1 | 10.4 | 15.7 | **7.4** | 9.2 | 14.0 |
| Village Bank | Midlothian | VA | **C** | C- | C | 537.7 | 4.88 | 8.4 | 6.7 | 14.7 | 8.7 | **7.1** | 9.7 | 12.6 |
| Village Bank & Trust, N.A. | Arlington Heights | IL | **B** | B | B- | 1850.0 | 18.24 | 41.9 | 10.4 | 3.7 | 14.2 | **5.6** | 9.0 | 11.4 |
| Vinings Bank | Smyrna | GA | **C+** | B- | B | 368.6 | 19.61 | 5.1 | 0.1 | 1.3 | 45.4 | **6.2** | 8.2 | 12.6 |
| ▲ Vintage Bank Kansas | Leon | KS | **B** | B | B | 144.6 | 12.44 | 7.7 | 2.9 | 15.5 | 21.8 | **9.0** | 10.4 | 15.3 |
| Vinton County National Bank | McArthur | OH | **B** | B | B | 1007.6 | 7.55 | 3.8 | 18.7 | 30.7 | 13.9 | **10.0** | 11.1 | 16.4 |
| Virginia Bank and Trust Co. | Danville | VA | **B** | B+ | B+ | 218.5 | 13.49 | 12.1 | 8.3 | 20.9 | 13.6 | **10.0** | 11.8 | 18.4 |
| Virginia Commonwealth Bank | Richmond | VA | **C+** | C+ | C | 1127.5 | 4.77 | 14.7 | 1.1 | 26.7 | 8.8 | **7.7** | 10.4 | 13.1 |
| ▲ Virginia National Bank | Charlottesville | VA | **A-** | B- | B | 702.7 | 9.02 | 11.5 | 10.0 | 14.3 | 16.2 | **9.6** | 10.7 | 15.0 |
| Virginia Partners Bank | Fredericksburg | VA | **C+** | C+ | C | 449.0 | 6.73 | 10.7 | 0.7 | 19.8 | 11.1 | **6.9** | 10.3 | 12.4 |
| Vision Bank, N.A. | Ada | OK | **B-** | B- | B- | 690.2 | 5.71 | 6.0 | 6.6 | 24.7 | 22.3 | **8.5** | 10.0 | 15.1 |
| VisionBank | Topeka | KS | **C+** | B- | B- | 190.5 | 6.76 | 24.5 | 2.1 | 18.9 | 2.0 | **5.1** | 8.6 | 11.0 |
| ▲ VisionBank | Saint Louis Park | MN | **A-** | B+ | B+ | 94.0 | 7.69 | 24.7 | 0.6 | 17.8 | 0.0 | **9.6** | 11.0 | 14.7 |
| VISIONBank | Fargo | ND | **D** | D | D | 200.9 | 2.75 | 24.1 | 4.7 | 19.3 | 0.0 | **7.3** | 10.2 | 12.8 |
| VisionBank of Iowa | Ames | IA | **B** | B- | B- | 541.9 | 8.28 | 5.3 | 0.1 | 9.8 | 0.9 | **7.4** | 10.5 | 12.9 |

| Asset Quality Index | Adjusted Non-Performing Loans as a % of Total Loans | Adjusted Non-Performing Loans as a % of Capital | Net Charge-Offs Avg Loans | Profitability Index | Net Income ($Mil) | Return on Assets (R.O.A.) | Return on Equity (R.O.E.) | Net Interest Spread | Overhead Efficiency Ratio | Liquidity Index | Liquidity Ratio | Hot Money Ratio | Stability Index |
|---|---|---|---|---|---|---|---|---|---|---|---|---|---|
| **6.9** | 0.24 | 1.5 | 0.07 | **6.8** | 5.2 | 1.12 | 9.49 | 4.04 | 61.4 | **1.2** | 28.7 | 42.3 | **9.0** |
| **3.6** | 1.79 | 5.3 | 1.49 | **5.2** | 718.7 | 0.86 | 8.61 | 5.18 | 75.9 | **5.1** | 47.9 | 4.5 | **8.2** |
| **10.0** | na | 0.0 | 0.00 | **9.5** | 223.3 | 14.24 | 74.82 | 2.05 | 71.4 | **3.8** | 105.3 | 55.7 | **7.0** |
| **3.9** | 1.50 | 10.7 | 0.05 | **6.0** | 4.6 | 1.08 | 10.53 | 3.70 | 52.6 | **0.6** | 12.0 | 43.3 | **7.2** |
| **6.2** | 0.96 | 3.9 | 0.00 | **9.5** | 2.4 | 2.74 | 17.81 | 5.85 | 54.3 | **5.6** | 34.0 | 3.5 | **9.7** |
| **5.6** | 1.84 | 8.2 | -0.08 | **3.7** | 4.0 | 0.63 | 7.21 | 3.50 | 84.7 | **3.7** | 32.1 | 13.8 | **5.3** |
| **8.1** | 0.72 | 3.1 | 0.00 | **9.5** | 4.4 | 2.51 | 24.70 | 4.06 | 41.2 | **6.6** | 61.8 | 6.3 | **7.5** |
| **4.4** | 1.93 | 11.3 | 0.05 | **8.2** | 2.4 | 1.89 | 17.19 | 5.07 | 56.4 | **1.7** | 24.1 | 23.1 | **6.6** |
| **2.3** | 3.51 | 9.7 | 0.08 | **3.6** | 0.7 | 0.53 | 4.98 | 4.43 | 81.3 | **4.9** | 36.7 | 8.9 | **6.2** |
| **1.6** | 6.07 | 24.3 | 0.04 | **5.0** | 0.9 | 0.86 | 7.93 | 4.71 | 76.3 | **5.7** | 38.4 | 4.9 | **6.7** |
| **9.0** | 0.48 | 1.2 | -0.02 | **1.5** | 0.0 | 0.01 | 0.04 | 3.30 | 99.2 | **1.3** | 8.4 | 16.6 | **7.1** |
| **9.1** | 0.00 | 0.0 | -0.07 | **4.3** | 0.6 | 0.90 | 7.54 | 3.36 | 64.3 | **6.8** | 67.3 | 4.3 | **6.1** |
| **3.3** | 0.97 | 4.9 | 0.06 | **5.3** | 357.7 | 1.07 | 9.50 | 2.98 | 54.9 | **1.1** | 6.8 | 14.4 | **9.4** |
| **5.9** | 0.36 | 5.3 | 0.00 | **4.7** | 1.2 | 1.08 | 10.82 | 3.50 | 70.3 | **5.5** | 40.9 | 7.1 | **6.6** |
| **8.4** | 0.00 | 0.0 | 0.00 | **5.7** | 10.5 | 1.22 | 11.97 | 3.43 | 54.5 | **4.4** | 22.5 | 7.3 | **6.7** |
| **8.9** | 0.12 | 1.0 | 0.04 | **4.2** | 1.1 | 0.89 | 5.15 | 3.32 | 63.1 | **1.7** | 35.6 | 35.7 | **8.1** |
| **6.7** | 0.68 | 3.3 | 0.10 | **4.9** | 1.3 | 1.01 | 7.53 | 4.18 | 66.0 | **1.7** | 20.1 | 20.9 | **7.2** |
| **8.2** | 0.06 | 0.5 | 0.00 | **6.6** | 2.3 | 1.52 | 16.29 | 4.11 | 64.0 | **0.8** | 15.3 | 41.5 | **6.4** |
| **3.9** | 0.57 | 5.2 | 0.27 | **3.5** | 2.6 | 0.59 | 6.52 | 3.89 | 79.3 | **0.5** | 11.0 | 40.9 | **5.2** |
| **9.0** | 0.00 | 0.0 | 0.01 | **7.9** | 1.5 | 1.73 | 19.03 | 3.61 | 69.3 | **0.7** | 15.6 | 43.2 | **5.7** |
| **9.1** | 0.00 | 0.0 | -0.02 | **8.7** | 5.0 | 2.06 | 19.14 | 4.55 | 61.4 | **5.2** | 39.4 | 8.5 | **7.1** |
| **9.9** | 0.07 | 0.4 | 0.00 | **2.7** | 0.5 | 0.43 | 2.02 | 2.71 | 81.0 | **3.2** | 44.3 | 20.4 | **7.6** |
| **10.0** | na | 0.0 | na | **10.0** | 19.4 | 19.99 | 24.37 | 2.22 | 65.9 | **4.0** | na | 0.0 | **6.7** |
| **8.1** | 0.00 | 0.0 | 0.00 | **4.6** | 0.3 | 1.07 | 11.29 | 4.06 | 77.1 | **2.5** | 9.4 | 15.8 | **3.7** |
| **4.8** | 0.89 | 5.9 | -0.02 | **6.4** | 23.7 | 1.20 | 8.48 | 4.50 | 64.5 | **1.6** | 19.9 | 25.6 | **9.2** |
| **5.3** | 0.31 | 4.4 | 0.34 | **4.2** | 4.4 | 0.67 | 6.50 | 3.56 | 71.5 | **0.8** | 19.3 | 46.6 | **6.5** |
| **0.9** | 3.95 | 25.3 | 0.33 | **3.4** | 1.4 | 0.69 | 6.26 | 2.51 | 58.8 | **0.6** | 18.0 | 69.0 | **6.1** |
| **5.9** | 0.79 | 4.3 | 0.09 | **5.2** | 24.6 | 1.05 | 10.26 | 4.02 | 69.8 | **5.0** | 23.8 | 6.2 | **8.3** |
| **7.3** | 0.03 | 5.0 | -0.04 | **3.0** | 0.2 | 0.44 | 2.80 | 2.82 | 80.3 | **3.7** | 66.4 | 22.8 | **7.3** |
| **4.3** | 0.51 | 4.3 | 0.19 | **6.7** | 100.0 | 1.26 | 8.60 | 4.05 | 53.0 | **1.6** | 17.4 | 20.8 | **10.0** |
| **3.7** | 3.78 | 15.5 | 0.31 | **5.9** | 1.6 | 1.35 | 12.79 | 4.30 | 63.7 | **3.2** | 34.1 | 16.9 | **6.5** |
| **7.2** | 0.02 | 0.3 | 0.00 | **8.1** | 2.5 | 1.95 | 11.45 | 3.71 | 44.2 | **2.0** | 16.3 | 19.4 | **9.5** |
| **7.5** | 0.99 | 3.4 | 0.06 | **9.8** | 13.7 | 2.41 | 15.15 | 3.52 | 33.7 | **5.6** | 51.2 | 9.5 | **10.0** |
| **0.5** | 6.24 | 32.0 | 2.07 | **0.7** | -0.4 | -1.20 | -11.74 | 3.45 | 84.7 | **0.6** | 14.6 | 52.1 | **4.9** |
| **9.3** | 0.00 | 0.0 | 0.00 | **4.5** | 0.5 | 0.89 | 4.34 | 3.59 | 67.4 | **2.7** | 25.0 | 16.4 | **7.5** |
| **7.3** | 0.00 | 0.0 | -0.01 | **9.8** | 5.5 | 2.04 | 15.42 | 4.25 | 40.3 | **1.2** | 10.2 | 9.6 | **9.4** |
| **2.2** | 2.27 | 8.2 | 0.00 | **5.1** | 0.3 | 0.83 | 4.60 | 3.85 | 61.2 | **4.1** | 70.4 | 18.0 | **8.1** |
| **6.6** | 0.12 | 1.3 | 0.13 | **5.0** | 2.6 | 1.00 | 10.78 | 4.38 | 67.4 | **3.5** | 11.6 | 10.9 | **5.2** |
| **7.1** | 0.77 | 4.1 | -0.11 | **9.5** | 6.2 | 3.57 | 24.30 | 3.30 | 50.2 | **1.4** | 17.8 | 27.5 | **9.7** |
| **7.1** | 0.79 | 3.3 | 0.06 | **4.6** | 3.6 | 0.92 | 9.85 | 3.34 | 69.2 | **3.7** | 35.4 | 14.9 | **5.7** |
| **7.7** | 0.97 | 3.7 | 0.17 | **2.1** | 0.3 | 0.15 | 0.93 | 2.32 | 92.3 | **3.6** | 77.6 | 32.4 | **7.2** |
| **5.1** | 0.25 | 2.9 | 0.10 | **6.2** | 2.7 | 1.46 | 9.44 | 4.22 | 59.2 | **2.7** | 18.0 | 16.0 | **9.3** |
| **9.0** | 0.09 | 1.0 | 0.04 | **6.0** | 1.0 | 1.38 | 11.94 | 3.68 | 61.9 | **4.0** | 24.1 | 10.1 | **7.6** |
| **7.7** | 0.19 | 2.7 | 0.13 | **5.5** | 1.2 | 1.33 | 14.04 | 3.52 | 62.2 | **5.8** | 39.9 | 4.8 | **5.0** |
| **8.9** | 0.37 | 2.2 | 0.00 | **4.4** | 10.3 | 0.84 | 7.74 | 3.06 | 65.2 | **1.0** | 16.5 | 34.2 | **9.0** |
| **3.6** | 2.33 | 10.6 | -0.24 | **5.5** | 3.2 | 1.10 | 12.17 | 4.35 | 77.3 | **3.7** | 28.6 | 12.9 | **7.1** |
| **3.1** | 2.01 | 9.4 | 0.00 | **4.6** | 5.2 | 0.98 | 10.23 | 3.88 | 75.4 | **2.3** | 13.8 | 17.4 | **6.6** |
| **5.4** | 0.87 | 5.5 | 0.27 | **6.5** | 22.0 | 1.31 | 12.02 | 3.33 | 44.7 | **1.8** | 21.1 | 17.4 | **8.4** |
| **6.6** | 1.00 | 4.4 | 0.12 | **3.7** | 4.0 | 1.17 | 13.19 | 3.38 | 83.3 | **4.8** | 27.2 | 5.8 | **5.1** |
| **6.0** | 0.90 | 5.0 | 0.00 | **5.5** | 1.8 | 1.28 | 11.39 | 4.47 | 62.5 | **3.5** | 14.5 | 10.1 | **7.0** |
| **6.3** | 0.46 | 3.2 | 0.14 | **4.7** | 9.0 | 0.92 | 7.82 | 3.82 | 71.5 | **2.1** | 12.0 | 18.3 | **9.2** |
| **6.5** | 1.15 | 3.9 | 0.15 | **4.6** | 1.9 | 0.90 | 7.81 | 4.24 | 72.3 | **5.2** | 32.1 | 5.5 | **6.7** |
| **5.8** | 0.96 | 5.0 | 0.17 | **3.9** | 9.0 | 0.82 | 7.48 | 3.58 | 69.1 | **1.4** | 13.1 | 25.4 | **7.3** |
| **6.4** | 0.43 | 1.9 | 0.39 | **6.1** | 7.6 | 1.15 | 10.35 | 3.56 | 60.6 | **3.4** | 20.4 | 12.7 | **7.6** |
| **7.6** | 0.10 | 0.8 | 0.00 | **4.6** | 1.6 | 2.97 | 29.15 | 25.75 | 83.0 | **0.7** | 14.1 | 40.6 | **6.0** |
| **4.5** | 1.41 | 8.5 | 0.30 | **4.9** | 8.0 | 1.17 | 11.93 | 4.22 | 72.6 | **1.6** | 7.2 | 20.2 | **7.3** |
| **4.6** | 0.84 | 6.6 | 1.00 | **3.4** | 0.8 | 0.44 | 4.78 | 3.85 | 66.1 | **1.4** | 5.0 | 23.4 | **5.5** |
| **8.3** | 0.14 | 0.5 | 0.04 | **8.3** | 1.6 | 1.79 | 16.84 | 4.13 | 54.8 | **0.6** | 11.1 | 54.7 | **7.7** |
| **1.1** | 4.14 | 26.6 | 0.82 | **3.9** | 1.2 | 0.63 | 6.02 | 4.07 | 74.3 | **1.4** | 10.3 | 24.6 | **6.5** |
| **6.4** | 0.38 | 2.8 | -0.01 | **5.1** | 6.4 | 1.27 | 11.86 | 3.29 | 63.1 | **1.5** | 17.5 | 12.2 | **7.1** |

| Name | City | State | Rating | 2018 Rating | 2017 Rating | Total Assets ($Mil) | One Year Asset Growth | Asset Mix (As a % of Total Assets) Comm-ercial Loans | Cons-umer Loans | Mort-gage Loans | Secur-ities | Capital-ization Index | Lever-age Ratio | Risk-Based Capital Ratio |
|---|---|---|---|---|---|---|---|---|---|---|---|---|---|---|
| ▲ VIST Bank | Wyomissing | PA | B+ | B | B | 1769.0 | 3.27 | 6.8 | 0.2 | 18.9 | 13.4 | 6.6 | 8.7 | 12.2 |
| Vista Bank | Dallas | TX | B- | B+ | B+ | 920.5 | 14.67 | 15.0 | 0.6 | 9.7 | 2.8 | 7.4 | 9.7 | 12.8 |
| Volunteer Federal Savings Bank | Madisonville | TN | B | B- | B- | 215.6 | 4.56 | 0.5 | 4.5 | 44.9 | 8.6 | 10.0 | 13.8 | 28.0 |
| ▲ Volunteer State Bank | Portland | TN | B | B | B+ | 766.1 | 10.02 | 8.1 | 0.6 | 11.3 | 1.3 | 6.8 | 9.7 | 12.3 |
| Wabash Savings Bank | Mount Carmel | IL | D- | D- | D | 8.8 | -2.65 | 1.8 | 7.9 | 30.2 | 9.5 | 10.0 | 13.2 | 29.6 |
| Wadena State Bank | Wadena | MN | B+ | A- | B+ | 175.7 | 4.44 | 10.4 | 3.1 | 16.3 | 21.5 | 8.9 | 10.3 | 15.8 |
| ▲ Waggoner National Bank of Vernon | Vernon | TX | A | A- | A+ | 295.3 | 0.34 | 7.9 | 5.1 | 6.9 | 28.3 | 10.0 | 13.9 | 20.1 |
| ▼ Wahoo State Bank | Wahoo | NE | C | B- | B- | 92.0 | 15.18 | 9.1 | 4.4 | 20.9 | 17.4 | 5.6 | 7.6 | 12.2 |
| Wake Forest Federal S&L Assn. | Wake Forest | NC | A | A- | A- | 101.8 | -2.39 | 0.0 | 0.4 | 34.8 | 1.9 | 10.0 | 23.6 | 40.7 |
| Wakefield Co-operative Bank | Wakefield | MA | C | C | C | 246.6 | 9.51 | 0.2 | 0.0 | 60.1 | 14.9 | 5.8 | 7.8 | 14.9 |
| Walcott Trust and Savings Bank | Walcott | IA | B- | B | B | 139.8 | 12.91 | 5.8 | 0.5 | 12.0 | 8.3 | 2.4 | 7.0 | 9.4 |
| ▲ Walden Savings Bank | Montgomery | NY | B | C+ | C | 594.0 | 4.08 | 8.3 | 0.6 | 35.4 | 13.5 | 8.7 | 10.1 | 16.5 |
| Waldo State Bank | Waldo | WI | B | B | B | 87.0 | 7.11 | 10.1 | 1.7 | 38.5 | 10.5 | 10.0 | 12.6 | 18.8 |
| Walker State Bank | Walker | IA | B | B- | B- | 42.9 | 1.81 | 4.3 | 1.7 | 10.6 | 21.6 | 10.0 | 11.1 | 16.3 |
| ▼ Wallis Bank | Wallis | TX | A- | A- | B+ | 796.7 | 10.78 | 8.5 | 0.4 | 1.4 | 1.5 | 9.8 | 11.4 | 14.9 |
| Wallkill Valley Federal S&L Assn. | Wallkill | NY | C | C- | C | 327.8 | 1.86 | 4.3 | 1.3 | 51.3 | 6.5 | 8.5 | 10.0 | 15.6 |
| Walpole Co-operative Bank | Walpole | MA | B | B | B | 514.4 | 4.39 | 2.4 | 0.0 | 22.1 | 11.3 | 10.0 | 18.6 | 23.4 |
| Walters Bank and Trust Co. | Walters | OK | B | B | B- | 53.6 | -2.81 | 3.0 | 5.2 | 21.0 | 30.7 | 10.0 | 23.2 | 54.9 |
| Walton State Bank | Walton | KS | D- | D- | D- | 9.2 | 2.15 | 4.0 | 4.9 | 12.1 | 29.8 | 5.6 | 7.6 | 22.0 |
| Wanda State Bank | Wanda | MN | B+ | B+ | B+ | 145.1 | 7.25 | 2.9 | 0.5 | 3.0 | 17.9 | 10.0 | 16.0 | 23.1 |
| Warren Bank and Trust Co. | Warren | AR | B- | B | B | 124.1 | 1.52 | 4.8 | 5.4 | 17.1 | 56.2 | 10.0 | 17.8 | 43.2 |
| Warren-Boynton State Bank | New Berlin | IL | A- | B+ | A- | 174.2 | 0.90 | 9.5 | 2.1 | 17.1 | 23.7 | 10.0 | 13.1 | 19.4 |
| Warrington Bank | Pensacola | FL | C | C- | C- | 88.0 | 5.49 | 0.0 | 0.3 | 1.8 | 47.9 | 10.0 | 18.3 | 49.4 |
| Warsaw Federal S&L Assn. | Cincinnati | OH | D | D | D+ | 55.5 | -9.97 | 0.0 | 0.0 | 51.0 | 20.8 | 10.0 | 12.4 | 23.1 |
| Washington Business Bank | Olympia | WA | B+ | B- | B | 91.1 | 4.65 | 29.7 | 0.0 | 14.5 | 0.1 | 10.0 | 11.4 | 15.2 |
| Washington County Bank | Blair | NE | B+ | B | B+ | 441.2 | 2.11 | 6.5 | 1.3 | 6.6 | 12.2 | 7.8 | 9.7 | 13.2 |
| Washington Federal Bank, N.A. | Seattle | WA | A- | A- | A- | 16420.3 | 1.42 | 6.6 | 0.7 | 34.8 | 17.5 | 9.1 | 10.4 | 15.0 |
| Washington Financial Bank | Washington | PA | B | B | B | 1212.2 | 3.11 | 5.3 | 0.6 | 34.0 | 13.9 | 10.0 | 12.6 | 21.0 |
| Washington Savings Bank | Effingham | IL | B- | B- | C+ | 384.3 | 5.14 | 5.7 | 1.5 | 26.1 | 25.4 | 10.0 | 16.7 | 27.1 |
| Washington Savings Bank | Lowell | MA | C | C | C | 252.6 | 0.64 | 0.6 | 0.1 | 56.1 | 8.9 | 7.3 | 9.2 | 16.4 |
| Washington Savings Bank | Philadelphia | PA | D | D+ | D+ | 163.9 | -0.20 | 1.3 | 2.4 | 58.6 | 1.9 | 6.0 | 8.0 | 12.6 |
| Washington State Bank | Washington | IA | A- | B+ | A- | 329.2 | 3.57 | 5.8 | 1.0 | 27.2 | 25.2 | 10.0 | 12.8 | 19.7 |
| Washington State Bank | Washington | IL | B- | C+ | C | 62.9 | 3.21 | 3.1 | 5.0 | 33.8 | 38.8 | 9.2 | 10.5 | 24.1 |
| Washington State Bank | Washington | LA | B- | B | B | 204.2 | 7.29 | 12.5 | 2.1 | 15.5 | 9.5 | 9.0 | 10.3 | 14.8 |
| Washington Trust Bank | Spokane | WA | A- | A- | B+ | 7151.9 | 9.31 | 16.9 | 1.9 | 9.8 | 26.6 | 8.6 | 10.1 | 13.9 |
| Washington Trust Co. of Westerly | Westerly | RI | B+ | B+ | B+ | 5291.9 | 5.59 | 4.3 | 0.3 | 28.3 | 17.0 | 7.0 | 9.0 | 12.9 |
| Washita State Bank | Burns Flat | OK | C+ | B | B | 89.4 | -15.76 | 6.1 | 4.6 | 11.8 | 36.2 | 10.0 | 11.0 | 23.9 |
| Washita Valley Bank | Fort Cobb | OK | B | B+ | B+ | 42.2 | 3.28 | 6.3 | 9.2 | 1.1 | 24.9 | 10.0 | 17.6 | 22.8 |
| Waterford Bank, N.A. | Toledo | OH | B+ | B | B+ | 772.6 | 5.95 | 26.8 | 1.2 | 4.3 | 5.5 | 7.5 | 11.0 | 13.0 |
| Waterford Commercial and Savings Bank | Waterford | OH | B | B | B | 44.5 | -0.08 | 2.6 | 12.2 | 36.7 | 26.2 | 10.0 | 14.4 | 25.9 |
| Waterman State Bank | Waterman | IL | C- | D+ | E+ | 33.7 | 0.37 | 13.0 | 1.7 | 5.9 | 29.9 | 9.9 | 10.9 | 17.4 |
| WaterStone Bank, SSB | Wauwatosa | WI | A | A | A | 1993.2 | 4.25 | 1.5 | 0.0 | 35.5 | 9.4 | 10.0 | 17.1 | 22.9 |
| Watertown Savings Bank | Watertown | MA | C+ | C+ | C+ | 1274.1 | 7.58 | 0.5 | 0.1 | 36.0 | 41.4 | 9.6 | 10.7 | 23.4 |
| Watertown Savings Bank | Watertown | NY | B | B- | B+ | 676.0 | 3.25 | 7.3 | 1.5 | 16.1 | 14.4 | 10.0 | 14.7 | 21.6 |
| Watkins Savings Bank | Watkins | IA | B+ | B+ | B+ | 69.8 | 2.88 | 0.5 | 1.1 | 6.7 | 51.5 | 10.0 | 17.8 | 34.0 |
| Wauchula State Bank | Wauchula | FL | B+ | B | B- | 725.0 | 9.98 | 2.5 | 0.6 | 15.1 | 22.9 | 10.0 | 11.7 | 19.4 |
| Waukesha State Bank | Waukesha | WI | A | A | A | 1027.2 | 5.36 | 8.7 | 0.7 | 19.0 | 20.5 | 10.0 | 12.3 | 16.3 |
| ▲ Waukon State Bank | Waukon | IA | A | A- | A | 300.9 | 8.16 | 8.9 | 2.1 | 17.1 | 11.9 | 10.0 | 12.3 | 15.9 |
| ▲ Waumandee State Bank | Waumandee | WI | B | B | C | 188.3 | 1.26 | 9.8 | 2.0 | 20.4 | 11.6 | 9.5 | 10.7 | 15.5 |
| Waycross Bank & Trust | Waycross | GA | B+ | B | B | 176.3 | 11.72 | 6.9 | 0.5 | 10.6 | 32.8 | 9.5 | 10.7 | 21.5 |
| Wayland State Bank | Mount Pleasant | IA | A- | A- | A- | 113.3 | 0.83 | 8.8 | 2.0 | 14.1 | 27.9 | 10.0 | 16.7 | 25.8 |
| Wayne Bank | Honesdale | PA | B+ | B+ | B | 1231.7 | 3.90 | 5.9 | 12.3 | 19.0 | 17.1 | 8.5 | 10.2 | 13.8 |
| Wayne Bank and Trust Co. | Cambridge City | IN | B- | B- | B- | 168.5 | -0.60 | 6.1 | 4.8 | 22.1 | 12.6 | 10.0 | 11.5 | 15.9 |
| Wayne County Bank | Waynesboro | TN | C+ | C+ | C+ | 315.6 | 1.23 | 10.4 | 7.6 | 17.0 | 9.3 | 10.0 | 14.8 | 20.1 |
| Wayne Savings Community Bank | Wooster | OH | B | B- | B- | 493.8 | 4.35 | 5.7 | 0.6 | 30.8 | 12.0 | 7.7 | 9.4 | 13.7 |
| Waypoint Bank | Cozad | NE | A- | B+ | A- | 273.4 | -1.55 | 8.8 | 1.8 | 1.6 | 15.4 | 10.0 | 12.4 | 15.1 |
| WCF Financial Bank | Webster City | IA | C | C | C | 134.5 | 2.98 | 0.0 | 4.6 | 40.5 | 30.3 | 10.0 | 16.1 | 35.4 |
| WebBank | Salt Lake City | UT | B+ | B+ | A | 960.7 | 10.23 | 31.3 | 49.8 | 0.0 | 4.0 | 10.0 | 18.3 | 19.5 |
| Webster Bank, N.A. | Waterbury | CT | B | B | B | 30412.3 | 10.13 | 19.6 | 0.7 | 18.9 | 27.3 | 6.5 | 8.5 | 12.6 |
| Webster Five Cents Savings Bank | Webster | MA | B | B | B | 897.8 | 5.70 | 5.7 | 1.2 | 25.4 | 14.9 | 10.0 | 12.3 | 15.9 |

| Asset Quality Index | Adjusted Non-Performing Loans as a % of Total Loans | Adjusted Non-Performing Loans as a % of Capital | Net Charge-Offs Avg Loans | Profitability Index | Net Income ($Mil) | Return on Assets (R.O.A.) | Return on Equity (R.O.E.) | Net Interest Spread | Overhead Efficiency Ratio | Liquidity Index | Liquidity Ratio | Hot Money Ratio | Stability Index |
|---|---|---|---|---|---|---|---|---|---|---|---|---|---|
| **5.7** | 0.60 | 3.6 | 0.26 | **4.1** | 15.3 | 0.88 | 8.01 | 3.22 | 68.0 | **4.1** | 8.4 | 6.4 | **7.8** |
| **6.1** | 0.62 | 3.1 | 0.03 | **4.5** | 9.2 | 1.12 | 11.23 | 4.36 | 66.0 | **1.7** | 24.5 | 20.6 | **5.0** |
| **9.0** | 0.08 | 1.8 | 0.01 | **4.3** | 1.8 | 0.87 | 6.40 | 3.81 | 72.7 | **3.6** | 28.0 | 13.0 | **7.5** |
| **6.2** | 0.33 | 0.6 | 0.01 | **5.1** | 6.4 | 0.84 | 5.36 | 5.09 | 77.2 | **1.9** | 22.6 | 18.5 | **9.7** |
| **5.6** | 0.66 | 8.7 | 0.23 | **0.0** | -0.1 | -0.81 | -6.15 | 3.05 | 124.1 | **3.1** | 59.0 | 22.8 | **4.5** |
| **4.8** | 2.40 | 7.6 | 0.03 | **7.0** | 2.9 | 1.69 | 15.17 | 4.18 | 58.1 | **4.9** | 37.8 | 9.6 | **8.3** |
| **7.3** | 1.12 | 4.3 | 0.07 | **9.8** | 8.0 | 2.75 | 20.16 | 4.38 | 45.6 | **2.2** | 17.9 | 18.5 | **9.8** |
| **5.4** | 1.97 | 6.2 | 0.01 | **2.9** | 0.3 | 0.34 | 4.12 | 3.60 | 89.9 | **4.9** | 28.0 | 5.6 | **4.2** |
| **9.4** | 0.00 | 0.0 | 0.00 | **7.4** | 1.6 | 1.50 | 6.54 | 3.64 | 46.3 | **2.3** | 41.3 | 31.0 | **8.5** |
| **5.9** | 0.74 | 7.2 | 0.00 | **3.0** | 1.2 | 0.51 | 6.54 | 2.92 | 75.8 | **1.1** | 17.6 | 25.8 | **4.3** |
| **4.8** | 0.59 | 3.4 | na | **2.1** | 0.1 | 0.07 | 0.58 | na | 68.3 | **2.0** | 29.5 | 19.6 | **6.7** |
| **4.7** | 2.86 | 12.1 | 0.02 | **4.7** | 5.7 | 0.96 | 9.92 | 3.85 | 71.6 | **4.6** | 17.6 | 4.9 | **6.6** |
| **5.8** | 2.45 | 10.2 | 0.07 | **4.3** | 0.7 | 0.86 | 6.94 | 3.73 | 70.6 | **0.9** | 21.7 | 27.0 | **7.0** |
| **8.6** | 0.00 | 0.0 | 0.00 | **6.1** | 0.6 | 1.35 | 12.25 | 3.51 | 58.0 | **4.2** | 41.6 | 14.3 | **6.5** |
| **5.0** | 1.42 | 5.0 | 0.08 | **10.0** | 20.1 | 2.70 | 22.63 | 5.24 | 53.7 | **1.3** | 26.0 | 32.1 | **8.9** |
| **3.5** | 2.63 | 10.9 | 0.06 | **3.8** | 2.5 | 0.78 | 6.82 | 4.07 | 73.7 | **1.8** | 10.4 | 16.9 | **6.4** |
| **6.0** | 1.37 | 4.4 | -0.02 | **3.3** | 2.8 | 0.56 | 2.97 | 3.18 | 75.3 | **0.7** | 12.6 | 36.0 | **8.7** |
| **8.8** | 0.00 | 0.4 | 0.01 | **3.9** | 0.5 | 0.91 | 4.00 | 3.73 | 78.3 | **5.0** | 37.8 | 9.2 | **7.2** |
| **3.0** | 4.76 | 18.9 | 0.00 | **1.8** | 0.0 | 0.24 | 3.10 | 3.24 | 92.6 | **5.6** | 59.5 | 8.0 | **1.0** |
| **7.5** | 0.20 | 0.9 | 0.12 | **4.2** | 1.1 | 0.81 | 4.80 | 3.07 | 60.0 | **3.4** | 38.6 | 17.4 | **8.1** |
| **8.2** | 3.94 | 4.4 | 0.04 | **2.9** | 0.6 | 0.51 | 2.92 | 2.88 | 82.9 | **3.5** | 50.3 | 20.4 | **8.0** |
| **7.2** | 1.86 | 5.4 | 0.01 | **6.0** | 2.0 | 1.17 | 8.43 | 3.88 | 62.4 | **1.7** | 14.2 | 21.0 | **8.6** |
| **9.6** | 0.00 | 0.0 | 0.01 | **2.6** | 0.3 | 0.39 | 2.09 | 2.61 | 81.5 | **7.2** | 83.9 | 4.1 | **6.2** |
| **7.6** | 2.46 | 6.6 | 0.00 | **0.0** | -0.9 | -1.57 | -11.60 | 2.55 | 145.1 | **2.5** | 45.0 | 30.2 | **5.7** |
| **8.2** | 0.00 | 0.0 | -0.01 | **5.7** | 1.1 | 1.20 | 10.89 | 4.22 | 63.6 | **0.9** | 12.0 | 32.2 | **7.0** |
| **7.7** | 0.14 | 1.1 | 0.07 | **6.7** | 5.6 | 1.31 | 13.41 | 3.62 | 54.6 | **3.8** | 14.9 | 10.1 | **6.8** |
| **7.5** | 0.52 | 2.2 | -0.04 | **6.5** | 223.4 | 1.36 | 11.24 | 3.13 | 51.1 | **1.9** | 19.6 | 20.1 | **10.0** |
| **8.7** | 0.56 | 2.9 | 0.05 | **4.0** | 10.5 | 0.88 | 7.02 | 3.34 | 67.6 | **4.6** | 16.1 | 5.5 | **9.2** |
| **8.6** | 0.32 | 2.1 | 0.03 | **3.3** | 2.0 | 0.52 | 3.03 | 2.63 | 77.8 | **4.1** | 37.2 | 13.6 | **7.6** |
| **6.1** | 1.01 | 6.0 | -0.01 | **3.3** | 1.5 | 0.58 | 6.67 | 3.07 | 77.9 | **1.1** | 14.0 | 25.0 | **5.3** |
| **7.8** | 0.52 | 4.7 | 0.01 | **0.8** | -0.5 | -0.32 | -3.83 | 2.78 | 107.3 | **2.6** | 14.2 | 16.1 | **4.0** |
| **7.7** | 0.42 | 3.0 | 0.17 | **6.5** | 4.4 | 1.33 | 10.40 | 3.60 | 55.5 | **1.9** | 29.4 | 20.3 | **8.0** |
| **5.0** | 0.62 | 11.3 | 0.08 | **4.1** | 0.5 | 0.79 | 7.41 | 2.81 | 63.7 | **3.9** | 26.0 | 10.9 | **4.8** |
| **4.6** | 2.29 | 14.9 | 0.55 | **3.8** | 1.6 | 0.77 | 7.36 | 4.23 | 72.0 | **1.3** | 17.3 | 28.0 | **7.0** |
| **8.5** | 0.32 | 1.9 | -0.06 | **6.5** | 84.5 | 1.28 | 13.24 | 3.97 | 62.9 | **6.3** | 32.6 | 2.0 | **8.9** |
| **7.5** | 0.45 | 3.2 | 0.04 | **6.9** | 70.2 | 1.36 | 14.02 | 2.78 | 54.5 | **1.7** | 13.2 | 13.0 | **9.3** |
| **5.0** | 3.16 | 9.9 | 3.04 | **1.1** | -0.2 | -0.21 | -1.59 | 1.73 | 67.2 | **1.4** | 31.8 | 41.9 | **5.7** |
| **7.1** | 0.64 | 4.0 | 0.31 | **6.4** | 0.4 | 1.00 | 5.72 | 5.26 | 57.4 | **2.6** | 31.5 | 19.3 | **6.3** |
| **4.7** | 1.00 | 5.7 | 0.00 | **6.3** | 9.9 | 1.28 | 12.06 | 3.67 | 60.4 | **2.9** | 14.9 | 10.9 | **7.9** |
| **7.9** | 0.13 | 3.2 | -0.04 | **4.9** | 0.5 | 1.07 | 7.77 | 4.26 | 73.4 | **3.9** | 13.7 | 9.5 | **6.9** |
| **4.6** | 5.59 | 11.9 | 0.01 | **1.8** | 0.1 | 0.19 | 1.77 | 3.40 | 98.0 | **2.2** | 25.9 | 19.5 | **3.1** |
| **8.6** | 0.62 | 2.4 | 0.00 | **9.5** | 35.8 | 1.81 | 10.03 | 3.00 | 74.5 | **1.5** | 15.2 | 26.4 | **10.0** |
| **9.8** | 0.55 | 2.2 | 0.00 | **2.9** | 5.4 | 0.44 | 4.20 | 2.71 | 79.8 | **4.3** | 50.3 | 18.5 | **7.5** |
| **4.9** | 1.58 | 8.3 | 0.24 | **5.7** | 7.8 | 1.16 | 7.33 | 3.95 | 60.6 | **4.7** | 14.4 | 4.0 | **8.6** |
| **9.1** | 0.00 | 0.0 | 0.00 | **5.0** | 0.8 | 1.06 | 6.08 | 2.88 | 53.4 | **3.7** | 63.1 | 20.7 | **8.2** |
| **4.8** | 2.58 | 12.7 | 0.09 | **9.3** | 15.4 | 2.23 | 18.46 | 4.38 | 50.6 | **3.7** | 36.8 | 15.3 | **8.6** |
| **8.9** | 0.32 | 1.3 | 0.00 | **8.0** | 17.6 | 1.77 | 14.73 | 4.30 | 65.1 | **5.2** | 16.8 | 1.2 | **10.0** |
| **8.4** | 0.00 | 0.0 | -0.01 | **9.0** | 5.7 | 1.99 | 15.85 | 3.61 | 44.0 | **2.7** | 24.1 | 16.3 | **9.6** |
| **7.7** | 0.24 | 0.8 | 0.14 | **4.7** | 1.6 | 0.87 | 7.92 | 3.92 | 68.0 | **2.2** | 21.7 | 18.5 | **6.6** |
| **6.6** | 0.75 | 3.3 | 0.01 | **7.0** | 2.9 | 1.69 | 15.49 | 3.34 | 70.7 | **4.6** | 41.5 | 12.5 | **7.3** |
| **7.5** | 1.28 | 3.7 | 0.06 | **6.6** | 1.5 | 1.37 | 7.89 | 3.77 | 47.2 | **6.0** | 49.8 | 6.4 | **8.5** |
| **7.6** | 0.09 | 0.6 | 0.13 | **5.7** | 14.6 | 1.21 | 11.32 | 3.53 | 59.5 | **1.5** | 6.2 | 22.6 | **8.6** |
| **6.4** | 0.62 | 4.6 | 0.13 | **3.0** | 0.8 | 0.47 | 4.08 | 4.06 | 89.3 | **2.8** | 19.4 | 7.4 | **6.6** |
| **3.4** | 4.62 | 18.2 | 0.34 | **5.4** | 2.9 | 0.91 | 6.22 | 4.42 | 67.0 | **0.9** | 23.7 | 38.8 | **7.1** |
| **5.7** | 0.81 | 5.8 | 0.05 | **6.4** | 6.6 | 1.35 | 14.02 | 3.63 | 55.6 | **2.8** | 12.4 | 10.5 | **6.0** |
| **5.5** | 1.35 | 6.3 | 0.01 | **7.6** | 4.5 | 1.69 | 13.00 | 4.07 | 55.9 | **3.0** | 19.4 | 13.9 | **9.4** |
| **8.9** | 0.55 | 2.5 | 0.10 | **1.9** | 0.2 | 0.19 | 1.23 | 2.74 | 91.4 | **3.3** | 52.2 | 24.3 | **7.2** |
| **5.0** | 0.00 | 3.8 | 3.81 | **10.0** | 50.0 | 5.58 | 32.19 | 11.66 | 28.0 | **0.5** | 14.0 | 6.1 | **9.1** |
| **5.3** | 1.41 | 6.3 | 0.21 | **6.9** | 404.9 | 1.39 | 13.38 | 3.57 | 55.9 | **4.2** | 21.5 | 6.9 | **9.1** |
| **8.4** | 0.35 | 1.8 | 0.02 | **4.2** | 6.9 | 0.80 | 6.39 | 3.57 | 74.6 | **3.6** | 12.2 | 3.6 | **7.8** |

| Name | City | State | Rating | 2018 Rating | 2017 Rating | Total Assets ($Mil) | One Year Asset Growth | Asset Mix (As a % of Total Assets) Commercial Loans | Consumer Loans | Mortgage Loans | Securities | Capitalization Index | Leverage Ratio | Risk-Based Capital Ratio |
|---|---|---|---|---|---|---|---|---|---|---|---|---|---|---|
| Welch State Bank of Welch, Oklahoma | Welch | OK | A- | A | A- | 279.7 | 3.68 | 5.2 | 2.8 | 14.7 | 18.8 | 8.9 | 10.2 | 15.0 |
| Welcome State Bank | Welcome | MN | B+ | C+ | B | 32.9 | 7.79 | 10.3 | 6.6 | 11.8 | 3.8 | 9.7 | 10.8 | 14.8 |
| Wellesley Bank | Wellesley | MA | B- | B- | B- | 940.1 | 8.12 | 10.3 | 0.0 | 41.7 | 3.2 | 5.8 | 8.4 | 11.6 |
| Wellington State Bank | Wellington | TX | B | B | B | 447.9 | 12.63 | 5.7 | 2.2 | 4.5 | 23.1 | 9.2 | 10.9 | 14.3 |
| Wellington Trust Co., N.A. | Boston | MA | U | U | U | 93.4 | -0.32 | 0.0 | 0.0 | 0.0 | 0.0 | 10.0 | 45.7 | 44.6 |
| Wells Bank | Platte City | MO | A- | A- | A- | 249.7 | 8.41 | 2.8 | 0.8 | 22.6 | 8.7 | 8.2 | 9.8 | 13.6 |
| Wells Fargo Bank South Central, N.A. | Houston | TX | A- | B | B- | 5630.2 | -21.12 | 0.0 | 0.0 | 97.8 | 0.0 | 10.0 | 13.5 | 27.0 |
| Wells Fargo Bank, Ltd. | Los Angeles | CA | U | U | U | 841.3 | -3.77 | 0.0 | 0.0 | 0.0 | 0.0 | 10.0 | 93.4 | 82.3 |
| Wells Fargo Bank, N.A. | Sioux Falls | SD | B | B | B- | 1712919.0 | 1.40 | 10.8 | 6.6 | 16.6 | 23.9 | 6.6 | 8.6 | 14.3 |
| Wells Fargo Delaware Trust Co., N.A. | Wilmington | DE | U | U | U | 232.7 | -39.17 | 0.0 | 0.0 | 0.0 | 0.0 | 10.0 | 95.9 | 486.4 |
| Wells Fargo National Bank West | Las Vegas | NV | A- | A- | B+ | 16012.9 | 60.69 | 0.0 | 0.0 | 72.7 | 0.0 | 8.5 | 10.0 | 22.6 |
| Wells Fargo Trust Co., N.A. | Salt Lake City | UT | U | U | B+ | 1291.7 | -0.71 | 0.0 | 0.0 | 0.0 | 0.9 | 10.0 | 94.2 | 416.5 |
| Wells River Savings Bank | Wells River | VT | C- | D+ | C- | 187.1 | 1.21 | 4.7 | 5.5 | 44.1 | 23.2 | 9.9 | 10.9 | 16.7 |
| Wenona State Bank | Wenona | IL | C+ | C+ | C+ | 35.7 | 9.72 | 9.3 | 3.8 | 4.8 | 29.3 | 10.0 | 14.1 | 22.8 |
| WesBanco Bank, Inc. | Wheeling | WV | A- | B+ | B | 15674.4 | 26.00 | 8.3 | 2.3 | 15.4 | 20.9 | 8.1 | 11.1 | 13.4 |
| West Alabama Bank & Trust | Reform | AL | A- | B+ | A- | 644.1 | 6.13 | 8.0 | 1.8 | 12.0 | 29.4 | 10.0 | 12.9 | 19.5 |
| West Bank | West Des Moines | IA | B+ | B+ | B+ | 2473.2 | 7.76 | 14.3 | 0.1 | 2.3 | 16.1 | 6.0 | 9.8 | 11.7 |
| ▲ West Central Bank | Ashland | IL | B- | C | C | 187.3 | 0.14 | 11.2 | 7.3 | 22.8 | 7.4 | 8.9 | 10.2 | 14.5 |
| ▲ West Central Georgia Bank | Thomaston | GA | A | A- | A- | 120.5 | -6.50 | 3.2 | 4.2 | 17.7 | 47.9 | 10.0 | 27.4 | 59.1 |
| West End Bank, S.B. | Richmond | IN | C | C- | C+ | 288.0 | -3.95 | 4.2 | 33.5 | 21.5 | 5.0 | 9.0 | 10.4 | 14.2 |
| West Gate Bank | Lincoln | NE | B+ | B+ | A- | 738.0 | 20.78 | 11.7 | 0.2 | 32.7 | 4.0 | 7.6 | 9.4 | 13.4 |
| West Iowa Bank | West Bend | IA | A- | B+ | A- | 135.8 | -3.97 | 7.5 | 1.1 | 8.9 | 19.4 | 10.0 | 13.1 | 18.5 |
| West Michigan Community Bank | Hudsonville | MI | B- | C+ | C+ | 595.8 | 15.00 | 24.5 | 0.7 | 9.8 | 7.9 | 5.9 | 10.3 | 11.7 |
| West Plains Bank | Ainsworth | NE | A- | B+ | A- | 115.9 | -3.36 | 19.3 | 1.7 | 0.5 | 14.3 | 10.0 | 14.3 | 18.1 |
| West Plains Bank and Trust Co. | West Plains | MO | A- | B+ | A- | 402.1 | 1.84 | 13.0 | 2.9 | 10.4 | 14.8 | 10.0 | 12.5 | 15.5 |
| West Plains S&L Assn. | West Plains | MO | B- | B | B | 82.3 | 5.42 | 1.5 | 1.1 | 61.5 | 10.3 | 10.0 | 21.8 | 43.3 |
| West Point Bank | Radcliff | KY | B | B+ | B+ | 284.9 | 9.97 | 0.4 | 2.0 | 32.6 | 29.0 | 6.7 | 8.7 | 12.5 |
| West Pointe Bank | Oshkosh | WI | C+ | C | C- | 293.1 | 2.45 | 14.0 | 0.2 | 18.2 | 12.1 | 10.0 | 17.5 | 20.5 |
| West Shore Bank | Ludington | MI | B- | B- | B- | 462.4 | 2.77 | 13.5 | 4.8 | 21.1 | 15.2 | 6.8 | 8.8 | 12.7 |
| West Suburban Bank | Lombard | IL | B- | B- | B- | 2304.5 | 2.38 | 16.4 | 0.3 | 5.9 | 38.4 | 7.8 | 9.5 | 15.0 |
| West Texas National Bank | Midland | TX | A- | B+ | B | 1392.7 | -2.65 | 26.3 | 0.6 | 12.1 | 25.5 | 9.5 | 10.7 | 16.3 |
| West Texas State Bank | Snyder | TX | B- | C- | D+ | 145.8 | 8.37 | 5.6 | 2.8 | 5.8 | 36.1 | 10.0 | 12.1 | 20.8 |
| West Town Bank & Trust | North Riverside | IL | B- | C | C | 279.1 | 6.79 | 34.1 | 0.0 | 15.6 | 4.0 | 10.0 | 12.7 | 16.2 |
| West Union Bank | West Union | WV | B- | C+ | C+ | 201.7 | 5.62 | 5.9 | 8.9 | 7.5 | 46.4 | 6.7 | 8.7 | 16.0 |
| West Valley National Bank | Goodyear | AZ | D- | D | D- | 81.1 | 39.98 | 13.8 | 0.2 | 4.0 | 3.2 | 7.4 | 9.3 | 14.9 |
| West View Savings Bank | Pittsburgh | PA | B- | C+ | C+ | 353.9 | 1.44 | 0.0 | 0.0 | 23.0 | 69.4 | 7.2 | 9.2 | 16.9 |
| WestAmerica Bank | San Rafael | CA | B+ | B+ | B | 5599.1 | 1.16 | 2.8 | 4.8 | 0.6 | 68.3 | 5.6 | 7.6 | 12.6 |
| Westbury Bank | West Bend | WI | B- | B- | C | 831.4 | -1.16 | 8.9 | 0.7 | 18.9 | 12.3 | 7.1 | 9.7 | 12.6 |
| Westchester Bank | White Plains | NY | A- | A- | B+ | 992.9 | 9.50 | 30.7 | 0.4 | 3.5 | 7.9 | 10.0 | 13.3 | 15.4 |
| Western Alliance Bank | Phoenix | AZ | A- | A- | A- | 26862.7 | 16.10 | 19.4 | 0.0 | 7.3 | 14.3 | 6.2 | 10.3 | 11.9 |
| ▲ Western Bank | Lordsburg | NM | A | B+ | A- | 193.5 | 6.25 | 4.5 | 1.8 | 6.5 | 50.2 | 10.0 | 11.5 | 25.7 |
| Western Bank | Lubbock | TX | B- | B- | B | 341.5 | 41.86 | 14.3 | 0.9 | 13.1 | 16.5 | 6.1 | 9.0 | 11.9 |
| Western Bank of Clovis | Clovis | NM | B+ | B+ | B+ | 74.9 | -26.96 | 3.0 | 0.5 | 2.4 | 16.3 | 10.0 | 13.3 | 20.5 |
| ▲ Western Bank, Artesia, New Mexico | Artesia | NM | B- | C+ | B | 219.7 | 0.39 | 29.6 | 1.4 | 2.3 | 34.4 | 7.5 | 9.3 | 17.7 |
| ▲ Western Commerce Bank | Carlsbad | NM | A- | B+ | B+ | 522.8 | 5.84 | 11.8 | 0.6 | 16.7 | 27.6 | 6.1 | 8.1 | 18.3 |
| ▲ Western Dakota Bank | Timber Lake | SD | C | D+ | D | 42.7 | 6.80 | 5.0 | 3.3 | 0.1 | 2.8 | 6.4 | 8.4 | 18.5 |
| Western Heritage Bank | Las Cruces | NM | C+ | C- | C | 243.7 | 18.29 | 22.3 | 1.3 | 7.4 | 2.9 | 9.5 | 11.1 | 14.6 |
| Western National Bank | Duluth | MN | C | C | B- | 104.7 | -4.62 | 10.1 | 2.7 | 18.9 | 1.5 | 9.1 | 10.4 | 15.7 |
| Western National Bank | Chester | NE | B | B | B | 133.4 | 0.91 | 7.9 | 2.5 | 13.6 | 0.2 | 7.1 | 9.1 | 12.7 |
| Western National Bank of Cass Lake | Cass Lake | MN | C | C | B- | 34.3 | -3.15 | 1.6 | 2.1 | 26.8 | 3.5 | 5.9 | 7.9 | 16.5 |
| Western Nebraska Bank | Curtis | NE | C- | D+ | C- | 126.3 | 2.75 | 15.3 | 2.0 | 6.3 | 10.2 | 5.2 | 9.8 | 11.1 |
| Western State Bank | Garden City | KS | A- | A | A | 491.5 | 2.63 | 10.3 | 0.4 | 5.2 | 22.6 | 10.0 | 12.1 | 17.6 |
| Western State Bank | Devils Lake | ND | B | B- | B | 1286.5 | 17.24 | 40.3 | 1.3 | 6.7 | 4.4 | 7.6 | 10.8 | 13.0 |
| ▲ Western States Bank | Laramie | WY | B- | C | B- | 471.1 | -4.16 | 11.1 | 0.8 | 9.7 | 11.3 | 10.0 | 12.3 | 16.9 |
| Westfield Bank | Westfield | MA | B- | B | B | 2179.4 | 2.98 | 10.9 | 0.2 | 30.5 | 10.5 | 7.9 | 9.9 | 13.2 |
| Westfield Bank, FSB | Westfield Center | OH | B | B | B | 1480.4 | 3.64 | 22.2 | 12.1 | 17.6 | 8.6 | 9.3 | 10.6 | 14.4 |
| ▼ Westmoreland Federal S&L Assn. | Latrobe | PA | C | C+ | C+ | 172.7 | 2.01 | 0.0 | 0.0 | 38.5 | 39.6 | 10.0 | 24.8 | 63.0 |
| ▲ WestSide Bank | Hiram | GA | B- | C- | D | 135.3 | 5.54 | 3.8 | 0.5 | 8.1 | 6.2 | 8.9 | 10.3 | 16.6 |
| Westside State Bank | Westside | IA | B- | B- | B- | 124.2 | 18.61 | 13.6 | 1.9 | 22.6 | 4.7 | 4.1 | 8.2 | 10.5 |
| WestStar Bank | El Paso | TX | A- | A- | A- | 1906.6 | 4.56 | 15.4 | 0.1 | 2.8 | 20.4 | 7.3 | 10.8 | 12.8 |

| Asset Quality Index | Adjusted Non-Performing Loans as a % of Total Loans | Adjusted Non-Performing Loans as a % of Capital | Net Charge-Offs Avg Loans | Profitability Index | Net Income ($Mil) | Return on Assets (R.O.A.) | Return on Equity (R.O.E.) | Net Interest Spread | Overhead Efficiency Ratio | Liquidity Index | Liquidity Ratio | Hot Money Ratio | Stability Index |
|---|---|---|---|---|---|---|---|---|---|---|---|---|---|
| **7.7** | 0.15 | 1.1 | 0.21 | **5.3** | 3.3 | 1.21 | 9.72 | 4.35 | 72.4 | **0.6** | 7.7 | 36.5 | **9.1** |
| **7.9** | 0.00 | 0.0 | -1.05 | **9.2** | 0.6 | 1.99 | 17.81 | 4.30 | 61.6 | **3.7** | 23.8 | 11.5 | **7.0** |
| **7.6** | 0.49 | 3.3 | 0.00 | **4.3** | 7.4 | 0.79 | 9.74 | 3.02 | 63.8 | **1.3** | 8.4 | 18.8 | **5.9** |
| **7.1** | 0.21 | 1.4 | 0.19 | **4.4** | 3.9 | 0.97 | 8.05 | 4.36 | 75.3 | **2.3** | 17.4 | 17.7 | **6.3** |
| **10.0** | na | 0.0 | na | **10.0** | 3.0 | 3.56 | 8.29 | na | 98.6 | **4.0** | 17.6 | 0.0 | **7.0** |
| **7.3** | 0.56 | 4.2 | 0.00 | **9.1** | 5.1 | 2.26 | 22.90 | 4.46 | 50.8 | **4.3** | 12.1 | 6.5 | **7.4** |
| **6.7** | 1.71 | 8.6 | -0.04 | **10.0** | 300.9 | 5.18 | 39.40 | 3.67 | 10.8 | **4.4** | 0.0 | 0.0 | **8.6** |
| **8.5** | na | 0.0 | na | **10.0** | 118.9 | 14.12 | 16.93 | 2.13 | 72.3 | **4.0** | na | 0.0 | **7.0** |
| **5.4** | 1.24 | 5.3 | 0.30 | **5.7** | 19553.0 | 1.16 | 11.69 | 3.08 | 63.5 | **5.4** | 39.4 | 4.1 | **9.2** |
| **10.0** | na | 0.0 | na | **10.0** | 8.5 | 3.27 | 3.36 | 2.31 | 30.0 | **4.0** | na | 0.0 | **7.0** |
| **10.0** | 0.03 | 0.4 | 0.00 | **9.5** | 304.7 | 2.07 | 21.73 | 2.57 | 14.3 | **2.5** | 28.3 | 0.0 | **7.9** |
| **10.0** | na | 0.0 | na | **5.5** | 72.8 | 5.65 | 6.06 | 2.78 | 73.4 | **4.0** | na | 0.0 | **8.1** |
| **6.4** | 0.29 | 2.8 | 0.08 | **2.3** | 0.6 | 0.32 | 2.87 | 3.85 | 89.3 | **3.7** | 29.9 | 3.7 | **5.5** |
| **5.5** | 2.79 | 8.5 | 0.13 | **3.1** | 0.2 | 0.62 | 4.30 | 3.45 | 75.8 | **4.6** | 47.8 | 8.4 | **6.2** |
| **5.9** | 0.48 | 2.2 | 0.09 | **6.5** | 169.0 | 1.32 | 7.97 | 3.69 | 58.1 | **3.7** | 11.1 | 10.2 | **9.9** |
| **6.9** | 1.23 | 3.1 | 0.18 | **5.9** | 7.2 | 1.15 | 8.28 | 3.53 | 62.4 | **1.6** | 30.9 | 30.8 | **8.7** |
| **7.3** | 0.03 | 0.2 | 0.00 | **6.5** | 30.2 | 1.27 | 13.18 | 3.03 | 49.7 | **2.1** | 14.5 | 12.5 | **9.3** |
| **4.2** | 0.22 | 6.7 | 0.43 | **4.0** | 1.7 | 0.93 | 8.66 | 4.06 | 77.6 | **1.7** | 20.1 | 23.3 | **6.0** |
| **9.3** | 0.00 | 0.0 | -0.02 | **6.4** | 1.6 | 1.29 | 5.00 | 3.82 | 62.1 | **6.1** | 74.3 | 11.3 | **8.4** |
| **2.6** | 0.91 | 10.6 | 0.71 | **2.8** | 1.0 | 0.35 | 3.41 | 4.16 | 80.1 | **1.2** | 3.7 | 26.4 | **5.2** |
| **7.8** | 0.11 | 0.8 | 0.03 | **7.9** | 11.2 | 1.61 | 15.99 | 4.82 | 66.0 | **1.6** | 6.7 | 15.6 | **7.9** |
| **8.3** | 0.00 | 0.0 | 0.00 | **6.4** | 1.8 | 1.29 | 9.89 | 3.72 | 54.2 | **3.9** | 18.2 | 9.8 | **8.0** |
| **6.2** | 0.31 | 1.3 | -0.01 | **5.8** | 6.8 | 1.23 | 12.08 | 3.93 | 60.8 | **2.2** | 9.2 | 14.5 | **6.7** |
| **6.2** | 1.94 | 4.3 | 0.00 | **7.8** | 1.6 | 1.40 | 9.73 | 4.09 | 53.5 | **2.4** | 19.0 | 17.2 | **9.1** |
| **6.9** | 0.96 | 4.6 | 0.02 | **7.4** | 6.6 | 1.69 | 13.87 | 3.89 | 61.3 | **2.0** | 6.9 | 9.7 | **9.1** |
| **6.2** | 2.19 | 9.2 | 0.00 | **3.3** | 0.5 | 0.57 | 2.63 | 3.20 | 67.1 | **1.3** | 29.8 | 38.6 | **7.7** |
| **6.9** | 0.99 | 6.1 | -0.01 | **4.4** | 2.5 | 0.88 | 10.50 | 2.79 | 64.0 | **1.3** | 4.0 | 14.2 | **6.4** |
| **2.2** | 5.47 | 19.9 | -0.52 | **6.2** | 3.6 | 1.27 | 7.26 | 3.76 | 51.1 | **0.6** | 15.7 | 54.7 | **7.2** |
| **4.4** | 1.37 | 8.8 | 0.05 | **3.9** | 3.6 | 0.77 | 8.45 | 3.79 | 83.5 | **3.1** | 10.8 | 13.3 | **5.4** |
| **5.4** | 1.97 | 8.7 | 0.09 | **4.0** | 15.8 | 0.69 | 7.26 | 3.25 | 73.7 | **6.4** | 42.1 | 4.8 | **7.8** |
| **7.6** | 0.26 | 4.3 | 0.89 | **6.7** | 20.8 | 1.55 | 14.21 | 3.96 | 48.2 | **6.4** | 45.2 | 5.6 | **9.6** |
| **3.3** | 5.47 | 14.9 | 0.26 | **5.5** | 2.0 | 1.48 | 11.77 | 3.70 | 62.2 | **3.8** | 32.5 | 13.5 | **6.3** |
| **1.4** | 5.13 | 26.6 | 0.53 | **8.3** | 3.9 | 1.46 | 11.46 | 4.57 | 65.2 | **0.6** | 11.0 | 28.6 | **8.7** |
| **7.9** | 0.21 | 1.0 | 0.00 | **5.2** | 2.2 | 1.12 | 12.48 | 3.81 | 62.8 | **5.6** | 32.9 | 2.9 | **4.5** |
| **8.6** | 0.05 | 0.3 | 0.02 | **0.3** | -0.5 | -0.65 | -6.30 | 4.71 | 109.6 | **5.2** | 40.4 | 9.1 | **4.0** |
| **10.0** | 0.00 | 0.0 | 0.00 | **4.1** | 2.9 | 0.82 | 8.99 | 2.06 | 48.3 | **2.8** | 41.7 | 13.7 | **5.3** |
| **8.3** | 0.66 | 1.1 | 0.16 | **7.2** | 81.6 | 1.47 | 14.84 | 3.10 | 47.6 | **7.7** | 68.3 | 1.7 | **8.6** |
| **4.7** | 1.36 | 10.2 | -0.01 | **4.2** | 7.4 | 0.88 | 9.19 | 3.28 | 66.4 | **3.6** | 12.8 | 10.5 | **6.7** |
| **7.1** | 0.29 | 1.8 | 0.00 | **7.6** | 13.8 | 1.52 | 11.87 | 3.90 | 49.2 | **2.7** | 13.5 | 9.5 | **8.1** |
| **7.7** | 0.43 | 2.3 | 0.02 | **10.0** | 501.3 | 2.01 | 17.89 | 4.60 | 43.9 | **3.6** | 14.2 | 6.7 | **10.0** |
| **7.6** | 2.12 | 4.0 | 0.03 | **8.3** | 4.7 | 2.51 | 20.68 | 4.05 | 58.1 | **6.6** | 58.5 | 5.7 | **8.0** |
| **8.5** | 0.00 | 0.0 | 0.00 | **4.7** | 3.3 | 1.09 | 12.53 | 4.42 | 70.0 | **0.6** | 6.8 | 32.5 | **5.5** |
| **8.4** | 1.81 | 3.8 | 0.00 | **5.7** | 0.9 | 1.12 | 9.03 | 4.11 | 61.6 | **4.0** | 27.7 | 10.7 | **6.6** |
| **4.9** | 2.10 | 8.6 | 0.07 | **9.6** | 5.2 | 2.37 | 24.47 | 3.91 | 38.3 | **5.9** | 57.1 | 9.6 | **7.5** |
| **9.3** | 0.39 | 0.8 | 0.01 | **8.7** | 11.6 | 2.21 | 29.47 | 4.37 | 47.2 | **5.1** | 38.4 | 8.9 | **7.6** |
| **8.9** | 0.00 | 0.0 | 0.02 | **3.4** | 0.3 | 0.69 | 8.50 | 3.57 | 78.7 | **6.5** | 64.3 | 5.4 | **3.1** |
| **8.0** | 0.18 | 1.1 | 0.07 | **3.9** | 1.8 | 0.80 | 6.60 | 4.47 | 75.5 | **1.9** | 25.6 | 22.4 | **5.8** |
| **2.7** | 1.95 | 13.1 | 0.81 | **3.2** | 0.5 | 0.42 | 3.30 | 4.53 | 77.5 | **0.6** | 14.3 | 35.2 | **6.5** |
| **6.6** | 0.01 | 0.1 | -0.11 | **5.8** | 1.8 | 1.34 | 12.22 | 3.52 | 56.9 | **0.7** | 14.6 | 40.3 | **7.4** |
| **7.3** | 0.43 | 2.8 | -0.04 | **3.3** | 0.2 | 0.58 | 6.16 | 3.70 | 85.3 | **1.6** | 36.0 | 26.7 | **4.3** |
| **4.1** | 0.69 | 5.0 | 1.10 | **2.2** | 0.2 | 0.12 | 1.25 | 3.74 | 78.7 | **0.8** | 7.6 | 21.6 | **5.9** |
| **5.1** | 2.04 | 9.3 | 0.63 | **9.3** | 9.6 | 2.06 | 16.44 | 4.85 | 48.6 | **2.9** | 17.0 | 14.6 | **9.3** |
| **4.8** | 1.70 | 10.0 | 0.30 | **9.2** | 19.4 | 1.62 | 15.20 | 4.83 | 52.4 | **1.5** | 13.5 | 19.0 | **9.8** |
| **4.5** | 3.54 | 12.0 | 0.03 | **5.7** | 5.9 | 1.25 | 10.19 | 4.00 | 67.3 | **2.7** | 24.1 | 16.3 | **7.1** |
| **6.5** | 0.62 | 4.4 | 0.04 | **3.8** | 14.9 | 0.70 | 6.80 | 2.93 | 67.8 | **1.7** | 10.4 | 20.2 | **8.3** |
| **5.2** | 0.76 | 4.4 | 0.08 | **4.5** | 14.2 | 0.95 | 8.39 | 3.24 | 65.6 | **2.6** | 12.1 | 16.2 | **9.3** |
| **9.3** | 2.04 | 3.2 | 0.00 | **2.0** | 0.2 | 0.14 | 0.55 | 1.67 | 90.4 | **5.0** | 79.5 | 17.6 | **7.5** |
| **7.8** | 0.20 | 0.9 | 0.27 | **4.8** | 4.2 | 3.10 | 31.56 | 4.92 | 81.9 | **3.4** | 30.2 | 15.0 | **5.5** |
| **7.0** | 0.00 | 0.0 | 0.07 | **3.7** | 0.8 | 0.72 | 8.28 | 3.86 | 78.9 | **1.6** | 20.6 | 22.4 | **5.2** |
| **6.6** | 0.21 | 0.9 | -0.02 | **9.8** | 49.4 | 2.62 | 20.23 | 4.32 | 47.2 | **4.2** | 22.3 | 10.4 | **10.0** |

| Name | City | State | Rating | 2018 Rating | 2017 Rating | Total Assets ($Mil) | One Year Asset Growth | Asset Mix (As a % of Total Assets) Comm-ercial Loans | Cons-umer Loans | Mort-gage Loans | Secur-ities | Capital-ization Index | Lever-age Ratio | Risk-Based Capital Ratio |
|---|---|---|---|---|---|---|---|---|---|---|---|---|---|---|
| WEX Bank | Midvale | UT | **B+** | B+ | B+ | 2729.6 | -0.46 | 80.0 | 0.0 | 0.0 | 0.0 | **8.3** | 10.9 | 13.5 |
| ▲ Wheatland Bank | Spokane | WA | **B+** | B- | B- | 460.0 | 5.91 | 5.4 | 0.5 | 3.5 | 8.0 | **7.7** | 10.6 | 13.1 |
| Wheaton Bank & Trust Co., N.A. | Wheaton | IL | **B** | B | B- | 2022.7 | 16.65 | 23.6 | 18.6 | 4.2 | 17.5 | **5.5** | 9.2 | 11.4 |
| Wheaton College Trust Co., N.A. | Wheaton | IL | **U** | U | U | 3.7 | 3.66 | 0.0 | 0.0 | 0.0 | 93.4 | **0.0** | 92.8 | 0.0 |
| Wheeler County State Bank | Alamo | GA | **B+** | B+ | B+ | 95.0 | 7.83 | 9.7 | 6.4 | 16.4 | 9.8 | **10.0** | 17.4 | 26.5 |
| Whitaker Bank, Inc. | Lexington | KY | **B** | B | B- | 1155.0 | -5.02 | 3.0 | 3.0 | 17.3 | 36.3 | **10.0** | 15.2 | 28.0 |
| White State Bank | South English | IA | **B** | B- | B- | 41.2 | 8.86 | 7.4 | 2.3 | 12.9 | 26.7 | **10.0** | 14.5 | 19.8 |
| Whitesville State Bank | Whitesville | WV | **C+** | B- | B- | 107.6 | 5.69 | 1.8 | 15.0 | 26.0 | 33.5 | **9.2** | 10.5 | 22.9 |
| ▲ Wilcox County State Bank | Abbeville | GA | **B** | C+ | B | 113.8 | 8.70 | 4.5 | 5.7 | 35.0 | 9.9 | **9.9** | 10.9 | 17.6 |
| Wilkinson County Bank | Irwinton | GA | **B** | B | B | 48.7 | -2.18 | 5.6 | 6.7 | 41.0 | 31.0 | **10.0** | 17.4 | 35.1 |
| Willamette Community Bank | Albany | OR | **C+** | B- | C+ | 150.6 | 1.68 | 13.3 | 0.1 | 2.2 | 9.4 | **9.2** | 13.1 | 14.3 |
| Willamette Valley Bank | Salem | OR | **A-** | B+ | A | 268.9 | 11.53 | 4.6 | 0.1 | 29.0 | 0.0 | **10.0** | 14.5 | 18.3 |
| ▼ William Penn Bank, | Bristol | PA | **B+** | B+ | B+ | 444.6 | 10.29 | 0.5 | 0.2 | 50.7 | 10.5 | **10.0** | 16.0 | 25.5 |
| Williamstown Bank, Inc. | Williamstown | WV | **B+** | B+ | A- | 165.6 | 2.09 | 9.3 | 15.2 | 37.3 | 8.0 | **10.0** | 12.8 | 18.5 |
| Williamsville State Bank & Trust | Williamsville | IL | **C** | C | C | 94.2 | -2.33 | 6.4 | 4.2 | 23.0 | 45.5 | **10.0** | 13.3 | 32.9 |
| ▲ Wilmington Savings Bank | Wilmington | OH | **B** | C+ | C+ | 173.4 | 11.41 | 1.2 | 1.4 | 57.2 | 4.6 | **10.0** | 19.0 | 26.8 |
| ▲ Wilmington Savings Fund Society, FSB | Wilmington | DE | **A-** | B+ | B+ | 12223.1 | 70.17 | 10.6 | 3.1 | 14.9 | 17.0 | **8.8** | 11.7 | 14.0 |
| Wilmington Trust, N.A. | Wilmington | DE | **B-** | B | B | 4658.2 | 7.77 | 0.0 | 0.0 | 0.9 | 0.1 | **10.0** | 13.1 | 56.5 |
| ▼ Wilson & Muir Bank & Trust Co. | Bardstown | KY | **B-** | B | B | 564.6 | 8.72 | 9.8 | 2.2 | 15.7 | 29.4 | **5.7** | 7.7 | 13.3 |
| Wilson Bank and Trust | Lebanon | TN | **A-** | A- | A- | 2780.3 | 10.11 | 3.6 | 1.3 | 19.4 | 15.2 | **9.9** | 11.9 | 14.9 |
| Wilson State Bank | Wilson | KS | **C+** | C | C | 87.6 | 0.46 | 18.4 | 3.0 | 22.2 | 12.6 | **5.5** | 8.8 | 11.4 |
| Winchester Co-operative Bank | Winchester | MA | **B** | B | B | 705.4 | 11.11 | 0.0 | 0.2 | 58.4 | 11.7 | **10.0** | 12.9 | 26.4 |
| Winchester Savings Bank | Winchester | MA | **C+** | C+ | C+ | 577.1 | 6.40 | 0.9 | 0.1 | 53.0 | 13.4 | **10.0** | 12.8 | 20.2 |
| Windsor Federal S&L Assn. | Windsor | CT | **B-** | B- | B- | 543.3 | 5.60 | 8.4 | 0.1 | 26.3 | 15.8 | **10.0** | 11.9 | 15.8 |
| WinFirst Bank | Winchester | KY | **B+** | B+ | A- | 149.4 | 2.92 | 0.6 | 0.4 | 53.2 | 10.7 | **10.0** | 13.5 | 21.3 |
| Winnsboro State Bank & Trust Co. | Winnsboro | LA | **C** | C+ | B- | 230.5 | 19.18 | 5.2 | 3.2 | 14.4 | 8.0 | **7.7** | 9.4 | 13.8 |
| Winter Hill Bank, FSB | Somerville | MA | **C** | C | C | 368.8 | 0.90 | 0.0 | 0.3 | 49.7 | 8.7 | **7.8** | 9.5 | 15.1 |
| Winter Park National Bank | Winter Park | FL | **B** | C | | 351.9 | 42.37 | 13.4 | 0.4 | 1.0 | 31.2 | **10.0** | 12.0 | 20.6 |
| Wintrust Bank, N.A. | Chicago | IL | **B** | B | B- | 6849.2 | 16.29 | 33.3 | 6.7 | 5.6 | 7.2 | **6.0** | 10.3 | 11.8 |
| Wisconsin Bank & Trust | Madison | WI | **B+** | B+ | B | 1090.7 | -2.13 | 16.9 | 1.2 | 5.8 | 16.4 | **9.0** | 10.8 | 14.1 |
| Wisconsin River Bank | Sauk City | WI | **B** | B- | B+ | 147.1 | 16.28 | 4.6 | 0.4 | 29.4 | 7.0 | **9.1** | 10.4 | 15.4 |
| WNB Financial, N.A. | Winona | MN | **B+** | B+ | B+ | 415.5 | 39.27 | 7.4 | 1.7 | 17.1 | 32.7 | **9.5** | 10.7 | 16.8 |
| Wolf River Community Bank | Hortonville | WI | **A-** | A- | A- | 195.4 | 5.43 | 9.9 | 1.9 | 25.7 | 12.7 | **10.0** | 12.6 | 17.2 |
| Wood & Huston Bank | Marshall | MO | **A-** | B+ | A- | 767.9 | 7.55 | 10.5 | 2.4 | 15.1 | 17.8 | **9.5** | 11.2 | 14.6 |
| Woodford State Bank | Monroe | WI | **B+** | B | B | 254.5 | 10.74 | 7.6 | 0.8 | 12.6 | 21.3 | **7.1** | 9.1 | 13.2 |
| Woodforest National Bank | The Woodlands | TX | **B+** | B+ | A- | 6444.9 | 8.80 | 31.0 | 1.0 | 8.8 | 15.2 | **7.1** | 9.5 | 12.6 |
| ▲ Woodland Bank | Grand Rapids | MN | **B** | B | B | 106.1 | 5.02 | 14.2 | 5.2 | 24.0 | 5.8 | **10.0** | 11.1 | 15.6 |
| Woodlands Bank | Williamsport | PA | **B-** | B- | B- | 415.6 | 0.95 | 10.1 | 0.3 | 26.6 | 15.6 | **9.3** | 10.5 | 14.7 |
| Woodlands National Bank | Onamia | MN | **A-** | B+ | A- | 207.9 | 13.40 | 17.0 | 4.6 | 5.9 | 22.6 | **10.0** | 12.4 | 20.2 |
| Woodruff Federal S&L Assn. | Woodruff | SC | **B-** | C+ | C+ | 103.4 | 17.20 | 0.0 | 0.0 | 43.8 | 2.9 | **10.0** | 31.4 | 70.9 |
| Woodsboro Bank | Woodsboro | MD | **C** | C | C | 262.7 | 4.47 | 7.0 | 0.6 | 18.6 | 28.7 | **6.8** | 8.9 | 13.9 |
| Woodsfield Savings Bank | Woodsfield | OH | **C-** | C- | C- | 70.3 | 9.25 | 3.0 | 8.4 | 37.5 | 17.3 | **6.2** | 8.2 | 16.9 |
| Woodsville Guaranty Savings Bank | Woodsville | NH | **C+** | C+ | C+ | 517.3 | 1.34 | 6.9 | 1.8 | 45.4 | 13.7 | **7.5** | 9.3 | 17.3 |
| ▲ WoodTrust Bank | Wisconsin Rapids | WI | **B** | B- | B- | 441.2 | 4.80 | 10.2 | 0.9 | 7.6 | 22.8 | **7.7** | 10.0 | 13.1 |
| Woori America Bank | New York | NY | **B+** | A- | B+ | 2033.6 | 4.51 | 7.4 | 0.1 | 18.5 | 9.1 | **10.0** | 13.7 | 18.1 |
| Worthington Federal Savings Bank, FSB | Worthington | MN | **B** | B | B | 77.6 | 3.49 | 0.9 | 2.8 | 65.6 | 11.8 | **10.0** | 16.3 | 39.3 |
| Worthington National Bank | Arlington | TX | **B** | B- | B- | 295.4 | 2.30 | 10.5 | 1.6 | 28.9 | 2.7 | **9.4** | 10.6 | 15.8 |
| ▲ Wray State Bank | Wray | CO | **C-** | D+ | C- | 159.3 | -3.89 | 8.6 | 3.3 | 9.7 | 7.3 | **8.4** | 10.2 | 13.7 |
| Wrentham Co-operative Bank | Wrentham | MA | **C+** | C+ | C+ | 116.6 | 2.12 | 0.1 | 2.1 | 58.0 | 4.4 | **10.0** | 14.1 | 31.7 |
| WSB Municipal Bank | Watertown | NY | **U** | U | U | 106.7 | -3.46 | 0.0 | 0.0 | 0.0 | 78.8 | **10.0** | 14.1 | 69.2 |
| Wyoming Bank & Trust | Cheyenne | WY | **A** | A- | A | 206.7 | 4.70 | 4.4 | 2.7 | 4.9 | 36.1 | **9.1** | 10.4 | 16.4 |
| Wyoming Community Bank | Riverton | WY | **B** | B | B | 153.7 | 2.26 | 8.1 | 4.6 | 8.5 | 30.0 | **8.0** | 9.6 | 15.8 |
| Yakima Federal S&L Assn. | Yakima | WA | **A-** | A- | B+ | 1799.4 | -4.83 | 0.0 | 0.0 | 36.7 | 40.3 | **10.0** | 25.9 | 69.8 |
| ▲ Yampa Valley Bank | Steamboat Springs | CO | **A-** | B- | B | 320.0 | 1.86 | 7.0 | 2.0 | 19.3 | 12.9 | **7.3** | 9.6 | 12.7 |
| Yellowstone Bank | Laurel | MT | **A** | A | A | 793.6 | 6.58 | 9.5 | 1.0 | 10.4 | 18.4 | **10.0** | 18.7 | 26.1 |
| YNB | Yukon | OK | **C+** | C | C- | 217.7 | -3.14 | 3.6 | 4.5 | 20.5 | 22.3 | **5.7** | 7.7 | 12.2 |
| Yoakum National Bank | Yoakum | TX | **A-** | A- | A- | 226.3 | 1.09 | 6.4 | 5.5 | 17.9 | 40.7 | **10.0** | 14.3 | 30.6 |
| ▲ York State Bank | York | NE | **B-** | C | B- | 151.5 | -0.49 | 8.7 | 1.9 | 4.4 | 6.7 | **7.7** | 10.9 | 13.1 |
| York Traditions Bank | York | PA | **B** | B- | B- | 542.4 | 12.32 | 12.5 | 0.1 | 20.4 | 14.5 | **9.2** | 10.4 | 15.6 |
| Yorktown Bank | Pryor | OK | **B-** | B- | B- | 113.8 | 15.75 | 13.1 | 1.5 | 24.0 | 0.1 | **9.1** | 10.4 | 16.6 |

| Asset Quality Index | Adjusted Non-Performing Loans as a % of Total Loans | Adjusted Non-Performing Loans as a % of Capital | Net Charge-Offs Avg Loans | Profitability Index | Net Income ($Mil) | Return on Assets (R.O.A.) | Return on Equity (R.O.E.) | Net Interest Spread | Overhead Efficiency Ratio | Liquidity Index | Liquidity Ratio | Hot Money Ratio | Stability Index |
|---|---|---|---|---|---|---|---|---|---|---|---|---|---|
| **5.5** | 0.05 | 7.7 | 1.39 | **10.0** | 272.1 | 9.19 | 83.18 | 22.19 | 63.3 | **0.7** | 17.0 | 1.6 | **9.1** |
| **7.4** | 0.08 | 0.3 | -0.01 | **6.2** | 5.4 | 1.23 | 11.90 | 4.89 | 72.2 | **4.8** | 22.4 | 4.1 | **6.7** |
| **6.6** | 0.36 | 1.9 | 0.42 | **6.7** | 23.1 | 1.24 | 10.33 | 3.36 | 43.9 | **2.5** | 12.0 | 11.9 | **8.6** |
| **10.0** | na | 0.0 | na | **8.7** | 0.1 | 2.10 | 2.23 | 2.25 | 91.2 | **4.0** | na | 0.0 | **0.0** |
| **6.5** | 1.25 | 5.0 | -0.07 | **5.1** | 1.1 | 1.15 | 6.64 | 4.38 | 73.6 | **1.8** | 20.8 | 22.0 | **8.2** |
| **4.0** | 5.76 | 14.1 | 0.11 | **4.8** | 12.8 | 1.09 | 6.87 | 3.86 | 73.8 | **5.3** | 31.9 | 8.8 | **7.9** |
| **7.9** | 0.00 | 0.0 | 0.01 | **7.8** | 0.7 | 1.84 | 11.05 | 3.92 | 47.8 | **4.1** | 43.4 | 14.9 | **7.0** |
| **6.4** | 0.58 | 2.8 | 0.36 | **3.8** | 0.7 | 0.72 | 6.89 | 3.96 | 83.1 | **3.4** | 50.8 | 20.7 | **5.2** |
| **4.9** | 1.52 | 7.1 | 0.18 | **6.8** | 1.3 | 1.21 | 11.27 | 4.57 | 65.6 | **1.3** | 17.4 | 28.6 | **7.0** |
| **6.8** | 2.54 | 7.4 | 0.18 | **6.9** | 0.6 | 1.28 | 7.68 | 4.57 | 62.3 | **3.8** | 21.5 | 10.5 | **6.3** |
| **3.4** | 1.30 | 7.0 | 0.00 | **3.2** | 0.7 | 0.47 | 3.61 | 4.37 | 83.5 | **4.1** | 9.8 | 7.6 | **7.1** |
| **7.5** | 0.40 | 2.4 | 0.00 | **10.0** | 12.1 | 4.69 | 36.87 | 4.08 | 70.2 | **0.7** | 7.6 | 30.3 | **9.2** |
| **6.8** | 1.15 | 3.9 | 0.05 | **5.0** | 4.4 | 1.06 | 5.93 | 3.54 | 67.4 | **2.2** | 23.5 | 19.0 | **7.7** |
| **7.4** | 0.25 | 2.9 | 0.17 | **5.0** | 1.6 | 0.97 | 7.67 | 4.47 | 72.4 | **3.4** | 13.7 | 12.0 | **7.7** |
| **4.5** | 4.94 | 17.6 | 0.49 | **1.0** | 0.0 | -0.04 | -0.29 | 2.95 | 99.7 | **6.0** | 55.7 | 7.1 | **6.6** |
| **4.9** | 5.70 | 14.1 | -0.18 | **4.2** | 1.4 | 0.86 | 4.55 | 2.95 | 76.9 | **2.5** | 24.7 | 17.6 | **6.4** |
| **6.5** | 0.43 | 1.7 | 0.22 | **6.7** | 141.8 | 1.23 | 8.28 | 4.37 | 68.2 | **4.0** | 15.5 | 6.6 | **9.9** |
| **10.0** | 4.43 | 0.8 | 0.20 | **4.4** | 17.1 | 0.42 | 2.91 | 4.79 | 93.0 | **8.7** | 108.4 | 0.1 | **8.0** |
| **3.7** | 1.40 | 15.3 | 1.05 | **7.4** | 8.8 | 1.63 | 19.47 | 4.27 | 50.9 | **5.1** | 28.5 | 4.6 | **7.4** |
| **7.5** | 0.31 | 2.0 | 0.02 | **7.4** | 36.9 | 1.38 | 11.71 | 3.62 | 59.2 | **2.7** | 12.7 | 15.7 | **9.9** |
| **3.5** | 1.38 | 9.6 | 0.39 | **4.2** | 0.8 | 0.90 | 8.80 | 4.13 | 70.6 | **1.7** | 9.3 | 18.6 | **6.1** |
| **7.7** | 0.29 | 4.3 | 0.00 | **3.8** | 4.2 | 0.64 | 4.84 | 2.36 | 64.4 | **1.4** | 30.6 | 35.3 | **7.6** |
| **9.3** | 0.33 | 2.1 | 0.00 | **2.8** | 1.9 | 0.35 | 2.88 | 2.63 | 83.2 | **1.6** | 25.4 | 26.9 | **7.3** |
| **5.7** | 2.14 | 8.1 | 0.00 | **3.7** | 3.7 | 0.72 | 6.09 | 3.41 | 75.1 | **3.4** | 20.2 | 12.7 | **7.5** |
| **7.2** | 1.17 | 6.4 | 0.00 | **5.3** | 1.7 | 1.26 | 9.09 | 3.31 | 61.9 | **0.7** | 15.0 | 41.4 | **8.5** |
| **3.6** | 1.31 | 15.2 | 0.31 | **4.2** | 2.0 | 0.92 | 9.83 | 4.12 | 72.1 | **1.0** | 17.1 | 31.8 | **5.2** |
| **9.0** | 0.24 | 1.0 | 0.00 | **2.6** | 1.4 | 0.37 | 3.96 | 3.05 | 87.8 | **1.4** | 14.6 | 16.0 | **5.6** |
| **9.0** | 0.00 | 0.0 | 0.00 | **4.8** | 4.2 | 1.33 | 9.81 | 2.98 | 47.2 | **6.3** | 41.9 | 2.2 | **5.8** |
| **6.0** | 0.43 | 3.7 | 0.04 | **8.6** | 99.0 | 1.62 | 14.83 | 3.56 | 52.2 | **3.4** | 18.0 | 10.5 | **8.3** |
| **3.7** | 2.56 | 10.6 | 0.11 | **6.7** | 13.5 | 1.30 | 9.71 | 4.14 | 63.9 | **5.3** | 25.6 | 4.9 | **8.3** |
| **3.7** | 3.02 | 20.7 | 0.00 | **5.0** | 1.3 | 0.96 | 9.04 | 3.39 | 56.2 | **0.7** | 15.6 | 38.7 | **6.7** |
| **6.5** | 0.67 | 2.0 | 0.08 | **4.8** | 5.3 | 1.26 | 9.83 | 3.86 | 73.4 | **4.4** | 27.9 | 8.6 | **8.0** |
| **6.3** | 2.08 | 7.5 | 0.00 | **5.9** | 2.3 | 1.21 | 9.80 | 4.20 | 63.3 | **3.5** | 12.4 | 11.3 | **8.0** |
| **8.3** | 0.07 | 0.4 | 0.10 | **7.2** | 10.9 | 1.50 | 12.93 | 3.74 | 65.1 | **2.2** | 12.0 | 17.6 | **9.2** |
| **7.1** | 0.43 | 2.2 | 0.00 | **7.6** | 4.2 | 1.76 | 19.25 | 3.99 | 58.5 | **3.7** | 30.5 | 13.5 | **7.0** |
| **5.8** | 1.26 | 4.6 | 0.32 | **8.7** | 135.2 | 2.16 | 22.84 | 3.86 | 78.8 | **6.4** | 30.4 | 1.1 | **8.9** |
| **5.5** | 1.51 | 7.7 | 0.01 | **4.6** | 0.8 | 0.79 | 7.21 | 4.58 | 77.7 | **1.5** | 10.0 | 22.5 | **6.8** |
| **4.3** | 2.19 | 12.5 | -0.10 | **5.9** | 5.4 | 1.29 | 12.48 | 3.87 | 67.5 | **4.1** | 10.7 | 7.4 | **6.9** |
| **6.3** | 0.19 | 0.4 | 0.07 | **6.4** | 2.5 | 1.22 | 9.13 | 4.05 | 62.6 | **5.9** | 39.2 | 3.5 | **7.5** |
| **7.8** | 3.08 | 4.1 | 0.00 | **3.2** | 0.6 | 0.62 | 1.86 | 2.70 | 71.3 | **2.5** | 51.7 | 46.6 | **7.2** |
| **6.5** | 0.56 | 3.0 | -0.02 | **3.2** | 1.3 | 0.50 | 5.73 | 3.55 | 83.8 | **4.2** | 31.9 | 11.1 | **5.0** |
| **4.4** | 1.80 | 12.5 | -0.01 | **3.0** | 0.3 | 0.44 | 5.37 | 3.50 | 81.4 | **4.8** | 37.5 | 10.1 | **3.9** |
| **7.6** | 0.23 | 1.7 | 0.04 | **3.7** | 3.7 | 0.74 | 7.88 | 3.42 | 76.8 | **3.4** | 18.6 | 10.6 | **6.1** |
| **4.8** | 2.20 | 10.4 | -0.05 | **10.0** | 14.1 | 3.47 | 30.86 | 3.63 | 44.0 | **5.6** | 32.8 | 2.7 | **7.6** |
| **7.5** | 0.03 | 0.2 | 0.03 | **4.6** | 17.5 | 0.86 | 6.34 | 3.31 | 67.2 | **1.3** | 17.7 | 25.3 | **9.4** |
| **9.6** | 0.29 | 1.3 | 0.00 | **4.1** | 0.6 | 0.72 | 4.45 | 3.24 | 66.7 | **4.2** | 31.9 | 11.4 | **8.0** |
| **8.6** | 0.03 | 0.2 | 0.00 | **4.9** | 3.0 | 1.04 | 10.38 | 4.24 | 69.9 | **1.8** | 20.9 | 21.7 | **6.4** |
| **2.1** | 3.54 | 14.8 | 0.21 | **5.9** | 1.8 | 1.14 | 10.22 | 4.57 | 62.4 | **1.6** | 11.8 | 22.4 | **6.6** |
| **9.8** | 0.42 | 1.0 | 0.00 | **2.6** | 0.4 | 0.38 | 2.68 | 2.86 | 84.1 | **3.9** | 34.4 | 13.4 | **7.3** |
| **10.0** | na | 0.0 | na | **6.0** | 1.5 | 1.35 | 10.96 | 1.74 | 2.8 | **4.7** | 24.2 | 5.3 | **7.0** |
| **8.4** | 0.02 | 0.3 | 0.05 | **9.4** | 5.1 | 2.56 | 21.73 | 3.79 | 81.3 | **5.4** | 41.5 | 5.1 | **8.9** |
| **7.7** | 0.58 | 2.0 | -0.02 | **4.8** | 1.6 | 1.08 | 11.20 | 3.95 | 74.7 | **3.2** | 30.4 | 15.9 | **6.7** |
| **10.0** | 0.20 | 0.3 | 0.00 | **5.5** | 21.1 | 1.18 | 4.62 | 2.51 | 45.7 | **3.7** | 73.7 | 32.8 | **10.0** |
| **6.9** | 0.20 | 1.2 | -0.09 | **10.0** | 7.9 | 2.50 | 25.91 | 4.82 | 51.1 | **4.0** | 19.2 | 9.4 | **8.4** |
| **7.2** | 0.22 | 0.4 | -0.79 | **10.0** | 24.3 | 3.19 | 16.91 | 4.67 | 44.0 | **4.5** | 24.5 | 6.6 | **10.0** |
| **7.0** | 0.38 | 2.4 | 0.04 | **3.4** | 1.7 | 0.71 | 9.47 | 3.82 | 82.2 | **2.9** | 10.9 | 14.3 | **4.5** |
| **8.9** | 0.03 | 0.1 | 0.00 | **5.6** | 3.0 | 1.34 | 9.25 | 2.89 | 55.4 | **3.0** | 47.2 | 25.1 | **8.6** |
| **4.8** | 0.30 | 2.0 | 0.04 | **5.6** | 1.8 | 1.16 | 8.58 | 3.90 | 62.5 | **2.4** | 9.3 | 13.9 | **7.9** |
| **6.2** | 0.64 | 3.2 | 0.04 | **5.1** | 5.2 | 1.02 | 9.69 | 3.56 | 71.4 | **3.0** | 14.4 | 12.2 | **6.7** |
| **7.6** | 0.00 | 0.0 | -0.01 | **4.5** | 1.0 | 0.83 | 6.24 | 3.70 | 69.2 | **1.4** | 29.7 | 33.0 | **7.6** |

| Name | City | State | Rating | 2018 Rating | 2017 Rating | Total Assets ($Mil) | One Year Asset Growth | Asset Mix (As a % of Total Assets) Commercial Loans | Consumer Loans | Mortgage Loans | Securities | Capitalization Index | Leverage Ratio | Risk-Based Capital Ratio |
|---|---|---|---|---|---|---|---|---|---|---|---|---|---|---|
| Young Americans Bank | Denver | CO | **D-** | D- | D- | 20.5 | 1.16 | 0.0 | 0.3 | 0.0 | 0.5 | **5.2** | 7.2 | 240.4 |
| Zapata National Bank | Zapata | TX | **B** | B- | B | 86.6 | 3.25 | 5.7 | 5.1 | 17.3 | 33.2 | **10.0** | 13.1 | 39.6 |
| Zavala County Bank | Crystal City | TX | **B+** | B+ | B+ | 75.2 | 15.96 | 2.0 | 4.2 | 0.3 | 54.8 | **10.0** | 12.9 | 48.9 |
| Zions BanCorp., N.A. | Salt Lake City | UT | **A-** | A- | B+ | 69171.6 | 0.62 | 18.2 | 1.0 | 11.5 | 20.7 | **7.3** | 9.2 | 13.2 |

| Asset Quality Index | Adjusted Non-Performing Loans as a % of Total Loans | Adjusted Non-Performing Loans as a % of Capital | Net Charge-Offs Avg Loans | Profitability Index | Net Income ($Mil) | Return on Assets (R.O.A.) | Return on Equity (R.O.E.) | Net Interest Spread | Overhead Efficiency Ratio | Liquidity Index | Liquidity Ratio | Hot Money Ratio | Stability Index |
|---|---|---|---|---|---|---|---|---|---|---|---|---|---|
| **10.0** | 0.00 | 0.2 | 3.80 | **0.0** | -1.3 | -6.20 | -82.37 | 2.48 | 343.5 | **8.1** | 106.1 | 0.5 | **0.9** |
| **4.4** | 8.31 | 16.9 | -0.01 | **5.7** | 1.0 | 1.20 | 8.74 | 3.13 | 66.4 | **1.7** | 36.3 | 48.2 | **8.4** |
| **9.4** | 0.06 | 0.0 | 0.04 | **4.2** | 0.7 | 0.98 | 7.23 | 3.00 | 72.4 | **5.6** | 60.2 | 10.6 | **7.0** |
| **6.7** | 0.66 | 3.5 | 0.08 | **6.3** | 816.1 | 1.17 | 10.82 | 3.52 | 61.4 | **4.7** | 23.5 | 2.8 | **9.9** |

# Section II

# Weiss Recommended Banks by State

A compilation of those

**U.S. Commercial Banks and Savings Banks**

receiving a Weiss Safety Rating
of A+, A, A-, or B+.

Institutions are ranked by Safety Rating
in each state where they have a branch location.

# Section II Contents

This section provides a list of Weiss Recommended Banks by State and contains all financial institutions receiving a Safety Rating of A+, A, A-, or B+. Recommended institutions are listed in each state in which they currently operate one or more branches. If a company is not on this list, it should not be automatically assumed that the firm is weak. Indeed, there are many firms that have not achieved a B+ or better rating but are in good condition with adequate resources to weather an average recession. Not being included in this list should not be construed as a recommendation to immediately withdraw deposits or cancel existing financial arrangements.

Institutions are ranked within each state by their Weiss Safety Rating, and then listed alphabetically by name. Institutions with the same rating should be viewed as having the same relative safety regardless of their ranking in this table.

- **State** — The state in which the institution currently operates one or more branches. With the adoption of interstate branching laws, some institutions operating in your area may actually be headquartered in another state. Even so, there are no restrictions on your ability to do business with an out-of-state institution.

- **Institution Name** — The name under which the institution was chartered. A bank's name can be very similar to, or the same as, the name of other banks which may not be on our Recommended List, so make sure you note the exact name.

- **Telephone** — The telephone number for the institution's headquarters, or main office.

- **Safety Rating** — Weiss rating assigned to the institution at the time of publication. Our ratings are designed to distinguish levels of insolvency risk and are measured on a scale from A to F based upon a wide range of factors. Highly rated companies are, in our opinion, less likely to experience financial difficulties than lower rated firms. See *About Weiss Safety Ratings* for more information and a description of what each rating means.

Weiss Safety Ratings are not deemed to be a recommendation concerning the purchase or sale of the securities of any bank that is publicly owned.

## Alabama

| Name | Telephone |
|---|---|
| **Rating: A+** | |
| First Bank of Boaz | (256) 593-8670 |
| **Rating: A** | |
| Cheaha Bank | (256) 835-8855 |
| Citizens Bank of Winfield | (205) 487-4277 |
| First Metro Bank | (256) 386-0600 |
| First National Bank | (205) 921-7435 |
| Metro City Bank | (770) 455-4989 |
| **Rating: A-** | |
| Armed Forces Bank, N.A. | (913) 682-9090 |
| AuburnBank | (334) 821-9200 |
| Bank of Vernon | (205) 695-7141 |
| Bank OZK | (501) 978-2265 |
| BankSouth | (334) 677-2265 |
| Bryant Bank | (205) 464-4646 |
| CCB Community Bank | (334) 222-2561 |
| Centennial Bank | (501) 328-4663 |
| Central State Bank | (205) 668-0711 |
| Citizens Bank | (334) 624-8888 |
| Citizens Bank & Trust, Inc. | (706) 657-5678 |
| Community Neighbor Bank | (334) 682-4215 |
| Cullman Savings Bank | (256) 734-1740 |
| Farmers and Merchants Bank | (334) 864-9941 |
| First Bank of Alabama | (256) 362-2334 |
| First Citizens Bank | (334) 335-3346 |
| First Jackson Bank, Inc. | (256) 437-2107 |
| First National Bank of Pulaski | (931) 363-2585 |
| FirstState Bank | (256) 396-2187 |
| HNB First Bank | (334) 693-3352 |
| HomeTown Bank of Alabama | (205) 625-4434 |
| Metro Bank | (205) 884-2265 |
| Oakworth Capital Bank | (205) 263-4700 |
| Pinnacle Bank | (205) 221-4111 |
| Renasant Bank | (800) 680-1601 |
| River Bank & Trust | (334) 290-1012 |
| Robertson Banking Co. | (334) 289-3564 |
| Samson Banking Co., Inc. | (334) 898-7107 |
| ServisFirst Bank | (205) 949-0302 |
| Town-Country National Bank | (334) 682-4155 |
| West Alabama Bank & Trust | (205) 375-6261 |
| **Rating: B+** | |
| Ameris Bank | (404) 814-8114 |
| BancorpSouth Bank | (662) 680-2000 |
| Brantley Bank and Trust Co. | (334) 527-3206 |
| Cadence Bank, N.A. | (800) 636-7622 |
| Capital City Bank | (850) 402-7700 |
| CenterState Bank, N.A. | (863) 293-3900 |
| Citizens Bank of Fayette | (205) 932-8911 |
| Citizens Trust Bank | (678) 406-4000 |
| Exchange Bank of Alabama | (205) 589-6334 |
| Farmers & Merchants Bank | (256) 766-2579 |
| Farmers & Merchants Bank | (256) 447-9041 |
| First Bank | (256) 395-2255 |
| First Community Bank of Central Alabama | (334) 567-0081 |
| First Southern State Bank | (256) 437-2171 |
| First State Bank of the South, Inc. | (205) 698-8116 |
| First, A National Banking Assn. | (601) 268-8998 |
| FirstBank | (615) 313-0080 |
| JPMorgan Chase Bank, N.A. | (614) 248-5800 |
| Merchants Bank of Alabama | (256) 734-8110 |
| MidSouth Bank | (334) 702-7774 |
| Phenix-Girard Bank | (334) 298-0691 |
| Southern Independent Bank | (334) 493-2265 |
| Synovus Bank | (706) 649-4900 |
| Traditions Bank | (256) 735-2121 |
| Troy Bank & Trust Co. | (334) 566-4000 |
| Truist Bank | (336) 776-5342 |
| Trustmark National Bank | (601) 208-5111 |
| Woodforest National Bank | (832) 375-2505 |

## Alaska

| Name | Telephone |
|---|---|
| **Rating: A** | |
| First National Bank Alaska | (907) 777-4362 |
| **Rating: A-** | |
| Mt. McKinley Bank | (907) 452-1751 |

## Arizona

| Name | Telephone |
|---|---|
| **Rating: A** | |
| Western Bank | (575) 542-3521 |
| **Rating: A-** | |
| Academy Bank, N.A. | (816) 472-0081 |
| Alerus Financial, N.A. | (701) 795-3200 |
| Armed Forces Bank, N.A. | (913) 682-9090 |
| Comerica Bank | (214) 462-4000 |
| First Savings Bank | (605) 763-2009 |
| FirstBank | (303) 232-2000 |
| Gateway Commercial Bank | (480) 358-1000 |
| Glacier Bank | (406) 756-4200 |
| Johnson Bank | (262) 619-2700 |
| KS StateBank | (785) 587-4000 |
| Metro Phoenix Bank | (602) 346-1800 |
| Pacific Premier Bank | (949) 864-8000 |
| Stearns Bank N.A. | (320) 253-6607 |
| Washington Federal Bank, N.A. | (206) 204-3446 |
| Western Alliance Bank | (602) 389-3500 |
| Zions BanCorp., N.A. | (801) 844-7637 |
| **Rating: B+** | |
| 1st Bank Yuma | (928) 783-3334 |
| Arizona Bank & Trust | (602) 381-2090 |
| Bank of America, N.A. | (704) 386-5681 |
| Bell Bank | (701) 298-1500 |
| BNC National Bank | (602) 508-3760 |
| CIT Bank, N.A. | (855) 462-2652 |
| Enterprise Bank & Trust | (314) 725-5500 |
| First National Bank Texas | (254) 554-4236 |
| First-Citizens Bank & Trust Co. | (919) 716-7050 |
| JPMorgan Chase Bank, N.A. | (614) 248-5800 |
| Meadows Bank | (702) 471-2265 |
| Northern Trust Co. | (312) 630-6000 |
| Republic Bank of Arizona | (602) 277-2500 |
| Sunwest Bank | (714) 730-4444 |
| TCF National Bank | (952) 745-2760 |
| TrustBank | (618) 395-4311 |

## Arkansas

| Name | Telephone |
|---|---|
| **Rating: A+** | |
| First Security Bank | (501) 279-3400 |
| **Rating: A** | |
| First National Bank of Izard County | (870) 297-3711 |
| FSNB, N.A. | (580) 357-9880 |
| Peoples Bank | (870) 942-5707 |
| **Rating: A-** | |
| Bank of Delight | (870) 379-2293 |
| Bank of Lake Village | (870) 265-2241 |
| Bank OZK | (501) 978-2265 |
| Centennial Bank | (501) 328-4663 |
| Citizens Bank & Trust Co. | (479) 474-1201 |
| Fidelity Bank | (870) 735-8700 |
| First National Bank | (870) 215-4000 |
| First National Bank of Fort Smith | (479) 782-2041 |
| First State Bank | (479) 498-2400 |
| Great Southern Bank | (417) 895-5234 |
| McGehee Bank | (870) 222-3151 |
| Petit Jean State Bank | (501) 354-4988 |
| Premier Bank of Arkansas | (870) 739-7300 |
| **Rating: B+** | |
| BancorpSouth Bank | (662) 680-2000 |
| Bank of America, N.A. | (704) 386-5681 |
| Bank of Bearden | (870) 687-2233 |
| Bank of England | (501) 842-2555 |
| Bank of Salem | (870) 895-2591 |
| Commercial National Bank of Texarkana | (903) 831-4561 |
| Connect Bank | (870) 628-4286 |
| Cross County Bank | (870) 238-8171 |
| Farmers & Merchants Bank | (870) 673-6911 |
| Farmers Bank | (479) 996-4171 |
| FBT Bank & Mortgage | (870) 352-3107 |
| First Financial Bank | (870) 863-7000 |
| First Missouri Bank of SEMO | (573) 717-7177 |
| First National Bank at Paris | (479) 963-2121 |
| First National Bank of Eastern Arkansas | (870) 633-3112 |
| First National Bank of Lawrence County | (870) 886-5959 |
| First National Bank Texas | (254) 554-4236 |
| First State Bank of DeQueen | (870) 642-4423 |
| Focus Bank | (573) 683-3712 |
| Grand Savings Bank | (918) 786-2203 |
| Logan County Bank | (479) 938-2511 |
| Security Bank | (870) 786-5416 |
| Simmons Bank | (870) 541-1000 |
| Southern Bank | (573) 778-1800 |
| Truist Bank | (336) 776-5342 |
| Union Bank of Mena | (479) 394-2211 |
| United Bank | (479) 756-8811 |

## California

### Rating: A

| Name | Telephone |
|---|---|
| Bank of Stockton | (209) 929-1600 |
| California First National Bank | (800) 735-2465 |
| Central Valley Community Bank | (559) 298-1775 |
| Exchange Bank | (707) 524-3000 |
| Home Bank of California | (858) 270-5881 |
| Pacific City Bank | (213) 210-2000 |
| Poppy Bank | (707) 636-9000 |
| Royal Business Bank | (213) 627-9888 |
| Santa Cruz County Bank | (831) 457-5000 |
| Savings Bank of Mendocino County | (707) 462-6613 |
| Sterling Bank and Trust, FSB | (248) 355-2400 |
| Tri Counties Bank | (530) 898-0300 |

### Rating: A-

| Name | Telephone |
|---|---|
| American Continental Bank | (626) 363-8988 |
| American First National Bank | (713) 596-2888 |
| American Plus Bank, N.A. | (626) 821-9188 |
| Armed Forces Bank, N.A. | (913) 682-9090 |
| Axos Bank | (858) 350-6200 |
| Bank of America California, N.A. | (925) 988-4801 |
| Bank of Feather River | (530) 755-3700 |
| Bank of Hemet | (951) 248-2000 |
| Bank of Marin | (415) 763-4520 |
| Bank of San Francisco | (415) 744-6700 |
| Bank of the Sierra | (559) 782-4900 |
| California Pacific Bank | (415) 399-8000 |
| Cathay Bank | (213) 625-4791 |
| Citizens Business Bank | (909) 980-4030 |
| Comerica Bank | (214) 462-4000 |
| Commonwealth Business Bank | (323) 988-3000 |
| Community Bank of Santa Maria | (805) 922-2900 |
| Community Valley Bank | (760) 352-7777 |
| CTBC Bank Corp. (USA) | (424) 277-4612 |
| East West Bank | (626) 768-6000 |
| Farmers & Merchants Bank | (209) 367-2300 |
| Farmers & Merchants Bank of Long Beach | (562) 437-0011 |
| First Commercial Bank (USA) | (626) 300-6000 |
| First General Bank | (626) 820-1234 |
| First Northern Bank of Dixon | (707) 678-3041 |
| FirstBank | (303) 232-2000 |
| Golden Bank, N.A. | (713) 777-3838 |
| Heritage Bank of Commerce | (408) 947-6900 |
| Malaga Bank F.S.B. | (310) 375-9000 |
| Mission Valley Bank | (818) 394-2300 |
| New OMNI Bank, N.A. | (626) 284-5555 |
| Open Bank | (213) 892-9999 |
| Pacific Coast Bankers' Bank | (415) 399-1900 |
| Pacific Premier Bank | (949) 864-8000 |
| Pinnacle Bank | (408) 842-8200 |
| Premier Valley Bank | (559) 438-2002 |
| Silicon Valley Bank | (408) 654-7400 |
| Silvergate Bank | (858) 362-6300 |
| Summit Bank | (510) 839-8800 |
| United Business Bank | (925) 476-1800 |
| US Metro Bank | (714) 620-8888 |
| Wallis Bank | (979) 478-6151 |
| Western Alliance Bank | (602) 389-3500 |
| Zions BanCorp., N.A. | (801) 844-7637 |

### Rating: B+

| Name | Telephone |
|---|---|
| 1st Capital Bank | (831) 264-4000 |
| Avidbank | (408) 200-7390 |
| Bank of America, N.A. | (704) 386-5681 |
| Bank of Santa Clarita | (661) 362-6000 |
| Banner Bank | (509) 527-3636 |
| C3bank, N.A. | (760) 759-1130 |
| Chino Commercial Bank, N.A. | (909) 393-8880 |
| CIT Bank, N.A. | (855) 462-2652 |
| Citibank, N.A. | (605) 370-6261 |
| City National Bank | (800) 773-7100 |
| CommerceWest Bank | (949) 251-6959 |
| Community Commerce Bank | (909) 450-2050 |
| EverTrust Bank | (626) 993-3800 |
| First Bank | (314) 995-8700 |
| First Choice Bank | (562) 345-9092 |
| First-Citizens Bank & Trust Co. | (919) 716-7050 |
| Five Star Bank | (916) 851-5440 |
| Flagstar Bank, FSB | (248) 312-5400 |
| Fremont Bank | (510) 505-5226 |
| Fresno First Bank | (559) 439-0200 |
| Golden Valley Bank | (530) 894-1000 |
| Habib American Bank | (212) 532-4444 |
| Hanmi Bank | (213) 382-2200 |
| International City Bank | (562) 436-9800 |
| Israel Discount Bank of New York | (212) 551-8500 |
| JPMorgan Chase Bank, N.A. | (614) 248-5800 |
| Merchants Bank of Commerce | (800) 421-2575 |
| Mission Bank | (661) 859-2500 |
| Mission National Bank | (415) 826-3627 |
| Montecito Bank & Trust | (805) 564-0256 |
| Murphy Bank | (559) 225-0225 |
| Northern California National Bank | (530) 879-5900 |
| Northern Trust Co. | (312) 630-6000 |

## California

| Name | Telephone |
|---|---|
| Oak Valley Community Bank | (209) 844-7500 |
| Pacific Alliance Bank | (626) 773-8888 |
| Pacific Western Bank | (310) 887-8500 |
| Preferred Bank | (213) 891-1188 |
| Redwood Capital Bank | (707) 444-9800 |
| River City Bank | (916) 567-2600 |
| Signature Bank | (646) 822-1500 |
| Southwestern National Bank | (713) 771-9700 |
| State Bank of India (California) | (213) 225-5700 |
| Suncrest Bank | (916) 830-3597 |
| Sunwest Bank | (714) 730-4444 |
| Umpqua Bank | (541) 440-3961 |
| United Security Bank | (559) 248-4944 |
| Valley Republic Bank | (661) 371-2000 |
| WestAmerica Bank | (415) 257-8057 |
| Woori America Bank | (212) 244-1500 |

## Colorado

| Name | Telephone |
|---|---|
| **Rating: A** | |
| Commerce Bank | (816) 234-2000 |
| Farmers Bank | (970) 834-2121 |
| First National Bank of Las Animas | (719) 456-1512 |
| North Valley Bank | (303) 452-5500 |
| **Rating: A-** | |
| 5Star Bank | (719) 574-2777 |
| Academy Bank, N.A. | (816) 472-0081 |
| Alamosa State Bank | (719) 589-2564 |
| Alpine Bank | (970) 945-2424 |
| AMG National Trust Bank | (303) 694-2190 |
| Armed Forces Bank, N.A. | (913) 682-9090 |
| Bank of Colorado | (970) 206-1160 |
| Bank of Estes Park | (970) 586-4485 |
| Bankers' Bank of the West | (303) 291-3700 |
| Champion Bank | (303) 840-8484 |
| Community State Bank | (719) 336-3272 |
| Dolores State Bank | (970) 882-7600 |
| Eastern Colorado Bank | (719) 767-5652 |
| Farmers State Bank of Brush | (970) 842-5101 |
| First National Bank | (605) 223-2521 |
| First National Bank of Hugo | (719) 743-2415 |
| First Pioneer National Bank | (970) 332-4824 |
| First State Bank | (308) 632-4158 |
| FirstBank | (303) 232-2000 |
| FirsTier Bank | (308) 235-4633 |
| FirstOak Bank | (620) 331-2265 |
| Frontier Bank | (719) 336-4351 |
| Glacier Bank | (406) 756-4200 |
| Gunnison Bank and Trust Co. | (970) 641-0320 |
| High Country Bank | (719) 539-2516 |
| High Plains Bank | (719) 765-4000 |
| Points West Community Bank | (970) 686-0878 |
| Redstone Bank | (720) 880-5000 |
| Solera National Bank | (303) 209-8600 |
| United Business Bank | (925) 476-1800 |
| Verus Bank of Commerce | (970) 204-1010 |
| Waypoint Bank | (308) 784-2515 |
| Yampa Valley Bank | (970) 879-2993 |
| Zions BanCorp., N.A. | (801) 844-7637 |
| **Rating: B+** | |
| Adams Bank & Trust | (308) 284-4071 |
| ANB Bank | (303) 394-5143 |
| Bank of America, N.A. | (704) 386-5681 |
| Bank of Burlington | (719) 346-5376 |
| Central Trust Bank | (573) 634-1302 |
| CIT Bank, N.A. | (855) 462-2652 |
| Citywide Banks | (303) 365-3800 |
| Colorado Bank and Trust Co. of La Junta | (719) 384-8131 |
| First-Citizens Bank & Trust Co. | (919) 716-7050 |
| FNB Bank | (785) 890-2000 |
| Golden Belt Bank, FSA | (785) 726-3157 |
| Grand Valley Bank | (435) 654-7400 |
| Independent Bank | (972) 562-9004 |
| JPMorgan Chase Bank, N.A. | (614) 248-5800 |
| Kirkpatrick Bank | (405) 341-8222 |
| Legacy Bank | (719) 829-4811 |
| Northern Trust Co. | (312) 630-6000 |
| Pacific Western Bank | (310) 887-8500 |
| Pueblo Bank and Trust Co. | (719) 545-1834 |
| Simmons Bank | (870) 541-1000 |
| TCF National Bank | (952) 745-2760 |
| United Fidelity Bank, FSB | (812) 424-0921 |

## Connecticut

| Name | Telephone |
|---|---|
| **Rating: A** | |
| Bessemer Trust Co., N.A. | (212) 708-9100 |
| **Rating: A-** | |
| Chelsea Groton Bank | (860) 823-4800 |
| Liberty Bank | (860) 638-2922 |
| Savings Bank of Danbury | (203) 743-3849 |
| Stafford Savings Bank | (860) 684-4261 |
| **Rating: B+** | |
| Bank of America, N.A. | (704) 386-5681 |
| Citibank, N.A. | (605) 370-6261 |
| JPMorgan Chase Bank, N.A. | (614) 248-5800 |
| Northern Trust Co. | (312) 630-6000 |
| Signature Bank | (646) 822-1500 |
| Union Savings Bank | (203) 830-4200 |
| Washington Trust Co. of Westerly | (401) 348-1200 |

## Delaware

| Name | Telephone |
|---|---|
| **Rating: A+** | |
| Deutsche Bank Trust Co. Delaware | (302) 636-3301 |
| **Rating: A** | |
| Applied Bank | (888) 839-7952 |
| Calvin B. Taylor Banking Co. | (410) 641-1700 |
| FSNB, N.A. | (580) 357-9880 |
| Morgan Stanley Private Bank, N.A. | (212) 762-1803 |
| **Rating: A-** | |
| Bank of Ocean City | (410) 213-0173 |
| Wilmington Savings Fund Society, FSB | (302) 792-6000 |
| **Rating: B+** | |
| Bank of America, N.A. | (704) 386-5681 |
| Bryn Mawr Trust Co. | (610) 581-4839 |
| Citibank, N.A. | (605) 370-6261 |
| JPMorgan Chase Bank, N.A. | (614) 248-5800 |
| Shore United Bank | (410) 822-1400 |

## District of Columbia

### Rating: A

| Name | Telephone |
|---|---|
| EagleBank | (240) 497-2075 |

### Rating: B+

| Name | Telephone |
|---|---|
| Bank of America, N.A. | (704) 386-5681 |
| Citibank, N.A. | (605) 370-6261 |
| City National Bank | (800) 773-7100 |
| FVCbank | (703) 436-4740 |
| John Marshall Bank | (703) 584-0840 |
| JPMorgan Chase Bank, N.A. | (614) 248-5800 |
| Northern Trust Co. | (312) 630-6000 |
| Truist Bank | (336) 776-5342 |

## Federated States of Micronesia

| Name | Telephone | Name | Telephone |
| --- | --- | --- | --- |

**Rating: A-**

Bank of the Federated States of Micronesia

## Florida

| Name | Telephone |
|---|---|
| **Rating: A+** | |
| Citizens First Bank | (352) 753-9515 |
| **Rating: A** | |
| Esquire Bank, N.A. | (516) 535-2002 |
| Hillsboro Bank | (813) 707-6506 |
| Metro City Bank | (770) 455-4989 |
| Paradise Bank | (561) 392-5444 |
| Southeastern Bank | (912) 437-4141 |
| **Rating: A-** | |
| 1st Source Bank | (574) 235-2000 |
| Amerasia Bank | (718) 463-3600 |
| American National Bank | (954) 491-7788 |
| Armed Forces Bank, N.A. | (913) 682-9090 |
| Bank OZK | (501) 978-2265 |
| Busey Bank | (217) 351-6500 |
| CCB Community Bank | (334) 222-2561 |
| Centennial Bank | (501) 328-4663 |
| Charlotte State Bank & Trust | (941) 624-5400 |
| Comerica Bank | (214) 462-4000 |
| Commerce National Bank & Trust | (407) 622-8181 |
| Community Bank of the South | (321) 452-0420 |
| Crews Bank & Trust | (863) 494-2220 |
| Drummond Community Bank | (352) 493-2277 |
| Englewood Bank & Trust | (941) 475-6771 |
| First Federal Bank | (386) 755-0600 |
| First National Bank of Mount Dora | (352) 383-2111 |
| Florida Business Bank | (321) 253-1555 |
| FNBT Bank | (850) 796-2000 |
| Heartland National Bank | (863) 386-1300 |
| Peoples Bank of Graceville | (850) 263-3267 |
| Raymond James Bank, N.A. | (727) 567-8000 |
| Renasant Bank | (800) 680-1601 |
| Republic Bank & Trust Co. | (502) 584-3600 |
| ServisFirst Bank | (205) 949-0302 |
| Stearns Bank N.A. | (320) 253-6607 |
| Sunrise Bank | (321) 784-8333 |
| TrustCo Bank | (518) 377-3311 |
| **Rating: B+** | |
| American Momentum Bank | (979) 774-1111 |
| Ameris Bank | (404) 814-8114 |
| BAC Florida Bank | (305) 789-7000 |
| BancorpSouth Bank | (662) 680-2000 |
| Bank of America, N.A. | (704) 386-5681 |
| Bank of Central Florida | (863) 701-2685 |
| Bank of Tampa | (813) 872-1216 |
| BankUnited, N.A. | (786) 313-1010 |
| Cadence Bank, N.A. | (800) 636-7622 |
| Capital City Bank | (850) 402-7700 |
| CenterState Bank, N.A. | (863) 293-3900 |
| CIT Bank, N.A. | (855) 462-2652 |
| Citibank, N.A. | (605) 370-6261 |
| City National Bank | (800) 773-7100 |
| First Home Bank | (727) 440-6848 |
| First National Bank Northwest Florida | (850) 769-3207 |
| First National Bank of Coffee County | (912) 384-1100 |
| First Port City Bank | (229) 246-6200 |
| First, A National Banking Assn. | (601) 268-8998 |
| First-Citizens Bank & Trust Co. | (919) 716-7050 |
| Flagler Bank | (561) 432-2122 |
| Interaudi Bank | (212) 833-1000 |
| Israel Discount Bank of New York | (212) 551-8500 |
| JPMorgan Chase Bank, N.A. | (614) 248-5800 |
| Lake Forest Bank & Trust Co., N.A. | (847) 234-2882 |
| MidSouth Bank | (334) 702-7774 |
| Northern Trust Co. | (312) 630-6000 |
| Ocean Bank | (305) 442-2660 |
| Prime Meridian Bank | (850) 907-2301 |
| Safra National Bank of New York | (212) 704-5500 |
| Seacoast National Bank | (772) 221-2760 |
| Synovus Bank | (706) 649-4900 |
| Truist Bank | (336) 776-5342 |
| Trustmark National Bank | (601) 208-5111 |
| United Fidelity Bank, FSB | (812) 424-0921 |
| Wauchula State Bank | (863) 773-4151 |
| Woodforest National Bank | (832) 375-2505 |

## Georgia

### Rating: A

| Name | Telephone |
|---|---|
| Commercial Bank | (706) 743-8184 |
| Douglas National Bank | (912) 384-2233 |
| Durden Banking Co., Inc. | (478) 763-2121 |
| Embassy National Bank | (770) 822-9111 |
| Farmers State Bank | (706) 359-3131 |
| First National Bank of Waynesboro | (706) 554-8100 |
| FNB South | (912) 632-7262 |
| FSNB, N.A. | (580) 357-9880 |
| Metro City Bank | (770) 455-4989 |
| Quantum National Bank | (770) 945-8300 |
| South Georgia Bank | (912) 654-1051 |
| Southeastern Bank | (912) 437-4141 |
| United Bank | (770) 567-7211 |
| West Central Georgia Bank | (706) 647-8951 |

### Rating: A-

| Name | Telephone |
|---|---|
| American Pride Bank | (478) 784-1448 |
| Armed Forces Bank, N.A. | (913) 682-9090 |
| Bank of Dade | (706) 657-6842 |
| Bank of Dawson | (229) 995-2141 |
| Bank of Dudley | (478) 277-1500 |
| Bank of Madison | (706) 342-1953 |
| Bank OZK | (501) 978-2265 |
| BankSouth | (706) 453-2943 |
| Century Bank of Georgia | (770) 387-1922 |
| Citizens Bank & Trust, Inc. | (706) 657-5678 |
| Citizens Community Bank | (229) 794-2111 |
| Commercial Banking Co. | (229) 242-7600 |
| Community Banking Co. of Fitzgerald | (229) 423-4321 |
| East West Bank | (626) 768-6000 |
| Exchange Bank | (478) 452-4531 |
| Farmers State Bank | (478) 275-3223 |
| First American Bank and Trust Co. | (706) 354-5000 |
| First Peoples Bank | (706) 663-2700 |
| First State Bank of Blakely | (229) 723-3711 |
| First Volunteer Bank | (423) 668-4509 |
| Glennville Bank | (912) 654-3471 |
| Northeast Georgia Bank | (706) 356-4444 |
| Peoples Bank of East Tennessee | (423) 442-7262 |
| PromiseOne Bank | (678) 385-0800 |
| RBC Bank (Georgia), N.A. | (919) 206-1060 |
| Renasant Bank | (800) 680-1601 |
| River City Bank | (706) 236-2123 |
| Security State Bank | (229) 868-6431 |
| ServisFirst Bank | (205) 949-0302 |
| South Georgia Banking Co. | (229) 382-4211 |
| South State Bank | (803) 771-2265 |
| Thomasville National Bank | (229) 226-3300 |
| United Community Bank | (706) 745-2151 |
| Wallis Bank | (979) 478-6151 |

### Rating: B+

| Name | Telephone |
|---|---|
| Ameris Bank | (404) 814-8114 |
| Atlantic Capital Bank, N.A. | (404) 995-6050 |
| Bank of Alapaha | (229) 532-6115 |
| Bank of America, N.A. | (704) 386-5681 |
| Bank of Camilla | (229) 336-5225 |
| Bank of Hancock County | (706) 444-5781 |
| Bank of Monticello | (706) 468-6418 |
| Cadence Bank, N.A. | (800) 636-7622 |
| Capital City Bank | (850) 402-7700 |
| CenterState Bank, N.A. | (863) 293-3900 |
| Citizens Bank of Americus | (229) 924-4011 |
| Citizens Bank of Swainsboro | (478) 237-7001 |
| Citizens Bank of The South | (478) 552-5116 |
| Citizens National Bank of Quitman | (229) 263-7575 |
| Citizens Trust Bank | (678) 406-4000 |
| City National Bank | (800) 773-7100 |
| F&M Bank | (706) 678-2187 |
| Family Bank | (229) 294-2821 |
| First Community Bank | (803) 951-2265 |
| First IC Bank | (770) 451-7200 |
| First National Bank of Coffee County | (912) 384-1100 |
| First Port City Bank | (229) 246-6200 |
| First, A National Banking Assn. | (601) 268-8998 |
| FirstBank | (615) 313-0080 |
| First-Citizens Bank & Trust Co. | (919) 716-7050 |
| Four County Bank | (478) 962-3221 |
| Greater Community Bank | (706) 295-9300 |
| Guardian Bank | (229) 241-9444 |
| JPMorgan Chase Bank, N.A. | (614) 248-5800 |
| Liberty First Bank | (770) 207-3000 |
| Northern Trust Co. | (312) 630-6000 |
| Oconee Federal S&L Assn. | (864) 882-2765 |
| Peach State Bank & Trust | (770) 536-1100 |
| Pinnacle Bank | (706) 283-2854 |
| Rabun County Bank | (706) 782-4571 |
| Southern First Bank | (864) 679-9000 |
| State Bank of Cochran | (478) 934-4501 |
| SunMark Community Bank | (478) 783-4036 |
| Synovus Bank | (706) 649-4900 |
| Truist Bank | (336) 776-5342 |
| Waycross Bank & Trust | (912) 283-0001 |

## Georgia

| Name | Telephone |
|---|---|
| Wheeler County State Bank | (912) 568-7191 |
| Woodforest National Bank | (832) 375-2505 |

## Guam

| Name | Telephone |
| --- | --- |
| **Rating: B+** | |
| First Hawaiian Bank | (808) 525-6340 |

## Hawaii

| Name | Telephone |
|---|---|
| **Rating: A-** | |
| Central Pacific Bank | (808) 544-0500 |
| **Rating: B+** | |
| American Savings Bank, F.S.B. | (808) 627-6900 |
| CIT Bank, N.A. | (855) 462-2652 |
| First Hawaiian Bank | (808) 525-6340 |
| Territorial Savings Bank | (808) 946-1400 |

## Idaho

### Rating: A

| Name | Telephone |
|---|---|
| Altabank | (801) 756-7681 |
| Bank of Commerce | (208) 525-9108 |
| Farmers Bank | (208) 543-4351 |

### Rating: A-

| Name | Telephone |
|---|---|
| bankcda | (208) 665-5999 |
| D.L. Evans Bank | (208) 678-8615 |
| First FSB of Twin Falls | (208) 733-4222 |
| Glacier Bank | (406) 756-4200 |
| Northwest Bank | (208) 332-0700 |
| Washington Federal Bank, N.A. | (206) 204-3446 |
| Washington Trust Bank | (509) 353-4204 |
| Zions BanCorp., N.A. | (801) 844-7637 |

### Rating: B+

| Name | Telephone |
|---|---|
| Bank of America, N.A. | (704) 386-5681 |
| Banner Bank | (509) 527-3636 |
| Bell Bank | (701) 298-1500 |
| Columbia State Bank | (253) 305-1900 |
| First Interstate Bank | (406) 255-5000 |
| Ireland Bank | (208) 766-2211 |
| JPMorgan Chase Bank, N.A. | (614) 248-5800 |
| Sunwest Bank | (714) 730-4444 |
| Twin River Bank | (208) 746-4848 |
| Umpqua Bank | (541) 440-3961 |

## Illinois

## Rating: A

| Name | Telephone |
|---|---|
| Commerce Bank | (816) 234-2000 |
| Farmers National Bank | (815) 537-2348 |
| Federal Savings Bank | (312) 738-8422 |
| First Eagle Bank | (312) 850-2900 |
| First Trust and Savings Bank of Watseka | (815) 432-2494 |
| Germantown Trust & Savings Bank | (618) 526-4202 |
| Grand Ridge National Bank | (815) 249-6414 |
| Lindell Bank & Trust Co. | (314) 645-7700 |
| Municipal Trust and Savings Bank | (815) 935-8000 |
| Park Ridge Community Bank | (847) 384-9200 |
| Reynolds State Bank | (309) 372-4242 |
| Royal Business Bank | (213) 627-9888 |
| Teutopolis State Bank | (217) 857-3166 |

## Rating: A-

| Name | Telephone |
|---|---|
| Albany Bank and Trust Co., N.A. | (773) 267-7300 |
| AMG National Trust Bank | (303) 694-2190 |
| Apple River State Bank | (815) 594-2351 |
| Armed Forces Bank, N.A. | (913) 682-9090 |
| Bank of Advance | (573) 722-3517 |
| Bank of Bourbonnais | (815) 933-0570 |
| Bank of O'Fallon | (618) 632-3595 |
| Bank of Pontiac | (815) 844-6155 |
| Blackhawk Bank & Trust | (309) 787-4451 |
| Bradford National Bank of Greenville | (618) 664-2200 |
| Buena Vista National Bank | (618) 826-2331 |
| Burling Bank | (312) 408-8400 |
| Busey Bank | (217) 351-6500 |
| Cathay Bank | (213) 625-4791 |
| Community Bank | (815) 367-5011 |
| Community Bank of Easton | (309) 562-7420 |
| Crossroads Bank | (217) 347-7751 |
| Farmers and Merchants National Bank | (618) 327-4401 |
| Farmers State Bank | (217) 285-5585 |
| Farmers State Bank of Western Illinois | (309) 629-4361 |
| First Community Bank and Trust | (708) 946-2246 |
| First Farmers State Bank | (309) 392-2623 |
| First Financial Bank, N.A. | (812) 238-6000 |
| First Merchants Bank | (765) 747-1500 |
| First National Bank | (605) 482-8293 |
| First National Bank in Pinckneyville | (618) 357-9393 |
| First National Bank in Taylorville | (217) 824-2241 |
| First National Bank of Beardstown | (217) 323-4105 |
| First National Bank of Brookfield | (708) 485-2770 |
| First National Bank of Pana | (217) 562-3961 |
| First National Bank of Sparta | (618) 443-2187 |
| First Nations Bank | (773) 594-5900 |
| First Southern Bank | (618) 997-4341 |
| Fisher National Bank | (217) 897-1136 |
| FNB Community Bank | (618) 283-1141 |
| Gold Coast Bank | (312) 587-3200 |
| Goodfield State Bank | (309) 965-2221 |
| Heartland Bank and Trust Co. | (309) 662-4444 |
| Lakeside Bank | (312) 435-5100 |
| Lisle Savings Bank | (630) 852-3710 |
| Milledgeville State Bank | (815) 225-7171 |
| Millennium Bank | (847) 296-9500 |
| Old Second National Bank | (630) 892-0202 |
| Petefish, Skiles & Co. | (217) 452-3041 |
| Poplar Grove State Bank | (815) 765-3333 |
| Prairie State Bank & Trust | (217) 993-6260 |
| Rushville State Bank | (217) 322-3323 |
| Signature Bank | (847) 268-1001 |
| State Bank of Cherry | (815) 894-2345 |
| State Bank of Lincoln | (217) 735-5551 |
| Sterling Bank | (573) 778-3333 |
| Town and Country Bank Midwest | (217) 222-0015 |
| Vermilion Valley Bank | (815) 686-2258 |
| Warren-Boynton State Bank | (217) 488-6091 |

## Rating: B+

| Name | Telephone |
|---|---|
| American Community Bank & Trust | (815) 338-2300 |
| Anna State Bank | (618) 833-2151 |
| Anna-Jonesboro National Bank | (618) 833-8506 |
| Bank of America, N.A. | (704) 386-5681 |
| Bank of Carbondale | (618) 549-2181 |
| BankChampaign, N.A. | (217) 351-2870 |
| BankFinancial, N.A. | (800) 894-6900 |
| CBI Bank & Trust | (563) 263-3131 |
| Central Bank Illinois | (309) 944-5601 |
| Central Bank of St. Louis | (314) 862-8300 |
| Citibank, N.A. | (605) 370-6261 |
| Citizens Community Bank | (618) 566-8800 |
| Du Quoin State Bank | (618) 542-2111 |
| Evergreen Bank Group | (630) 413-9580 |
| Fairfield National Bank | (618) 842-2107 |
| Farmers & Mechanics Bank | (309) 343-7141 |
| First Bank | (314) 995-8700 |
| First Federal S&L Assn. of Central Illinois, S.B. | (217) 774-3322 |
| First Financial Bank | (877) 322-9530 |
| First Mid Bank & Trust, N.A. | (217) 234-7454 |
| First National Bank in Olney | (618) 395-8541 |
| First National Bank of Litchfield | (217) 324-2105 |

## Illinois

| Name | Telephone |
|---|---|
| First National Bank of Steeleville | (618) 965-3441 |
| First State Bank of Beecher City | (618) 487-5161 |
| First State Bank of Campbell Hill | (618) 426-3396 |
| First State Bank of St. Peter | (618) 349-8343 |
| Forreston State Bank | (815) 938-3121 |
| Frederick Community Bank | (815) 457-2111 |
| H. F. Gehant Banking Co. | (815) 628-3121 |
| Hanmi Bank | (213) 382-2200 |
| Hometown National Bank | (815) 223-7300 |
| Illinois Bank & Trust | (815) 637-7000 |
| Ipava State Bank | (309) 753-8202 |
| Itasca Bank & Trust Co. | (630) 773-0350 |
| Jersey State Bank | (618) 498-6466 |
| JPMorgan Chase Bank, N.A. | (614) 248-5800 |
| Lake Forest Bank & Trust Co., N.A. | (847) 234-2882 |
| Lena State Bank | (815) 369-4901 |
| Liberty Bank | (217) 645-3434 |
| Mason City National Bank | (217) 482-3246 |
| Midland Community Bank | (217) 237-4324 |
| Northern Trust Co. | (312) 630-6000 |
| Old Exchange National Bank of Okawville | (618) 243-5234 |
| Peoples National Bank of Kewanee | (309) 853-3333 |
| Peoples State Bank of Colfax | (309) 723-2111 |
| Philo Exchange Bank | (217) 684-2600 |
| Providence Bank & Trust | (708) 333-0700 |
| Quad City Bank and Trust Co. | (563) 344-0600 |
| Republic Bank of Chicago | (630) 570-7700 |
| Royal Savings Bank | (773) 768-4800 |
| Shelby County State Bank | (217) 774-3911 |
| Simmons Bank | (870) 541-1000 |
| Southern Bank | (573) 778-1800 |
| Southern Illinois Bank | (618) 983-8433 |
| Spring Valley City Bank | (815) 663-2211 |
| State Bank | (815) 297-0900 |
| State Bank of Davis | (815) 865-5125 |
| State Bank of Herscher | (815) 426-2156 |
| State Bank of St. Jacob | (618) 644-5555 |
| State Bank of Texas | (972) 252-6000 |
| TCF National Bank | (952) 745-2760 |
| TrustBank | (618) 395-4311 |
| Union National Bank | (847) 888-7500 |
| United Fidelity Bank, FSB | (812) 424-0921 |
| Villa Grove State Bank | (217) 832-2631 |
| Woodforest National Bank | (832) 375-2505 |

| Name | Telephone |
|---|---|

## Indiana

| Name | Telephone |
|---|---|
| **Rating: A** | |
| Kentland Bank | (219) 474-5155 |
| Stock Yards Bank & Trust Co. | (502) 582-2571 |
| **Rating: A-** | |
| 1st Source Bank | (574) 235-2000 |
| Alliance Bank | (219) 567-9151 |
| Bank of Wolcott | (219) 279-2185 |
| Busey Bank | (217) 351-6500 |
| CentreBank | (765) 294-2228 |
| Civista Bank | (419) 625-4121 |
| Community State Bank | (260) 897-3361 |
| Farmers & Merchants State Bank | (419) 446-2501 |
| Farmers and Merchants Bank | (260) 637-5546 |
| First Financial Bank, N.A. | (812) 238-6000 |
| First Merchants Bank | (765) 747-1500 |
| Fountain Trust Co. | (765) 793-2237 |
| Fowler State Bank | (765) 884-1200 |
| Freedom Bank | (812) 683-8998 |
| Friendship State Bank | (812) 667-5101 |
| German American Bank | (812) 482-1314 |
| Greenfield Banking Co. | (317) 462-1431 |
| Lake City Bank | (574) 267-6144 |
| Logansport Savings Bank | (574) 722-3855 |
| Morris Plan Co. of Terre Haute, Inc. | (812) 238-6063 |
| Napoleon State Bank | (812) 852-4002 |
| Republic Bank & Trust Co. | (502) 584-3600 |
| Union Savings Bank | (513) 247-0300 |
| WesBanco Bank, Inc. | (304) 234-9000 |
| **Rating: B+** | |
| Bank of America, N.A. | (704) 386-5681 |
| Centier Bank | (219) 755-6100 |
| DeMotte State Bank | (219) 987-4141 |
| Farmers State Bank | (260) 463-7111 |
| FCN Bank, N.A. | (765) 647-4116 |
| First Bank of Berne | (260) 589-2151 |
| First Financial Bank | (877) 322-9530 |
| First Harrison Bank | (812) 738-2198 |
| First Savings Bank | (812) 283-0724 |
| First State Bank of Middlebury | (574) 825-2166 |
| First State Bank of Porter | (219) 926-2136 |
| Flagstar Bank, FSB | (248) 312-5400 |
| Greenville National Bank | (937) 548-1114 |
| Horizon Bank | (219) 874-9245 |
| JPMorgan Chase Bank, N.A. | (614) 248-5800 |
| Merchants Bank of Indiana | (317) 324-4660 |
| New Washington State Bank | (812) 293-3321 |
| Providence Bank & Trust | (708) 333-0700 |
| STAR Financial Bank | (260) 467-5500 |
| State Bank and Trust Co. | (419) 783-8950 |
| State Bank of Lizton | (317) 994-5115 |
| Truist Bank | (336) 776-5342 |
| United Fidelity Bank, FSB | (812) 424-0921 |
| Woodforest National Bank | (832) 375-2505 |

## Iowa

### Rating: A

| Name | Telephone |
|---|---|
| Bank 1st | (563) 422-3883 |
| Citizens First National Bank | (712) 732-5440 |
| Farmers State Bank | (319) 377-4891 |
| Farmers Trust & Savings Bank | (319) 668-2525 |
| First State Bank | (641) 843-4411 |
| Hills Bank and Trust Co. | (319) 679-2291 |
| Iowa State Bank | (515) 288-0111 |
| Iowa Trust and Savings Bank | (641) 437-4500 |
| Liberty Trust & Savings Bank | (563) 785-4441 |
| Midwest Heritage Bank, FSB | (515) 278-6541 |
| New Albin Savings Bank | (563) 544-4214 |
| Pinnacle Bank | (641) 752-2393 |
| Security National Bank of Omaha | (402) 344-7300 |
| United Bank and Trust Co. | (641) 456-5587 |
| Waukon State Bank | (563) 568-3451 |

### Rating: A-

| Name | Telephone |
|---|---|
| Bellevue State Bank | (563) 872-4911 |
| Blackhawk Bank & Trust | (309) 787-4451 |
| Boone Bank & Trust Co. | (515) 432-6200 |
| Breda Savings Bank | (712) 673-2321 |
| Chelsea Savings Bank | (319) 444-3144 |
| Citizens Savings Bank | (563) 427-3255 |
| Citizens Savings Bank | (563) 562-3674 |
| Citizens Savings Bank | (319) 462-3561 |
| Citizens State Bank | (319) 465-5921 |
| Citizens State Bank | (712) 324-2519 |
| Decorah Bank & Trust Co. | (563) 382-9661 |
| Farmers Savings Bank | (641) 752-2525 |
| Farmers Savings Bank & Trust | (319) 478-2148 |
| Farmers State Bank | (515) 295-7221 |
| Farmers State Bank | (641) 424-3053 |
| Farmers Trust and Savings Bank | (641) 562-2696 |
| First Bank Hampton | (641) 456-4793 |
| First Central State Bank | (563) 659-3141 |
| First Citizens Bank | (641) 423-1600 |
| First National Bank | (605) 482-8293 |
| First National Bank, Ames, Iowa | (515) 232-5561 |
| First Security Bank | (712) 881-1131 |
| First State Bank | (641) 527-2535 |
| First State Bank | (515) 832-2520 |
| Great Southern Bank | (417) 895-5234 |
| Heartland Bank | (515) 467-5561 |
| Home Federal Savings Bank | (507) 535-1309 |
| Iowa State Bank | (515) 295-3595 |
| Iowa State Bank | (712) 662-4721 |
| Iowa State Bank | (712) 439-1025 |
| Lee County Bank | (319) 372-2243 |
| Leighton State Bank | (641) 628-1566 |
| Manufacturers Bank & Trust Co. | (641) 585-2825 |
| Maquoketa State Bank | (563) 652-2491 |
| Maynard Savings Bank | (563) 637-2289 |
| Mount Vernon Bank and Trust Co. | (319) 895-8835 |
| Northeast Security Bank | (563) 578-3251 |
| NorthStar Bank | (712) 362-3322 |
| Northwestern Bank | (712) 737-4911 |
| NSB Bank | (641) 423-7638 |
| Ohnward Bank & Trust | (563) 852-7696 |
| Pilot Grove Savings Bank | (319) 469-3951 |
| Readlyn Savings Bank | (319) 279-3321 |
| Savings Bank | (712) 957-6815 |
| Security National Bank of Sioux City, Iowa | (712) 277-6500 |
| Security Savings Bank | (515) 352-3333 |
| Security State Bank | (319) 352-3500 |
| Security State Bank | (515) 295-9501 |
| Solon State Bank | (319) 624-3405 |
| South Ottumwa Savings Bank | (641) 682-7541 |
| St. Ansgar State Bank | (641) 713-4501 |
| State Bank & Trust Co. | (515) 382-2191 |
| Templeton Savings Bank | (712) 669-3322 |
| United Bank of Iowa | (712) 364-3393 |
| Victor State Bank | (319) 647-2231 |
| Washington State Bank | (319) 653-2151 |
| Wayland State Bank | (319) 385-8189 |
| West Iowa Bank | (515) 887-7811 |

### Rating: B+

| Name | Telephone |
|---|---|
| American Savings Bank | (319) 882-4279 |
| American State Bank | (641) 342-2175 |
| Atkins Savings Bank & Trust | (319) 446-7700 |
| Audubon State Bank | (712) 563-2644 |
| Availa Bank | (712) 792-3567 |
| Bank of America, N.A. | (704) 386-5681 |
| BankFirst | (402) 371-8005 |
| Bridge Community Bank | (319) 895-8200 |
| BTC Bank | (660) 425-7285 |
| CBI Bank & Trust | (563) 263-3131 |
| Cedar Rapids Bank and Trust Co. | (319) 862-2728 |
| Charter Bank | (515) 331-2265 |
| Clear Lake Bank and Trust Co. | (641) 357-7121 |
| Community State Bank | (515) 331-3100 |
| Community State Bank | (712) 262-3030 |
| Corydon State Bank | (641) 872-2212 |

## Iowa

| Name | Telephone |
|---|---|
| CUSB Bank | (563) 547-2040 |
| Danville State Savings Bank | (319) 392-4261 |
| Dubuque Bank and Trust Co. | (563) 589-2000 |
| F&M Bank | (402) 372-5331 |
| Farmers & Merchants State Bank | (515) 462-4242 |
| Farmers Bank of Northern Missouri | (660) 947-2474 |
| Farmers State Bank | (712) 376-4154 |
| Farmers Trust & Savings Bank | (712) 747-2000 |
| First Iowa State Bank | (641) 932-2144 |
| First Iowa State Bank | (319) 293-3794 |
| First National Bank | (319) 352-1340 |
| First National Bank in Creston | (641) 782-2195 |
| First National Bank of Manning | (712) 655-3557 |
| First Security Bank-Sleepy Eye | (507) 794-3911 |
| First State Bank | (641) 435-4943 |
| First Whitney Bank and Trust | (712) 243-3195 |
| FNB Bank | (641) 745-2141 |
| GNB Bank | (319) 824-5431 |
| Home State Bank | (712) 933-5511 |
| Home Trust & Savings Bank | (641) 732-3763 |
| Iowa Trust & Savings Bank | (712) 852-3451 |
| Laurens State Bank | (712) 845-2627 |
| Liberty National Bank | (712) 224-4425 |
| Luana Savings Bank | (563) 539-2166 |
| Maxwell State Bank | (515) 387-1175 |
| MetaBank | (605) 361-4347 |
| Northwest Bank | (712) 580-4100 |
| Pocahontas State Bank | (712) 335-3567 |
| Principal Bank | (800) 672-3343 |
| Quad City Bank and Trust Co. | (563) 344-0600 |
| Reliance State Bank | (515) 733-4396 |
| Security State Bank | (712) 446-3324 |
| Sloan State Bank | (712) 428-3344 |
| State Savings Bank | (515) 457-9533 |
| United Bank & Trust N.A. | (641) 753-5900 |
| Watkins Savings Bank | (319) 227-7773 |
| West Bank | (515) 222-2300 |

## Kansas

### Rating: A

| Name | Telephone |
|---|---|
| Bank7 | (405) 810-8600 |
| CBW Bank | (620) 396-8221 |
| City National B&T Co. of Lawton, Oklahoma | (866) 385-3444 |
| Commerce Bank | (816) 234-2000 |
| Community State Bank | (620) 251-1313 |
| Farmers Bank & Trust | (620) 792-2411 |
| Garden Plain State Bank | (316) 721-1500 |

### Rating: A-

| Name | Telephone |
|---|---|
| Academy Bank, N.A. | (816) 472-0081 |
| Armed Forces Bank, N.A. | (913) 682-9090 |
| Bank of Prairie Village | (913) 713-0300 |
| Bank of Tescott | (785) 283-4217 |
| Citizens State Bank | (785) 562-2186 |
| Citizens State Bank and Trust Co. | (785) 742-2101 |
| Community National Bank | (785) 336-6143 |
| Country Club Bank | (816) 931-4060 |
| Denison State Bank | (785) 364-3131 |
| Eastern Colorado Bank | (719) 767-5652 |
| Exchange Bank & Trust | (913) 367-6000 |
| Farmers & Merchants Bank of Colby | (785) 460-3321 |
| Farmers and Drovers Bank | (620) 767-5138 |
| Farmers National Bank | (785) 543-6541 |
| Farmers State Bank | (620) 241-3090 |
| Farmers State Bank of Aliceville, Kansas | (785) 489-2468 |
| Farmers State Bank of Oakley, Kansas | (785) 672-3251 |
| Fidelity State Bank and Trust Co. | (620) 227-8586 |
| First National Bank in Fredonia | (620) 378-2151 |
| First National Bank of Hutchinson | (620) 663-1521 |
| First National Bank of Louisburg | (913) 837-5191 |
| First State B&T Co. of Larned | (620) 285-6931 |
| FirstOak Bank | (620) 331-2265 |
| Flint Hills Bank | (785) 449-2266 |
| Great Southern Bank | (417) 895-5234 |
| Kaw Valley State Bank and Trust Co. | (785) 456-2021 |
| Kearny County Bank | (620) 355-6222 |
| KS StateBank | (785) 587-4000 |
| Mutual Savings Assn. | (913) 682-3491 |
| Pinnacle Bank | (402) 434-3127 |
| Security Bank of Kansas City | (913) 281-3165 |
| Security State Bank | (620) 872-7224 |
| Solomon State Bank | (785) 655-2941 |
| Stanley Bank | (913) 681-8800 |
| State Bank of Bern | (785) 336-6121 |
| TriCentury Bank | (913) 583-3222 |
| Union Bank and Trust Co. | (402) 323-1828 |
| United Bank & Trust | (785) 562-2333 |
| Western State Bank | (620) 275-4128 |

### Rating: B+

| Name | Telephone |
|---|---|
| Adams Bank & Trust | (308) 284-4071 |
| Alliance Bank | (785) 271-1800 |
| ANB Bank | (303) 394-5143 |
| Bank of America, N.A. | (704) 386-5681 |
| Bank of Blue Valley | (913) 338-1000 |
| Bankers' Bank of Kansas | (316) 681-2265 |
| Bankwest of Kansas | (785) 899-2342 |
| Central Bank of the Midwest | (816) 525-5300 |
| CIT Bank, N.A. | (855) 462-2652 |
| Citizens State Bank | (620) 836-2888 |
| Citizens State Bank | (620) 345-6317 |
| City Bank | (806) 792-7101 |
| Commercial Bank | (620) 421-1000 |
| Community Bank | (785) 440-4400 |
| Community First Bank | (913) 371-1242 |
| Cornerstone Bank | (913) 239-8100 |
| Emprise Bank | (316) 383-4301 |
| Enterprise Bank & Trust | (314) 725-5500 |
| Exchange Bank | (308) 468-5741 |
| Farmers State Bank | (785) 457-3316 |
| Farmers State Bank | (785) 364-4691 |
| First Bank | (620) 278-2161 |
| First Bank Kansas | (785) 825-2211 |
| First Commerce Bank | (785) 562-5558 |
| First Kansas Bank | (620) 653-4921 |
| First State Bank | (785) 798-3347 |
| First-Citizens Bank & Trust Co. | (919) 716-7050 |
| FNB Bank | (785) 890-2000 |
| FNB Washington | (785) 325-2221 |
| Golden Belt Bank, FSA | (785) 726-3157 |
| Howard State Bank | (620) 374-2127 |
| JPMorgan Chase Bank, N.A. | (614) 248-5800 |
| Kansas State Bank | (785) 242-3600 |
| Kansas State Bank Overbrook Kansas | (785) 665-7121 |
| Labette Bank | (620) 784-5311 |
| NBKC Bank | (816) 965-1400 |
| Peoples Bank | (620) 582-2166 |
| Peoples Bank and Trust Co. | (620) 241-2100 |
| Silver Lake Bank | (785) 232-0102 |
| Simmons Bank | (870) 541-1000 |
| Solutions North Bank | (785) 425-6721 |
| Stockgrowers State Bank | (620) 635-4032 |
| Stockgrowers State Bank | (785) 256-4241 |

## Kentucky

### Rating: A

| Name | Telephone |
|---|---|
| Cumberland Security Bank, Inc. | (606) 679-9361 |
| Farmers Bank and Trust Co. | (270) 365-5526 |
| Jackson County Bank | (606) 287-8484 |
| Kentucky Farmers Bank Corp. | (606) 929-5000 |
| Stock Yards Bank & Trust Co. | (502) 582-2571 |
| Town & Country Bank and Trust Co. | (502) 348-3911 |
| United Community Bank of W Kentucky | (270) 389-3232 |

### Rating: A-

| Name | Telephone |
|---|---|
| Armed Forces Bank, N.A. | (913) 682-9090 |
| Bank of the Bluegrass & Trust Co. | (859) 233-4500 |
| Central Bank & Trust Co. | (859) 253-6013 |
| Citizens Deposit Bank of Arlington, Inc. | (270) 655-6921 |
| Edmonton State Bank | (270) 432-3231 |
| Elkton Bank & Trust Co. | (270) 265-9841 |
| First Financial Bank, N.A. | (812) 238-6000 |
| First National Bank of Grayson | (606) 474-2000 |
| First United Bank and Trust Co. | (270) 821-5555 |
| Franklin Bank & Trust Co. | (270) 586-7121 |
| German American Bank | (812) 482-1314 |
| Lincoln National Bank | (270) 358-4116 |
| Magnolia Bank | (270) 324-3226 |
| Paducah Bank and Trust Co. | (270) 575-5700 |
| Peoples Bank MT. Washington | (502) 538-7301 |
| Republic Bank & Trust Co. | (502) 584-3600 |
| Sacramento Deposit Bank | (270) 736-2212 |
| Springfield State Bank | (859) 336-3939 |
| Taylor County Bank | (270) 465-4196 |
| Traditional Bank, Inc. | (859) 498-0414 |
| United Citizens Bank of Southern Kentucky, Inc. | (270) 384-2265 |
| Victory Community Bank | (859) 341-2265 |
| WesBanco Bank, Inc. | (304) 234-9000 |

### Rating: B+

| Name | Telephone |
|---|---|
| Bank of Clarkson | (270) 242-2111 |
| Bank of Maysville | (606) 564-4001 |
| Casey County Bank, Inc. | (606) 787-8394 |
| Cecilian Bank | (270) 862-3294 |
| Citizens National Bank of Somerset | (606) 679-6341 |
| City National Bank of West Virginia | (304) 769-1100 |
| Commercial Bank | (423) 869-5151 |
| Farmers Bank and Trust Co. | (270) 965-3106 |
| Farmers National Bank of Danville | (859) 236-2926 |
| First Financial Bank | (877) 322-9530 |
| First Harrison Bank | (812) 738-2198 |
| First National Bank of Kentucky | (502) 732-4406 |
| First State Bank | (270) 547-2271 |
| FirstBank | (615) 313-0080 |
| Fredonia Valley Bank | (270) 545-3301 |
| Guardian Savings Bank, F.S.B. | (513) 942-3500 |
| Independence Bank of Kentucky | (270) 686-1776 |
| JPMorgan Chase Bank, N.A. | (614) 248-5800 |
| Kentucky Bank | (859) 987-1795 |
| Lewisburg Banking Co. | (270) 755-4818 |
| Meade County Bank | (270) 422-4141 |
| PBK Bank, Inc. | (606) 365-7098 |
| Peoples Bank | (502) 477-2244 |
| Peoples Bank & Trust Co. | (502) 484-3466 |
| Planters Bank, Inc. | (270) 886-9030 |
| River City Bank, Inc. | (502) 585-4600 |
| Security Bank and Trust Co. | (606) 564-3304 |
| Security Bank and Trust Co. | (731) 642-6644 |
| South Central Bank, Inc. | (270) 651-7466 |
| Truist Bank | (336) 776-5342 |
| United Citizens Bank & Trust Co. | (502) 532-7392 |
| United Southern Bank | (270) 885-0056 |
| WinFirst Bank | (859) 744-1900 |
| Woodforest National Bank | (832) 375-2505 |

## Louisiana

| Name | Telephone |
|---|---|
| **Rating: A** | |
| First American Bank and Trust | (225) 265-2265 |
| First National Bank of Louisiana | (337) 783-4014 |
| FSNB, N.A. | (580) 357-9880 |
| Rayne State Bank & Trust Co. | (337) 334-3191 |
| **Rating: A-** | |
| American Bank & Trust Co. | (337) 948-3056 |
| Exchange Bank and Trust Co. | (318) 352-8141 |
| First National Bank of Benton | (318) 965-9691 |
| First National Bank USA | (985) 785-8411 |
| Guaranty Bank and Trust Co. | (225) 638-8621 |
| Gulf Coast Bank | (337) 893-7733 |
| Jonesboro State Bank | (318) 259-4411 |
| Mississippi River Bank | (504) 392-1111 |
| Pedestal Bank | (985) 580-2265 |
| Red River Bank | (318) 561-4000 |
| South Louisiana Bank | (985) 851-3434 |
| Southern Heritage Bank | (318) 339-8505 |
| The Bank | (337) 824-0033 |
| **Rating: B+** | |
| BancorpSouth Bank | (662) 680-2000 |
| Bank of Sunset and Trust Co. | (337) 662-5222 |
| Beauregard Federal Savings Bank | (337) 463-4493 |
| Citizens National Bank, N.A. | (318) 747-6000 |
| Cottonport Bank | (318) 253-9612 |
| Cross Keys Bank | (318) 766-3246 |
| Evangeline Bank and Trust Co. | (337) 363-5541 |
| Feliciana Bank & Trust Co. | (225) 683-8565 |
| First, A National Banking Assn. | (601) 268-8998 |
| Franklin State Bank & Trust Co. | (318) 435-3711 |
| Guaranty Bank & Trust Co. of Delhi | (318) 878-3703 |
| Home Federal Bank | (318) 841-1170 |
| JD Bank | (337) 824-3424 |
| JPMorgan Chase Bank, N.A. | (614) 248-5800 |
| Sabine State Bank and Trust Co. | (318) 256-7000 |
| Tensas State Bank | (318) 467-5401 |
| Woodforest National Bank | (832) 375-2505 |

## Maine

| Name | Telephone |
|---|---|
| **Rating: A** | |
| Bath Savings Institution | (207) 442-7711 |
| Norway Savings Bank | (207) 743-7986 |
| **Rating: A-** | |
| Kennebec Savings Bank | (207) 622-5801 |
| **Rating: B+** | |
| Bank of America, N.A. | (704) 386-5681 |
| Camden National Bank | (207) 236-8821 |
| Franklin Savings Bank | (207) 778-3339 |
| Machias Savings Bank | (207) 255-3347 |
| NBT Bank, N.A. | (607) 337-6416 |
| Partners Bank of New England | (207) 324-2285 |
| Skowhegan Savings Bank | (207) 474-9511 |

## Maryland

| Name | Telephone |
|---|---|
| **Rating: A** | |
| Calvin B. Taylor Banking Co. | (410) 641-1700 |
| EagleBank | (240) 497-2075 |
| **Rating: A-** | |
| 1880 Bank | (410) 228-5600 |
| ACNB Bank | (717) 334-3161 |
| Bank of Ocean City | (410) 213-0173 |
| Cathay Bank | (213) 625-4791 |
| Clear Mountain Bank | (304) 379-2265 |
| Queenstown Bank of Maryland | (410) 827-8881 |
| Severn Savings Bank, FSB | (410) 260-2000 |
| Sonabank | (804) 528-4754 |
| WesBanco Bank, Inc. | (304) 234-9000 |
| **Rating: B+** | |
| Atlantic Union Bank | (804) 327-5720 |
| Bank of America, N.A. | (704) 386-5681 |
| Chesapeake Bank & Trust Co. | (410) 778-1600 |
| Citibank, N.A. | (605) 370-6261 |
| Essex Bank | (804) 419-4329 |
| First-Citizens Bank & Trust Co. | (919) 716-7050 |
| FVCbank | (703) 436-4740 |
| John Marshall Bank | (703) 584-0840 |
| JPMorgan Chase Bank, N.A. | (614) 248-5800 |
| PeoplesBank, A Codorus Valley Co. | (717) 846-1970 |
| Revere Bank | (301) 841-9600 |
| Shore United Bank | (410) 822-1400 |
| Truist Bank | (336) 776-5342 |
| Woodforest National Bank | (832) 375-2505 |
| Woori America Bank | (212) 244-1500 |

## Massachusetts

| Name | Telephone |
|---|---|
| **Rating: A** | |
| Leader Bank, N.A. | (781) 646-3900 |
| **Rating: A-** | |
| Boston Trust Walden Co. | (617) 726-7250 |
| Cape Ann Savings Bank | (978) 283-0246 |
| Cathay Bank | (213) 625-4791 |
| East West Bank | (626) 768-6000 |
| Hingham Institution for Savings | (781) 749-2200 |
| Institution for Savings | (978) 462-3106 |
| Lowell Five Cent Savings Bank | (978) 452-1300 |
| MutualOne Bank | (508) 820-4000 |
| National Grand Bank of Marblehead | (781) 631-6000 |
| Northmark Bank | (978) 686-9100 |
| Salem Five Cents Savings Bank | (978) 745-5555 |
| TrustCo Bank | (518) 377-3311 |
| **Rating: B+** | |
| Bank of America, N.A. | (704) 386-5681 |
| Cambridge Trust Co. | (617) 876-5500 |
| Community Bank, N.A. | (315) 445-2282 |
| Eastern Bank | (617) 897-1100 |
| Everett Co-operative Bank | (617) 387-1110 |
| JPMorgan Chase Bank, N.A. | (614) 248-5800 |
| Martha's Vineyard Savings Bank | (774) 310-2001 |
| Mechanics Cooperative Bank | (508) 823-7744 |
| NBT Bank, N.A. | (607) 337-6416 |
| Northern Bank & Trust Co. | (781) 937-5400 |
| Northern Trust Co. | (312) 630-6000 |
| Patriot Community Bank | (781) 935-3318 |
| Provident Bank | (978) 834-8555 |
| Rockland Trust Co. | (781) 982-6110 |
| State Street Bank and Trust Co. | (617) 786-3000 |

## Michigan

### Rating: A

| Name | Telephone |
|---|---|
| Chelsea State Bank | (734) 475-1355 |
| Macatawa Bank | (616) 820-1444 |
| Sterling Bank and Trust, FSB | (248) 355-2400 |

### Rating: A-

| Name | Telephone |
|---|---|
| 1st Source Bank | (574) 235-2000 |
| Alden State Bank | (231) 331-4481 |
| Bank of Ann Arbor | (734) 662-1600 |
| Comerica Bank | (214) 462-4000 |
| Exchange State Bank | (810) 657-9333 |
| First Merchants Bank | (765) 747-1500 |
| Mercantile Bank of Michigan | (616) 242-7760 |
| Peoples State Bank of Munising | (906) 387-2006 |
| Superior National Bank & Trust Co. | (906) 482-0404 |
| Tri-County Bank | (810) 346-2745 |
| Upper Peninsula State Bank | (906) 789-7000 |

### Rating: B+

| Name | Telephone |
|---|---|
| Bank of America, N.A. | (704) 386-5681 |
| Charlevoix State Bank | (231) 547-4411 |
| ChoiceOne Bank | (616) 887-7366 |
| Farmers State Bank | (260) 463-7111 |
| First Community Bank | (231) 526-2114 |
| Flagstar Bank, FSB | (248) 312-5400 |
| Horizon Bank | (219) 874-9245 |
| JPMorgan Chase Bank, N.A. | (614) 248-5800 |
| Lakestone Bank & Trust | (810) 664-2977 |
| Nicolet National Bank | (920) 430-1400 |
| Northern Trust Co. | (312) 630-6000 |
| Port Austin State Bank | (989) 738-5235 |
| State Bank | (810) 629-2263 |
| TCF National Bank | (952) 745-2760 |
| University Bank | (734) 741-5858 |
| Waterford Bank, N.A. | (419) 720-3900 |

## Minnesota

| Name | Telephone |
|---|---|
| **Rating: A+** | |
| Vermillion State Bank | (651) 437-4433 |
| **Rating: A** | |
| Bank of Alma | (608) 685-4461 |
| Charter Bank | (715) 832-4254 |
| Eagle Bank | (320) 634-4545 |
| First National Bank North | (218) 547-1160 |
| First National Bank of Bemidji | (218) 751-2430 |
| First State Bank Southwest | (507) 376-9747 |
| Lake Central Bank | (320) 274-8216 |
| Liberty Bank Minnesota | (320) 252-2841 |
| **Rating: A-** | |
| 1st United Bank | (507) 334-2201 |
| Alerus Financial, N.A. | (701) 795-3200 |
| American Heritage National Bank | (320) 732-6131 |
| Bank of Maple Plain | (763) 479-1931 |
| Bridgewater Bank | (952) 893-6868 |
| Castle Rock Bank | (651) 463-7590 |
| Center National Bank | (320) 693-3255 |
| Citizens National Bank of Park Rapids | (218) 732-3393 |
| Community First Bank | (218) 564-4171 |
| Community Resource Bank | (507) 645-4441 |
| CornerStone State Bank | (507) 364-2265 |
| Farmers Trust and Savings Bank | (641) 562-2696 |
| Fidelity Bank | (952) 831-6600 |
| First Bank Blue Earth | (507) 526-3241 |
| First Citizens Bank | (641) 423-1600 |
| First Minnetonka City Bank | (952) 935-8663 |
| First National Bank | (605) 482-8293 |
| First National Bank of Henning | (218) 367-2735 |
| First National Bank of Le Center | (507) 357-2273 |
| First National Bank of Milaca | (320) 983-3101 |
| First National Bank of Moose Lake | (218) 485-4441 |
| First State Bank of Sauk Centre | (320) 352-5771 |
| First State Bank of Wyoming | (651) 462-7611 |
| Gateway Bank | (651) 209-4800 |
| Granite Falls Bank | (320) 564-2111 |
| Great Southern Bank | (417) 895-5234 |
| Home Federal Savings Bank | (507) 535-1309 |
| HomeTown Bank | (507) 637-1000 |
| Lake Elmo Bank | (651) 777-8365 |
| Manufacturers Bank & Trust Co. | (641) 585-2825 |
| Neighborhood National Bank | (320) 679-3100 |
| North American Banking Co. | (651) 636-9654 |
| Northeast Bank | (612) 379-8811 |
| PrinsBank | (320) 978-6351 |
| Red Rock Bank | (507) 648-3871 |
| Security State Bank of Aitkin | (218) 927-3765 |
| Security State Bank of Marine | (651) 433-2424 |
| State Bank of Wheaton | (320) 563-8142 |
| Stearns Bank Holdingford N.A. | (320) 746-2261 |
| Stearns Bank N.A. | (320) 253-6607 |
| Stearns Bank Upsala N.A. | (320) 573-2111 |
| VisionBank | (952) 920-8400 |
| Woodlands National Bank | (320) 384-6191 |
| **Rating: B+** | |
| 21st Century Bank | (763) 479-2178 |
| Arlington State Bank | (507) 964-2256 |
| Bank of America, N.A. | (704) 386-5681 |
| Bank of Elk River | (763) 441-1000 |
| Bank of Zumbrota | (507) 732-7555 |
| BANKWEST | (763) 477-5231 |
| Bell Bank | (701) 298-1500 |
| BNC National Bank | (602) 508-3760 |
| Bremer Bank, N.A. | (651) 288-3751 |
| Choice Financial Group | (701) 356-9700 |
| Citizens State Bank of Roseau | (218) 463-2135 |
| Citizens State Bank of Waverly | (763) 658-4417 |
| City National Bank | (800) 773-7100 |
| Elysian Bank | (507) 267-4326 |
| Farmers State Bank of Hartland | (507) 845-2233 |
| First Bank & Trust | (605) 696-2265 |
| First Farmers & Merchants Bank | (507) 263-3030 |
| First National Bank of Fairfax | (507) 426-7242 |
| First Security Bank - Canby | (507) 223-7231 |
| First Security Bank-Hendricks | (507) 275-3141 |
| First Security Bank-Sleepy Eye | (507) 794-3911 |
| First State Bank of Le Center | (507) 357-2225 |
| Home State Bank | (320) 593-2001 |
| Janesville State Bank | (507) 234-5108 |
| JPMorgan Chase Bank, N.A. | (614) 248-5800 |
| Lake Community Bank | (952) 473-7347 |
| Midwest Bank | (218) 847-4771 |
| Minnesota National Bank | (320) 352-5211 |
| Minnwest Bank | (507) 637-5731 |
| North Star Bank | (651) 489-8811 |
| Northern State Bank | (715) 682-2772 |
| Northern State Bank of Thief River Falls | (218) 681-4020 |
| Northern Trust Co. | (312) 630-6000 |
| Ormsby State Bank | (507) 736-2941 |
| Pine Country Bank | (320) 632-9740 |

## Minnesota

| Name | Telephone |
|---|---|
| Pine Island Bank | (507) 356-8328 |
| Produce State Bank | (507) 889-4311 |
| Security Bank & Trust Co. | (320) 864-3107 |
| Security Bank Minnesota | (507) 373-1481 |
| Security Bank USA | (218) 751-1510 |
| Security State Bank of Fergus Falls | (218) 736-5485 |
| Security State Bank of Oklee | (218) 796-5157 |
| Security State Bank of Wanamingo | (507) 824-2265 |
| St. Clair State Bank (Inc.) | (507) 245-3636 |
| State Bank of Danvers | (320) 843-3828 |
| TCF National Bank | (952) 745-2760 |
| Think Mutual Bank | (507) 288-3425 |
| United Community Bank | (218) 346-5700 |
| Wadena State Bank | (218) 631-1860 |
| Wanda State Bank | (507) 550-1678 |
| Welcome State Bank | (507) 728-8251 |
| West Bank | (515) 222-2300 |
| WNB Financial, N.A. | (507) 454-8800 |

## Mississippi

| Name | Telephone |
|---|---|
| **Rating: A** | |
| FSNB, N.A. | (580) 357-9880 |
| **Rating: A-** | |
| Bank of Commerce | (662) 453-4142 |
| Bank of Franklin | (601) 384-2305 |
| Bank of Vernon | (205) 695-7141 |
| Bank OZK | (501) 978-2265 |
| BNA Bank | (662) 534-8171 |
| Citizens National Bank of Meridian | (601) 484-5269 |
| Cleveland State Bank | (662) 843-9461 |
| Commerce Bank | (662) 286-5577 |
| Farmers and Merchants Bank | (662) 365-1200 |
| First Choice Bank | (662) 489-1631 |
| First Security Bank | (662) 563-9311 |
| Jefferson Bank | (662) 332-7545 |
| Renasant Bank | (800) 680-1601 |
| **Rating: B+** | |
| BancorpSouth Bank | (662) 680-2000 |
| Bank of Brookhaven | (601) 835-3033 |
| Bank of Forest | (601) 469-3663 |
| Bank of Kilmichael | (662) 262-7844 |
| Bank of Morton | (601) 732-8944 |
| Bank of Wiggins | (601) 928-5233 |
| BankPlus | (662) 247-1811 |
| Cadence Bank, N.A. | (800) 636-7622 |
| Citizens Bank | (662) 838-2146 |
| First Financial Bank | (870) 863-7000 |
| First National Bank of Clarksdale | (662) 627-3261 |
| First Southern Bank | (601) 736-6378 |
| First State Bank | (601) 735-3124 |
| First, A National Banking Assn. | (601) 268-8998 |
| FNB Oxford Bank | (662) 234-2821 |
| Grand Bank for Savings, FSB | (601) 264-1467 |
| Pike National Bank | (601) 684-7575 |
| RiverHills Bank | (601) 636-1445 |
| Truist Bank | (336) 776-5342 |
| Trustmark National Bank | (601) 208-5111 |
| Woodforest National Bank | (832) 375-2505 |

## Missouri

### Rating: A

| Name | Telephone |
|---|---|
| Bank of Old Monroe | (636) 665-5601 |
| Cass Commercial Bank | (314) 506-5544 |
| Central Bank of Kansas City | (816) 483-1210 |
| Commerce Bank | (816) 234-2000 |
| Community Bank of El Dorado Springs | (417) 876-6811 |
| HNB National Bank | (573) 221-0050 |
| Lindell Bank & Trust Co. | (314) 645-7700 |
| Nodaway Valley Bank | (660) 562-3232 |
| Senath State Bank | (573) 738-2646 |
| St. Clair County State Bank | (417) 646-8128 |

### Rating: A-

| Name | Telephone |
|---|---|
| Academy Bank, N.A. | (816) 472-0081 |
| Adrian Bank | (816) 297-2194 |
| Armed Forces Bank, N.A. | (913) 682-9090 |
| Bank Northwest | (816) 583-2154 |
| Bank of Advance | (573) 722-3517 |
| Bank of Grain Valley | (816) 373-1905 |
| Bank of Monticello | (573) 767-5264 |
| Bank of New Madrid | (573) 748-5551 |
| Bank of St. Elizabeth | (573) 493-2313 |
| Busey Bank | (217) 351-6500 |
| Century Bank of the Ozarks | (417) 679-3321 |
| Citizens Bank of Charleston | (573) 683-3373 |
| Citizens Bank of Eldon | (573) 392-3381 |
| Community First Banking Co. | (417) 255-2265 |
| Country Club Bank | (816) 931-4060 |
| Exchange Bank & Trust | (913) 367-6000 |
| Farmers and Merchants Bank of St. Clair | (636) 629-2225 |
| Farmers Bank of Lincoln | (660) 547-3311 |
| First State Bank and Trust Co., Inc. | (573) 333-1700 |
| First State Bank of St. Charles, Missouri | (636) 940-5555 |
| Great Southern Bank | (417) 895-5234 |
| Hawthorn Bank | (573) 761-6100 |
| Home Exchange Bank | (660) 684-6114 |
| Kearney Trust Co. | (816) 628-6666 |
| Lamar Bank and Trust Co. | (417) 682-3348 |
| Legends Bank | (573) 897-2204 |
| Maries County Bank | (573) 422-3323 |
| Mercantile Bank of Louisiana, Missouri | (573) 754-6221 |
| Mid America Bank | (573) 635-0019 |
| Missouri Bank | (636) 456-3441 |
| Missouri Bank II | (660) 827-5520 |
| New Era Bank | (573) 783-3336 |
| North American Savings Bank, F.S.B. | (866) 599-9800 |
| Northeast Missouri State Bank | (660) 665-6161 |
| Peoples Community Bank | (573) 224-3267 |
| Pinnacle Bank | (402) 434-3127 |
| Progressive Ozark Bank | (573) 729-4146 |
| Rockwood Bank | (636) 938-9222 |
| Security Bank of Kansas City | (913) 281-3165 |
| Sterling Bank | (573) 778-3333 |
| Town & Country Bank | (573) 729-3155 |
| Town and Country Bank Midwest | (217) 222-0015 |
| Wells Bank | (816) 858-2121 |
| West Plains Bank and Trust Co. | (417) 256-2147 |
| Wood & Huston Bank | (660) 886-6825 |

### Rating: B+

| Name | Telephone |
|---|---|
| Alliance Bank | (573) 334-1010 |
| Alliant Bank | (660) 291-3041 |
| Alton Bank | (417) 778-7211 |
| BancorpSouth Bank | (662) 680-2000 |
| Bank of America, N.A. | (704) 386-5681 |
| Bank of Blue Valley | (913) 338-1000 |
| Bank of Kirksville | (660) 665-7766 |
| Bank of Missouri | (573) 547-6541 |
| Bank of Odessa | (816) 230-4512 |
| Bloomsdale Bank | (573) 483-2514 |
| BTC Bank | (660) 425-7285 |
| Central Bank of Boone County | (573) 874-8100 |
| Central Bank of Branson | (417) 334-4125 |
| Central Bank of Lake of the Ozarks | (573) 348-2761 |
| Central Bank of Sedalia | (660) 827-3333 |
| Central Bank of St. Louis | (314) 862-8300 |
| Central Bank of the Midwest | (816) 525-5300 |
| Central Bank of the Ozarks | (417) 881-3100 |
| Central Trust Bank | (573) 634-1302 |
| Citizens Bank of Edina | (660) 397-2266 |
| Citizens-Farmers Bank of Cole Camp | (660) 668-4416 |
| Commercial Bank of Oak Grove | (816) 690-4416 |
| Commercial Trust Co. of Fayette | (660) 248-2222 |
| Community Bank of Missouri | (816) 470-2265 |
| Community Bank of Pleasant Hill | (816) 540-2525 |
| Community Bank of Raymore | (816) 322-2100 |
| Community National Bank | (417) 235-2265 |
| Community State Bank of Missouri | (573) 324-2233 |
| Concordia Bank | (660) 463-7911 |
| Enterprise Bank & Trust | (314) 725-5500 |
| Exchange Bank of Missouri | (660) 248-3388 |
| Farmers Bank of Northern Missouri | (660) 947-2474 |
| First Bank | (314) 995-8700 |
| First Community Bank of the Ozarks | (417) 336-6310 |

## Missouri

| Name | Telephone |
|---|---|
| First Mid Bank & Trust, N.A. | (217) 234-7454 |
| First Missouri Bank of SEMO | (573) 717-7177 |
| First Missouri State Bank | (573) 785-6800 |
| First State Community Bank | (573) 756-4547 |
| First-Citizens Bank & Trust Co. | (919) 716-7050 |
| Focus Bank | (573) 683-3712 |
| Investors Community Bank | (660) 646-3733 |
| Jefferson Bank of Missouri | (573) 634-0888 |
| JPMorgan Chase Bank, N.A. | (614) 248-5800 |
| La Monte Community Bank | (660) 347-5656 |
| Landmark Bank | (573) 499-7333 |
| Metz Banking Co. | (417) 667-4550 |
| Midwest Independent Bank | (573) 636-9555 |
| NBKC Bank | (816) 965-1400 |
| Northern Trust Co. | (312) 630-6000 |
| Parkside Financial Bank & Trust | (314) 290-8600 |
| Peoples Bank | (573) 885-2511 |
| Peoples Bank of Wyaconda | (660) 727-2941 |
| Security Bank of Southwest Missouri | (417) 847-4794 |
| Silex Banking Co. | (573) 384-5221 |
| Simmons Bank | (870) 541-1000 |
| Southern Bank | (573) 778-1800 |
| Springfield First Community Bank | (417) 882-8111 |
| State Street Bank and Trust Co. | (617) 786-3000 |
| Stifel Bank and Trust | (314) 342-2000 |
| TPNB Bank | (660) 327-4181 |
| United Security Bank | (573) 386-2233 |

## Montana

| Name | Telephone |
|---|---|
| **Rating: A** | |
| Bank of Commerce | (208) 525-9108 |
| First State Bank of Shelby | (406) 434-5567 |
| Yellowstone Bank | (406) 628-7951 |
| **Rating: A-** | |
| 1st Bank | (406) 436-2611 |
| American Bank | (406) 587-1234 |
| Bank of Montana | (406) 829-2662 |
| Glacier Bank | (406) 756-4200 |
| Independence Bank | (406) 265-1241 |
| Stockman Bank of Montana | (406) 234-8420 |
| **Rating: B+** | |
| Eagle Bank | (406) 883-2940 |
| First Interstate Bank | (406) 255-5000 |
| First Security Bank of Deer Lodge | (406) 846-2300 |
| Manhattan Bank | (406) 284-3255 |
| Three Rivers Bank of Montana | (406) 755-4271 |
| TrailWest Bank | (406) 273-2400 |

## Nebraska

| Name | Telephone |
|---|---|
| **Rating: A** | |
| American Interstate Bank | (402) 289-2551 |
| First Westroads Bank, Inc. | (402) 330-7200 |
| Heritage Bank | (308) 583-2262 |
| Minden Exchange Bank & Trust Co. | (308) 832-1600 |
| Security National Bank of Omaha | (402) 344-7300 |
| **Rating: A-** | |
| Auburn State Bank | (402) 274-4342 |
| Bank of Prague | (402) 663-4317 |
| Bankers' Bank of the West | (303) 291-3700 |
| Cattle Bank & Trust | (402) 643-3636 |
| First National Bank of Chadron | (308) 432-5552 |
| First Northeast Bank of Nebraska | (402) 687-2640 |
| First Savings Bank | (605) 763-2009 |
| First State Bank | (308) 569-2311 |
| First State Bank | (308) 632-4158 |
| FirsTier Bank | (308) 235-4633 |
| Five Points Bank | (308) 384-5350 |
| Five Points Bank of Hastings | (402) 462-2228 |
| Great Southern Bank | (417) 895-5234 |
| Horizon Bank | (402) 786-2555 |
| Madison County Bank | (402) 454-6511 |
| Nebraska State Bank | (308) 772-3234 |
| Pinnacle Bank | (402) 434-3127 |
| Pinnacle Bank - Wyoming | (307) 532-2181 |
| Platte Valley Bank | (402) 652-3221 |
| Points West Community Bank | (970) 686-0878 |
| Scribner Bank | (402) 664-2561 |
| Security Bank | (402) 256-3247 |
| South Central State Bank | (402) 756-8601 |
| State Nebraska Bank & Trust | (402) 375-1130 |
| Town & Country Bank | (308) 452-3225 |
| Union Bank and Trust Co. | (402) 323-1828 |
| Waypoint Bank | (308) 784-2515 |
| West Plains Bank | (402) 387-2381 |
| **Rating: B+** | |
| Adams Bank & Trust | (308) 284-4071 |
| Adams State Bank | (402) 988-2255 |
| Bank of Dixon County | (402) 755-2224 |
| Bank of Elgin | (402) 843-2228 |
| BankFirst | (402) 371-8005 |
| Chambers State Bank | (402) 482-5222 |
| CIT Bank, N.A. | (855) 462-2652 |
| Clarkson Bank | (402) 892-3411 |
| Commercial State Bank | (308) 799-3995 |
| Cornerstone Bank | (402) 363-7411 |
| Exchange Bank | (308) 468-5741 |
| F&M Bank | (402) 372-5331 |
| F&M Bank | (402) 245-2491 |
| First Bank and Trust of Fullerton | (308) 536-2492 |
| First National Bank of Gordon | (308) 282-0050 |
| First Nebraska Bank | (402) 359-2281 |
| First State Bank | (402) 337-0323 |
| First State Bank & Trust Co. | (402) 721-2500 |
| FirstBank of Nebraska | (402) 443-4117 |
| Hershey State Bank | (308) 368-5555 |
| Homestead Bank | (308) 784-2000 |
| Jones Bank | (402) 643-3602 |
| JPMorgan Chase Bank, N.A. | (614) 248-5800 |
| Midwest Bank N.A. | (402) 329-6221 |
| Northwest Bank | (712) 580-4100 |
| Premier Bank | (402) 558-8000 |
| Springfield State Bank | (402) 253-2222 |
| Two Rivers Bank | (402) 426-9500 |
| Washington County Bank | (402) 426-2111 |
| West Gate Bank | (402) 434-3453 |

## Nevada

### Rating: A

| Name | Telephone |
|---|---|
| Bank of George | (702) 851-4200 |
| First Security Bank of Nevada | (702) 853-0900 |
| Royal Business Bank | (213) 627-9888 |

### Rating: A-

| Name | Telephone |
|---|---|
| American First National Bank | (713) 596-2888 |
| Armed Forces Bank, N.A. | (913) 682-9090 |
| Cathay Bank | (213) 625-4791 |
| Eaglemark Savings Bank | (775) 886-3000 |
| East West Bank | (626) 768-6000 |
| First Savings Bank | (605) 763-2009 |
| Glacier Bank | (406) 756-4200 |
| Pacific Premier Bank | (949) 864-8000 |
| Washington Federal Bank, N.A. | (206) 204-3446 |
| Wells Fargo National Bank West | (702) 952-6650 |
| Western Alliance Bank | (602) 389-3500 |
| Wilmington Savings Fund Society, FSB | (302) 792-6000 |
| Zions BanCorp., N.A. | (801) 844-7637 |

### Rating: B+

| Name | Telephone |
|---|---|
| Bank of America, N.A. | (704) 386-5681 |
| Charles Schwab Bank | (775) 689-6800 |
| CIT Bank, N.A. | (855) 462-2652 |
| Citibank, N.A. | (605) 370-6261 |
| City National Bank | (800) 773-7100 |
| First National Bank of Ely | (775) 289-4441 |
| JPMorgan Chase Bank, N.A. | (614) 248-5800 |
| Kirkwood Bank of Nevada | (702) 912-0700 |
| Meadows Bank | (702) 471-2265 |
| Northern Trust Co. | (312) 630-6000 |
| Town & Country Bank | (702) 252-8777 |
| Umpqua Bank | (541) 440-3961 |

## New Hampshire

### Rating: A-

| Name | Telephone |
|---|---|
| Lowell Five Cent Savings Bank | (978) 452-1300 |

### Rating: B+

| Name | Telephone |
|---|---|
| Bank of America, N.A. | (704) 386-5681 |
| Cambridge Trust Co. | (617) 876-5500 |
| Camden National Bank | (207) 236-8821 |
| Eastern Bank | (617) 897-1100 |
| JPMorgan Chase Bank, N.A. | (614) 248-5800 |
| Ledyard National Bank | (802) 649-2050 |
| NBT Bank, N.A. | (607) 337-6416 |
| Partners Bank of New England | (207) 324-2285 |
| Provident Bank | (978) 834-8555 |

## New Jersey

| Name | Telephone |
|---|---|
| **Rating: A** | |
| Bessemer Trust Co. | (212) 708-9100 |
| Metro City Bank | (770) 455-4989 |
| Pacific City Bank | (213) 210-2000 |
| Parke Bank | (856) 256-2500 |
| **Rating: A-** | |
| AMG National Trust Bank | (303) 694-2190 |
| Armed Forces Bank, N.A. | (913) 682-9090 |
| Cathay Bank | (213) 625-4791 |
| Cenlar FSB | (609) 883-3900 |
| Cross River Bank | (201) 808-7000 |
| CTBC Bank Corp. (USA) | (424) 277-4612 |
| NewBank | (718) 353-9100 |
| TrustCo Bank | (518) 377-3311 |
| Unity Bank | (908) 730-7630 |
| Wilmington Savings Fund Society, FSB | (302) 792-6000 |
| **Rating: B+** | |
| Bank of America, N.A. | (704) 386-5681 |
| Bank of Princeton | (609) 921-1700 |
| Bryn Mawr Trust Co. | (610) 581-4839 |
| Citibank, N.A. | (605) 370-6261 |
| First IC Bank | (770) 451-7200 |
| Firstrust Savings Bank | (610) 238-5001 |
| Habib American Bank | (212) 532-4444 |
| Hanmi Bank | (213) 382-2200 |
| Israel Discount Bank of New York | (212) 551-8500 |
| JPMorgan Chase Bank, N.A. | (614) 248-5800 |
| Lakeland Bank | (973) 697-2000 |
| Lusitania Savings Bank | (973) 344-5125 |
| Peapack-Gladstone Bank | (908) 234-0700 |
| State Street Bank and Trust Co. | (617) 786-3000 |
| Sumitomo Mitsui Trust Bank (U.S.A.) Ltd. | (201) 420-9470 |
| Truist Bank | (336) 776-5342 |
| William Penn Bank, | (215) 269-1200 |
| Woori America Bank | (212) 244-1500 |

## New Mexico

| Name | Telephone |
|---|---|
| **Rating: A** | |
| First American Bank | (575) 746-8000 |
| First New Mexico Bank | (575) 546-2691 |
| First New Mexico Bank of Silver City | (575) 388-3121 |
| First New Mexico Bank, Las Cruces | (575) 556-3000 |
| Valley Bank of Commerce | (575) 623-2265 |
| Western Bank | (575) 542-3521 |
| **Rating: A-** | |
| AimBank | (806) 385-4441 |
| Bank of Clovis | (575) 769-9000 |
| Bank of Colorado | (970) 206-1160 |
| Centinel Bank of Taos | (575) 758-6700 |
| Citizens Bank | (806) 350-5600 |
| Citizens Bank | (505) 599-0100 |
| Citizens Bank of Clovis | (575) 769-1911 |
| Citizens Bank of Las Cruces | (575) 647-4100 |
| First National Bank | (575) 437-4880 |
| First Savings Bank | (605) 763-2009 |
| James Polk Stone Community Bank | (575) 356-6601 |
| Lea County State Bank | (575) 397-4511 |
| New Mexico Bank & Trust | (505) 830-8100 |
| United Business Bank | (925) 476-1800 |
| Washington Federal Bank, N.A. | (206) 204-3446 |
| Western Commerce Bank | (575) 887-6686 |
| WestStar Bank | (915) 532-1000 |
| Zions BanCorp., N.A. | (801) 844-7637 |
| **Rating: B+** | |
| American Heritage Bank | (575) 762-2800 |
| Bank of America, N.A. | (704) 386-5681 |
| Century Bank | (505) 995-1200 |
| City Bank | (806) 792-7101 |
| CNB Bank | (575) 234-2500 |
| Enterprise Bank & Trust | (314) 725-5500 |
| First National Bank Texas | (254) 554-4236 |
| First-Citizens Bank & Trust Co. | (919) 716-7050 |
| Main Bank | (505) 880-1700 |
| Western Bank of Clovis | (575) 769-1975 |

## New York

| Name | Telephone |
|---|---|
| **Rating: A** | |
| Alpine Capital Bank | (212) 328-2555 |
| Bessemer Trust Co., N.A. | (212) 708-9100 |
| Deutsche Bank Trust Co. Americas | (212) 250-2500 |
| Esquire Bank, N.A. | (516) 535-2002 |
| Fulton Savings Bank | (315) 592-4201 |
| Metro City Bank | (770) 455-4989 |
| Morgan Stanley Private Bank, N.A. | (212) 762-1803 |
| Pacific City Bank | (213) 210-2000 |
| Royal Business Bank | (213) 627-9888 |
| Sterling Bank and Trust, FSB | (248) 355-2400 |
| **Rating: A-** | |
| Amerasia Bank | (718) 463-3600 |
| Armed Forces Bank, N.A. | (913) 682-9090 |
| Bank of Utica | (315) 797-2700 |
| Bank OZK | (501) 978-2265 |
| Cathay Bank | (213) 625-4791 |
| Centennial Bank | (501) 328-4663 |
| Citizens & Northern Bank | (570) 724-3411 |
| CTBC Bank Corp. (USA) | (424) 277-4612 |
| East West Bank | (626) 768-6000 |
| First National Bank of Groton | (607) 898-5871 |
| Genesee Regional Bank | (585) 249-1540 |
| Hamlin Bank and Trust Co. | (814) 887-5555 |
| Maspeth Federal S&L Assn. | (718) 335-1300 |
| Metropolitan Commercial Bank | (212) 659-0600 |
| NewBank | (718) 353-9100 |
| Steuben Trust Co. | (607) 324-5010 |
| Tioga State Bank | (607) 589-7000 |
| TrustCo Bank | (518) 377-3311 |
| Westchester Bank | (914) 368-9919 |
| **Rating: B+** | |
| Bank of America, N.A. | (704) 386-5681 |
| Bank of Greene County | (518) 943-2600 |
| BankUnited, N.A. | (786) 313-1010 |
| BNB Bank | (631) 537-8834 |
| Canandaigua National Bank and Trust Co. | (585) 394-4260 |
| Citibank, N.A. | (605) 370-6261 |
| City National Bank | (800) 773-7100 |
| Community Bank, N.A. | (315) 445-2282 |
| First IC Bank | (770) 451-7200 |
| First National Bank of Dryden | (607) 844-8141 |
| Glens Falls National Bank and Trust Co. | (518) 793-4121 |
| Habib American Bank | (212) 532-4444 |
| Hanmi Bank | (213) 382-2200 |
| Hanover Community Bank | (516) 248-4868 |
| Interaudi Bank | (212) 833-1000 |
| Israel Discount Bank of New York | (212) 551-8500 |
| Jeff Bank | (845) 482-4000 |
| JPMorgan Chase Bank, N.A. | (614) 248-5800 |
| Lakeland Bank | (973) 697-2000 |
| NBT Bank, N.A. | (607) 337-6416 |
| Northern Trust Co. | (312) 630-6000 |
| Peoples Security Bank and Trust Co. | (570) 955-1700 |
| Preferred Bank | (213) 891-1188 |
| Safra National Bank of New York | (212) 704-5500 |
| Saratoga National Bank and Trust Co. | (518) 583-3114 |
| Signature Bank | (646) 822-1500 |
| Spring Bank | (718) 879-5000 |
| Tompkins Trust Co. | (607) 273-3210 |
| Wayne Bank | (570) 253-1455 |
| Woodforest National Bank | (832) 375-2505 |
| Woori America Bank | (212) 244-1500 |

## North Carolina

| Name | Telephone |
|---|---|
| **Rating: A** | |
| FSNB, N.A. | (580) 357-9880 |
| Peoples Bank | (828) 464-5620 |
| Wake Forest Federal S&L Assn. | (919) 556-5146 |
| **Rating: A-** | |
| Bank OZK | (501) 978-2265 |
| Benchmark Community Bank | (434) 676-9054 |
| BlueHarbor Bank | (704) 662-7700 |
| CresCom Bank | (855) 273-7266 |
| Farmers & Merchants Bank | (704) 633-1772 |
| Fidelity Bank | (919) 552-2242 |
| First FSB of Lincolnton | (704) 735-0416 |
| Live Oak Banking Co. | (910) 790-5867 |
| Providence Bank | (252) 443-9477 |
| South State Bank | (803) 771-2265 |
| Southern Bank and Trust Co. | (919) 658-7000 |
| Surrey Bank & Trust | (336) 783-3900 |
| TowneBank | (757) 638-7500 |
| United Community Bank | (706) 745-2151 |
| **Rating: B+** | |
| American National Bank and Trust Co. | (434) 792-5111 |
| Atlantic Union Bank | (804) 327-5720 |
| Bank of America, N.A. | (704) 386-5681 |
| First Bank | (910) 692-6222 |
| First-Citizens Bank & Trust Co. | (919) 716-7050 |
| JPMorgan Chase Bank, N.A. | (614) 248-5800 |
| Morganton Savings Bank, S.S.B. | (828) 437-1426 |
| Pacific Western Bank | (310) 887-8500 |
| Pinnacle Bank | (615) 744-3705 |
| Roxboro Savings Bank, SSB | (336) 599-2137 |
| Signature Bank | (646) 822-1500 |
| Southern First Bank | (864) 679-9000 |
| Truist Bank | (336) 776-5342 |
| Woodforest National Bank | (832) 375-2505 |

## North Dakota

| Name | Telephone |
|---|---|
| **Rating: A** | |
| Ramsey National Bank | (701) 662-4024 |
| **Rating: A-** | |
| Alerus Financial, N.A. | (701) 795-3200 |
| Citizens State Bank of Finley | (701) 524-1921 |
| Commercial Bank of Mott | (701) 824-2593 |
| First Security Bank - West | (701) 873-4301 |
| First State Bank & Trust | (701) 577-2113 |
| First State Bank of Golva | (701) 872-3656 |
| Grant County State Bank | (701) 622-3491 |
| Liberty State Bank | (701) 464-5421 |
| Sargent County Bank | (701) 724-3216 |
| Security First Bank of North Dakota | (701) 794-8758 |
| Stock Growers Bank | (701) 754-2226 |
| **Rating: B+** | |
| American State Bank & Trust Co | (701) 774-4100 |
| Bell Bank | (701) 298-1500 |
| BNC National Bank | (602) 508-3760 |
| Bremer Bank, N.A. | (651) 288-3751 |
| Choice Financial Group | (701) 356-9700 |
| Dakota Community Bank & Trust, N.A. | (701) 878-4416 |
| Dakota Western Bank | (701) 523-5803 |
| Horizon Financial Bank | (701) 682-5331 |
| Peoples State Bank | (701) 245-6407 |
| Security State Bank, Wishek, North Dakota | (701) 452-2314 |
| Starion Bank | (701) 223-6050 |

## Northern Mariana Islands

| Name | Telephone |
|---|---|
| **Rating: B+** | |
| First Hawaiian Bank | (808) 525-6340 |

## Ohio

| Name | Telephone |
|---|---|
| **Rating: A+** | |
| FDS Bank | (513) 573-2265 |
| **Rating: A** | |
| Peoples Bank Co. | (419) 678-2385 |
| Perpetual Federal Savings Bank | (937) 653-1700 |
| St. Henry Bank | (419) 678-2358 |
| Stock Yards Bank & Trust Co. | (502) 582-2571 |
| **Rating: A-** | |
| Buckeye Community Bank | (440) 233-8800 |
| Citizens Bank Co. | (740) 984-2381 |
| Civista Bank | (419) 625-4121 |
| Farmers & Merchants State Bank | (419) 446-2501 |
| Farmers Savings Bank | (330) 648-2441 |
| First Merchants Bank | (765) 747-1500 |
| Hamler State Bank | (419) 274-3955 |
| Heartland Bank | (614) 416-4601 |
| Killbuck Savings Bank Co. | (330) 276-4881 |
| Miami Savings Bank | (513) 353-1339 |
| North Side Bank and Trust Co. | (513) 542-7800 |
| Ottoville Bank Co. | (419) 453-3313 |
| Republic Bank & Trust Co. | (502) 584-3600 |
| Settlers Bank | (740) 373-9200 |
| Signature Bank, N.A. | (419) 841-7773 |
| Spring Valley Bank | (513) 761-6688 |
| Union Savings Bank | (513) 247-0300 |
| WesBanco Bank, Inc. | (304) 234-9000 |
| **Rating: B+** | |
| Bank of America, N.A. | (704) 386-5681 |
| City National Bank of West Virginia | (304) 769-1100 |
| Commercial & Savings Bank of Millersburg | (330) 674-9015 |
| Corn City State Bank | (419) 278-0015 |
| Croghan Colonial Bank | (419) 332-7301 |
| Fahey Banking Co. | (740) 382-8231 |
| Farmers & Merchants Bank | (937) 866-2455 |
| Farmers National Bank of Canfield | (330) 533-3341 |
| FCN Bank, N.A. | (765) 647-4116 |
| First Bank of Berne | (260) 589-2151 |
| First Bank of Ohio | (419) 448-9740 |
| First Commonwealth Bank | (724) 463-8555 |
| First Financial Bank | (877) 322-9530 |
| First National Bank in New Bremen | (419) 629-2761 |
| First National Bank of Blanchester | (937) 783-2451 |
| Flagstar Bank, FSB | (248) 312-5400 |
| Greenville National Bank | (937) 548-1114 |
| Guardian Savings Bank, F.S.B. | (513) 942-3500 |
| JPMorgan Chase Bank, N.A. | (614) 248-5800 |
| Liberty National Bank | (419) 634-5015 |
| Minster Bank | (419) 628-2351 |
| Northern Trust Co. | (312) 630-6000 |
| Osgood State Bank | (419) 582-2681 |
| State Bank and Trust Co. | (419) 783-8950 |
| TCF National Bank | (952) 745-2760 |
| Truist Bank | (336) 776-5342 |
| Unified Bank | (740) 633-0445 |
| Union Banking Co. | (937) 355-6511 |
| Waterford Bank, N.A. | (419) 720-3900 |
| Woodforest National Bank | (832) 375-2505 |

## Oklahoma

### Rating: A

| Name | Telephone |
|---|---|
| Bank of Hydro | (405) 663-2214 |
| Bank of the West | (580) 661-3541 |
| Bank7 | (405) 810-8600 |
| City National B&T Co. of Lawton, Oklahoma | (866) 385-3444 |
| Commerce Bank | (816) 234-2000 |
| Community National Bank of Okarche | (405) 263-7491 |
| Farmers and Merchants National Bank | (580) 227-3773 |
| First Bank of Okarche | (405) 263-7215 |
| FSNB, N.A. | (580) 357-9880 |
| Payne County Bank | (405) 547-2436 |
| Sooner State Bank | (405) 381-2326 |
| Stock Exchange Bank | (580) 256-3314 |

### Rating: A-

| Name | Telephone |
|---|---|
| American Bank and Trust Co. | (918) 481-3000 |
| BancFirst | (405) 270-1086 |
| Bank of the Panhandle | (580) 338-2593 |
| Bank, N.A. | (918) 423-2265 |
| Community Bank | (918) 367-3343 |
| Community Bank | (580) 327-5500 |
| Exchange Bank | (918) 396-2345 |
| F&M Bank | (405) 715-1100 |
| First Bank | (580) 526-3332 |
| First Bank & Trust Co. | (580) 336-5562 |
| First Bank of Owasso | (918) 272-5301 |
| First National Bank & Trust of Elk City | (580) 225-2580 |
| First National Bank of Fort Smith | (479) 782-2041 |
| First Texoma National Bank | (580) 924-4242 |
| Great Southern Bank | (417) 895-5234 |
| International Bank of Commerce Oklahoma | (405) 841-2100 |
| Liberty National Bank | (580) 351-2265 |
| McClain Bank | (405) 527-6503 |
| McCurtain County National Bank | (580) 584-6262 |
| Oklahoma Bank and Trust Co. | (580) 323-2345 |
| Oklahoma State Bank | (918) 256-5585 |
| Peoples National Bank of Checotah | (918) 473-2237 |
| Prime Bank | (405) 340-2775 |
| Prosperity Bank | (979) 543-2200 |
| Security First National Bank of Hugo | (580) 326-9641 |
| Security State Bank | (580) 497-3354 |
| Shamrock Bank, N.A. | (580) 927-2311 |
| Welch State Bank of Welch, Oklahoma | (918) 788-3373 |

### Rating: B+

| Name | Telephone |
|---|---|
| American Exchange Bank | (405) 756-3101 |
| Anchor D Bank | (580) 423-7541 |
| Bank of America, N.A. | (704) 386-5681 |
| Bank of Commerce | (918) 696-7745 |
| Bank of Commerce | (918) 789-2567 |
| Bank of Cordell | (580) 832-5600 |
| Bank of Cushing | (918) 225-2010 |
| Central National Bank of Poteau | (918) 647-2233 |
| Fairview S&L Assn. | (580) 227-3735 |
| First Bank & Trust Co. | (580) 255-1810 |
| First Bank of Thomas | (580) 661-3515 |
| First National B&T Co. of Weatherford | (580) 772-5574 |
| First National Bank | (918) 653-3200 |
| First National Bank and Trust Co. | (405) 224-2200 |
| First National Bank of Fletcher | (580) 549-6106 |
| First National Bank of Lindsay | (405) 756-4433 |
| First State Bank | (580) 623-4945 |
| First-Citizens Bank & Trust Co. | (919) 716-7050 |
| Grand Savings Bank | (918) 786-2203 |
| Idabel National Bank | (580) 286-7656 |
| JPMorgan Chase Bank, N.A. | (614) 248-5800 |
| Kirkpatrick Bank | (405) 341-8222 |
| Landmark Bank | (573) 499-7333 |
| Oklahoma State Bank | (580) 735-2545 |
| Security National Bank of Enid | (580) 234-5151 |
| Simmons Bank | (870) 541-1000 |
| Southwest Bank of Weatherford | (580) 774-0900 |
| State Bank of Wynnewood | (405) 665-2001 |

## Oregon

| Name | Telephone |
|---|---|
| **Rating: A** | |
| Citizens Bank | (541) 752-5161 |
| Clackamas County Bank | (503) 668-5501 |
| Pioneer Trust Bank, N.A. | (503) 363-3136 |
| Riverview Community Bank | (360) 693-6650 |
| **Rating: A-** | |
| Bank of the Pacific | (360) 537-4052 |
| Northwest Bank | (208) 332-0700 |
| Oregon Coast Bank | (541) 265-9000 |
| Washington Federal Bank, N.A. | (206) 204-3446 |
| Washington Trust Bank | (509) 353-4204 |
| Willamette Valley Bank | (503) 485-2222 |
| Zions BanCorp., N.A. | (801) 844-7637 |
| **Rating: B+** | |
| Baker-Boyer National Bank | (509) 525-2000 |
| Bank of America, N.A. | (704) 386-5681 |
| Banner Bank | (509) 527-3636 |
| Columbia State Bank | (253) 305-1900 |
| Community Bank | (541) 432-9050 |
| First Interstate Bank | (406) 255-5000 |
| First-Citizens Bank & Trust Co. | (919) 716-7050 |
| Heritage Bank | (360) 943-1500 |
| JPMorgan Chase Bank, N.A. | (614) 248-5800 |
| Lewis & Clark Bank | (503) 212-3200 |
| Oregon Pacific Banking Co. | (541) 997-7121 |
| Umpqua Bank | (541) 440-3961 |

## Pennsylvania

| Name | Telephone |
|---|---|
| **Rating: A** | |
| Haverford Trust Co. | (610) 995-8700 |
| Parke Bank | (856) 256-2500 |
| **Rating: A-** | |
| ACNB Bank | (717) 334-3161 |
| Citizens & Northern Bank | (570) 724-3411 |
| Fidelity Deposit and Discount Bank | (570) 342-8281 |
| First Columbia Bank & Trust Co. | (570) 784-1660 |
| Hamlin Bank and Trust Co. | (814) 887-5555 |
| Honesdale National Bank | (570) 253-3355 |
| Neffs National Bank | (610) 767-3875 |
| Port Richmond Savings | (215) 634-7000 |
| Slovenian S&L Assn. of Canonsburg | (724) 745-5000 |
| Union Savings Bank | (513) 247-0300 |
| Unity Bank | (908) 730-7630 |
| WesBanco Bank, Inc. | (304) 234-9000 |
| Wilmington Savings Fund Society, FSB | (302) 792-6000 |
| **Rating: B+** | |
| American Bank | (610) 366-1800 |
| Apollo Trust Co. | (724) 478-3151 |
| Bank of America, N.A. | (704) 386-5681 |
| Bank of Landisburg | (717) 789-3213 |
| Bank of Princeton | (609) 921-1700 |
| Bryn Mawr Trust Co. | (610) 581-4839 |
| Centric Bank | (717) 657-7727 |
| Commercial Bank & Trust of PA | (724) 539-3501 |
| Community Bank, N.A. | (315) 445-2282 |
| Elderton State Bank | (724) 354-2111 |
| Farmers and Merchants Trust Co. | (717) 264-6116 |
| Farmers National Bank of Canfield | (330) 533-3341 |
| First Commonwealth Bank | (724) 463-8555 |
| First National B&T Co. of Newtown | (215) 860-9100 |
| Firstrust Savings Bank | (610) 238-5001 |
| JPMorgan Chase Bank, N.A. | (614) 248-5800 |
| National Bank of Malvern | (610) 647-0100 |
| NBT Bank, N.A. | (607) 337-6416 |
| NexTier Bank, N.A. | (724) 543-1125 |
| Peoples Security Bank and Trust Co. | (570) 955-1700 |
| PeoplesBank, A Codorus Valley Co. | (717) 846-1970 |
| Philadelphia Trust Co. | (215) 979-3434 |
| Susquehanna Community Bank | (570) 568-6851 |
| Truist Bank | (336) 776-5342 |
| Turbotville National Bank | (570) 649-5118 |
| VIST Bank | (610) 208-0966 |
| Wayne Bank | (570) 253-1455 |
| William Penn Bank, | (215) 269-1200 |
| Woodforest National Bank | (832) 375-2505 |
| Woori America Bank | (212) 244-1500 |

## Puerto Rico

| Name | Telephone |
|---|---|
| **Rating: B+** | |
| Citibank, N.A. | (605) 370-6261 |

## Rhode Island

| Name | Telephone |
|---|---|
| **Rating: B+** | |
| Bank of America, N.A. | (704) 386-5681 |
| BankNewport | (401) 846-3400 |
| JPMorgan Chase Bank, N.A. | (614) 248-5800 |
| Washington Trust Co. of Westerly | (401) 348-1200 |

## South Carolina

### Rating: A

| Name | Telephone |
|---|---|
| Bank of Clarendon | (803) 433-4451 |
| Bank of South Carolina | (843) 724-1500 |
| First Piedmont Federal S&L Assn. of Gaffney | (864) 489-6046 |
| Palmetto State Bank | (803) 943-2671 |

### Rating: A-

| Name | Telephone |
|---|---|
| Bank OZK | (501) 978-2265 |
| Carolina Bank & Trust Co. | (843) 413-9978 |
| Commercial Bank | (864) 369-7326 |
| CresCom Bank | (855) 273-7266 |
| First Federal Bank | (386) 755-0600 |
| ServisFirst Bank | (205) 949-0302 |
| South State Bank | (803) 771-2265 |
| United Community Bank | (706) 745-2151 |

### Rating: B+

| Name | Telephone |
|---|---|
| Ameris Bank | (404) 814-8114 |
| Arthur State Bank | (864) 427-1213 |
| Bank of America, N.A. | (704) 386-5681 |
| Bank of Greeleyville | (843) 426-2161 |
| Bank of Travelers Rest | (864) 834-9031 |
| Bank of York | (803) 684-4249 |
| Citizens Building and Loan, SSB | (864) 877-2054 |
| Conway National Bank | (843) 248-5721 |
| Farmers and Merchants Bank | (803) 496-3430 |
| First Bank | (910) 692-6222 |
| First Community Bank | (803) 951-2265 |
| First Palmetto Bank | (803) 432-2265 |
| First-Citizens Bank & Trust Co. | (919) 716-7050 |
| JPMorgan Chase Bank, N.A. | (614) 248-5800 |
| Oconee Federal S&L Assn. | (864) 882-2765 |
| Pinnacle Bank | (615) 744-3705 |
| Southern First Bank | (864) 679-9000 |
| Synovus Bank | (706) 649-4900 |
| Truist Bank | (336) 776-5342 |
| Woodforest National Bank | (832) 375-2505 |

## South Dakota

| Name | Telephone |
|---|---|
| **Rating: A** | |
| First Premier Bank | (605) 357-3000 |
| Pioneer Bank & Trust | (605) 717-2265 |
| Security National Bank of South Dakota | (605) 232-6060 |
| **Rating: A-** | |
| Dakota Prairie Bank | (605) 223-2337 |
| First National Bank | (605) 223-2521 |
| First National Bank | (605) 482-8293 |
| First National Bank in Philip | (605) 859-2525 |
| First National Bank in Sioux Falls | (605) 335-5200 |
| First Savings Bank | (605) 763-2009 |
| First State Bank of Roscoe | (605) 287-4451 |
| First Western Federal Savings Bank | (605) 341-1203 |
| Quoin Financial Bank | (605) 853-2473 |
| **Rating: B+** | |
| Bryant State Bank | (605) 628-2171 |
| Citibank, N.A. | (605) 370-6261 |
| Department Stores National Bank | |
| First Bank & Trust | (605) 978-9300 |
| First Bank & Trust | (605) 696-2265 |
| First Fidelity Bank | (605) 775-2641 |
| First Interstate Bank | (406) 255-5000 |
| Liberty National Bank | (712) 224-4425 |
| MetaBank | (605) 361-4347 |
| Minnwest Bank | (507) 637-5731 |
| Richland State Bank | (605) 627-5671 |
| Security State Bank | (605) 449-4261 |
| TCF National Bank | (952) 745-2760 |

## Tennessee

### Rating: A

| Name | Telephone |
|---|---|
| Citizens Bank | (615) 735-1490 |
| Citizens Bank | (423) 543-2265 |
| Citizens National Bank | (865) 453-9031 |
| Elizabethton Federal Savings Bank | (423) 543-5050 |
| First Bank and Trust Co. | (276) 889-4622 |
| FSNB, N.A. | (580) 357-9880 |
| Truxton Trust Co. | (615) 515-1700 |

### Rating: A-

| Name | Telephone |
|---|---|
| Andrew Johnson Bank | (423) 783-1000 |
| Bank of Cleveland | (423) 478-5656 |
| Bank of Lincoln County | (931) 433-1708 |
| Bank of Marion | (276) 783-3116 |
| Bank of Waynesboro | (931) 722-2265 |
| Citizens B&T Co. of Grainger County | (865) 828-5237 |
| Citizens Bank | (615) 374-2265 |
| Commercial Bank & Trust Co. | (731) 642-3341 |
| Farmers Bank | (615) 325-2265 |
| Financial Federal Bank | (901) 756-2848 |
| First Federal Bank | (615) 446-2822 |
| First Financial Bank, N.A. | (812) 238-6000 |
| First Jackson Bank, Inc. | (256) 437-2107 |
| First National Bank of Manchester | (931) 728-3518 |
| First National Bank of Middle Tennessee | (931) 473-4402 |
| First National Bank of Oneida | (423) 569-8586 |
| First National Bank of Pulaski | (931) 363-2585 |
| First National Bank of Tennessee | (931) 823-1261 |
| First Volunteer Bank | (423) 668-4509 |
| Peoples Bank | (731) 858-2661 |
| Peoples Bank & Trust Co. | (931) 728-3381 |
| Peoples Bank of East Tennessee | (423) 442-7262 |
| Peoples Bank of Middle Tennessee | (931) 684-7222 |
| Putnam 1st Mercantile Bank | (931) 528-6372 |
| Renasant Bank | (800) 680-1601 |
| Republic Bank & Trust Co. | (502) 584-3600 |
| Security FSB of McMinnville | (931) 473-4483 |
| ServisFirst Bank | (205) 949-0302 |
| Tennessee State Bank | (865) 453-0873 |
| United Community Bank | (706) 745-2151 |
| Wilson Bank and Trust | (615) 444-2265 |

### Rating: B+

| Name | Telephone |
|---|---|
| BancorpSouth Bank | (662) 680-2000 |
| Bank of America, N.A. | (704) 386-5681 |
| Bank of Crockett | (731) 663-2031 |
| Bank of Frankewing | (931) 363-1796 |
| Bank of Gleason | (731) 648-5506 |
| Cadence Bank, N.A. | (800) 636-7622 |
| CapStar Bank | (615) 732-6400 |
| Citizens Bank of Lafayette | (615) 666-2195 |
| Citizens Community Bank | (931) 967-3342 |
| City National Bank | (800) 773-7100 |
| Commercial Bank | (423) 869-5151 |
| First Century Bank | (423) 626-7261 |
| First Citizens National Bank | (731) 285-4410 |
| First Community Bank of Tennessee | (931) 684-5800 |
| First Farmers and Merchants Bank | (931) 388-3145 |
| First National Bank of Eastern Arkansas | (870) 633-3112 |
| First Vision Bank of Tennessee | (931) 454-0500 |
| FirstBank | (615) 313-0080 |
| First-Citizens Bank & Trust Co. | (919) 716-7050 |
| JPMorgan Chase Bank, N.A. | (614) 248-5800 |
| Legends Bank | (931) 503-1234 |
| Mountain Commerce Bank | (865) 694-5725 |
| Pinnacle Bank | (615) 744-3705 |
| Planters Bank, Inc. | (270) 886-9030 |
| Security Bank and Trust Co. | (731) 642-6644 |
| Simmons Bank | (870) 541-1000 |
| Southern Bank of Tennessee | (615) 758-6600 |
| Synovus Bank | (706) 649-4900 |
| Truist Bank | (336) 776-5342 |
| Trustmark National Bank | (601) 208-5111 |
| Union Bank & Trust Co. | (931) 823-1247 |

## Texas

| Name | Telephone |
|---|---|
| **Rating: A+** | |
| Citizens 1st Bank | (903) 581-1900 |
| **Rating: A** | |
| Austin Bank, Texas N.A. | (903) 586-1526 |
| Bank7 | (405) 810-8600 |
| Bessemer Trust Co., N.A. | (212) 708-9100 |
| Commerce Bank | (956) 724-1616 |
| Commercial National Bank of Brady | (325) 597-2961 |
| Community Bank | (903) 236-4422 |
| Crockett National Bank | (210) 467-5391 |
| Crossroads Bank | (361) 293-3572 |
| Falcon International Bank | (956) 723-2265 |
| First Financial Bank, N.A. | (325) 627-7200 |
| First State Bank of Bedias | (936) 395-2141 |
| First State Bank of Odem | (361) 368-2651 |
| FSNB, N.A. | (580) 357-9880 |
| International Bank of Commerce | (956) 765-8361 |
| International Bank of Commerce | (956) 547-1000 |
| International Bank of Commerce | (956) 722-7611 |
| Mason Bank | (325) 347-5911 |
| Metro City Bank | (770) 455-4989 |
| Muenster State Bank | (940) 759-2257 |
| Sanger Bank | (940) 458-4600 |
| Security State Bank & Trust | (830) 997-7575 |
| Texas Community Bank | (956) 722-8333 |
| Texas Exchange Bank, SSB | (817) 297-4331 |
| Texas State Bank | (325) 949-3721 |
| TexasBank | (325) 649-9200 |
| ValueBank Texas | (361) 888-4451 |
| Waggoner National Bank of Vernon | (940) 552-2511 |
| **Rating: A-** | |
| AimBank | (806) 385-4441 |
| American First National Bank | (713) 596-2888 |
| American National Bank of Mount Pleasant | (903) 572-1776 |
| Amistad Bank | (830) 775-0295 |
| Armed Forces Bank, N.A. | (913) 682-9090 |
| Arrowhead Bank | (325) 247-5741 |
| Bank of DeSoto, N.A. | (972) 780-7777 |
| Bank of Texas | (432) 221-6100 |
| Bank OZK | (501) 978-2265 |
| Big Bend Banks, N.A. | (432) 729-4344 |
| BOC Bank | (806) 373-1720 |
| Brenham National Bank | (979) 836-4571 |
| BTH Bank, N.A. | (903) 763-2264 |
| Buckholts State Bank | (254) 593-3661 |
| Cathay Bank | (213) 625-4791 |
| Central National Bank | (254) 776-3800 |
| Citizens Bank | (806) 350-5600 |
| Citizens Bank of Las Cruces | (575) 647-4100 |
| Citizens Bank, N.A. | (325) 695-3000 |
| Citizens National Bank at Brownwood | (325) 643-3545 |
| Citizens State Bank | (936) 398-2566 |
| Citizens State Bank | (979) 885-3571 |
| Citizens State Bank | (325) 468-3311 |
| City National Bank of Sulphur Springs | (903) 885-7523 |
| City National Bank of Taylor | (512) 671-2265 |
| Comerica Bank | (214) 462-4000 |
| Commonwealth Business Bank | (323) 988-3000 |
| Community Bank & Trust, Waco, Texas | (254) 753-1521 |
| Community National B&T of Texas | (903) 654-4500 |
| CommunityBank of Texas, N.A. | (409) 861-7200 |
| Cowboy Bank of Texas | (972) 435-2131 |
| East West Bank | (626) 768-6000 |
| First Command Bank | (888) 763-7600 |
| First Community Bank | (361) 888-9310 |
| First Liberty National Bank | (936) 336-6471 |
| First National Bank | (806) 659-5544 |
| First National Bank of Albany | (325) 762-2222 |
| First National Bank of Bastrop | (512) 321-2561 |
| First National Bank of Burleson | (817) 295-0461 |
| First National Bank of Eldorado | (325) 853-2561 |
| First National Bank of Floydada | (806) 983-3717 |
| First National Bank of Granbury | (817) 573-2655 |
| First National Bank of Hebbronville | (361) 527-3221 |
| First Savings Bank | (605) 763-2009 |
| First State Bank | (903) 676-1900 |
| First State Bank | (979) 648-2691 |
| First State Bank | (806) 396-5521 |
| First State Bank and Trust Co. | (903) 693-6606 |
| First State Bank of Ben Wheeler, Texas | (903) 833-5861 |
| First State Bank of Burnet | (512) 756-2191 |
| First State Bank of Paint Rock | (325) 732-4386 |
| First Texas Bank | (512) 556-3691 |
| First Texoma National Bank | (580) 924-4242 |
| First United Bank | (806) 647-4151 |
| Frost Bank | (210) 220-4011 |
| Golden Bank, N.A. | (713) 777-3838 |
| Grandview Bank | (817) 866-3316 |
| Happy State Bank | (806) 558-2265 |
| HomeBank Texas | (972) 287-2030 |
| HomeTown Bank, N.A. | (409) 763-1271 |
| International Bank of Commerce Oklahoma | (405) 841-2100 |

## Texas

| Name | Telephone |
|---|---|
| Inwood National Bank | (214) 358-5281 |
| Johnson City Bank | (830) 868-7131 |
| Liberty Capital Bank | (469) 375-6600 |
| Liberty National Bank in Paris | (903) 785-5555 |
| Llano National Bank | (325) 247-5701 |
| Marion State Bank | (830) 420-2331 |
| Moody National Bank | (409) 632-5016 |
| Open Bank | (213) 892-9999 |
| Pearland State Bank | (281) 485-3211 |
| Pegasus Bank | (214) 353-3000 |
| Peoples Bank | (806) 794-0044 |
| Peoples State Bank | (830) 683-2119 |
| Perryton National Bank | (806) 435-9641 |
| Pinnacle Bank | (817) 810-9110 |
| PlainsCapital Bank | (214) 525-9100 |
| PromiseOne Bank | (678) 385-0800 |
| Prosperity Bank | (979) 543-2200 |
| Roscoe State Bank | (325) 766-3311 |
| Round Top State Bank | (979) 249-3151 |
| Schertz Bank & Trust | (210) 945-7400 |
| Security Bank | (432) 570-9330 |
| Security State Bank | (806) 481-3327 |
| Security State Bank | (830) 334-3606 |
| Shelby Savings Bank, SSB | (936) 598-5688 |
| Southside Bank | (903) 531-7111 |
| SouthStar Bank, S.S.B. | (361) 596-4611 |
| State National Bank of Big Spring | (432) 264-2100 |
| Tejas Bank | (432) 943-4230 |
| Texas Bank and Trust Co. | (903) 237-5500 |
| Texas Financial Bank | (325) 869-5511 |
| Texas First Bank | (409) 948-1990 |
| Texas Republic Bank, N.A. | (972) 334-0700 |
| Texas Security Bank | (469) 398-4800 |
| Titan Bank, N.A. | (940) 325-9821 |
| Tolleson Private Bank | (214) 252-3033 |
| Trinity Bank, N.A. | (817) 763-9966 |
| Wallis Bank | (979) 478-6151 |
| Washington Federal Bank, N.A. | (206) 204-3446 |
| Wells Fargo Bank South Central, N.A. | (713) 802-2717 |
| West Texas National Bank | (432) 685-6500 |
| WestStar Bank | (915) 532-1000 |
| Yoakum National Bank | (361) 293-5225 |
| Zions BanCorp., N.A. | (801) 844-7637 |

## Rating: B+

| Name | Telephone |
|---|---|
| Amarillo National Bank | (806) 378-8000 |
| American Momentum Bank | (979) 774-1111 |
| American National Bank of Texas | (972) 524-3411 |
| Anahuac National Bank | (409) 267-3106 |
| Austin Capital Bank SSB | (512) 693-3600 |
| Austin County State Bank | (979) 865-4200 |
| BancorpSouth Bank | (662) 680-2000 |
| Bandera Bank | (830) 796-3711 |
| Bank and Trust, SSB | (830) 774-2555 |
| Bank of America, N.A. | (704) 386-5681 |
| Benchmark Bank | (972) 673-4000 |
| Brazos National Bank | (979) 265-1911 |
| Broadway National Bank | (210) 283-6500 |
| Burton State Bank | (979) 289-3151 |
| Cadence Bank, N.A. | (800) 636-7622 |
| Capital Bank of Texas | (830) 876-5221 |
| Cendera Bank, N.A. | (903) 965-7755 |
| Central Bank | (832) 485-2300 |
| CIT Bank, N.A. | (855) 462-2652 |
| Citibank, N.A. | (605) 370-6261 |
| Citizens National Bank of Crosbyton | (806) 675-2376 |
| Citizens National Bank of Hillsboro | (254) 582-2531 |
| Citizens State Bank | (903) 322-4256 |
| Citizens State Bank | (979) 596-1421 |
| City Bank | (806) 792-7101 |
| Coleman County State Bank | (325) 625-2172 |
| Commercial National Bank of Texarkana | (903) 831-4561 |
| Community National Bank | (830) 426-3066 |
| Community National Bank | (432) 262-1600 |
| Dilley State Bank | (830) 965-1511 |
| Ennis State Bank | (972) 875-9676 |
| Farmers State Bank | (254) 729-3272 |
| Fidelity Bank of Texas | (254) 755-6555 |
| First Bank & Trust | (806) 788-0800 |
| First Bank and Trust of Memphis | (806) 259-3556 |
| First IC Bank | (770) 451-7200 |
| First National Bank of Alvin | (281) 331-3151 |
| First National Bank of Aspermont | (940) 989-3505 |
| First National Bank of Bellville | (979) 865-3181 |
| First National Bank of Bosque County | (254) 932-5345 |
| First National Bank of Central Texas | (254) 772-9330 |
| First National Bank of Dublin | (254) 445-4400 |
| First National Bank of Evant | (254) 471-5531 |
| First National Bank of Huntsville | (936) 295-5701 |
| First National Bank of Livingston | (936) 327-1234 |
| First National Bank of McGregor | (254) 840-2836 |
| First National Bank of Shiner | (361) 594-3317 |
| First National Bank of Stanton | (432) 756-3361 |
| First National Bank of Winnsboro | (903) 342-5275 |

## Texas

| Name | Telephone |
|---|---|
| First National Bank Texas | (254) 554-4236 |
| First State Bank | (940) 549-8880 |
| First State Bank | (940) 665-1711 |
| First State Bank of Uvalde | (830) 278-6231 |
| First Texas Bank | (512) 863-2567 |
| FirstBank Southwest | (806) 355-9661 |
| First-Citizens Bank & Trust Co. | (919) 716-7050 |
| Fort Hood National Bank | (254) 532-1026 |
| Frontier Bank of Texas | (512) 281-1500 |
| Guadalupe Bank | (830) 792-1950 |
| Guaranty Bank & Trust, N.A. | (903) 572-9881 |
| Hanmi Bank | (213) 382-2200 |
| Hondo National Bank | (830) 426-3355 |
| Horizon Bank, SSB | (512) 637-5730 |
| Independent Bank | (972) 562-9004 |
| Industry State Bank | (979) 357-4437 |
| Jacksboro National Bank | (940) 567-5551 |
| Jefferson Bank | (210) 734-4311 |
| JPMorgan Chase Bank, N.A. | (614) 248-5800 |
| Landmark Bank | (573) 499-7333 |
| Legend Bank, N.A. | (940) 872-2221 |
| Lone Star National Bank | (956) 984-2991 |
| Lytle State Bank of Lytle, Texas | (830) 709-3601 |
| NexBank SSB | (972) 934-4700 |
| Northern Trust Co. | (312) 630-6000 |
| Pointbank | (940) 686-7000 |
| Sabine State Bank and Trust Co. | (318) 256-7000 |
| Sage Capital Bank | (830) 672-8585 |
| Santa Anna National Bank | (325) 348-3108 |
| Simmons Bank | (870) 541-1000 |
| Southwest Bank | (432) 552-5000 |
| Southwestern National Bank | (713) 771-9700 |
| Spirit of Texas Bank, SSB | (936) 538-1000 |
| Spring Hill State Bank | (903) 759-0751 |
| State Bank of De Kalb | (903) 667-2553 |
| State Bank of Texas | (972) 252-6000 |
| Stockmens National Bank in Cotulla | (830) 879-2331 |
| Sundown State Bank | (806) 229-2111 |
| T Bank, N.A. | (972) 720-9000 |
| Texas Bank Financial | (817) 596-9998 |
| Texas Brand Bank | (214) 219-0003 |
| TexStar National Bank | (210) 659-4000 |
| Truist Bank | (336) 776-5342 |
| Trustmark National Bank | (601) 208-5111 |
| UBank | (936) 639-5566 |
| Woodforest National Bank | (832) 375-2505 |
| Zavala County Bank | (830) 374-5866 |

## Utah

| Name | Telephone |
|---|---|
| **Rating: A+** | |
| Green Dot Bank | (801) 344-7020 |
| Optum Bank, Inc. | (866) 234-8913 |
| **Rating: A** | |
| Altabank | (801) 756-7681 |
| Bank of Utah | (801) 409-5000 |
| Central Bank | (801) 375-1000 |
| LCA Bank Corp. | (435) 658-4824 |
| Morgan Stanley Bank, N.A. | (801) 236-3600 |
| State Bank of Southern Utah | (435) 865-2300 |
| UBS Bank USA | (801) 741-0310 |
| **Rating: A-** | |
| BMW Bank of North America | (801) 461-6500 |
| Brighton Bank | (801) 943-6500 |
| D.L. Evans Bank | (208) 678-8615 |
| Finwise Bank | (801) 545-6000 |
| First Electronic Bank | (801) 572-4004 |
| Glacier Bank | (406) 756-4200 |
| Holladay Bank & Trust | (801) 272-4275 |
| Home Savings Bank | (801) 523-3878 |
| Marlin Business Bank | (888) 479-9111 |
| Pitney Bowes Bank, Inc. | (801) 832-4440 |
| Utah Independent Bank | (435) 529-7459 |
| Washington Federal Bank, N.A. | (206) 204-3446 |
| Zions BanCorp., N.A. | (801) 844-7637 |
| **Rating: B+** | |
| Ally Bank | (801) 790-5000 |
| Bank of America, N.A. | (704) 386-5681 |
| Celtic Bank | (801) 363-6500 |
| EnerBank USA | (801) 832-0700 |
| Grand Valley Bank | (435) 654-7400 |
| JPMorgan Chase Bank, N.A. | (614) 248-5800 |
| Rock Canyon Bank | (801) 426-0150 |
| Sunwest Bank | (714) 730-4444 |
| WebBank | (801) 456-8350 |
| WEX Bank | (801) 568-4345 |

## Vermont

| Name | Telephone |
|---|---|
| **Rating: A-** | |
| TrustCo Bank | (518) 377-3311 |
| **Rating: B+** | |
| Community Bank, N.A. | (315) 445-2282 |
| Ledyard National Bank | (802) 649-2050 |
| NBT Bank, N.A. | (607) 337-6416 |

## Virgin Islands of the U.S.

| Name | Telephone |
|---|---|
| **Rating: B+** | |
| United Fidelity Bank, FSB | (812) 424-0921 |

## Virginia

| Name | Telephone |
|---|---|
| **Rating: A** | |
| Bank of Southside Virginia | (434) 246-5211 |
| Calvin B. Taylor Banking Co. | (410) 641-1700 |
| EagleBank | (240) 497-2075 |
| First Bank and Trust Co. | (276) 889-4622 |
| Metro City Bank | (770) 455-4989 |
| National Bank of Blacksburg | (540) 951-6205 |
| **Rating: A-** | |
| AMG National Trust Bank | (303) 694-2190 |
| Armed Forces Bank, N.A. | (913) 682-9090 |
| Bank of Charlotte County | (434) 542-5111 |
| Bank of Marion | (276) 783-3116 |
| Benchmark Community Bank | (434) 676-9054 |
| Citizens and Farmers Bank | (804) 843-2360 |
| Citizens Bank and Trust Co. | (434) 292-8100 |
| Farmers & Merchants Bank | (540) 864-5156 |
| Farmers and Miners Bank | (276) 546-4692 |
| Fidelity Bank | (919) 552-2242 |
| First Bank | (540) 465-9121 |
| Sonabank | (804) 528-4754 |
| South State Bank | (803) 771-2265 |
| Southern Bank and Trust Co. | (919) 658-7000 |
| Surrey Bank & Trust | (336) 783-3900 |
| TowneBank | (757) 638-7500 |
| Virginia National Bank | (434) 817-8621 |
| **Rating: B+** | |
| American National Bank and Trust Co. | (434) 792-5111 |
| Atlantic Union Bank | (804) 327-5720 |
| Bank of America, N.A. | (704) 386-5681 |
| Bank of Clarke County | (540) 955-2510 |
| Chesapeake Bank | (804) 435-1181 |
| Citibank, N.A. | (605) 370-6261 |
| City National Bank of West Virginia | (304) 769-1100 |
| Essex Bank | (804) 419-4329 |
| Farmers Bank | (757) 242-6111 |
| Farmers Bank of Appomattox | (434) 352-7171 |
| First-Citizens Bank & Trust Co. | (919) 716-7050 |
| FVCbank | (703) 436-4740 |
| Hanmi Bank | (213) 382-2200 |
| Highlands Community Bank | (540) 962-2265 |
| John Marshall Bank | (703) 584-0840 |
| JPMorgan Chase Bank, N.A. | (614) 248-5800 |
| Lee Bank and Trust Co. | (276) 546-2211 |
| MainStreet Bank | (703) 481-4567 |
| MVB Bank, Inc. | (304) 363-4800 |
| Pinnacle Bank | (615) 744-3705 |
| Shore United Bank | (410) 822-1400 |
| Summit Community Bank, Inc. | (304) 530-1000 |
| Truist Bank | (336) 776-5342 |
| Woodforest National Bank | (832) 375-2505 |
| Woori America Bank | (212) 244-1500 |

## Washington

| Name | Telephone |
|---|---|
| **Rating: A** | |
| 1st Security Bank of Washington | (800) 683-0973 |
| Bessemer Trust Co., N.A. | (212) 708-9100 |
| Cashmere Valley Bank | (509) 782-2624 |
| Riverview Community Bank | (360) 693-6650 |
| Security State Bank | (360) 736-0763 |
| Sterling Bank and Trust, FSB | (248) 355-2400 |
| Timberland Bank | (360) 533-4747 |
| **Rating: A-** | |
| American Continental Bank | (626) 363-8988 |
| Armed Forces Bank, N.A. | (913) 682-9090 |
| Bank of the Pacific | (360) 537-4052 |
| Cathay Bank | (213) 625-4791 |
| Coastal Community Bank | (425) 257-9000 |
| Commencement Bank | (253) 284-1800 |
| East West Bank | (626) 768-6000 |
| Glacier Bank | (406) 756-4200 |
| Islanders Bank | (360) 378-3658 |
| Kitsap Bank | (360) 876-7834 |
| Northwest Bank | (208) 332-0700 |
| Pacific Premier Bank | (949) 864-8000 |
| Peoples Bank | (360) 715-4200 |
| UniBank | (425) 275-9700 |
| United Business Bank | (925) 476-1800 |
| Washington Federal Bank, N.A. | (206) 204-3446 |
| Washington Trust Bank | (509) 353-4204 |
| Yakima Federal S&L Assn. | (509) 248-2634 |
| Zions BanCorp., N.A. | (801) 844-7637 |
| **Rating: B+** | |
| Baker-Boyer National Bank | (509) 525-2000 |
| Bank of America, N.A. | (704) 386-5681 |
| Banner Bank | (509) 527-3636 |
| Columbia State Bank | (253) 305-1900 |
| Community Bank | (541) 432-9050 |
| Community First Bank | (509) 783-3435 |
| First Financial Northwest Bank | (425) 255-4400 |
| First Interstate Bank | (406) 255-5000 |
| First-Citizens Bank & Trust Co. | (919) 716-7050 |
| Heritage Bank | (360) 943-1500 |
| JPMorgan Chase Bank, N.A. | (614) 248-5800 |
| Lamont Bank of St. John | (509) 648-3636 |
| Northern Trust Co. | (312) 630-6000 |
| Pacific Crest Savings Bank | (425) 670-9600 |
| Sound Banking Co. | (253) 588-0100 |
| Twin River Bank | (208) 746-4848 |
| Umpqua Bank | (541) 440-3961 |
| Washington Business Bank | (360) 754-1945 |
| Wheatland Bank | (509) 458-2265 |

## West Virginia

| Name | Telephone |
|---|---|
| **Rating: A-** | |
| Bank of Monroe | (304) 772-3034 |
| Clay County Bank, Inc. | (304) 587-4221 |
| Clear Mountain Bank | (304) 379-2265 |
| Mountain Valley Bank, N.A. | (304) 637-2265 |
| WesBanco Bank, Inc. | (304) 234-9000 |
| **Rating: B+** | |
| Citizens Bank of Weston, Inc. | (304) 269-2862 |
| City National Bank of West Virginia | (304) 769-1100 |
| Community Bank of Parkersburg | (304) 485-7991 |
| Fayette County National Bank of Fayetteville | (304) 574-1212 |
| First-Citizens Bank & Trust Co. | (919) 716-7050 |
| JPMorgan Chase Bank, N.A. | (614) 248-5800 |
| MVB Bank, Inc. | (304) 363-4800 |
| Summit Community Bank, Inc. | (304) 530-1000 |
| Truist Bank | (336) 776-5342 |
| Union Bank, Inc. | (304) 758-2191 |
| Williamstown Bank, Inc. | (304) 375-6262 |
| Woodforest National Bank | (832) 375-2505 |

## Wisconsin

| Name | Telephone |
|---|---|
| **Rating: A+** | |
| Bank of Prairie Du Sac | (608) 643-3393 |
| **Rating: A** | |
| Bank of Alma | (608) 685-4461 |
| Bank of Mauston | (608) 847-6200 |
| Charter Bank | (715) 832-4254 |
| Farmers State Bank Hillsboro | (608) 489-2621 |
| First National Bank of Bangor | (608) 486-2386 |
| Intercity State Bank | (715) 359-4231 |
| National Exchange Bank and Trust | (920) 921-7700 |
| Northwestern Bank | (715) 723-4461 |
| Oregon Community Bank | (608) 835-3168 |
| WaterStone Bank, SSB | (414) 761-1000 |
| Waukesha State Bank | (262) 549-8500 |
| **Rating: A-** | |
| Advantage Community Bank | (715) 654-5100 |
| American National Bank-Fox Cities | (920) 739-1040 |
| Apple River State Bank | (815) 594-2351 |
| Badger Bank | (920) 563-2478 |
| Bank of Cashton | (608) 654-5121 |
| Bank of Deerfield | (608) 764-5411 |
| Bank of Lake Mills | (920) 648-8336 |
| Bank of Wisconsin Dells | (608) 253-1111 |
| BLC Community Bank | (920) 788-4141 |
| Bluff View Bank | (608) 582-2233 |
| Capitol Bank | (608) 836-1616 |
| DMB Community Bank | (608) 846-3711 |
| Farmers State Bank of Waupaca | (715) 258-1400 |
| First Citizens State Bank | (262) 473-2112 |
| First Community Bank | (608) 868-7644 |
| First National Bank of River Falls | (715) 425-2401 |
| Home Federal Savings Bank | (507) 535-1309 |
| Hometown Bank | (920) 907-0788 |
| International Bank of Amherst | (715) 824-3325 |
| John Deere Financial, F.S.B. | (608) 821-2000 |
| Johnson Bank | (262) 619-2700 |
| McFarland State Bank | (608) 838-3141 |
| Nekoosa Port Edwards State Bank | (715) 886-3104 |
| Park Bank | (414) 466-8000 |
| Peoples Community Bank | (608) 795-2120 |
| Shell Lake State Bank | (715) 468-7858 |
| State Bank of Newburg | (262) 675-2306 |
| Timberwood Bank | (608) 372-2265 |
| Tri City National Bank | (414) 761-1610 |
| TSB Bank | (920) 269-7777 |
| Wolf River Community Bank | (920) 779-7000 |
| **Rating: B+** | |
| Bank of Brodhead | (608) 897-2121 |
| Bay Bank | (920) 490-7600 |
| Black River Country Bank | (715) 284-9448 |
| Bonduel State Bank | (715) 758-2141 |
| Bremer Bank, N.A. | (651) 288-3751 |
| Citizens Bank | (262) 363-6500 |
| Citizens State Bank of Loyal | (715) 255-8526 |
| Clare Bank, N.A. | (608) 348-2727 |
| Community First Bank | (608) 375-4117 |
| Cumberland Federal Bank, FSB | (715) 822-2249 |
| First National Bank at Darlington | (608) 776-4071 |
| First-Citizens Bank & Trust Co. | (919) 716-7050 |
| Flagstar Bank, FSB | (248) 312-5400 |
| Great Midwest Bank, S.S.B. | (262) 784-4400 |
| Headwaters State Bank | (715) 547-3383 |
| Hustisford State Bank | (920) 349-3241 |
| JPMorgan Chase Bank, N.A. | (614) 248-5800 |
| Nicolet National Bank | (920) 430-1400 |
| Northern State Bank | (715) 682-2772 |
| Northern Trust Co. | (312) 630-6000 |
| Oostburg State Bank | (920) 564-2336 |
| Paper City Savings Assn. | (715) 423-8100 |
| Partners Bank | (715) 659-2430 |
| Peoples State Bank | (715) 842-2191 |
| Pineries Bank | (715) 341-5600 |
| River Falls State Bank | (715) 425-6782 |
| Royal Bank | (608) 462-8401 |
| Starion Bank | (701) 223-6050 |
| TCF National Bank | (952) 745-2760 |
| Wisconsin Bank & Trust | (608) 203-1200 |
| WNB Financial, N.A. | (507) 454-8800 |
| Woodford State Bank | (608) 325-7766 |

## Wyoming

| Name | Telephone |
| --- | --- |
| **Rating: A** | |
| RSNB Bank | (307) 362-8801 |
| Wyoming Bank & Trust | (307) 632-7733 |
| **Rating: A-** | |
| AMG National Trust Bank | (303) 694-2190 |
| Bank of Commerce | (307) 324-2265 |
| First State Bank | (308) 632-4158 |
| FirsTier Bank | (308) 235-4633 |
| Glacier Bank | (406) 756-4200 |
| Hilltop National Bank | (307) 265-2740 |
| Lusk State Bank | (307) 334-2500 |
| Pinnacle Bank - Wyoming | (307) 532-2181 |
| Points West Community Bank | (970) 686-0878 |
| Zions BanCorp., N.A. | (801) 844-7637 |
| **Rating: B+** | |
| ANB Bank | (303) 394-5143 |
| Bank of Star Valley | (307) 885-0000 |
| Converse County Bank | (307) 358-5300 |
| First Interstate Bank | (406) 255-5000 |
| Rocky Mountain Bank | (307) 739-9000 |

# Section III

# Rating Upgrades and Downgrades

A list of all

**U.S. Commercial Banks and Savings Banks**

receiving a rating upgrade or downgrade
during the current quarter.

# Section III Contents

This section identifies those institutions receiving a rating change since the previous edition of this publication, whether it be a rating upgrade, rating downgrade, newly-rated company or the withdrawal of a rating. A rating upgrade or downgrade may entail a change from one letter grade to another, or it may mean the addition or deletion of a plus or minus sign within the same letter grade previously assigned to the company. Ratings are normally updated once each quarter of the year. In some instances, however, an institution's rating may be downgraded outside of the normal updates due to overriding circumstances.

1. **Institution Name** The name under which the institution was chartered. A company's name can be very similar to, or the same as, that of another, so verify the company's exact name, city, and state to make sure you are looking at the correct company.

2. **New Safety Rating** Weiss rating assigned to the institution at the time of publication. Our ratings are designed to distinguish levels of insolvency risk and are measured on a scale from A to F based upon a wide range of factors. Highly rated companies are, in our opinion, less likely to experience financial difficulties than lower rated firms. See *About Weiss Safety Ratings* for more information and a description of what each rating means.

3. **State** The state in which the institution's headquarters or main office is located.

4. **Date of Change** Date that rating was finalized.

## New Ratings

| Name | State | Date of Change |
|---|---|---|
| **Rating: B** | | |
| Peoples Bank Midwest | WI | 03/09/20 |
| Pioneer Bank | NY | 03/09/20 |

## Rating Upgrades

### Rating: A+

| Name | State | Date of Change |
|---|---|---|
| Citizens First Bank | FL | 03/09/20 |
| Green Dot Bank | UT | 03/09/20 |

### Rating: A

| Name | State | Date of Change |
|---|---|---|
| Bank 1st | IA | 03/09/20 |
| Bank of George | NV | 03/09/20 |
| Bank of Hydro | OK | 03/09/20 |
| Bank of Mauston | WI | 03/09/20 |
| Bank of Southside Virginia | VA | 03/09/20 |
| Bath Savings Institution | ME | 03/09/20 |
| Bessemer Trust Co. | NY | 03/09/20 |
| Cass Commercial Bank | MO | 03/09/20 |
| Central Bank | UT | 03/09/20 |
| City National B&T Co. of Lawton, Oklahoma | OK | 03/09/20 |
| Community Bank of El Dorado Springs | MO | 03/09/20 |
| Crockett National Bank | TX | 03/09/20 |
| Crossroads Bank | TX | 03/09/20 |
| Douglas National Bank | GA | 03/09/20 |
| Esquire Bank, N.A. | NY | 03/09/20 |
| Farmers Bank | ID | 03/09/20 |
| First National Bank of Bangor | WI | 03/09/20 |
| First State Bank of Odem | TX | 03/09/20 |
| First State Bank Southwest | MN | 03/09/20 |
| FNB South | GA | 03/09/20 |
| Fulton Savings Bank | NY | 03/09/20 |
| Garden Plain State Bank | KS | 03/09/20 |
| Germantown Trust & Savings Bank | IL | 03/09/20 |
| Grand Ridge National Bank | IL | 03/09/20 |
| HNB National Bank | MO | 03/09/20 |
| Home Bank of California | CA | 03/09/20 |
| Intercity State Bank | WI | 03/09/20 |
| Iowa Trust and Savings Bank | IA | 03/09/20 |
| Jackson County Bank | KY | 03/09/20 |
| LCA Bank Corp. | UT | 03/09/20 |
| Minden Exchange Bank & Trust Co. | NE | 03/09/20 |
| Muenster State Bank | TX | 03/09/20 |
| Nodaway Valley Bank | MO | 03/09/20 |
| Oregon Community Bank | WI | 03/09/20 |
| Palmetto State Bank | SC | 03/09/20 |
| Park Ridge Community Bank | IL | 03/09/20 |
| Parke Bank | NJ | 03/09/20 |
| Pinnacle Bank | IA | 03/09/20 |
| Ramsey National Bank | ND | 03/09/20 |
| Security National Bank of South Dakota | SD | 03/09/20 |
| Senath State Bank | MO | 03/09/20 |
| St. Clair County State Bank | MO | 03/09/20 |
| Sterling Bank and Trust, FSB | MI | 03/09/20 |
| TexasBank | TX | 03/09/20 |
| United Community Bank of W Kentucky | KY | 03/09/20 |
| Valley Bank of Commerce | NM | 03/09/20 |
| ValueBank Texas | TX | 03/09/20 |
| Waggoner National Bank of Vernon | TX | 03/09/20 |
| Waukon State Bank | IA | 03/09/20 |
| West Central Georgia Bank | GA | 03/09/20 |
| Western Bank | NM | 03/09/20 |

### Rating: A-

| Name | State | Date of Change |
|---|---|---|
| 1880 Bank | MD | 03/09/20 |
| Adrian Bank | MO | 03/09/20 |
| Albany Bank and Trust Co., N.A. | IL | 03/09/20 |
| Alden State Bank | MI | 03/09/20 |
| Amerasia Bank | NY | 03/09/20 |
| American National Bank | FL | 03/09/20 |
| Apple River State Bank | IL | 03/09/20 |
| Bank of Bourbonnais | IL | 03/09/20 |
| Bank of Cleveland | TN | 03/09/20 |
| Bank of Commerce | MS | 03/09/20 |
| Bank of Dawson | GA | 03/09/20 |
| Bank of DeSoto, N.A. | TX | 03/09/20 |
| Bank of Dudley | GA | 03/09/20 |
| Bank of Feather River | CA | 03/09/20 |
| Bank of Hemet | CA | 03/09/20 |
| Bank of Lake Village | AR | 03/09/20 |
| Bank of Madison | GA | 03/09/20 |
| Bank of Maple Plain | MN | 03/09/20 |
| Bank of Pontiac | IL | 03/09/20 |
| Bank of Prague | NE | 03/09/20 |
| Bank of Utica | NY | 03/09/20 |
| Bank of Wisconsin Dells | WI | 03/09/20 |
| Bank of Wolcott | IN | 03/09/20 |
| Bluff View Bank | WI | 03/09/20 |
| Bradford National Bank of Greenville | IL | 03/09/20 |
| Brenham National Bank | TX | 03/09/20 |
| Buckeye Community Bank | OH | 03/09/20 |
| Carolina Bank & Trust Co. | SC | 03/09/20 |
| CCB Community Bank | AL | 03/09/20 |
| Centennial Bank | AR | 03/09/20 |
| Central Bank & Trust Co. | KY | 03/09/20 |
| CentreBank | IN | 03/09/20 |
| Century Bank of the Ozarks | MO | 03/09/20 |
| Citizens B&T Co. of Grainger County | TN | 03/09/20 |
| Citizens Bank | TN | 03/09/20 |
| Citizens Bank | TX | 03/09/20 |
| Citizens Bank of Las Cruces | NM | 03/09/20 |
| Citizens Bank, N.A. | TX | 03/09/20 |
| Citizens Community Bank | GA | 03/09/20 |
| Citizens National Bank of Park Rapids | MN | 03/09/20 |
| Citizens Savings Bank | IA | 03/09/20 |

## Rating Upgrades

| Name | State | Date of Change |
|---|---|---|
| Citizens State Bank | TX | 03/09/20 |
| Citizens State Bank Midwest | ND | 03/09/20 |
| Citizens State Bank of Finley | ND | 03/09/20 |
| City National Bank of Sulphur Springs | TX | 03/09/20 |
| Commencement Bank | WA | 03/09/20 |
| Community Bank | IL | 03/09/20 |
| Community Bank of Easton | IL | 03/09/20 |
| Community Bank of the South | FL | 03/09/20 |
| Community National B&T of Texas | TX | 03/09/20 |
| Community National Bank | KS | 03/09/20 |
| Cross River Bank | NJ | 03/09/20 |
| Crossroads Bank | IL | 03/09/20 |
| Dakota Prairie Bank | SD | 03/09/20 |
| DMB Community Bank | WI | 03/09/20 |
| Exchange Bank | GA | 03/09/20 |
| F&M Bank | OK | 03/09/20 |
| Farmers & Merchants Bank | NC | 03/09/20 |
| Farmers State Bank | IA | 03/09/20 |
| Fidelity Deposit and Discount Bank | PA | 03/09/20 |
| First Bank | VA | 03/09/20 |
| First Columbia Bank & Trust Co. | PA | 03/09/20 |
| First Community Bank | WI | 03/09/20 |
| First Electronic Bank | UT | 03/09/20 |
| First National Bank | TX | 03/09/20 |
| First National Bank of Albany | TX | 03/09/20 |
| First National Bank of Chadron | NE | 03/09/20 |
| First National Bank of Grayson | KY | 03/09/20 |
| First National Bank of Hebbronville | TX | 03/09/20 |
| First National Bank of Hutchinson | KS | 03/09/20 |
| First Nations Bank | IL | 03/09/20 |
| First Security Bank | IA | 03/09/20 |
| First State Bank | IA | 03/09/20 |
| First State Bank & Trust | ND | 03/09/20 |
| First State Bank of Blakely | GA | 03/09/20 |
| First State Bank of Golva | ND | 03/09/20 |
| First State Bank of Paint Rock | TX | 03/09/20 |
| First Texas Bank | TX | 03/09/20 |
| Freedom Bank | IN | 03/09/20 |
| Genesee Regional Bank | NY | 03/09/20 |
| Granite Falls Bank | MN | 03/09/20 |
| Gulf Coast Bank | LA | 03/09/20 |
| Hamler State Bank | OH | 03/09/20 |
| Hawthorn Bank | MO | 03/09/20 |
| Hingham Institution for Savings | MA | 03/09/20 |
| Hometown Bank | WI | 03/09/20 |
| Institution for Savings | MA | 03/09/20 |
| Jefferson Bank | MS | 03/09/20 |
| Johnson City Bank | TX | 03/09/20 |
| Kennebec Savings Bank | ME | 03/09/20 |
| Lake Elmo Bank | MN | 03/09/20 |
| Lamar Bank and Trust Co. | MO | 03/09/20 |
| Leighton State Bank | IA | 03/09/20 |
| Llano National Bank | TX | 03/09/20 |
| Lowell Five Cent Savings Bank | MA | 03/09/20 |
| Lusk State Bank | WY | 03/09/20 |
| Maries County Bank | MO | 03/09/20 |
| McFarland State Bank | WI | 03/09/20 |
| Milledgeville State Bank | IL | 03/09/20 |
| Mission Valley Bank | CA | 03/09/20 |
| Mutual Savings Assn. | KS | 03/09/20 |
| Napoleon State Bank | IN | 03/09/20 |
| Pacific Coast Bankers' Bank | CA | 03/09/20 |
| Park Bank | WI | 03/09/20 |
| Pegasus Bank | TX | 03/09/20 |
| Peoples Bank MT. Washington | KY | 03/09/20 |
| Peoples Community Bank | WI | 03/09/20 |
| Pinnacle Bank | CA | 03/09/20 |
| Pinnacle Bank | TX | 03/09/20 |
| PrinsBank | MN | 03/09/20 |
| Providence Bank | NC | 03/09/20 |
| Queenstown Bank of Maryland | MD | 03/09/20 |
| RBC Bank (Georgia), N.A. | NC | 03/09/20 |
| River Bank & Trust | AL | 03/09/20 |
| Rockwood Bank | MO | 03/09/20 |
| Security Bank | NE | 03/09/20 |
| Security Bank | TX | 03/09/20 |
| Security Savings Bank | IA | 03/09/20 |
| Security State Bank | IA | 03/09/20 |
| Slovenian S&L Assn. of Canonsburg | PA | 03/09/20 |
| South Ottumwa Savings Bank | IA | 03/09/20 |
| Spring Valley Bank | OH | 03/09/20 |
| Stafford Savings Bank | CT | 03/09/20 |
| State Bank of Cherry | IL | 03/09/20 |
| State Bank of Newburg | WI | 03/09/20 |
| State Bank of Wheaton | MN | 03/09/20 |
| Texas First Bank | TX | 03/09/20 |
| Town-Country National Bank | AL | 03/09/20 |
| TrustCo Bank | NY | 03/09/20 |
| Union Bank and Trust Co. | NE | 03/09/20 |
| US Metro Bank | CA | 03/09/20 |
| Virginia National Bank | VA | 03/09/20 |
| VisionBank | MN | 03/09/20 |
| Western Commerce Bank | NM | 03/09/20 |
| Wilmington Savings Fund Society, FSB | DE | 03/09/20 |
| Yampa Valley Bank | CO | 03/09/20 |

### Rating: B+

| Name | State | Date of Change |
|---|---|---|
| 1st Bank Yuma | AZ | 03/09/20 |
| 21st Century Bank | MN | 03/09/20 |
| American State Bank | IA | 03/09/20 |

## Rating Upgrades

| Name | State | Date of Change |
|---|---|---|
| Apollo Trust Co. | PA | 03/09/20 |
| Arlington State Bank | MN | 03/09/20 |
| Audubon State Bank | IA | 03/09/20 |
| Bank of Bearden | AR | 03/09/20 |
| Bank of Commerce | OK | 03/09/20 |
| Bank of Cordell | OK | 03/09/20 |
| Bank of Dixon County | NE | 03/09/20 |
| Bank of Elgin | NE | 03/09/20 |
| Bank of Frankewing | TN | 03/09/20 |
| Bank of Greeleyville | SC | 03/09/20 |
| Bank of Monticello | GA | 03/09/20 |
| Bloomsdale Bank | MO | 03/09/20 |
| BNC National Bank | AZ | 03/09/20 |
| BTC Bank | MO | 03/09/20 |
| Burton State Bank | TX | 03/09/20 |
| Capital City Bank | FL | 03/09/20 |
| CapStar Bank | TN | 03/09/20 |
| Casey County Bank, Inc. | KY | 03/09/20 |
| Celtic Bank | UT | 03/09/20 |
| Central Bank Illinois | IL | 03/09/20 |
| Central National Bank of Poteau | OK | 03/09/20 |
| ChoiceOne Bank | MI | 03/09/20 |
| Citizens Bank | WI | 03/09/20 |
| Citizens Bank of Edina | MO | 03/09/20 |
| Citizens Bank of Swainsboro | GA | 03/09/20 |
| Citizens Community Bank | TN | 03/09/20 |
| Citizens National Bank of Somerset | KY | 03/09/20 |
| Citizens State Bank | KS | 03/09/20 |
| Citizens State Bank | KS | 03/09/20 |
| Clarkson Bank | NE | 03/09/20 |
| Coleman County State Bank | TX | 03/09/20 |
| Commercial & Savings Bank of Millersburg | OH | 03/09/20 |
| Commercial Bank | TN | 03/09/20 |
| Community Bank | KS | 03/09/20 |
| Dakota Western Bank | ND | 03/09/20 |
| Eagle Bank | MT | 03/09/20 |
| Elysian Bank | MN | 03/09/20 |
| Ennis State Bank | TX | 03/09/20 |
| Essex Bank | VA | 03/09/20 |
| Evangeline Bank and Trust Co. | LA | 03/09/20 |
| Family Bank | GA | 03/09/20 |
| Farmers and Merchants Trust Co. | PA | 03/09/20 |
| Farmers Bank | VA | 03/09/20 |
| Farmers State Bank | KS | 03/09/20 |
| Farmers State Bank of Hartland | MN | 03/09/20 |
| Farmers Trust & Savings Bank | IA | 03/09/20 |
| First Bank of Ohio | OH | 03/09/20 |
| First Commerce Bank | KS | 03/09/20 |
| First Fidelity Bank | SD | 03/09/20 |
| First Harrison Bank | IN | 03/09/20 |
| First Iowa State Bank | IA | 03/09/20 |
| First National B&T Co. of Weatherford | OK | 03/09/20 |
| First National Bank and Trust Co. | OK | 03/09/20 |
| First National Bank in Olney | IL | 03/09/20 |
| First National Bank of Evant | TX | 03/09/20 |
| First National Bank of Huntsville | TX | 03/09/20 |
| First National Bank of Winnsboro | TX | 03/09/20 |
| First State Bank of Middlebury | IN | 03/09/20 |
| First Whitney Bank and Trust | IA | 03/09/20 |
| FirstBank of Nebraska | NE | 03/09/20 |
| Five Star Bank | CA | 03/09/20 |
| Flagler Bank | FL | 03/09/20 |
| GNB Bank | IA | 03/09/20 |
| Golden Belt Bank, FSA | KS | 03/09/20 |
| Grand Savings Bank | OK | 03/09/20 |
| Guardian Savings Bank, F.S.B. | OH | 03/09/20 |
| Homestead Bank | NE | 03/09/20 |
| Horizon Financial Bank | ND | 03/09/20 |
| Howard State Bank | KS | 03/09/20 |
| Jones Bank | NE | 03/09/20 |
| Kansas State Bank | KS | 03/09/20 |
| Kirkpatrick Bank | OK | 03/09/20 |
| Lake Community Bank | MN | 03/09/20 |
| Lamont Bank of St. John | WA | 03/09/20 |
| Ledyard National Bank | VT | 03/09/20 |
| Lee Bank and Trust Co. | VA | 03/09/20 |
| Legend Bank, N.A. | TX | 03/09/20 |
| Legends Bank | TN | 03/09/20 |
| Lewis & Clark Bank | OR | 03/09/20 |
| Liberty Bank | IL | 03/09/20 |
| Liberty National Bank | IA | 03/09/20 |
| Machias Savings Bank | ME | 03/09/20 |
| Meadows Bank | NV | 03/09/20 |
| Merchants Bank of Alabama | AL | 03/09/20 |
| Merchants Bank of Commerce | CA | 03/09/20 |
| Midwest Bank | MN | 03/09/20 |
| Morganton Savings Bank, S.S.B. | NC | 03/09/20 |
| NBT Bank, N.A. | NY | 03/09/20 |
| New Washington State Bank | IN | 03/09/20 |
| Northern Bank & Trust Co. | MA | 03/09/20 |
| Northern State Bank | WI | 03/09/20 |
| Oostburg State Bank | WI | 03/09/20 |
| Partners Bank of New England | ME | 03/09/20 |
| Peoples Bank & Trust Co. | KY | 03/09/20 |
| Peoples Bank of Wyaconda | MO | 03/09/20 |
| Phenix-Girard Bank | AL | 03/09/20 |
| Pine Country Bank | MN | 03/09/20 |
| Pineries Bank | WI | 03/09/20 |
| Pointbank | TX | 03/09/20 |
| Produce State Bank | MN | 03/09/20 |

## Rating Upgrades

| Name | State | Date of Change |
|---|---|---|
| Providence Bank & Trust | IL | 03/09/20 |
| Quad City Bank and Trust Co. | IA | 03/09/20 |
| Rabun County Bank | GA | 03/09/20 |
| Redwood Capital Bank | CA | 03/09/20 |
| RiverHills Bank | MS | 03/09/20 |
| Sabine State Bank and Trust Co. | LA | 03/09/20 |
| Sage Capital Bank | TX | 03/09/20 |
| Security Bank | AR | 03/09/20 |
| Security Bank USA | MN | 03/09/20 |
| Security State Bank | IA | 03/09/20 |
| Security State Bank | SD | 03/09/20 |
| Security State Bank, Wishek, North Dakota | ND | 03/09/20 |
| Springfield First Community Bank | MO | 03/09/20 |
| SunMark Community Bank | GA | 03/09/20 |
| T Bank, N.A. | TX | 03/09/20 |
| Tensas State Bank | LA | 03/09/20 |
| Texas Bank Financial | TX | 03/09/20 |
| Traditions Bank | AL | 03/09/20 |
| TrailWest Bank | MT | 03/09/20 |
| TrustBank | IL | 03/09/20 |
| Turbotville National Bank | PA | 03/09/20 |
| Twin River Bank | ID | 03/09/20 |
| Union Bank & Trust Co. | TN | 03/09/20 |
| Union Bank of Mena | AR | 03/09/20 |
| United Southern Bank | KY | 03/09/20 |
| VIST Bank | PA | 03/09/20 |
| Wheatland Bank | WA | 03/09/20 |

## Rating: B

| Name | State | Date of Change |
|---|---|---|
| Affiliated Bank, N.A. | TX | 03/09/20 |
| American State Bank & Trust Co. | KS | 03/09/20 |
| Auburn Banking Co. | KY | 03/09/20 |
| BAC Community Bank | CA | 03/09/20 |
| Bank of Botetourt | VA | 03/09/20 |
| Bank of Columbia | KY | 03/09/20 |
| Bank of Coushatta | LA | 03/09/20 |
| Bank of Edmonson County | KY | 03/09/20 |
| Bank of Hays | KS | 03/09/20 |
| Bank of Jackson Hole | WY | 03/09/20 |
| Bank of New England | NH | 03/09/20 |
| Bank of Ontario | WI | 03/09/20 |
| Bank of Southern California, N.A. | CA | 03/09/20 |
| Bank of the Prairie | KS | 03/09/20 |
| BankTennessee | TN | 03/09/20 |
| Beacon Business Bank, N.A. | CA | 03/09/20 |
| Bippus State Bank | IN | 03/09/20 |
| Black Hills Community Bank, N.A. | SD | 03/09/20 |
| Bruning Bank | NE | 03/09/20 |
| Capon Valley Bank | WV | 03/09/20 |
| Carroll Bank and Trust | TN | 03/09/20 |
| Central Bank | IA | 03/09/20 |
| CFBank, N.A. | OH | 03/09/20 |
| Charter West Bank | NE | 03/09/20 |
| Citizens Bank | IN | 03/09/20 |
| Citizens Bank | AL | 03/09/20 |
| Citizens Bank & Trust Co. | LA | 03/09/20 |
| Citizens Bank & Trust Co. | LA | 03/09/20 |
| Citizens State Bank | IL | 03/09/20 |
| Clay County State Bank | IL | 03/09/20 |
| Clinton Savings Bank | MA | 03/09/20 |
| Colorado Federal Savings Bank | CO | 03/09/20 |
| Commercial Bank & Trust Co. | AR | 03/09/20 |
| Commercial Bank of California | CA | 03/09/20 |
| Community Bank of the Midwest | KS | 03/09/20 |
| Community First Bank | LA | 03/09/20 |
| Cortland Savings and Banking Co. | OH | 03/09/20 |
| Crossroads Bank | IN | 03/09/20 |
| Deerwood Bank | MN | 03/09/20 |
| F & M Community Bank, N.A. | MN | 03/09/20 |
| Farmers & Stockmens Bank | NM | 03/09/20 |
| Farmers Bank and Savings Co. | OH | 03/09/20 |
| Farmers Bank of Willards | MD | 03/09/20 |
| Farmers National Bank of Lebanon | KY | 03/09/20 |
| First Colony Bank of Florida | FL | 03/09/20 |
| First Commercial Bank, N.A. | TX | 03/09/20 |
| First Federal Bank & Trust | WY | 03/09/20 |
| First National B&T Co. of Broken Arrow | OK | 03/09/20 |
| First National B&T Co. of McAlester | OK | 03/09/20 |
| First National B&T Co. of Miami | OK | 03/09/20 |
| First National Bank | TX | 03/09/20 |
| First National Bank and Trust | KS | 03/09/20 |
| First National Bank in Frankfort | KS | 03/09/20 |
| First National Bank in Howell | MI | 03/09/20 |
| First National Bank of Cokato | MN | 03/09/20 |
| First National Bank of Gillette | WY | 03/09/20 |
| First National Bank of Hooker | OK | 03/09/20 |
| First National Bank of Hughes Springs | TX | 03/09/20 |
| First National Bank of McIntosh | MN | 03/09/20 |
| First National Bank of North Arkansas | AR | 03/09/20 |
| First National Bank of Quitaque | TX | 03/09/20 |
| First National Bank of Scott City | KS | 03/09/20 |
| First National Bank, Cortez | CO | 03/09/20 |
| First Security Bank of Helena | MT | 03/09/20 |
| First Security State Bank | TX | 03/09/20 |
| First Southern National Bank | KY | 03/09/20 |
| First State Bank Nebraska | NE | 03/09/20 |
| Flagship Bank Minnesota | MN | 03/09/20 |
| Garrison State Bank and Trust | ND | 03/09/20 |
| Georgia Community Bank | GA | 03/09/20 |
| Goose River Bank | ND | 03/09/20 |

## Rating Upgrades

| Name | State | Date of Change |
|---|---|---|
| Goppert Financial Bank | MO | 03/09/20 |
| Grant County Bank | WV | 03/09/20 |
| Grant County State Bank | IN | 03/09/20 |
| Halstead Bank | KS | 03/09/20 |
| Hamilton Bank | MO | 03/09/20 |
| Hardin County Savings Bank | IA | 03/09/20 |
| Harleysville Bank | PA | 03/09/20 |
| Hicksville Bank | OH | 03/09/20 |
| High Plains Bank | OK | 03/09/20 |
| Highland State Bank | WI | 03/09/20 |
| Hodge Bank & Trust Co. | LA | 03/09/20 |
| INSOUTH Bank | TN | 03/09/20 |
| Integrity Bank & Trust | CO | 03/09/20 |
| Interstate Bank | TX | 03/09/20 |
| Jonesburg State Bank | MO | 03/09/20 |
| Karnes County National Bank | TX | 03/09/20 |
| Kennett Trust Bank | MO | 03/09/20 |
| Kress National Bank | TX | 03/09/20 |
| Lake Area Bank | MN | 03/09/20 |
| Lake Bank | MN | 03/09/20 |
| Legacy Bank of Florida | FL | 03/09/20 |
| Lincoln Savings Bank | IA | 03/09/20 |
| Merchants & Farmers Bank | MS | 03/09/20 |
| Merchants & Farmers Bank & Trust Co. | LA | 03/09/20 |
| Mountain Valley Bank | CO | 03/09/20 |
| MutualBank | IN | 03/09/20 |
| National Bank of Commerce | WI | 03/09/20 |
| National United | TX | 03/09/20 |
| NorthEast Community Bank | NY | 03/09/20 |
| Northview Bank | MN | 03/09/20 |
| Northway Bank | NH | 03/09/20 |
| Oak Bank | WI | 03/09/20 |
| Ohio Valley Bank Co. | OH | 03/09/20 |
| One World Bank | TX | 03/09/20 |
| Opportunity Bank of Montana | MT | 03/09/20 |
| Owen County State Bank | IN | 03/09/20 |
| Oxford Bank | MI | 03/09/20 |
| Ozona National Bank | TX | 03/09/20 |
| Pacific Valley Bank | CA | 03/09/20 |
| Paragon Bank | TN | 03/09/20 |
| Park State Bank | MN | 03/09/20 |
| Patriots Bank | KS | 03/09/20 |
| People's Bank of Commerce | OR | 03/09/20 |
| Piedmont Bank | GA | 03/09/20 |
| Pioneer Bank | VA | 03/09/20 |
| Platte Valley Bank | WY | 03/09/20 |
| Plumas Bank | CA | 03/09/20 |
| Port Washington State Bank | WI | 03/09/20 |
| PremierBank | WI | 03/09/20 |
| PrimeSouth Bank | GA | 03/09/20 |
| Profinium, Inc. | MN | 03/09/20 |
| Putnam County State Bank | MO | 03/09/20 |
| Quontic Bank | NY | 03/09/20 |
| Resource Bank | LA | 03/09/20 |
| Riverside Bank | AR | 03/09/20 |
| Roundbank | MN | 03/09/20 |
| Salisbury Bank and Trust Co. | CT | 03/09/20 |
| Scott State Bank | IL | 03/09/20 |
| Security State Bank | SD | 03/09/20 |
| Sherburne State Bank | MN | 03/09/20 |
| Southwest Georgia Bank | GA | 03/09/20 |
| State Bank of Arcadia | WI | 03/09/20 |
| State Bank of Canton | KS | 03/09/20 |
| State Bank of Whittington | IL | 03/09/20 |
| State Street Bank and Trust Co. | IL | 03/09/20 |
| Stephenson National Bank and Trust | WI | 03/09/20 |
| Stillman BancCorp, N.A. | IL | 03/09/20 |
| Sunrise Banks, N.A. | MN | 03/09/20 |
| Synergy Bank | LA | 03/09/20 |
| The Bank of Soperton | GA | 03/09/20 |
| Unison Bank | ND | 03/09/20 |
| United Community Bank | IA | 03/09/20 |
| United Community Bank of North Dakota | ND | 03/09/20 |
| United Farmers State Bank | MN | 03/09/20 |
| United State Bank | MO | 03/09/20 |
| University National Bank of Lawrence | KS | 03/09/20 |
| Vantage Bank Texas | TX | 03/09/20 |
| Viking Bank | MN | 03/09/20 |
| Village Bank | IL | 03/09/20 |
| Vintage Bank Kansas | KS | 03/09/20 |
| Volunteer State Bank | TN | 03/09/20 |
| Walden Savings Bank | NY | 03/09/20 |
| Waumandee State Bank | WI | 03/09/20 |
| Wilcox County State Bank | GA | 03/09/20 |
| Wilmington Savings Bank | OH | 03/09/20 |
| Woodland Bank | MN | 03/09/20 |
| WoodTrust Bank | WI | 03/09/20 |

## Rating: B-

| Name | State | Date of Change |
|---|---|---|
| 1st State Bank | MI | 03/09/20 |
| All America Bank | OK | 03/09/20 |
| American Bank of the North | MN | 03/09/20 |
| American Commerce Bank, N.A. | GA | 03/09/20 |
| Asian Bank | PA | 03/09/20 |
| Atlanta National Bank | IL | 03/09/20 |
| Banco Santander Puerto Rico | PR | 03/09/20 |
| Bank of Baker | MT | 03/09/20 |
| Bank of Grandin | MO | 03/09/20 |
| Bank of Kremlin | OK | 03/09/20 |
| Bank of Little Rock | AR | 03/09/20 |

## Rating Upgrades

| Name | State | Date of Change | Name | State | Date of Change |
|---|---|---|---|---|---|
| Bank of Wrightsville | GA | 03/09/20 | Frontier Bank | SD | 03/09/20 |
| Bank Plus | IA | 03/09/20 | Gateway Bank | AR | 03/09/20 |
| Basile State Bank | LA | 03/09/20 | Geo. D. Warthen Bank | GA | 03/09/20 |
| Blue Grass Federal S&L Assn. | KY | 03/09/20 | Gogebic Range Bank | MI | 03/09/20 |
| Caldwell Bank & Trust Co. | LA | 03/09/20 | Grand Bank | OK | 03/09/20 |
| California Bank of Commerce | CA | 03/09/20 | Guthrie County State Bank | IA | 03/09/20 |
| Capital Community Bank | UT | 03/09/20 | Heartland State Bank | ND | 03/09/20 |
| Century Bank | MS | 03/09/20 | Heartland State Bank | SD | 03/09/20 |
| Ciera Bank | TX | 03/09/20 | Heritage Bank of Schaumburg | IL | 03/09/20 |
| Citizens Bank & Trust Co. | MN | 03/09/20 | HomeTrust Bank | NC | 03/09/20 |
| Citizens National Bank of Bluffton | OH | 03/09/20 | Huron National Bank | MI | 03/09/20 |
| Claremont Savings Bank | NH | 03/09/20 | INB, N.A. | IL | 03/09/20 |
| Columbus Bank and Trust Co. | NE | 03/09/20 | Independent Bank | TN | 03/09/20 |
| Commerce State Bank | WI | 03/09/20 | Iroquois Federal S&L Assn. | IL | 03/09/20 |
| Commercial Bank | MI | 03/09/20 | Jefferson Security Bank | WV | 03/09/20 |
| Community Partners Savings Bank | IL | 03/09/20 | Kaw Valley State Bank | KS | 03/09/20 |
| Community State Bank | IL | 03/09/20 | Kerndt Brothers Savings Bank | IA | 03/09/20 |
| Community State Bank | MO | 03/09/20 | Kleberg Bank, N.A. | TX | 03/09/20 |
| County Bank | DE | 03/09/20 | KS Bank, Inc. | NC | 03/09/20 |
| CrossFirst Bank | KS | 03/09/20 | Lake Region Bank | MN | 03/09/20 |
| Dundee Bank | NE | 03/09/20 | Lauderdale County Bank | TN | 03/09/20 |
| Enterprise Bank | NE | 03/09/20 | M C Bank & Trust Co. | LA | 03/09/20 |
| Ergo Bank | WI | 03/09/20 | Main Street Bank | MI | 03/09/20 |
| Evolve Bank & Trust | TN | 03/09/20 | Merchants and Farmers Bank | AR | 03/09/20 |
| Farmers and Merchants State Bank | MN | 03/09/20 | MidCountry Bank | MN | 03/09/20 |
| Farmers Bank, Frankfort, Indiana, Inc. | IN | 03/09/20 | Midstates Bank, N.A. | IA | 03/09/20 |
| Farmers National Bank of Emlenton | PA | 03/09/20 | Minnesota Lakes Bank | MN | 03/09/20 |
| Fidelity Bank | IA | 03/09/20 | Monona Bank | WI | 03/09/20 |
| First Bank & Trust | TX | 03/09/20 | Murphy-Wall State Bank and Trust Co. | IL | 03/09/20 |
| First Bank of Baldwin | WI | 03/09/20 | New Frontier Bank | MO | 03/09/20 |
| First Bank of the Palm Beaches | FL | 03/09/20 | Normangee State Bank | TX | 03/09/20 |
| First Enterprise Bank | OK | 03/09/20 | North Alabama Bank | AL | 03/09/20 |
| First Federal Bank of Wisconsin | WI | 03/09/20 | Northern Sky Bank | MN | 03/09/20 |
| First Freedom Bank | TN | 03/09/20 | Northwest Bank & Trust Co. | IA | 03/09/20 |
| First Midwest Bank of Dexter | MO | 03/09/20 | Park Bank | WI | 03/09/20 |
| First Midwest Bank of Poplar Bluff | MO | 03/09/20 | People's B&T Co. of Clinton County | KY | 03/09/20 |
| First Midwest Bank of the Ozarks | MO | 03/09/20 | People's B&T Co. of Pickett County | TN | 03/09/20 |
| First National Bank of Mertzon | TX | 03/09/20 | Peoples Bank | MD | 03/09/20 |
| First Northern Bank of Wyoming | WY | 03/09/20 | Peoples Bank | IN | 03/09/20 |
| First Secure Bank and Trust Co. | IL | 03/09/20 | Peoples State Bank of Wells | MN | 03/09/20 |
| First Security Trust and Savings Bank | IL | 03/09/20 | Premier Bank | MN | 03/09/20 |
| First Sentinel Bank | VA | 03/09/20 | Premier Community Bank | WI | 03/09/20 |
| First State Bank | NE | 03/09/20 | Randall State Bank | MN | 03/09/20 |
| First State Bank | TX | 03/09/20 | Range Bank, N.A. | MI | 03/09/20 |
| First State Bank and Trust | KS | 03/09/20 | Republic Bank & Trust | OK | 03/09/20 |
| First State Bank of DeKalb County | AL | 03/09/20 | RiverHills Bank | OH | 03/09/20 |
| First State Bank of Healy | KS | 03/09/20 | Royal Banks of Missouri | MO | 03/09/20 |
| First State Bank of Purdy | MO | 03/09/20 | Sabal Palm Bank | FL | 03/09/20 |
| First Utah Bank | UT | 03/09/20 | Savings Bank | MA | 03/09/20 |
| FNB Bank | AL | 03/09/20 | Seacoast Commerce Bank | CA | 03/09/20 |

## Rating Upgrades

| Name | State | Date of Change |
|---|---|---|
| Sentry Bank | MN | 03/09/20 |
| Shelby County State Bank | IA | 03/09/20 |
| Sound Community Bank | WA | 03/09/20 |
| South Porte Bank | IL | 03/09/20 |
| Spring Bank | WI | 03/09/20 |
| State Bank of Bottineau | ND | 03/09/20 |
| State Bank of Southwest Missouri | MO | 03/09/20 |
| State Bank of Taunton | MN | 03/09/20 |
| Stroud National Bank | OK | 03/09/20 |
| TCM Bank, N.A. | FL | 03/09/20 |
| Touchstone Bank | VA | 03/09/20 |
| Tri-County Trust Co. | MO | 03/09/20 |
| Union Bank & Trust Co. | AR | 03/09/20 |
| Union S&L Assn. | IN | 03/09/20 |
| Union State Bank of Browns Valley | MN | 03/09/20 |
| United Valley Bank | ND | 03/09/20 |
| West Central Bank | IL | 03/09/20 |
| Western Bank, Artesia, New Mexico | NM | 03/09/20 |
| Western States Bank | WY | 03/09/20 |
| WestSide Bank | GA | 03/09/20 |
| York State Bank | NE | 03/09/20 |

## Rating: C+

| Name | State | Date of Change |
|---|---|---|
| 1st Bank of Sea Isle City | NJ | 03/09/20 |
| Alliance Bank & Trust Co. | NC | 03/09/20 |
| American Metro Bank | IL | 03/09/20 |
| Americana Community Bank | MN | 03/09/20 |
| America's Community Bank | MO | 03/09/20 |
| Bank of Newington | GA | 03/09/20 |
| Bank of Perry County | TN | 03/09/20 |
| BankGloucester | MA | 03/09/20 |
| Beal Bank USA | NV | 03/09/20 |
| Belmont Bank & Trust Co. | IL | 03/09/20 |
| Blue Grass Valley Bank | VA | 03/09/20 |
| Boundary Waters Bank | MN | 03/09/20 |
| Brattleboro S&L Assn. | VT | 03/09/20 |
| Cedar Valley Bank & Trust | IA | 03/09/20 |
| Centreville Bank | RI | 03/09/20 |
| CFG Community Bank | MD | 03/09/20 |
| Citizens First State Bank of Walnut | IL | 03/09/20 |
| Citizens Tri-County Bank | TN | 03/09/20 |
| CLB The Community Bank | LA | 03/09/20 |
| CNB Bank & Trust, N.A. | IL | 03/09/20 |
| Community 1st Bank Las Vegas | NM | 03/09/20 |
| Community Bank of Pickens County | GA | 03/09/20 |
| Community West Bank, N.A. | CA | 03/09/20 |
| Crown Bank | NJ | 03/09/20 |
| Equitable Bank | NE | 03/09/20 |
| Farmers State Bank of Bucklin, Kansas | KS | 03/09/20 |
| Financial Security Bank | MN | 03/09/20 |
| First Commerce Bank | NJ | 03/09/20 |
| First FarmBank | CO | 03/09/20 |
| First Reliance Bank | SC | 03/09/20 |
| First Resource Bank | PA | 03/09/20 |
| First Security Bank | MN | 03/09/20 |
| First Security State Bank | IA | 03/09/20 |
| First State Bank | IA | 03/09/20 |
| First State Bank of Bloomington | IL | 03/09/20 |
| First State Bank of Dongola | IL | 03/09/20 |
| First United Bank | ND | 03/09/20 |
| FMS Bank | CO | 03/09/20 |
| Freedom Bank | MT | 03/09/20 |
| Georgia Primary Bank | GA | 03/09/20 |
| Golden State Bank | CA | 03/09/20 |
| Heartland Bank | NE | 03/09/20 |
| Idaho First Bank | ID | 03/09/20 |
| Jonestown Bank and Trust Co. | PA | 03/09/20 |
| Lamar National Bank | TX | 03/09/20 |
| Leaders Bank | IL | 03/09/20 |
| Lee Bank | MA | 03/09/20 |
| Lowry State Bank | MN | 03/09/20 |
| Main Street Bank | MA | 03/09/20 |
| Main Street Bank Corp. | WV | 03/09/20 |
| Mediapolis Savings Bank | IA | 03/09/20 |
| Merchants & Planters Bank | AR | 03/09/20 |
| Morris Bank | GA | 03/09/20 |
| Mountain Valley Bank | TN | 03/09/20 |
| New Buffalo Savings Bank | MI | 03/09/20 |
| New Haven Bank | CT | 03/09/20 |
| Oxford Bank & Trust | IL | 03/09/20 |
| Peoples Bank of Kankakee County | IL | 03/09/20 |
| Peoples State Bank | KS | 03/09/20 |
| Premier Bank | IA | 03/09/20 |
| Provident Savings Bank, F.S.B. | CA | 03/09/20 |
| Security Bank of Crawford | TX | 03/09/20 |
| Security First Bank | NE | 03/09/20 |
| Small Business Bank | KS | 03/09/20 |
| State Bank | IA | 03/09/20 |
| State Bank & Trust Co. | LA | 03/09/20 |
| State Bank of Cross Plains | WI | 03/09/20 |
| State Farm Bank, FSB | IL | 03/09/20 |
| Stockmans Bank | OK | 03/09/20 |
| Stride Bank, N.A. | OK | 03/09/20 |
| Swedish-American State Bank | KS | 03/09/20 |
| Tilden Bank | NE | 03/09/20 |
| Town Center Bank | IL | 03/09/20 |
| Ulster Savings Bank | NY | 03/09/20 |
| United Bank of Michigan | MI | 03/09/20 |
| United Community Bank | LA | 03/09/20 |
| United Prairie Bank | MN | 03/09/20 |

## Rating Upgrades

### Rating: C

| Name | State | Date of Change |
|---|---|---|
| 1st National Bank | OH | 03/09/20 |
| American Eagle Bank of Chicago | IL | 03/09/20 |
| Bank of Delmarva | MD | 03/09/20 |
| Bank of Eastman | GA | 03/09/20 |
| Bank of Glen Burnie | MD | 03/09/20 |
| Blue Ridge Bank and Trust Co. | MO | 03/09/20 |
| Carver State Bank | GA | 03/09/20 |
| Community Bank Mankato | MN | 03/09/20 |
| Community Federal Savings Bank | NY | 03/09/20 |
| Congressional Bank | MD | 03/09/20 |
| Earlham Savings Bank | IA | 03/09/20 |
| Envision Bank | MA | 03/09/20 |
| Farmington State Bank | WA | 03/09/20 |
| First Bank of the Lake | MO | 03/09/20 |
| First Capital Bank | TX | 03/09/20 |
| First Progressive Bank | AL | 03/09/20 |
| Florida Capital Bank, N.A. | FL | 03/09/20 |
| Goldwater Bank, N.A. | AZ | 03/09/20 |
| Green Belt Bank & Trust | IA | 03/09/20 |
| Heritage Bank, N.A. | MN | 03/09/20 |
| Kindred State Bank | ND | 03/09/20 |
| Merchants Commercial Bank | VI | 03/09/20 |
| Midwest Regional Bank | MO | 03/09/20 |
| Morris County National Bank | TX | 03/09/20 |
| Mutual Federal Bank | IL | 03/09/20 |
| Optus Bank | SC | 03/09/20 |
| Pee Dee Federal Savings Bank | SC | 03/09/20 |
| Peoples Bank, Biloxi, Mississippi | MS | 03/09/20 |
| Plains State Bank | TX | 03/09/20 |
| Regional Missouri Bank | MO | 03/09/20 |
| Rivers Edge Bank | SD | 03/09/20 |
| Savoy Bank | NY | 03/09/20 |
| Southwest Capital Bank | NM | 03/09/20 |
| SpiritBank | OK | 03/09/20 |
| State Bank of Bellingham | MN | 03/09/20 |
| Summit National Bank | WY | 03/09/20 |
| Trust Bank | GA | 03/09/20 |
| Western Dakota Bank | SD | 03/09/20 |

### Rating: C-

| Name | State | Date of Change |
|---|---|---|
| American Eagle Bank | IL | 03/09/20 |
| Bank of Okolona | MS | 03/09/20 |
| BlackRidgeBANK | ND | 03/09/20 |
| Carroll Community Bank | MD | 03/09/20 |
| Cedar Rapids State Bank | NE | 03/09/20 |
| Citizens National Bank of Hammond | NY | 03/09/20 |
| Citizens State Bank | TX | 03/09/20 |
| Coastal States Bank | SC | 03/09/20 |
| Eagle State Bank | NE | 03/09/20 |
| Farm Bureau Bank, FSB | NV | 03/09/20 |
| Farmers and Merchants State Bank | MN | 03/09/20 |
| First Chatham Bank | GA | 03/09/20 |
| First Community National Bank | MO | 03/09/20 |
| First National Bank of Chisholm | MN | 03/09/20 |
| First National Bank of Harveyville | KS | 03/09/20 |
| First National Bank of Proctor | MN | 03/09/20 |
| Frost State Bank | MN | 03/09/20 |
| Gifford State Bank | IL | 03/09/20 |
| Hillsboro State Bank | KS | 03/09/20 |
| Industrial Bank | DC | 03/09/20 |
| Legacy State Bank | GA | 03/09/20 |
| Paramount Bank | MO | 03/09/20 |
| Peoples Bank | TN | 03/09/20 |
| Powell State Bank | TX | 03/09/20 |
| Prairie Sun Bank | MN | 03/09/20 |
| Signature Bank of Georgia | GA | 03/09/20 |
| South Lafourche Bank & Trust Co. | LA | 03/09/20 |
| State Bank of Eagle Butte | SD | 03/09/20 |
| Talbot State Bank | GA | 03/09/20 |
| Wray State Bank | CO | 03/09/20 |

### Rating: D+

| Name | State | Date of Change |
|---|---|---|
| Bank of Fincastle | VA | 03/09/20 |
| Best Hometown Bank | IL | 03/09/20 |
| Camp Grove State Bank | IL | 03/09/20 |
| Citizens State Bank and Trust Co. | KS | 03/09/20 |
| Community National Bank in Monmouth | IL | 03/09/20 |
| Corn Growers State Bank | NE | 03/09/20 |
| Cornerstone Bank | NJ | 03/09/20 |
| Farmers-Merchants Bank & Trust Co. | LA | 03/09/20 |
| First Security Bank | IL | 03/09/20 |
| FMB Bank | MO | 03/09/20 |
| Great Plains Bank | SD | 03/09/20 |
| State Bank of Colon | NE | 03/09/20 |
| State Exchange Bank | OK | 03/09/20 |
| Valley Bank of Nevada | NV | 03/09/20 |

### Rating: D

| Name | State | Date of Change |
|---|---|---|
| Alma Bank | NY | 03/09/20 |
| Community Bank & Trust - Alabama | AL | 03/09/20 |
| Cowboy State Bank | WY | 03/09/20 |
| Equitable Bank, S.S.B. | WI | 03/09/20 |
| Garfield County Bank | MT | 03/09/20 |
| Gateway Bank, F.S.B. | CA | 03/09/20 |
| Millennial Bank | AL | 03/09/20 |

### Rating: D-

| Name | State | Date of Change |
|---|---|---|
| Beach Community Bank | FL | 03/09/20 |

## Rating Upgrades

| Name | State | Date of Change |
|---|---|---|
| Cogent Bank | FL | 03/09/20 |

### Rating: E+

| Name | State | Date of Change |
|---|---|---|
| Lafayette State Bank | FL | 03/09/20 |
| McHenry Savings Bank | IL | 03/09/20 |
| Peoples Bank | GA | 03/09/20 |
| United Trust Bank | IL | 03/09/20 |

## Rating Downgrades

### Rating: A-

| Name | State | Date of Change |
|---|---|---|
| California Pacific Bank | CA | 03/09/20 |
| First National Bank in Taylorville | IL | 03/09/20 |
| Five Points Bank | NE | 03/09/20 |
| Five Points Bank of Hastings | NE | 03/09/20 |
| Kaw Valley State Bank and Trust Co. | KS | 03/09/20 |
| Poplar Grove State Bank | IL | 03/09/20 |
| Wallis Bank | TX | 03/09/20 |

### Rating: B+

| Name | State | Date of Change |
|---|---|---|
| Commercial State Bank | NE | 03/09/20 |
| EverTrust Bank | CA | 03/09/20 |
| First Bank & Trust Co. | OK | 03/09/20 |
| First Choice Bank | CA | 03/09/20 |
| Industry State Bank | TX | 03/09/20 |
| Platte Valley Bank of Missouri | MO | 03/09/20 |
| Reliance State Bank | IA | 03/09/20 |
| United Bank & Trust N.A. | IA | 03/09/20 |
| William Penn Bank, | PA | 03/09/20 |

### Rating: B

| Name | State | Date of Change |
|---|---|---|
| Bank of Holyrood | KS | 03/09/20 |
| Bank of Sun Prairie | WI | 03/09/20 |
| Burke & Herbert Bank & Trust Co. | VA | 03/09/20 |
| Campbell County Bank, Inc. | SD | 03/09/20 |
| Dearborn Federal Savings Bank | MI | 03/09/20 |
| First Farmers & Merchants National Bank | MN | 03/09/20 |
| First Farmers & Merchants State Bank | MN | 03/09/20 |
| First National Bank in DeRidder | LA | 03/09/20 |
| First National Bank of Northfield | MN | 03/09/20 |
| First State Bank | OK | 03/09/20 |
| Goldman Sachs Bank USA | NY | 03/09/20 |
| Graham S&L, SSB | TX | 03/09/20 |
| Marion County State Bank | IA | 03/09/20 |
| Marquette Savings Bank | PA | 03/09/20 |

### Rating: B-

| Name | State | Date of Change |
|---|---|---|
| American Bank of Baxter Springs | KS | 03/09/20 |
| Atlantic Community Bankers Bank | PA | 03/09/20 |
| Banesco USA | FL | 03/09/20 |
| Bank of the Orient | CA | 03/09/20 |
| Cayuga Lake National Bank | NY | 03/09/20 |
| Central Savings Bank | MI | 03/09/20 |
| Dime Community Bank | NY | 03/09/20 |
| Essex Savings Bank | CT | 03/09/20 |
| Exchange Bank and Trust Co. | OK | 03/09/20 |
| Executive National Bank | FL | 03/09/20 |
| First American Bank, N.A. | WI | 03/09/20 |
| First National Bank of Pawnee | OK | 03/09/20 |
| First Western Bank & Trust | ND | 03/09/20 |
| Gouverneur S&L Assn. | NY | 03/09/20 |
| Grove Bank & Trust | FL | 03/09/20 |
| Lamesa National Bank | TX | 03/09/20 |
| Marion Bank and Trust Co. | AL | 03/09/20 |
| Melvin Savings Bank | IA | 03/09/20 |
| NobleBank & Trust | AL | 03/09/20 |
| Patterson State Bank | LA | 03/09/20 |
| State Savings Bank | IA | 03/09/20 |
| Wilson & Muir Bank & Trust Co. | KY | 03/09/20 |

### Rating: C+

| Name | State | Date of Change |
|---|---|---|
| 1st State Bank of Mason City | IL | 03/09/20 |
| American Bank and Trust Co., N.A. | IA | 03/09/20 |
| Bank of Eufaula | OK | 03/09/20 |
| BankPacific, Ltd | GU | 03/09/20 |
| Blue Foundry Bank | NJ | 03/09/20 |
| Bogota Savings Bank | NJ | 03/09/20 |
| CalPrivate Bank | CA | 03/09/20 |
| CornerStone Bank, N.A. | VA | 03/09/20 |
| ESB Financial | KS | 03/09/20 |
| Escambia County Bank | AL | 03/09/20 |
| Farmers and Merchants State Bank | SD | 03/09/20 |
| First Federal S&L Assn. | MS | 03/09/20 |
| First Neighborhood Bank | WV | 03/09/20 |
| First Service Bank | AR | 03/09/20 |
| First State Bank in Temple | OK | 03/09/20 |
| FNB Community Bank | OK | 03/09/20 |
| Hendricks County Bank and Trust Co. | IN | 03/09/20 |
| Heritage Bank Minnesota | MN | 03/09/20 |
| Jarrettsville Federal S&L Assn. | MD | 03/09/20 |
| Lakeside Bank | TX | 03/09/20 |
| Mercer County State Bank | PA | 03/09/20 |
| Midwest Bank | IL | 03/09/20 |
| Settlers bank | WI | 03/09/20 |
| Tarboro Savings Bank, SSB | NC | 03/09/20 |
| Time Federal Savings Bank | WI | 03/09/20 |
| Titonka Savings Bank | IA | 03/09/20 |
| Union Bank | TN | 03/09/20 |
| Valley National Bank | NJ | 03/09/20 |

### Rating: C

| Name | State | Date of Change |
|---|---|---|
| Alva State Bank & Trust Co. | OK | 03/09/20 |
| Arundel Federal Savings Bank | MD | 03/09/20 |
| Central State Bank | IL | 03/09/20 |
| CIBM Bank | IL | 03/09/20 |
| Citizens Bank of Newburg | MO | 03/09/20 |
| Community National Bank | TN | 03/09/20 |
| Dalhart Federal S&L Assn., SSB | TX | 03/09/20 |
| Farmers and Merchants State Bank | SD | 03/09/20 |

## Rating Downgrades

| Name | State | Date of Change |
|---|---|---|
| First Savings Bank | IL | 03/09/20 |
| First Summit Bank | OK | 03/09/20 |
| Flatwater Bank | NE | 03/09/20 |
| Freedom Bank | TX | 03/09/20 |
| Greenville Federal | OH | 03/09/20 |
| Liberty Savings Assn., FSA | KS | 03/09/20 |
| Longview Bank | IL | 03/09/20 |
| Melrose Bank | MA | 03/09/20 |
| Pioneer Savings Bank | OH | 03/09/20 |
| Prairie Community Bank | IL | 03/09/20 |
| Star Bank | MN | 03/09/20 |
| UNICO Bank | MO | 03/09/20 |
| Union State Bank of Hazen | ND | 03/09/20 |
| Wahoo State Bank | NE | 03/09/20 |
| Westmoreland Federal S&L Assn. | PA | 03/09/20 |

### Rating: C-

| Name | State | Date of Change |
|---|---|---|
| Bank of Moundville | AL | 03/09/20 |
| Citizens Bank & Trust Co. | TN | 03/09/20 |
| Crown Bank | MN | 03/09/20 |
| Dallas Capital Bank, N.A. | TX | 03/09/20 |
| Farmers & Merchants Bank & Trust | IA | 03/09/20 |
| Farmers State Bank | KS | 03/09/20 |
| First State Bank | OK | 03/09/20 |
| First Trust and Savings Bank | IA | 03/09/20 |
| Horicon Bank | WI | 03/09/20 |
| InterBank | OK | 03/09/20 |
| Liberty Bay Bank | WA | 03/09/20 |
| Marquette Farmers State Bank | KS | 03/09/20 |
| Merchants & Planters Bank | AR | 03/09/20 |
| Peoples State Bank | KS | 03/09/20 |
| Valley Central Bank | OH | 03/09/20 |

### Rating: D+

| Name | State | Date of Change |
|---|---|---|
| Amory Federal S&L Assn. | MS | 03/09/20 |
| Emerald Bank | KS | 03/09/20 |
| Ericson State Bank | NE | 03/09/20 |
| Fairport Savings Bank | NY | 03/09/20 |
| First National Bank of Gilbert | MN | 03/09/20 |
| First Security Bank | OK | 03/09/20 |
| FNNB Bank | IA | 03/09/20 |
| Great North Bank | WI | 03/09/20 |
| HomeBank of Arkansas | AR | 03/09/20 |
| Intercredit Bank, N.A. | FL | 03/09/20 |
| M.Y. Safra Bank, FSB | NY | 03/09/20 |
| Oklahoma State Bank | OK | 03/09/20 |
| Sawyer Savings Bank | NY | 03/09/20 |
| Valley Bank of Ronan | MT | 03/09/20 |

### Rating: D

| Name | State | Date of Change |
|---|---|---|
| Greenfield Banking Co. | TN | 03/09/20 |
| Security State Bank of Warroad | MN | 03/09/20 |
| State Bank of Nauvoo | IL | 03/09/20 |

### Rating: D-

| Name | State | Date of Change |
|---|---|---|
| DR Bank | CT | 03/09/20 |
| Enterprise Bank | PA | 03/09/20 |
| Farmers Bank | OK | 03/09/20 |
| First National Bank of Hope | KS | 03/09/20 |
| Iowa State Bank | IA | 03/09/20 |
| Rolette State Bank | ND | 03/09/20 |

### Rating: E+

| Name | State | Date of Change |
|---|---|---|
| Community Bank & Trust - West Georgia | GA | 03/09/20 |
| First Citizens Bank of Polson, N.A. | MT | 03/09/20 |
| Sidney Federal S&L Assn. | NE | 03/09/20 |

### Rating: E-

| Name | State | Date of Change |
|---|---|---|
| Brighton Bank | TN | 03/09/20 |

# Appendix

# RECENT BANK FAILURES
# 2020

| Institution | Headquarters | Date of Failure | At Date of Failure | |
|---|---|---|---|---|
| | | | Total Assets ($Mil) | Safety Rating |
| Ericson State Bank | Ericson, NE | 2/14/20 | 113.02 | C- (Fair) |

# 2019

| Institution | Headquarters | Date of Failure | At Date of Failure | |
|---|---|---|---|---|
| | | | Total Assets ($Mil) | Safety Rating |
| City National Bank of NJ | Newark, NJ | 11/1/19 | 142.5 | E- (Very Weak) |
| Resolute Bank | Maumee, OH | 10/25/19 | 27.1 | E+ (Very Weak) |
| Enloe State Bank | Cooper, TX | 5/31/19 | 36.5 | C (Fair) |

# 2017

| Institution | Headquarters | Date of Failure | At Date of Failure | |
|---|---|---|---|---|
| | | | Total Assets ($Mil) | Safety Rating |
| Washington Federal Banks for Savings | Chicago, IL | 12/15/17 | 166.4 | A (Excellent) |
| Farmers & Merchants State Bk of Argonia | Argonia, KS | 10/13/17 | 34.2 | E- (Very Weak) |
| Fayette County Bank | Saint Elmo, IL | 05/26/17 | 34.8 | E- (Very Weak) |
| Guaranty Bank (MHC) | Milwaukee, WI | 05/05/17 | 1,010.0 | E- (Very Weak) |
| First NBC Bank | New Orleans, LA | 04/28/17 | 4,740.0 | E- (Very Weak) |
| Proficio Bank | Cottonwood Heights, UT | 03/03/17 | 80.3 | E- (Very Weak) |
| Seaway Bank and Trust Co | Chicago, IL | 01/27/17 | 361.2 | E- (Very Weak) |
| Harvest Community Bank | Pennsville, NJ | 01/13/17 | 126.4 | E- (Very Weak) |

# 2016

| Institution | Headquarters | Date of Failure | At Date of Failure | |
|---|---|---|---|---|
| | | | Total Assets ($Mil) | Safety Rating |
| Allied Bank | Mulberry, AR | 09/23/16 | 66.3 | E- (Very Weak) |
| Woodbury Banking Company | Woodbury, GA | 08/19/16 | 22.5 | E- (Very Weak) |
| First Cornerstone Bank | King of Prussia, PA | 05/06/16 | 107.0 | E- (Very Weak) |
| Trust Co Bank | Memphis, TN | 04/29/16 | 20.7 | E- (Very Weak) |
| North Milwaukee State Bank | Milwaukee, WI | 03/11/16 | 67.1 | E- (Very Weak) |

# 2015

| Institution | Headquarters | Date of Failure | At Date of Failure | |
|---|---|---|---|---|
| | | | Total Assets ($Mil) | Safety Rating |
| Bramble Savings Bank | Milford, OH | 12/17/15 | 47.5 | E- (Very Weak) |
| Bank of Georgia | Peachtree City, GA | 10/02/15 | 294.2 | E- (Very Weak) |
| Hometown National Bank | Longview, WA | 10/02/15 | 4.9 | E+ (Very Weak) |
| Premier Bank | Denever, CO | 07/10/15 | 31.7 | E- (Very Weak) |
| Edgebrook Bank | Chicago, IL | 05/08/15 | 90.0 | E- (Very Weak) |
| Doral Bank | San Juan, PR | 02/27/15 | 5,900.0 | E+ (Very Weak) |
| Capitol City Bank & Trust Co | Atlanta, GA | 02/13/15 | 272.3 | E- (Very Weak) |
| Highland Community Bank | Chicago, IL | 01/23/15 | 54.7 | E- (Very Weak) |
| First National Bank of Crestview | Crestview, FL | 01/16/15 | 79.7 | E- (Very Weak) |

# 2014

| Institution | Headquarters | Date of Failure | At Date of Failure | |
|---|---|---|---|---|
| | | | Total Assets ($Mil) | Safety Rating |
| Northern Star Bank | Makato, MN | 12/19/14 | 18.8 | E- (Very Weak) |
| Frontier Bank, FSB | Palm Desert, CA | 11/07/14 | 86.4 | E- (Very Weak) |
| National Republic Bk of Chicago | Chicago, IL | 10/24/14 | 954.4 | E- (Very Weak) |
| NBRS Financial | Rising Sun, MD | 10/17/14 | 188.2 | E- (Very Weak) |
| Greenchoice Bank FSB | Chicago, IL | 07/25/14 | 72.9 | E- (Very Weak) |
| Eastside Commercial Bank | Conyers, GA | 07/18/14 | 169.0 | E- (Very Weak) |
| Freedom State Bank | Freedom, OK | 06/27/14 | 22.8 | D (Weak) |
| Valley Bank | Moline, IL | 06/20/14 | 456.4 | E+ (Very Weak) |
| Valley Bank | Fort Lauderdale, FL | 06/20/14 | 81.8 | E- (Very Weak) |
| Slavie Federal Savings Bank | Bel Air, MD | 05/30/14 | 140.1 | E- (Very Weak) |
| Columbia Savings Bank | Cincinnati, OH | 05/23/14 | 36.5 | E- (Very Weak) |
| AztecAmerica Bank | Berwyn, IL | 05/16/14 | 66.3 | E- (Very Weak) |
| Allendale County Bank | Fairfax, SC | 04/25/14 | 54.5 | E- (Very Weak) |
| Millennium Bank NA | Sterling, VA | 02/28/14 | 130.3 | E- (Very Weak) |
| Vantage Point Bank | Horsham, PA | 02/28/14 | 63.5 | E- (Very Weak) |
| Syringa Bank | Boise, ID | 01/31/14 | 153.4 | E- (Very Weak) |
| Bank of Union | El Reno, OK | 01/24/14 | 331.4 | D- (Weak) |
| DuPage National Bank | West Chicago, IL | 01/17/14 | 61.7 | E- (Very Weak) |

# How Do Banks and Credit Unions Differ?

Since credit unions first appeared in 1946, they have been touted as a low-cost, friendly alternative to banks. But with tightening margins, pressure to compete in technology, branch closures, and the introduction of a host of service fees — some even higher than those charged by banks — the distinction between banks and credit unions has been gradually narrowing. Following are the key differences between today's banks and credit unions.

| | Banks | Credit Unions |
|---|---|---|
| **Access** | Practically anyone is free to open an account or request a loan from any bank. There are no membership requirements. | Credit unions are set up to serve the needs of a specific group who share a "common bond." In order to open an account or request a loan, you must demonstrate that you meet the credit union's common bond requirements. |
| **Ownership** | Banks are owned by one or more investors who determine the bank's policies and procedures. A bank's customers do not have direct input into how the bank is operated. | Although they may be sponsored by a corporation or other entity, credit unions are owned by their members through their funds on deposit. Therefore, each depositor has a voice in how the credit union is operated. |
| **Dividends and Fees** | Banks are for-profit organizations where the profits are used to pay dividends to the bank's investors or are reinvested in an effort to increase the bank's value to investors. In an effort to generate more profits, bank services and fees are typically more costly. | Credit unions are not-for-profit organizations. Any profits generated are returned to the credit union's members in the form of higher interest rates on deposits, lower loan rates, and free or low-cost services. |
| **Management and Staffing** | A bank's management and other staff are employees of the bank, hired directly or indirectly by its investors. | Credit unions are frequently run using elected members, volunteer staff, and staff provided by the credit union's sponsor. This helps to hold down costs. |
| **Insurance** | Banks are insured by the Federal Deposit Insurance Corporation, an agency of the federal government. | Credit unions are insured by the National Credit Union Share Insurance Fund, which is managed by the National Credit Union Administration, an agency of the federal government. |

# Glossary

This glossary contains the most important terms used in this publication.

**ARM** Adjustable-Rate Mortgage. This is a loan whose interest rate is tied to an index and is adjusted at a predetermined frequency. An ARM is subject to credit risk if interest rates rise and the borrower is unable to make the mortgage payment.

**Average Recession** A recession involving a decline in real GDP that is approximately equivalent to the average of the postwar recessions of 1957-58, 1960, 1970, 1974-75, 1980, 1981-82, 1990-1991, 2001, and 2007-2009. It is assumed, however, that in today's market, the financial losses suffered from a recession of that magnitude would be greater than those experienced in previous decades. (See also "Severe Recession.")

**Bank Holding Company** A company that holds stock in one or more banks and possibly other companies.

**Bank Insurance Fund (BIF)** A unit of Federal Deposit Insurance Corporation (FDIC) that provided deposit insurance for banks, other than thrifts. BIF was formed as part of the 1989 savings and loan association bailout bill to keep separate the administration of the bank and thrift insurance programs. There were thus two distinct insurance entities under the FDIC: BIF and savings association insurance fund (SAIF). (See also Federal Deposit Insurance Corporation.")

**Brokered Deposits** Deposits that are brought into an institution through a broker. They are relatively costly, volatile funds that are more readily withdrawn from the institution if there is a loss of confidence or intense interest rate competition. Reliance on brokered deposits is usually a sign that the institution is having difficulty attracting deposits from its local geographic markets and could be a warning signal if other institutions in the same areas are not experiencing similar difficulties.

**Capital** The cushion an institution has of its own resources to help withstand losses. The basic component of capital is stockholder's equity which consists of common and preferred stock and retained earnings. (See also "Core Capital")

**Cash & Equivalents** Cash plus highly liquid assets which can be readily converted to cash.

**Core (Tier 1) Capital** A measurement of capital defined by the federal regulatory agencies for evaluating an institution's degree of leverage. Core capital consists of the following: common stockholder's equity, preferred stockholder's equity up to certain limits, and retained earnings net of any intangible assets.

**Critical Ranges** Guidelines developed to help you evaluate the levels of each index contributing to a company's Weiss Safety Rating. The sum or average of these grades does not necessarily have a one-to-one correspondence with the final rating for an institution because the rating is derived from a wider range of more complex calculations.

**Deposit Insurance Fund (DIF)** In 2005 Congress passed legislation merging the SAIF and BIF into one insurance fund called the deposit insurance fund (DIF). The same law also raised the federal deposit insurance level from $100,000 to $250,000. (See also "Emergency Economic Stabilization Act.")

**Emergency Stabilization Act** In 2008 Congress passed the Emergency Economic Stabilization Act that temporarily increased the basic limit on deposit insurance for all ownership categories from $100,000 to $250,000. This increase was set to expire in 2013 but has been extended permanently.

**Equity** Total assets minus total liabilities. This is the "capital cushion" the institution has to fall back on in times of trouble. (See also "Capital.")

**FDIC** Federal Deposit Insurance Corporation. The provider of insurance on deposits. This agency also plays an active role when banks are found to be insolvent or in need of federal assistance. It is the governing body of the Deposit Insurance Fund (DIF) that now incorporates both the Bank Insurance Fund (BIF) and the Savings Association Insurance Fund (SAIF). (See also "Deposit Insurance Fund.")

**Federal Home Loan Bank (FHLB)** A quasi-governmental agency (reporting to the Federal Housing Finance Board) whose chartered purpose is to promote the issuance of mortgage loans by providing increased liquidity to lenders. This agency raises money by issuing notes and bonds and then lends the money to banks and other mortgage lenders.

**Federal Reserve** America's central bank, regulating all banks that offer transaction accounts. It works hand-in-hand with the FDIC, providing examination and regulation of its member banks.

**Safety Rating** Weiss Safety Ratings, which grade institutions on a scale from A (Excellent) to F (Failed). Ratings are based on many factors, emphasizing capitalization, asset quality, profitability, liquidity, and stability.

**FSB** Federal Savings Bank. A thrift institution operating under a federal charter.

**Goodwill** The value of an institution as a going concern, meaning the value which exceeds book value on a balance sheet. It generally represents the value of a well-respected business name, good customer relations, high employee morale and other intangible factors which would be expected to translate into greater than normal earning power. In a bank acquisition, goodwill is the value paid by a buyer of the institution in excess of the value of the institution's equity because of these intangible factors.

**Hot Money** Individual deposits of $100,000 or more plus those deposits received through a broker. These types of deposits are considered "hot money" because they tend to chase whoever is offering the best interest rates at the time and are thus relatively costly and fairly volatile sources of funds.

**Loan Loss Reserves** The amount of capital an institution sets aside to cover any potential losses due to the nonrepayment of loans.

**N.A.** National Association. A commercial bank operating under a federal charter.

**Net Charge-offs** The amount of foreclosed loans written off the institution's books since the beginning of the year, less any previous write-offs that were recovered during the year.

**Net Interest Spread** The difference between the interest income earned on the institution's loans and investments and the interest expense paid on its interest-bearing deposits and borrowings. This "spread" is most commonly analyzed as a percentage of average earning assets to show the institution's net return on income-generating assets.

Since the margin between interest earned and interest paid is generally where the company generates the majority of its income, this figure provides insight into the company's ability to effectively manage interest spreads. A low Net Interest Spread can be the result of poor loan and deposit pricing, high levels of nonaccruing loans, or poor asset/liability management.

**Net Profit or Loss** The bottom line income or loss the institution has sustained in its most recent reporting period.

**Nonaccruing Loans** Loans for which payments are past due and full repayment is doubtful. Interest income on these loans is no longer recorded on the income statement. (See also "Past Due Loans.")

**Nonperforming Loans** The sum of loans past due 90 days or more and nonaccruing loans. These are loans the institution made where full repayment is now doubtful. (See also "Past Due Loans" and "Nonaccruing Loans.")

**Past Due Loans** Loans for which payments are at least 90 days in arrears. The institution continues to record income on these loans, even though none is actually being received, because it is expected that the borrower will eventually repay the loan in full. It is likely, however, that at least a portion of these loans will move into nonaccruing status. (See also "Nonaccruing Loans.")

**OCC** Office of the Comptroller of the Currency. This agency of the U.S. Treasury Department is the primary regulator of national banks.

**Overhead Expense** Expenses of the institution other than interest expense, such as salaries and benefits of employees, rent and utility expenses, and data processing expenses. A certain amount of "fixed" overhead is required to operate a bank, so it is important that the institution leverage that overhead to the fullest extent in supporting its revenue-generating activities.

**RBCR** See "Risk-Based Capital Ratio."

**Resolution Trust Corp. (RTC)** The now-defunct federal agency that was formed to handle the liquidation of insolvent savings and loans.

**Restructured Loans** Loans whose terms have been modified in order to enable the borrower to make payments which he otherwise would be unable to make. Modifications could include a reduction in the interest rate or a lengthening of the time to maturity.

| | |
|---|---|
| **Risk-Based Capital Ratio** | A ratio originally developed by the International Committee on Banking as a means of assessing the adequacy of an institution's capital in relation to the amount of credit risk on and off its balance sheet. (See also "Risk-weighted Assets.") |
| **Risk-Weighted Assets** | The sum of assets and certain off-balance sheet items after they have been individually adjusted for the level of credit risk they pose to the institution. Assets with close to no risk are weighted 0%; those with minor risk are weighted 20%; those with low risk, 50%; and those with normal or high risk, 100%. |
| **R.O.A** | Return on Assets calculated as net profit or loss as a percentage of average assets. This is the most commonly used measure of bank profitability. |
| **R.O.E.** | Return on Equity calculated as net profit or loss as a percentage of average equity. This represents the rate of return on the shareholders' investment. |
| **S.A.** | Savings Association. |
| **Savings and Loan (S&L)** | A financial institution that traditionally offered primarily home mortgages to individuals and served small depositors. However, in 1980, savings and loans were given power to diversify into other areas of lending. Also known as a thrift. |
| **Savings and Loan Holding Company** | A company that holds stock in one or more savings and loans and possibly other companies. |
| **Savings Association Insurance Fund (SAIF)** | Fund created in 1989 by Congress to replace the FSLIC as the provider of deposit insurance to thrifts. This fund is administered by the Federal Deposit Insurance Corporation (FDIC). (See also "Bank Insurance Fund.") |
| **Savings Bank** | A financial institution created to serve primarily the small saver and to lend mortgage money to individuals. Though savings banks have expanded their services, they are still primarily engaged in providing consumer mortgages and accepting consumer deposits. Also known as a thrift. |
| **Severe Recession** | A drop in real GDP which is significantly greater than that of an average postwar recession. (See also "Average Recession.") |
| **Stockholder's Equity** | See "Equity." |
| **Thrift** | Generic term for an institution formed primarily as a depository for consumer savings and a lender for home mortgages, such as a savings and loan or a savings bank. |
| **Total Assets** | Total resources of an institution, primarily composed of cash, securities (such as municipal and treasury bonds), loans, and fixed assets (such as real estate, buildings, and equipment). |
| **Total Equity** | See "Equity." |

**Total Liabilities** All debts owed by an institution. Normally, the largest liability of a bank is its deposits.

**Trust Company** A financial institution chartered to provide trust services (legal agreements to act for the benefit of another party), which may also be authorized to provide banking services.